SCHAUM'S OUTLINE OF

THEORY AND PROBLEMS

OF

PROGRAMMING

WITH

C

.

Second Edition

.

BYRON S. GOTTFRIED, Ph.D.

Professor of Industrial Engineering
University of Pittsburgh

SCHAUM'S OUTLINE SERIES
McGRAW-HILL

New York St. Louis San Francisco Auckland Bogotá Caracas
Lisbon London Madrid Mexico City Milan Montreal
New Delhi San Juan Singapore
Sydney Tokyo Toronto

In memory of Sidney Gottfried:
father, teacher and friend

BYRON S. GOTTFRIED is a Professor of Industrial Engineering and Academic Director of the Freshman Engineering Program at the University of Pittsburgh. He received his Ph.D. from Case-Western Reserve University in 1962, and has been a member of the Pitt faculty since 1970. His primary interests are in the areas of computer simulation, software engineering, and the use of new educational paradigms. He is the author of eleven college textbooks, including *Programming with C*, *Programming with Pascal* and *Programming with Structured BASIC* in the Schaum's Outline Series.

DEC is a registered trademark of Digital Equipment Corporation.
IBM is a registered trademark of International Business Machines Corporation.
IBM PC-AT is a trademark of International Business Machines Corporation.
Microsoft is a registered trademark of Microsoft Corporation.
Quick C and MS-DOS are registered trademarks of Microsoft Corporation.
Turbo C and Turbo C++ are registered trademarks of Borland International, Inc.
VAX is a trademark of Digital Equipment Corporation.
VMS is a trademark of Digital Equipment Corporation.

Schaum's Outline of Theory and Problems of
PROGRAMMING WITH C

3 4 5 6 7 8 9 10 11 12 13 14 15 16 17 18 19 20 PRS PRS 9 0 1 0 9 8 7

ISBN 0–07–024035–3

Sponsoring Editors: John Aliano, Arthur Biderman
Production Supervisor: Suzanne Rapcavage
Editing Supervisor: Maureen Walker

Library of Congress Cataloging-in-Publication Data
Gottfried, Byron S., date
    Schaum's outline of theory and problems of programming with C /
    Byron S. Gottfried. -- 2nd ed.
        p.   cm. -- (Schaum's outline series)
    ISBN 0-07-024035-3
    1. C (Computer program language)   I. Title.   II. Series.
    QA76.73.C15G67 1996
    005.13'3--dc20   96-2724
                                                        CIP

McGraw-Hill

A Division of The McGraw·Hill Companies

Preface

C has continued to increase in popularity since the publication of the first edition of this book in 1990. Most newer compilers provide numerous extensions to the 1989 ANSI standard, as well as a full-feature graphical programming environment including a debugger, a project manager, and extensive on-line help. Moreover, interest in C has not been diminished by the emergence of C++, since the features found in this newer programming language require a solid background in C.

This second edition provides instruction in the use of the C language, within the context of contemporary C programming style. It includes complete and understandable explanations of the commonly used features of C, including most of the features included in the current ANSI standard. In addition, the book presents a contemporary approach to programming, stressing the importance of clarity, legibility, modularity and efficiency in program design. Thus, the reader is exposed to the principles of good programming practice as well as the specific rules of C. Complete C programs are presented throughout the text, beginning with the first chapter. The use of an interactive programming style is emphasized throughout the text.

The book can be used by a wide reader audience, ranging from beginning programmers to practicing professionals. It is particularly well suited for advanced secondary or beginning college-level students as a textbook for an introductory programming course, as a supplementary text, or as an effective independent-study guide.

Many examples are included as an integral part of the text. These include numerous programming examples of varying complexity, as well as illustrative drill-type problems. The sample programs conform to the ANSI C standard. Many are solved using other programming languages in the companion Schaum's Outlines, thus providing the reader with a basis of comparison among several popular languages.

Sets of review questions and drill problems are provided at the end of each chapter. The review questions enable readers to test their recall of the material presented within each chapter. They also provide an effective chapter summary. The drill problems reinforce the principles presented within each chapter. The reader should solve as many of these problems as possible. Answers to most of the drill problems are provided at the end of the book.

In addition, problems that require the writing of complete C programs are presented at the end of each chapter, beginning with Chap. 5. The reader is encouraged to write and execute as many of these programs as possible. This will greatly enhance the reader's self-confidence and stimulate interest in the subject. (Computer programming is a demanding skill, much like creative writing or playing a musical instrument. As such, it cannot be learned simply by reading a textbook!)

Most of these programming problems require no special mathematical or technical background. Hence, they can be solved by a broad range of readers. When using this book in a programming course, the instructor may wish to supplement these problems with additional programming exercises that reflect particular disciplinary interests.

A number of changes have been made to the earlier edition. Chapter 5 has been rewritten, illustrating the use of C within Borland International's Turbo C++ programming environment, and the material on debugging techniques has been rewritten and expanded. The topics in Chap. 6 have been rearranged to correspond to the order in which they are presented in most introductory programming courses, with branching preceding looping. Some earlier material on the use of functions, reflecting an older programming style, has been removed from Chap. 7, and a section on dynamic memory allocation has been added to Chap. 10. Stylistic changes have been made in most programming examples; in particular, programs involving functions now emphasize full function prototyping, as recommended by the current ANSI standard.

All of the programming examples and many of the end-of-chapter programming problems have been solved on an Intel-type ("IBM-compatible") personal computer, using several different versions of Borland International's Turbo C++ compiler. In addition, some of the examples were run on a Digital Equipment VAX computer, using the versions of C provided by DEC for their VMS operating system.

The principal features of C are summarized in Appendixes A through H at the end of the book. This material should be used frequently for ready reference and quick recall. It is particularly helpful when writing or debugging a new program.

BYRON S. GOTTFRIED

Contents

Complete Programming Examples

The programming examples are listed in the order in which they first appear within the text. The examples vary from very simple to moderately complex. Multiple versions are presented for many of the programs, particularly the simpler programs.

1. *Area of a Circle* — Examples 1.6 – 1.13
2. *Lowercase to Uppercase Character Conversion* — Examples 3.31, 7.1
3. *Lowercase to Uppercase Text Conversion* — Examples 4.4, 6.9, 6.12, 6.16, 9.2
4. *Reading and Writing a Line of Text* — Examples 4.19, 4.31
5. *Averaging Student Exam Scores* — Example 4.32
6. *Compound Interest Calculations* — Examples 5.1 – 5.4, 8.13
7. *Syntactic Errors* — Example 5.5
8. *Execution Errors (Real Roots of a Quadratic Equation)* — Example 5.6
9. *Debugging a Program* — Example 5.7
10. *Debugging with an Interactive Debugger* — Example 5.8
11. *Generating Consecutive Integer Quantities* — Examples 6.8, 6.11, 6.14, 6.15
12. *Averaging a List of Numbers* — Examples 6.10, 6.13, 6.17, 6.31
13. *Repeated Averaging of a List of Numbers* — Example 6.18
14. *Converting Several Lines of Text to Uppercase* — Examples 6.19, 6.34
15. *Encoding a String of Characters* — Example 6.20
16. *Repeated Compound Interest Calculations with Error Trapping* — Example 6.21
17. *Solution of an Algebraic Equation* — Example 6.22
18. *Calculating Depreciation* — Examples 6.26, 7.13
19. *Searching for Palindromes* — Example 6.32
20. *Largest of Three Integer Quantities* — Example 7.9
21. *Calculating Factorials* — Examples 7.10, 7.14, 8.2
22. *Simulation of a Game of Chance (Shooting Craps)* — Examples 7.11, 8.9
23. *Printing Backwards* — Example 7.15
24. *The Towers of Hanoi* — Example 7.16
25. *Average Length of Several Lines of Text* — Examples 8.3, 8.5
26. *Search for a Maximum* — Examples 8.4, 8.11
27. *Generating Fibonacci Numbers* — Examples 8.7, 8.12, 13.2
28. *Deviations About an Average* — Examples 9.8, 9.9
29. *Reordering a List of Numbers* — Examples 9.13, 10.16
30. *A Piglatin Generator* — Example 9.14
31. *Adding Two Tables of Numbers* — Examples 9.19, 10.22, 10.24
32. *Reordering a List of Strings* — Examples 9.20, 10.26
33. *Analyzing a Line of Text* — Example 10.8
34. *Displaying the Day of the Year* — Example 10.28
35. *Future Value of Monthly Deposits (Compound Interest Calculations)* — Examples 10.30, 14.13
36. *Updating Customer Records* — Examples 11.14, 11.28
37. *Locating Customer Records* — Example 11.26
38. *Processing a Linked List* — Example 11.32
39. *Raising a Number to a Power* — Examples 11.37, 14.5
40. *Creating a Data File (Lowercase to Uppercase Text Conversion)* — Example 12.3
41. *Reading a Data File* — Examples 12.4, 14.9
42. *Creating a File Containing Customer Records* — Example 12.5
43. *Updating a File Containing Customer Records* — Example 12.6
44. *Creating an Unformatted Data File Containing Customer Records* — Example 12.7
45. *Updating an Unformatted Data File Containing Customer Records* — Example 12.8
46. *Displaying Bit Patterns* — Example 13.16
47. *Data Compression (Storing Names and Birthdates)* — Example 13.23

Chapter 1

Introductory Concepts

This book offers instruction in computer programming using a popular, structured programming language called C. We will learn how programs can be written in C. In addition, we will see how problems that are initially described in very general terms can be analyzed, outlined and finally transformed into well-organized C programs. These concepts are demonstrated in detail by the many sample problems that are included in the text.

1.1 INTRODUCTION TO COMPUTERS

Today's computers come in many different forms. They range from massive, multipurpose *mainframes* and *supercomputers* to desktop-size *personal computers*. Between these extremes is a vast middle ground of *minicomputers* and *workstations*. Large minicomputers approach mainframes in computing power, whereas workstations are powerful personal computers.

Mainframes and large minicomputers are used by many businesses, universities, hospitals and government agencies to carry out sophisticated scientific and business calculations. These computers are expensive (large computers can cost millions of dollars) and may require a sizeable staff of supporting personnel and a special, carefully controlled environment.

Personal computers, on the other hand, are small and inexpensive. In fact, portable, battery-powered "laptop" computers weighing less than 5 or 6 pounds are now widely used by many students and traveling professionals. Personal computers are used extensively in most schools and businesses and they are rapidly becoming common household items. Most students use personal computers when learning to program with C.

Figure 1.1 shows a student using a laptop computer.

Fig. 1.1

1

Despite their small size and low cost, modern personal computers approach minicomputers in computing power. They are now used for many applications that formerly required larger, more expensive computers. Moreover, their performance continues to improve dramatically as their cost continues to drop. The design of a personal computer permits a high level of interaction between the user and the computer. Most applications (e.g., word processors, graphics programs, spreadsheets and database management programs) are specifically designed to take advantage of this feature, thus providing the skilled user with a wide variety of creative tools to write, draw or carry out numerical computations. Applications involving high-resolution graphics are particularly common.

Many organizations connect personal computers to larger computers or to other personal computers, thus permitting their use either as stand-alone devices or as terminals within a computer *network*. Connections over telephone lines are also common. When viewed in this context, we see that personal computers often *complement*, rather than *replace*, the use of larger computers.

1.2 COMPUTER CHARACTERISTICS

All digital computers, regardless of their size, are basically electronic devices that can transmit, store, and manipulate *information* (i.e., *data*). Several different types of data can be processed by a computer. These include *numeric data*, *character data* (names, addresses, etc.), *graphic data* (charts, drawings, photographs, etc.), and *sound* (music, speech patterns, etc.). The two most common types, from the standpoint of a beginning programmer, are numeric data and character data. Scientific and technical applications are concerned primarily with numeric data, whereas business applications usually require processing of both numeric and character data.

To process a particular set of data, the computer must be given an appropriate set of instructions called a *program*. These instructions are entered into the computer and then stored in a portion of the computer's *memory*.

A stored program can be *executed* at any time. This causes the following things to happen.

1. A set of information, called the *input data*, will be entered into the computer (from the keyboard, a floppy disk, etc.) and stored in a portion of the computer's memory.

2. The input data will be processed to produce certain desired results, known as the *output data*.

3. The output data, and perhaps some of the input data, will be printed onto a sheet of paper or displayed on a *monitor* (a television receiver specially designed to display computer output).

This three-step procedure can be repeated many times if desired, thus causing a large quantity of data to be processed in rapid sequence. It should be understood, however, that each of these steps, particularly steps 2 and 3, can be lengthy and complicated.

EXAMPLE 1.1   A computer has been programmed to calculate the area of a circle using the formula $a = \pi r^2$, given a numeric value for the radius r as input data. The following steps are required.

1. Read the numeric value for the radius of the circle.

2. Calculate the value of the area using the above formula. This value will be stored, along with the input data, in the computer's memory.

3. Print (display) the values of the radius and the corresponding area.

4. Stop.

Each of these steps will require one or more instructions in a computer program.

The foregoing discussion illustrates two important characteristics of a digital computer: *memory* and *capability to be programmed*. A third important characteristic is its *speed and reliability*. We will say more about memory, speed and reliability in the next few paragraphs. Programmability will be discussed at length throughout the remainder of this book.

Memory

Every piece of information stored within the computer's memory is encoded as some unique combination of zeros and ones. These zeros and ones are called *bits* (*bi*nary dig*its*). Each bit is represented by an electronic device that is, in some sense, either "off" (zero) or "on" (one).

Small computers have memories that are organized into 8-bit multiples called *bytes*, as illustrated in Fig. 1.2. Notice that the individual bits are numbered, beginning with 0 (for the rightmost bit) and extending to 7 (the leftmost bit). Normally, a single character (e.g., a letter, a single digit or a punctuation symbol) will occupy one byte of memory. An instruction may occupy 1, 2 or 3 bytes. A single numeric quantity may occupy 1 to 8 bytes, depending on its *precision* (i.e., the number of significant figures) and its *type* (integer, floating-point, etc.).

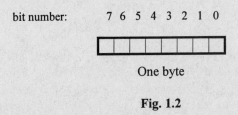

One byte

Fig. 1.2

The size of a computer's memory is usually expressed as some multiple of $2^{10} = 1024$ bytes. This is referred to as 1K. Modern small computers have memories whose sizes typically range from 4 to 16 megabytes, where 1 megabyte (1M) is equivalent to $2^{10} \times 2^{10}$ bytes, or 2^{10} K = 1024K bytes.

EXAMPLE 1.2   The memory of a personal computer has a capacity of 16M bytes. Thus, as many as $16 \times 1024 \times 1024 = 16,777,216$ characters and/or instructions can be stored in the computer's memory. If the entire memory is used to represent character data (which is actually quite unlikely), then over 200,000 names and addresses can be stored within the computer at any one time, assuming 80 characters for each name and address.

If the memory is used to represent numeric data rather than names and addresses, then more than 4 million individual numbers can be stored at any one time, assuming each numeric quantity requires 4 bytes of memory.

Large computers have memories that are organized into *words* rather than bytes. Each word will consist of a relatively large number of bits—typically 32 or 36. The bit-wise organization of a 32-bit word is illustrated in Fig. 1.3. Notice that the bits are numbered, beginning with 0 (for the rightmost bit) and extending to 31 (the leftmost bit).

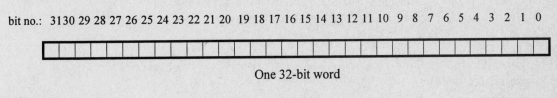

One 32-bit word

Fig. 1.3

Figure 1.4 shows the same 32-bit word organized into 4 consecutive bytes. The bytes are numbered in the same manner as the individual bits, ranging from 0 (for the rightmost byte) to 3 (the leftmost byte).

The use of a 32- or a 36-bit word permits one numeric quantity, or a small *group* of characters (typically 4 or 5), to be represented within a single word of memory. Large computers commonly have several million words (i.e., several megawords) of memory.

bit no.:   31 30 29 28 27 26 25 24 23 22 21 20 19 18 17 16 15 14 13 12 11 10 9   8   7   6   5   4   3   2   1   0

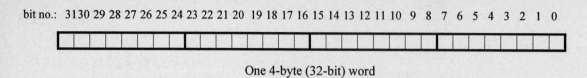

One 4-byte (32-bit) word

Fig. 1.4

EXAMPLE 1.3   The memory of a large computer has a capacity of 32M (32,768K) words, which is equivalent to $32 \times 1024 \times 1024 = 33,554,432$ words. If the entire memory is used to represent numeric data (which is unlikely), then more than 33 million numbers can be stored within the computer at any one time, assuming each numeric quantity requires one word of memory.

If the memory is used to represent characters rather than numeric data, then about 130 million characters can be stored at any one time, based upon 4 characters per word. This is enough memory to store the contents of several large books.

Most computers also employ *auxiliary storage devices* (e.g., magnetic tapes, disks, optical memory devices) in addition to their primary memories. These devices can store more than 1 gigabyte (1G = 1024M bytes) of information. Moreover, they allow information to be recorded permanently, since they can often be physically disconnected from the computer and stored when not in use. However, the access time (i.e., the time required to store or retrieve information) is considerably greater for these auxiliary devices than for the computer's primary memory.

Speed and Reliability

Because of its extremely high speed, a computer can carry out calculations within minutes that might require many days, perhaps even months or years, if carried out by hand. For example, the end-of-semester grades for all students in a large university can typically be processed in just a few minutes on a large computer.

The time required to carry out simple computational tasks, such as adding two numbers, is usually expressed in terms of *microseconds* (1 μsec = 10^{-6} sec) or *nanoseconds* (1 nsec = 10^{-3} μsec = 10^{-9} sec). Thus, if a computer can add two numbers in 10 nanoseconds (typical of a modern medium-speed computer), 100 million (10^8) additions will be carried out in one second.

This very high speed is accompanied by an equally high level of reliability. Thus, computers never make mistakes of their own accord. Highly publicized "computer errors," such as a person's receiving a tax refund of several million dollars, are the result of programming errors or data entry errors rather than errors caused by the computer itself.

1.3 MODES OF OPERATION

There are two different ways that a large computer can be shared by many different users. These are the *batch mode* and the *interactive mode*. Each has its own advantages for certain types of problems.

Batch Processing

In *batch processing*, a number of jobs are entered into the computer, stored internally, and then processed sequentially. (A *job* refers to a computer program and its associated sets of input data.) After the job is processed, the output, along with a listing of the computer program, is printed on multiple sheets of paper by a high-speed printer. Typically, the user will pick up the printed output at some convenient time, after the job has been processed.

In *classical batch processing* (which is now obsolete), the program and the data were recorded on *punched cards*. This information was read into the computer by means of a mechanical card reader and then processed. In the early days of computing, all jobs were processed in this manner.

Modern batch processing is generally tied into a timesharing system (see below). Thus, the program and the data are typed into the computer via a *timesharing terminal* or a personal computer acting as a terminal. The information is then stored within the computer's memory and processed in its proper sequence. This form of batch processing is preferable to classical batch processing, since it eliminates the need for punched cards and allows the input information (program and data) to be edited while it is being entered.

Large quantities of information (both programs and data) can be transmitted into and out of the computer very quickly in batch processing. Furthermore, the user need not be present while the job is being processed. Therefore, this mode of operation is well-suited to jobs that require large amounts of computer time or are physically lengthy. On the other hand, the total time required for a job to be processed in this manner may vary from several minutes to several hours, even though the job may require only a second or two of actual computer time. (Each job must wait its turn before it can be read, processed, and the results displayed.) Thus, batch processing is undesirable when processing small, simple jobs that must be returned as quickly as possible (as, for example, when learning computer programming).

Timesharing

Timesharing allows many different users to use a single computer simultaneously. The host computer may be a mainframe, a minicomputer or a large desktop computer. The various users communicate with the computer through their own individual terminals. In a modern timesharing network, personal computers are often used as timesharing terminals. Since the host computer operates much faster than a human sitting at a terminal, the host computer can support many terminals at the same time. Thus, each user will be unaware of the presence of any other users and will seem to have the host computer at his or her own disposal.

An individual timesharing terminal may be wired directly to the host computer, or it may be connected to the computer over telephone lines, a microwave circuit, or even an earth satellite. Thus, the terminal can be located far—perhaps hundreds of miles—from its host computer. Systems in which personal computers are connected to large mainframes over telephone lines are particularly common. Such systems make use of *modems* (i.e., *mo*dulator/*dem*odulator devices) to convert the digitized computer signals into analog telephone signals and vice versa. Through such an arrangement a person working at home, on his or her own personal computer, can easily access a remote computer at school or at the office.

Timesharing is best suited for processing relatively simple jobs that do not require extensive data transmission or large amounts of computer time. Many applications that arise in schools and commercial offices have these characteristics. Such applications can be processed quickly, easily, and at minimum expense using timesharing.

EXAMPLE 1.4   A major university has a computer timesharing capability consisting of 200 hard-wired timesharing terminals and 80 additional telephone connections. The timesharing terminals are located at various places around the campus and are wired directly to a large mainframe computer. Each terminal is able to transmit information to or from the central computer at a maximum speed of 960 characters per second.

The telephone connections allow students who are not on campus to connect their personal computers to the central computer. Each personal computer can transmit data to or from the central computer at a maximum speed of 240 characters per second. Thus, all 280 terminals and personal computers can interact with the central computer at the same time, though each student will be unaware that others are simultaneously sharing the computer.

Interactive Computing

Interactive computing is a type of computing environment that originated with commercial timesharing systems and has been refined by the widespread use of personal computers. In an interactive computing environment, the user and the computer interact with each other during the computational session. Thus, the user may periodically be asked to provide certain information that will determine what subsequent actions are to be taken by the computer and vice versa.

EXAMPLE 1.5   A student wishes to use a personal computer to calculate the radius of a circle whose area has a value of 100. A program is available that will calculate the area of a circle, given the radius. (Note that this is just the opposite of what the student wishes to do.) This program isn't exactly what is needed, but it does allow the student to obtain an answer by trial and error. The procedure will be to guess a value for the radius and then calculate a corresponding area. This trial-and-error procedure continues until the student has found a value for the radius that yields an area sufficiently close to 100.

Once the program execution begins, the message

```
Radius = ?
```

is displayed. The student then enters a value for the radius. Let us assume that the student enters a value of 5 for the radius. The computer will respond by displaying

```
Area = 78.5398

Do you wish to repeat the calculation?
```

The student then types either yes or no. If the student types yes, the message

```
Radius = ?
```

again appears, and the entire procedure is repeated. If the student types no, the message

```
Goodbye
```

is displayed and the computation is terminated.

Shown below is a printed copy of the information displayed during a typical interactive session using the program described above. In this session, an approximate value of $r = 5.6$ was determined after only three calculations. The information typed by the student is underlined.

```
Radius = ? 5
Area = 78.5398

Do you wish to repeat the calculation? yes

Radius = ? 6
Area = 113.097

Do you wish to repeat the calculation? yes

Radius = ? 5.6
Area = 98.5204

Do you wish to repeat the calculation? no

Goodbye
```

Notice the manner in which the student and the computer appear to be conversing with one another. Also, note that the student waits until he or she sees the calculated value of the area before deciding whether or not to carry out another calculation. If another calculation is initiated, the new value for the radius supplied by the student will depend on the previously calculated results.

Programs designed for interactive computing environments are sometimes said to be *conversational* in nature. Computerized games are excellent examples of such interactive applications. This includes fast-action, graphical arcade games, even though the user's responses may be reflexive rather than numeric or verbal.

1.4 TYPES OF PROGRAMMING LANGUAGES

There are many different languages can be used to program a computer. The most basic of these is *machine language*—a collection of very detailed, cryptic instructions that control the computer's internal circuitry. This is the natural dialect of the computer. Very few computer programs are actually written in machine language, however, for two significant reasons: First, because machine language is very cumbersome to work with and second, because every different type of computer has its own unique instruction set. Thus, a machine-language program written for one type of computer cannot be run on another type of computer without significant alterations.

Usually, a computer program will be written in some *high-level* language, whose instruction set is more compatible with human languages and human thought processes. Most of these are *general-purpose* languages such as C. (Some other popular general-purpose languages are Pascal, Fortran and BASIC.) There are also various *special-purpose* languages that are specifically designed for some particular type of application. Some common examples are CSMP and SIMAN, which are special-purpose *simulation* languages, and LISP, a *list-processing* language that is widely used for artificial intelligence applications.

As a rule, a single instruction in a high-level language will be equivalent to several instructions in machine language. This greatly simplifies the task of writing complete, correct programs. Furthermore, the rules for programming in a particular high-level language are much the same for all computers, so that a program written for one computer can generally be run on many different computers with little or no alteration. Thus, we see that a high-level language offers three significant advantages over machine language: *simplicity, uniformity* and *portability* (i.e., machine independence).

A program that is written in a high-level language must, however, be translated into machine language before it can be executed. This is known as *compilation* or *interpretation*, depending on how it is carried out. (Compilers translate the entire program into machine language before executing any of the instructions. Interpreters, on the other hand, proceed through a program by translating and then executing single instructions or small groups of instructions.) In either case, the translation is carried out automatically within the computer. In fact, inexperienced programmers may not even be aware that this process is taking place, since they typically see only their original high-level program, the input data, and the calculated results. Most implementations of C operate as compilers.

A compiler or interpreter is itself a computer program. It accepts a program written in a high-level language (e.g., C) as input, and generates a corresponding machine-language program as output. The original high-level program is called the *source* program, and the resulting machine-language program is called the *object* program. Every computer must have its own compiler or interpreter for a particular high-level language.

It is generally more convenient to develop a new program using an interpreter rather than a compiler. Once an error-free program has been developed, however, a compiled version will normally execute much faster than an interpreted version. The reasons for this are beyond the scope of our present discussion.

1.5 INTRODUCTION TO C

C is a general-purpose, structured programming language. Its instructions consist of terms that resemble algebraic expressions, augmented by certain English *keywords* such as if, else, for, do and while. In this respect C resembles other high-level structured programming languages such as Pascal and Fortran. C also contains certain additional features, however, that allow it to be used at a lower level, thus bridging the gap between machine language and the more conventional high-level languages. This flexibility allows C to be used for *systems programming* (e.g., for writing operating systems) as well as for *applications programming* (e.g., for writing a program to solve a complicated system of mathematical equations, or for writing a program to bill customers).

C is characterized by the ability to write very concise source programs, due in part to the large number of operators included within the language. It has a relatively small instruction set, though actual implementations include extensive *library functions* which enhance the basic instructions. Furthermore, the language encourages users to write additional library functions of their own. Thus the features and capabilities of the language can easily be extended by the user.

C compilers are commonly available for computers of all sizes, and C interpreters are becoming increasingly common. The compilers are usually compact, and they generate object programs that are small and highly efficient when compared with programs compiled from other high-level languages. The interpreters are less efficient, though they are easier to use when developing a new program. Many programmers begin with an interpreter, and then switch to a compiler once the program has been debugged (i.e., once all of the programming errors have been removed).

Another important characteristic of C is that its programs are highly portable, even more so than with other high-level languages. The reason for this is that C relegates most computer-dependent features to its library functions. Thus, every version of C is accompanied by its own set of library functions, which are written for the particular characteristics of the host computer. These library functions are relatively standardized, however, and each individual library function is generally accessed in the same manner from one version of C to another. Therefore, most C programs can be processed on many different computers with little or no alteration.

History of C

C was originally developed in the 1970s by Dennis Ritchie at Bell Telephone Laboratories, Inc. (now a part of AT&T). It is an outgrowth of two earlier languages, called BCPL and B, which were also developed at Bell Laboratories. C was largely confined to use within Bell Laboratories until 1978, when Brian Kernighan and Ritchie published a definitive description of the language.[*] The Kernighan and Ritchie description is commonly referred to as "K&R C."

Following the publication of the K&R description, computer professionals, impressed with C's many desirable features, began to promote the use of the language. By the mid 1980s, the popularity of C had become widespread. Numerous C compilers and interpreters had been written for computers of all sizes, and many commercial application programs had been developed. Moreover, many commercial software products that were originally written in other languages were rewritten in C in order to take advantage of its efficiency and its portability.

Early commercial implementations of C differed somewhat from Kernighan and Ritchie's original definition, resulting in minor incompatibilities between different implementations of the language. These differences diminished the portability that the language attempted to provide. Consequently, the American National Standards Institute[**] (ANSI committee X3J11) has developed a standardized definition of the C language. Virtually all commercial C compilers and interpreters now adhere to the ANSI standard. Many also provide additional features of their own.

In the early 1980s, another high-level programming language, called C++, was developed by Bjarne Stroustrup[***] at the Bell Laboratories. C++ is built upon C, and hence all standard C features are available within C++. However, C++ is not merely an extension of C. Rather, it incorporates several new fundamental concepts that form a basis for *object-oriented programming*—a new programming paradigm that is of interest to professional programmers. We will not describe C++ in this book, except to mention that a knowledge of C is an excellent starting point for learning C++.

This book describes the features of C that are included in the ANSI standard and are supported by commercial C compilers and interpreters. The reader who has mastered this material should have no difficulty in customizing a C program to any particular implementation of the language.

Structure of a C Program

Every C program consists of one or more modules called *functions*. One of the functions must be called `main`. The program will always begin by executing the `main` function, which may access other functions. Any other function definitions must be defined separately, either ahead of or after `main` (more about this later, in Chaps. 7 and 8).

---

[*] Brian W. Kernighan and Dennis M. Ritchie, *The C Programming Language*, Prentice-Hall, 1978.

[**] ANSI Standard X3.159-1989. American National Standards Institute, 1430 Broadway, New York, NY, 10018. (See also Brian W. Kernighan and Dennis M. Ritchie, *The C Programming Language*, 2d ed., Prentice-Hall, 1988.)

[***] Stroustrup, Bjarne, *The C++ Programming Language*, 2d ed., Addison-Wesley, 1991.

Each function must contain:

1. A function *heading*, which consists of the function name, followed by an optional list of *arguments*, enclosed in parentheses.

2. A list of argument *declarations*, if arguments are included in the heading.

3. A *compound statement*, which comprises the remainder of the function.

The arguments are symbols that represent information being passed between the function and other parts of the program. (Arguments are also referred to as *parameters*.)

Each compound statement is enclosed within a pair of braces, i.e., { }. The braces may contain one or more elementary statements (called *expression statements*) and other compound statements. Thus compound statements may be nested, one within another. Each expression statement must end with a semicolon (;).

Comments (remarks) may appear anywhere within a program, as long as they are placed within the delimiters /* and */ (e.g., /* this is a comment */). Such comments are helpful in identifying the program's principal features or in explaining the underlying logic of various program features.

These program components will be discussed in much greater detail later in this book. For now, the reader should be concerned only with an overview of the basic features that characterize most C programs.

EXAMPLE 1.6 Area of a Circle   Here is an elementary C program that reads in the radius of a circle, calculates its area and then writes the calculated result.

```
/* program to calculate the area of a circle */      /* TITLE (COMMENT) */

#include <stdio.h>                                    /* LIBRARY FILE ACCESS */

main()                                                /* FUNCTION HEADING */

{
    float radius, area;                               /* VARIABLE DECLARATIONS */

    printf("Radius = ? ");                            /* OUTPUT STATEMENT (PROMPT) */
    scanf("%f", &radius);                             /* INPUT STATEMENT */
    area = 3.14159 * radius * radius;                 /* ASSIGNMENT STATEMENT */
    printf("Area = %f", area);                        /* OUTPUT STATEMENT */
}
```

The comments at the end of each line have been added in order to emphasize the overall program organization. Normally a C program will not look like this. Rather, it might appear as shown below.

```
/* program to calculate the area of a circle */

#include <stdio.h>

main()

{
    float radius, area;

    printf("Radius = ? ");
    scanf("%f", &radius);
    area = 3.14159 * radius * radius;
    printf("Area = %f", area);
}
```

The following features should be pointed out in this last program.

1. The program is typed in lowercase. Either upper- or lowercase can be used, though it is customary to type ordinary instructions in lowercase. Most comments are also typed in lowercase, though comments are sometimes typed in uppercase for emphasis, or to distinguish certain comments from the instructions.

(Uppercase and lowercase characters are not equivalent in C. Later in this book we will see some special situations that are characteristically typed in uppercase.)

2. The first line is a comment that identifies the purpose of the program.

3. The second line contains a reference to a special file (called `stdio.h`) which contains information that must be included in the program when it is compiled. The inclusion of this required information will be handled automatically by the compiler.

4. The third line is a heading for the function `main`. The empty parentheses following the name of the function indicate that this function does not include any arguments.

5. The remaining five lines of the program are indented and enclosed within a pair of braces. These five lines comprise the compound statement within `main`.

6. The first indented line is a *variable declaration*. It establishes the symbolic names `radius` and `area` as *floating-point variables* (more about this in the next chapter).

7. The remaining four indented lines are expression statements. The second indented line (`printf`) generates a request for information (namely, a value for the radius). This value is entered into the computer via the third indented line (`scanf`).

8. The fourth indented line is a particular type of expression statement called an *assignment statement*. This statement causes the area to be calculated from the given value of the radius. Within this statement the asterisks (*) represent multiplication signs.

9. The last indented line (`printf`) causes the calculated value for the area to be displayed. The numerical value will be preceded by a brief label.

10. Notice that each expression statement within the compound statement ends with a semicolon. This is required of all expression statements.

11. Finally, notice the liberal use of spacing and indentation, creating *whitespace* within the program. The blank lines separate different parts of the program into logically identifiable components, and the indentation indicates subordinate relationships among the various instructions. These features are not grammatically essential, but their presence is strongly encouraged as a matter of good programming practice.

Execution of the program results in an interactive dialog such as that shown below. The user's response is underlined, for clarity.

```
Radius = ? 3
Area = 28.274309
```

1.6 SOME SIMPLE C PROGRAMS

In this section we present several C programs that illustrate some commonly used features of the language. All of the programs are extensions of Example 1.6; that is, each program calculates the area of a circle, or the areas of several circles. Each program illustrates a somewhat different approach to this problem.

The reader should not attempt to understand the syntactic details of these examples, though experienced programmers will recognize features similar to those found in other programming languages. Beginners should focus their attention only on the overall program logic. The details will be provided later in this book.

EXAMPLE 1.7 Area of a Circle   Here is a variation of the program given in Example 1.6 for calculating the area of a circle.

```
/* program to calculate the area of a circle */

#include <stdio.h>

#define PI 3.14159

float process(float radius);          /* function prototype */
```

```
main()

{
    float radius, area;              /* variable declaration */

    printf("Radius = ? ");
    scanf("%f", &radius);
    area = process(radius);
    printf("Area = %f", area);
}

float process(float r)               /* function definition */

{
    float a;                         /* local variable declaration */

    a = PI * r * r;
    return(a);
}
```

This version utilizes a separate programmer-defined function, called process, to carry out the actual calculations (i.e., to process the data). Within this function, r is an argument (also called a *parameter*) that represents the value of the radius supplied to process from main, and a is the calculated result that is returned to main. A reference to the function appears in main, within the statement

```
    area = process(radius);
```

The main function is preceded by a *function declaration*, which indicates that process accepts a floating-point argument and returns a floating-point value. The use of functions will be discussed in detail in Chap. 7.

This program also contains a *symbolic constant*, PI, that represents the numerical value 3.14159. This is a form of shorthand that exists for the programmer's convenience. When the program is actually compiled, the symbolic constant will automatically be replaced by its equivalent numerical value.

When this program is executed, it behaves in the same manner as the program shown in Example 1.6.

EXAMPLE 1.8 Area of a Circle with Error Checking   Here is a variation of the program given in Example 1.7.

```
    /* program to calculate the area of a circle, with error checking */

    #include <stdio.h>

    #define PI 3.14159

    float process(float radius);        /* function prototype */


    main()

    {
        float radius, area;              /* variable declaration */

        printf("Radius = ? ");
        scanf("%f", &radius);

        if (radius < 0)
           area = 0;
        else
           area = process(radius);

        printf("Area = %f", area);
    }
```

```
float process(float r)        /* function definition */
{
    float a;                  /* local variable declaration */

    a = PI * r * r;
    return(a);
}
```

This program again calculates the area of a circle. It includes the function process, and the symbolic constant PI, as discussed in the previous example. Now, however, we have added a simple error correction routine, which tests to see if the value of the radius is less than zero. (Mathematically, a negative value for the radius does not make any sense.) The test is carried out within main, using an if - else statement (see Sec. 6.6). Thus, if radius has a negative value, a value of zero is assigned to area; otherwise, the value for area is calculated within process, as before.

EXAMPLE 1.9 Areas of Several Circles The following program expands the previous sample programs by calculating the areas of several circles.

```
/* program to calculate the areas of circles, using a for loop */
#include <stdio.h>
#define PI 3.14159

float process(float radius);         /* function prototype */

main()
{
    float radius, area;              /* variable declaration */
    int count, n;                    /* variable declaration */

    printf("How many circles? ");
    scanf("%d", &n);

    for (count = 1; count <= n; ++count)   {
        printf("\nCircle no. %d:   Radius = ? ", count);
        scanf("%f", &radius);

        if (radius < 0)
            area = 0;
        else
            area = process(radius);

        printf("Area = %f\n", area);
    }
}

float process(float r)        /* function definition */
{
    float a;                  /* local variable declaration */

    a = PI * r * r;
    return(a);
}
```

In this case the total number of circles, represented by the integer variable n, must be entered into the computer before any calculation is carried out. The for statement is then used to calculate the areas repeatedly, for all n circles (see Sec. 6.4).

Note the use of the variable count, which is used as a counter within the for loop (i.e., within the repeated portion of the program). The value of count will increase by 1 during each pass through the loop. Also, notice the expression ++count which appears in the for statement. This is a shorthand notation for increasing the value of the counter by 1; i.e., it is equivalent to count = count + 1 (see Sec. 3.2).

When the program is executed, it generates an interactive dialog, such as that shown below. The user's responses are again underlined.

```
How many circles? 3

Circle no. 1:    Radius = ? 3
Area = 28.274309

Circle no. 2:    Radius = ? 4
Area = 50.265442

Circle no. 3:    Radius = ? 5
Area = 78.539749
```

EXAMPLE 1.10 Areas of an Unspecified Number of Circles   The previous program can be improved by processing an unspecified number of circles, where the calculations continue until a value of zero is entered for the radius. This avoids the need to count, and then specify, the number of circles in advance. This feature is especially helpful when there are many sets of data to be processed.

Here is the complete program.

```c
/* program to calculate the areas of circles, using a for loop;
   the number of circles is unspecified */

#include <stdio.h>

#define PI 3.14159

float process(float radius);          /* function prototype */


main()

{
    float radius, area;               /* variable declaration */
    int count;                        /* variable declaration */

    printf("To STOP, enter 0 for the radius\n");
    printf("\nRadius = ? ");
    scanf("%f", &radius);

    for (count = 1; radius != 0; ++count)    {

        if (radius < 0)
           area = 0;
        else
           area = process(radius);

        printf("Area = %f\n", area);

        printf("\nRadius = ? ");
        scanf("%f", &radius);

    }

}
```

```
float process(float r)          /* function definition */

{
    float a;                    /* local variable declaration */

    a = PI * r * r;
    return(a);
}
```

Notice that this program will display a message at the beginning of the program execution, telling the user how to end the computation.

The dialog resulting from a typical execution of this program is shown below. Once again, the user's responses are underlined.

```
To STOP, enter 0 for the radius

Radius = ? 3
Area = 28.274309

Radius = ? 4
Area = 50.265442

Radius = ? 5
Area = 78.539749

Radius = ? 0
```

EXAMPLE 1.11 Areas of an Unspecified Number of Circles Here is a variation of the program shown in the previous example.

```
/* program to calculate the areas of circles, using a while loop;
   number of circles is unspecified */

#include <stdio.h>

#define PI 3.14159

float process(float radius);        /* function declaration */

main()

{
    float radius, area;              /* variable declaration */

    printf("To STOP, enter 0 for the radius\n");
    printf("\nRadius = ? ");
    scanf("%f", &radius);

    while (radius != 0)   {

        if (radius < 0)
            area = 0;
        else
            area = process(radius);

        printf("Area = %f\n", area);

        printf("\nRadius = ? ");
        scanf("%f", &radius);
    }
}
```

```
float process(float r)          /* function definition */

{
    float a;                    /* local variable declaration */

    a = PI * r * r;
    return(a);
}
```

This program includes the same features as the program shown in the previous example. Now, however, we use a `while` statement rather than a `for` statement to carry out the repeated program execution (see Sec. 6.2). The `while` statement will continue to execute as long as the value assigned to `radius` is not zero.

In more general terms, the `while` statement will continue to execute as long as the expression contained within the parentheses is considered to be *true*. Therefore, the first line of the `while` statment can be written more briefly as

```
while (radius)    {
```

rather than

```
while (radius != 0)    {
```

because any nonzero value for `radius` will be interpreted as a *true* condition.

Some problems are better suited to the use of the `for` statement, while others are better suited to the use of `while`. The `while` statement is somewhat simpler in this particular application. There is also a third type of looping statement, called do - while, which is similar to the `while` statement shown above. (More about this in Chap. 6).

When this program is executed, it generates an interactive dialog that is identical to that shown in Example 1.10.

EXAMPLE 1.12 Calculating and Storing the Areas of Several Circles   Some problems require that a series of calculated results be stored within the computer, perhaps for recall in a later calculation. The corresponding input data may also be stored internally, along with the calculated results. This can be accomplished through the use of *arrays*.

The following program utilizes two arrays, called `radius` and `area`, to store the radius and the area for as many as 100 different circles. Each array can be thought of as a list of numbers. The individual numbers within each list are referred to as *array elements*. The array elements are numbered, beginning with 0. Thus, the radius of the first circle will be stored within the array element `radius[0]`, the radius of the second circle will be stored within `radius[1]`, and so on. Similarly, the corresponding areas will be stored in `area[0]`, `area[1]`, etc.

Here is the complete program.

```
/* program to calculate the areas of circles, using a while loop;
   the results are stored in an array; the number of circles is unspecified */

#include <stdio.h>

#define PI 3.14159

float process(float radius);           /* function prototype */

main()

{
    int n, i = 0;                      /* variable declaration */
    float radius[100], area[100];      /* array declaration    */

    printf("To STOP, enter 0 for the radius\n\n");
    printf("Radius = ? ");
    scanf("%f", &radius[i]);
```

```
        while (radius[i])   {

            if (radius[i] < 0)
                area[i] = 0;
            else
                area[i] = process(radius[i]);

            printf("Radius = ? ");
            scanf("%f", &radius[++i]);
        }

        n = --i;          /* tag the highest value of i */

        /* display the array elements */
        printf("\nSummary of Results\n\n");
        for (i = 0; i <= n; ++i)
            printf("Radius = %f   Area = %f\n", radius[i], area[i]);
    }


    float process(float r)      /* function definition */

    {
        float a;              /* local variable declaration */

        a = PI * r * r;
        return(a);
    }
```

An unspecified number of radii will be entered into the computer, as before. As each value for the radius is entered (i.e., as the ith value is entered), it is stored within radius[i]. Its corresponding area is then calculated and stored within area[i]. This process will continue until all of the radii have been entered, i.e., until a value of zero is entered for a radius. The entire set of stored values (i.e., the array elements whose values are nonzero) will then be displayed.

Notice the expression ++i, which appears twice within the program. Each of these expressions causes the value of i to increase by 1; i.e., they are equivalent to i = i + 1. Similarly, the statement

```
    n = --i;
```

causes the current value of i to be decreased by 1 and the new value assigned to n. In other words, the statement is equivalent to

```
    n = i - 1;
```

Expressions such as ++i and --i are discussed in detail in Chap. 3 (see Sec. 3.2).

When the program is executed it results in an interactive dialog, such as that shown below. The user's responses are once again underlined.

```
        To STOP, enter 0 for the radius

        Radius = ? 3
        Radius = ? 4
        Radius = ? 5
        Radius = ? 0

        Summary of Results

        Radius = 3.000000   Area = 28.274309
        Radius = 4.000000   Area = 50.265442
        Radius = 5.000000   Area = 78.539749
```

This simple program does not make any use of the values that have been stored within the arrays. Its only purpose is to demonstrate the mechanics of utilizing arrays. In a more complex example, we might want to determine an average value for the areas, and then compare each individual area with the average. To do this we would have to recall the individual areas (i.e., the individual array elements area[0], area[1], . . ., etc.).

The use of arrays is discussed briefly in Chap. 2, and extensively in Chap. 9.

EXAMPLE 1.13 Calculating and Storing the Areas of Several Circles   Here is a more sophisticated approach to the problem described in the previous example.

```c
/* program to calculate the areas of circles, using a while loop;
   the results are stored in an array of structures;
   the number of circles is unspecified;
   a string is entered to identify each data set */

#include <stdio.h>

#define PI 3.14159

float process(float radius);        /* function prototype */

main()

{
    int n, i = 0;                     /* variable declaration */

    struct   {
                char text[20];
                float radius;
                float area;
    } circle[10];                     /* structure variable declaration */

    printf("To STOP, enter END for the identifier\n");
    printf("\nIdentifier: ");
    scanf("%s", circle[i].text);
    while (circle[i].text[0] != 'E' || circle[i].text[1] != 'N'
                                    || circle[i].text[2] != 'D')   {
            printf("Radius: ");
            scanf("%f", &circle[i].radius);

            if (circle[i].radius < 0)
                circle[i].area = 0;
            else
                circle[i].area = process(circle[i].radius);

            ++i;
            printf("\nIdentifier: ");          /* next set of data */
            scanf("%s", circle[i].text);
    }

    n = --i;        /* tag the highest value of i */

    /* display the array elements */
    printf("\n\nSummary of Results\n\n");
    for (i = 0; i <= n; ++i)
        printf("%s   Radius = %f   Area = %f\n", circle[i].text,
                                            circle[i].radius,
                                            circle[i].area);

}
```

```
float process(float r)        /* function definition */

{

    float a;                  /* local variable declaration */

    a = PI * r * r;
    return(a);

}
```

In this program we enter a one-word *descriptor*, followed by a value of the radius, for each circle. The characters that comprise the descriptor are stored in an array called `text`. Collectively, these characters are referred to as a *string constant* (see Sec. 2.4). In this program, the maximum size of each string constant is 20 characters.

The descriptor, the radius and the corresponding area of each circle are defined as the components of a *structure* (see Chap. 11). We then define `circle` as an array of structures. That is, each element of `circle` will be a structure containing the descriptor, the radius and the area. For example, `circle[0].text` refers to the descriptor for the first circle, `circle[0].radius` refers to the radius of the first circle, and `circle[0].area` refers to the area of the first circle. (Remember that the numbering system for array elements begins with 0, not 1.)

When the program is executed, a descriptor is entered for each circle, followed by a value of the radius. This information is stored within `circle[i].text` and `circle[i].radius`. The corresponding area is then calculated and stored in `circle[i].area`. This procedure continues until the descriptor END is entered. All of the information stored within the array elements (i.e., the descriptor, the radius and the area for each circle) will then be displayed, and the execution will stop.

Execution of this program results in an interactive dialog, such as that shown below. Note that the user's responses are once again underlined.

```
To STOP, enter END for the identifier

Identifier: RED
Radius: 3

Identifier: WHITE
Radius: 4

Identifier: BLUE
Radius: 5

Identifier: END


Summary of Results

RED    Radius = 3.000000    Area = 28.274309
WHITE    Radius = 4.000000    Area = 50.265442
BLUE    Radius = 5.000000    Area = 78.539749
```

1.7 DESIRABLE PROGRAM CHARACTERISTICS

Before concluding this chapter let us briefly examine some important characteristics of well-written computer programs. These characteristics apply to programs that are written in *any* programming language, not just C. They can provide us with a useful set of guidelines later in this book, when we start writing our own C programs.

1. *Integrity*. This refers to the accuracy of the calculations. It should be clear that all other program enhancements will be meaningless if the calculations are not carried out correctly. Thus, the integrity of the calculations is an absolute necessity in any computer program.

2. *Clarity* refers to the overall readability of the program, with particular emphasis on its underlying logic. If a program is clearly written, it should be possible for another programmer to follow the program logic without undue effort. It should also be possible for the original author to follow his or her own program after being away from the program for an extended period of time. One of the objectives in the design of C is the development of clear, readable programs through an orderly and disciplined approach to programming.

3. *Simplicity.* The clarity and accuracy of a program are usually enhanced by keeping things as simple as possible, consistent with the overall program objectives. In fact, it may be desirable to sacrifice a certain amount of computational efficiency in order to maintain a relatively simple, straightforward program structure.

4. *Efficiency* is concerned with execution speed and efficient memory utilization. These are generally important goals, though they should not be obtained at the expense of clarity or simplicity. Many complex programs require a tradeoff between these characteristics. In such situations, experience and common sense are key factors.

5. *Modularity.* Many programs can be broken down into a series of identifiable subtasks. It is good programming practice to implement each of these subtasks as a separate program module. In C, such modules are written as functions. The use of a modular programming structure enhances the accuracy and clarity of a program, and it facilitates future program alterations.

6. *Generality.* Usually we will want a program to be as general as possible, within reasonable limits. For example, we may design a program to read in the values of certain key parameters rather than placing fixed values into the program. As a rule, a considerable amount of generality can be obtained with very little additional programming effort.

Review Questions

1.1   What is a mainframe computer? Where can mainframes be found? What are they generally used for?

1.2   What is a personal computer? How do personal computers differ from mainframes?

1.3   What is a supercomputer? A minicomputer? A workstation? How do these computers differ from one another? How do they differ from mainframes and personal computers?

1.4   Name four different types of data.

1.5   What is meant by a computer program? What, in general, happens when a computer program is executed?

1.6   What is computer memory? What kinds of information are stored in a computer's memory?

1.7   What is a bit? What is a byte? What is the difference between a byte and a word of memory?

1.8   What terms are used to describe the size of a computer's memory? What are some typical memory sizes?

1.9   Name some typical auxiliary memory devices. How does this type of memory differ from the computer's main memory?

1.10 What time units are used to express the speed with which elementary tasks are carried out by a computer?

1.11 What is the difference between batch processing and timesharing? What are the relative advantages and disadvantages of each?

1.12 What is meant by interactive computing? For what types of applications is interactive computing best suited?

1.13 What is machine language? How does machine language differ from high-level languages?

1.14 Name some commonly used high-level languages. What are the advantages of using high-level languages?

1.15 What is meant by compilation? What is meant by interpretation? How do these two processes differ?

1.16 What is a source program? An object program? Why are these concepts important?

1.17 What are the general characteristics of C?

1.18   Where was C originally developed and by whom? What has been done to standardize the language?

1.19   What is C++? What is the relationship between C and C++?

1.20   What are the major components of a C program? What significance is attached to the name `main`?

1.21   Describe the composition of a function in C.

1.22   What are arguments? Where do arguments appear within a C program? What other term is sometimes used for an argument?

1.23   What is a compound statement? How is a compound statement written?

1.24   What is an expression statement? Can an expression statement be included in a compound statement? Can a compound statement be included in an expression statement?

1.25   How can comments (remarks) be included within a C program? Where can comments be placed?

1.26   Are C programs required to be typed in lowercase? Is uppercase ever used in a C program? Explain.

1.27   What is an assignment statement? What is the relationship between an assignment statement and an expression statement?

1.28   What item of punctuation is used at the end of most C statements? Do all statements end this way?

1.29   Why are some of the statements within a C program indented? Why are empty lines included within a typical C program?

1.30   Summarize the meaning of each of the following program characteristics: integrity, clarity, simplicity, efficiency, modularity and generality. Why is each of these characteristics important?

Problems

1.31   Determine, as best you can, the purpose of each of the following C programs. Identify all variables within each program. Identify all input and output statements, all assignment statements, and any other special features that you recognize.

(*a*) `main()`

```
    {
        printf("Welcome to the Wonderful World of Computing!\n");
    }
```

(*b*) `#define MESSAGE "Welcome to the Wonderful World of Computing!\n"`

```
    main()

    {
        printf(MESSAGE);
    }
```

(*c*) `main()`

```
    {
        float base, height, area;

        printf("Base: ");
        scanf("%f", &base);
        printf("Height: ");
        scanf("%f", &height);
        area = (base * height) / 2.;
        printf("Area: %f", area);
    }
```

(*d*)
```
main()
{
    float gross, tax, net;

    printf("Gross salary: ");
    scanf("%f", &gross);
    tax = 0.14 * gross;
    net = gross - tax;
    printf("Taxes withheld: %.2f\n", tax);
    printf("Net salary: %.2f", net);
}
```

(*e*)
```
int smaller(int a, int b);

main()
{
    int a, b, min;

    printf("Please enter the first number: ");
    scanf("%d", &a);
    printf("Please enter the second number: ");
    scanf("%d", &b);

    min = smaller(a, b);

    printf("\nThe smaller number is: %d", min);
}

int smaller(int a, int b)
{
    if (a <= b)
        return(a);
    else
        return(b);
}
```

(*f*)
```
int smaller(int a, int b);

main()
{
    int count, n, a, b, min;

    printf("How many pairs of numbers? ");
    scanf("%d", &n);

    for (count = 1; count <= n; ++count)    {
        printf("\nPlease enter the first number: ");
        scanf("%d", &a);
        printf("Please enter the second number: ");
        scanf("%d", &b);

        min = smaller(a, b);

        printf("\nThe smaller number is: %d\n", min);
    }
}
```

```
    int smaller(int a, int b)

    {
        if (a <= b)
            return(a);
        else
            return(b);
    }
```

(g)   int smaller(int a, int b);

```
    main()

    {
        int a, b, min;

        printf("To STOP, enter 0 for each number\n");

        printf("\nPlease enter the first number: ");
        scanf("%d", &a);
        printf("Please enter the second number: ");
        scanf("%d", &b);

        while (a != 0 || b != 0)    {

            min = smaller(a, b);
            printf("\nThe smaller number is: %d\n", min);

            printf("\nPlease enter the first number: ");
            scanf("%d", &a);
            printf("Please enter the second number: ");
            scanf("%d", &b);

        }
    }

    int smaller(int a, int b)

    {
        if (a <= b)
            return(a);
        else
            return(b);
    }
```

(h)   int smaller(int, int);

```
    main()

    {
        int n, i = 0;
        int a[100], b[100], min[100];

        printf("To STOP, enter 0 for each number\n");

        printf("\nPlease enter the first number: ");
        scanf("%d", &a[i]);
        printf("Please enter the second number: ");
        scanf("%d", &b[i]);
```

```
            while (a[i] || b[i])   {

                min[i] = smaller(a[i], b[i]);

                printf("\nPlease enter the first number: ");
                scanf("%d", &a[++i]);
                printf("Please enter the second number: ");
                scanf("%d", &b[i]);

            }

            n = --i;

            printf("\nSummary of Results\n\n");
            for (i = 0; i <= n; ++i)
                printf("a = %d   b = %d   min = %d\n", a[i], b[i], min[i]);
        }

    int smaller(int a, int b)

    {
        if (a <= b)
            return(a);
        else
            return(b);
    }
```

Chapter 2

C Fundamentals

This chapter is concerned with the basic elements used to construct simple C statements. These elements include the C character set, identifiers and keywords, data types, constants, variables and arrays, declarations, expressions and statements. We will see how these basic elements can be combined to form more comprehensive program components.

Some of this material is rather detailed and therefore somewhat difficult to absorb, particularly by an inexperienced programmer. Remember, however, that the purpose of this material is to introduce certain basic concepts and to provide some necessary definitions for the topics that follow in the next few chapters. Therefore, when reading this material for the first time, you need only acquire a general familiarity with the individual topics. A more comprehensive understanding will come later, from repeated references to this material in subsequent chapters.

2.1 THE C CHARACTER SET

C uses the uppercase letters A to Z, the lowercase letters a to z, the digits 0 to 9, and certain special characters as building blocks to form basic program elements (e.g., constants, variables, operators, expressions, etc.). The special characters are listed below.

+	–	*	/	=	%	&	#
!	?	^	"	'	~	\	|
<	>	(	)	[	]	{	}
:	;	.	,	_	(blank space)		

Most versions of the language also allow certain other characters, such as @ and $, to be included within strings and comments.

C uses certain combinations of these characters, such as \b, \n and \t, to represent special conditions such as backspace, newline and horizontal tab, respectively. These character combinations are known as *escape sequences*. We will discuss escape sequences in Sec. 2.4. For now we simply mention that each escape sequence represents a single character, even though it is written as two or more characters.

2.2 IDENTIFIERS AND KEYWORDS

Identifiers are names that are given to various program elements, such as variables, functions and arrays. Identifiers consist of letters and digits, in any order, except that *the first character must be a letter*. Both upper- and lowercase letters are permitted, though common usage favors the use of lowercase letters for most types of identifiers. Upper- and lowercase letters are not interchangeable (i.e., an uppercase letter is *not* equivalent to the corresponding lowercase letter.) The underscore character (_) can also be included, and is considered to be a letter. An underscore is often used in the middle of an identifier. An identifier may also begin with an underscore, though this is rarely done in practice.

EXAMPLE 2.1 The following names are valid identifiers.

```
x              y12          sum_1          _temperature
names          area         tax_rate       TABLE
```

24

The following names are *not* valid identifiers for the reasons stated.

`4th`	The first character must be a letter.
`"x"`	Illegal characters (`"`).
`order-no`	Illegal character (–).
`error flag`	Illegal character (blank space).

An identifier can be arbitrarily long. Some implementations of C recognize only the first eight characters, though most implementations recognize more (typically, 31 characters). Additional characters are carried along for the programmer's convenience.

EXAMPLE 2.2   The identifiers `file_manager` and `file_management` are both grammatically valid. Some compilers may be unable to distinguish between them, however, because the first eight letters are the same for each identifier. Therefore, only one of these identifiers should be used in a single C program.

As a rule, an identifier should contain enough characters so that its meaning is readily apparent. On the other hand, an excessive number of characters should be avoided.

EXAMPLE 2.3   A C program is being written to calculate the future value of an investment. The identifiers `value` or `future_value` are appropriate symbolic names. However, `v` or `fv` would probably be too brief, since the intended representation of these identifiers is not clear. On the other hand, the identifier `future_value_of_an_investment` would be unsatisfactory because it is too long and cumbersome.

There are certain reserved words, called *keywords*, that have standard, predefined meanings in C. These keywords can be used only for their intended purpose; they cannot be used as programmer-defined identifiers.
The standard keywords are

`auto`	`extern`	`sizeof`
`break`	`floatn`	`static`
`case`	`for`	`struct`
`char`	`goto`	`switch`
`const`	`if`	`typedef`
`continue`	`int`	`union`
`default`	`long`	`unsigned`
`do`	`register`	`void`
`double`	`return`	`volatile`
`else`	`short`	`while`
`enum`	`signed`	

Some compilers may also include some or all of the following keywords.

`ada`	`far`	`near`
`asm`	`fortran`	`pascal`
`entry`	`huge`	

Some C compilers may recognize other keywords. Consult a reference manual to obtain a complete list of keywords for your particular compiler.
Note that the keywords are all lowercase. Since uppercase and lowercase characters are not equivalent, it is possible to utilize an uppercase keyword as an identifier. Normally, however, this is not done, as it is considered a poor programming practice.

2.3 DATA TYPES

C supports several different types of data, each of which may be represented differently within the computer's memory. The basic data types are listed below. Typical memory requirements are also given. (The memory requirements for each data type will determine the permissible range of values for that data type. Note that the memory requirements for each data type may vary from one C compiler to another.)

Data Type	Description	Typical Memory Requirements
int	integer quantity	2 bytes or one word (varies from one compiler to another)
char	single character	1 byte
float	floating-point number (i.e., a number containing a decimal point and/or an exponent)	1 word (4 bytes)
double	double-precision floating-point number (i.e., more significant figures, and an exponent which may be larger in magnitude)	2 words (8 bytes)

C compilers written for personal computers or small minicomputers (i.e., computers whose natural word size is less than 32 bits) generally represent a word as 4 bytes (32 bits).

The basic data types can be augmented by the use of the data type *qualifiers* short, long, signed and unsigned. For example, integer quantities can be defined as short int, long int or unsigned int (these data types are usually written simply as short, long or unsigned, and are understood to be integers). The interpretation of a qualified integer data type will vary from one C compiler to another, though there are some commonsense relationships. Thus, a short int may require less memory than an ordinary int or it may require the same amount of memory as an ordinary int, but it will never exceed an ordinary int in word length. Similarly, a long int may require the same amount of memory as an ordinary int or it may require more memory, but it will never be less than an ordinary int.

If short int and int both have the same memory requirements (e.g., 2 bytes), then long int will generally have double the requirements (e.g., 4 bytes). Or if int and long int both have the same memory requiremements (e.g., 4 bytes) then short int will generally have half the memory requirements (e.g., 2 bytes). Remember that the specifics will vary from one C compiler to another.

An unsigned int has the same memory requirements as an ordinary int. However, in the case of an ordinary int (or a short int or a long int), the leftmost bit is reserved for the sign. With an unsigned int, all of the bits are used to represent the numerical value. Thus, an unsigned int can be approximately twice as large as an ordinary int (though, of course, negative values are not permitted). For example, if an ordinary int can vary from −32,768 to +32,767 (which is typical for a 2-byte int), then an unsigned int will be allowed to vary from 0 to 65,535. The unsigned qualifier can also be applied to other qualified ints, e.g., unsigned short int or unsigned long int.

The char type is used to represent individual characters. Hence, the char type will generally require only one byte of memory. Each char type has an equivalent integer interpretation, however, so that a char is a really a special kind of short integer (see Sec. 2.4). With most compilers, a char data type will permit a range of values extending from 0 to 255. Some compilers represent the char data type as having a range of values extending from −128 to +127. There may also be unsigned char data (with typical values ranging from 0 to 255), or signed char data (with values ranging from −128 to +127).

Some compilers permit the qualifier long to be applied to float or to double, e.g., long float, or long double. However, the meaning of these data types will vary from one C compiler to another. Thus, long float may be equivalent to double. Moreover, long double may be equivalent to double, or it may refer to a separate, "extra-large" double-precision data type requiring more than two words of memory.

Two additional data types, void and enum, will be introduced later in this book (void is discussed in Sec. 7.2; enum is discussed in Sec. 14.1).

Every identifier that represents a number or a character within a C program must be associated with one of the basic data types before the identifier appears in an executable statement. This is accomplished via a *type declaration*, as described in Sec. 2.6.

2.4 CONSTANTS

There are four basic types of constants in C. They are *integer constants*, *floating-point constants*, *character constants* and *string constants* (there are also *enumeration constants*, which are discussed in Sec. 14.1). Moreover, there are several different kinds of integer and floating-point constants, as discussed below.

Integer and floating-point constants represent numbers. They are often referred to collectively as *numeric-type* constants. The following rules apply to all numeric-type constants.

1. Commas and blank spaces cannot be included within the constant.

2. The constant can be preceded by a minus (–) sign if desired. (Actually the minus sign is an *operator* that changes the sign of a positive constant, though it can be thought of as a part of the constant itself.)

3. The value of a constant cannot exceed specified minimum and maximum bounds. For each type of constant, these bounds will vary from one C compiler to another.

Let us consider each type of constant individually.

Integer Constants

An *integer constant* is an integer-valued number. Thus it consists of a sequence of digits. Integer constants can be written in three different number systems: decimal (base 10), octal (base 8) and hexadecimal (base 16). Beginning programmers rarely, however, use anything other than decimal integer constants.

A *decimal* integer constant can consist of any combination of digits taken from the set 0 through 9. If the constant contains two or more digits, the first digit must be something other than 0.

EXAMPLE 2.4   Several valid decimal integer constants are shown below.

    0   1   743   5280   32767   9999

The following decimal integer constants are written incorrectly for the reasons stated.

    12,245   illegal character (,).
    36.0   illegal character (.).
    10 20 30   illegal character (blank space).
    123-45-6789   illegal character (-).
    0900   the first digit cannot be a zero.

An *octal* integer constant can consist of any combination of digits taken from the set 0 through 7. However the first digit must be 0, in order to identify the constant as an octal number.

EXAMPLE 2.5   Several valid octal integer constants are shown below.

    0   01   0743   077777

The following octal integer constants are written incorrectly for the reasons stated.

    743   Does not begin with 0.
    05280   Illegal digit (8).
    0777.777   Illegal character (.).

A *hexadecimal* integer constant must begin with either Ox or OX. It can then be followed by any combination of digits taken from the sets 0 through 9 and a through f (either upper- or lowercase). Note that the letters a through f (or A through F) represent the (decimal) quantities 10 through 15, respectively.

EXAMPLE 2.6   Several valid hexadecimal integer constants are shown below.

        Ox   OX1   OX7FFF   Oxabcd

The following hexadecimal integer constants are written incorrectly for the reasons stated.

OX12.34	Illegal character (.).
OBE38	Does not begin with Ox or OX.
Ox.4bff	Illegal character (.).
OXDEFG	Illegal character (G).

The magnitude of an integer constant can range from zero to some maximum value that varies from one computer to another (and from one compiler to another, on the same computer). A typical maximum value for most personal computers and many minicomputers is 32767 decimal (equivalent to 77777 octal or 7fff hexadecimal), which is $2^{15} - 1$. Mainframe computers generally permit larger values, such as 2,147,483,647 (which is $2^{31} - 1$).[*] You should determine the appropriate value for the version of C used with your particular computer.

Unsigned and Long Integer Constants

Unsigned integer constants may exceed the magnitude of ordinary integer constants by approximately a factor of 2, though they may not be negative.[*] An unsigned integer constant can be identified by appending the letter U (either upper- or lowercase) to the end of the constant.

Long integer constants may exceed the magnitude of ordinary integer constants, but require more memory within the computer. With some computers (and/or some compilers), a long integer constant will automatically be generated simply by specifying a quantity that exceeds the normal maximum value. It is *always* possible, however, to create a long integer constant by appending the letter L (either upper- or lowercase) to the end of the constant.

An unsigned long integer may be specified by appending the letters UL to the end of the constant. The letters may be written in either upper- or lowercase. However, the U must precede the L.

EXAMPLE 2.7   Several unsigned and long integer constants are shown below.

Constant	*Number System*
50000U	decimal (unsigned)
123456789L	decimal (long)
123456789UL	decimal (unsigned long)
0123456L	octal (long)
0777777U	octal (unsigned)
OX50000U	hexadecimal (unsigned)
OXFFFFFUL	hexadecimal (unsigned long)

---

[*] Suppose a particular computer uses a *w*-bit word. Then an ordinary integer quantity may fall within the range -2^{w-1} to $+2^{w-1} - 1$, whereas an unsigned integer quantity may vary from 0 to $2^w - 1$. A short integer may substitute $w/2$ for w, and a long integer may substitute $2w$ for w. These rules may vary from one computer to another.

The maximum permissible values of unsigned and long integer constants will vary from one computer (and one compiler) to another. With some computers, the maximum permissible value of a long integer constant may be the same as that for an ordinary integer constant; other computers may allow a long integer constant to be much larger than an ordinary integer constant. You are again advised to determine the appropriate values for your particular version of C.

Floating-Point Constants

A *floating-point constant* is a base-10 number that contains either a decimal point or an exponent (or both).

EXAMPLE 2.8 Several valid floating-point constants are shown below.

0.	1.	0.2	827.602
50000.	0.000743	12.3	315.0066
2E-8	0.006e-3	1.6667E+8	.12121212e12

The following are *not* valid floating-point constants for the reasons stated.

1	Either a decimal point or an exponent must be present.
1,000.0	Illegal character (,).
2E+10.2	The exponent must be an integer quantity (it cannot contain a decimal point).
3E 10	Illegal character (blank space) in the exponent.

If an exponent is present, its effect is to shift the location of the decimal point to the right, if the exponent is positive, or to the left, if the exponent is negative. If a decimal point is not included within the number, it is assumed to be positioned to the right of the last digit.

The interpretation of a floating-point constant with an exponent is essentially the same as scientific notation, except that the base 10 is replaced by the letter E (or e). Thus, the number 1.2×10^{-3} would be written as 1.2E-3 or 1.2e-3. This is equivalent to 0.12e-2, or 12e-4, etc.

EXAMPLE 2.9 The quantity 3×10^5 can be represented in C by any of the following floating-point constants.

300000.	3e5	3e+5	3E5	3.0e+
.3e6	0.3E6	30E4	30.E+4	300e3

Similarly, the quantity 5.026×10^{-17} can be represented by any of the following floating-point constants.

5.026E-17	.5026e-16	50.26e-18	.0005026E-13

Floating-point constants have a much greater range than integer constants. Typically, the magnitude of a floating-point constant might range from a minimum value of approximately 3.4E-38 to a maximum of 3.4E+38. Some versions of the language permit floating-point constants that cover a wider range, such as 1.7E-308 to 1.7E+308. Also, the value 0.0 (which is less than either 3.4E-38 or 1.7E-308) is a valid floating-point constant. You should determine the appropriate values for the version of C used on your particular computer.

Floating-point constants are normally represented as double-precision quantities in C. Hence, each floating-point constant will typically occupy 2 words (8 bytes) of memory. Some versions of C permit the specification of a "single-precision," floating-point constant, by appending the letter F (in either upper- or lowercase) to the end of the constant (e.g., 3E5F). Similarly, some versions of C permit the specification of a "long" floating-point constant, by appending the letter L (upper- or lowercase) to the end of the constant (e.g., 0.123456789E-33L).

The precision of floating-point constants (i.e, the number of significant figures) will vary from one version of C to another. Virtually all versions of the language permit at least six significant figures, and some versions permit as many as eighteen significant figures. You should determine the appropriate number of significant figures for your particular version of C.

Numerical Accuracy

It should be understood that integer constants are exact quantities, whereas floating-point constants are approximations. The reasons for this are beyond the current scope of discussion. However, you should understand that the floating-point constant 1.0 might be represented within the computer's memory as 0.99999999..., even though it might appear as 1.0 when it is displayed (because of automatic rounding). Therefore floating-point values cannot be used for certain purposes, such as counting, indexing, etc., where exact values are required. We will discuss these restrictions as they arise, in later chapters of this book.

Character Constants

A *character constant* is a single character, enclosed in apostrophes (i.e., single quotation marks).

EXAMPLE 2.10   Several character constants are shown below.

'A'   'x'   '3'   '?'   ' '

Notice that the last constant consists of a blank space, enclosed in apostrophes.

Character constants have integer values that are determined by the computer's particular character set. Thus, the value of a character constant may vary from one computer to another. The constants themselves, however, are independent of the character set. This feature eliminates the dependence of a C program on any particular character set (more about this later).

Most computers, and virtually all personal computers, make use of the ASCII (i.e., American Standard Code for Information Interchange) character set, in which each individual character is numerically encoded with its own unique 7-bit combination (hence a total of $2^7 = 128$ different characters). Table 2-1 contains the ASCII character set, showing the decimal equivalent of the 7 bits that represent each character. Notice that the characters are ordered as well as encoded. In particular, the digits are ordered consecutively in their proper numerical sequence (0 to 9), and the letters are arranged consecutively in their proper alphabetical order, with uppercase characters preceding lowercase characters. This allows character-type data items to be compared with one another, based upon their relative order within the character set.

EXAMPLE 2.11   Several character constants and their corresponding values, as defined by the ASCII character set, are shown below.

Constant	Value
'A'	65
'x'	120
'3'	51
'?'	63
' '	32

These values will be the same for all computers that utilize the ASCII character set. The values will be different, however, for computers that utilize an alternate character set.

IBM mainframe computers, for example, utilize the EBCDIC (i.e., Extended Binary Coded Decimal Information Code) character set, in which each individual character is numerically encoded with its own unique 8-bit combination. The EBCDIC character set is distinctly different from the ASCII character set.

Table 2-1   The ASCII Character Set

ASCII Value	Character	ASCII Value	Character	ASCII Value	Character	ASCII Value	Character
0	NUL	32	(blank)	64	@	96	`
1	SOH	33	!	65	A	97	a
2	STX	34	"	66	B	98	b
3	ETX	35	#	67	C	99	c
4	EOT	36	$	68	D	100	d
5	ENQ	37	%	69	E	101	e
6	ACK	38	&	70	F	102	f
7	BEL	39	'	71	G	103	g
8	BS	40	(	72	H	104	h
9	HT	41	)	73	I	105	i
10	LF	42	*	74	J	106	j
11	VT	43	+	75	K	107	k
12	FF	44	,	76	L	108	l
13	CR	45	−	77	M	109	m
14	SO	46	.	78	N	110	n
15	SI	47	/	79	O	111	o
16	DLE	48	0	80	P	112	p
17	DC1	49	1	81	Q	113	q
18	DC2	50	2	82	R	114	r
19	DC3	51	3	83	S	115	s
20	DC4	52	4	84	T	116	t
21	NAK	53	5	85	U	117	u
22	SYN	54	6	86	V	118	v
23	ETB	55	7	87	W	119	w
24	CAN	56	8	88	X	120	x
25	EM	57	9	89	Y	121	y
26	SUB	58	:	90	Z	122	z
27	ESC	59	;	91	[	123	{
28	FS	60	<	92	\	124		
29	GS	61	=	93	]	125	}
30	RS	62	>	94	^	126	~
31	US	63	?	95	_	127	DEL

The first 32 characters and the last character are control characters. Usually, they are not displayed. However, some versions of C (some computers) support special graphics characters for these ASCII values. For example, 001 may represent the character ▣, 002 may represent ▨, and so on.

Escape Sequences

Certain nonprinting characters, as well as the backslash (\) and the apostrophe ('), can be expressed in terms of *escape sequences*. An escape sequence always begins with a backward slash and is followed by one or more special characters. For example, a line feed (LF), which is referred to as a *newline* in C, can be represented as \n. Such escape sequences always represent single characters, even though they are written in terms of two or more characters.

The commonly used escape sequences are listed below.

Character	Escape Sequence	ASCII Value
bell (alert)	\a	007
backspace	\b	008
horizontal tab	\t	009
vertical tab	\v	011
newline (line feed)	\n	010
form feed	\f	012
carriage return	\r	013
quotation mark (")	\"	034
apostrophe (')	\'	039
question mark (?)	\?	063
backslash (\)	\\	092
null	\0	000

EXAMPLE 2.12   Shown below are several character constants, expressed in terms of escape sequences.

```
'\n'        '\t'        '\b'        '\''        '\\'        '\"'
```

Note that the last three escape sequences represent an apostrophe, a backslash and a quotation mark, respectively.

Of particular interest is the escape sequence \0. This represents the *null character* (ASCII 000), which is used to indicate the end of a *string* (see below). Note that the null character constant '\0' is *not* equivalent to the character constant '0'.

An escape sequence can also be expressed in terms of one, two or three octal digits which represent single-character bit patterns. The general form of such an escape sequence is \ooo, where each o represents an octal digit (0 through 7). Some versions of C also allow an escape sequence to be expressed in terms of one or more hexadecimal digits, preceded by the letter x. The general form of a hexadecimal escape sequence is \xhh, where each h represents a hexadecimal digit (0 through 9 and a through f). The letters can be either upper- or lowercase. The use of an octal or hexadecimal escape sequence is usually less desirable than writing the character constant directly, however, since the bit patterns may be dependent upon some particular character set.

EXAMPLE 2.13   The letter A is represented by the decimal value 065 in the ASCII character set. This value is equivalent to the octal value 101. (The equivalent binary bit pattern is 001 000 001.) Hence the character constant 'A' can be expressed as the octal escape sequence '\101'.

In some versions of C, the letter A can also be expressed as a hexadecimal escape sequence. The hexadecimal equivalent of the decimal value 65 is 41. (The equivalent binary bit pattern is 0100 0001.) Hence the character constant 'A' can be expressed as '\x41', or as '\X41'.

It should be understood that the preferred way to represent this character constant is simply 'A'. In this form, the character constant is not dependent upon its equivalent ASCII representation.

Escape sequences can only be written for certain special characters, such as those listed above, or in terms of octal or hexadecimal digits. If a backslash is followed by any other character, the result may be unpredictable. Usually, however, it will simply be ignored.

String Constants

A *string constant* consists of any number of consecutive characters (including none), enclosed in (double) quotation marks.

EXAMPLE 2.14 Several string constants are shown below.

```
"green"          "Washington, D.C. 20005"     "270-32-3456"

"$19.95"         "THE CORRECT ANSWER IS:"      "2*(I+3)/J"

"     "          "Line 1\nLine 2\nLine 3"      ""
```

Note that the string constant `"Line 1\nLine 2\nLine 3"` extends over three lines, because of the newline characters that are embedded within the string. Thus, this string would be displayed as

```
Line 1
Line 2
Line 3
```

Also, notice that the string `""` is a *null* (empty) string.

Sometimes certain special characters (e.g., a backslash or a quotation mark) must be included as a part of a string constant. These characters *must* be represented in terms of their escape sequences. Similarly, certain nonprinting characters (e.g., tab, newline) can be included in a string constant if they are represented in terms of their corresponding escape sequences.

EXAMPLE 2.15 The following string constant includes three special characters that are represented by their corresponding escape sequences.

```
"\tTo continue, press the \"RETURN\" key\n"
```

The special characters are `\t` (horizontal tab), `\"` (double quotation marks, which appears twice), and `\n` (newline).

The compiler automatically places a null character (`\0`) at the end of every string constant, as the last character within the string (before the closing double quotation mark). This character is not visible when the string is displayed. However, we can easily examine the individual characters within a string, and test to see whether or not each character is a null character (we will see how this is done in Chap. 6). Thus, the end of every string can be readily identified. This is very helpful if the string is scanned on a character-by-character basis, as is required in many applications. Also, in many situations this end-of-string designation eliminates the need to specify a maximum string length.

EXAMPLE 2.16 The string constant shown in Example 2.15 actually contains 38 characters. This includes five blank spaces, four special characters (horizontal tab, two quotation marks and newline) represented by escape sequences, and the null character (`\0`) at the end of the string.

Remember that a character constant (e.g., `'A'`) and the corresponding single-character string constant (`"A"`) are not equivalent. Also remember that a character constant has an equivalent integer value, whereas a single-character string constant does not have an equivalent integer value and, in fact, consists of two characters — the specified character followed by the null character (`\0`).

EXAMPLE 2.17 The character constant `'w'` has an integer value of 119 in the ASCII character set. It does not have a null character at the end. In contrast, the string constant `"w"` actually consists of two characters — the lowercase letter w and the null character `\0`. This constant does not have a corresponding integer value.

2.5 VARIABLES AND ARRAYS

A *variable* is an identifier that is used to represent some specified type of information within a designated portion of the program. In its simplest form, a variable is an identifier that is used to represent a single data item; i.e., a numerical quantity or a character constant. The data item must be assigned to the variable at some point in the program. The data item can then be accessed later in the program simply by referring to the variable name.

A given variable can be assigned different data items at various places within the program. Thus, the information represented by the variable can change during the execution of the program. However, the data type associated with the variable cannot change.

EXAMPLE 2.18   A C program contains the following lines.

```
int a, b, c;
char d;
. . .
a = 3;
b = 5;
c = a + b;
d = 'a';

. . .
a = 4;
b = 2;
c = a - b;
d = 'W';
```

The first two lines are *type declarations*, which state that a, b and c are integer variables, and that d is a char-type variable. Thus a, b and c will each represent an integer-valued quantity, and d will represent a single character. These type declarations will apply throughout the program (more about this in Sec. 2.6).

The next four lines cause the following things to happen: the integer quantity 3 is assigned to a, 5 is assigned to b, and the quantity represented by the sum a + b (i.e., 8) is assigned to c. The character 'a' is then assigned to d.

In the third line within this group, notice that the values of the variables a and b are accessed simply by writing the variables on the right-hand side of the equal sign.

The last four lines redefine the values assigned to the variables as follows: the integer quantity 4 is assigned to a, replacing the earlier value, 3; then 2 is assigned to b, replacing the earlier value, 5; then the difference between a and b (i.e., 2) is assigned to c, replacing the earlier value, 8. Finally, the character 'W' is assigned to d, replacing the earlier character, 'a'.

The *array* is another kind of variable that is used extensively in C. An array is an identifier that refers to a *collection* of data items that all have the same name. The data items must all be of the same type (e.g., all integers, all characters, etc.). The individual data items are represented by their corresponding *array_elements* (i.e., the first data item is represented by the first array element, etc.). The individual array elements are distinguished from one another by the value that is assigned to a *subscript*.

EXAMPLE 2.19   Suppose that x is a 10-element array. The first element is referred to as x[0], the second as x[1], and so on. The last element will be x[9].

The subscript associated with each element is shown in square braces. Thus, the value of the subscript for the first element is 0, the value of the subscript for the second element is 1, and so on. For an n-element array, the subscripts always range from 0 to n–1.

There are several different ways to categorize arrays (e.g., integer arrays, character arrays, one-dimensional arrays, multi-dimensional arrays). For now, we will confine our attention to only one type of array: the one-dimensional, char-type array (often called a one-dimensional *character* array). This type of array is generally used to represent a string. Each array element will represent one character within the string. Thus, the entire array can be thought of as an ordered list of characters.

Since the array is one-dimensional, there will be a single *subscript* (sometimes called an *index*) whose value refers to individual array elements. If the array contains n elements, the subscript will be an integer quantity whose values range from 0 to n–1. Note that an n-character string will require an (n+1)-element array, because of the null character (\0) that is automatically placed at the end of the string.

EXAMPLE 2.20 Suppose that the string "California" is to be stored in a one-dimensional character array called letter. Since "California" contains 10 characters, letter will be an 11-element array. Thus, letter[0] will represent the letter C, letter[1] will represent a, and so on, as summarized below. Note that the last (i.e., the 11th) array element, letter[10], represents the null character which signifies the end of the string.

Element Number	Subscript Value	Array Element	Corresponding Data Item (String Character)
1	0	letter[0]	C
2	1	letter[1]	a
3	2	letter[2]	l
4	3	letter[3]	i
5	4	letter[4]	f
6	5	letter[5]	o
7	6	letter[6]	r
8	7	letter[7]	n
9	8	letter[8]	i
10	9	letter[9]	a
11	10	letter[10]	\0

From this list we can determine, for example, that the 5th array element, letter[4], represents the letter f, and so on. The array elements and their contents are shown schematically in Fig. 2.1.

C	a	l	i	f	o	r	n	i	a	\0

Subscript: 0   1   2   3   4   5   6   7   8   9   10

An 11-element character array

Fig. 2.1

We will discuss arrays in much greater detail in Chaps. 9 and 10.

2.6 DECLARATIONS

A *declaration* associates a group of variables with a specific data type. All variables must be declared before they can appear in executable statements.

A declaration consists of a data type, followed by one or more variable names, ending with a semicolon. (Recall that the permissible data types are discussed in Sec. 2.3.) Each array variable must be followed by a pair of square brackets, containing a positive integer which specifies the size (i.e., the number of elements) of the array.

EXAMPLE 2.21 A C program contains the following type declarations.

```
int   a, b, c;
float root1, root2;
char  flag, text[80];
```

Thus, a, b and c are declared to be integer variables, root1 and root2 are floating-point variables, flag is a char-type variable and text is an 80-element, char-type array. Note the square brackets enclosing the size specification for text.

These declarations could also have been written as follows.

```
int a;
int b;
int c;
float root1;
float root2;
char flag;
char text[80];
```

This form may be useful if each variable is to be accompanied by a comment explaining its purpose. In small programs, however, items of the same type are usually combined in a single declaration.

Integer-type variables can be declared to be *short integer* for smaller integer quantities, or *long integer* for larger integer quantities. (Recall that some C compilers allocate less storage space to short integers, and additional storage space to long integers.) Such variables are declared by writing `short int` and `long int`, or simply `short` and `long`, respectively.

EXAMPLE 2.22   A C program contains the following type declarations.

```
short int a, b, c;
long  int r, s, t;
int   p, q;
```

Some compilers will allocate less storage space to the short integer variables a, b and c than to the integer variables p and q. Typical values are two bytes for each short integer variable, and four bytes (one word) for each ordinary integer variable. The maximum permissible values of a, b and c will be smaller than the maximum permissible values of p and q when using a compiler of this type.

Similarly, some compilers will allocate additional storage space to the long integer variables r, s and t than to the integer variables p and q. Typical values are two words (8 bytes) for each long integer variable, and one word (4 bytes) for each ordinary integer variable. The maximum permissible values of r, s and t will be larger than the maximum permissible values of p and q when using one of these compilers.

The above declarations could have been written as

```
short a, b, c;
long  r, s, t;
int   p, q;
```

Thus, `short` and `short int` are equivalent, as are `long` and `long int`.

An integer variable can also be declared to be *unsigned*, by writing `unsigned int`, or simply `unsigned`, as the type indicator. Unsigned integer quantities can be larger than ordinary integer quantities (approximately twice as large), but they cannot be negative.

EXAMPLE 2.23   A C program contains the following type declarations.

```
int a, b;
unsigned x, y;
```

The unsigned variables x and y can represent values that are twice as large as the values represented by a and b. However, x and y cannot represent negative quantities. For example, if the computer uses 2 bytes for each integer quantity, then a and b may take on values that range from −32768 to +32767, whereas the values of x and y may vary from 0 to +65535.

Floating-point variables can be declared to be *double precision* by using the type indicator `double` or `long float` rather than `float`. In most versions of C, the exponent within a double-precision quantity is larger in magnitude than the exponent within an ordinary floating-point quantity. Hence, the quantity represented by a double-precision variable can fall within a greater range. Moreover, a double-precision quantity will usually be expressed in terms of more significant figures.

EXAMPLE 2.24   A C program contains the following type declarations.

```
float  c1, c2, c3;
double root1, root2;
```

With a particular C compiler, the double-precision variables `root1` and `root2` represent values that can vary (in magnitude) from approximately 1.7×10^{-308} to $1.7 \times 10^{+308}$. However, the floating-point variables `c1`, `c2` and `c3` are restricted (in magnitude) to the range 3.4×10^{-38} to 3.4×10^{38}. Furthermore, the values represented by `root1` and `root2` will each be expressed in terms of 18 significant figures, whereas the values represented by `c1`, `c2` and `c3` will each be expressed in terms of only 6 significant figures.

The last declaration could have been written

```
long float root1, root2;
```

though the original form (i.e., `double root1, root2;`) is more common.

Initial values can be assigned to variables within a type declaration. To do so, the declaration must consist of a data type, followed by a variable name, an equal sign (=) and a constant of the appropriate type. A semicolon must appear at the end, as usual.

EXAMPLE 2.25   A C program contains the following type declarations.

```
int    c = 12;
char   star = '*';
float  sum = 0.;
double factor = 0.21023e-6;
```

Thus, `c` is an integer variable whose initial value is 12, `star` is a char-type variable initially assigned the character `'*'`, `sum` is a floating-point variable whose initial value is `0.`, and `factor` is a double-precision variable whose initial value is 0.21023×10^{-6}.

A character-type array can also be initialized within a declaration. To do so, the array is usually written without an explicit size specification (the square brackets are empty). The array name is then followed by an equal sign, the string (enclosed in quotes), and a semicolon. This is a convenient way to assign a string to a character-type array.

EXAMPLE 2.26   A C program contains the following type declaration.

```
char text[] = "California";
```

This declaration will cause `text` to be an 11-element character array. The first 10 elements will represent the 10 characters within the word `California`, and the 11th element will represent the null character (`\0`) which is automatically added at the end of the string.

The declaration could also have been written

```
char text[11] = "California";
```

where the size of the array is explicitly specified. In such situations it is important, however, that the size be specified correctly. If the size is too small, e.g.,

```
char text[10] = "California";
```

the characters at the end of the string (in this case, the null character) will be lost. If the size is too large, e.g.,

```
char text[20] = "California";
```

the extra array elements may be assigned zeros, or they may be filled with meaningless characters.

Array declarations that include the assignment of initial values can only appear in certain places within a C program (see Chap. 9).

In Chap. 8 we shall see that variables can be categorized by *storage class* as well as by data type. The storage class specifies the portion of the program within which the variables are recognized. Moreover, the storage class associated with an array determines whether or not the array can be initialized. This is explained in Chap. 9.

2.7 EXPRESSIONS

An *expression* represents a single data item, such as a number or a character. The expression may consist of a single entity, such as a constant, a variable, an array element or a reference to a function. It may also consist of some combination of such entities, interconnected by one or more *operators*. The use of expressions involving operators is particularly common in C, as in most other programming languages.

Expressions can also represent logical conditions that are either true or false. However, in C the conditions *true* and *false* are represented by the integer values 1 and 0, respectively. Hence logical-type expressions really represent numerical quantities.

EXAMPLE 2.27   Several simple expressions are shown below.

```
a + b
x = y
c = a + b
x <= y
x == y
++i
```

The first expression involves use of the *addition operator* (+). This expression represents the sum of the values assigned to the variables a and b.

The second expression involves the *assignment operator* (=). In this case, the expression causes the value represented by y to be assigned to x. We have already encountered the use of this operator in several earlier examples (see Examples 1.6 through 1.13, 2.25 and 2.26). C includes several additional assignment operators, as discussed in Sec. 3.4.

In the third line, the value of the expression (a + b) is assigned to the variable c. Note that this combines the features of the first two expressions (addition and assignment).

The fourth expression will have the value 1 (true) if the value of x is less than or equal to the value of y. Otherwise, the expression will have the value 0 (false). In this expression, <= is a *relational operator* that compares the values of the variables x and y.

The fifth expression is a test for equality (compare with the second expression, which is an assignment expression). Thus, the expression will have the value 1 (true) if the value of x is equal to the value of y. Otherwise, the expression will have the value 0 (false).

The last expression causes the value of the variable i to be increased by 1 (i.e., *incremented*). Thus, the expression is equivalent to

```
i = i + 1
```

The operator ++, which indicates incrementing, is called a *unary* operator because it has only one *operand* (in this case, the variable i). C includes several other operators of this type, as discussed in Sec. 3.2.

The C language includes many different kinds of operators and expressions. Most are described in detail in Chap. 3. Others will be discussed elsewhere in this book, as the need arises.

2.8 STATEMENTS

A *statement* causes the computer to carry out some action. There are three different classes of statements in C. They are *expression statements*, *compound statements* and *control statements*.

An expression statement consists of an expression followed by a semicolon. The execution of an expression statement causes the expression to be evaluated.

EXAMPLE 2.28   Several expression statements are shown below.

```
a = 3;
c = a + b;
++i;
printf("Area = %f", area);
;
```

The first two expression statements are assignment-type statements. Each causes the value of the expression on the right of the equal sign to be assigned to the variable on the left. The third expression statement is an incrementing-type statement, which causes the value of i to increase by 1.

The fourth expression statement causes the printf function to be evaluated. This is a standard C library function that writes information out of the computer (more about this in Sec. 3.6). In this case, the message Area = will be displayed, followed by the current value of the variable area. Thus, if area represents the value 100., the statement will generate the message

```
Area = 100.
```

The last expression statement does nothing, since it consists of only a semicolon. It is simply a mechanism for providing an empty expression statement in places where this type of statement is required. Consequently, it is called a *null statement*.

A compound statement consists of several individual statements enclosed within a pair of braces { }. The individual statements may themselves be expression statements, compound statements or control statements. Thus, the compound statement provides a capability for embedding statements within other statements. Unlike an expression statement, a compound statement does *not* end with a semicolon.

EXAMPLE 2.29   A typical compound statement is shown below.

```
{
    pi = 3.141593;
    circumference = 2. * pi * radius;
    area = pi * radius * radius;
}
```

This particular compound statement consists of three assignment-type expression statements, though it is considered a single entity within the program in which it appears. Note that the compound statement does not end with a semicolon after the brace.

Control statements are used to create special program features, such as logical tests, loops and branches. Many control statements require that other statements be embedded within them, as illustrated in the following example.

EXAMPLE 2.30 The following control statement creates a conditional loop in which several actions are executed repeatedly, until some particular condition is satisfied.

```
while (count <= n)   {
    printf("x = ");
    scanf("%f", &x);
    sum += x;
    ++count;
}
```

This statement contains a compound statement, which in turn contains four expression statements. The compound statement will continue to be executed as long as the value of count does not exceed the value of n. Note that count increases in value during each pass through the loop.

Chapter 6 presents a detailed discussion of control statements.

2.9 SYMBOLIC CONSTANTS

A *symbolic constant* is a name that substitutes for a sequence of characters. The characters may represent a numeric constant, a character constant or a string constant. Thus, a symbolic constant allows a name to appear in place of a numeric constant, a character constant or a string. When a program is compiled, each occurrence of a symbolic constant is replaced by its corresponding character sequence.

Symbolic constants are usually defined at the beginning of a program. The symbolic constants may then appear later in the program in place of the numeric constants, character constants, etc. that the symbolic constants represent.

A symbolic constant is defined by writing

```
#define  name  text
```

where *name* represents a symbolic name, typically written in uppercase letters, and *text* represents the sequence of characters that is associated with the symbolic name. Note that *text* does not end with a semicolon, since a symbolic constant definition is not a true C statement. Moreover, if *text* were to end with a semicolon, this semicolon would be treated as though it were a part of the numeric constant, character constant or string constant that is substituted for the symbolic name.

EXAMPLE 2.31 A C program contains the following symbolic constant definitions.

```
#define  TAXRATE  0.23

#define  PI  3.141593

#define  TRUE  1
#define  FALSE  0

#define  FRIEND  "Susan"
```

Notice that the symbolic names are written in uppercase, to distinguish them from ordinary C identifiers. Also, note that the definitions do not end with semicolons.

Now suppose that the program contains the statement

```
area = PI * radius * radius;
```

During the compilation process, each occurrence of a symbolic constant will be replaced by its corresponding text. Thus, the above statement will become

```
area = 3.141593 * radius * radius;
```

Now suppose that a semicolon had been (incorrectly) included in the definition for PI, i.e.,

```
#define  PI  3.141593;
```

The assignment statement for area would then become

```
area = 3.141593; * radius * radius;
```

Note the semicolon preceding the first asterisk. This is clearly incorrect, and it will cause an error in the compilation.

The substitution of text for a symbolic constant will be carried out anywhere beyond the #define statement, *except* within a string. Thus, any text enclosed by (double) quotation marks will be unaffected by this substitution process.

EXAMPLE 2.32   A C program contains the following statements.

```
#define  CONSTANT  6.023E23
int c;
. . . . .
printf("CONSTANT = %f", c);
```

The printf statement will be unaffected by the symbolic constant definition, since the term "CONSTANT = %f" is a string constant. If, however, the printf statement were written as

```
printf("CONSTANT = %f", CONSTANT);
```

then the printf statement would become

```
printf("CONSTANT = %f", 6.023E23);
```

during the compilation process.

Symbolic constants are not required when writing C programs. Their use is recommended, however, since they contribute to the development of clear, orderly programs. For example, symbolic constants are more readily identified than the information that they represent, and the symbolic names usually suggest the significance of their associated data items. Furthermore, it is much easier to change the value of a single symbolic constant than to change every occurrence of some numerical constant that may appear in several places within the program.

The #define feature, which is used to define symbolic constants, is one of several features included in the C *preprocessor* (i.e., a program that provides the first step in the translation of a C program into machine language). A detailed discussion of the C preprocessor is included in Chap. 14 (see Sec. 14.6).

Review Questions

2.1   Which characters comprise the C character set?

2.2   Summarize the rules for naming identifiers. Are uppercase letters equivalent to lowercase letters? Can digits be included in an identifier name? Can any special characters be included?

2.3   How many characters can be included in an identifier name? Are all of these characters equally significant?

2.4   What are the keywords in C? What restrictions apply to their use?

2.5   Name and describe the four basic data types in C.

2.6   Name and describe the four data-type qualifiers. To which data types can each qualifier be applied?

2.7   Name and describe the four basic types of constants in C.

2.8   Summarize the rules that apply to all numeric-type constants.

2.9   What special rules apply to integer constants?

2.10 When writing integer constants, how are decimal constants, octal constants and hexadecimal constants distinguished from one another?

2.11 Typically, what is the largest permissible magnitude of an integer constant? State your answer in decimal, octal and hexadecimal.

2.12 What are unsigned integer constants? What are long integer constants? How do these constants differ from ordinary integer constants? How can they be written and identified?

2.13 Describe two different ways that floating-point constants can be written. What special rules apply in each case?

2.14 What is the purpose of the (optional) exponent in a floating-point constant?

2.15 Typically, what is the largest permissible magnitude of a floating-point constant? Compare with an integer constant.

2.16 How can "single-precision" and "long" floating-point constants be written and identified?

2.17 Typically, how many significant figures are permitted in a floating-point constant?

2.18 Describe the differences in accuracy between integer and floating-point constants. Under what circumstances should each type of constant be used?

2.19 What is a character constant? How do character constants differ from numeric-type constants? Do character constants represent numerical values?

2.20 What is the ASCII character set? How common is its use?

2.21 What is an escape sequence? What is its purpose?

2.22 Summarize the standard escape sequences in C. Describe other, nonstandard escape sequences that are commonly available.

2.23 What is a string constant? How do string constants differ from character constants? Do string constants represent numerical values?

2.24 Can escape sequences be included in a string constant? Explain.

2.25 What is a variable? How can variables be characterized?

2.26 What is an array variable? How does an array variable differ from an ordinary variable?

2.27 What restriction must be satisfied by all of the data items represented by an array?

2.28 How can individual array elements be distinguished from one another?

2.29 What is a subscript? What range of values is permitted for the subscript of a one-dimensional, n-element array?

2.30 What is the purpose of a type declaration? What does a type declaration consist of?

2.31 Must all variables appearing within a C program be declared?

2.32 How are initial values assigned to variables within a type declaration? How are strings assigned to one-dimensional, character-type arrays?

2.33 What is an expression? What kind of information is represented by an expression?

2.34 What is an operator? Describe several different types of operators that are included within the C language.

2.35 Name the three different classes of statements in C. Describe the composition of each.

2.36 Can statements be embedded within other statements? Explain.

2.37 What is a symbolic constant? How is a symbolic constant defined? How is the definition written? Where must a symbolic constant definition be placed within a C program?

2.38 During the compilation process, what happens to symbolic constants that appear within a C program?

Problems

2.39 Determine which of the following are valid identifiers. If invalid, explain why.

    (a) `record1`

    (b) `1record`

    (c) `file_3`

    (d) `return`

    (e) `$tax`

    (f) `name`

    (g) `name and address`

    (h) `name_and_address`

    (i) `name-and-address`

    (j) `123-45-6789`

2.40 Assume that your version of C can recognize only the first 8 characters of an identifier name, though identifier names may be arbitrarily long. Which of the following pairs of identifier names are considered to be identical and which are distinct?

    (a) `name, names`

    (b) `address, Address`

    (c) `identifier_1, identifier_2`

    (d) `list1, list2`

    (e) `answer, ANSWER`

    (f) `char1, char_1`

2.41 Determine which of the following numerical values are valid constants. If a constant is valid, specify whether it is integer or real. Also, specify the base for each valid integer constant.

    (a) `0.5`

    (b) `27,822`

    (c) `9.3e12`

    (d) `9.3e-12`

    (e) `12345678`

    (f) `12345678L`

    (g) `0.8E+0.8`

    (h) `0.8E 8`

    (i) `0515`

    (j) `018CDF`

    (k) `0XBCFDAL`

    (l) `0x87e3ha`

2.42 Determine which of the following are valid character constants.

    (a) `'a'`

    (b) `'$'`

    (c) `'\n'`

    (d) `'/n'`

    (e) `'\\'`

    (f) `'\a'`

    (g) `'T'`

    (h) `'\0'`

    (i) `'xyz'`

    (j) `'\052'`

2.43 Determine which of the following are valid string constants.

    (a) `'8:15 P.M.'`

    (b) `"Red, White and Blue"`

    (c) `"Name:`

    (d) `"Chap. 3 (Cont\'d)"`

    (e) `"1.3e-12"`

    (f) `"NEW YORK, NY 10020"`

    (g) `"The professor said, "Please don't sleep in class"`

2.44 Write appropriate declarations for each group of variables and arrays.

    (a) Integer variables: `p, q`
         Floating-point variables: `x, y, z`
         Character variables: `a, b, c`

    (b) Floating-point variables: `root1, root2`
         Long integer variable: `counter`
         Short integer variable: `flag`

   (c)   Integer variable: `index`
        Unsigned integer variable: `cust_no`
        Double-precision variables: `gross, tax, net`

   (d)   Character variables: `current, last`
        Unsigned integer variable: `count`
        Floating-point variable: `error`

   (e)   Character variables: `first, last`
        80-element character array: `message`

2.45   Write appropriate declarations and assign the given initial values for each group of variables and arrays.

   (a)   Floating-point variables: $a = -8.2$, $b = 0.005$
        Integer variables: $x = 129$, $y = 87$, $z = -22$
        Character variables: `c1 = 'w'`, `c2 = '&'`

   (b)   Double-precision variables: $d1 = 2.88 \times 10^{-8}$, $d2 = -8.4 \times 10^5$
        Integer variables: $u = 711$ (octal), $v = $ `ffff` (hexadecimal)

   (c)   Long integer variable: `big` $= 123456789$
        Double-precision variable: $c = 0.3333333333$
        Character variable: `eol` = *newline character*

   (d)   One-dimensional character array: `message = "ERROR"`

2.46   Explain the purpose of each of the following expressions.

   (a)   `a - b`   (d)   `a >= b`   (f)   `a < (b / c)`

   (b)   `a * (b + c)`   (e)   `(a % 5) == 0`   (g)   `--a`

   (c)   `d = a * (b + c)`

2.47   Identify whether each of the following statements is an expression statement, a compound statement or a control statement.

   (a)   `a * (b + c);`

   (b)
```
while (a < 100)   {
      d = a * (b + c);
      ++a;
}
```

   (c)
```
if (x > 0)
      y = 2.0;
else
      y = 3.0;
```

   (d)
```
{
    ++x;
    if (x > 0)
        y = 2.0;
    else
        y = 3.0;
    printf("%f", y);
}
```

   (e)
```
{
    ++x;
    if (x > 0)   {
        y = 2.0;
        z = 6.0;
    }
    else   {
        y = 3.0;
        z = 9.0;
    }
}
```

2.48   Write an appropriate definition for each of the following symbolic constants, as it would appear within a C program.

	Constant	*Text*
(a)	FACTOR	−18
(b)	ERROR	0.0001
(c)	BEGIN	{
	END	}
(d)	NAME	"Sharon"
(e)	EOLN	'\n'
(f)	COST	"$19.95"

Chapter 3

Operators and Expressions

We have already seen that individual constants, variables, array elements and function references can be joined together by various operators to form expressions. We have also mentioned that C includes a large number of operators which fall into several different categories. In this chapter we examine certain of these categories in detail. Specifically, we will see how arithmetic operators, unary operators, relational and logical operators, assignment operators and the conditional operator are used to form expressions.

The data items that operators act upon are called *operands*. Some operators require two operands, while others act upon only one operand. Most operators allow the individual operands to be expressions. A few operators permit only single variables as operands (more about this later).

3.1 ARITHMETIC OPERATORS

There are five *arithmetic operators* in C. They are

Operator	*Purpose*
+	addition
–	subtraction
*	multiplication
/	division
%	remainder after integer division

The % operator is sometimes referred to as the *modulus operator*.

There is no exponentiation operator in C. However, there is a *library function* (pow) to carry out exponentiation (see Sec. 3.6).

The operands acted upon by arithmetic operators must represent numeric values. Thus, the operands can be integer quantities, floating-point quantities or characters (remember that character constants represent integer values, as determined by the computer's character set). The remainder operator (%) requires that both operands be integers and the second operand be nonzero. Similarly, the division operator (/) requires that the second operand be nonzero.

Division of one integer quantity by another is referred to as *integer division*. This operation always results in a truncated quotient (i.e., the decimal portion of the quotient will be dropped). On the other hand, if a division operation is carried out with two floating-point numbers, or with one floating-point number and one integer, the result will be a floating-point quotient.

EXAMPLE 3.1 Suppose that a and b are integer variables whose values are 10 and 3, respectively. Several arithmetic expressions involving these variables are shown below, together with their resulting values.

Expression	*Value*
a + b	13
a – b	7
a * b	30
a / b	3
a % b	1

Notice the truncated quotient resulting from the division operation, since both operands represent integer quantities. Also, notice the integer remainder resulting from the use of the modulus operator in the last expression.

Now suppose that v1 and v2 are floating-point variables whose values are 12.5 and 2.0, respectively. Several arithmetic expressions involving these variables are shown below, together with their resulting values.

Expression	*Value*
v1 + v2	14.5
v1 - v2	10.5
v1 * v2	25.0
v1 / v2	6.25

Finally, suppose that c1 and c2 are character-type variables that represent the characters P and T, respectively. Several arithmetic expressions that make use of these variables are shown below, together with their resulting values (based upon the ASCII character set).

Expression	*Value*
c1	80
c1 + c2	164
c1 + c2 + 5	169
c1 + c2 + '5'	217

Note that P is encoded as (decimal) 80, T is encoded as 84, and 5 is encoded as 53 in the ASCII character set, as shown in Table 2-1.

If one or both operands represent negative values, then the addition, subtraction, multiplication and division operations will result in values whose signs are determined by the usual rules of algebra. Integer division will result in truncation toward zero; i.e., the resultant will always be smaller in magnitude than the true quotient.

The interpretation of the remainder operation is unclear when one of the operands is negative. Most versions of C assign the sign of the first operand to the remainder. Thus, the condition

        a = ((a / b) * b) + (a % b)

will always be satisfied, regardless of the signs of the values represented by a and b.

Beginning programmers should exercise care in the use of the remainder operation when one of the operands is negative. In general, it is best to avoid such situations.

EXAMPLE 3.2 Suppose that a and b are integer variables whose values are 11 and −3, respectively. Several arithmetic expressions involving these variables are shown below, together with their resulting values.

Expression	*Value*
a + b	8
a - b	14
a * b	−33
a / b	−3
a % b	2

If a had been assigned a value of −11 and b had been assigned 3, then the value of a / b would still be −3 but the value of a % b would be −2. Similarly, if a and b had both been assigned negative values (−11 and −3, respectively), then the value of a / b would be 3 and the value of a % b would be −2.

Note that the condition

```
a = ((a / b) * b) + (a % b)
```

will be satisfied in each of the above cases. Most versions of C will determine the sign of the remainder in this manner, though this feature is unspecified in the formal definition of the language.

EXAMPLE 3.3   Here is an illustration of the results that are obtained with floating-point operands having different signs. Let $r1$ and $r2$ be floating-point variables whose assigned values are -0.66 and 4.50. Several arithmetic expressions involving these variables are shown below, together with their resulting values.

Expression	Value
r1 + r2	3.84
r1 - r2	-5.16
r1 * r2	-2.97
r1 / r2	-0.1466667

Operands that differ in type may undergo type conversion before the expression takes on its final value. In general, the final result will be expressed in the highest precision possible, consistent with the data types of the operands. The following rules apply when neither operand is unsigned.

1.   If both operands are floating-point types whose precisions differ (e.g., a float and a double), the lower-precision operand will be converted to the precision of the other operand, and the result will be expressed in this higher precision. Thus, an operation between a float and a double will result in a double; a float and a long double will result in a long double; and a double and a long double will result in a long double. (Note: In some versions of C, all operands of type float are automatically converted to double.)

2.   If one operand is a floating-point type (e.g., float, double or long double) and the other is a char or an int (including short int or long int), the char or int will be converted to the floating-point type and the result will be expressed as such. Hence, an operation between an int and a double will result in a double.

3.   If neither operand is a floating-point type but one is a long int, the other will be converted to long int and the result will be long int. Thus, an operation between a long int and an int will result in a long int.

4.   If neither operand is a floating-point type or a long int, then both operands will be converted to int (if necessary) and the result will be int. Thus, an operation between a short int and an int will result in an int.

A detailed summary of these rules is given in Appendix D. Conversions involving unsigned operands are also explained in Appendix D.

EXAMPLE 3.4   Suppose that i is an integer variable whose value is 7, f is a floating-point variable whose value is 5.5, and c is a character-type variable that represents the character w. Several expressions which include the use of these variables are shown below. Each expression involves operands of two different types. Assume that the ASCII character set is being used.

Expression	Value	Type
i + f	12.5	double-precision
i + c	126	integer
i + c - '0'	78	integer
(i + c) - (2 * f / 5)	123.8	double-precision

Note that w is encoded as (decimal) 119 and 0 is encoded as 48 in the ASCII character set, as shown in Table 2-1.

The value of an expression can be converted to a different data type if desired. To do so, the expression must be preceded by the name of the desired data type, enclosed in parentheses, i.e.,

```
(data type) expression
```

This type of construction is known as a *cast*.

EXAMPLE 3.5   Suppose that i is an integer variable whose value is 7, and f is a floating-point variable whose value is 8.5. The expression

```
(i + f) % 4
```

is invalid, because the first operand (i + f) is floating-point rather than integer. However, the expression

```
((int) (i + f)) % 4
```

forces the first operand to be an integer and is therefore valid, resulting in the integer remainder 3.

Note that the explicit type specification applies only to the first operand, not the entire expression.

The data type associated with the expression itself is not changed by a cast. Rather, it is the *value* of the expression that undergoes type conversion wherever the cast appears. This is particularly relevant when the expression consists of only a single variable.

EXAMPLE 3.6   Suppose that f is a floating-point variable whose value is 5.5. The expression

```
((int) f) % 2
```

contains two integer operands and is therefore valid, resulting in the integer remainder 1. Note, however, that f remains a floating-point variable whose value is 5.5, even though the value of f was converted to an integer (5) when carrying out the remainder operation.

The operators within C are grouped hierarchically according to their *precedence* (i.e., order of evaluation). Operations with a higher precedence are carried out before operations having a lower precedence. The natural order of evaluation can be altered, however, through the use of parentheses, as illustrated in Example 3.5.

Among the arithmetic operators, *, / and % fall into one precedence group, and + and – fall into another. The first group has a higher precedence than the second. Thus, multiplication, division and remainder operations will be carried out before addition and subtraction.

Another important consideration is the *order* in which consecutive operations within the same precedence group are carried out. This is known as *associativity*. Within each of the precedence groups described above, the associativity is left to right. In other words, consecutive addition and subtraction operations are carried out from left to right, as are consecutive multiplication, division and remainder operations.

EXAMPLE 3.7   The arithmetic expression

```
a - b / c * d
```

is equivalent to the algebraic formula $a - [(b / c) \times d]$. Thus, if the floating-point variables a, b, c and d have been assigned the values 1., 2., 3. and 4., respectively, the expression would represent the value $-1.666666 \cdots$, since

$$1. - [(2. / 3.) \times 4.] = 1. - [0.666666 \cdots \times 4.] = 1. - 2.666666 \cdots = -1.666666 \cdots$$

Notice that the division is carried out first, since this operation has a higher precedence than subtraction. The resulting quotient is then multiplied by 4., because of left-to-right associativity. The product is then subtracted from 1., resulting in the final value of $-1.666666 \cdots$.

The natural precedence of operations can be altered through the use of parentheses, thus allowing the arithmetic operations within an expression to be carried out in any desired order. In fact, parentheses can be *nested*, one pair within another. In such cases the innermost operations are carried out first, then the next innermost operations, and so on.

EXAMPLE 3.8   The arithmetic expression

```
(a - b) / (c * d)
```

is equivalent to the algebraic formula $(a - b) / (c \times d)$. Thus, if the floating-point variables a, b, c and d have been assigned the values 1., 2., 3. and 4., respectively, the expression would represent the value $-0.08333333\cdots$, since

$$(1. - 2.) / (3. \times 4.) = -1. / 12. = -0.08333333\cdots$$

Compare this result with that obtained in Example 3.7.

Sometimes it is a good idea to use parentheses to clarify an expression, even though the parentheses may not be required. On the other hand, the use of overly complex expressions, such as that shown in the next example, should be avoided if at all possible. Such expressions are difficult to read, and they are often written incorrectly because of unbalanced parentheses.

EXAMPLE 3.9   Consider the arithmetic expression

```
2 * ((i % 5) * (4 + (j - 3) / (k + 2)))
```

where i, j and k are integer variables. If these variables are assigned the values 8, 15 and 4, respectively, then the given expression would be evaluated as

$$2 \times ((8 \% 5) \times (4 + (15 - 3) / (4 + 2))) = 2 \times (3 \times (4 + (12/6))) = 2 \times (3 \times (4 + 2)) = 2 \times (3 \times 6) = 2 \times 18 = 36$$

Suppose the value of this expression will be assigned to the integer variable w; i.e.,

```
w = 2 * ((i % 5) * (4 + (j - 3) / (k + 2)));
```

It is generally better to break this long arithmetic expression up into several shorter expressions, such as

```
u = i % 5;
v = 4 + (j - 3) / (k + 2);
w = 2 * (u * v);
```

where u and v are integer variables. These equivalent expressions are much more likely to be written correctly than the original lengthy expression.

Assignment expressions will be discussed in greater detail in Sec. 3.4.

3.2 UNARY OPERATORS

C includes a class of operators that act upon a single operand to produce a new value. Such operators are known as *unary operators*. Unary operators usually precede their single operands, though some unary operators are written after their operands.

Perhaps the most common unary operation is *unary minus*, where a numerical constant, variable or expression is preceded by a minus sign. (Some programming languages allow a minus sign to be included as a part of a numeric constant. In C, however, all numeric constants are positive. Thus, a negative number is actually an expression, consisting of the unary minus operator, followed by a positive numeric constant.)

Note that the unary minus operation is distinctly different from the arithmetic operator which denotes subtraction (–). The subtraction operator requires two separate operands.

EXAMPLE 3.10   Here are several examples which illustrate the use of the unary minus operation.

```
-743            -0X7FFF         -0.2            -5E-8

-root1          -(x + y)        -3 * (x + y)
```

In each case the minus sign is followed by a numerical operand which may be an integer constant, a floating-point constant, a numeric variable or an arithmetic expression.

There are two other commonly used unary operators: The *increment operator*, ++, and the *decrement operator*, --. The increment operator causes its operand to be increased by 1, whereas the decrement operator causes its operand to be decreased by 1. The operand used with each of these operators must be a single variable.

EXAMPLE 3.11   Suppose that i is an integer variable that has been assigned a value of 5. The expression ++i, which is equivalent to writing i = i + 1, causes the value of i to be increased to 6. Similarly, the expression --i, which is equivalent to i = i - 1, causes the (original) value of i to be decreased to 4.

The increment and decrement operators can each be utilized two different ways, depending on whether the operator is written before or after the operand. If the operator precedes the operand (e.g., ++i), then the operand will be altered in value *before* it is utilized for its intended purpose within the program. If, however, the operator *follows* the operand (e.g., i++), then the value of the operand will be altered *after* it is utilized.

EXAMPLE 3.12   A C program includes an integer variable i whose initial value is 1. Suppose the program includes the following three printf statements. (See Example 1.6 for a brief explanation of the printf statement.)

```
printf("i = %d\n", i);
printf("i = %d\n", ++i);
printf("i = %d\n", i);
```

These printf statements will generate the following three lines of output. (Each printf statement will generate one line.)

```
i = 1
i = 2
i = 2
```

The first statement causes the original value of i to be displayed. The second statement increments i and then displays its value. The final value of i is displayed by the last statement.

Now suppose that the program includes the following three printf statements, rather than the three statements given above.

```
printf("i = %d\n", i);
printf("i = %d\n", i++);
printf("i = %d\n", i);
```

The first and third statements are identical to those shown above. In the second statement, however, the unary operator follows the integer variable rather than precedes it.

These statements will generate the following three lines of output.

```
i = 1
i = 1
i = 2
```

The first statement causes the original value of i to be displayed, as before. The second statement causes the current value of i (1) to be displayed and then incremented (to 2). The final value of i (2) is displayed by the last statement.

We will say much more about the use of the printf statement in Chap. 4. For now, simply note the distinction between the expression ++i in the first group of statements, and the expression i++ in the second group.

Another unary operator that is worth mentioning at this time is the `sizeof` operator. This operator returns the size of its operand, in bytes. The `sizeof` operator always precedes its operand. The operand may be an expression, or it may be a cast.

Elementary programs rarely make use of the `sizeof` operator. However, this operator allows a determination of the number of bytes allocated to various types of data items. This information can be very useful when transferring a program to a different computer or to a new version of C. It is also used for dynamic memory allocation, as explained in Sec. 10.4.

EXAMPLE 3.13 Suppose that i is an integer variable, x is a floating-point variable, d is a double-precision variable, and c is a character-type variable. The statements

```
printf("integer: %d\n", sizeof i);
printf("float: %d\n", sizeof x);
printf("double: %d\n", sizeof d);
printf("character: %d\n", sizeof c);
```

might generate the following output.

```
integer: 2
float: 4
double: 8
character: 1
```

Thus, we see that this version of C allocates 2 bytes to each integer quantity, 4 bytes to each floating-point quantity, 8 bytes to each double-precision quantity, and 1 byte to each character. These values may vary from one version of C to another, as explained in Sec. 2.3.

Another way to generate the same information is to use a cast rather than a variable within each `printf` statement. Thus, the `printf` statements could have been written as

```
printf("integer: %d\n", sizeof (integer));
printf("float: %d\n", sizeof (float));
printf("double: %d\n", sizeof (double));
printf("character: %d\n", sizeof (char));
```

These `printf` statements will generate the same output as that shown above. Note that each cast is enclosed in parentheses, as described in Sec. 3.1.

Finally, consider the array declaration

```
char text[] = "California";
```

The statement

```
printf("Number of characters = %d", sizeof text);
```

will generate the following output.

```
Number of characters = 11
```

Thus we see that the array `text` contains 11 characters, as explained in Example 2.26.

A *cast* is also considered to be a unary operator (see Example 3.5 and the preceding discussion). In general terms, a reference to the cast operator is written as (*type*). Thus, the unary operators that we have encountered so far in this book are –, ++, ––, `sizeof` and (*type*).

Unary operators have a higher precedence than arithmetic operators. Hence, if a unary minus operator acts upon an arithmetic expression that contains one or more arithmetic operators, the unary minus operation will be carried out first (unless, of course, the arithmetic expression is enclosed in parentheses). Also, the associativity of the unary operators is right to left, though consecutive unary operators rarely appear in elementary programs.

EXAMPLE 3.14 Suppose that x and y are integer variables whose values are 10 and 20, respectively. The value of the expression –x + y will be –10 + 20 = 10. Note that the unary minus operation is carried out before the addition.

Now suppose that parentheses are introduced, so that the expression becomes –(10 + 20). The value of this expression is –(10 + 20) = –30. Note that the addition now *precedes* the unary minus operation.

C includes several other unary operators. They will be discussed in later sections of this book, as the need arises.

3.3 RELATIONAL AND LOGICAL OPERATORS

There are four *relational operators* in C. They are

Operator	Meaning
<	less than
<=	less than or equal to
>	greater than
>=	greater than or equal to

These operators all fall within the same precedence group, which is lower than the arithmetic and unary operators. The associativity of these operators is left to right.

Closely associated with the relational operators are the following two *equality operators.*

Operator	Meaning
==	equal to
!=	not equal to

The equality operators fall into a separate precedence group, beneath the relational operators. These operators also have a left-to-right associativity.

These six operators are used to form logical expressions, which represent conditions that are either true or false. The resulting expressions will be of type integer, since *true* is represented by the integer value 1 and *false* is represented by the value 0.

EXAMPLE 3.15 Suppose that i, j and k are integer variables whose values are 1, 2 and 3, respectively. Several logical expressions involving these variables are shown below.

Expression	Interpretation	Value
i < j	true	1
(i + j) >= k	true	1
(j + k) > (i + 5)	false	0
k != 3	false	0
j == 2	true	1

When carrying out relational and equality operations, operands that differ in type will be converted in accordance with the rules discussed in Sec. 3.1.

EXAMPLE 3.16 Suppose that i is an integer variable whose value is 7, f is a floating-point variable whose value is 5.5, and c is a character variable that represents the character 'w'. Several logical expressions that make use of these variables are shown below. Each expression involves two different type operands. (Assume that the ASCII character set applies.)

Expression	Interpretation	Value
f > 5	true	1
(i + f) <= 10	false	0
c == 119	true	1
c != 'p'	true	1
c >= 10 * (i + f)	false	0

In addition to the relational and equality operators, C contains two *logical operators* (also called *logical connectives*). They are

Operator	Meaning
&&	and
||	or

These operators are referred to as *logical and* and *logical or*, respectively.

The logical operators act upon operands that are themselves logical expressions. The net effect is to combine the individual logical expressions into more complex conditions that are either true or false. The result of a *logical and* operation will be true only if both operands are true, whereas the result of a *logical or* operation will be true if either operand is true or if both operands are true. In other words, the result of a *logical or* operation will be false only if both operands are false.

In this context it should be pointed out that *any* nonzero value, not just 1, is interpreted as true.

EXAMPLE 3.17 Suppose that i is an integer variable whose value is 7, f is a floating-point variable whose value is 5.5, and c is a character variable that represents the character 'w'. Several complex logical expressions that make use of these variables are shown below.

Expression	Interpretation	Value
(i >= 6) && (c == 'w')	true	1
(i >= 6) || (c == 119)	true	1
(f < 11) && (i > 100)	false	0
(c != 'p') || ((i + f) <= 10)	true	1

The first expression is true because both operands are true. In the second expression, both operands are again true; hence the overall expression is true. The third expression is false because the second operand is false. And finally, the fourth expression is true because the first operand is true.

Each of the logical operators falls into its own precedence group. *Logical and* has a higher precedence than *logical or*. Both precedence groups are lower than the group containing the equality operators. The associativity is left to right. The precedence groups are summarized below.

C also includes the unary operator ! that negates the value of a logical expression; i.e., it causes an expression that is originally true to become false, and vice versa. This operator is referred to as the *logical negation* (or *logical not*) operator.

EXAMPLE 3.18   Suppose that i is an integer variable whose value is 7, and f is a floating-point variable whose value is 5.5. Several logical expressions which make use of these variables and the logical negation operator are shown below.

Expression	_Interpretation_	_Value_
f > 5	true	1
!(f > 5)	false	0
i <= 3	false	0
!(i <= 3)	true	1
i > (f + 1)	true	1
!(i > (f + 1))	false	0

We will see other examples illustrating the use of the logical negation operator in later chapters of this book.

The hierarchy of operator precedences covering all of the operators discussed so far has become extensive. These operator precedences are summarized below, from highest to lowest.

Operator category	_Operators_	_Associativity_
unary operators	− ++ −− ! sizeof (_type_)	R → L
arithmetic multiply, divide and remainder	* / %	L → R
arithmetic add and subtract	+ −	L → R
relational operators	< <= > >=	L → R
equality operators	== !=	L → R
logical _and_	&&	L → R
logical _or_	||	L → R

A more complete listing is given in Table 3-1, later in this chapter.

EXAMPLE 3.19   Consider once again the variables i, f and c, as described in Examples 3.16 and 3.17; i.e., i = 7, f = 5.5 and c = 'w'. Some logical expressions that make use of these variables are shown below.

Expression	_Interpretation_	_Value_
i + f <= 10	false	0
i >= 6 && c == 'w'	true	1
c != 'p' || i + f <= 10	true	1

Each of these expressions has been presented before (the first in Example 3.16, and the other two in Example 3.17), though pairs of parentheses were included in the previous examples. The parentheses are not necessary because of the natural operator precedences. Thus, the arithmetic operations will automatically be carried out before the relational or equality operations, and the relational and equality operations will automatically be carried out before the logical connectives.

Consider the last expression in particular. The first operation to be carried out will be addition (i.e., i + f); then the relational comparison (i.e., i + f <= 10); then the equality comparison (i.e., c != 'p'); and finally, the _logical or_ condition.

Complex logical expressions that consist of individual logical expressions joined together by the logical operators && and || are evaluated left to right, but only until the overall true/false value has been established. Thus, a complex logical expression will not be evaluated in its entirety if its value can be established from its constituent operands.

EXAMPLE 3.20   Consider the complex logical expression shown below.

```
error > .0001 && count < 100
```

If error > .0001 is false, then the second operand (i.e., count < 100) will not be evaluated, because the entire expression will be considered false.

On the other hand, suppose the expression had been written

```
error > .0001 || count < 100
```

If error > .0001 is true, then the entire expression will be true. Hence, the second operand will not be evaluated. If error > .0001 is false, however, then the second expression (i.e., count < 100) must be evaluated to determine if the entire expression is true or false.

3.4 ASSIGNMENT OPERATORS

There are several different assignment operators in C. All of them are used to form *assignment expressions*, which assign the value of an expression to an identifier.

The most commonly used assignment operator is =. Assignment expressions that make use of this operator are written in the form

```
identifier = expression
```

where *identifier* generally represents a variable, and *expression* represents a constant, a variable or a more complex expression.

EXAMPLE 3.21   Here are some typical assignment expressions that make use of the = operator.

```
a = 3
x = y
delta = 0.001
sum = a + b
area = length * width
```

The first assignment expression causes the integer value 3 to be assigned to the variable a, and the second assignment causes the value of y to be assigned to x. In the third assignment, the floating-point value 0.001 is assigned to delta. The last two assignments each result in the value of an arithmetic expression being assigned to a variable (i.e., the value of a + b is assigned to sum, and the value of length * width is assigned to area).

Remember that the *assignment operator* = and the *equality operator* == are *distinctly different*. The assignment operator is used to assign a value to an identifier, whereas the equality operator is used to determine if two expressions have the same value. These operators cannot be used in place of one another. Beginning programmers often incorrectly use the assignment operator when they want to test for equality. This results in a logical error that is usually difficult to detect.

Assignment expressions are often referred to as *assignment statements*, since they are usually written as complete statements. However, assignment expressions can also be written as expressions that are included within other statements (more about this in later chapters).

If the two operands in an assignment expression are of different data types, then the value of the expression on the right (i.e., the right-hand operand) will automatically be converted to the type of the identifier on the left. The entire assignment expression will then be of this same data type.

Under some circumstances, this automatic type conversion can result in an alteration of the data being assigned. For example:

- A floating-point value may be truncated if assigned to an integer identifier.
- A double-precision value may be rounded if assigned to a floating-point (single-precision) identifier.
- An integer quantity may be altered if assigned to a shorter integer identifier or to a character identifier (some high-order bits may be lost).

Moreover, the value of a character constant assigned to a numeric-type identifier will be dependent upon the particular character set in use. This may result in inconsistencies from one version of C to another.

The careless use of type conversions is a frequent source of error among beginning programmers.

EXAMPLE 3.22 In the following assignment expressions, suppose that i is an integer-type variable.

Expression	Value
i = 3.3	3
i = 3.9	3
i = -3.9	-3

Now suppose that i and j are both integer-type variables, and that j has been assigned a value of 5. Several assignment expressions that make use of these two variables are shown below.

Expression	Value	
i = j	5	
i = j / 2	2	
i = 2 * j / 2	5	(left-to-right associativity)
i = 2 * (j / 2)	4	(truncated division, followed by multiplication)

Finally, assume that i is an integer-type variable, and that the ASCII character set applies.

Expression	Value
i = 'x'	120
i = '0'	48
i = ('x' - '0') / 3	24
i = ('y' - '0') / 3	24

Multiple assignments of the form

        identifier 1 = identifier 2 = ··· = expression

are permissible in C. In such situations, the assignments are carried out from right to left. Thus, the multiple assignment

        identifier 1 = identifier 2 = expression

is equivalent to

        identifier 1 = (identifier 2 = expression)

and so on, with right-to-left nesting for additional multiple assignments.

EXAMPLE 3.23   Suppose that i and j are integer variables. The multiple assignment expression

```
i = j = 5
```

will cause the integer value 5 to be assigned to both i and j. (To be more precise, 5 is first assigned to j, and the value of j is then assigned to i.)

Similarly, the multiple assignment expression

```
i = j = 5.9
```

will cause the integer value 5 to be assigned to both i and j. Remember that truncation occurs when the floating-point value 5.9 is assigned to the integer variable j.

C contains the following five additional assignment operators: +=, −=, *=, /= and %=. To see how they are used, consider the first operator, +=. The assignment expression

expression 1 += expression 2

is equivalent to

expression 1 = expression 1 + expression 2

Similarly, the assignment expression

expression 1 −= expression 2

is equivalent to

expression 1 = expression 1 − expression 2

and so on for all five operators.

Usually, *expression 1* is an identifier, such as a variable or an array element.

EXAMPLE 3.24   Suppose that i and j are integer variables whose values are 5 and 7, and f and g are floating-point variables whose values are 5.5 and −3.25. Several assignment expressions that make use of these variables are shown below. Each expression utilizes the *original* values of i, j, f and g.

Expression	*Equivalent Expression*	*Final value*
i += 5	i = i + 5	10
f −= g	f = f − g	8.75
j *= (i − 3)	j = j * (i − 3)	14
f /= 3	f = f / 3	1.833333
i %= (j − 2)	i = i % (j − 2)	0

Assignment operators have a lower precedence than any of the other operators that have been discussed so far. Therefore unary operations, arithmetic operations, relational operations, equality operations and logical operations are all carried out before assignment operations. Moreover, the assignment operations have a right-to-left associativity.

The hierarchy of operator precedences presented in the last section can now be modified as follows to include assignment operators.

Operator category	Operators	Associativity
unary operators	$-$ ++ $--$! sizeof (*type*)	R → L
arithmetic multiply, divide and remainder	* / %	L → R
arithmetic add and subtract	+ $-$	L → R
relational operators	< <= > >=	L → R
equality operators	== !=	L → R
logical *and*	&&	L→ R
logical *or*	||	L → R
assignment operators	= += $-=$ *= /= %=	R → L

See Table 3-1 later in this chapter for a more complete listing.

EXAMPLE 3.25　Suppose that x, y and z are integer variables which have been assigned the values 2, 3 and 4, respectively. The expression

```
x *= -2 * (y + z) / 3
```

is equivalent to the expression

```
x = x * (-2 * (y + z) / 3)
```

Either expression will cause the value −8 to be assigned to x.

　　Consider the order in which the operations are carried out in the first expression. The arithmetic operations precede the assignment operation. Therefore the expression (y + z) will be evaluated first, resulting in 7. Then the value of this expression will be multiplied by −2, yielding −14. This product will then be divided by 3 and truncated, resulting in −4. Finally, this truncated quotient is multiplied by the original value of x (i.e., 2) to yield the final result of −8.

　　Note that all of the explicit arithmetic operations are carried out before the final multiplication and assignment are made.

　　C contains other assignment operators, in addition to those discussed above. We will discuss them in Chap. 13.

3.5 THE CONDITIONAL OPERATOR

Simple conditional operations can be carried out with the *conditional operator* (? :). An expression that makes use of the conditional operator is called a *conditional expression*. Such an expression can be written in place of the more traditional if-else statement, which is discussed in Chap. 6.

　　A conditional expression is written in the form

```
expression 1 ? expression 2 : expression 3
```

　　When evaluating a conditional expression, *expression 1* is evaluated first. If *expression 1* is true (i.e., if its value is nonzero), then *expression 2* is evaluated and this becomes the value of the conditional expression. However, if *expression 1* is false (i.e., if its value is zero), then *expression 3* is evaluated and this becomes the value of the conditional expression. Note that only one of the embedded expressions (either *expression 2* or *expression 3*) is evaluated when determining the value of a conditional expression.

EXAMPLE 3.26　In the conditional expression shown below, assume that i is an integer variable.

```
(i < 0) ? 0 : 100
```

The expression (i < 0) is evaluated first. If it is true (i.e., if the value of i is less than 0), the entire conditional expression takes on the value 0. Otherwise (if the value of i is not less than 0), the entire conditional expression takes on the value 100.

In the following conditional expression, assume that f and g are floating-point variables.

```
(f < g) ? f : g
```

This conditional expression takes on the value of f if f is less than g; otherwise, the conditional expression takes on the value of g. In other words, the conditional expression returns the value of the smaller of the two variables.

If the operands (i.e., *expression 2* and *expression 3*) differ in type, then the resulting data type of the conditional expression will be determined by the rules given in Sec. 3.1.

EXAMPLE 3.27   Now suppose that i is an integer variable, and f and g are floating-point variables. The conditional expression

```
(f < g) ? i : g
```

involves both integer and floating-point operands. Thus, the resulting expression will be floating-point, even if the value of i is selected as the value of the expression (because of rule 2 in Sec. 3.1).

Conditional expressions frequently appear on the right-hand side of a simple assignment statement. The resulting value of the conditional expression is assigned to the identifier on the left.

EXAMPLE 3.28   Here is an assignment statement that contains a conditional expression on the right-hand side.

```
flag = (i < 0) ? 0 : 100
```

If the value of i is negative, then 0 will be assigned to flag. If i is not negative, however, then 100 will be assigned to flag.

Here is another assignment statement that contains a conditional expression on the right-hand side.

```
min = (f < g) ? f : g
```

This statement causes the value of the smaller of f and g to be assigned to min.

The conditional operator has its own precedence, just above the assignment operators. The associativity is right to left.

Table 3-1 summarizes the precedences for all of the operators discussed in this chapter.

Table 3-1   Operator Precedence Groups

Operator category	Operators						Associativity
unary operators	−	++	−−	!	sizeof	(*type*)	R → L
arithmetic multiply, divide and remainder			*	/	%		L → R
arithmetic add and subtract			+	−			L → R
relational operators		<	<=	>	>=		L → R
equality operators			==	!=			L → R
logical *and*			&&				L → R
logical *or*			||				L → R
conditional operator			? :				R → L
assignment operators	=	+=	−=	*=	/=	%=	R → L

A complete listing of all C operators, which is more extensive than that given in Table 3-1, is shown in Appendix C.

EXAMPLE 3.29 In the following assignment statement, a, b and c are assumed to be integer variables. The statement includes operators from six different precedence groups.

```
c += (a > 0 && a <= 10) ? ++a : a/b;
```

The statement begins by evaluating the complex expression

```
(a > 0 && a <= 10)
```

If this expression is true, the expression ++a is evaluated. Otherwise, the expression a/b is evaluated. Finally, the assignment operation (+=) is carried out, causing the value of c to be increased by the value of the conditional expression.

If, for example, a, b and c have the values 1, 2 and 3, respectively, then the value of the conditional expression will be 2 (because the expression ++a will be evaluated), and the value of c will increase to 5 (c = 3 + 2). On the other hand, if a, b and c have the values 50, 10 and 20, respectively, then the value of the conditional expression will be 5 (because the expression a/b will be evaluated), and the value of c will increase to 25 (c = 20 + 5).

3.6 LIBRARY FUNCTIONS

The C language is accompanied by a number of *library functions* that carry out various commonly used operations or calculations. These library functions are not a part of the language per se, though all implementations of the language include them. Some functions return a data item to their access point; others indicate whether a condition is true or false by returning a 1 or a 0, respectively; still others carry out specific operations on data items but do not return anything. Features which tend to be computer-dependent are generally written as library functions.

For example, there are library functions that carry out standard input/output operations (e.g., read and write characters, read and write numbers, open and close files, test for end of file, etc.), functions that perform operations on characters (e.g., convert from lower- to uppercase, test to see if a character is uppercase, etc.), functions that perform operations on strings (e.g., copy a string, compare strings, concatenate strings, etc.), and functions that carry out various mathematical calculations (e.g., evaluate trigonometric, logarithmic and exponential functions, compute absolute values, square roots, etc.). Other kinds of library functions are also available.

Library functions that are functionally similar are usually grouped together as (compiled) object programs in separate library files. These library files are supplied as a part of each C compiler. All C compilers contain similar groups of library functions, though they lack precise standardization. Thus there may be some variation in the library functions that are available in different versions of the language.

A typical set of library functions will include a fairly large number of functions that are common to most C compilers, such as those shown in Table 3-2 below. Within this table, the column labeled "type" refers to the data type of the quantity that is returned by the function. The *void* entry shown for function srand indicates that nothing is returned by this function.

A more extensive list, which includes all of the library functions that appear in the programming examples presented in this book, is shown in Appendix H. For complete list, see the programmer's reference manual that accompanies your particular version of C.

A library function is accessed simply by writing the function name, followed by a list of *arguments* that represent information being passed to the function. The arguments must be enclosed in parentheses and separated by commas. The arguments can be constants, variable names, or more complex expressions. The parentheses must be present, even if there are no arguments.

A function that returns a data item can appear anywhere within an expression, in place of a constant or an identifier (i.e., in place of a variable or an array element). A function that carries out operations on data items but does not return anything can be accessed simply by writing the function name, since this type of function reference constitutes an expression statement.

Table 3-2   Some Commonly Used Library Functions

Function	Type	Purpose
`abs(i)`	int	Return the absolute value of `i`.
`ceil(d)`	double	Round up to the next integer value (the smallest integer that is greater than or equal to `d`).
`cos(d)`	double	Return the cosine of `d`.
`cosh(d)`	double	Return the hyperbolic cosine of `d`.
`exp(d)`	double	Raise e to the power `d` ($e = 2.7182818 \cdots$ is the base of the natural (Naperian) system of logarithms).
`fabs(d)`	double	Return the absolute value of `d`.
`floor(d)`	double	Round down to the next integer value (the largest integer that does not exceed `d`).
`fmod(d1,d2)`	double	Return the remainder (i.e., the noninteger part of the quotient) of `d1/d2`, with same sign as `d1`.
`getchar()`	int	Enter a character from the standard input device.
`log(d)`	double	Return the natural logarithm of `d`.
`pow(d1,d2)`	double	Return `d1` raised to the `d2` power.
`printf(...)`	int	Send data items to the standard output device (arguments are complicated — see Chap. 4).
`putchar(c)`	int	Send a character to the standard output device.
`rand()`	int	Return a random positive integer.
`sin(d)`	double	Return the sine of `d`.
`sqrt(d)`	double	Return the square root of `d`.
`srand(u)`	void	Initialize the random number generator.
`scanf(...)`	int	Enter data items from the standard input device (arguments are complicated — see Chap. 4).
`tan(d)`	double	Return the tangent of `d`.
`toascii(c)`	int	Convert value of argument to ASCII.
`tolower(c)`	int	Convert letter to lowercase.
`toupper(c)`	int	Convert letter to uppercase.

Note: *Type* refers to the data type of the quantity that is returned by the function.

c denotes a character-type argument

i denotes an integer argument

d denotes a double-precision argument

u denotes an unsigned integer argument

EXAMPLE 3.30   Shown below is a portion of a C program that solves for the roots of the quadratic equation

$$ax^2 + bx + c = 0$$

using the well-known quadratic formula

$$x = \frac{-b \pm \sqrt{b^2 - 4ac}}{2a}$$

This program uses the `sqrt` library function to evaluate the square root.

```
main()   /* solution of a quadratic equation */
{
    double a,b,c,root,x1,x2;

    /* read values for a, b and c */

    root = sqrt(b * b - 4 * a * c);
    x1 = (-b + root) / (2 * a);
    x2 = (-b - root) / (2 * a);

    /* display values for a, b, c, x1 and x2 */
}
```

In order to use a library function it may be necessary to include certain specific information within the main portion of the program. For example, forward function declarations and symbolic constant definitions are usually required when using library functions (see Secs. 7.3, 8.5 and 8.6). This information is generally stored in special files which are supplied with the compiler. Thus, the required information can be obtained simply by accessing these special files. This is accomplished with the preprocessor statement #include; i.e.,

```
#include <filename>
```

where *filename* represents the name of a special file.

The names of these special files are specified by each individual implementation of C, though there are certain commonly used file names such as `stdio.h`, `stdlib.h` and `math.h`. The suffix "h" generally designates a "header" file, which indicates that it is to be included at the beginning of the program. (Header files are discussed in Sec. 8.6.)

Note the similarity between the preprocessor statement #include and the preprocessor statement #define, which was discussed in Sec. 2.9.

EXAMPLE 3.31 Lowercase to Uppercase Character Conversion   Here is a complete C program that reads in a lowercase character, converts it to uppercase and then displays the uppercase equivalent.

```
/* read a lowercase character and display its uppercase equivalent */

#include <stdio.h>
#include <ctype.h>

main()
{
    int lower, upper;

    lower = getchar();
    upper = toupper(lower);
    putchar(upper);
}
```

This program contains three library functions: `getchar`, `toupper` and `putchar`. The first two functions each return a single character (`getchar` returns a character that is entered from the keyboard, and `toupper` returns the uppercase equivalent of its argument). The last function (`putchar`) causes the value of the argument to be displayed. Notice that the last two functions each have one argument but the first function does not have any arguments, as indicated by the empty parentheses.

Also, notice the preprocessor statements `#include <stdio.h>` and `#include <ctype.h>`, which appear at the start of the program. These statements cause the contents of the files `stdio.h` and `ctype.h` to be inserted into the program the compilation process begins. The information contained in these files is essential for the proper functioning of the library functions `getchar`, `putchar` and `toupper`.

Review Questions

3.1   What is an expression? What are its components?

3.2   What is an operator? Describe several different types of operators that are included in C.

3.3   What is an operand? What is the relationship between operators and operands?

3.4   Describe the five arithmetic operators in C. Summarize the rules associated with their use.

3.5   Summarize the rules that apply to expressions whose operands are of different types.

3.6   How can the value of an expression be converted to a different data type? What is this called?

3.7   What is meant by operator precedence? What are the relative precedences of the arithmetic operators?

3.8   What is meant by associativity? What is the associativity of the arithmetic operators?

3.9   When should parentheses be included within an expression? When should the use of parentheses be avoided?

3.10   In what order are the operations carried out within an expression that contains nested parentheses?

3.11   What are unary operators? How many operands are associated with a unary operator?

3.12   Describe the six unary operators discussed in this chapter. What is the purpose of each?

3.13   Describe two different ways to utilize the increment and decrement operators. How do the two methods differ?

3.14   What is the relative precedence of the unary operators compared with the arithmetic operators? What is their associativity?

3.15   How can the number of bytes allocated to each data type be determined for a particular C compiler?

3.16   Describe the four relational operators included in C. With what type of operands can they be used? What type of expression is obtained?

3.17   Describe the two equality operators included in C. How do they differ from the relational operators?

3.18   Describe the two logical operators included in C. What is the purpose of each? With what type of operands can they be used? What type of expression is obtained?

3.19   What are the relative precedences of the relational, equality and logical operators with respect to one another and with respect to the arithmetic and unary operators? What are their associativities?

3.20   Describe the *logical not* (logical negation) operator. What is its purpose? Within which precedence group is it included? How many operands does it require? What is its associativity?

3.21   Describe the six assignment operators discussed in this chapter. What is the purpose of each?

3.22   How is the type of an assignment expression determined when the two operands are of different data types? In what sense is this situation sometimes a source of programming errors?

3.23   How can multiple assignments be written in C? In what order will the assignments be carried out?

3.24   What is the precedence of assignment operators relative to other operators? What is their associativity?

3.25   Describe the use of the conditional operator to form conditional expressions. How is a conditional expression evaluated?

3.26   How is the type of a conditional expression determined when its operands differ in type?

3.27   How can the conditional operator be combined with the assignment operator to form an "if - else" type statement?

3.28   What is the precedence of the conditional operator relative to the other operators described in this chapter? What is its associativity?

3.29   Describe, in general terms, the kinds of operations and calculations that are carried out by the C library functions.

3.30   Are the library functions actually a part of the C language? Explain.

3.31   How are the library functions usually packaged within a C compiler?

3.32   How are library functions accessed? How is information passed to a library function from the access point?

3.33   What are arguments? How are arguments written? How is a call to a library function written if there are no arguments?

3.34   How is specific information that may be required by the library functions stored? How is this information entered into a C program?

3.35   In what general category do the #define and #include statements fall?

Problems

3.36 Suppose a, b and c are integer variables that have been assigned the values a = 8, b = 3 and c = –5. Determine the value of each of the following arithmetic expressions.

(a)	a + b + c	(f)	a % c
(b)	2 * b + 3 * (a – c)	(g)	a * b / c
(c)	a / b	(h)	a * (b / c)
(d)	a % b	(i)	(a * c) % b
(e)	a / c	(j)	a * (c % b)

3.37 Suppose x, y and z are floating-point variables that have been assigned the values x = 8.8, y = 3.5 and z = –5.2. Determine the value of each of the following arithmetic expressions.

(a)	x + y + z	(e)	x / (y + z)
(b)	2 * y + 3 * (x – z)	(f)	(x / y) + z
(c)	x / y	(g)	2 * x / 3 * y
(d)	x % y	(h)	2 * x / (3 * y)

3.38 Suppose c1, c2 and c3 are character-type variables that have been assigned the characters E, 5 and ?, respectively. Determine the numerical value of the following expressions, based upon the ASCII character set (see Table 2-1).

(a)	c1	(f)	c1 % c3
(b)	c1 – c2 + c3	(g)	'2' + '2'
(c)	c2 – 2	(h)	(c1 / c2) * c3
(d)	c2 – '2'	(i)	3 * c2
(e)	c3 + '#'	(j)	'3' * c2

3.39 A C program contains the following declarations:

```
int i, j;
long ix;
short s;
float x;
double dx;
char c;
```

Determine the data type of each of the following expressions.

(a)	i + c	(f)	s + j
(b)	x + c	(g)	ix + j
(c)	dx + x	(h)	s + c
(d)	((int) dx) + ix	(i)	ix + c
(e)	i + x		

3.40 A C program contains the following declarations and initial assignments:

```
int i = 8, j = 5;
float x = 0.005, y = –0.01;
char c = 'c', d = 'd';
```

Determine the value of each of the following expressions. Use the values initially assigned to the variables for each expression.

(a)	(3 * i – 2 * j) % (2 * d – c)
(b)	2 * ((i / 5) + (4 * (j – 3)) % (i + j – 2))

(c)   (i - 3 * j) % (c + 2 * d) / (x - y)

(d)   -(i + j)

(e)   ++i

(f)   i++

(g)   —j

(h)   ++x

(i)   y—

(j)   i <= j

(k)   c > d

(l)   x >= 0

(m)   x < y

(n)   j != 6

(o)   c == 99

(p)   5 * (i + j) > 'c'

(q)   (2 * x + y) == 0

(r)   2 * x + (y == 0)

(s)   2 * x + y == 0

(t)   !(i <= j)

(u)   !(c == 99)

(v)   !(x > 0)

(w)   (i > 0) && (j < 5)

(x)   (i > 0) !! (j < 5)

(y)   (x > y) && (i > 0) !! (j < 5)

(z)   (x > y) && (i > 0) && (j < 5)

3.41   A C program contains the following declarations and initial assignments:

```
int i = 8, j = 5, k;
float x = 0.005, y = -0.01, z;
char a, b, c = 'c', d = 'd';
```

Determine the value of each of the following assignment expressions. Use the values originally assigned to the variables for each expression.

(a)	k = (i + j)	(l)	y -= x
(b)	z = (x + y)	(m)	x *= 2
(c)	i = j	(n)	i /= j
(d)	k = (x + y)	(o)	i %= j
(e)	k = c	(p)	i += (j - 2)
(f)	z = i / j	(q)	k = (j == 5) ? i : j
(g)	a = b = d	(r)	k = (j > 5) ? i : j
(h)	i = j = 1.1	(s)	z = (x >= 0) ? x : 0
(i)	z = k = x	(t)	z = (y >= 0) ? y : 0
(j)	k = z = x	(u)	a = (c < d) ? c : d
(k)	i += 2	(v)	i -= (j > 0) ? j : 0

3.42   Each of the following expressions involves the use of a library function. Identify the purpose of each expression. (See Appendix H for an extensive list of library functions.)

(a)	`abs(i - 2 * j)`	(l)	`sqrt(x*x + y*y)`
(b)	`fabs(x + y)`	(m)	`isalnum(10 * j)`
(c)	`isprint(c)`	(n)	`isalpha(10 * j)`
(d)	`isdigit(c)`	(o)	`isascii(10 * j)`
(e)	`toupper(d)`	(p)	`toascii(10 * j)`
(f)	`ceil(x)`	(q)	`fmod(x, y)`
(g)	`floor(x + y)`	(r)	`tolower(65)`
(h)	`islower(c)`	(s)	`pow(x - y, 3.0)`
(i)	`isupper(j)`	(t)	`sin(x - y)`
(j)	`exp(x)`	(u)	`strlen("hello\0")`
(k)	`log(x)`	(v)	`strpos("hello\0", 'e')`

3.43   A C program contains the following declarations and initial assignments:

```
int i = 8, j = 5;
double x = 0.005, y = -0.01;
char c = 'c', d = 'd';
```

Determine the value of each of the following expressions, which involve the use of library functions. (See Appendix H for an extensive list of library functions.)

(a)	`abs(i - 2 * j)`	(n)	`log(exp(x))`
(b)	`fabs(x + y)`	(o)	`sqrt(x*x + y*y)`
(c)	`isprint(c)`	(p)	`isalnum(10 * j)`
(d)	`isdigit(c)`	(q)	`isalpha(10 * j)`
(e)	`toupper(d)`	(r)	`isascii(10 * j)`
(f)	`ceil(x)`	(s)	`toascii(10 * j)`
(g)	`ceil(x + y)`	(t)	`fmod(x, y)`
(h)	`floor(x)`	(u)	`tolower(65)`
(i)	`floor(x + y)`	(v)	`pow(x - y, 3.0)`
(j)	`islower(c)`	(w)	`sin(x - y)`
(k)	`isupper(j)`	(x)	`strlen("hello\0")`
(l)	`exp(x)`	(y)	`strpos("hello\0", 'e')`
(m)	`log(x)`	(z)	`sqrt(sin(x) + cos(y))`

3.44   Determine which of the library functions shown in Appendix H are available for your particular version of C. Are some of the functions available under a different name? What header files are required?

Chapter 4

Data Input and Output

We have already seen that the C language is accompanied by a collection of library functions, which includes a number of input/output functions. In this chapter we will make use of six of these functions: `getchar`, `putchar`, `scanf`, `printf`, `gets` and `puts`. These six functions permit the transfer of information between the computer and the standard input/output devices (e.g., a keyboard and a TV monitor). The first two functions, `getchar` and `putchar`, allow single characters to be transferred into and out of the computer; `scanf` and `printf` are the most complicated, but they permit the transfer of single characters, numerical values and strings; `gets` and `puts` facilitate the input and output of strings. Once we have learned how to use these functions, we will be able to write a number of complete, though simple, C programs.

4.1 PRELIMINARIES

An input/output function can be accessed from anywhere within a program simply by writing the function name, followed by a list of arguments enclosed in parentheses. The arguments represent data items that are sent to the function. Some input/output functions do not require arguments, though the empty parentheses must still appear.

The names of those functions that return data items may appear within expressions, as though each function reference were an ordinary variable (e.g., `c = getchar();`), or they may be referenced as separate statements (e.g., `scanf(. . .);`). Some functions do not return any data items. Such functions are referenced as though they were separate statements (e.g., `putchar(. . .);`).

Most versions of C include a collection of header files that provide necessary information (e.g., symbolic constants) in support of the various library functions. Each file generally contains information in support of a group of related library functions. These files are entered into the program via an `#include` statement at the beginning of the program. As a rule, the header file required by the standard input/output library functions is called `stdio.h` (see Sec. 8.6 for more information about the contents of these header files).

EXAMPLE 4.1 Here is an outline of a typical C program that makes use of several input/output routines from the standard C library.

```
/* sample setup illustrating the use of input/output library functions */

#include <stdio.h>

main()
{
        char c,d;                       /* declarations */
        float x,y;
        int i,j,k;

        c = getchar();                  /* character input */
        scanf("%f", &x);                /* floating-point input */
        scanf("%d %d", &i, &j);         /* integer input */
        . . .                           /* action statements */
        putchar(d);                     /* character output */
        printf("%3d %7.4f", k, y);      /* numerical output */
}
```

The program begins with the preprocessor statement #include <stdio.h>. This statement causes the contents of the header file stdio.h to be included within the program. The header file supplies required information to the library functions scanf and printf. (The syntax of the #include statement may vary from one version of C to another; some versions of the language use quotes instead of angle-brackets, e.g., #include "stdio.h".)

Following the preprocessor statement is the program heading main() and some variable declarations. Several input/output statements are shown in the skeletal outline that follows the declarations. In particular, the assignment statement c = getchar(); causes a single character to be entered from the keyboard and assigned to the character variable c. The first reference to scanf causes a floating-point value to be entered from the keyboard and assigned to the floating-point variable x, whereas the second reference to scanf causes two decimal integer quantities to be entered from the keyboard and assigned to the integer variables i and j, respectively.

The output statements behave in a similar manner. Thus, the reference to putchar causes the value of the character variable d to be displayed. Similarly, the reference to printf causes the values of the integer variable k and the floating-point variable y to be displayed.

The details of each input/output statement will be discussed in subsequent sections of this chapter. For now, you should consider only a general overview of the input/output statements appearing in this typical C program.

4.2 SINGLE CHARACTER INPUT — THE getchar FUNCTION

Single characters can be entered into the computer using the C library function getchar. We have already encountered the use of this function in Chaps. 1 and 2, and in Example 4.1. Let us now examine it more thoroughly.

The getchar function is a part of the standard C I/O library. It returns a single character from a standard input device (typically a keyboard). The function does not require any arguments, though a pair of empty parentheses must follow the word getchar.

In general terms, a function reference would be written as

character variable = getchar();

where *character variable* refers to some previously declared character variable.

EXAMPLE 4.2   A C program contains the following statements.

```
char c;
. . . . .
c = getchar();
```

The first statement declares that c is a character-type variable. The second statement causes a single character to be entered from the standard input device (usually a keyboard) and then assigned to c.

If an *end-of-file* condition is encountered when reading a character with the getchar function, the value of the symbolic constant EOF will automatically be returned. (This value will be assigned within the stdio.h file. Typically, EOF will be assigned the value −1, though this may vary from one compiler to another.) The detection of EOF in this manner offers a convenient way to detect an end of file, whenever and wherever it may occur. Appropriate corrective action can then be taken. Both the detection of the EOF condition and the corrective action can be carried out using the if - else statement described in Chap. 6.

The getchar function can also be used to read multicharacter strings, by reading one character at a time within a multipass loop. We will see one illustration of this in Example 4.4 below. Additional examples will be presented in later chapters of this book.

4.3 SINGLE CHARACTER OUTPUT — THE putchar FUNCTION

Single characters can be displayed (i.e, written out of the computer) using the C library function putchar. This function is complementary to the character input function getchar, which we discussed in the last section.   We have already seen illustrations of the use of these two functions in Chaps. 1 and 2, and in Example 4.1. We now examine the use of putchar in more detail.

The putchar function, like getchar, is a part of the standard C I/O library. It transmits a single character to a standard output device (typically a TV monitor). The character being transmitted will normally be represented as a character-type variable. It must be expressed as an argument to the function, enclosed in parentheses, following the word putchar.

In general, a function reference would be written as

```
putchar(character variable)
```

where *character variable* refers to some previously declared character variable.

EXAMPLE 4.3   A C program contains the following statements.

```
char c;
. . . . .
putchar(c);
```

The first statement declares that c is a character-type variable. The second statement causes the current value of c to be transmitted to the standard output device (e.g., a TV monitor) where it will be displayed. (Compare with Example 4.2, which illustrates the use of the getchar function.)

The putchar function can be used to output a string constant by storing the string within a one-dimensional, character-type array, as explained in Chap. 2. Each character can then be written separately within a loop. The most convenient way to do this is to utilize a for statement, as illustrated in the following example. (The for statement is discussed in detail in Chap. 6.)

EXAMPLE 4.4 Lowercase to Uppercase Text Conversion   Here is a complete program that reads a line of lowercase text, stores it within a one-dimensional, character-type array, and then displays it in uppercase.

```
/* read in a line of lowercase text and display it in uppercase */

#include <stdio.h>
#include <ctype.h>

main()
{
    char letter[80];
    int count, tag;

    /* enter the text */

    for (count = 0; (letter[count] = getchar()) != '\n'; ++count)
        ;

    /* tag the character count */

    tag = count;

    /* display the line in uppercase */

    for (count = 0; count < tag; ++count)
        putchar(toupper(letter[count]));
}
```

Notice the declaration

```
        char letter[80];
```

This declares `letter` to be an 80-element, character-type array whose elements will represent the individual characters within the line of text.

Now consider the statement

```
        for (count = 0; (letter[count] = getchar()) != '\n'; ++count)
            ;
```

This statement creates a loop that causes the individual characters to be read into the computer and assigned to the array elements. The loop begins with a value of `count` equal to zero. A character is then read into the computer from the standard input device, and assigned to `letter[0]` (the first element in `letter`). The value of `count` is then incremented, and the process is repeated for the next array element. This looping action continues as long as a *newline* character (i.e., `'\n'`) is not encountered. The *newline* character will signify the end of the line, and will therefore terminate the process.

Once all of the characters have been entered, the value of `count` corresponding to the last character is assigned to `tag`. Another `for` loop is then initiated, in which the uppercase equivalents of the original characters are displayed on the standard output device. Characters that were originally uppercase, digits, punctuation characters, etc., will be displayed in their original form. Thus, if the message

```
Now is the time for all good men to come to the aid of their country!
```

is entered as input, the corresponding output will be

```
NOW IS THE TIME FOR ALL GOOD MEN TO COME TO THE AID OF THEIR COUNTRY!
```

Note that `tag` will be assigned the value 69 after all of the characters have been entered, since the 69th character will be the newline character following the exclamation point.

Chapter 6 contains more detailed information on the use of the `for` statement to control a character array. For now, you should seek only a general understanding of what is happening.

4.4 ENTERING INPUT DATA — THE scanf FUNCTION

Input data can be entered into the computer from a standard input device by means of the C library function `scanf`. This function can be used to enter any combination of numerical values, single characters and strings. The function returns the number of data items that have been entered successfully.

In general terms, the `scanf` function is written as

```
        scanf(control string, arg1, arg2, . . . , argn)
```

where *control string* refers to a string containing certain required formatting information, and *arg1, arg2, . . . , argn* are arguments that represent the individual input data items. (Actually, the arguments represent *pointers* that indicate the *addresses* of the data items within the computer's memory. More about this later, in Chap. 10.)

The control string consists of individual groups of characters, with one character group for each input data item. Each character group must begin with a percent sign (%). In its simplest form, a single character group will consist of the percent sign, followed by a *conversion character* which indicates the type of the corresponding data item.

Within the control string, multiple character groups can be contiguous, or they can be separated by whitespace characters (i.e., blank spaces, tabs or newline characters). If whitespace characters are used to separate multiple character groups in the control string, then all consecutive whitespace characters in the input data will be read but ignored. The use of blank spaces as character-group separators is very common.

The more frequently used conversion characters are listed in Table 4-1.

Table 4-1   Commonly Used Conversion Characters for Data Input

Conversion Character	Meaning
c	data item is a single character
d	data item is a decimal integer
e	data item is a floating-point value
f	data item is a floating-point value
g	data item is a floating-point value
h	data item is a short integer
i	data item is a decimal, hexadecimal or octal integer
o	data item is an octal integer
s	data item is a string followed by a whitespace character (the null character \0 will automatically be added at the end)
u	data item is an unsigned decimal integer
x	data item is a hexadecimal integer
[. . .]	data item is a string which may include whitespace characters (see explanation below)

The arguments are written as variables or arrays, whose types match the corresponding character groups in the control string. *Each variable name must be preceded by an ampersand* (&). (The arguments are actually pointers that indicate where the data items are stored in the computer's memory, as explained in Chap. 10.) However, array names should *not* begin with an ampersand.

EXAMPLE 4.5   Here is a typical application of a scanf function.

```
#include <stdio.h>

main()

{
    char item[20];
    int partno;
    float cost;

    . . . . .

    scanf("%s %d %f", item, &partno, &cost);

    . . . . .

}
```

Within the scanf function, the control string is "%s %d %f". It contains three character groups. The first character group, %s, indicates that the first argument (item) represents a string. The second character group, %d, indicates that the second argument (&partno) represents a decimal integer value, and the third character group, %f, indicates that the third argument (&cost) represents a floating-point value.

Notice that the numerical variables partno and cost are preceded by ampersands within the scanf function. An ampersand does not precede item, however, since item is an array name.

Notice also that the scanf function could have been written

```
scanf("%s%d%f", item, &partno, &cost);
```

with no whitespace characters in the control string. This is also valid, though the input data could be interpreted differently when using c-type conversions (more about this later in this chapter).

The actual data items are numeric values, single characters or strings, or some combination thereof. They are entered from a standard input device (typically a keyboard). The data items must correspond to the arguments in the scanf function in number, in type and in order. Numeric data items are written in the same form as numeric constants (see Sec. 2.4), though octal values need not be preceded by a 0, and hexadecimal values need not be preceded by 0x or 0X. Floating-point values must include either a decimal point or an exponent (or both).

If two or more data items are entered, they must be separated by whitespace characters. (A possible exception to this rule occurs with c-type conversions, as described in Sec. 4.5) The data items may continue onto two or more lines, since the newline character is considered to be a whitespace character and can therefore separate consecutive data items.

Moreover, if the control string begins by reading a character-type data item, it is generally a good idea to precede the first conversion character with a blank space. This causes the scanf function to ignore any extraneous characters that may have been entered earlier (for example, by pressing the Enter key after entering a previous line of data).

EXAMPLE 4.6   Consider once again the skeletal outline of a C program shown in Example 4.5; i.e.,

```
#include <stdio.h>

main()

{
    char item[20];
    int partno;
    float cost;

    . . . . .
    scanf(" %s %d %f", item, &partno, &cost);

    . . . . .
}
```

Notice the blank space that precedes %s. This prevents any previously entered extraneous characters from being assigned to item.

The following data items could be entered from the standard input device when the program is executed.

```
fastener 12345 0.05
```

Thus, the characters that make up the string fastener would be assigned to the first eight elements of the array item; the integer value 12345 would be assigned to partno, and the floating-point value 0.05 would be assigned to cost.

Note that the individual data items are entered on one line, separated by blank spaces. The data items could also be entered on separate lines, however, since newline characters are also whitespace characters. Therefore, the data items could also be entered in any of the following ways:

```
fastener              fastener              fastener    12345
12345                 12345     0.05        0.05
0.05
```

Note that the s-type conversion character applies to a string that is terminated by a whitespace character. Therefore, a string that *includes* whitespace characters cannot be entered in this manner. There are ways, however, to work with strings that include whitespace characters. One way is to use the getchar function within a loop, as illustrated in Example 4.4. It is also possible to use the scanf function to enter such strings. To do so, the s-type conversion character within the control string is replaced by a sequence of characters enclosed in square brackets, designated as [. . .]. Whitespace characters may be included within the brackets, thus accommodating strings that contain such characters.

When the program is executed, successive characters will continue to be read from the standard input device as long as each input character matches one of the characters enclosed within the brackets. The order of the characters within the square brackets need not correspond to the order of the characters being entered. Input characters may be repeated. The string will terminate, however, once an input character is encountered that does not match any of the characters within the brackets. A null character (\0) will then automatically be added to the end of the string.

EXAMPLE 4.7   This example illustrates the use of the scanf function to enter a string consisting of uppercase letters and blank spaces. The string will be of undetermined length, but it will be limited to 79 characters (actually, 80 characters including the null character that is added at the end). Notice the blank space that precedes the % sign.

```
#include <stdio.h>

main()

{
    char line[80];

    . . . . .

    scanf(" %[ ABCDEFGHIJKLMNOPQRSTUVWXYZ]", line);

    . . . . .

}
```

If the string

```
NEW YORK CITY
```

is entered from the standard input device when the program is executed, the entire string will be assigned to the array line since the string is comprised entirely of uppercase letters and blank spaces. If the string were written as

```
New York City
```

however, then only the single letter N would be assigned to line, since the first lowercase letter (in this case, e) would be interpreted as the first character beyond the string. It would, of course, be possible to include both uppercase and lowercase characters within the brackets, but this becomes cumbersome.

A variation of this feature which is often more useful is to precede the characters within the square brackets by a *circumflex* (i.e., ^). This causes the subsequent characters within the brackets to be interpreted in the opposite manner. Thus, when the program is executed, successive characters will continue to be read from the standard input device as long as each input character *does not* match one of the characters enclosed within the brackets.

If the characters within the brackets are simply the circumflex followed by a newline character, then the string entered from the standard input device can contain any ASCII characters except the newline character (line feed). Thus, the user may enter whatever he or she wishes and then press the Enter key. The Enter key will issue the newline character, thus signifying the end of the string.

EXAMPLE 4.8   Suppose a C program contains the following statements.

```
#include <stdio.h>

main()
{
    char line[80];

    . . . . .

    scanf(" %[^\n]", line);

    . . . . .
}
```

Notice the blank space preceding `%[^\n]`, to ignore any unwanted characters that may have been entered previously.

When the `scanf` function is executed, a string of undetermined length (but not more than 79 characters) will be entered from the standard input device and assigned to `line`. There will be no restrictions on the characters that comprise the string, except that they all fit on one line. For example, the string

```
The PITTSBURGH STEELERS is one of America's favorite football teams!
```

could be entered from the keyboard and assigned to `line`.

4.5 MORE ABOUT THE scanf FUNCTION

This section contains some additional details about the `scanf` function. Beginning C programmers may wish to skip over this material for the time being.

The consecutive nonwhitespace characters that define a data item collectively define a *field*. It is possible to limit the number of such characters by specifying a maximum *field width* for that data item. To do so, an unsigned integer indicating the field width is placed within the control string, between the percent sign (%) and the conversion character.

The data item may contain fewer characters than the specified field width. However, the number of characters in the actual data item cannot exceed the specified field width. Any characters that extend beyond the specified field width will not be read. Such leftover characters may be incorrectly interpreted as the components of the next data item.

EXAMPLE 4.9   The skeletal structure of a C program is shown below.

```
#include <stdio.h>

main()
{
    int a, b, c;

    . . . . .

    scanf("%3d %3d %3d", &a, &b, &c);

    . . . . .
}
```

When the program is executed, three integer quantities will be entered from the standard input device (the keyboard). Suppose the input data items are entered as

1 2 3

Then the following assignments will result:

```
a = 1,    b = 2,    c = 3
```

If the data had been entered as

```
123 456 789
```

Then the assignments would be

```
a = 123,        b = 456,   c = 789
```

Now suppose that the data had been entered as

```
123456789
```

Then the assignments would be

```
a = 123,        b = 456,   c = 789
```

as before, since the first three digits would be assigned to a, the next three digits to b, and the last three digits to c.
Finally, suppose that the data had been entered as

```
1234 5678 9
```

The resulting assignments would now be

```
a = 123,        b = 4,   c = 567
```

The remaining two digits (8 and 9) would be ignored, unless they were read by a subsequent scanf statement.

EXAMPLE 4.10   Consider a C program that contains the following statements.

```
#include <stdio.h>

main()
{
    int i;
    float x;
    char c;

    . . . . .

    scanf("%3d %5f %c", &i, &x, &c);

    . . . . .
}
```

If the data items are entered as

```
10 256.875 T
```

when the program is executed, then 10 will be assigned to i, 256.8 will be assigned to x and the character 7 will be assigned to c. The remaining two input characters (5 and T) will be ignored.

Most versions of C allow certain conversion characters within the control string to be preceded by a single-letter *prefix*, which indicates the length of the corresponding argument. For example, an l (lowercase L) is used to indicate either a signed or unsigned long integer argument, or a double-precision argument. Similarly, an h is used to indicate a signed or unsigned short integer. Also, some versions of of C permit the use of an uppercase L to indicate a long double.

EXAMPLE 4.11 Suppose the following statements are included in a C program.

```
#include <stdio.h>

main()

{
    short ix,iy;
    long lx,ly;
    double dx,dy;

    . . . . .

    scanf("%hd %ld %lf", &ix, &lx, &dx);

    . . . . .

    scanf("%3ho %7lx %15le", &iy, &ly, &dy);

    . . . . .

}
```

The control string in the first scanf function indicates that the first data item will be assigned to a short decimal integer variable, the second will be assigned to a long decimal integer variable, and the third will be assigned to a double-precision variable. The control string in the second scanf function indicates that the first data item will have a maximum field width of 3 characters and it will be assigned to a short octal integer variable, the second data item will have a maximum field width of 7 characters and it will be assigned to a long hexadecimal integer variable, and the third data item will have a maximum field width of 15 characters and it will be assigned to a double-precision variable.

Some versions of C permit the use of uppercase conversion characters to indicate long integers (signed or unsigned). This feature may be available in addition to the prefix "l", or it may replace the use of the prefix.

EXAMPLE 4.12 Consider once again the skeletal outline of the C program given in Example 4.11. With some versions of C, it may be possible to write the scanf functions somewhat differently, as follows.

```
#include <stdio.h>

main()

{
    short ix,iy;
    long lx,ly;
    double dx,dy;

    . . . . .

    scanf("%hd %D %f", &ix, &lx, &dx);

    . . . . .

    scanf("%3ho %7X %15e", &iy, &ly, &dy);

    . . . . .

}
```

Notice the use of uppercase conversion characters (in the scanf functions) to indicate long integers. The interpretation of the scanf functions will be the same as in the previous example.

In most versions of C it is possible to skip over a data item, without assigning it to the designated variable or array. To do so, the % sign within the appropriate control group is followed by an asterisk (*). This feature is referred to as *assignment suppression*.

EXAMPLE 4.13   Here is a variation of the scanf features shown in Example 4.6.

```
#include <stdio.h>

main()

{
    char item[20];
    int partno;
    float cost;

    . . . . .

    scanf(" %s %*d %f", item, &partno, &cost);

    . . . . .
}
```

Notice the asterisk in the second character group.
If the corresponding data items are

```
fastener 12345 0.05
```

then fastener will be assigned to item and 0.05 will be assigned to cost. However 12345 will not be assigned to partno because of the asterisk, which is interpreted as an assignment suppression character.
Note that the integer quantity 12345 will be read into the computer along with the other data items, even though it is not assigned to its corresponding variable.

If the control string contains multiple character groups without interspersed whitespace characters, then some care must be taken with c-type conversion. In such cases a whitespace character within the input data will be interpreted as a data item. To skip over such whitespace characters and read the next nonwhitespace character, the conversion group %1s should be used.

EXAMPLE 4.14   Consider the following skeletal outline of a C program.

```
#include <stdio.h>

main()

{
    char c1,c2,c3;

    . . . . .

    scanf(" %c%c%c", &c1, &c2, &c3);

    . . . . .
}
```

If the input data consisted of

```
    a b c
```

(with blank spaces between the letters), then the following assignments would result:

```
    c1 = a,          c2 = <blank space>,          c3 = b
```

If the scanf function were written as

```
    scanf(" %c%1s%1s", &c1, &c2, &c3)
```

however, then the same input data would result in the following assignments:

```
    c1 = a,          c2 = b,          c3 = c
```

as intended.

Note that there are some other ways around this problem. We could have written the scanf function as

```
    scanf(" %c %c %c", &c1, &c2, &c3);
```

with blank spaces separating the %c terms, or we could have used the original scanf function but written the input data as consecutive characters without blanks; i.e., abc.

Unrecognized characters within the control string are expected to be matched by the same characters in the input data. Such input characters will be read into the computer, but not assigned to an identifier. Execution of the scanf function will terminate if a match is not found.

EXAMPLE 4.15   Consider the following skeletal outline.

```
    #include <stdio.h>

    main()

    {
        int i;
        float x;

        . . . . .

        scanf("%d a %f", &i, &x);

        . . . . .
    }
```

If the input data consist of

```
    1 a 2.0
```

then the decimal integer 1 will be read in and assigned to i, the character a will be read in but subsequently ignored, and the floating-point value 2.0 will be read in and assigned to x.

On the other hand, if the input were entered simply as

```
    1 2.0
```

then the scanf function would stop executing once the expected character (a) is not found. Therefore, i would be assigned the value 1 but x would automatically represent the value 0.

You should understand that there is some variation in the features supported by the scanf function from one version of C to another. The features described above are quite common and are available in virtually all versions of the language. However, there may be slight differences in their implementation. Moreover, additional features may be available in some versions of the language.

4.6 WRITING OUTPUT DATA — THE printf FUNCTION

Output data can be written from the computer onto a standard output device using the library function printf. This function can be used to output any combination of numerical values, single characters and strings. It is similar to the input function scanf, except that its purpose is to display data rather than to enter it into the computer. That is, the printf function moves data from the computer's memory to the standard output device, whereas the scanf function enters data from the standard input device and stores it in the computer's memory.

In general terms, the printf function is written as

```
printf(control string, arg1, arg2, . . . , argn)
```

where *control string* refers to a string that contains formatting information, and *arg1*, *arg2*, . . . , *argn* are arguments that represent the individual output data items. The arguments can be written as constants, single variable or array names, or more complex expressions. Function references may also be included. In contrast to the scanf function discussed in the last section, the arguments in a printf function do *not* represent memory addresses and therefore are *not* preceded by ampersands.

The control string consists of individual groups of characters, with one character group for each output data item. Each character group must begin with a percent sign (%). In its simplest form, an individual character group will consist of the percent sign, followed by a *conversion character* indicating the type of the corresponding data item.

Multiple character groups can be contiguous, or they can be separated by other characters, including whitespace characters. These "other" characters are simply transferred directly to the output device, where they are displayed. The use of blank spaces as character-group separators is particularly common.

Several of the more frequently used conversion characters are listed in Table 4-2.

Table 4-2   Commonly Used Conversion Characters for Data Output

Conversion Character	Meaning
c	Data item is displayed as a single character
d	Data item is displayed as a signed decimal integer
e	Data item is displayed as a floating-point value with an exponent
f	Data item is displayed as a floating-point value without an exponent
g	Data item is displayed as a floating-point value using either e-type or f-type conversion, depending on value. Trailing zeros and trailing decimal point will not be displayed.
i	Data item is displayed as a signed decimal integer
o	Data item is displayed as an octal integer, without a leading zero
s	Data item is displayed as a string
u	Data item is displayed as an unsigned decimal integer
x	Data item is displayed as a hexadecimal integer, without the leading 0x

Note that some of these characters are interpreted differently than with the scanf funtion (see Table 4-1).

EXAMPLE 4.16   Here is a simple program that makes use of the printf function.

```
#include <stdio.h>
#include <math.h>

main()   /* print several floating-point numbers */
{
    float i = 2.0, j = 3.0;
    printf("%f %f %f %f", i, j, i+j, sqrt(i+j));
}
```

Notice that the first two arguments within the printf function are single variables, the third argument is an arithmetic expression, and the last argument is a function reference that has a numeric expression as an argument.

Executing the program produces the following output:

```
2.000000 3.000000 5.000000 2.236068
```

EXAMPLE 4.17   The following skeletal outline indicates how several different types of data can be displayed using the printf function.

```
#include <stdio.h>

main()
{
    char item[20];
    int partno;
    float cost;

    . . . . .

    printf("%s %d %f", item, partno, cost);

    . . . . .

}
```

Within the printf function, the control string is "%s %d %f". It contains three character groups. The first character group, %s, indicates that the first argument (item) represents a string. The second character group, %d, indicates that the second argument (partno) represents a decimal integer value, and the third character group, %f, indicates that the third argument (cost) represents a floating-point value.

Notice that the arguments are not preceded by ampersands. This differs from the scanf function, which requires ampersands for all arguments other than array names (see Example 4.5).

Now suppose that name, partno and cost have been assigned the values fastener, 12345 and 0.05, respectively, within the program. When the printf statement is executed, the following output will be generated.

```
fastener 12345 0.050000
```

The single space between data items is generated by the blank spaces that appear within the control string in the printf statement.

Suppose the printf statement had been written as

```
printf("%s%d%f", item, partno, cost);
```

This printf statement is syntactically valid, though it causes the output items to run together; i.e.,

```
fastener123450.050000
```

The f-type conversion and the e-type conversion are both used to output floating-point values. However, the latter causes an exponent to be included in the output, whereas the former does not.

EXAMPLE 4.18   The following program generates the same floating-point output in two different forms.

```
#include <stdio.h>

main()    /* display floating-point output 2 different ways */
{
    double x = 5000.0, y = 0.0025;

    printf("%f %f %f %f\n\n", x, y, x*y, x/y);
    printf("%e %e %e %e", x, y, x*y, x/y);
}
```

Both printf statements have the same arguments. However, the first printf statement makes use of f-type conversion, whereas the second printf statement uses e-type conversion. Also, notice the repeated newline character in the first printf statement. This causes the output to be double-spaced, as shown below.

When the program is executed, the following output is generated.

```
5000.000000 0.002500 12.500000 2000000.000000

5.000000e+03 2.500000e-03 1.250000e+01 2.000000e+06
```

The first line of output shows the quantities represented by x, y, x*y and x/y in standard floating-point format, without exponents. The second line of output shows these same quantities in a form resembling scientific notation, with exponents.

Notice that six decimal places are shown for each value. The number of decimal places can be altered, however, by specifying the *precision* as a part of each character group within the control string (more about this in Sec. 4.7).

The printf function interprets s-type conversion differently than the scanf function. In the printf function, s-type conversion is used to output a string that is terminated by the null character (\0). Whitespace characters may be included within the string.

EXAMPLE 4.19 Reading and Writing a Line of Text   Here is a short C program that will read in a line of text and then write it back out, just as it was entered. The program illustrates the syntactic differences in reading and writing a string that contains a variety of characters, including whitespace characters.

```
#include <stdio.h>

main()          /* read and write a line of text */
{
    char line[80];

    scanf(" %[^\n]", line);
    printf("%s", line);
}
```

Notice the difference in the control strings within the scanf function and the printf function.

Now suppose that the following string is entered from the standard input device when the program is executed.

```
The PITTSBURGH STEELERS is one of America's favorite football teams!
```

This string contains lowercase characters, uppercase characters, punctuation characters and whitespace characters. The entire string can be entered with the single scanf function, as long as it is terminated by a newline character (by pressing the Enter key). The printf function will then cause the entire string to be displayed on the standard output device, just as it had been entered. Thus, the message

```
The PITTSBURGH STEELERS is one of America's favorite football teams!
```

would be generated by the computer.

A *minimum* field width can be specified by preceding the conversion character by an unsigned integer. If the number of characters in the corresponding data item is less than the specified field width, then the data item will be preceded by enough leading blanks to fill the specified field. If the number of characters in the data item exceeds the specified field width, however, then additional space will be allocated to the data item, so that the entire data item will be displayed. This is just the opposite of the field width indicator in the scanf function, which specifies a *maximum* field width.

EXAMPLE 4.20   The following C program illustrates the use of the minimum field width feature.

```
#include <stdio.h>

main()        /* minimum field width specifications */

{
    int i = 12345;
    float x = 345.678;

    printf("%3d %5d %8d\n\n", i, i, i);
    printf("%3f %10f %13f\n\n", x, x, x);
    printf("%3e %13e %16e", x, x, x);
}
```

Notice the double newline characters in the first two printf statements. They will cause the lines of output to be double spaced, as shown below.

When the program is executed, the following output is generated.

```
12345 12345    12345

345.678000 345.678000    345.678000

3.456780e+02   3.456780e+02     3.456780e+02
```

The first line of output displays a decimal integer using three different minimum field widths (three characters, five characters and eight characters). The entire integer value is displayed within each field, even if the field width is too small (as with the first field in this example).

The second value in the first line is preceded by one blank space. This is generated by the blank space separating the first two character groups within the control string.

The third value is preceded by four blank spaces. One blank space comes from the blank space separating the last two character groups within the control field. The other three blank spaces fill the minimum field width, which exceeds the number of characters in the output value (the minimum field width is eight, but only five characters are displayed).

A similar situation is seen in the next two lines, where the floating-point value is displayed using f-type conversion (in line 2) and e-type conversion (line 3).

EXAMPLE 4.21   Here is a variation of the program presented in Example 4.20, which makes use of g-type conversion.

```
#include <stdio.h>

main()        /* minimum field width specifications */

{
    int i = 12345;
    float x = 345.678;

    printf("%3d %5d %8d\n\n", i, i, i);
    printf("%3g %10g %13g\n\n", x, x, x);
    printf("%3g %13g %16g", x, x, x);
}
```

Execution of this program causes the following output to be displayed.

```
12345 12345     12345

   345.678       345.678          345.678

   345.678       345.678          345.678
```

The floating-point values are displayed with an f-type conversion, since this results in a shorter display. The minimum field widths conform to the specifications within the control string.

4.7 MORE ABOUT THE printf FUNCTION

This section contains additional details about the printf function. Beginning C programmers may wish to skip over this material for the time being.

We have already learned how to specify a minimum field width in a printf function. It is also possible to specify the maximum number of decimal places for a floating-point value, or the maximum number of characters for a string. This specification is known as *precision*. The precision is an unsigned integer that is always preceded by a decimal point. If a minimum field width is specified in addition to the precision (as is usually the case), then the precision specification follows the field width specification. Both of these integer specifications precede the conversion character.

A floating-point number will be *rounded* if it must be shortened to conform to a precision specification.

EXAMPLE 4.22 Here is a program that illustrates the use of the precision feature with floating-point numbers.

```
#include <stdio.h>

main()   /* display a floating-point number with several different precisions */

{
    float x = 123.456;

    printf("%7f %7.3f %7.1f\n\n", x, x, x);
    printf("%12e %12.5e %12.3e", x, x, x);
}
```

When this program is executed, the following output is generated.

```
123.456000 123.456    123.5

1.234560e+02  1.23456e+02    1.235e+02
```

The first line is produced by f-type conversion. Notice the rounding that occurs in the third number because of the precision specification (one decimal place). Also, notice the leading blanks that are added to fill the specified minimum field width (seven characters).

The second line, produced by e-type conversion, has similar characteristics. Again, we see that the third number is rounded to conform to the specified precision (three decimal places). Also, note the leading blanks that are added to fill the specified minimum field width (12 characters).

A minimum field width specification need not necessarily accompany the precision specification. It is possible to specify the precision without the minimum field width, though the precision must still be preceded by a decimal point.

EXAMPLE 4.23 Now let us rewrite the program shown in the last example without any minimum field width specifications, but with precision specifications.

```
#include <stdio.h>

main()   /* display a floating-point number with several different precisions */

{
    float x = 123.456;

    printf("%f %.3f %.1f\n\n", x, x, x);
    printf("%e %.5e %.3e", x, x, x);
}
```

Execution of this program produces the following output.

```
123.456000 123.456 123.5

1.234560e+02 1.23456e+02 1.235e+02
```

Notice that the third number in each line does not have multiple leading blanks, since there is no minimum field width that must be satisfied. In all other respects, however, this output is the same as the output generated in the last example.

Minimum field width and precision specifications can be applied to character data as well as numerical data. When applied to a string, the minimum field width is interpreted in the same manner as with a numerical quantity; i.e., leading blanks will be added if the string is shorter than the specified field width, and additional space will be allocated if the string is longer than the specified field width. Hence, the field width specification will not prevent the entire string from being displayed.

However, the precision specification will determine the maximum number of characters that can be displayed. If the precision specification is less than the total number of characters in the string, the excess right-most characters will not be displayed. This will occur even if the minimum field width is larger than the entire string, resulting in the addition of leading blanks to the truncated string.

EXAMPLE 4.24 The following program outline illustrates the use of field width and precision specifications in conjunction with string output.

```
#include <stdio.h>

main()

{
    char line[12];

    . . . . .

    printf("%10s %15s %15.5s %.5s", line, line, line, line);
}
```

Now suppose that the string hexadecimal is assigned to the character array line. When the program is executed, the following output will be generated.

```
hexadecimal     hexadecimal          hexad hexad
```

The first string is shown in its entirety, even though this string consists of 11 characters but the field width specification is only 10 characters. Thus, the first string overrides the minimum field width specification. The second string is padded with four leading blanks to fill out the 15-character minimum; hence, the second string is *right justified* within its field. The third string consists of only five nonblank characters because of the five-character precision specification; however, 10 leading blanks are added to fill out the minimum field width specification, which is 15 characters. The last string also consists of five nonblank characters. Leading blanks are not added, however, because there is no minimum field width specification.

Most versions of C permit the use of prefixes within the control string to indicate the length of the corresponding argument. The allowable prefixes are the same as the prefixes used with the scanf function. Thus, an l (lowercase) indicates a signed or unsigned integer argument, or a double-precision argument; an h indicates a signed or unsigned short integer. Some versions of C permit an L (uppercase) to indicate a long double.

EXAMPLE 4.25   Suppose the following statements are included in a C program.

```
#include <stdio.h>

main ()

{
    short a, b;
    long c, d;

    . . . . .

    printf("%5hd %6hx %8lo %lu", a, b, c, d);

    . . . . .

}
```

The control string indicates that the first data item will be a short decimal integer, the second will be a short hexadecimal integer, the third will be a long octal integer, and the fourth will be a long unsigned (decimal) integer. Note that the first three fields have minimum field width specifications, but the fourth does not.

Some versions of C allow the conversion characters X, E and G to be written in uppercase. These uppercase conversion characters cause any letters within the output data to be displayed in uppercase. (Note that this use of uppercase conversion characters is distinctly different than with the scanf function.)

EXAMPLE 4.26   The following program illustrates the use of uppercase conversion characters in the printf function.

```
#include <stdio.h>

main()       /* use of uppercase conversion characters */

{
    int a = 0x80ec;
    float b = 0.3e-12;

    printf("%4x %10.2e\n\n", a, b);
    printf("%4X %10.2E", a, b);
}
```

Notice that the first printf statement contains lowercase conversion characters, whereas the second printf statement contains uppercase conversion characters.

When the program is executed, the following output is generated.

```
80ec   3.00e-13

80EC   3.00E-13
```

The first quantity on each line is a hexadecimal number. Note that the letters ec (which are a part of the hexadecimal number) are shown in lowercase on the first line, and in uppercase on the second line.

The second quantity on each line is a decimal floating-point number which includes an exponent. Notice that the letter e, which indicates the exponent, is shown in lowercase on the first line and uppercase on the second.

You are again reminded that the use of uppercase conversion characters is not supported by all compilers.

In addition to the field width, the precision and the conversion character, each character group within the control string can include a *flag*, which affects the appearance of the output. The flag must be placed immediately after the percent sign (%). Some compilers allow two or more flags to appear consecutively, within the same character group. The more commonly used flags are listed in Table 4-3.

Table 4-3   Commonly Used Flags

Flag	Meaning
–	Data item is left justified within the field (blank spaces required to fill the minimum field width will be added *after* the data item rather than *before* the data item).
+	A sign (either + or –) will precede each signed numerical data item. Without this flag, only negative data items are preceded by a sign.
0	Causes leading zeros to appear instead of leading blanks. Applies only to data items that are right justified within a field whose minimum size is larger than the data item. (*Note:* Some compilers consider the zero flag to be a part of the field width specification rather than an actual flag. This assures that the 0 is processed last, if multiple flags are present.)
' ' (*blank space*)	A blank space will precede each positive signed numerical data item. This flag is overridden by the + flag if both are present.
# (*with* o- *and* x-*type conversion*)	Causes octal and hexadecimal data items to be preceded by 0 and 0x, respectively.
# (*with* e-, f- *and* g-*type conversion*)	Causes a decimal point to be present in all floating-point numbers, even if the data item is a whole number. Also prevents the truncation of trailing zeros in g-type conversion.

EXAMPLE 4.27   Here is a simple C program that illustrates the use of flags with integer and floating-point quantities.

```
#include <stdio.h>

main()     /* use of flags with integer and  floating-point numbers */
{
    int i = 123;
    float x = 12.0, y = -3.3;

    printf(":%6d %7.0f %10.1e:\n\n", i, x, y);
    printf(":%-6d %-7.0f %-10.1e:\n\n", i, x, y);
    printf(":%+6d %+7.0f %+10.1e:\n\n", i, x, y);
    printf(":%-+6d %-+7.0f %-+10.1e:\n\n", i, x, y);
    printf(":%7.0f %#7.0f %7g %#7g:", x, x, y, y);
}
```

When the program is executed, the following output is produced. (The colons indicate the beginning of the first field and the end of the last field in each line.)

```
:   123      12   -3.3e+00:

:123     12       -3.3e+00  :

:  +123     +12   -3.3e+00:

:+123    +12      -3.3e+00  :

:     12     12.    -3.3 -3.30000:
```

The first line illustrates how integer and floating-point numbers appear without any flags. Each number is right justified within its respective field. The second line shows the same numbers, using the same conversions, with a – flag included within each character group. Note that the numbers are now left justified within their respective fields. The third line shows the effect of using a + flag. The numbers are now right justified, as in the first line, but each number (whether positive or negative) is preceded by an appropriate sign.

The fourth line shows the effect of combining a – and a + flag. The numbers are now left justified and preceded by an appropriate sign. Finally, the last line shows two floating-point numbers, each displayed first without and then with the # flag. Note that the effect of the flag is to include a decimal point in the number 12. (which is printed with f-type conversion), and to include the trailing zeros in the number –3.300000 (printed with g-type conversion).

EXAMPLE 4.28 Now consider the following program, which displays decimal, octal and hexadecimal numbers.

```
#include <stdio.h>

main()   /* use of flags with unsigned decimal,       octal and hexadecimal numbers */
{
    int i = 1234, j = 01777, k = 0xa08c;

    printf(":%8u %8o %8x:\n\n", i, j, k);
    printf(":%-8u %-8o %-8x:\n\n", i, j, k);
    printf(":%#8u %#8o %#8X:\n\n", i, j, k);
    printf(":%08u %08o %08X:\n\n", i, j, k);
}
```

Execution of this program results in the following output. (The colons indicate the beginning of the first field and the end of the last field in each line.)

```
:    1234     1777     a08c:

:1234     1777     a08c     :

:    1234    01777   0XA08C:

:00001234 00001777 0000A08C:
```

The first line illustrates the display of unsigned integer, octal and hexadecimal output without any flags. Note that the numbers are right justified within their respective fields. The second line shows what happens when you include a – flag within each character group. Now the numbers are left justified within their respective fields.

In the third line we see what happens when the # flag is used. This flag causes the octal number 1777 to be preceded by a 0 (appearing as 01777), and the hexadecimal number to be preceded by 0X (i.e., 0XA08C). Notice that the unsigned decimal integer 1234 is unaffected by this flag. Also, notice that the hexadecimal number now contains uppercase characters, since the conversion character was written in uppercase (X).

The last line illustrates the use of the 0 flag. This flag causes the fields to be filled with leading 0s rather than leading blanks. We again see uppercase hexadecimal characters, in response to the uppercase conversion character (X).

EXAMPLE 4.29 The following program outline illustrates the use of flags with string output.

```
#include <stdio.h>

main()
{
    char line[12];

    . . . . .

    printf(":%15s %15.5s %.5s:\n\n", line, line, line);
    printf(":%-15s %-15.5s %-.5s:", line, line, line);
}
```

Now suppose that the string lower-case is assigned to the character array line. The following output will be generated when the program is executed.

```
    :       lower-case            lower lower:

    :lower-case      lower            lower:
```

The first line illustrates how strings are displayed when flags are not present, as explained in Example 4.24. The second line shows the same strings, left justified, in response to the – flag in each character group.

Unrecognized characters within the control string will be displayed just as they appear. This feature allows us to include labels and messages with the output data items, if we wish.

EXAMPLE 4.30 The following program illustrates how printed output can be labeled.

```c
#include <stdio.h>

main()     /* labeling of floating-point numbers */

{
    float a = 2.2, b = -6.2, x1 = .005, x2 = -12.88;

    printf("$%4.2f   %7.1f%%\n\n", a, b);
    printf("x1=%7.3f    x2=%7.3f", x1, x2);
}
```

This program causes the value of a (2.2) to be preceded by a dollar sign ($), and the value of b (-6.2) to be followed by a percent sign (%). Note the two consecutive percent signs in the first printf statement. The first percent sign indicates the start of a character group, whereas the second percent sign is interpreted as a label.

The second printf statement causes the value of x1 to be preceded by the label x1=, and the value of x2 to be preceded by the label x2=. Three blank spaces will separate these two labeled data items.

The actual output is shown below.

```
$2.20      -6.2%

x1=  0.005   x2=-12.880
```

Remember that there is some variation in the features supported by the printf function in different versions of C. The features described in this section are very common, though there may be differences in the way these features are implemented. Additional features are also available in many versions of the language.

4.8 THE gets AND puts FUNCTIONS

C contains a number of other library functions that permit some form of data transfer into or out of the computer. We will encounter several such functions in Chap. 12, where we discuss data files. Before leaving this chapter, however, we mention the gets and puts functions, which facilitate the transfer of strings between the computer and the standard input/output devices.

Each of these functions accepts a single argument. The argument must be a data item that represents a string. (e.g., a character array). The string may include whitespace characters. In the case of gets, the string will be entered from the keyboard, and will terminate with a newline character (i.e., the string will end when the user presses the Enter key).

The gets and puts functions offer simple alternatives to the use of scanf and printf for reading and displaying strings, as illustrated in the following example.

EXAMPLE 4.31 Reading and Writing a Line of Text   Here is another version of the simple program originally presented in Example 4.19, that reads a line of text into the computer and then writes it back out in its original form.

```c
#include <stdio.h>

main()          /* read and write a line of text */

{
    char line[80];

    gets(line);
    puts(line);
}
```

This program utilizes gets and puts, rather than scanf and printf, to transfer the line of text into and out of the computer. Note that the syntax is simpler in the present program (compare carefully with the program shown in Example 4.19). On the other hand, the scanf and printf functions in the earlier program can be expanded to include additional data items, whereas the present program cannot.

When this program is executed, it will behave in exactly the same manner as the program shown in Example 4.19.

4.9 INTERACTIVE (CONVERSATIONAL) PROGRAMMING

Many modern computer programs are designed to create an interactive dialog between the computer and the person using the program (the "user"). These dialogs usually involve some form of question-answer interaction, where the computer asks the questions and the user provides the answers, or vice versa. The computer and the user thus appear to be carrying on some limited form of conversation.

In C, such dialogs can be created by alternate use of the scanf and printf functions. The actual programming is straightforward, though sometimes confusing to beginners, since the printf function is used both when entering data (to create the computer's questions) and when displaying results. On the other hand, scanf is used only for actual data entry.

The basic ideas are illustrated in the following example.

EXAMPLE 4.32 Averaging Student Exam Scores   This example presents a simple, interactive C program that reads in a student's name and three exam scores, and then calculates an average score. The data will be entered interactively, with the computer asking the user for information and the user supplying the information in a free format, as requested. Each input data item will be entered on a separate line. Once all of the data have been entered, the computer will compute the desired average and write out all of the data (both the input data and the calculated average).

The actual program is shown below.

```c
#include <stdio.h>

main()      /* sample interactive program */

{
    char name[20];
    float score1, score2, score3, avg;

    printf("Please enter your name: ");          /* enter name */
    scanf(" %[^\n]", name);

    printf("Please enter the first score:  ");  /* enter 1st score */
    scanf("%f", &score1);

    printf("Please enter the second score:  ");  /* enter 2nd score */
    scanf("%f", &score2);

    printf("Please enter the third score:  ");  /* enter 3rd score */
```

```
        scanf("%f", &score3);

        avg = (score1+score2+score3)/3;          /* calculate avg */

        printf("\n\nName: %-s\n\n", name);        /* write output */
        printf("Score 1: %-5.1f\n", score1);
        printf("Score 2: %-5.1f\n", score2);
        printf("Score 3: %-5.1f\n\n", score3);
        printf("Average: %-5.1f\n\n", avg);
}
```

Notice that two statements are associated with each input data item. The first is a `printf` statement, which generates a request for the item. The second statement, a `scanf` function, causes the data item to be entered from the standard input device (i.e., the keyboard).

After the student's name and all three exam scores have been entered, an average exam score is calculated. The input data and the calculated average are then displayed, as a result of the group of `printf` statements at the end of the program.

A typical interactive session is shown below. To illustrate the nature of the dialog, the user's responses have been underlined.

```
        Please enter your name: Robert Smith
        Please enter the first score:  88
        Please enter the second score: 62.5
        Please enter the third score:  90


        Name: Robert Smith

        Score 1:     88.0
        Score 2:     62.5
        Score 3:     90.0

        Average:     80.2
```

Additional interactive programs will be seen in many of the programming examples presented in later chapters of this book.

Review Questions

4.1   What are the commonly used input/output functions in C? How are they accessed?

4.2   What is the standard input/output header file called in most versions of C? How is the file included within a program?

4.3   What is the purpose of the `getchar` function? How is it used within a C program?

4.4   What happens when an end-of-file condition is encountered when reading characters with the `getchar` function? How is the end-of-file condition recognized?

4.5   How can the `getchar` function be used to read multicharacter strings?

4.6   What is the purpose of the `putchar` function? How is it used within a C program? Compare with the `getchar` function.

4.7   How can the `putchar` function be used to write multicharacter strings?

4.8   What is a character-type array? What does each element of a character-type array represent? How are character-type arrays used to represent multicharacter strings?

4.9   What is the purpose of the `scanf` function? How is it used within a C program? Compare with the `getchar` function.

4.10   What is the purpose of the control string in a scanf function? What type of information does it convey? Of what is the control string composed?

4.11   How is each character group within the control string identified? What are the constituent characters within a character group?

4.12   If a control string within a scanf function contains multiple character groups, how are the character groups separated? Are whitespace characters required?

4.13   If whitespace characters are present within a control string, how are they interpreted?

4.14   Summarize the meaning of the more commonly used conversion characters within the control string of a scanf function.

4.15   What special symbol must be included with the arguments, other than the control string, in a scanf function? In what way are array names treated differently than other arguments?

4.16   When entering data via the scanf function, what relationships must there be between the data items and the corresponding arguments? How are multiple data items separated from one another?

4.17   When entering data via the scanf function, must octal data be preceded by 0? Must hexadecimal data be preceded by 0x (or 0X)? How must floating-point data be written?

4.18   When entering a string via the scanf function using an s-type conversion factor, how is the string terminated?

4.19   When entering a string via the scanf function, how can a single string which includes whitespace characters be entered?

4.20   Summarize a convenient method for entering a string of undetermined length, which may contain whitespace characters and all printable characters, and which is terminated by a carriage return. Answer this question relative to the type of conversion required within the control string of a scanf function.

4.21   What is meant by a field?

4.22   How can the maximum field width for a data item be specified within a scanf function?

4.23   What happens if an input data item contains more characters than the maximum allowable field width? What if the data item contains fewer characters?

4.24   How can short integer, long integer and double-precision arguments be indicated within the control string of a scanf function?

4.25   How can long double arguments be indicated within the control string of a scanf function? Is this feature available in most versions of C?

4.26   How can the assignment of an input data item to its corresponding argument be suppressed?

4.27   If the control string within a scanf function contains multiple character groups without interspersed whitespace characters, what difficulty can arise when using c-type conversion? How can this difficulty be avoided?

4.28   How are unrecognized characters within the control string of a scanf function interpreted?

4.29   What is the purpose of the printf function? How is it used within a C program? Compare with the putchar function.

4.30   In what ways does the control string within a printf function differ from the control string within a scanf function?

4.31   If the control string within a printf function contains multiple character groups, how are the character groups separated? How are the separators interpreted?

4.32   Summarize the meaning of the more commonly used conversion characters within the control string of a printf function. Compare with the conversion characters that are used in a scanf function.

4.33   In a printf function, must the arguments (other than the control string) be preceded by ampersands? Compare with the scanf function and explain any differences.

4.34   What is the difference between f-type conversion, e-type conversion and g-type conversion when outputting floating-point data with a printf function?

4.35   Compare the use of s-type conversion in the printf and the scanf functions. How does s-type conversion differ when processing strings containing whitespace characters?

4.36   How can the minimum field width for a data item be specified within the `printf` function?

4.37   What happens if an output data item contains more characters than the minimum field width? What if the data item contains fewer characters? Contrast with the field width specifications in the `scanf` function.

4.38   What is meant by the precision of an output data item? To what types of data does this apply?

4.39   How can the precision be specified within a `printf` function?

4.40   What happens to a floating-point number if it must be shortened to conform to a precision specification? What happens to a string?

4.41   Must a precision specification be accompanied by a minimum field width specification in a `printf` function?

4.42   How can short integer, long integer and double-precision arguments be indicated within the control string of a `printf` function? How can long double arguments be indicated?

4.43   How are uppercase conversion characters interpreted differently than the corresponding lowercase conversion characters in a `printf` function? To what types of conversion does this feature apply? Do all versions of C recognize this distinction?

4.44   Summarize the purpose of the flags that are commonly used within the `printf` function.

4.45   Can two or more flags appear consecutively within the same character group?

4.46   How are unrecognized characters within the control string of a `printf` function interpreted?

4.47   How can labeled data items be generated by the `printf` function?

4.48   Summarize the use of the `gets` and `puts` functions to transfer strings between the computer and the standard input/output devices. Compare the use of these functions with the string transfer features in the `scanf` and `printf` statements.

4.49   Explain, in general terms, how an interactive dialog can be generated by repeated use of pairs of `scanf` and `printf` functions.

Problems

4.50   A C program contains the following statements:

```
#include <stdio.h>

char a, b, c;
```

(*a*)   Write appropriate `getchar` statements that will allow values for a, b and c to be entered into the computer.

(*b*)   Write appropriate `putchar` statements that will allow the current values of a, b and c to be written out of the computer (i.e., to be displayed).

4.51   Solve Prob. 4.50 using a single `scanf` function and a single `printf` function rather than the `getchar` and `putchar` statements. Compare your answer with the solution to Prob. 4.50.

4.52   A C program contains the following statements:

```
#include <stdio.h>

char text[80];
```

(*a*)   Write a `for` statement that will permit a 60-character message to be entered into the computer and stored in the character array `text`. Include a reference to the `getchar` function in the `for` loop, as in Example 4.4.

(*b*)   Write a `for` statement that will permit the first 60 characters of the character array `text` to be displayed. Include a reference to the `putchar` function in the `for` loop, as in Example 4.4.

4.53   Modify the solution to Prob. 4.52(*a*) so that a character array whose length is unspecified can be read into the computer. Assume that the message does not exceed 79 characters, and that it is automatically terminated by a *newline* character (\n). (See Example 4.4.)

4.54 Solve Prob. 4.53 using a `scanf` statement in place of a `for` statement (see Example 4.8). What additional information is provided by the method described in Prob. 4.53?

4.55 A C program contains the following statements:

```
#include <stdio.h>

int i, j, k;
```

Write an appropriate `scanf` function to enter numerical values for i, j and k, assuming

(a)   The values for i, j and k will be decimal integers.

(b)   The value for i will be a decimal integer, j an octal integer and k a hexadecimal integer.

(c)   The values for i and j will be hexadecimal integers and k will be an octal integer.

4.56 A C program contains the following statements:

```
#include <stdio.h>

int i, j, k;
```

Write an appropriate `scanf` function to enter numerical values for i, j and k into the computer, assuming

(a)   The values for i, j and k will be decimal integers not exceeding six characters each.

(b)   The value for i will be a decimal integer, j an octal integer and k a hexadecimal integer, with each quantity not exceeding 8 characters.

(c)   The values for i and j will be hexadecimal integers and k will be an octal integer. Each quantity will be 7 or fewer characters.

4.57 Interpret the meaning of the control string in each of the following `scanf` functions.

(a)   `scanf("%12ld %5hd %15lf %15le", &a, &b, &c, &d);`

(b)   `scanf("%10lx %6ho %5hu %14lu", &a, &b, &c, &d);`

(c)   `scanf("%12D %hd %15f %15e", &a, &b, &c, &d);`

(d)   `scanf("%8d %*d %12lf %12lf", &a, &b, &c, &d);`

4.58 A C program contains the following statements:

```
#include <stdio.h>

int i, j;
long ix;
short s;
unsigned u;
float x;
double dx;
char c;
```

For each of the following groups of variables, write a `scanf` function that will allow a set of data items to be read into the computer and assigned to the variables. Assume that all integers will be read in as decimal quantities.

(a)   i, j, x and dx   (c)   i, u and c

(b)   i, ix, j, x and u   (d)   c, x, dx and s

4.59 A C program contains the following statements:

```
#include <stdio.h>

int i, j;
long ix;
short s;
unsigned u;
float x;
double dx;
char c;
```

Write an appropriate `scanf` function to accommodate each of the following situations, assuming that all integers will be read in as decimal quantities.

(a)   Enter values for `i`, `j`, `x` and `dx`, assuming that each integer quantity does not exceed four characters, the floating-point quantity does not exceed eight characters, and the double-precision quantity does not exceed 15 characters.

(b)   Enter values for `i`, `ix`, `j`, `x` and `u`, assuming that each integer quantity does not exceed five characters, the long integer does not exceed 12 characters, and the floating-point quantity does not exceed 10 characters.

(c)   Enter values for `i`, `u` and `c`, assuming that each integer quantity does not exceed six characters.

(d)   Enter values for `c`, `x`, `dx` and `s`, assuming that the floating-point quantity does not exceed nine characters, the double-precision quantity does not exceed 16 characters and the short integer does not exceed six characters.

4.60   A C program contains the following statements:

```
#include <stdio.h>

char text[80];
```

Write a `scanf` function that will allow a string to be read into the computer and assigned to the character array `text`. Assume that the string does not contain any whitespace characters.

4.61   Solve Prob. 4.60 assuming that the string contains only lowercase letters, blank spaces and newline characters.

4.62   Solve Prob. 4.60 assuming that the string contains only uppercase letters, digits, dollar signs and blank spaces.

4.63   Solve Prob. 4.60 assuming that the string contains anything other than an asterisk (i.e., assume that an asterisk will be used to indicate the end of the string).

4.64   A C program contains the following statements.

```
#include <stdio.h>

char a, b, c;
```

Suppose that $ is to be entered into the computer and assigned to `a`, * assigned to `b` and @ assigned to `c`. Show how the input data must be entered for each of the following `scanf` functions.

(a)   `scanf("%c%c%c", &a, &b, &c);`

(b)   `scanf("%c %c %c", &a, &b, &c);`

(c)   `scanf("%s%s%s", &a, &b, &c);`

(d)   `scanf("%s %s %s", &a, &b, &c);`

(e)   `scanf("%1s%1s%1s", &a, &b, &c);`

4.65   A C program contains the following statements.

```
#include <stdio.h>

int a, b;
float x, y;
```

Suppose the value 12 is to be entered into the computer and assigned to `a`, −8 assigned to `b`, 0.011 assigned to `x` and -2.2×10^6 assigned to `y`. Show how the input data might most conveniently be entered for each of the following `scanf` functions.

(a)   `scanf("%d %d %f %f", &a, &b, &x, &y);`

(b)   `scanf("%d %d %e %e", &a, &b, &x, &y);`

(c)   `scanf("%2d %2d %5f %6e", &a, &b, &x, &y);`

(d)   `scanf("%3d %3d %8f %8e", &a, &b, &x, &y);`

4.66   A C program contains the following statements:

```
#include <stdio.h>

int i, j, k;
```

Write a `printf` function for each of the following groups of variables or expressions. Assume all variables represent decimal integers.

(*a*)   i, j and k

(*b*)   (i + j), (i - k)

(*c*)   sqrt(i + j), abs(i - k)

4.67   A C program contains the following statements:

```
#include <stdio.h>

int i, j, k;
```

Write a `printf` function for each of the following groups of variables or expressions. Assume all variables represent decimal integers.

(*a*)   i, j and k, with a minimum field width of three characters per quantity.

(*b*)   (i + j), (i - k), with a minimum field width of five characters per quantity.

(*c*)   sqrt(i + j), abs(i - k), with a minimum field width of nine characters for the first quantity, and seven characters for the second quantity.

4.68   A C program contains the following statements:

```
#include <stdio.h>

float x, y, z;
```

Write a `printf` function for each of the following groups of variables or expressions.

(*a*)   x, y and z

(*b*)   (x + y), (x - z)

(*c*)   sqrt(x + y), fabs(x - z)

4.69   A C program contains the following statements:

```
#include <stdio.h>

float x, y, z;
```

Write a `printf` function for each of the following groups of variables or expressions, using `f`-type conversion for each floating-point quantity.

(*a*)   x, y and z, with a minimum field width of six characters per quantity.

(*b*)   (x + y), (x - z), with a minimum field width of eight characters per quantity.

(*c*)   sqrt(x + y), abs(x - z), with a minimum field width of 12 characters for the first quantity and nine characters for the second.

4.70   Repeat the previous problem using e-type conversion.

4.71   A C program contains the following statements:

```
#include <stdio.h>

float x, y, z;
```

Write a `printf` function for each of the following groups of variables or expressions, using `f`-type conversion for each floating-point quantity.

(*a*)   x, y and z, with a minimum field width of eight characters per quantity, with no more than four decimal places.

(b)   (x + y), (x − z), with a minimum field width of nine characters per quantity, with no more than three decimal places.

(c)   sqrt(x + y), abs(x − z), with a minimum field width of 12 characters for the first quantity and 10 characters for the second. Display a maximum of four decimal places for each quantity.

4.72   A C program contains the following statements:

```
#include <stdio.h>

float x, y, z;
```

Write a printf function for each of the following groups of variables or expressions, using e-type conversion for each floating-point quantity.

(a)   x, y and z, with a minimum field width of 12 characters per quantity, with no more than four decimal places.

(b)   (x + y), (x − z), with a minimum field width of 14 characters per quantity, with no more than five decimal places.

(c)   sqrt(x + y), abs(x − z), with a minimum field width of 12 characters for the first quantity and 15 characters for the second. Display a maximum of seven decimal places for each quantity.

4.73   A C program contains the following statements:

```
#include <stdio.h>

int a = 0177, b = 055, c = 0xa8, d = 0x1ff;
```

Write a printf function for each of the following groups of variables or expressions.

(a)   a, b, c and d

(b)   (a + b), (c − d)

4.74   A C program contains the following statements:

```
#include <stdio.h>

int i, j;
long ix;
unsigned u;
float x;
double dx;
char c;
```

For each of the following groups of variables, write a printf function that will allow the values of the variables to be displayed.   Assume that all integers will be shown as decimal quantities.

(a)   i, j, x and dx   (c)   i, u and c

(b)   i, ix, j, x and u   (d)   c, x, dx and ix

4.75   A C program contains the following statements:

```
#include <stdio.h>

int i, j;
long ix;
unsigned u;
float x;
double dx;
char c;
```

Write an appropriate printf function for each of the following situations, assuming that all integers will be displayed as decimal quantities.

(a)   Display the values of i, j, x and dx, assuming that each integer quantity will have a minimum field width of four characters and each floating-point quantity is displayed in exponential notation with a total of at least 14 characters and no more than eight decimal places.

(b)   Repeat part (a), displaying each quantity on a separate line.

(c)   Display the values of i, ix, j, x and u, assuming that each integer quantity will have a minimum field width of five characters, the long integer will have a minimum field width of 12 characters and the floating-point quantity will be have at least 10 characters with a maximum of five decimal places. Do not include an exponent.

(d)   Repeat part (c), displaying the first three quantities on one line, followed by a blank line and then the remaining two quantities on the next line.

(e)   Display the values of i, u and c, with a minimum field width of six characters for each integer quantity. Place three blank spaces between each output quantity.

(f)   Display the values for j, u and x. Display the integer quantities with a minimum field width of five characters. Display the floating-point quantity using f-type conversion, with a minimum field width of 11 and a maximum of four decimal places.

(g)   Repeat part (f), with each data item left justified within its respective field.

(h)   Repeat part (f), with a sign (either + or −) preceding each signed data item.

(i)   Repeat part (f), with leading zeros filling out the field for each of the integer quantities.

(j)   Repeat part (f), with a provision for a decimal point in the value of x regardless of its value.

4.76   Assume that i, j and k are integer variables, and that i represents an octal quantity, j represents a decimal quantity and k represents a hexadecimal quantity. Write an appropriate printf function for each of the following situations.

(a)   Display the values for i, j and k, with a minimum field width of eight characters for each value.

(b)   Repeat part (a) with each output data item left justified within its respective field.

(c)   Repeat part (a) with each output data item preceded by zeros (0x, in the case of the hexadecimal quantity).

4.77   A C program contains the following variable declarations.

```
int i = 12345, j = -13579, k = -24680;
long ix = 123456789;
short sx = -2222;
unsigned ux = 5555;
```

Show the output resulting from each of the following printf statements.

(a)   printf("%d %d %d %ld %d %u", i, j, k, ix, sx, ux);

(b)   printf("%3d %3d %3d\n\n%3ld %3d %3u", i, j, k, ix, sx, ux);

(c)   printf("%8d %8d %8d\n\n%15ld %8d %8u", i, j, k, ix, sx, ux);

(d)   printf("%-8d %-8d\n%-8d %-15ld\n%-8d %-8u", i, j, k, ix, sx, ux);

(e)   printf("%+8d %+8d\n%+8d %+15ld\n%+8d %8u", i, j, k, ix, sx, ux);

(f)   printf("%08d %08d\n%08d %015ld\n%08d %08u", i, j, k, ix, sx, ux);

4.78   A C program contains the following variable declarations.

```
int i = 12345, j = 0xabcd9, k = 077777;
```

Show the output resulting from each of the following printf statements.

(a)   printf("%d %x %o", i, j, k);

(b)   printf("%3d %3x %3o", i, j, k);

(c)   printf("%8d %8x %8o", i, j, k);

(d)   printf("%-8d %-8x %-8o", i, j, k);

    (e)   `printf("%+8d %+8x %+8o", i, j, k);`

    (f)   `printf("%08d %#8x %#8o", i, j, k);`

4.79 A C program contains the following variable declarations.

       `float a = 2.5, b = 0.0005, c = 3000.;`

Show the output resulting from each of the following `printf` statements.

    (a)   `printf("%f %f %f", a, b, c);`

    (b)   `printf("%3f %3f %3f", a, b, c);`

    (c)   `printf("%8f %8f %8f", a, b, c);`

    (d)   `printf("%8.4f %8.4f %8.4f", a, b, c);`

    (e)   `printf("%8.3f %8.3f %8.3f", a, b, c);`

    (f)   `printf("%e %e %e", a, b, c);`

    (g)   `printf("%3e %3e %3e", a, b, c);`

    (h)   `printf("%12e %12e %12e", a, b, c);`

    (i)   `printf("%12.4e %12.4e %12.4e", a, b, c);`

    (j)   `printf("%8.2e %8.2e %8.2e", a, b, c);`

    (k)   `printf("%-8f %-8f %-8f", a, b, c);`

    (l)   `printf("%+8f %+8f %+8f", a, b, c);`

    (m) `printf("%08f %08f %08f", a, b, c);`

    (n)   `printf("%#8f %#8f %#8f", a, b, c);`

    (o)   `printf("%g %g %g", a, b, c);`

    (p)   `printf("%#g %#g %#g", a, b, c);`

4.80 A C program contains the following variable declarations.

       `char c1 = 'A', c2 = 'B', c3 = 'C';`

Show the output resulting from each of the following `printf` statements.

    (a)   `printf("%c %c %c", c1, c2, c3);`

    (b)   `printf("%c%c%c", c1, c2, c3);`

    (c)   `printf("%3c %3c %3c", c1, c2, c3);`

    (d)   `printf("%3c%3c%3c", c1, c2, c3);`

    (e)   `printf("c1=%c c2=%c c3=%c", c1, c2, c3);`

4.81 A C program contains the following statements.

       `#include <stdio.h>`

       `char text[80];`

Write a `printf` function that will allow the contents of `text` to be displayed in the following ways.

    (a)   Entirely on one line.

    (b)   Only the first eight characters.

    (c)   The first eight characters, preceded by five blanks.

    (d)   The first eight characters, followed by five blanks.

4.82 A C program contains the following array declaration.

       `char text[80];`

Suppose that the following string has been assigned to `text`.

```
Programming with C can be a challenging creative activity.
```

Show the output resulting from the following printf statements.

(a)   printf("%s", text);   (d)   printf("%18.7s", text);

(b)   printf("%18s", text);   (e)   printf("%-18.7s", text);

(c)   printf("%.18s", text);

4.83   Write the necessary scanf or printf statements for each of the following situations.

(a)   Generate the message

```
Please enter your name:
```

Then enter the name on the same line. Assign the name to a character-type array called name.

(b)   Suppose that x1 and x2 are floating-point variables whose values are 8.0 and –2.5, respectively. Display
the values of x1 and x2, with appropriate labels; i.e., generate the message

```
x1 =   8.0    x2 = -2.5
```

(c)   Suppose that a and b are integer variables. Prompt the user for input values of these two variables, then
display their sum. Label the output accordingly.

4.84   Determine which conversion characters are available with your particular version of C. Also, determine which
flags are available for data output.

Chapter 5

Preparing and Running a Complete C Program

By now we have learned enough about C to write complete, though simple, C programs. We will therefore pause briefly from our coverage of new features and devote some attention to the planning, writing and execution of a complete C program. In addition, we will discuss some methods for detecting and correcting the different types of errors that can occur in improperly written programs.

Our attention will be directed toward the use of Version 4.5 of Borland International's Turbo C++, running within the Windows operating environment (remember that C++ includes a full implementation of standard ANSI C, as discussed in Sec. 1.5). We emphasize this particular version of C because of its widespread popularity on personal computers, its low cost, and because it is representative of contemporary C usage on many different computers.

5.1 PLANNING A C PROGRAM

It is essential that the overall program strategy be completely mapped out before any of the detailed programming actually begins. This permits you to concentrate on the general program logic, without being concerned with the syntactic details of the actual instructions. Once the overall program strategy has been clearly established, the details associated with the individual program statements can be considered. This approach is generally referred to as "top-down" programming. With large programs, this entire process might be repeated several times, with more programming detail added at each stage.

Top-down program organization is normally carried out by developing an informal outline, consisting of phrases or sentences that are part English and part C. In the initial stages of program development the amount of C is minimal, consisting only of major program components, such as function headings, function references, braces defining compound statements, and portions of control statements describing major program structures. Additional detail is then provided by descriptive English material which is inserted between these elements, often in the form of program comments. The resulting outline is usually referred to as *pseudocode*.

EXAMPLE 5.1 Compound Interest A common problem in personal finance is that of determining how much money will accumulate in a bank account after n years if a known amount, P, is deposited initially and the account collects interest at a rate of r percent per year, compounded annually. The answer to this question can be determined by the well-known formula

$$F = P(1 + i)^n$$

where F represents the future accumulation of money (including the original sum, P, which is known as the *principal*) and i is the decimal representation of the interest rate; i.e., $i = r/100$ (for example, an interest rate of $r = 5\%$ would correspond to $i = 0.05$).

Consider the organization of a C program that will solve this problem. The program will be based upon the following general outline.

1. Declare the required program variables.

2. Read in values for the principal (P), the interest rate (r) and the number of years (n).

3. Calculate the decimal representation of the interest rate (i), using the formula

$$i = r/100$$

4. Determine the future accumulation (F) using the formula

$$F = P(1 + i)^n$$

5. Display the calculated value for F.

Here is the program outline in the form of pseudocode.

```
/* compound interest calculations */

main()

{
    /* declare the program variables */

    /* read in values for P, r and n */

    /* calculate a value for i */

    /* calculate a value for F */

    /* display the calculated value for F */
}
```

Each of these steps appears very simple when viewed from the top. However, some steps require more detail before they can actually be programmed. For example, the data input step will be carried out interactively. This will require some dialog generated by pairs of printf and scanf statements, as explained in the Chap. 4. Moreover, C does not have an exponentiation operator. Therefore, some additional detail will be required in order to evaluate the formula

$$F = P(1 + i)^n$$

Here is a more detailed version of the above outline.

```
/* compound interest calculations */

main()

{
    /* declare p, r, n, i and f to be floating-point variables */

    /* write a prompt for p and then read in its value */
    /* write a prompt for r and then read in its value */
    /* write a prompt for n and then read in its value */

    /* calculate i = r/100 */

    /* calculate f = p (1 + i)ⁿ as follows:

        f = p * pow((1+i),n)

        where pow is a library function for exponentiation */

    /* display the value for f, with an accompanying label */
}
```

This outline involves more detail than is actually necessary for a program this simple, though it does illustrate the top-down approach to program development.

We will consider the detailed development and implementation of this program later in this chapter, in Examples 5.2, 5.4 and 5.5.

Another method that is sometimes used when planning a C program is the "bottom-up" approach. This method may be useful for programs that make use of self-contained program modules (e.g., user-defined functions). The bottom-up approach involves the detailed development of these program modules early in the planning process. The overall program development is then based upon the known characteristics of these available program modules.

In practice we often use both approaches: top-down for the overall program planning, bottom-up in developing individual modules before the main part of the program, and top-down with respect to the development of each individual module.

5.2 WRITING A C PROGRAM

Once an overall program strategy has been formulated and a program outline has been written, attention can be given to the detailed development of a working C program. At this point the emphasis becomes one of translating each step of the program outline (or each portion of the pseudocode) into one or more equivalent C instructions. This should be a straightforward activity provided the overall program strategy has been thought through carefully and in enough detail.

You should understand, however, that there is more to writing a complete C program than simply arranging the individual declarations and statements in the right order and then punctuating them correctly. Attention should also be given to including certain additional features that will improve the readability of the program and its resulting output. These features include the logical sequencing of the statements, the use of indentation and whitespace, the inclusion of comments and the generation of clearly labeled output.

The selection of the program statements and their logical sequencing within the program is, to a large extent, determined by the underlying program logic. Often, however, there will be several different choices available for obtaining the same end result. This is particularly true of more complex programs that involve the use of conditional or repeated program segments. In such cases, the manner in which the program is organized can have a major effect on the logical clarity of the program and the efficiency of execution. Therefore it is important that the statements be selected and sequenced in the most effective manner. We will say more about this in Chap. 6, where we discuss the various types of conditional and repetitive features that are available in C.

The use of indentation is closely related to the sequencing of groups of statements within a program. Whereas sequencing affects the order in which a group of operations is carried out, indentation illustrates the subordinate nature of individual statements within a group. In addition, blank lines are sometimes used to separate related groups of statements. The value of the indentation and the blank lines should be obvious, even in the simple programs presented earlier in this book. This will become even more apparent later, as we encounter C programs whose structure is more complex.

Comments should always be included within a C program. If written properly, comments can provide a useful overview of the general program logic. They can also delineate major segments of a program, identify certain key items within the program and provide other useful information about the program. Generally, the comments need not be extensive; a few well-placed comments can shed a great deal of light on an otherwise obscure program. Such comments can be of great use to the original programmer as well as to other persons trying to read and understand a program, since most programmers do not remember the details of their own programs over a period of time. This is especially true of programs that are long and complicated.

Another important characteristic of a well-written program is its ability to generate clear, legible output. Two factors contribute to this legibility. The first is labeling of the output data, as we have discussed in Chap. 4. The second is the appearance of some of the input data along with the output, so that each instance of program execution (if there are more than one) can be clearly identified. The manner in which this is accomplished depends upon the environment in which the C program will be executed. In an interactive environment the input data is displayed on the screen at the time of data entry, during program execution. Hence the input data need not be displayed again.

When executing an interactive program, the *user* (someone other than the programmer) may not know how to enter the required input data. For example, the user may not know what data items are required, when the data items should be entered, or the order in which they should be entered. Thus a well-written interactive program should generate *prompts* at appropriate times during the program execution in order to provide this information.

EXAMPLE 5.2 Compound Interest   Let us now consider an interactive C program corresponding to the outline presented in Example 5.1.

```
/* simple compound interest problem */

#include <stdio.h>
#include <math.h>

main()

{
    float p, r, n, i, f;

    /* read input data (including prompts) */

    printf("Please enter a value for the principal (P): ");
    scanf("%f", &p);
    printf("Please enter a value for the interest rate (r): ");
    scanf("%f", &r);
    printf("Please enter a value for the number of years (n): ");
    scanf("%f", &n);

    /* calculate i, then f */

    i = r/100;
    f = p * pow((1 + i),n);

    /* display the output */

    printf("\nThe final value (F) is: %.2f\n", f);
}
```

The program shown in this example is logically very straightforward. Thus we did not have to concern ourselves with alternate ways to sequence the statements. There are, however, some other desirable features that might have been included. For example, we might want to execute the program repetitively, for several different sets of input data. Or, we might want to add error traps that prevent the user from entering negative values for any of the input parameters. In Chap. 6 we will see how these features can be added.

5.3 ENTERING THE PROGRAM INTO THE COMPUTER

Once the program has been written, it must be entered into the computer before it can be compiled and executed. In older versions of C this was done by typing the program into a text file on a line-by-line basis, using a text editor or a word processor.

Most contemporary versions of C or C++ include a *screen editor* that is used for this purpose. The editor is usually integrated into the software environment. Thus, to access the editor, you must first enter the C or C++ programming environment. The manner in which this accomplished varies from one implementation of C to another.

Consider, for example, Version 4.5 Turbo C++, running under Windows on an IBM-compatible personal computer. To enter Turbo C++, open the Turbo C++ group and then click on the Turbo C++ icon. This will result in the near-empty window shown in Fig. 5.1. Within this window, the first line (containing `Turbo C++ -[noname00.cpp]`), is the *title bar*, and the second line (containing `File Edit Search View`, etc.) is the *menu bar*. Selecting one of the items in the menu bar will cause a *drop-down menu* to appear, with a number of choices related to the menu bar selection. For example, the `File` menu includes choices that allow you to open a new program, retrieve an existing program, save a program, print a program listing, or exit from Turbo C++. We will discuss some of these drop-down menu selections later in this chapter.

Usually a pointing device, such as a *mouse*, is used to select a menu item. This is accomplished by moving the cursor over the desired item and then "clicking" on the item; i.e., pressing a button on the pointing device.

The large clear space beneath the menu bar is an *editing area* where a new program can be entered or an existing program displayed. Portions of the program listed in this area can be changed, deleted, copied or moved to another part of the program. Some of these changes are made directly in the editing area, while others are made by *highlighting* (i.e., selecting) a part of the program and then copying, moving or deleting the highlighted material using the selections provided in the Edit menu. Highlighting is usually carried out by holding down a mouse button and then dragging the mouse across the material to be highlighted.

Scroll bars are present beneath and to the right of the editing area. The scroll bars allow you to move quickly to other parts of the program if the program listing extends beyond the confines of the screen. Thus, you can move vertically through the program listing by clicking along the right scroll bar, or by dragging the small square scroll button up or down. Similarly, you can move horizontally across the program listing by clicking along the bottom scroll bar, or by dragging the scroll button to the right or the left.

Finally, the last line is the *status bar*, which indicates the current status of the editing area, or the purpose of the currently highlighted menu selection. Figure 5.1 indicates that the editing window is in the *insert* mode, meaning that text can be inserted anywhere within the window.

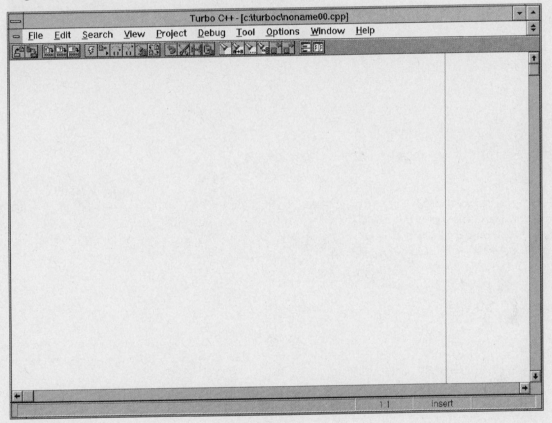

Fig. 5.1

To enter a new program in Turbo C++, you simply type the program into the editing area on a line-by-line basis and press the Enter key at the end of each line. To edit a line, use the mouse or the cursor movement (arrow) keys to locate the beginning of the edit area. Then use the Backspace or Delete keys to remove unwanted characters. You may also insert additional characters, as required.

You may *delete* one or more lines simply by highlighting the lines and then selecting Cut from the Edit menu, or by pressing the Delete key. A block of lines can be *moved* to another location using the Cut and Paste selections in the Edit menu. Similarly, a block of lines can be *copied* to another location using the Copy and Paste selections in the Edit menu. Additional editing instructions are provided in the Turbo C++ User's Manual.

Once the program has been entered, it should be saved before it is executed. In Turbo C++, this is accomplished by selecting Save As from the File menu, and then supplying a program name, such as INTEREST.C. (The extension C will be added automatically if an extension is not included as a part of the file name.) Once the program has been saved and a name has been provided, it can again be saved at some later time (with, for example, any recent editing changes), simply by selecting Save from the File menu.

A program that has been saved can later be recalled by selecting Open from the File menu, and then either typing the program name or selecting the program name from a list of stored programs. A printed listing of the current program (called a "hard copy") can be obtained at any time by selecting Print from the File menu.

EXAMPLE 5.3 Compound Interest   Suppose you have entered the compound interest program shown in Example 5.2 into an IBM-compatible personal computer using Turbo C++. After all typing corrections have been made, the screen will appear as shown in Fig. 5.2. You can then save the program by selecting Save As from the File menu, as shown in Fig. 5.3.

Once you select Save As, a dialog box will appear, requesting the name of the program being saved. Respond by entering the program name INTEREST.C. You may then conclude the session by selecting Exit from the File menu.

```
/* simple compound interest problem */

#include <stdio.h>
#include <math.h>

main()

{

    float p, r, n, i, f;

    /* prompt for input data */

    printf("Please enter a value for the principal (P): ");
    scanf("%f", &p);
    printf("Please enter a value for the interest rate (r): ");
    scanf("%f", &r);
    printf("Please enter a value for the number of years (n): ");
    scanf("%f", &n);

    /* calculate i, then f */

    i = r / 100;
    f = p * pow((1 + i), n);

    /* display the output */

    printf("\nThe final value (F) is: %.2f\n", f);
}
```

Fig. 5.2

5.4 COMPILING AND EXECUTING THE PROGRAM

Once the program has been entered into the computer, edited and saved, it can be compiled and executed by selecting Run from the Debug menu. A new window will then be opened, and an attempt will be made to compile the current program. If the program does not compile successfully, a list of error messages will appear in a separate window. Each error message indicates the line number where the error was detected as well as the type of error. If the program does compile successfully, however, it will immediately begin to execute, prompting for input, displaying output, etc., within the new window.

EXAMPLE 5.4 Compound Interest   Suppose you reenter Turbo C++ after concluding the session described in Example 5.3. Start by loading the previous program, INTEREST.C, into the computer's memory, by selecting Open from the File menu. Then select Run from the Debug menu, as shown in Fig. 5.4.

Turbo C++ - [c:\turboc\interest.c]
File Edit Search View Project Debug Tool Options Window Help
New
Open...
Save Ctrl+K s
Save as...
Save all
Print...
Printer setup...
Exit
1 c:\turboc\roots.c
problem */
/* prompt for input data */
printf("Please enter a value for the principal (P): ");
scanf("%f", &p);
printf("Please enter a value for the interest rate (r): ");
scanf("%f", &r);
printf("Please enter a value for the number of years (n): ");
scanf("%f", &n);
/* calculate i, then f */
i = r / 100;
f = p * pow((1 + i), n);
/* display the output */
printf("\nThe final value (F) is: %.2f\n", f);
}
Save the file in the active window under a new name

Fig. 5.3

Turbo C++ - [c:\turboc\interest.c]
File Edit Search View Project Debug Tool Options Window Help
Run Ctrl+F9
Step over F8
Trace into F7
Toggle breakpoint F5
Find execution point
Pause program
Terminate program Ctrl+F2
Add watch... Ctrl+F5
Add breakpoint...
Evaluate/Modify... Ctrl+F7
Inspect...
Load symbol table...
/* simple compound interest probl
#include <stdio.h>
#include <math.h>
main()
{
float p, r, n, i, f;
/* prompt for input data */
printf("Please enter a value
scanf("%f", &p);
printf("Please enter a value for the interest rate (r): ");
scanf("%f", &r);
printf("Please enter a value for the number of years (n): ");
scanf("%f", &n);
/* calculate i, then f */
i = r / 100;
f = p * pow((1 + i), n);
/* display the output */
printf("\nThe final value (F) is: %.2f\n", f);
}
Make and run the current program

Fig. 5.4

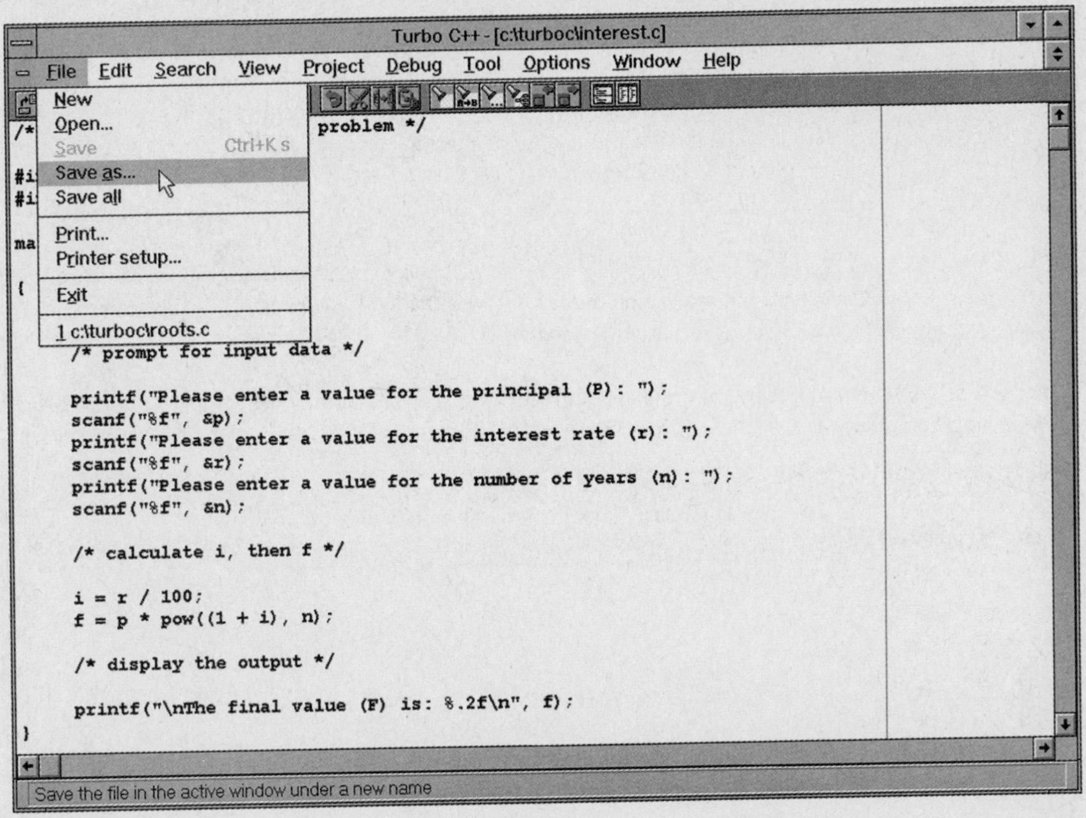

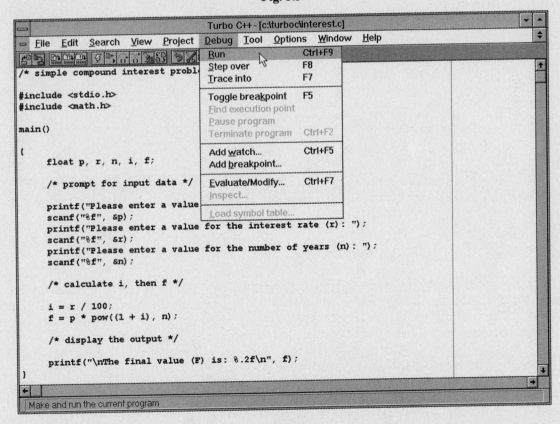

```
Turbo C++ - [c:\turboc\interest.c]
File  Edit  Search  View  Project  Debug  Tool  Options  Window  Help

/* simple compound interest problem */

#include <stdio.h>
#include <math.h>

main()                    ┌──────── C:\TURBOC\INTEREST.EXE ────────┐
                          │Please enter a value for the principal (P): 1000
{                         │Please enter a value for the interest rate (r): 6
    float p, r,           │Please enter a value for the number of years (n): 20
                          │
    /* prompt fo          │
                          │
    printf("Plea          │
    scanf("%f",           │
    printf("Plea          │
    scanf("%f",           │
    printf("Plea          │
    scanf("%f",           │
                          │
    /* calculate          └────────────────────────────────────────┘

    i = r / 100;
    f = p * pow((1 + i), n);

    /* display the output */

    printf("\nThe final value (F) is: %.2f\n", f);
}

Program running
```

Fig. 5.5

```
Turbo C++ - [c:\turboc\interest.c]
File  Edit  Search  View  Project  Debug  Tool  Options  Window  Help

/* simple compound interest problem */

#include <stdio.h>
#include <math.h>

main()                 ┌──────── (Inactive C:\TURBOC\INTEREST.EXE) ────────┐
                       │Please enter a value for the principal (P): 1000
{                      │Please enter a value for the interest rate (r): 6
    float p, r,        │Please enter a value for the number of years (n): 20
                       │
    /* prompt fo       │The final value (F) is: 3207.14
                       │
    printf("Plea       │
    scanf("%f",        │
    printf("Plea       │
    scanf("%f",        │
    printf("Plea       │
    scanf("%f",        │
                       │
    /* calculate       └──────────────────────────────────────────────────┘

    i = r / 100;
    f = p * pow((1 + i), n);

    /* display the output */

    printf("\nThe final value (F) is: %.2f\n", f);
}

Program running
```

Fig. 5.6

The program is compiled successfully and immediately begins to execute. A new window, showing the input/output dialog, appears on top of the original window containing the program listing. This is shown in Fig. 5.5 for the values $P = 1000$, $r = 6$ and $n = 20$. These values have been entered by the user, in response to the input prompts.

Once the last input quantity has been entered ($n = 20$), the program resumes execution, resulting in the final output shown in Fig. 5.6. Thus, we see that a value of $F = 3207.14$ is obtained for the given input quantities.

5.5 ERROR DIAGNOSTICS

Programming errors often remain undetected until an attempt is made to compile or execute the program. The presence of *syntactic* (or *grammatical*) errors will become readily apparent once the Run command has been issued, since these errors will prevent the program from being compiled or executed successfully. Some particularly common errors of this type are improperly declared variables, a reference to an undeclared variable, incorrect punctuation, etc.

Most C compilers will generate *diagnostic messages* when syntactic errors have been detected during the compilation process. These diagnostic messages are not always straightforward in their meaning and they may not correctly identify where the error occurred (though they may attempt to do so). Nevertheless, they are helpful in identifying the nature and the approximate location of the errors.

If a program includes several different syntactic errors, they may not all be detected on the first pass through the compiler. Thus, it may be necessary to correct some syntactic errors before others can be found. This process could repeat itself through several cycles before all of the syntactic errors have been identified and corrected.

EXAMPLE 5.5 Syntactic Errors   Here is another version of the compound interest program shown in Examples 5.2 through 5.4.

```
/* simple compound interest problem */

#include <stdio.h>
include <math.h>

main()

{
    float p, r, n, i, f;

    /* read input data (including prompts) */

    printf("Please enter a value for the principal (P): ");
    scanf("%f", &p);
    printf("Please enter a value for the interest rate (r): );
    scanf("%f", &r);
    printf("Please enter a value for the number of years (n): ");
    scanf("%f", &n)

    /* calculate i, then f */

    i = r/100;
    f = p * pow(1 + i),n);

    /* write output /*

    printf("\nThe final value (F) is: %.2f\n", f);
}
```

This version of the program contains five different syntactic errors. The errors are as follows:

1. The second `include` statement does not begin with a `#` sign.

2. The control string in the second `printf` statement does not have a closing quotation mark.

3. The last `scanf` statement does not end with a semicolon.

4. The assignment statement for `f` contains unbalanced parentheses.

5. The last comment closes improperly (it ends with `/*` instead of `*/`).

When a compilation was attempted (by selecting either Run from the Debug menu or Compile from the Project menu), the error messages shown in Fig. 5.7 were obtained within a separate message window.

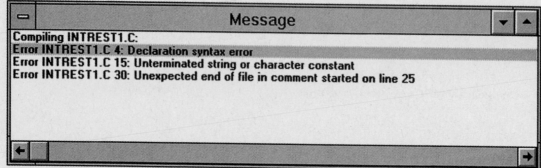

Fig. 5.7

The first message refers to the missing # sign in line 4 (the line numbers include empty lines). The second message refers to the missing double quote (") at the end of the second printf statement (line 15), and the third message refers to the improper ending of the last comment (line 25). Notice that the error messages are somewhat cryptic. Thus, some ingenuity may be required to determine what they mean.

When these three errors were correctly identified and corrected, another attempt was made to compile the program. This resulted in the new set of error messages shown in Fig. 5.8.

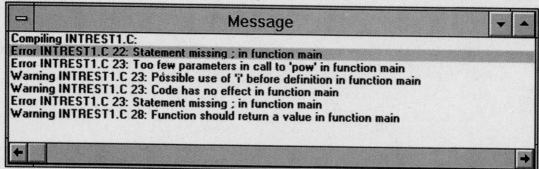

Fig. 5.8

The first error message refers to the missing semicolon at the end of the last scanf statement (which actually occurs in line 18, not line 22). The second message refers to the missing left parenthesis in second assignment statement (line 23). The following two warnings and the third error message are also a result of this one error.

When these remaining two errors were corrected, the program compiled correctly and began to execute, as shown in Fig. 5.5.

You should understand that the specific error messages and warnings will vary from one version of C to another. Some compilers may generate messages that are longer or more informative than those shown in this example, though the messages shown here are typical.

Another type of error that is quite common is the *execution* error. Execution errors occur during program execution, after a successful compilation. For example, some common execution errors are a *numerical overflow* of *underflow* (exceeding the largest or smallest permissible number that can be stored in the computer), division by zero, attempting to compute the logarithm or the square root of a negative number, etc. Diagnostic messages will often be generated in situations of this type, making it easy to identify and correct the errors. These diagnostics are sometimes called *execution* messages or *run-time* messages, to distinguish them from the *compilation* messages described earlier.

EXAMPLE 5.6 Real Roots of a Quadratic Equation Suppose we want to calculate the real roots of the quadratic equation

$$ax^2 + bx + c = 0$$

using the quadratic formula

$$x = \frac{-b \pm \sqrt{b^2 - 4ac}}{2a}$$

Here is a C program that will carry out these calculations.

```c
/* real roots of a quadratic equation */

#include <stdio.h>
#include <math.h>

main()

{
    float a, b, c, d, x1, x2;

    /* read input data */

    printf("a = ");
    scanf("%f", &a);
    printf("b = ");
    scanf("%f", &b);
    printf("c = ");
    scanf("%f", &c);

    /* carry out the calculations */

    d = sqrt(b * b - 4 * a * c);
    x1 = (-b + d) / (2 * a);
    x2 = (-b - d) / (2 * a);

    /* display the output */

    printf("\nx1 = %e     x2 = %e", x1, x2);
}
```

This program is completely free of syntactic errors, but it is unable to accommodate negative values for $b^2 - 4ac$. Furthermore, numerical difficulties may be encountered if the variable a has a very small or a very large numerical value, or if $a = 0$. A separate error message will be generated for each of these errors.

Suppose, for example, the program is run with Turbo C++ using the following input values:

```
a=1.0     b=2.0     c=3.0
```

The program compiles without any difficulty. When the object program is executed, however, the following error message is generated, after the input values have been entered into the computer.

```
sqrt: DOMAIN error
```

Everything then comes to a halt, since the program execution cannot continue beyond this point. Figure 5.9 illustrates the appearance of the screen in Turbo C++.

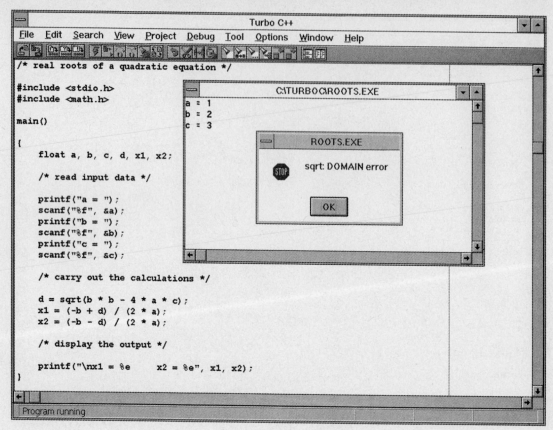

Fig. 5.9

Similarly, suppose the program is run with the input values

```
a=1E-30        b=1E10        c=1E36
```

The system now generates the error message

```
Floating Point: Overflow
```

when an attempt is made to execute the program. Figure 5.10 shows the appearance of the screen in Turbo C++.

5.6 DEBUGGING TECHNIQUES

We now know that syntactic errors and execution errors usually produce error messages when compiling or executing a program. Syntactic errors are relatively easy to find and correct, even if the resulting error messages are unclear. Execution errors, on the other hand, can be much more troublesome. When an execution error occurs, we must first determine its location (*where* it occurs) within the program. Once the location of the execution error has been identified, the source of the error (*why* it occurs) must be determined. Knowing where the error occurred often assists, however, in recognizing and correcting the error.

Closely related to execution errors are *logical* errors. Here the program executes correctly, carrying out the programmer's wishes, but the programmer has supplied the computer with instructions that are logically incorrect. Logical errors can be very difficult to detect, since the output resulting from a logically incorrect program may appear to be error-free. Moreover, logical errors are often hard to locate even when they are known to exist (as, for example, when the computed results are obviously incorrect).

Fortunately, methods are available for finding the location of execution errors and logical errors within a program. Such methods are generally referred to as *debugging techniques*. Some of the more commonly used debugging techniques are described below.

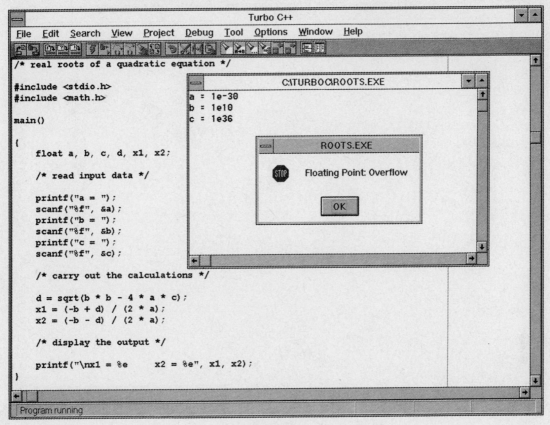

Fig. 5.10

Error Isolation

Error isolation is useful for locating an error resulting in a diagnostic message. If the general location of the error is not known, it can frequently be found by temporarily deleting a portion of the program and then rerunning the program to see if the error disappears. The temporary deletion is accomplished by surrounding the instructions with comment markers (/* and */), causing the enclosed instructions to become comments. If the error message then disappears, the deleted portion of the program contains the source of the error.

A closely related technique is that of inserting several unique `printf` statements, such as

```
printf("Debugging - line 1\n");

printf("Debugging - line 2\n");
```

etc.

at various places within the program. When the program is executed, the debug messages will indicate the approximate location of the error. Thus, the source of the error will lie somewhere between the last `printf` statement whose message *did* appear, and the first `printf` statement whose message *did not* appear.

Tracing

Tracing involves the use of `printf` statements to display the values assigned to certain key variables, or to display the values that are calculated internally at various locations within the program. This information serves several purposes. For example, it verifies that the values actually assigned to certain variables really are (or are not) the values that should be assigned to those values. It is not uncommon to find that the actual assigned values are different than those expected. In addition, this information allows you to monitor the progress of the computation as the program executes. In many situations, you will be able to identify a particular place where things begin to go wrong because the values generated will be obviously incorrect.

EXAMPLE 5.7 Debugging a Program   Consider once again the program for calculating the real roots of a quadratic equation, originally shown in Example 5.6. We saw that the program generates the execution error

```
Floating Point: Overflow
```

when it was executed with the input values a = 1E-30, b = 1E10 and c = 1E36. Let us now apply error isolation and tracing techniques to determine the source of the error.

It is reasonable to assume that the error is generated in one of the three assignment statements following the last scanf statement. Therefore, let us temporarily remove these three statements by placing exaggerated comment markers around them, as shown in the following program listing.

```
/* real roots of a quadratic equation */

#include <stdio.h>
#include <math.h>

main()

{
    float a, b, c, d, x1, x2;

    /* read input data */

    printf("a = ");
    scanf("%f", &a);
    printf("b = ");
    scanf("%f", &b);
    printf("c = ");
    scanf("%f", &c);

    /* carry out the calculations */

    /******************************* error isolation ************************
    d = sqrt(b * b - 4 * a * c);
    x1 = (-b + d) / (2 * a);
    x2 = (-b - d) / (2 * a);
    ******************************* end error isolation *********************/

    /* display the output */

    printf("\nx1 = %e     x2 = %e", x1, x2);
}
```

When the altered program was executed with the same three input values, the error message did not appear (though the displayed values for x1 and x2 did not make any sense). Thus, it is clear that the source of the original error message lies in one of these three statements.

We now remove the comment markers, but precede each assignment statement with a printf statement, as shown below.

```
/* real roots of a quadratic equation */

#include <stdio.h>
#include <math.h>

main()

{
    float a, b, c, d, x1, x2;
```

```
    /* read input data */

    printf("a = ");
    scanf("%f", &a);
    printf("b = ");
    scanf("%f", &b);
    printf("c = ");
    scanf("%f", &c);

    /* carry out the calculations */

    printf("Debugging - Line 1\n");          /* temporary debugging statement */
    d = sqrt(b * b - 4 * a * c);
    printf("Debugging - Line 2\n");          /* temporary debugging statement */
    x1 = (-b + d) / (2 * a);
    printf("Debugging - Line 3\n");          /* temporary debugging statement */
    x2 = (-b - d) / (2 * a);

    /* display the output */

    printf("\nx1 = %e      x2 = %e", x1, x2);
}
```

When the program was executed, again using the same three input values, all three debug messages appeared; i.e.,

```
Debugging - Line 1
Debugging - Line 2
Debugging - Line 3
```

Hence, we conclude that the overflow occurred in the last assignment statement, since this statement follows the third printf statement.

We might normally conclude our debugging efforts at this point. To be complete, however, let us remove these three debugging statements and replace them with three other printf statements (i.e., three *tracing* statements). The first printf statement will display the values of a, b, c and d, the second will display the value of (−b + d), and the last will display the value of (−b − d), as shown below. (Notice the placement of the three printf statements, together after the calculation of d but before the calculation of x1 and x2. Also, notice the e-type formats in the printf statements.)

```
    /* real roots of a quadratic equation */

    #include <stdio.h>
    #include <math.h>

    main()

    {
        float a, b, c, d, x1, x2;
        /* read input data */

        printf("a = ");
        scanf("%f", &a);
        printf("b = ");
        scanf("%f", &b);
        printf("c = ");
        scanf("%f", &c);

        /* carry out the calculations */

        d = sqrt(b * b - 4 * a * c);
```

```
        printf("a = %e   b = %e    c = %e    d = %e\n", a, b, c, d);   /* tracing statement */
        printf("-b + d = %e\n", (-b + d));                             /* tracing statement */
        printf("-b - d = %e\n", (-b - d));                             /* tracing statement */

        x1 = (-b + d) / (2 * a);
        x2 = (-b - d) / (2 * a);

        /* display the output */

        printf("\nx1 = %e     x2 = %e", x1, x2);
    }
```

Execution of this program resulted in the following output:

```
    a = 1.000000e-30   b = 1.000000e+10   c = 1.000000e+36   d = 1.000000e+10
    -b + d = 0.000000e+00
    -b - d = -2.000000e+10
```

From these results we can now determine that the value of x2 should be

$$x2 = (-b - d) / (2 * a) = (-2.000000e+10) / (2 \times 1.000000e-30) = -1.000000e+40$$

The resulting value, -1.000000e+40, exceeds (in magnitude) the largest floating-point number that can be stored within the computer's memory (see Sec. 2.4). Hence, the overflow.

Most contemporary C compilers include an *interactive debugger*, which provides the ability to set *watch values* and *breakpoints*, and allows *stepping* through a program one instruction at a time. Watch values are usually used with breakpoints or with stepping to provide detailed monitoring of the program as it executes. The use of these features offers greater flexibility and convenience than the simple error isolation and tracing techniques described previously. Each of these features is described in more detail below.

Watch Values

A *watch value* is the value of a variable or an expression which is displayed continuously as the program executes. Thus, you can see the changes in a watch value as they occur, in response to the program logic. By monitoring a few carefully selected watch values, you can often determine where the program begins to generate incorrect or unexpected values.

In Turbo C++, watch values can be defined by selecting Add Watch from the Debug menu (see Fig. 5.4 earlier in this chapter), and then specifying one or more variables or expressions in the resulting dialog box. The watch values will then be displayed within a separate window as the program executes.

Breakpoints

A *breakpoint* is a temporary stopping point within a program. Each breakpoint is associated with a particular instruction within the program. When the program is executed, the program execution will temporarily stop at the breakpoint, *before* the instruction is executed. The execution may then be resumed, until the next breakpoint is encountered. Breakpoints are often used in conjunction with watch values, by observing the current watch value at each breakpoint as the program executes.

To set a breakpoint in Turbo C++, select Add Breakpoint from the Debug menu (see Fig. 5.4), and then provide the requested information in the resulting dialog box. Or, select a particular line within the program and designate it a breakpoint by pressing function key F5. The breakpoint may later be disabled by again pressing F5. (Function key F5 is called a "toggle" in this context, since it turns the breakpoint on or off by successively pressing the key.)

Stepping

Stepping refers to the execution of one instruction at a time, typically by pressing a function key to execute each instruction. In Turbo C++, for example, stepping can be carried out by pressing either function key F7 or F8. (F8 steps over subordinate functions, whereas F7 steps through the functions.) By stepping through an entire program, you can determine which instructions produce erroneous results or generate error messages.

Stepping is often used with watch values, allowing you to trace the entire history of a program as it executes. Thus, you can observe changes to watch values as they happen. This allows you to determine which instructions generate erroneous results.

EXAMPLE 5.8 Debugging with an Interactive Debugger   Let us again consider the program given in Examples 5.6 and 5.7, for calculating the real roots of a quadratic equation. We will now use the interactive debugger in Turbo C++ to determine the source of error when the program is executed with the input values a = 1E–30, b = 1E10 and c = 1E36, as before.

Figure 5.11 shows the program within the Turbo C++ editing window. Three watch values have been selected for the quantities –b+d, –b–d and 2*a. Each watch value was selected by choosing Add Watch from the Debug menu. The watch values can be seen in the Watch window, which is superimposed over the program listing.

In addition, a breakpoint has been defined at the first assignment statement, i.e., d = sqrt(b*b – 4*a*c). The breakpoint was defined by placing the cursor on the desired statement and then pressing function key F5. The breakpoint is shown highlighted in Fig. 5.11.

Note that Fig. 5.11 shows the status of the program *before* it has begun to execute. That is why the message <No process running> appears after each watch value.

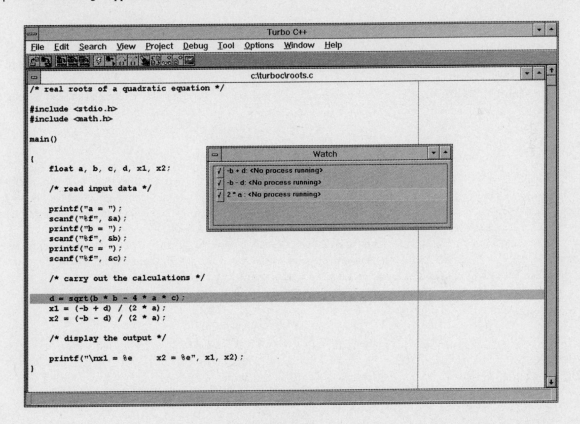

Fig. 5.11

Once the program execution begins (by selecting Run from the Debug menu), the values for a, b and c are entered from the keyboard and the execution continues as far as the break point. The program then temporarily stops, as shown in

Fig. 5.12. Note that the first assignment statement has not yet been executed, so that d has not yet been assigned a value. Hence, the first two watch values are undefined. However, the last watch value is obtained directly from the input data. Its value is shown in the watch window in Fig. 5.12 as 2e–30.

```
/* real roots of a quadratic equation */

#include <stdio.h>
#include <math.h>

main()

{
    float a, b, c, d, x1, x2;

    /* read input data */

    printf("a = ");
    scanf("%f", &a);
    printf("b = ");
    scanf("%f", &b);
    printf("c = ");
    scanf("%f", &c);

    /* carry out the calculations */

    d = sqrt(b * b - 4 * a * c);
    x1 = (-b + d) / (2 * a);
    x2 = (-b - d) / (2 * a);

    /* display the output */

    printf("\nx1 = %e     x2 = %e", x1, x2);
}
```

Fig. 5.12

We could resume the execution, continuing to the end of the program, by again selecting Run from the Debug menu. Instead, however, let us step through the program by pressing function key F8 two times. Figure 5.13 shows the status of the program at this point. Note that the breakpoint remains highlighted. In addition, the third assignment statement (i.e., x2 = (–b – d) / (2 * a)) is also highlighted. This last highlight indicates the next statement to be executed.

Within the watch window, we now see the current values for all of the watch values. It is now easy to see that the value to be assigned to x2, which is the quotient of the second watch value divided by the third watch value, will produce an overflow. Indeed, if we resume the program execution, either by selecting Run from the Debug menu or by stepping, the overflow message shown in Fig. 5.10 will appear.

Sometimes an error simply cannot be located, despite the most elaborate debugging techniques. On such occasions beginning programmers are often inclined to suspect a problem that is beyond their control, such as a hardware error or an error in the compiler. However, the problem almost always turns out to be some subtle error in the program logic. In such situations, you should resist the temptation to blame the computer and not look further for that elusive programming error. Though computer errors do occur *on rare occasions*, they usually produce very bizarre results, such as the computer "locking up" or displaying random, unintelligible characters.

Finally, you should recognize that some logical errors are inescapable in computer programming, no matter how carefully you may attempt to minimize their occurrence. You should therefore anticipate the need for some logical debugging when writing realistic, meaningful C programs.

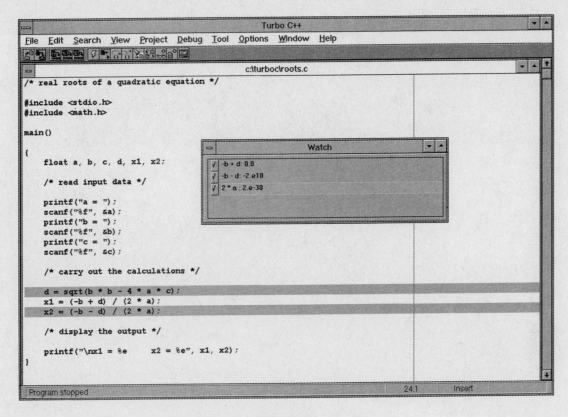

Fig. 5.13

Review Questions

5.1   What is meant by "top-down" programming? What are its advantages? How is it carried out?

5.2   What is pseudocode? What advantage is there in using pseudocode to plan a new program?

5.3   What is meant by "bottom-up" programming? How does it differ from top-down programming?

5.4   How much flexibility does the programmer have in the logical sequencing of the statements within a C program?
Explain.

5.5   Why are some statements indented within a C program? Is this indentation absolutely necessary?

5.6   What are the reasons for placing comments within a C program? How extensive should these comments be?

5.7   Name two factors that contribute to the generation of clear, legible output data.

5.8   What useful information is provided by prompts?

5.9   How is a program entered into the computer in most contemporary C programming environments?

5.10   What is a program name extension?

5.11   What is a syntactic error? Name some common syntactic errors.

5.12   What is an execution error? Name some common execution errors.

5.13   How do syntactic errors and execution errors differ from one another?

5.14   What is a logical error? How do logical errors differ from syntactic and execution errors?

5.15   What are diagnostic messages?

5.16   What is the difference between compilation messages and execution messages? Name some situations in which
each type of diagnostic message would be generated.

5.17   What is error isolation? For what is it used? How is error isolation carried out?

5.18   What is tracing? For what is it used? How is tracing carried out?

5.19   What is an interactive debugger? What special features are made available by a debugger?

5.20   What are watch values? For what are they used? In general terms, how are watch values defined?

5.21   What are breakpoints? For what are they used? In general terms, how are breakpoints defined?

5.22   What is stepping? For what is it used? In general terms, how is stepping carried out?

5.23   Describe how watch values can be used with breakpoints and stepping to monitor the progress of a program's execution.

Problems

The following questions are concerned with information gathering rather than actual problem solving.

5.24   For the personal computers at your school or office, obtain answers to the following questions.

     (*a*)   Exactly what equipment is available (printers, auxiliary memory devices, etc.)?

     (*b*)   What operating systems are available?

     (*c*)   How can files (programs) be saved, displayed, and transferred from one memory device to another?

     (*d*)   What is the approximate cost of a complete personal computer system?

5.25   For the C compiler at your school or office, obtain answers to the following questions.

     (*a*)   What version of C is available? What operating system does it require?

     (*b*)   How is the C compiler accessed? Once the compiler is active, how is a C program accessed? How is the program displayed? How is it saved?

     (*c*)   How are normal editing functions (e.g., insert, delete, etc.) carried out?

     (*d*)   How is a C program compiled and executed?

     (*e*)   Does your compiler include an interactive debugger? If so, what features are supported by the debugger? How are the more common features utilized?

     (*f*)   What is the cost of the C compiler?

Programming Problems

5.26   Example 1.6 presents a C program for calculating the area of a circle, given its radius. Enter this program into your computer and make any necessary modifications, such as #include <stdio.h>. Be sure to correct any typing errors. List the program after it has been stored within the computer. When you are sure that it is correct, compile the program and then execute the object program using several different values for the radius. Verify that the computed answers are correct by comparing them with hand calculations.

5.27   Enter, compile and execute the C programs given in Examples 1.7 through 1.13. Verify that they run correctly with your particular version of C. (If any of the programs do not run, try to determine why.)

5.28   Repeat Prob. 5.27 for a few of the programs given in Prob. 1.31.

5.29   Example 5.2 presents a C program for determining the future value of a savings account if the interest is allowed to accumulate and compound annually. Enter this program into the computer and save it, then run the program using several different sets of input data. Verify that the calculated results are correct by comparing them with calculations carried out by hand, with the aid of a calculator.

5.30   Write a complete C program for each of the following problem situations. Enter each program into the computer, being sure to correct any typing errors. When you are sure that it has been entered correctly, save the program, then compile and execute. Be sure to include prompts for all input data, and label all output.

(a) Print HELLO! at the beginning of a line.

(b) Have the computer print

HI, WHAT'S YOUR NAME?

on one line. The user then enters his or her name immediately after the question mark. The computer then skips two lines and prints

WELCOME (*name*)
LET'S BE FRIENDS!

on two consecutive lines. Use a character-type array to represent the user's name. Assume the name contains fewer than 20 characters.

(c) Convert a temperature reading in degrees Fahrenheit to degrees Celsius, using the formula

$$C = (5/9) \times (F - 32)$$

Test the program with the following values: 68, 150, 212, 0, −22, −200 (degrees Fahrenheit).

(d) Determine how much money (in dollars) is in a piggy bank that contains several half-dollars, quarters, dimes, nickels and pennies. Use the following values to test your program: 11 half-dollars, 7 quarters, 3 dimes, 12 nickels and 17 pennies. (*Answer*: $8.32).

(e) Calculate the volume and area of a sphere using the formulas

$$V = 4\pi r^3/3$$

$$A = 4\pi r^2$$

Test the program using the following values for the radius: 1, 6, 12.2, 0.2.

(f) Calculate the mass of air in an automobile tire, using the formula

$$PV = 0.37m(T + 460)$$

where P = pressure, pounds per square inch (psi)
        V = volume, cubic feet
        m = mass of air, pounds
        T = temperature, degrees Fahrenheit

The tire contains 2 cubic feet of air. Assume that the pressure is 32 psi at room temperature.

(g) Read a five-letter word into the computer, then encode the word on a letter-by-letter basis by subtracting 30 from the numerical value that is used to represent each letter. Thus if the ASCII character set is being used, the letter a (which is represented by the value 97) would become a C (represented by the value 67), etc.

      Write out the encoded version of the word. Test the program with the following words: white, roses, Japan, zebra.

(h) Read into the computer a five-letter word that has been encoded using the scheme described above. Decode the word by reversing the above procedure, then write out the decoded word.

(i) Read an entire line of text into the computer, encoding it as it is read in, using the method described in part (g). Display the entire line of text in encoded form. Then decode the text and write it out (displaying the text as it originally appeared), using the method described in part (h).

(j) Read into the computer a line of text containing both uppercase and lowercase letters. Write out the text with the uppercase and lowercase letters reversed, but all other characters intact. (*Hint*: Use the conditional operator ?: and the library functions islower, tolower and toupper.)

Chapter 6

Control Statements

In most of the C programs we have encountered so far, the instructions were executed in the same order in which they appeared within the program. Each instruction was executed once and only once. Programs of this type are unrealistically simple, since they do not include any logical control structures. Thus, these programs did not include tests to determine if certain conditions are true or false, they did not require the repeated execution of groups of statements, and they did not involve the execution of individual groups of statements on a selective basis. Most C programs that are of practical interest make extensive use of features such as these.

For example, a realistic C program may require that a logical test be carried out at some particular point within the program. One of several possible actions will then be carried out, depending on the outcome of the logical test. This is known as *branching*. There is also a special kind of branching, called *selection*, in which one group of statements is selected from several available groups. In addition, the program may require that a group of instructions be executed repeatedly, until some logical condition has been satisfied. This is known as *looping*. Sometimes the required number of repetitions is known in advance; and sometimes the computation continues indefinitely until the logical condition becomes true.

All of these operations can be carried out using the various control statements included in C. We will see how this is accomplished in this chapter. The use of these statements will open the door to programming problems that are much broader and more interesting than those considered earlier.

6.1 PRELIMINARIES

Before considering the detailed control statements available in C, let us review some concepts presented in Chaps. 2 and 3 that must be used in conjunction with these statements. Understanding these concepts is essential in order to proceed further.

First, we will need to form logical expressions that are either true or false. To do so, we can use the four *relational operators*, <, <=, >, >=, and the two *equality operators*, == and != (see Sec. 3.3).

EXAMPLE 6.1   Several logical expressions are shown below.

```
count <= 100

sqrt(a+b+c) > 0.005

answer == 0

balance >= cutoff

ch1 < 'T'

letter != 'x'
```

The first four expressions involve numerical operands. Their meaning should be readily apparent.

In the fifth expression, ch1 is assumed to be a char-type variable. This expression will be true if the character represented by ch1 comes before T in the character set, i.e., if the numerical value used to encode the character is less than the numerical value used to encode the letter T.

The last expression makes use of the char-type variable letter. This expression will be true if the character represented by letter is something other than x.

122

In addition to the relational and equality operators, C contains two *logical connectives* (also called *logical operators*), && (AND) and || (OR), and the *unary negation operator* ! (see Sec. 3.3). The logical connectives are used to combine logical expressions, thus forming more complex expressions. The negation operator is used to reverse the meaning of a logical expression (e.g., from true to false).

EXAMPLE 6.2 Here are some logical expressions that illustrate the use of the logical connectives and the negation operator.

```
(count <= 100) && (ch1 != '*')

(balance < 1000.0) || (status == 'R')

(answer < 0) || ((answer > 5.0) && (answer <= 10.0))

!((pay >= 1000.0) && (status == 's'))
```

Note that ch1 and status are assumed to be char-type variables in these examples. The remaining variables are assumed to be numeric (either integer or floating-point).

Since the relational and equality operators have a higher precedence than the logical operators, some of the parentheses are not needed in the above expressions (see Table 3-1 in Sec. 3.5). Thus, we could have written these expressions as

```
count <= 100 && ch1 != '*'

balance < 1000.0 || status == 'R'

answer < 0 || answer > 5.0 && answer <= 10.0

!(pay >= 1000.0 && status == 's')
```

It is a good idea, however, to include pairs of parentheses if there is any doubt about the operator precedences. This is particularly true of expressions that are relatively complicated, such as the third expression above.

The *conditional operator* ?: also makes use of an expression that is either true or false (see Sec. 3.5). An appropriate value is selected, depending on the outcome of this logical expression. This operator is equivalent to a simple *if - else* structure (see Sec. 6.6).

EXAMPLE 6.3 Suppose status is a char-type variable and balance is a floating-point variable. We wish to assign the character C (current) to status if balance has a value of zero, and O (overdue) if balance has a value that is greater than zero. This can be accomplished by writing

```
status = (balance == 0) ? 'C' : 'O'
```

Finally, recall that there are three different kinds of statements in C: *expression statements, compound statements* and *control statements* (see Sec. 2.8). An expression statement consists of an expression, followed by a semicolon (see Sec. 2.7). A compound statement consists of a sequence of two or more consecutive statements enclosed in braces ({ and }). The enclosed statements can be expression statements, other compound statements or control statements. Most control statements contain expression statements or compound statements, including embedded compound statements.

EXAMPLE 6.4 Here is an elementary compound statement which we have seen before, in Example 3.31.

```
{
    int lower, upper;

    lower = getchar();
    upper = toupper(lower);
    putchar(upper);
}
```

Here is a more complicated compound statement

```
{
    float sum = 0, sumsq = 0, sumsqrt = 0, x;

    scanf("%f", &x);
    while (x != 0)  {
            sum += x;
            sumsq += x*x;
            sumsqrt += sqrt(x);
            scanf("%f", &x);
    }
}
```

This last example contains one compound statement embedded within another.

The control statements presented within this chapter make extensive use of logical expressions and compound statements. *Assignment operators*, such as the one used in the above example (i.e., +=), will also be utilized.

6.2 BRANCHING: THE if - else STATEMENT

The if - else statement is used to carry out a logical test and then take one of two possible actions, depending on the outcome of the test (i.e., whether the outcome is true or false).

The else portion of the if - else statement is optional. Thus, in its simplest general form, the statement can be written as

```
if (expression) statement
```

The *expression* must be placed in parentheses, as shown. In this form, the *statement* will be executed only if the *expression* has a nonzero value (i.e., if *expression* is true). If the *expression* has a value of zero (i.e., if *expression* is false), then the *statement* will be ignored.

The *statement* can be either simple or compound. In practice, it is often a compound statement which may include other control statements.

EXAMPLE 6.5 Several representative if statements are shown below.

```
if (x < 0) printf("%f", x);

if (pastdue > 0)
    credit = 0;

if (x <= 3.0)   {
    y = 3 * pow(x, 2);
    printf("%f\n", y);
}

if ((balance < 1000.) || (status == 'R'))
    printf("%f", balance);

if ((a >= 0) && (b <= 5))   {
    xmid = (a + b) / 2;
    ymid = sqrt(xmid);
}
```

The first statement causes the value of the floating-point variable x to be printed (displayed) if its value is negative. In the second statement, a value of zero is assigned to credit if the value of pastdue exceeds zero. The third statement involves a compound statement, in which y is evaluated and then displayed if the value of x does not exceed 3. In the fourth statement we see a complex logical expression, which causes the value of balance to be displayed if its value is less than 1000 *or* if status has been assigned the character 'R'.

The last statement involves both a complex logical expression and a compound statement. Thus, the variables xmid and ymid will both be assigned appropriate values if the current value of a is nonnegative *and* the current value of b does not exceed 5.

The general form of an if statement which includes the else clause is

> if (*expression*) *statement 1* else *statement 2*

If the *expression* has a nonzero value (i.e., if *expression* is true), then *statement 1* will be executed. Otherwise (i.e., if *expression* is false), *statement 2* will be executed.

EXAMPLE 6.6   Here are several examples illustrating the full if - else statement.

```
if (status == 'S')
   tax = 0.20 * pay;
else
   tax = 0.14 * pay;

if (pastdue > 0)    {
   printf("account number %d is overdue", accountno);
   credit = 0;
}
else
   credit = 1000.0;

if (x <= 3)
   y = 3 * pow(x, 2);
else
   y = 2 * pow(x - 3), 2);
printf("%f\n", balance);

if (circle)  {
   scanf("%f", &radius);
   area = 3.14159 * radius * radius;
   printf("Area of circle = %f", area);
}
else  {
   scanf("%f %f", &length, &width);
   area = length * width;
   printf("Area of rectangle = %f", area);
}
```

In the first example the value of tax is determined in one of two possible ways, depending on the character that has been assigned to the variable status. Notice the semicolon at the end of each statement, particularly the first statement (tax = 0.2 * pay;). A more concise way to accomplish the same thing is to write

```
tax = (status == 'S') ? (0.20 * pay) : (0.14 * pay);
```

though this approach is not as clear.

The second example examines the past-due status of an account. If the value of `pastdue` exceeds zero, a message is displayed and the credit limit is set at zero; otherwise, the credit limit is set at 1000.0. In the third example, the value of y is computed differently, depending on whether or not the corresponding value of x exceeds 3.

The fourth example shows how an area can be calculated for either of two different geometric figures. If `circle` is assigned a nonzero value, the radius of a circle is read into the computer, the area is calculated and then displayed. If the value of `circle` is zero, however, then the length and width of a rectangle are read into the computer, the area is calculated and then displayed. In each case, the type of geometric figure is included in the label that accompanies the value of the area.

It is possible to *nest* (i.e., embed) `if - else` statements, one within another. There are several different forms that nested `if - else` statements can take. The most general form of two-layer nesting is

```
if e1 if e2 s1
        else s2
else   if e3 s3
        else s4
```

where *e1*, *e2* and *e3* represent logical expressions and *s1*, *s2*, *s3* and *s4* represent statements. Now, one complete `if - else` statement will be executed if *e1* is nonzero (true), and another complete `if - else` statement will be executed if *e1* is zero (false). It is, of course, possible that *s1*, *s2*, *s3* and *s4* will contain other `if - else` statements. We would then have multilayer nesting.

Some other forms of two-layer nesting are

```
if e1 s1
else if e2 s2


if e1 s1
else if e2 s2
        else s3


if e1 if e2 s1
        else s2
else s3


if e1 if e2 s1
        else s2
```

In the first three cases the association between the `else` clauses and their corresponding expressions is straightforward. In the last case, however, it is not clear which expression (*e1* or *e2*) is associated with the `else` clause. The answer is *e2*. The rule is that the `else` clause is always associated with the closest preceding unmatched (i.e., `else`-less) `if`. This is suggested by the indentation, though the indentation itself is not the deciding factor. Thus, the last example is equivalent to

```
if e1  {
    if e2 s1 else s2
}
```

If we wanted to associate the `else` clause with *e1* rather than *e2*, we could do so by writing

```
if e1  {
    if e2 s1
}
else s2
```

This type of nesting must be carried out carefully in order to avoid possible ambiguities.

In some situations it may be desirable to nest multiple if - else statements, in order to create a situation in which one of several different courses of action will be selected. For example, the general form of four nested if - else statements could be written as

```
if e1 s1
else if e2 s2
     else if e3 s3
          else if e4 s4
               else s5
```

When a logical expression is encountered whose value is nonzero (true), the corresponding statement will be executed and the remainder of the nested if - else statements will be bypassed. Thus, control will be transferred out of the entire nest once a true condition is encountered.

The final else clause will apply if none of the expressions is true. It can be used to provide a default condition or an error message.

EXAMPLE 6.7   Here is an illustration of three nested if - else statements.

```
if ((time >= 0.) && (time < 12.)) printf("Good Morning");
else if ((time >= 12.) && (time < 18.)) printf("Good Afternoon");
     else if ((time >= 18.) && (time < 24.)) printf("Good Evening");
          else printf("Time is out of range");
```

This example causes a different message to be displayed at various times of the day. Specifically, the message Good Morning will be displayed if time has a value between 0 and 12; Good Afternoon will be displayed if time has a value between 12 and 18; and Good Evening will be displayed if time has a value between 18 and 24. An error message (Time is out of range) will be displayed if the value of time is less than zero, or greater than or equal to 24.

6.3 LOOPING: THE while STATEMENT

The while statement is used to carry out looping operations, in which a group of statements is executed repeatedly, until some condition has been satisfied.

The general form of the while statement is

```
while (expression) statement
```

The *statement* will be executed repeatedly, as long as the *expression* is true (i.e., as long *expression* has a nonzero value). This *statement* can be simple or compound, though it is usually a compound statement. It must include some feature that eventually alters the value of the *expression*, thus providing a stopping condition for the loop.

EXAMPLE 6.8 Consecutive Integer Quantities   Suppose we want to display the consecutive digits 0, 1, 2, . . . , 9, with one digit on each line. This can be accomplished with the following program.

```
#include <stdio.h>

main()     /* display the integers 0 through 9 */

{
    int digit = 0;

    while (digit <= 9)  {
          printf("%d\n", digit);
          ++digit;
    }
}
```

Initially, `digit` is assigned a value of 0. The `while` loop then displays the current value of `digit`, increases its value by 1 and then repeats the cycle, until the value of `digit` exceeds 9. The net effect is that the body of the loop will be repeated 10 times, resulting in 10 consecutive lines of output. Each line will contain a successive integer value, beginning with 0 and ending with 9. Thus, when the program is executed, the following output will be generated.

```
0
1
2
3
4
5
6
7
8
9
```

This program can be written more concisely as

```c
#include <stdio.h>

main()      /* display the integers 0 through 9 */
{
    int digit = 0;

    while (digit <= 9)
        printf("%d\n", digit++);
}
```

When executed, this program will generate the same output as the first program.

In some looping situations, the number of passes through the loop is known in advance. The previous example illustrates this type of loop. Sometimes, however, the number of passes through the loop is not known in advance. Rather, the looping action continues indefinitely, until the specified logical condition has been satisfied. The `while` statement is particularly well suited for this second type of loop.

EXAMPLE 6.9 Lowercase to Uppercase Text Conversion   In this example we will read a line of lowercase text character-by-character and store the characters in a char-type array called `letter`. The program will continue reading input characters until an end-of-line (EOF) character has been read. The characters will then be converted to uppercase, using the library function `toupper`, and displayed.

Two separate `while` loops will be used. The first will read the text from the keyboard. Note that the number of passes through this loop is not known in advance. The second `while` loop will perform the conversion and write out the converted text. It will make a known number of passes, since the number of characters to be displayed will be determined by counting the number of passes through the first loop.

The complete program is shown below.

```c
/* convert a line of lowercase text to uppercase */

#include <stdio.h>
#include <ctype.h>

#define EOL  '\n'

main()
{
    char letter[80];
    int tag, count = 0;
```

```
        /* read in the lowercase text */
        while ((letter[count] = getchar()) != EOL)  ++count;
        tag = count;

        /* display the uppercase text */
        count = 0;
        while (count < tag)  {
               putchar(toupper(letter[count]));
               ++count;
        }
}
```

Notice that count is initially assigned a value of zero. Its value increases by 1 during each pass through the first loop. The final value of count, at the conclusion of the first loop, is then assigned to tag. The value of tag determines the number of passes through the second loop.

The first while loop, i.e.,

```
        while ((letter[count] = getchar()) != EOL)  ++count;
```

is written very concisely. This single-statement loop is equivalent to the following:

```
    letter[count] = getchar();
    while (letter[count] != EOL)  {
         count = count + 1;
         letter[count] = getchar();
    }
```

This latter form will be more familiar to those readers experienced with other high-level programming languages, such as Pascal or BASIC. Either form is correct, though the original form is more representative of typical C programming style.

When the program is executed, any line of text entered into the computer will be displayed in uppercase. Suppose, for example, that the following line of text had been entered:

```
Fourscore and seven years ago our fathers brought forth . . .
```

The computer would respond by printing

```
FOURSCORE AND SEVEN YEARS AGO OUR FATHERS BROUGHT FORTH . . .
```

EXAMPLE 6.10 Averaging a List of Numbers   Let us now use a while statement to calculate the average of a list of n numbers. Our strategy will be based on the use of a partial sum that is initially set equal to zero, then updated as each new number is read into the computer. Thus, the problem very naturally lends itself to the use of a while loop.

The calculations will be carried out in the following manner.

1. Assign a value of 1 to the integer variable count. This variable will be used as a loop counter.

2. Assign a value of 0 to the floating-point variable sum.

3. Read in the value for the integer variable n.

4. Carry out the following steps repeatedly, as long as count does not exceed n.
   (a) Read in one of the numbers in the list. Each number will be represented by the floating-point variable x.
   (b) Add the value of x to the current value of sum.
   (c) Increase the value of count by 1.

5. Divide the value of sum by n to obtain the desired average.

6. Write out the calculated value for the average.

Here is the actual C program. Notice that the input operations are all accompanied by prompts that ask the user for the required information.

```
/* calculate the average of n numbers */

#include <stdio.h>

main()

{
    int n, count = 1;
    float x, average, sum = 0;

    /* initialize and read in a value for n */
    printf("How many numbers? ");
    scanf("%d", &n);

    /* read in the numbers */
    while (count <= n)  {
            printf("x = ");
            scanf("%f", &x);
            sum += x;
            ++count;
    }

    /* calculate the average and display the answer */
    average = sum/n;
    printf("\nThe average is %f\n", average);
}
```

Notice that the while loop contains a compound statement which, among other things, causes the value of count to increase. Eventually, this will cause the logical expression

```
count <= n
```

to become false, thus terminating the loop. Also, note that the loop will not be executed at all if n is assigned a value that is less than 1 (which, of course, would make no sense).

Now suppose that the program will be used to process the following six values: 1, 2, 3, 4, 5, 6. Execution of the program will produce the following interactive dialog. (Note that the user's responses have been underlined.)

```
How many numbers? 6
x = 1
x = 2
x = 3
x = 4
x = 5
x = 6

The average is 3.500000
```

6.4 MORE LOOPING: THE do - while STATEMENT

When a loop is constructed using the while statement described in Sec. 6.3, the test for continuation of the loop is carried out at the *beginning* of each pass. Sometimes, however, it is desirable to have a loop with the test for continuation at the *end* of each pass. This can be accomplished by means of the do - while statement.

The general form of the do - while statement is

```
do statement while (expression);
```

The *statement* will be executed repeatedly, as long as the value of *expression* is true (i.e., is nonzero). Notice that *statement* will always be executed at least once, since the test for repetition does not occur until the end of the first pass through the loop. The *statement* can be either simple or compound, though most applications will require it to be a compound statement. It must include some feature that eventually alters the value of *expression* so the looping action can terminate.

For many applications it is more natural to test for continuation of a loop at the beginning rather than at the end of the loop. For this reason, the do - while statement is used less frequently than the while statement described in Sec. 6.3. For illustrative purposes, however, the programming examples shown in Sec. 6.3 are repeated below using the do - while statement for the conditional loops.

EXAMPLE 6.11 Consecutive Integer Quantities   In Example 6.8 we saw two complete C programs that use the while statement to display the consecutive digits 0, 1, 2, . . . , 9. Here is another program to do the same thing, using the do - while statement in place of the while statement.

```
#include <stdio.h>

main()     /* display the integers 0 through 9 */
{
    int digit = 0;

    do
    printf("%d\n", digit++);
    while (digit <= 9);
}
```

As in the earlier example, digit is initially assigned a value of 0. The do - while loop displays the current value of digit, increases its value by 1, and then tests to see if the current value of digit exceeds 9. If so, the loop terminates; otherwise, the loop continues, using the new value of digit. Note that the test is carried out at the end of each pass through the loop. The net effect is that the loop will be repeated 10 times, resulting in 10 successive lines of output. Each line will appear exactly as shown in Example 6.8.

Comparing this program with the second program presented in Example 6.8, we see about the same level of complexity in both programs. Neither of the conditional looping structures (i.e., while or do - while) appears more desirable than the other.

EXAMPLE 6.12 Lowercase to Uppercase Text Conversion   Now let us rewrite the program shown in Example 6.9, which converts lowercase text to uppercase, so that the two while loops are replaced by do - while loops. As in the earlier program, our overall strategy will be to read in a line of lowercase text on a character-by-character basis, store the characters in a char-type array called letter, and then write them out in uppercase using the library function toupper. We will make use of a do - while statement to read in the text on a character-by-character basis, and another do - while statement to convert the characters to uppercase and then write them out.

Here is the complete C program.

```
/* convert a line of lowercase text to uppercase */

#include <stdio.h>
#include <ctype.h>

#define EOL   '\n'

main()
{
    char letter[80];
    int tag, count = -1;

    /* read in the lowercase text */
    do ++count; while ((letter[count] = getchar()) != EOL);
    tag = count;
```

```
        /* display the uppercase text */
        count = 0;
        do {
                putchar(toupper(letter[count]));
                ++count;
        } while (count < tag);
    }
```

We again see two different types of loops, even though they are both written as do - while loops. In particular, the number of passes through the first loop will not be known in advance, but the second loop will execute a known number of passes, as determined by the value assigned to tag.

Notice that the first loop, i.e.,

```
        do ++count; while ((letter[count] = getchar()) != EOL);
```

is simple and concise, but the second loop,

```
        do {
                putchar(toupper(letter[count]));
                ++count;
        } while (count < tag);
```

is somewhat more complex. Both loops resemble the corresponding while loops presented in Example 6.9. Note, however, that the first loop in the present program begins with a value of −1 assigned to count, whereas the initial value of count was 0 in Example 6.9.

When the program is executed, it behaves in exactly the same way as the program shown in Example 6.9.

Before leaving this example, we mention that the last loop could have been written more concisely as

```
        do
            putchar(toupper(letter[count++]));
        while (count < tag);
```

This may appear a bit strange to beginners, though it is characteristic of the programming style that is commonly used by experienced C programmers.

EXAMPLE 6.13 Averaging a List of Numbers   The program shown in Example 6.10 can easily be rewritten to illustrate the use of the do - while statement. The logic will be the same, except that the test to determine if all n numbers have been entered into the computer will not be made until the end of the loop rather than the beginning. Thus the program will always make at least one pass through the loop, even if n is assigned a value of 0 (which would make no sense).

Here is the modified version of the program.

```
    /* calculate the average of n numbers */

    #include <stdio.h>

    main()
    {
        int n, count = 1;
        float x, average, sum = 0;

        /* initialize and read in a value for n */
        printf("How many numbers? ");
        scanf("%d", &n);
```

```
        /* read in the numbers */
        do {
              printf("x = ");
              scanf("%f", &x);
              sum += x;
              ++count;
        } while (count <= n);

        /* calculate the average and display the answer */
        average = sum/n;
        printf("\nThe average is %f\n", average);
}
```

When the program is executed it will behave exactly the same way as the earlier version shown in Example 6.10.

6.5 STILL MORE LOOPING: THE for STATEMENT

The for statement is the third and perhaps the most commonly used looping statement in C. This statement includes an expression that specifies an initial value for an index, another expression that determines whether or not the loop is continued, and a third expression that allows the index to be modified at the end of each pass.

The general form of the for statement is

```
        for (expression 1; expression 2; expression 3) statement
```

where *expression 1* is used to initialize some parameter (called an *index*) that controls the looping action, *expression 2* represents a condition that must be true for the loop to continue execution, and *expression 3* is used to alter the value of the parameter initially assigned by *expression 1*. Typically, *expression 1* is an assignment expression, *expression 2* is a logical expression and *expression 3* is a unary expression or an assignment expression.

When the for statement is executed, *expression 2* is evaluated and tested at the *beginning* of each pass through the loop, and *expression 3* is evaluated at the *end* of each pass. Thus, the for statement is equivalent to

```
        expression 1;
        while (expression 2)  {
           statement
           expression 3;
        }
```

The looping action will continue as long as the value of *expression 2* is not zero, that is, as long as the logical condition represented by *expression 2* is true.

The for statement, like the while and the do - while statements, can be used to carry out looping actions where the number of passes through the loop is not known in advance. Because of the features that are built into the for statement, however, it is particularly well suited for loops in which the number of passes *is* known in advance. As a rough rule of thumb, while loops are generally used when the number of passes is *not* known in advance, and for loops are generally used when the number of passes *is* known in advance.

EXAMPLE 6.14 Consecutive Integer Quantities   We have already seen several different versions of a C program that will display the consecutive digits 0, 1, 2, ... , 9, with one digit on each line (see Examples 6.8 and 6.11). Here is another program which does the same thing. Now, however, we will make use of the for statement rather than the while statement or the do - while statement, as in the earlier examples.

```
#include <stdio.h>

main()   /* display the numbers 0 through 9 */

{
    int digit;

    for (digit = 0; digit <= 9; ++digit)
        printf("%d\n", digit);
}
```

The first line of the for statement contains three expressions, enclosed in parentheses. The first expression assigns an initial value 0 to the integer variable digit; the second expression continues the looping action as long as the current value of digit does not exceed 9 at the *beginning* of each pass; and the third expression increases the value of digit by 1 at the *end* of each pass through the loop. The printf function, which is included in the for loop, produces the desired output, as shown in Example 6.8.

From a syntactic standpoint all three expressions need not be included in the for statement, though the semicolons must be present. However, the consequences of an omission should be clearly understood. The first and third expressions may be omitted if other means are provided for initializing the index and/or altering the index. If the second expression is omitted, however, it will be assumed to have a permanent value of 1 (true); thus, the loop will continue indefinitely unless it is terminated by some other means, such as a break or a return statement (see Secs. 6.8 and 7.2). As a practical matter, most for loops include all three expressions.

EXAMPLE 6.15 Consecutive Integer Quantities Revisited   Here is still another example of a C program that generates the consecutive integers 0, 1, 2, . . . , 9, with one digit on each line. We now use a for statement in which two of the three expressions are omitted.

```
#include <stdio.h>

main()   /* display the numbers 0 through 9 */

{
    int digit = 0;

    for (; digit <= 9; )
        printf("%d\n", digit++);
}
```

This version of the program is more obscure than that shown in Example 6.14, and hence less desirable.

Note the similarity between this program and the second program in Example 6.8, which makes use of a while loop.

EXAMPLE 6.16 Lowercase to Uppercase Text Conversion   Here once again is a C program that converts lowercase text to uppercase. We have already seen other programs that do this, in Examples 6.9 and 6.12. Now, however, we make use of a for loop rather than a while loop or a do - while loop.

As before, our overall strategy will be to read in a line of lowercase text on a character-by-character basis, store the characters in a char-type array called letter, and then write them out in uppercase using the library function toupper. Two separate loops will be required: one to read and store the lowercase characters, the other to display the characters in uppercase. Note that we will now use a for statement to build a loop in which the number of passes is not known in advance.

Here is the complete C program.

```
/* convert a line of lowercase text to uppercase */

#include <stdio.h>
#include <ctype.h>

#define EOL  '\n'

main()

{
    char letter[80];
    int tag, count;

    /* read in the lowercase text */
    for (count = 0; (letter[count] = getchar()) != EOL; ++count)
    ;
    tag = count;

    /* display the uppercase text */
    for (count = 0; count < tag; ++count)
        putchar(toupper(letter[count]));
}
```

Comparing this program with the corresponding programs given in Examples 6.9 and 6.12, we see that the loops can be written more concisely using the for statement than with while or do-while statements.

EXAMPLE 6.17 Averaging a List of Numbers   Now let us modify the program given in Example 6.10, which calculates the average of a list of n numbers, so that the looping action is accomplished by means of a for statement. The logic will be essentially the same, though some of the steps will be carried out in a slightly different order. In particular:

1. Assign a value of 0 to the floating-point variable sum.

2. Read in a value for the integer variable n.

3. Assign a value of 1 to the integer variable count, where count is an index that counts the number of passes through the loop.

4. Carry out the following steps repeatedly, as long as the value of count does not exceed n.

    (a) Read in one of the numbers in the list. Each number will be represented by the floating-point variable x.

    (b) Add the value of x to the current value of sum.

    (c) Increase the value of count by 1.

5. Divide the value of sum by n to obtain the desired average.

6. Write out the calculated value for the average.

Here is the complete C program. Notice that steps 3 and 4 are combined in the for statement, and that steps 3 and 4(c) are both carried out in the first line (first and third expressions, respectively). Also, notice that the input operations are all accompanied by prompts that ask the user for the desired information.

```
/* calculate the average of n numbers */

#include <stdio.h>

main()

{
    int n, count;
    float x, average, sum = 0;

    /* initialize and read in a value for n */
    printf("How many numbers? ");
    scanf("%d", &n);
```

```
/* read in the numbers */
for (count = 1; count <= n; ++count)  {
    printf("x = ");
    scanf("%f", &x);
    sum += x;
}

/* calculate the average and display the answer */
average = sum/n;
printf("\nThe average is %f\n", average);
}
```

Comparing this program to the corresponding programs shown in Examples 6.10 and 6.13, we again see a more concise loop specification when the for statement is used rather than while or do - while. Now, however, the for statement is somewhat more complex than in the preceding programming examples. In particular, notice that the *statement* part of the loop is now a compound statement. Moreover, we must assign an initial value to sum explicitly, before entering the for loop.

When the program is executed it will behave exactly as the earlier versions, presented in Examples 6.10 and 6.13.

6.6 NESTED CONTROL STRUCTURES

Loops, like if - else statements, can be *nested*, one within another. The inner and outer loops need not be generated by the same type of control structure. It is essential, however, that one loop be completely embedded within the other — there can be no overlap. Each loop must be controlled by a different index.

Moreover, nested control structures can involve both loops and if - else statements. Thus, a loop can be nested within an if - else statement, and an if - else statement can be nested within a loop. The nested structures may be as complex as necessary, as determined by the program logic.

EXAMPLE 6.18 Repeated Averaging of a List of Numbers   Suppose we want to calculate the average of several consecutive lists of numbers. If we know in advance how many lists are to be averaged, then we can use a for statement to control the number of times that the inner (averaging) loop is executed. The actual averaging can be accomplished using any of the three methods presented earlier, in Examples 6.10, 6.13 and 6.17 (using a while, a do - while, or a for loop).

Let us arbitrarily use the for statement to carry out the averaging, as in Example 6.17. Thus, we will proceed in the following manner.

1.   Read in a value of loops, an integer quantity that indicates the number of lists that will be averaged.

2.   Repeatedly read in a list of numbers and determine its average. That is, calculate the average of a list of numbers for each successive value of loopcount ranging from 1 to loops. Follow the steps given in Example 6.14 to calculate each average.

Here is the actual C program.

```
/* calculate averages for several different lists of numbers */

#include <stdio.h>

main()

{
    int n, count, loops, loopcount;
    float x, average, sum;

    /* read in the number of lists */
    printf("How many lists? ");
    scanf("%d", &loops);
```

```
      /* outer loop (process each list of numbers */
      for (loopcount = 1; loopcount <= loops; ++loopcount)  {

          /* initialize and read in a value for n */
          sum = 0;
          printf("\nList number %d\nHow many numbers? ", loopcount);
          scanf("%d", &n);

          /* read in the numbers */
          for (count = 1; count <= n; ++count)  {
              printf("x = ");
              scanf("%f", &x);
              sum += x;
          }    /* end inner loop */

          /* calculate the average and display the answer */
          average = sum/n;
          printf("\nThe average is %f\n", average);

      }    /* end outer loop */
}
```

This program contains several interesting features. First, it contains two for statements, one embedded within the other. Each for statement includes a compound statement, consisting of several individual statements enclosed in braces. Also, a different index is used in each for statement (the indices are loopcount and count, respectively).

Note that sum must now be initialized within the outer loop, rather than within the declaration. This allows sum to be reset to zero each time a new set of data is encountered (i.e., at the beginning of each pass through the outer loop).

The input data operations are all accompanied by prompts, indicating to the user what data are required. Thus, we see pairs of printf and scanf functions at several places throughout the program. Two of the printf functions contain multiple newline characters, to control the line spacing of the output. This causes the output associated with each set of data (each pass through the outer loop) to be easily identified.

Finally, note that the program is organized into separate identifiable segments, with each segment preceded by a blank space and a comment.

When the program is executed using three simple sets of data, the following dialog is generated. As usual, the user's responses to the input prompts have been underlined.

```
How many lists? 3

List number 1
How many numbers? 4
x = 1.5
x = 2.5
x = 6.2
x = 3.0

The average is 3.300000

List number 2
How many numbers? 3
x = 4
x = -2
x = 7

The average is 3.000000
```

```
List number 3
How many numbers? 5
x = 5.4
x = 8.0
x = 2.2
x = 1.7
x = -3.9


The average is 2.680000
```

EXAMPLE 6.19 Converting Several Lines of Text to Uppercase   This example illustrates the use of two different types of loops, one nested within the other. Let us extend the lowercase to uppercase conversion programs presented in Examples 6.9, 6.12 and 6.16 so that multiple lines of lowercase text can be converted to uppercase, with the conversion taking place one line at a time. In other words, we will read in a line of lowercase text, display it in uppercase, then process another line, and so on. The procedure will continue until a line is detected in which the first character is an asterisk.

We will use nested loops to carry out the computation. The outer loop will be used to process multiple lines of text. Two separate inner loops will be embedded within the outer loop. The first will read in a line of text, and the second will display the converted uppercase text. Note that these inner loops are not nested. Let us arbitrarily utilize a while statement for the outer loop, and a for statement for each of the inner loops.

In general terms, the computation will proceed as follows.

1.   Assign an initial value of 1 to the outer loop index (linecount).

2.   Carry out the following steps repeatedly, for each successive line of text, as long as the first character in the line is not an asterisk.

   (a)   Read in a line of text and assign the individual characters to the elements of the char-type array letter. A line will be defined as a succession of characters that is terminated by an end-of-line (newline) designation.

   (b)   Assign the character count (including the end-of-line character) to tag.

   (c)   Display the line in uppercase, using the library function toupper to carry out the conversion. Then write out two newline characters so that the next line of input will be separated from the current output by a blank line, and increment the line counter (linecount).

3.   Once an asterisk has been detected as the first character of a new line, write out Good bye and terminate the computation.

Here is the complete C program.

```
/* convert several lines of text to uppercase
   continue the conversion until the first character in a line is an asterisk (*) */

#include <stdio.h>
#include <ctype.h>

#define EOL '\n'

main()
{
    char letter[80];
    int tag, count;

    while((letter[0] = getchar()) != '*')   {

        /* read in a line of text */
        for (count = 1; (letter[count] = getchar()) != EOL; ++count)
            ;
        tag = count;
```

```
            /* display the line of text */
            for (count = 0; count < tag; ++count)
                putchar(toupper(letter[count]));
            printf("\n\n");
  }     /* end outer loop */

     printf("Good bye");
  }
```

A typical interactive session, illustrating the execution of the program, is shown below. Note that the input text supplied by the user is underlined, as usual.

```
Now is the time for all good men to come to the aid . . .
NOW IS THE TIME FOR ALL GOOD MEN TO COME TO THE AID . . .


Fourscore and seven years ago our fathers brought forth . . .
FOURSCORE AND SEVEN YEARS AGO OUR FATHERS BROUGHT FORTH . . .


*
Good bye
```

It should be understood that the decision to use a `while` statement for the outer loop and `for` statements for the inner loops is arbitrary. Other loop structures could also have been selected.

Many programs involve both looping and branching. The various control structures are often nested, one within another, as illustrated in the following three examples.

EXAMPLE 6.20 Encoding a String of Characters   Let us write a simple C program that will read in a sequence of ASCII characters and write out a sequence of encoded characters in its place. If a character is a letter or a digit, we will replace it with the next character in the character set, except that Z will be replaced by A, z by a, and 9 by 0. Thus 1 becomes 2, C becomes D, p becomes q, and so on. Any character other than a letter or a digit will be replaced by a period (.).

The computation will begin by reading in the characters. The `scanf` function will be used for this purpose. All the characters, up to but not including the newline (\n) character that is used to terminate the input, will be entered and stored in an 80-element, character-type array called `line`.

The characters will then be encoded and displayed individually within a `for` loop. The loop will process each of the characters in `line`, until the escape character \0, which designates the end of the character sequence, is encountered. (Recall that the escape sequence \0 is automatically added at the end of each string.) Several nested `if - else` statements will be included within the loop, to carry out the appropriate encoding. Each encoded character will then be displayed using the `putchar` function.

The complete C program is shown below.

```
/* read in a string, then replace each character with an equivalent encoded character */

#include <stdio.h>

main()

{
    char line[80];
    int count;

    /* read in the entire string */

    printf("Enter a line of text below:\n");
    scanf("%[^\n]", line);
```

```
/* encode each individual character and display it */

for (count = 0; line[count] != '\0'; ++count)  {
    if (((line[count] >= '0') && (line[count] < '9')) ||
        ((line[count] >= 'A') && (line[count] < 'Z')) ||
        ((line[count] >= 'a') && (line[count] < 'z')))
            putchar(line[count] + 1);
    else if (line[count] == '9') putchar('0');
        else if (line[count] == 'Z') putchar('A');
            else if (line[count] == 'z') putchar('a');
                else putchar('.');
}
}
```

Execution of this program generates the following representative dialog. The input provided by the user is again underlined.

```
Enter a line of text below:
The White House, 1600 Pennsylvania Avenue, Washington, DC
Uif.Xijuf.Ipvtf..2711.Qfootzmwbojb.Bwfovf..Xbtijohupo..ED
```

EXAMPLE 6.21 Repeated Compound Interest Calculations with Error Trapping   In Example 5.2 we saw a complete C program to carry out simple compound interest calculations, as outlined in Example 5.1. However, the program in Example 5.2 did not allow for repetitive execution (i.e., for several successive calculations, using different input data for each calculation), nor did it attempt to detect errors in the input data. Let us now add these features to the earlier program.

In particular, let us embed the earlier calculations within a while statement, which will continue to execute as long as the value entered for the principal (P) is positive. Thus, a zero value for P will be interpreted as a stopping condition. We will include a message explaining the stopping condition when prompting for the value of P.

In addition, let us include an *error trap* that will test the value of each input quantity to determine if it is negative, since a negative value would not make any sense and should be interpreted as an error. Each test will be carried out with a separate if statement. If an error (i.e., a negative value) is detected, a message will be written asking the user to reenter the data.

Here is the entire C program.

```
/* simple compound interest problem */

#include <stdio.h>
#include <math.h>

main()

{
    float p,r,n,i,f;

    /* read initial value for the principal */

    printf("Please enter a value for the principal (P) ");
    printf("\n(To end program, enter 0 for the principal): ");
    scanf("%f", &p);
    if (p < 0)   {
        printf("\nERROR - Please try again: ");
        scanf("%f", &p);
    }
```

```
    while (p > 0)   {      /* main loop */

        /* read remaining input data */

        printf("\nPlease enter a value for the interest rate (r): ");
        scanf("%f", &r);
        if (r < 0)   {
            printf("\nERROR - Please try again: ");
            scanf("%f", &r);
        }
        printf("\nPlease enter a value for the number of years (n): ");
        scanf("%f", &n);
        if (n < 0)   {
            printf("\nERROR - Please try again: ");
            scanf("%f", &n);
        }

        /* calculate i, then f */

        i = r/100;
        f = p * pow((1 + i), n);

        /* display the output */

        printf("\nThe final value (F) is: %.2f\n", f);

        /* read principal for next pass */

        printf("\n\nPlease enter a value for the principal (P) ");
        printf("\n(To end program, enter 0 for the principal): ");
        scanf("%f", &p);
        if (p < 0)   {
            printf("\nERROR - Please try again: ");
            scanf("%f", &p);
        }
    }   /* end while loop */
}
```

A typical interactive session is shown below. Note that the user's responses are underlined.

```
Please enter a value for the principal (P)
(To end program, enter 0 for the principal): 1000

Please enter a value for the interest rate (r): 6

Please enter a value for the number of years (n): 20


The final value (F) is: 3207.14


Please enter a value for the principal (P)
(To end program, enter 0 for the principal): 5000

Please enter a value for the interest rate (r): -7.5

ERROR - Please try again: 7.5
```

```
Please enter a value for the number of years (n): 12

The final value (F) is: 11908.90


Please enter a value for the principal (P)
(To end program, enter 0 for the principal): 0
```

Notice that two sets of input data are provided. The first set of data is entered correctly, resulting in a calculated future value of 3207.14 (as in Example 5.4). In the second data set, a negative value is initially supplied for the interest rate (r). This is detected as an error, resulting in an error message and a request for another value. Once the corrected value is supplied, the remaining program execution proceeds as expected.

After the second data set has been processed, the user enters a value of 0 for the principal, in response to the prompt. This causes the execution of the program to terminate.

Remember that the error trapping used in this program applies only to negative floating-point quantities entered as input data. Another type of error occurs if a letter or punctuation mark is entered for one of the required input quantities. This will produce a type mismatch in the scanf function, resulting in an input error. Individual compilers deal with this type of error differently, thus preventing a simple, general error trap.

The following program is more comprehensive in nature. It includes most of the programming features that we have encountered earlier in this book.

EXAMPLE 6.22 Solution of an Algebraic Equation   For the more mathematically inclined reader, this example illustrates how computers can be used to solve algebraic equations, including those that cannot be solved by more direct methods. Consider, for example, the equation

$$x^5 + 3x^2 - 10 = 0.$$

This equation cannot be rearranged to yield an exact solution for x. However, we can determine the solution by a repeated trial-and-error procedure (called an *iterative* procedure) that successively refines an initial guess.

We begin by rearranging the equation into the form

$$x = (10 - 3x^2)^{1/5}$$

Our procedure will then be to guess a value for x, substitute this value into the right-hand side of the rearranged equation, and thus calculate a new value for x. If this new value is equal (or very nearly equal) to the old value, then we will have obtained a solution to the equation. Otherwise, this new value will be substituted into the right-hand side and still another value obtained for x, and so on. This procedure will continue until either the successive values of x have become sufficiently close (i.e., until the computation has *converged*), or until a specified number of iterations has been exceeded. This last condition prevents the computation from continuing indefinitely in the event that the computed results do not converge.

To see how the method works, suppose we choose an initial value of $x = 1.0$. Substituting this value into the right-hand side of the equation, we obtain

$$x = [10 - 3(1.0)^2]^{0.2} = 1.47577$$

We then substitute this new value of x into the equation, resulting in

$$x = [10 - 3(1.47577)^2]^{0.2} = 1.28225$$

Continuing this procedure, we obtain

$$x = [10 - 3(1.28225)^2]^{0.2} = 1.38344$$

$$x = [10 - 3(1.38344)^2]^{0.2} = 1.33613$$

and so on. Notice that the successive values of x appear to be converging to some final answer.

The success of the method depends on the value chosen for the initial guess. If this value is too large in magnitude, then the quantity in brackets will be negative, and a negative value cannot be raised to a fractional power. Therefore we should test for a negative value of $10 - 3x^2$ whenever we substitute a new value of x into the right-hand side.

In order to write a program outline, let us define the following symbols.

count = an iteration counter (count will increase by 1 at each successive iteration)

guess = the value of x substituted into the right-hand side of the equation

root = the newly calculated value of x

test = the quantity $(10 - 3x^2)$

error = the absolute difference between root and guess

flag = an integer variable that signifies whether or not to continue the iteration

We will continue the computation until one of the following conditions is satisfied.

1.   The value of error becomes less than 0.00001, in which case we have obtained a satisfactory solution.

2.   Fifty iterations have been completed (i.e., count = 50).

3.   The variable test takes on a negative value, in which case the computation cannot be continued.

Let us monitor the progress of the computation by writing out each successive value of root.

We can now write the following program outline.

1.   For convenience, define the symbolic constants TRUE and FALSE.

2.   Declare all variables, and initialize the integer variables flag and count (assign TRUE to flag and 0 to count).

3.   Read in a value for the initial guess.

4.   Carry out the following looping procedure, while flag remains TRUE.

   (*a*)   Increase the value of count by 1.

   (*b*)   Assign FALSE to flag if the new value of count equals 50. This will signify the last pass through the loop.

   (*c*)   Examine the value of test. If its value is positive, proceed as follows.

      (*i*)   Calculate a new value for root; then write out the current value for count, followed by the current value for root.

      (*ii*)   Evaluate error, which is the absolute value of the difference between root and guess. If this value is greater than 0.00001, assign the current value of root to guess and proceed with another iteration. Otherwise write out the current values of root and count, and set flag to FALSE. The current value of root will be considered to be the desired solution.

   (*d*)   If the current value of test is not positive, then the computation cannot proceed. Hence, write an appropriate error message (e.g., Numbers out of range) and set flag to FALSE.

5.   Upon completion of step 4, write an appropriate error message (e.g., Convergence not obtained) if count has a value of 50 and the value of error is greater than 0.00001.

Now let us express the program outline in the form of pseudocode, in order to simplify the transition from a general outline to a working C program.

```
#include files

#define symbolic constants

main()

{
    /* variable declarations and initialization */

    /* read input parameters */
```

```
    while (flag)  {

        /* increment count */

        /* flag becomes FALSE if count = 50 */

        /* evaluate test */

        if (test > 0)  {
           /* evaluate root */
           /* display count and loop */
           /* evaluate error */

           if (error > 0.00001) guess = root;
           else  {
              /* flag becomes FALSE */
              /* display the final answer (root and count) */
           }
        }

        else  {
           /* flag becomes FALSE */
           /* numbers out of range - write error message */
        }

    }   /* end while */

    if ((count == 50) && (error > 0.00001))
       /* convergence not obtained - write error message */
}
```

Here is the complete C program.

```
/* determine the roots of an algebraic equation using an iterative procedure */

#include <stdio.h>
#include <math.h>

#define TRUE 1
#define FALSE 0

main()

{
    int flag = TRUE, count = 0;
    float guess, root, test, error;

    /* read input parameters */

    printf("Initial guess: ");
    scanf("%f", &guess);
    while (flag)   {                                    /* begin the main loop */
        ++count;
        if (count == 50) flag = FALSE;
        test = 10. - 3. * guess * guess;
        if (test > 0)   {                               /* another iteration */
           root = pow(test, 0.2);
           printf("\nIteration number: %2d", count);
           printf("    x= %7.5f", root);
           error = fabs(root - guess);
```

```
                    if (error > 0.00001) guess = root;          /* repeat the calculation */
                    else   {                                     /* display the final answer */
                       flag = FALSE;
                       printf("\n\nRoot= %7.5f", root);
                       printf("    No. of iterations= %2d", count);
                    }
                 }
                 else   {                                        /* error message */
                    flag = FALSE;
                    printf("\nNumbers out of range - try another initial guess");
                 }
              }
              if ((count == 50) && (error > 0.00001))            /* another error message */
                 printf("\n\nConvergence not obtained after 50 iterations");

}
```

Notice that the program contains a while statement and several if - else statements. A for statement could easily have been used instead of the while statement. Also, notice the nested if - else statements near the middle of the program.

The output that is generated for an initial guess of x = 1 is shown below, with the user's responses underlined. Notice that the computation has converged to the solution x = 1.35195 after 16 iterations. The printed output shows the successive values of x becoming closer and closer, leading to the final solution.

```
Initial guess: 1

Iteration number:  1   x=     1.47577
Iteration number:  2   x=     1.28225
Iteration number:  3   x=     1.38344
Iteration number:  4   x=     1.33613
Iteration number:  5   x=     1.35951
Iteration number:  6   x=     1.34826
Iteration number:  7   x=     1.35375
Iteration number:  8   x=     1.35109
Iteration number:  9   x=     1.35238
Iteration number: 10   x=     1.35175
Iteration number: 11   x=     1.35206
Iteration number: 12   x=     1.35191
Iteration number: 13   x=     1.35198
Iteration number: 14   x=     1.35196
Iteration number: 15   x=     1.35196
Iteration number: 16   x=     1.35195

Root= 1.35195    No. of iterations= 16
```

Now suppose that a value of x = 10 had been selected as an initial guess. This value generates a negative number for test in the first iteration. Therefore the output would appear as follows.

```
Initial guess: 10
Numbers out of range - try another initial guess
```

It is interesting to see what happens when the initial guess is once again chosen as x = 1, but the maximum number of iterations is changed from 50 to 10. You are encouraged to try this and observe the result.

you should underdstand that there are many other iterative methods for solving algebraic equations. Most converge faster than the method described above (i.e., they require fewer iterations to obtain a solution), though the mathematics is more complicated.

6.7 THE switch STATEMENT

The switch statement causes a particular group of statements to be chosen from several available groups. The selection is based upon the current value of an expression which is included within the switch statement.

The general form of the switch statement is

```
switch (expression) statement
```

where *expression* results in an integer value. Note that *expression* may also be of type char, since individual characters have equivalent integer values.

The embedded *statement* is generally a compound statement that specifies alternate courses of action. Each alternative is expressed as a group of one or more individual statements within the overall embedded *statement*.

For each alternative, the first statement within the group must be preceded by one or more *case labels* (also called *case prefixes*). The case labels identify the different groups of statements (i.e., the different alternatives) and distinguish then from one another. The case labels must therefore be unique within a given switch statement.

In general terms, each group of statements is written as

```
case expression :
    statement 1
    statement 2
    . . . . .
    statement n
```

or, when multiple case labels are required,

```
case expression 1 :
case expression 2 :
    . . . . .
case expression m :
    statement 1
    statement 2
    . . . . .
    statement n
```

where *expression 1*, *expression 2*, . . . , *expression m* represent constant, integer-valued expressions. Usually, each of these expressions will be written as either an integer constant or a character constant. Each individual *statement* following the case labels may be either simple or complex.

When the switch statement is executed, the *expression* is evaluated and control is transferred directly to the group of statements whose case-label value matches the value of the *expression*. If none of the case-label values matches the value of the *expression*, then none of the groups within the switch statement will be selected. In this case control is transferred directly to the statement that follows the switch statement.

EXAMPLE 6.23 A simple switch statement is illustrated below. In this example, choice is assumed to be a char-type variable.

```
switch (choice = getchar())  {
case 'r':
case 'R':
    printf("RED");
    break;
```

```
    case 'w':
    case 'W':
        printf("WHITE");
        break;

    case 'b':
    case 'B':
        printf("BLUE");
    }
```

Thus, RED will be displayed if choice represents either r or R, WHITE will be displayed if choice represents either w or W, and BLUE will be displayed if choice represents either b or B. Nothing will be displayed if any other character has been assigned to choice.

Notice that each group of statements has two case labels, to account for either upper or lowercase. Also, note that each of the first two groups ends with the break statement (see Sec. 6.8). The break statement causes control to be transferred out of the switch statement, thus preventing more than one group of statements from being executed.

One of the labeled groups of statements within the switch statement may be labeled default. This group will be selected if none of the case labels matches the value of the *expression*. (This is a convenient way to generate error messages or error correction routines.) The default group may appear anywhere within the switch statement—it need not necessarily be placed at the end. If none of the case labels matches the value of the *expression* and the default group is not present (as in the above example), then no action will be taken by the switch statement.

EXAMPLE 6.24   Here is a variation of the switch statement presented in Example 6.23.

```
    switch (choice = toupper(getchar()))  {

    case 'R':
        printf("RED");
        break;

    case 'W':
        printf("WHITE");
        break;

    case 'B':
        printf("BLUE");
        break;

    default:
        printf("ERROR");
    }
```

The switch statement now contains a default group (consisting of only one statement), which generates an error message if none of the case labels matches the original *expression*.

Each of the first three groups of statements now has only one case label. Multiple case labels are not necessary in this example, since the library function toupper causes all incoming characters to be converted to uppercase. Hence, choice will always be assigned an uppercase character.

EXAMPLE 6.25   Here is another typical switch statement. In this example flag is assumed to be an integer variable, and x and y are assumed to be floating-point variables.

```
switch (flag)  {

case -1:
      y = abs(x);
      break;

case 0:
      y = sqrt(x);
      break;

case 1:
      y = x;
      break;

case 2:
case 3:
      y = 2 * (x - 1);
      break;

default:
      y = 0;
}
```

In this example y will be assigned some value that is related to the value of x if **flag** equals –1, 0, 1, 2 or 3. The exact relationship between y and x will depend upon the particular value of **flag**. If **flag** represents some other value, however, then y will be assigned a value of 0.

Notice that the case labels are numeric in this example. Also, note that the third group of statements has two case labels, whereas each of the other groups have only one case label. And finally, notice that a default group (consisting of only one statement) is included within this **switch** statement.

In a practical sense, the **switch** statement may be thought of as an alternative to the use of nested **if** - **else** statements, though it can only replace those **if** - **else** statements that test for equality. In such situations, the use of the **switch** statement is generally much more convenient.

EXAMPLE 6.26 Calculating Depreciation   Let us consider how to calculate the yearly depreciation for some depreciable item, such as a building, a machine, etc. There are three commonly used methods for calculating depreciation, known as the *straight-line* method, the *double-declining-balance* method, and the *sum-of-the-years'-digits* method. We wish to write a C program that will allow us to select any one of these methods for each set of calculations.

The computation will begin by reading in the original (undepreciated) value of the item, the life of the item (i.e., the number of years over which it will be depreciated) and an integer that indicates which method will be used. The yearly depreciation and the remaining (undepreciated) value of the item will then be calculated and written out for each year.

The *straight-line* method is the easiest to use. In this method the original value of the item is divided by its life (total number of years). The resulting quotient will be the amount by which the item depreciates each year. For example, if an $8000 item is to be depreciated over 10 years, then the annual depreciation would be $8000/10 = $800. Therefore, the value of the item would decrease by $800 each year. Notice that the annual depreciation is the same each year when using straight-line depreciation.

When using the *double-declining-balance* method, the value of the item will decrease by a constant *percentage* each year. Hence the actual amount of the depreciation, in dollars, will vary from one year to the next. To obtain the depreciation factor, we divide 2 by the life of the item. The depreciation factor is multiplied by the value of the item *at the beginning of each year* (not the original value of the item) to obtain the annual depreciation.

Suppose, for example, that we wish to depreciate an $8000 item over 10 years, using the double-declining-balance method. The depreciation factor will be 2/10 = 0.20. Hence the depreciation for the first year will be 0.20 × $8000 = $1600.   The second year's depreciation will be 0.20 × ($8000 – $1600) = 0.20 × $6400 = $1280; the third year's depreciation will be 0.20 × $5120 = $1024, and so on.

In the *sum-of-the-years'-digits* method the value of the item will decrease by a percentage that is *different* each year. The depreciation factor will be a fraction whose denominator is the sum of the digits from 1 to n, where n represents the life of the item. If, for example, we consider a 10-year lifetime, the denominator will be $1 + 2 + 3 + \cdots + 10 = 55$. For the first year the numerator will be n, for the second year it will be $(n - 1)$, for the third year $(n - 2)$, and so on. The yearly depreciation is obtained by multiplying the depreciation factor by the original value of the item.

To see how the sum-of-the-years'-digits method works, we again depreciate an $8000 item over 10 years. The depreciation for the first year will be $(10/55) \times \$8000 = \$1454.55$; for the second year it will be $(9/55) \times \$8000 = \$1309.09$; and so on.

Now let us define the following symbols, so that we can write the actual program.

      `val` = the current value of the item

      `tag` = the original value of the item (i.e., the original value of `val`)

  `deprec` = the annual depreciation

        `n` = the number of years over which the item will be depreciated

    `year` = a counter ranging from 1 to n

`choice` = an integer indicating which method to use

Our C program will follow the outline presented below.

1. Declare all variables, and initialize the integer variable `choice` to 0 (actually, we can assign any value other than 4 to `choice`).

2. Repeat all of the following steps as long as the value of `choice` is not equal to 4.

    (*a*) Read a value for `choice` which indicates the type of calculation to be carried out. This value can only be 1, 2, 3 or 4. (Any other value will be an error.)

    (*b*) If choice is assigned a value of 1, 2 or 3, read values for `val` and `n`.

    (*c*) Depending on the value assigned to `choice`, branch to the appropriate part of the program and carry out the indicated calculations. In particular,

        (*i*) If `choice` is assigned a value of 1, 2 or 3, calculate the yearly depreciation and the new value of the item on a year-by-year basis, using the appropriate method indicated by the value of `choice`. Print out the results as they are calculated, on a year-by-year basis.

        (*ii*) If `choice` is assigned a value of 4, write out a "goodbye" message and end the computation by terminating the `while` loop.

        (*iii*) If `choice` is assigned any value other than 1, 2, 3 or 4, write out an error message and begin another pass through the `while` loop.

Now let us express this outline in pseudocode.

```
#include files

main()

{
    /* variable declarations and initialization */

    while (choice != 4)  {

        /* generate menu and read choice */

        if (choice >= 1 && choice <= 3)
           /* read val and n */

        switch (choice)  {

        case  1:        /* straight-line method */

              /* write out title */
```

```
                        /* calculate depreciation */

                        /* for each year:
                                calculate a new value
                                write out year, depreciation, value */

             case   2:         /* double-declining-balance method */

                        /* write out title */

                        /* for each year:
                                calculate depreciation
                                calculate a new value
                                write out year, depreciation, value */

             case   3:         /* sum-of-the-years'-digits method */

                        /* write out title */

                        /* tag original value */

                        /* for each year:
                                calculate depreciation
                                calculate a new value
                                write out year, depreciation, value */

             case   4:         /* end of computation */

                        /* write "goodbye" message */

                        /* write out title */

             default:          /* generate error message */

                        /* write error message */
             }
        }
}
```

Most of the pseudocode is straightforward, though a few comments are in order. First, we see that a while statement is used to repeat the entire set of calculations. Within this overall loop, the switch statement is used to select a particular depreciation method. Each depreciation method uses a for statement to carry out the required calculations.

At this point it is not difficult to write a complete C program, as shown below.

```
/* calculate depreciation using one of three different methods */

#include <stdio.h>

main()
{
    int n, year, choice = 0;
    float val, tag, deprec;

    while (choice != 4)  {

        /* read input data */

        printf("\nMethod: (1-SL  2-DDB  3-SYD  4-End) ");
        scanf("%d", &choice);
        if (choice >= 1 && choice <= 3)  {
            printf("Original value: ");
            scanf("%f", &val);
```

```
        printf("Number of years: ");
        scanf("%d", &n);
    }

    switch (choice)  {

    case 1:          /* straight-line method */

        printf("\nStraight-Line Method\n\n");
        deprec = val/n;
        for (year = 1; year <= n; ++year)  {
            val -= deprec;
            printf("End of Year %2d", year);
            printf("  Depreciation: %7.2f", deprec);
            printf("  Current Value: %8.2f\n", val);
        }
        break;

    case 2:          /* double-declining-balance method */

        printf("\nDouble-Declining-Balance Method\n\n");
        for (year = 1; year <= n; ++year)  {
            deprec = 2*val/n;
            val -= deprec;
            printf("End of Year %2d", year);
            printf("  Depreciation: %7.2f", deprec);
            printf("  Current Value: %8.2f\n", val);
        }
        break;

    case 3:          /* sum-of-the-years'-digits method */

        printf("\nSum-Of-The-Years\'-Digits Method\n\n");
        tag = val;
        for (year = 1; year <= n; ++year)  {
            deprec = (n-year+1)*tag / (n*(n+1)/2);
            val -= deprec;
            printf("End of Year %2d", year);
            printf("  Depreciation: %7.2f", deprec);
            printf("  Current Value: %8.2f\n", val);
        }
        break;

    case 4:          /* end of computation */

        printf("\nGoodbye, have a nice day!\n");
        break;

    default:         /* generate error message */

        printf("\nIncorrect data entry - please try again\n");
    }    /* end switch */
}    /* end while */
}
```

The calculation of the depreciation for the sum-of-the-years'-digits method may be somewhat obscure. In particular, the term (n-year+1) in the numerator requires some explanation. This quantity is used to count *backward* (from n down to 1) as year progresses *forward* (from 1 to n). These declining values are required by the sum-of-the-years'-digits method. We could, of course, have set up a backward-counting loop instead, i.e.

```
for (year = n; year >= 1; --year)
```

but then we would have required a corresponding forward-counting loop to write out the results of the calculations on a yearly basis. Also, the term $(n*(n+1)/2)$ which appears in the denominator is a formula for the sum of the first n digits; i.e., $1 + 2 + . . . + n$.

The program is designed to be run interactively, with prompts for the required input data. Notice that the program generates a *menu* with four choices, to calculate the depreciation using one of the three methods or to end the computation. The computer will continue to accept new sets of input data, and carry out the appropriate calculations for each data set, until a value of 4 is selected from the menu. The program automatically generates an error message and returns to the menu if some value other than 1, 2, 3 or 4 is entered in response to the menu request.

Some representative output is shown below. In each case, an $8000 item is depreciated over a 10-year period, using one of the three methods. The error message that is generated by an incorrect data entry is also illustrated. Finally, the computation is terminated in response to the last menu selection.

```
Method: (1-SL  2-DDB  3-SYD  4-End) 1
Original value: 8000
Number of years: 10


Straight-Line Method


End of Year  1  Depreciation: 800.00  Current Value: 7200.00
End of Year  2  Depreciation: 800.00  Current Value: 6400.00
End of Year  3  Depreciation: 800.00  Current Value: 5600.00
End of Year  4  Depreciation: 800.00  Current Value: 4800.00
End of Year  5  Depreciation: 800.00  Current Value: 4000.00
End of Year  6  Depreciation: 800.00  Current Value: 3200.00
End of Year  7  Depreciation: 800.00  Current Value: 2400.00
End of Year  8  Depreciation: 800.00  Current Value: 1600.00
End of Year  9  Depreciation: 800.00  Current Value:  800.00
End of Year 10  Depreciation: 800.00  Current Value:    0.00


Method: (1-SL  2-DDB  3-SYD  4-End) 2
Original value: 8000
Number of years: 10


Double-Declining-Balance Method


End of Year  1  Depreciation:1600.00  Current Value: 6400.00
End of Year  2  Depreciation:1280.00  Current Value: 5120.00
End of Year  3  Depreciation:1024.00  Current Value: 4096.00
End of Year  4  Depreciation: 819.20  Current Value: 3276.80
End of Year  5  Depreciation: 655.36  Current Value: 2621.44
End of Year  6  Depreciation: 524.29  Current Value: 2097.15
End of Year  7  Depreciation: 419.43  Current Value: 1677.72
End of Year  8  Depreciation: 335.54  Current Value: 1342.18
End of Year  9  Depreciation: 268.44  Current Value: 1073.74
End of Year 10  Depreciation: 214.75  Current Value:  858.99


Method: (1-SL  2-DDB  3-SYD  4-End) 3
Original value: 8000
Number of years: 10


Sum-of-the-Years'-Digits Method
```

```
End of Year  1  Depreciation:1454.55  Current Value: 6545.45
End of Year  2  Depreciation:1309.09  Current Value: 5236.36
End of Year  3  Depreciation:1163.64  Current Value: 4072.73
End of Year  4  Depreciation:1018.18  Current Value: 3054.55
End of Year  5  Depreciation: 872.73  Current Value: 2181.82
End of Year  6  Depreciation: 727.27  Current Value: 1454.55
End of Year  7  Depreciation: 581.82  Current Value:  872.73
End of Year  8  Depreciation: 436.36  Current Value:  436.36
End of Year  9  Depreciation: 290.91  Current Value:  145.45
End of Year 10  Depreciation: 145.45  Current Value:    0.00


Method: (1-SL  2-DDB  3-SYD  4-End) 5


Incorrect data entry - please try again


Method: (1-SL  2-DDB  3-SYD  4-End) 4


Goodbye, have a nice day!
```

Notice that the double-declining-balance method and the sum-of-the-years'-digits method result in a large annual depreciation during the early years, but a very small annual depreciation in the last few years of the item's lifetime. Also, we see that the item has a value of zero at the end of its lifetime when using the straight-line method and the sum-of-the-years'-digits method, but a small value remains undepreciated when using the double-declining-balance method.

6.8 THE break STATEMENT

The break statement is used to terminate loops or to exit from a switch. It can be used within a for, while, do - while, or switch statement.

The break statement is written simply as

```
break;
```

without any embedded expressions or statements.

We have already seen several examples of the use of the break statement within a switch statement, in Sec. 6.7. The break statement causes a transfer of control out of the entire switch statement, to the first statement following the switch statement.

EXAMPLE 6.27   Consider once again the switch statement originally presented in Example 6.24.

```c
switch (choice = toupper(getchar()))  {

case 'R':
    printf("RED");
    break;

case 'W':
    printf("WHITE");
    break;

case 'B':
    printf("BLUE");
    break;

default:
    printf("ERROR");
    break;
}
```

Notice that each group of statements ends with a break statement, in order to transfer control out of the switch statement. The break statement is required within each of the first three groups, in order to prevent the succeeding groups of statements from executing. The last group does not require a break statement, since control will automatically be transferred out of the switch statement after the last group has been executed. This last break statement is included, however, as a matter of good programming practice, so that it will be present if another group of statements is added later.

If a break statement is included in a while, do - while or for loop, then control will immediately be transferred out of the loop when the break statement is encountered. This provides a convenient way to terminate the loop if an error or other irregular condition is detected.

EXAMPLE 6.28 Here are some illustrations of loops that contain break statements. In each situation, the loop will continue to execute as long as the current value for the floating-point variable x does not exceed 100. However, the computation will break out of the loop if a negative value for x is detected.

First, consider a while loop.

```
scanf("%f", &x);
while (x <= 100)  {
     if (x < 0)    {
         printf("ERROR - NEGATIVE VALUE FOR X");
         break;
     }

     /* process the nonnegative value of x */
     . . . . .
     scanf("%f", &x);
}
```

Now consider a do − while loop that does the same thing.

```
do  {
     scanf("%f", &x);
     if (x < 0)  {
         printf("ERROR - NEGATIVE VALUE FOR X");
         break;
     }

    /* process the nonnegative value of x */
    . . . . .
} while (x <= 100);
```

Finally, here is a for loop that is similar.

```
for (count = 1; x <= 100; ++count)    {
    scanf("%f", &x);
    if (x < 0)  {
        printf("ERROR - NEGATIVE VALUE FOR X");
        break;
    }

    /* process the nonnegative value of x */
    . . . . .
}
```

In the event of several nested `while`, `do - while`, `for` or `switch` statements, a `break` statement will cause a transfer of control out of the immediate enclosing statement, but not out of the outer surrounding statements. We have seen one illustration of this in Example 6.26, where a `switch` statement is embedded within a `while` statement. Another illustration is shown below.

EXAMPLE 6.29   Consider the following outline of a `while` loop embedded within a `for` loop.

```
for (count = 0; count <= n; ++count)  {
    . . . . .
    while (c = getchar() != '\n')  {
        if (c = '*')  break;
        . . . . .
    }
}
```

If the character variable c is assigned an asterisk (*), then the `while` loop will be terminated. However, the `for` loop will continue to execute. Thus, if the value of count is less than n when the breakout occurs, the computer will increment count and make another pass through the `for` loop.

6.9 THE `continue` STATEMENT

The `continue` statement is used to *bypass* the remainder of the current pass through a loop. The loop does *not* terminate when a `continue` statement is encountered. Rather, the remaining loop statements are skipped and the computation proceeds directly to the next pass through the loop. (Note the distinction between `continue` and `break`.)

The `continue` statement can be included within a `while`, a `do - while` or a `for` statement. It is written simply as

```
continue;
```

without any embedded statements or expressions.

EXAMPLE 6.30   Here are some illustrations of loops that contain `continue` statements.

First, consider a `do - while` loop.

```
do  {
     scanf("%f", &x);
     if (x < 0)  {
        printf("ERROR - NEGATIVE VALUE FOR X");
        continue;
     };

     /* process the nonnegative value of x */

     . . . . .
} while (x <= 100);
```

Here is a similar `for` loop.

```
for (count = 1; x <= 100; ++count)    {
    scanf("%f", &x);
    if (x < 0)  {
       printf("ERROR - NEGATIVE VALUE FOR X");
       continue;
    }
```

```
    /* process the nonnegative value of x */

    . . . . .
}
```

In each case, the processing of the current value of x will be bypassed if the value of x is negative. Execution of the loop will then continue with the next pass.

It is interesting to compare these structures with those shown in Example 6.28, which make use of the break statement instead of the continue statement. (Why is a modification of the while loop shown in Example 6.28 not included in this example?)

EXAMPLE 6.31 Averaging a List of Nonnegative Numbers   In Example 6.17 we saw a complete C program that uses a for loop to calculate the average of a list of n numbers. Let us now modify this program so that it processes only nonnegative numbers.

The earlier program requires two minor changes to accommodate this modification. First, the for loop must include an if statement to determine whether or not each new value of x is nonnegative. A continue statement will be included in the if statement to bypass the processing of negative values of x. Secondly, we require a special counter (navg) to determine how many nonnegative numbers have been processed. This counter will appear in the denominator when the average is calculated (i.e., the average will be determined as average = sum/navg).

Here is the actual C program. It is interesting to compare it with the program shown in Example 6.17.

```
/* calculate the average of the nonnegative numbers in a list of n numbers */

#include <stdio.h>

main()

{
    int n, count, navg = 0;
    float x, average, sum = 0;

    /* initialize and read in a value for n */
    printf("How many numbers? ");
    scanf("%d", &n);

    /* read in the numbers */
    for (count = 1; count <= n; ++count)  {
        printf("x = ");
        scanf("%f", &x);
        if (x < 0) continue;
        sum += x;
        ++navg;
    }

    /* calculate the average and write out the answer */
    average = sum/navg;
    printf("\nThe average is %f\n", average);
}
```

When the program is executed with nonnegative values for x, it behaves exactly like the earlier version presented in Example 6.17. When some of the x's are assigned negative values, however, the negative values are ignored in the calculation of the average.

A sample interactive session is shown below. As usual, the user's responses are underlined.

```
How many numbers? 6
x = 1
x = -1
x = 2
x = -2
x = 3
x = -3


The average is 2.000000
```

This is the correct average of the positive numbers. Note that the average would be zero if all of the numbers had been averaged.

6.10 THE COMMA OPERATOR

We now introduce the comma operator (,) which is used primarily in conjunction with the for statement. This operator permits two different expressions to appear in situations where only one expression would ordinarily be used. For example, it is possible to write

for (*expression 1a*, *expression 1b*; *expression 2*; *expression 3*) *statement*

where *expression 1a* and *expression 1b* are the two expressions, separated by the comma operator, where only one expression (*expression 1*) would normally appear. These two expressions would typically initialize two separate indices that would be used simultaneously within the for loop.

Similarly, a for statement might make use of the comma operator in the following manner.

for (*expression 1*; *expression 2*; *expression 3a*, *expression 3b*) *statement*

Here *expression 3a* and *expression 3b*, separated by the comma operator, appear in place of the usual single expression. In this application the two separate expressions would typically be used to alter (e.g., increment or decrement) two different indices that are used simultaneously within the loop. For example, one index might count forward while the other counts backward.

EXAMPLE 6.32 Searching for Palindromes   A *palindrome* is a word, phrase or sentence that reads the same way either forward or backward. For example, words such as *noon*, *peep*, and *madam* are palindromes. If we disregard punctuation and blank spaces, then the sentence *Rise to vote, sir*! is also a palindrome.

Let us write a C program that will enter a line of text containing a word, a phrase or a sentence, and determine whether or not the text is a palindrome. To do so, we will compare the first character with the last, the second character with the next to last, and so on, until we have reached the middle of the text. The comparisons will include punctuation and blank spaces.

In order to outline a computational strategy, let us define the following variables.

- letter = a character-type array containing as many as 80 elements. These elements will be the characters in the line of text.

- tag = an integer variable indicating the number of characters assigned to letter, excluding the escape character \0 at the end.

- count = an integer variable used as an index when moving forward through letter.

- countback = an integer variable used as an index when moving backward through letter.

- flag = an integer variable that will be used to indicate a true/false condition. True will indicate that a palindrome has been found.

- loop = an integer variable whose value will always equal 1, thus appearing always to be true. The intent here is to continue execution of a main loop, until a particular stopping condition causes a breakout.

We can now outline our overall strategy as follows.

1. Define the symbolic constants EOL (end-of-line), TRUE and FALSE.

2. Declare all variables and initialize loop (i.e., assign TRUE to loop).

3. Enter the main loop.

    (*a*)   Assign TRUE to flag, in anticipation of finding a palindrome.

    (*b*)   Read in the line of text on a character-by-character basis, and store in letter.

    (*c*)   Test to see if the uppercase equivalents of the first three characters are E, N and D, respectively. If so, break out of the main loop and exit the program.

    (*d*)   Assign the final value of count, less 1, to tag. This value will indicate the number of characters in the line of text, not including the final escape character \0.

    (*e*)   Compare each character in the first half of letter with the corresponding character in the second half. If a mismatch is found, assign FALSE to flag and break out of the (inner) comparison loop.

    (*f*)   If flag is TRUE, display a message indicating that a palindrome has been found. Otherwise, display a message indicating that a palindrome has not been found.

4. Repeat step 3 (i.e., make another pass through the outer loop), thus processing another line of text.

Here is the corresponding pseudocode.

```
#include files

#define symbolic constants

main()

{

    /* declare all variables and initialize as required */

    while (loop)  {

        flag = TRUE;    /* anticipating a palindrome */

        /* read in a line of text and store in letter */

        /* break out of while loop if first three characters
           of letter spell END (test uppercase equivalents) */

        /* assign number of characters in text to tag */

        for ((count = 0, countback = tag); count <= (tag - 1)/ 2;(++count, --countback)) {

            if (letter[count] != letter[countback])  {
                flag = FALSE;

                /* not a palindrome - break out of for loop */
            }
        }

        /* display a message indicating whether or not letter contains a palindrome */

    }
}
```

The program utilizes the comma operator within a for loop to compare each character in the first half of letter with the corresponding character in the second half. Thus, as count increases from 0 to (tag - 1) / 2, countback decreases from tag to (tag / 2) + 1. Note that integer division (resulting in a truncated quotient) is involved in establishing these limiting values.

Also, observe that there will be two distinct comma operators within the for statement. Each comma operator and its associated operands are enclosed in parentheses. This is not necessary, but it does emphasize that each operand pair comprises one argument within the for statement.

The complete C program is shown below.

```
/* search for a palindrome */

#include <stdio.h>
#include <ctype.h>

#define EOL  '\n'
#define TRUE 1
#define FALSE 0

main()
{
    char letter[80];
    int tag, count, countback, flag, loop = TRUE;

    /* main loop */

    while (loop)   {
       flag = TRUE;

       /* read the text */

       printf("Please enter a word, phrase or sentence below:\n");
       for (count = 0; (letter[count] = getchar()) != EOL; ++count)
            ;
       if ((toupper(letter[0]) == 'E') && (toupper(letter[1]) == 'N') &&
           (toupper(letter[2]) == 'D')) break;
       tag = count - 1;

       /* carry out the search */

       for ((count = 0, countback = tag); count <= tag/2;
           (++count, --countback))   {

               if (letter[count] != letter[countback])   {
                   flag = FALSE;
                   break;
               }
       }

       /* display message */

       for (count = 0; count <= tag; ++count)
           putchar(letter[count]);
       if (flag) printf(" IS a palindrome\n\n");
       else printf(" is NOT a palindrome\n\n");
    }
}
```

A typical interactive session is shown below, indicating the type of output that is generated when the program is executed. As usual, the user's responses are underlined.

```
Please enter a word, phrase or sentence below:
TOOT

TOOT IS a palindrome
```

```
Please enter a word, phrase or sentence below:
FALSE

FALSE is NOT a palindrome

Please enter a word, phrase or sentence below:
PULLUP

PULLUP IS a palindrome

Please enter a word, phrase or sentence below:
ABLE WAS I ERE I SAW ELBA

ABLE WAS I ERE I SAW ELBA IS a palindrome

Please enter a word, phrase or sentence below:
END
```

Remember that the comma operator accepts two distinct expressions as operands. These expressions will be evaluated from left to right. In situations that require the evaluation of the overall expression (i.e., the expression formed by the two operands and the comma operator), the type and value of the overall expression will be determined by the type and value of the right operand.

Within the collection of C operators, the comma operator has the lowest precedence. Thus, the comma operator falls within its own unique precedence group, beneath the precedence group containing the various assignment operators (see Appendix C). Its associativity is left to right.

6.11 THE goto STATEMENT

The goto statement is used to alter the normal sequence of program execution by transferring control to some other part of the program. In its general form, the goto statement is written as

goto *label*;

where *label* is an identifier that is used to label the target statement to which control will be transferred.

Control may be transferred to any other statement within the program. (To be more precise, control may be transferred anywhere within the current *function*. We will introduce functions in the next chapter, and discuss them thoroughly in Chapter 7.) The target statement must be labeled, and the label must be followed by a colon. Thus, the target statement will appear as

label: *statement*

Each labeled statement within the program (more precisely, within the current function) must have a unique label; i.e., no two statements can have the same label.

EXAMPLE 6.33 The following skeletal outline illustrates how the goto statement can be used to transfer control out of a loop if an unexpected condition arises.

```
/* main loop */

scanf("%f", &x);
while (x <= 100)   {
     . . . . .
     if (x < 0) goto errorcheck;
     . . . . .
     scanf("%f", &x);
}
```

```
             . . . . .

    /* error detection routine */

    errorcheck: {
                   printf("ERROR - NEGATIVE VALUE FOR X");
                   . . . . .
               }
```

In this example control is transferred out of the while loop, to the compound statement whose label is errorcheck, if a negative value is detected for the input variable x.

The same thing could have been accomplished using the break statement, as illustrated in Example 6.28. The use of the break statement is actually the preferred approach. The use of the goto statement is presented here only to illustrate the syntax.

All of the popular general-purpose programming languages contain a goto statement, though modern programming practice discourages its use. The goto statement was used extensively, however, in early versions of some older languages, such as Fortran and BASIC. The most common applications were:

1. Branching around statements or groups of statements under certain conditions.

2. Jumping to the end of a loop under certain conditions, thus bypassing the remainder of the loop during the current pass.

3. Jumping completely out of a loop under certain conditions, thus terminating the execution of a loop.

The structured features in C enable all of these operations to be carried out without resorting to the goto statement. For example, branching around statements can be accomplished with the if - else statement; jumping to the end of a loop can be carried out with the continue statement; and jumping out of a loop is easily accomplished using the break statement. The use of these structured features is preferrable to the use of the goto statement, because the use of goto tends to encourage (or at least, not discourage) logic that skips all over the program whereas the structured features in C require that the entire program be written in an orderly, sequential manner. For this reason, *use of the* goto *statement should generally be avoided.*

Occasional situations do arise, however, in which the goto statement can be useful. Consider, for example, a situation in which it is necessary to jump out of a doubly nested loop if a certain condition is detected. This can be accomplished with two if - break statements, one within each loop, though this is awkward. A better solution in this particular situation might make use of the goto statement to transfer out of both loops at once. The procedure is illustrated in the following example.

EXAMPLE 6.34 Converting Several Lines of Text to Uppercase   Example 6.19 presents a program to convert several successive lines of text to uppercase, processing one line of text at a time, until the first character in a new line is an asterisk (*). Let us now modify this program to detect a break condition, as indicated by two successive dollar signs ($$) anywhere within a line of text. If the break condition is encountered, the program will print the line of text containing the dollar signs, followed by an appropriate message. Execution of the program will then terminate.

The logic will be the same as that given in Example 6.19, except that an additional loop will now be added to test for two consecutive dollar signs. Thus the program will proceed as follows.

1. Assign an initial value of 1 to the outer loop index (linecount).

2. Carry out the following steps repeatedly, for successive lines of text, as long as the first character in the line is not an asterisk.

    (*a*) Read in a line of text and assign the individual characters to the elements of the char-type array letter. A line will be defined as a succession of characters that is terminated by an end-of-line (i.e, a *newline*) designation.

    (*b*) Assign the character count, including the end-of-line character, to tag.

    (*c*)   Display the line in uppercase, using the library function `toupper` to carry out the conversion. Then display two newline characters (so that the next line of input will be separated from the current output by a blank line), and increment the line counter (`linecount`).

    (*d*)   Test all successive characters in the line for two successive dollar signs. If two successive dollar signs are detected, then display a message indicating that a break condition has been found and jump to the terminating condition at the end of the program (see below).

3.   Once an asterisk has been detected as the first character of a new line, write out "Good bye." and terminate the computation.

Here is the complete C program.

```
/* convert several lines of text to uppercase

   Continue conversion until the first character in a line is an asterisk (*).
   Break out of the program sooner if two successive dollar signs ($$) are detected */

#include <stdio.h>
#include <ctype.h>

#define EOL '\n'

main()

{
    char letter[80];
    int tag, count, linecount = 1;

    while ((letter[0] = getchar()) != '*')   {

        /* read in a line of text */
        for (count = 1; (letter[count] = getchar()) != EOL; ++count)
            ;
        tag = count;

        /* display the line of text */
        for (count = 0; count < tag; ++count)
            putchar(toupper(letter[count]));
        printf("\n\n");
        ++linecount;

        /* test for a break condition */
        for (count=1; count < tag; ++count)
            if (letter[count-1] == '$' && letter[count] == '$')   {
                printf("BREAK CONDITION DETECTED - TERMINATE EXECUTION\n\n");
                goto end;
            }
    }
    end: printf("Good bye");
}
```

It is interesting to compare this program with the corresponding program presented earlier, in Example 6.19. The present program contains an additional `for` loop embedded at the end of the `while` loop. This `for` loop examines consecutive pairs of characters for a break condition ($$), after the entire line has already been written out in uppercase. If a break condition is encountered, then control is transferred to the final `printf` statement (`"Good bye"`) which is now labeled `end`. Note that this transfer of control causes a breakout from the `if` statement, the current `for` loop, and the outer `while` loop.

You should run this program, using both the regular terminating condition (an asterisk at the start of a new line) and the breakout condition. Compare the results obtained with the output shown in Example 6.19.

Review Questions

6.1   What is meant by branching?

6.2   What is meant by selection?

6.3   What is meant by looping? Describe two different forms of looping.

6.4   Summarize the rules associated with the use of the four relational operators, the two equality operators, the two logical connectives and the unary negation operator. What types of operands are used with each type of operator?

6.5   How are char-type constants and char-type variables interpreted when used as operands with a relational operator?

6.6   How do expression statements differ from compound statements? Summarize the rules associated with each.

6.7   What is the purpose of the `if - else` statement?

6.8   Describe the two different forms of the `if - else` statement. How do they differ?

6.9   Compare the use of the `if - else` statement with the use of the `?:` operator. In particular, in what way can the `?:` operator be used in place of an `if - else` statement?

6.10 Summarize the syntactic rules associated with the `if - else` statement

6.11 How are nested `if - else` statements interpreted? In particular, how is the following interpreted?

```
if e1 if e2 s1
    else s2
```

Which logical expression is associated with the `else` clause?

6.12 What happens when an expression is encountered whose value is nonzero within a group of nested `if - else` statements?

6.13 What is the purpose of the `while` statement? When is the logical expression evaluated? What is the minimum number of times that a `while` loop can be executed?

6.14 How is the execution of a `while` loop terminated?

6.15 Summarize the syntactic rules associated with the `while` statement.

6.16 What is the purpose of the `do - while` statement? How does it differ from the `while` statement?

6.17 What is the minimum number of times that a `do - while` loop can be executed? Compare with a `while` loop and explain the reasons for the differences.

6.18 Summarize the syntactic rules associated with the `do - while` statement. Compare with the `while` statement.

6.19 What is the purpose of the `for` statement? How does it differ from the `while` statement and the `do - while` statement?

6.20 How many times will a `for` loop be executed? Compare with the `while` loop and the `do - while` loop.

6.21 What is the purpose of the index in a `for` statement?

6.22 Can any of the three initial expressions in the `for` statement be omitted? If so, what are the consequences of each omission?

6.23 Summarize the syntactic rules associated with the `for` statement.

6.24 What rules apply to the nesting of loops? Can one type of loop be embedded within another?

6.25 Can loops be nested within `if - else` statements? Can `if - else` statements be nested within loops?

6.26 What is the purpose of the `switch` statement? How does this statement differ from the other statements described in this chapter?

6.27 What are case labels (case prefixes)? What type of expression must be used to represent a case label?

6.28 Summarize the syntactic rules associated with the use of the `switch` statement. Can multiple case labels be associated with one alternative?

6.29 What happens when the value of the expression in the `switch` statement matches the value of one of the case labels? What happens when the value of this expression does not match any of the case labels?

6.30   Can a default alternative be defined within a switch statement? If so, how would the default alternative be labeled?

6.31   Compare the use of the switch statement with the use of nested if - else statements. Which is more convenient?

6.32   What is the purpose of the break statement? Within which control statements can the break statement be included?

6.33   Suppose a break statement is included within the innermost of several nested control statements. What happens when the break statement is executed?

6.34   What is the purpose of the continue statement? Within which control statements can the continue statement be included? Compare with the break statement.

6.35   What is the purpose of the comma operator? Within which control statement does the comma operator usually appear?

6.36   In situations that require the evaluation of an expression containing the comma operator, which operand will determine the type and the value of the entire expression (i.e., the expression to the left of the comma operator or the expression to the right)?

6.37   What is the precedence of the comma operator compared with other C operators?

6.38   What is the purpose of the goto statement? How is the associated target statement identified?

6.39   Are there any restrictions that apply to where control can be transferred within a given C program?

6.40   Summarize the syntactic rules associated with the goto statement.

6.41   Compare the syntax associated with statement labels with that of case labels (case prefixes).

6.42   Why is the use of the goto statement generally discouraged? Under what conditions might the goto statement be helpful? What types of usage should be avoided, and why? Discuss thoroughly.

Problems

6.43   Explain what happens when the following statement is executed.

```
if (abs(x) < xmin) x = (x > 0) ? xmin : -xmin;
```

Is this a compound statement? Is a compound statement embedded within this statement?

6.44   Identify all compound statements that appear within the following program segment.

```
{
    sum = 0;
    do  {
            scanf("%d", &i);
            if (i < 0)    {
                i = -i;
                ++flag;
            }
            sum += i;
    } while (i != 0);
}
```

6.45   Write a loop that will calculate the sum of every third integer, beginning with $i = 2$ (i.e, calculate the sum $2 + 5 + 8 + 11 + \cdots$) for all values of i that are less than 100. Write the loop three different ways.

(*a*)   Using a while statement.

(*b*)   Using a do - while statement.

(*c*)   Using a for statement.

6.46   Repeat Prob. 6.45 calculating the sum of every nth integer, beginning with the value assigned to `nstart` (i.e., for `i = nstart, nstart + n, nstart + 2*n, nstart + 3*n`, etc.). Continue the looping process for all values of `i` that do not exceed `nstop`.

6.47   Write a loop that will examine each character in a character-type array called `text`, and write out the ASCII equivalent (i.e, the numerical value) of each character. Assume that the number of characters in the array is specified in advance by the integer variable `n`. Write the loop three different ways.

(*a*)   Using a while statement.

(*b*)   Using a do - while statement.

(*c*)   Using a for statement.

6.48   Repeat Prob. 6.47 assuming that the number of characters in the array is not specified in advance. Continue the looping action until an asterisk (`*`) is encountered. Write the loop three different ways, as before.

6.49   Generalize Prob. 6.45 by generating a *series* of loops, each loop generating the sum of every jth integer, where `j` ranges from 2 to 13. Begin each loop with a value of `i = 2`, and increase `i` by `j` until `i` takes on the largest possible value that is less than 100. (In other words, the first loop will calculate the sum $2 + 4 + 6 + \cdots + 98$; the second loop will calculate the sum $2 + 5 + 8 + \cdots + 98$; the third loop will calculate the sum $2 + 6 + 10 + \cdots + 98$; and so on. The last loop will calculate the sum $2 + 15 + 28 + \cdots + 93$.) Display the value of each complete sum.

Use a nested loop structure to solve this problem, with one loop embedded within another. Calculate each sum with the inner loop, and let the outer loop control the value of `j` that is used by each pass through the inner loop. Use a for statement to structure the outer loop, and use each of the three different loop statements (while, do - while and for) for the inner loop. Develop a separate solution for each type of inner loop.

6.50   Write a loop that will generate every third integer, beginning with `i = 2` and continuing for all integers that are less than 100. Calculate the sum of those integers that are evenly divisible by 5. Use two different methods to carry out the test.

(*a*)   Use the conditional operator (`?:`).

(*b*)   Use an if - else statement.

6.51   Generalize Prob. 6.50 by generating every nth integer, beginning with `nstart` (i.e., `i = nstart, nstart + n, nstart + 2*n, nstart + 3*n`, etc.). Continue the looping process for all values of `i` that do not exceed `nstop`. Calculate the sum of those integers that are evenly divisible by `k`, where `k` represents some positive integer.

6.52   Write a loop that will examine each character in a character-type array called `text` and determine how many of the characters are letters, how many are digits, how many are whitespace characters, and how many are other kinds of characters (e.g., punctuation characters). Assume that `text` contains 80 characters.

6.53   Write a loop that will examine each character in a character-type array called `text` and determine how many of the characters are vowels and how many are consonants. (*Hint*: First determine whether or not a character is a letter; if so, determine the type of letter.) Assume that `text` contains 80 characters.

6.54   Write a switch statement that will examine the value of an integer variable called `flag` and print one of the following messages, depending on the value assigned to `flag`.

(*a*)   HOT, if `flag` has a value of 1

(*b*)   LUKE WARM, if `flag` has a value of 2

(*c*)   COLD, if `flag` has a value of 3

(*d*)   OUT OF RANGE if `flag` has any other value

6.55   Write a switch statement that will examine the value of a char-type variable called `color` and print one of the following messages, depending on the character assigned to `color`.

(*a*)   RED, if either r or R is assigned to `color`,

(*b*)   GREEN, if either g or G is assigned to `color`,

(c)   BLUE, if either b or B is assigned to color,

(d)   BLACK, if color is assigned any other character.

6.56   Write an appropriate control structure that will examine the value of a floating-point variable called temp and print one of the following messages, depending on the value assigned to temp.

(a)   ICE, if the value of temp is less than 0.

(b)   WATER, if the value of temp lies between 0 and 100.

(c)   STEAM, if the value of temp exceeds 100.

Can a switch statement be used in this instance?

6.57   Write a for loop that will read the characters in a character-type array called text and write the characters backwards into another character-type array called backtext. Assume that text contains 80 characters. Use the comma operator within the for loop.

6.58   Describe the output that will be generated by each of the following C programs. (Note the similarities in the programs that are shown across from each other.)

(a)
```
#include <stdio.h>

main()

{
    int i = 0, x = 0;

    while (i < 20)   {
      if (i % 5 == 0)   {
        x += i;
        printf("%d ", x);
      }
      ++i;
    }
    printf("\nx = %d", x);
}
```

(b)
```
#include <stdio.h>

main()

{
    int i = 0, x = 0;

    do  {
        if (i % 5 == 0)   {
          x++;
          printf("%d ", x);
        }
        ++i;
    }   while (i < 20);
    printf("\nx = %d", x);
}
```

(c)
```
#include <stdio.h>

main()

{
    int i = 0, x = 0;

    for (i = 1; i < 10; i *= 2)   {
        x++;
        printf("%d ", x);
    }
    printf("\nx = %d", x);
}
```

(d)
```
#include <stdio.h>

main()

{
    int i = 0, x = 0;

    for (i = 1; i < 10; ++i)   {
        if (i % 2 == 1)
          x += i;
        else
          x--;
        printf("%d ", x);
    }
    printf("\nx = %d", x);
}
```

(e)
```c
#include <stdio.h>

main()

{
    int i = 0, x = 0;

    for (i = 1; i < 10; ++i)   {
        if (i % 2 == 1)
            x += i;
        else
            x--;
        printf("%d ", x);
        continue;
    }
    printf("\nx = %d", x);
}
```

(f)
```c
#include <stdio.h>

main()

{
    int i = 0, x = 0;

    for (i = 1; i < 10; ++i)   {
        if (i % 2 == 1)
            x += i;
        else
            x--;
        printf("%d ", x);
        break;
    }
    printf("\nx = %d", x);
}
```

(g)
```c
#include <stdio.h>

main()

{
    int i, j, x = 0;

    for (i = 0; i < 5; ++i)
        for (j = 0; j < i; ++j)   {
            x += (i + j - 1);
            printf("%d ", x);
        }
    printf("\nx = %d", x);
}
```

(h)
```c
#include <stdio.h>

main()

{
    int i, j, x = 0;

    for (i = 0; i < 5; ++i)
        for (j = 0; j < i; ++j)   {
            x += (i + j - 1);
            printf("%d ", x);
            break;
        }
    printf("\nx = %d", x);
}
```

(i)
```c
#include <stdio.h>

main()

{
    int i, j, x = 0;

    for (i = 0; i < 5; ++i)   {
        for (j = 0; j < i; ++j)
            x += (i + j - 1);
            printf("%d ", x);
        break;
    }
    printf("\nx = %d", x);
}
```

(*j*)
```c
#include <stdio.h>

main()

{
    int i, j, k, x = 0;

    for (i = 0; i < 5; ++i)
        for (j = 0; j < i; ++j)   {
            k = (i + j - 1);
            if (k % 2 == 0)
                x += k;
            else
                if (k % 3 == 0)
                    x += k - 2;
            printf("%d ", x);
        }
    printf("\nx = %d", x);
}
```

(*k*)
```c
#include <stdio.h>

main()

{
    int i, j, k, x = 0;

    for (i = 0; i < 5; ++i)
        for (j = 0; j < i; ++j)   {
            switch (i + j - 1)   {

            case -1:
            case  0:
                x += 1;
                break;

            case  1:
            case  2:
            case  3:
                x += 2;
                break;

            default:
                x += 3;
            }
            printf("%d ", x);
        }
    printf("\nx = %d", x);
}
```

(*l*)
```c
#include <stdio.h>

main()

{
    int i, j, k, x = 0;

    for (i = 0; i < 5; ++i)
        for (j = 0; j < i; ++j)   {
            switch (i + j - 1)   {

            case -1:
            case  0:
                x += 1;
                break;

            case  1:
            case  2:
            case  3:
                x += 2;

            default:
                x += 3;
            }
            printf("%d ", x);
        }
    printf("\nx = %d", x);
}
```

Programming Problems

6.59 Modify the programs given in Examples 6.9, 6.12 and 6.16 so that each program does the following:

(a) Read in a line of uppercase text, store it in an appropriate array, and then write it out in lowercase.

(b) Read in a line of mixed text, store it in an appropriate array, and then write it out with all lowercase and uppercase letters reversed, all digits replaced by 0s, and all other characters (nonletters and nondigits) replaced by asterisks (*).

6.60 Compile and execute the programs given in Examples 6.10, 6.13 and 6.17, using the following 10 numbers:

$$27.5, \quad 13.4, \quad 53.8, \quad 29.2, \quad 74.5, \quad 87.0, \quad 39.9, \quad 47.7, \quad 8.1, \quad 63.2$$

6.61 Compile and execute the program given in Example 6.31 using the following 10 numbers:

$$27.5, \quad -13.4, \quad 53.8, \quad -29.2, \quad 74.5, \quad 87.0, \quad 39.9, \quad -47.7, \quad -8.1, \quad 63.2$$

Compare the calculated result with the results obtained for the last problem.

6.62 Modify the program given in Example 6.10 so that the size of the list of numbers being averaged is not specified in advance. Continue looping (i.e., reading in a new value for x and adding it to sum) until a value of zero is entered. Thus, x = 0 will signal a stopping condition.

6.63 Repeat Problem 6.62 for the program given in Example 6.17.

6.64 Rewrite the depreciation program given in Example 6.26 to use the if - else statement instead of the switch statement. Test the program using the data given in Example 6.26. Which version do you prefer? Why?

6.65 The equation

$$x^5 + 3x^2 - 10 = 0$$

which was presented in Example 6.22, can be rearranged into the form

$$x = \sqrt{(10 - x^5)/3}$$

Rewrite the program presented in Example 6.22 to make use of the above form of the equation. Run the program and compare the calculated results with those presented in Example 6.22. Why are the results different? (Do computers always generate correct answers?)

6.66 Modify the program given in Example 6.22, which solves for the roots of an algebraic equation, so that the while statement is replaced by a do - while statement. Which structure is best suited for this particular problem?

6.67 Modify the program given in Example 6.22, which solves for the roots of an algebraic equation, so that the while statement is replaced by a for statement. Compare the use of the for, while and do - while statements. Which version do you prefer, and why?

6.68 Add an error-trapping routine similar to that given in Example 6.21 to the depreciation program in Example 6.26. The routine should generate an error message, followed by a request to reenter the data, whenever a nonpositive input value is detected.

6.69 Write a complete C program for each of the problems presented below. Use whatever control structures are most appropriate for each problem. Begin with a detailed outline. Rewrite the outline in pseudocode if the translation into a working C program is not obvious. Be sure to use good programming style (comments, indentation, etc.).

(a) Calculate the *weighted average* of a list of *n* numbers, using the formula

$$x_{avg} = f_1 x_1 + f_2 x_2 + \cdots + f_n x_n$$

where the *f*'s are fractional *weighting factors*, i.e.,

$$0 \le f_i < 1, \text{ and } f_1 + f_2 + \cdots + f_n = 1.$$

Test your program with the following data:

$i = 1$	$f = 0.06$	$x = 27.5$
2	0.08	13.4
3	0.08	53.8
4	0.10	29.2
5	0.10	74.5
6	0.10	87.0
7	0.12	39.9
8	0.12	47.7
9	0.12	8.1
10	0.12	63.2

(b)   Calculate the cumulative product of a list of n numbers. Test your program with the following six data items: 6.2, 12.3, 5.0, 18.8, 7.1, 12.8.

(c)   Calculate the *geometric average* of a list of numbers, using the formula

$$x_{avg} = [x_1 x_2 x_3 \cdots x_n]^{1/n}$$

Test your program using the values of x given in part (b) above. Compare the results obtained with the arithmetic average of the same data. Which average is larger?

(d)   Determine the roots of the quadratic equation

$$ax^2 + bx + c = 0$$

using the well-known quadratic formula

$$x = \frac{-b \pm \sqrt{b^2 - 4ac}}{2a}$$

(see Example 5.6). Allow for the possibility that one of the constants has a value of zero, and that the quantity $b^2 - 4ac$ is less than or equal to zero. Test the program using the following sets of data:

$a = 2$	$b = 6$	$c = 1$
3	3	0
1	3	1
0	12	−3
3	6	3
2	−4	3

(e)   The *Fibonacci numbers* are members of an interesting sequence in which each number is equal to the sum of the previous two numbers. In other words,

$$F_i = F_{i-1} + F_{i-2}$$

where F_i refers to the ith Fibonacci number. By definition, the first two Fibonacci numbers equal 1; i.e.,

$$F_1 = F_2 = 1.$$

Hence,

$$F_3 = F_2 + F_1 = 1 + 1 = 2$$
$$F_4 = F_3 + F_2 = 2 + 1 = 3$$
$$F_5 = F_4 + F_3 = 3 + 2 = 5$$

and so on.

Write a program that will determine the first n Fibonacci numbers. Test the program with $n = 7$, $n = 10$, $n = 17$ and $n = 23$.

(f)   A *prime number* is a positive integer quantity that is evenly divisible (without a remainder) only by 1 or by itself. For example, 7 is a prime number, but 6 is not.

Calculate and tabulate the first n prime numbers. (*Hint*: A number, n, will be a prime if the remainders of $n/2$, $n/3$, $n/4$, ..., $n/\sqrt{n}$ are all nonzero.) Test your program by calculating the first 100 prime numbers.

(g)   Write an interactive program that will read in a positive integer value and determine the following:

(i)   If the integer is a prime number.

(ii)   If the integer is a Fibonacci number.

Write the program in such a manner that it will execute repeatedly, until a zero value is detected for the input quantity. Test the program with several integer values of your choice.

(h)   Calculate the sum of the first n odd integers (i.e., $1 + 3 + 5 + \cdots + 2n - 1$). Test the program by calculating the sum of the first 100 odd integers (note that the last integer will be 199).

(i)   The sine of x can be calculated approximately by summing the first n terms of the infinite series

$$\sin x = x - x^3/3! + x^5/5! - x^7/7! + \cdots$$

where x is expressed in radians (*Note*: π radians = 180°).

Write a C program that will read in a value for x and then calculate its sine. Write the program two different ways:

(i)   Sum the first n terms, where n is a positive integer that is read into the computer along with the numerical value for x.

(ii)   Continue adding successive terms in the series until the value of the next term becomes smaller (in magnitude) than 10^{-5}.

Test the program for $x = 1$, $x = 2$ and $x = -3$. In each case, display the number of terms used to obtain the final answer.

(j)   Suppose that P dollars are borrowed from a bank, with the understanding that A dollars will be repaid each month until the entire loan has been repaid. Part of the monthly payment will be interest, calculated as i percent of the current unpaid balance. The remainder of the monthly payment will be applied toward reducing the unpaid balance.

Write a C program that will determine the following information:

(i)   The amount of interest paid each month.

(ii)   The amount of money applied toward the unpaid balance each month.

(iii)   The cumulative amount of interest that has been paid at the end of each month.

(iv)   The amount of the loan that is still unpaid at the end of each month.

(v)   The number of monthly payments required to repay the entire loan.

(vi)   The amount of the last payment (since it will probably be less than A).

Test your program using the following data: $P = \$40,000$; $A = \$2,000$; $i = 1\%$ per month.

(k)   A class of students earned the following grades for the six examinations taken in a C programming course.

Name	Exam Scores (percent)					
Adams	45	80	80	95	55	75
Brown	60	50	70	75	55	80
Davis	40	30	10	45	60	55
Fisher	0	5	5	0	10	5
Hamilton	90	85	100	95	90	90

Name			*Exam Scores (percent)*			
Jones	95	90	80	95	85	80
Ludwig	35	50	55	65	45	70
Osborne	75	60	75	60	70	80
Prince	85	75	60	85	90	100
Richards	50	60	50	35	65	70
Smith	70	60	75	70	55	75
Thomas	10	25	35	20	30	10
Wolfe	25	40	65	75	85	95
Zorba	65	80	70	100	60	95

Write an interactive C program that will accept each student's name and exam grades as input, determine an average grade for each student, and then display the student's name, the individual exam grades and the calculated average.

(*l*)　Modify the program written for part (*k*) above to allow for unequal weighting of the individual exam grades. In particular, assume that each of the first four exams contributes 15 percent to the final score, and each of the last two exams contributes 20 percent.

(*m*)　Extend the program written for part (*l*) above so that an overall class average is determined in addition to the individual student averages.

(*n*)　Write a C program that will allow the computer to be used as an ordinary desk calculator. Consider only the common arithmetic operations (addition, subtraction, multiplication and division). Include a memory that can store one number.

(*o*)　Generate the following "pyramid" of digits, using nested loops.

1

232

34543

4567654

567898765

67890109876

7890123210987

890123454321098

90123456765432109

0123456789876543210

Do *not* simply write out 10 multidigit strings. Instead, develop a formula to *generate* the appropriate output for each line.

(*p*)　Generate a plot of the function

$$y = e^{-0.1t} \sin 0.5t$$

on a printer, using an asterisk (*) for each of the points that makes up the plot. Have the plot run vertically down the page, with one point (one asterisk) per line. (*Hint*: Each printed line should consist of one asterisk, preceded by an appropriate number of blank spaces. Determine the position of the asterisk by rounding the value of y to the nearest integer, scaled to the maximum number of characters per line.)

(*q*)　Write an interactive C program that will convert a positive integer quantity to a roman numeral (e.g., 12 will be converted to XII, 14 will be converted to XIV, and so on). Design the program so that it will execute repeatedly, until a value of zero is read in from the keyboard.

(r) Write an interactive C program that will convert a date, entered in the form `mm-dd-yy` (example: 4-12-99) into an integer that indicates the number of days beyond January 1, 1980. If the year does not extend beyond 1999 (i.e., if yy ≤ 99), we can make use of the following relationships:

(*i*) The day of the current year can be determined approximately as

$$\text{day} = \text{(int) (30.42 * (mm - 1)) + dd}$$

(*ii*) If `mm == 2` (February), *increase* the value of day by 1.

(*iii*) If `mm > 2` and `mm < 8` (March, April, May, June or July), *decrease* the value of day by 1.

(*iv*) If `yy % 4 == 0` and `mm > 2` (leap year), *increase* the value of day by 1.

(*v*) *Increase* the value of day by 1461 for each full 4-year cycle beyond 1-1-80.

(*vi*) *Increase* day by 365 for each additional full year beyond the completion of the last full 4-year cycle, then add 1 (for the most recent leap year).

Test the program with today's date, or any other date of your choice.

(s) Extend part (r) above to accommodate calendar years beyond the year 1999 (Example 10.28 presents a solution to a more advanced version of this problem).

Chapter 7

Functions

We have already seen that C supports the use of library functions, which are used to carry out a number of commonly used operations or calculations (see Sec. 3.6). However, C also allows programmers to define their own functions for carrying out various individual tasks. This chapter concentrates on the creation and utilization of such programmer-defined functions.

The use of programmer-defined functions allows a large program to be broken down into a number of smaller, self-contained components, each of which has some unique, identifiable purpose. Thus a C program can be *modularized* through the intelligent use of such functions. (C does not support other forms of modular program development, such as the procedures in Pascal or the subroutines in Fortran.)

There are several advantages to this modular approach to program development. For example, many programs require that a particular group of instructions be accessed repeatedly, from several different places within the program. The repeated instructions can be placed within a single function, which can then be accessed whenever it is needed. Moreover, a different set of data can be transferred to the function each time it is accessed. Thus, *the use of a function avoids the need for redundant (repeated) programming of the same instructions*.

Equally important is the *logical clarity* resulting from the decomposition of a program into several concise functions, where each function represents some well-defined part of the overall problem. Such programs are easier to write and easier to debug, and their logical structure is more apparent than programs which lack this type of structure. This is especially true of lengthy, complicated programs. Most C programs are therefore modularized in this manner, even though they may not involve repeated execution of the same tasks. In fact the decomposition of a program into individual program modules is generally considered to be an important part of good programming practice.

The use of functions also enables a programmer to build a *customized library* of frequently used routines or of routines containing system-dependent features. Each routine can be programmed as a separate function and stored within a special library file. If a program requires a particular routine, the corresponding library function can be accessed and attached to the program during the compilation process. Hence a single function can be utilized by many different programs. This avoids repetitive programming between programs. It also promotes *portability* since programs can be written that are independent of system-dependent features.

In this chapter we will see how functions are defined and how they are accessed from various places within a C program. We will then consider the manner in which information is passed to a function. Our discussion will include the use of *function prototypes*, as recommended by the current ANSI standard. And finally, we will discuss an interesting and important programming technique known as *recursion*, in which a function can access itself repeatedly.

7.1 A BRIEF OVERVIEW

A *function* is a self-contained program segment that carries out some specific, well-defined task. Every C program consists of one or more functions (see Sec. 1.5). One of these functions must be called `main`. Execution of the program will always begin by carrying out the instructions in `main`. Additional functions will be subordinate to `main`, and perhaps to one another.

If a program contains multiple functions, their definitions may appear in any order, though they must be independent of one another. That is, one function definition cannot be embedded within another.

A function will carry out its intended action whenever it is *accessed* (i.e., whenever the function is "called") from some other portion of the program. The same function can be accessed from several different places within a program. Once the function has carried out its intended action, control will be returned to the point from which the function was accessed.

Generally, *a function will process information that is passed to it from the calling portion of the program, and return a single value.* Information is passed to the function via special identifiers called *arguments* (also called *parameters*), and returned via the return statement. Some functions, however, accept information but do not return anything (as, for example, the library function printf), whereas other functions (e.g., the library function scanf) return multiple values.

EXAMPLE 7.1 Lowercase to Uppercase Character Conversion   In Example 3.31 we saw a simple C program that read in a single lowercase character, converted it to uppercase using the library function toupper, and then displayed the uppercase equivalent. We now consider a similar program, though we will define and utilize our own function for carrying out the lowercase to uppercase conversion.

Our purpose in doing this is to illustrate the principal features involved in the use of functions. Hence, you should concentrate on the overall logic, and not worry about the details of each individual statement just yet.

Here is the complete program.

```
/* convert a lowercase character to uppercase using a programmer-defined function */

#include <stdio.h>

char lower_to_upper(char c1)            /* function definition */

{
    char c2;

    c2 = (c1 >= 'a' && c1 <= 'z') ? ('A' + c1 - 'a') : c1;
    return(c2);
}

main()

{
    char lower, upper;

    printf("Please enter a lowercase character: ");
    scanf("%c", &lower);
    upper = lower_to_upper(lower);
    printf("\nThe uppercase equivalent is %c\n\n", upper);
}
```

This program consists of two functions—the required main function, preceded by the programmer-defined function lower_to_upper. Note that lower_to_upper carries out the actual character conversion. This function converts only lowercase letters; all other characters are returned intact. A lowercase letter is transferred into the function via the argument c1, and the uppercase equivalent, c2, is returned to the calling portion of the program (i.e., to main) via the return statement.

Now consider the main function, which follows lower_to_upper. This function reads in a character (which may or may not be a lowercase letter) and assigns it to the char-type variable lower. Function main then calls the function lower_to_upper, transferring the lowercase character (lower) to lower_to_upper, and receiving the equivalent uppercase character (upper) from lower_to_upper. The uppercase character is then displayed, and the program ends. Notice that the variables lower and upper in main correspond to the variables c1 and c2 within lower_to_upper.

We will consider the rules associated with function definitions and function accesses in the remainder of this chapter.

7.2 DEFINING A FUNCTION

A function definition has two principal components: the *first line* (including the *argument declarations*), and the *body* of the function.

The first line of a function definition contains the type specification of the value returned by the function, followed by the function name, and (optionally) a set of arguments, separated by commas and enclosed in parentheses. Each argument is preceded by its associated type declaration. An empty pair of parentheses must follow the function name if the function definition does not include any arguments.

In general terms, the first line can be written as

$$\textit{data-type}\;\;\textit{name}(\textit{type 1}\;\;\textit{arg 1},\;\;\textit{type 2}\;\;\textit{arg 2},\;\;\ldots,\;\;\textit{type n arg n})$$

where *data-type* represents the data type of the item that is returned by the function, *name* represents the function name, and *type 1*, *type 2*,..., *type n* represent the data types of the arguments *arg 1*, *arg 2*, ..., *arg n*. The data types are assumed to be of type int if they are not shown explicitly. However, the omission of the data types is considered poor programming practice, even if the data items are integers.

The arguments are called *formal arguments*, because they represent the names of data items that are transferred into the function from the calling portion of the program. They are also known as *parameters* or *formal parameters*. (The corresponding arguments in the function *reference* are called *actual arguments*, since they define the data items that are actually transferred. Some textbooks refer to actual arguments simply as *arguments*, or as *actual parameters*.) The identifiers used as formal arguments are "local" in the sense that they are not recognized outside of the function. Hence, the names of the formal arguments need not be the same as the names of the actual arguments in the calling portion of the program. Each formal argument must be of the same *data type*, however, as the data item it receives from the calling portion of the program.

The remainder of the function definition is a compound statement that defines the action to be taken by the function. This compound statement is sometimes referred to as the *body* of the function. Like any other compound statement, this statement can contain expression statements, other compound statements, control statements, and so on. It should include one or more return statements, in order to return a value to the calling portion of the program.

A function can access other functions. In fact, it can even access itself (this process is known as *recursion* and is discussed in Sec. 7.6).

EXAMPLE 7.2   Consider the function lower_to_upper, which was originally presented in Example 7.1.

```
char lower_to_upper(char c1)        /* programmer-defined conversion function */
{
    char c2;

    c2 = (c1 >= 'a' && c1 <= 'z') ? ('A' + c1 - 'a') : c1;
    return(c2);
}
```

The first line contains the function name, lower_to_upper, followed by the formal argument c1, enclosed in parentheses. The *function name* is preceded by the data type char, which describes the data item that is returned by the function. In addition, the *formal argument* c1 is preceded by the data type char. This later data type, which is included within the pair of parentheses, refers to the formal argument. The formal argument, c1, represents the lowercase character that is transferred *to* the function from the calling portion of the program.

The body of the function begins on the second line, with the declaration of the local char-type variable c2. (Note the distinction between the *formal argument* c1, and the *local variable* c2.) Following the declaration of c2 is a statement that tests whether c1 represents a lowercase letter and then carries out the conversion. The original character is returned intact if it is not a lowercase letter. Finally, the return statement (see below) causes the converted character to be returned to the calling portion of the program.

Information is returned from the function to the calling portion of the program via the `return` statement. The `return` statement also causes the program logic to return to the point from which the function was accessed.

In general terms, the `return` statement is written as

```
return expression;
```

The value of the *expression* is returned to the calling portion of the program, as in Example 7.2 above. The *expression* is optional. If the *expression* is omitted, the `return` statement simply causes control to revert back to the calling portion of the program, without any transfer of information.

Only one expression can be included in the `return` statement. Thus, a function can return only one value to the calling portion of the program via `return`.

A function definition can include multiple `return` statements, each containing a different expression. Functions that include multiple branches often require multiple returns.

EXAMPLE 7.3 Here is a variation of the function `lower_to_upper`, which appeared in Examples 7.1 and 7.2.

```
char lower_to_upper(char c1)            /* programmer-defined conversion function */

{
    if (c1 >= 'a' && c1 <= 'z')
        return('A' + c1 - 'a');
    else
        return(c1);
}
```

This function utilizes the `if - else` statement rather than the conditional operator. It is somewhat less compact than the original version, though the logic is clearer. In addition, note that this form of the function does not require the local variable c2.

This particular function contains two different `return` statements. The first returns an expression that represents the uppercase equivalent of the lowercase character ; the second returns the original lowercase character, unchanged.

The `return` statement can be absent altogether from a function definition, though this is generally regarded as poor programming practice. If a function reaches the end without encountering a `return` statement, control simply reverts back to the calling portion of the program without returning any information. The presence of an empty `return` statement (without the accompanying expression) is recommended in such situations, to clarify the logic and to accommodate future modifications to the function.

EXAMPLE 7.4 The following function accepts two integer quantities and determines the larger value, which is then displayed. The function does not return any information to the calling program.

```
maximum(int x, int y)            /* determine the larger of two integer quantities */

{
    int z;

    z = (x >= y) ? x : y;
    printf("\n\nMaximum value = %d", z);
    return;
}
```

Notice that an empty `return` statement is included, as a matter of good programming practice. The function would still work properly, however, if the `return` statement were not present.

EXAMPLE 7.5   The *factorial* of a positive integer quantity, *n*, is defined as $n! = 1 \times 2 \times 3 \times \cdots \times n$. Thus, $2! = 1 \times 2 = 2$; $3! = 1 \times 2 \times 3 = 6$; $4! = 1 \times 2 \times 3 \times 4 = 24$; and so on.

The function shown below calculates the factorial of a given positive integer n. The factorial is returned as a long integer quantity, since factorials grow in magnitude very rapidly as n increases. (For example, 8! = 40,320. This value, expressed as an ordinary integer, may be too large for some computers.)

```
long int factorial(int n)         /* calculate the factorial of n */

{
    int i;
    long int prod = 1;

    if (n > 1)
        for (i = 2; i <= n; ++i)
            prod *= i;
    return(prod);
}
```

Notice the `long int` type specification that is included in the first line of the function definition. The local variable `prod` is declared to be a long integer within the function. It is assigned an initial value of 1, though its value is recalculated within a `for` loop. The final value of `prod`, which is returned by the function, represents the desired value of *n* factorial.

If the data type specified in the first line is inconsistent with the expression appearing in the `return` statement, the compiler will attempt to convert the quantity represented by the expression to the data type specified in the first line. This could result in a compilation error, or it may involve a partial loss of data (e.g., due to truncation). In any event, inconsistencies of this type should be avoided.

EXAMPLE 7.6   The following function definition is identical to that in Example 7.5 except that the first line does not include a type specification for the value that is returned by the function.

```
factorial(int n)          /* calculate the factorial of n */

{
    int i;
    long int prod = 1;

    if (n > 1)
        for (i = 2; i <= n; ++i)
            prod *= i;
    return(prod);
}
```

The function expects to return an ordinary integer quantity, since there is no explicit type declaration in the first line of the function definition. However the quantity being returned (`prod`) is declared as a long integer within the function. This inconsistency can result in an error. (Some compilers will generate a diagnostic error and then stop without completing the compilation.) The problem can be avoided, however, by adding a `long int` type declaration to the first line of the function definition, as in Example 7.5.

The keyword `void` can be used as a type specifier when defining a function that does not return anything, or when the function definition does not include any arguments. The presence of this keyword is not mandatory, but it is good programming practice to make use of this feature.

EXAMPLE 7.7   Consider once again the function presented in Example 7.4, which accepts two integer quantities and displays the larger of the two. Recall that this function does not return anything to the calling portion of the program. Therefore, the function can be written as

```
    void maximum(x, y)         /* determine the larger of two integer quantities */

    int x, y;

    {
        int z;

        z = (x >= y) ? x : y;
        printf("\n\nMaximum value = %d", z);
        return;
    }
```

This function is identical to that shown in Example 7.4 except that the keyword void has been added to the first line, indicating that the function does not return anything.

7.3 ACCESSING A FUNCTION

A function can be *accessed* (i.e., *called*) by specifying its name, followed by a list of arguments enclosed in parentheses and separated by commas. If the function call does not require any arguments, an empty pair of parentheses must follow the name of the function. The function call may be a part of a simple expression (such as an assignment statement), or it may be one of the operands within a more complex expression.

The arguments appearing in the function call are referred to as *actual arguments*, in contrast to the formal arguments that appear in the first line of the function definition. (They are also known simply as *arguments*, or as *actual parameters*.) In a normal function call, there will be one actual argument for each formal argument. The actual arguments may be expressed as constants, single variables, or more complex expressions. However, each actual argument must be of the same data type as its corresponding formal argument. Remember that it is the *value* of each actual argument that is transferred into the function and assigned to the corresponding formal argument.

If the function returns a value, the function access is often written as an assignment statement; e.g.,

```
    y = polynomial(x);
```

This function access causes the value returned by the function to be assigned to the variable y.

On the other hand, if the function does not return anything, the function access appears by itself; e.g.,

```
    display(a, b, c);
```

This function access causes the values of a, b and c to be processed internally (i.e., displayed) within the function.

EXAMPLE 7.8 Consider once again the program originally shown in Example 7.1, which reads in a single lowercase character, converts it to uppercase using a programmer-defined function, and then displays the uppercase equivalent.

```
    /* convert a lowercase character to uppercase using a programmer-defined function */

    #include <stdio.h>

    char lower_to_upper(char c1)         /* function definition */

    {
        char c2;

        c2 = (c1 >= 'a' && c1 <= 'z') ? ('A' + c1 - 'a') : c1;
        return(c2);
    }
```

```
void main(void)

{
    char lower, upper;

    printf("Please enter a lowercase character: ");
    scanf("%c", &lower);
    upper = lower_to_upper(lower);
    printf("\nThe uppercase equivalent is %c\n\n", upper);
}
```

Within this program, main contains only one call to the programmer-defined function lower_to_upper. The call is a part of the assignment expression upper = lower_to_upper(lower).

The function call contains one actual argument, the char-type variable lower. Note that the corresponding formal argument, c1, within the function definition is also a char-type variable.

When the function is accessed, the value of lower to be transferred to the function. This value is represented by c1 within the function. The value of the uppercase equivalent, c2, is then determined and returned to the calling portion of the program, where it is assigned to the char-type variable upper.

The last two statements in main can be combined to read

```
    printf("\nThe uppercase equivalent is %c\n\n", lower_to_upper(lower));
```

The call to lower_to_upper is now an actual argument for the library function printf. Also, note that the variable upper is no longer required.

Finally, notice the manner in which the first line of main is written, i.e., void main(void). This is permitted under the ANSI standard, though some compilers do not accept the void return type. Hence, many authors (and many programmers) write the first line of main as main(void), or simply main(). We will follow the latter designation throughout the remainder of this book.

There may be several different calls to the same function from various places within a program. The actual arguments may differ from one function call to another. Within each function call, however, *the actual arguments must correspond to the formal arguments in the function definition; i.e., the number of actual arguments must be the same as the number of formal arguments, and each actual argument must be of the same data type as its corresponding formal argument.*

EXAMPLE 7.9 Largest of Three Integer Quantities The following program determines the largest of three integer quantities. This program makes use of a function that determines the larger of two integer quantities. The function is similar to that defined in Example 7.4, except that the present function returns the larger value to the calling program rather than displaying it.

The overall strategy is to determine the larger of the first two quantities, and then compare this value with the third quantity. The largest quantity is then displayed by the main part of the program.

```
/* determine the largest of three integer quantities */

#include <stdio.h>


int maximum(int x, int y)        /* determine the larger of two integer quantities */

{
    int z;

    z = (x >= y) ? x : y;
    return(z);
}
```

```
main()
{
    int a, b, c, d;

    /* read the integer quantities */
    printf("\na = ");
    scanf("%d", &a);
    printf("\nb = ");
    scanf("%d", &b);
    printf("\nc = ");
    scanf("%d", &c);

    /* calculate and display the maximum value */

    d = maximum(a, b);
    printf("\n\nmaximum = %d", maximum(c, d));
}
```

The function `maximum` is accessed from two different places in `main`. In the first call to `maximum` the actual arguments are the variables `a` and `b`, whereas the arguments are `c` and `d` in the second call (`d` is a temporary variable representing the maximum value of `a` and `b`).

Note the two statements in `main` that access `maximum`, i.e.,

```
    d = maximum(a, b);
    printf("\n\nmaximum = %d", maximum(c, d));
```

These two statements can be replaced by a single statement; e.g.,

```
    printf("\n\nmaximum = %d", maximum(c, maximum(a, b)));
```

In this statement we see that one of the calls to `maximum` is an argument for the other call. Thus the calls are embedded, one within the other, and the intermediary variable, `d`, is not required. Such embedded function calls are permissible, though their logic may be unclear. Hence, they should generally be avoided by beginning programmers.

7.4 FUNCTION PROTOTYPES

In the programs that we have examined earlier in this chapter, the programmer-defined function has always *preceded* `main`. Thus, when these programs are compiled, the programmer-defined function will have been defined before the first function access. However, many programmers prefer a "top-down" approach, in which `main` appears ahead of the programmer-defined function definition. In such situations the function access (within `main`) will precede the function definition. This can be confusing to the compiler, unless the compiler is first alerted to the fact that the function being accessed will be defined later in the program. A *function prototype* is used for this purpose.

Function prototypes are usually written at the beginning of a program, ahead of any programmer-defined functions (including `main`). The general form of a function prototype is

data-type name(*type 1 arg 1*, *type 2 arg 2*, . . ., *type n arg n*);

where *data-type* represents the data type of the item that is returned by the function, *name* represents the function name, and *type 1*, *type 2*, . . ., *type n* represent the data types of the arguments *arg 1*, *arg 2*, . . ., *arg n*. Notice that a function prototype resembles the first line of a function definition (though a function prototype ends with a semicolon).

The names of the arguments within the function prototype need not be declared elsewhere in the program, since these are "dummy" argument names that are recognized only within the prototype. In fact, the argument names can be omitted (though it is not a good idea to do so); however, the argument *data types* are essential.

In practice, the argument names are usually included and are often the same as the names of the actual arguments appearing in one of the function calls. The data types of the actual arguments must conform to the data types of the arguments within the prototype.

Function prototypes are not mandatory in C. They are desirable, however, because they further facilitate error checking between the calls to a function and the corresponding function definition.

EXAMPLE 7.10 Calculating Factorials   Here is a complete program to calculate the factorial of a positive integer quantity. The program utilizes the function factorial, defined in Example 7.5. Note that the function definition precedes main, as in the earlier programming examples within this chapter.

```
/* calculate the factorial of an integer quantity */

#include <stdio.h>

long int factorial(int n)

/* calculate the factorial of n */

{
    int i;
    long int prod = 1;

    if (n > 1)
       for (i = 2; i <= n; ++i)
           prod *= i;
    return(prod);
}


main()

{
    int n;

    /* read in the integer quantity */

    printf("\nn = ");
    scanf("%d", &n);

    /* calculate and display the factorial */

    printf("\nn! = %ld", factorial(n));
}
```

The programmer-defined function (factorial) makes use of an integer argument (n) and two local variables—an ordinary integer (i) and a long integer (prod). Since the function returns a long integer, the type declaration long int appears in the first line of the function definition.

Here is another version of the program, written top-down (i.e, with main appearing ahead of factorial). Notice the presence of the function prototype at the beginning of the program. The function prototype indicates that a function called factorial, which accepts an integer quantity and returns a long integer quantity, will be defined later in the program.

```
/* calculate the factorial of an integer quantity */

#include <stdio.h>

long int factorial(int n);       /* function prototype */
```

```
main()

{
    int n;

    /* read in the integer quantity */

    printf("\nn = ");
    scanf("%d", &n);

    /* calculate and display the factorial */

    printf("\nn! = %ld", factorial(n));
}

long int factorial(int n)

/* calculate the factorial of n */

{
    int i;
    long int prod = 1;

    if (n > 1)
        for (i = 2; i <= n; ++i)
            prod *= i;
    return(prod);
}
```

Function calls can span several levels within a program. That is, function A can call function B, which can call function C, etc. Also, function A can call function C directly, and so on.

EXAMPLE 7.11 Simulation of a Game of Chance (Shooting Craps)   Here is an interesting programming problem that includes multiple function calls at several different levels. Both library functions and programmer-defined functions are required.

Craps is a popular dice game in which you throw a pair of dice one or more times until you either win or lose. The game can be simulated on a computer by generating random numbers rather than actually throwing the dice.

There are two ways to win in craps. You can throw the dice once and obtain a score of either 7 or 11; or you can obtain a 4, 5, 6, 8, 9 or 10 on the first throw and then repeat the same score on a subsequent throw before obtaining a 7. Conversely, there are two ways to lose. You can throw the dice once and obtain a 2, 3 or 12; or you can obtain a 4, 5, 6, 8, 9 or 10 on the first throw and then obtain a 7 on a subsequent throw before repeating your original score.

We will develop the game interactively, so that one throw of the dice will be simulated each time you press the Enter key. A message will then appear indicating the outcome of each throw. At the end of each game, you will be asked whether or not you want to continue to play.

Our program will require a random number generator that produces uniformly distributed integers between 1 and 6. (By *uniformly distributed* we mean that any integer between 1 and 6 is just as likely to appear as any other integer.) Most versions of C include a random number generator in their library routines. These random number generators typically return a floating-point number that is uniformly distributed between 0 and 1, or an integer quantity that is uniformly distributed between 0 and some very large integer value.

We will employ a random number generation routine called rand, which returns a uniformly distributed integer between 0 and $2^{15} - 1$ (i.e., between 0 and 32,767). We then convert each random integer quantity to a floating-point number, x, which varies from 0 to 0.99999···. To do so, we write

```
x = rand() / 32768.0
```

Note that the denominator is written as a floating-point constant. This forces the quotient, and hence x, to be a floating-point quantity.

The expression

```
(int) (6 * x)
```

will result in a truncated integer whose value will be uniformly distributed between 0 and 5. Thus, we obtain the desired value simply by adding 1; i.e.,

```
n = 1 + (int) (6 * x)
```

This value will represent the random outcome of rolling one die. If we repeat this process a second time and add the results, we obtain the result of rolling two dice.

The following function utilizes the above strategy to simulate one throw of a pair of dice.

```
int throw(void)    /* simulate one throw of a pair of dice */

{
    float x1, x2;   /* random floating-point numbers between 0 and 1 */
    int n1, n2;     /* random integers between 1 and 6 */

    x1 = rand() / 32768.0;
    x2 = rand() / 32768.0;

    n1 = 1 + (int) (6 * x1);    /* simulate first die */
    n2 = 1 + (int) (6 * x2);    /* simulate second die */

    return(n1 + n2);            /* score is sum of two dice */
}
```

The function returns the result of each throw (an integer quantity whose value varies between 2 and 12). Note that this final result will *not* be uniformly distributed, even though the individual values of n1 and n2 are.

Now let us define another function, called play, which can simulate one complete game of craps. Thus, the dice will be thrown as many times as is necessary to establish either a win or a loss. This function will therefore access throw. The complete rules of craps will also be built into this function.

In pseudocode, we can write the function play as

```
void play(void)    /* simulate one complete game */
{
    int score1, score2;

    /* instruct the user to throw the dice */

    /* initialize the random number generator */

    score1 = throw();

    switch (score1)   {

    case 7:
    case 11:

        /* display a message indicating a win on the first throw */

    case 2:
    case 3:
    case 12:

        /* display a message indicating a loss on the first throw */
```

```
         case 4:
         case 5:
         case 6:
         case 8:
         case 9:
         case 10:

              do   {
                         /* instruct the user to throw the dice again */

                         score2 = throw();

              }   while (score2 != score1 && score2 != 7);

              if (score2 == score1)

                  /* display a message indicating a win */

              else

                  /* display a message indicating a loss */

         }

     return;

}
```

The main routine will control the execution of the game. This routine will consist of a `while` loop containing some interactive input/output and a call to `play`. Thus, we can write the pseudocode for `main` as

```
main()
{
    /* declarations */

    /* initialize the random number generator */

    /* generate a welcoming message */

    while ( /* player wants to continue */ )   {

        play();

        /* ask if player wants to continue */

    }

    /*  generate a sign-off message */

}
```

The library function `srand` will be used to initialize the random number generator. This function requires a positive integer, called a *seed*, which establishes the sequence of random numbers generated by `rand`. A different sequence will be generated for each seed. For convenience, we can include a value for the seed as a symbolic constant within the program. (If the program is executed repeatedly with the same seed, the same sequence of random numbers will be generated each time. This is helpful when debugging the program.)

Here is the complete C program, written top-down.

```
/* simulation of a craps game */

#include <stdio.h>
#include <stdlib.h>
#include <ctype.h>

#define  SEED   12345
```

```c
void play(void);                /* function prototype */
int throw(void);                /* function prototype */

main()

{
    char answer = 'Y';

    printf("Welcome to the Game of CRAPS\n\n");
    printf("To throw the dice, press Enter\n\n");

    srand(SEED);   /* initialize the random number generator */

    /* main loop */

    while (toupper(answer) != 'N')   {
        play();
        printf("\nDo you want to play again? (Y/N) ");
        scanf(" %c", &answer);
        printf("\n");
    }
    printf("Bye, have a nice day");
}

void play(void)    /* simulate one complete game */

{
    int score1, score2;
    char dummy;

    printf("\nPlease throw the dice . . .");
    scanf("%c", &dummy);
    printf("\n");
    score1 = throw();
    printf("\n%2d", score1);

    switch (score1)  {

    case 7:    /* win on first throw */
    case 11:

        printf(" - Congratulations!  You WIN on the first throw\n");
        break;

    case 2:    /* lose on first throw */
    case 3:
    case 12:

        printf(" - Sorry, you LOSE on the first throw\n");
        break;

    case 4:    /* additional throws are required */
    case 5:
    case 6:
    case 8:
    case 9:
    case 10:
```

```
        do   {
                    printf(" - Throw the dice again . . .");
                    scanf("%c", &dummy);
                    score2 = throw();
                    printf("\n%2d", score2);
            } while (score2 != score1 && score2 != 7);

            if (score2 == score1)
                printf(" - You WIN by matching your first score\n");
            else
                printf(" - You LOSE by failing to match your first score\n");
            break;
        }

    return;
}

int throw(void)    /* simulate one throw of a pair of dice */

{
    float x1, x2;  /* random floating-point numbers between 0 and 1 */
    int n1, n2;    /* random integers between 1 and 6 */

    x1 = rand() / 32768.0;
    x2 = rand() / 32768.0;

    n1 = 1 + (int) (6 * x1);   /* simulate first die */
    n2 = 1 + (int) (6 * x2);   /* simulate second die */

    return(n1 + n2);           /* score is sum of two dice */
}
```

Notice that main calls srand and play. One argument is passed to srand (the value of the seed), but no arguments are passed to play. Also, note that play calls throw from two different places, and throw calls rand from two different places. There are no arguments passed from play to throw or from throw to rand. However, rand returns a random integer to throw, and throw returns the value of an integer expression (the outcome of one throw of the dice) to play. Notice that play does not return any information to main.

Within play, there are two references to the scanf function, each of which enters a value for the variable dummy. It should be understood that dummy is not actually used within the program. The scanf functions are present simply to halt the program temporarily, until the user presses the Enter key (to simulate a new throw of the dice).

This program is designed to run in an interactive environment, such as on a personal computer. A typical set of output is shown below. The user's responses are underlined for clarity.

```
Welcome to the Game of CRAPS

To throw the dice, press Enter (Enter)


Please throw the dice . . .

 6 - Throw the dice again . . .

10 - Throw the dice again . . .

 7 - You LOSE by failing to match your first score
```

```
Do you want to play again? (Y/N) y


Please throw the dice . . .

 7 - Congratulations!  You WIN on the first throw

Do you want to play again? (Y/N) y


Please throw the dice . . .

11 - Congratulations!  You WIN on the first throw

Do you want to play again? (Y/N) y


Please throw the dice . . .

 8 - Throw the dice again . . .

 5 - Throw the dice again . . .

 7 - You LOSE by failing to match your first score

Do you want to play again? (Y/N) y


Please throw the dice . . .

 6 - Throw the dice again . . .

 4 - Throw the dice again . . .

 6 - You WIN by matching your first score

Do you want to play again? (Y/N) y


Please throw the dice . . .

 3 - Sorry, you LOSE on the first throw

Do you want to play again? (Y/N) n

Bye, have a nice day
```

7.5 PASSING ARGUMENTS TO A FUNCTION

When a single value is passed to a function via an actual argument, the value of the actual argument is *copied* into the function. Therefore, *the value of the corresponding formal argument can be altered within the function, but the value of the actual argument within the calling routine will not change.* This procedure for passing the value of an argument to a function is known as *passing by value.*

EXAMPLE 7.12   Here is a simple C program containing a function that alters the value of its argument.

```
#include <stdio.h>

void modify(int a);        /* function prototype */

main()
{
    int a = 2;

    printf("\na = %d  (from main, before calling the function)", a);
    modify(a);
    printf("\n\na = %d  (from main, after calling the function)", a);
}

void modify(int a)
{
    a *= 3;
    printf("\n\na = %d  (from the function, after being modified)", a);
    return;
}
```

The original value of a (i.e., a = 2) is displayed when main begins execution. This value is then passed to the function modify, where it is multiplied by 3 and the new value displayed. Note that it is the *altered* value of the formal argument that is displayed within the function. Finally, the value of a within main (i.e., the actual argument) is again displayed, after control is transferred back to main from modify.

When the program is executed, the following output is generated.

```
a = 2  (from main, before calling the function)

a = 6  (from the function, after being modified)

a = 2  (from main, after calling the function)
```

These results show that a is *not* altered within main, even though the corresponding value of a *is* changed within modify.

Passing an argument by value has advantages and disadvantages. On the plus side, it allows a single-valued actual argument to be written as an expression rather than being restricted to a single variable. Moreover, if the actual argument is expressed simply as a single variable, it protects the value of this variable from alterations within the function. On the other hand, it does not allow information to be transferred back to the calling portion of the program via arguments. Thus, *passing by value is restricted to a one-way transfer of information.*

EXAMPLE 7.13 Calculating Depreciation   Let us consider a variation of the depreciation program presented in Example 6.26. The overall objective is to calculate depreciation as a function of time using any one of three different commonly used methods, as before. Now, however, we will rewrite the program so that a separate function is used for each method. This approach offers us a cleaner way to organize the program into its logical components. In addition, we will move a block of repeated output instructions into a separate function, thus eliminating some redundant programming from the original version of the program.

We will also expand the generality of the program somewhat, by permitting different sets of depreciation calculations to be carried out on the same input data. Thus, at the end of each set of calculations the user will be asked if another set of calculations is desired. If the answer is yes, then the user will be asked whether or not to enter new data.

Here is the new version of the program, written top-down.

```c
/* calculate depreciation using one of three different methods */

#include <stdio.h>
#include <ctype.h>

void sl(float val, int n);                              /* funct prototype */
void ddb(float val, int n);                             /* funct prototype */
void syd(float val, int n);                             /* funct prototype */
void writeoutput(int year, float depreciation, float value);   /* funct prototype */

main()

{
    int n, choice = 0;
    float val;
    char answer1 = 'Y', answer2 = 'Y';

    while (toupper(answer1) != 'N')   {

        /* read input data */

        if (toupper(answer2) != 'N')   {
            printf("\nOriginal value: ");
            scanf("%f", &val);
            printf("Number of years: ");
            scanf("%d", &n);
        }
        printf("\nMethod: (1-SL  2-DDB  3-SYD) ");
        scanf("%d", &choice);

        switch (choice)  {

        case 1:     /* straight-line method */

            printf("\nStraight-Line Method\n\n");
            sl(val, n);
            break;

        case 2:     /* double-declining-balance method */

            printf("\nDouble-Declining-Balance Method\n\n");
            ddb(val, n);
            break;

        case 3:     /* sum-of-the-years'-digits method */

            printf("\nSum-Of-The-Years\'-Digits Method\n\n");
            syd(val, n);
        }

        printf("\n\nAnother calculation? (Y/N) ");
        scanf("%1s", &answer1);
        if (toupper(answer1) != 'N')   {
            printf("Enter a new set of data? (Y/N) ");
            scanf("%1s", &answer2);
        }
    }

    printf("\nGoodbye, have a nice day!\n");

}
```

```c
void sl(float val, int n)      /* straight-line method */

{
    float deprec;
    int year;

    deprec = val/n;
    for (year = 1; year <= n; ++year)   {
        val -= deprec;
        writeoutput(year, deprec, val);
    }
    return;
}

void ddb(float val, int n)      /* double-declining-balance method */

{
    float deprec;
    int year;

    for (year = 1; year <= n; ++year)  {
        deprec = 2*val/n;
        val -= deprec;
        writeoutput(year, deprec, val);
    }
    return;
}

void syd(float val, int n)      /* sum-of-the-years'-digits method */

{
    float tag, deprec;
    int year;

    tag = val;
    for (year = 1; year <= n; ++year)   {
        deprec = (n-year+1)*tag / (n*(n+1)/2);
        val -= deprec;
        writeoutput(year, deprec, val);
    }
    return;
}

void writeoutput(int year, float depreciation, float value)      /* display output data */

{
    printf("End of Year %2d", year);
    printf("  Depreciation: %7.2f", depreciation);
    printf("  Current Value: %8.2f\n", value);
    return;
}
```

Notice that the switch statement is still employed, as in Example 6.26, though there are now only three choices rather than four. (The fourth choice, which ended the computation in the previous version, is now handled through interactive dialog at the end of each set of calculations.) A separate function is now provided for each type of calculation. In particular, the straight-line calculations are carried out within function sl, the double-declining-balance calculations within ddb, and the sum-of-the-years'-digits calculations within syd. Each of these functions includes the formal arguments val and n, which represent the original value of the item and its lifetime, respectively. Note that the value of val is altered within each function, although the original value assigned to val remains unaltered within main. It is this feature that allows repeated sets of calculations with the same input data.

The last function, writeoutput, causes the results of each set of calculations to be displayed on a year-by-year basis. This function is accessed from sl, ddb and syd. In each call to writeoutput, the *altered* value of val is transferred as an actual argument, along with the current year (year) and the current year's depreciation (deprec). Note that these quantities are called value, year and depreciation, respectively, within writeoutput.

A sample interactive session which makes use of this program is shown below.

```
Original value: 8000
Number of years: 10


Method: (1-SL   2-DDB   3-SYD) 1


Straight-Line Method


End of Year  1  Depreciation:  800.00  Current Value:  7200.00
End of Year  2  Depreciation:  800.00  Current Value:  6400.00
End of Year  3  Depreciation:  800.00  Current Value:  5600.00
End of Year  4  Depreciation:  800.00  Current Value:  4800.00
End of Year  5  Depreciation:  800.00  Current Value:  4000.00
End of Year  6  Depreciation:  800.00  Current Value:  3200.00
End of Year  7  Depreciation:  800.00  Current Value:  2400.00
End of Year  8  Depreciation:  800.00  Current Value:  1600.00
End of Year  9  Depreciation:  800.00  Current Value:   800.00
End of Year 10  Depreciation:  800.00  Current Value:     0.00



Another calculation? (Y/N) y
Enter a new set of data? (Y/N) n


Method: (1-SL   2-DDB   3-SYD) 2


Double-Declining-Balance Method


End of Year  1  Depreciation: 1600.00  Current Value:  6400.00
End of Year  2  Depreciation: 1280.00  Current Value:  5120.00
End of Year  3  Depreciation: 1024.00  Current Value:  4096.00
End of Year  4  Depreciation:  819.20  Current Value:  3276.80
End of Year  5  Depreciation:  655.36  Current Value:  2621.44
End of Year  6  Depreciation:  524.29  Current Value:  2097.15
End of Year  7  Depreciation:  419.43  Current Value:  1677.72
End of Year  8  Depreciation:  335.54  Current Value:  1342.18
End of Year  9  Depreciation:  268.44  Current Value:  1073.74
End of Year 10  Depreciation:  214.75  Current Value:   858.99



Another calculation? (Y/N) y
Enter a new set of data? (Y/N) n


Method: (1-SL   2-DDB   3-SYD) 3


Sum-Of-The-Years'-Digits Method
```

```
End of Year  1  Depreciation: 1454.55  Current Value:  6545.45
End of Year  2  Depreciation: 1309.09  Current Value:  5236.36
End of Year  3  Depreciation: 1163.64  Current Value:  4072.73
End of Year  4  Depreciation: 1018.18  Current Value:  3054.55
End of Year  5  Depreciation:  872.73  Current Value:  2181.82
End of Year  6  Depreciation:  727.27  Current Value:  1454.55
End of Year  7  Depreciation:  581.82  Current Value:   872.73
End of Year  8  Depreciation:  436.36  Current Value:   436.36
End of Year  9  Depreciation:  290.91  Current Value:   145.45
End of Year 10  Depreciation:  145.45  Current Value:     0.00


Another calculation? (Y/N) y
Enter a new set of data? (Y/N) y


Original value: 5000
Number of years: 4


Method: (1-SL  2-DDB  3-SYD) 1

Straight-Line Method

End of Year  1  Depreciation: 1250.00  Current Value:  3750.00
End of Year  2  Depreciation: 1250.00  Current Value:  2500.00
End of Year  3  Depreciation: 1250.00  Current Value:  1250.00
End of Year  4  Depreciation: 1250.00  Current Value:     0.00


Another calculation? (Y/N) y
Enter a new set of data? (Y/N) n


Method: (1-SL  2-DDB  3-SYD) 2

Double-Declining-Balance Method

End of Year  1  Depreciation: 2500.00  Current Value:  2500.00
End of Year  2  Depreciation: 1250.00  Current Value:  1250.00
End of Year  3  Depreciation:  625.00  Current Value:   625.00
End of Year  4  Depreciation:  312.50  Current Value:   312.50


Another calculation? (Y/N) n

Goodbye, have a nice day!
```

Notice that two different sets of input data are processed. Depreciation is calculated for the first set using all three methods, and for the second set using only the first two methods. Thus, it is not necessary to reenter the input data simply to recalculate the depreciation using a different method.

Array arguments are passed differently than single-valued data items. If an array name is specified as an actual argument, the individual array elements are not copied. Instead, the *location* of the array (i.e., the location of the first element) is passed to the function. If an element of the array is then accessed within the function, the access will refer to the location of that array element relative to the location of the first element.

Thus, *any alteration to an array element within the function will carry over to the calling routine.* We will discuss this in greater detail in Chap. 9, when we formally consider arrays.

There are also other kinds of data structures that can be passed as arguments to a function. We will discuss the transfer of such arguments in later chapters, as the additional data structures are introduced.

7.6 RECURSION

Recursion is a process by which a function calls itself repeatedly, until some specified condition has been satisfied. The process is used for repetitive computations in which each action is stated in terms of a previous result. Many iterative (i.e., repetitive) problems can be written in this form.

In order to solve a problem recursively, two conditions must be satisfied. First, the problem must be written in a recursive form, and second, the problem statement must include a stopping condition. Suppose, for example, we wish to calculate the factorial of a positive integer quantity. We would normally express this problem as $n! = 1 \times 2 \times 3 \times \cdots \times n$, where n is the specified positive integer (see Example 7.5). However, we can also express this problem in another way, by writing $n! = n \times (n - 1)!$ This is a recursive statement of the problem, in which the desired action (the calculation of $n!$) is expressed in terms of a previous result [the value of $(n - 1)!$, which is assumed to be known]. Also, we know that $1! = 1$ by definition. This last expression provides a stopping condition for the recursion.

EXAMPLE 7.14 Calculating Factorials   In Example 7.10 we saw two versions of a program that calculates the factorial of a given input quantity, using a nonrecursive function to perform the actual calculations. Here is a program that carries out this same calculation using recursion.

```c
/* calculate the factorial of an integer quantity using recursion */

#include <stdio.h>

long int factorial(int n);        /* function prototype */

main()

{
    int n;
    long int factorial(int n);

    /* read in the integer quantity */

    printf("n = ");
    scanf("%d", &n);

    /* calculate and display the factorial */

    printf("n! = %ld\n",  factorial(n));
}

long int factorial(int n)        /* calculate the factorial */

{
    if (n <= 1)
        return(1);
    else
        return(n * factorial(n - 1));
}
```

The main portion of the program simply reads the integer quantity n and then calls the long-integer recursive function `factorial`. (Recall that we use long integers for this calculation because factorials are such large integer quantities, even for modest values of n.) The function `factorial` calls itself recursively, with an actual argument (n - 1) that decreases in magnitude for each successive call. The recursive calls terminate when the value of the actual argument becomes equal to 1.

Notice that the present form of `factorial` is simpler than the function presented in Example 7.10. The close correspondence between this function and the original problem definition, in recursive terms, should be readily apparent. In particular, note that the `if-else` statement includes a termination condition that becomes active when the value of n is less than or equal to 1. (Note that the value of n will never be less than 1 unless an improper initial value is entered into the computer.)

When the program is executed, the function `factorial` will be accessed repeatedly, once in `main` and $(n - 1)$ times within itself, though the person using the program will not be aware of this. Only the final answer will be displayed; for example,

```
n = 10
```

```
n! = 3628800
```

When a recursive program is executed, the recursive function calls are not executed immediately. Rather, they are placed on a *stack* until the condition that terminates the recursion is encountered.[*] The function calls are then executed in reverse order, as they are "popped" off the stack. Thus, when evaluating a factorial recursively, the function calls will proceed in the following order.

$$n! = n \times (n - 1)!$$
$$(n - 1)! = (n - 1) \times (n - 2)!$$
$$(n - 2)! = (n - 2) \times (n - 3)!$$
$$\cdots\cdots\cdots\cdots\cdots\cdots\cdots\cdots$$
$$2! = 2 \times 1!$$

The actual values will then be returned in the following reverse order.

$$1! = 1$$
$$2! = 2 \times 1! = 2 \times 1 = 2$$
$$3! = 3 \times 2! = 3 \times 2 = 6$$
$$4! = 4 \times 3! = 4 \times 6 = 24$$
$$\cdots\cdots\cdots\cdots\cdots\cdots\cdots$$
$$n! = n \times (n - 1)! = \cdots$$

This reversal in the order of execution is a characteristic of all functions that are executed recursively.

If a recursive function contains local variables, a *different* set of local variables will be created during each call. The names of the local variables will, of course, always be the same, as declared within the function. However, the variables will represent a different set of values each time the function is executed. Each set of values will be stored on the stack, so that they will be available as the recursive process "unwinds," i.e., as the various function calls are "popped" off the stack and executed.

EXAMPLE 7.15 Printing Backwards   The following program reads in a line of text on a character-by-character basis, and then displays the characters in reverse order. The program utilizes recursion to carry out the reversal of the characters.

---

[*] A *stack* is a *last-in*, *first-out* data structure in which successive data items are "pushed down" upon preceding data items. The data items are later removed (i.e., they are "popped") from the stack in reverse order, as indicated by the last-in, first-out designation.

```
/* read a line of text and write it out backwards, using recursion */

#include <stdio.h>

#define EOLN  '\n'

void reverse(void);          /* function prototype */

main()

{
    printf("Please enter a line of text below\n");
    reverse();
}

void reverse(void)

/* read a line of characters and write it out backwards */

{
    char c;

    if ((c = getchar()) != EOLN) reverse();
    putchar(c);
    return;
}
```

The main portion of this program simply displays a prompt and then calls the function reverse, thus initiating the recursion. The recursive function reverse then proceeds to read single characters until an end-of-line designation (\n) is encountered. Each function call causes a new character (a new value for c) to be pushed onto the stack. Once the end of line is encountered, the successive characters are popped off the stack and displayed on a last-in, first-out basis. Thus, the characters are displayed in reverse order.

Suppose the program is executed with the following line of input:

```
Now is the time for all good men to come to the aid of their country!
```

Then the corresponding output will be

```
!yrtnuoc rieht fo dia eht ot emoc ot nem doog lla rof emit eht si woN
```

Sometimes a complicated repetitive process can be programmed very concisely using recursion, though the logic may be tricky. The following example provides a well-known illustration.

EXAMPLE 7.16 The Towers of Hanoi   The *Towers of Hanoi* is a well-known children's game, played with three poles and a number of different-sized disks. Each disk has a hole in the center, allowing it to be stacked around any of the poles. Initially, the disks are stacked on the leftmost pole in the order of decreasing size, i.e., the largest on the bottom and the smallest on the top, as illustrated in Fig. 7.1.

The object of the game is to transfer the disks from the leftmost pole to the rightmost pole, without ever placing a larger disk on top of a smaller disk. Only one disk may be moved at a time, and each disk must always be placed around one of the poles.

The general strategy is to consider one of the poles to be the origin, and another to be the destination. The third pole will be used for intermediate storage, thus allowing the disks to be moved without placing a larger disk over a smaller one. Assume there are n disks, numbered from smallest to largest, as in Fig. 7.1. If the disks are initially stacked on the left pole, the problem of moving all n disks to the right pole can be stated in the following recursive manner.

1.   Move the top $n - 1$ disks from the left pole to the center pole.

2.   Move the nth disk (the largest disk) to the right pole.

3.   Move the $n-1$ disks on the center pole to the right pole.

The problem can be solved in this manner for any value of n greater than 0 ($n = 0$ represents a stopping condition).

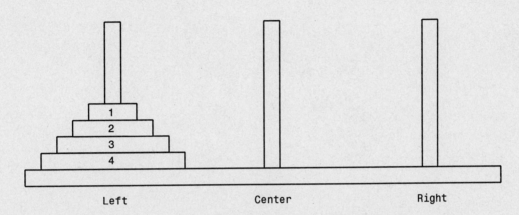

Left   Center   Right

Fig. 7.1

In order to program this game we first label the poles so that the left pole is represented as L, the center pole as C and the right pole as R. We then construct a recursive function called `transfer` that will transfer n disks from one pole to another. Let us refer to the individual poles with the char-type variables `from`, `to` and `temp` for the origin, destination, and temporary storage, respectively. Thus, if we assign the character L to `from`, R to `to` and C to `temp`, we will in effect be specifying the movement of n disks from the leftmost pole to the rightmost pole, using the center pole for intermediate storage.

With this notation, the function will have the following skeletal structure.

```
void transfer(int n, char from, char to, char temp)
/*    n = number of disks
   from = origin
     to = destination
   temp = temporary storage */

{
   if (n > 0)   {

      /* move n-1 disks from their origin to the temporary pole */

      /* move the nth disk from its origin to its destination */

      /* move the n-1 disks from the temporary pole to their destination */

   }
}
```

The transfer of the $n-1$ disks can be accomplished by a recursive call to `transfer`. Thus, we can write

```
transfer(n-1, from, temp, to);
```

for the first transfer, and

```
        transfer(n-1, temp, to, from);
```

for the second. (*Note the order of the arguments in each call.*) The movement of the *n*th disk from the origin to the destination simply requires writing out the current values of from and to. Hence, the complete function can be written as follows.

```
    void transfer(int n, char from, char to, char temp)

    /* transfer n disks from one pole to another */

    /* n    = number of disks
       from = origin
       to   = destination
       temp = temporary storage */

    {
       if (n > 0)   {
          /* move n-1 disks from origin to temporary */
          transfer(n-1, from, temp, to);

          /* move nth disk from origin to destination */
          printf("Move disk %d from %c to %c\n", n, from, to);

          /* move n-1 disks from temporary to destination */
          transfer(n-1, temp, to, from);
       }
       return;
    }
```

It is now a simple matter to add the main portion of the program, which merely reads in a value for *n* and then initiates the computation by calling transfer. In this first function call, the actual parameters will be specified as character constants, i.e.,

```
        transfer(n, 'L', 'R', 'C');
```

This function call specifies the transfer of all *n* disks from the leftmost pole (the origin) to the rightmost pole (the destination), using the center pole for intermediate storage.

Here is the complete program.

```
    /* the TOWERS OF HANOI - solved using recursion */

    #include <stdio.h>

    void transfer(int n, char from, char to, char temp);        /* function prototype */

    main()
    {
       int n;

       printf("Welcome to the TOWERS OF HANOI\n\n");
       printf("How many disks? ");
       scanf("%d", &n);
       printf("\n");
       transfer(n,'L','R','C');
    }
```

```
    void transfer(int n, char from, char to, char temp)

    /* transfer n disks from one pole to another */

    /* n    = number of disks
       from = origin
       to   = destination
       temp = temporary storage */

    {
        if (n > 0)   {
            /* move n-1 disks from origin to temporary */
            transfer(n-1, from, temp, to);

            /* move nth disk from origin to destination */
            printf("Move disk %d from %c to %c\n", n, from, to);

            /* move n-1 disks from temporary to destination */
            transfer(n-1, temp, to, from);
        }
        return;
    }
```

It should be understood that the function transfer receives a different set of values for its arguments each time the function is called. These sets of values will be pushed onto the stack independently of one another, and then popped from the stack at the proper time during the execution of the program. It is this ability to store and retrieve these independent sets of values that allows the recursion to work.

When the program is executed for the case where $n = 3$, the following output is obtained.

```
Welcome to the TOWERS OF HANOI

How many disks? 3

Move disk 1 from L to R
Move disk 2 from L to C
Move disk 1 from R to C
Move disk 3 from L to R
Move disk 1 from C to L
Move disk 2 from C to R
Move disk 1 from L to R
```

You should study these moves carefully to verify that the solution is indeed correct. The logic is very tricky, despite the apparent simplicity of the program.

We will see another programming example that utilizes recursion in Chap. 11, when we discuss linked lists.

The use of recursion is not necessarily the best way to approach a problem, even though the problem definition may be recursive in nature. A nonrecursive implementation may be more efficient, in terms of memory utilization and execution speed. Thus, the use of recursion may involve a tradeoff between simplicity and performance. Each problem should therefore be judged on its own individual merits.

Review Questions

7.1   What is a function? Are functions required when writing a C program?

7.2   State three advantages to the use of functions.

7.3   What is meant by a function call? From what parts of a program can a function be called?

7.4   What are arguments? What is their purpose? What other term is sometimes used for an argument?

7.5   What is the purpose of the `return` statement?

7.6   What are the two principal components of a function definition?

7.7   How is the first line of a function definition written? What is the purpose of each item, or group of items?

7.8   What are formal arguments? What are actual arguments? What is the relationship between formal arguments and actual arguments?

7.9   Describe some alternate terms that are used in place of *formal argument* and *actual argument*.

7.10 Can the names of the formal arguments within a function coincide with the names of other variables defined outside of the function? Explain.

7.11 Can the names of the formal arguments within a function coincide with the names of other variables defined within the function? Explain, and compare your answer with the answer to the last question.

7.12 Summarize the rules governing the use of the `return` statement. Can multiple expressions be included in a `return` statement? Can multiple `return` statements be included in a function?

7.13 What relationship must exist between the data type appearing at the beginning of the the first line of the function definition and the value returned by the `return` statement?

7.14 Why might a `return` statement be included in a function that does not return any value?

7.15 What is the purpose of the keyword `void`? Where is this keyword used?

7.16 Summarize the rules that apply to a function call. What relationships must be maintained between the actual arguments and the corresponding formal arguments in the function definition? Are the actual arguments subject to the same restrictions as the formal arguments?

7.17 Can a function be called from more than one place within a program?

7.18 What are function prototypes? What is their purpose? Where within a program are function prototypes normally placed?

7.19 Summarize the rules associated with function prototypes. What is the purpose of each item or group of items?

7.20 How are argument data types specified in a function prototype? What is the value of including argument data types in a function prototype?

7.21 When a function is accessed, must the names of the actual arguments agree with the names of the arguments in the corresponding function prototype?

7.22 Suppose function F1 calls function F2 within a C program. Does the order of the function definitions make any difference? Explain.

7.23 Describe the manner in which an actual argument passes information to a function. What name is associated with this process? What are the advantages and disadvantages to passing arguments in this manner?

7.24 What are differences between passing an array to a function and passing a single-valued data item to a function?

7.25 Suppose an array is passed to a function as an argument. If the value of an array element is altered within the function, will this change be recognized within the calling portion of the program?

7.26 What is recursion? What advantage is there in its use?

7.27 Explain why some problems can be solved either with or without recursion.

7.28 What is a stack? In what order is information added to and removed from a stack?

7.29 Explain what happens when a program containing recursive function calls is executed, in terms of information being added to and removed from the stack.

7.30   When a program containing recursive function calls is executed, how are the local variables within the recursive function interpreted?

7.31   If a repetitive process is programmed recursively, will the resulting program necessarily be more efficient than a nonrecursive version?

Problems

7.32   Explain the meaning of each of the following function prototypes.

(*a*)   `int f(int a);`
(*b*)   `double f(double a, int b);`
(*c*)   `void f(long a, short b, unsigned c);`
(*d*)   `char f(void);`
(*e*)   `unsigned f(unsigned a, unsigned b);`

7.33   Each of the following is the first line of a function definition. Explain the meaning of each.

(*a*)   `float f(float a, float b)`   (*c*)   `void f(int a)`
(*b*)   `long f(long a)`   (*d*)   `char f(void)`

7.34   Write an appropriate function call (function access) for each of the following functions.

(*a*)   `float formula(float x)`   (*b*)   `void display(int a, int b)`
```
        {                                            {
            float y;                                     int c;

            y = 3 * x - 1;                               c = sqrt(a * a + b * b);
            return(y);                                   printf("c = %i\n", c);
        }                                            }
```

7.35   Write the first line of the function definition, including the formal argument declarations, for each of the situations described below.

(*a*)   A function called `sample` generates and returns an integer quantity.

(*b*)   A function called `root` accepts two integer arguments and returns a floating-point result.

(*c*)   A function called `convert` accepts a character and returns another character.

(*d*)   A function called `transfer` accepts a long integer and returns a character.

(*e*)   A function called `inverse` accepts a character and returns a long integer.

(*f*)   A function called `process` accepts an integer and two floating-point quantities (in that order), and returns a double-precision quantity.

(*g*)   A function called `value` accepts two double-precision quantities and a short-integer quantity (in that order). The input quantities are processed to yield a double-precision value which is displayed as a final result.

7.36   Write appropriate function prototypes for each of the skeletal outlines shown below.

(*a*)   `main()`
```
        {
            int a, b, c;

            . . .

            c = funct1(a, b);

            . . .

        }
```

```
    int funct1(int x, int y)
    {
        int z;

        z = . . .;
        return(z);
    }
```

(b)
```
    main()
    {
        double a, b, c;

        . . .

        c = funct1(a, b);

        . . .
    }
```

```
    double funct1(double x, double y)
    {
        double z;

        z = . . .;
        return(z);
    }
```

(c)
```
    main()
    {
        int a;
        float b;
        long int c;

        . . .

        c = funct1(a, b);

        . . .
    }
```

```
    long int funct1(int x, float y)
    {
        long int z;

        z = . . .;
        return(z);
    }
```

(d)
```
    main()
    {
        double a, b, c, d;

        . . .

        c = funct1(a, b);

        . . .

        d = funct2(a + b, a + c);
    }
```

```
double funct1(double x, double y)
{
   double z;

   . . .

   z = 10 * funct2(x, y);
   return(z);
}


double funct2(double x, double y)
{
   double z;

   z = . . .;
   return(z);
}
```

7.37 Describe the output generated by each of the following programs.

(a)
```
#include <stdio.h>

int funct(int count);

main()
{
   int a, count;

   for (count = 1; count <= 5; ++count)   {
       a = funct1(count);
       printf("%d  ", a);
   }
}


int funct1(int x)
{
   int y;

   y = x * x;
   return(y);
}
```

(b)   Show how the preceding program can be written more concisely.

(c)
```
#include <stdio.h>

int funct1(int n);

main()
{
   int n = 10;

   printf("%d", funct1(n));
}


int funct1(int n)
{
   if (n > 0) return(n + funct1(n - 1));
}
```

(d)   ```
       #include <stdio.h>

       int funct1(int n);

       main()
       {
          int n = 10;

          printf("%d", funct1(n));
       }

       int funct1(int n)
       {
          if (n > 0) return(n + funct1(n - 2));
       }
       ```

**7.38**  Express each of the following algebraic formulas in a recursive form.

(a)    $y = (x_1 + x_2 + \cdots + x_n)$

(b)    $y = 1 - x + x^2/2 - x^3/6 + x^4/24 + \cdots + (-1)^n x^n/n!$

(c)    $p = (f_1 * f_2 * \cdots * f_t)$

## Programming Problems

**7.39**  Write a function that will calculate and display the real roots of the quadratic equation

$$ax^2 + bx + c = 0$$

using the quadratic formula

$$x = \frac{-b \pm \sqrt{b^2 - 4ac}}{2a}$$

Assume that $a$, $b$ and $c$ are floating-point arguments whose values are given, and that $x_1$ and $x_2$ are floating-point variables. Also, assume that $b^2 > 4*a*c$, so that the calculated roots will always be real.

**7.40**  Write a complete C program that will calculate the real roots of the quadratic equation

$$ax^2 + bx + c = 0$$

using the quadratic formula, as described in the previous problem. Read the coefficients $a$, $b$ and $c$ in the main portion of the program. Then access the function written for the preceding problem in order to obtain the desired solution. Finally, display the values of the coefficients, followed by the calculated values of $x_1$ and $x_2$. Be sure that all of the output is clearly labeled.

Test the program using the following data:

| $a$ | $b$ | $c$ |
|---|---|---|
| 2 | 6 | 1 |
| 3 | 3 | 0 |
| 1 | 3 | 1 |

**7.41**  Modify the function written for Prob. 7.39 so that *all* roots of the quadratic equation

$$ax^2 + bx + c = 0$$

will be calculated, given the values of $a$, $b$ and $c$. Note that the roots will be repeated (i.e., there will only be one real root) if $b^2 = 4*a*c$. Also, the roots will be complex if $b^2 < 4*a*c$. In this case, the real part of each root will be determined as
       ```

$$-b/(2*a)$$

and the imaginary parts will be calculated as

$$\pm\left(\sqrt{4ac - b^2}\right)i$$

where i represents $\sqrt{-1}$

7.42 Modify the C program written for Prob. 7.40 so that *all* roots of the quadratic equation

$$ax^2 + bx + c = 0$$

will be calculated, using the function written for Prob. 7.41. Be sure that all of the output is clearly labeled. Test the program using the following data:

a	b	c
2	6	1
3	3	0
1	3	1
0	12	−3
3	6	3
2	−4	3

7.43 Write a function that will allow a floating-point number to be raised to an integer power. In other words, we wish to evaluate the formula

$$y = x^n$$

where y and x are floating-point variables and n is an integer variable.

7.44 Write a complete C program that will read in numerical values for x and n, evaluate the formula

$$y = x^n$$

using the function written for Prob. 7.43, and then display the calculated result. Test the program using the following data:

x	n	x	n
2	3	1.5	3
2	12	1.5	10
2	−5	1.5	−5
−3	3	0.2	3
−3	7	0.2	5
−3	−5	0.2	−5

7.45 Expand the function written for Prob. 7.43 so that positive values of x can be raised to *any* power, integer or floating-point. (*Hint*: Use the formula

$$y = x^n = e^{(n \ln x)}.$$

Remember to include a test for inappropriate values of x.)

Include this function in the program written for Prob. 7.44. Test the program using the data given in Prob. 7.44, and the following additional data.

x	n	x	n
2	0.2	1.5	0.2
2	−0.8	1.5	−0.8
−3	0.2	0.2	0.2
−3	−0.8	0.2	−0.8
		0.2	0.0

7.46   Modify the program for calculating the solution of an algebraic equation, given in Example 6.22, so that each iteration is carried out within a separate function. Compile and execute the program to be sure that it runs correctly.

7.47   Modify the program for averaging a list of numbers, given in Example 6.17, so that it makes use of a function to read in the numbers and return their sum. Test the program using the following 10 numbers:

27.5	87.0
13.4	39.9
53.8	47.7
29.2	8.1
74.5	63.2

7.48   Modify the program for carrying out compound interest calculations given in Example 5.2 so that the actual calculations are carried out in a programmer-defined function. Write the function so that the values of P, r and n are entered as arguments, and the calculated value of F is returned. Test the program using the following data.

P	r	n
1000	6	20
1000	6.25	20
333.33	8.75	20
333.33	8.75	22.5

7.49   For each of the following problems, write a complete C program that includes a recursive function.

(a)   The *Legendre polynomials* can be calculated by means of the formulas $P_0 = 1$, $P_1 = x$,

$$P_n = [(2n - 1) / n] \, x \, P_{n-1} - [(n - 1) / n] \, P_{n-2}$$

where $n = 2, 3, 4, \ldots$ and x is any floating-point number between -1 and 1. (Note that the Legendre polynomials are floating-point quantities.)

Generate the first n Legendre polynomials. Let the values of n and x be input parameters.

(b)   Determine the cumulative sum of n floating-point numbers [see Prob. 7.38(a)]. Read a new number into the computer during each call to the recursive function.

(c)   Evaluate the first n terms in the series specified in Prob. 7.38(b). Enter n as an input parameter.

(d)   Determine the cumulative product of n floating-point numbers [see Prob. 7.38(c)]. Read a new number into the computer during each call to the recursive function.

Additional programming problems involving the use of functions can be found at the end of Chap. 8.

Chapter 8

Program Structure

This chapter is concerned with the structure of programs consisting of more than one function. We will first consider the distinction between "local" variables that are recognized only within a single function, and "global" variables that are recognized in two or more functions. We will see how global variables are defined and utilized in this chapter.

We will also consider the issue of static vs. dynamic retention of information by a local variable. That is, a local variable normally does not retain its value once control has been transferred out of its defining function. In some circumstances, however, it may be desirable to have certain local variables retain their values, so that the function can be reentered at a later time and the computation resumed.

And finally, it may be desirable to develop a large, multifunction program in terms of several independent files, with a small number of functions (perhaps only one) defined within each file. In such programs the individual functions can be defined and accessed locally within a single file, or globally within multiple files. This is similar to the definition and use of local vs. global variables in a multifunction, single-file program.

8.1 STORAGE CLASSES

We have already mentioned that there are two different ways to characterize variables: by *data type*, and by *storage class* (see Sec. 2.6). Data type refers to the type of information represented by a variable, e.g., integer number, floating-point number, character, etc. Storage class refers to the permanence of a variable, and its *scope* within the program, i.e., the portion of the program over which the variable is recognized.

There are four different storage-class specifications in C: *automatic*, *external*, *static* and *register*. They are identified by the keywords `auto`, `extern`, `static`, and `register`, respectively. We will discuss the *automatic*, *external* and *static* storage classes within this chapter. The *register* storage class will be discussed in Sec. 13.1.

The storage class associated with a variable can sometimes be established simply by the location of the variable declaration within the program. In other situations, however, the keyword that specifies a particular storage class must be placed at the beginning of the variable declaration.

EXAMPLE 8.1 Shown below are several typical variable declarations that include the specification of a storage class.

```
auto int a, b, c;

extern float root1, root2;

static int count = 0;

extern char star;
```

The first declaration states that `a`, `b` and `c` are automatic integer variables, and the second declaration establishes `root1` and `root2` as external floating-point variables. The third declaration states that `count` is a static integer variable whose initial value is 0, and the last declaration establishes `star` as an external character-type variable.

The exact procedure for establishing a storage class for a variable depends upon the particular storage class, and the manner in which the program is organized (i.e., single file vs. multiple file). We will consider these rules in the next few sections of this chapter.

8.2 AUTOMATIC VARIABLES

Automatic variables are always declared within a function and are local to the function in which they are declared; that is, their scope is confined to that function. Automatic variables defined in different functions will therefore be independent of one another, even though they may have the same name.

Any variable declared within a function is interpreted as an automatic variable unless a different storage-class specification is shown within the declaration. This includes formal argument declarations. All of the variables in the programming examples encountered earlier in this book have been automatic variables.

Since the location of the variable declarations within the program determines the automatic storage class, the keyword auto is not required at the beginning of each variable declaration. There is no harm in including an auto specification within a declaration, though this is normally not done.

EXAMPLE 8.2 Calculating Factorials   Consider once again the program for calculating factorials, originally shown in Example 7.10. Within main, n is an automatic variable. Within factorial, i and prod, as well as the formal argument n, are automatic variables.

The storage-class designation auto could have been included explicitly in the variable declarations if we had wished. Thus, the program could have been written as follows.

```
#/* calculate the factorial of an integer quantity */

include <stdio.h>

long int factorial(int n);

main()
{
    auto int n;

    /* read in the integer quantity */

    printf("\nn = ");
    scanf("%d", &n);

    /* calculate and display the factorial */

    printf("\nn! = %ld", factorial(n));
}

long int factorial(auto int n)         /* calculate the factorial */
{
    auto int i;
    auto long int prod = 1;

    if (n > 1)
       for (i = 2; i <= n; ++i)
           prod *= i;
    return(prod);
}
```

Either method is acceptable. As a rule, however, the auto designation is not included in variable or formal argument declarations, since this is the default storage class. Thus, the program shown in Example 7.10 represents a more common programming style.

Automatic variables can be assigned initial values by including appropriate expressions within the variable declarations, as in the above example, or by explicit assignment expressions elsewhere in the function. Such values will be reassigned each time the function is reentered. If an automatic variable is not initialized in some manner, however, its initial value will be unpredictable, and probably unintelligible.

An automatic variable does not retain its value once control is transferred out of its defining function. Therefore, any value assigned to an automatic variable within a function will be lost once the function is exited. If the program logic requires that an automatic variable be assigned a particular value each time the function is executed, that value will have to be reset whenever the function is reentered (i.e., whenever the function is accessed).

EXAMPLE 8.3 Average Length of Several Lines of Text   Let us now write a C program that will read several lines of text and determine the average number of characters (including punctuation and blank spaces) in each line. We will structure the program in such a manner that it continues to read additional lines of text until an empty line (i.e., a line whose first character is \n) is encountered.

We will utilize a function (linecount) that reads a single line of text and counts the number of characters, excluding the newline character (\n) that signifies the end of the line. The calling routine (main) will maintain a cumulative sum, as well as a running total of the number of lines that have been read. The function will be called repeatedly (thus reading a new line each time), until an empty line is encountered. The program will then divide the cumulative number of characters by the total number of lines to obtain an average.

Here is the entire program.

```
/* read several lines of text and determine the average number of characters per line */

#include <stdio.h>

int linecount(void);

main()

{
    int n;                      /* number of chars in given line */
    int count = 0;              /* number of lines */
    int sum = 0;                /* total number of characters */
    float avg;                  /* average number of chars per line */

    printf("Enter the text below\n");

    /* read a line of text and update the cumulative counters */

    while ((n = linecount()) > 0)   {
        sum += n;
        ++count;
    }

    avg = (float) sum / count;
    printf("\nAverage number of characters per line: %5.2f", avg);
}

int linecount(void)

/* read a line of text and count the number of characters */

{
    char line[80];
    int count = 0;

    while ((line[count] = getchar()) != '\n')
        ++count;
    return (count);
}
```

We see that `main` contains four automatic variables: `n, count, sum` and `avg`, whereas `linecount` contains two: `line` and `count`. (Notice that `line` is an 80-element character array, representing the contents of one line of text.) Three of these automatic variables are assigned initial values of zero.

Also, note that `count` has different meanings within each function. Within `linecount, count` represents the number of characters in a single line, whereas within `main, count` represents the total number of lines that have been read. Moreover, `count` is reset to zero within `linecount` whenever the function is accessed. This does not affect the value of `count` within `main`, since the variables are independent of one another. It would have been clearer if we had named these variables differently, e.g., `count` and `lines`, or perhaps `chars` and `lines`. We have used the same name for both variables to illustrate the independence of automatic variables within different functions.)

A sample interactive session, resulting from execution of this program, is shown below. As usual, the user's responses are underlined.

```
Enter the text below
Now is the time for all good men
to come to the aid of their country.

Average number of characters per line: 34.00
```

The scope of an automatic variable can be smaller than an entire function if we wish. In fact, automatic variables can be declared within a single compound statement. With small, simple programs there is usually no advantage in doing this, but it may be desirable in larger programs.

8.3 EXTERNAL (GLOBAL) VARIABLES

External variables, in contrast to automatic variables, are not confined to single functions. Their scope extends from the point of definition through the remainder of the program. Hence, they usually span two or more functions, and often an entire program. They are often referred to as *global variables*.

Since external variables are recognized globally, they can be accessed from any function that falls within their scope. They retain their assigned values within this scope. Therefore an external variable can be assigned a value within one function, and this value can be used (by accessing the external variable) within another function.

The use of external variables provides a convenient mechanism for transferring information back and forth between functions. In particular, we can transfer information into a function without using arguments. This is especially convenient when a function requires numerous input data items. Moreover, we now have a way to transfer multiple data items out of a function, since the `return` statement can return only one data item. (We will see another way to transfer information back and forth between functions in Chap. 10, where we discuss pointers.)

When working with external variables, we must distinguish between external variable *definitions* and external variable *declarations*. An external variable *definition* is written in the same manner as an ordinary variable declaration. It must appear outside of, and usually before, the functions that access the external variables. An external variable definition will automatically allocate the required storage space for the external variables within the computer's memory. The assignment of initial values can be included within an external variable definition if desired (more about this later).

The storage-class specifier `extern` is not required in an external variable definition, since the external variables will be identified by the location of their definition within the program. In fact, many C compilers forbid the use of `extern` within an external variable definition. We will follow this convention within this book.

If a function requires an external variable that has been defined earlier in the program, then the function may access the external variable freely, without any special declaration within the function. (Remember, however, that *any alteration to the value an external variable within a function will be recognized within the entire scope of the external variable*.) On the other hand, if the function definition *precedes* the external variable definition, then the function must include a *declaration* for that external variable. The function definitions within a large program often include external variable declarations, whether they are needed or not, as a matter of good programming practice.

An external variable *declaration* must begin with the storage-class specifier `extern`. The name of the external variable and its data type must agree with the corresponding external variable definition that appears outside of the function. Storage space for external variables will *not* be allocated as a result of an external variable declaration. Moreover, an external variable declaration *cannot* include the assignment of initial values. These distinctions between an external variable *definition* and an external variable *declaration* are very important.

EXAMPLE 8.4 Search for a Maximum　　　Suppose we wish to find the particular value of x that causes the function

$$y = x \cos(x)$$

to be maximized within the interval bounded by $x = 0$ on the left and $x = \pi$ on the right. We will require that the maximizing value of x be known very accurately. We will also require that the search scheme be relatively efficient in the sense that the function $y = x \cos(x)$ should be evaluated as few times as possible.

One obvious way to solve this problem would be to generate a large number of closely spaced trial functions (that is, evaluate the function at $x = 0$, $x = 0.0001$, $x = 0.0002$, . . . , $x = 3.1415$, and $x = 3.1416$) and determine the largest of these by visual inspection. This would not be very efficient, however, and it would require human intervention to obtain the final result. Instead let us use the following *elimination scheme*, which is a highly efficient computational procedure for all functions that have only one maximum (i.e., only one "peak") within the search interval.

The computation will be carried out as follows. We begin with two search points at the center of the search interval, located a very small distance from each other, as shown in Fig. 8.1.

The following notation is used.

　　　　a　= left end of the search interval
　　　xl　= left-hand interior search point
　　　xr　= right-hand interior search point
　　　　b　= right end of the search interval
　　sep　= distance between xl and xr.

If a, b and sep are known, then the interior points can be calculated as

```
xl = a + .5 * (b - a - sep)

xr = a + .5 * (b - a + sep) = xl + sep
```

Let us evaluate the function y = x cos(x) at xl and at xr. We will call these values yl and yr, respectively. Suppose yl turns out to be greater than yr. Then the maximum will lie somewhere between a and xr. Hence we retain only that portion of the search interval which ranges from x = a to x = xr. We will now refer to the old point xr as b, since it is now the right end of the new search interval, and generate two *new* search points, xl and xr. These points will be located at the center of the new search interval, a distance sep apart, as shown in Fig. 8.2.

On the other hand, suppose now that in our *original* search interval the value of yr turned out to be greater than yl. This would indicate that our new search interval should lie between xl and b. Hence we rename the point which was originally called xl to be a and we generate two *new* search points, xl and xr, at the center of the new search interval, as shown in Fig. 8.3.

We continue to generate a new pair of search points at the center of each new interval, compare the respective values of y, and eliminate a portion of the search interval until the new search interval becomes smaller than 3 * sep. Once this happens we can no longer distinguish the interior points from the boundaries. Hence the search is ended.

Each time we make a comparison between yl and yr, we eliminate that portion of the search interval that contains the smaller value of y. If both interior values of y should happen to be identical (which can happen, though it is unusual), then the search procedure stops, and the maximum is assumed to occur at the center of the last two interior points.

Once the search has ended, either because the search interval has become sufficiently small or because the two interior points yield identical values of y, we can calculate the approximate location of the maximum as

```
xmax = 0.5 * (xl + xr)
```

The corresponding maximum value of the function can then be obtained as xmax cos(xmax).

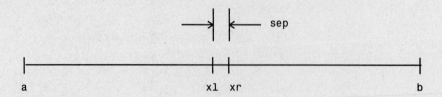

Fig. 8.1

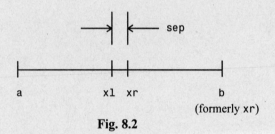

Fig. 8.2

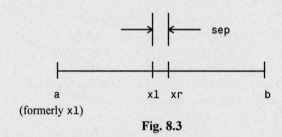

Fig. 8.3

Let us consider a program outline for the general case where a and b are input quantities but sep has a fixed value of 0.0001.

1. Assign a value of sep = 0.0001.

2. Read in the values of a and b.

3. Repeat the following until either yl becomes equal to yr (the desired maximum will be at the midpoint), or the most recent value of (b − a) becomes less than or equal to (3 * sep):

    (*a*)   Generate the two interior points, xl and xr.

    (*b*)   Calculate the corresponding values of yl and yr, and determine which is larger.

    (*c*)   Reduce the search interval, by eliminating that portion that does not contain the larger value of y.

4. Evaluate xmax and ymax.

5. Display the values of xmax and ymax, and stop.

To translate this outline into a program, we first create a programmer-defined function to evaluate the mathematical function y = x cos(x). Let us call this function curve. This function can easily be written as follows.

```
/*  evaluate the function y = x * cos(x)  */

double curve(double x)

{
    return (x * cos(x));
}
```

Note that cos(x) is a call to a C library function.

Now consider step 3 in the above outline, which carries out the interval reduction. This step can also be programmed as a function, which we will call reduce. Notice, however, that the values represented by the variables a, b, xl, xr, yl and yr, which change through the course of the computation, must be transferred back and forth between this function and main. Therefore, let these variables be external variables whose scope includes both reduce and main.

Function reduce can be written as

```c
/* interval reduction routine */

void reduce(void)
{
    xl = a + 0.5 * (b - a - CNST);
    xr = xl + CNST;
    yl = curve(xl);
    yr = curve(xr);

    if (yl > yr)   {     /* retain left interval */
       b = xr;
       return;
    }
    if (yl < yr)         /* retain right interval */
       a = xl;
    return;
}
```

Notice that the parameter that we have referred to earlier as sep is now represented as the character constant CNST. Also, notice that this function does not include any formal arguments, and it does not return anything via the return statement. All of the information transfers involve external variables.

It is now quite simple to write the main portion of the program, which calls the two functions defined above. Here is the entire program.

```c
/* find the maximum of a function within a specified interval */

#include <stdio.h>
#include <math.h>

#define  CNST  0.0001

double a, b, xl, yl, xr, yr;       /* global variables */

void reduce(void);                 /* function prototype */
double curve(double xl);           /* function prototype */

main()
{
    double xmax, ymax;

    /* read input data (interval end points) */

    printf("\na = ");
    scanf("%lf", &a);
    printf("b = ");
    scanf("%lf", &b);

    /* interval reduction loop */

    do
       reduce();
    while ((yl != yr) && ((b - a) > 3 * CNST));
```

```
/* calculate xmax and ymax, and display the results */

    xmax = 0.5 * (xl + xr);
    ymax = curve(xmax);
    printf("\nxmax = %8.6lf   ymax = %8.6lf", xmax, ymax);
}


/* interval reduction routine */

void reduce(void)

{
    xl = a + 0.5 * (b - a - CNST);
    xr = xl + CNST;
    yl = curve(xl);
    yr = curve(xr);

    if (yl > yr)   {      /* retain left interval */
       b = xr;
       return;
    }
    if (yl < yr)        /* retain right interval */
       a = xl;
    return;
}


/*  evaluate the function y = x * cos(x)  */

double curve(double x)

{
    return (x * cos(x));
}
```

The variables a, b, xl, yl, xr and yr are defined as external variables whose scope includes the entire program. Notice that these variables are declared before main begins.

Execution of the program, with a = 0 and b = 3.141593, produces the following interactive session. The user's responses are underlined, as usual.

```
a = 0
b = 3.141593

xmax = 0.860394   ymax = 0.561096
```

Thus, we have obtained the location and the value of the maximum within the given original interval.

External variables can be assigned initial values as a part of the variable definitions, but the initial values must be expressed as *constants* rather than expressions. These initial values will be assigned only once, at the beginning of the program. The external variables will then retain these initial values unless they are later altered during the execution of the program.

If an initial value is not included in the definition of an external variable, the variable will automatically be assigned a value of zero. Thus, external variables are never left dangling with undefined, garbled values. Nevertheless, it is good programming practice to assign an explicit initial value of zero when required by the program logic.

EXAMPLE 8.5 Average Length of Several Lines of Text   Shown below is a modification of the program previously presented in Example 8.3, for determining the average number of characters in several lines of text. The present version makes use of external variables to represent the total (cumulative) number of characters read, and the total number of lines.

```c
/* read several lines of text and determine the average number of characters per line */

#include <stdio.h>

int sum = 0;                  /* total number of characters */
int lines = 0;                /* total number of lines */

int linecount(void);


main()

{
    int n;                    /* number of chars in given line */
    float avg;                /* average number of chars per line */

    printf("Enter the text below\n");

    /* read a line of text and update the cumulative counters */

    while ((n = linecount()) > 0)   {
        sum += n;
        ++lines;
    }

    avg = (float) sum / lines;
    printf("\nAverage number of characters per line: %5.2f", avg);
}


/* read a line of text and count the number of characters */

int linecount(void)

{
    char line[80];
    int count = 0;

    while ((line[count] = getchar()) != '\n')
        ++count;
    return (count);
}
```

Notice that sum and lines are external variables that represent the total (cumulative) number of characters read and the total number of lines, respectively. Both of these variables are assigned initial values of zero. These values are successively modified within main, as additional lines of text are read.

Also, recall that the earlier version of the program used two different automatic variables, each called count in different parts of the program. In the present version of the program, however, the variables that represent the same quantities have different names, since one of the variables (lines) is now an external variable.

You should understand that sum and lines need not be assigned zero values explicitly, since external variables are always set equal to zero unless some other initial value is designated. We include the explicit zero initialization in order to clarify the program logic.

Arrays can also be declared either automatic or external, though automatic arrays cannot be initialized. We will see how initial values are assigned to array elements in Chap. 9.

Finally, it should be pointed out that there are inherent dangers in the use of external variables, since an alteration in the value of an external variable within a function will be carried over into other parts of the program. Sometimes this happens inadvertently, as a *side effect* of some other action. Thus, there is the possibility that the value of an external value will be changed unexpectedly, resulting in a subtle programming error. You should decide carefully which storage class is most appropriate for each particular programming situation.

8.4 STATIC VARIABLES

In this section and the next, we make the distinction between a *single-file* program, in which the entire program is contained within a single source file, and a *multifile* program, where the functions that make up the program are contained in separate source files. The rules governing the static storage class are different in each situation.

In a single-file program, static variables are defined within individual functions and therefore have the same scope as automatic variables; i.e., they are local to the functions in which they are defined. Unlike automatic variables, however, static variables retain their values throughout the life of the program. Thus, if a function is exited and then re-entered at a later time, the static variables defined within that function will retain their former values. This feature allows functions to retain information permanently throughout the execution of a program.

Static variables are defined within a function in the same manner as automatic variables, except that the variable declaration must begin with the `static` storage-class designation. Static variables can be utilized within the function in the same manner as other variables. They cannot, however, be accessed outside of their defining function.

It is not unusual to define automatic or static variables having the same names as external variables. In such situations the local variables will take precedence over the external variables, though the values of the external variables will be unaffected by any manipulation of the local variables. Thus the external variables maintain their independence from locally defined automatic and static variables. The same is true of local variables within one function that have the same names as local variables within another function.

EXAMPLE 8.6 Shown below is the skeletal structure of a C program that includes variables belonging to several different storage classes.

```
float a, b, c;

void dummy(void);

main()
{
    static float a;

    . . . . .
}

void dummy(void)
{
    static int a;
    int b;

    . . . . .
}
```

Within this program a, b and c are external, floating-point variables. However, a is redefined as a *static* floating-point variable within `main`. Therefore, b and c are the only external variables that will be recognized within `main`. Note that the static *local* variable a will be independent of the *external* variable a.

Similarly, a and b are redefined as integer variables within dummy. Note that a is a static variable, but b is an automatic variable. Thus, a will retain its former value whenever dummy is reentered, whereas b will lose its value whenever control is transferred out of dummy. Furthermore, c is the only *external* variable that will be recognized within dummy.

Since a and b are local to dummy, they will be independent of the external variables a, b and c, and the static variable a defined within main. The fact that a and b are declared as integer variables within dummy and floating-point variables elsewhere is therefore immaterial.

Initial values can be included in the static variable declarations. The rules associated with the assignment of these values are essentially the same as the rules associated with the initialization of external variables, even though the static variables are defined locally within a function. In particular:

1. The initial values must be expressed as constants, not expressions.

2. The initial values are assigned to their respective variables at the beginning of program execution. The variables retain these values throughout the life of the program, unless different values are assigned during the course of the computation.

3. Zeros will be assigned to all static variables whose declarations do not include explicit initial values. Hence, static variables will always have assigned values.

EXAMPLE 8.7 Generating Fibonacci Numbers   The Fibonacci numbers form an interesting sequence in which each number is equal to the sum of the previous two numbers. In other words,

$$F_i = F_{i-1} + F_{i-2}$$

where F_i refers to the ith Fibonacci number. The first two Fibonacci numbers are defined to equal 1; i.e.,

$$F_1 = F_2 = 1$$

Hence

$$F_3 = F_2 + F_1 = 1 + 1 = 2$$
$$F_4 = F_3 + F_2 = 2 + 1 = 3$$
$$F_5 = F_4 + F_3 = 3 + 2 = 5$$

and so on.

Let us write a C program that generates the first n Fibonacci numbers, where n is a value specified by the user. The main portion of the program will read in a value for n, and then enter a loop that generates and writes out each of the Fibonacci numbers. A function called fibonacci will be used to calculate each Fibonacci number from its two preceding values. This function will be called once during each pass through the main loop.

When fibonacci is entered, the computation of the current Fibonacci number, f, is very simple provided the two previous values are known. These values can be retained from one function call to the next if we assign them to the static variables f1 and f2, which represent F_{i-1} and F_{i-2}, respectively. (We could, of course, have used external variables for this purpose, but it is better to use local variables, since F_{i-1} and F_{i-2} are required only within the function.) We then calculate the desired Fibonacci number as

```
f = f1 + f2
```

and update the values of f2 and f1 using the formulas

```
f2 = f1
```

and

```
f1 = f
```

Here is the complete C program.

```
/* program to calculate successive Fibonacci numbers */

#include <stdio.h>

long int fibonacci(int count);

main()

{
    int count, n;

    printf("How many Fibonacci numbers? ");
    scanf("%d", &n);
    printf("\n");

    for (count = 1; count <= n; ++count)
        printf("\ni = %2d   F = %ld", count, fibonacci(count));
}


long int fibonacci(int count)

/* calculate a Fibonacci number using the formulas

   F = 1 for i < 3, and F = F1 + F2 for i >= 3 */

{
    static long int f1 = 1, f2 = 1;
    long int f;

    f = (count < 3) ? 1 : f1 + f2;
    f2 = f1;
    f1 = f;
    return(f);
}
```

Notice that long integers are used to represent the Fibonacci numbers. Also, note that f1 and f2 are static variables that are each assigned an initial value of 1. These initial values are assigned only once, at the beginning of the program execution. The subsequent values are retained between successive function calls, as they are assigned. You should understand that f1 and f2 are strictly local variables, even though they retain their values from one function call to another.

The output corresponding to a value of n = 30 is shown below. As usual, the user's response is underlined.

```
How many Fibonacci numbers? 30

i =  1      F = 1
i =  2      F = 1
i =  3      F = 2
i =  4      F = 3
i =  5      F = 5
i =  6      F = 8
i =  7      F = 13
i =  8      F = 21
i =  9      F = 34
i = 10      F = 55
i = 11      F = 89
i = 12      F = 144
i = 13      F = 233
```

```
i = 14      F =  377
i = 15      F =  610
i = 16      F =  987
i = 17      F =  1597
i = 18      F =  2584
i = 19      F =  4181
i = 20      F =  6765
i = 21      F =  10946
i = 22      F =  17711
i = 23      F =  28657
i = 24      F =  46368
i = 25      F =  75025
i = 26      F =  121393
i = 27      F =  196418
i = 28      F =  317811
i = 29      F =  514229
i = 30      F =  832040
```

It is possible to define and initialize static arrays as well as static single-valued variables. The use of arrays will be discussed in the next chapter.

8.5 MULTIFILE PROGRAMS

A *file* is a collection of information stored as a separate entity within the computer or on an auxiliary storage device. A file can be a collection of data, a source program, a portion of a source program, an object program, etc. In this chapter we will consider a file to be either an entire C program or a portion of a C program, i.e., one or more functions. (See Chap. 12 for a discussion of data files, and their relationship to C programs.)

Until now, we have restricted our attention to C programs that are contained entirely within a single file. Many programs, however, are composed of multiple files. This is especially true of programs that make use of lengthy functions, where each function may occupy a separate file. Or, if there are many small related functions within a program, it may be desirable to place a few functions within each of several files. The individual files will be compiled separately, and then linked together to form one executable object program (see Sec. 5.4). This facilitates the editing and debugging of the program, since each file can be maintained at a manageable size.

Multifile programs allow greater flexibility in defining the scope of both functions and variables. The rules associated with the use of storage classes become more complicated, however, because they apply to functions as well as variables, and more options are available for both external and static variables.

Functions

Let us begin by considering the rules associated with the use of functions. Within a multifile program, a function definition may be either *external* or *static*. An external function will be recognized throughout the entire program, whereas a static function will be recognized only within the file in which it is defined. In each case, the storage class is established by placing the appropriate storage-class designation (i.e., either `extern` or `static`) at the beginning of the function definition. The function is assumed to be *external* if a storage-class designation does not appear.

In general terms, the first line of a function definition can be written as

storage-class *data-type* *name*(*type 1 arg 1*, *type 2 arg 2*, . . .,

type n arg n)

where *storage-class* refers to the storage-class associated with the function, *data-type* refers to the data-type of the value returned by the function, *name* refers to the function name, *type 1, type 2, . . ., type n* refer to the formal argument types, and *arg 1, arg 2, . . ., arg n* refer to the formal arguments themselves. Remember that the storage-class, the data-type, and the formal arguments need not all be present in every function definition.

When a function is defined in one file and accessed in another, the latter file must include a function *declaration*. This declaration identifies the function as an external function whose definition appears elsewhere. Such declarations are usually placed at the beginning of the file, ahead of any function definitions.

It is good programming practice to begin the declaration with the storage-class specifier `extern`. This storage-class specifier is not absolutely necessary, however, since the function will be assumed to be external if a storage-class specifier is not present.

In general terms, a function *declaration* can be written as

storage-class data-type name(argument type 1, argument type 2, . . .,

argument type n);

A function declaration can also be written using full function prototyping (see Sec. 7.4) as

storage-class data-type name(type 1 arg 1, type 2 arg 2, . . .,

type n arg n);

Remember that the storage-class, the data-type and the argument types need not all be present in every function declaration.

To execute a multifile program, each individual file must be compiled and the resulting object files linked together. To do so, we usually combine the source files within a *project*. We then *build* the project (i.e., compile all of the source files and link the resulting object files together into a single executable program). If some of the source files are later changed, we *make* another executable program (i.e., compile the new source files and link the resulting object files, with the unchanged object files, into a new executable program). The details of how this is done will vary from one version of C to another.

EXAMPLE 8.8   Here is a simple program that generates the message "Hello, there!" from within a function. The program consists of two functions: `main` and `output`. Each function appears in a separate file.

First file:

```
/* simple, multifile program to write "Hello, there!" */

#include <stdio.h>

extern void output(void);      /* function prototype */

main()
{
    output();
}
```

Second file:

```
extern void output(void)      /* external function definition */
{
    printf("Hello, there!");
    return;
}
```

Notice that output is assigned the storage class extern, since it must be accessed from a file other than the one in which it is defined; it must therefore be an external function. Hence, the keyword extern is included in both the function declaration (in the first file) and the function definition (in the second file). Since extern is a default storage class, however, we could have omitted the keyword extern from both the function declaration and the function definition. Thus, the program could be written as follows:

First file:

```
/* simple, multifile program to write "Hello, there!" */

#include <stdio.h>

void output(void);      /* function prototype */

main()
{
    output();
}
```

Second file:

```
void output(void)      /* external function definition */
{
    printf("Hello, there!");
    return;
}
```

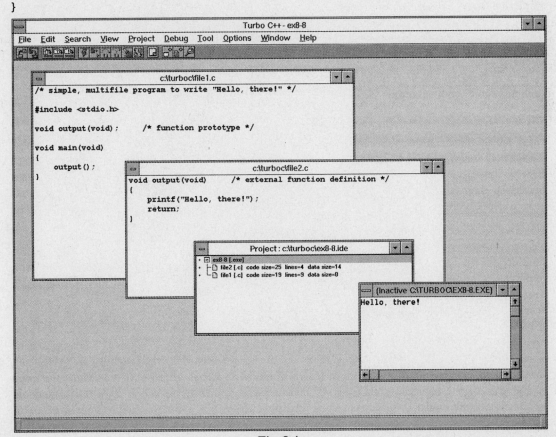

Fig. 8.4

Let us now build a Turbo C++ project corresponding to this multifile program. To do so, we first enter the source code shown in the first file, and save it in a file called FILE1.C. We then enter the source code shown in the second file, and save it in a file called FILE2.C. These two files are shown within separate windows in Fig. 8.4.

Next, we select New from the Project menu, and specify EX8-8.IDE as the project name. This will result in the Project window being opened, as shown near the center of Fig. 8.4. Within this window, we see that the project will result in an executable program called EX8-8.EXE. This executable program will be obtained from the previous two source files, FILE1.C and FILE2.C.

The program can now be executed by selecting Run from the Debug menu, as explained in Chap. 5 (see Example 5.4). The resulting message, Hello, there!, is displayed in the output window, as shown in the lower right portion of Fig. 8.4.

If a file contains a static function, it may be necessary to include the storage class static within the function declaration or the function prototype.

EXAMPLE 8.9 Simulation of a Game of Chance (Shooting Craps)   Here is another version of the craps game simulation, originally presented in Example 7.11. In this version the program consists of two separate files. The first file contains main, whereas the second file contains the functions play and throw.

First file:

```c
/* simulation of a craps game */

#include <stdio.h>
#include <stdlib.h>
#include <ctype.h>

#define  SEED   12345

extern void play(void);      /* function prototype */

main()
{
    char answer = 'Y';

    printf("Welcome to the Game of CRAPS\n\n");
    printf("To throw the dice, press RETURN\n\n");

    srand(SEED);      /* initialize the random number generator */

    /* main loop */

    while (toupper(answer) != 'N')   {
        play();
        printf("\nDo you want to play again? (Y/N) ");
        scanf(" %c", &answer);
        printf("\n");
    }
    printf("Bye, have a nice day");
}
```

Second file:

```c
#include <stdio.h>
#include <stdlib.h>

static int throw(void);           /* function prototype */
extern void play(void)            /* external function definition */
```

```
    /* simulate one complete game */

    {
        int score1, score2;
        char dummy;

        printf("\nPlease throw the dice . . .");
        scanf("%c", &dummy);
        printf("\n");
        score1 = throw();
        printf("\n%2d", score1);

        switch (score1)    {

        case 7:    /* win on first throw */
        case 11:

            printf(" - Congratulations!  You WIN on the first throw\n");
            break;

        case 2:     /* lose on first throw */
        case 3:
        case 12:

            printf(" - Sorry, you LOSE on the first throw\n");
            break;

        case 4:     /* additional throws are required */
        case 5:
        case 6:
        case 8:
        case 9:
        case 10:

            do    {
                    printf(" - Throw the dice again . . .");
                    scanf("%c", &dummy);
                    score2 = throw();
                    printf("\n%2d", score2);
            }  while (score2 != score1 && score2 != 7);

            if (score2 == score1)
               printf(" - You WIN by matching your first score\n");
            else
               printf(" - You LOSE by failing to match your first score\n");
            break;
        }

        return;
    }


    /* simulate one throw of a pair of dice */

    static int throw(void)       /* static function definition */

    {
        float x1, x2;              /* random floating-point numbers between 0 and 1 */
        int n1, n2;                /* random integers between 1 and 6 */
```

```
    x1 = rand() / 32768.0;
    x2 = rand() / 32768.0;

    n1 = 1 + (int) (6 * x1);      /* simulate first die */
    n2 = 1 + (int) (6 * x2);      /* simulate second die */

    return(n1 + n2);              /* score is sum of two dice */
}
```

Notice that play is defined as an external function, so it can be accessed from main (because main and play are defined in separate files). Therefore, play is declared an external function within the first file. On the other hand, throw is accessed only by play. Both throw and play are defined in the second file. Hence throw need not be recognized in the first file. We can therefore define throw to be a static function, confining its scope to the second file.

Also, notice that each file has a separate set of #include statements for the header files stdio.h and stdlib.h. This ensures that the necessary declarations for the library functions are included in each file.

When the individual files are compiled and linked, and the resulting executable program is run, the program generates a dialog identical to that shown in Example 7.11, as expected.

Variables

Within a multifile program, external (global) variables can be defined in one file and accessed in another. We again emphasize the distinction between the *definition* of an external variable and its *declarations*. An external variable *definition* can appear in only one file. Its location within the file must be external to any function definition. Usually, it will appear at the beginning of the file, ahead of the first function definition.

External variable definitions may include initial values. Any external variable that is not assigned an initial value will automatically be initialized to zero. The storage-class specifier extern is not required within the definition; in fact, many versions of C specifically forbid the appearance of this storage-class specifier in external variable *definitions*. Thus, external variable definitions are recognized by their location within the defining files and by their appearance. We will follow this convention in this book.

In order to access an external variable in another file, the variable must first be *declared* within that file. This declaration may appear anywhere within the file. Usually, however, it will be placed at the beginning of the file, ahead of the first function definition. The declaration *must* begin with the storage-class specifier extern. Initial values *cannot* be included in external variable declarations.

The value assigned to an external variable may be altered within any file in which the variable is recognized. Such changes *will* be recognized in all other files that fall within the scope of the variable. Thus, external variables provide a convenient means of transferring information between files.

EXAMPLE 8.10   Shown below is a skeletal outline of a two-file C program that makes use of external variables.

First file:

```
int a = 1, b = 2, c = 3;      /* external variable DEFINITION */
extern void funct1(void);     /* external function DECLARATION */

main()                        /* function DEFINITION */
{
    . . . . .
}
```

Second file:

```
extern int a, b, c              /* external variable DECLARATION */

extern void funct1(void)        /* external function DEFINITION */
{
     . . . . .
}
```

The variables a, b and c are defined as external variables within the first file, and assigned the initial values 1, 2 and 3, respectively. The first file also contains a *definition* of the function main, and a *declaration* for the external function funct1, which is defined elsewhere. Within the second file we see the *definition* of funct1, and a *declaration* for the external variables a, b and c.

Notice that the storage-class specifier extern appears in both the *definition* and the *declaration* of the external function funct1. This storage-class specifier is also present in the *declaration* of the external *variables* (in the second file), but it does *not* appear in the *definition* of the external variables (in the first file).

The scope of a, b and c is the entire program. Therefore these variables can be accessed, and their values altered, in either file, i.e., in either main or funct1.

EXAMPLE 8.11 Search for a Maximum   In Example 8.4 we presented a C program that determines the value of x which causes the function

$$y = x \cos(x)$$

to be maximized within a specified interval. We now present another version of this program, in which each of the three required functions is placed in a separate file.

First file:

```
/* find the maximum of a function within a specified interval */

#include <stdio.h>

double a, b, xl, yl, xr, yr, cnst = 0.0001;    /* external variable definition */

extern void reduce(void);                       /* external function prototype */
extern double curve(double xl);                 /* external function prototype */


main()                                          /* function definition */

{
    double xmax, ymax;

    /* read input data (interval end points) */

    printf("\na = ");
    scanf("%lf", &a);
    printf("b = ");
    scanf("%lf", &b);

    /* interval reduction loop */

    do
        reduce();
    while ((yl != yr) && ((b - a) > 3 * cnst));
```

```
        /* calculate xmax and ymax, and display the results */

        xmax = 0.5 * (xl + xr);
        ymax = curve(xmax);
        printf("\nxmax = %8.6lf   ymax = %8.6lf", xmax, ymax);
}
```

Second file:

```
/* interval reduction routine */

extern double a, b, xl, yl, xr, yr, cnst;        /* external variable declaration */

extern double curve(double xl);                  /* external function prototype */


extern void reduce(void)                         /* external function definition */

{
    xl = a + 0.5 * (b - a - cnst);
    xr = xl + cnst;
    yl = curve(xl);
    yr = curve(xr);

    if (yl > yr)    {       /* retain left interval */
        b = xr;
        return;
    }
    if (yl < yr)            /* retain right interval */
        a = xl;
    return;
}
```

Third file:

```
/*  evaluate the function y = x * cos(x)  */

#include <math.h>

extern double curve(double x)                    /* external function definition */

{
    return (x * cos(x));
}
```

The external function reduce, which is defined in the second file, is declared in the first file. Therefore its scope is the first two files. Similarly, the external function curve, which is defined in the third file, is declared in the first and second files. Hence, its scope is the entire program. Notice that the storage-class specifier extern appears in both the function definitions and the function prototypes.

Now consider the external variables a, b, xl, yl, xr, yr and cnst, which are defined in the first file. Observe that cnst is assigned an initial value within the definition. These variables are utilized, and hence declared, in the second file, but not in the third file. Note that the variable *declaration* (in the second file) includes the storage-class specifier extern, but the variable *definition* (in the first file) does not include a storage-class specifier.

Finally, notice the #include <math.h> statement at the beginning of the third file. This statement causes the header file math.h to be included in the third source file, in support of the cos library function.

Execution of this program results in output that is identical to that shown in Example 8.4.

Within a file, external variables can be defined as static. To do so, the storage-class specifier static is placed at the beginning of the definition. The scope of a static external variable will be the remainder of the file in which it is defined. It will not be recognized elsewhere in the program (i.e, in other files). Thus, the use of static external variables within a file permits a group of variables to be "hidden" from the remainder of a program. Other external variables having the same names can be defined in the remaining files. (Usually, however, it is not be a good idea to use identical variable names. Such identically named variables may cause confusion in understanding the program logic, even though they will not conflict with one another syntactically.)

EXAMPLE 8.12 Generating Fibonacci Numbers   Let us return to the problem of calculating Fibonacci numbers, which we originally considered in Example 8.7. If we rewrite the program as a two-file program employing static external variables, we obtain the following complete program.

First file:

```
/* program to calculate successive Fibonacci numbers */

#include <stdio.h>

extern long int fibonacci(int count);     /* external function prototype */

main()                                     /* function definition */
{
    int count, n;

    printf("How many Fibonacci numbers? ");
    scanf("%d", &n);
    printf("\n");

    for (count = 1; count <= n; ++count)
        printf("\ni = %2d   F = %ld", count, fibonacci(count));
}
```

Second file:

```
/* calculate a Fibonacci number (F = 1 for i < 3, and F = F1 + F2 for i >= 3) */

static long int f1 = 1, f2 = 1;            /* static external variable definition */

long int fibonacci(int count)              /* external function definition */
{
    long int f;

    f = (count < 3) ? 1 : f1 + f2;
    f2 = f1;
    f1 = f;
    return(f);
}
```

In this program the function fibonacci is defined in the second file and declared in the first file, so that its scope is the entire program. On the other hand, the variables f1 and f2 are defined as static external variables in the second file. Their scope is therefore confined to the second file. Note that the variable definition in the second file includes the assignment of initial values.

Execution of this program results in output that is identical to that shown in Example 8.7.

8.6 MORE ABOUT LIBRARY FUNCTIONS

Our discussion of multifile programs can provide additional insight into the use of library functions. Recall that library functions are prewritten routines that carry out various commonly used operations or calculations (see Sec. 3.6). They are contained within one or more library files that accompany each C compiler.

During the process of converting a C source program into an executable object program, the compiled source program may be linked with one or more *library files* to produce the final executable program. Thus, the final program may be assembled from two or more separate files, even though the original source program may have been contained within a single file. The source program must therefore include declarations for the library functions, just as it would for programmer-defined functions that are placed in separate files.

One way to provide the necessary library-function declarations is to write them explicitly, as in the multifile programs presented in the last section. This can become tedious, however, since a small program may make use of several library functions. We wish to simplify the use of library functions to the greatest extent possible. C offers us a clever way to do this, by placing the required library-function declarations in special source files, called *header files*.

Most C compilers include several header files, each of which contains declarations that are functionally related (see Appendix H). For example, stdio.h is a header file containing declarations for input/output routines; math.h contains declarations for certain mathematical functions; and so on. The header files also contain other information related to the use of the library functions, such as symbolic constant definitions.

The required header files must be merged with the source program during the compilation process. This is accomplished by placing one or more #include statements at the beginning of the source program (or at the beginning of the individual program files). We have been following this procedure in all of the programming examples presented in this book.

EXAMPLE 8.13 Compound Interest   Example 5.2 originally presented the following C program for carrying out simple compound interest calculations.

```c
/* simple compound interest problem */

#include <stdio.h>
#include <math.h>

main()

{
    float p,r,n,i,f;

    /* read input data (including prompts) */

    printf("Please enter a value for the principal (P): ");
    scanf("%f", &p);
    printf("Please enter a value for the interest rate (r): ");
    scanf("%f", &r);
    printf("Please enter a value for the number of years (n): ");
    scanf("%f", &n);

    /* calculate i, then f */

    i = r / 100;
    f = p * pow((1 + i),n);

    /* display the output */

    printf("\nThe final value (F) is: %.2f\n", f);
}
```

This program makes use of two header files, stdio.h and math.h. The first header file contains declarations for the printf and scanf functions, whereas the second header file contains a declaration for the power function, pow.

We can rewrite the program if we wish, removing the #include statements and adding our own function declarations, as follows.

```
/* simple compound interest problem */

extern int printf();                    /* library function declaration */
extern int scanf();                     /* library function declaration */
extern double pow(double, double);      /* library function declaration */

main()

{
    float p,r,n,i,f;

    /* read input data (including prompts) */

    printf("Please enter a value for the principal (P): ");
    scanf("%f", &p);
    printf("Please enter a value for the interest rate (r): ");
    scanf("%f", &r);
    printf("Please enter a value for the number of years (n): ");
    scanf("%f", &n);

    /* calculate i, then f */

    i = r / 100;
    f = p * pow((1 + i),n);

    /* display the output */

    printf("\nThe final value (F) is: %.2f\n", f);
}
```

This version of the program is compiled in the same way as the earlier version, and it will generate the same output when executed. In practice the use of such programmer-supplied function declarations is not done, however, as it is more complicated and it provides additional sources of error. Moreover, the error checking that occurs during the compilation process will be less complete, because the argument types are not specified for the printf and scanf function. (Note that the number of arguments in printf and scanf can vary from one function call to another. The manner in which argument types are specified under these conditions is beyond the scope of our present discussion.)

Platform independence (i.e., *machine independence*) is a significant advantage in this approach to the use of library functions and header files. Thus, machine-dependent features can be provided as library functions, or as character constants or *macros* (see Sec. 14.4) that are included within the header files. A typical C program will therefore run on many different kinds of computers without alteration, provided the appropriate library functions and header files are utilized. The portability resulting from this approach is a major contributor to the popularity of C.

Review Questions

8.1   What is meant by the storage class of a variable?

8.2   Name the four storage-class specifications included in C.

8.3   What is meant by the scope of a variable within a program?

8.4   What is the purpose of an automatic variable? What is its scope?

8.5   How is an automatic variable defined? How is it initialized? What happens if an automatic variable is not explicitly initialized within a function?

8.6   Does an automatic variable retain its value once control is transferred out of its defining function?

8.7   What is the purpose of an external variable? What is its scope?

8.8   Summarize the distinction between an external variable definition and an external variable declaration.

8.9   How is an external variable defined? How is it initialized? What happens if an external variable definition does not include the assignment of an initial value? Compare your answers with those for automatic variables.

8.10 Suppose an external variable is defined outside of function A and accessed within the function. Does it matter whether the external variable is defined before or after the function? Explain.

8.11 In what way is the initialization of an external variable more restricted than the initialization of an automatic variable?

8.12 What is meant by side effects?

8.13 What inherent dangers are there in the use of external variables?

8.14 What is the purpose of a static variable in a single-file program? What is its scope?

8.15 How is a static variable defined in a single-file program? How is a static variable initialized? Compare with automatic variables.

8.16 Under what circumstances might it be desirable to have a program composed of several different files?

8.17 Compare the definition of functions within a multifile program with the definition of functions within a single-file program. What additional options are available in the multifile case?

8.18 In a multifile program, what is the default storage class for a function if a storage class is not explicitly included in the function definition?

8.19 What is the purpose of a static function in a multifile program?

8.20 Compare the definition of external variables within a multifile program with the definition of external variables within a single-file program. What additional options are available in the multifile case?

8.21 Compare external variable definitions with external variable declarations in a multifile program. What is the purpose of each? Can an external variable declaration include the assignment of an initial value?

8.22 Under what circumstances can an external variable be defined to be static? What advantage might there be in doing this?

8.23 What is the scope of a static external variable?

8.24 What is the purpose of a header file? Is the use of a header file absolutely necessary?

Problems

8.25 Describe the output generated by each of the following programs.

(*a*)
```
#include <stdio.h>

int funct1(int count);

main()
{
    int a, count;

    for (count = 1; count <= 5; ++count)   {
        a = funct1(count);
        printf("%d  ", a);
    }
}
```

```
        funct1(int x)
        {
            int y = 0;

            y += x;
            return(y);
        }
```

(b) ```
     #include <stdio.h>

     int funct1(int count);

     main()
     {
         int a, count;

         for (count = 1; count <= 5; ++count)   {
             a = funct1(count);
             printf("%d ", a);
         }
     }

     funct1(int x)
     {
         static int y = 0;

         y += x;
         return(y);
     }
     ```

(c)  ```
     #include <stdio.h>

     int funct1(int a);
     int funct2(int a);

     main()
     {
         int a = 0, b = 1, count;

         for (count = 1; count <= 5; ++count)   {
             b += funct1(a) + funct2(a);
             printf("%d  ", b);
         }
     }

     funct1(int a)
     {
         int b;

         b = funct2(a);
         return(b);
     }

     funct2(int a)
     {
         static int b = 1;

         b += 1;
         return(b + a);
     }
     ```

8.26 Write the first line of the function definition for each of the situations described below.

   (*a*) The second file of a two-file program contains a function called `solver` which accepts two floating-point quantities and returns a floating-point argument. The function will be called by other functions which are defined in both files.

   (*b*) The second file of a two-file program contains a function called `solver` which accepts two floating-point quantities and returns a floating-point argument, as in the preceding problem. Recognition of this function is to remain local within the second file.

8.27 Add the required (or suggested) function declarations for each of the skeletal outlines shown below.

   (*a*) This is a two-file program.

   First file:

```
main()
{
    double x, y, z;

    . . . . .

z = funct1(x, y);

    . . . . .

}
```

   Second file:

```
double funct1(double a, double b)
{
    . . . . .
}
```

   (*b*) This is a two-file program.

   First file:

```
main()
{
    double x, y, z;

    . . . . .

    z = funct1(x, y);

    . . . . .

}
```

   Second file:

```
double funct1(double a, double b)
{
    double c;

    c = funct2(a, b);

    . . . . .

}
```

```
            static double funct2(double a, double b)
            {

                . . . . .

            }
```

8.28   Describe the output generated by each of the following programs.

(a)   ```
       #include <stdio.h>

       int a = 3;

       int funct1(int count);

       main()
       {
           int count;

           for (count = 1; count <= 5; ++count)   {
               a = funct1(count);
               printf("%d ", a);
           }
       }

       funct1(int x)
       {
           a += x;
           return(a);
       }
       ```

(b)    ```
       #include <stdio.h>

       int a = 100, b = 200;

       int funct1(int a, int b);

       main()
       {
           int count, c, d;

           for (count = 1; count <= 5; ++count)   {
               c = 20 * (count - 1);
               d = 4 * count * count;
               printf("%d  %d  ", funct1(a, c), funct1(b, d));
           }
       }

       funct1(int x, int y)
       {
           return(x - y);
       }
       ```

(c)   ```
       #include <stdio.h>

       int a = 100, b = 200;

       int funct1(int c);
       ```
       ```

```
main()
{
    int count, c;

    for (count = 1; count <= 5; ++count)   {
        c = 4 * count * count;
        printf("%d  ", funct1(c));
    }
}


funct1(int x)
{
    int c;

    c = (x < 50) ? (a + x) : (b - x);
    return(c);
}
```

(d)   ```
       #include <stdio.h>

       int a = 100, b = 200;

       int funct1(int count);
       int funct2(int c);

       main()
       {
           int count;

           for (count = 1; count <= 5; ++count)
               printf("%d ", funct1(count));
       }

       funct1(int x)
       {
           int c, d;

           c = funct2(x);
           d = (c < 100) ? (a + c) : b;
           return(d);
       }

       funct2(int x)
       {
           static int prod = 1;

           prod *= x;
           return(prod);
       }
       ```

(e)    ```
       #include <stdio.h>

       int funct1(int a);
       int funct2(int b);
       ```

```
    main()
    {
        int a = 0, b = 1, count;

        for (count = 1; count <= 5; ++count)   {
            b += funct1(a + 1) + 1;
            printf("%d  ", b);
        }
    }


    funct1(int a)
    {
        int b;

        b = funct2(a + 1) + 1;
        return(b);
    }


    funct2(int a)
    {
        return(a + 1);
    }
```

(f)   ```
    #include <stdio.h>

    int a = 0, b = 1;

    int funct1(int a);
    int funct2(int b);

    main()
    {
        int count;

        for (count = 1; count <= 5; ++count)   {
            b += funct1(a + 1) + 1;
            printf("%d ", b);
        }
    }

    funct1(int a)
    {
        int b;

        b = funct2(a + 1) + 1;
        return(b);
    }

    funct2(int a)
    {
        return(a + 1);
    }
```
```

(g)
```
#include <stdio.h>

int a = 0, b = 1;

int funct1(int a);
int funct2(int b);

main()
{
    int count;

    for (count = 1; count <= 5; ++count)    {
        b += funct1(a + 1) + 1;
        printf("%d  ", b);
    }
}

funct1(int a)
{
    b = funct2(a + 1) + 1;
    return(b);
}

funct2(int a)
{
    return(b + a);
}
```

(h)
```
#include <stdio.h>

int count = 0;

void funct1(void);

main()
{
    printf("Please enter a line of text below\n");
    funct1();
    printf("%d", count);
}

void funct1(void)
{
    char c;

    if ((c = getchar()) != '\n')    {
        ++count;
        funct1();
    }
    return;
}
```

Programming Problems

8.29 The program given in Example 8.4 can easily be modified to *minimize* a function of *x*. This minimization procedure can provide us with a highly effective technique for calculating the roots of a nonlinear algebraic equation. For example, suppose we want to find the particular value of x that causes some function $f(x)$ to equal zero. A typical function of this nature might be

$$f(x) = x + \cos(x) - 1 - \sin(x).$$

If we let $y(x) = f(x)^2$, then the function $y(x)$ will always be positive, except for those values of x that are roots of the given function [i.e., for which $f(x)$, and hence $y(x)$, will equal zero]. Therefore, any value of x that causes $y(x)$ to be minimized will also be a root of the equation $f(x) = 0$.

Modify the program shown in Example 8.4 to minimize a given function. Use the program to obtain the roots of the following equations:

(a) $x + \cos(x) = 1 + \sin(x)$, $\quad \pi/2 < x < \pi$

(b) $x^5 + 3x^2 + 10$, $\quad 0 <= x <= 3$ (see Example 6.21)

8.30 Modify the program shown in Example 7.11 so that a sequence of craps games will be simulated automatically, in a noninteractive manner. Enter the total number of games as an input variable. Include within the program a counter that will determine the total number of wins. Use the program to simulate a large number of games (e.g., 1000). Estimate the probability of coming out ahead when playing multiple games of craps. This value, expressed as a decimal, is equal to the number of wins divided by the total number of games played. If the probability exceeds 0.500, it favors the player; otherwise it favors the house.

8.31 Rewrite each of the following programs so that it includes at least one programmer-defined function, in addition to the main function. Be careful with your choice of arguments and (if necessary) external variables.

(a) Calculate the weighted average of a list of numbers [see Prob. 6.69(a)].

(b) Calculate the cumulative product of a list of numbers [see Prob. 6.69(b)].

(c) Calculate the geometric average of a list of numbers [see Prob. 6.69(c)].

(d) Calculate and tabulate a list of prime numbers [see Prob. 6.69(f)].

(e) Compute the sine of x, using the method described in Prob. 6.69(i).

(f) Compute the repayments on a loan [see Prob. 6.69(j)].

(g) Determine the average exam score for each student in a class, as described in Prob. 6.69(k).

8.32 Write a complete C program to solve each of the problems described below. Utilize programmer-defined functions wherever appropriate. Compile and execute each program using the data given in the problem description.

(a) Suppose you place a given sum of money, A, into a savings account at the beginning of each year for n years. If the account earns interest at the rate of i percent annually, then the amount of money that will have accumulated after n years, F, is given by

$$F = A\,[(1 + i/100) + (1 + i/100)^2 + (1 + i/100)^3 + \cdots + (1 + i/100)^n]$$

Write a conversational-style C program to determine the following.

(i) How much money will accumulate after 30 years if \$1000 is deposited at the beginning of each year and the interest rate is 6 percent per year, compounded annually?

(ii) How much money must be deposited at the beginning of each year in order to accumulate \$100,000 after 30 years, again assuming that the interest rate is 6 percent per year, with annual compounding?

In each case, first determine the unknown amount of money. Then create a table showing the total amount of money that will have accumulated at the end of each year. Use the function written for Prob. 7.43 to carry out the exponentiation.

(b) Modify the above program to accommodate quarterly rather than annual compounding of interest. Compare the calculated results obtained for both problems. *Hint*: The proper formula is

$$F = A\,[(1 + i/100m)^m + (1 + i/100m)^{2m} + (1 + i/100m)^{3m} + \cdots + (1 + i/100m)^{nm}]$$

where m represents the number of interest periods per year.

(c)   Home mortgage costs are determined in such a manner that the borrower pays the same amount of money
        to the lending institution each month throughout the life of the mortgage. The fraction of the total monthly
        payment that is required as an interest payment on the outstanding balance of the loan varies, however,
        from month to month. Early in the life of the mortgage most of the monthly payment is required to pay
        interest, and only a small fraction of the total monthly payment is applied toward reducing the amount of
        the loan. Gradually, the outstanding balance becomes smaller, which causes the monthly interest payment
        to decrease, and the amount available to reduce the outstanding balance therefore increases. Hence the
        balance of the loan is reduced at an accelerated rate.

        Typically, prospective home buyers know how much money they must borrow and the time required for
        repayment. They then ask a lending institution how much their monthly payment will be at the prevailing
        interest rate. They should also be concerned with how much of each monthly payment is charged to
        interest, how much total interest they have paid since they first borrowed the money, and how much money
        they still owe the lending institution at the end of each month.

        Write a C program that can be used by a lending institution to provide a potential customer with this
        information. Assume that the amount of the loan, the annual interest rate and the duration of the loan are
        specified. The amount of the monthly payment is calculated as

$$A = iP(1 + i)^n / [(1 + i)^n - 1]$$

        where A = monthly payment, dollars

               P = total amount of the loan, dollars

               i = monthly interest rate, expressed as a decimal (e.g., 1/2 percent would be written 0.005)

               n = total number of monthly payments

        The monthly interest payment can then be calculated from the formula

$$I = iB$$

        where I = monthly interest payment, dollars

                B = current outstanding balance, dollars

        The current outstanding balance is simply equal to the original amount of the loan, less the sum of the
        previous payments toward principal. The monthly payment toward principal (i.e., the amount which is used
        to reduce the outstanding balance) is simply

$$T = A - I$$

        where T = monthly payment toward principal.

            Use the program to calculate the cost of a 25-year, $50,000 mortgage at an annual interest rate of 8
        percent. Then repeat the calculations for an annual interest rate of 8.5 percent. Make use of the function
        written for Prob. 7.43 to carry out the exponentiation. How significant is the additional 0.5 percent in the
        interest rate over the entire life of the mortgage?

(d)   The method used to calculate the cost of a home mortgage in the previous problem is known as a *constant
        payment* method, since each monthly payment is the same. Suppose instead that the monthly payments
        were computed by the method of simple interest. That is, suppose that the same amount is applied toward
        reducing the loan each month. Hence

$$T = P / n$$

        However, the monthly interest will depend on the amount of the outstanding balance; that is,

$$I = iB$$

        Thus the total monthly payment, $A = T + I$, will decrease each month as the outstanding balance diminishes.

            Write a C program to calculate the cost of a home mortgage using this method of repayment. Label the
        output clearly. Use the program to calculate the cost of a 25-year, $50,000 loan at 8 percent annual interest.
        Compare the results with those obtained in part (c) above.

(e)   Suppose we are given a number of discrete points (x_1, y_1), (x_2, y_2), . . . , (x_n, y_n) read from a curve $y = f(x)$, where x is bounded between x_1 and x_n. We wish to approximate the area under the curve by breaking up the curve into a number of small rectangles and calculating the area of these rectangles. (This is known as the *trapezoidal rule*.) The appropriate formula is

$$A = (y_1 + y_2)(x_2 - x_1)/2 + (y_2 + y_3)(x_3 - x_2)/2 + \cdots + (y_{n-1} + y_n)(x_n - x_{n-1})/2$$

Notice that the average height of each rectangle is given by $(y_i + y_{i+1})/2$ and the width of each rectangle is equal to $(x_{i+1} - x_i)$; $i = 1, 2, \ldots, n - 1$.

Write a C program to implement this strategy, using a function to evaluate the formula $y = f(x)$. Use the program to calculate the area under the curve $y = x^3$ between the limits $x = 1$ and $x = 4$. Solve this problem first with 16 evenly spaced points, then with 61 points, and finally with 301 points. Note that the accuracy of the solution will improve as the number of points increases. (The exact answer to this problem is 63.75.)

(f)   Part (e) above describes a method known as the *trapezoidal rule* for calculating the area under a curve $y(x)$, where a set of tabulated values (x_1, y_1), (x_2, y_2), . . . , (x_n, y_n) is used to describe the curve. If the tabulated values of x are equally spaced, then the equation given in the preceding problem can be simplified to read

$$A = (y_1 + 2y_2 + 2y_3 + 2y_4 + \cdots + 2y_{n-1} + y_n)h/2$$

where h is the distance between successive values of x.

Another technique that applies when there is an even number of equally spaced intervals (i.e., an odd number of data points) is *Simpson's rule*. The computational equation for implementing Simpson's rule is

$$A = (y_1 + 4y_2 + 2y_3 + 4y_4 + 2y_5 + \cdots + 4y_{n-1} + y_n)h/3$$

For a given value of h, this method will yield a more accurate result than the trapezoidal rule. (Note that the method requires about the same amount of computational complexity as the trapezoidal rule.)

Write a C program for calculating the area under a curve using either of the above techniques, assuming an odd number of equally spaced data points. Implement each method with a separate function, and utilize another independent function to evaluate $y(x)$.

Use the program to calculate the area under the curve

$$y = e^{-x}$$

where x ranges from 0 to 1. Calculate the area using each method, and compare the results with the correct answer of $A = 0.7468241$.

(g)   Still another technique for calculating the area under a curve is to employ the *Monte Carlo* method, which makes use of randomly generated numbers. Suppose that the curve $y = f(x)$ is positive for any value of x between the specified lower and upper limits $x = a$ and $x = b$. Let the largest value of y within these limits be y^*. The Monte Carlo method proceeds as follows.

(i)   Begin with a counter set equal to zero.

(ii)   Generate a random number, r_x, whose value lies between a and b.

(iii) Evaluate $y(r_x)$.

(iv)   Generate a second random number, r_y, whose value lies between 0 and y^*.

(v)   Compare r_y with $y(r_x)$. If r_y is less than or equal to $y(r_x)$, then this point will fall on or under the given curve. Hence the counter is incremented by 1.

(vi)   Repeat steps (ii) through (v) a large number of times. Each time will be called a *cycle*.

(vii) When a specified number of cycles has been completed, the fraction of points that fell on or under the curve, F, is computed as the value of the counter divided by the total number of cycles. The area under the curve is then obtained as

$$A = Fy^*(b - a).$$

Write a C program to implement this strategy. Use this program to find the area under the curve $y = e^{-x}$ between the limits $a = 0$ and $b = 1$. Determine how many cycles are required to obtain an answer that is accurate to three significant figures. Compare the computer time required for this problem with the time required for the preceding problem. Which method is better?

(h)   A normally distributed random variate x, with mean μ and standard deviation σ, can be generated from the formula

$$x = \mu + \sigma \frac{\sum\limits_{i=1}^{N} r_i - N/2}{\sqrt{N/12}}$$

where r_i is a uniformly distributed random number whose value lies between 0 and 1. A value of $N = 12$ is frequently selected when using this formula. The underlying basis for the formula is the *central limit theorem*, which states that a set of mean values of uniformly distributed random variates will tend to be normally distributed.

    Write a C program that will generate a specified number of normally distributed random variates with a given mean and a given standard deviation. Let the number of random variates, the mean and the standard deviation be input quantities to the program. Generate each random variate within a function that accepts the mean and standard deviation as arguments.

(i)   Write a C program that will allow a person to play a game of tic-tac-toe against the computer. Write the program in such a manner that the computer can be either the first or the second player. If the computer is the first player, let the first move be generated randomly. Write out the complete status of the game after each move. Have the computer acknowledge a win by either player when it occurs.

(j)   Write a complete C program that includes a recursive function to determine the value of the nth Fibonacci number, F_n, where $F_n = F_{n-1} + F_{n-2}$ and $F_1 = F_2 = 1$ (see Example 8.7). Let the value of n be an input quantity.

Chapter 9

Arrays

Many applications require the processing of multiple data items that have common characteristics (e.g., a set of numerical data, represented by $x_1, x_2, \ldots, x_n$). In such situations it is often convenient to place the data items into an *array*, where they will all share the same name (e.g., x). The individual data items can be characters, integers, floating-point numbers, etc. However, they must all be of the same type and the same storage class.

Each array element (i.e., each individual data item) is referred to by specifying the array name followed by one or more *subscripts*, with each subscript enclosed in square brackets. Each subscript must be expressed as a nonnegative integer. In an *n*-element array, the array elements are x[0], x[1], x[2], ..., x[n − 1], as illustrated in Fig. 9.1. The value of each subscript can be expressed as an integer constant, an integer variable or a more complex integer expression.

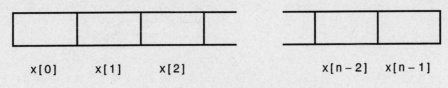

| x[0]   x[1]   x[2]   x[n − 2]   x[n − 1]

x is an n-element, one-dimensional array

Fig. 9.1

The number of subscripts determines the dimensionality of the array. For example, x[i] refers to an element in the one-dimensional array x. Similarly, y[i][j] refers to an element in the two-dimensional array y. (We can think of a two-dimensional array as a table, where y[i][j] is the *j*th element of the *i*th row.) Higher-dimensional arrays can be also be formed, by adding additional subscripts in the same manner (e.g., z[i][j][k]).

Recall that we have used one-dimensional character arrays earlier in this book, in conjunction with the processing of strings and lines of text. Thus, arrays are not entirely new, even though our previous references to them were somewhat casual. We will now consider arrays in greater detail. In particular, we will discuss the manner in which arrays are defined and processed, the passing of arrays to functions, and the use of multidimensional arrays. Both numerical and character-type arrays will be considered. Initially we will concentrate on one-dimensional arrays, though multidimensional arrays will be considered in Sec. 9.4.

9.1 DEFINING AN ARRAY

Arrays are defined in much the same manner as ordinary variables, except that each array name must be accompanied by a size specification (i.e., the number of elements). For a one-dimensional array, the size is specified by a positive integer expression, enclosed in square brackets. The expression is usually written as a positive integer constant.

In general terms, a one-dimensional array definition may be expressed as

storage-class data-type array[*expression*] ;

241

where *storage-class* refers to the storage class of the array, *data-type* is the data type, *array* is the array name, and *expression* is a positive-valued integer expression which indicates the number of array elements. The *storage-class* is optional; default values are automatic for arrays that are defined within a function or a block, and external for arrays that are defined outside of a function.

EXAMPLE 9.1   Several typical one-dimensional array definitions are shown below.

```
int x[100];
char text[80];
static char message[25];
static float n[12];
```

The first line states that x is a 100-element integer array, and the second defines text to be an 80-element character array. In the third line, message is defined as a static 25-element character array, whereas the fourth line establishes n as a static 12-element floating-point array.

It is sometimes convenient to define an array size in terms of a symbolic constant rather than a fixed integer quantity. This makes it easier to modify a program that utilizes an array, since all references to the maximum array size (e.g., within for loops as well as in array definitions) can be altered simply by changing the value of the symbolic constant.

EXAMPLE 9.2 Lowercase to Uppercase Text Conversion   Here is a complete program that reads in a one-dimensional character array, converts all of the elements to uppercase, and then displays the converted array. Similar programs are shown in Examples 4.4, 6.9, 6.12 and 6.16.

```
/* read in a line of lowercase text to uppercase */

#include <stdio.h>
#include <ctype.h>

#define  SIZE  80

main()
{
    char letter[SIZE];
    int count;

    /* read in the line */

    for (count = 0; count < SIZE; ++count)
        letter[count] = getchar();

    /* display the line in upper case */

    for (count = 0; count < SIZE; ++count)
        putchar(toupper(letter[count]));
}
```

Notice that the symbolic constant SIZE is assigned a value of 80. This symbolic constant, rather than its value, appears in the array definition and in the two for statements. (Remember that *the value of the symbolic constant will be substituted for the constant itself during the compilation process*.) Therefore, in order to alter the program to accommodate a different size array, only the #define statement must be changed.

For example, to alter the above program so that it will process a 60-element array, the original #define statement is simply replaced by

```
#define  SIZE  60
```

This one change accommodates all of the necessary program alterations; there is no possibility that some required program modification will be overlooked.

Automatic arrays, unlike automatic variables, cannot be initialized. However, external and static array definitions can include the assignment of initial values if desired. The initial values must appear in the order in which they will be assigned to the individual array elements, enclosed in braces and separated by commas. The general form is

storage-class data-type array[expression] = {value 1, value 2, . . ., value n};

where *value 1* refers to the value of the first array element, *value 2* refers to the value of the second element, and so on. The appearance of the *expression*, which indicates the number of array elements, is optional when initial values are present.

EXAMPLE 9.3 Shown below are several array definitions that include the assignment of initial values.

```
int digits[10] = {1, 2, 3, 4, 5, 6, 7, 8, 9, 10};
static float x[6] = {0, 0.25, 0, -0.50, 0, 0};
char color[3] = {'R', 'E', 'D'};
```

Note that x is a static array. The other two arrays (digits and color) are assumed to be external arrays by virtue of their placement within the program.

The results of these initial assignments, in terms of the individual array elements, are as follows. (Remember that the subscripts in an n-element array range from 0 to n − 1.)

```
digits[0] = 1            x[0] =  0            color[0] = 'R'
digits[1] = 2            x[1] =  0.25         color[1] = 'E'
digits[2] = 3            x[2] =  0            color[2] = 'D'
digits[3] = 4            x[3] = -0.50
digits[4] = 5            x[4] =  0
digits[5] = 6            x[5] =  0
digits[6] = 7
digits[7] = 8
digits[8] = 9
digits[9] = 10
```

All individual array elements that are not assigned explicit initial values will automatically be set to zero. This includes the remaining elements of an array in which some elements have been assigned nonzero values.

EXAMPLE 9.4 Consider the following array definitions.

```
int digits[10] = {3, 3, 3};
static float x[6] = {-0.3, 0 , 0.25};
```

The results, on an element-by-element basis, are as follows.

```
digits[0] = 3            x[0] = -0.3
digits[1] = 3            x[1] =  0
digits[2] = 3            x[2] =  0.25
digits[3] = 0            x[3] =  0
digits[4] = 0            x[4] =  0
digits[5] = 0            x[5] =  0
digits[6] = 0
digits[7] = 0
digits[8] = 0
digits[9] = 0
```

In each case, all of the array elements are automatically set to zero except those that have been explicitly initialized within the array definitions. Note that the repeated values (i.e., 3, 3, 3) must be shown individually.

The array size need not be specified explicitly when initial values are included as a part of an array definition. With a numerical array, the array size will automatically be set equal to the number of initial values included within the definition.

EXAMPLE 9.5 Consider the following array definitions, which are variations of the definitions shown in Examples 9.3 and 9.4.

```
int digits[] = {1, 2, 3, 4, 5, 6};
static float x[] = {0, 0.25, 0, -0.5};
```

Thus, digits will be a six-element integer array, and x will be a static, four-element floating-point array. The individual elements will be assigned the following values. (*Note the empty brackets in the array declarations.*)

```
        digits[0] = 1         x[0] =  0
        digits[1] = 2         x[1] =  0.25
        digits[2] = 3         x[2] =  0
        digits[3] = 4         x[3] = -0.5
        digits[4] = 5
        digits[5] = 6
```

Strings (i.e., character arrays) are handled somewhat differently, as discussed in Sec. 2.6. In particular, when a string constant is assigned to an external or a static character array as a part of the array definition, the array size specification is usually omitted. The proper array size will be assigned automatically. This will include a provision for the null character \0, which is automatically added at the end of every string (see Example 2.26).

EXAMPLE 9.6 Consider the following two character array definitions. Each includes the initial assignment of the string constant "RED". However, the first array is defined as a three-element array, whereas the size of the second array is unspecified.

```
char color[3] = "RED";

char color[] = "RED";
```

The results of these initial assignments are not the same because of the null character, \0, which is automatically added at the end of the second string. Thus, the elements of the first array are

```
color[0] = 'R'
color[1] = 'E'
color[2] = 'D'
```

whereas the elements of the second array are

```
color[0] = 'R'
color[1] = 'E'
color[2] = 'D'
color[3] = '\0'
```

Thus, the first form is incorrect, since the null character \0 is not included in the array.

The array definition could also have been written as

```
char color[4] = "RED";
```

This definition is correct, since we are now defining a four-element array which includes an element for the null character. However, many programmers prefer the earlier form, which omits the size specifier.

If a program requires a one-dimensional array *declaration* (because the array is defined elsewhere in the program), the declaration is written in the same manner as the array definition with the following exceptions.

1. The square brackets may be empty, since the array size will have been specified as a part of the array definition. Array declarations are customarily written in this form.

2. Initial values cannot be included in the declaration.

These rules apply to formal argument declarations within functions as well as external variable declarations. However, the rules for defining *multidimensional* formal arguments are more complex (see Sec. 9.4).

EXAMPLE 9.7 Here is a skeletal outline of a two-file C program that makes use of external arrays.

First file:

```
int c[] = {1, 2, 3};        /* external array DEFINITION */
char message[] = "Hello!";  /* external array DEFINITION */
extern void funct1(void);   /* function prototype */
main()
{
    . . . . .
}
```

Second file:

```
extern int c[];             /* external array DECLARATION */
extern char message[];      /* external array DECLARATION */
extern void funct1(void)    /* function definition */
{
    . . . . .
}
```

This program outline includes two external arrays, c and message. The first array (c) is a three-element integer array that is defined and initialized in the first file. The second array (message) is a character array that is also defined and initialized in the first file. The arrays are then *declared* in the second file, because they are global arrays that must be recognized throughout the entire program.

Neither the array definitions in the first file nor the array declarations in the second file include explicit size specifications. Such size specifications are permissible in the first file, but are omitted because of the initialization. Moreover, array size specifications serve no useful purpose within the second file, since the array sizes have already been established.

9.2 PROCESSING AN ARRAY

Single operations which involve entire arrays are not permitted in C. Thus, if a and b are similar arrays (i.e., same data type, same dimensionality and same size), assignment operations, comparison operations, etc. must be carried out on an element-by-element basis. This is usually accomplished within a loop, where each pass through the loop is used to process one array element. The number of passes through the loop will therefore equal the number of array elements to be processed.

We have already seen several examples in which the individual elements of a character array are processed in one way or another (see Examples 4.4, 4.19, 6.9, 6.12, 6.16, 6.19, 6.20, 6.32, 6.34, 8.3, 8.5 and 9.2). Numerical arrays are processed in much the same manner. In a numerical array, each array element represents a single numerical quantity, as illustrated in the example below.

EXAMPLE 9.8 Deviations About an Average   Suppose we want to read a list of n floating-point quantities and then calculate their average, as in Example 6.17. In addition to simply calculating the average, however, we will also compute the *deviation* of each numerical quantity about the average, using the formula

$$d = x_i - avg$$

where x_i represents each of the given quantities, $i = 1, 2, \cdots, n$, and *avg* represents the calculated average.

In order to solve this problem we must store each of the given quantities in a one-dimensional, floating-point array. This is an essential part of the program. The reason, which must be clearly understood, is as follows.

In all of the earlier examples where we calculated the average of a list of numbers, each number was replaced by its successor in the given list (see Examples 6.10, 6.13, 6.17 and 6.31). Hence each individual number was no longer available for subsequent calculations once the next number had been entered. Now, however, these individual quantities must be retained within the computer in order to calculate their corresponding deviations after the average has been determined. We therefore store them in a one-dimensional array, which we shall call list.

Let us define list to be a 100-element, floating-point array. However, we need not make use of all 100 elements. Rather, we shall specify the actual number of elements by entering a positive integer quantity (not exceeding 100) for the integer variable n.

Here is the complete C program.

```
/* calculate the average of n numbers,
   then compute the deviation of each number about the average */

#include <stdio.h>

main()
{
    int n, count;
    float avg, d, sum = 0;
    float list[100];

    /* read a value for n */
    printf("\nHow many numbers will be averaged? ");
    scanf("%d", &n);
    printf("\n");

    /* read the numbers and calculate their sum */
    for (count = 0; count < n; ++count)   {
        printf("i = %d   x = ", count + 1);
        scanf("%f", &list[count]);
        sum += list[count];
    }

    /* calculate and display the average */
    avg = sum / n;
    printf("\nThe average is %5.2f\n\n", avg);
```

```
        /* calculate and display the deviations about the average */
        for (count = 0; count < n; ++count)   {
            d = list[count] - avg;
            printf("i = %d   x = %5.2f   d = %5.2f\n", count + 1, list[count], d);
        }
    }
```

Note that the second scanf function (within the first for loop) includes an ampersand (&) in front of list[count], since we are entering a single array element rather than an entire array (see Sec. 4.4).

Now suppose the program is executed using the following five numerical quantities: $x_1 = 3$, $x_2 = -2$, $x_3 = 12$, $x_4 = 4.4$, $x_5 = 3.5$. The interactive session, including the data entry and the calculated results, is shown below. The user's responses are underlined.

```
How many numbers will be averaged? 5
i = 1    x = 3
i = 2    x = -2
i = 3    x = 12
i = 4    x = 4.4
i = 5    x = 3.5

The average is  4.18

i = 1    x =  3.00    d = -1.18
i = 2    x = -2.00    d = -6.18
i = 3    x = 12.00    d =  7.82
i = 4    x =  4.40    d =  0.22
i = 5    x =  3.50    d = -0.68
```

In some applications it may be desirable to assign initial values to the elements of an array. This requires that the array either be defined globally, or locally (within the function) as a static array. The next example illustrates the use of a global array definition.

EXAMPLE 9.9 Deviations About an Average Revisited   Let us again calculate the average of a given set of numbers and then compute the deviation of each number about the average, as in Example 9.8. Now, however, let us assign the given numbers to the array within the array definition. To do so, let us move the definition of the array list outside of the main portion of the program. Thus, list will become an external array. Moreover, we will remove the explicit size specification from the definition, since the number of initial values will now determine the array size.

The initial values included in the following program are the same five values that were specified as input data for the previous example. To be consistent, we will also assign an initial value for n. This can be accomplished by defining n as either an automatic variable within main, or as an external variable. We have chosen the latter method, so that all of the initial assignments that might otherwise be entered as input data are grouped together.

Here is the complete program.

```
/* calculate the average of n numbers,
   then compute the deviation of each number about the average */

#include <stdio.h>

int n = 5;
float list[] = {3, -2, 12, 4.4, 3.5};

main()

{
    int count;
    float avg, d, sum = 0;
```

```
    /* calculate and display the average */
    for (count = 0; count < n; ++count)
        sum += list[count];
    avg = sum / n;
    printf("\nThe average is %5.2f\n\n", avg);

    /* calculate and display the deviations about the average */
    for (count = 0; count < n; ++count)   {
        d = list[count] - avg;
        printf("i = %d x = %5.2f   d = %5.2f\n", count + 1, list[count], d);
    }
}
```

Note that this version of the program does not require any input data.

Execution of this program will generate the following output.

```
The average is  4.18

i = 1   x =   3.00   d = -1.18
i = 2   x = -2.00   d = -6.18
i = 3   x = 12.00   d =  7.82
i = 4   x =  4.40   d =  0.22
i = 5   x =  3.50   d = -0.68
```

9.3 PASSING ARRAYS TO FUNCTIONS

An entire array can be passed to a function as an argument. The manner in which the array is passed differs markedly, however, from that of an ordinary variable.

To pass an array to a function, the array name must appear by itself, without brackets or subscripts, as an actual argument within the function call. The corresponding formal argument is written in the same manner, though it must be declared as an array within the formal argument declarations. When declaring a one-dimensional array as a formal argument, the array name is written with a pair of empty square brackets. The size of the array is not specified within the formal argument declaration.

Some care is required when writing function prototypes that include array arguments. An empty pair of square brackets must follow the name of each array argument, thus indicating that the argument is an array. If argument names are not included in a function declaration, then an empty pair of square brackets must follow the array argument data type.

EXAMPLE 9.10 The following program outline illustrates the passing of an array from the main portion of the program to a function.

```
float average(int a, float x[]);      /* function prototype */

main()
{
    int n;                          /* variable DECLARATION */
    float avg;                      /* variable DECLARATION */
    float list[100];                /* array DEFINITION */

    . . . . .

    avg = average(n, list);

    . . . . .
}
```

```
float average(int a, float x[])        /* function DEFINITION */
{
    . . . . .
}
```

Within main we see a call to the function average. This function call contains two actual arguments — the integer variable n, and the one-dimensional, floating-point array list. Notice that list appears as an ordinary variable within the function call; i.e., the square brackets are not included.

The first line of the function definition includes two formal arguments, a and x. The formal argument declarations establish a as an integer variable and x as a one-dimensional, floating-point array. Thus, there is a correspondence between the actual argument n and the formal argument a. Similarly, there is a correspondence between the actual argument list and the formal argument x. Note that the size of x is not specified within the formal argument declaration.

Note that the function prototype could have been written without argument names, as

```
float average(int, float[]);           /* function declaration */
```

Either form is valid.

We have already discussed the fact that arguments are passed to a function by value when the arguments are ordinary variables (see Sec. 7.5). When an array is passed to a function, however, the values of the array elements *are not* passed to the function. Rather, the array name is interpreted as the *address* of the first array element (i.e., the address of the memory location containing the first array element). This address is assigned to the corresponding formal argument when the function is called. The formal argument therefore becomes a *pointer* to the first array element (more about this in the next chapter). Arguments that are passed in this manner are said to be passed *by reference* rather than by value.

When a reference is made to an array element within the function, the value of the element's subscript is added to the value of the pointer to indicate the address of the specified array element. Therefore any array element can be accessed from within the function. Moreover, *if an array element is altered within the function, the alteration will be recognized in the calling portion of the program* (actually, throughout the entire scope of the array).

EXAMPLE 9.11 Here is a simple C program that passes a three-element integer array to a function, where the array elements are altered. The values of the array elements are displayed at three different places in the program, thus illustrating the effects of the alterations.

```
#include <stdio.h>

void modify(int a[]);          /* function prototype */

main()
{
    int count, a[3];           /* array definition */

    printf("\nFrom main, before calling the function:\n");
    for (count = 0; count <= 2; ++count)   {
        a[count] = count + 1;
        printf("a[%d] = %d\n", count, a[count]);
    }

    modify(a);

    printf("\nFrom main, after calling the function:\n");
    for (count = 0; count <=2; ++count)
        printf("a[%d] = %d\n", count, a[count]);
}
```

```
void modify(int a[])            /* function definition */
{
    int count;

    printf("\nFrom the function, after modifying the values:\n");
    for (count = 0; count <= 2; ++count)   {
        a[count] = -9;
        printf("a[%d] = %d\n", count, a[count]);
    }
    return;
}
```

The array elements are assigned the values a[0] = 1, a[1] = 2 and a[2] = 3 within the first loop appearing in main. These values are displayed as soon as they are assigned. The array is then passed to the function modify, where each array element is assigned the value –9. These new values are then displayed from within the function. Finally, the values of the array elements are again displayed from main, after control has been transferred back to main from modify.

When the program is executed, the following output is generated.

```
From main, before calling the function:
a[0] = 1
a[1] = 2
a[2] = 3

From the function, after modifying the values:
a[0] = –9
a[1] = –9
a[2] = –9

From main, after calling the function:
a[0] = –9
a[1] = –9
a[2] = –9
```

These results show that the elements of a are altered within main as a result of the changes that were made within modify.

EXAMPLE 9.12   We now consider a variation of the previous program. The present program includes the use of a global variable, and the transfer of both a local variable and an array to the function.

```
#include <stdio.h>

int a = 1;                      /* global variable */
void modify(int b, int c[]);    /* function prototype */

main()
{
    int b = 2;              /* local variable */
    int count, c[3];        /* array definition */

    printf("\nFrom main, before calling the function:\n");
    printf("a = %d   b = %d\n", a, b);
    for (count = 0; count <= 2; ++count)   {
        c[count] = 10 * (count + 1);
        printf("c[%d] = %d\n", count, c[count]);
    }
```

```
    modify(b, c);                /* function access */
    printf("\nFrom main, after calling the function:\n");
    printf("a = %d   b = %d\n", a, b);
    for (count = 0; count <=2; ++count)
        printf("c[%d] = %d\n", count, c[count]);
}


void modify(int b, int c[])         /* function definition */
{
    int count;

    printf("\nFrom the function, after modifying the values:\n");
    a = -999;
    b = -999;
    printf("a = %d   b = %d\n", a, b);
    for (count = 0; count <= 2; ++count)   {
        c[count] = -9;
        printf("c[%d] = %d\n", count, c[count]);
    }
    return;
}
```

When the program is executed, the following output is generated.

```
From main, before calling the function:
a = 1   b = 2
c[0] = 10
c[1] = 20
c[2] = 30

From the function, after modifying the values:
a = -999   b = -999
c[0] = -9
c[1] = -9
c[2] = -9

From main, after calling the function:
a = -999   b = 2
c[0] = -9
c[1] = -9
c[2] = -9
```

We now see that the value of a and the elements of c are altered within main as a result of the changes that were made in modify. However, the change made to b is confined to the function, as expected. (Compare with the results obtained in the last example, and in Example 7.12.)

The ability to alter an array globally within a function provides a convenient mechanism for moving multiple data items back and forth between the function and the calling portion of the program. Simply pass the array to the function and then alter its elements within the function. Or, if the original array must be preserved, copy the array (element-by-element) within the calling portion of the program, pass the copy to the function, and perform the alterations. You should exercise some caution in altering an array within a function, however, since it is very easy to unintentionally alter the array outside of the function.

EXAMPLE 9.13 Reordering a List of Numbers   Consider the well-known problem of rearranging (i.e., *sorting*) a list of n integer quantities into a sequence of increasing values. Let us write a sorting program in such a manner that unnecessary storage will not be used. Therefore the program will contain only one array—a one-dimensional, integer array called x, which will be rearranged one element at a time.

The rearrangement will begin by scanning the entire array for the smallest number. This number will then be interchanged with the first number in the array, thus placing the smallest number at the top of the list. Next the remaining $n - 1$ numbers will be scanned for the smallest, which will be exchanged with the second number. The remaining $n - 2$ numbers will then be scanned for the smallest, which will be interchanged with the third number, and so on, until the entire array has been rearranged. The complete rearrangement will require a total of $n - 1$ passes through the array, though the length of each scan will become progressively smaller with each pass.

In order to find the smallest number within each pass, we sequentially compare each number in the array, x[i], with the starting number, x[item], where item is an integer variable that is used to identify a particular array element. If x[i] is smaller than x[item], then we interchange the two numbers; otherwise we leave the two numbers in their original positions. Once this procedure has been applied to the entire array, the first number in the array will be the smallest. We then repeat the entire procedure $n - 2$ times, for a total of $n - 1$ passes (item = 0, 1, . . . , $n - 2$).

The only remaining question is how the two numbers are actually interchanged. To carry out the interchange, we first temporarily save the value of x[item] for future reference. Then we assign the current value of x[i] to x[item]. Finally, we assign the *original* value of x[item], which has temporarily been saved, to x[i]. The interchange is now complete.

The strategy described above can be written in C as follows.

```
/* reorder all array elements */
for (item = 0; item < n - 1; ++item)
    /* find the smallest of all remaining elements */
    for (i = item + 1; i < n; ++i)
        if (x[i] < x[item])   {
            /* interchange two elements */
            temp = x[item];
            x[item] = x[i];
            x[i] = temp;
        }
```

We are assuming that item and i are integer variables that are used as counters, and that temp is an integer variable that is used to temporarily store the value of x[item].

It is now a simple matter to add the required variable and array definitions, and the required input/output statements. Here is a complete C program.

```
/* reorder a one-dimensional, integer array from smallest to largest */

#include <stdio.h>

#define  SIZE  100

void reorder(int n, int x[]);

main()
{
    int i, n, x[SIZE];

    /* read in a value for n */
    printf("\nHow many numbers will be entered? ");
    scanf("%d", &n);
    printf("\n");

    /* read in the list of numbers */
```

```
        for (i = 0; i < n; ++i)    {
            printf("i = %d    x = ", i + 1);
            scanf("%d", &x[i]);
        }

        /* reorder all array elements */
        reorder(n, x);

        /* display the reordered list of numbers */
        printf("\n\nReordered List of Numbers:\n\n");
        for (i = 0; i < n; ++i)
            printf("i = %d    x = %d\n", i + 1, x[i]);
    }


    void reorder(int n, int x[])    /* rearrange the list of numbers */

    {
        int i, item, temp;

        for (item = 0; item < n - 1; ++item)
            /* find the smallest of all remaining elements */
            for (i = item + 1; i < n; ++i)
                if (x[i] < x[item])    {
                    /* interchange two elements */
                    temp = x[item];
                    x[item] = x[i];
                    x[i] = temp;
                }
        return;
    }
```

In this program x is defined initially as a 100-element integer array. (Notice the use of the symbolic constant SIZE to define the size of x.) A value for n is first read into the computer, followed by numerical values for the first n elements of x (i.e., $x[0]$, $x[1]$, . . . , $x[n - 1]$). Following the data input, n and x are passed to the function reorder, where the first n elements of x are rearranged into ascending order. The reordered elements of x are then displayed from main at the conclusion of the program.

The declaration for reorder appearing in main is written as a function prototype, as a matter of good programming practice. Notice the manner in which the function arguments are written. In particular, note that the second argument is identified as an integer array by the empty square brackets that follow the array name, i.e., int x[]. The square brackets are a required part of this argument specification.

Now suppose that the program is used to reorder the following six numbers: 595 78 –1505 891 –29 –7. The program will generate the following interactive dialog. (The user's responses are underlined, as usual.)

```
How many numbers will be entered? 6

i = 1    x = 595
i = 2    x = 78
i = 3    x = -1505
i = 4    x = 891
i = 5    x = -29
i = 6    x = -7


Reordered list of numbers:
```

```
i = 1    x = -1505
i = 2    x = -29
i = 3    x = -7
i = 4    x = 78
i = 5    x = 595
i = 6    x = 891
```

It should be mentioned that *the* `return` *statement cannot be used to return an array*, since `return` can pass only a *single-valued* expression back to the calling portion of the program. Therefore, if the elements of an array are to be passed back to the calling portion of the program, the array must either be defined as an external array whose scope includes both the function and the calling portion of the program, or it must be passed to the function as a formal argument.

EXAMPLE 9.14 A Piglatin Generator   Piglatin is an encoded form of English that is often used by children as a game. A piglatin word is formed from an English word by transposing the first sound (usually the first letter) to the end of the word, and then adding the letter "a". Thus, the word "dog" becomes "ogda," "computer" becomes "omputerca," "piglatin" becomes "iglatinpa" (or "igpa atinla," if spelled as two separate words), and so on.

Let us write a C program that will accept a line of English text and then print out the corresponding text in piglatin. We will assume that each textual message can be typed on one 80-column line, with a single blank space between successive words. (Actually, we will require that the *piglatin* message not exceed 80 characters. Therefore the original message must be somewhat less than 80 characters, since the corresponding piglatin message will be lengthened by the addition of the letter "a" after each word.) For simplicity, we will transpose only the first letter (not the first sound) of each word. Also, we will ignore any special consideration that might be given to capital letters and to punctuation marks.

We will use two character arrays in this program. One array will contain the original line of English text, and the other will contain the translated piglatin.

The overall computational strategy will be straightforward, consisting of the following major steps.

1.   Initialize both arrays by assigning blank spaces to all of the elements.

2.   Read in an entire line of text (several words).

3.   Determine the number of words in the line (by counting the number of single blank spaces that are followed by a nonblank space).

4.   Rearrange the words into piglatin, on a word-by-word basis, as follows:
     (*a*) Locate the end of the word.
     (*b*) Transpose the first letter to the end of the word and then add an "a."
     (*c*) Locate the beginning of the next word.

5.   Display the entire line of piglatin.

We will continue this procedure repetitively, until the computer reads a line of text whose first three letters are "end" (or "END").

In order to implement this strategy we will make use of two markers, called `m1` and `m2`, respectively. The first marker (`m1`) will indicate the position of the beginning of a particular word within the original line of text. The second marker (`m2`) will indicate the end of the word. Note that the character in the column preceding column number `m1` will be a blank space (except for the first word). Also, note that the character in the column beyond column number `m2` will be a blank space.

This program lends itself to the use of a function for carrying out each of the major tasks. Before discussing the individual functions, however, we define the following program variables.

   `english` = a one-dimensional character array that represents the original line of text

   `piglatin` = a one-dimensional character array that represents the new line of text (i.e., the piglatin)

      `words` = an integer variable that indicates the number of words in the given line of text

         `n` = an integer variable that is used as a word counter (n = 1, 2, . . . , `words`)

     `count` = an integer variable that is used as a character counter within each line (`count` = 0, 1, 2, . . . , 79)

We will also make use of the integer variables `m1` and `m2` discussed earlier.

Now let us return to the overall program outline presented above. The first step, array initialization, can be carried out in a straightforward manner with the following function.

```
/* initialize the character arrays with blank spaces */

void initialize(char english[], char piglatin[])

{
    int count;

    for (count = 0; count < 80; ++count)
        english[count] = piglatin[count] = ' ';
    return;
}
```

Step 2 can also be carried out with a simple function. This procedure will contain a while loop that will continue to read characters from the keyboard until an end of line is detected. This sequence of characters will become the elements of the character array english. Here is the complete function.

```
/* read one line of English text */

void readinput(char english[])

{
    int count = 0;
    char c;

    while ((c = getchar()) != '\n')   {
            english[count] = c;
            ++count;
    }
    return;
}
```

Step 3 of the overall outline is equally straightforward. We simply scan the original line for occurrences of single blank characters followed by nonblank characters. The word counter (words) is then incremented each time a single blank character is encountered. Here is the word-count routine.

```
/* scan the English text and determine the number of words */

int countwords(char english[])

{
    int count, words = 1;

    for (count = 0; count < 79; ++count)
    if (english[count] == ' ' && english[count + 1] != ' ')
        ++words;
    return (words);
}
```

Now consider step 4 (rearrange the English text into piglatin), which is really the heart of the program. The logic for carrying this out is rather involved since it requires three separate, though related, operations. We must first identify the end of each word by finding the first blank space beyond m1. We then assign the characters that make up the word to the character array piglatin, with the first character at the end of the word. Finally, we must reset the initial marker, to identify the beginning of the next word.

The logic must be handled carefully, since the new line of text will be longer than the original line (because of the latter "a" added at the end). Hence, the characters in the first piglatin word will occupy locations m1 to m2+1. The characters in the second word will occupy locations m1+1 to m2+2 (note that these are new values for m1 and m2), and so on. These rules can be generalized as follows.

First, for word number n, transfer all characters except the first from the original line to the new line. This can be accomplished by writing

```
for (count = m1; count < m2; ++count)
    piglatin[count + (n - 1)] = english[count + 1];
```

The last two characters (i.e., the first character in the original word plus the letter "a") can then be added in the following manner.

```
piglatin[m2 + (n - 1)] = english[m1];
piglatin[m2 + n] = 'a';
```

We then reset the value of m1, i.e.,

```
m1 = m2 + 2;
```

in preparation for the next word. This entire group of calculations is repeated for each word in the original line.

Here is the function that accomplishes all of this.

```
/* convert each word into piglatin */

void convert(int words, char english[], char piglatin[])

{
    int n, count;
    int m1 = 0;              /* marker -> beginning of word */
    int m2;                  /* marker -> end of word       */

    /* convert each word */
    for (n = 1; n <= words; ++n)   {

        /* locate the end of the current word */
        count = m1;
        while (english[count] != ' ')
            m2 = count++;

        /* transpose the first letter and add 'a' */
        for (count = m1; count < m2; ++count)
            piglatin[count + (n - 1)] = english[count + 1];
        piglatin[m2 + (n - 1)] = english[m1];
        piglatin[m2 + n] = 'a';

        /* reset the initial marker */
        m1 = m2 + 2;
    }
    return;
}
```

Step 5 (display the piglatin) requires little more than a for loop. The complete function can be written as

```
/* display the line of text in piglatin */

void writeoutput(char piglatin[])
{
    int count = 0;

    for (count = 0; count < 80; ++count)
        putchar(piglatin[count]);
    printf("\n");
    return;
}
```

Now consider the main portion of the program. This is nothing more than a group of definitions and declarations, an initial message, a do - while loop that allows for repetitious program execution (until the word "end" is detected, in either upper or lowercase, as the first word in the english text), and a closing message. The do - while loop can be made to continue indefinitely by using the test (words >= 0) at the end of the loop. Since words is assigned an initial value of 1 and its value does not decrease, the test will always be true.

The complete program is shown below.

```
/* convert English to piglatin, one line at a time */

#include <stdio.h>
#include <stdlib.h>
#include <ctype.h>

void initialize(char english[], char piglatin[]);
void readinput(char english[]);
int countwords(char english[]);
void convert(int words, char english[], char piglatin[]);
void writeoutput(char piglatin[]);

main()
{
    char english[80], piglatin[80];
    int words;

    printf("Welcome to the Piglatin Generator\n\n");
    printf("Type \'END\' when finished\n\n");

    do {  /* process a new line of text */

            initialize(english, piglatin);
            readinput(english);

            /* test for stopping condition */
            if (toupper(english[0]) == 'E' &&
                toupper(english[1]) == 'N' &&
                toupper(english[2]) == 'D')   break;

            /* count the number of words in the line */
            words = countwords(english);

            /* convert english into piglatin */
            convert(words, english, piglatin);
            writeoutput(piglatin);
    }
    while (words >= 0);

    printf("\naveHa aa icena ayda  (Have a nice day)\n");
}
```

```
/* initialize the character arrays with blank spaces */

void initialize(char english[], char piglatin[])

{
    int count;

    for (count = 0; count < 80; ++count)
        english[count] = piglatin[count] = ' ';
    return;
}

/* read one line of English text */

void readinput(char english[])

{
    int count = 0;
    char c;

    while ((c = getchar()) != '\n')   {
            english[count] = c;
            ++count;
    }
    return;
}

/* scan the English text and determine the number of words */

int countwords(char english[])

{
    int count, words = 1;

    for (count = 0; count < 79; ++count)
        if (english[count] == ' ' && english[count + 1] != ' ')
            ++words;
    return (words);
}

/* convert each word into piglatin */

void convert(int words, char english[], char piglatin[])

{
    int n, count;
    int m1 = 0;            /* marker -> beginning of word */
    int m2;                /* marker -> end of word        */

    /* convert each word */
    for (n = 1; n <= words; ++n)   {

        /* locate the end of the current word */
        count = m1;
        while (english[count] != ' ')
                m2 = count++;

        /* transpose the first letter and add 'a' */
        for (count = m1; count < m2; ++count)
            piglatin[count + (n - 1)] = english[count + 1];
        piglatin[m2 + (n - 1)] = english[m1];
        piglatin[m2 + n] = 'a';
```

```
        /* reset the initial marker */
        m1 = m2 + 2;
    }
    return;
}


/* display the line of text in piglatin */

void writeoutput(char piglatin[])

{
    int count = 0;

    for (count = 0; count < 80; ++count)
        putchar(piglatin[count]);
    printf("\n");
    return;
}
```

Notice that each function requires at least one array as an argument. In countwords and writeoutput, the array arguments simply provide input to the functions. In convert, however, one array argument provides input to the function and the other provides output to main. And in initialize and readinput, the arrays represent information that is returned to main.

The function declarations within main are written as full function prototypes. Note that each array argument is identified by an empty pair of square brackets following the array name.

Now consider what happens when the program is executed. Here is a typical interactive session, in which the user's entries are underlined.

```
Welcome to the Piglatin Generator

Type 'END' when finished

C is a popular structured programming language
Ca sia aa opularpa tructuredsa rogrammingpa anguagela

baseball is the great American pastime,
aseballba sia heta reatga mericanAa astime,pa

though there are many who prefer football
houghta hereta reaa anyma howa referpa ootballfa

please do not sneeze in the computer room
leasepa oda otna neezesa nia heta omputerca oomra

end

aveHa aa icena ayda   (Have a nice day)
```

The program does not include any special accommodations for punctuation marks, uppercase letters, or double-letter sounds (e.g., "th" or "sh"). These refinements are left as exercises for the reader.

9.4 MULTIDIMENSIONAL ARRAYS

Multidimensional arrays are defined in much the same manner as one-dimensional arrays, except that a separate pair of square brackets is required for each subscript. Thus, a two-dimensional array will require two pairs of square brackets, a three-dimensional array will require three pairs of square brackets, and so on.

In general terms, a multidimensional array definition can be written as *storage-class data-type*   array[*expression 1*][*expression 2*] . . .[*expression n*];

where *storage-class* refers to the storage class of the array, *data-type* is its data type, *array* is the array name, and *expression 1,   expression 2, . . .,   expression n* are positive-valued integer expressions that indicate the number of array elements associated with each subscript. Remember that the *storage-class* is optional; the default values are *automatic* for arrays that are defined inside of a function, and *external* for arrays defined outside of a function.

We have already seen that an n-element, one-dimensional array can be thought of as a *list* of values, as illustrated in Fig. 9.1. Similarly, an m × n, two-dimensional array can be thought of as a *table* of values having m rows and n columns, as illustrated in Fig. 9.2. Extending this idea, a three-dimensional array can be visualized as a *set* of tables (e.g., a book in which each page is a table), and so on.

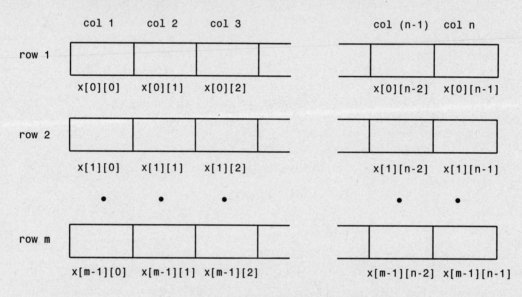

x is a m × n, two-dimensional array

Fig. 9.2

EXAMPLE 9.15   Several typical multidimensional array definitions are shown below.

```
float table[50][50];

char page[24][80];

static double records[100][66][255];

static double records[L][M][N];
```

The first line defines table as a floating-point array having 50 rows and 50 columns (hence 50 × 50 = 2500 elements), and the second line establishes page as a character array with 24 rows and 80 columns (24 × 80 = 1920 elements). The third array can be thought of as a set of 100 static, double-precision tables, each having 66 lines and 255 columns (hence 100 × 66 × 255 = 1,683,000 elements).

The last definition is similar to the preceding definition except that the array size is defined by the symbolic constants L, M and N. Thus, the values assigned to these symbolic constants will determine the actual size of the array.

Some care must be given to the order in which initial values are assigned to multidimensional array elements. (Remember, *only external and static arrays can be initialized.*) The rule is that the last (rightmost) subscript increases most rapidly, and the first (leftmost) subscript increases least rapidly. Thus, the elements of a two-dimensional array will be assigned by rows; i.e., the elements of the first row will be assigned, then the elements of the second row, and so on.

EXAMPLE 9.16 Consider the following two-dimensional array definition.

```
int values[3][4] = {1, 2, 3, 4, 5, 6, 7, 8, 9, 10, 11, 12};
```

Note that `values` can be thought of as a table having 3 rows and 4 columns (4 elements per row). Since the initial values are assigned by rows (i.e., last subscript increasing most rapidly), the results of this initial assignment are as follows.

```
values[0][0] = 1    values[0][1] = 2    values[0][2] = 3    values[0][3] = 4
values[1][0] = 5    values[1][1] = 6    values[1][2] = 7    values[1][3] = 8
values[2][0] = 9    values[2][1] = 10   values[2][2] = 11   values[2][3] = 12
```

Remember that the first subscript ranges from 0 to 2, and the second subscript ranges from 0 to 3.

The natural order in which the initial values are assigned can be altered by forming groups of initial values enclosed within braces (i.e., { . . . }). The values within each innermost pair of braces will be assigned to those array elements whose last subscript changes most rapidly. In a two-dimensional array, for example, the values within an inner pair of braces will be assigned to the elements of a row, since the second (column) subscript increases most rapidly. If there are too few values within a pair of braces, the remaining elements of that row will be assigned zeros. However, the number of values within each pair of braces cannot exceed the defined row size.

EXAMPLE 9.17 Here is a variation of the two-dimensional array definition presented in the last example.

```
int values[3][4] = {
                     {1, 2, 3, 4},
                     {5, 6, 7, 8},
                     {9, 10, 11, 12}
                   };
```

This definition results in the same initial assignments as in the last example. Thus, the four values in the first inner pair of braces are assigned to the array elements in the first row, the values in the second inner pair of braces are assigned to the array elements in the second row, etc. Note that an outer pair of braces is required, containing the inner pairs.

Now consider the following two-dimensional array definition.

```
int values[3][4] = {
                     {1, 2, 3},
                     {4, 5, 6},
                     {7, 8, 9}
                   };
```

This definition assigns values only to the first three elements in each row. Therefore, the array elements will have the following initial values.

```
values[0][0] = 1    values[0][1] = 2    values[0][2] = 3    values[0][3] = 0
values[1][0] = 4    values[1][1] = 5    values[1][2] = 6    values[1][3] = 0
values[2][0] = 7    values[2][1] = 8    values[2][2] = 9    values[2][3] = 0
```

Notice that the last element in each row is assigned a value of zero.

If the preceding array definition is written as

```
int values[3][4] = {1, 2, 3, 4, 5, 6, 7, 8, 9};
```

then three of the array elements will again be assigned zeros, though the order of the assignments will be different. In particular, the array elements will have the following initial values.

```
values[0][0] = 1    values[0][1] = 2    values[0][2] = 3    values[0][3] = 4
values[1][0] = 5    values[1][1] = 6    values[1][2] = 7    values[1][3] = 8
values[2][0] = 9    values[2][1] = 0    values[2][2] = 0    values[2][3] = 0
```

Now the initial values are assigned with the last subscript increasing most rapidly, on a row-by-row basis, until all of the initial values have been assigned. Without the inner pairs of braces, however, the initial values cannot be grouped for assignment to specific rows.

Finally, consider the array definition

```
int values[3][4] = {
                        {1, 2, 3, 4, 5},
                        {6, 7, 8, 9, 10},
                        {11, 12, 13, 14, 15}
                    };
```

This will result in a compilation error, since the number of values in each inner pair of braces (five values in each pair) exceeds the defined array size (four elements in each row).

The use of embedded groups of initial values can be generalized to higher dimensional arrays.

EXAMPLE 9.18   Consider the following three-dimensional array definition.

```
int t[10][20][30] = {
                    {                       /* table 1 */
                        {1, 2, 3, 4},       /* row 1 */
                        {5, 6, 7, 8},       /* row 2 */
                        {9, 10, 11, 12}     /* row 3 */
                    },

                    {                       /* table 2 */
                        {21, 22, 23, 24},   /* row 1 */
                        {25, 26, 27, 28},   /* row 2 */
                        {29, 30, 31, 32}    /* row 3 */
                    }
                };
```

Think of this array as a collection of 10 tables, each having 20 rows and 30 columns. The groups of initial values will result in the assignment of the following nonzero values in the first two tables.

```
t[0][0][0] = 1     t[0][0][1] = 2     t[0][0][2] = 3     t[0][0][3] = 4
t[0][1][0] = 5     t[0][1][1] = 6     t[0][1][2] = 7     t[0][1][3] = 8
t[0][2][0] = 9     t[0][2][1] = 10    t[0][2][2] = 11    t[0][2][3] = 12

t[1][0][0] = 21    t[1][0][1] = 22    t[1][0][2] = 23    t[1][0][3] = 24
t[1][1][0] = 25    t[1][1][1] = 26    t[1][1][2] = 27    t[1][1][3] = 28
t[1][2][0] = 29    t[1][2][1] = 30    t[1][2][2] = 31    t[1][2][3] = 32
```

All of the remaining array elements will be assigned zeros.

Multidimensional arrays are processed in the same manner as one-dimensional arrays, on an element-by-element basis. However, some care is required when passing multidimensional arrays to a function. In particular, the formal argument declarations within the function definition *must* include explicit size specifications in all of the subscript positions *except the first*. These size specifications must be consistent with the corresponding size specifications in the calling program. The first subscript position may be written as an empty pair of square brackets, as with a one-dimensional array. The corresponding function prototypes must be written in the same manner.

EXAMPLE 9.19 Adding Two Tables of Numbers   Suppose we want to read two tables of integers into the computer, calculate the sums of the corresponding elements, i.e.,

```
c[i][j] = a[i][j] + b[i][j]
```

and then display the new table containing these sums. We will assume that all of the tables contain the same number of rows and columns, not exceeding 20 rows and 30 columns.

Let us make use of the following variable and array definitions.

   a, b, c = two-dimensional arrays, each having the same number of rows and the same number of columns, not
                    exceeding 20 rows and 30 columns

     nrows = an integer variable indicating the actual number of rows in each table

     ncols = an integer variable indicating the actual number of columns in each table

       row = an integer counter that indicates the row number

       col = an integer counter that indicates the column number

The program will be modularized by writing separate functions to read in an array, calculate the sum of the array elements, and display an array. Let us call these functions readinput, computesums and writeoutput, respectively.

The logic within each function is quite straightforward. Here is a complete C program for carrying out the computation.

```
/* calculate the sum of the elements in two tables of integers */

#include <stdio.h>

#define MAXROWS  20
#define MAXCOLS  30

void readinput(int a[][MAXCOLS], int nrows, int ncols);
void computesums(int a[][MAXCOLS], int b[][MAXCOLS],
                 int c[][MAXCOLS], int nrows, int ncols);
void writeoutput(int c[][MAXCOLS], int nrows, int ncols);


main()

{
    int nrows, ncols;

    /* array definitions */
    int a[MAXROWS][MAXCOLS], b[MAXROWS][MAXCOLS], c[MAXROWS][MAXCOLS];

    printf("How many rows? ");
    scanf("%d", &nrows);
    printf("How many columns? ");
    scanf("%d", &ncols);

    printf("\n\nFirst table:\n");
    readinput(a, nrows, ncols);

    printf("\n\nSecond table:\n");
    readinput(b, nrows, ncols);

    computesums(a, b, c, nrows, ncols);
```

```
        printf("\n\nSums of the elements:\n\n");
        writeoutput(c, nrows, ncols);
    }


    /* read in a table of integers */

    void readinput(int a[][MAXCOLS], int m, int n)

    {
        int row, col;

        for (row = 0; row < m; ++row)    {
            printf("\nEnter data for row no. %2d\n", row + 1);
            for (col = 0; col < n; ++col)
                scanf("%d", &a[row][col]);
        }
        return;
    }


    /* add the elements of two integer tables */

    void computesums(int a[][MAXCOLS], int b[][MAXCOLS],
                     int c[][MAXCOLS], int m, int n)

    {
        int row, col;

        for (row = 0; row < m; ++row)
            for (col = 0; col < n; ++col)
                c[row][col] = a[row][col] + b[row][col];
        return;
    }


    /* display a table of integers */

    void writeoutput(int a[][MAXCOLS], int m, int n)

    {
        int row, col;

        for (row = 0; row < m; ++row)    {
            for (col = 0; col < n; ++col)
                printf("%4d", a[row][col]);
            printf("\n");
        }
        return;
    }
```

The array definitions are expressed in terms of the symbolic constants MAXROWS and MAXCOLS, whose values are specified as 20 and 30, respectively, at the beginning of the program.

Notice the manner in which the formal argument declarations are written within each function definition. For example, the first line of function readinput is written as

```
        void readinput(int a[][MAXCOLS], int m, int n)
```

The array name, a, is followed by two pairs of square brackets. The first pair is empty, because the number of rows need not be specified explicitly. However, the second pair contains the symbolic constant MAXCOLS, which provides an explicit size specification for the number of columns. The array names appearing in the other function definitions (i.e., in functions computesums and writeoutput) are written in the same manner.

Also, notice the function prototypes at the beginning of the program. Each prototype is analogous to the first line of the corresponding function definition. In particular, each array name is followed by two pairs of brackets, the first of which is empty. The second pair of brackets contains the size specification for the number of columns, as required.

Now suppose the program is used to sum the following two tables of numbers.

	First table				*Second table*			
1	2	3	4		10	11	12	13
5	6	7	8		14	15	16	17
9	10	11	12		18	19	20	21

Execution of the program will generate the following dialog. (The user's responses are underlined, as usual.)

```
How many rows? 3
How many columns? 4

First table:

Enter data for row no.   1
1 2 3 4

Enter data for row no.   2
5 6 7 8

Enter data for row no.   3
9 10 11 12

Second table:

Enter data for row no.   1
10 11 12 13

Enter data for row no.   2
14 15 16 17

Enter data for row no.   3
18 19 20 21

Sums of the elements:

11   13   15   17
19   21   23   25
27   29   31   33
```

Some C compilers are unable to pass sizeable multidimensional arrays to functions. In such situations it may be possible to redesign the program so that the multidimensional arrays are defined as external (global) arrays. Hence, the arrays need not be passed to functions as arguments. This strategy will not always work, however, because some programs (such as the program shown in the last example) use the same function to process different arrays. Problems of this type can usually be circumvented through the use of pointers, as discussed in the next chapter.

9.5 ARRAYS AND STRINGS

We have already seen that a string can be represented as a one-dimensional character-type array. Each character within the string will be stored within one element of the array. Some problems require that the

characters within a string be processed individually (e.g., the piglatin generator shown in Example 9.14).
However, there are many other problems which require that strings be processed as complete entities. Such
problems can be simplified considerably through the use special string-oriented library functions.

For example, most C compilers include library functions that allow strings to be compared, copied or
concatenated (i.e., combined, one behind another). Other library functions permit operations on individual
characters within strings; e.g., they allow individual characters to be located within strings, and so on. The
following example illustrates the use of some of these library functions.

EXAMPLE 9.20 Reordering a List of Strings   Suppose we wish to enter a list of strings into the computer, rearrange
them into alphabetical order, and then display the rearranged list. The strategy for doing this is very similar to that shown
in Example 9.13, where we rearranged a list of numbers into ascending order. Now, however, there is the additional
complication of comparing entire strings, rather than single numerical values. We will therefore store the strings within a
two-dimensional character array. Each string will be stored in a separate row within the array.

To simplify the computation, let us make use of the library functions strcmp and strcpy. These functions are used
to compare two strings and to copy one string to another, respectively. (Some compilers also include the strcmpi
function, which is a variation of the more common strcmp. The use of strcmpi is sometimes more convenient, since it
does not distinguish between upper- and lowercase. However, it is not supported by the ANSI standard.)

The strcmp function accepts two strings as arguments and returns an integer value, depending upon the relative
order of the two strings, as follows:

1.   A negative value if the first string precedes the second string alphabetically.

2.   A value of zero if the first string and the second string are identical (disregarding case).

3.   A positive value if the second string precedes the first string alphabetically.

Therefore, if strcmp(*string1, string2*) returns a positive value, it would indicate that *string2* must be moved,
placing it ahead of *string1* in order to alphabetize the two strings properly.

The strcpy function also accepts two strings as arguments. Its first argument is generally an identifier that
represents a string. The second argument can be a string constant or an identifier representing another string. The
function copies the value of *string2* to *string1*. Hence, it effectively causes one string to be assigned to another.

The complete program is very similar to the numerical reordering program presented in Example 9.13. Now,
however, we will allow the program to accept an unspecified number of strings, until a string is entered whose first three
characters are END (in either upper- or lowercase). The program will count the strings as they are entered, ignoring the last
string, which contains END.

Here is the entire program.

```
/* sort a list of strings alphabetically using a two-dimensional character array */

#include <stdio.h>
#include <stdlib.h>
#include <string.h>

void reorder(int n, char x[][12]);        /* function prototype */

main()
{
    int i, n = 0;
    char x[10][12];

    printf("Enter each string on a separate line below\n\n");
    printf("Type \'END\' when finished\n\n");

    /* read in the list of strings */
    do {
            printf("string %d: ", n + 1);
            scanf("%s", x[n]);
        } while (strcmp(x[n++], "END"));
```

```
        /* adjust the value of n */

        n--;
        /* reorder the list of strings */
        reorder(n, x);

        /* display the reordered list of strings */
        printf("\n\nReordered List of Strings:\n");
        for (i = 0; i < n; ++i)
            printf("\nstring %d: %s", i + 1, x[i]);
}


void reorder(int n, char x[][12])      /* rearrange the list of strings */

{
    char temp[12];
    int i, item;

    for (item = 0; item < n - 1; ++item)

        /* find the lowest of all remaining strings */
        for (i = item + 1; i < n; ++i)

            if (strcmp(x[item], x[i]) > 0)   {
                /* interchange the two strings */
                strcpy(temp, x[item]);
                strcpy(x[item], x[i]);
                strcpy(x[i], temp);
            }
    return;
}
```

The strcmp function appears in two different places within this program: in main, when testing for a stopping condition, and in rearrange, when testing for the need to interchange two strings. The actual string interchange is carried out using strcpy.

The dialog resulting from a typical execution of the program is shown below. The user's responses are underlined, as usual.


```
Enter each string on a separate line below

Type 'END' when finished

string 1: PACIFIC
string 2: ATLANTIC
string 3: INDIAN
string 4: CARIBBEAN
string 5: BERING
string 6: BLACK
string 7: RED
string 8: NORTH
string 9: BALTIC
string 10: CASPIAN
string 11: END
```

```
Reordered List of Strings:

string 1: ATLANTIC
string 2: BALTIC
string 3: BERING
string 4: BLACK
string 5: CARIBBEAN
string 6: CASPIAN
string 7: INDIAN
string 8: NORTH
string 9: PACIFIC
string 10: RED
```

In the next chapter we will see a different way to represent lists of strings, which is more efficient in terms of its memory requirements.

Review Questions

9.1   In what way does an array differ from an ordinary variable?

9.2   What conditions must be satisfied by all of the elements of any given array?

9.3   How are individual array elements identified?

9.4   What are subscripts? How are they written? What restrictions apply to the values that can be assigned to subscripts?

9.5   Suggest a practical way to visualize one-dimensional arrays and two-dimensional arrays.

9.6   How does an array definition differ from that of an ordinary variable?

9.7   Summarize the rules for writing a one-dimensional array definition.

9.8   What advantage is there in defining an array size in terms of a symbolic constant rather than a fixed integer quantity?

9.9   Can initial values be specified within an external array definition? Can they be specified within a static array definition? Can they be specified within an automatic array definition?

9.10 How are initial values written in a one-dimensional array definition? Must the entire array be initialized?

9.11 What value is automatically assigned to those array elements that are not explicitly initialized?

9.12 Describe the manner in which an initial string constant is most commonly assigned to a one-dimensional character array. Can a similar procedure be used to assign values to a one-dimensional numerical array?

9.13 When a one-dimensional character array of unspecified length is assigned an initial value, what extra character is automatically added to the end of the string?

9.14 When are array declarations (in contrast to array definitions) required in a C program? How do such declarations differ from array definitions?

9.15 How are arrays usually processed in C? Can entire arrays be processed with single instructions, without repetition?

9.16 When passing an array to a function, how must the array argument be written? How is the corresponding formal argument written?

9.17 How is an array name interpreted when it is passed to a function?

9.18 Suppose a function declaration includes argument type specifications, and one of the arguments is an array. How must the array type specification be written?

9.19 When passing an argument to a function, what is the difference between passing by value and passing by reference? To what types of arguments does each apply?

9.20 If an array is passed to a function and several of its elements are altered within the function, are these changes recognized in the calling portion of the program? Explain.

9.21 Can an array be passed from a function to the calling portion of the program via a `return` statement?

9.22 How are multidimensional arrays defined? Compare with the manner in which one-dimensional arrays are defined.

9.23 State the rule that determines the order in which initial values are assigned to multidimensional array elements.

9.24 When assigning initial values to the elements of a multidimensional array, what advantage is there to forming groups of initial values, where each group is enclosed in its own set of braces?

9.25 When a multidimensional array is passed to a function, how are the formal argument declarations written? Compare with one-dimensional arrays.

9.26 How can a list of strings be stored within a two-dimensional array? How can the individual strings be processed? What library functions are available to simplify string processing?

Problems

9.27 Describe the array that is defined in each of the following statements.

(a) `char name[30];`

(b) `float c[6];`

(c) `#define  N  50`

     `. . . . .`

     `int a[N];`

(d) `int params[5][5];`

(e) `#define  A  66`

     `#define  B  132`

     `. . . . .`

     `char memo[A][B];`

(f) `double accounts[50][20][80];`

9.28 Describe the array that is defined in each of the following statements. Indicate what values are assigned to the individual array elements.

(a) `float c[8] = {2., 5., 3., -4., 12., 12., 0., 8.};`

(b) `float c[8] = {2., 5., 3., -4.};`

(c) `int z[12] = {0, 0, 8, 0, 0, 6};`

(d) `char flag[4] = {'T', 'R', 'U', 'E'};`

(e) `char flag[5] = {'T', 'R', 'U', 'E'};`

(f) `char flag[] = "TRUE";`

(g) `char flag[] = "FALSE";`

(h) `int p[2][4] = {1, 3, 5, 7};`

(i) `int p[2][4] = {1, 1, 3, 3, 5, 5, 7, 7};`

(j) `int p[2][4] = {`
          `{1, 3, 5, 7},`
          `{2, 4, 6, 8}`
   `};`

(k) `int p[2][4] = {`
          `{1, 3},`
          `{5, 7}`
   `};`

```
(l)     int c[2][3][4] = {

                        {
                            {1, 2, 3},
                            {4, 5},
                            {6, 7, 8, 9}
                        },
                        {
                            {10, 11},
                            {},
                            {12, 13, 14}
                        }
                    };

(m)   char colors[3][6] = {
                            {'R', 'E', 'D'},
                            {'G', 'R', 'E', 'E', 'N'},
                            {'B', 'L', 'U', 'E'}
                    };
```

9.29   Write an appropriate array definition for each of the following problem situations.

(a)   Define a one-dimensional, 12-element integer array called c. Assign the values 1, 4, 7, 10, . . . , 34 to the array elements.

(b)   Define a one-dimensional character array called point. Assign the string "NORTH" to the array elements. End the string with the null character.

(c)   Define a one-dimensional, four-element character array called letters. Assign the characters 'N', 'S', 'E' and 'W' to the array elements.

(d)   Define a one-dimensional, six-element floating-point array called consts. Assign the following values to the array elements:

$$0.005 \qquad -0.032 \qquad 1e{-}6 \qquad 0.167 \qquad -0.3e8 \qquad 0.015$$

(e)   Define a two-dimensional, 3×4 integer array called n. Assign the following values to the array elements:

10	12	14	16
20	22	24	26
30	32	34	36

(f)   Define a two-dimensional, 3×4 integer array called n. Assign the following values to the array elements:

10	12	14	0
0	20	22	0
0	30	32	0

(g)   Define a two-dimensional, 3×4 integer array called n. Assign the following values to the array elements:

10	12	14	16
20	22	0	0
0	0	0	0

9.30   In each of the following situations, write the definitions and declarations required to transfer the indicated. variables and arrays from main to a function called sample (see Examples 9.10 and 9.11). In each case, assign the value returned from the function to the floating-point variable x.

(a)   Transfer the floating-point variables a and b, and the one-dimensional, 20-element integer array jstar.

(b)   Transfer the integer variable n, the character variable c and the one-dimensional, 50-element double-precision array values.

(c)   Transfer the two-dimensional, 12×80 character array text.

(d)   Transfer the one-dimensional, 40-element character array message, and the two-dimensional, 50×100 floating-point array accounts.

9.31   Describe the output generated by each of the following programs.

(*a*)
```c
#include <stdio.h>

main()
{
    int a, b = 0;
    static int c[10] = {1, 2, 3, 4, 5, 6, 7, 8, 9, 0};

    for (a = 0; a < 10; ++a)
        if ((c[a] % 2) == 0) b += c[a];
    printf("%d", b);
}
```

(*b*)
```c
#include <stdio.h>

main()
{
    int a, b = 0;
    static int c[10] = {1, 2, 3, 4, 5, 6, 7, 8, 9, 0};

    for (a = 0; a < 10; ++a)
        if ((a % 2) == 0) b += c[a];
    printf("%d", b);
}
```

(*c*)
```c
#include <stdio.h>

main()
{
    int a, b = 0;
    int c[10] = {1, 2, 3, 4, 5, 6, 7, 8, 9, 0};

    for (a = 0; a < 10; ++a)
        b += c[a];
    printf("%d", b);
}
```

(*d*)
```c
#include <stdio.h>

int c[10] = {1, 2, 3, 4, 5, 6, 7, 8, 9, 0};

main()
{
    int a, b = 0;

    for (a = 0; a < 10; ++a)
        if ((c[a] % 2) == 1) b += c[a];
    printf("%d", b);
}
```

(*e*)
```c
#include <stdio.h>

#define  ROWS    3
#define  COLUMNS  4

int z[ROWS][COLUMNS] = {1, 2, 3, 4, 5, 6, 7, 8, 9, 10, 11, 12};

main()
{
    int a, b, c = 999;
```

```
            for (a = 0; a < ROWS; ++a)
                for (b = 0;  b < COLUMNS;  ++b)
                    if (z[a][b] < c) c = z[a][b];
            printf("%d", c);
        }


(f)    #include <stdio.h>

       #define  ROWS  3
       #define  COLUMNS  4

       int z[ROWS][COLUMNS] = {1, 2, 3, 4, 5, 6, 7, 8, 9, 10, 11, 12};

       main()
       {
           int a, b, c;

           for (a = 0; a < ROWS; ++a)   {
               c = 999;
               for (b = 0; b < COLUMNS; ++b)
                   if (z[a][b] < c) c = z[a][b];
               printf("%d  ", c);
           }
       }

(g)    #include <stdio.h>

       #define  ROWS  3
       #define  COLUMNS  4

       void sub1(int z[][COLUMNS]);

       main()
       {
           static int z[ROWS][COLUMNS] = {1, 2, 3, 4, 5, 6, 7, 8, 9, 10, 11, 12};

           sub1(z);
       }

       void sub1(int x[][4])
       {
           int a, b, c;

           for (b = 0; b < COLUMNS; ++b)   {
               c = 0;
               for (a = 0; a < ROWS; ++a)
                   if (x[a][b] > c) c = x[a][b];
               printf("%d  ", c);
           }
           return;
       }

(h)    #include <stdio.h>

       #define  ROWS  3
       #define  COLUMNS  4

       void sub1(int z[][COLUMNS]);
```

```
main()
{
    int a, b;
    static int z[ROWS][COLUMNS] = {1, 2, 3, 4, 5, 6, 7, 8, 9, 10, 11, 12};

    sub1(z);

    for (a = 0; a < ROWS; ++a)   {
        for (b = 0; b < COLUMNS; ++b)
            printf("%d  ", z[a][b]);
        printf("\n");
    }
}

void sub1(int x[][COLUMNS])
{
    int a, b;

    for (a = 0; a < ROWS; ++a)
        for (b = 0; b < COLUMNS; ++b)
            if ((x[a][b] % 2) == 1) x[a][b]--;
    return;
}
```

(*i*)   ```
         #include <stdio.h>

         main()
         {
             int a;
             static char c[] = "Programming with C can be great fun!";

             for (a = 0; c[a] != '\0'; ++a)
                 if ((a % 2) == 0)
                     printf("%c%c", c[a], c[a]);
         }
         ```

## Programming Problems

**9.32**  Modify the program given in Example 9.8 (deviations about an average) to include two additional functions. Have the first function read in the numbers to be averaged, calculating their sum as they are entered. The second function should calculate the deviations about the average. All remaining program features (reading in a value for n, calculating a value for the average, displaying the calculated average and displaying the deviations about the average) should be carried out in the main portion of the program.

**9.33**  Modify the program given in Example 9.9 (deviations about an average revisited) to include two additional functions. Calculate and display the average in the first function. Calculate and display the deviations about the average in the second function.

**9.34**  Modify the program given in Example 9.13 (reordering a list of numbers) so that the numbers are rearranged into a sequence of *decreasing* values (i.e., from largest to smallest). Test the program using the data given in Example 9.13.

**9.35**  Modify the program given in Example 9.13 (reordering a list of numbers) so that any one of the following rearrangements can be carried out:

(*a*)    Smallest to largest, by magnitude

(*b*)    Smallest to largest, algebraic (by sign)
         ```

(c)   Largest to smallest, by magnitude

(d)   Largest to smallest, algebraic

Include a menu that will allow the user to select which rearrangement will be used each time the program is executed. Test the program using the following 10 values.

4.7	−8.0
−2.3	11.4
12.9	5.1
8.8	−0.2
6.0	−14.7

9.36 Modify the piglatin generator given in Example 9.14 so that it can accommodate punctuation marks, uppercase letters and double-letter sounds.

9.37 Modify the program given in Example 9.19 (adding two tables of numbers) so that it calculates the differences rather than the sums of the corresponding elements in two tables of integer numbers. Test the program using the data given in Example 9.19.

9.38 Modify the program given in Example 9.19 (adding two tables of numbers) so that it utilizes 1 three-dimensional array rather than 3 two-dimensional arrays. Let the first subscript refer to one of the three tables. The second subscript will refer to the row number, and the third subscript will refer to the column number.

9.39 Write a C program that will enter a line of text, store it in an array and then display it backwards. Allow the length of the line to be unspecified (terminated by pressing the Enter key), but assume that it will not exceed 80 characters.

Test the program with any line of text of your own choosing. Compare with the program given in Example 7.15, which makes use of recursion rather than an array. Which approach is better, and why?

9.40 Write an interactive C program to process the exam scores for a group of students in a C programming course. Begin by specifying the number of exam scores for each student (assume this value is the same for all students in the class). Then enter each student's name and exam scores. Calculate an average score for each student, and an overall class average (an average of the individual student averages). Display the overall class average, followed by the name, the individual exam scores and the average score for each student.

Store the student names in a two-dimensional character array, and store the exam scores in a two-dimensional floating-point array. Make the program as general as possible. Label the output clearly.

Test the program using the following set of student exam grades.

Name	*Exam Scores (percent)*					
Adams	45	80	80	95	55	75
Brown	60	50	70	75	55	80
Davis	40	30	10	45	60	55
Fisher	0	5	5	0	10	5
Hamilton	90	85	100	95	90	90
Jones	95	90	80	95	85	80
Ludwig	35	50	55	65	45	70
Osborne	75	60	75	60	70	80
Prince	85	75	60	85	90	100
Richards	50	60	50	35	65	70
Smith	70	60	75	70	55	75
Thomas	10	25	35	20	30	10
Wolfe	25	40	65	75	85	95
Zorba	65	80	70	100	60	95

Compare with the program written for Prob. 6.69(k).

9.41 Modify the program written for the previous problem to allow for unequal weighting of the individual exam scores. In particular, assume that each of the first four exams contributes 15 percent to the final score, and each of the last two exams contributes 20 percent [see Prob. 6.69(*l*)].

9.42 Extend the program written for the preceding problem so that the deviation of each student's average about the overall class average will be determined. Display the class average, followed by each student's name, individual exam scores, final score, and the deviation about the class average. Be sure that the output is logically organized and clearly labeled.

9.43 Write a C program that will generate a table of values for the equation

$$y = 2e^{-0.1t} \sin 0.5t$$

where *t* varies between 0 and 60. Allow the size of the *t*-increment to be entered as an input parameter.

9.44 Write a complete C program that will generate a table of compound interest factors, *F/P*, where

$$F/P = (1 + i/100)^n$$

In this formula *F* represents the future value of a given sum of money, *P* represents its present value, *i* represents the annual interest rate, expressed as a percentage, and *n* represents the number of years.

    Let each row in the table correspond to a different value of *n*, with *n* ranging from 1 to 30 (hence 30 rows). Let each column represent a different interest rate. Include the following interest rates: 4, 4.5, 5, 5.5, 6, 6.5, 7, 7.5, 8, 8.5, 9, 9.5, 10, 11, 12 and 15 percent (hence a total of 16 columns). Be sure to label the rows and columns appropriately.

9.45 Consider the following foreign currencies and their equivalents to one U.S. dollar.

British pound:	0.65 pound per U.S. dollar
Canadian dollar:	1.4 dollars per U.S. dollar
Dutch guilder:	1.7 guilders per U.S. dollar
French franc:	5.3 francs per U.S. dollar
German mark:	1.5 marks per U.S. dollar
Italian lira:	1570 lira per U.S. dollar
Japanese yen:	98 yen per U.S. dollar
Mexican peso:	3.4 pesos per U.S. dollar
Swiss franc:	1.3 francs per U.S. dollar

Write an interactive, menu-driven program that will accept two different currencies and return the value of the second currency per one unit of the first currency. (For example, if the two currencies are Japanese yen and Mexican pesos, the program will return the number of Mexican pesos equivalent to one Japanese yen.) Use the data given above to carry out the conversions. Design the program so that it executes repeatedly, until a stopping condition is selected from the menu.

9.46 Consider the following list of countries and their capitals.

Canada	Ottawa
England	London
France	Paris
Germany	Bonn
India	New Delhi
Israel	Jerusalem
Italy	Rome
Japan	Tokyo
Mexico	Mexico City
People's Republic of China	Beijing
Russia	Moscow
United States	Washington

Write an interactive C program that will accept the name of a country as input and display the corresponding capital, and vice versa. Design the program so that it executes repeatedly, until the word End is entered as input.

9.47   Write a complete C program for each of the problems presented below. Include the most appropriate types of arrays for each problem. Be sure to modularize each program, label the output clearly, and make use of natural data types and efficient control structures.

(*a*)   Suppose we are given a table of integers, A, having m rows and n columns, and a list of integers, X, having n elements. We wish to generate a new list of integers, Y, that is formed by carrying out the following operations.

```
Y[1] = A[1][1]*X[1] + A[1][2]*X[2] + . . . + A[1][n]*X[n]

Y[2] = A[2][1]*X[1] + A[2][2]*X[2] + . . . + A[2][n]*X[n]

    . . . . .

Y[m] = A[m][1]*X[1] + A[m][2]*X[2] + . . . + A[m][n]*X[n]
```

Display the input data (i.e., the values of the elements A and X), followed by the values of the elements of Y. Use the program to process the following data.

$$
A = \begin{bmatrix}
1 & 2 & 3 & 4 & 5 & 6 & 7 & 8 \\
2 & 3 & 4 & 5 & 6 & 7 & 8 & 9 \\
3 & 4 & 5 & 6 & 7 & 8 & 9 & 10 \\
4 & 5 & 6 & 7 & 8 & 9 & 10 & 11 \\
5 & 6 & 7 & 8 & 9 & 10 & 11 & 12 \\
6 & 7 & 8 & 9 & 10 & 11 & 12 & 13
\end{bmatrix}
\qquad
X = \begin{bmatrix}
1 \\ -8 \\ 3 \\ -6 \\ 5 \\ -4 \\ 7 \\ -2
\end{bmatrix}
$$

(*b*)   Suppose A is a table of floating-point numbers having k rows and m columns, and B is a table of floating-point numbers having m rows and n columns. We wish to generate a new table, C, where each element of C is determined by

```
C[i][j] = A[i][1]*B[1][j] + A[i][2]*B[2][j] + . . . + A[i][m]*B[m][j]
```

where $i = 1, 2, \ldots, k$ and $j = 1, 2, \ldots, n$. (This operation is known as *matrix multiplication.*)
Use the program to process the following set of data.

$$
A = \begin{bmatrix}
2 & -1/3 & 0 & 2/3 & 4 \\
1/2 & 3/2 & 4 & -2 & 1 \\
0 & 3 & -9/7 & 6/7 & 4/3
\end{bmatrix}
\qquad
B = \begin{bmatrix}
6/5 & 0 & -2 & 1/3 \\
5 & 7/2 & 3/4 & -3/2 \\
0 & -1 & 1 & 0 \\
9/2 & 3/7 & -3 & 3 \\
4 & -1/2 & 0 & 3/4
\end{bmatrix}
$$

Display the elements of A, B and C. Be sure that everything is clearly labeled.

(*c*)   Read in the first *m* elements of a one-dimensional floating-point array. Calculate the sum of these elements, the mean, the deviations, the standard deviation, the algebraic maximum and the algebraic minimum.
The *mean* is defined as

$$
\bar{x} = \frac{x_1 + x_2 + \cdots + x_m}{m}
$$

the *deviation about the mean* is

$$d_i = (x_i - \bar{x}), \quad i = 1, 2, \ldots, m$$

and the *standard deviation* is

$$s = \sqrt{(d_1{}^2 + d_2{}^2 + \cdots + d_m{}^2)/m}$$

Use the program to process the following set of data.

27.5	87.0
13.4	39.9
53.8	47.7
29.2	8.1
74.5	63.2

Repeat the computation for k different lists of numbers. Calculate the overall mean, the overall standard deviation, the absolute (largest) maximum and the absolute (algebraically smallest) minimum.

(*d*)   Suppose we are given a set of tabulated values for y versus x, i.e.,

y_0	y_1	y_2	$\cdots$	y_n
x_0	x_1	x_2	$\cdots$	x_n

and we wish to obtain a value of y at some specified value of x that lies between two of the tabulated values. This problem is commonly solved by *interpolation*, i.e., by passing a polynomial $y(x)$ through n points such that $y(x_0) = y_0, y(x_1) = y_1, \ldots, y(x_n) = y_n$ and then evaluating y at the desired value of x.

A common way to carry out the interpolation is to use the *Lagrange form* of the interpolation polynomial. To do this we write

$$y(x) = f_0(x)\, y_0 + f_1(x)\, y_1 + \cdots + f_n(x)\, y_n$$

where $f_i(x)$ is a polynomial such that

$$f_i(x) = \left[\frac{(x - x_0)(x - x_1) \cdots (x - x_{i-1})(x - x_{i+1}) \cdots (x - x_n)}{(x_i - x_0)(x_i - x_1) \cdots (x_i - x_{i-1})(x_i - x_{i+1}) \cdots (x_i - x_n)} \right]$$

Notice that $f_i(x_i) = 1$ and $f_i(x_j) = 0$, where x_j is a tabulated value of x different from x_i. Therefore we are assured that $y(x_i) = y_i$.

Write a C program to read in n pairs of data, where n does not exceed 10, and then obtain an interpolated value of y at one or more specified values of x. Use the program to obtain interpolated values of y at $x = 13.7$, $x = 37.2$, $x = 112$ and $x = 147$ from the data listed below. Determine how many tabulated pairs of data are required in each calculation in order to obtain reasonably accurate interpolated y-values.

$y =$ 0.21073	$x =$ 0
0.45482	20
0.49011	30
0.50563	40
0.49245	50
0.47220	60
0.43433	80
0.33824	120
0.19390	180

9.48   The following problems are concerned with games of chance (gambling games). Each problem requires the use of random numbers, as described in Example 7.11. The program written for each problem will require the use of an array. The programs should be interactive and they should be modularized.

(a)   Write a C program that will simulate a game of *blackjack* between two players. The computer will not be a participant in this game, but will simply deal the cards to each player and then provide each player with one or more "hits" (additional cards) when requested.

       The cards are dealt in order, first one card to each player, then a second card to each player. Additional hits may then be requested.

       The object of the game is to obtain 21 points, or as many points as possible without exceeding 21 points, on each hand. A player is automatically disqualified if his or her hand exceeds 21 points. Picture cards count 10 points, and an ace can count either 1 point or 11 points. Thus a player can obtain 21 points (blackjack!) if he or she is dealt an ace and either a picture card or a 10. If the player has a low score with his (her) first two cards, he (she) may request one or more hits, as long as his (her) total score does not exceed 21.

       Use random numbers to simulate dealing the cards. Be sure to include a provision that the same card is not dealt more than once.

(b)   *Roulette* is played with a wheel containing 38 different squares along its circumference. Two of these squares, numbered 0 and 00, are green; 18 squares are red, and 18 are black. The red and black squares alternate in color, and are numbered 1 through 36 in a random order.

       A small marble is spun within the wheel, which eventually comes to rest within a groove beneath one of the squares. The game is played by betting on the outcome of each spin, in any one of the following ways.

    (i)   By selecting a single red or black square, at 35-to-1 odds. Thus, if a player were to bet $1.00 and win, he or she would receive a total of $36.00: the original $1.00, plus an additional $35.00.

    (ii)   By selecting a color, either red or black, at 1-to-1 odds. Thus if a player chose red on a $1.00 bet, he or she would receive $2.00 if the marble came to rest beneath any red square.

    (iii) By selecting either the odd or the even numbers (excluding 0 and 00), at 1-to-1 odds.

    (iv)   By selecting either the low 18 or the high 18 numbers at 1-to-1 odds.

The player will automatically lose if the marble comes to rest beneath one of the green squares (0 or 00).

       Write an interactive C program that will simulate a roulette game. Allow the players to select whatever type of bets they wish by choosing from a menu. Then print the outcome of each game followed by an appropriate message indicating whether each player has won or lost.

(c)   Write an interactive C program that will simulate a game of *BINGO*. Print each letter-number combination as it is drawn (randomly generated). Be sure that no combination is drawn more than once. Remember that each of the letters B-I-N-G-O corresponds to a certain range of numbers, as indicated below.

         B: 1 – 15
         I :   16 – 30
         N: 31 – 45
         G: 46 – 60
         O: 61 – 75

Each player will have a card with five columns, labeled B-I-N-G-O. Each column will contain five numbers, within the ranges indicated above. No two players will have the same card. The first player to have one entire line of numbers drawn (either vertically, horizontally or diagonally) wins.

       Note: the center position of each card is sometimes covered before the game begins (a "free" call). Also, the game is sometimes played such that a player must have *all* of the numbers on his or her card drawn before he (she) can win.

9.49 Write an interactive C program that will encode or decode a line of text. To encode a line of text, proceed as follows.

  1.   Convert each character, including blank spaces, to its ASCII equivalent.

  2.   Generate a positive random integer. Add this integer to the ASCII equivalent of each character. The same random integer will be used for the entire line of text.

3.   Suppose that N1 represents the lowest permissible value in the ASCII code, and N2 represents the highest permissible value. If the number obtained in step 2 above (i.e., the original ASCII equivalent plus the random integer) exceeds N2, then subtract the largest possible multiple of N2 from this number, and add the remainder to N1. Hence the encoded number will always fall between N1 and N2, and will therefore always represent some ASCII character.

4.   Display the characters that correspond to the encoded ASCII values.

The procedure is reversed when decoding a line of text. Be certain, however, that the same random number is used in decoding as was used in encoding.

Chapter 10

Pointers

A *pointer* is a variable that represents the *location* (rather than the *value*) of a data item, such as a variable or an array element. Pointers are used frequently in C, as they have a number of useful applications. For example, pointers can be used to pass information back and forth between a function and its reference point. In particular, pointers provide a way to return multiple data items from a function via function arguments. Pointers also permit references to other functions to be specified as arguments to a given function. This has the effect of passing functions as arguments to the given function.

Pointers are also closely associated with arrays and therefore provide an alternate way to access individual array elements. Moreover, pointers provide a convenient way to represent multidimensional arrays, allowing a single multidimensional array to be replaced by a lower-dimensional array of pointers. This feature permits a group of strings to be represented within a single array, though the individual strings may differ in length.

10.1 FUNDAMENTALS

Within the computer's memory, every stored data item occupies one or more contiguous memory cells (i.e., adjacent words or bytes). The number of memory cells required to store a data item depends on the type of data item. For example, a single character will typically be stored in one byte (8 bits) of memory; an integer usually requires two contiguous bytes; a floating-point number may require four contiguous bytes; and a double-precision quantity may require eight contiguous bytes. (See Chap. 2 and Appendix D.)

Suppose v is a variable that represents some particular data item. The compiler will automatically assign memory cells for this data item. The data item can then be accessed if we know the location (i.e., the *address*) of the first memory cell.[*] The address of v's memory location can be determined by the expression &v, where & is a unary operator, called the *address operator*, that evaluates the address of its operand.

Now let us assign the address of v to another variable, pv. Thus,

    pv = &v

This new variable is called a *pointer* to v, since it "points" to the location where v is stored in memory. Remember, however, that pv represents v's *address*, not its value. Thus, pv is referred to as a *pointer variable*. The relationship between pv and v is illustrated in Fig. 10.1.

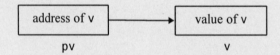

Fig. 10.1 Relationship between pv and v (where pv = &v and v = *pv)

The data item represented by v (i.e., the data item stored in v's memory cells) can be accessed by the expression *pv, where * is a unary operator, called the *indirection operator*, that operates only on a pointer

---

[*] Adjacent memory cells within a computer are numbered consecutively, from the beginning to the end of the memory area. The number associated with each memory cell is known as the memory cell's *address*. Most computers use a hexadecimal numbering system to designate the addresses of consecutive memory cells, though some computers use an octal numbering system (see Appendix A).

280

variable. Therefore, *pv and v both represent the same data item (i.e., the contents of the same memory cells). Furthermore, if we write pv = &v and u = *pv, then u and v will both represent the same value; i.e., the value of v will indirectly be assigned to u. (It is assumed that u and v are of the same data type.)

EXAMPLE 10.1   Shown below is a simple program that illustrates the relationship between two integer variables, their corresponding addresses and their associated pointers.

```
#include <stdio.h>

main()
{
    int u = 3;
    int v;
    int *pu;        /* pointer to an integer */
    int *pv;        /* pointer to an integer */

    pu = &u;        /* assign address of u to pu */
    v = *pu;        /* assign value of u to v */
    pv = &v;        /* assign address of v to pv */

    printf("\nu=%d    &u=%X    pu=%X    *pu=%d", u, &u, pu, *pu);
    printf("\n\nv=%d    &v=%X    pv=%X    *pv=%d", v, &v, pv, *pv);
}
```

Note that pu is a pointer to u, and pv is a pointer to v. Therefore pu represents the address of u, and pv represents the address of v. (Pointer declarations will be discussed in the next section.)

Execution of this program results in the following output.

```
u=3    &u=F8E    pu=F8E    *pu=3

v=3    &v=F8C    pv=F8C    *pv=3
```

In the first line, we see that u represents the value 3, as specified in the declaration statement. The address of u is determined automatically by the compiler as F8E (hexadecimal). The pointer pu is assigned this value; hence, pu also represents the (hexadecimal) address F8E. Finally, the value to which pu points (i.e., the value stored in the memory cell whose address is F8E) is 3, as expected.

Similarly, the second line shows that v also represents the value 3. This is expected, since we have assigned the value *pu to v. The address of v, and hence the value of pv, is F8C. Notice that u and v have different addresses. And finally, we see that the value to which pv points is 3, as expected.

The relationships between pu and u, and pv and v, are shown in Fig. 10.2. Note that the memory locations of the pointer variables (i.e., address EC7 for pu, and EC5 for pv) are not displayed by the program.

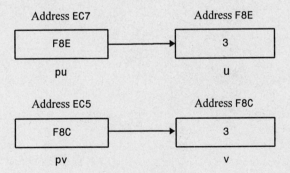

Fig. 10.2

The unary operators & and * are members of the same precedence group as the other unary operators, i.e., –, ++, --, !, sizeof and (type), which were presented in Chap. 3. Remember that this group of operators has a higher precedence than the groups containing the arithmetic operators, and that the associativity of the unary operators is right to left (see Appendix C).

The address operator (&) must act upon operands that are associated with unique addresses, such as ordinary variables or single array elements. Thus *the address operator cannot act upon arithmetic expressions*, such as 2 * (u + v).

The indirection operator (*) can only act upon operands that are pointers (e.g., pointer variables). However, if pv points to v (i.e., pv = &v), then an expression such as *pv can be used interchangeably with its corresponding variable v. Thus, an indirect reference (e.g., *pv) can appear in place of an ordinary variable (e.g., v) within a more complicated expression.

EXAMPLE 10.2   Consider the simple C program shown below.

```
#include <stdio.h>

main()
{
    int u1, u2;
    int v = 3;
    int *pv;                /* pv points to v */

    u1 = 2 * (v + 5);       /* ordinary expression */

    pv = &v;
    u2 = 2 * (*pv + 5);     /* equivalent expression */

    printf("\nu1=%d    u2=%d", u1, u2);
}
```

This program involves the use of two integer expressions. The first, 2 * (v + 5), is an ordinary arithmetic expression whereas the second, 2 * (*pv + 5), involves the use of a pointer. The expressions are equivalent, since v and *pv each represent the same integer value.

The following output is generated when the program is executed.

```
u1=16    u2=16
```

An indirect reference can also appear on the left side of an assignment statement. This provides another method for assigning a value to a variable or an array element.

EXAMPLE 10.3   A simple C program is shown below.

```
#include <stdio.h>

main()
{
    int v = 3;
    int *pv;

    pv = &v;                                /* pv points to v */
    printf("\n*pv=%d    v=%d", *pv, v);

    *pv = 0;                                /* reset v indirectly */
    printf("\n\n*pv=%d    v=%d", *pv, v);
}
```

The program begins by assigning an initial value of 3 to the integer variable v, and then assigns the address of v to the pointer variable pv. Thus, pv becomes a pointer to v. The expression *pv therefore represents the value 3. The first printf statement is intended to illustrate this by displaying the current values of *pv and v.

Following the first printf statement, the value of *pv is reset to 0. Therefore, v will be reassigned the value 0. This is illustrated by the second printf statement, which causes the new values of *pv and v to be displayed.

When the program is executed, the following output is generated.

```
*pv=3    v=3

*pv=0    v=0
```

Thus, the value of v has been altered by assigning a new value to *pv.

Pointer variables can point to numeric or character variables, arrays, functions or other pointer variables. (They can also point to certain other data structures that will be discussed later in this book.) Thus, a pointer variable can be assigned the address of an ordinary variable (e.g., pv = &v). Also, a pointer variable can be assigned the value of another pointer variable (e.g., pv = px), provided both pointer variables point to data items of the same type. Moreover, a pointer variable can be assigned a *null* (zero) value, as explained in Sec. 10.2 below. On the other hand, *ordinary* variables *cannot* be assigned arbitrary addresses (i.e., an expression such as &x cannot appear on the left-hand side of an assignment statement).

Section 10.5 presents additional information concerning those operations that can be carried out on pointers.

10.2 POINTER DECLARATIONS

Pointer variables, like all other variables, must be declared before they may be used in a C program. The interpretation of a pointer declaration differs, however, from the interpretation of other variable declarations. When a pointer variable is declared, the variable name must be preceded by an asterisk (*). This identifies the fact that the variable is a pointer. The data type that appears in the declaration refers to the *object* of the pointer, i.e., the data item that is stored in the address represented by the pointer, rather than the pointer itself.

Thus, a pointer declaration may be written in general terms as

```
data-type  *ptvar;
```

where *ptvar* is the name of the pointer variable, and *data-type* refers to the data type of the pointer's object. Remember that an asterisk must precede *ptvar*.

EXAMPLE 10.4   A C program contains the following declarations.

```
float u, v;
float *pv;
```

The first line declares u and v to be floating-point variables. The second line declares pv to be a pointer variable whose object is a floating-point quantity; i.e., pv points to a floating-point quantity. Note that pv represents an *address*, not a floating-point quantity. (Some additional pointer declarations are shown in Examples 10.1 to 10.3.)

Within a variable declaration, a pointer variable can be initialized by assigning it the address of another variable. Remember that the variable whose address is assigned to the pointer variable must have been declared earlier in the program.

EXAMPLE 10.5   A C program contains the following declarations.

```
float u, v;
float *pv = &v;
```

The variables u and v are declared to be floating-point variables and pv is declared as a pointer variable that points to a floating-point quantity, as in Example 10.4. In addition, the address of v is initially assigned to pv.

This terminology can be confusing. Remember that these declarations are equivalent to writing

```
float u, v;        /* floating-point variable declarations */
float *pv;         /* pointer variable declaration */
. . . . .
pv = &v;           /* assign v's address to pv */
```

Note that an asterisk is not included in the assignment statement.

In general, it does not make sense to assign an integer value to a pointer variable. An exception, however, is an assignment of 0, which is sometimes used to indicate some special condition. In such situations the recommended programming practice is to define a symbolic constant NULL which represents 0, and to use NULL in the pointer initialization. This practice emphasizes the fact that the zero assignment represents a special situation.

EXAMPLE 10.6   A C program contains the following symbolic constant definitions and array declarations.

```
#define  NULL  0
float u, v;
float *pv = NULL;
```

The variables u and v are declared to be floating-point variables and pv is declared as a pointer variable that points to a floating-point quantity. In addition, pv is initially assigned a value of 0 to indicate some special condition dictated by the logic of the program (which is not shown in this example). The use of the symbolic constant NULL suggests that this initial assignment is something other than the assignment of an ordinary integer value.

We will see other kinds of pointer declarations later in this chapter.

10.3 PASSING POINTERS TO A FUNCTION

Pointers are often passed to a function as arguments. This allows data items within the calling portion of the program to be accessed by the function, altered within the function, and then returned to the calling portion of the program in altered form. We refer to this use of pointers as passing arguments by *reference* (or by *address* or by *location*), in contrast to passing arguments by *value* as discussed in Chap. 7.

When an argument is passed by value, the data item is *copied* to the function. Thus, any alteration made to the data item within the function is not carried over into the calling routine (see Sec. 7.5). When an argument is passed by reference, however (i.e., when a pointer is passed to a function), the *address* of a data item is passed to the function. The contents of that address can be accessed freely, either within the function or within the calling routine. Moreover, any change that is made to the data item (i.e., to the contents of the address) will be recognized in both the function and the calling routine. Thus, the use of a pointer as a function argument permits the corresponding data item to be altered globally from within the function.

When pointers are used as arguments to a function, some care is required with the formal argument declarations within the function. Specifically, formal pointer arguments that must each be preceded by an asterisk. Function prototypes are written in the same manner. If a function declaration does not include variable names, the data type of each pointer argument must be followed by an asterisk. The use of pointer arguments is illustrated in the following example.

EXAMPLE 10.7   Here is a simple C program that illustrates the difference between ordinary arguments, which are passed by value, and pointer arguments, which are passed by reference.

```
#include <stdio.h>

void funct1(int u, int v);            /* function prototype */
void funct2(int *pu, int *pv);        /* function prototype */


main()
{
    int u = 1;
    int v = 3;

    printf("\nBefore calling funct1:   u=%d    v=%d", u, v);
    funct1(u, v);
    printf("\nAfter calling funct1:    u=%d    v=%d", u, v);

    printf("\n\nBefore calling funct2:   u=%d    v=%d", u, v);
    funct2(&u, &v);
    printf("\nAfter calling funct2:    u=%d    v=%d", u, v);
}


void funct1(int u, int v)

{
    u = 0;
    v = 0;
    printf("\nWithin funct1:           u=%d    v=%d", u, v);
    return;
}


void funct2(int *pu, int *pv)

{
    *pu = 0;
    *pv = 0;
    printf("\nWithin funct2:           *pu=%d *pv=%d", *pu, *pv);
    return;
}
```

This program contains two functions, called funct1 and funct2. The first function, funct1, receives two integer variables as arguments. These variables are originally assigned the values 1 and 3, respectively. The values are then changed, to 0, 0 within funct1. The new values are not recognized in main, however, because the arguments were passed by value, and any changes to the arguments are local to the function in which the changes occur.

Now consider the second function, funct2. This function receives two *pointers* to integer variables as its arguments. The arguments are identified as pointers by the indirection operators (i.e., the asterisks) that appear in the argument declaration. In addition, the argument declaration indicates that the pointers contain the addresses of *integer* quantities.

Within funct2, the contents of the pointer addresses are reassigned the values 0, 0. Since the addresses are recognized in both funct2 and main, the reassigned values will be recognized within main after the call to funct2. Therefore, the integer variables u and v will have their values changed from 1, 3 to 0, 0.

The six printf statements illustrate the values of u and v, and their associated values *pu and *pv, within main and within the two functions. Hence, the following output is generated when the program is executed.

```
Before calling funct1:   u=1    v=3
Within funct1:           u=0    v=0
After calling funct1:    u=1    v=3
```

```
Before calling funct2:   u=1    v=3
Within funct2:          *pu=0 *pv=0
After calling funct2:    u=0    v=0
```

Notice that the values of u and v are unchanged within main after the call to funct1, though the values of these variables *are* changed within main after the call to funct2. Thus, the output illustrates the local nature of the alterations within funct1, and the global nature of the alterations within funct2.

This example contains some additional features that should be pointed out. Notice, for example, the function prototype

```
void funct2(int *pu, int *pv);
```

The items in parentheses identify the arguments as pointers to integer quantities. The pointer variables, pu and pv, have not been declared elsewhere in main. This is permitted in the function prototype, however, because pu and pv are dummy arguments rather than actual arguments. The function declaration could also have been written without any variable names, as

```
void funct2(int *, int *);
```

Now consider the declaration of the formal arguments within the first line of funct2, i.e.,

```
void funct2(int *pu, int *pv)
```

The formal arguments pu and pv are consistent with the dummy arguments in the function prototype. In this example the corresponding variable names are the same, though this is generally not required.

Finally, notice the manner in which u and v are accessed within funct2, i.e.,

```
*pu = 0;
*pv = 0;
```

Thus, u and v are accessed indirectly, by referencing the contents of the addresses represented by the pointers pu and pv. This is necessary because the variables u and v are not recognized as such within funct2.

We have already mentioned the fact that an array name is actually a pointer to the array; i.e., the array name represents the address of the first element in the array (see Sec. 9.3). Therefore, an array name is treated as a pointer when it is passed to a function. However, it is not necessary to precede the array name with an ampersand within the function call.

An array name that appears as a formal argument within a function definition can be declared either as a pointer or as an array of unspecified size, as shown in Sec. 9.3. The choice is a matter of personal preference, though it will often be determined by the manner in which the individual array elements are accessed within the function (more about this in the next section).

EXAMPLE 10.8 Analyzing a Line of Text   Suppose we wish to analyze a line of text by examining each of the characters and determinining into which of several different categories it falls. In particular, suppose we count the number of vowels, consonants, digits, whitespace characters and "other" characters (punctuation, operators, brackets, etc.) This can easily be accomplished by reading in a line of text, storing it in a one-dimensional character array, and then analyzing the individual array elements. An appropriate counter will be incremented for each character. The value of each counter (number of vowels, number of consonants, etc.) can then be written out after all of the characters have been analyzed.

Let us write a complete C program that will carry out such an analysis. To do so, we first define the following symbols.

        line   = an 80-element character array containing the line of text

     vowels   = an integer counter indicating the number of vowels

  consonants   = an integer counter indicating the number of consonants

     digits   = an integer counter indicating the number of digits whitespc = an integer counter indicating the number of whitespace characters (blank spaces or tabs)

other = an integer counter indicating the number of characters that do not fall into any of the preceding categories

Notice that newline characters are not included in the "whitespace" category, because there can be no newline characters within a single line of text.

We will structure the program so that the line of text is read into the main portion of the program, and then passed to a function where it will be analyzed. The function will return the value of each counter after all of the characters have been analyzed. The results of the analysis (i.e., the value of each counter) will then be displayed from the main portion of the program.

The actual analysis can be carried out by creating a loop to examine each of the characters. Within the loop we first convert each character that is a letter to uppercase. This avoids the need to distinguish between uppercase and lowercase letters. We can then categorize the character using a nest of if - else statements. Once the proper category has been identified, the corresponding counter is incremented. The entire process is repeated until the string termination character (\0) has been found.

The complete C program is shown below.

```
/* count the number of vowels, consonants, digits, whitespace characters,
   and "other" characters in a line of text                              */

#include <stdio.h>
#include <ctype.h>

/* function prototype */
void scan_line(char line[], int *pv, int *pc, int *pd, int *pw, int *po);

main()
{
    char line[80];              /* line of text */
    int vowels = 0;             /* vowel counter */
    int consonants = 0;         /* consonant counter */
    int digits = 0;             /* digit counter */
    int whitespc = 0;           /* whitespace counter */
    int other = 0;              /* remaining character counter */

    printf("Enter a line of text below:\n");
    scanf("%[^\n]", line);

    scan_line(line, &vowels, &consonants, &digits, &whitespc, &other);

    printf("\nNo. of vowels: %d", vowels);
    printf("\nNo. of consonants: %d", consonants);
    printf("\nNo. of digits: %d", digits);
    printf("\nNo. of whitespace characters: %d", whitespc);
    printf("\nNo. of other characters: %d", other);
}


void scan_line(char line[], int *pv, int *pc, int *pd, int *pw, int *po)

/* analyze the characters in a line of text */

{
    char c;                     /* uppercase character */
    int count = 0;              /* character counter */
```

```
        while ((c = toupper(line[count])) != '\0')   {

            if (c == 'A' || c == 'E' || c == 'I' || c == 'O' || c == 'U')
                ++ *pv;                               /* vowel */
            else if (c >= 'A' && c <= 'Z')
                    ++ *pc;                           /* consonant */
                else if (c >= '0' && c <= '9')
                        ++ *pd;                       /* digit */
                    else if (c == ' ' || c == '\t')
                            ++ *pw;                   /* whitespace */
                        else
                            ++ *po;                   /* other */

            ++count;
        }
        return;
    }
```

Notice the function prototype for scan_line that appears at the beginning of the program. In particular, notice the use of the void data type, and notice the manner in which the argument data types are specified. Note the distinction between the array argument and the remaining pointer arguments.

Also, observe the manner in which the actual arguments are written in the call to scan_line. The array argument, line, is not preceded by an ampersand, since arrays are, by definition, pointers. Each of the remaining arguments must be preceded by an ampersand so that its address, rather than its value, is passed to the function.

Now consider the function scan_line. All of the formal arguments, including line, are pointers. However, line is declared as an array whose size is unspecified, whereas the remaining arguments are specifically declared as pointers. It is possible (and quite common) to declare line as a pointer rather than an array. Thus, the first line of scan_line could have been written as

```
void scan_line(char *line, int *pv, int *pc, int *pd, int *pw, int *po)
```

rather than as shown in the program listing. To be consistent, the corresponding function prototype would then be written in a similar manner.

Incrementing the various counters also requires some explanation. First, note that it is the *content* of each address (i.e., the *object* of each pointer) that is incremented. Second, note that each indirection expression (e.g., *pv) is *preceded* by the unary operator ++. Since the unary operators are evaluated from right to left, we are assured that the content of each address, rather than the address itself, is increased in value.

Here is a typical dialog that might be encountered when the program is executed. (The line of text entered by the user is underlined.)

```
    Enter a line of text below:
    Personal computers with memories in excess of 4096 KB are now quite common.
```

The corresponding output is:

```
    No. of vowels: 23
    No. of consonants: 35
    No. of digits: 4
    No. of whitespace characters: 12
    No. of other characters: 1
```

Thus, we see that this particular line of text contains 23 vowels, 35 consonants, 4 digits, 12 whitespace characters (blank spaces), and one other character (the period).

Recall that the scanf function requires those arguments that are ordinary variables to be preceded by ampersands (see Sec. 4.4). However, array names are exempted from this requirement. This may have seemed somewhat mysterious back in Chap. 4 but it should now make sense, considering what we now know about array names and addresses. Thus, the scanf function requires that the *addresses* of the data items being entered into the computer's memory be specified. The ampersands provide a means for accessing the addresses of ordinary single-valued variables. Ampersands are not required with array names, since array names themselves represent addresses.

EXAMPLE 10.9   The skeletal structure of a C program is shown below (repeated from Example 4.5).

```
#include <stdio.h>

main()
{
    char item[20];
    int partno;
    float cost;

    . . . . .

    scanf("%s %d %f", item, &partno, &cost);

    . . . . .

}
```

The scanf statement causes a character string, an integer quantity and a floating-point quantity to be entered into the computer and stored in the addresses associated with item, partno and cost, respectively. Since item is the name of an array, it is understood to represent an address. Hence, item need not (cannot) be preceded by an ampersand within the scanf statement. On the other hand, partno and cost are conventional variables. Therefore they must be written as &partno and &cost within the scanf statement. The ampersands are required in order to access the *addresses* of these variables rather than their values.

If the scanf function is used to enter a single array element rather than an entire array, the name of the array element must be preceded by an ampersand, as shown below (from Example 9.8)l

```
    scanf("%f", &list[count]);
```

It is possible to pass a *portion* of an array, rather than an entire array, to a function. To do so, the address of the first array element to be passed must be specified as an argument. The remainder of the array, starting with the specified array element, will then be passed to the function.

EXAMPLE 10.10   The skeletal structure of a C program is shown below.

```
#include <stdio.h>

void process(float z[]);

main()
{
    float z[100];
    . . . . .
    /* enter values for elements of z */

    . . . . .

    process(&z[50]);

    . . . . .

}
```

```
void process(float f[])
{

    . . . . .

    /* process elements of f */

    . . . . .

    return;
}
```

Within `main`, `z` is declared to be a 100-element, floating-point array. After the elements of `z` are entered into the computer, the address of `z[50]` (i.e., `&z[50]`) is passed to the function `process`. Hence, the last 50 elements of `z` (i.e., the elements `z[50]` through `z[99]`) will be available to `process`.

In the next section we will see that the address of `z[50]` can be written as `z + 50` rather than `&z[50]`. Therefore, the call to `process` can appear as `process(z + 50)` rather than `process(&z[50])`, as shown above. Either method may be used, depending on the programmer's preferences.

Within `process`, the corresponding array is referred to as `f`. This array is declared to be a floating-point array whose size is unspecified. Thus, the fact that the function receives only a portion of `z` is immaterial; if all of the array elements are altered within `process`, only the last 50 elements will be affected within `main`.

Within `process`, it may be desirable to declare the formal argument `f` as a pointer to a floating-point quantity rather than an array name. Thus, the outline of `process` may be written as

```
void process(float *f)
{
    . . . . .
    /* process elements of f */
    . . . . .
    return;
}
```

Notice the difference between the formal argument declarations in the two function outlines. Both declarations are valid.

A function can also return a pointer to the calling portion of the program. To do so, the function definition and any corresponding function declarations must indicate that the function will return a pointer. This is accomplished by preceding the function name by an asterisk. The asterisk must appear in both the function definition and the function declarations.

EXAMPLE 10.11 Shown below is the skeletal structure of a C program that transfers a double-precision array to a function and returns a pointer to one of the array elements.

```
#include <stdio.h>

double *scan(double z[]);

main()
{
    double z[100];          /* array declaration */
    double *pz;             /* pointer declaration */

    /* enter values for elements of z */

    . . . . .

    pz = scan(z);

    . . . . .

}
```

```
double *scan(double f[])
{
    double *pf;              /* pointer declaration */

    . . . . .

    /* process elements of f */

    pf = . . . . .;

    return(pf);
}
```

Within main we see that z is declared to be a 100-element, double-precision array, and pz is a pointer to a double-precision quantity. We also see a declaration for the function scan. Note that scan will accept a double-precision array as an argument, and it will return a pointer to (i.e., the address of) a double-precision quantity. The asterisk preceding the function name (*scan) indicates that the function will return a pointer.

Within the function definition, the first line indicates that scan accepts one formal parameter (f[]) and returns a pointer to a double-precision quantity. The formal parameter will be a one-dimensional, double-precision array. The outline suggests that the address of one of the array elements is assigned to the pointer pf during or after the processing of the array elements. This address is then returned to main, where it is assigned to the pointer variable pz.

10.4 POINTERS AND ONE-DIMENSIONAL ARRAYS

Recall that an array name is really a pointer to the first element in the array. Therefore, if x is a one-dimensional array, then the address of the first array element can be expressed as either &x[0] or simply as x. Moreover, the address of the second array element can be written as either &x[1] or as (x + 1), and so on. In general, the address of array element $(i + 1)$ can be expressed as either &x[i] or as (x + i). Thus we have two different ways to write the address of any array element: We can write the actual array element, preceded by an ampersand; or we can write an expression in which the subscript is added to the array name.

In the latter case, it should be understood that we are dealing with a very special and unusual type of expression. In the expression (x + i), for example, x represents an address, whereas i represents an integer quantity. Moreover, x is the name of an array whose elements may be characters, integers, floating-point quantities, etc. (though all of the the array elements must be of the same data type). Thus, we are not simply adding numerical values. Rather, we are specifying an address that is a certain number of memory cells beyond the address of the first array element. Or, in simpler terms, we are specifying a location that is i array elements beyond the first. Hence, the expression (x + i) is a symbolic representation for an address specification rather than an arithmetic expression.

Recall that the number of memory cells associated with an array element will depend upon the data type of the array as well as the particular computer's architecture. With some computers, for example, an integer quantity occupies two bytes (two memory cells), a floating-point quantity requires four bytes, and a double-precision quantity requires eight bytes of memory. With other computers, an integer quantity may require four bytes, and floating-point and double-precision quantities may each require eight bytes. And so on.

When writing the address of an array element in the form (x + i), however, you need not be concerned with the number of memory cells associated with each type of array element; the C compiler adjusts for this automatically. You must specify only the address of the first array element (i.e., the name of the array) and the number of array elements beyond the first (i.e., a value for the subscript). The value of i is sometimes referred to as an *offset* when used in this manner.

Since &x[i] and (x + i) both represent the address of the *i*th element of x, it would seem reasonable that x[i] and *(x + i) both represent the contents of that address, i.e., the *value* of the *i*th element of x. This is indeed the case. The two terms are interchangeable. Hence, either term can be used in any particular application. The choice depends upon your individual preferences.

EXAMPLE 10.12   Here is a simple program that illustrates the relationship between array elements and their addresses.

```
#include <stdio.h>

main()
{
    static int x[10] = {10, 11, 12, 13, 14, 15, 16, 17, 18, 19};
    int i;

    for (i = 0; i <= 9; ++i)   {
        /* display an array element */
        printf("\ni= %d     x[i]= %d     *(x+i)= %d", i, x[i], *(x+i));

        /* display the corresponding array address */
        printf("     &x[i]= %X     x+i= %X", &x[i], (x+i));
    }
}
```

This program defines a one-dimensional, 10-element integer array x, whose elements are assigned the values 10, 11, . . . , 19. The action portion of the program consists of a loop that displays the value and the corresponding address of each array element. Note that the value of each array element is specified in two different ways, as x[i] and as *(x+i), in order to illustrate their equivalence. Similarly, the address of each array element is specified in two different ways, as &x[i] and as (x+i), for the same reason. Therefore the value and the address of each array element should appear twice.

Execution of this program results in the following output.

```
i= 0     x[i]= 10     *(x+i)= 10     &x[i]= 72     x+i= 72
i= 1     x[i]= 11     *(x+i)= 11     &x[i]= 74     x+i= 74
i= 2     x[i]= 12     *(x+i)= 12     &x[i]= 76     x+i= 76
i= 3     x[i]= 13     *(x+i)= 13     &x[i]= 78     x+i= 78
i= 4     x[i]= 14     *(x+i)= 14     &x[i]= 7A     x+i= 7A
i= 5     x[i]= 15     *(x+i)= 15     &x[i]= 7C     x+i= 7C
i= 6     x[i]= 16     *(x+i)= 16     &x[i]= 7E     x+i= 7E
i= 7     x[i]= 17     *(x+i)= 17     &x[i]= 80     x+i= 80
i= 8     x[i]= 18     *(x+i)= 18     &x[i]= 82     x+i= 82
i= 9     x[i]= 19     *(x+i)= 19     &x[i]= 84     x+i= 84
```

The output clearly illustrates the distinction between x[i], which represents the value of the *i*th array element, and &x[i], which represents its address. Moreover, we see that the value of the *i*th array element can be represented by either x[i] or *(x+i), and the address of the *i*th element can be represented by either &x[i] or x+i. Thus we see another comparison, between *(x+i), which also represents the value of the *i*th element, and x+i, which also represents its address.

Notice, for example, that the first array element (corresponding to i = 0) has been assigned a value of 10 and a (hexadecimal) address of 72. The second array element has a value of 11 and an address of 74, etc. Thus, memory location 72 will contain the integer value 10, location 74 will contain 11, and so on.

You should understand that these addresses are assigned automatically by the compiler.

When assigning a *value* to an array element such as x[i], the left side of the assignment statement may be written as either x[i] or as *(x + i). Thus, a value may be assigned directly to an array element, or it may be assigned to the memory area whose address is that of the array element.

On the other hand, it is sometimes necessary to assign an *address* to an identifier. In such situations, a pointer variable must appear on the left side of the assignment statement. It is *not* possible to assign an arbitrary address to an array name or to an array element. Thus, expressions such as x, (x + i) and &x[i] cannot appear on the left side of an assignment statement. Moreover, the address of an array cannot arbitrarily be altered, so that expressions such as ++x are not permitted.

EXAMPLE 10.13 Consider the skeletal structure of the C program shown below.

```
#include <stdio.h>

main()
{
    int line[80];
    int *pl;

    . . . . .

    /* assign values */
    line[2] = line[1];
    line[2] = *(line + 1);
    *(line + 2) = line[1];
    *(line + 2) = *(line + 1);

    /* assign addresses */
    pl = &line[1];
    pl = line + 1;
}
```

Each of the first four assignment statements assigns the value of the second array element (i.e, line[1]) to the third array element (line[2]). Thus, the four statements are all equivalent. An experienced programmer would probably choose either the first or the fourth, however, in order that the notation be consistent.

The last two assignment statements each assigns the *address* of the second array element to the pointer pl. We might choose to do this in an actual program if it were necessary to "tag" the address of line[1] for some reason.

Note that *the address of one array element cannot be assigned to some other array element*. Thus we *cannot* write a statement such as

```
&line[2] = &line[1];
```

On the other hand, we *can* assign the *value* of one array element to another through a pointer if we wish, e.g.,

```
pl = &line[1];
line[2] = *pl;
```

or

```
pl = line + 1;
*(line + 2) = *pl;
```

If a numerical array is defined as a pointer variable, the array elements cannot be assigned initial values. Therefore, a conventional array definition is required if initial values will be assigned to the elements of a numerical array. However, a *character-type* pointer variable can be assigned an entire string as a part of the variable declaration. Thus, a string can conveniently be represented by either a one-dimensional character array or a character pointer.

EXAMPLE 10.14 Shown below is a simple C program in which two strings are represented as one-dimensional character arrays.

```
#include <stdio.h>

char x[] = "This string is declared externally\n\n";
```

```
main()
{
    static char y[] = "This string is declared within main";

    printf("%s", x);
    printf("%s", y);
}
```

The first string is assigned to the external array x[]. The second string is assigned to the static array y[], which is defined within main. This second definition occurs within a function; therefore y[] must be defined as a static array so that it can be initialized.

Here is a different version of the same program. The strings are now assigned to pointer variables rather than to one-dimensional arrays.

```
#include <stdio.h>

char *x = "This string is declared externally\n\n";

main()
{
    char *y = "This string is declared within main";

    printf("%s", x);
    printf("%s", y);
}
```

The external pointer variable x points to the beginning of the first string, whereas the pointer variable y, declared within main, points to the beginning of the second string. Note that y can now be initialized without being declared static.

Execution of either program produces the following output.

```
This string is declared externally

This string is declared within main
```

Syntactically, of course, it is possible to declare a pointer variable static. However, there is no reason to do so in this example.

10.5 DYNAMIC MEMORY ALLOCATION

Since an array name is actually a pointer to the first element within the array, it should be possible to define the array as a pointer variable rather than as a conventional array. Syntactically, the two definitions are equivalent. However, a conventional array definition results in a fixed block of memory being reserved at the beginning of program execution, whereas this does not occur if the array is represented in terms of a pointer variable. Therefore, the use of a pointer variable to represent an array requires some type of initial memory assignment before the array elements are processed. This is known as *dynamic memory allocation*. Generally, the malloc library function is used for this purpose, as illustrated in the next example.

EXAMPLE 10.15 Suppose x is a one-dimensional, 10-element array of integers. It is possible to define x as a pointer variable rather than an array. Thus, we can write

```
int *x;
```

rather than

```
int x[10];
```

or

```
#define SIZE 10
int x[SIZE];
```

However, x is not automatically assigned a memory block when it is defined as a pointer variable, though a block of memory large enough to store 10 integer quantities will be reserved in advance when x is defined as an array.

To assign sufficient memory for x, we can make use of the library function `malloc`, as follows.

```
x = (int *) malloc(10 * sizeof(int));
```

This function reserves a block of memory whose size (in bytes) is equivalent to 10 integer quantities. As written, the function returns a pointer to an integer. This pointer indicates the beginning of the memory block. In general, the type cast preceding `malloc` must be consistent with the data type of the pointer variable. Thus, if y were defined as a pointer to a double-precision quantity and we wanted enough memory to store 10 double-precision quantities, we would write

```
y = (double *) malloc(10 * sizeof(double));
```

If the declaration is to include the assignment of initial values, however, then x must be defined as an array rather than a pointer variable. For example,

```
int x[10] = {1, 2, 3, 4, 5, 6, 7, 8, 9, 10};
```

or

```
int x[] = {1, 2, 3, 4, 5, 6, 7, 8, 9, 10};
```

When programming in C, it is not unusual to use pointer expressions rather than references to individual array elements. The resulting programs may appear strange at first, though they are straightforward once you become comfortable accessing values that are stored in specified addresses. Generally, a small amount of practice is all that is required.

EXAMPLE 10.16 Reordering a List of Numbers To illustrate the use of pointers with dynamic memory allocation, let us once again consider the problem of reordering a list of integers, as described in Example 9.13. Now, however, we will utilize pointer expressions to access numerical values rather than refer explicitly to individual array elements. In all other respects, we present a program that is identical to that given in Example 9.13.

Here is the complete C program.

```
/* reorder a one-dimensional, integer array from smallest to largest,
   using pointer notation                                           */

#include <stdio.h>
#include <stdlib.h>

void reorder(int n, int *x);

main()
{
    int i, n, *x;

    /* read in a value for n */
    printf("\nHow many numbers will be entered? ");
    scanf("%d", &n);
    printf("\n");

    /* allocate memory */
    x = (int *) malloc(n * sizeof(int));
```

```
        /* read in the list of numbers */
        for (i = 0; i < n; ++i)   {
            printf("i = %d   x = ", i + 1);
            scanf("%d", x + i);
        }

        /* reorder all array elements */
        reorder(n, x);

        /* display the reordered list of numbers */
        printf("\n\nReordered List of Numbers:\n\n");
        for (i = 0; i < n; ++i)
            printf("i = %d   x = %d\n", i + 1, *(x + i));
    }

    void reorder(int n, int *x)     /* rearrange the list of numbers */

    {
        int i, item, temp;

        for (item = 0; item < n - 1; ++item)

            /* find the smallest of all remaining elements */
            for (i = item + 1; i < n; ++i)

                if (*(x + i) < *(x + item))   {

                    /* interchange two elements */
                    temp = *(x + item);
                    *(x + item) = *(x + i);
                    *(x + i) = temp;
                }
        return;
    }
```

In this program, the integer array is defined as a pointer to an integer. Memory is initially assigned to the pointer variable via the `malloc` library function. Elsewhere in the program, pointer notation is used to process the individual array elements. For example, the function prototype now specifies that the second argument is a pointer to an integer quantity rather than an integer array. This pointer will identify the beginning of the integer array.

We also see that the `scanf` function now specifies the address of the ith element as `x + i` rather than `&x[i]`. Similarly, the `printf` function now represents the value of the ith element as `*(x + i)` rather than `x[i]`. The call to reorder, however, is the same as in the earlier program—namely, `reorder(n, x);`.

Within the function `reorder`, we see that the second formal argument is now defined as a pointer variable rather than an integer array. This is consistent with the function prototype. Even more pronounced, however, are the differences in the `if` statement. In particular, notice that each reference to an array element is now written as the contents of an address. Thus `x[i]` is now written as `*(x + i)`, and `x[item]` is now written as `*(x + item)`. This compound `if` statement can be viewed as a conditional interchange involving the contents of two different addresses, rather than an interchange of two different elements within a conventional array.

You should compare this program with that shown in Example 9.13 in order to appreciate the differences. Both programs will generate identical results with the same input data. However, you should understand the syntactic differences between the two programs.

An important advantage of dynamic memory allocation is the ability to reserve as much memory as may be required during program execution, and then release this memory when it is no longer needed. Moreover, this process may be repeated many times during execution of a program. The library functions `malloc` and `free` are used for these purposes, as illustrated in Example 11.32 (see Sec. 11.6).

10.6 OPERATIONS ON POINTERS

In Sec. 10.4 we saw that an integer value can be added to an array name in order to access an individual array element. The integer value is interpreted as an array subscript; it represents the location of the desired array element relative to the first element in the array. This works because all of the array elements are of the same data type, and therefore each array element occupies the same number of memory cells (i.e., the same number of bytes or words). The actual number of memory cells that separate the two array elements will depend on the data type of the array, though this is taken care of automatically by the compiler and therefore need not concern you directly.

This concept can be extended to pointer variables in general. Thus, an integer value can be added to or subtracted from a pointer variable, though the resulting expression must be interpreted very carefully. Suppose, for example, that px is a pointer variable that represents the address of some variable x. We can write expressions such as ++px, --px, (px + 3), (px + i), and (px - i), where i is an integer variable. Each expression will represent an address that is located some distance from the original address represented by px. The exact distance will be the product of the integer quantity and the number of bytes or words associated with the data item to which px points. Suppose, for example, that px points to an integer quantity, and each integer quantity requires two bytes of memory. Then the expression (px + 3) will result in an address that is six bytes beyond the integer to which px points, as illustrated in Fig. 10.3. It should be understood, however, that this new address will *not* necessarily represent the address of another data item, particularly if the data items stored between the two addresses involve different data types.

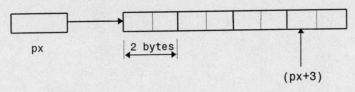

Fig. 10.3

EXAMPLE 10.17   Consider the simple C program shown below.

```
#include <stdio.h>

main()

{
    int *px;              /* pointer to an integer */
    int i = 1;
    float f = 0.3;
    double d = 0.005;
    char c = '*';

    px = &i;
    printf("Values:    i=%i    f=%f    d=%f    c=%c\n\n", i, f, d, c);
    printf("Addresses:    &i=%X    &f=%X    &d=%X    &c=%X\n\n", &i, &f, &d, &c);
    printf("Pointer values:    px=%X    px + 1=%X    px + 2=%X    px + 3=%X",
                                          px, px + 1, px + 2, px + 3);

}
```

This program displays the values and addresses associated with four different types of variables: i, an integer variable; f, a floating-point variable; d, a double-precision variable; and c, a character variable. The program also makes use of a pointer variable, px, which represents the address of i. The values of px, px + 1, px + 2 and px + 3 are also displayed, so that they may be compared with the addresses of the different variables.

Execution of the program results in the following output.

```
Values:    i=1    f=0.300000    d=0.005000    c=*

Addresses:    &i=117E    &f=1180    &d=1186    &c=118E

Pointer values:    px=117E    px + 1=1180    px + 2=1182    px + 3=1184
```

The first line simply displays the values of the variables, and the second line displays their addresses, as assigned by the compiler. Notice that the number of bytes associated with each data item is different. Thus, the integer value represented by i requires two bytes (specifically, addresses 117E and 117F). The floating-point value represented by f appears to be assigned six bytes (addresses 1180 through 1185), though only four bytes (addresses 1180 through 1183) are actually used for this purpose. (Compilers allocate memory space according to their own rules.) However, eight bytes are required for the double-precision value represented by d (addresses 1186 through 118D). And finally, the character represented by c begins in address 118E. Only one byte is required to store this single character, though the output does not indicate the number of bytes between this character and the next data item.

Now consider the third line of output, which contains the addresses represented by the pointer expressions. Clearly, px represents the address of i (i.e., 117E). This comes as no surprise, since this address was explicitly assigned to px by the expression px = &i. However, px + 1 moves over only two bytes, to 1180, and px + 2 moves over another two bytes, to 1182, and so on. The reason is that px points to an integer quantity, and integer quantities each require two bytes with this particular C compiler. Therefore, when integer constants are added to px, the constants are interpreted in terms of two-byte multiples.

If px is defined as a pointer to a different type of object (e.g., a character or a floating-point quantity), then any integer constant that is added to or subtracted from the pointer will be interpreted differently. In particular, each integer value will represent an equivalent number of individual bytes if px points to a character, or a corresponding number of four-byte multiples if px points to a floating-point quantity. You are encouraged to verify this on your own.

One pointer variable can be subtracted from another provided both variables point to elements of the same array. The resulting value indicates the number of words or bytes separating the corresponding array elements.

EXAMPLE 10.18   In the program shown below, two different pointer variables point to the first and the last elements of an integer array.

```
#include <stdio.h>

main()
{
    int *px, *py;          /* integer pointers */
    static int a[6] = {1, 2, 3, 4, 5, 6};

    px = &a[0];
    py = &a[5];
    printf("px=%X    py=%X", px, py);
    printf("\n\npy - px=%X", py - px);
}
```

In particular, the pointer variable px points to a[0], and py points to a[5]. The difference, py - px, should be 5, since a[5] is the fifth element beyond a[0].

Execution of the program results in the following output.

```
px=52    py=5C

py - px=5
```

The first line indicates that the address of a[0] is 52, and the address of a[5] is 5C. The difference between these two hexadecimal numbers is 10 (when converted to decimal). Thus, a[5] is stored at an address which is 10 bytes beyond the address of a[0]. Since each integer quantity occupies two bytes, we would expect the difference between py and px to be 10/2 = 5. The second line of output confirms this value.

Pointer variables can be compared provided both variables are of the same data type. Such comparisons can be useful when both pointer variables point to elements of the same array. The comparisons can test for either equality or inequality. Moreover, a pointer variable can be compared with zero (which is usually expressed as NULL when used in this manner, as explained in Sec. 10.2).

EXAMPLE 10.19 Suppose px and py are pointer variables that point to elements of the same array. Several logical expressions involving these two variables are shown below. All of the expressions are syntactically correct.

```
(px < py)

(px >= py)

(px == py)

(px != py)

(px == NULL)
```

These expressions can be used as any other logical expression. For example,

```
if (px < py)
    printf("px < py");
else
    printf("px >= py");
```

Expressions such as (px < py) indicate whether or not the element associated with px is ranked ahead of the element associated with py (i.e., whether or not the subscript associated with *px is less than the subscript associated with *py).

You should understand that the operations discussed previously are the *only* operations that can be carried out on pointers. These permissible operations are summarized below.

1. A pointer variable can be assigned the address of an ordinary variable (e.g., pv = &v).

2. A pointer variable can be assigned the value of another pointer variable (e.g., pv = px) provided both pointers point to objects of the same data type .

3. A pointer variable can be assigned a null (zero) value (e.g., pv = NULL, where NULL is a symbolic constant that represents the value 0).

4. An integer quantity can be added to or subtracted from a pointer variable (e.g., pv + 3, ++pv, etc.)

5. One pointer variable can be subtracted from another provided both pointers point to elements of the same array.

6. Two pointer variables can be compared provided both pointers point to objects of the same data type.

Other arithmetic operations on pointers are not allowed. Thus, a pointer variable cannot be multiplied by a constant; two pointer variables cannot be added; and so on. Also, you are again reminded that an ordinary variable cannot be assigned an arbitrary address (i.e., an expression such as &x cannot appear on the left side of an assignment statement).

10.7 POINTERS AND MULTIDIMENSIONAL ARRAYS

Since a one-dimensional array can be represented in terms of a pointer (the array name) and an offset (the subscript), it is reasonable to expect that a multidimensional array can also be represented with an equivalent pointer notation. This is indeed the case. A two-dimensional array, for example, is actually a collection of one-dimensional arrays.   Therefore, we can define a two-dimensional array as a pointer to a group of contiguous one-dimensional arrays. Thus, a two-dimensional array declaration can be written as

> *data-type*   (**ptvar*)[*expression 2*];

rather than

> *data-type*   *array*[*expression 1*][*expression 2*];

This concept can be generalized to higher-dimensional arrays; that is,

> *data-type*   (**ptvar*)[*expression 2*][*expression 3*] . . . [*expression n*];

replaces

> *data-type*   *array*[*expression 1*][*expression 2*] . . . [*expression n*];

In these declarations *data-type* refers to the data type of the array, *ptvar* is the name of the pointer variable, *array* is the corresponding array name, and *expression 1*, *expression 2*, . . ., *expression n* are positive-valued integer expressions that indicate the maximum number of array elements associated with each subscript.

Notice the parentheses that surround the array name and the preceding asterisk in the pointer version of each declaration. These parentheses must be present. Without them we would be defining an array of pointers rather than a pointer to a group of arrays, since these particular symbols (i.e., the square brackets and the asterisk) would normally be evaluated right to left. We will say more about this in the next section.

EXAMPLE 10.20   Suppose x is a two-dimensional integer array having 10 rows and 20 columns. We can declare x as

```
int (*x)[20];
```

rather than

```
int x[10][20];
```

In the first declaration, x is defined to be a pointer to a group of contiguous, one-dimensional, 20-element integer arrays. Thus, x points to the first 20-element array, which is actually the first row (i.e., row 0) of the original two-dimensional array. Similarly, (x + 1) points to the second 20-element array, which is the second row (row 1) of the original two-dimensional array, and so on, as illustrated in Fig. 10.4.

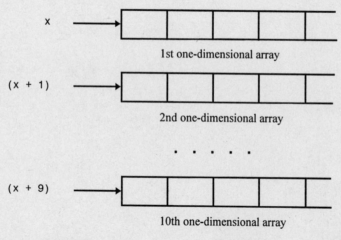

Fig. 10.4

Now consider a three-dimensional floating-point array t. This array can be defined as

```
float (*t)[20][30];
```

rather than

```
float t[10][20][30];
```

In the first declaration, t is defined as a pointer to a group of contiguous two-dimensional, 20 × 30 floating-point arrays. Hence, t points to the first 20 × 30 array, (t + 1) points to the second 20 × 30 array, and so on.

An individual array element within a multidimensional array can be accessed by the repeated use of the indirection operator. Usually, however, this procedure is more awkward than the conventional method for accessing an array element. The following example illustrates the use of the indirection operator.

EXAMPLE 10.21   Suppose x is a two-dimensional integer array having 10 rows and 20 columns, as declared in the previous example. The item in row 2, column 5 can be accessed by writing either

```
x[2][5]
```

or

```
*(*(x + 2) + 5)
```

The second form requires some explanation. First, note that (x + 2) is a pointer to row 2. Therefore the object of this pointer, *(x + 2), refers to the entire row. Since row 2 is a one-dimensional array, *(x + 2) is actually a pointer to the first element in row 2. We now add 5 to this pointer. Hence, (*(x + 2) + 5) is a pointer to element 5 (i.e., the sixth element) in row 2. The object of this pointer, *(*(x + 2) + 5), therefore refers to the item in column 5 of row 2, which is x[2][5]. These relationships are illustrated in Fig. 10.5.

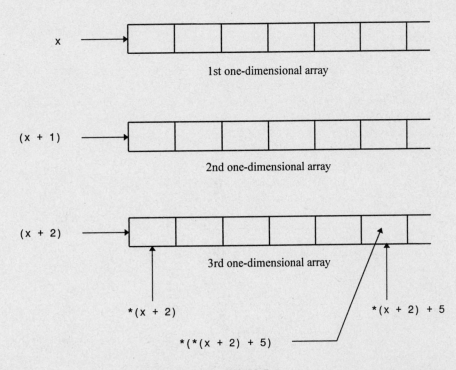

Fig. 10.5

Programs that make use of multidimensional arrays can be written in several different ways. In particular, there are different ways to define the arrays, and different ways to process the individual array elements. The choice of one method over another is often a matter of personal preference. In applications involving numerical arrays, it is often easier to define the arrays in the conventional manner, thus avoiding any possible subtleties associated with initial memory assignments. The following example, however, illustrates the use of pointer notation to process multidimensional numerical arrays.

EXAMPLE 10.22 Adding Two Tables of Numbers   In Example 9.19 we developed a C program to calculate the sum of the corresponding elements of two tables of integers. That program required three separate two-dimensional arrays, which were defined and processed in the conventional manner. Here is a variation of the program, in which each two-dimensional array is defined as an array of pointers to a set of one-dimensional integer arrays.

```
/* calculate the sum of the elements in two tables of integers */

/* each 2-dimensional array is processed as an array
   of pointers to a set of 1-dimensional integer arrays */

#include <stdio.h>
#include <stdlib.h>

#define MAXROWS  20

/* function prototypes */
void readinput  (int *a[MAXROWS], int nrows, int ncols);
void computesums(int *a[MAXROWS], int *b[MAXROWS],
                 int *c[MAXROWS], int nrows, int ncols);
void writeoutput(int *c[MAXROWS], int nrows, int ncols);

main()
{
    int row, nrows, ncols;

    /* pointer definitions */
    int *a[MAXROWS], *b[MAXROWS], *c[MAXROWS];

    printf("How many rows? ");
    scanf("%d", &nrows);
    printf("How many columns? ");
    scanf("%d", &ncols);

    /* allocate initial memory */
    for (row = 0; row < nrows; ++row)   {
        a[row] = (int *) malloc (ncols * sizeof(int));
        b[row] = (int *) malloc (ncols * sizeof(int));
        c[row] = (int *) malloc (ncols * sizeof(int));
    }

    printf("\n\nFirst table:\n");
    readinput(a, nrows, ncols);

    printf("\n\nSecond table:\n");
    readinput(b, nrows, ncols);

    computesums(a, b, c, nrows, ncols);

    printf("\n\nSums of the elements:\n\n");
    writeoutput(c, nrows, ncols);
}
```

```
    void readinput(int *a[MAXROWS], int m, int n)
    /* read in a table of integers */

    {
        int row, col;

        for (row = 0; row < m; ++row)   {
            printf("\nEnter data for row no. %2d\n", row + 1);
            for (col = 0; col < n; ++col)
                scanf("%d", (*(a + row) + col));
        }
        return;
    }


    void computesums(int *a[MAXROWS], int *b[MAXROWS], int *c[MAXROWS], int m, int n)
    /* add the elements of two integer tables */

    {
        int row, col;

        for (row = 0; row < m; ++row)
            for (col = 0; col < n; ++col)
                *(*(c + row) + col) = *(*(a + row) + col) + *(*(b + row) + col);
        return;
    }


    void writeoutput(int *a[MAXROWS], int m, int n)
    /* write out a table of integers */

    {
        int row, col;

        for (row = 0; row < m; ++row)   {
            for (col = 0; col < n; ++col)
                printf("%4d", *(*(a + row) + col));
            printf("\n");
        }
        return;
    }
```

In this program a, b and c are each defined as an array of pointers to integers. Each array has a maximum of MAXROWS elements. The function prototypes and the formal argument declarations within the subordinate functions also represent the arrays in this manner.

Since each element of a, b and c is a pointer, we must provide each pointer with enough memory for each row of integer quantities, using the malloc function as described in Sec. 10.5. These memory allocations appear in main, after the values for nrows and ncols have been entered. Consider the first memory allocation; i.e.,

```
        a[row] = (int *) malloc(ncols *sizeof(int));
```

In this statement a[0] points to the the first row. Similarly, a[1] points to the second row, a[2] points to the third row, and so on. Thus, each array element points to a block of memory large enough to store one row of integer quantities (ncols integer quantities). Similar memory allocations are written for the other two arrays.

The individual array elements are processed by repeated use of the indirection operator. In readinput, for example, each array element is referenced as

```
scanf("%d", (*(a + row) + col));
```

Similarly, the addition of the array elements within computesums is written as

```
*(*(c + row) + col) = *(*(a + row) + col) + *(*(b + row) + col);
```

and the first printf statement within writeoutput is written as

```
printf("%4d", *(*(a + row) + col));
```

We could, of course, have used the more conventional notation within the functions. Thus, in readinput we could have written

```
scanf("%d", a[row][col]);
```

instead of

```
scanf("%d", (*(a + row) + col));
```

Similarly, in computesums we could have written

```
c[row][col] = a[row][col] + b[row][col];
```

instead of

```
*(*(c + row) + col) = *(*(a + row) + col) + *(*(b + row) + col);
```

and in writeoutput we could have written

```
printf("%4d", a[row][col]);
```

rather than

```
printf("%4d", *(*(a + row) + col));
```

This program will generate output identical to that shown in Example 9.19 when executed with the same input data.

10.8 ARRAYS OF POINTERS

A multidimensional array can be expressed in terms of an array of pointers rather than a pointer to a group of contiguous arrays. In such situations the newly defined array will have one less dimension than the original multidimensional array. Each pointer will indicate the beginning of a separate $(n-1)$-dimensional array.

In general terms, a two-dimensional array can be defined as a one-dimensional array of pointers by writing

> *data-type *array[expression 1];*

rather than the conventional array definition,

> *data-type array[expression 1][expression 2];*

Similarly, an n-dimensional array can be defined as an $(n-1)$-dimensional array of pointers by writing

> *data-type *array[expression 1][expression 2] . . . [expression n-1];*

rather than

> *data-type array[expression 1][expression 2] . . . [expression n];*

In these declarations *data-type* refers to the data type of the original *n*-dimensional array, *array* is the array name, and *expression 1, expression 2, . . ., expression n* are positive-valued integer expressions that indicate the maximum number of elements associated with each subscript.

Notice that the array name and its preceding asterisk are *not* enclosed in parentheses in this type of declaration. (Compare carefully with the pointer declarations presented in the last section.) Thus, a right-to-left rule first associates the pairs of square brackets with *array*, defining the named object as an array. The preceding asterisk then establishes that the array will contain pointers.

Moreover, note that the *last* (i.e., the rightmost) expression is omitted when defining an array of pointers, whereas the *first* (i.e., the leftmost) expression is omitted when defining a pointer to a group of arrays. (Again, compare carefully with the declarations presented in the last section.) You should understand the distinction between this type of declaration and that presented in the last section.

When an *n*-dimensional array is expressed in this manner, an individual array element within the *n*-dimensional array can be accessed by a single use of the indirection operator. The following example illustrates how this is done.

EXAMPLE 10.23 Suppose x is a two-dimensional integer array having 10 rows and 20 columns, as in Example 10.20. We can define x as a one-dimensional array of pointers by writing

```
int *x[10];
```

Hence, x[0] points to the beginning of the first row, x[1] points to the beginning of the second row, and so on. Note that the number of elements within each row is not explicitly specified.

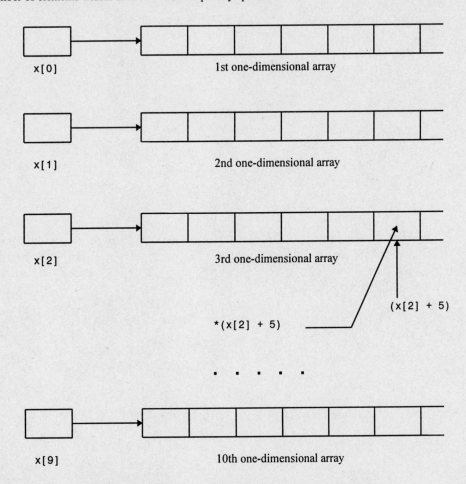

Fig. 10.6

An individual array element, such as x[2][5], can be accessed by writing

```
*(x[2] + 5)
```

In this expression, x[2] is a pointer to the first element in row 2, so that (x[2] + 5) points to element 5 (actually, the sixth element) within row 2. The object of this pointer, *(x[2] + 5), therefore refers to x[2][5]. These relationships are illustrated in Fig. 10.6.

Now consider a three-dimensional floating-point array t. Suppose the dimensionality of t is $10 \times 20 \times 30$. This array can be expressed as a two-dimensional array of pointers by writing

```
float *t[10][20];
```

Therefore we have 200 pointers (10 rows, 20 columns), each pointing to a one-dimensional array.

An individual array element, such as t[2][3][5], can be accessed by writing

```
*(t[2][3] + 5)
```

In this expression, t[2][3] is a pointer to the first element in the one-dimensional array represented by t[2][3]. Hence, (t[2][3] + 5) points to element 5 (the sixth element) within this array. The object of this pointer, *(t[2][3] + 5), therefore represents t[2][3][5]. This situation is directly analogous to the two-dimensional case described above.

EXAMPLE 10.24 Adding Two Tables of Numbers   Here is yet another version of the programs presented in Examples 9.19 and 10.22, which calculate the sum of the corresponding elements of two tables of integers. Now each two-dimensional array is represented as an array of pointers to one-dimensional arrays. Each one-dimensional array will correspond to one row within the original two-dimensional array.

```
/* calculate the sum of the elements in two tables of integers */

/* each 2-dimensional array is represented as an array of pointers
   each pointer indicates a row in the original 2-dimensional array */

#include <stdio.h>
#include <stdlib.h>

#define MAXROWS  20
#define MAXCOLS  30

/* function prototypes */
void readinput(int *a[MAXROWS], int nrows, int ncols);
void computesums(int *a[MAXROWS], int *b[MAXROWS],
                 int *c[MAXROWS], int nrows, int ncols);
void writeoutput(int *c[MAXROWS], int nrows, int ncols);


main()

{
    int row, nrows, ncols;

    /* array definitions */
    int *a[MAXROWS], *b[MAXROWS], *c[MAXROWS];

    printf("How many rows? ");
    scanf("%d", &nrows);
    printf("How many columns? ");
    scanf("%d", &ncols);
```

```
    /* allocate initial memory */
    for (row = 0; row <= nrows; row++)   {
        a[row] = (int *) malloc(ncols * sizeof(int));
        b[row] = (int *) malloc(ncols * sizeof(int));
        c[row] = (int *) malloc(ncols * sizeof(int));
    }

    printf("\n\nFirst table:\n");
    readinput(a, nrows, ncols);

    printf("\n\nSecond table:\n");
    readinput(b, nrows, ncols);

    computesums(a, b, c, nrows, ncols);

    printf("\n\nSums of the elements:\n\n");
    writeoutput(c, nrows, ncols);
}

void readinput(int *a[MAXROWS], int m, int n)
/* read in a table of integers */

{
    int row, col;

    for (row = 0; row < m; ++row)   {
        printf("\nEnter data for row no. %2d\n", row + 1);
        for (col = 0; col < n; ++col)
            scanf("%d", (a[row] + col));
    }
    return;
}

void computesums(int *a[MAXROWS], int *b[MAXROWS],
                 int *c[MAXROWS], int m, int n)
/* add the elements of two integer tables */

{
    int row, col;

    for (row = 0; row < m; ++row)
        for (col = 0; col < n; ++col)
            *(c[row] + col) = *(a[row] + col) + *(b[row] + col);
    return;
}

void writeoutput(int *a[MAXROWS], int m, int n)
/* write out a table of integers */

{
    int row, col;

    for (row = 0; row < m; ++row)   {
        for (col = 0; col < n; ++col)
            printf("%4d", *(a[row] + col));
        printf("\n");
    }
    return;
}
```

Notice that a, b and c are now defined as one-dimensional arrays of pointers. Each array will contain MAXROWS elements (i.e., MAXROWS pointers). Each array element will point to a one-dimensional array of integers. The function prototypes and the formal argument declarations within the subordinate functions also represent the arrays in this manner.

Each one-dimensional array that is the object of a pointer (i.e., each row within each of the tables) must be allocated an initial block of memory. The `malloc` function accomplishes this. For example, each row within the first table is allocated an initial block of memory in the following manner.

```
a[row] = (int *) malloc(ncols * sizeof(int));
```

This statement associates a block of memory large enough to store `ncols` integer quantities with each pointer (i.e., with each element of a). Similar memory allocations are written for b and c. These `malloc` statements are placed within a `for` loop in order to allocate a block of memory for each of the nonzero rows within the three tables.

Notice the way the individual array elements are processed, using a combination of array and pointer notation. For example, in `readinput` each array element is now referenced as

```
scanf("%d", (a[row] + col));
```

Similarly, in `computesums` and `writeoutput` the individual array elements are referenced as

```
*(c[row] + col) = *(a[row] + col) + *(b[row] + col);
```

and

```
printf("%4d", *(a[row] + col));
```

respectively. These statements could also have been written using conventional two-dimensional array notation.

This program, as well as the program presented in Example 10.22, will generate output that is identical to that shown in Example 9.19 when executed with the same input data. You may wish to verify this on your own. If this problem were being programmed from scratch, however, the conventional approach shown in Example 9.19, using two-dimensional arrays, would most likely be chosen.

Pointer arrays offer a particularly convenient method for storing strings. In this situation, each array element is a character-type pointer that indicates the beginning of a separate string. Thus, an n-element array can point to n different strings. Each individual string can be accessed by referring to its corresponding pointer.

EXAMPLE 10.25   Suppose the following strings are to be stored in a character-type array.

```
PACIFIC
ATLANTIC
INDIAN
CARIBBEAN
BERING
BLACK
RED
NORTH
BALTIC
CASPIAN
```

These strings can be stored in a two-dimensional character-type array; e.g.,

```
char names[10][12];
```

Note that `names` contains 10 rows, to accommodate the 10 strings. Each row must be large enough to store at least 10 characters, since `CARIBBEAN` contains 9 letters plus the null character (\0) at the end. To provide for larger strings, we are allowing each row to contain as many as 12 characters.

A better way to do this is to define a 10-element array of pointers; i.e.

```
char *names[10];
```

Thus, names[0] will point to PACIFIC, names[1] will point to ATLANTIC, and so on. Note that it is not necessary to include a maximum string size within the array declaration. However, a specified amount of memory will have to be allocated for each string later in the program, e.g.,

```
names[i] = (char *) malloc(12 * sizeof(char));
```

Just as individual strings can be accessed by referring to the corresponding pointer (i.e., the corresponding array element), so can individual string elements be accessed through the use of the indirection operator. For example, *(*(names + 2) + 3) refers to the fourth character (i.e., character number 3) in the third string (row number 2) of the array names, as defined in the preceding example.

Rearrangement of the strings can be accomplished simply by reassigning the pointers (i.e., by reassigning the elements in an array of pointers). The strings themselves need not be moved.

EXAMPLE 10.26 Reordering a List of Strings   Consider once again the problem of entering a list of strings into the computer and rearranging them into alphabetical order. We saw one approach to this problem in Example 9.20, where the list of strings was stored in a two-dimensional array. Let us now approach this problem using a one-dimensional array of pointers, where each pointer indicates the beginning of a string. The string interchanges can now be carried out simply by reassigning the pointers, as required.

The complete program is presented below.

```
/* sort a list of strings into alphabetical order using an array of pointers */

#include <stdio.h>
#include <stdlib.h>
#include <string.h>

void reorder(int n, char *x[]);

main()
{
    int i, n = 0;
    char *x[10];

    printf("Enter each string on a separate line below\n\n");
    printf("Type \'END\' when finished\n\n");

    /* read in the list of strings */
    do   {
            /* allocate memory */
            x[n] = (char *) malloc(12 * sizeof(char));

            printf("string %d: ", n + 1);
            scanf("%s", x[n]);
        }
    while (strcmp(x[n++], "END"));

    /* reorder the list of strings */
    reorder(--n, x);

    /* display the reordered list of strings */
    printf("\n\nReordered List of Strings:\n");
    for (i = 0; i < n; ++i)
        printf("\nstring %d: %s", i + 1, x[i]);
}
```

```
void reorder(int n, char *x[])     /* rearrange the list of strings */

{
    char *temp;
    int i, item;

    for (item = 0; item < n - 1; ++item)

    /* find the lowest of all remaining strings */
    for (i = item + 1; i < n; ++i)

        if (strcmp(x[item], x[i]) > 0)   {
            /* interchange the two strings */
            temp = x[item];
            x[item] = x[i];
            x[i] = temp;
        }
    return;
}
```

The logic is essentially the same as that shown in Example 9.20, though the array containing the strings is now defined as an array of pointers. Notice that the second formal argument in the function reorder is declared in the same manner. Also, notice the string interchange routine (i.e., the if statement) within reorder. It is now the pointers, not the actual strings, that are interchanged. Hence the library function strcpy, which was used in Example 9.20, is not required. The program will therefore run somewhat faster than the earlier version.

Execution of this program will generate the same dialog as that shown in Example 9.20.

If the elements of an array are string pointers, a set of initial values can be specified as a part of the array declaration. In such cases the initial values will be strings, where each string corresponds to a separate array element. Remember, however, that an array must be declared static if it is initialized within a function.

An advantage to this scheme is that a fixed block of memory need not be reserved in advance, as is done when initializing a conventional array. Thus, if the initial declaration includes many strings and some of them are relatively short, there may be a substantial savings in memory allocation. Moreover, if some of the strings are particularly long, there is no need to worry about the possibility of exceeding some maximum specified string length (i.e., the maximum number of characters per row). Arrays of this type are often referred to as *ragged arrays*.

EXAMPLE 10.27 The following array declaration appears within a function.

```
static char *names[10] = {
                            "PACIFIC",
                            "ATLANTIC",
                            "INDIAN",
                            "CARIBBEAN",
                            "BERING",
                            "BLACK",
                            "RED",
                            "NORTH",
                            "BALTIC",
                            "CASPIAN"
                        };
```

In this example, names is a 10-element array of pointers. Thus, the first array element (i.e., the first pointer) will point to PACIFIC, the second array element will point to ATLANTIC, and so on.

Notice that the array is declared as static so that it can be initialized within the function. If the array declaration were external to all program functions, the static storage class designation would not be necessary.

Since the array declaration includes initial values, it is really not necessary to include an explicit size designation within the declaration. The size of the array will automatically be set equal to the number of strings that are present. Thus, the above declaration can be written as

```
static char *names[] = {
                        "PACIFIC",
                        "ATLANTIC",
                        "INDIAN",
                        "CARIBBEAN",
                        "BERING",
                        "BLACK",
                        "RED",
                        "NORTH",
                        "BALTIC",
                        "CASPIAN"
                };
```

It should be understood that the ragged-array concept refers only to the *initialization* of string arrays, not the assignment of individual strings that may be read into the computer via the scanf function. Thus, applications requiring that strings be read into the computer and then processed, as in Example 10.26, still require the allocation of a specified amount of memory for each array element.

Initialized string values can be accessed by referring to their corresponding pointers (i.e., their corresponding array elements), in the usual manner. These pointers can be reassigned other string constants elsewhere in the program if necessary.

EXAMPLE 10.28 Displaying the Day of the Year   Let us develop a program that will accept three integer quantities, indicating the month, day and year, and then display the corresponding day of the week, the month, the day and the year in a more legible manner. For example, suppose we were to enter the date 5 24 1997; this would produce the output Saturday, May 24, 1997. Programs of this type are often used to display information that is stored in a computer's internal memory in an encoded format.

Our basic strategy will be to enter a date into the computer, in the form *month, day, year* (mm dd yyyy), and then convert this date into the number of days relative to some base date. The day of the week corresponding to the specified date can then be determined quite easily, provided we know the day of the week corresponding to the base date. Let us arbitrarily choose Monday, January 1, 1900 as the base date. We will then convert any date beyond January 1, 1900 (actually, any date between January 1, 1900 and December 31, 2099) into an equivalent day of the week.

The computation can be carried out using the following empirical rules.

1. Enter numerical values for the variables mm, dd and yy, which represent the month, day and year, respectively (e.g., 5 24 1997).

2. Determine the approximate day of the current year, as

    ndays = (long) (30.42 * (mm - 1)) + dd;

3. If mm == 2 (February), increase the value of ndays by 1.

4. If mm > 2 and mm < 8 (March, April, May, June or July), decrease the value of ndays by 1.

5. Convert the year into the number of years beyond the base date; i.e., yy -= 1900. Then test for a leap year as follows: If (yy % 4) == 0 and mm > 2, increase the value of ndays by 1.

6. Determine the number of complete 4-year cycles beyond the base date as yy / 4. For each complete 4-year cycle, add 1461 to ndays.

7. Determine the number of full years beyond the last complete 4-year cycle as yy % 4. For each full year, add 365 to ndays. Then add 1, because the first year beyond a full 4-year cycle will be a leap year.

8. If ndays > 59 (i.e., if the date is any day beyond February 28, 1900), decrease the value of ndays by 1, because 1900 is not a leap year. (Note that the last year of each century is not a leap year, except those years that are evenly divisible by 400. Therefore 1900, the last year of the ninteenth century, is *not* a leap year, but 2000, the last year of the twentieth century, *is* a leap year.)

9. Determine the numerical day of the week corresponding to the specified date as day = (ndays % 7).

Note that day == 1 corresponds either to the base date, which is a Monday, or another date that also occurs on a Monday. Hence, day == 2 will refer to a Tuesday, day == 3 will refer to a Wednesday, . . . , day == 6 will refer to a Saturday, and day == 0 will refer to a Sunday.

Here is a complete function, called convert, that carries out steps 2 through 9. Note that convert accepts the integers mm, dd and yy as input parameters, and returns the integer quantity (ndays % 7). Also, notice that ndays and ncycles are long integer variables, whereas all other variables are ordinary integers.

```c
int convert(int mm, int dd, int yy)    /* convert date to numerical day of week */

{
    long ndays;         /* number of days from start of 1900 */
    long ncycles;       /* number of 4-year cycles beyond 1900 */
    int nyears;         /* number of years beyond last 4-year cycle */
    int day;            /* day of week (0, 1, 2, 3, 4, 5 or 6) */

    /* numerical conversions */
    yy -= 1900;
    ndays = (long) (30.42 * (mm - 1)) + dd;    /* approximate day of year */

    if (mm == 2) ++ndays;                       /* adjust for February */
    if ((mm > 2) && (mm < 8)) --ndays;          /* adjust for March - July */
    if ((yy % 4 == 0) && (mm > 2)) ++ndays;     /* adjust for leap year */

    ncycles = yy / 4;                           /* 4-year cycles beyond 1900 */
    ndays += ncycles * 1461;                    /* add days for 4-year cycles */

    nyears = yy % 4;            /* years beyond last 4-year cycle */
    if (nyears > 0)             /* add days for yrs beyond last 4-year cycle */
       ndays += 365 * nyears + 1;

    if (ndays > 59) --ndays;   /* adjust for 1900 (NOT a leap year) */

    day = ndays % 7;

    return(day);
}
```

The names of the days of the week can be stored as strings in a 7-element array; i.e.,

```c
static char *weekday[] = {"Sunday", "Monday", "Tuesday", "Wednesday",
                          "Thursday", "Friday", "Saturday"};
```

Each day corresponds to the value assigned to day, where day = (ndays % 7). The days begin with Sunday because Sunday corresponds to day == 0, as explained above. If the base date were not a Monday, this particular ordering of the days of the week would have to be changed.

Similarly, the names of the months can be stored as strings in a 12-element array; i.e.,

```c
static char *month[] = {"January", "February", "March", "April", "May", "June", "July",
                        "August", "September", "October", "November", "December"};
```

Each month corresponds to the value of mm - 1.

Here is an entire C program that will carry out the conversion interactively.

```c
/* convert a numerical date (mm dd yyyy) into "day of week, month, day, year"
          (e.g., 5 24 1997 -> Saturday, May 24, 1997") */

#include <stdio.h>

void readinput(int *pm, int *pd, int *py);      /* function prototype */
int convert(int mm, int dd, int yy);            /* function prototype */


main()

{
    int mm, dd, yy;
    int day_of_week;    /* day of the week (0 -> Sunday,
                                            1 -> Monday,

                                               . . .

                                            6 -> Saturday)  */

    static char *weekday[] = {"Sunday", "Monday", "Tuesday", "Wednesday",
                              "Thursday", "Friday", "Saturday"};

    static char *month[] = {"January", "February", "March", "April",
                            "May", "June", "July", "August", "September",
                            "October", "November", "December"};

    /* opening message */
    printf("Date Conversion Routine\nTo STOP, enter 0 0 0");

    readinput(&mm, &dd, &yy);

    /* convert date to numerical day of week */
    while (mm > 0)    {
        day_of_week = convert(mm, dd, yy);
        printf("\n%s, %s %d, %d", weekday[day_of_week], month[mm-1], dd, yy);

        readinput(&mm, &dd, &yy);
    }
}


void readinput(int *pm, int *pd, int *py)   /* read in the numerical date */

{
    printf("\n\nEnter mm dd yyyy: ");
    scanf("%d %d %d", pm, pd, py);
    return;
}


int convert(int mm, int dd, int yy)   /* convert date to numerical day of week */

{
    long ndays;         /* number of days from start of 1900 */
    long ncycles;       /* number of 4-year cycles beyond 1900 */
    int nyears;         /* number of years beyond last 4-year cycle */
    int day;            /* day of week (0, 1, 2, 3, 4, 5 or 6) */
```

```
        /* numerical conversions */
        yy -= 1900;
        ndays = (long) (30.42 * (mm - 1)) + dd;    /* approximate day of year */

        if (mm == 2) ++ndays;                      /* adjust for February */
        if ((mm > 2) && (mm < 8)) --ndays;         /* adjust for March - July */
        if ((yy % 4 == 0) && (mm > 2)) ++ndays;    /* adjust for leap year */

        ncycles = yy / 4;                          /* 4-year cycles beyond 1900 */
        ndays += ncycles * 1461;                   /* add days for 4-year cycles */

        nyears = yy % 4;            /* years beyond last 4-year cycle */
        if (nyears > 0)            /* add days for yrs beyond last 4-year cycle */
           ndays += 365 * nyears + 1;

        if (ndays > 59) --ndays;   /* adjust for 1900 (NOT a leap year) */

        day = ndays % 7;

        return(day);
}
```

This program includes a loop that repeatedly accepts a date in the form of three integers (i.e., mm dd yyyy) and returns the corresponding day and date in a more legible form. The program will continue to run until a value of 0 is entered for mm. Note that the prompt indicates that three zeros must be entered in order to stop the program execution; i.e., 0 0 0. Actually, however, the program only checks the value of mm.

A typical interactive session is shown below. As usual, the user's responses are underlined.

```
Date Conversion Routine
To STOP, enter 0 0 0

Enter mm dd yyyy: 10 29 1929

Tuesday, October 29, 1929

Enter mm dd yyyy: 8 15 1945

Wednesday, August 15, 1945

Enter mm dd yyyy: 7 20 1969

Sunday, July 20, 1969

Enter mm dd yyyy: 5 24 1997

Saturday, May 24, 1997

Enter mm dd yyyy: 8 30 2010

Monday, August 30, 2010

Enter mm dd yyyy: 4 12 2069

Friday, April 12, 2069

Enter mm dd yyyy: 0 0 0
```

10.9 PASSING FUNCTIONS TO OTHER FUNCTIONS

A pointer to a function can be passed to another function as an argument. This allows one function to be transferred to another, as though the first function were a variable. Let us refer to the first function as the *guest function*, and the second function as the *host function*. Thus, the guest is passed to the host, where it can be accessed. Successive calls to the host function can pass different pointers (i.e., different guest functions) to the host.

When a host function accepts the name of a guest function as an argument, the formal argument declaration must identify that argument as a pointer to the guest function. In its simplest form, the formal argument declaration can be written as

```
data-type (*function-name)()
```

where *data-type* refers to the data type of the quantity returned by the guest and *function-name* is the name of the guest. The formal argument declaration can also be written as

```
data-type (*function-name)(type 1,  type 2, . . .)
```

or as

```
data-type (*function-name)(type 1 arg 1,  type 2 arg 2, . . .)
```

where *type 1, type 2, . . .* refer to the data types of the arguments associated with the guest, and *arg 1, arg 2, . . .* refer to the names of the arguments associated with the guest.

The guest function can be accessed within the host by means of the indirection operator. To do so, the indirection operator must precede the guest function name (i.e., the formal argument). Both the indirection operator and the guest function name must be enclosed in parentheses; i.e.,

```
(*function-name)(argument 1,  argument 2,  . . .,  argument n);
```

where *argument 1, argument 2, . . ., argument n* refer to the arguments that are required in the function call.

Now consider the function declaration for the host function. It may be written as

```
funct-data-type  funct-name(arg-data-type  (*)(type 1,  type 2, . . . ),
```
|←———   *pointer to guest function*   ———→|

```
                                             data types of other funct args);
```

where *funct-data-type* refers to the data type of the quantity returned by the host function; *funct-name* refers to the name of the host function; *arg-data-type* refers to the data type of the quantity returned by the guest function, and *type 1, type 2, . . .* refer to the data types of guest function's arguments. Notice that the indirection operator appears in parentheses, to indicate a pointer to the guest function. Moreover, the data types of the guest function's arguments follow in a separate pair of parentheses, to indicate that they are function arguments.

When full function prototyping is used, the host function declaration is expanded as follows.

```
funct-data-type  funct-name
            (arg-data-type  (*pt-var)(type 1  arg 1,  type 2  arg 2, . . . ),
```
|←———   *pointer to guest function*   ———→|

```
            data types and names of other funct args);
```

The notation is the same as above, except that *pt-var* refers to the pointer variable pointing to the guest function, and *type 1 arg 1, type 2 arg 2, . . .* refer to the data types and the corresponding names of the guest function's arguments.

EXAMPLE 10.29   The skeletal outline of a C program is shown below. This program consists of four functions: `main`, `process`, `funct1` and `funct2`. Note that `process` is a host function for `funct1` and `funct2`. Each of the three subordinate functions returns an integer quantity.

```
int process(int (*)(int, int));     /* function declaration (host)  */
int funct1(int, int);               /* function declaration (guest) */
int funct2(int, int);               /* function declaration (guest) */

main()
{
    int i, j;
    . . . . .
    i = process(funct1);   /* pass funct1 to process; return a value for i */

    . . . . .
    j = process(funct2);   /* pass funct2 to process; return a value for j */

    . . . . .
}

process(int (*pf)(int, int))        /* host function definition */
                                    /* (formal argument is a pointer to a function) */
{
    int a, b, c;

    . . . . .
    c = (*pf)(a, b);       /* access the function passed to this function;
                              return a value for c */

    . . . . .
    return(c);
}

funct1(a, b)            /* guest function definition */
int a, b;
{
    int c;

    c = . . .           /* use a and b to evaluate c */

    return(c);
}

funct2(x, y)            /* guest function definition */
int x, y;
{
    int z;

    z = . . .           /* use x and y to evaluate z */

    return(z);
}
```

Notice that this program contains three function declarations. The declarations for funct1 and funct2 are straightforward. However the declaration for process requires some explanation. This declaration states that process is a host function that returns an integer quantity and has one argument. The argument is a pointer to a guest function that returns an integer quantity and has two integer arguments. The argument designation for the guest function is written as

```
int (*)(int, int)
```

Notice the way the argument designation fits into the entire host function declaration; i.e.,

```
int process(int (*)(int, int));
```

Now consider the formal argument declaration that appears within process; i.e.,

```
int (*pf)(int, int);
```

This declaration states that pf is a pointer to a guest function. The guest function will return an integer quantity, and it requires two integer arguments.

Here is another version of this same outline, utilizing full function prototyping. The changes are shown in boldface.

```
int process(int (*pf)(int a, int b));    /* function prototype (host)  */
int funct1(int a, int b);                /* function prototype (guest) */
int funct2(int a, int b);                /* function prototype (guest) */

main()
{
    int i, j;
    . . . . .
    i = process(funct1);   /* pass funct1 to process; return a value for i */

    . . . . .
    j = process(funct2);   /* pass funct2 to process; return a value for j */

    . . . . .
}

process(int (*pf)(int a, int b))     /* host function definition */
{
    int a, b, c;

    . . . . .
    c = (*pf)(a, b);       /* access the function passed to this function;
                              return a value for c */

    . . . . .
    return(c);
}

funct1(int a, int b)       /* guest function definition */
{
    int c;
    c = . . .              /* use a and b to evaluate c */
    return(c);
}
```

```
funct2(int x, int y)        /* guest function definition */
{
    int z;

    z = . . .               /* use x and y to evaluate z */

    return(z);
}
```

The function prototypes include argument names as well as argument data types. Moreover, the prototype for process now includes the name of the variable (pf) that points to the guest function. Notice that the declaration of the formal argument pf within process is consistent with the function prototype.

Some programming applications can be formulated quite naturally in terms of one function being passed to another. For example, one function might represent a mathematical equation, and the other might contain a computational strategy to process the equation. In such cases the function representing the equation might be passed to the function that processes the equation. This is particularly useful if the program contains several different mathematical equations, one of which is selected by the user each time the program is executed.

EXAMPLE 10.30 Future Value of Monthly Deposits (Compound Interest Calculations)   Suppose a person decides to save a fixed amount of money at the end of every month for n years. If the money earns interest at i percent per year, then it is natural to ask how much money will accumulate after n years (i.e., after $12n$ monthly deposits). The answer, of course, depends upon how much money is deposited each month, the interest rate, and the frequency with which the interest is compounded. For example, if the interest is compounded annually, semiannually, quarterly or monthly, the future amount of money that will accumulate after n years is given by

$$F = \frac{12A}{m}\left[\frac{(1+i/m)^{mn}-1}{i/m}\right] = 12A\left[\frac{(1+i/m)^{mn}-1}{i}\right]$$

where F is the future accumulation, A is the amount of money deposited each month, i is the annual interest rate (expressed as a decimal), and m is the number of compounding periods per year (e.g., $m = 1$ for annual compounding, $m = 2$ for semiannual compounding, $m = 4$ for quarterly compounding and $m = 12$ for monthly compounding).

If the compounding periods are shorter than the payment periods, such as in the case of daily compounding, then the future amount of money is determined by

$$F = A\left[\frac{(1+i/m)^{mn}-1}{(1+i/m)^{m/12}-1}\right]$$

Note that m is customarily assigned a value of 360 when the interest is compounded daily.

Finally, in the case of continuous compounding, the future amount of money is determined as

$$F = A\left[\frac{e^{in}-1}{e^{i/12}-1}\right]$$

Suppose we wish to determine F as a function of the annual interest rate i, for given values of A, m and n. Let us develop a program that will read the required input data into main, and then carry out the calculations within a separate function, called table. Each of the three formulas for determining the ratio F/A will be placed in one of three independent functions, called md1, md2 and md3, respectively. Thus, the program will consist of five different functions.

When table is called from main, one of the arguments passed to table will be the name of the function containing the appropriate formula, as indicated by an input parameter (freq). The values of A, m and n that are read into main will also be passed to table as arguments. A loop will then be initiated within table, in which values of F are determined

for interest rates ranging from 0.01 (i.e., 1 percent per year) to 0.20 (20 percent per year). The calculated values will be
displayed as they are generated. The entire program is shown below.

```c
/* personal finance calculations */

#include <stdio.h>
#include <stdlib.h>
#include <ctype.h>
#include <math.h>

/* function prototypes */
void table (double (*pf)(double i, int m, double n), double a, int m, double n);
double md1(double i, int m, double n);
double md2(double i, int m, double n);
double md3(double i, int m, double n);


main()      /* calculate the future value of a series of monthly deposits */
{
    int m;        /* number of compounding periods per year */
    double n;     /* number of years */
    double a;     /* amount of each monthly payment */
    char freq;    /* frequency of compounding indicator */

    /* enter input data */
    printf("\nFUTURE VALUE OF A SERIES OF MONTHLY DEPOSITS\n\n");
    printf("Amount of Each Monthly Payment: ");
    scanf("%lf", &a);
    printf("Number of Years: ");
    scanf("%lf", &n);

    /* enter frequency of compounding */
    do   {
            printf("Frequency of Compounding (A, S, Q, M, D, C): ");
            scanf("%1s", &freq);
            freq = toupper(freq);     /* convert to upper case */
            if (freq == 'A')   {
               m = 1;
               printf("\nAnnual Compounding\n");
            }
            else if (freq == 'S')   {
               m = 2;
               printf("\nSemiannual Compounding\n");
            }
            else if (freq == 'Q')   {
               m = 4;
               printf("\nQuarterly Compounding\n");
            }
            else if (freq == 'M')   {
               m = 12;
               printf("\nMonthly Compounding\n");
            }
            else if (freq == 'D')   {
               m = 360;
               printf("\nDaily Compounding\n");
            }
```

```
                    else if (freq == 'C')    {
                        m = 0;
                        printf("\nContinuous Compounding\n");
                    }
                    else
                        printf("\nERROR - Please Repeat\n\n");
            } while (freq != 'A' && freq != 'S' && freq != 'Q' &&
                    freq != 'M' && freq != 'D' && freq != 'C');

        /* carry out the calculations */
        if (freq == 'C')
            table(md3, a, m, n);    /* continuous compounding */
        else if (freq == 'D')
            table(md2, a, m, n);    /* daily compounding */
        else
            table(md1, a, m, n);    /* annual, semiannual, quarterly or monthly compounding */
}

void table (double (*pf)(double i, int m, double n), double a, int m, double n)
/* table generator (this function accepts a pointer to another function as an argument)

    NOTE:    double (*pf)(double i, int m, double n)    is a POINTER TO A FUNCTION */

{
    int count;      /* loop counter */
    double i;       /* annual interest rate */
    double f;       /* future value */

    printf("\nInterest Rate    Future Amount\n\n");
    for (count = 1; count <= 20; ++count)    {
        i = 0.01 * count;
        f = a * (*pf)(i, m, n);     /* ACCESS THE FUNCTION PASSED AS A POINTER */
        printf("      %2d                %.2f\n", count, f);
    }
    return;
}

double md1(double i, int m, double n)
/* monthly deposits, periodic compounding */

{
    double factor, ratio;

    factor = 1 + i/m;
    ratio = 12 * (pow(factor, m*n) - 1) / i;
    return(ratio);
}

double md2(double i, int m, double n)
/* monthly deposits, daily compounding */

{
    double factor, ratio;

    factor = 1 + i/m;
    ratio = (pow(factor, m*n) - 1) / (pow(factor, m/12) - 1);
    return(ratio);
}
```

```
double md3(double i, int dummy, double n)
/* monthly deposits, continuous compounding */

{
    double ratio;

    ratio = (exp(i*n) - 1) / (exp(i/12) - 1);
    return(ratio);
}
```

Notice the function prototypes, particularly the prototype for `table`. The first argument passed to `table` is a pointer to a guest function that receives two double-precision arguments and an integer argument, and returns a double-precision quantity. This pointer is intended to represent `md1`, `md2` or `md3`. The prototypes for these three functions follow the prototype for `table`. Each of these functions accepts two double-precision arguments and an integer argument, and returns a double-precision quantity, as required.

An interactive dialog for the input data is generated within `main`. In particular, the program accepts numerical values for `a` and `n`. It also accepts a one-character string for the character variable `freq`, which indicates the frequency of compounding. The only allowable characters that can be assigned to `freq` are A, S, Q, M, D or C (for Annual, Semiannual, Quarterly, Monthly, Daily or Continuous compounding, respectively). This character can be entered in either upper- or lowercase, since it is converted to uppercase within the program. Note that the program contains an error trap preventing characters other than A, S, Q, M, D or C from being entered.

An appropriate numerical value is assigned to `m` as soon as the frequency of compounding is determined. The program then accesses `table`, passing either `md1`, `md2` or `md3` as an argument, as determined by the character assigned to `freq`. (See the multiple `if - else` statement at the end of `main`.)

Now examine the host function `table`. The last three formal arguments (a, m and n) are declared as ordinary double-precision or integer variables. However, the first formal argument (`pf`) is declared as a pointer to a guest function that accepts two double-precision arguments and an integer argument, and returns a double-precision quantity. These formal argument declarations are consistent with the function prototype for `table`.

The values for `i` (i.e., the interest rates) are generated internally within `table`. These values are determined as `0.01 * count`. Since `count` ranges from 1 to 20, we see that the interest rates range from 0.01 to 0.20, as required.

Notice the manner in which the values for `f` are calculated within `table`; i.e.,

```
f = a * (*pf)(i, m, n);
```

The expression (`*pf`) refers to the guest function whose name is passed to `table` (i.e., either `md1`, `md2` or `md3`). This is accompanied by the required list of arguments, containing the current values for `i`, `m` and `n`. The value returned by the guest function is then multiplied by `a`, and the product is assigned to `f`.

The three remaining functions, `md1`, `md2` and `md3`, are straightforward. Notice that the second argument in `md3` is called `dummy`, because the value of this argument is not utilized within the function. We could have done this with `md2` as well, since the value of `m` is always 360 in the case of daily compounding.

Execution of the program produces the following representative dialog.

```
FUTURE VALUE OF A SERIES OF MONTHLY DEPOSITS

Amount of Each Monthly Payment: 100
Number of Years: 3
Frequency of Compounding (A, S, Q, M, D, C): p

ERROR - Please Repeat

Frequency of Compounding (A, S, Q, M, D, C): m

Monthly Compounding
```

Interest Rate	Future Amount
1	3653.00
2	3707.01
3	3762.06
4	3818.16
5	3875.33
6	3933.61
7	3993.01
8	4053.56
9	4115.27
10	4178.18
11	4242.31
12	4307.69
13	4374.33
14	4442.28
15	4511.55
16	4582.17
17	4654.18
18	4727.60
19	4802.45
20	4878.78

10.10 MORE ABOUT POINTER DECLARATIONS

Before leaving this chapter we mention that pointer declarations can become complicated, and some care is required in their interpretation. This is especially true of declarations that involve functions or arrays.

One difficulty is the dual use of parentheses. In particular, parentheses are used to indicate functions, and they are used for nesting purposes (to establish precedence) within more complicated declarations. Thus, the declaration

```
int *p(int a);
```

indicates a function that accepts an integer argument, and returns a pointer to an integer. On the other hand, the declaration

```
int (*p)(int a);
```

indicates a *pointer to a function* that accepts an integer argument and returns an integer. In this last declaration, the first pair of parentheses is used for nesting, and the second pair is used to indicate a function.

The interpretation of more complex declarations can be increasingly troublesome. For example, consider the declaration

```
int *(*p)(int (*a)[]);
```

In this declaration, (*p)(. . .) indicates a pointer to a function. Hence, int *(*p)(. . .) indicates a pointer to a function that returns a pointer to an integer. Within the last pair of parentheses (the function's argument specification), (*a)[] indicates a pointer to an array. Therefore, int (*a)[] represents a pointer to an array of integers. Putting the pieces together, (*p)(int (*a)[]) represents a pointer to a function whose argument is a pointer to an array of integers. And finally, the entire declaration

```
int *(*p)(int (*a)[]);
```

represents a pointer to a function that accepts a pointer to an array of integers as an argument, and returns a pointer to an integer.

Remember that a left parenthesis immediately following an identifier name indicates that the identifier represents a function. Similarly, a left square bracket immediately following an identifier name indicates that the identifier represents an array. Parentheses that identify functions and square brackets that identify arrays have a higher precedence than the unary indirection operator (see Appendix C). Therefore, additional parentheses are required when declaring a pointer to a function or a pointer to an array.

The following example provides a number of illustrations.

EXAMPLE 10.31 Several declarations involving pointers are shown below. The individual declarations range from simple to complex.

```
int *p;                 /* p is a pointer to an integer quantity */

int *p[10];             /* p is a 10-element array of pointers to integer quantities */

int (*p)[10];           /* p is a pointer to a 10-element integer array */

int *p(void);           /* p is a function that
                           returns a pointer to an integer quantity */

int p(char *a);         /* p is a function that
                           accepts an argument which is a pointer to a character and
                           returns an integer quantity */

int *p(char a*);        /* p is a function that
                           accepts an argument which is a pointer to a character
                           returns a pointer to an integer quantity */

int (*p)(char *a);      /* p is a pointer to a function that
                           accepts an argument which is a pointer to a character
                           returns an integer quantity */

int (*p(char *a))[10];  /* p is a function that
                           accepts an argument which is a pointer to a character
                           returns a pointer to a 10-element integer array */

int p(char (*a)[]);     /* p is a function that
                           accepts an argument which is a pointer to a character array
                           returns an integer quantity */

int p(char *a[]);       /* p is a function that
                           accepts an argument which is an array of pointers to
                             characters
                           returns an integer quantity */

int *p(char a[]);       /* p is a function that
                           accepts an argument which is a character array
                           returns a pointer to an integer quantity */

int *p(char (*a)[]);    /* p is a function that
                           accepts an argument which is a pointer to a character array
                           returns a pointer to an integer quantity */

int *p(char *a[]);      /* p is a function that
```

```
                              accepts an argument which is an array of pointers to
                                 characters
                              returns a pointer to an integer quantity */

int (*p)(char (*a)[]);     /* p is a pointer to a function that
                              accepts an argument which is a pointer to a character array
                              returns an integer quantity */

int *(*p)(char (*a)[]);    /* p is pointer to a function that
                              accepts an argument which is a pointer to a character array
                              returns a pointer to an integer quantity */

int *(*p)(char *a[]);      /* p is a pointer to a function that
                              accepts an argument which is an array of pointers to
                                 characters
                              returns a pointer to an integer quantity */

int (*p[10])(void);        /* p is a 10-element array of pointers to functions;
                              each function returns an integer quantity */

int (*p[10])(char a);      /* p is a 10-element array of pointers to functions;
                              each function accepts an argument which is a character, and
                              returns an integer quantity */

int *(*p[10])(char a);     /* p is a 10-element array of pointers to functions;
                              each function accepts an argument which is a character, and
                              returns a pointer to an integer quantity */

int *(*p[10])(char *a);    /* p is a 10-element array of pointers to functions;
                              each function accepts an argument which is a pointer to a
                                 character, and
                              returns a pointer to an integer quantity */
```

Review Questions

10.1   For the version of C available on your particular computer, how many memory cells are required to store a single character? An integer quantity? A long integer? A floating-poing quantity? A double-precision quantity?

10.2   What is meant by the address of a memory cell? How are addresses usually numbered?

10.3   How is a variable's address determined?

10.4   What kind of information is represented by a pointer variable?

10.5   What is the relationship between the address of a variable v and the corresponding pointer variable pv?

10.6   What is the purpose of the indirection operator? To what type of operand must the indirection operator be applied?

10.7   What is the relationship between the data item represented by a variable v and the corresponding pointer variable pv?

10.8   What precedence is assigned to the unary operators compared with the multiplication, division and remainder operators? In what order are the unary operators evaluated?

10.9   Can the address operator act upon an arithmetic expression, such as 2 * (u + v)? Explain the reasons for your answer.

10.10 Can an expression involving the indirection operator appear on the left side of an assignment statement? Explain.

10.11   What kinds of objects can be associated with pointer variables?

10.12   How is a pointer variable declared? What is the purpose of the data type included in the declaration?

10.13   In what way can the assignment of an initial value be included in the declaration of a pointer variable?

10.14   Are integer values ever assigned to pointer variables? Explain.

10.15   Why is it sometimes desirable to pass a pointer to a function as an argument?

10.16   Suppose a function receives a pointer as an argument. Explain how the function prototype is written. In particular, explain how the data type of the pointer argument is represented.

10.17   Suppose a function receives a pointer as an argument. Explain how the pointer argument is declared within the function definition.

10.18   What is the relationship between an array name and a pointer? How is an array name interpreted when it appears as an argument to a function?

10.19   Suppose a formal argument within a function definition is an array. How can the array be declared within the function?

10.20   How can a portion of an array be passed to a function?

10.21   How can a function return a pointer to its calling routine?

10.22   Describe two different ways to specify the address of an array element.

10.23   Why is the value of an array subscript sometimes referred to as an offset when the subscript is a part of an expression indicating the address of an array element?

10.24   Describe two different ways to access an array element. Compare your answer to that of question 10.22.

10.25   Can an address be assigned to an array name or an array element? Can an address be assigned to a pointer variable whose object is an array?

10.26   Suppose a numerical array is defined in terms of a pointer variable. Can the individual array elements be initialized?

10.27   Suppose a character-type array is defined in terms of a pointer variable. Can the individual array elements be initialized? Compare your answer with that of the previous question.

10.28   What is meant by dynamic memory allocation? What library function is used to allocate memory dynamically? How is the size of the memory block specified? What kind of information is returned by the library function?

10.29   Suppose an integer quantity is added to or subtracted from a pointer variable. How will the sum or difference be interpreted?

10.30   Under what conditions can one pointer variable be subtracted from another? How will this difference be interpreted?

10.31   Under what conditions can two pointer variables be compared? Under what conditions are such comparisons useful?

10.32   How is a multidimensional array defined in terms of a pointer to a collection of contiguous arrays of lower dimensionality?

10.33   How can the indirection operator be used to access a multidimensional array element?

10.34   How is a multidimensional array defined in terms of an array of pointers? What does each pointer represent? How does this definition differ from a pointer to a collection of contiguous arrays of lower dimensionality?

10.35   How can a one-dimensional array of pointers be used to represent a collection of strings?

10.36   If several strings are stored within a one-dimensional array of pointers, how can an individual string be accessed?

10.37   If several strings are stored within a one-dimensional array of pointers, what happens if the strings are reordered? Are the strings actually moved to different locations within the array?

10.38   Under what conditions can the elements of a multidimensional array be initialized if the array is defined in terms of an array of pointers?

10.39   When transferring one function to another, what is meant by the guest function? What is the host function?

10.40 Suppose a formal argument within a host function definition is a pointer to another function. How is the formal argument declared? Within the declaration, to what does the data type refer?

10.41 Suppose a formal argument within the definition of the host function p is a pointer to the guest function q. How is the formal argument declared within p? In this declaration, to what does the data type refer? How is function q accessed within function p?

10.42 Suppose that p is a host function, and one of p's arguments is a pointer to function q. How would the declaration for p be written if full function prototyping is used?

10.43 For what types of applications is it particularly useful to pass one function to another?

Problems

10.44 Explain the meaning of each of the following declarations.

(a)   `int *px;`

(b)   `float a, b;`
        `float *pa, *pb;`

(c)   `float a = −0.167;`
        `float *pa = &a;`

(d)   `char c1, c2, c3;`
        `char *pc1, *pc2, *pc3 = &c1;`

(e)   `double funct(double *a, double *b, int *c);`

(f)   `double *funct(double *a, double *b, int *c);`

(g)   `double (*a)[12];`

(h)   `double *a[12];`

(i)   `char *a[12];`

(j)   `char *d[4] = {"north", "south", "east", "west"};`

(k)   `long (*p)[10][20];`

(l)   `long *p[10][20];`

(m)   `char sample(int (*pf)(char a, char b));`

(n)   `int (*pf)(void);`

(o)   `int (*pf)(char a, char b);`

(p)   `int (*pf)(char *a, char *b);`

10.45 Write an appropriate declaration for each of the following situations.

(a)   Declare two pointers whose objects are the integer variables i and j.

(b)   Declare a pointer to a floating-point quantity, and a pointer to a double-precision quantity.

(c)   Declare a funtion that accepts two integer arguments and returns a pointer to a long integer.

(d)   Declare a function that accepts two arguments and returns a long integer. Each argument will be a pointer to an integer quantity.

(e)   Declare a one-dimensional floating-point array using pointer notation.

(f)   Declare a two-dimensional floating-point array, with 15 rows and 30 columns, using pointer notation.

(g)   Declare an array of strings whose initial values are "red," "green" and "blue."

(h)   Declare a function that accepts another function as an argument and returns a pointer to a character. The function passed as an argument will accept an integer argument and return an integer quantity.

(i)   Declare a pointer to a function that accepts three integer arguments and returns a floating-point quantity.

(j)   Declare a pointer to a function that accepts three pointers to integer quantities as arguments and returns a pointer to a floating-point quantity.

10.46 A C program contains the following statements.

```
char u, v = 'A';
char *pu, *pv = &v;

. . . . .

*pv = v + 1;
u = *pv + 1;
pu = &u;
```

Suppose each character occupies 1 byte of memory. If the value assigned to u is stored in (hexadecimal) address F8C and the value assigned to v is stored in address F8D, then

(a)   What value is represented by &v?

(b)   What value is assigned to pv?

(c)   What value is represented by *pv?

(d)   What value is assigned to u?

(e)   What value is represented by &u?

(f)   What value is assigned to pu?

(g)   What value is represented by *pu?

10.47 A C program contains the following statements.

```
int i, j = 25;
int *pi, *pj = &j;

. . . . .

*pj = j + 5;
i = *pj + 5;
pi = pj;
*pi = i + j;
```

Suppose each integer quantity occupies 2 bytes of memory. If the value assigned to i begins at (hexadecimal) address F9C and the value assigned to j begins at address F9E, then

(a)   What value is represented by &i?

(b)   What value is represented by &j?

(c)   What value is assigned to pj?

(d)   What value is assigned to *pj?

(e)   What value is assigned to i?

(f)   What value is represented by pi?

(g)   What final value is assigned to *pi?

(h)   What value is represented by (pi + 2)?

(i)   What value is represented by the expression (*pi + 2)?

(j)   What value is represented by the expression *(pi + 2)?

10.48 A C program contains the following statements.

```
float a = 0.001, b = 0.003;
float c, *pa, *pb;

pa = &a;
*pa = 2 * a;
pb = &b;
c = 3 * (*pb - *pa);
```

Suppose each floating-point number occupies 4 bytes of memory. If the value assigned to a begins at (hexadecimal) address 1130, the value assigned to b begins at address 1134, and the value assigned to c begins at 1138, then

(a)   What value is assigned to &a?

(b)   What value is assigned to &b?

(c)   What value is assigned to &c?

(d)   What value is assigned to pa?

(e)   What value is represented by *pa?

(f)   What value is represented by &(*pa)?

(g)   What value is assigned to pb?

(h)   What value is represented by *pb?

(i)   What value is assigned to c?

10.49 The skeletal structure of a C program is shown below.

```
int funct1(char a, char b);
int funct2(char *pa, char *pb);

main()
{
    char a = 'X';
    char b = 'Y';
    int i, j;

    . . . . .

    i = funct1(a, b);
    printf("a=%c   b=%c\n", a, b);

    . . . . .

    j = funct2(&a, &b);
    printf("a=%c   b=%c", a, b);
}

int funct1(char c1, char c2)
{
    c1 = 'P';
    c2 = 'Q';

    . . . . .

    return((c1 < c2) ? c1 : c2);
}

int funct2(char *c1, char *c2)
{
    *c1 = 'P';
    *c2 = 'Q';

    . . . . .

    return((*c1 == *c2) ? *c1 : *c2);
}
```

(a)   Within main, what value is assigned to i?

(b)   What value is assigned to j?

(c)   What values are displayed by the first `printf` statement?

(d)   What values are displayed by the second `printf` statement?

Assume ASCII characters.

10.50 The skeletal structure of a C program is shown below.

```
void funct(int *p);

main()
{
    static int a[5] = {10, 20, 30, 40, 50};

    . . . . .

    funct(a);

    . . . . .

}

void funct(int *p)
{
    int i, sum = 0;
    for (i = 0; i < 5; ++i)
        sum += *(p + i);
    printf("sum=%d", sum);
    return;
}
```

(a)   What kind of argument is passed to `funct`?

(b)   What kind of information is returned by `funct`?

(c)   What kind of formal argument is defined within `funct`?

(d)   What is the purpose of the `for` loop that appears within `funct`?

(e)   What value is displayed by the `printf` statement within `funct`?

10.51 The skeletal structure of a C program is shown below.

```
void funct(int *p);

main()
{
    static int a[5] = {10, 20, 30, 40, 50};

    . . . . .

    funct(a + 3);

    . . . . .

}

void funct(int *p)
{
    int i, sum = 0;
    for (i = 3; i < 5; ++i)
        sum += *(p + i);
    printf("sum=%d", sum);
    return;
}
```

(a)   What kind of argument is passed to funct?

(b)   What kind of information is returned by funct?

(c)   What information is actually passed to funct?

(d)   What is the purpose of the for loop that appears within funct?

(e)   What value is displayed by the printf statement within funct?

Compare your answers with those of the previous problem. In what ways do these two skeletal outlines differ?

10.52   The skeletal structure of a C program is shown below.

```
int *funct(int *p);

main()
{
    static int a[5] = {10, 20, 30, 40, 50};
    int *ptmax;

    . . . . .

    ptmax = funct(a);
    printf("max=%d", *ptmax);

    . . . . .

}

int *funct(int *p)
{
    int i, imax, max = 0;
    for (i = 0; i < 5; ++i)
        if (*(p + i) > max)    {
            max = *(p + i);
            imax = i;
        }
    return(p + imax);
}
```

(a)   Within main, what is ptmax?

(b)   What kind of information is returned by funct?

(c)   What is assigned to ptmax when the function is accessed?

(d)   What is the purpose of the for loop that appears within funct?

(e)   What value is displayed by the printf statement within main?

Compare your answers with those of the previous two problems. In what ways are the skeletal outlines different?

10.53   A C program contains the following declaration.

```
static int x[8] = {10, 20, 30, 40, 50, 60, 70, 80};
```

(a)   What is the meaning of x?

(b)   What is the meaning of (x + 2)?

(c)   What is the value of *x?

(d)   What is the value of (*x + 2)?

(e)   What is the value of *(x + 2)?

10.54 A C program contains the following declaration.

```
static float table[2][3] = {
                              {1.1, 1.2, 1.3},
                              {2.1, 2.2, 2.3}
                     };
```

(a)   What is the meaning of `table`?

(b)   What is the meaning of `(table + 1)`?

(c)   What is the meaning of `*(table + 1)`?

(d)   What is the meaning of `(*(table + 1) + 1)`?

(e)   What is the meaning of `(*(table) + 1)`?

(f)   What is the value of `*(*(table + 1) + 1)`?

(g)   What is the value of `*(*(table) + 1)`?

(h)   What is the value of `*(*(table + 1))`?

(i)   What is the value of `*(*(table) + 1) + 1`?

10.55 A C program contains the following declaration.

```
static char *color[6] = {"red", "green", "blue", "white", "black", "yellow"};
```

(a)   What is the meaning of `color`?

(b)   What is the meaning of `(color + 2)`?

(c)   What is the value of `*color`?

(d)   What is the value of `*(color + 2)`?

(e)   How do `color[5]` and `*(color + 5)` differ?

10.56 The skeletal structure of a C program is shown below.

```
float one(float x, float y);
float two(float x, float y);
float three(float (*pt)(float x, float y));

main()
{
    float a, b;

    . . . . .

    a = three(one);

    . . . . .

    b = three(two);

    . . . . .
}

float one(float x, float y)
{
    float z;

    z = . . . . .

    return(z);
}
```

```
float two(float p, float q)
{
    float r;

    r = . . . . .

    return(r);
}


float three(float (*pt)(float x, float y))
{
    float a, b, c;

    . . . . .

    c = (*pt)(a, b);

    . . . . .

    return(c);
}
```

(a) Interpret each of the function prototypes.

(b) Interpret the definitions of the functions one and two.

(c) Interpret the definition of the function three. How does three differ from one and two?

(d) What happens within main each time three is accessed?

10.57 The skeletal structure of a C program is shown below.

```
float one(float *px, float *py);
float two(float *px, float *py);
float *three(float (*pt)(float *px, float *py));

main()
{
    float *pa, *pb;

    . . . . .

    pa = three(one);

    . . . . .

    pb = three(two);

    . . . . .
}


float one(float *px, float *py)
{
    float z;

    z = . . . . .

    return(z);
}
```

```
      float two(float *pp, float *pq)
      {
          float r;

          r = . . . . .

          return(r);
      }

      float *three(float (*pt)(float *px, float *py))
      {
          float a, b, c;

          . . . . .

          c = (*pt)(&a, &b);

          . . . . .

          return(&c);
      }
```

(a) Interpret each of the function prototypes.

(b) Interpret the definitions of the functions one and two.

(c) Interpret the definition of the function three. How does three differ from one and two?

(d) What happens within main each time three is accessed?

(e) How does this program outline differ from the outline shown in the last example?

10.58 Explain the purpose of each of the following declarations.

(a) `float (*x)(int *a);`

(b) `float (*x(int *a))[20];`

(c) `float x(int (*a)[]);`

(d) `float x(int *a[]);`

(e) `float *x(int a[]);`

(f) `float *x(int (*a)[]);`

(g) `float *x(int *a[]);`

(h) `float (*x)(int (*a)[]);`

(i) `float *(*x)(int *a[]);`

(j) `float (*x[20])(int a);`

(k) `float *(*x[20])(int *a);`

10.59 Write an appropriate declaration for each of the following situations involving pointers.

(a) Declare a function that accepts an argument which is a pointer to an integer quantity and returns a pointer to a six-element character array.

(b) Declare a function that accepts an argument which is a pointer to an integer array and returns a character.

(c) Declare a function that accepts an argument which is an array of pointers to integer quantities and returns a character.

(d) Declare a function that accepts an argument which is an integer array and returns a pointer to a character.

(e) Declare a function that accepts an argument which is a pointer to an integer array and returns a pointer to a character.

(f) Declare a function that accepts an argument which is an array of pointers to integer quantities and returns a pointer to a character.

(g) Declare a pointer to a function that accepts an argument which is a pointer to an integer array and returns a character.

(h) Declare a pointer to a function that accepts an argument which is a pointer to an integer array and returns a pointer to a character.

(i) Declare a pointer to a function that accepts an argument which is an array of pointers to integer quantities and returns a pointer to a character.

(j) Declare a 12-element array of pointers to functions. Each function will accept two double-precision quantities as arguments and will return a double-precision quantity.

(k) Declare a 12-element array of pointers to functions. Each function will accept two double-precision quantities as arguments and will return a pointer to a double-precision quantity.

(l) Declare a 12-element array of pointers to functions. Each function will accept two pointers to double-precision quantities as arguments and will return a pointer to a double-precision quantity.

Programming Problems

10.60 Modify the program shown in Example 10.1 as follows.

(a) Use floating-point data rather than integer data. Assign an initial value of 0.3 to u.

(b) Use double-precision data rather than integer data. Assign an initial value of 0.3×10^{45} to u.

(c) Use character data rather than integer data. Assign an initial value of 'C' to u.

Execute each modification and compare the results with those given in Example 10.1. Be sure to modify the printf statements accordingly.

10.61 Modify the program shown in Example 10.3 as follows.

(a) Use floating-point data rather than integer data. Assign an initial value of 0.3 to v.

(b) Use double-precision data rather than integer data. Assign an initial value of 0.3×10^{45} to v.

(c) Use character data rather than integer data. Assign an initial value of 'C' to v.

Execute each modification and compare the results with those given in Example 10.3. Be sure to modify the printf statements accordingly.

10.62 Modify the program shown in Example 10.7 so that a single one-dimensional, character-type array is passed to funct1. Delete funct2 and all references to funct2. Initially, assign the string "red" to the array within main. Then reassign the string "green" to the array within funct1. Execute the program and compare the results with those shown in Example 10.7. Remember to modify the printf statements accordingly.

10.63 Modify the program shown in Example 10.8 (analyzing a line of text) so that it also counts the number of words and the total number of characters in the line of text. (*Note*: A new word can be recognized by the presence of a blank space followed by a nonwhitespace character.) Test the program using the text given in Example 10.8.

10.64 Modify the program shown in Example 10.8 (analyzing a line of text) so that it can process multiple lines of text. First enter and store all lines of text. Then determine the number of vowels, consonants, digits, whitespace characters and "other" characters for each line. Finally, determine the average number of vowels per line, consonants per line, etc. Write and execute the program two different ways.

(a) Store the multiple lines of text in a two-dimensional array of characters.

(b) Store the multiple lines of text as individual strings whose maximum length is unspecified. Maintain a pointer to each string within a one-dimensional array of pointers.

In each case, identify the last line of text in some predetermined manner (e.g., by entering the string "END"). Test the program using several lines of text of your own choosing.

10.65 Modify the program shown in Example 10.12 so that the elements of x are long integers rather than ordinary integers. Execute the program and compare the results with those shown in Example 10.12. (Remember to modify the printf statement to accommodate the long integer quantities.)

10.66   Modify the program shown in Example 10.16 so that any one of the following rearrangements can be carried out:

   (a)   Smallest to largest, by magnitude

   (b)   Smallest to largest, algebraic

   (c)   Largest to smallest, by magnitude

   (d)   Largest to smallest, algebraic

   Use pointer notation to represent individual integer quantities, as in Example 10.16. (Recall that an array version of this problem was presented in Example 9.13.)   Include a menu that will allow the user to select which rearrangement will be used each time the program is executed. Test the program using the following 10 values.

4.7	−8.0
−2.3	11.4
12.9	5.1
8.8	−0.2
6.0	−14.7

10.67   Modify the program shown in Example 10.22 (adding two tables of numbers) so that each element in the table c is the larger of the corresponding elements in tables a and b (rather than the sum of the corresponding elements in a and b). Represent each table (each array) as a pointer to a group of one-dimensional arrays, as in Example 10.22. Use pointer notation to access the individual table elements. Test the program using the tabular data provided in Example 9.19. (You may wish to experiment with this program, using several different ways to represent the arrays and the individual array elements.)

10.68   Repeat the previous problem, representing each table (each array) as a one-dimensional array of pointers, as discussed in Example 10.24.

10.69   Modify the program shown in Example 10.26 (reordering a list of strings) so that the list of strings can be rearranged into either alphabetical or reverse-alphabetical order. Use pointer notation to represent the beginning of each string. Include a menu that will allow the user to select which rearrangement will be used each time the program is executed. Test the program using the data provided in Example 9.20.

10.70   Modify the program shown in Example 10.28 (displaying the day of the year) so that it can determine the number of days between two dates, assuming both dates are beyond the base date of January 1, 1900. (*Hint*: Determine the number of days between the first specified date and the base date; then determine the number of days between the second specified date and the base date. Finally, determine the difference between these two calculated values.)

10.71   Modify the program shown in Example 10.30 (compound interest calculations) so that it generates a table of F-values for various interest rates, using different compounding frequencies. Assume that A and n are input values. Display the output in the following manner.

```
                         A = . . .
                         n = . . .


Interest rate =    5%    6%    7%    8%    9%   10%   11%   12%   13%   14%   15%

Frequency of
Compounding


Annual             —     —     —     —     —     —     —     —     —     —     —
Semiannual         —     —     —     —     —     —     —     —     —     —     —
Quarterly          —     —     —     —     —     —     —     —     —     —     —
Monthly            —     —     —     —     —     —     —     —     —     —     —
Daily              —     —     —     —     —     —     —     —     —     —     —
Continuously       —     —     —     —     —     —     —     —     —     —     —
```

   Notice that the first four rows are generated by one function with different arguments, and each of the last two rows is generated by a different function.

10.72 Modify the program shown in Example 10.30 (compound interest calculations) so that it generates a table of F-values for various time periods, using different compounding frequencies. Assume that A and i are input values. Display the output in the following manner.

```
                                   A = . . .
                                   i = . . .


Time period (n) =   1     2     3     4     5     6     7     8     9     10

Frequency of
Compounding


Annual             —     —     —     —     —     —     —     —     —     —
Semiannual         —     —     —     —     —     —     —     —     —     —
Quarterly          —     —     —     —     —     —     —     —     —     —
Monthly            —     —     —     —     —     —     —     —     —     —
Daily              —     —     —     —     —     —     —     —     —     —
Continuously       —     —     —     —     —     —     —     —     —     —
```

Notice that the first four rows are generated by one function with different arguments, and each of the last two rows is generated by a different function.

10.73 Repeat the previous problem, but transpose the table so that each row represents a different value for n and each column represents a different compounding frequency. Consider integer values of n ranging from 1 to 50. Note that this table will consist of 50 rows and 6 columns. (*Hint*: Generate the table by columns, storing each column in a two-dimensional array. Display the entire array after all the values have been generated.)

  Compare the programming effort required for this problem with the programming effort required for the preceding problem.

10.74 Examples 9.8 and 9.9 present programs to calculate the average of a list of numbers and then calculate the deviations about the average. Both programs make use of one-dimensional, floating-point arrays. Modify both programs so that they utilize pointer notation. (Note that the program shown in Example 9.9 includes the assignment of initial values to individual array elements.) Test both programs using the data given in the examples.

10.75 Modify the program given in Example 9.14 (piglatin generator) so that it uses character-type arrays. Modify the program so that is uses pointer notation. Test the program using several lines of text of your own choosing.

10.76 Write a complete C program, using pointer notation in place of arrays, for each of the following problems taken from the end of Chap. 9.

(*a*) Problem 9.39 (read a line of text, store it within the computer's memory, and then display it backwards).

(*b*) Problem 9.40 (process a set of student exam scores). Test the program using the data given in Prob. 9.40.

(*c*) Problem 9.42 (process a set of weighted student exam scores, and calculate the deviation of each student's average about the overall class average). Test the program using the data given in Prob. 9.40.

(*d*) Problem 9.44 (generate a table of compound interest factors).

(*e*) Problem 9.45 (convert from one foreign currency to another).

(*f*) Problem 9.46 (determine the capital for a specified country, or the country whose capital is specified). Test the program using the list of countries and their capitals given in Prob. 9.46.

(*g*) Problem 9.47(*a*) (matrix/vector multiplication). Test the program using the data given in Prob. 9.47(*a*).

(*h*) Problem 9.47(*b*) (matrix multiplication). Test the program using the data given in Prob. 9.47(*b*).

(*i*) Problem 9.47(*d*) (Lagrange interpolation). Test the program using the data given in Prob. 9.47(*d*).

(*j*) Problem 9.48(*a*) (blackjack).

      (*k*)   Problem 9.48(*b*) (roulette).

      (*l*)   Problem 9.48(*c*) (BINGO).

      (*m*)   Problem 9.49 (encode and decode a line of text).

10.77 Write a complete C program, using pointer notation, that will generate a table containing the following three columns:

$$t \qquad ae^{bt} \sin ct \qquad ae^{bt} \cos ct$$

Structure the program in the following manner: write two special functions, f1 and f2, where f1 evaluates the quantity $ae^{bt} \sin ct$ and f2 evaluates $ae^{bt} \cos ct$. Have main enter the values of a, b and c, and then call a function, table_gen, which will generate the actual table. Pass f1 and f2 to table_gen as arguments.

    Test the program using the values $a = 2$, $b = -0.1$, $c = 0.5$ where the values of t are 1, 2, 3, ... , 60.

Chapter 11

Structures and Unions

In Chap. 9 we studied the array, which is a data structure whose elements are all of the same data type. We now turn our attention to the *structure*, in which the individual elements can differ in type. Thus, a single structure might contain integer elements, floating-point elements and character elements. Pointers, arrays and other structures can also be included as elements within a structure. The individual structure elements are referred to as *members*.

This chapter is concerned with the use of structures within a C program. We will see how structures are defined, and how their individual members are accessed and processed within a program. The relationships between structures and pointers, arrays and functions will also be examined.

Closely associated with the structure is the *union*, which also contains multiple members. Unlike a structure, however, the members of a union share the same storage area, even though the individual members may differ in type. Thus, a union permits several different data items to be stored in the same portion of the computer's memory at different times. We will see how unions are defined and utilized within a C program.

11.1 DEFINING A STRUCTURE

Structure declarations are somewhat more complicated than array declarations, since a structure must be defined in terms of its individual members. In general terms, the composition of a structure may be defined as

```
struct  tag {
     member 1;
     member 2;
     . . . . .
     member m;
};
```

In this declaration, `struct` is a required keyword; *tag* is a name that identifies structures of this type (i.e., structures having this composition); and *member 1*, *member 2*, . . . , *member m* are individual member declarations. (*Note*: There is no formal distinction between a structure *definition* and a structure *declaration*; the terms are used interchangeably.)

The individual members can be ordinary variables, pointers, arrays, or other structures. The member names within a particular structure must be distinct from one another, though a member name can be the same as the name of a variable that is defined outside of the structure. A storage class, however, cannot be assigned to an individual member, and individual members cannot be initialized within a structure type declaration.

Once the composition of the structure has been defined, individual structure-type variables can be declared as follows:

> *storage-class* struct *tag variable 1, variable 2, . . ., variable n*;

where *storage-class* is an optional storage class specifier, `struct` is a required keyword, *tag* is the name that appeared in the structure declaration, and *variable 1, variable 2, . . ., variable n* are structure variables of type *tag*.

EXAMPLE 11.1   A typical structure declaration is shown below.

```
struct account  {
      int acct_no;
      char acct_type;
      char name[80];
      float balance;
};
```

This structure is named `account` (i.e., the tag is `account`). It contains four members: an integer quantity (`acct_no`), a single character (`acct_type`), an 80-element character array (`name[80]`), and a floating-point quantity (`balance`). The composition of this account is illustrated schematically in Fig. 11.1.

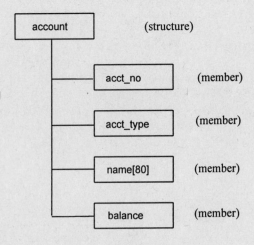

Fig. 11.1

We can now declare the structure variables `oldcustomer` and `newcustomer` as follows.

```
struct  account  oldcustomer, newcustomer;
```

Thus, `oldcustomer` and `newcustomer` are variables of type `account`. In other words, `oldcustomer` and `newcustomer` are structure-type variables whose composition is identified by the tag `account`.

It is possible to combine the declaration of the structure composition with that of the structure variables, as shown below.

```
storage-class struct  tag {
        member 1;
        member 2;
        . . . . .
        member m;
} variable 1,  variable 2,  . . .,  variable n;
```

The *tag* is optional in this situation.

EXAMPLE 11.2   The following single declaration is equivalent to the two declarations presented in the previous example.

```
struct account  {
      int acct_no;
      char acct_type;
      char name[80];
      float balance;
} oldcustomer, newcustomer;
```

Thus, `oldcustomer` and `newcustomer` are structure variables of type `account`.

Since the variable declarations are now combined with the declaration of the structure type, the tag (i.e., `account`) need not be included. Thus, the above declaration can also be written as

```
struct  {
      int acct_no;
      char acct_type;
      char name[80];
      float balance;
} oldcustomer, newcustomer;
```

A structure variable may be defined as a member of another structure. In such situations, the declaration of the embedded structure must appear before the declaration of the outer structure.

EXAMPLE 11.3 A C program contains the following structure declarations.

```
struct date  {
      int month;
      int day;
      int year;
};

struct account  {
      int acct_no;
      char acct_type;
      char name[80];
      float balance;
      struct date lastpayment;
} oldcustomer, newcustomer;
```

The second structure (`account`) now contains another structure (`date`) as one of its members. Note that the declaration of `date` precedes the declaration of `account`. The composition of `account` is shown schematically in Fig. 11.2.

The members of a structure variable can be assigned initial values in much the same manner as the elements of an array. The initial values must appear in the order in which they will be assigned to their corresponding structure members, enclosed in braces and separated by commas. The general form is

> *storage-class* struct *tag variable* = {*value 1, value 2, . . ., value m*};

where *value 1* refers to the value of the first member, *value 2* refers to the value of the second member, and so on. A structure variable, like an array, can be initialized only if its storage class is either `external` or `static`.

EXAMPLE 11.4 This example illustrates the assignment of initial values to the members of a structure variable.

```
struct date  {
      int month;
      int day;
      int year;
};
```

```
struct account  {
    int acct_no;
    char acct_type;
    char name[80];
    float balance;
    struct date lastpayment;
};
```

```
static  struct  account  customer = {12345, 'R', "John W. Smith", 586.30, 5, 24, 90};
```

Thus, customer is a static structure variable of type account, whose members are assigned initial values. The first member (acct_no) is assigned the integer value 12345, the second member (acct_type) is assigned the character 'R', the third member (name[80]) is assigned the string "John W. Smith", and the fourth member (balance) is assigned the floating-point value 586.30. The last member is itself a structure that contains three integer members (month, day and year). Therefore, the last member of customer is assigned the integer values 5, 24 and 90.

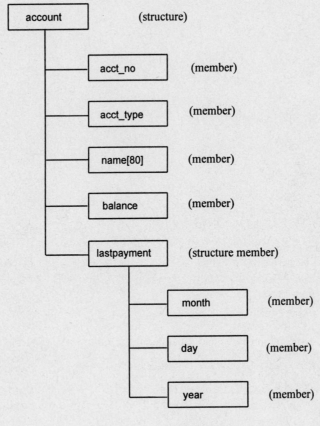

Fig. 11.2

It is also possible to define an array of structures; i.e., an array in which each element is a structure. The procedure is illustrated in the following example.

EXAMPLE 11.5   A C program contains the following structure declarations.

```
struct date  {
     int month;
     int day;
     int year;
};

struct account  {
     int acct_no;
     char acct_type;
     char name[80];
     float balance;
     struct date lastpayment;
} customer[100];
```

In this declaration `customer` is a 100-element array of structures. Hence, each element of `customer` is a separate structure of type `account` (i.e., each element of `customer` represents an individual customer record).

Note that each structure of type `account` includes an array (`name[80]`) and another structure (`date`) as members. Thus, we have an array and a structure embedded within another structure, which is itself an element of an array.

It is, of course, also permissible to define `customer` in a separate declaration, as shown below.

```
struct date  {
     int month;
     int day;
     int year;
};

struct account  {
     int acct_no;
     char acct_type;
     char name[80];
     float balance;
     struct date lastpayment;
};

struct  account  customer[100];
```

An array of structures can be assigned initial values just as any other array. Remember that each array element is a structure that must be assigned a corresponding set of initial values, as illustrated below.

EXAMPLE 11.6   A C program contains the following declarations.

```
struct date  {
     char name[80];
     int month;
     int day;
     int year;
};

static  struct  date  birthday[] = {"Amy", 12, 30, 73,
                                    "Gail", 5, 13, 66,
                                    "Marc", 7, 15, 72,
                                    "Marla", 11, 29, 70,
                                    "Megan", 2, 4, 77,
                                    "Sharon", 12, 29, 63,
                                    "Susan", 4, 12, 69};
```

In this example `birthday` is an array of structures whose size is unspecified. The initial values will define the size of the array, and the amount of memory required to store the array.

Notice that each row in the variable declaration contains four constants. These constants represent the initial values, i.e., the name, month, day and year, for one array element. Since there are 7 rows (7 sets of constants), the array will contain 7 elements, numbered 0 to 6.

Some programmers may prefer to embed each set of constants within a separate pair of braces, in order to delineate the individual array elements more clearly. This is entirely permissible. Thus, the array declaration can be written

```
static  struct  date  bi.thday[] = {
                                    {"Amy", 12, 30, 73},
                                    {"Gail", 5, 13, 66},
                                    {"Marc", 7, 15, 72},
                                    {"Marla", 11, 29, 70},
                                    {"Megan", 2, 4, 77},
                                    {"Sharon", 12, 29, 63},
                                    {"Susan", 4, 12, 69}
                           };
```

Remember that each structure is a self-contained entity with respect to member definitions. Thus, the same member name can be used in different structures to represent different data. In other words, the scope of a member name is confined to the particular structure within which it is defined.

EXAMPLE 11.7   Two different structures, called `first` and `second`, are declared below.

```
struct first  {
     float a;
     int b;
     char c;
};

struct second  {
     char a;
     float b, c;
};
```

Notice that the individual member names a, b and c appear in both structure declarations, but the associated data types are different. Thus, a represents a floating-point quantity in `first` and a character in `second`. Similarly, b represents an integer quantity in `first` and a floating-point quantity in `second`, whereas c represents a character in `first` and a floating-point quantity in `second`. This duplication of member names is permissible, since the scope of each set of member definitions is confined to its respective structure. Within each structure the member names are distinct, as required.

11.2 PROCESSING A STRUCTURE

The members of a structure are usually processed individually, as separate entities. Therefore, we must be able to access the individual structure members. A structure member can be accessed by writing

variable.member

where *variable* refers to the name of a structure-type variable, and *member* refers to the name of a member within the structure. Notice the period (.) that separates the variable name from the member name. This period is an operator; it is a member of the highest precedence group, and its associativity is left to right (see Appendix C).

EXAMPLE 11.8 Consider the following structure declarations.

```
struct date  {
      int month;
      int day;
      int year;
};

struct account  {
      int acct_no;
      char acct_type;
      char name[80];
      float balance;
      struct date lastpayment;
}  customer;
```

In this example `customer` is a structure variable of type `account`. If we wanted to access the customer's account number, we would write

```
customer.acct_no
```

Similarly, the customer's name and the customer's balance can be accessed by writing

```
customer.name
```

and

```
customer.balance
```

Since the period operator is a member of the highest precedence group, this operator will take precedence over the unary operators as well as the various arithmetic, relational, logical and assignment operators. Thus, an expression of the form `++variable.member` is equivalent to `++(variable.member)`; i.e., the `++` operator will apply to the structure member, not the entire structure variable. Similarly, the expression `&variable.member` is equivalent to `&(variable.member)`; thus, the expression accesses the address of the structure member, not the starting address of the structure variable.

EXAMPLE 11.9 Consider the structure declarations given in Example 11.8; i.e.,

```
struct date  {
      int month;
      int day;
      int year;
};

struct account  {
      int acct_no;
      char acct_type;
      char name[80];
      float balance;
      struct date lastpayment;
}  customer;
```

Several expressions involving the structure variable `customer` and its members are given below.

Expression	_Interpretation_
++customer.balance	Increment the value of customer.balance
customer.balance++	Increment the value of customer.balance after accessing its value
--customer.acct_no	Decrement the value of customer.acct_no
&customer	Access the beginning address of customer
&customer.acct_no	Access the address of customer.acctno

More complex expressions involving the repeated use of the period operator may also be written. For example, if a structure member is itself a structure, then a member of the embedded structure can be accessed by writing

> _variable.member.submember_

where _member_ refers to the name of the member within the outer structure, and _submember_ refers to the name of the member within the embedded structure. Similarly, if a structure member is an array, then an individual array element can be accessed by writing

> _variable.member[expression]_

where _expression_ is a nonnegative value that indicates the array element.

EXAMPLE 11.10   Consider once again the structure declarations presented in Example 11.8.

```
struct date  {
    int month;
    int day;
    int year;
};
struct account  {
    int acct_no;
    char acct_type;
    char name[80];
    float balance;
    struct date lastpayment;
} customer;
```

The last member of customer is customer.lastpayment, which is itself a structure of type date. To access the month of the last payment, we would therefore write

> customer.lastpayment.month

Moreover, this value can be incremented by writing

> ++customer.lastpayment.month

Similarly, the third member of customer is the character array customer.name. The third character within this array can be accessed by writing

> customer.name[2]

This character's address can be obtained as

> &customer.name[2]

The use of the period operator can be extended to arrays of structures, by writing

```
array[expression].member
```

where *array* refers to the array name, and *array[expression]* is an individual array element (a structure variable). Therefore *array[expression].member* will refer to a specific member within a particular structure.

EXAMPLE 11.11 Consider the following structure declarations, which were originally presented in Example 11.5.

```
struct date  {
    int month;
    int day;
    int year;
};

struct account  {
    int acct_no;
    char acct_type;
    char name[80];
    float balance;
    struct date lastpayment;
}  customer[100];
```

In this example customer is an array that may contain as many as 100 elements. Each element is a structure of type account. Thus, if we wanted to access the account number for the 14th customer (i.e., customer[13], since the subscripts begin with 0), we would write customer[13].acct_no. Similarly, this customer's balance can be accessed by writing customer[13].balance. The corresponding address can be obtained as &customer[13].balance.

The 14th customer's name can be accessed by writing customer[13].name. Moreover, we can access an individual character within the name by specifying a subscript. For example, the 8th character within the customer's name can be accessed by writing customer[13].name[7]. In a similar manner we can access the month, day and year of the 14th customer's last payment by specifying the individual members of customer[13].lastpayment, i.e., customer[13].lastpayment.month, customer[13].lastpayment.day, customer[13].lastpayment.year. Moreover, the expression ++customer[13].lastpayment.day causes the value of the day to be incremented.

Structure members can be processed in the same manner as ordinary variables of the same data type. Single-valued structure members can appear in expressions, they can be passed to functions, and they can be returned from functions, as though they were ordinary single-valued variables. Complex structure members are processed in the same way as ordinary data items of that same type. For example, a structure member that is an array can be processed in the same manner as an ordinary array, and with the same restrictions. Similarly, a structure member that is itself a structure can be processed on a member-by-member basis (the members here refer to the embedded structure), the same as any other structure.

EXAMPLE 11.12 Several statements or groups of statements that access individual structure members are shown below. All of the structure members conform to the declarations given in Example 11.8.

```
customer.balance = 0;

customer.balance -= payment;

customer.lastpayment.month = 12;

printf("Name: %s\n", customer.name);

if (customer.acct_type == 'P')
    printf("Preferred account no.: %d\n", customer.acct_no);
else
    printf("Regular account no.: %d\n", customer.acct_no);
```

The first statement assigns a value of zero to `customer.balance`, whereas the second statement causes the value of `customer.balance` to be decreased by the value of `payment`. The third statement causes the value 12 to be assigned to `customer.lastpayment.month`. Note that `customer.lastpayment.month` is a member of the embedded structure `customer.lastpayment`.

The fourth statement passes the array `customer.name` to the `printf` function, causing the customer name to be displayed. Finally, the last example illustrates the use of structure members in an `if - else` statement. Also, we see a situation in which the structure member `customer.acct_no` is passed to a function as an argument.

In some older versions of C, structures must be processed on a member-by-member basis. With this restriction, the only permissible operation on an entire structure is to take its address (more about this later). However, the current ANSI standard permits entire structures to be assigned to one another provided the structures have the same composition.

EXAMPLE 11.13   Suppose `oldcustomer` and `newcustomer` are structure variables having the same composition; i.e.,

```
struct date  {
     int month;
     int day;
     int year;
};

struct account  {
     int acct_no;
     char acct_type;
     char name[80];
     float balance;
     struct date lastpayment;
} oldcustomer, newcustomer;
```

as declared in Example 11.8. Let us assume that all of the members of `oldcustomer` have been assigned individual values. In most newer versions of C, it is possible to copy these values to `newcustomer` simply by writing

```
newcustomer = oldcustomer;
```

On the other hand, some older versions of C may require that the values be copied individually, member by member; for example,

```
newcustomer.acct_no = oldcustomer.acct_no;
newcustomer.acct_type = oldcustomer.acct_type;

. . . . .

newcustomer.lastpayment.year = oldcustomer.lastpayment.year;
```

It is also possible to pass entire structures to and from functions, though the way this is done varies from one version of C to another. Older versions of C allow only pointers to be passed, whereas the ANSI standard allows passing of the structures themselves. We will discuss this further in Sec. 11.5. Before moving on to the relationship between structures and pointers and the methods for passing structures to functions, however, let us consider a more comprehensive example that involves the processing of structure members.

EXAMPLE 11.14 Updating Customer Records   To illustrate further how the individual members of a structure can be processed, consider a very simple customer billing system. In this system the customer records will be stored within an array of structures. Each record will be stored as an individual structure (i.e., as an array element) containing the customer's name, street address, city and state, account number, account status (current, overdue or delinquent), previous balance, current payment, new balance and payment date.

The overall strategy will be to enter each customer record into the computer, updating it as soon as it is entered, to reflect current payments. All of the updated records will then be displayed, along with the current status of each account. The account status will be based upon the size of the current payment relative to the customer's previous balance.

The structure declarations are shown below.

```
struct date  {
    int month;
    int day;
    int year;
};

struct account  {
    char name[80];
    char street[80];
    char city[80];
    int acct_no;
    char acct_type;
    float oldbalance;
    float newbalance;
    float payment;
    struct date lastpayment;
} customer[100];
```

Notice that `customer` is a 100-element array of structures. Thus, each array element (each structure) will represent one customer record. Each structure includes three members that are character-type arrays (`name`, `street` and `city`), and one member that is another structure (`lastpayment`).

The status of each account will be determined in the following manner:

1. If the current payment is greater than zero but less than 10 percent of the previous outstanding balance, the account will be overdue.

2. If there is an outstanding balance and the current payment is zero, the account will be delinquent.

3. Otherwise, the account will be current.

The overall program strategy will be as follows.

1. Specify the number of customer accounts (i.e., the number of structures) to be processed.

2. For each customer, read in the following items.

(a)	name	(e)	previous balance
(b)	street	(f)	current payment
(c)	city	(g)	payment date
(d)	account number		

3. As each customer record is read into the computer, update it in the following manner.

   (a) Compare the current payment with the previous balance and determine the appropriate account status.

   (b) Calculate a new account balance by subtracting the current payment from the previous balance (a negative balance will indicate a credit).

4. After all of the customer records have been entered and processed, write out the following information for each customer.

(a)	name	(e)	old balance
(b)	account number	(f)	current payment
(c)	street	(g)	new balance
(d)	city	(h)	account status

Let us write the program in a modular manner, with one function to enter and update each record and another function to display the updated data. Ideally, we would like to pass every customer record (i.e., every array element) to each of these functions. Since each customer record is a structure, however, and we have not yet discussed how to pass a structure to or from a function, we will define the array of structures as an external array. This will allow us to access the array elements, and the individual structure members, directly from all of the functions.

The individual program modules are straightforward, though some care is required in reading the individual structure members into the computer. Here is the entire program.

```c
/* update a series of customer accounts (simplified billing system) */
/* maintain the customer accounts as an external array of structures */

#include <stdio.h>

void readinput(int i);
void writeoutput(int i);

struct date  {
     int month;
     int day;
     int year;
};

struct account  {
     char name[80];
     char street[80];
     char city[80];
     int acct_no;              /* (positive integer) */
     char acct_type;           /* C (current), O (overdue), or D (delinquent) */
     float oldbalance;         /* (nonnegative quantity) */
     float newbalance;         /* (nonnegative quantity) */
     float payment;            /* (nonnegative quantity) */
     struct date lastpayment;
} customer[100];               /* maintain as many as 100 customers */

main()

{
     int i, n;

     printf("CUSTOMER BILLING SYSTEM\n\n");
     printf("How many customers are there? ");
     scanf("%d", &n);

     for (i = 0; i < n; ++i)   {
          readinput(i);

          /* determine account status */

          if (customer[i].payment > 0)
             customer[i].acct_type =
                 (customer[i].payment < 0.1 * customer[i].oldbalance) ? 'O' : 'C';
          else
             customer[i].acct_type =
                 (customer[i].oldbalance > 0) ? 'D' : 'C';

          /* adjust account balance */

          customer[i].newbalance = customer[i].oldbalance - customer[i].payment;
     };
     for (i = 0; i < n; ++i)
          writeoutput(i);
}
```

```
void readinput(int i)

/* read input data and update record for each customer */

{
    printf("\nCustomer no. %d\n", i + 1);
    printf("   Name: ");
    scanf(" %[^\n]", customer[i].name);
    printf("   Street: ");
    scanf(" %[^\n]", customer[i].street);
    printf("   City: ");
    scanf(" %[^\n]", customer[i].city);
    printf("   Account number: ");
    scanf("%d", &customer[i].acct_no);
    printf("   Previous balance: ");
    scanf("%f", &customer[i].oldbalance);
    printf("   Current payment: ");
    scanf("%f", &customer[i].payment);
    printf("   Payment date (mm/dd/yyyy): ");
    scanf("%d/%d/%d", &customer[i].lastpayment.month,
                      &customer[i].lastpayment.day,
                      &customer[i].lastpayment.year);
    return;
}


void writeoutput(int i)

/* display current information for each customer */

{
    printf("\nName:   %s", customer[i].name);
    printf("   Account number: %d\n", customer[i].acct_no);
    printf("Street: %s\n", customer[i].street);
    printf("City:   %s\n\n", customer[i].city);
    printf("Old balance: %7.2f", customer[i].oldbalance);
    printf("   Current payment: %7.2f", customer[i].payment);
    printf("   New balance: %7.2f\n\n", customer[i].newbalance);
    printf("Account status: ");

    switch (customer[i].acct_type)  {
    case 'C':
                printf("CURRENT\n\n");
                break;
    case 'O':
                printf("OVERDUE\n\n");
                break;
    case 'D':
                printf("DELINQUENT\n\n");
                break;
    default:
                printf("ERROR\n\n");
    }
    return;
}
```

Now suppose the program is used to process four fictitious customer records. The input dialog is shown below, with the user's responses underlined.

```
CUSTOMER BILLING SYSTEM

How many customers are there? 4

Customer no. 1
    Name: Steve Johnson
    Street: 123 Mountainview Drive
    City: Denver, CO
    Account number: 4208
    Previous balance: 247.88
    Current payment: 25.00
    Payment date (mm/dd/yyyy): 6/14/1998

Customer no. 2
    Name: Susan Richards
    Street: 4383 Alligator Blvd
    City: Fort Lauderdale, FL
    Account number: 2219
    Previous balance: 135.00
    Current payment: 135.00
    Payment date (mm/dd/yyyy): 8/10/2000

Customer no. 3
    Name: Martin Peterson
    Street: 1787 Pacific Parkway
    City: San Diego, CA
    Account number: 8452
    Previous balance: 387.42
    Current payment: 35.00
    Payment date (mm/dd/yyyy): 9/22/1999

Customer no. 4
    Name: Phyllis Smith
    Street: 1000 Great White Way
    City: New York, NY
    Account number: 711
    Previous balance: 260.00
    Current payment: 0
    Payment date (mm/dd/yyyy): 11/27/2001
```

The program will then generate the following output data:

```
Name:   Steve Johnson      Account number: 4208
Street: 123 Mountainview Drive
City:   Denver, CO

Old balance: 247.88  Current payment:   25.00  New balance:   222.88

Account status: CURRENT
```

```
Name:    Susan Richards      Account number: 2219
Street: 4383 Alligator Blvd
City:    Fort Lauderdale, FL


Old balance:  135.00  Current payment:  135.00  New balance:    0.00


Account status: CURRENT



Name:    Martin Peterson     Account number: 8452
Street: 1787 Pacific Parkway
City:    San Diego, CA


Old balance:  387.42  Current payment:   35.00  New balance:  352.42


Account status: OVERDUE



Name:    Phyllis Smith     Account number: 711
Street: 1000 Great White Way
City:    New York, NY


Old balance:  260.00  Current payment:    0.00  New balance:  260.00


Account status: DELINQUENT
```

You should understand that this example is unrealistic from a practical standpoint, for two reasons. First, the array of structures (customer) is defined to be external to all of the functions within the program. It would be preferrable to declare customer within main, and then pass it to or from readinput or writeouput as required. We will learn how to do this in Sec. 11.5.

A more serious problem is the fact that a real customer billing system will store the customer records within a data file on an auxiliary memory device, such as a hard disk or a magnetic tape. To update a record we would access the record from the data file, change the data where necessary, and then write the updated record back to the data file. The use of data files will be discussed in Chap. 12. Since the present example does not make use of data files, we must reenter all of the customer records whenever the program is run. This is rather contrived, though it does provide a simple example illustrating the manner in which structures can be processed on a member-by-member basis.

It is sometimes useful to determine the number of bytes required by an array or a structure. This information can be obtained through the use of the sizeof operator, originally discussed in Sec. 3.2. For example, the size of a structure can be determined by writing either sizeof *variable* or sizeof (struct *tag*).

EXAMPLE 11.15   An elementary C program is shown below.

```
#include <stdio.h>

main()   /* determine the size of a structure */
{
    struct date  {
        int month;
        int day;
        int year;
    };
```

```
        struct account  {
             int acct_no;
             char acct_type;
             char name[80];
             float balance;
             struct date lastpayment;
        } customer;

        printf("%d\n", sizeof customer);
        printf("%d", sizeof (struct account));
}
```

This program makes use of the `sizeof` operator to determine the number of bytes associated with the structure variable `customer` (or equivalently, the structure `account`). The two `printf` statements illustrate different ways to utilize the `sizeof` operator. Both `printf` statements will produce the same output.

Execution of the program will result in the following output.

```
93
93
```

Thus, the structure variable `customer` (or the structure `account`) will occupy 93 bytes. This value is obtained as follows.

Structure member	Number of bytes
acct_no	2
acct_type	1
name	80
balance	4
lastpayment	6
Total	93

Some compilers may assign two bytes to `acct_type` in order to maintain an even number of bytes. Hence, the total byte count may be 94 rather than 93.

11.3 USER-DEFINED DATA TYPES (`typedef`)

The `typedef` feature allows users to define new data-types that are equivalent to existing data types. Once a user-defined data type has been established, then new variables, arrays, structures, etc. can be declared in terms of this new data type.

In general terms, a new data type is defined as

```
typedef  type  new-type;
```

where *type* refers to an existing data type (either a standard data type, or previous user-defined data type), and *new-type* refers to the new user-defined data type. It should be understood, however, that the new data type will be new in name only. In reality, this new data type will not be fundamentally different from one of the standard data types.

EXAMPLE 11.16   Here is a simple declaration involving the use of `typedef`.

```
typedef  int  age;
```

In this declaration `age` is a user-defined data type, which is equivalent to type `int`. Hence, the variable declaration

```
        age  male, female;
```

is equivalent to writing

```
        int  male, female;
```

In other words, `male` and `female` are regarded as variables of type `age`, though they are actually integer-type variables.
       Similarly, the declarations

```
        typedef  float  height[100];
        height  men, women;
```

define `height` as a 100-element, floating-point array type—hence, men and women are 100-element, floating-point arrays. Another way to express this is

```
        typedef  float  height;
        height  men[100], women[100];
```

though the former declaration is somewhat simpler.

       The `typedef` feature is particularly convenient when defining structures, since it eliminates the need to repeatedly write `struct` *tag* whenever a structure is referenced. Hence, the structure can be referenced more concisely. In addition, the name given to a user-defined structure type often suggests the purpose of the structure within the program.
       In general terms, a user-defined structure type can be written as

```
        typedef  struct  {
             member 1;
             member 2;
               . . . . .
             member m;
        }  new-type;
```

where *new-type* is the user-defined structure type. Structure variables can then be defined in terms of the new data type.

EXAMPLE 11.17 The following declarations are comparable to the structure declarations presented in Examples 11.1 and 11.2. Now, however, we introduce a user-defined data type to describe the structure.

```
        typedef  struct  {
             int acct_no;
             char acct_type;
             char name[80];
             float balance;
        }  record;

        record oldcustomer, newcustomer;
```

The first declaration defines `record` as a user-defined data type. The second declaration defines `oldcustomer` and `newcustomer` as structure variables of type `record`.

       The `typedef` feature can be used repeatedly, to define one data type in terms of other user-defined data types.

EXAMPLE 11.18   Here are some variations of the structure declarations presented in Example 11.5.

```
typedef struct  {
      int month;
      int day;
      int year;
} date;

typedef struct  {
      int acct_no;
      char acct_type;
      char name[80];
      float balance;
      date lastpayment;
} record;

record customer[100];
```

In this example date and record are user-defined stucture types, and customer is a 100-element array whose elements are structures of type record. (Recall that date was a tag rather than an actual data type in Example 11.5.) The individual members within the *i*th element of customer can be written as customer[i].acct_no, customer[i].name, customer[i].lastpayment.month, etc., as before.

There are, of course, variations on this theme. Thus, an alternate declaration can be written as

```
typedef struct  {
      int month;
      int day;
      int year;
} date;

typedef struct  {
      int acct_no;
      char acct_type;
      char name[80];
      float balance;
      date lastpayment;
} record[100];

record customer;
```

or simply

```
typedef struct  {
      int month;
      int day;
      int year;
} date;

struct  {
      int acct_no;
      char acct_type;
      char name[80];
      float balance;
      date lastpayment;
} customer[100];
```

All three sets of declarations are equivalent.

11.4 STRUCTURES AND POINTERS

The beginning address of a structure can be accessed in the same manner as any other address, through the use of the address (&) operator. Thus, if *variable* represents a structure-type variable, then *&variable* represents the starting address of that variable. Moreover, we can declare a pointer variable for a structure by writing

```
type *ptvar;
```

where *type* is a data type that identifies the composition of the structure, and *ptvar* represents the name of the pointer variable. We can then assign the beginning address of a structure variable to this pointer by writing

```
ptvar = &variable;
```

EXAMPLE 11.19 Consider the following structure declaration, which is a variation of the declaration presented in Example 11.1.

```
typedef struct  {
     int acct_no;
     char acct_type;
     char name[80];
     float balance;
}  account;

account  customer, *pc;
```

In this example customer is a structure variable of type account, and pc is a pointer variable whose object is a structure variable of type account. Thus, the beginning address of customer can be assigned to pc by writing

```
pc = &customer;
```

The variable and pointer declarations can be combined with the structure declaration by writing

```
struct  {
     member 1;
     member 2;
     . . . . .
     member m;
}  variable,  *ptvar;
```

where *variable* again represents a structure-type variable, and *ptvar* represents the name of a pointer variable.

EXAMPLE 11.20 The following single declaration is equivalent to the two declarations presented in the previous example.

```
struct  {
     int acct_no;
     char acct_type;
     char name[80];
     float balance;
}  customer, *pc;
```

The beginning address of customer can be assigned to pc by writing

```
pc = &customer;
```

as in the previous example.

An individual structure member can be accessed in terms of its corresponding pointer variable by writing

```
ptvar->member
```

where *ptvar* refers to a structure-type pointer variable and the operator -> is comparable to the period (.) operator discussed in Sec. 11.2. Thus, the expression

```
ptvar->member
```

is equivalent to writing

```
variable.member
```

where *variable* is a structure-type variable, as discussed in Sec. 11.2. The operator -> falls into the highest precedence group, like the period operator (.). Its associativity is left to right (see Appendix C).

The -> operator can be combined with the period operator to access a submember within a structure (i.e., to access a member of a structure that is itself a member of another structure). Hence, a submember can be accessed by writing

```
ptvar->member.submember
```

Similarly, the -> operator can be used to access an element of an array that is a member of a structure. This is accomplished by writing

```
ptvar->member[expression]
```

where *expression* is a nonnegative integer that indicates the array element.

EXAMPLE 11.21   Here is a variation of the declarations shown in Example 11.8.

```
typedef struct  {
      int month;
      int day;
      int year;
} date;

struct  {
      int acct_no;
      char acct_type;
      char name[80];
      float balance;
      date lastpayment;
} customer, *pc = &customer;
```

Notice that the pointer variable pc is initialized by assigning it the beginning address of the structure variable customer. In other words, pc will point to customer.

If we wanted to access the customer's account number, we could write any of the following:

```
customer.acct_no        pc->acct_no        (*pc).acct_no
```

The parentheses are required in the last expression because the period operator has a higher precedence than the indirection operator (*). Without the parentheses the compiler would generate an error, because pc (a pointer) is not directly compatible with the dot operator.

Similarly, the customer's balance can be accessed by writing any of the following:

    customer.balance   pc->balance   (*pc).balance

and the month of the last payment can be accessed by writing any of the following:

    customer.lastpayment.month   pc->lastpayment.month   (*pc).lastpayment.month

Finally, the customer's name can be accessed by writing any of the following:

    customer.name   pc->name   (*pc).name

Therefore, the third character of the customer's name can be accessed by writing any of the following (see Sec. 10.4).

    customer.name[2]   pc->name[2]   (*pc).name[2]

    *(customer.name + 2)   pc->(name + 2)   *((*pc).name + 2)

A structure can also include one or more pointers as members. Thus, if *ptmember* is both a pointer and a member of *variable*, then *variable.ptmember* will access the value to which *ptmember* points. Similarly, if *ptvar* is a pointer variable that points to a structure and *ptmember* is a member of that structure, then *ptvar->ptmember* will access the value to which *ptmember* points.

EXAMPLE 11.22   Consider the simple C program shown below.

```
#include <stdio.h>

main()

{
    int n = 3333;
    char t = 'C';
    float b = 99.99;

    typedef struct  {
        int month;
        int day;
        int year;
    }  date;

    struct  {
        int *acct_no;
        char *acct_type;
        char *name;
        float *balance;
        date lastpayment;
    }  customer, *pc = &customer;

    customer.acct_no = &n;
    customer.acct_type = &t;
    customer.name = "Smith";
    customer.balance = &b;

    printf("%d %c %s %.2f\n", *customer.acct_no, *customer.acct_type,
                              customer.name, *customer.balance);
    printf("%d %c %s %.2f", *pc->acct_no, *pc->acct_type,
                            pc->name, *pc->balance);
}
```

Within the second structure, the members `acct_no`, `acct_type`, `name` and `balance` are written as pointers. Thus, the value to which `acct_no` points can be accessed by writing either `*customer.acct_no` or `*pc->acct_no`. The same is true for `acct_type` and `balance`. Moreover, recall that a string can be assigned directly to a character-type pointer. Therefore, if `name` points to the beginning of a string, then the string can be accessed by writing either `customer.name` or `pc->name`.

Execution of this simple program results in the following two lines of output.

```
3333 C Smith 99.99
3333 C Smith 99.99
```

The two lines of output are identical, as expected.

Since the `->` operator is a member of the highest precedence group, it will be given the same high priority as the period (`.`) operator, with left-to-right associativity. Moreover, this operator, like the period operator, will take precedence over any unary, arithmetic, relational, logical or assignment operators that may appear in an expression. We have already discussed this point, as it applies to the period operator, in Sec. 11.2. However, some additional consideration should be given to certain unary operators, such as `++`, as they apply to structure-type pointer variables.

We already know that expressions such as `++ptvar->member` and `++ptvar->member.submember` are equivalent to `++(ptvar->member)` and `++(ptvar->member.submember)`, respectively. Thus, such expressions will cause the value of the member or the submember to be incremented, as discussed in Sec. 11.2. On the other hand, the expression `++ptvar` will cause the value of *ptvar* to increase by whatever number of bytes is associated with the structure to which *ptvar* points. (The number of bytes associated with a particular structure can be determined through the use of the `sizeof` operator, as illustrated in Example 11.15.) Hence, the address represented by *ptvar* will change as a result of this expression. Similarly, the expression `(++ptvar).member` will cause the value of *ptvar* to increase by this number of bytes before accessing *member*. There is some danger in attempting operations like these, because *ptvar* may no longer point to a structure variable once its value has been altered.

EXAMPLE 11.23   Here is a variation of the simple C program shown in Example 11.15.

```c
#include <stdio.h>

main()
{
    typedef struct  {
        int month;
        int day;
        int year;
    }  date;

    struct  {
        int acct_no;
        char acct_type;
        char name[80];
        float balance;
        date lastpayment;
    }  customer, *pt = &customer;

    printf("Number of bytes (dec): %d\n", sizeof *pt);
    printf("Number of bytes (hex): %x\n\n", sizeof *pt);
    printf("Starting address (hex): %x\n", pt);
    printf("Incremented address (hex): %x", ++pt);
}
```

Notice that pt is a pointer variable whose object is the structure variable customer.

The first printf statement causes the number of bytes associated with customer to be displayed as a decimal quantity. The second printf statement displays this same value as a hexadecimal quantity. The third printf statement causes the value of pt (i.e., the starting address of customer) to be displayed in hexadecimal, whereas the fourth printf statement shows what happens when pt is incremented.

Execution of the program causes the following output to be generated.

```
Number of bytes (dec): 93
Number of bytes (hex): 5d

Starting address (hex): f72
Incremented address (hex): fcf
```

Thus, we see that customer requires 93 decimal bytes, which is 5d in hexadecimal. The initial value assigned to pt (i.e., the starting address of customer) is f72, in hexadecimal. When pt is incremented, its value increases by 5d hexadecimal bytes, to fcf.

It is interesting to alter this program by replacing the character array member name[80] with the character pointer *name, and then execute the program. What do you think will happen?

11.5 PASSING STRUCTURES TO FUNCTIONS

There are several different ways to pass structure-type information to or from a function. Structure members can be transferred individually, or entire structures can be transferred. The mechanics for carrying out the transfers vary, depending on the type of transfer (individual members or complete structures) and the particular version of C.

Individual structure members can be passed to a function as arguments in the function call, and a single structure member can be returned via the return statement. To do so, each structure member is treated the same as an ordinary single-valued variable.

EXAMPLE 11.24 The skeletal outline of a C program is shown below. This outline makes use of the structure declarations presented earlier.

```
float adjust(char name[], int acct_no, float balance);      /* funct prototype */

main()
{
    typedef struct  {                     /* structure declaration */
        int month;
        int day;
        int year;
    }  date;

    struct  {                             /* structure declaration */
        int acct_no;
        char acct_type;
        char name[80];
        float balance;
        date lastpayment;
    }  customer;

    . . . . .

    customer.balance = adjust(customer.name, customer.acct_no, customer.balance);

    . . . . .

}
```

```
      float adjust(char name[], int acct_no, float balance)

      {
          float newbalance;                    /* local variable declaration */

          . . . . .

          newbalance = . . . . .;              /* adjust value of balance */

          . . . . .

          return(newbalance);
      }
```

This program outline illustrates the manner in which structure members can be passed to a function. In particular, `customer.name`, `customer.acct_no` and `customer.balance` are passed to the function `adjust`. Within `adjust`, the value assigned to `newbalance` presumably makes use of the information passed to the function. This value is then returned to `main`, where it is assigned to the structure member `customer.balance`.

Notice the function declaration in `main`. This declaration could also have been written without the argument names, as follows:

```
      float adjust(char [], int, float);
```

Some programmers prefer this form, since it avoids the specification of dummy argument names for data items that are actually structure members. We will continue to utilize full function prototypes, however, to take advantage of the resulting error checking.

A complete structure can be transferred to a function by passing a structure-type pointer as an argument. In principle, this is similar to the procedure used to transfer an array to a function. However, we must use explicit pointer notation to represent a structure that is passed as an argument.

You should understand that a structure passed in this manner will be passed by *reference* rather than by *value*. Hence, if any of the structure members are altered within the function, the alterations will be recognized outside of the function. Again, we see a direct analogy with the transfer of arrays to a function.

EXAMPLE 11.25   Consider the simple C program shown below.

```
      #include <stdio.h>

      typedef struct {
          char *name;
          int acct_no;
          char acct_type;
          float balance;
      } record;

      main()   /* transfer a structure-type pointer to a function */
      {
          void adjust(record *pt);        /* function declaration */

          static record customer = {"Smith", 3333, 'C', 33.33};

          printf("%s %d %c %.2f\n", customer.name, customer.acct_no,
                                    customer.acct_type, customer.balance);
          adjust(&customer);
          printf("%s %d %c %.2f\n", customer.name, customer.acct_no,
                                    customer.acct_type, customer.balance);

      }
```

```
void adjust(record *pt)          /* function definition */

{
    pt->name = "Jones";
    pt->acct_no = 9999;
    pt->acct_type = 'R';
    pt->balance = 99.99;
    return;
}
```

This program illustrates the transfer of a structure to a function by passing the structure's address (a pointer) to the function. In particular, customer is a static structure of type record, whose members are assigned an initial set of values. These initial values are displayed when the program begins to execute. The structure's address is then passed to the function adjust, where different values are assigned to the members of the structure.

Within adjust, the formal argument declaration defines pt as a pointer to a structure of type record. Also, notice the empty return statement; i.e., nothing is explicitly returned from adjust to main.

Within main, we see that the current values assigned to the members of customer are displayed a second time, after adjust has been accessed. Thus, the program illustrates whether or not the changes made in adjust carry over to the calling portion of the program.

Execution of the program results in the following output.

```
Smith 3333 C 33.33
Jones 9999 R 99.99
```

Thus, the values assigned to the members of customer within adjust are recognized within main, as expected.

A pointer to a structure can be returned from a function to the calling portion of the program. This feature may be useful when several structures are passed to a function, but only one structure is returned.

EXAMPLE 11.26 Locating Customer Records   Here is a simple C program that illustrates how an array of structures is passed to a function, and how a pointer to a particular structure is returned.

Suppose we specify an account number for a particular customer and then locate and display the complete record for that customer. Each customer record will be maintained in a structure, as in the last example. Now, however, the entire set of customer records will be stored in an array called customer. Each element of customer will be an independent structure.

The basic strategy will be to enter an account number, and then transfer both the account number and the array of records to a function called search. Within search, the specified account number will be compared with the account number that is stored within each customer record until a match is found, or until the entire list of records has been searched. If a match is found, a pointer to that array element (the structure containing the desired customer record) is returned to main, and the contents of the record are displayed.

If a match is not found after searching the entire array, then the function returns a value of NULL (zero) to main. The program then displays an error message requesting that the user reenter the account number. This overall search procedure will continue until a value of zero is entered for the account number.

The complete program is shown below. Within this program, customer is an array of structures of type record, and pt is a pointer to a structure of this same type. Also, search is a function that accepts two arguments and returns a pointer to a structure of type record. The arguments are an array of structures of type record and an integer quantity, respectively. Within search, the quantity returned is either the address of an array element, or NULL (zero).

```
/* find a customer record that corresponds to a specified account number */

#include <stdio.h>

#define N   3
#define NULL   0
```

```
typedef struct {
    char *name;
    int acct_no;
    char acct_type;
    float balance;
} record;

record *search(record table[], int acctn);     /* function prototype */

main()

{
    static record customer[N] = {
                                {"Smith", 3333, 'C', 33.33},
                                {"Jones", 6666, 'O', 66.66},
                                {"Brown", 9999, 'D', 99.99}
                            };                      /* array of structures */

    int acctn;                                  /* variable declaration */
    record *pt;                                 /* pointer declaration */

    printf("Customer Account Locator\n");
    printf("To END, enter O for the account number\n");
    printf("\nAccount no.: ");                  /* enter first account number */
    scanf("%d", &acctn);

    while (acctn != 0)   {
        pt = search(customer, acctn);

        if (pt != NULL)   {        /* found a match */
            printf("\nName: %s\n", pt->name);
            printf("Account no.: %d\n", pt->acct_no);
            printf("Account type: %c\n", pt->acct_type);
            printf("Balance: %.2f\n", pt->balance);
        }
        else
            printf("\nERROR - Please try again\n");

        printf("\nAccount no.: ");              /* enter next account number */
        scanf("%d", &acctn);
    }
}


record *search(record table[N], int acctn)      /* function definition */

/* accept an array of structures and an account number,
   return a pointer to a particular structure (an array element)
   if the account number matches a member of that structure */

{
    int count;

    for (count = 0; count < N; ++count)
        if (table[count].acct_no == acctn)                  /* found a match */
            return(&table[count]);      /* return pointer to array element */

    return(NULL);
}
```

The array size is expressed in terms of the symbolic constant N. For this simple example we have selected a value of N = 3. That is, we are storing only three sample records within the array. In a more realistic example, N would have a much greater value.

Finally, it should be mentioned that there are much better ways to search through a set of records than examining each record sequentially. We have selected this simple though inefficient procedure in order to concentrate on the mechanics of transferring structures between main and its subordinate function search.

Shown below is a typical dialog that might result from execution of the program. The user's responses are underlined, as usual.

```
Customer Account Locator
To END, enter 0 for the account number

Account no.: 3333

Name: Smith
Account no.: 3333
Account type: C
Balance: 33.33


Account no.: 9999

Name: Brown
Account no.: 9999
Account type: D
Balance: 99.99


Account no.: 666

ERROR - Please try again

Account no.: 6666

Name: Jones
Account no.: 6666
Account type: O
Balance: 66.66


Account no.: 0
```

Newer versions of C permit an entire structure to be transferred directly to a function as an argument, and returned directly from a function via the return statement. (Notice the contrast with arrays, which *cannot* be returned via the return statement.) These features are included in the current ANSI standard.

When a structure is passed directly to a function, the transfer is by value rather than by reference. This is consistent with other direct (nonpointer) transfers in C. Therefore, if any of the structure members are altered within the function, the alterations *will not* be recognized outside of the function. However, if the altered structure is returned to the calling portion of the program, then the changes *will* be recognized within this broader scope.

EXAMPLE 11.27 In Example 11.25 we saw a program that transferred a structure-type pointer to a function. Two different printf statements within main illustrated the fact that transfers of this type are by reference; i.e., alterations made to the structure within the function are recognized within main. A similar program is shown below. However, the present program transfers a complete structure, rather than a structure-type pointer, to the function.

```
#include <stdio.h>

typedef struct {
    char *name;
    int acct_no;
    char acct_type;
    float balance;
} record;

void adjust(record customer);          /* function prototype*/

main()    /* transfer a structure to a function */

{
    static record customer = {"Smith", 3333, 'C', 33.33};

    printf("%s %d %c %.2f\n", customer.name, customer.acct_no,
                            customer.acct_type, customer.balance);
    adjust(customer);
    printf("%s %d %c %.2f\n", customer.name, customer.acct_no,
                            customer.acct_type, customer.balance);

}


void adjust(record cust)          /* function definition */

{
    cust.name = "Jones";
    cust.acct_no = 9999;
    cust.acct_type = 'R';
    cust.balance = 99.99;
    return;
}
```

Notice that the function `adjust` now accepts a structure of type `record` as an argument, rather than a pointer to a structure of type `record`, as in Example 11.25. Nothing is returned from `adjust` to `main` in either program.

When the program is executed, the following output is obtained.

```
Smith 3333 C 33.33
Smith 3333 C 33.33
```

Thus, the new assignments made within `adjust` are not recognized within `main`. This is expected, since the transfer of the structure `customer` from `main` to `adjust` is by value rather than by reference. (Compare with the output shown in Example 11.25.)

Now suppose we modify this program so that the altered structure is returned from `adjust` to `main`. Here is the modified program.

```
#include <stdio.h>

typedef struct {
    char *name;
    int acct_no;
    char acct_type;
    float balance;
} record;

    record adjust(record customer);          /* function prototype */
```

```
main()   /* transfer a structure to a function and return the structure */

{
    static record customer = {"Smith", 3333, 'C', 33.33};

    printf("%s %d %c %.2f\n", customer.name, customer.acct_no,
                              customer.acct_type, customer.balance);
    customer = adjust(customer);
    printf("%s %d %c %.2f\n", customer.name, customer.acct_no,
                              customer.acct_type, customer.balance);
}


record adjust(record cust)                    /* function definition */

{
    cust.name = "Jones";
    cust.acct_no = 9999;
    cust.acct_type = 'R';
    cust.balance = 99.99;
    return(cust);
}
```

Notice that adjust now returns a structure of type record to main. The return statement is modified accordingly. Execution of this program results in the following output.

```
Smith 3333 C 33.33
Jones 9999 R 99.99
```

Thus, the alterations that were made within adjust are now recognized within main. This is expected, since the altered structure is now returned directly to the calling portion of the program. (Compare with the output shown in Example 11.25 as well as the output shown earlier in this example.)

Most versions of C allow complicated data structures to be transferred freely between functions. We have already seen examples involving the transfer of individual structure members, entire structures, pointers to structures and arrays of structures. As a practical matter, however, there are some limitations on the complexity of data structures that can easily be transferred to or from a function. In particular, some compilers may have difficulty executing programs that involve complex data structure transfers, because of certain memory restrictions. Beginning programmers should be aware of these limitations, though the details of this topic are beyond the scope of the current text.

EXAMPLE 11.28 Updating Customer Records   Example 11.14 presented a simple customer billing system illustrating the use of structures to maintain and update customer records. In that example the customer records were stored within a global (external) array of structures. We now consider two variations of that program. In each program the array of structures is maintained locally, within main. The individual array elements (i.e., individual customer records) are transferred back and forth between functions, as required.

In the first program, complete structures are transferred between the functions. In particular, the function readinput allows information defining each customer record to be entered into the computer. When an entire record has been entered, the corresponding structure is returned to main, where it is stored within the 100-element array called customer and adjusted for the proper account type. After all the records have been entered and adjusted, they are transferred individually to the function writeoutput, where certain information is displayed for each customer.

The entire program is shown below.

```
/* update a series of customer accounts (simplified billing system) */

#include <stdio.h>

/* maintain the customer accounts as an array of structures,
   transfer complete structures to and from functions              */

typedef struct  {
    int month;
    int day;
    int year;
} date;

typedef struct  {
    char name[80];
    char street[80];
    char city[80];
    int acct_no;          /* (positive integer) */
    char acct_type;       /* C (current), O (overdue), or D (delinquent) */
    float oldbalance;     /* (nonnegative quantity) */
    float newbalance;     /* (nonnegative quantity) */
    float payment;        /* (nonnegative quantity) */
    date lastpayment;
} record;

record readinput(int i);              /* function prototype */
void writeoutput(record customer);    /* function prototype */


main()

/* read customer accounts, process each account, and display output */

{
    int i, n;                 /* variable declarations */
    record customer[100];     /* array declaration (array of structures) */

    printf("CUSTOMER BILLING SYSTEM\n\n");
    printf("How many customers are there? ");
    scanf("%d", &n);

    for (i = 0; i < n; ++i)   {
        customer[i] = readinput(i);

        /* determine account status */

        if (customer[i].payment > 0)
            customer[i].acct_type =
                (customer[i].payment < 0.1 * customer[i].oldbalance) ? 'O' : 'C';
        else
            customer[i].acct_type =
                (customer[i].oldbalance > 0) ? 'D' : 'C';

        /* adjust account balance */

        customer[i].newbalance = customer[i].oldbalance - customer[i].payment;
    }

    for (i = 0; i < n; ++i)
        writeoutput(customer[i]);
}
```

```
record readinput(int i)

/* read input data for a customer */

{
    record customer;

    printf("\nCustomer no. %d\n", i + 1);
    printf("   Name: ");
    scanf(" %[^\n]", customer.name);
    printf("   Street: ");
    scanf(" %[^\n]", customer.street);
    printf("   City: ");
    scanf(" %[^\n]", customer.city);
    printf("   Account number: ");
    scanf("%d", &customer.acct_no);
    printf("   Previous balance: ");
    scanf("%f", &customer.oldbalance);
    printf("   Current payment: ");
    scanf("%f", &customer.payment);
    printf("   Payment date (mm/dd/yyyy): ");
    scanf("%d/%d/%d", &customer.lastpayment.month,
                      &customer.lastpayment.day,
                      &customer.lastpayment.year);
    return(customer);
}


void writeoutput(record customer)

/* display current information for a customer */

{
    printf("\nName:   %s", customer.name);
    printf("     Account number: %d\n", customer.acct_no);
    printf("Street: %s\n", customer.street);
    printf("City:   %s\n\n", customer.city);
    printf("Old balance: %7.2f", customer.oldbalance);
    printf("   Current payment: %7.2f", customer.payment);
    printf("   New balance: %7.2f\n\n", customer.newbalance);
    printf("Account status: ");

    switch (customer.acct_type)   {
      case 'C':
                printf("CURRENT\n\n");
                break;
      case 'O':
                printf("OVERDUE\n\n");
                break;
      case 'D':
                printf("DELINQUENT\n\n");
                break;
      default:
                printf("ERROR\n\n");
    }
    return;
}
```

The next program is very similar to the previous program. Now, however, the transfers involve pointers to structures rather than the structures themselves. Thus, the structures are now transferred by reference, whereas they were transferred by value in the previous program.

For brevity, this program is outlined rather than listed in its entirety. The missing blocks are identical to the corresponding portions of the previous program.

```
/* update a series of customer accounts (simplified billing system) */

#include <stdio.h>

/* maintain the customer accounts as an array of structures,
   transfer pointers to structures to and from functions     */


/* (structure definitions) */

record *readinput(int i);          /* function prototype */
void writeoutput(record *cust);    /* function prototype */


main()

/* read customer accounts, process each account, and display output */

{
    int i, n;                  /* variable declarations */
    record customer[100];      /* array declaration (array of structures) */

    . . . . .

    for (i = 0; i < n; ++i)   {
        customer[i] = *readinput(i);

        /* determine account status */

        . . . . .

        /* adjust account balance */

        . . . . .
    }

    for (i = 0; i < n; ++i)
        writeoutput(&customer[i]);
}


record *readinput(int i)

/* read input data for a customer */

{
    record customer;

    /* enter input data */

    return(&customer);
}
```

```
void writeoutput(record *pt)

/* display current information for a customer */

{
    record customer;

    customer = *pt;

    /* display output data */

    return;
}
```

Both of these programs will behave in the same manner as the program given in Example 11.14 when executed. Because of the complexity of the data structure (i.e., the array of structures, where each structure contains embedded arrays and embedded structures), however, the compiled programs may not be executable with certain compilers. In particular, a stack overflow condition (a type of inadequate memory condition) may be experienced with some compilers.

This problem would not exist if the program were more realistic; i.e., if the customer records were stored within a file on an auxiliary memory device, rather than in an array that is stored within the computer's memory. We will discuss this problem in Chap. 12, where we consider the use of data files for situations such as this.

11.6 SELF-REFERENTIAL STRUCTURES

It is sometimes desirable to include within a structure one member that is a pointer to the parent structure type. In general terms, this can be expressed as

```
struct  tag  {
      member 1;
      member 2;
      . . . . .
      struct  tag  *name;
};
```

where *name* refers to the name of a pointer variable. Thus, the structure of type *tag* will contain a member that points to another structure of type *tag*. Such structures are known as *self-referential* structures.

EXAMPLE 11.29   A C program contains the following structure declaration.

```
struct  list_element  {
          char item[40];
          struct  list_element  *next;
};
```

This is a structure of type list_element. The structure contains two members: a 40-element character array, called item, and a pointer to a structure of the same type (i.e., a pointer to a structure of type list_element), called next. Therefore this is a self-referential structure.

Self-referential structures are very useful in applications that involve linked data structures, such as lists and trees. We will see a comprehensive example illustrating the processing of a linked list in Example 11.32. First, however, we present a brief summary of linked data structures.

The basic idea of a linked data structure is that each component within the structure includes a pointer indicating where the next component can be found. Therefore, the relative order of the components can easily be changed simply by altering the pointers. In addition, individual components can easily be added or deleted, again by altering the pointers. As a result, a linked data structure is not confined to some maximum number of components. Rather, the data structure can expand or contract in size as required.

EXAMPLE 11.30 Figure 11.3(*a*) illustrates a linked list containing three components. Each component consists of two data items: a string, and a pointer that references the next component within the list. Thus, the first component contains the string red, the second contains green and the third contains blue. The beginning of the list is indicated by a separate pointer, which is labeled start. Also, the end of the list is indicated by a special pointer, called NULL.

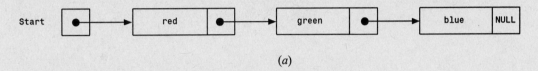

(*a*)

Now let us add another component, whose value is white, between red and green. To do so we merely change the pointers, as illustrated in Fig. 11.3(*b*). Similarly, if we choose to delete the component whose value is green, we simply change the pointer associated with the second component, as shown in Fig. 11.3(*c*).

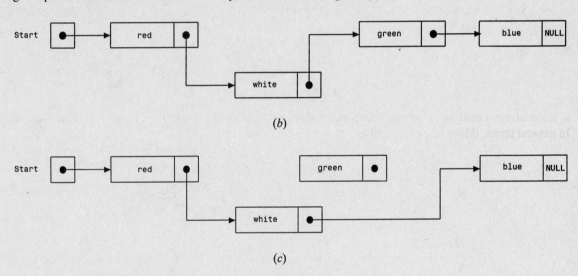

(*b*)

(*c*)

Fig. 11.3

There are several different kinds of linked data structures, including *linear* linked lists, in which the components are all linked together sequentially; linked lists with *multiple pointers*, which permit forward and backward traversal within the list; *circular* linked lists, which have no beginning and no ending; and *trees*, in which the components are arranged in a hierarchical structure. We have already seen an illustration of a linear linked list in Example 11.30. Other kinds of linked lists are illustrated in the next example.

EXAMPLE 11.31 Figure 11.4 shows a linear linked list that is similar to that shown in Fig. 11.3(*a*). Now, however, we see that there are *two* pointers associated with each component: a forward pointer, and a backward pointer. This double set of pointers allows us to traverse the list in either direction, i.e., from beginning to end, or from end to beginning.

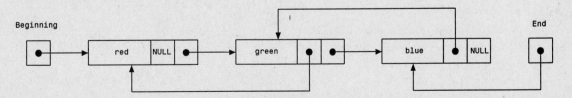

Fig. 11.4

Now consider the list shown in Fig. 11.5. This list is similar to that shown in Fig. 11.3(*a*), except that the last data item (blue) points to the first data item (red). Hence, this list has no beginning and no ending. Such lists are referred to as *circular lists*.

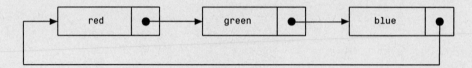

Fig. 11.5

Finally, in Fig. 11.6(*a*) we see an example of a *tree*. Trees consist of nodes and branches, arranged in some hierarchical manner which indicates a corresponding hierarchical structure within the data. (A *binary tree* is a tree in which every node has no more than two branches.)

In Fig. 11.6(*a*) the *root node* has the value screen, and the associated branches lead to the nodes whose values are foreground and background, respectively. Similarly, the branches associated with foreground lead to the nodes whose values are white, green and amber, and the branches associated with background lead to the nodes whose values are black, blue and white.

Figure 11.6(*b*) illustrates the manner in which pointers are used to construct the tree.

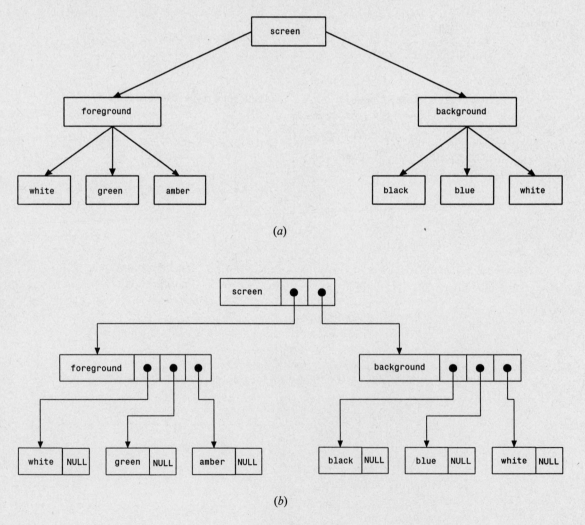

Fig. 11.6

Self-referential structures are ideally suited for applications involving linked data structures.   Each structure will represent a single component (i.e., one node) within the linked data structure.   The self-referential pointer will indicate the location of the next component.

EXAMPLE 11.32 Processing a Linked List   We now present an interactive C program that allows us to create a linear linked list, add a new component to the linked list, or delete an existing component from the linked list. Each component will consist of a string, and a pointer to the next component. The program will be menu-driven to facilitate its use by nonprogrammers. We will include a provision to display the list after the selection of any menu item (i.e., after any change has been made to the list).

This program is somewhat more complex than the preceding example programs. It utilizes both *recursion* (see Sec. 7.6) and *dynamic memory allocation* (see Sec. 10.5, and Examples 10.15, 10.22, 10.24 and 10.26).

The entire program is shown below. Following the program listing, the individual functions are discussed in detail.

```c
/* menu-driven program to process a linked list of strings */

#include <stdio.h>
#include <stdlib.h>
#include <string.h>

#define  NULL  0

struct list_element  {
          char item[40];                 /* data item for this node */
          struct list_element *next;     /* pointer to the next node */
};

typedef struct list_element node;        /* structure type declaration */

int menu(void);                          /* function prototype */
void create(node *pt);                   /* function prototype */
node *insert(node *pt);                  /* function prototype */
node *remove(node *pt);                  /* function prototype */
void display(node *pt);                  /* function prototype */


main()

{
    node *start;                         /* pointer to beginning of list*/
    int choice;                          /* local variable declaration */

    do   {
          choice = menu();
          switch (choice)  {

          case 1:    /* create the linked list */
              start = (node *) malloc(sizeof(node));   /* allocate space, 1st node */
              create(start);
              printf("\n");
              display(start);
              continue;

          case 2:    /* add one component */
              start = insert(start);
              printf("\n");
              display(start);
              continue;
```

```
            case 3:      /* delete one component */
                start = remove(start);
                printf("\n");
                display(start);
                continue;

            default:     /* terminate computation */
                printf("End of computation\n");
            }
    }   while (choice != 4);
}


int menu(void)      /* generate the main menu */

{
    int choice;

    do   {
            printf("\nMain menu:\n");
            printf("  1 - CREATE the linked list\n");
            printf("  2 - ADD a component\n");
            printf("  3 - DELETE a component\n");
            printf("  4 - END\n");
            printf("Please enter your choice (1, 2, 3 or 4) -> ");
            scanf("%d", &choice);
            if (choice < 1 || choice > 4)
                printf("\nERROR - Please try again\n");
    }   while (choice < 1 || choice > 4);
    printf("\n");
    return(choice);
}


void create(node *record)      /* create a linked list */

/* argument points to the current node */

{
    printf("Data item (type \'END\' when finished): ");
    scanf(" %[^\n]", record->item);

    if (strcmp(record->item, "END") == 0)
        record->next = NULL;
    else   {
        /* allocate space for next node */
        record->next = (node *) malloc(sizeof(node));

        /* create the next node */
        create(record->next);
    }
    return;
}


void display(node *record)      /* display the linked list */

/* argument points to the current node */
```

```
{
    if (record->next != NULL)   {
        printf("%s\n", record->item);           /* display this data item */
        display(record->next);                  /* get the next data item */
    }
    return;
}


node *insert(node *first)     /* add one component to the linked list
                                 return a pointer to beginning of the modified list */

/* argument points to the first node */

{
    node *locate(node*, char[]);     /* function declaration */
    node *newrecord;                 /* pointer to new node */
    node *tag;                       /* pointer to node BEFORE target node */
    char newitem[40];                /* new data item */
    char target[40];                 /* data item following the new entry */

    printf("New data item: ");
    scanf(" %[^\n]", newitem);
    printf("Place before (type \'END\' if last): ");
    scanf(" %[^\n]", target);

    if (strcmp(first->item, target) == 0)   {
        /* new node is first in list */

        /* allocate space for the new node */
        newrecord = (node *) malloc(sizeof(node));

        /* assign the new data item to newrecord->item */
        strcpy(newrecord->item, newitem);

        /* assign the current pointer to newrecord->next */
        newrecord->next = first;

        /* new pointer becomes the beginning of the list */
        first = newrecord;
    }

    else   {
        /* insert new node after an existing node */

        /* locate the node PRECEDING the target node */
        tag = locate(first, target);

        if (tag == NULL)
            printf("\nMatch not found - Please try again\n");
        else   {
            /* allocate space for the new node */
            newrecord = (node *) malloc(sizeof(node));

            /* assign the new data item to newrecord->item */
            strcpy(newrecord->item, newitem);

            /* assign the next pointer to newrecord->next */
            newrecord->next = tag->next;
```

```
                        /* assign the new pointer to tag->next */
                        tag->next = newrecord;
                    }
                }
            return(first);
    }


    node *locate(node *record, char target[])        /* locate a node */

    /* return a pointer to the node BEFORE the target node
       The first argument points to the current node
       The second argument is the target string            */

    {
        if (strcmp(record->next->item, target) == 0)        /* found a match */
            return(record);
        else
            if (record->next->next == NULL)                 /* end of list */
                return(NULL);
            else
                locate(record->next, target);               /* try next node */
    }


    node *remove(node *first)      /* remove (delete) one component from the linked list
                                      return a pointer to beginning of the modified list */

    /* argument points to the first node */

    {
        node *locate(node*, char[]);        /* function declaration */
        node *tag;                          /* pointer to node BEFORE target node */
        node *temp;                         /* temporary pointer */
        char target[40];                    /* data item to be deleted */

        printf("Data item to be deleted: ");
        scanf(" %[^\n]", target);

        if (strcmp(first->item, target) == 0)   {
            /* delete the first node */

            /* mark the node following the target node */
            temp = first->next;

            /* free space for the target node */
            free(first);

            /* adjust the pointer to the first node */
            first = temp;
        }

        else   {
            /* delete a data item other than the first */

            /* locate the node PRECEDING the target node */
            tag = locate(first, target);

            if (tag == NULL)
                printf("\nMatch not found - Please try again\n");
```

```
            else   {
                /* mark the node following the target node */
                temp = tag->next->next;

                /* free space for the target node */
                free(tag->next);

                /* adjust the link to the next node */
                tag->next = temp;
            }
        }
        return(first);
    }
```

The program begins with the usual #include statements and a definition of the symbolic constant NULL to represent the value 0. Following these statements is a declaration for the self-referential structure list_element. This structure declaration is the same as that shown in Example 11.29. Thus, list_element identifies a structure consisting of two members: a 40-element character array (item), and a pointer (next) to another structure of the same type. The character array will represent a string, and the pointer will identify the location of the next component in the linked list.

The data type node is then defined, identifying structures having composition list_element. This definition is followed by the function prototypes. Within the function prototypes, notice that start is a pointer to a structure of type node. This pointer will indicate the beginning of the linked list. The remaining function prototypes identify several additional functions that are called from main. Note that these declarations and function prototypes are external. They will therefore be recognized throughout the program.

The main function consists of a do - while loop that permits repetitive execution of the entire process. This loop calls the function menu, which generates the main menu, and returns a value for choice, indicating the user's menu selection. A switch statement then calls the appropriate functions, in accordance with the user's selection. Notice that the program will stop executing if choice is assigned a value of 4.

If choice is assigned a value of 1, indicating that a new linked list will be created, a block of memory must be allocated for the first data item before calling the function create. This is accomplished using the library function malloc, as discussed in Sec. 10.5. Thus, memory allocation statement

```
    start = (node *) malloc(sizeof(node));
```

reserves a block of memory whose size (in bytes) is sufficient for one node. The statement returns a pointer to a structure of type node. This pointer indicates the beginning of the linked list. Thus, it is passed to create as an argument.

Note that the type cast (node *) is required as a part of the memory allocation statement. Without it, the malloc function would return a pointer to a char rather than a pointer to a structure of type node.

Now consider the function menu, which is used to generate the main menu. This function accepts a value for choice after the menu has been generated. The only permissible values for choice are 1, 2, 3 or 4. An error trap, in the form of a do - while statement, causes an error message to be displayed and a new menu to be generated if a value other than 1, 2, 3 or 4 is entered in response to the menu.

The linked list is created by the function create. This is a recursive function that accepts a pointer to the current node (i.e., the node that is being created) as an argument. The pointer variable is called record.

The create function begins by prompting for the current data item; i.e., the string that is to reside in the current node. If the user enters the string END (in either upper- or lowercase), then NULL is assigned to the pointer that indicates the location of the next node and the recursion stops. If the user enters any string other than END, however, memory is allocated for the next node via the malloc function and the function calls itself recursively. Thus, the recursion will continue until the user has entered END for one of the data items.

Once the linked list has been created, it is displayed via the function display. This function is called from main, after the call to create. Notice that display accepts a pointer to the current node as an argument. The function then executes recursively, until it receives a pointer whose value is NULL. The recursion therefore causes the entire linked list to be displayed.

Now consider the function insert, which is used to add a new component (i.e., a new node) to the linked list. This function asks the user where the insertion is to occur. Note that the function accepts a pointer to the beginning of the list as an argument, and then returns a pointer to the beginning of the list, after the insertion has been made. These two pointers will be the same, unless the insertion is made at the beginning of the list.

The insert function does not execute recursively. It first prompts for the new data item (newitem), followed by a prompt for the existing data item that will follow the new data item (the existing data item is called target). If the insertion is to be made at the *beginning of the list*, then memory is allocated for the new node, newitem is assigned to the first member, and the pointer originally indicating the beginning of the linked list (first) is assigned to the second member. The pointer returned by malloc, which indicates the beginning of the new node, is then assigned to first. Hence, the beginning of the new node becomes the beginning of the entire list.

If the insertion is to be made *after an existing node*, then function locate is called to determine the location of the insertion. This function returns a pointer to the node *preceding* the target node. The value returned is assigned to the pointer tag. Hence, tag points to the node that will precede the new node. If locate cannot find a match between the value entered for target and an existing data item, it will return NULL.

If a match is found by locate, then the insertion is made in the following manner: memory is allocated for the new node, newitem is assigned to the first member of newrecord (i.e., tonewrecord->item), and the pointer to the target node (i.e., tag->next) is assigned to the second member of newrecord (i.e., newrecord->next). The pointer returned by malloc, which indicates the beginning of the new node, is then assigned to tag->next. Hence, the pointer in the preceding node will point to the new node, and the pointer in the new node will point to the target node.

Now consider the function locate. this is a simple recursive function that accepts a pointer to the current node and the target string as arguments, and returns a pointer to the node that *precedes* the current node. Therefore, if the data item in the node following the current node matches the target string, the function will return the pointer to the current node. Otherwise, one of two possible actions will be taken. If the pointer in the node following the current node is NULL, indicating the end of the linked list, a match has not been found. Therefore, the function will return NULL. But, if the pointer in the node following the current node is something other than NULL, the function will call itself recursively, thus testing the next node for a match.

Finally, consider the function remove, which is used to delete an existing component (i.e., an existing node) from the linked list. This function is similar to insert, though somewhat simpler. It accepts a pointer to the beginning of the linked list as an argument, and returns a pointer to the beginning of the linked list after the deletion has been made.

The remove function begins by prompting for the data item to be deleted (target). If this is the first data item, then the pointers are adjusted as follows: The pointer indicating the location of the second node is temporarily assigned to the pointer variable temp; the memory utilized by the first node is freed, using the library function free; and the location of the second node (which is now the first node, because of the deletion) is assigned to first. Hence, the beginning of the (former) second node becomes the beginning of the entire list.

If the data item to be deleted is *not* the first data item in the list, then locate is called to determine the location of the deletion. This function will return a pointer to the node *preceding* the target node. The value returned is assigned to the pointer variable tag. If this value is NULL, a match cannot be found. An error message is then generated, requesting that the user try again.

If locate returns a value other than NULL, the target node is deleted in the following manner: The pointer to the node following the target node is temporarily assigned to the pointer variable temp; the memory utilized by the target node is then freed, using the library function free; and the value of temp is then assigned to tag->next. Hence, the pointer in the preceding node will point to the node following the target node.

Let us now utilize this program to create a linked list containing the following cities: Boston, Chicago, Denver, New York, Pittsburgh, San Francisco. We will then add several cities and delete several cities, thus illustrating all of the program's features. We will maintain the list of cities in alphabetical order throughout the exercise. (We could, of course, have the computer do the sorting for us, though this would further complicate an already complex program.)

The entire interactive session is shown below. As usual, the user's responses have been underlined.

```
Main menu:
    1 - CREATE the linked list
    2 - ADD a component
    3 - DELETE a component
    4 - END
```

```
Please enter your choice (1, 2, 3 or 4) -> 1

Data item (type 'END' when finished): BOSTON
Data item (type 'END' when finished): CHICAGO
Data item (type 'END' when finished): DENVER
Data item (type 'END' when finished): NEW YORK
Data item (type 'END' when finished): PITTSBURGH
Data item (type 'END' when finished): SAN FRANCISCO
Data item (type 'END' when finished): END


BOSTON
CHICAGO
DENVER
NEW YORK
PITTSBURGH
SAN FRANCISCO

Main menu:
   1 - CREATE the linked list
   2 - ADD a component
   3 - DELETE a component
   4 - END
Please enter your choice (1, 2, 3 or 4) -> 2

New data item: ATLANTA
Place before (type 'END' if last): BOSTON


ATLANTA
BOSTON
CHICAGO
DENVER
NEW YORK
PITTSBURGH
SAN FRANCISCO


Main menu:
   1 - CREATE the linked list
   2 - ADD a component
   3 - DELETE a component
   4 - END
Please enter your choice (1, 2, 3 or 4) -> 2

New data item: SEATTLE
Place before (type 'END' if last): END


ATLANTA
BOSTON
CHICAGO
DENVER
NEW YORK
PITTSBURGH
SAN FRANCISCO
SEATTLE
```

```
Main menu:
  1 - CREATE the linked list
  2 - ADD a component
  3 - DELETE a component
  4 - END
Please enter your choice (1, 2, 3 or 4) -> 3


Data item to be deleted: NEW YORK


ATLANTA
BOSTON
CHICAGO
DENVER
PITTSBURGH
SAN FRANCISCO
SEATTLE


Main menu:
  1 - CREATE the linked list
  2 - ADD a component
  3 - DELETE a component
  4 - END
Please enter your choice (1, 2, 3 or 4) -> 2


New data item: WASHINGTON
Place before (type 'END' if last): WILLIAMSBURG


Match not found - Please try again


ATLANTA
BOSTON
CHICAGO
DENVER
PITTSBURGH
SAN FRANCISCO
SEATTLE


Main menu:
  1 - CREATE the linked list
  2 - ADD a component
  3 - DELETE a component
  4 - END
Please enter your choice (1, 2, 3 or 4) -> 2


New data item: WASHINGTON
Place before (type 'END' if last): END


ATLANTA
BOSTON
CHICAGO
DENVER
PITTSBURGH
SAN FRANCISCO
```

```
SEATTLE
WASHINGTON

Main menu:
  1 - CREATE the linked list
  2 - ADD a component
  3 - DELETE a component
  4 - END
Please enter your choice (1, 2, 3 or 4) -> 3

Data item to be deleted: ATLANTA

BOSTON
CHICAGO
DENVER
PITTSBURGH
SAN FRANCISCO
SEATTLE
WASHINGTON

Main menu:
  1 - CREATE the linked list
  2 - ADD a component
  3 - DELETE a component
  4 - END
Please enter your choice (1, 2, 3 or 4) -> 2

New data item: DALLAS
Place before (type 'END' if last): DENVER

BOSTON
CHICAGO
DALLAS
DENVER
PITTSBURGH
SAN FRANCISCO
SEATTLE
WASHINGTON

Main menu:
  1 - CREATE the linked list
  2 - ADD a component
  3 - DELETE a component
  4 - END
Please enter your choice (1, 2, 3 or 4) -> 3

Data item to be deleted: MIAMI

Match not found - Please try again

BOSTON
CHICAGO
DALLAS
```

```
DENVER
PITTSBURGH
SAN FRANCISCO
SEATTLE
WASHINGTON

Main menu:
  1 - CREATE the linked list
  2 - ADD a component
  3 - DELETE a component
  4 - END
Please enter your choice (1, 2, 3 or 4) -> 3

Data item to be deleted: WASHINGTON

BOSTON
CHICAGO
DALLAS
DENVER
PITTSBURGH
SAN FRANCISCO
SEATTLE

Main menu:
  1 - CREATE the linked list
  2 - ADD a component
  3 - DELETE a component
  4 - END
Please enter your choice (1, 2, 3 or 4) -> 5

ERROR - Please try again

Main menu:
  1 - CREATE the linked list
  2 - ADD a component
  3 - DELETE a component
  4 - END
Please enter your choice (1, 2, 3 or 4) -> 4

End of computation
```

11.7 UNIONS

Unions, like structures, contain members whose individual data types may differ from one another. However, the members within a union all share the same storage area within the computer's memory, whereas each member within a structure is assigned its own unique storage area. Thus, unions are used to conserve memory. They are useful for applications involving multiple members, where values need not be assigned to all of the members at any one time.

Within a union, the bookkeeping required to store members whose data types are different (having different memory requirements) is handled automatically by the compiler. However, the user must keep track of what type of information is stored at any given time. An attempt to access the wrong type of information will produce meaningless results.

In general terms, the composition of a union may be defined as

```
union  tag  {
    member 1;
    member 2;
    . . . . .
    member m;
};
```

where `union` is a required keyword and the other terms have the same meaning as in a structure definition (see Sec. 11.1). Individual union variables can then be declared as

```
storage-class union  tag variable 1,  variable 2,  . . .,  variable n;
```

where *storage-class* is an optional storage class specifier, union is a required keyword, *tag* is the name that appeared in the union definition, and *variable 1*, *variable 2*, . . ., *variable n* are union variables of type *tag*.

The two declarations may be combined, just as we did with structures. Thus, we can write

```
storage-class union  tag  {
        member 1;
        member 2;
        . . . . .
        member m;
}  variable 1,  variable 2,  . . .,  variable n;
```

The *tag* is optional in this type of declaration.

EXAMPLE 11.33   A C program contains the following union declaration.

```
union id  {
    char color[12];
    int size;
}  shirt, blouse;
```

Here we have two union variables, `shirt` and `blouse`, of type `id`. Each variable can represent either a 12-character string (`color`) or an integer quantity (`size`) at any one time.

The 12-character string will require more storage area within the computer's memory than the integer quantity. Therefore, a block of memory large enough for the 12-character string will be allocated to each union variable. The compiler will automatically distinguish between the 12-character array and the integer quantity within the given block of memory, as required.

A union may be a member of a structure, and a structure may be a member of a union. Moreover, structures and unions may be freely mixed with arrays.

EXAMPLE 11.34   A C program contains the following declarations.

```
union id  {
    char color[12];
    int size;
};
struct clothes  {
    char manufacturer[20];
    float cost;
    union id description;
}  shirt, blouse;
```

Now shirt and blouse are structure variables of type clothes. Each variable will contain the following members: a string (manufacturer), a floating-point quantity (cost), and a union (description). The union may represent either a string (color) or an integer quantity (size).

Another way to declare the structure variables shirt and blouse is to combine the preceding two declarations, as follows.

```
struct clothes {
    char manufacturer[20];
    float cost;
    union {
        char color[12];
        int size;
    } description;
} shirt, blouse;
```

This declaration is more concise, though perhaps less straightforward, than the original declarations.

An individual union member can be accessed in the same manner as an individual structure member, using the operators . and -> . Thus, if *variable* is a union variable, then *variable.member* refers to a member of the union. Similarly, if *ptvar* is a pointer variable that points to a union, then *ptvar->member* refers to a member of that union.

EXAMPLE 11.35   Consider the simple C program shown below.

```
#include <stdio.h>

main()

{
    union id {
        char color;
        int size;
    };

    struct {
        char manufacturer[20];
        float cost;
        union id description;
    } shirt, blouse;

    printf("%d\n", sizeof(union id));

    /* assign a value to color */
    shirt.description.color = 'w';
    printf("%c %d\n", shirt.description.color, shirt.description.size);

    /* assign a value to size */
    shirt.description.size = 12;
    printf("%c %d\n", shirt.description.color, shirt.description.size);
}
```

This program contains declarations similar to those shown in Example 11.34. Notice, however, that the first member of the union is now a single character rather than the 12-character array shown in the previous example. This change is made to simplify the assignment of appropriate values to the union members.

Following the declarations and the initial printf statement, we see that the character 'w' is assigned to the union member shirt.description.color. Note that the other union member, shirt.description.size, will not have a meaningful value. The values of both union members are then displayed.

We then assign the value 12 to `shirt.description.size`, thus overwriting the single character previously assigned to `shirt.description.color`. The values of both union members are then displayed once more.

Execution of the program results in the following output.

```
2
w -24713
@ 12
```

The first line indicates that the union is allocated two bytes of memory, to accommodate an integer quantity. In line 2, the first data item (w) is meaningful, but the second (-24713) is not. In line 3, the first data item (@) is meaningless, but the second data item (12) has meaning. Thus, each line of output contains one meaningful value, in accordance with the assignment statement preceding each `printf` statement.

A union variable can be initialized provided its storage class is either external or static. Remember, however, that *only one member of a union can be assigned a value at any one time*. Most compilers will accept an initial value for only one union member, and they will assign this value to the first member within the union.

EXAMPLE 11.36   Shown below is a simple C program that includes the assignment of initial values to a structure variable.

```c
#include <stdio.h>

main()

{
    union id  {
        char color[12];
        int size;
    };

    struct clothes {
        char manufacturer[20];
        float cost;
        union id description;
    };

    static struct clothes shirt = {"American", 25.00, "white"};

    printf("%d\n", sizeof(union id));
    printf("%s %5.2f ", shirt.manufacturer, shirt.cost);
    printf("%s %d\n", shirt.description.color, shirt.description.size);

    shirt.description.size = 12;
    printf("%s %5.2f ", shirt.manufacturer, shirt.cost);
    printf("%s %d\n", shirt.description.color, shirt.description.size);
}
```

Notice that `shirt` is a static structure variable of type `clothes`. One of its members is `description`, which is a union of type `id`. This union consists of two members: a 12-character array and an integer quantity.

The structure variable declaration includes the assignment of the following initial values: `"American"` is assigned to the array member `shirt.manufacturer`; 25.00 is assigned to the integer member `shirt.cost`, and `"white"` is assigned to the union member `shirt.description.color`. Notice that the second union member within the structure, i.e., `shirt.description.size`, remains unspecified.

The program first displays the size of the memory block allocated to the union, and the value of each member of `shirt`. Then 12 is assigned to `shirt.description.size`, and the value of each member of `shirt` is again displayed.

When the program is executed, the following output is generated.

```
12
American 25.00 white 26743
American 25.00 ~ 12
```

The first line indicates that 12 bytes of memory are allocated to the union, in order to accommodate the 12-character array. The second line shows the values initially assigned to `shirt.manufacturer`, `shirt.cost` and `shirt.description.color`. The value shown for `shirt.description.size` is meaningless. In the third line we see that `shirt.manufacturer` and `shirt.cost` are unchanged. Now, however, the reassignment of the union members causes `shirt.description.color` to have a meaningless value, but `shirt.description.size` shows the newly assigned value of 12.

   In all other respects, unions are processed in the same manner, and with the same restrictions, as structures. Thus, individual union members can be processed as though they were ordinary variables of the same data type, and pointers to unions can be passed to or from functions (by reference). Moreover, most C compilers permit an entire union to be assigned to another, provided both unions have the same composition. These compilers also permit entire unions to be passed to or from functions (by value), in accordance with the ANSI standard.

EXAMPLE 11.37 Raising a Number to a Power   This example is a bit contrived, though it does illustrate how a union can be used to pass information to a function. The problem is to raise a number to a power. Thus, we wish to evaluate the formula $y = x^n$, where x and y are floating-point values, and n can be either integer or floating point.

   If n is an integer, then y can be evaluated by multiplying x by itself an appropriate number of times. For example, the quantity x^3 could be expressed in terms of the product $(x)(x)(x)$. On the other hand, if n is a floating-point value, we can write $\log y = n \log x$, or $y = e^{(n \log x)}$. In the latter case x must be a positive quantity, since we cannot take the log of zero or a negative quantity.

   Now let us introduce the following declarations:

```
typedef  union  {
    float fexp;        /* floating-point exponent */
    int nexp;          /* integer exponent */
} nvals;

typedef  struct  {
float x;               /* value to be raised to a power */
    char flag;         /* 'f' if exponent is floating-point,
                          'i' if exponent is integer */
    nvals exp;         /* union containing exponent */
} values;

values a;
```

Thus, `nvals` is a user-defined union type, consisting of the floating-point member `fexp` and the integer member `nexp`. These two members represent the two possible types of exponents in the expression $y = x^n$. Similarly, `values` is a user-defined structure type, consisting of a floating-point member `x`, a character member `flag` and a union of type `nvals` called `exp`. Note that `flag` indicates the type of exponent currently represented by the union. If `flag` represents `'i'`, the union will represent an integer exponent (`nexp` will currently be assigned a value); and if `flag` represents `'f'`, the union will represent a floating-point exponent (`fexp` will currently be assigned a value). Finally, we see that `a` is a structure variable of type `values`.

   With these declarations, it is easy to write a function that will evaluate the formula $y = x^n$, as follows.

```
    float power(values a)      /* carry out the exponentiation */


    {
        int i;
        float y = a.x;

        if (a.flag == 'i')  {       /* integer exponent */
           if (a.exp.nexp == 0)
              y = 1.0;               /* zero exponent */
           else  {
              for (i = 1; i < abs(a.exp.nexp); ++i)
                 y *= a.x;
              if (a.exp.nexp < 0)
                 y = 1./y;           /* negative integer exponent */
           }
        }
        else                        /* floating-point exponent */
           y = exp(a.exp.fexp * log(a.x));

        return(y);
    }
```

This function accepts a structure variable (a) of type `values` as an argument. The method used to carry out the calculations depends on the value assigned to `a.flag`. If `a.flag` is assigned the character `'i'`, then the exponentiation is carried out by multiplying `a.x` by itself an appropriate number of times. Otherwise, the exponentiation is carried out using the formula $y = e^{(n \log x)}$. Notice that the function contains corrections to accommodate a zero exponent ($y = 1.0$), and for a negative integer exponent.

Let us add a `main` function which prompts for the values of x and n, determines whether or not n is an integer (by comparing n with its truncated value), assigns appropriate values to `a.flag` and `a.exp`, calls `power`, and then writes out the result. We also include a provision for generating an error message if n is a floating-point exponent and the value of x is less than or equal to zero.

Here is the entire program.

```
    /* program to raise a number to a power */

    #include <stdio.h>
    #include <math.h>

    typedef  union  {
        float fexp;            /* floating-point exponent */
        int nexp;              /* integer exponent */
    } nvals;

    typedef  struct  {
        float x;               /* value to be raised to a power */
        char flag;             /* 'f' if exponent is floating-point,
                                 'i' if exponent is integer */
        nvals exp;             /* union containing exponent */
    } values;

    float power(values a);     /* function prototype */
```

```
main()

{
    values a;                    /* structure containing x, flag and fexp/nexp */
    int i;
    float n, y;

    /* enter input data */
    printf("y = x^n\n\nEnter a value for x: ");
    scanf("%f", &a.x);
    printf("Enter a value for n: ");
    scanf("%f", &n);

    /* determine type of exponent */
    i = (int) n;
    a.flag = (i == n) ? 'i' : 'f';
    if (a.flag == 'i')
        a.exp.nexp = i;
    else
        a.exp.fexp = n;

    /* raise x to the appropriate power and display the result */
    if (a.flag == 'f' && a.x <= 0.0)   {
        printf("\nERROR - Cannot raise a non-positive number to a ");
        printf("floating-point power");
    }
    else  {
        y = power(a);
        printf("\ny = %.4f", y);
    }
}


float power(values a)      /* carry out the exponentiation */

{
    int i;
    float y = a.x;

    if (a.flag == 'i') {       /* integer exponent */
        if (a.exp.nexp == 0)
            y = 1.0;                /* zero exponent */
        else  {
            for (i = 1; i < abs(a.exp.nexp); ++i)
                y *= a.x;
            if (a.exp.nexp < 0)
                y = 1./y;           /* negative integer exponent */
        }
    }
    else                       /* floating-point exponent */
        y = exp(a.exp.fexp * log(a.x));

    return(y);
}
```

Notice that the union and structure declarations are external to the program functions, but the structure variable a is defined locally within each function.

The program does not execute repetitiously. Several typical dialogs, each representing a separate program execution, are shown below. As usual, the user's responses are underlined.

```
Enter a value for x: 2
Enter a value for n: 3

y = 8.0000

Enter a value for x: -2
Enter a value for n: 3

y = -8.0000

Enter a value for x: 2.2
Enter a value for n: 3.3

y = 13.4895

Enter a value for x: -2.2
Enter a value for n: 3.3

ERROR - cannot raise a non-positive number to a floating-point power
```

It should be pointed out that most C compilers include the library function pow, which is used to raise a number to a power. We have used pow in several earlier programming examples (see Examples 5.2, 5.4, 6.21, 8.13 and 10.30). The present program is not meant to replace pow; it is presented only to illustrate the use of a union in a representative programming situation.

Review Questions

11.1 What is a structure? How does a structure differ from an array?

11.2 What is a structure member? What is the relationship between a structure member and a structure?

11.3 Describe the syntax for defining the composition of a structure. Can individual members be initialized within a structure type declaration?

11.4 How can structure variables be declared? How do structure variable declarations differ from structure type declarations?

11.5 What is a tag? Must a tag be included in a structure type definition? Must a tag be included in a structure variable declaration? Explain fully.

11.6 Can a structure variable be defined as a member of another structure? Can an array be included as a member of a structure? Can an array have structures as elements?

11.7 How are the members of a structure variable assigned initial values? What restrictions apply to the structure's storage class when initial values are assigned?

11.8 How is an array of structures initialized?

11.9 What is the scope of a member name? What does this imply with respect to the naming of members within different structures?

11.10 How is a structure member accessed? How can a structure member be processed?

11.11 What is the precedence of the period (.) operator? What is its associativity?

11.12 Can the period operator be used with an array of structures? Explain.

11.13 What is the only operation that can be applied to an entire structure in some older versions of C? How is this rule modified in newer versions that conform to the current ANSI standard?

11.14 How can the size of a structure be determined? In what units is the size reported?

11.15 What is the purpose of the `typedef` feature? How is this feature used in conjuction with structures?

11.16 How is a structure-type pointer variable declared? To what does this type of variable point?

11.17 How can an individual structure member be accessed in terms of its corresponding pointer variable?

11.18 What is the precedence of the `->` operator? What is its associativity? Compare with the answers to question 11.11.

11.19 Suppose a pointer variable points to a structure that contains another structure as a member. How can a member of the embedded structure be accessed?

11.20 Suppose a pointer variable points to a structure that contains an array as a member. How can an element of the embedded array be accessed?

11.21 Suppose a member of a structure is a pointer variable. How can the object of the pointer be accessed, in terms of the structure variable name and the member name?

11.22 What happens when a pointer to a structure is incremented? What danger is associated with this type of operation?

11.23 How can an entire structure be passed to a function? Describe fully, both for older and newer versions of C.

11.24 How can an entire structure be returned from a function? Describe fully, both for older and newer versions of C.

11.25 What is a self-referential structure? For what kinds of applications are self-referential structures useful?

11.26 What is the basic idea behind a linked data structure? What advantages are there in the use of linked data structures?

11.27 Summarize several types of commonly used linked data structures.

11.28 What is a union? How does a union differ from a structure?

11.29 For what kinds of applications are unions useful?

11.30 In what sense can unions, structures and arrays be intermixed?

11.31 How is a union member accessed? How can a union member be processed? Compare with your answers to question 11.10.

11.32 How is a member of a union variable assigned an initial value? In what way does the initialization of a union variable differ from the initialization of a structure variable?

11.33 Summarize the rules that apply to processing unions. Compare with the rules that apply to processing structures.

Problems

11.34 Define a structure consisting of two floating-point members, called `real` and `imaginary`. Include the tag `complex` within the definition.

11.35 Declare the variables `x1`, `x2` and `x3` to be structures of type `complex`, as described in the preceding problem.

11.36 Combine the structure definition and the variable declarations described in Probs. 11.34 and 11.35 into one declaration.

11.37 Declare a variable `x` to be a structure variable of type `complex`, as described in Prob. 11.34. Assign the initial values 1.3 and −2.2 to the members `x.real` and `x.imaginary`, respectively.

11.38 Declare a pointer variable, `px`, which points to a structure of type `complex`, as described in Prob. 11.34. Write expressions for the structure members in terms of the pointer variable.

11.39 Declare a one-dimensional, 100-element array called `cx` whose elements are structures of type `complex`, as described in Prob. 11.34.

11.40 Combine the structure definition and the array declaration described in Probs. 11.34 and 11.39 into one declaration.

11.41 Suppose that `cx` is a one-dimensional, 100-element array of structures, as described in Prob. 11.39. Write expressions for the members of the 18*th* array element (i.e., element number 17).

11.42 Define a structure that contains the following three members:

    (*a*)   an integer quantity called `won`

    (*b*)   an integer quantity called `lost`

    (*c*)   a floating-point quantity called `percentage`

Include the user-defined data type `record` within the definition.

11.43 Define a structure that contains the following two members:

    (*a*)   a 40-element character array called `name`

    (*b*)   a structure named `stats`, of type `record`, as defined in Prob. 11.42

Include the user-defined data type `team` within the definition.

11.44 Declare a variable `t` to be a structure variable of type `team`, as described in Prob. 11.43. Write an expression for each member and submember of `t`.

11.45 Declare a variable `t` to be a structure variable of type `team`, as in the previous problem. Now, however, initialize `t` as follows.

```
name : Chicago Bears
won : 14
lost : 2
percentage : 87.5
```

11.46 Write a statement that will display the size of the memory block associated with the variable `t` which was described in Prob. 11.44.

11.47 Declare a pointer variable `pt`, which points to a structure of type `team`, as described in Prob. 11.43. Write an expression for each member and submember within the structure.

11.48 Declare a one-dimensional, 48-element array called `league` whose elements are structures of type `team`, as described in Prob. 11.43. Write expressions for the name and percentage of the 5th team in the league (i.e., team number 4).

11.49 Define a self-referential structure containing the following three members:

    (*a*)   a 40-element character array called `name`

    (*b*)   a structure named `stats`, of type `record`, as defined in Prob. 11.42

    (*c*)   a pointer to another structure of this same type, called `next`

Include the tag `team` within the structure definition. Compare your solution with that of Prob. 11.43.

11.50 Declare `pt` to be a pointer to a structure whose composition is described in the previous problem. Then write a statement that will allocate an appropriate block of memory, with `pt` pointing to the beginning of the memory block.

11.51 Define a structure of type `hms` containing three integer members, called `hour`, `minute` and `second`, respectively. Then define a union containing two members, each a structure of type `hms`. Call the union members `local` and `home`, respectively. Declare a pointer variable called `time` that points to this union.

11.52 Define a union of type `ans` which contains the following three members:

    (*a*)   an integer quantity called `ians`

    (*b*)   a floating-point quantity called `fans`

    (*c*)   a double-precision quantity called `dans`

Then define a structure which contains the following four members:

    (*a*)   a union of type `ans`, called `answer`

    (*b*)   a single character called `flag`

    (*c*)   integer quantities called `a` and `b`

Finally, declare two structure variables, called `x` and `y`, whose composition is as described above.

11.53 Declare a structure variable called `v` whose composition is as described in Prob. 11.52. Assign the following initial values within the declaration:

```
answer : 14
flag : 'i'
a : -2
b : 5
```

11.54 Modify the structure definition described in Prob. 11.52 so that it contains an additional member, called `next`, which is a pointer to another structure of the same type. (Note that the structure will now be self-referential.) Add a declaration of two variables, called x and px, where x is a structure variable and px is a pointer to a structure variable. Assign the starting address of x to px within the declaration.

11.55 Describe the output generated by each of the following programs. Explain any differences between the programs.

(*a*)
```c
#include <stdio.h>

typedef struct {
    char *a;
    char *b;
    char *c;
} colors;

void funct(colors sample);

main()
{
    static colors sample = {"red", "green", "blue"};

    printf("%s %s %s\n", sample.a, sample.b, sample.c);
    funct(sample);
    printf("%s %s %s\n", sample.a, sample.b, sample.c);
}

void funct(colors sample)
{
    sample.a = "cyan";
    sample.b = "magenta";
    sample.c = "yellow";
    printf("%s %s %s\n", sample.a, sample.b, sample.c);
    return;
}
```

(*b*)
```c
#include <stdio.h>

typedef struct {
    char *a;
    char *b;
    char *c;
} colors;

void funct(colors *pt);

main()
{
    static colors sample = {"red", "green", "blue"};

    printf("%s %s %s\n", sample.a, sample.b, sample.c);
    funct(&sample);
    printf("%s %s %s\n", sample.a, sample.b, sample.c);
}
```

```
            void funct(colors *pt)
            {
                pt->a = "cyan";
                pt->b = "magenta";
                pt->c = "yellow";
                printf("%s %s %s\n", pt->a, pt->b, pt->c);
                return;
            }
```

(c)   `#include <stdio.h>`

```
        typedef struct {
            char *a;
            char *b;
            char *c;
        } colors;

        colors funct(colors sample);

        main()
        {
            static colors sample = {"red", "green", "blue"};

            printf("%s %s %s\n", sample.a, sample.b, sample.c);
            sample = funct(sample);
            printf("%s %s %s\n", sample.a, sample.b, sample.c);
        }

        colors funct(colors sample)
        {
            sample.a = "cyan";
            sample.b = "magenta";
            sample.c = "yellow";
            printf("%s %s %s\n", sample.a, sample.b, sample.c);
            return(sample);
        }
```

11.56 Describe the output generated by the following program. Distinguish between meaninful and meaningless output.

```
        #include <stdio.h>

        main()
        {
            union {
                int i;
                float f;
                double d;
            } u;
            printf("%d\n", sizeof u);
            u.i = 100;
            printf("%d %f %f\n", u.i, u.f, u.d);
            u.f = 0.5;
            printf("%d %f %f\n", u.i, u.f, u.d);
            u.d = 0.0166667;
            printf("%d %f %f\n", u.i, u.f, u.d);
        }
```

11.57 Describe the output generated by the following programs. Explain any differences between them.

(a)
```c
#include <stdio.h>

typedef union {
    int i;
    float f;
} udef;

void funct(udef u);

main()
{
    udef u;

    u.i = 100;
    u.f = 0.5;
    funct(u);
    printf("%d %f\n", u.i, u.f);
}


void funct(udef u)
{
    u.i = 200;
    printf("%d %f\n", u.i, u.f);
    return;
}
```

(b)
```c
#include <stdio.h>

typedef union {
    int i;
    float f;
} udef;

void funct(udef u);

main()
{
    udef u;

    u.i = 100;
    u.f = 0.5;
    funct(u);
    printf("%d %f\n", u.i, u.f);
}


void funct(udef u)
{
    u.f = -0.3;
    printf("%d %f\n", u.i, u.f);
    return;
}
```

```
(c)     #include <stdio.h>

        typedef union {
            int i;
            float f;
        } udef;

        udef funct(udef u);

        main()
        {
            udef u;

            u.i = 100;
            u.f = 0.5;
            u = funct(u);
            printf("%d %f\n", u.i, u.f);
        }

        udef funct(udef u)
        {
            u.f = -0.3;
            printf("%d %f\n", u.i, u.f);
            return(u);
        }
```

Programming Problems

11.58 Answer the following questions as they pertain to your particular C compiler or interpreter.

    (*a*)   Can an entire structure variable (or union variable) be assigned to another structure (union) variable, provided both variables have the same composition?

    (*b*)   Can an entire structure variable (or union variable) be passed to a function as an argument?

    (*c*)   Can an entire structure variable (or union variable) be returned from a function to its calling routine?

    (*d*)   Can a pointer to a structure (or a union) be passed to a function as an argument?

    (*e*)   Can a pointer to a structure (or a union) be returned from a function to its calling routine?

11.59 Modify the program given in Example 11.26 (locating customer records) so that the function `search` returns a complete structure rather than a pointer to a structure. (Do not attempt this problem if your version of C does not support the return of entire structures from a function.)

11.60 Modify the billing program shown in Example 11.28 so that any of the following reports can be displayed:

    (*a*)   Status of all customers (now generated by the program)

    (*b*)   Status of overdue and delinquent customers only

    (*c*)   Status of delinquent customers only

Include a provision for generating a menu when the program is executed, from which the user may choose which report will be generated. Have the program return to the menu after printing each report, thus allowing for the possibility of generating several different reports.

11.61 Modify the billing program shown in Example 11.28 so that the structure of type `record` now includes a union containing the members `office_address` and `home_address`. Each union member should itself be a structure consisting of two 80-character arrays, called `street` and `city`, respectively. Add another member to the primary structure (of type `record`), which is a single character called `flag`. This member should be assigned a character (e.g., `'o'` or `'h'`) to indicate which type of address is currently stored in the union.

    Modify the remainder of the program so that the user is asked which type of address will be supplied for each customer. Then display the appropriate address, with a corresponding label, along with the rest of the output.

11.62 Modify the program given in Example 11.37 so that a number raised to a floating-point power can be executed in either single precision or double precision, as specified by the user in response to a prompt. The union type nvals should now contain a third member, which should be a double-precision quantity called dexp.

11.63 Rewrite each of the following C programs so that it makes use of structure variables.

(*a*) The depreciation program presented in Example 7.20.
(*b*) The program given in Example 10.28 for displaying the day of the year
(*c*) The program for determining the future value of monthly deposits, given in Example 10.31

11.64 Modify the piglatin generator presented in Example 9.14 so that it will accept multiple lines of text. Represent each line of text with a separate structure. Include the following three members within each structure:

(*a*) The original line of text
(*b*) The number of words within the line
(*c*) The modified line of text (i.e., the piglatin equivalent of the original text)

Include the enhancements described in Prob. 9.36 (i.e., provisions for punctuation marks, uppercase letters and double-letter sounds).

11.65 Write a C program that reads several different names and addresses into the computer, rearranges the names into alphabetical order, and then writes out the alphabetized list. (See Examples 9.20 and 10.26.) Make use of structure variables within the program.

11.66 For each of the following programming problems described in earlier chapters, write a complete C program that makes use of structure variables.

(*a*) The student exam score averaging problem described in Prob. 9.40.
(*b*) The more comprehensive version of the student exam score averaging problem described in Prob. 9.42.
(*c*) The problem that matches the names of countries with their corresponding capitals, described in Prob. 9.46.
(*d*) The text encoding-decoding problem as described in Prob. 9.49, but extended to accommodate multiple lines of text.

11.67 Write a C program that will accept the following information for each team in a baseball or a football league.

1. Team name, including the city (e.g., Pittsburgh Steelers)
2. Number of wins
3. Number of losses

For a baseball team, add the following information:

4. Number of hits
5. Number of runs
6. Number of errors
7. Number of extra-inning games

Similarly, add the following information for a football team:

4. Number of ties
5. Number of touchdowns
6. Number of field goals
7. Number of turnovers
8. Total yards gained (season total)
9. Total yards given up to opponents

Enter this information for all of the teams in the league. Then reorder and print the list of teams according to their win-lose records, using the reordering techniques described in Examples 9.13 and 10.16 (see also Examples 9.21 and 10.26). Store the information in an array of structures, where each array element (i.e., each structure) contains the information for a single team. Make use of a union to represent the variable information (either baseball or football) that is included as a part of the structure. This union should itself contain two structures, one for baseball-related statistics and the other for football-related statistics.

Test the program using a current set of league statistics. (Ideally, the program should be tested using both baseball and football statistics.)

11.68   Modify the program given in Example 11.32 so that it makes use of each of the following linked structures.

    (*a*)   A linear linked list with two sets of pointers: one set pointing in the forward direction, the other pointing backwards.

    (*b*)   A circular linked list. Be sure to include a pointer to identify the beginning of the circular list.

11.69   Modify the program given in Example 11.32 so that each node contains the following information:

    (*a*)   Name
    (*b*)   Street address
    (*c*)   City/State/ZIP code
    (*d*)   Account number
    (*e*)   Account status (a single character indicating current, overdue or delinquent status)

11.70   Write a complete C program that will allow you to enter and maintain a computerized version of your family tree. Begin by specifying the number of generations (i.e., the number of levels within the tree). Then enter the names and nationalities in a hierarchical fashion, beginning with your own name and nationality. Include capabilities for modifying the tree and for adding new names (new nodes) to the tree. Also, include a provision for displaying the entire tree automatically after each update.

    Test the program, including at least three generations if possible (you, your parents and your grandparents). Obviously, the tree becomes more interesting as the number of generations increases.

11.71   An RPN calculator utilizes a scheme whereby each new numerical value is followed by the operation that is to be performed between the new value and its predecessor. (RPN stands for "reverse Polish notation.") Thus, adding two numbers, say 3.3 and 4.8, would require the following keystrokes:

```
3.3  <enter>
4.8  +
```

The sum, 8.1, would then be displayed in the calculator's single visible register.

    RPN calculators make use of a *stack*, typically containing four registers (four components), as illustrated in Fig. 11.7. Each new number is entered into the *X* register, causing all previously entered values to be pushed up in the stack. If the top register (i.e., the *T* register) was previously occupied, then the old number will be lost (it will be overwritten by the value that is pushed up from the *Z* register).

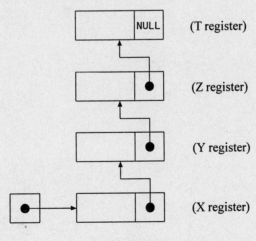

Fig. 11.7

    Arithmetic operations are always carried out between the numbers in the *X* and *Y* registers. The result of such an operation will always be displayed in the *X* register, causing everything in the upper registers to drop down one level (thus "popping" the stack). This procedure is illustrated in Fig. 11.8(*a*) to (*c*) for the addition of the values 3.3 and 4.8, as described above.

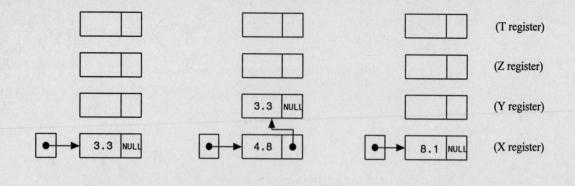

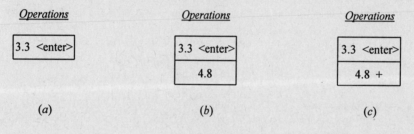

Fig. 11.8

Write an interactive C program that will simulate an RPN calculator. Display the contents of the stack after each operation, as in Fig. 11.8(a) to (c). Include a provision for carrying out each of the following operations.

Operation	Keystrokes
enter new data	(value) <enter>
addition	(value) +
subtraction	(value) –
multiplication	(value) *
division	(value) /

Test the program using any numerical data of your choice.

Chapter 12

Data Files

Many applications require that information be written to or read from an auxiliary memory device. Such information is stored on the memory device in the form of a *data file*. Thus, data files allow us to store information permanently, and to access and alter that information whenever necessary.

In C, an extensive set of library functions is available for creating and processing data files. Unlike other programming languages, C does not distinguish between sequential and direct access (random access) data files. However, there are two different types of data files, called *stream-oriented* (or *standard*) data files, and *system-oriented* (or *low-level*) data files. Stream-oriented data files are generally easier to work with and are therefore more commonly used.

Stream-oriented data files can be subdivided into two categories. In the first category are *text* files, consisting of consecutive characters. These characters can be interpreted as individual data items, or as components of strings or numbers. The manner in which these characters are interpreted is determined either by the particular library functions used to transfer the information, or by format specifications within the library functions, as in the scanf and printf functions discussed in Chap. 4.

The second category of stream-oriented data files, often referred to as *unformatted* data files, organizes data into blocks containing contiguous bytes of information. These blocks represent more complex data structures, such as arrays and structures. A separate set of library functions is available for processing stream-oriented data files of this type. These library functions provide single instructions that can transfer entire arrays or structures to or from data files.

System-oriented data files are more closely related to the computer's operating system than stream-oriented data files. They are somewhat more complicated to work with, though their use may be more efficient for certain kinds of applications. A separate set of procedures, with accompanying library functions, is required to process system-oriented data files.

This chapter is concerned only with stream-oriented data files. The overall approach is relatively standardized, though the details may vary from one version of C to another. Thus, the examples presented in this chapter may not apply to all versions of the language in exactly the manner shown. Nevertheless, readers should have little difficulty in relating this material to their particular version of C.

12.1 OPENING AND CLOSING A DATA FILE

When working with a stream-oriented data file, the first step is to establish a *buffer area*, where information is temporarily stored while being transferred between the computer's memory and the data file. This buffer area allows information to be read from or written to the data file more rapidly than would otherwise be possible. The buffer area is established by writing

    FILE *ptvar;

where FILE (uppercase letters required) is a special structure type that establishes the buffer area, and *ptvar* is a pointer variable that indicates the beginning of the buffer area. The structure type FILE is defined within a system include file, typically stdio.h. The pointer *ptvar* is often referred to as a *stream pointer*, or simply a *stream*.

A data file must be *opened* before it can be created or processed. This associates the file name with the buffer area (i.e., with the stream). It also specifies how the data file will be utilized, i.e., as a read-only file, a write-only file, or a read/write file, in which both operations are permitted.

The library function fopen is used to open a file. This function is typically written as

> *ptvar* = fopen(*file-name*, *file-type*);

where *file-name* and *file-type* are strings that represent the name of the data file and the manner in which the data file will be utilized. The name chosen for the *file-name* must be consistent with the rules for naming files, as determined by the computer's operating system. The *file-type* must be one of the strings shown in Table 12-1.

Table 12-1   File-Type Specifications

File-Type	*Meaning*
"r"	Open an existing file for reading only.
"w"	Open a new file for writing only. If a file with the specified *file-name* currently exists, it will be destroyed and a new file created in its place.
"a"	Open an existing file for appending (i.e., for adding new information at the end of the file). A new file will be created if the file with the specified *file-name* does not exist.
"r+"	Open an existing file for both reading and writing.
"w+"	Open a new file for both reading and writing. If a file with the specified *file-name* currently exists, it will be destroyed and a new file created in its place.
"a+"	Open an existing file for both reading and appending. A new file will be created if the file with the specified *file-name* does not exist.

The fopen function returns a pointer to the beginning of the buffer area associated with the file. A NULL value is returned if the file cannot be opened as, for example, when an existing data file cannot be found.

Finally, a data file must be *closed* at the end of the program. This can be accomplished with the library function fclose. The syntax is simply

> fclose(*ptvar*);

It is good programming practice to close a data file explicitly using the fclose function, though most C compilers will automatically close a data file at the end of program execution if a call to fclose is not present.

EXAMPLE 12.1   A C program contains the following statements.

```
#include <stdio.h>

FILE *fpt;

fpt = fopen("sample.dat", "w");

. . . . .

fclose(fpt);
```

The first statement causes the header file stdio.h to be included in the program. The second statement defines a pointer called fpt which will point to a structure of type FILE, indicating the beginning of the data-file buffer area. Note that FILE is defined in stdio.h.

The third statement opens a new data file called sample.dat as a write-only file. Moreover, the fopen function returns a pointer to the beginning of the buffer area and assigns it to the pointer variable fpt. Thus, fpt points to the buffer area associated with the data file sample.dat. All subsequent file processing statements (which are not shown explicitly in this example) will access the data file via the pointer variable fpt rather than by the file name.

Finally, the last statement closes the data file. Note that the argument is the pointer variable fpt, not the file name sample.dat.

The value returned by the fopen function can be used to generate an error message if a data file cannot be opened, as illustrated in the next example.

EXAMPLE 12.2   A C program contains the following statements.

```
#include <stdio.h>
#define  NULL  0

main()
{
    FILE *fpt;

    fpt = fopen("sample.dat", "r+");

    if (fpt == NULL)
        printf("\nERROR - Cannot open the designated file\n");
    else  {

        . . . . .

        fclose (fpt);
    }
}
```

This program attempts to open an existing data file called sample.dat for both reading and writing. An error message will be generated if this data file cannot be found. Otherwise the data file will be opened and processed, as indicated.

The fopen and the if statments are often combined, as follows.

```
    if ((fpt = fopen("sample.dat", "r+")) == NULL)
        printf("\nERROR - Cannot open the designated file\n");
```

Either method is acceptable.

12.2 CREATING A DATA FILE

A data file must be created before it can be processed. A *stream-oriented* data file can be created in two ways. One is to create the file directly, using a text editor or a word processor. The other is to write a program that enters information into the computer and then writes it out to the data file. *Unformatted* data files can only be created with such specially written programs.

When creating a new data file with a specially written program, the usual approach is to enter the information from the keyboard and then write it out to the data file. If the data file consists of individual characters, the library functions getchar and putc can be used to enter the data from the keyboard and to write it out to the data file. We have already discussed the use of getchar in Sec. 4.2. The putc function is new, though its use is analogous to putchar, which we discussed in Sec. 4.3.

EXAMPLE 12.3 Creating a Data File (Lowercase to Uppercase Text Conversion)   Here is a variation of several earlier programs, which read a line of lowercase text into the computer and write it out in uppercase (see Examples 4.4, 6.9, 6.12, 6.16 and 9.2). In this example we will read the text into the computer on a character-by-character basis using the getchar function, and then write it out to a data file using putc. The lowercase to uppercase conversion will be carried out by the library function toupper, as before.

The program begins by defining the stream pointer fpt, indicating the beginning of the data-file buffer area. A new data file, called sample.dat, is then opened for writing only. Next, a do - while loop reads a series of characters from the keyboard and writes their uppercase equivalents to the data file. The putc function is used to write each character to the data file. Notice that putc requires specification of the stream pointer fpt as an argument.

The loop continues as long as a newline character ('\n') is not entered from the keyboard. Once a newline character is detected, the loop ceases and the data file is closed.

```c
/* read a line of lowercase text and store in uppercase within a data file */

#include <stdio.h>
#include <ctype.h>

main()
{
    FILE *fpt;    /* define a pointer to predefined structure type FILE */

    char c;

    /* open a new data file for writing only */
    fpt = fopen("sample.dat", "w");

    /* read each character and write its uppercase equivalent to the data file */
    do
        putc(toupper(c = getchar()), fpt);
    while (c != '\n');

    /* close the data file */
    fclose(fpt);
}
```

After the program has been executed, the data file `sample.dat` will contain an uppercase equivalent of the line of text entered into the computer from the keyboard. For example, if the original line of text had been

```
We, the people of the United States
```

the data file would contain the text

```
WE, THE PEOPLE OF THE UNITED STATES
```

A data file that has been created in this manner can be viewed in several different ways. For example, the data file can be viewed directly, using an operating system command such as `print` or `type`. The data file can also be examined using a text editor or a word processor.

Another approach is to write a program that will read the data file and display its contents. Such a program will, in a sense, be a mirror image of the one described above; i.e., the library function `getc` will read the individual characters from the data file, and `putchar` will display them on the screen. This is a more complicated way to display a data file but it offers a great deal of flexibility, since the individual data items can be processed as they are read.

EXAMPLE 12.4 Reading a Data File   The following program will read a line of text from a data file on a character-by-character basis, and display the text on the screen. The program makes use of the library functions `getc` and `putchar` (see Sec. 4.3) to read and display the data. It complements the program presented in Example 12.3.

The logic is directly analogous to that of the program shown in Example 12.3. However, this program opens the data file `sample.dat` as a read-only file, whereas the previous program opened `sample.dat` as a write-only file. An error message is generated if `sample.dat` cannot be opened. Also, notice that `getc` requires the stream pointer `fpt` to be specified as an argument.

```c
/* read a line of text from a data file and display it on the screen */

#include <stdio.h>

#define  NULL  0
```

```
    main()

    {

        FILE *fpt;    /* define a pointer to predefined structure type FILE */

        char c;

        if ((fpt = fopen("sample.dat", "r")) == NULL)
            /* open the data file for reading only */
            printf("\nERROR - Cannot open the designated file\n");

        else    /* read and display each character from the data file */
            do
                putchar(c = getc(fpt));
            while (c != '\n');

        /* close the data file */
        fclose(fpt);
    }
```

Data files consisting entirely of strings can often be created and read more easily with programs that utilize special string-oriented library functions. Some commonly used functions of this type are gets, puts, fgets and fputs. The functions gets and puts read or write strings to or from the standard output devices, whereas fgets and fputs exchange strings with data files. Since the use of these functions is straightforward, we will not pursue this topic further. You may wish to experiment with these functions, however, by reprogramming some of the character-oriented read/write programs presented earlier.

Many data files consist of complex data structures, such as structures that contain various combinations of numeric and character information. Such data files can be processed using the library functions fscanf and fprintf, which are analogous to the functions scanf and printf discussed in Chap. 4 (see Secs. 4.4 and 4.6). Thus, the fscanf function permits formatted data to be read from a data file associated with a particular stream, and fprintf permits formatted data to be written to the data file. The actual format specifications are the same as those used with the scanf and printf functions.

EXAMPLE 12.5 Creating a File Containing Customer Records   The last chapter presented three programs that supposedly were used to create and update customer records (see Examples 11.14 and 11.28). When describing the programs we remarked that the examples were unrealistic, because data files should be used for applications of this type. We now turn our attention to a program that creates such a data file for a series of customer records whose composition is as follows.

```
    typedef struct  {
        int month;
        int day;
        int year;
    } date;

    typedef struct  {
        char name[80];
        char street[80];
        char city[80];
        int acct_no;
        char acct_type;
        float oldbalance;
        float newbalance;
        float payment;
        struct date lastpayment;
    } record;
```

The overall strategy will be to provide the current date, and then enter a loop that will process a series of customer records.   For each customer, the customer's name, street, city, account number (acct_no) and initial balance (oldbalance) will be read into the computer.   An initial value of 0 will then be assigned to the structure members newbalance and payment, the character 'C' will be assigned to acct_type (indicating a current status), and the current date assigned to lastpayment. Each customer record will then be written to a write-only data file called records.dat.

The procedure will continue until a customer name is encountered whose first three characters are END (in either upper- or lowercase). When END is encountered, it will be written to the data file, indicating an end-of-file condition.

Here is the complete C program.

```
/* create a data file containing customer records */

#include <stdio.h>
#include <string.h>

#define  TRUE  1

typedef struct  {
    int month;
    int day;
    int year;
}  date;

typedef struct  {
    char name[80];
    char street[80];
    char city[80];
    int acct_no;                      /* (positive integer) */
    char acct_type;                   /* C (current), O (overdue), or D (delinquent) */
    float oldbalance;                 /* (nonnegative quantity) */
    float newbalance;                 /* (nonnegative quantity) */
    float payment;                    /* (nonnegative quantity) */
    date lastpayment;
}  record;

record readscreen(record customer);   /* function prototype */
void writefile(record customer);      /* function prototype */

FILE *fpt;                            /* pointer to predefined structure FILE */

main()
{
    int flag = TRUE;                  /* variable declaration */
    record customer;                  /* structure variable declaration */

    /* open a new data file for writing only */
    fpt = fopen("records.dat", "w");

    /* enter date and assign initial values */
    printf("CUSTOMER BILLING SYSTEM - INITIALIZATION\n\n");
    printf("Please enter today\'s date (mm/dd/yyyy): ");
    scanf("%d/%d/%d", &customer.lastpayment.month,
                      &customer.lastpayment.day,
                      &customer.lastpayment.year);
    customer.newbalance = 0;
    customer.payment = 0;
    customer.acct_type = 'C';
```

```
        /* main loop */
        while (flag)  {
                        /* enter customer's name and write to data file */
                        printf("\nName (enter \'END\' when finished): ");
                        scanf(" %[^\n]", customer.name);
                        fprintf(fpt, "\n%s\n", customer.name);

                        /* test for stopping condition */
                        if (strcmp(customer.name, "END") == 0)
                           break;

                        customer = readscreen(customer);
                        writefile(customer);
        }

        fclose(fpt);
}


record readscreen(record customer)      /* read remaining data */

{
    printf("Street: ");
    scanf(" %[^\n]", customer.street);
    printf("City: ");
    scanf(" %[^\n]", customer.city);
    printf("Account number: ");
    scanf("%d", &customer.acct_no);
    printf("Current balance: ");
    scanf("%f", &customer.oldbalance);
    return(customer);
}


void writefile(record customer)      /* write remaining data to a data file */

{
    fprintf(fpt, "%s\n", customer.street);
    fprintf(fpt, "%s\n", customer.city);
    fprintf(fpt, "%d\n", customer.acct_no);
    fprintf(fpt, "%c\n", customer.acct_type);
    fprintf(fpt, "%.2f\n", customer.oldbalance);
    fprintf(fpt, "%.2f\n", customer.newbalance);
    fprintf(fpt, "%.2f\n", customer.payment);
    fprintf(fpt, "%d/%d/%d\n", customer.lastpayment.month,
                            customer.lastpayment.day,
                            customer.lastpayment.year);
    return;
}
```

The program begins by defining the composition of each customer record and the stream pointer fpt. Within main, a new data file, called records.dat, is then opened for writing only. Next, the program prompts for the current date, and initial values are assigned to the structure members newbalance, payment and acct_type.

The program then enters a while loop, which prompts for a customer name and writes the name to the data file. Next, the program tests to see if the name that has been entered is END (upper- or lowercase). If so, the program breaks out of the loop, the data file is closed, and the computation terminates. Otherwise, the remaining information for the current customer is entered via function readscreen, and then written to the data file via function writefile.

Within `main` and `readscreen` we see that the various data items are entered interactively, using the familiar formatted `printf` and `scanf` functions. On the other hand, within `main` and `writefile` the data are written to the data file via the `fprintf` function. The syntax governing the use of this function is the same as the syntax used with `printf`, except that a stream pointer must be included as an additional argument. Notice that the control string makes use of the same character groups (i.e., the same formatting features) as the `printf` function described in Chap. 4.

When the program is executed, the information for each customer record is entered interactively, as shown below for four fictitious customers. As usual, the user's responses are underlined.

```
CUSTOMER BILLING SYSTEM - INITIALIZATION

Please enter today's date (mm/dd/yyyy): 5/24/1998

Name (enter 'END' when finished): Steve Johnson
Street: 123 Mountainview Drive
City: Denver, CO
Account number: 4208
Current Balance: 247.88

Name (enter 'END' when finished): Susan Richards
Street: 4383 Alligator Blvd
City: Fort Lauderdale, FL
Account number: 2219
Current Balance: 135.00

Name (enter 'END' when finished): Martin Peterson
Street: 1787 Pacific Parkway
City: San Diego, CA
Account number: 8452
Current Balance: 387.42

Name (enter 'END' when finished): Phyllis Smith
Street: 1000 Great White Way
City: New York, NY
Account number: 711
Current Balance: 260.00


Name (enter 'END' when finished): END
```

After the program has been executed, the data file `records.dat` will have been created, containing the following information.

```
Steve Johnson
123 Mountainview Drive
Denver, CO
4208
C
247.88
0.00
0.00
5/24/1998
```

```
Susan Richards
4383 Alligator Blvd
Beechview, OH
2219
C
135.00
0.00
0.00
5/24/1998

Martin Peterson
1787 Pacific Parkway
San Diego, CA
8452
C
387.42
0.00
0.00
5/24/1998

Phyllis Smith
1000 Great White Way
New York, NY
711
C
260.00
0.00
0.00
5/24/1998

END
```

In the next section we will see a program that updates the information contained in this file.

12.3 PROCESSING A DATA FILE

Most data file applications require that a data file be altered as it is being processed. For example, in an application involving the processing of customer records, it may be desirable to add new records to the file (either at the end of the file or interspersed among the existing records), to delete existing records, to modify the contents of existing records, or to rearrange the records. These requirements in turn suggest several different computational strategies.

Consider, for example, the problem of updating the records within a data file. There are several approaches to this problem. Perhaps the most obvious approach is to read each record from a data file, update the record as required, and then write the updated record to the same data file. However, there are some problems with this strategy. In particular, it is difficult to read and write formatted data to the same data file without disrupting the arrangement of the data items within the file. Moreover, the original set of records may become inaccessible if something goes wrong during the program execution.

Another approach is to work with two different data files — an old file (a *source*) and a new file. Each record is read from the old file, updated as necessary, and then written to the new file. When all of the records have been updated, the old file is deleted or placed into archival storage and the new file renamed. Hence, the new file will become the source for the next round of updates.

Historically, the origin of this method goes back to the early days of computing, when data files were maintained on magnetic tapes. The method is still used, however, because it provides a series of old source files that can be used to generate a customer history. The most recent source file can also be used to recreate the current file if the current file is damaged or destroyed.

EXAMPLE 12.6 Updating a File Containing Customer Records   Example 12.5 presents a program to create a data file called records.dat that contains customer records. We now present a program to update the records within this data file. The program will make use of the two-file update procedure described above. Hence, we will assume that the previously created data file records.dat has been renamed records.old. This will be the source file.

Our overall strategy will be similar to that described in Example 12.5. That is, we will first provide the current date, and then enter a loop that will read a series of customer records from records.old, and write the corresponding updated records to a new data file called records.new. Each pass through the loop will read one record, update it if necessary, and then write the record to records.new. By following this procedure, all of the records will be written to records.new, whether updated or not.

The procedure will continue until the customer name END has been read from the source file (in either upper- or lowercase). Once this happens, END will be written to the new data file, indicating an end-of-file condition.

The complete program is given below. The program begins by defining the composition of each customer record, using the same definitions presented in Example 12.5. These definitions are followed by definitions of the stream pointers ptold and ptnew.

Within the main function, records.old is opened as an existing read-only file, and records.new is opened as a new write-only file. An error message is generated if records.old cannot be opened. Otherwise, the program enters a while loop that reads successive customer records from records.old (actually, from stream ptold), updates each record as required, and writes each record to records.new (to stream ptnew).

```
/* update a data file containing customer records */

#include <stdio.h>
#include <string.h>

#define  NULL  0
#define  TRUE  1

typedef struct  {
    int month;
    int day;
    int year;
}  date;

typedef struct  {
    char name[80];
    char street[80];
    char city[80];
    int acct_no;                      /* (positive integer) */
    char acct_type;                   /* C (current), O (overdue), or D (delinquent) */
    float oldbalance;                 /* (nonnegative quantity) */
    float newbalance;                 /* (nonnegative quantity) */
    float payment;                    /* (nonnegative quantity) */
    date lastpayment;
}  record;

record readfile(record customer);     /* function prototype */
record update(record customer);       /* function prototype */
void writefile(record customer);      /* function prototype */

FILE *ptold, *ptnew;                  /* pointers to predefined structure FILE */
int month, day, year;                 /* global variable declarations */
```

```
    main()

    {
    int flag = TRUE;                    /* local variable declaration */
        record customer;                /* structure variable declaration */

        /* open data files */
        if ((ptold = fopen("records.old", "r")) == NULL)
           printf("\nERROR - Cannot open the designated read file\n");
        else   {
           ptnew = fopen("records.new", "w");

           /* enter current date */
           printf("CUSTOMER BILLING SYSTEM - UPDATE\n\n");
           printf("Please enter today\'s date (mm/dd/yyyy): ");
           scanf("%d/%d/%d", &month, &day, &year);

           /* main loop */
           while (flag)  {
                /* read a name from old data file and write to new data file */
                fscanf(ptold, " %[^\n]", customer.name);
                fprintf(ptnew, "\n%s\n", customer.name);

                /* test for stopping condition */
                if (strcmp(customer.name, "END") == 0)
                   break;

                /* read remaining data from old data file */
                customer = readfile(customer);

                /* prompt for updated information */
                customer = update(customer);

                /* write updated information to new data file */
                writefile(customer);
           }
           fclose(ptold);
           fclose(ptnew);
        }  /* end else */
    }


    record readfile(record customer)   /* read remaining data from the old data file */

    {
        fscanf(ptold, " %[^\n]", customer.street);
        fscanf(ptold, " %[^\n]", customer.city);
        fscanf(ptold, " %d", &customer.acct_no);
        fscanf(ptold, " %c", &customer.acct_type);
        fscanf(ptold, " %f", &customer.oldbalance);
        fscanf(ptold, " %f", &customer.newbalance);
        fscanf(ptold, " %f", &customer.payment);
        fscanf(ptold, " %d/%d/%d", &customer.lastpayment.month,
                                   &customer.lastpayment.day,
                                   &customer.lastpayment.year);

        return(customer);
    }
```

```
record update(record customer)   /* prompt for new information, update records and    '
                                                          display summary data */


{
    printf("\n\nName:   %s", customer.name);
    printf("     Account number: %d\n", customer.acct_no);
    printf("\nOld balance: %7.2f", customer.oldbalance);
    printf("   Current payment: ");
    scanf("%f", &customer.payment);

    if (customer.payment > 0)   {
       customer.lastpayment.month = month;
       customer.lastpayment.day = day;
       customer.lastpayment.year = year;
       customer.acct_type = (customer.payment < 0.1 * customer.oldbalance) ? 'O' : 'C';
    }
    else
       customer.acct_type = (customer.oldbalance > 0) ? 'D' : 'C';

    customer.newbalance = customer.oldbalance - customer.payment;
    printf("New balance: %7.2f", customer.newbalance);

    printf("    Account status: ");
    switch (customer.acct_type)   {
       case 'C':
                 printf("CURRENT\n");
                 break;
       case 'O':
                 printf("OVERDUE\n");
                 break;
       case 'D':
                 printf("DELINQUENT\n");
                 break;
       default:
                 printf("ERROR\n");
    }

    return(customer);
}


void writefile(record customer)   /* write updated information to the new data file */


{
    fprintf(ptnew, "%s\n", customer.street);
    fprintf(ptnew, "%s\n", customer.city);
    fprintf(ptnew, "%d\n", customer.acct_no);
    fprintf(ptnew, "%c\n", customer.acct_type);
    fprintf(ptnew, "%.2f\n", customer.oldbalance);
    fprintf(ptnew, "%.2f\n", customer.newbalance);
    fprintf(ptnew, "%.2f\n", customer.payment);
    fprintf(ptnew, "%d/%d/%d\n", customer.lastpayment.month,
                                 customer.lastpayment.day,
                                 customer.lastpayment.year);
    return;
}
```

Each customer name is read from the source file and then written to the new file within main. The remaining information for each record is then read from the source file, updated, and written to the new file within the functions readfile, update, and writefile, respectively. This process continues until a record is encountered containing the customer name END, as discussed above. Both data files are then closed, and the computation terminates.

The function readfile reads additional information for each customer record from the source file. The various data items are represented as members of the structure variable customer. This structure variable is passed to the function as an argument. The library function fscanf is used to read each data item, using a syntax that is essentially identical to that used with the scanf function, as described in Chap. 4. With fscanf, however, the stream pointer ptold must be included as an additional argument within each function call. Once all of the information has been read from the source file, the customer record is returned to main.

The function update is similar, though it requires that a value for customer.payment be entered from the keyboard. Additional information is then assigned to customer.lastpayment, customer.acct_type and customer.newbalance. The values assigned depend on the value provided for customer.payment. The updated record is then returned to main.

The remaining function, writefile, simply accepts each customer record as an argument and writes it to the new data file. Within writefile, the library function fprintf is used to transfer the information to the new data file, using the same procedures shown in Example 12.5.

When the program is executed, the name, account number and old balance are displayed for each customer. The user is then prompted for a value for the current payment. Once this value has been entered, the customer's new balance and current account status are shown.

A typical interactive session, based upon the data file created in Example 12.5, is shown below. The user's responses are underlined, as usual.

```
CUSTOMER BILLING SYSTEM - UPDATE

Please enter today's date (mm/dd/yyyy): 12/29/1998

Name:   Steve Johnson     Account number: 4208

Old balance:  247.88    Current payment: 25.00
New balance:  222.88    Account status: CURRENT


Name:   Susan Richards    Account number: 2219

Old balance:  135.00    Current payment: 135.00
New balance:    0.00    Account status: CURRENT


Name:   Martin Peterson    Account number: 8452

Old balance:  387.42    Current payment: 35.00
New balance:  352.42    Account status: OVERDUE


Name:   Phyllis Smith     Account number: 711

Old balance:  260.00    Current payment: 0
New balance:  260.00    Account status: DELINQUENT
```

After all of the customer records have been processed the new data file records.new will have been created, containing the following information.

```
      Steve Johnson
      123 Mountainview Drive
      Denver, CO
      4208
      C
      247.88
      222.88
      25.00
      12/29/1998

      Susan Richards
      4383 Alligator Blvd
      Fort Lauderdale, FL
      2219
      C
      135.00
      0.00
      135.00
      12/29/1998

      Martin Peterson
      1787 Pacific Parkway
      San Diego, CA
      8452
      O
      387.42
      352.42
      35.00
      12/29/1998

      Phyllis Smith
      1000 Great White Way
      New York, NY
      711
      D
      260.00
      260.00
      0.00
      5/24/1998

      END
```

Note that the old data file, records.old, is still available in its original form; hence, it can be stored for archival purposes. Before this program can be run again, however, the new data file will have to be renamed records.old. (Usually, this is done at the operating system level, before entering the update program.)

12.4 UNFORMATTED DATA FILES

Some applications involve the use of data files to store blocks of data, where each block consists of a fixed number of contiguous bytes. Each block will generally represent a complex data structure, such as a structure or an array. For example, a data file may consist of multiple structures having the same composition, or it may contain multiple arrays of the same type and size. For such applications it may be desirable to read the entire block from the data file, or write the entire block to the data file, rather than reading or writing the individual components (i.e., structure members or array elements) within each block separately.

The library functions `fread` and `fwrite` are intended to be used in situations of this type. These functions are often referred to as *unformatted* read and write functions. Similarly, data files of this type are often referred to as unformatted data files.

Each of these functions requires four arguments: a pointer to the data block, the size of the data block, the number of data blocks being transferred, and the stream pointer. Thus, a typical `fwrite` function might be written as

```
fwrite(&customer, sizeof(record), 1, fpt);
```

where `customer` is a structure variable of type `record`, and `fpt` is the stream pointer associated with a data file that has been opened for output.

EXAMPLE 12.7 Creating an Unformatted Data File Containing Customer Records   Consider a variation of the program presented in Example 12.5, for creating a data file containing customer records. Now, however, we will write each customer record to the data file `data.bin` as a single, unformatted block of information. This is in contrast to the earlier program, where we wrote the items within each record (i.e., the individual structure members) as separate, formatted data items.

Here is the complete program.

```c
/* create an unformatted data file containing customer records */

#include <stdio.h>
#include <string.h>

#define  TRUE   1

typedef struct  {
    int month;
    int day;
    int year;
}  date;

typedef struct  {
    char name[80];
    char street[80];
    char city[80];
    int acct_no;                        /* (positive integer) */
    char acct_type;                     /* C (current), O (overdue), or D (delinquent) */
    float oldbalance;                   /* (nonnegative quantity) */
    float newbalance;                   /* (nonnegative quantity) */
    float payment;                      /* (nonnegative quantity) */
    date lastpayment;
}  record;

record readscreen(record customer);     /* function prototype */

FILE *fpt;                              /* pointer to predefined structure FILE */


main()

{
    int flag = TRUE;                    /* variable declaration */
    record customer;                    /* structure variable declaration */
```

```
        /* open a new data file for writing only */
        fpt = fopen("data.bin", "w");

        /* enter date and assign initial values */
        printf("CUSTOMER BILLING SYSTEM - INITIALIZATION\n\n");
        printf("Please enter today\'s date (mm/dd/yyyy): ");
        scanf("%d/%d/%d", &customer.lastpayment.month,
                          &customer.lastpayment.day,
                          &customer.lastpayment.year);
        customer.newbalance = 0;
        customer.payment = 0;
        customer.acct_type = 'C';

        /* main loop */
        while (flag)  {
            /* enter customer's name */
            printf("\nName (enter \'END\' when finished): ");
            scanf(" %[^\n]", customer.name);

            /* test for stopping condition */
            if (strcmp(customer.name, "END") == 0)
               break;

            /* enter remaining data and write to data file */
            customer = readscreen(customer);
            fwrite(&customer, sizeof(record), 1, fpt);

            /* erase strings */
            strset(customer.name, ' ');
            strset(customer.street, ' ');
            strset(customer.city, ' ');
        }

        fclose(fpt);
}


record readscreen(record customer)      /* read remaining data */

{
    printf("Street: ");
    scanf(" %[^\n]", customer.street);
    printf("City: ");
    scanf(" %[^\n]", customer.city);
    printf("Account number: ");
    scanf("%d", &customer.acct_no);
    printf("Current balance: ");
    scanf("%f", &customer.oldbalance);
    return(customer);
}
```

Comparing this program with that shown in Example 12.5, we see that the two programs are very similar. Within main, the present program reads each customer name and tests for a stopping condition (END), but does not write the customer name to the data file, as in the earlier program. Rather, if a stopping condition is not indicated, the present program reads the remainder of the customer record interactively, and then writes the entire customer record to the data file with the single fwrite statement

```
        fwrite(&customer, sizeof(record), 1, fpt);
```

Note that the data file created by this program is called `data.bin`, as indicated by the first argument within the call to the `fopen` function.

The programmer-defined `writefile` function shown in Example 12.5 is not required in this program, since the `fwrite` library function takes its place. On the other hand, both programs make use of the same programmer-defined function `readscreen`, which causes the information for a given customer record to be entered into the computer interactively.

After each record has been written to the data file, the string members `customer.name`, `customer.street` and `customer.city` are cleared (i.e., replaced with blanks), so that none of the previous information will be included in each new record. The library function `strset` is used for this purpose. Thus, the statement

```
strset(customer.name, ' ');
```

causes the contents of `customer.name` to be replaced with repeated blank characters, as indicated by `' '`. Note that the header file `string.h` is included in this program, in support of the `strset` function.

Execution of this program produces the same interactive dialog as that shown in Example 12.5. Thus, during program execution the user cannot tell whether the data file being created is formatted or unformatted. Once the new data file `data.bin` has been created, however, its contents will not be legible unless the file is read by a specially written program. Such a program will be presented in the next example.

Once an unformatted data file has been created, the question arises as to how to detect an end-of-file condition. The library function `feof` is available for this purpose. (Actually, `feof` will indicate an end-of-file condition for *any* stream-oriented data file, not just an unformatted data file.) This function returns a non-zero value (TRUE) if an end-of-file condition has been detected, and a value of zero (FALSE) if an end of file is *not* detected. Hence, a program that reads an unformatted data file can utilize a loop that continues to read successive records, as long as the value returned by `feof` is not TRUE.

EXAMPLE 12.8 Updating an Unformatted Data File Containing Customer Records   We now consider a program for reading and updating the unformatted data file created in Example 12.7. We will again make use of a two-file update procedure, as in Example 12.6. Now, however, the files will be called `data.old` and `data.new`. Therefore, the file created in the previous example, called `data.bin`, will have to be renamed `data.old` before the present program can be run.

The overall program logic is similar to that presented in Example 12.6. That is, a record is read from `data.old`, updated interactively, and then written to `data.new`. This procedure continues until an end-of-file condition has been detected during the most recent `fread` operation. Note the manner in which the end-of-file test is built into the specification of the `while` loop, i.e., `while (!feof(ptold))`.

This program, however, will make use of the library functions `fread` and `fwrite` to read unformatted customer records from `data.old`, and to write the updated records to `data.new`. Therefore the present program will not make use of programmer-defined functions `readfile` and `writefile`, as in Example 12.6.

The updating of each record is carried out interactively, via the user-defined function `update`. This function is identical to that shown in Example 12.6.

The entire C program is shown below.

```
/* update an unformatted data file containing customer records */

#include <stdio.h>

#define  NULL  0

typedef struct  {
    int month;
    int day;
    int year;
} date;
```

```
typedef struct  {
    char name[80];
    char street[80];
    char city[80];
    int acct_no;                    /* (positive integer) */
    char acct_type;                 /* C (current), O (overdue), or D (delinquent) */
    float oldbalance;               /* (nonnegative quantity) */
    float newbalance;               /* (nonnegative quantity) */
    float payment;                  /* (nonnegative quantity) */
    date lastpayment;
}  record;

record update(record customer);     /* function prototype */

FILE *ptold, *ptnew;            .......\* pointers to pre-defined structure FILE */
int month, day, year;           .......\* global variable declarations */


main()

{
    record customer;                    /* structure variable declaration */

    /* open data files */
    if ((ptold = fopen("data.old", "r")) == NULL)
        printf("\nERROR - Cannot open the designated read file\n");
    else   {
        ptnew = fopen("data.new", "w");

        /* enter current date */
        printf("CUSTOMER BILLING SYSTEM - UPDATE\n\n");
        printf("Please enter today\'s date (mm/dd/yyyy): ");
        scanf("%d/%d/%d", &month, &day, &year);

        /* read the first record from old data file */
        fread(&customer, sizeof(record), 1, ptold);

        /* main loop (continue until end-of-file is detected) */
        while (!feof(ptold))  {
            /* prompt for updated information */
            customer = update(customer);

            /* write updated information to new data file */
            fwrite(&customer, sizeof(record), 1, ptnew);

            /* read next record from old data file */
            fread(&customer, sizeof(record), 1, ptold);
        }

        fclose(ptold);
        fclose(ptnew);
    } /* end else */
}
```

```
record update(record customer)    /* prompt for new information, update records and
                                      display summary data */

{
    printf("\n\nName:    %s", customer.name);
    printf("    Account number: %d\n", customer.acct_no);
    printf("\nOld balance: %7.2f", customer.oldbalance);
    printf("    Current payment: ");
    scanf("%f", &customer.payment);

    if (customer.payment > 0)    {
        customer.lastpayment.month = month;
        customer.lastpayment.day = day;
        customer.lastpayment.year = year;
        customer.acct_type = (customer.payment < 0.1 * customer.oldbalance) ? 'O' : 'C';
    }
    else
        customer.acct_type = (customer.oldbalance > 0) ? 'D' : 'C';

    customer.newbalance = customer.oldbalance - customer.payment;
    printf("New balance: %7.2f", customer.newbalance);

    printf("    Account status: ");
    switch (customer.acct_type)    {
        case 'C':
                printf("CURRENT\n");
                break;
        case 'O':
                printf("OVERDUE\n");
                break;
        case 'D':
                printf("DELINQUENT\n");
                break;
        default:
                printf("ERROR\n");
    }

    return(customer);
}
```

Execution of the program results in the same interactive dialog as that shown in Example 12.6.

We will not pursue the use of data files further within this book. Remember, however, that most versions of C contain many different library functions for carrying out various file-oriented operations. Some of these functions are intended to be used with standard input/output devices (i.e., reading from the keyboard and writing to the screen), some are intended for stream-oriented data files, and others are available for use with system-oriented data files. Thus, we have only scratched the surface of this important topic within the present chapter. You should find out what file-related functions are available for your particular version of the language.

Review Questions

12.1   What is the primary advantage to using a data file?

12.2   Describe the different ways in which data files can be categorized in C.

12.3   What is the purpose of a buffer area when working with a stream-oriented data file? How is a buffer area defined?

12.4 When defining a buffer area for use with a stream-oriented data file, what does the symbol FILE represent? Where is FILE defined?

12.5 What is a stream pointer? What is the relationship between a stream pointer and a buffer area?

12.6 What is meant by opening a data file? How is this accomplished?

12.7 Summarize the rules governing the use of the fopen function. Describe the information that is returned by this function.

12.8 Summarize the different file types that can be specified by the fopen function.

12.9 What is the purpose of the fclose function? Must a call to this function appear within a program that utilizes a data file?

12.10 Describe a commonly used programming construct in which a provision for an error message accompanies a call to the fopen function.

12.11 Describe two different methods for creating a stream-oriented data file. Can both methods be used with unformatted data files?

12.12 Describe the general procedure for creating a stream-oriented data file using a specially written C program. What file-oriented library functions might be used within the program?

12.13 How can a stream-oriented data file be viewed once it has been created? Does your answer apply to unformatted data files?

12.14 Describe the general procedure for reading a stream-oriented data file using a specially written C program. What file-oriented library functions might be used within the program? Compare your answer with the answer to Prob. 12.12.

12.15 Describe two different approaches to updating a data file. Which approach is better, and why?

12.16 Contrast the use of the fscanf and fprintf functions with the use of the scanf and printf functions described in Chap. 4. How do the grammatical rules differ?

12.17 For what kinds of applications are unformatted data files well suited?

12.18 Contrast the use of the fread and fwrite functions with the use of the fscanf and fprintf functions. How do the grammatical rules differ? For what kinds of applications is each group of functions well suited?

12.19 What is the purpose of the library function strset? Why might strset be included in a program that creates an unformatted data file?

12.20 What is the purpose of the library function feof? How might the feof function be utilized within a program that updates an unformatted data file?

Problems

12.21 Associate the stream pointer pointr with a new stream-oriented data file called students.dat. Open the data file for writing only.

12.22 Associate the stream pointer pointr with an existing stream-oriented data file called students.dat. Open the data file so that new information can be appended to the end of the file.

12.23 Associate the stream pointer pointr with a new stream-oriented data file called sample.dat. Open the data file so that information can either be read from or written to the file. Show how the data file can be closed at the end of the program.

12.24 Associate the stream pointer pointr with an existing stream-oriented data file called sample.dat. Open the data file so that information can either be read from or written to the file. Show how the data file can be closed at the end of the program.

12.25 Repeat Prob. 12.24, adding a provision for generating an error message in the event that the data file cannot be opened (if, for example, the data file is not present).

12.26 The skeletal outline of a C program is shown below.

```
#include <stdio.h>

main()
{
    FILE *fpt;

    int a;
    float b;
    char c;

    fpt = fopen("sample.dat", "w");

    . . . . .

    fclose(fpt);
}
```

Enter values for a, b and c from the keyboard, in response to prompts generated by the program. Then write the values to the data file. Format the floating-point value so that not more than two decimals are written to the data file.

12.27 The skeletal outline of a C program is shown below.

```
#include <stdio.h>

main()
{
    FILE *fpt;

    int a;
    float b;
    char c;

    fpt = fopen("sample.dat", "r");

    . . . . .

    fclose(fpt);
}
```

Read the values of a, b and c from the data file and display them on the screen.

12.28 The skeletal outline of a C program is shown below.

```
#include <stdio.h>

main()
{
    FILE *pt1, *pt2;

    int a;
    float b;
    char c;

    pt1 = fopen("sample.old", "r");
    pt2 = fopen("sample.new", "w");

    . . . . .

    fclose(pt1);
    fclose(pt2);
}
```

(a) Read the values of a, b and c from the data file `sample.old`.

(b) Display each value on the screen and enter an updated value.

(c) Write the new values to the data file `sample.new`. Format the floating-point value so that not more than two decimals are written to `sample.new`.

12.29 The skeletal outline of a C program is shown below.

```
#include <stdio.h>

main()
{
    FILE *pt1, *pt2;

    char name[20];

    pt1 = fopen("sample.old", "r");
    pt2 = fopen("sample.new", "w");

    . . . . .

    fclose(pt1);
    fclose(pt2);
}
```

(a) Read the string represented by name from the data file `sample.old`.

(b) Display it on the screen.

(c) Enter an updated string.

(d) Write the new string to the data file `sample.new`.

12.30 The skeletal outline of a C program is shown below.

```
#include <stdio.h>

main()
{
    struct  {
        int a;
        float b;
        char c;
        char name[20];
    } values;

    pt1 = fopen("data.old", "r+");
    pt2 = fopen("data.new", "w+");

    . . . . .

    fclose(pt1);
    fclose(pt2);
}
```

(a) Read the value of `values.name` from the formatted data file `data.old` and display it on the screen.

(b) Enter values for `values.a`, `values.b` and `values.c` from the keyboard, in response to programmed prompts.

(c) Write the values of `values.name`, `values.a`, `values.b` and `values.c` to the formatted data file `data.new`.

12.31 Repeat Prob. 12.30, treating the two data files as unformatted data files. (Read an entire record from `data.old`, and write an entire updated record to `data.new`.)

Programming Problems

12.32 Modify the program given in Example 12.3 (read in a line of lowercase text and write uppercase equivalent to data file) so that each character entered from the keyboard is tested to determine its case, and is then written to the data file in the opposite case. (Hence, lowercase is converted to uppercase, and uppercase is converted to lowercase.) Use the library function `isupper` or `islower` to test case of each incoming character, and use the functions `toupper` and `tolower` to carry out the conversions.

12.33 Modify the programs given in Examples 12.3 and 12.4 so that multiple lines of text can be processed. As a stopping condition, check for END (either upper- or lowercase) in the first three characters within each line.

12.34 Modify the program given in Example 12.6 (updating a file containing customer records) so that it uses only one file; i.e., each updated customer record replaces the original record. Use the library function `ftell` to determine the current file position, and the function `fseek` to change the file position, as needed. Be sure to open a data file of the proper type.

12.35 Expand the program given in Example 12.6 so that new customer records can be added, old records can be deleted, and existing records can be modified. Be sure to maintain the records in alphabetical order. Allow the user to choose which option will be executed before each record is processed.

12.36 Modify the program given in Example 12.8 (updating an unformatted data file containing customer records) so that it uses only one file; i.e., each updated customer record replaces the original record. Use the library function `ftell` to determine the current file position, and the function `fseek` to change the file position, as needed. Be sure to open a data file of the proper type.

12.37 Write a program that will read successive records from the new data file created in Example 12.8 and display each record on the screen in an appropriately formatted form.

12.38 Expand the program described in Prob. 12.36 so that new customer records can be added, old records can be deleted, and existing records can be modified. Be sure to maintain the records in alphabetical order. Allow the user to choose which option will be executed before each record is processed.

12.39 Write an interactive C program that will encode and decode multiple lines of text, using the encoding/decoding procedure described in Prob. 9.49. Store the encoded text within a data file, so that it can be retrieved and decoded at any time. The program should include the following features:

(a) Enter text from the keyboard, encode the text and store the encoded text in a data file.
(b) Retrieve the encoded text and display it in its encoded form.
(c) Retrieve the encoded text, decode it and then display the decoded text.
(d) End the computation.

Test the program using several lines of text of your choice.

12.40 Extend the program described in Prob. 12.39 so that multiple random integers can be generated, where each successive integer is used to encode each consecutive line. Thus, the first random integer will be used to encode the first line of text, the second random integer will be used to encode the second line of text, and so on. Include a provision for reproducing the sequence of random integers, so that the same random integers can be used to decode the text. Test the program using several lines of text of your choice.

12.41 Modify the craps game simulator given in Example 7.11 so that it simulates a specified number of games and saves the outcome of each game in a data file. At the end of the simulation, read the data file to determine the percentage of wins and losses that the player has experienced.

Test the program by simulating 500 consecutive games. Based upon these results, estimate the odds of winning when playing craps.

12.42 Modify the piglatin generator presented in Example 9.14 so that multiple lines of text can be entered from the keyboard. Save the entire English text in a data file, and save the corresponding piglatin in another data file.

Include within the program a provision for generating a menu that will allow the user to select any one of the following features:

(a) Enter new text, convert to piglatin and save. (Save both the original text and the piglatin, as described above.)
(b) Read previously entered text from a data file and display.
(c) Read the piglatin equivalent of previously entered text and display.
(d) End the computation.

Test the program using several arbitrary lines of text.

12.43 Write a complete C program that will generate a data file containing the student exam data presented in Prob. 6.69(k). Let each file component be a structure containing the name and exam scores for a single student. Run the program, creating a data file for use in the next problem.

12.44 Write a file-oriented C program that will process the student exam scores given in Prob. 6.69(k). Read the data from the data file created in the previous problem. Then create a report containing the name, exam scores and average grade for each student.

12.45 Extend the program written for Prob. 12.44 so that an overall class average is determined, followed by the deviation of each student's average about the class average. Write the output onto a new data file. Then display the output in the form of a well-labeled report.

12.46 Write an interactive, file-oriented C program that will maintain a list of names, addresses and telephone numbers in alphabetical order (by last names). Process the information associated with each name as a separate record. Represent each record as a structure.

Include a menu that will allow the user to select any of the following features:

(a) Add a new record.
(b) Delete a record.
(c) Modify an existing record.
(d) Retrieve and display an entire record for a given name.
(e) Generate a complete list of all names, addresses and telephone numbers.
(f) End the computation.

Be sure to rearrange the records whenever a new record is added or a record is deleted, so that the records are always maintained in alphabetical order. Utilize a linear linked list, as described in Example 11.32.

12.47 Write a program that will generate a data file containing the list of countries and their corresponding capitals given in Prob. 9.46. Place the name of each country and its corresponding capital in a separate structure. Treat each structure as a separate record. Run the program, creating a data file for use in the next problem.

12.48 Write an interactive, menu-driven C program that will access the data file generated in the preceding problem and then allow one of the following operations to be executed:

(a) Determine the capital of a specified country.
(b) Determine the country whose capital is specified.
(c) Terminate the computation.

12.49 Extend the program written for Prob. 12.48 to include the following additional features:

(a) Add a new record (i.e., a new country and its corresponding capital).
(b) Delete a record.
(c) Generate a listing of all of the countries and their corresponding capitals.

12.50 Write a complete C program that can be used as a simple line-oriented text editor. This program must have the following capabilities:

(a) Enter several lines of text and store in a data file.
(b) List the data file.
(c) Retrieve and display a particular line, determined by line number.
(d) Insert n lines.
(e) Delete n lines.
(f) Save the newly edited text and end the computation.

Carry out each of these tasks in response to a one-letter command, preceded by a dollar sign ($). The find (retrieve) command should be followed by an unsigned integer to indicate which line should be retrieved. Also, the insert and delete commands can be followed by an optional unsigned integer if several consecutive lines are to be inserted or deleted.

Each command should appear on a line by itself, thus providing a means of distinguishing commands from lines of text. (A command line will begin with a dollar sign, followed by a single-letter command, an optional unsigned integer, and a newline designation.)

The following commands are recommended:

$E — enter new text.

$L — list the entire block of text.

$F*k* — find (retrieve) line number *k*.

$I*n* — insert *n* lines after line number *k*.

$D*n* — delete *n* lines after line number *k*.

$S — save the edited block of text and end the computation.

12.51 Extend the program described in Prob. 11.67 so that the team information is maintained in a data file rather than an array. Each file component should be a structure containing the data for one team. Include provisions for each of the following operations:

(*a*) Entering new records (adding new teams)
(*b*) Updating existing records
(*c*) Deleting records (removing teams)
(*d*) Generating a summary report for all of the teams in the league

Chapter 13

Low-Level Programming

From the material presented in the first 12 chapters of this book, it should be clear that C is a full-fledged, high-level programming language. However, C also possesses certain "low-level" features that allow the programmer to carry out operations normally available only in assembly language or machine language. For example, it is possible to store the values of certain variables within the central processing unit's registers. This will usually speed up any computation associated with these values.

C also permits the manipulation of individual bits within a word. Thus, bits can be shifted to the left or the right, *inverted* (1s and 0s reversed), or *masked* (extracted selectively). Applications requiring these operations are familiar to assembly language programmers. Furthermore, C allows the bits within a word of memory to be organized into individual groups. This permits multiple data items to be packed within a single word.

This chapter shows how to carry out low-level operations in C. Readers who lack background in this area may wish to skip some of this material, particularly Sec. 13.2.

13.1 REGISTER VARIABLES

In Chap. 8 we mentioned that there are four different storage class specifications in C, and we examined three of them — automatic, external and static — in detail. We now turn our attention to the last of these, which is the *register* storage class.

Registers are special storage areas within the computer's central processing unit. The actual arithmetic and logical operations that comprise a program are carried out within these registers. Normally, these operations are carried out by transferring information from the computer's memory to these registers, carrying out the indicated operations, and then transferring the results back to the computer's memory. This general procedure is repeated many times during the course of a program's execution.

For some programs, the execution time can be reduced considerably if certain values can be stored within these registers rather than in the computer's memory. Such programs may also be somewhat smaller in size (i.e., they may require fewer instructions), since fewer data transfers will be required. Usually, however, the size reduction will not be dramatic and will be less significant than the savings in execution time.

In C, the values of *register variables* are stored within the registers of the central processing unit. A variable can be assigned this storage class simply by preceding the type declaration with the keyword `register`. There can, however, be only a few register variables (typically, two or three) within any one function. The exact number depends upon the particular computer, and the specific C compiler. Usually, only integer variables are assigned the `register` storage class (more about this later in this section).

The `register` and `automatic` storage classes are closely related. In particular, their visibility (i.e., their scope) is the same. Thus, `register` variables, like `automatic` variables, are local to the function in which they are declared. Furthermore, the rules governing the use of `register` variables are the same as those for `automatic` variables (see Sec. 8.2), except that the address operator (&) cannot be applied to register variables.

The similarities between `register` and `automatic` variables is not coincidental, because the `register` storage class can be assigned only to variables that would otherwise have the storage class `automatic`. Moreover, declaring certain variables to be `register` variables does not guarantee that they will be actually be treated as `register` variables. The declaration will be valid only if the requested register space is available. If a `register` declaration is not honored, the variables will be treated as having the storage class `automatic`.

EXAMPLE 13.1   A C program contains the variable declaration

```
register int a, b, c;
```

This declaration specifies that the variables a, b and c will be integer variables with storage class `register`. Hence, the values of a, b and c will be stored within the registers of the computer's central processing unit rather than in memory, provided the register space is available.

If the register space is not available, then the variables will be treated as integer variables with storage class `automatic`. This is equivalent to the declaration

```
auto int a, b, c;
```

or simply

```
int a, b, c;
```

as explained in Sec. 8.2.

Unfortunately, there is no way to determine whether a `register` declaration will be honored, other than to run a program with and without the declaration and compare the results. A program that makes use of `register` variables should run faster than the corresponding program without `register` variables. It may also be somewhat smaller in size.

EXAMPLE 13.2 Generating Fibonacci Numbers   The program presented below is a variation of that shown in Example 8.7, for generating a series of Fibonacci numbers.

```c
/* calculate the first 23 Fibonacci numbers 10,000,000 times,
   to illustrate the use of register variables */

#include <stdio.h>
#include <time.h>

main()

{
    time_t start, finish;                   /* start and finish times */
    int count, n = 23;
    long int loop, loopmax = 10000000;
    register int f, f1, f2;

    /* tag the starting time */
    time(&start);

    /* do multiple loops */
    for (loop = 1; loop <= loopmax; ++loop)  {
        f1 = 1;
        f2 = 1;

        /* generate the first n Fibonacci numbers */
        for (count = 1; count <= n; ++count)  {
            f = (count < 3) ? 1 : f1 + f2;
            f2 = f1;
            f1 = f;
        }
    }
```

```
/* adjust the counter and tag the completion time */
--count;
time(&finish);

/* display the output */
printf("i = %d    F = %d\n", count, f);
printf("elapsed time: %.0lf seconds", difftime(finish, start));
}
```

This program includes three integer variables that have the `register` storage class. Only 23 Fibonacci numbers will be calculated, since the Fibonacci numbers are represented as ordinary integer variables (higher Fibonacci numbers would generate an integer overflow).

The calculation of the Fibonacci numbers is repeated 10,000,000 times, in order to obtain a reasonably accurate assessment of the time required to execute the program. The only output generated is the value of the 23rd Fibonacci number, calculated at the end of the last loop. Thus the program is computationally intensive (minimal input/output), in order to emphasize the advantage in using the `register` storage class.

Note that the program includes its own timing mechanism. In particular, the program makes use of the library function `time`, which assigns the current time (in seconds) to the variables `start` and `finish`. These variables are of type `time_t`, as defined in the header file `time.h`. The program also makes use of the library function `difftime`, which returns the time difference defined by the variables `finish` and `start`.

When executed on a Pentium-class desktop computer, the following results were obtained:

```
i = 23    F = 28657
elapsed time: 37 seconds
```

If the program is rerun without the `register` declaration (i.e., if the variables `f`, `f1` and `f2` are declared as ordinary integer variables), the output is essentially the same. Hence, use of the `register` class did not provide any noticeable advantage. When run with an older desktop computer, however, the use of the register class resulted in a 36 percent reduction in computer time. However, the sizes of the compiled object programs, with and without `register` variables, are not significantly different with either computer.

Though the `register` storage class is usually associated with integer variables, some compilers allow the `register` storage class to be associated with other types of variables having the same word size (e.g., `short` or `unsigned` integers). Moreover, *pointers* to such variables may also be permitted.

The `register` storage class specification can be included as a part of a formal argument declaration within a function, or as a part of an argument type specification within a function prototype. (*Note that* `register` *is the only storage class specifier that can be used in this manner.*)

EXAMPLE 13.3 The skeletal outline of a C program is shown below.

```
void funct(register unsigned u, register int *pt);     /* function prototype */

main()

{
    register unsigned u;        /* variable declaration */
    register int *pt;           /* pointer declaration */

    u = 5;                      /* assign an integer quantity */
    *pt = 12;                   /* assign an integer quantity */

    funct(u, pt);
}
```

```
    void funct(register unsigned u, register int *pt)     /* function definition */

    {
        . . . . .

        return;
    }
```

The function prototype indicates that the first argument transferred to funct is an unsigned integer having the register storage class, and the second argument is a pointer to an integer having this same storage class. Notice that the function prototype is consistent with the argument specifications shown in the function definition.

Within main, we see that u is an unsigned integer, and pt is a pointer to an integer. Both of these variables are assigned the register storage class. Thus, u will represent an unsigned integer that is stored within one register of the computer's central processing unit, and pt will point to the contents of another such register. In both cases, the use of the computer's registers will be contingent upon their availability.

Following the declarations, a value of 5 is assigned to u, and a value of 12 is assigned to the location to which pt points. These values will be stored in the computer's registers, provided the registers are available. The variables u and pt are then passed to funct, where they are processed in some unspecified manner.

13.2 BITWISE OPERATIONS

Some applications require the manipulation of individual bits within a word of memory. Assembly language or machine language is normally required for operations of this type. However, C contains several special operators that allow such bitwise operations to be carried out easily and efficiently. These bitwise operators can be divided into three general categories: the one's complement operator, the logical bitwise operators, and the shift operators. C also contains several operators that combine bitwise operations with ordinary assignment. Each category is discussed separately below.

The One's Complement Operator

The *one's complement operator* (~) is a unary operator that causes the bits of its operand to be inverted (i.e., reversed) so that 1s become 0s and 0s become 1s. This operator always precedes its operand. The operand must be an integer-type quantity (including integer, long, short, unsigned, char, etc.). Generally, the operand will be an unsigned octal or an unsigned hexadecimal quantity, though this is not a firm requirement.

EXAMPLE 13.4   Consider the hexadecimal number 07ff. The corresponding bit pattern, expressed in terms of a 16-bit word, is 0000 0111 1111 1111 (see Appendix A). The one's complement of this bit pattern is 1111 1000 0000 0000, which corresponds to the hexadecimal number f800. Thus, we see that the value of the expression ~0x7ff is 0xf800. (Note that the bit patterns in this example have been arranged into groups of 4 for convenience only.)

Several other expressions which make use of the one's complement operator, and their corresponding values, are shown below. All results are expressed in terms of a 16-bit word.

Expression	*Value*	
~0xc5	0xff3a	(hexadecimal constants)
~0x1111	0xeeee	(hexadecimal constants)
~0xffff	0	(hexadecimal constants)
~052	0177725	(octal constants)
~0177777	0	(octal constants)

In the last two expressions, the leftmost octal digit is equivalent to only one bit (otherwise, the total bit pattern would exceed 16 bits).

You are encouraged to show the validity of these expressions by writing out the equivalent bit patterns, as shown above.

The one's complement operator is sometimes referred to as the *complementation operator*. It is a member of the same precedence group as the other unary operators. Thus, its associativity is right to left.

EXAMPLE 13.5   Consider the simple C program shown below.

```
#include <stdio.h>

main()
{
    unsigned i = 0x5b3c;

    printf("hexadecimal values:  i = %x   ~i = %x\n", i, ~i);
    printf("decimal equivalents: i = %u   ~i = %u", i, ~i);
}
```

Executing this program on a computer with a 16-bit word size results in the following output.

```
hexadecimal values:  i = 5b3c   ~i = a4c3
decimal equivalents: i = 23356   ~i = 42179
```

To understand these results, first consider the bit patterns corresponding to the values for i and ~i.

```
i = 0101 1011 0011 1100
~i = 1010 0100 1100 0011
```

The decimal equivalent of the first bit pattern can be determined by writing

$$i = 0{\times}2^{15} + 1{\times}2^{14} + 0{\times}2^{13} + 1{\times}2^{12} + 1{\times}2^{11} + 0{\times}2^{10} + 1{\times}2^{9} + 1{\times}2^{8} +$$
$$0{\times}2^{7} + 0{\times}2^{6} + 1{\times}2^{5} + 1{\times}2^{4} + 1{\times}2^{3} + 1{\times}2^{2} + 0{\times}2^{1} + 0{\times}2^{0} =$$
$$16384 + 4096 + 2048 + 512 + 256 + 32 + 16 + 8 + 4 = 23356$$

Thus, the decimal equivalent of 0x5b3c is 23356.

Similarly, the decimal equivalent of the second bit pattern can be determined by writing

$$\sim i = 1{\times}2^{15} + 0{\times}2^{14} + 1{\times}2^{13} + 0{\times}2^{12} + 0{\times}2^{11} + 1{\times}2^{10} + 0{\times}2^{9} + 0{\times}2^{8} +$$
$$1{\times}2^{7} + 1{\times}2^{6} + 0{\times}2^{5} + 0{\times}2^{4} + 0{\times}2^{3} + 0{\times}2^{2} + 1{\times}2^{1} + 1{\times}2^{0} =$$
$$32768 + 8192 + 1024 + 128 + 64 + 2 + 1 = 42179$$

Thus, we see that the decimal equivalent of 0xa4c3 is 42179.

The Logical Bitwise Operators

There are three logical bitwise operators: *bitwise and* (&), *bitwise exclusive or* (^), and *bitwise or* (|). Each of these operators requires two integer-type operands. The operations are carried out independently on each pair of corresponding bits within the operands. Thus, the least significant bits (i.e., the rightmost bits) within the two operands will be compared, then the next least significant bits, and so on, until all of the bits have been compared. The results of these comparisons are:

- A *bitwise and* expression will return a 1 if both bits have a value of 1 (i.e., if both bits are true). Otherwise, it will return a value of 0.

- A *bitwise exclusive or* expression will return a 1 if one of the bits has a value of 1 and the other has a value of 0 (one bit is true, the other false). Otherwise, it will return a value of 0.

- A *bitwise or* expression will return a 1 if one or more of the bits have a value of 1 (one or both bits are true). Otherwise, it will return a value of 0.

These results are summarized in Table 13-1. In this table, *b1* and *b2* represent the corresponding bits within the first and second operands, respectively.

Table 13-1   Logical Bitwise Operations

b1	b2	b1 & b2	b1 ^ b2	b1 | b2
1	1	1	0	1
1	0	0	1	1
0	1	0	1	1
0	0	0	0	0

EXAMPLE 13.6 Suppose a and b are unsigned integer variables whose values are 0x6db7 and 0xa726, respectively. The results of several bitwise operations on these variables are shown below.

```
~a = 0x9248

~b = 0x58d9

a & b = 0x2526

a ^ b = 0xca91

a | b = 0xefb7
```

The validity of these expressions can be verified by expanding each of the bit patterns. Thus,

```
    a = 0110 1101 1011 0111
       ─────────────────────
   ~a = 1001 0010 0100 1000
      = 0x9248


    b = 1010 0111 0010 0110
       ─────────────────────
   ~b = 0101 1000 1101 1001
      = 0x58d9


    a = 0110 1101 1011 0111
    b = 1010 0111 0010 0110
       ─────────────────────
a & b = 0010 0101 0010 0110
      = 0x2526


    a = 0110 1101 1011 0111
    b = 1010 0111 0010 0110
       ─────────────────────
a ^ b = 1100 1010 1001 0001
      = 0xca91


    a = 0110 1101 1011 0111
    b = 1010 0111 0010 0110
       ─────────────────────
a | b = 1110 1111 1011 0111
      = 0xefb7
```

Each of the logical bitwise operators has its own precedence. The *bitwise and* (&) operator has the highest precedence, followed by *bitwise exclusive or* (^), then *bitwise or* (|). *Bitwise and* follows the equality operators (== and !=). *Bitwise or* is followed by *logical and* (&&). The associativity for each bitwise operator is left to right. (See Appendix C for a summary of all C operators, showing their precedences and associativities.)

Masking

Masking is a process in which a given bit pattern is transformed into another bit pattern by means of a logical bitwise operation. The original bit pattern is one of the operands in the bitwise operation. The second operand, called the *mask*, is a specially selected bit pattern that brings about the desired transformation.

There are several different kinds of masking operations. For example, a portion of a given bit pattern can be copied to a new word, while the remainder of the new word is filled with 0s. Thus, part of the original bit pattern will be "masked off" from the final result. The *bitwise and* operator (&) is used for this type of masking operation, as illustrated below.

EXAMPLE 13.7   Suppose a is an unsigned integer variable whose value is 0x6db7. Extract the rightmost 6 bits of this value and assign them to the unsigned integer variable b. Assign 0s to the 10 leftmost bits of b.

To carry out this operation, we write the bitwise expression

```
b = a & 0x3f;
```

The second operand (the hexadecimal constant 0x3f) will serve as a mask. Thus, the resulting value of b will be 0x37. The validity of this result can be established by examining the corresponding bit patterns.

```
   a = 0110 1101 1011 0111
mask = 0000 0000 0011 1111
       ─────────────────────
   b = 0000 0000 0011 0111
     = 0x37.
```

The mask prevents the leftmost 10 bits from being copied from a to b.

The mask in the last example contained 1s in the rightmost bit positions (i.e., the least significant bit positions) and 0s in the leftmost bit positions (the most significant bit positions). Such masks are independent of the word length, since 0s are used to fill the remainder of the word after the required 1s have been placed in the low-order bit positions. If 1s were required in the leftmost bit positions, the mask would be related to the length of the word. (Remember that the rightmost bit position always represents 2^0, whereas the leftmost bit position represents 2^{n-1}, where n is the number of bits in the word.) Such dependence can often be removed, however, by writing the mask in terms of its one's complement.

EXAMPLE 13.8   Suppose once again that a is an unsigned integer variable whose value is 0x6db7. Now extract the *leftmost* 6 bits of this value and assign them to the unsigned integer variable b. Assign 0s to the 10 rightmost bits of b.

To carry out this operation, we can write the bitwise expression

```
b = a & 0xfc00;
```

Thus, the hexadecimal constant 0xfc00 will serve as a mask. The resulting value of b will be 0x6c00. The validity of this result can be established by again examining the corresponding bit patterns.

```
   a = 0110 1101 1011 0111
mask = 1111 1100 0000 0000
       ─────────────────────
   b = 0110 1100 0000 0000
     = 0x6c00.
```

The mask now blocks the rightmost 10 bits in a.

The mask is dependent on the 16-bit word size in this situation, since the 1s appear in the leftmost bit positions. If the mask is written in terms of its one's complement, however, the 1s appear in the rightmost bit positions, and the remaining bit positions are filled with 0s. The mask therefore becomes independent of the word size.

The one's complement of the original mask is the hexadecimal constant 0x3ff. We can therefore express this masking operation as

```
b = a & ~0x3ff;
```

The resulting value of b will be 0x6c00, as before.

The validity of this result can be seen by examining the corresponding bit patterns shown below.

```
       0x3ff = 0000 0011 1111 1111
                _____
      ~0x3ff = 1111 1100 0000 0000 = 0xfc00   (the original mask)

           a = 0110 1101 1011 0111
      ~0x3ff = 1111 1100 0000 0000
                _____
           b = 0110 1100 0000 0000
             = 0x6c00.
```

Another type of masking operation allows a portion of a given bit pattern to be copied to a new word, while the remainder of the new word is filled with 1s. The *bitwise or* operator is used for this purpose. (Note the distinction between this and the previous masking operation, which allowed a portion of a bit pattern to be copied to a new word, while the remainder of the new word was filled with 0s.)

EXAMPLE 13.9 Suppose that a is an unsigned integer variable whose value is 0x6db7, as before. Transform the corresponding bit pattern into another bit pattern in which the rightmost 8 bits are all 1s, and the leftmost 8 bits retain their original value. Assign this new bit pattern to the unsigned integer variable b.

This operation is carried out with the bitwise expression

```
b = a | 0xff;
```

The hexadecimal constant 0xff is the mask. The resulting value of b will be 0x6dff.

Now let us examine the corresponding bit patterns, in order to verify the accuracy of this result.

```
        a = 0110 1101 1011 0111
     mask = 0000 0000 1111 1111
             _____
        b = 0110 1101 1111 1111
          = 0x6dff
```

Remember that the bitwise operation is now *bitwise or*, not *bitwise and*, as in the previous examples. Thus, when each of the rightmost 8 bits in a is compared with the corresponding 1 in the mask, the result is always 1. When each of the leftmost 8 bits in a is compared with the corresponding 0 in the mask, however, the result will be the same as the original bit in a.

Now suppose we wish to transform the bit pattern of a into another bit pattern in which the *leftmost* 8 bits are all 1s, and the *rightmost* 8 bits retain their original value. This can be accomplished by either of the following two expressions.

```
b = a | 0xff00;
```

or

```
b = a | ~0xff;
```

In either case, the resulting value of b will be 0xffb7. The second expression is preferable because it is independent of the word size.

You should verify the accuracy of these results by expanding the corresponding bit patterns and carrying out the indicated bitwise operations.

A portion of a given bit pattern can be copied to a new word, while the remainder of the original bit pattern is inverted within the new word. This type of masking operation makes use of *bitwise exclusive or*. The details are illustrated in the following example.

EXAMPLE 13.10 Suppose that a is an unsigned integer variable whose value is 0x6db7, as in the last several examples. Now let us reverse the rightmost 8 bits, and preserve the leftmost 8 bits. This new bit pattern will be assigned to the unsigned integer variable b.

To do this, we make use of the *bitwise exclusive or* operation.

```
b = a ^ 0xff;
```

The hexadecimal constant 0xff is the mask. This expression will result in the value 0x6d48 being assigned to b.

Here are the corresponding bit patterns.

```
   a = 0110 1101 1011 0111
mask = 0000 0000 1111 1111
     ─────────────────────
   b = 0110 1101 0100 1000
     = 0x6d48
```

Remember that the bitwise operation is now *bitwise exclusive or* rather than *bitwise and* or *bitwise or*. Therefore, when each of the rightmost 8 bits in a is compared with the corresponding 1 in the mask, the resulting bit will be the opposite of the bit originally in a. On the other hand, when each of the leftmost 8 bits in a is compared with the corresponding 0 in the mask, the resulting bit will be the same as the bit originally in a.

If we wanted to invert the leftmost 8 bits in a while preserving the original rightmost 8 bits, we could write either

```
b = a ^ 0xff00;
```

or the more desirable expression (because it is independent of the word size)

```
b = a ^ ~0xff;
```

The resulting value of each expression is 0x92b7.

The *exclusive or* operation can be used repeatedly as a *toggle*, to change the value of a particular bit within a word. In other words, if a particular bit has a value of 1, the *exclusive or* operation will change its value to 0, and vice versa. Such operations are particularly common in programs that interact closely with the computer's hardware.

EXAMPLE 13.11 Suppose that a is an unsigned integer variable whose value is 0x6db7, as in the previous examples. The expression

```
a ^ 0x4
```

will invert the value of bit number 2 (the third bit from the right) within a. If this operation is carried out repeatedly, the value of a will alternate between 0x6db7 and 0x6db3. Thus, the repeated use of this operation will toggle the third bit from the right on and off.

The corresponding bit patterns are shown below.

```
0x6db7 = 0110 1101 1011 0111
  mask = 0000 0000 0000 0100
       ─────────────────────
0x6db3 = 0110 1101 1011 0011
  mask = 0000 0000 0000 0100
       ─────────────────────
0x6db7 = 0110 1101 1011 0111
```

The Shift Operators

The two bitwise shift operators are *shift left* (<<) and *shift right* (>>). Each operator requires two operands. The first is an integer-type operand that represents the bit pattern to be shifted. The second is an unsigned integer that indicates the number of displacements (i.e., whether the bits in the first operand will be shifted by 1 bit position, 2 bit positions, 3 bit positions, etc.). This value cannot exceed the number of bits associated with the word size of the first operand.

The left shift operator causes all of the bits in the first operand to be shifted to the left by the number of positions indicated by the second operand. The leftmost bits (i.e., the overflow bits) in the original bit pattern will be lost. The rightmost bit positions that become vacant will be filled with 0s.

EXAMPLE 13.12   Suppose a is an unsigned integer variable whose value is 0x6db7. The expression

        b = a << 6;

will shift all bits of a six places to the left and assign the resulting bit pattern to the unsigned integer variable b. The resulting value of b will be 0x6dc0.

To see how the final result was obtained, let us write out the corresponding bit patterns.

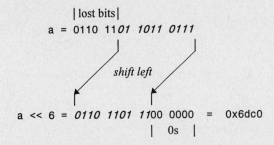

All of the bits originally assigned to a are shifted to the left 6 places, as indicated by the italicized digits. The leftmost 6 bits (originally 0110 11) are lost. The rightmost 6 bit positions are filled with 00 0000.

The right shift operator causes all of the bits in the first operand to be shifted to the right by the number of positions indicated by the second operand. The rightmost bits (i.e., the underflow bits) in the original bit pattern will be lost. If the bit pattern being shifted represents an *unsigned* integer, then the leftmost bit positions that become vacant will be filled with 0s. Hence, the behavior of the right shift operator is similar to that of the left shift operator when the first operand is an unsigned integer.

EXAMPLE 13.13   Suppose a is an unsigned integer variable whose value is 0x6db7. The expression

        b = a >> 6;

will shift all bits of a 6 places to the right and assign the resulting bit pattern to the unsigned integer variable b. The resulting value of b will be 0x1b6.

To see how the final result was obtained, let us once again write out the corresponding bit patterns.

```
            | lost bits |
a =  0110 1101 1011 0111

         shift right

a >> 6 = 0000 0001 1011 0110   =   0x1b6
         |  0s  |
```

We see that all of the bits originally assigned to a are shifted to the right 6 places, as indicated by the italicized bits. The rightmost 6 bits (originally 11 0111) are lost. The leftmost 6 bit positions are filled with 00 0000.

If the bit pattern representing a *signed* integer is shifted to the right, the outcome of the shift operation may depend on the value of the leftmost bit (the sign bit). Most compilers will fill the vacant bit positions with the contents of this bit. (Negative integers have a 1 in this position, whereas positive integers have a 0 here.) However, some compilers will fill the vacant bit positions with 0s, regardless of the sign of the original integer quantity. You should determine how your particular compiler will handle this situation.

EXAMPLE 13.14   Here is a simple C program that illustrates the use of the right-shift operator.

```
#include <stdio.h>

main()
{
    unsigned a = 0xf05a;
    int b = a;

    printf("%u %d\n", a, b);
    printf("%x\n", a >> 6);
    printf("%x\n", b >> 6);
}
```

Notice that a represents an unsigned integer quantity, whereas b represents an ordinary (signed) integer. Both variables are initially assigned the (hexadecimal) value 0xf05a. Since the leftmost bit position will contain a 1, the signed integer (b) will interpret this value as a negative number.

The program displays the decimal values represented by the bit patterns assigned to a and b. We therefore see the result of a 6-bit right-shift operation for each quantity. Thus, if the program is run with a compiler that copies the contents of the sign bit into the vacated bit positions, the following output will be obtained.

```
61530 -4006
3c1
ffc1
```

The first line shows that the hexadecimal quantity 0xf05a is equivalent to the unsigned decimal quantity 61530, and the signed decimal quantity -4006. When the *unsigned* integer is shifted 6 places to the right, the vacated bit positions are filled with zeros. Hence, the hexadecimal equivalent of the resulting bit pattern is 0x3c1. When the *signed* integer is shifted 6 places to the right, however, the vacated bit positions are filled with 1s (the value of the sign bit). Therefore, the hexadecimal equivalent of the resulting bit pattern in this case is ffc1.

The actual bit patterns, before and after the right-shift operations, are shown below.

```
    a = 1111 0000 0101 1010

a >> 6 = 0000 0011 1100 0001  =  0x3c1

    b = 1111 0000 0101 1010

b >> 6 = 1111 1111 1100 0001  =  0xffc1
```

The Bitwise Assignment Operators

C also contains the following *bitwise assignment* operators.

```
    &=     ^=     |=     <<=     >>=
```

These operators combine the preceding bitwise operations with ordinary assignment. The left operand must be an assignable integer-type identifier (e.g., an integer variable), and the right operand must be a bitwise expression. The left operand is interpreted as the first operand in the bitwise expression. The value of the bitwise expression is then assigned to the left operand. For example, the expression a &= 0x7f is equivalent to a = a & 0x7f.

The bitwise assignment operators are members of the same precedence group as the other assignment operators in C. Their associativity is right to left (see Appendix C).

EXAMPLE 13.15 Several bitwise assignment expressions are shown below. In each expression, assume that a is an unsigned integer variable whose initial value is 0x6db7.

Expression	*Equivalent Expression*	*Final Value*
a &= 0x7f	a = a & 0x7f	0x37
a ^= 0x7f	a = a ^ 0x7f	0x6dc8
a |= 0x7f	a = a | 0x7f	0x6dff
a <<= 5	a = a << 5	0xb6e0
a >>= 5	a = a >> 5	0x36d

Many applications involve the use of multiple bitwise operations. In fact, two or more bitwise operations may be combined in the same expression.

EXAMPLE 13.16 Displaying Bit Patterns   Most versions of C do not include a library function to convert a decimal integer into a binary bit pattern. A complete C program to carry out this conversion is shown below. The program will display the bit pattern corresponding to either a positive or a negative integer quantity.

```
/* display the bit pattern corresponding to a signed decimal integer */

#include <stdio.h>

main()
{
    int a, b, m, count, nbits;
    unsigned mask;

    /* determine the word size in bits and set the initial mask */
    nbits = 8 * sizeof(int);
    m = 0x1 << (nbits - 1);                    /* place 1 in leftmost position */

    /* main loop */
    do   {
            /* read a signed integer */
            printf("\n\nEnter an integer value (0 to stop): ", a);
            scanf("%d", &a);

            /* output the bit pattern */
            mask = m;
            for (count = 1; count <= nbits; count++)  {
                b = (a & mask) ? 1 : 0;   /* set display bit on or off */
                printf("%x", b);          /* print display bit */
                if (count % 4 == 0)
                    printf(" ");          /* blank space after every 4th digit */
                mask >>= 1;               /* shift mask 1 position to the right */
            }
    } while (a != 0);
}
```

The program is written so that it is independent of the integer word size. Therefore it can be used on any computer. It begins by determining the word size, in bits. It then assigns an appropriate initial value to the integer variable m. This value will be used as a mask in a *bitwise and* operation. Notice that m contains a 1 in the leftmost bit position, and 0s in all of the other bit positions.

The main part of the program is a do - while loop that allows multiple integer quantities to be converted into equivalent bit patterns. Each pass through the loop causes one integer quantity to be entered into the computer and converted into an equivalent bit pattern, which is then displayed. The computation continues until a value of 0 is entered into the computer and converted into a succession of 0 bits.

Once an integer quantity has been entered into the computer, the mask is assigned the initial value defined at the beginning of the program. A for loop is then used to examine the integer quantity on a bit-by-bit basis, beginning with the most significant bit (i.e., the leftmost bit). A masking operation, based upon the use of *bitwise and*, is used to examine each bit position. The content of the bit position is then displayed. Finally, the 1 within the mask is shifted one bit position to the right, in anticipation of examining the next bit.

Note that all of the bits are displayed on the same line. A blank space is displayed after every group of 4 bits, to enhance the legibility of the display.

The interactive dialog resulting from a typical program execution is shown below. The user's responses are underlined.

```
Enter an integer value (0 to stop): 1
0000 0000 0000 0001

Enter an integer value (0 to stop): -1
1111 1111 1111 1111

Enter an integer value (0 to stop): 129
0000 0000 1000 0001

Enter an integer value (0 to stop): -129
1111 1111 0111 1111

Enter an integer value (0 to stop): 1024
0000 0100 0000 0000

Enter an integer value (0 to stop): -1024
1111 1100 0000 0000

Enter an integer value (0 to stop): 7033
0001 1011 0111 1001

Enter an integer value (0 to stop): -7033
1110 0100 1000 0111

Enter an integer value (0 to stop): 32767
0111 1111 1111 1111

Enter an integer value (0 to stop): -32768
1000 0000 0000 0000

Enter an integer value (0 to stop): 0
0000 0000 0000 0000
```

Notice that each positive number has a 0 in the leftmost bit position, and each negative number has a 1 in this position. (Actually, the bit pattern for a negative number is the *two's complement* of the bit pattern for a positive number. To obtain the two's complement, form the one's complement and then add 1 to the rightmost bit position.)

13.3 BIT FIELDS

In some applications it may be desirable to work with data items that consist of only a few bits (e.g., a single-bit flag to indicate a true/false condition, a 3-bit integer whose values can range from 0 through 7, or a 7-bit ASCII character.) Several such data items can be packed into an individual word of memory. To do so, the word is subdivided into individual *bit fields*. These bit fields are defined as members of a structure. Each bit field can then be accessed individually, like any other member of a structure.

In general terms, the decomposition of a word into distinct bit fields can be written as

```
struct  tag  {
                member 1;
                member 2;
                . . . . .
                member m;
};
```

where the individual elements have the same meaning as in a structure declaration. Each member declaration must now include a specification indicating the size of the corresponding bit field. To do so, the member name must be followed by a colon and an unsigned integer indicating the field size.

The interpretation of these bit fields may vary from one C compiler to another. For example, some C compilers may order the bit fields from right to left, whereas other C compilers will order them from left to right. We will assume right-to-left ordering in the examples shown below.

EXAMPLE 13.17   A C program contains the following declarations.

```
struct  sample  {
                  unsigned a : 1;
                  unsigned b : 3;
                  unsigned c : 2;
                  unsigned d : 1;
};

struct  sample  v;
```

The first declaration defines a structure which is subdivided into four bit fields, called a, b, c and d. These bit fields have widths of 1 bit, 3 bits, 2 bits and 1 bit, respectively. Hence, the bit fields occupy a total of 7 bits within a word of memory. Any additional bits within the word will remain uncommitted.

Fig. 13.1 illustrates the layout of the bit fields within the word, assuming a 16-bit word with the fields ordered from right to left.

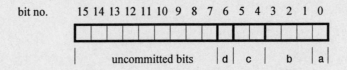

Fig. 13.1 Bit fields within a 16-bit word

The second declaration states that v is a structure variable of type `sample`. Thus, v.a is a field within v whose width is 1 bit. Similarly, v.b is a field whose width is 3 bits; and so on.

A bit field can only be defined as a portion of an `integer` or an `unsigned` word. (Some compilers also permit a bit field to be a portion of a `char` or a `long` word.) In all other respects, however, the rules for defining bit fields are the same as the rules that govern other kinds of structures.

EXAMPLE 13.18   The declarations in Example 13.17 can be combined to read

```
struct  sample  {
                  unsigned a : 1;
                  unsigned b : 3;
                  unsigned c : 2;
                  unsigned d : 1;
   } v;
```

The interpretation of the variable v is the same as that given in Example 13.17. Moreover, the tag can be omitted, so that the above declaration can be further shortened to

```
struct  {
          unsigned a : 1;
          unsigned b : 3;
          unsigned c : 2;
          unsigned d : 1;
   } v;
```

A field within a structure cannot overlap a word within the computer's memory. This issue does not arise if the sum of the field widths does not exceed the size of an unsigned integer quantity. If the sum of the field widths does exceed this word size, however, then any overlapping field will automatically be forced to the beginning of the next word.

EXAMPLE 13.19   Consider the simple C program shown below.

```
#include <stdio.h>

main()
{
    static struct  {
                  unsigned a : 5;        /* begin first word */
                  unsigned b : 5;
                  unsigned c : 5;
                  unsigned d : 5;        /* forced to second word */
    } v = {1, 2, 3, 4};

    printf("v.a = %d   v.b = %d   v.c = %d   v.d = %d\n", v.a, v.b, v.c, v.d);
    printf("v requires %d bytes\n", sizeof(v));
}
```

The four fields within v require a total of 20 bits. If the computer only allows 16 bits for an unsigned integer quantity, this structure declaration will require two words of memory. The first three fields will be stored in the first word. Since the last field will straddle the word boundary, it is automatically forced to the beginning of the second word.

Fig. 13.2 shows the layout of the bit fields within the two 16-bit words.

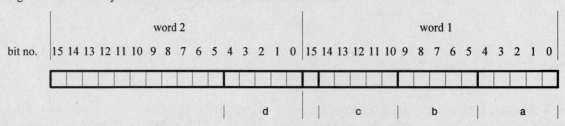

Fig. 13.2 Four bit fields within two 16-bit words

Execution of this program will produce the following output.

```
v.a = 1    v.b = 2    v.c = 3    v.d = 4
v requires 4 bytes
```

The second line verifies the need for two words, since each word is equivalent to 2 bytes. (With some compilers, v will require only 3 bytes; i.e., 24 bits.)

Unnamed fields can be used to control the alignment of bit fields within a word of memory. Such fields provide padding within the word. The size of the unnamed field determines the extent of the padding.

EXAMPLE 13.20   Consider the simple C program shown below.

```
#include <stdio.h>

main()
{
    static struct  {
                     unsigned a : 5;
                     unsigned b : 5;
                     unsigned c : 5;
    } v = {1, 2, 3};

    printf("v.a = %d    v.b = %d    v.c = %d\n", v.a, v.b, v.c);
    printf("v requires %d bytes\n", sizeof(v));
}
```

This program is similar to that shown in the previous example. Now, however, only three fields (15 bits) are defined within v. Hence, only one word of memory is required to store this structure.

Execution of this program results in the following output.

```
v.a = 1    v.b = 2    v.c = 3
v requires 2 bytes
```

The second line of output verifies that all three fields can be stored within a single unsigned word (2 bytes).

Let us alter this program by adding an unnamed field whose field width is 6 bits; i.e.,

```
#include <stdio.h>

main()
{
    static struct  {
                     unsigned a : 5;     /* begin first word */
                     unsigned b : 5;
                     unsigned   : 6;     /* fill out first word */
                     unsigned c : 5;     /* begin second word */
    } v = {1, 2, 3};

    printf("v.a = %d    v.b = %d    v.c = %d\n", v.a, v.b, v.c);
    printf("v requires %d bytes\n", sizeof(v));
}
```

Now two words of memory will be required. The first two fields will be stored within the first word, followed by 6 vacant bits (for a total of 16 bits, thus filling the first word). The last field will therefore be aligned with the beginning of the second word, as illustrated in Fig. 13.3.

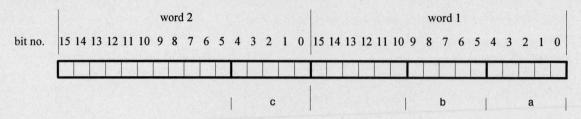

Fig. 13.3 Three bit fields within two 16-bit words

When this program is executed, the following output is produced.

```
v.a = 1   v.b = 2   v.c = 3
v requires 4 bytes
```

From the last line of output, we see that two words (4 bytes) are now required to store the three fields because of the additional padding.

Another way to control the alignment of bit fields is to include an unnamed field whose width is zero. This will automatically force the next field to be aligned with the beginning of a new word.

EXAMPLE 13.21   Consider the simple C program shown below.

```
#include <stdio.h>

main()
{
    static struct  {
                    unsigned a : 5;        /* begin first word */
                    unsigned b : 5;
                    unsigned   : 0;        /* force alignment with second word */
                    unsigned c : 5;        /* begin second word */
    } v = {1, 2, 3};
    printf("v.a = %d   v.b = %d   v.c = %d\n", v.a, v.b, v.c);
    printf("v requires %d bytes\n", sizeof(v));
}
```

This program is similar to the second program shown in the last example. Now, however, the structure declaration includes an unnamed bit field whose field width is zero. This will automatically force the last field to the beginning of a new word, as illustrated previously in Fig. 13.3.

When this program is executed, the following output is generated.

```
v.a = 1   v.b = 2   v.c = 3
v requires 4 bytes
```

The last line verifies that two words (4 bytes) are required to store the three fields, as defined above. (With some compilers, v will require only 3 bytes; i.e., 24 bits.)

Remember that some compilers order bit fields from right to left (i.e., from low-order bits to high-order bits) within a word, whereas other compilers order the fields from left to right (high-order to low-order bits). Check your programmer's reference manual to determine how this is done on your particular computer.

EXAMPLE 13.22   Consider the first structure declaration presented in Example 13.20; i.e.,

```
static struct   {
                unsigned a : 5;
                unsigned b : 5;
                unsigned c : 5;
} v = {1, 2, 3};
```

With some computers, the first field (v.a) will occupy the rightmost 5 bits (i.e., bits 0 through 4), the second field (v.b) will occupy the next 5 bits (bits 5 through 9), and the last field (v.c) will occupy bits 10 through 14. The leftmost bit (i.e, bit 15, which is the most significant bit) will be unoccupied, as shown in Fig. 13.4(a).

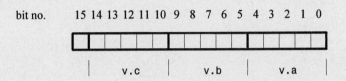

Fig. 13.4 (a) Bit fields with right-to-left ordering

With other computers, however, the first field (v.a) will occupy the leftmost 5 bits (bits 11 through 15), the second field (v.b) will occupy bits 6 through 10, and the last field (v.c) will occupy bits 1 through 5. The rightmost bit (i.e., bit 0, which is the least significant bit) will be unoccupied, as shown in Fig. 13.4(b). Thus, a program written for one type of computer may produce incorrect results when run on the other type of computer.

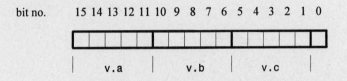

Fig. 13.4 (b) Bit fields with left-to-right ordering

Bit fields are accessed in the same manner as other structure members, and they may appear within arithmetic expressions as unsigned integer quantities. There are, however, several restrictions on their use. In particular, arrays of bit fields are not permitted; the address operator (&) cannot be applied to a bit field; a pointer cannot access a bit field; and a function cannot return a bit field.

EXAMPLE 13.23 Data Compression (Storing Names and Birthdates)   This example presents a program that stores the names and birthdates of several students within an array. The overall strategy will be to first enter each student's name and birthdate. The program will then display the name, birthday (i.e., day of the week that the student was born) and date of birth for each student. The birthdays will be determined using the method described in Example 10.28.

Each birthdate will consist of three integer quantities: the month, day and year of birth. (The year will be stored as a 3-digit integer, representing the number of years since 1900, as described in Example 10.28. Thus, the year 1999 will be entered as 1999 but stored simply as 99. Similarly, the year 2010 will be entered as 2010 and stored as 110.) To conserve memory, these three integer quantities will be stored in bit fields within a single 16-bit word, as shown below.

```
typedef struct   {
                unsigned month : 4;
                unsigned day   : 5;
                unsigned year  : 7;
} date;
```

The month will be stored as a 4-bit unsigned integer whose values can range from 0 to 15 (note that $2^4 - 1 = 15$). Of course, we will be concerned only with the values 1 through 12. Similarly, the day will be stored as a 5-bit unsigned integer. Its values can range from 0 to 31 (note that $2^5 - 1 = 31$). And the year will be stored as a 7-bit integer, whose values can range from 0 to 127 (note that $2^7 - 1 = 127$). Hence, we will be able to accommodate birthdates ranging from the year 1900 to the year 2027.

Here is the entire program.

```c
/* Store students' names and birthdates within an array, using bit fields
   for the birthdates.

   When finished, display each student's name and birthdate.
   Display each birthdate as follows: day_of_week, month, day, year    */

#include <stdio.h>
#include <string.h>

int convert(int mm, int dd, int yy);        /* function prototype */

main()
{
    int mm, dd, yy, count = 0;
    int day_of_week;    /* day of the week (0 -> Sunday, 1 -> Monday, etc.) */

    typedef struct   {
                        unsigned month : 4;
                        unsigned day   : 5;
                        unsigned year  : 7;
    } date;

    struct   {
                char name[30];
                date birthdate;
    } student[40];

    static char *weekday[] = {"Sunday", "Monday", "Tuesday", "Wednesday",
                              "Thursday", "Friday", "Saturday"};

    static char *month[] = {"January", "February", "March", "April",
                            "May", "June", "July", "August", "September",
                            "October", "November", "December"};

    /* opening message */
    printf("Data Entry Routine\nType \'END\' when finished\n");
    printf("\nName: ");
    scanf(" %[^\n]", student[count].name);

    /* enter data for all students */
    while (strcmp(student[count].name, "END") != 0)   {
            printf("Birthdate (mm dd yyyy): ");
            scanf("%d %d %d", &mm, &dd, &yy);

            /* assign integer input data to bit fields */
            student[count].birthdate.month = mm;
            student[count].birthdate.day = dd;
            student[count].birthdate.year = yy - 1900;

            printf("\nName: ");
            scanf(" %[^\n]", student[++count].name);
    }
```

```
        /* convert birthdates and display output for all students */
        count = 0;
        while (strcmp(student[count].name, "END") != 0)    {
                day_of_week = convert(student[count].birthdate.month,
                                      student[count].birthdate.day,
                                      student[count].birthdate.year);
                printf("\n%s     ", student[count].name);
                printf("%s %s %d, %d\n", weekday[day_of_week],
                                        month[student[count].birthdate.month-1],
                                        student[count].birthdate.day,
                                        student[count].birthdate.year + 1900);
                                        ++count;

        }
}


int convert(int mm, int dd, int yy)      /* convert date to numerical day of week */
{
    long ndays;          /* number of days from start of 1900 */
    long ncycles;        /* number of 4-year cycles beyond 1900 */
    int nyears;          /* number of years beyond last 4-year cycle */
    int day;             /* day of week (0, 1, . . ., 6) */

    /* numerical conversions */
    ndays = (long) (30.42 * (mm - 1)) + dd; /* approximate day of year */

    if (mm == 2) ++ndays;                      /* adjust for February */
    if ((mm > 2) && (mm < 8)) --ndays;       /* adjust for March - July */
    if ((yy % 4 == 0) && (mm > 2)) ++ndays; /* adjust for leap year */

    ncycles = yy / 4;                          /* 4-year cycles beyond 1900 */
    ndays += ncycles * 1461;                   /* add days for 4-year cycles */

    nyears = yy % 4;             /* years beyond last 4-year cycle */
    if (nyears > 0)              /* add days for yrs beyond last 4-yr cycle */
       ndays += 365 * nyears + 1;

    if (ndays > 59) --ndays;    /* adjust for 1900 (NOT a leap year) */

    day = ndays % 7;

    return(day);
}
```

Within this program, we see that student is a 40-element array of structures. Each array element (i.e., each structure) consists of a 30-element character array (name) that represents the student's name, and another structure (birthdate) that contains the student's date of birth. This last structure is comprised of the three bit fields birthdate.month, birthdate.day and birthdate.year as members.

The program also contains two arrays of strings, whose elements represent the days of the week and the months of the year, respectively. These arrays are discussed in Example 10.28. In addition, the program includes the function convert, which is used to convert any date between January 1, 1900 and December 31, 2099 into an equivalent (integer-valued) day of the week. This function differs only slightly from the function described in Example 10.28. (Within convert, the statement yy $-=$ 1900, which was present in Example 10.28, is now absent.)

The main function consists essentially of two while loops. The first loop is used to enter and store input data for all the students. Each pass through the loop will enter and store data for a different student. This process will continue until the word "END" has been detected for a student name (in either upper- or lowercase). Notice the manner in which values are assigned to the bit fields in this loop.

The second loop causes each student's birthdate to be converted into a day of the week and then displayed, along with the student's name and date of birth. The details governing the birthdate conversion and the display of information are given in Example 10.28, and need not be repeated here. Notice the manner in which the bit fields are accessed within the function calls.

The input dialog and the corresponding output resulting from a typical program execution are shown below. As usual, the user's responses are underlined.

```
Data Entry Routine
Type 'END' when finished

Name: Rob Smith
Birthdate (mm dd yy): 7 20 1972

Name: Judy Thompson
Birthdate (mm dd yy): 11 27 1983

Name: Jim Williams
Birthdate (mm dd yy): 12 29 1998

Name: Mort Davis
Birthdate (mm dd yy): 6 10 2010

Name: END

Rob Smith      Thursday July 20, 1972

Judy Thompson    Sunday November 27, 1983

Jim Williams    Tuesday December 29, 1998

Mort Davis     Thursday June 10, 2010
```

Before leaving this example, a few additional observations are in order. First, it should be pointed out that the memory savings resulting from the use of bit fields has not been dramatic. However, the benefit of this data compression technique would be greater if the dimensionality of the student array were to increase.

Second, some additional data compression could be realized by storing eight 7-bit ASCII characters in seven bytes of memory, using the bitwise shift operators. Each byte would then contain one complete character, plus one bit from the eighth character. This would result in a 12.5 percent reduction in the memory requirements. The details of this technique are beyond the scope of our present discussion, though you may wish to experiment with this technique on your own. (See Prob. 13.55 at the end of this chapter.)

Review Questions

13.1   What is meant by low-level programming?

13.2   What are registers? In general terms, what are registers used for?

13.3   What is the purpose of the `register` storage class? What benefits are obtained from the use of this storage class? What types of variables can be assigned this storage class?

13.4   What is the scope of register variables?

13.5   Summarize the rules for using register variables.

13.6   Why might a `register` declaration not be honored? If a `register` declaration is not honored, how are the register variables treated?

13.7   How can a programmer tell if a `register` declaration is honored within a program?

13.8   What is meant by bitwise operations?

13.9   What is the purpose of the one's complement operator? To what types of operands does it apply? To what precedence group does it belong? What is its associativity?

13.10   Describe the three logical bitwise operators. What is the purpose of each?

13.11   What types of operands are required by each of the logical bitwise operators?

13.12   Summarize the values that are returned by each of the logical bitwise operations. Consider all possible operand values in your answer.

13.13   Describe the precedence and the associativity for each of the logical bitwise operators.

13.14   What is a masking operation? What is the purpose of each operand? Which operand is the mask, and how is it chosen?

13.15   Describe a masking operation in which a portion of a given bit pattern is copied while the remaining bits are all set to 0. Which logical bitwise operation is used for this operation? How is the mask selected?

13.16   Describe a masking operation in which a portion of a given bit pattern is copied while the remaining bits are all set to 1. Which logical bitwise operation is used for this operation? How is the mask defined? Compare your answer with the answer to the previous question.

13.17   Describe a masking operation in which a portion of a given bit pattern is copied while the remaining bits are inverted. Which logical bitwise operation is used for this operation? How is the mask defined? Compare your answer with the answers to the previous two questions.

13.18   Why is the one's complement operator sometimes used in a masking operation? Under what conditions is its use desirable?

13.19   How can a particular bit be toggled on and off repeatedly? Which logical bitwise operation is used for this purpose?

13.20   Describe the two bitwise shift operators. What requirement must the operands satisfy? What is the purpose of each operand?

13.21   Describe the precedence and the associativity for the bitwise shift operators.

13.22   When shifting bits to the left or to the right, what happens to the bits shifted out of the original word position?

13.23   When shifting bits to the left, what value fills the rightmost bit positions that are vacated by the shifting bits?

13.24   When shifting bits to the right, what value fills the leftmost bit positions that are vacated by the shifting bits? Does the type of operand being shifted affect this value? Explain fully. Compare your answer with the answer to the last question.

13.25   Do all C compilers handle right-shift operations in the same manner? Explain fully.

13.26   List the bitwise assignment operators and describe their purpose.

13.27   Describe each of the operands in a bitwise assignment operation.

13.28   Describe the precedence and the associativity for the bitwise assignment operators.

13.29   What are bit fields? To what type of data structure do bit fields belong? How are individual bit fields accessed?

13.30   Summarize the rules for defining bit fields.

13.31   What data type must be associated with each bit field?

13.32   What happens if a bit field overlaps a word within the computer's memory?

13.33   Within a bit field declaration, what interpretation is given to an unnamed bit field? What interpretation is given to a zero-width field?

13.34   In what order are the bit fields arranged within a word? Is this convention uniform among all compilers?

13.35   What restrictions apply to the use of bit fields within a program, after they have been properly declared?

Problems

13.36 Declare the variables u and v to be unsigned integer variables with the `register` storage class.

13.37 Declare the variables u, v, x and y to be integer variables whose initial values are 1, 2, 3 and 4, respectively. Assume that u and v will be automatic variables. Assign the `register` storage class to x and y.

13.38 Suppose that `funct` is a function that accepts a pointer to an unsigned integer register variable as an argument, and returns a pointer to an unsigned integer. Write a skeletal outline of the `main` calling routine and `funct`, illustrating how these features are defined.

13.39 Suppose that a is an unsigned integer whose value is (hexadecimal) `0xa2c3`. Write the corresponding bit pattern for this value. Then evaluate each of the following bitwise expressions, first showing the resulting bit pattern and then the equivalent hexadecimal value. Utilize the original value of a in each expression. Assume that a is stored in a 16-bit word.

(*a*) ~a   (*h*) a >> 3   (*o*) a & ~(0x3f06 << 8)

(*b*) a & 0x3f06   (*i*) a << 5   (*p*) a ^ ~0x3f06 << 8

(*c*) a ^ 0x3f06   (*j*) a & ~a   (*q*) (a ^ ~0x3f06) << 8

(*d*) a | 0x3f06   (*k*) a ^ ~a   (*r*) a ^ ~(0x3f06 << 8)

(*e*) a & ~0x3f06   (*l*) a | ~a   (*s*) a | ~0x3f06 << 8

(*f*) a ^ ~0x3f06   (*m*) a & ~0x3f06 << 8   (*t*) (a | ~0x3f06) << 8

(*g*) a | ~0x3f06   (*n*) (a & ~0x3f06) << 8   (*u*) a | ~(0x3f06 << 8)

13.40 Rewrite each of the following bitwise expressions in the form of a bitwise assignment statement, where the value of each expression is assigned to the variable a.

(*a*) Prob. 13.39 (*b*)   (*d*) Prob. 13.39 (*h*)   (*g*) Prob. 13.39 (*o*)

(*b*) Prob. 13.39 (*c*)   (*e*) Prob. 13.39 (*i*)

(*c*) Prob. 13.39 (*g*)   (*f*) Prob. 13.39 (*k*)

13.41 Define a mask and write the appropriate masking operation for each of the situations described below.

(*a*) Copy the odd bits (bits 1, 3, 5, . . . , 15) and place zeros in the even bit locations (bits 0, 2, 4, . . . , 14) of a 16-bit, unsigned integer quantity represented by the variable v. Assume that bit 0 is the rightmost bit.

(*b*) Strip the most significant bit (the leftmost bit) from an 8-bit character represented by the variable c. (Certain word processors use this bit to control the formatting of the text within a document. Stripping this bit, i.e., setting it to zero, can transform the word processor document into a text file consisting of ordinary ASCII characters.)

(*c*) Copy the odd bits (bits 1, 3, 5, . . . , 15) and place one's in the even bit locations (bits 0, 2, 4, . . . , 14) of a 16-bit, unsigned integer quantity represented by the variable v. Assume that bit 0 is the rightmost bit.

(*d*) Toggle (invert) the values of bits 1 and 6 of a 16-bit, unsigned integer quantity represented by the variable v, while preserving all of the remaining bits. Assign the new bit pattern to v. Assume that bit 0 is the rightmost bit.

13.42 (*a*) Suppose that v is a signed, 16-bit integer quantity whose hexadecimal value is `0x369c`. Evaluate each of the following shift expressions. (Utilize the original value of v in each expression.)

(*i*) v << 4

(*ii*) v >> 4

(*b*) Now suppose the value of v is changed to `0xc369`. Evaluate each of the following shift expressions, and compare the results with those obtained in part (*a*). Explain any differences.

(*i*) v << 4

(*ii*) v >> 4

13.43 Describe the composition of each of the following structures. Assume a 16-bit integer word.

(*a*)
```
struct  {
            unsigned u : 3;
            unsigned v : 1;
            unsigned w : 7;
            unsigned x : 5;
};
```

(*b*)
```
static struct  {
                unsigned u : 3;
                unsigned v : 1;
                unsigned w : 7;
                unsigned x : 5;
} a = {2, 1, 16, 8};
```

(*c*)
```
struct  {
            unsigned u : 7;
            unsigned v : 7;
            unsigned w : 7;
} a;
```

(*d*)
```
struct  {
            unsigned u : 7;
            unsigned   : 9;
            unsigned v : 7;
            unsigned   : 2;
            unsigned w : 7;
};
```

(*e*)
```
struct  {
            unsigned u : 7;
            unsigned   : 0;
            unsigned v : 7;
            unsigned   : 0;
            unsigned w : 7;
}
```

13.44 Write a structure declaration for each of the following situations. Assume a 16-bit integer word.

(*a*) Define three bit fields, called a, b and c, whose widths are 6 bits, 4 bits and 6 bits, respectively.

(*b*) Declare a structure-type variable v having the composition defined in part (*a*) above. Assign the initial values 3, 5 and 7, respectively, to the three bit fields. Are the bit fields large enough to accommodate these values?

(*c*) What are the largest values that can be assigned to each of the bit fields defined in part (*a*) above?

(*d*) Define three bit fields, called a, b and c, whose widths are 8 bits, 6 bits and 5 bits, respectively. How will these fields be stored within the computer's memory?

(*e*) Define three bit fields, called a, b and c, whose widths are 8 bits, 6 bits and 5 bits, respectively. Separate a and b with 2 vacant bits.

(*f*) Define three bit fields, called a, b and c, whose widths are 8 bits, 6 bits and 5 bits, respectively. Force b to the beginning of a second word of storage. Separate b and c with 2 vacant bits.

Programming Problems

13.45 Modify the program presented in Example 13.2 (repeated calculation of a sequence of Fibonacci numbers) so that f, f1 and f2 are pointers to integer quantities stored within registers.

13.46   Problem 6.69(*f*) describes a method for calculating prime numbers, and suggests writing a program to calculate the first *n* prime numbers, where *n* is a specified quantity (e.g., *n* = 100). Modify this problem statement so that the list of *n* prime numbers is generated 10,000,000 times. Display the list only once, after the last pass through the loop.

Solve the problem with and without the `register` storage class specification. Compare the execution times and the sizes of the compiled object programs.

13.47   Another way to generate a list of prime numbers is to use the famous *sieve of Eratosthenes*. This method proceeds as follows.

(*a*) Generate an ordered list of integers ranging from 2 to *n*.

(*b*) For some particular integer, *i*, within the list, carry out the following operations:

    (*i*)   Tag the integer as a prime (you may wish to place it in an array, or write it out to a data file).

    (*ii*) Then remove all succeeding integers that are multiples of *i*.

(*c*) Repeat part (*b*) for each successive value of i within the list, beginning with *i* = 2 and ending with the last remaining integer.

Write a C program that uses this method to determine the primes within a list of numbers ranging from 1 to *n*, where *n* is an input quantity. Repeat the calculation 30,000 times, displaying the list of prime numbers at the end of the last pass through the loop.

Solve the problem with and without the `register` storage class specification. Compare the execution times and the sizes of the compiled object programs.

13.48   Write a C program that will accept a hexadecimal number as input, and then display a menu that will permit any of the following operations to be carried out:

(*a*) Display the hexadecimal equivalent of the one's complement.

(*b*) Carry out a masking operation and then display the hexadecimal equivalent of the result.

(*c*) Carry out a bit shifting operation and then display the hexadecimal equivalent of the result.

(*d*) Exit.

If the masking operation is selected, prompt the user for the type of operation (*bitwise and, bitwise exclusive or,* or *bitwise or*), and then a (hexadecimal) value for the mask. If the bit shifting operation is selected, prompt the user for the type of shift (left or right), and then the number of bits.

Test the program with several different (hexadecimal) input values of your own choice.

13.49   Modify the program written for Prob. 13.48 above so that binary bit patterns are displayed in addition to hexadecimal values. Use a separate function, patterned after the program shown in Example 13.16, to display the binary bit patterns.

13.50   Modify the program written for Prob. 13.49 so that the input quantity can be a decimal, hexadecimal or octal constant. Begin by displaying a menu that allows the user to specify the type of number (i.e., the desired number system) before entering the actual value. Then display the input value in the other two number systems and in terms of its equivalent binary bit pattern.

After the input quantity has been entered and displayed, generate the main menu prompting for the type of operation, as described in Prob. 13.48. If a masking operation is selected, enter the mask as either a hexadecimal or an octal constant. Display the result of each operation in decimal, hexadecimal, octal and binary.

13.51   Write a C program that will illustrate the equivalence between

(*a*) Shifting a binary number to the left *n* bits and multiplying the binary number by 2^n.

(*b*) Shifting a binary number to the right *n* bits and dividing the binary number by 2^n (or equivalently, multiplying the binary number by 2^{-n}).

Choose the initial binary number carefully, so that bits will not be lost as a result of the shifting operation. (For the shift left, choose a relatively small number so that there will be several leading zeros in the leftmost bit positions. For the shift right, choose a relatively large number, with zeros in the rightmost bit positions.)

13.52 Write a complete C program that will encode and decode the contents of a text file (i.e., a character-oriented data file) by replacing each character with its one's complement. Note that the one's complement of a one's complement is the original character. Hence, the process of obtaining the one's complement can be used either to encode the original text or to decode the encoded text.

Include the following features in your program:

(a) Enter the contents of an ordinary text file from the keyboard.

(b) Save the current text file in its present state (either encoded or decoded).

(c) Retrieve a text file that has been saved (either encoded or decoded).

(d) Encode or decode the current text file (i.e., reverse its current state by obtaining the one's complement of each of the characters).

(e) Display the current text file in its present state (either encoded or decoded).

Generate a menu that will allow the user to select any of these features, as desired.

13.53 Alter the program written for Prob. 13.52 so that the encoding and decoding is carried out using a *bitwise exclusive or* masking operation rather than the one's complement operation. Include a provision which will allow the user to specify a *key* (i.e., a mask, which will be the second operand in the *exclusive or* operation). Since *exclusive or* provides a toggling operation, it can be used either to encode the original text or to decode the encoded text. The same key must be used for both the encoding and the decoding.

13.54 Modify the data compression program shown in Example 13.23 so that it displays each student's age (in years), in addition to the output that is presently generated. Then add the following capabilities, as separate features:

(a) Display the age of a student whose name is specified as an input item.

(b) Display the names of all students whose age is specified by the user.

(c) Display the names of all students who are the same age or younger than a certain value specified by the user.

(d) Display the names of all students who are the same age or older than a certain value specified by the user.

Generate a menu that will allow the user to select any of these features, as desired.

13.55 Modify the program presented in Example 10.8 (analyzing a line of text) so that the 80 characters within each line of text are stored within a 70-byte character array. (Assume 7-bit ASCII characters.) To do so, use the bitwise shift operators in such a manner that a group of eight characters is stored in seven consecutive array elements (i.e., seven bytes). Each array element will contain one complete character, plus one bit from another character.

Include a provision to display the contents of the 70-byte array (using hexadecimal constants) in compressed form and in the equivalent uncompressed form.

Use the program to analyze the following line of text:

```
Personal computers with memories in excess of 8192 KB have become very common.
```

(Note that this line of text, including punctuation and blank spaces between the words, contains a total of 78 characters.) Examine the hexadecimal output as well as the results of the analysis to verify that the program executes correctly.

Chapter 14

Some Additional Features of C

In this last chapter we consider several new, unrelated features of C, and we present some additional information about certain other features that have already been discussed. We begin with a discussion of enumerations—a data type that defines a set of integer-type identifiers which can be assigned to corresponding enumeration variables. Enumeration variables are useful in programs that require flags to identify various internal logical conditions.

We then consider command line arguments, which allow parameters to be transferred to a program when the compiled object program is executed from the operating system. File names, for example, can easily be transferred to a program in this manner.

A discussion of the C library functions is then presented, in which the library functions provided by most commercial C compilers are viewed from a broader perspective. This is followed by a discussion of macros, which provide an alternative to the use of library functions. The use of macros may be more desirable than the use of library functions in certain situations. The chapter concludes with a discussion of the C preprocessor, which is a set of special commands that are carried out at the beginning of the compilation process.

14.1 ENUMERATIONS

An *enumeration* is a data type, similar to a structure or a union. Its members are constants that are written as identifiers, though they have signed integer values. These constants represent values that can be assigned to corresponding enumeration variables.

In general terms, an enumeration may be defined as

        enum   *tag*   {*member 1*,   *member 2*,   . . . ,   *member m*};

where enum is a required keyword; *tag* is a name that identifies enumerations having this composition; and *member 1*, *member 2*, . . . , *member m* represent the individual identifiers that may be assigned to variables of this type (see below). The member names must differ from one another, and they must be distinct from other identifiers whose scope is the same as that of the enumeration.

Once the enumeration has been defined, corresponding enumeration variables can declared as

        storage-class enum   *tag*   *variable 1*,   *variable 2*,   . . .,   *variable n*;

where *storage-class* is an optional storage class specifier, enum is a required keyword, *tag* is the name that appeared in the enumeration definition, and *variable 1*, *variable 2*, . . . , *variable n* are enumeration variables of type *tag*.

The enumeration definition can be combined with the variable declarations, as indicated below.

        storage-class enum   *tag*   {*member 1*,   *member 2*,   . . .,   *member m*}
                                   variable 1,   *variable 2*,   . . . ,   *variable n*;

The *tag* is optional in this situation.

EXAMPLE 14.1   A C program contains the following declarations.

```
enum  colors  {black, blue, cyan, green, magenta, red, white, yellow};

colors  foreground, background;
```

The first line defines an enumeration named `colors` (i.e., the tag is `colors`). The enumeration consists of eight constants whose names are `black`, `blue`, `cyan`, `green`, `magenta`, `red`, `white` and `yellow`.

The second line declares the variables `foreground` and `background` to be enumeration variables of type `colors`. Thus, each variable can be assigned any one of the constants `black`, `blue`, `cyan`, . . . , `yellow`.

The two declarations can be combined if desired, resulting in

```
enum  colors  {black, blue, cyan, green, magenta, red, white, yellow}
                                                  foreground, background;
```

or, without the tag, simply

```
enum  {black, blue, cyan, green, magenta, red, white, yellow} foreground, background;
```

Enumeration constants are automatically assigned equivalent integer values, beginning with 0 for the first constant, with each successive constant increasing by 1. Thus, *member 1* will automatically be assigned the value 0, *member 2* will be assigned 1, and so on.

EXAMPLE 14.2   Consider the enumeration defined in Example 14.1, i.e.,

```
enum  colors  {black, blue, cyan, green, magenta, red, white, yellow};
```

The enumeration constants will represent the following integer values.

```
black       0
blue        1
cyan        2
green       3
magenta     4
red         5
white       6
yellow      7
```

These automatic assignments can be overridden within the definition of the enumeration. That is, some of the constants can be assigned explicit integer values which differ from the default values. To do so, each constant (i.e., each member) which is assigned an explicit value is expressed as an ordinary assignment expression; i.e., *member = int*, where *int* represents a signed integer quantity. Those constants that are not assigned explicit values will automatically be assigned values which increase successively by 1 from the last explicit assignment. This may cause two or more enumeration constants to have the same integer value.

EXAMPLE 14.3   Here is a variation of the enumeration defined in Examples 14.1 and 14.2.

```
enum  colors  {black = -1, blue, cyan, green, magenta, red = 2, white, yellow};
```

The enumeration constants will now represent the following integer values.

```
black        -1
blue          0
cyan          1
green         2
magenta       3
red           2
white         3
yellow        4
```

The constants black and red are now assigned the explicit values −1 and 2, respectively. The remaining enumeration constants are automatically assigned values that increase successively by 1 from the last explicit assignment. Thus, blue, cyan, green and magenta are assigned the values 0, 1, 2 and 3, respectively. Similarly, white and yellow are assigned the values 3 and 4. Notice that there are now duplicate assignments; i.e., green and red both represent 2, whereas magenta and white both represent 3.

Enumeration variables can be processed in the same manner as other integer variables. Thus, they can be assigned new values, compared, etc. It should be understood, however, that enumeration variables are generally used internally, to indicate various conditions that can arise within a program. Hence, there are certain restrictions associated with their use. In particular, *an enumeration constant cannot be read into the computer and assigned to an enumeration variable.* (It is possible to enter an *integer* and assign it to an enumeration variable, though this is generally not done.) Moreover, *only the integer value of an enumeration variable can be written out of the computer.*

EXAMPLE 14.4   Consider once again the declarations presented in Example 14.1, i.e.,

```
enum  colors  {black, blue, cyan, green, magenta, red, white, yellow};
colors  foreground, background;
```

Several statements involving the use of the enumeration variables foreground and background are shown below.

```
foreground = white;

background = blue;

if (background == blue)
   foreground = yellow;
else
   foreground = white;

if (foreground == background)
   foreground = (enum colors)  (++background % 8);

switch (background)  {
case black:
          foreground = white;
          break;
case blue:
          blue:
          cyan:
          green:
          magenta:
          red:
          foreground = yellow;
          break;
```

```
    case white:
            foreground = black;
            break;

    case yellow:
            foreground = blue;
            break;

    case default:
            printf("ERROR IN SELECTION OF BACKGROUND COLOR\n");
    }
```

The use of enumeration variables within a program can often increase the logical clarity of that program. Enumeration variables are particularly useful as flags, to indicate various options for carrying out a calculation, or to identify various conditions that may have arisen as a result of previous internal calculations. From this perspective, the use of enumeration variables within a complex program is encouraged. It should be understood, however, that ordinary integer variables can always be used in place of enumeration variables. Thus, enumeration variables do not provide any fundamentally new capabilities.

EXAMPLE 14.5 Raising a Number to a Power   In Example 11.37 we saw a C program to evaluate the formula $y = x^n$, where x and y are floating-point values and n is either an integer or a floating-point exponent. That program made use of the following data structures.

```
    typedef  union  {
        float fexp;             /* floating-point exponent */
        int nexp;               /* integer exponent */
    } nvals;

    typedef  struct  {
        float x;                /* value to be raised to a power */
        char flag;              /* 'f' if exponent is floating-point,
                                   'i' if exponent is integer */
        nvals exp;              /* union containing exponent */
    } values;
```

Note that the union contains the value of the exponent, which may be either an integer or a floating-point quantity. The structure includes the value of x, a flag (a single character), which indicates the nature of the exponent, and the union, which contains the exponent.

We now present another version of this program, in which the single-character flag is replaced with an enumeration variable. The data structures are therefore modified as follows.

```
    typedef  enum  {floating_exp, integer_exp}  exp_type;

    typedef  union  {
        float fexp;             /* floating-point exponent */
        int nexp;               /* integer exponent */
    } nvals;

    typedef  struct  {
        float x;                /* value to be raised to a power */
        exp_type flag;          /* flag indicating type of exponent */
        nvals exp;              /* union containg exponent */
    } values;
```

Notice that flag, which is a member of the structure of type values, is now an enumeration variable of type exp_type. This variable can take on the value floating_exp or integer_exp, indicating either a floating-point exponent or an integer exponent, respectively.

The calculations will be carried out differently, depending on the nature of the exponent. In particular, the exponentiation will be carried out by repeated multiplication in the case of an integer exponent, and by utilizing logarithms in the case of a floating-point exponent.

Here is the modified version of the program.

```c
/* program to raise a number to a power */

#include <stdio.h>
#include <math.h>

typedef  enum  {floating_exp, integer_exp}  exp_type;

typedef  union  {
    float fexp;             /* floating-point exponent */
    int nexp;               /* integer exponent */
} nvals;

typedef  struct  {
    float x;                /* value to be raised to a power */
    exp_type flag;          /* flag indicating type of exponent */
    nvals exp;              /* union containing exponent */
} values;

float power(values a);    /* function prototype*/

main()
{
    values a;              /* structure containing x, flag and fexp/nexp */
    int i;
    float n, y;

    /* enter input data */
    printf("y = x^n\n\n\nEnter a value for x: ");
    scanf("%f", &a.x);
    printf("Enter a value for n: ");
    scanf("%f", &n);

    /* determine type of exponent */
    i = (int) n;
    a.flag = (i == n) ? integer_exp : floating_exp;
    if (a.flag == integer_exp)
       a.exp.nexp = i;
    else
       a.exp.fexp = n;

    /* raise x to the appropriate power and display the result */
    if (a.flag == floating_exp && a.x <= 0.0)        {
       printf("\nERROR - Cannot raise a non-positive number to a ");
       printf("floating-point power");
    }
    else {
       y = power(a);
       printf("\ny = %.4f", y);
    }
}
```

```
        float power(values a)  /* carry out the exponentiation */
        {
            int i;
            float y = a.x;

            if (a.flag == integer_exp)  {  /* integer exponent */
                if (a.exp.nexp == 0)
                    y = 1.0;                    /* zero exponent */
                else  {
                    for (i = 1; i < abs(a.exp.nexp); ++i)
                        y *= a.x;
                    if (a.exp.nexp < 0)
                        y = 1./y;               /* negative integer exponent */
                }
            }
            else                            /* floating-point exponent */
                y = exp(a.exp.fexp * log(a.x));

            return(y);
        }
```

When executed, this program behaves in exactly the same manner as the earlier version. You may wish to verify this by executing the program using the input values shown in Example 11.37.

This version of the program does not represent a dramatic improvement over the earlier version. The advantage in using enumeration variables becomes clearer, however, in programs that include more complicated options.

An enumeration variable can be initialized, in much the same manner as other variables in C. The initialization can be accomplished by assigning either an enumeration constant or an integer value to the variable. Usually, however, the variable will be assigned an enumeration constant, as illustrated below (also, see Example 14.13).

EXAMPLE 14.6 A C program contains the following declarations.

```
        enum  colors  {black, blue, cyan, green, magenta, red, white, yellow};

        colors  foreground = yellow, background = red;
```

Thus, the enumeration variables foreground and background are assigned the initial values yellow and red, respectively. These initialization assignments are equivalent to writing

```
        foreground = 7;

        background = 5;
```

However, enumeration variables are usually assigned enumeration constants rather than their equivalent integer values.

14.2 COMMAND LINE PARAMETERS

You may have been wondering about the empty parentheses in the first line of the main function, i.e., main(). These parentheses may contain special arguments that allow parameters to be passed to main from the operating system. Most versions of C permit two such arguments, which are traditionally called argc and argv, respectively. The first of these, argc, must be an integer variable, while the second, argv, is an array of pointers to characters; i.e., an array of strings. Each string in this array will represent a parameter that is passed to main. The value of argc will indicate the number of parameters passed.

EXAMPLE 14.7   The following outline indicates how the arguments `argc` and `argv` are defined within `main`.

```
void main(int argc, char *argv[])
{
    . . . . .
}
```

The first line can be written without the keyword `void`, i.e.,

```
main(int argc, char *argv[])
```

A program is normally executed by specifying the name of the program within a menu-driven environment, as explained in Sec. 5.4. Some compilers also allow a program to be executed by specifying the name of the program (actually, the name of the file containing the compiled object program) at the *operating system level*. The program name is then interpreted as an operating system command. Hence, the line in which it appears is generally referred to as a *command line*.

In order to pass one or more parameters to the program when it is executed from the operating system, the parameters must follow the program name on the command line, e.g.,

```
program-name   parameter 1   parameter 2   . . .   parameter n
```

The individual items must be separated from one another either by blank spaces or by tabs. Some operating systems permit blank spaces to be included within a parameter provided the entire parameter is enclosed in quotation marks.

The program name will be stored as the first item in `argv`, followed by each of the parameters. Hence, if the program name is followed by n parameters, there will be $(n + 1)$ entries in `argv`, ranging from `argv[0]` to `argv[n]`. Moreover, `argc` will automatically be assigned the value $(n + 1)$. Note that the value for `argc` is not supplied explicitly from the command line.

EXAMPLE 14.8   Consider the following simple C program, which will be executed from a command line.

```
#include <stdio.h>

main(int argc, char *argv[])
{
    int count;

    printf("argc = %d\n", argc);

    for (count = 0; count < argc; ++count)
        printf("argv[%d] = %s\n", count, argv[count]);
}
```

This program allows an unspecified number of parameters to be entered from the command line. When the program is executed, the current value for `argc` and the elements of `argv` will be displayed as separate lines of output.

Suppose, for example, that the program name is `sample`, and the command line initiating the program execution is

```
sample   red   white   blue
```

Then the program will be executed, resulting in the following output.

```
argc = 4
argv[0] = sample.exe
argv[1] = red
argv[2] = white
argv[3] = blue
```

The output tells us that four separate items have been entered from the command line. The first is the program name, `sample.exe`, followed by the three parameters, `red`, `white` and `blue`. Each item is an element in the array `argv`. (Note that `sample.exe` is the name of the object file resulting from the compilation of the source code `sample.c`.)

Similarly, if the command line is

```
sample  red  "white  blue"
```

the resulting output will be

```
argc = 3
argv[0] = sample.exe
argv[1] = red
argv[2] = white  blue
```

In this case the string `"white  blue"` will be interpreted as a single parameter, because of the quotation marks.

Once the parameters have been entered, they can be utilized within the program in any desired manner. One particularly common application is to specify the names of data files as command line parameters, as illustrated below.

EXAMPLE 14.9 Reading a Data File   Here is a variation of the program shown in Example 12.4, which reads a line of text from a data file on a character-by-character basis, and displays the text on the screen. In its original form, the program read the text from a data file called `sample.dat`; i.e., the name of the data file was built into the program. Now, however, the file name is entered as a command line parameter. Thus, the program is applicable to *any* data file; it is no longer confined to `sample.dat`.

Here is the entire program.

```
/* read a line of text from a data file and display it on the screen */

#include <stdio.h>

#define  NULL  0

main(int argc, char *argv[])

{
    FILE *fpt;    /* define a pointer to pre-defined structure type FILE */

    char c;

    /* open the data file for reading only */
    if ((fpt = fopen(argv[1], "r")) == NULL)
        printf("\nERROR - Cannot open the designated file\n");

    else          /* read and display each character from the data file */
        do
            putchar(c = getc(fpt));
        while (c != '\n');

    /* close the data file */
    fclose(fpt);
}
```

Notice that the `main` function now includes the formal arguments `argc` and `argv`, defined in the manner described earlier. Also, the `fopen` statement now reads

```
fopen(argv[1], "r")
```

rather than

```
fopen("sample.dat", "r")
```

as in the earlier version of the program.

Now suppose that the program name is `readfile`. To execute this program and read the data file `sample.dat`, the command line would be written

```
readfile  sample.dat
```

The program will then behave in exactly the same manner as the earlier version shown in Example 12.4.

14.3 MORE ABOUT LIBRARY FUNCTIONS

By now we have learned that the C library functions are extensive, both in number and in purpose. We have seen evidence of this in the programming examples presented earlier in this book, and in the list of commonly used library functions given in Appendix H. Throughout this book we have used these library functions freely, wherever they were needed.

You should be aware, however, that all of the library functions presented in this book fall into a few basic categories. In particular, they facilitate various input/output operations, mathematical function evaluations, data conversions, character classifications and conversions, string manipulations, dynamic memory allocation, and certain miscellaneous operations associated with clock time.

Most commercial C compilers include many additional library functions. Some of these functions fall into the categories described above, while others fall into new categories that have not been described elsewhere in this book. For example, most compilers include library functions that can manipulate buffer areas (i.e., blocks of memory in which arrays of characters are stored temporarily), facilitate file handling and file management, and provide capabilities for carrying out searching and sorting. In addition, there may be library functions that provide access to certain operating system commands, and to the computer's internal hardware (especially instructions embedded in the computer's read-only memory). Some compilers also include library functions for more specialized applications, such as process control and computer graphics.

These library functions simplify the writing of comprehensive C programs in a number of important areas. For example, C is used to write operating systems, as well as office automation applications such as word processors, spreadsheets and data base management programs. The well known UNIX operating system is written primarily in C. So are many commercial office automation programs.

The process control functions permit applications in which programs are executed simultaneously, in a hierchical manner. Similarly, the graphics functions facilitate the writing of various graphics applications, such as "paint" programs and computer-aided design (CAD) applications. The use of C for other types of commercial applications appears to be increasing rapidly.

Detailed discussions of such comprehensive programming applications are well beyond the scope of the present text. However, you should understand that it is practical to write such applications in C, largely because of the availability of the extensive C library. To pursue these topics further, you should familiarize yourself with the library functions that accompany your particular C compiler.

14.4 MACROS

We have already seen that the `#define` statement can be used to define symbolic constants within a C program. At the beginning of the compilation process, all symbolic constants are replaced by their equivalent text (see Sec. 2.9). Thus, symbolic constants provide a form of shorthand notation that can simplify the organization of a program.

The `#define` statement can be used for more, however, than simply defining symbolic constants. In particular, it can be used to define *macros*; i.e., single identifiers that are equivalent to expressions, complete statements or groups of statements. Macros resemble functions in this sense. They are defined in an altogether different manner than functions, however, and they are treated differently during the compilation process.

EXAMPLE 14.10   Consider the simple C program shown below.

```
#include <stdio.h>

#define  area  length * width


main()
{
    int length, width;

    printf("length = ");
    scanf("%d", &length);
    printf("width = ");
    scanf("%d", &width);

    printf("\narea = %d", area);
}
```

This program contains the macro area, which represents the expression length * width. When the program is compiled, the expression length * width will replace the identifier area within the printf statement, so that the printf statement will become

```
printf("\narea = %d", length * width);
```

Note that the format string "\narea = %d" is unaffected by the #define statement (see Sec. 2.9).

When the program is executed, the values for length and width are entered interactively from the keyboard, and the corresponding value for area is displayed. A typical interactive session is shown below. The user's responses are underlined, as usual.

```
length = 3
width = 4

area = 12
```

Macro definitions are customarily placed at the beginning of a file, ahead of the first function definition. The scope of a macro definition extends from its point of definition to the end of the file. However, a macro defined in one file is not recognized within another file.

Multiline macros can be defined by placing a backward slash (\) at the end of each line except the last. This feature permits a single macro (i.e., a single identifier) to represent a compound statement.

EXAMPLE 14.11   Here is another simple C program that contains a macro.

```
#include <stdio.h>

#define  loop  for (lines = 1; lines <= n; lines++)  {       \
                    for (count = 1; count <= n - lines; count++)   \
                        putchar(' ');                          \
                    for (count = 1; count <= 2 * lines - 1; count++)   \
                        putchar('*');                          \
                    printf("\n");                              \
                }
```

```
main()
{
    int count, lines, n;

    printf("number of lines = ");
    scanf("%d", &n);
    printf("\n");

    loop
}
```

This program contains a multiline macro, which represents a compound statement. The compound statement consists of several embedded for loops. Notice the backward slash (\) at the end of each line, except the last.

When this program is compiled, the reference to the macro is actually replaced by the statements contained within the macro definition. Thus, the above program becomes

```
#include <stdio.h>

main()
{
    int count, lines, n;

    printf("number of lines = ");
    scanf("%d", &n);
    printf("\n");

    for (lines = 1; lines <= n; lines++)  {
        for (count = 1; count <= n - lines; count++)
            putchar(' ');
        for (count = 1; count <= 2 * lines - 1; count++)
            putchar('*');
        printf("\n");
    }
}
```

When the program is executed it displays a triangle of asterisks, whose size, in terms of the number of lines, is determined by a user-supplied value (i.e., the value for n). The result of a typical execution is shown below. Again, the user's response is underlined.

```
number of lines = 6

     *
    ***
   *****
  *******
 *********
***********
```

A macro definition may include arguments, which are enclosed in parentheses. The left parenthesis must appear immediately after the macro name; i.e., there can be no space separating the macro name from the left parenthesis. When a macro is defined in this manner, its appearance within a program resembles a function call.

EXAMPLE 14.12   Here is another variation of the program shown in Example 14.11.

```
#include <stdio.h>

#define  loop(n)  for (lines = 1; lines <= n; lines++)  {              \
                      for (count = 1; count <= n - lines; count++)      \
                          putchar(' ');                                 \
                      for (count = 1; count <= 2 * lines - 1; count++)  \
                          putchar('*');                                 \
                      printf("\n");                                     \
                  }

main()
{
    int count, lines, n;

    printf("number of lines = ");
    scanf("%d", &n);
    printf("\n");

    loop(n)
}
```

The program now passes the value of n to the macro, as though it were an actual argument in a function call.

When executed, the program behaves in exactly the same manner as the program shown in Example 14.11.

Macros are sometimes used in place of functions within a program. The use of a macro in place of a function eliminates the time delays associated with function calls. If a program contains many repeated function calls, the time savings resulting from the use of macros can become significant.

On the other hand, macro substitution will take place wherever a reference to a macro appears within a program. Thus, a program that contains several references to the same macro may become unreasonably long. We are therefore faced with a tradeoff between execution speed and size of the compiled object program. The use of a macro is most advantageous in applications where there are relatively few function calls but the function is called repeatedly (e.g., a single function call within a loop).

EXAMPLE 14.13 Future Value of Monthly Deposits (Compound Interest Calculations)   In Example 10.30 we saw a C program that generates the future value of a given sum of money over a specified time period for various interest rates. The program was originally structured in a manner that illustrates how one function can be passed as an argument to another function. In particular, main passed another function, either md1, md2 or md3, to table, which generated a table of future value vs. interest rate.

We now present two variations of that program. The first version utilizes function calls directly from main, whereas the second version makes use of macro substitution. Here is the first version.

```
/* personal finance calculations, using function calls */

#include <stdio.h>
#include <stdlib.h>
#include <ctype.h>
#include <math.h>

/* function prototypes */
double md1(double i, int m, double n);
double md2(double i, int m, double n);
double md3(double i, double n);
```

```c
main()    /* calculate the future value of a series of monthly deposits */
{
    enum {A = 1, S = 2, Q = 4, M = 12, D = 360, C} m;
                    /* number of compounding periods per year */

    int count;      /* loop counter */
    double n;       /* number of years */
    double a;       /* amount of each monthly payment */
    double i;       /* annual interest rate */
    double f;       /* future value */
    char freq;      /* frequency of compounding indicator */

    /* enter input data */
    printf("\nFUTURE VALUE OF A SERIES OF MONTHLY DEPOSITS\n\n");
    printf("Amount of Each Monthly Payment: ");
    scanf("%lf", &a);
    printf("Number of Years: ");
    scanf("%lf", &n);

    /* enter frequency of compounding */
    do  {
            printf("Frequency of Compounding (A, S, Q, M, D, C): ");
            scanf("%1s", &freq);
            freq = toupper(freq);   /* convert to uppercase */
            if (freq == 'A')   {
                m = A;
                printf("\nAnnual Compounding\n");
            }
            else if (freq == 'S')   {
                m = S;
                printf("\nSemiannual Compounding\n");
            }
            else if (freq == 'Q')   {
                m = Q;
                printf("\nQuarterly Compounding\n");
            }
            else if (freq == 'M')   {
                m = M;
                printf("\nMonthly Compounding\n");
            }
            else if (freq == 'D')   {
                m = D;
                printf("\nDaily Compounding\n");
            }
            else if (freq == 'C')   {
                m = C;
                printf("\nContinuous Compounding\n");
            }
            else
                printf("\nERROR - Please Repeat\n\n");
    } while (freq != 'A' && freq != 'S' && freq != 'Q' &&
            freq != 'M' && freq != 'D' && freq != 'C');

    /* carry out the calculations */
    printf("\nInterest Rate    Future Amount\n\n");
```

```
     for (count = 1; count <= 20; ++count)    {
         i = 0.01 * count;
         if (m == C)
             f = a * md3(i, n);        /* continuous compounding */
         else if (m == D)
             f = a * md2(i, m, n);     /* daily compounding */
         else
             f = a * md1(i, m, n);     /* annual, semiannual, quarterly or
                                                     monthly compounding */
         printf("    %2d            %.2f\n", count, f);
     }
}


double md1(double i, int m, double n)
/* monthly deposits, periodic compounding */

{
    double factor, ratio;

    factor = 1 + i/m;
    ratio = 12 * (pow(factor, m*n) - 1) / i;
    return(ratio);
}


double md2(double i, int m, double n)
/* monthly deposits, daily compounding */

{
    double factor, ratio;

    factor = 1 + i/m;
    ratio = (pow(factor, m*n) - 1) / (pow(factor, m/12) - 1);
    return(ratio);
}


double md3(double i, double n)
/* monthly deposits, continuous compounding */

{
    double ratio;

    ratio = (exp(i*n) - 1) / (exp(i/12) - 1);
    return(ratio);
}
```

Notice that the function table, which was included in the original program, is now combined with main, thus avoiding the need to pass one function to another. The present program utilizes an enumeration to simplify the internal bookkeeping somewhat.

Here is the second version, which utilizes macro substitution in place of the functions

```
/* personal finance calculations, using macro substitutions */

#include <stdio.h>
#include <stdlib.h>
#include <ctype.h>
#include <math.h>
```

```c
#define  md1(i, m, n)  {    /* monthly deposits, periodic compounding */    \
                factor = 1 + i/m;                                           \
                ratio = (12/m) * (pow(factor, m*n) - 1) / (i/m);           \
        }

#define  md2(i, m, n)  {    /* monthly deposits, daily compounding */       \
                factor = 1 + i/m;                                           \
                ratio = (pow(factor, m*n) - 1) / (pow(factor, m/12) - 1);  \
        }

#define  md3(i, n)     {    /* monthly deposits, continuous compounding */  \
                ratio = (exp(i*n) - 1) / (exp(i/12) - 1);                  \
        }


main()   /* calculate the future value of a series of monthly deposits */
{
    enum {A = 1, S = 2, Q = 4, M = 12, D = 360, C} m;
                            /* number of compounding periods per year */
    int count;              /* loop counter */
    double n;               /* number of years */
    double a;               /* amount of each monthly payment */
    double i;               /* annual interest rate */
    double f;               /* future value */
    double factor, ratio;   /* internal parameters */
    char freq;              /* frequency of compounding indicator */

    /* enter input data */
    printf("\nFUTURE VALUE OF A SERIES OF MONTHLY DEPOSITS\n\n");
    printf("Amount of Each Monthly Payment: ");
    scanf("%lf", &a);
    printf("Number of Years: ");
    scanf("%lf", &n);

    /* enter frequency of compounding */
    do   {
            printf("Frequency of Compounding (A, S, Q, M, D, C): ");
            scanf("%1s", &freq);
            freq = toupper(freq);   /* convert to uppercase */
            if (freq == 'A')   {
               m = A;
               printf("\nAnnual Compounding\n");
            }
            else if (freq == 'S')   {
               m = S;
               printf("\nSemiannual Compounding\n");
            }
            else if (freq == 'Q')   {
               m = Q;
               printf("\nQuarterly Compounding\n");
            }
            else if (freq == 'M')   {
               m = M;
               printf("\nMonthly Compounding\n");
            }
```

```
                    else if (freq == 'D')    {
                       m = D;
                       printf("\nDaily Compounding\n");
                    }
                    else if (freq == 'C')    {
                       m = C;
                       printf("\nContinuous Compounding\n");
                    }
                    else
                       printf("\nERROR - Please Repeat\n\n");
            } while (freq != 'A' && freq != 'S' && freq != 'Q' &&
                     freq != 'M' && freq != 'D' && freq != 'C');

         /* carry out the calculations */
         printf("\nInterest Rate    Future Amount\n\n");
         for (count = 1; count <= 20; ++count)    {
            i = 0.01 * count;

            if (m == C)
               md3(i, n)                     /* continuous compounding */

            else if (m == D)
               md2(i, m, n)                  /* daily compounding */

            else
               md1(i, m, n)                  /* annual, semiannual, quarterly or
                                                        monthly compounding */

            f = a * ratio;
            printf("      %2d              %.2f\n", count, f);
         }
      }
```

Examine these two programs carefully, comparing the use of macro substitution in place of the functions. In particular, notice the manner in which the functions are accessed in the first program, compared with the references to the macros in the second program (refer to the if - else statement at the end of main).

When executed, both of these programs behave in exactly the same manner as the original program given in Example 10.30.

Many commercial C compilers offer certain library functions both as macros and as true functions. The macros are defined in the various header files. You may then choose which form is most appropriate for each particular application. Keep in mind, however, that there are certain disadvantages associated with the use of macros in place of functions, aside from the potentially significant increase in program length. In particular:

1. When passing arguments to a macro, the number of arguments will be checked, but their data types will not. Thus, there is less error checking than with a function call.

2. A macro identifier is not associated with an address, so that a macro cannot be utilized as a pointer. Thus, a macro identifier cannot be passed to a function as an argument, in the same sense that a function can be passed to another function as an argument (see Sec. 10.9). Moreover, a macro cannot call itself recursively.

3. There are possible undesirable side effects associated with the use of macros, particularly when calling arguments are involved.

EXAMPLE 14.14   Consider the macro definition

```
#define  root(a, b)  sqrt(a*a + b*b)
```

Now suppose that this macro is utilized within a program in the following manner.

```
root(a+1, b+2)
```

The intent, of course, is to evaluate the formula

```
sqrt((a+1)*(a+1) + (b+2)*(b+2))
```

However, each appearance of a is replaced by the expression a + 1 (without parentheses), and each appearance of b is replaced by b + 1. Therefore, the result of the macro substitution will be

```
sqrt(a+1*a+1 + b+2*b+2)
```

This expression is equivalent to

```
sqrt(2*a+1 + 3*b+2) = sqrt(2*a + 3*b + 3)
```

which is clearly incorrect. The source of error can be corrected, however, by placing additional parentheses within the macro definition; i.e.,

```
#define  root(a, b)  sqrt((a)*(a) + (b)*(b))
```

A more subtle error occurs if we write

```
root(a++, b++)
```

The macro substitution results in the expression

```
sqrt(a*(a+1) + b*(b+1))
```

rather than

```
sqrt(a*a + b*b)
```

as intended. This is an example of an undesired side effect. The placement of additional parentheses within the macro definition will not correct this problem.

14.5 THE C PREPROCESSOR

The C preprocessor is a collection of special statements, called *directives*, that are executed at the beginning of the compilation process. The #include and #define statements considered earlier in this book are preprocessor directives. Additional preprocessor directives are #if, #elif, #else, #endif, #ifdef, #ifndef, #line and #undef. The preprocessor also includes three special operators: defined, #, and ##.

Preprocessor directives usually appear at the beginning of a program, though this is not a firm requirement. Thus, a preprocessor directive may appear anywhere within a program. However, the directive will apply only to the portion of the program following its appearance.

For the beginning programmer, some of the preprocessor directives are relatively unimportant. Hence, we will not describe each preprocessor feature in detail. The more important features are discussed below.

The #if, #elif, #else and #endif directives are used most frequently. They permit conditional compilation of the source program, depending on the value of one or more true/false conditions. They are sometimes used in conjunction with the defined operator, which is used to determine whether or not a symbolic constant or a macro identifier has been defined within a program.

EXAMPLE 14.15 The following preprocessor directives illustrate the conditional compilation of a C program. The conditional compilation depends on the status of the symbolic constant FOREGROUND.

```
#if  defined(FOREGROUND)
    #define  BACKGROUND  0
#else
    #define  FOREGROUND  0
    #define  BACKGROUND  7
#endif
```

Thus, if FOREGROUND has already been defined, the symbolic constant BACKGROUND will represent the value 0. Otherwise, FOREGROUND and BACKGROUND will represent the values 0 and 7, respectively.

Here is another way to accomplish the same thing.

```
#ifdef  FOREGROUND
    #define  BACKGROUND  0
#else
    #define  FOREGROUND  0
    #define  BACKGROUND  7
#endif
```

The directive #ifdef is equivalent to #if defined(). Similarly, the directive #ifndef is equivalent to #if !defined(), i.e., "if not defined." The original approach, in which the defined operator appears explicitly, is the preferred form.

In each of these examples, the last directive is #endif. The preprocessor requires that any set of directives beginning with #if, #ifdef or #ifndef must end with #endif.

The directive #elif is analogous to an else - if clause using ordinary C control statements. An #if directive can be followed by any number of #elif directives, though there can be only one #else directive. The appearance of the #else directive is optional, as determined by the required program logic.

EXAMPLE 14.16 Here is another illustration of conditional compilation. In this situation the conditional compilation will depend on the value that is represented by the symbolic constant BACKGROUND.

```
#if BACKGROUND == 7
    #define  FOREGROUND  0
#elif BACKGROUND == 6
    #define  FOREGROUND  1
#else
    #define  FOREGROUND  6
#endif
```

In this example we see that FOREGROUND will represent 0 if BACKGROUND represents 7, and FOREGROUND will represent 1 if BACKGROUND represents 6. Otherwise, FOREGROUND will represent 6.

The #undef directive "undefines" a symbolic constant or a macro identifier; i.e., it negates the effect of a #define directive that may have appeared earlier in the program.

EXAMPLE 14.17   The following example illustrates the use of the #undefine directive within a C program.

```
#define   FOREGROUND   7
#define   BACKGROUND   O

main()

{

    . . . . .

    #undef   FOREGROUND

    . . . . .

    #undef   BACKGROUND

    . . . . .

}
```

The symbolic constants FOREGROUND and BACKGROUND are defined by the first two directives. These definitions are then negated by the #undef directives, when they appear later in the program. Prior to the #undef directives, any references to FOREGROUND or BACKGROUND will be associated with the values 7 and 0, respectively. After the #undef directives, any references to the corresponding identifiers will be ignored.

The "stringizing" operator # allows a formal argument within a macro definition to be converted to a string. If a formal argument in a macro definition is preceded by this operator, the corresponding actual argument will automatically be enclosed in double quotes. Consecutive whitespace characters inside the actual argument will be replaced by a single blank space, and any special characters, such as ', " and \, will be replaced by their corresponding escape sequences; e.g., \', \" and \\. In addition, the resulting string will automatically be concatenated (i.e., combined) with any adjacent strings.

EXAMPLE 14.18   Here is an illustration of the use of the "stringizing" operator, #.

```
#define   display(text)   printf(#text "\n")

main()
{
    . . . . .
    display(Please do not sleep in class.);
    . . . . .
    display(Please   -   don't snore during the professor's lecture!);
}
```

Within main, the macros are equivalent to

```
printf("Please do not sleep in class.\n");
```

and

```
printf("Please - don\'t snore during the professor\'s lecture!\n");
```

Notice that each actual argument is converted to a string within the printf function. Each argument is concatenated with a newline character (\n), which is written as a separate string within the macro definition. Also, notice that the consecutive blank spaces appearing in the second argument are replaced by single blank spaces, and each apostrophe (') is replaced by its corresponding escape sequence (\').

Execution of this program will result in the following output:

```
Please do not sleep in class.

Please - don't snore during the professor's lecture!
```

The "token-pasting" operator ## causes individual items within a macro definition to be concatenated, thus forming a single item. The various rules governing the use of this operator are somewhat complicated. However, the general purpose of the token-pasting operator is illustrated in the following example.

EXAMPLE 14.19   A C program contains the following macro definition.

```
#define  display(i)  printf("x" #i " = %f\n", x##i)
```

Suppose this macro is accessed by writing

```
display(3);
```

The result will be

```
printf("x3 = %f\n", x3);
```

Thus, the expression x##i becomes the variable x3, since 3 is the current value of the argument i.

Notice that this example illustrates the use of both the stringizing operator (#) and the token-pasting operator (##).

Refer to the programmer's reference manual for your particular C compiler for more information on the use of the C preprocessor.

Review Questions

14.1   What is an enumeration? How is an enumeration defined?

14.2   What are enumeration constants? In what form are they written?

14.3   Summarize the rules for assigning names to enumeration constants.

14.4   Summarize the rules for assigning numerical values to enumeration constants. What default values are assigned to enumeration constants?

14.5   Can two or more enumeration constants have the same numerical value? Explain.

14.6   What are enumeration variables? How are they declared?

14.7   In what ways can enumeration variables be processed? What restrictions apply to the processing of enumeration variables?

14.8   What advantage is there in using enumeration variables within a program?

14.9   Summarize the rules for assigning initial values to enumeration variables. Compare your answer with that for Prob. 14.4.

14.10   Most C programs recognize two formal arguments in the definition of function main. What are they traditionally called? What are their respective data types?

14.11   Describe the information represented by each formal argument in function main. Is information passed explicitly to each argument?

14.12   When parameters are passed to a program from the command line, how is the program execution initiated? Where do the parameters appear?

14.13   What useful purpose can be served by command line parameters when executing a program involving the use of data files?

14.14   The library functions discussed in earlier chapters of this book are all members of a few broad categories of library functions. Describe each category, in general terms.

14.15   Describe, in general terms, some additional categories of library functions that are provided with most commercial C compilers. What is the purpose of each category?

14.16   What is a macro? Summarize the similarities and differences between macros and functions.

14.17   How is a multiline macro defined?

14.18   Describe the use of arguments within a macro.

14.19   What is the principal advantage in the use of a macro rather than a function? What is the principal disadvantage? What other disadvantages are there?

14.20   Summarize the various preprocessor directives, other than `#include` and `#define`. Indicate the purpose of the more commonly used directives.

14.21   What is the scope of a preprocessor directive within a program file?

14.22   Summarize the special preprocessor operators # and ##. What is the purpose of each?

14.23   What is meant by conditional compilation? In general terms, how is conditional compilation carried out? What preprocessor directives are available for this purpose?

Problems

14.24   Define an enumeration type called `flags`, having the following members: `first`, `second`, `third`, `fourth` and `fifth`.

14.25   Define an enumeration variable called `event`, of type `flags` (see the preceding problem).

14.26   Define two enumeration variables, called `soprano` and `bass`, whose members are as follows: `do`, `re`, `mi`, `fa`, `sol`, `la` and `ti`. Assign the following integer values to these members:

```
do      1
re      2
mi      3
fa      4
sol     5
la      6
ti      7
```

14.27   Define an enumeration type called `money`, having the following members: `penny`, `nickel`, `dime`, `quarter`, `half` and `dollar`. Assign the following integer values to these members:

```
penny     1
nickel    5
dime     10
quarter  25
half     50
dollar  100
```

14.28   Define an enumeration variable called `coins`, of type `money` (see the preceding problem). Assign the initial value `dime` to `coins`.

14.29 In the following enumeration declaration, determine the value of each member.

```
enum  compass  {north = 2, south, east = 1, west};
```

14.30 Determine the value associated with each of the following enumeration variables (see the preceding problem).

```
enum  compass  move_1 = south, move_2 = north;
```

14.31 Explain the purpose of the following program outline.

```
int score = 0;
enum compass move;

. . . . .

switch (move)  {

case north:
        score += 10;
        break;

case south:
        score += 20;
        break;

case east:
        score += 30;
        break;

case west:
        score += 40;
        break;

default:
        printf("ERROR - Please try again\n");
}
```

14.32 The outline of a C program is shown below.

```
main(int argc, char *argv[])
{

    . . . . .

}
```

(a) Suppose the compiled object program is stored in a file called demo.exe, and the following commands are issued to initiate the execution of the program.

```
demo  debug  fast
```

Determine the value of argc and the non-empty elements of argv.

(b) Suppose the command line is written as

```
demo  "debug  fast"
```

How will this change affect the values of argc and argv?

14.33   Describe the purpose of the C program shown below.

```c
#include <stdio.h>
#include <string.h>

main(int argc, char *argv[])
{
     char letter[80];
     int count, tag;

     for (count = 0; (letter[count] = getchar()) != '\n'; ++count)
        ;

     tag = count;
     for (count = 0; count < tag; ++count)
        if (strcmp(argv[1], "upper") == 0)
           putchar(toupper(letter[count]));
        else if (strcmp(argv[1], "lower") == 0)
              putchar(tolower(letter[count]));
        else {
           puts("ERROR IN COMMAND LINE - PLEASE TRY AGAIN");
           break;
        }
}
```

14.34   Consider the program shown below, which reads a line of text from an existing data file, displays it on the screen, and writes it out to a new data file.

```c
/* read a line of text from a data file, display it on the screen
                                 and write it to a new data file */
#include <stdio.h>

#define  NULL  0

main(int argc, char *argv[])
{
     FILE *fpt1, *fpt2;

     char c;

     /* open the old data file for reading only */
     if ((fpt1 = fopen(argv[1], "r")) == NULL)
        printf("\nERROR - Cannot open the designated file\n");

     else
        /* read, display and write each character from the old data file */
        fpt2 = fopen(argv[2], "w");
        do {
              putchar(c = getc(fpt1));
              putc(c, fpt2);
        } while (c != '\n');

     /* close the data files */
     fclose(fpt1);
     fclose(fpt2);
}
```

Suppose the program is stored in a file called `transfer.exe`, the old data file is called `data.old` and the new data file is called `data.new`. How should the command line be written in order to execute this program?

14.35 Write a symbolic constant or a macro definition for each of the following situations. Do not include arguments unless the problem asks you to do so.

(*a*) Define the symbolic constant PI to represent the value 3.1415927.

(*b*) Define a macro called AREA, which will calculate the area of a circle in terms of its radius. Use the constant PI, defined in part (*a*), in the calculation.

(*c*) Rewrite the macro described in the preceding problem so that the radius is expressed as an argument.

(*d*) Define a macro called CIRCUMFERENCE, which will calculate the circumference of a circle in terms of its radius. Use the constant PI, defined in part (*a*), in the calculation.

(*e*) Rewrite the macro described in the preceding problem so that the radius is expressed as an argument.

(*f*) Write a multiline macro called interest, which will evaluate the compound interest formula

$$F = P(1 + i)^n$$

where F is the future amount of money that will accumulate after n years, P is the principal (i.e., the original amount of money), $i = 0.01r$, and r is the annual interest rate, expressed as a percentage.

Evaluate i on one line of the macro, and evaluate F on a separate line. Assume that all of the symbols represent floating-point quantities.

(*g*) Rewrite the macro described in the preceding problem so that P, r and n are expressed as arguments.

(*h*) Write a macro called max that utilizes the conditional operator (? :) to determine the maximum of a and b, where a and b are integer quantities.

(*i*) Rewrite the macro described in the preceding problem so that a and b are expressed as arguments.

14.36 Explain the purpose of each of the following groups of preprocessor directives.

(*a*)
```
#if !defined(FLAG)
     #define  FLAG  1
#endif
```

(*b*)
```
#if defined(PASCAL)
     #define  BEGIN  {
     #define  END    }
#endif
```

(*c*)
```
#ifdef  CELSIUS
     #define  temperature(t)  0.5555555 * (t - 32)
#else
     #define  temperature(t)  1.8 * t + 32
#endif
```

(*d*)
```
#ifndef  DEBUG
     #define  out  printf("x = %f\n", x)
#elif  LEVEL == 1
     #define  out  printf("i = %d   y = %f\n", i, y[i])
#else
     #define  out  for (count = 1; count <= n; ++count)        \
                        printf("i = %d   y = %f\n", i, y[i])
#endif
```

(*e*)
```
#if defined(DEBUG)
     #undef  DEBUG
#endif
```

(*f*)
```
#ifdef  ERROR_CHECKS
     #define  message(line)  printf(#line)
#endif
```

(*g*)
```
#if defined(ERROR_CHECKS)
     #define  message(n)  printf("%s\n", message##n)
#endif
```

14.37   Write one or more preprocessor directives for each of the following situations.

     (*a*)   If the symbolic constant BOOLEAN has been defined, define the symbolic constants TRUE and FALSE so that their values are 1 and 0, respectively, and negate the definitions of the symbolic constants YES and NO.

     (*b*)   If flag has a value of 0, define the symbolic constant COLOR to have a value of 1. Otherwise, if the value of flag is less than 3, define COLOR to have a value of 2; and if the value of flag equals or exceeds 3, define COLOR to have a value of 3.

     (*c*)   If the symbolic constant SIZE has the same value as the symbolic constant WIDE, define the symbolic constant WIDTH to have a value of 132; otherwise, define WIDTH to have a value of 80.

     (*d*)   Use the "stringizing" operator to define a macro called error(text) that will display text as a string.

     (*e*)   Use the "token-pasting" operator to define a macro called error(i) that will print the value of the string variable errori (e.g., error1).

14.38   Familiarize yourself with the library functions and the header files that accompany your particular C compiler. Are some functions available both as macros and as true functions?

14.39   Does the library accompanying your particular C compiler include graphics or process control routines? Are other special routines included? If so, what are they?

Programming Problems

14.40   Modify the programs given in Example 14.13 (future value of monthly deposits) so that they accept a command line parameter indicating the frequency of compounding. The command line parameter should be a single character, selected from A, S, Q, M, D or C (either upper- or lowercase), as explained in the example.

14.41   Modify the program given in Example 6.22 (solution of an algebraic equation) so that flag is an enumeration variable whose value is either true or false.

14.42   Modify the program given in Example 6.32 (searching for palindromes) so that flag is an enumeration variable whose value is either true or false.

14.43   Modify the program given in Example 7.9 (largest of three integer quantities) so that the function maximum is written as a multiline macro.

14.44   Modify the program given in Example 7.10 (calculating factorials) so that the function factorial is written as a multiline macro.

14.45   Modify the program given in Example 7.11 (shooting craps) so that the function throw is written as a multiline macro. Can an enumeration variable be used effectively in this particular problem?

14.46   Write a complete C program to solve the problem described in Prob. 7.42 (roots of a quadratic equation). Include an enumeration variable within the program.

14.47   Write a complete C program to solve the problem described in Prob. 9.46 (names of countries and their capitals). Use an enumeration variable to distinguish between the two program options (i.e., find the name of a capital for a specified country, or find the country whose capital is specified).

14.48   Modify the program given in Example 10.28 (displaying the day of the year) so that it makes use of an enumeration variable to represent the months of the year.

14.49   Write a complete C program to solve the problem described in Prob. 11.67 (maintaining baseball/football team statistics). Include an enumeration variable to distinguish between baseball and football.

14.50   Write a complete C program to solve the problem described in Prob. 11.71 (an RPN calculator). Include an enumeration variable to identify the types of arithmetic operations that will be carried out by the calculator.

14.51   Repeat Prob. 14.50, utilizing macros in place of functions.

14.52   Modify the program given in each of the following examples so that the required file name is entered as a command line parameter.

     (*a*)   Example 12.3 (creating a data file)

     (*b*)   Example 12.4 (reading a data file)

14.53 Modify the program given in each of the following examples so that the required file names are entered as command line parameters. Utilize an enumeration variable to represent internal true/false conditions within each program.

(a) Example 12.5 (creating a file containing customer records)

(b) Example 12.6 (updating a file containing customer records)

(c) Example 12.7 (creating an unformatted data file containing customer records)

(d) Example 12.8 (updating an unformatted data file containing customer records)

14.54 Write a complete C program to solve each of the following problems.

(a) Prob. 12.50 (line-oriented text editor).

(b) Prob. 12.51 (maintaining baseball/football team statistics in a data file).

For each program, enter the required file names as command line parameters.

14.55 Each of the following problems requires that one or more numerical values be specified as command line parameters. Use the library functions atoi and atof to convert the command line parameters into integers and floating-point values, respectively.

(a) Write a complete C program to solve the problem described in Prob. 7.49(a) (recursive generation of Legendre polynomials). Enter the values of n and x as command line parameters.

(b) Write a complete C program to solve the problem described in Prob. 7.49(b) (calculate the sum of n floating-point numbers recursively). Enter the value of n as a command line parameter (but enter the individual floating-point numbers interactively, as before).

(c) Write a complete C program to solve the problem described in Prob. 7.49(c) (calculate the first n terms of a series recursively). Enter the value of n as a command line parameter.

(d) Write a complete C program to solve the problem described in Prob. 7.49(d) (calculate the product of n floating-point numbers recursively). Enter the value of n as a command line parameter. (Enter the individual floating-point numbers interactively, however, as before.)

(e) Modify the program given in Example 8.4 (search for a maximum) in the following ways.

(i) Enter values for CNST, a and b as command line parameters.

(ii) Write the function curve as a macro.

(f) Modify the program given in Example 8.7 (generating Fibonacci numbers) so that the value for n is entered as a command line parameter.

(g) Modify the program given in Example 9.13 (reordering a list of numbers) so that the value for n is entered as a command line parameter.

(h) Modify the program given in Example 9.19 (adding two tables of numbers) so that the values of nrows and ncols are entered as command line parameters.

14.56 Write a complete C program to generate the table described in Prob. 9.43. Use a macro to evaluate the formula

$$y = 2e^{-0.1t} \sin 0.5t$$

14.57 Write a complete C program to generate the table described in Prob. 9.44. Use a macro to evaluate the formula

$$F/P = (1 + i/100)^n$$

14.58 Write a complete C program to solve the problem described in Prob. 7.44 (evaluating the formula $y = x^n$). Use a multiline macro in place of the function to carry out the exponentiation.

Appendix A

Number Systems

Decimal	Binary	Octal	Hexadecimal
0	0000	0	0
1	0001	1	1
2	0010	2	2
3	0011	3	3
4	0100	4	4
5	0101	5	5
6	0110	6	6
7	0111	7	7
8	1000	10	8
9	1001	11	9
10	1010	12	A
11	1011	13	B
12	1100	14	C
13	1101	15	D
14	1110	16	E
15	1111	17	F

Notice that there are eight octal digits and 16 hexadecimal digits. The octal digits range from 0 to 7; the hexadecimal digits range from 0 to 9, and then A to F.

Each octal digit is equivalent to three binary digits (3 bits), and each hexadecimal digit is equivalent to four binary digits (4 bits). Thus, octal and hexadecimal numbers offer a convenient and concise way to represent binary bit patterns. For example, the bit pattern 10110111 can be represented in hexadecimal as B7. To see this relationship more clearly, rearrange the bits into groups of 4 and represent each group by a single hexadecimal digit; e.g., 1011 0111 is represented as B 7.

Similarly, this same bit pattern (10110111) can be represented in octal as 267. To see this relationship more clearly, add leading zeros (so that the number of bits in the bit pattern will be some multiple of 3), rearrange the bits into groups of three, and represent each group by a single octal digit; e.g., 010 110 111 is represented as 2 6 7.

Most computers use hexadecimal numbers to represent bit patterns, though some computers use octal numbers for this purpose.

Appendix B

Escape Sequences

Character	Escape Sequence	ASCII Value
bell (alert)	\a	007
backspace	\b	008
horizontal tab	\t	009
newline (line feed)	\n	010
vertical tab	\v	011
form feed	\f	012
carriage return	\r	013
quotation mark (")	\"	034
apostrophe (')	\'	039
question mark (?)	\?	063
backslash (\)	\\	092
null	\0	000

octal number   \ooo   (o represents an octal digit)

    Usually, not more than 3 octal digits are permitted.

    Examples: \5,   \005,   \123,   \177

hexadecimal number   \xhh   (h represents a hexadecimal digit)

    Usually, any number of hexadecimal digits are permitted.

    Examples: \x5,   \x05,   \x53,   \x7f

Most compilers permit the apostrophe (') and the question mark (?) to appear within a string constant as either an ordinary character or an escape sequence.

Appendix C

Operator Summary

Precedence Group	Operators					Associativity
function, array, structure member, pointer to structure member	( )	[ ]	.	->		L → R
unary operators	− ++ − − ! ~ * & sizeof (*type*)					R → L
arithmetic multiply, divide and remainder	*	/	%			L → R
arithmetic add and subtract	+	−				L → R
bitwise shift operators	<<	>>				L → R
relational operators	<	<=	>	>=		L → R
equality operators	==	!=				L → R
bitwise *and*	&					L → R
bitwise *exclusive or*	^					L → R
bitwise *or*	|					L → R
logical *and*	&&					L → R
logical *or*	||					L → R
conditional operator	? :					R → L
assignment operators	= += −= *= /= %= &= ^= |= <<= >>=					R → L
comma operator	,					L → R

Note: The precedence groups are listed from highest to lowest. Some C compilers also include a unary plus (+) operator, to complement the unary minus (−) operator. However, a unary plus expression is equivalent to the value of its operand; i.e., +v has the same value as v.

Appendix D

Data Types and Data Conversion Rules

Data Type	Description	Typical Memory Requirements
int	Integer quantity	2 bytes or 1 word (varies from one computer to another)
short	Short integer quantity (may contain fewer digits than int)	2 bytes or 1word (varies from one computer to another)
long	Long integer quantity (may contain more digits than int)	1 or 2 words (varies from one computer to another)
unsigned	Unsigned (positive) integer quantity (maximum permissible quantity is approximately twice as large as int)	2 bytes or 1 word (varies from one computer to another)
char	Single character	1 byte
signed char	Single character, with numerical values ranging from −128 to +127	1 byte
unsigned char	Single character, with numerical values ranging from 0 to 255	1 byte
float	Floating-point number (i.e., a number containing a decimal point and/or an exponent)	1 word
double	Double-precision floating-point number (i.e., more significant figures, and an exponent that may be larger in magnitude)	2 words
long double	Double-precision floating-point number (may be higher precision than double)	2 or more words (varies from one computer to another)
void	Special data type for functions that do not return any value	(not applicable)
enum	Enumeration constant (special type of int)	2 bytes or 1 word (varies from one computer to another)

Note: The qualifier unsigned may appear with short int or long int, e.g., unsigned short int (or unsigned short), or unsigned long int (or unsigned long).

CONVERSION RULES

These rules apply to arithmetic operations between two operators with dissimilar data types. There may be some variation from one version of C to another.

1.   If one of the operands is `long double`, the other will be converted to `long double` and the result will be `long double`.

2.   Otherwise, if one of the operands is `double`, the other will be converted to `double` and the result will be `double`.

3.   Otherwise, if one of the operands is `float`, the other will be converted to `float` and the result will be `float`.

4.   Otherwise, if one of the operands is `unsigned long int`, the other will be converted to `unsigned long int` and the result will be `unsigned long int`.

5.   Otherwise, if one of the operands is `long int` and the other is `unsigned int`, then:

    (*a*)   If `unsigned int` can be converted to `long int`, the `unsigned int` operand will be converted as such and the result will be `long int`.

    (*b*)   Otherwise, both operands will be converted to `unsigned long int` and the result will be `unsigned long int`.

6.   Otherwise, if one of the operands is `long int`, the other will be converted to `long int` and the result will be `long int`.

7.   Otherwise, if one of the operands is `unsigned int`, the other will be converted to `unsigned int` and the result will be `unsigned int`.

8.   If none of the above conditions applies, then both operands will be converted to `int` (if necessary), and the result will be `int`.

Note that some versions of C automatically convert all floating-point operands to double-precision.

ASSIGNMENT RULES

If the two operands in an assignment expression are of different data types, then the value of the right-hand operand will automatically be converted to the type of the operand on the left. The entire assignment expression will then be of this same data type. In addition,

1.   A floating-point value may be truncated if assigned to an integer identifier.

2.   A double-precision value may be rounded if assigned to a floating-point (single-precision) identifier.

3.   An integer quantity may be altered (some high-order bits may be lost) if it is assigned to a shorter integer identifier or to a character identifier .

Appendix E

The ASCII Character Set

ASCII Value	Character	ASCII Value	Character	ASCII Value	Character	ASCII Value	Character
0	NUL	32	(blank)	64	@	96	`
1	SOH	33	!	65	A	97	a
2	STX	34	"	66	B	98	b
3	ETX	35	#	67	C	99	c
4	EOT	36	$	68	D	100	d
5	ENQ	37	%	69	E	101	e
6	ACK	38	&	70	F	102	f
7	BEL	39	'	71	G	103	g
8	BS	40	(	72	H	104	h
9	HT	41	)	73	I	105	i
10	LF	42	*	74	J	106	j
11	VT	43	+	75	K	107	k
12	FF	44	,	76	L	108	l
13	CR	45	–	77	M	109	m
14	SO	46	.	78	N	110	n
15	SI	47	/	79	O	111	o
16	DLE	48	0	80	P	112	p
17	DC1	49	1	81	Q	113	q
18	DC2	50	2	82	R	114	r
19	DC3	51	3	83	S	115	s
20	DC4	52	4	84	T	116	t
21	NAK	53	5	85	U	117	u
22	SYN	54	6	86	V	118	v
23	ETB	55	7	87	W	119	w
24	CAN	56	8	88	X	120	x
25	EM	57	9	89	Y	121	y
26	SUB	58	:	90	Z	122	z
27	ESC	59	;	91	[	123	{
28	FS	60	<	92	\	124		
29	GS	61	=	93	]	125	}
30	RS	62	>	94	^	126	~
31	US	63	?	95	_	127	DEL

The first 32 characters and the last character are control characters. Usually, they are not displayed. However, some versions of C (some computers) support special graphics characters for these ASCII values. For example, 001 may represent the character ☺, 002 may represent ☻, and so on.

Appendix F

Control Statement Summary

Statement	General Form	Example

break	break;	```for (n = 1; n <= 100; ++n) {```
		``` scanf("%f", &x);```
		``` if (x < 0) {```
		``` printf("ERROR - NEGATIVE VALUE FOR X");```
		``` break;```
		``` }```
		``` . . . . .```
		```}```

continue	continue;	```for (n = 1; n <= 100; ++n) {```
		``` scanf("%f", &x);```
		``` if (x < 0) {```
		``` printf("ERROR - NEGATIVE VALUE FOR X");```
		``` continue;```
		``` }```
		``` . . . . .```
		```}```

do - while	```do```
	``` statement```
	```while (expression);```
		```do```
		``` printf("%d\n", digit++);```
		```while (digit <= 9);```

for	```for (exp 1; exp 2; exp 3)``` ``` statement```	```for (digit = 0; digit <= 9; ++digit)``` ``` printf("%d\n", digit);```

goto	```goto label;```
	```. . . . .```
	```label: statement```
		```if (x < 0)```
		``` goto flag;```
		```. . . . .```
		```flag: printf("ERROR");```

if	```if (expression)``` ``` statement```	```if (x < 0)``` ``` printf("%f", x);```

Statement	*General Form*	*Example*

if - else	if (*expression*)
	    statement 1
	else
	    statement 2
		if (status == 'S')
		    tax = 0.20 * pay;
		else
		    tax = 0.14 * pay;

return	return *expression*;	return (n1 + n2);

switch	switch (*expression*) {
	
	case *expression 1*:
	    statement 1
	    statement 2
	    . . . . .
	    statement m
	    break;
	
	case *expression 2*:
	    statement 1
	    statement 2
	    . . . . .
	    statement n
	    break;
	
	    . . . . .
	
	default:
	    statement 1
	    statement 2
	    . . . . .
	    statement k
	}
		switch (choice = getchar()) {
		
		case 'R':
		    printf("RED");
		    break;
		
		case 'W':
		    printf("WHITE");
		    break;
		
		case 'B';
		    printf("BLUE");
		    break;
		
		default:
		    printf("ERROR");
		}

while	while (*expression*)
	    statement
		while (digit <= 9)
		    printf(%d\n", digit++);

Appendix G

Commonly Used *scanf* and *printf* Conversion Characters

scanf Conversion Characters

Conversion Character	Meaning
c	Data item is a single character
d	Data item is a decimal integer
e	Data item is a floating-point value
f	Data item is a floating-point value
g	Data item is a floating-point value
h	Data item is a short integer
i	Data item is a decimal, hexadecimal, or octal integer
o	Data item is an octal integer
s	Data item is a string followed by a whitespace character (the null character ' \0 ' will automatically be added at the end)
u	Data item is an unsigned decimal integer
x	Data item is a hexadecimal integer
[. . .]	Data item is a string which may include whitespace characters

A *prefix* may precede certain conversion characters.

Prefix	Meaning
h	Short data item (short integer or short unsigned integer)
l	Long data item (long integer, long unsigned integer or double)
L	Long data item (long double)

Example:

```
int a;
short b;
long c;
unsigned d;
double x;
char str[80];

scanf("%5d  %3hd  %12ld  %12lu  %15lf", &a, &b, &c, &d, &x);

scanf("%[^\n]", str);
```

printf **Conversion Characters**

Conversion Character	Meaning
c	Data item is displayed as a single character
d	Data item is displayed as a signed decimal integer
e	Data item is displayed as a floating-point value with an exponent
f	Data item is displayed as a floating-point value without an exponent
g	Data item is displayed as a floating-point value using either e-type or f-type conversion, depending on value; trailing zeros, trailing decimal point will not be displayed.
i	Data item is displayed as a signed decimal integer
o	Data item is displayed as an octal integer, without a leading zero
s	Data item is displayed as a string
u	Data item is displayed as an unsigned decimal integer
x	Data item is displayed as a hexadecimal integer, without leading 0x

Some of these characters are interpreted differently than with the scanf funtion.

A *prefix* may precede certain conversion characters.

Prefix	Meaning
h	Short data item (short integer or short unsigned integer)
l	Long data item (long integer, long unsigned integer or double)
L	Long data item (long double)

Example:

```
int a;
short b;
long c;
unsigned d;
double x;
char str[80];

printf("%5d  %3hd  %12ld  %12lu  %15.7le\n", a, b, c, d, x);

printf("%40s\n", str);
```

Flags

Flag	Meaning
-	Data item is left justified within the field (blank spaces required to fill the minimum field-width will be added *after* the data item rather than *before* the data item.)
+	A sign (either + or -) will precede each signed numerical data item. Without this flag, only negative data items are preceded by a sign.
0	Causes leading zeros to appear instead of leading blanks. Applies only to data items that are right justified within a field whose minimum size is larger than the data item. (*Note*: Some compilers consider the zero flag to be a part of the field-width specification rather than an actual flag. This assures that the 0 is processed last, if multiple flags are present.)
' ' (*blank space*)	A blank space will precede each positive signed numerical data item. This flag is over-ridden by the + flag if both are present.
# (*with* o- *and* x- *type conversion*)	Causes octal and hexadecimal data items to be preceded by 0 and 0x, respectively.
# e-, f- *and* g- *type conversion*)	Causes a decimal point to be present in all floating-point numbers, even if the data item (*with* is a whole number. Also prevents the truncation of trailing zeros in g-type conversion.

Example:

```
int a;
short b;
long c;
unsigned d;
double x;

printf("%+5d  %+5hd  %+12ld  %-12lu  %#15.7le\n", a, b, c, d, x);
```

Appendix H

Library Functions

Function	Type	Purpose	include *File*
abs(i)	int	Return the absolute value of i.	stdlib.h
acos(d)	double	Return the arc cosine of d.	math.h
asin(d)	double	Return the arc sine of d.	math.h
atan(d)	double	Return the arc tangent of d.	math.h
atan2(d1,d2)	double	Return the arc tangent of d1/d2.	math.h
atof(s)	double	Convert string s to a double-precision quantity.	stdlib.h
atoi(s)	int	Convert string s to an integer.	stdlib.h
atol(s)	long	Convert string s to a long integer.	stdlib.h
calloc(u1,u2)	void*	Allocate memory for an array having u1 elements, each of length u2 bytes. Return a pointer to the beginning of the allocated space.	malloc.h, or stdlib.h
ceil(d)	double	Return a value rounded up to the next higher integer.	math.h
cos(d)	double	Return the cosine of d.	math.h
cosh(d)	double	Return the hyperbolic cosine of d.	math.h
difftime(l1,l2)	double	Return the time difference l1 − l2, where l1 and l2 represent elapsed times beyond a designated base time (see the time function).	time.h
exit(u)	void	Close all files and buffers, and terminate the program. (Value of u is assigned by function, to indicate termination status.)	stdlib.h
exp(d)	double	Raise *e* to the power d ($e = 2.7182818 \cdots$ is the base of the natural (Naperian) system of logarithms).	math.h
fabs(d)	double	Return the absolute value of d.	math.h
fclose(f)	int	Close file f. Return 0 if file is successfully closed.	stdio.h
feof(f)	int	Determine if an end-of-file condition has been reached. If so, return a nonzero value; otherwise, return 0.	stdio.h
fgetc(f)	int	Enter a single character from file f.	stdio.h
fgets(s,i,f)	char*	Enter string s, containing i characters, from file f.	stdio.h
floor(d)	double	Return a value rounded down to the next lower integer.	math.h
fmod(d1,d2)	double	Return the remainder of d1/d2 (with same sign as d1).	math.h
fopen(s1,s2)	file*	Open a file named s1 of type s2. Return a pointer to the file.	stdio.h
fprintf(f,...)	int	Send data items to file f (remaining arguments are complicated — see Appendix G).	stdio.h
fputc(c,f)	int	Send a single character to file f.	stdio.h
fputs(s,f)	int	Send string s to file f.	stdio.h

Function	*Type*	*Purpose*	include *File*
`fread(s,i1,i2,f)`	int	Enter i2 data items, each of size i1 bytes, from file f to string s.	`stdio.h`
`free(p)`	void	Free a block of allocated memory whose beginning is indicated by p.	`malloc.h`, or `stdlib.h`
`fscanf(f,...)`	int	Enter data items from file f (remaining arguments are complicated — see Appendix G)	`stdio.h`
`fseek(f,l,i)`	int	Move the pointer for file f a distance l bytes from location i (i may represent the beginning of the file, the current pointer position, or the end of the file).	`stdio.h`
`ftell(f)`	long int	Return the current pointer position within file f.	`stdio.h`
`fwrite(s,i1,i2,f)`	int	Send i2 data items, each of size i1 bytes, from string s to file f.	`stdio.h`
`getc(f)`	int	Enter a single character from file f.	`stdio.h`
`getchar()`	int	Enter a single character from the standard input device.	`stdio.h`
`gets(s)`	char*	Enter string s from the standard input device.	`stdio.h`
`isalnum(c)`	int	Determine if argument is alphanumeric. Return a nonzero value if true; 0 otherwise.	`ctype.h`
`isalpha(c)`	int	Determine if argument is alphabetic. Return a nonzero value if true; 0 otherwise.	`ctype.h`
`isascii(c)`	int	Determine if argument is an ASCII character. Return a nonzero value if true; 0 otherwise.	`ctype.h`
`iscntrl(c)`	int	Determine if argument is an ASCII control character. Return a nonzero value if true; 0 otherwise.	`ctype.h`
`isdigit(c)`	int	Determine if argument is a decimal digit. Return a nonzero value if true; 0 otherwise.	`ctype.h`
`isgraph(c)`	int	Determine if argument is a graphic ASCII character (hex 0x21–0x7e; octal 041–176). Return a nonzero value if true; 0 otherwise.	`ctype.h`
`islower(c)`	int	Determine if argument is lowercase. Return a nonzero value if true; 0 otherwise.	`ctype.h`
`isodigit(c)`	int	Determine if argument is an octal digit. Return a nonzero value if true; 0 otherwise.	`ctype.h`
`isprint(c)`	int	Determine if argument is a printing ASCII character (hex 0x20–0x7e; octal 040–176). Return a nonzero value if true; 0 otherwise.	`ctype.h`
`ispunct(c)`	int	Determine if argument is a punctuation character. Return a nonzero value if true; 0 otherwise.	`ctype.h`
`isspace(c)`	int	Determine if argument is a whitespace character. Return a nonzero value if true; 0 otherwise.	`ctype.h`
`isupper(c)`	int	Determine if argument is uppercase. Return a nonzero value if true; 0 otherwise.	`ctype.h`
`isxdigit(c)`	int	Determine if argument is a hexadecimal digit. Return a nonzero value if true; 0 otherwise.	`ctype.h`
`labs(l)`	long int	Return the absolute value of l.	`math.h`
`log(d)`	double	Return the natural logarithm of d.	`math.h`

Function	Type	Purpose	include *File*
log10(d)	double	Return the logarithm (base 10) of d.	math.h
malloc(u)	void*	Allocate u bytes of memory. Return a pointer to the beginning of the allocated space.	malloc.h, or stdlib.h
pow(d1,d2)	double	Return d1 raised to the d2 power.	math.h
printf(...)	int	Send data items to the standard output device (arguments are complicated — see Appendix G).	stdio.h
putc(c,f)	int	Send a single character to file f.	stdio.h
putchar(c)	int	Send a single character to the standard output device.	stdio.h
puts(s)	int	Send string s to the standard output device.	stdio.h
rand()	int	Return a random positive integer.	stdlib.h
rewind(f)	void	Move the pointer to the beginning of file f.	stdio.h
scanf(...)	int	Enter data items from the standard input device (arguments are complicated — see Appendix G).	stdio.h
sin(d)	double	Return the sine of d.	math.h
sinh(d)	double	Return the hyperbolic sine of d.	math.h
sqrt(d)	double	Return the square root of d.	math.h
srand(u)	void	Initialize the random number generator.	stdlib.h
strcmp(s1,s2)	int	Compare two strings lexicographically. Return a negative value if s1 < s2; 0 if s1 and s2 are identical; and a positive value if s1 > s2.	string.h
strcmpi(s1,s2)	int	Compare two strings lexicographically, without regard to case. Return a negative value if s1 < s2; 0 if s1 and s2 are identical; and a positive value if s1 > s2.	string.h
strcpy(s1,s2)	char*	Copy string s2 to string s1.	string.h
strlen(s)	int	Return the number of characters in a string.	string.h
strset(s,c)	char*	Set all characters within s to c (excluding the terminating null character \0).	string.h
system(s)	int	Pass command s to the operating system. Return 0 if the command is successfully executed; otherwise, return a nonzero value, typically −1.	stdlib.h
tan(d)	double	Return the tangent of d.	math.h
tanh(d)	double	Return the hyperbolic tangent of d.	math.h
time(p)	long int	Return the number of seconds elapsed beyond a designated base time.	time.h
toascii(c)	int	Convert value of argument to ASCII.	ctype.h
tolower(c)	int	Convert letter to lowercase.	ctype.h, or stdlib.h
toupper(c)	int	Convert letter to uppercase.	ctype.h, or stdlib.h

Notes: *Type* refers to the data type of the quantity that is returned by the function. An asterisk (*) denotes a pointer.

c denotes a character-type argument

d denotes a double-precision argument

f denotes a file argument

i denotes an integer argument

l denotes a long integer argument

p denotes a pointer argument

s denotes a string argument

u denotes an unsigned integer argument

Most commercial C compilers are accompanied by many more library functions. Consult the C reference manual for your particular compiler for more detailed information on each of the above functions, and for a listing of additional functions.

Answers to Selected Problems

Chapter 1

1.31   (*a*)   This program prints the message `Welcome to the Wonderful World of Computing!`. The program does not contain any variables. The line containing `printf` is an output statement. There are no assignment or input statements.

      (*b*)   This program also prints the message `Welcome to the Wonderful World of Computing!`. The program does not contain any variables. (`MESSAGE` is a symbolic constant, not a variable.) The line containing `printf` is an output statement. There are no assignment or input statements.

      (*c*)   This program calculates the area of a triangle from its base and height. The variables are `base`, `height` and `area`. The alternating `printf` - `scanf` statements provide interactive input. The final `printf` statement is an output statement. The statement that begins with `area` = is an assignment statement.

      (*d*)   This program calculates net (after tax) salary, given the gross salary and the tax rate (which is expressed as a constant 14%). The variables are `gross`, `tax` and `net`. The initial `printf` - `scanf` statements provide interactive input. The final two `printf` statements are output statements. Note that the statements containing `tax` = and `net` = are assignment statements.

      (*e*)   This program uses a function to determine the smaller of two integer quantities. The variables are `a`, `b` and `min`. The alternating pairs of `printf` - `scanf` statements provide interactive input. The final `printf` statement is an output statement. The statement `min` = `smaller(a, b)` references the function, which is called `smaller`. This function contains an `if` - `else` statement that returns the smaller of the two quantities to the `main` portion of the program.

      (*f*)   This program processes n pairs of integer quantities, and determines the smaller of each pair. A `for` loop is used to process the multiple pairs of integer quantities. In all other respects, this program is similar to that shown in part (*e*).

      (*g*)   This program processes an unspecified number of pairs of integer quantities, and determines the smaller of each pair. The computation continues until a pair of zeros are entered into the computer. A `while` loop is used to process the multiple pairs of integer quantities. In all other respects, this program is similar to that shown in part (*f*).

      (*h*)   This program processes an unspecified number of pairs of integer quantities, and determines the smaller of each pair. The original values and the corresponding minimum values are stored in the arrays `a`, `b` and `min`. Each array can store as many as 100 integer values.

            After all of the data have been entered and all of the minimum values have been determined, the number of data sets is "tagged" with the assignment statement `n` = `--i`; then a `for` loop is used to display the data. In all other respects, this program is similar to that shown in part (*g*).

Chapter 2

2.39   (*a*)   Valid
      (*b*)   An identifier must begin with a letter.
      (*c*)   Valid
      (*d*)   `return` is a reserved word.
      (*e*)   An identifier must begin with a letter.
      (*f*)   Valid
      (*g*)   Blank spaces are not allowed.
      (*h*)   Valid
      (*i*)   Dash (minus sign) is not allowed.
      (*j*)   An identifier must begin with a letter or an underscore.

2.40   (*a*)   Distinct   (*c*)   Identical   (*e*)   Distinct
      (*b*)   Distinct   (*d*)   Distinct   (*f*)   Distinct

2.41   (*a*)   Valid (real)
      (*b*)   Illegal character (,)
      (*c*)   Valid (real)

(d)   Valid (real)

(e)   Valid (decimal integer)

(f)   Valid (long integer)

(g)   Valid (real)

(h)   Illegal character (blank space)

(i)   Valid (octal constant)

(j)   Illegal characters (C, D, F), if intended as an octal constant. If intended as a hexadecimal constant, an X or an x must be included (i.e., 0X18CDF).

(k)   Valid (hexadecimal long integer)

(l)   Illegal character (h)

2.42 (a)   Valid

(b)   Valid

(c)   Valid

(d)   Escape sequences must be written with a backward slash.

(e)   Valid

(f)   Valid

(g)   Valid

(h)   Valid (null-character escape sequence).

(i)   A character constant cannot consist of multiple   characters.

(j)   Valid (octal escape sequence). Note that octal 52 is equivalent to decimal 42. In the ASCII character set, this value represents an asterisk (*).

2.43 (a)   A string constant must be enclosed in double quotation marks.

(b)   Valid

(c)   Trailing quotation mark is missing.

(d)   Valid

(e)   Valid

(f)   Valid

(g)   Quotation marks and (optionally) the apostrophe within the string must be expressed as escape sequences; i.e., "The professor said, \"Please don\'t sleep in class\""

2.44 (a)
```
int p, q;
float x, y, z;
char a, b, c;
```
(d)
```
char current, last;
unsigned count;
float error;
```

(b)
```
float root1, root2;
long counter;
short flag;
```
(e)
```
char first, last;
char message[80];
```

(c)
```
int index;
unsigned cust_no;
double gross, tax, net;
```

2.45 (a)
```
float a = -8.2, b = 0.005;
int x = 129, y = 87, z = -22;
char c1 = 'w', c2 = '&';
```
(c)
```
long big = 123456789L;
double c = 0.3333333333;
char eol = '\n';
```

(b)
```
double d1 = 2.88e-8, d2 = -8.4e5;
int u = 0711, v = 0xffff;
```
(d)
```
char message[] = "ERROR";
```

2.46 (a)   Subtract the value of b from the value of a.

(b)   Add the values of b and c, then multiply the sum by the value of a.

(c)   Add the values of b and c and multiply the sum by the value of a. Then assign the result to d.

(d)   Determine whether or not the value of a is greater than or equal to the value of b. The result will be either true or false, represented by the value 1 (true) or 0 (false).

(e)   Divide the value of a by 5, and determine whether or not the remainder is equal to zero. The result will be either true or false.

(f)   Divide the value of b by the value of c, and determine whether or not the value of a is less than the quotient. The result will be either true or false.

(g)   Decrement the value of a; i.e., decrease the value of a by 1.

2.47 (a)   Expression statement

(b)   Control statement containing a compound statement. (The compound statement is enclosed in braces.)

    (c)   Control statement

    (d)   Compound statement containing expression statements and a control statement.

    (e)   Compound statement containing an expression statement and a control statement. The control statement itself contains two compound statements.

2.48

(a)	`#define FACTOR -18`	
(b)	`#define ERROR 0.0001`	
(c)	`#define BEGIN {` `#define END   }`	

(d)	`#define NAME "Sharon"`
(e)	`#define EOLN '\n'`
(f)	`#define COST "$19.95"`

Chapter 3

3.36
- (a) 6
- (b) 45
- (c) 2
- (d) 2
- (e) −1
- (f) 3
- (g) −4
- (h) 0 (because b / c is zero)
- (i) −1
- (j) −16

3.37
- (a) 7.1
- (b) 49
- (c) 2.51429
- (d) The remainder operation is not defined for floating-point operands.
- (e) −5.17647
- (f) −2.68571
- (g) 20.53333
- (h) 1.67619

3.38
- (a) 69
- (b) 79
- (c) 51
- (d) 3
- (e) 98
- (f) 6
- (g) 100
- (h) 63
- (i) 159
- (j) 2703

3.39
- (a) integer
- (b) float (some versions of C will convert to double-precision)
- (c) double-precision
- (d) long integer
- (e) float (or double-precision)
- (f) integer
- (g) long integer
- (h) integer
- (i) long integer

3.40
- (a) 14
- (b) 18
- (c) −466.6667
- (d) −13
- (e) 9
- (f) 9
- (g) 4
- (h) 1.005
- (i) −1.01

(j)	0
(k)	0
(l)	1
(m)	0
(n)	1
(o)	1
(p)	0
(q)	1
(r)	0.01
(s)	1
(t)	1
(u)	0
(v)	0
(w)	0
(x)	1
(y)	1
(z)	0

3.41

(a)	k = 13
(b)	z = -0.005
(c)	i = 5
(d)	k = 0
(e)	k = 99
(f)	z = 1.0
(g)	b = 100, a = 100 (Note that 100 is the encoded value for 'd' in the ASCII character set.)
(h)	j = 1, i = 1
(i)	k = 0, z = 0.0
(j)	z = 0.005, k = 0 [compare with (i) above]
(k)	i = 10
(l)	y = -0.015
(m)	x = 0.010
(n)	i = 1
(o)	i = 3
(p)	i = 11
(q)	k = 8
(r)	k = 5
(s)	z = 0.005
(t)	z = 0.0
(u)	a = 'c'
(v)	i = 3

3.42

(a) Return the absolute value of the integer expression (i - 2 * j).

(b) Return the absolute value of the floating-point expression (x + y).

(c) Determine if the character represented by c is a printing ASCII character.

(d) Determine if the character represented by c is a decimal digit.

(e) Convert the character represented by c to uppercase.

(f) Round the value of x up to the next higher integer.

(g) Round the value of (x + y) down to the next lower integer.

(h) Determine if the character represented by c is lowercase.

(i) Determine if the character represented by j is uppercase.

(j) Return the value e^x.

(k) Return the natural logarithm of x.

(l) Return the square root of the expression (x*x + y*y).

(m) Determine if the value of the expression (10 * j) can be interpreted as an alphanumeric character.

(n) Determine if the value of the expression (10 * j) can be interpreted as an alphabetic character.

(o) Determine if the value of the expression (10 * j) can be interpreted as an ASCII character.

(p) Convert the value of the expression (10 * j) to an ASCII character.

(q) Divide the value of x by the value of y, and return the remainder with the same sign as x.

(r) Convert the ASCII character whose numerical code is 65 to lowercase.

(s) Determine the difference between the value of x and the value of y, then raise this difference to the 3.0 power.

(t) Evaluate the expression (x - y) and return its sine.

(u) Return the number of characters in the string "hello".

(v) Return the position of the first occurrence of the letter e in the string "hello".

3.43 (a) 2
(b) 0.005
(c) 1
(d) 0
(e) 'D'
(f) 1.0
(g) 0.0
(h) 0.0
(i) −1.0
(j) 1
(k) 0
(l) 1.005013
(m) −5.298317
(n) 0.005
(o) 0.011180
(p) 1
(q) 0
(r) 1
(s) '2'
(t) 0.005
(u) 'a'
(v) 3.375e−6
(w) 0.014999
(x) 5
(y) 1 (0 indicates first position)
(z) 1.002472

Chapter 4

4.50 (a)
```
a = getchar();
b = getchar();
c = getchar();
```
(b)
```
putchar(a);
putchar(b);
putchar(c);
```

4.51 (a)
```
scanf("%c%c%c", &a, &b, &c);
or  scanf("%c %c %c", &a, &b, &c);
```
(b)
```
printf("%c%c%c", a, b, c);
or  printf("%c %c %c", a, b, c);
```

4.52 (a)
```
for (count = 0; count < 60; ++count)
text[count] = getchar();
```
(b)
```
for (count = 0; count < 60; ++count)
putchar(text[count]);
```
(Note: count is assumed to be an integer variable.)

4.53
```
for (count = 0; (text[count] = getchar()) != '\n'; ++count)
    ;
```

4.54
```
scanf("%[^\n]", text);
```
The method used in Prob. 4.53 indicates the number of characters that have been read.

4.55 (a) `scanf("%d %d %d", &i, &j, &k);`
(b) `scanf("%d %o %x", &i, &j, &k);`
(c) `scanf("%x %x %o", &i, &j, &k);`

4.56 (*a*) `scanf("%6d %6d %6d", &i, &j, &k);`
  (*b*) `scanf("%8d %8o %8x", &i, &j, &k);`
  (*c*) `scanf("%7x %7x %7o", &i, &j, &k);`

4.57 (*a*) a will be assigned a long decimal integer with a maximum field-width of 12; b will be assigned a short decimal integer with a maximum field-width of 5; c and d will be assigned double-precision quantities with maximum field-widths of 15.

  (*b*) a will be assigned a long hexadecimal integer with a maximum field-width of 10; b will be assigned a short octal integer with a maximum field-width of 6; c will be assigned a short unsigned integer with a maximum field-width of 6; and d will be assigned a long unsigned integer with a maximum field-width of 14.

  (*c*) a will be assigned a long decimal integer with a maximum field-width of 12; b will be assigned a short decimal integer whose maximum field-width is unspecified; c and d will be assigned floating-point quantities with maximum field-widths of 15.

  (*d*) a will be assigned a decimal integer with a maximum field-width of 8; another decimal integer will then be read into the computer but not assigned; c and d will then be assigned double-precision quantities with maximum field-widths of 12.

4.58 (*a*) `scanf("%d %d %e %le", &i, &j, &x, &dx);`
   or `scanf("%d %d %f %lf", &i, &j, &x, &dx);`
  (*b*) `scanf("%d %ld %d %f %u", &i, &ix, &j, &x, &u);`
  (*c*) `scanf("%d %u %c", &i, &u, &c);`
  (*d*) `scanf("%c %f %lf %hd", &c, &x, &dx, &s);`
   or `scanf("%c %e %le %hd", &c, &x, &dx, &s);`

4.59 (*a*) `scanf("%4d %4d %8e %15le", &i, &j, &x, &dx);`
   or `scanf("%4d %4d %8f %15lf", &i, &j, &x, &dx);`
  (*b*) `scanf("%5d %12ld %5d %10f %5u", &i, &ix, &j, &x, &u);`
  (*c*) `scanf("%6d %6u %c", &i, &u, &c);`
  (*d*) `scanf("%c %9f %16lf %6hd", &c, &x, &dx, &s);`
   or `scanf("%c %9e %16le %6hd", &c, &x, &dx, &s);`

4.60 `scanf("%s", text);`

4.61 `scanf("%[ abcdefghijklmnopqrstuvwxyz\n]", text);`

4.62 `scanf("%[ ABCDEFGHIJKLMNOPQRSTUVWXYZ1234567890$ ]", text);`

4.63 `scanf("%[^*]", text);`

4.64 (*a*) $*@ (no spaces separating the characters)
  (*b*) $ * @ (one or more blank spaces between the characters)
  (*c*) $ * @ (one or more whitespace characters between the input characters)
  (*d*) $ * @ (one or more blank spaces between the characters. Other whitespace characters may also appear with the blank spaces.)
  (*e*) $*@ (no spaces separating the characters)

4.65 (*a*) 12 –8 0.011 –2.2e6
  (*b*) 12 –8 0.011 –2.2e6
  (*c*) 12 –8 0.011 –2.2e6
  (*d*) 12 –8 0.011 –2.2e6

  Note that the specified field-widths cannot be exceeded, and that one or more blank spaces must separate the successive numerical quantities. The most convenient representation of the floating-point values is as shown, irrespective of the particular conversion characters in each `scanf` function.

4.66 (*a*) `printf("%d %d %d", i, j, k);`
  (*b*) `printf("%d %d", (i + j), (i - k));`
  (*c*) `printf("%f %d", sqrt(i + j), abs(i - k));`

4.67 (*a*) `printf("%3d %3d %3d", i, j, k);`
  (*b*) `printf("%5d %5d", (i + j), (i - k));`
  (*c*) `printf("%9f %7d", sqrt(i + j), abs(i - k));`

4.68 (*a*) `printf("%f %f %f", x, y, z);`
  (*b*) `printf("%f %f", (x + y), (x - z));`
  (*c*) `printf("%f %f", sqrt(x + y), fabs(x - z));`

Note: e- or g-type conversion could also be used, e.g.,

```
printf("%e %e %e", x, y, z);
```

4.69   (*a*)   `printf("%6f %6f %6f", x, y, z);`

        (*b*)   `printf("%8f %8f", (x + y), (x - z));`

        (*c*)   `printf("%12f %9f", sqrt(x + y), abs(x - z));`

4.70   (*a*)   `printf("%6e %6e %6e", x, y, z);`

        (*b*)   `printf("%8e %8e", (x + y), (x - z));`

        (*c*)   `printf("%12e %9e", sqrt(x + y), abs(x - z));`

In each case, the numerical values will include exponents.

4.71   (*a*)   `printf("%8.4f %8.4f %8.4f", x, y, z);`

        (*b*)   `printf("%9.3f %9.3f", (x + y), (x - z));`

        (*c*)   `printf("%12.4f %10.4f", sqrt(x + y), abs(x - z));`

4.72   (*a*)   `printf("%12.4e %12.4e %12.4e", x, y, z);`

        (*b*)   `printf("%14.5e %14.5e", (x + y), (x - z));`

        (*c*)   `printf("%12.7e %15.7e", sqrt(x + y), abs(x - z));`

4.73   (*a*)   `printf("%o %o %x %X", a, b, c, d);`

        (*b*)   `printf("%o %x", (a + b), (c - d));`

4.74   (*a*)   `printf("%d %d %g %g", i, j, x, dx);`

        (*b*)   `printf("%d %ld %d %g %u", i, ix, j, x, u);`

        (*c*)   `printf("%d %u %c", i, u, c);`

        (*d*)   `printf("%c %g %g %ld", c, x, dx, ix);`

Note: e- or f-type conversion may be used in place of the g-type conversion.

4.75   (*a*)   `printf("%4d %4d %14.8e %14.8e", i, j, x, dx);`

        (*b*)   `printf("%4d\n %4d\n %14.8e\n %14.8e", i, j, x, dx);`

        (*c*)   `printf("%5d %12ld %5d %10.5f %5u", i, ix, j, x, u);`

        (*d*)   `printf("%5d %12ld %5d\n\n %10.5f %5u", i, ix, j, x, u);`

        (*e*)   `printf("%6d   %6u   %c", i, u, c);`

        (*f*)   `printf("%5d %5u %11.4f", j, u, x);`

        (*g*)   `printf("%-5d %-5u %-11.4f", j, u, x);`

        (*h*)   `printf("%+5d %5u %+11.4f", j, u, x);`

        (*i*)   `printf("%05d %05u %11.4f", j, u, x);`

        (*j*)   `printf("%5d %5u %#11.4f", j, u, x);`

4.76   (*a*)   `printf("%8o %8d %8x", i, j, k);`

        (*b*)   `printf("%-8o %-8d %-8x", i, j, k);`

        (*c*)   `printf("%#8o %08d %#8x", i, j, k);`

4.77   (*a*)   `12345 -13579 -24680 123456789 -2222 5555`

        (*b*)   `12345 -13579 -24680`

                `123456789 -2222 5555`

        (*c*)   `   12345    -13579    -24680`

                `   123456789    -2222    5555`

        (*d*)   `12345    -13579`

                 `-24680    123456789`

                 `-2222    5555`

        (*e*)   `+12345    -13579`

                 `-24680        +123456789`

                 `-2222    5555`

        (*f*)   `00012345 -0013579`

               `-0024680 000000123456789`

               `-0002222 00005555`

4.78   (*a*)   `12345 abcd9 77777`

        (*b*)   `12345 abcd9 77777`

        (*c*)   `   12345    abcd9    77777`

        (*d*)   `12345    abcd9    77777`

(e)		+12345 abcd9 77777
(f)		00012345 0xabcd9 077777

4.79

(a)		2.500000 0.000500 3000.000000
(b)		2.500000 0.000500 3000.000000
(c)		2.500000 0.000500 3000.000000
(d)		2.5000 0.0005 3000.0000
(e)		2.500 0.001 3000.000
(f)		2.500000e+000 5.000000e-004 3.000000e+003
(g)		2.500000e+000 5.000000e-004 3.000000e+003
(h)		2.500000e+000 5.000000e-004 3.000000e+003
(i)		2.5000e+000 5.0000e-004 3.0000e+003
(j)		2.50e+000 5.00e-004 3.00e+003
(k)		2.500000 0.000500 3000.000000
(l)		+2.500000 +0.000500 +3000.000000
(m)		2.500000 0.000500 3000.000000
(n)		2.500000 0.000500 3000.000000
(o)		2.5 0.0005 3000
(p)		2.500000 0.000500 3000.000000

4.80

(a)		A B C
(b)		ABC
(c)		A B C
(d)		A B C
(e)		c1=A c2=B c3=C

4.81

(a)		printf("%s", text);
(b)		printf("%.8s", text);
(c)		printf("%13.8s", text);
(d)		printf("%-13.8s", text);

4.82

(a)		Programming with C can be a challenging creative activity.
(b)		Programming with C can be a challenging creative activity.
(c)		Programming with C
(d)		Program
(e)		Program

4.83

(a)
```
printf("Please enter your name: ");
scanf("%[^\n]", name);
```

(b)
```
printf("x1 = %4.1f   x2 = %4.1f", x1, x2);
```

(c)
```
printf("Please enter a value for a: ");
scanf("%d", &a);
printf("Please enter a value for b: ");
scanf("%d", &b);
printf("\nThe sum is %d", (a + b));
```

The last statement can also be written as
```
printf("\n%s %d", "The sum is", (a + b));
```

Chapter 5

5.31 (a)
```
/* "HELLO!" program */

#include <stdio.h>

main()
{
    printf("%s", "HELLO!");
}
```

(b)
```c
/* "WELCOME - LET'S BE FRIENDS" program */

#include <stdio.h>

main()
{
    char name[20];

    printf("%s", "HI, WHAT\'S YOUR NAME? ");
    scanf("%[^\n]", name);
    printf("\n\n%s%s\n%s", "WELCOME ", name, "LET\'S BE FRIENDS!");
}
```

(c)
```c
/* temperature conversion - fahrenheit to celsius */

#include <stdio.h>

main()
{
    float c, f;

    printf("%s", "Please enter a value for the temperature in degrees F: ");
    scanf("%f", &f);

    c = (5. / 9.) * (f - 32.);

    printf("\n%s%5.1f", "The corresponding value for C is: ", c);
}
```

(d)
```c
/* piggy-bank problem */

#include <stdio.h>

main()
{
    int halfs, quarters, dimes, nickels, pennies;
    float dollars;

    printf("%s", "How many half-dollars? ");
    scanf("%d", &halfs);
    printf("%s", "How many quarters? ");
    scanf("%d", &quarters);
    printf("%s", "How many dimes? ");
    scanf("%d", &dimes);
    printf("%s", "How many nickels? ");
    scanf("%d", &nickels);
    printf("%s", "How many pennies? ");
    scanf("%d", &pennies);

    dollars = 0.5 * halfs + 0.25 * quarters + 0.1 * dimes +
                          0.05 * nickels + 0.01 * pennies;

    printf("\n%s%6.2f%s", "The total is ", dollars, " dollars");
}
```

(e)
```c
/* volume and area of a sphere */

#include <stdio.h>

#define PI 3.1415927

main()
{
    float radius, volume, area;

    printf("%s", "Please enter a value for the radius: ");
    scanf("%f", &radius);

    volume = (4. / 3.) *  PI * radius * radius * radius;
    area  = 4. * PI * radius * radius;

    printf("\n%s%.3e\n%s%.3e", "The volume is ", volume, "The area is ", area);
}
```

(f)   ```
        /* mass of air in an automobile tire */
        #include <stdio.h>
        main()
        {
            float p, v, m, t;

            printf("%s", "Please enter a value for the volume, in cubic feet: ");
            scanf("%f", &v);
            printf("%s", "Please enter a value for the pressure, in psi: ");
            scanf("%f", &p);
            printf("%s", "Please enter a value for the temperature, in degrees F: ");
            scanf("%f", &t);

            m = (p * v) / (0.37 * (t + 460.));
            printf("\nMass of air: %g pounds", m);
        }
        ```

*(g)*    ```
        /* encoding of a 5-letter word */
        #include <stdio.h>
        main()
        {
            char c1, c2, c3, c4, c5;

            printf("%s", "Please enter a 5-letter word: ");
            scanf("%c%c%c%c%c", &c1, &c2, &c3, &c4, &c5);
            printf("%c%c%c%c%c", (c1-30), (c2-30), (c3-30), (c4-30), (c5-30));
        }
        ```

(h)   ```
        /* decoding of a 5-letter word */
        #include <stdio.h>
        main()
        {
            char c1, c2, c3, c4, c5;

            printf("%s", "Please enter the encoded 5-letter word: ");
            scanf("%c%c%c%c%c", &c1, &c2, &c3, &c4, &c5);
            printf("%c%c%c%c%c", (c1+30), (c2+30), (c3+30), (c4+30), (c5+30));
        }
        ```

*(i)*    ```
        /* encoding and decoding a line of text */
        #include <stdio.h>
        main()
        {
            int count, tag;
            char text[80];

            /* read and encode the line of text */
            printf("%s", "Please enter a line of text below: \n");
            for (count = 0; (text[count] = getchar() - 30) != ('\n' - 30); ++count)
                ;
            tag = count;

            /* write out the encoded text */
            printf("\nEncoded text:\n");
            for (count = 0; count < tag; ++count)
                putchar(text[count]);

            /* decode and write out, returning the original text */
            printf("\n\nDecoded (original) text:\n");
            for (count = 0; count < tag; ++count)
                putchar(text[count] + 30);
        }
        ```

```
(j)    /* reversing uppercase and lowercase letters in a line of text */

       #include <stdio.h>
       #include <ctype.h>

       main()
       {
           int count, tag;
           char c, text[80];

           /* read a line of input */

           printf("%s", "Please enter a line of text below: \n");
           for (count = 0; (text[count] = getchar()) != '\n'; ++count)
               ;
           tag = count;

           /* write the reversed line of output */

           for (count = 0; count < tag; ++count)    {
               c = islower(text[count]) ? toupper(text[count])
                                        : tolower(text[count]);
               putchar(c);
           }
       }
```

Chapter 6

6.43 If the value of x is smaller in magnitude than the value of xmin, then the value of xmin is assigned to x if x has a positive value, and the value of -xmin is assigned to x if x has a negative value or if x equals zero. This is not a compound statement, and there are no embedded compound statements.

6.44 (1) The program segment itself is a compound statement.
        (2) The do - while statement, which is embedded in the program segment, contains a compound statement.
        (3) The if statement, which is embedded in the do - while statement, contains a compound statement.

6.45 (a)
```
sum = 0;
i = 2;
while (i < 100)    {
    sum += i;
    i += 3;
}
```
     (c)
```
sum = 0;
for (i = 2; i < 100; i += 3)
    sum += i;
```

    (b)
```
sum = 0;
i = 2;
do {
    sum += i;
    i += 3;
} while (i < 100);
```

6.46 (a)
```
sum = 0;
i = nstart;
while (i <= nstop)    {
    sum += i;
    i += n;
}
```
     (c)
```
sum = 0;
for (i = nstart; i <= nstop; i += n)
    sum += i;
```

    (b)
```
sum = 0;
i = nstart;
do {
    sum += i;
    i += n;
} while (i <= nstop);
```

6.47 (a)
```
count = 0;                              or    count = 0;
while (count < n)   {                         while (count < n)
    printf("%d ", text[count]);                   printf("%d ", text[count++]);
    ++count;
}
```

(b)
```
count = 0;                              or    count = 0;
do {                                          do
    printf("%d ", text[count]);                   printf("%d ", text[count++]);
    ++count;                                  while (count < n);
} while (count < n);
```

(c)
```
for (count = 0; count < n; ++count)
    printf("%d ", text[count]);
```

6.48 (a)
```
count = 0;                              or    count = 0;
while (text[count] != '*')   {                while (text[count] != '*')
    printf("%d ", text[count]);                   printf("%d ", text[count++]);
    ++count;
}
```

(b)
```
count = 0;                              or    count = 0;
do {                                          do
    printf("%d ", text[count]);                   printf("%d ", text[count++]);
    ++count;                                  while (text[count]) != '*');
} while (text[count] != '*');
```

(c)
```
for (count = 0; text[count] != '*'; ++count)
    printf("%d ", text[count]);
```

6.49 (a)
```
for (j = 2; j <= 13; ++j)   {           (c)   for (j = 2; j <= 13; ++j)   {
    sum = 0;                                      sum = 0;
    i = 2;                                        for (i = 2; i < 100; i += j)
    while (i < 100)   {                               sum += i;
        sum += i;                                 printf("%d", sum);
        i += j;                               }
    }
    printf("%d", sum);
}
```

(b)
```
for (j = 2; j <= 13; ++j)   {
    sum = 0;
    i = 2;
    do {
        sum += i;
        i += j;
    } while (i < 100);
    printf("%d", sum);
}
```

6.50 (a)
```
sum = 0;                                (b)   sum = 0;
for (i = 2; i < 100; i += 3)                  for (i = 2; i < 100; i += 3)
    sum = (i % 5 == 0) ? += i : += 0;             if (i % 5 == 0) sum += i;
```

6.51 (a)
```
sum = 0;
for (i = nstart; i <= nstop; i += n)
    sum = (i % k == 0) ? += i : += 0;
```

(b)
```
sum = 0;
for (i = nstart; i <= nstop; i += n)
    if (i % k == 0) sum += i;
```

6.52
```
letters = digits = whitesp = other = 0;
for (count = 0; count < 80; ++count)   {
    if ((text[count] >= 'a' && text[count] <= 'z') ||
        (text[count] >= 'A' && text[count] <= 'Z'))
            ++letters;
    else if (text[count] >= '0' && text[count] <= '9')
            ++digits;
        else if (text[count] == ' ' || text[count] == '\n' || text[count] == '\t')
                ++whitesp;
            else ++other;
}
```

6.53
```
vowels = consonants = 0;
for (count = 0; count < 80; ++count)   {
    if (isalpha(text[count])
        if (text[count] == 'a' || text[count] == 'A' ||
            text[count] == 'e' || text[count] == 'E' ||
            text[count] == 'i' || text[count] == 'I' ||
            text[count] == 'o' || text[count] == 'O' ||
            text[count] == 'u' || text[count] == 'U')
                ++vowels;
    else ++consonants;
}
```

The loop can also be written as

```
vowels = consonants = 0;
for (count = 0; count < 80; ++count)   {
    if (isalpha(text[count])
        if (tolower(text[count]) == 'a' ||
            tolower(text[count]) == 'e' ||
            tolower(text[count]) == 'i' ||
            tolower(text[count]) == 'o' ||
            tolower(text[count]) == 'u')
                ++vowels;
    else ++consonants;
}
```

6.54
```
switch (flag)   {

case 1:  printf("HOT");
        break;

case 2:  printf("LUKE WARM");
        break;

case 3:  printf("COLD");
        break;

default: printf("OUT OF RANGE");
}
```

6.55
```
switch (color)   {
case 'r':
case 'R':
        printf("RED");
        break;

case 'g':
case 'G':
        printf("GREEN");
        break;
```

```
                 case 'b':
                 case 'B':
                            printf("BLUE");
                            break;

                 default:
                            printf("BLACK");
                            break;
                 }
```

6.56
```
        if (temp < 0.)
           printf("ICE");
        else if (temp <= 100.)
                printf("WATER");
            else
                printf("STEAM");
```
A switch statement cannot be used because:

(*a*)   The tests involve floating-point quantities rather than integer quantities.

(*b*)   The tests involve ranges of values rather than exact values.

6.57
```
        for (i = 0, j = 79; i < 80; ++i, --j)
            backtext[j] = text[i];
```

6.58   (*a*)   0 5 15 30   (*g*)   0 1 3 5 8 12 15 19 24 30
                   x = 30   x = 30

      (*b*)   1 2 3 4   (*h*)   0 1 3 6
                   x = 4   x = 6

      (*c*)   1 2 3 4   (*i*)   0
                   x = 4   x = 0

      (*d*)   1 0 3 2 7 6 13 12 21   (*j*)   0 0 2 4 5 9 10 14 14 20
                   x = 21   x = 20

      (*e*)   1 0 3 2 7 6 13 12 21   (*k*)   1 3 5 7 9 12 14 17 20 23
                   x = 21   x = 23

      (*f*)   1   (*l*)   1 6 11 16 21 24 29 32 35 38
                   x = 1   x = 38

Chapter 7

7.32   (*a*)   f accepts an integer argument and returns an integer quantity.

      (*b*)   f accepts two arguments and returns a double-precision quantity. The first argument is a double-precision quantity, and the second is an integer.

      (*c*)   f accepts three arguments and returns nothing. The first function is a long integer, the second is a short integer and the third is an unsigned integer.

      (*d*)   f does not accept any argument but returns a single character.

      (*e*)   f accepts two unsigned integer arguments and returns an unsigned integer.

7.33   (*a*)   f accepts two floating-point arguments and returns a floating-point value.

      (*b*)   f accepts a long integer and returns a long integer.

      (*c*)   f accepts an integer and returns nothing.

      (*d*)   f accepts nothing but returns a character.

7.34   (*a*)   `y = formula(x);`

      (*b*)   `display(a, b);`

7.35   (*a*)   `int sample(void)`

      (*b*)   `float root(int a, int b);`

      (*c*)   `char convert(char c)`

      (*d*)   `char transfer(long i)`

      (*e*)   `long inverse(char c)`

    (f)   `double process(int i, float a, float b)`

    (g)   `void value(double x, double y, short i)`

7.36   (a)   `int funct1(int a, int b);`

    (b)   `double funct1(double a, double b);`

    (c)   `long int funct1(int a, float b);`

    (d)   `double funct1(double a, double b);`

            `double funct2(double a, double b);`

7.37   (a)   `1  4  9  16  25`

    (b)
```
#include <stdio.h>

int funct1(int count);

main()
{
    int count;

    for (count = 1; count <= 5; ++count)
        printf("%d  ", funct1(count));
}

int funct1(int x)
{
    return(x * x);
}
```

    (c)   `55`

    (d)   `30`

7.38   (a) $y = x_n + \sum_{i=1}^{n-1} x_i$ or

            $y_1 = x_1,$ and $y_n = x_n + y_{n-1}$ for $n > 1$

    (b) $y = (-1)^n x^n / n! + \sum_{i=0}^{n-1} (-1)^i x^i / i!$ or

            $y_0 = 1,$ and $y_n = (-1)^n x^n/n! + y_{n-1}$ for $n > 0$

    (c) $p = f_t * \prod_{j=1}^{t-1} f_j$ or

            $p_1 = f_1,$ and $p_t = f_t * p_{t-1}$ for $n > 1$

Chapter 8

8.25   (a)   `1  2  3  4  5`

    (b)   `1  3  6  10  15`

    (c)   `6  15  28  45  66`

8.26   (a)   `extern float solver(float a, float b)`

            Note that `extern` can be omitted; i.e., the first line can be written as

            `float solver(float a, float b)`

    (b)   `static float solver(float a, float b)`

8.27   (a)   *First file*:

```
extern double funct1(double a, double b);   /* added */

main()
{
    double x, y, z;

    . . . . .
```

```
        z = funct1(x, y);

        . . . . .
}
```

Second file:

```
double funct1(double a, double b)
{
        . . . . .
}
```

(b)   *First file*:

```
extern double funct1(double x, double y);   /* added */
extern double funct2(double x, double y);   /* added */

main()
{
    double x, y, z;

        . . . . .

    z = funct1(x, y);

        . . . . .
}
```

Second file:

```
double funct1(double a, double b)
{
    double c;

    c = funct2(a, b);

        . . . . .
}

static double funct2(double a, double b)
{
        . . . . .
}
```

8.28 (a)   4   6   9   13   18
       (b)   100   196   80   184   60   164   40   136   20   100
       (c)   104   116   136   136   100
       (d)   101   102   106   124   200
       (e)   6   11   16   21   26
       (f)   6   11   16   21   26
       (g)   9   25   57   121   249
       (h)   This program will return the number of characters within a line of text entered from the keyboard. The terminating newline character will not be included in the sum.

Chapter 9

9.27 (a)   name is a one-dimensional, 30-element character array.
       (b)   c is a one-dimensional, 6-element floating-point array.
       (c)   a is a one-dimensional, 50-element integer array.
       (d)   params is a two-dimensional, 25-element integer array (5 rows, 5 columns).
       (e)   memo is a two-dimensional, 8712-element character array (66 rows, 132 columns).
       (f)   accounts is a three-dimensional, 80,000-element double-precision array (50 pages, 20 rows, 80 columns).

9.28 (a)   c is a one-dimensional, 8-element floating-point array.

```
c[0] = 2.        c[1] = 5.        c[2] = 3.        c[3] = -4.
c[4] = 12.       c[5] = 12.       c[6] = 0.        c[7] = 8.
```

(b)   c is a one-dimensional, 8-element floating-point array.

c[0] = 2.   c[1] = 5.   c[2] = 3.   c[3] = -4.
c[4] = 0.   c[5] = 0.   c[6] = 0.   c[7] = 0.

(c)   z is a one-dimensional, 12-element integer array.

z[2] = 8   z[5] = 6 All other elements are assigned zeros

(d)   flag is a one-dimensional, 4-element character array.

flag[0] = 'T' flag[1] = 'R' flag[2] = 'U' flag[3] = 'E'

(e)   flag is a one-dimensional, 5-element character array.

flag[0] = 'T' flag[1] = 'R' flag[2] = 'U' flag[3] = 'E'
flag[4] is assigned zero.

(f)   flag is a one-dimensional, 5-element character array.

flag[0] = 'T' flag[1] = 'R' flag[2] = 'U' flag[3] = 'E'
flag[4] = '\0'

(g)   flag is a one-dimensional, 6-element character array.

flag[0] = 'F' flag[1] = 'A' flag[2] = 'L' flag[3] = 'S'
flag[4] = 'E' flag[5] = '\0'

(h)   p is a two-dimensional, 2 × 4 integer array.

p[0][0] = 1   p[0][1] = 3   p[0][2] = 5   p[0][3] = 7
p[1][0] = 0   p[1][1] = 0   p[1][2] = 0   p[1][3] = 0

(i)   p is a two-dimensional, 2 × 4 integer array.

p[0][0] = 1   p[0][1] = 1   p[0][2] = 3   p[0][3] = 3
p[1][0] = 5   p[1][1] = 5   p[1][2] = 7   p[1][3] = 7

(j)   p is a two-dimensional, 2 × 4 integer array.

p[0][0] = 1   p[0][1] = 3   p[0][2] = 5   p[0][3] = 7
p[1][0] = 2   p[1][1] = 4   p[1][2] = 6   p[1][3] = 8

(k)   p is a two-dimensional, 2 × 4 integer array.

p[0][0] = 1   p[0][1] = 3   p[0][2] = 0   p[0][3] = 0
p[1][0] = 5   p[1][1] = 7   p[1][2] = 0   p[1][3] = 0

(l)   c is a three-dimensional, 2 × 3 × 4 integer array.

c[0][0][0] = 1   c[0][0][1] = 2   c[0][0][2] = 3   c[0][0][3] = 0
c[0][1][0] = 4   c[0][1][1] = 5   c[0][1][2] = 0   c[0][1][3] = 0
c[0][2][0] = 6   c[0][2][1] = 7   c[0][2][2] = 8   c[0][2][3] = 9
c[1][0][0] = 10   c[1][0][1] = 11   c[1][0][2] = 0   c[1][0][3] = 0
c[1][1][0] = 0   c[1][1][1] = 0   c[1][1][2] = 0   c[1][1][3] = 0
c[1][2][0] = 12   c[1][2][1] = 13   c[1][2][2] = 14   c[1][2][3] = 0

(m)   colors is a two-dimensional, 3 × 6 character array.

colors[0][0] = 'R'   colors[0][1] = 'E'   colors [0][2] = 'D'
colors[0][3] = 0   colors[0][4] = 0   colors[0][5] = 0
colors[1][0] = 'G'   colors[1][1] = 'R'   colors [1][2] = 'E'
colors[1][3] = 'E'   colors[1][4] = 'N'   colors[1][5] = 0
colors[2][0] = 'B'   colors[2][1] = 'L'   colors [2][2] = 'U'
colors[2][3] = 'E'   colors[2][4] = 0   colors[2][5] = 0

9.29   (a)   int c[12] = {1, 4, 7, 10, 13, 16, 19, 22, 25, 28, 31, 34};
       (b)   char point[] = "NORTH";
       (c)   char letters[4] = {'N', 'S', 'E', 'W'};

(*d*)   `float consts[6] = {0.005, -0.032, 1e-6, 0.167, -0.3e8, 0.015};`

(*e*)   `int n[3][4] = {10, 12, 14, 16, 20, 22, 24, 26, 30, 32, 34, 36};`

Another way to assign the initial values is as follows.

```
int n[3][4] = {
                {10, 12, 14, 16},
                {20, 22, 24, 26},
                {30, 32, 34, 36}
            };
```

(*f*)   `int n[3][4] = {10, 12, 14, 0, 0, 20, 22, 0, 0, 30, 32, 0};`

or

```
int n[3][4] = {
                {10, 12, 14},
                {0, 20, 22},
                {0, 30, 32}
            };
```

(*g*)   `int n[3][4] = {10, 12, 14, 16, 20, 22};`

9.30 (*a*)   `float sample(float a, float b, int jstar[]);`

```
main()
{
    float a, b, x;
    int jstar[20];

    . . . . .

    x = sample(a, b, jstar);

    . . . . .
}

float sample(float a, float b, int jstar[])
{
    . . . . .
}
```

(*b*)   `float sample(int n, char c, double values[]);`

```
main()
{
    int n;
    char c;
    float x;
    double values[50];

    . . . . .

    x = sample(n, c, values);

    . . . . .
}

float sample(int n, char c, double values[])
{
    . . . . .
}
```

(c)
```
float sample(char text[][80]);

main()
{
    float x;
    char text[12][80];

    . . . . .

    x = sample(text);

    . . . . .
}

float sample(char text[][80])
{
    . . . . .
}
```

(d)
```
float sample(char message[], float accounts[][100]);

main()
{
    float x;
    char message[40];
    float accounts[50][100];

    . . . . .

    x = sample(message, accounts);

    . . . . .
}

float sample(char message[], float accounts[][100])
{
    . . . . .
}
```

9.31 (a) 20 (sum of the array elements whose values are even)
(b) 25 (sum of the even array elements)
(c) Will not run (automatic arrays cannot be initialized).
(d) 25 (sum of the external array elements whose values are odd)
(e) 1 (smallest value)
(f) 1 5 9 (smallest value within each row)
(g) 9 10 11 12 (largest value within each column)
(h) 0 2 2 4
4 6 6 8
8 10 10 12 (if the value of an element is odd, reduce its value by 1; then display the entire array)
(i) PPoorrmmiiggwwtt   aa eeggeettffnn (skip the even-numbered array elements; print each odd-numbered array element twice)

Chapter 10

10.44 (a) px is a pointer to an integer quantity.
(b) a and b are floating-point variables; pa and pb are pointers to floating-point quantities (though not necessarily to a and b).
(c) a is a floating-point variable whose initial value is −0.167; pa is a pointer to a floating-point quantity; the address of a is assigned to pa as an initial value.
(d) c1, c2 and c3 are char-type variables; pc1, pc2 and pc3 are pointers to characters; the address of c1 is assigned to pc3.
(e) funct is a function that accepts three arguments and returns a double-precision quantity. The first two arguments are pointers to double-precision quantities; the third argument is a pointer to an integer quantity.

(*f*)   `funct` is a function that accepts three arguments and returns a pointer to a double-precision quantity. The first two arguments are pointers to double-precision quantities; the third argument is a pointer to an integer quantity.

(*g*)   `a` is a pointer to a group of contiguous, one-dimensional, double-precision arrays; this is equivalent to `double a[][12];`

(*h*)   `a` is a one-dimensional array of pointers to double-precision quantities (equivalent to a two-dimensional array of double-precision quantities).

(*i*)   `a` is a one-dimensional array of pointers to single characters or strings (equivalent to a two-dimensional array of characters).

(*j*)   `d` is a one-dimensional array of pointers to the strings `"north"`, `"south"`, `"east"` and `"west"`.

(*k*)   `p` is a pointer to a group of contiguous, two-dimensional, long-integer arrays; equivalent to `p[][10][20];`

(*l*)   `p` is a two-dimensional array of pointers to long-integer quantities (equivalent to a three-dimensional array of long integers).

(*m*)   `sample` is a function that accepts an argument which is a function and returns a character. The function passed as an argument accepts two character arguments and returns an integer quantity.

(*n*)   `pf` is a pointer to a function that accepts no arguments but returns an integer quantity.

(*o*)   `pf` is a pointer to a function that accepts two character arguments and returns an integer quantity.

(*p*)   `pf` is a pointer to a function that accepts two pointers to characters as arguments and returns an integer quantity.

10.45 (*a*)
```
int i, j;
int *pi = &i;
int *pj = &j;
```
      (*b*)
```
float *pf;
double *pd;
```
      (*c*)   `long *funct(int a, int b);`
      (*d*)   `long funct(int *a, int *b);`
      (*e*)   `float *x;`
      (*f*)   `float (*x)[30];` or `float *x[15];`
      (*g*)   `char *color[3] = {"red", "green", "blue"};`
      (*h*)   `char *funct(int (*pf)(int a));`
      (*i*)   `float (*pf)(int a, int b, int c);`
      (*j*)   `float *(*pf)(int *a, int *b, int *c);`

10.46 (*a*) F8D   (*c*) `'B'`   (*e*) F8C   (*g*) `'C'`
       (*b*) F8D   (*d*) `'C'`   (*f*) F8C

10.47 (*a*) F9C   (*f*) F9E
       (*b*) F9E   (*g*) (i + j) = 35 + 30 = 65
       (*c*) F9E   (*h*) FA2
       (*d*) 30 (note that this changes the value of j)   (*i*) 67
       (*e*) 35   (*j*) unspecified

10.48 (*a*) 1130   (*d*) 1130   (*g*) 1134
       (*b*) 1134   (*e*) 0.002   (*h*) 0.003
       (*c*) 1138   (*f*) &(*pa) = pa = 1130   (*i*) 0.003

10.49 (*a*) 80   (*c*) a=88 b=89
       (*b*) 81   (*d*) a=80 b=81

10.50 (*a*) A pointer to an integer.
       (*b*) Nothing is returned.
       (*c*) A pointer to an integer quantity.
       (*d*) Calculate the sum of the elements of p (p is a five-element integer array).
       (*e*) sum=150

10.51 (*a*) A pointer to an integer.
       (*b*) Nothing is returned.
       (*c*) The last two elements of a five-element integer array.
       (*d*) Calculate the sum of the last two elements of the five-element integer array.
       (*e*) sum=90

10.52 (a) A pointer to an integer quantity.

(b) A pointer to an integer quantity.

(c) The address of the element of p whose value is the largest (p is actually a five-element integer array).

(d) Determine the largest value of the elements of p.

(e) `max=50`

10.53 (a) Address of `x[0]`   (d) `12` (i.e., `10 + 2`)

(b) Address of `x[2]`   (e) `30` (this is the value of `x[2]`)

(c) `10`

10.54 (a) Address of `table[0][0]`

(b) Address of row 1 (the second row) of `table`

(c) Address of `table[1][0]`

(d) Address of `table[1][1]`

(e) Address of `table[0][1]`

(f) `2.2` (i.e., `1.2 + 1`)

(g) `1.2`

(h) `2.1`

(i) `2.2`

10.55 (a) Address of `color[0]` (the beginning of the first string)

(b) Address of `color[2]` (the beginning of the third string)

(c) `"red"`

(d) `"blue"`

(e) They both refer to the same array element (pointer to `"yellow"`)

10.56 (a) a and b are ordinary floating-point variables. one, two and three are functions, each of which returns a floating-point quantity. one and two each accept two floating-point quantities as arguments. three accepts a function as an argument; the argument function will accept two floating-point quantities as its own arguments, and it will return a floating-point quantity. (Note that either one or two can appear as an argument to three).

(b) one and two are conventional function definitions. Each accepts two floating-point quantities and returns a floating-point quantity which is calculated within the function.

(c) three accepts a pointer to a function as an argument. The argument function accepts two floating-point quantities and returns a floating-point quantity. Within three, the argument function is accessed and the calculated result is assigned to c. The value of c is then returned to main.

(d) A different function is passed to three each time it is accessed. Therefore, the value that is returned by three will be calculated differently each time three is accessed.

10.57 (a) a and b are pointers to floating-point quantities. one, two and three are functions; one and two each return a floating-point quantity, and three returns a pointer to a floating-point quantity. one and two each accept two pointers to floating-point quantities as arguments. three accepts a function as an argument; the argument function will accept two pointers to floating-point quantities as its own arguments, and it will return a floating-point quantity. (Note that either one or two can appear as an argument to three).

(b) one and two are conventional function definitions. Each accepts two pointers to floating-point quantities and returns a floating-point quantity which is calculated within the function.

(c) three accepts a pointer to a function as an argument. The argument function accepts two pointers to floating-point quantities and returns a floating-point quantity. Within three, the argument function is accessed and the calculated result is assigned to c. The address of c is then returned to main.

(d) A different function is passed to three each time it is accessed. Therefore, the value whose address is returned by three will be calculated differently each time three is accessed.

(e) In this outline one and two accept pointers as arguments, whereas one and two accept ordinary floating-point variables as arguments in the previous outline. Also, in this outline three returns a pointer whereas three returns an ordinary floating-point quantity in the previous outline.

10.58 (a) x is a pointer to a function that accepts an argument which is a pointer to an integer quantity and returns a floating-point quantity.

(b) x is a function that accepts an argument which is a pointer to an integer quantity and returns a pointer to a 20-element floating-point array.

(c) x is a function that accepts an argument which is a pointer to an integer array and returns a floating-point quantity.

(d)   x is a function that accepts an argument that is an array of pointers to integer quantities and returns a floating-point quantity.

(e)   x is a function that accepts an argument which is an integer array and returns a pointer to a floating-point quantity.

(f)   x is a function that accepts an argument which is a pointer to an integer array and returns a pointer to a floating-point quantity.

(g)   x is a function that accepts an argument which is an array of pointers to integer quantities and returns a pointer to a floating-point quantity.quantity.

(h)   x is a pointer to a function that accepts an argument which is a pointer to an integer array and returns a floating-point quantity.

(i)   x is a pointer to a function that accepts an argument which is an array of pointers to integer quantities and returns a pointer to a floating-point quantity.

(j)   x is a 20-element array of pointers to functions; each function accepts an argument which is an integer quantity and returns a floating-point quantity.

(k)   x is a 20-element array of pointers to functions; each function accepts an argument which is a pointer to an integer quantity and returns a pointer to a floating-point quantity.

10.59 (a) `char (*p(int *a))[6];`   (g) `char (*p)(int (*a)[]);`
       (b) `char p(int (*a)[]);`   (h) `char *(*p)(int (*a)[]);`
       (c) `char p(int *a[]);`   (i) `char *(*p)(int *a[]);`
       (d) `char *p(int a[]);`   (j) `double (*f[12])(double a, double b);`
       (e) `char *p(int (*a)[]);`   (k) `double *(*f[12])(double a, double b);`
       (f) `char *p(int *a[]);`   (l) `double *(*f[12])(double *a, double *b);`

Chapter 11

11.34
```
struct  complex  {
     float real;
     float imaginary;
};
```

11.35 `struct  complex  x1, x2, x3;`

11.36
```
struct  complex  {
     float real;
     float imaginary;
}  x1, x2, x3;
```

Including the tag (complex) is optional in this situation.

11.37 `struct  complex  x = {1.3, –2.2};`

Remember that x must be either static or external.

11.38 `struct  complex  *px;`

The structure members are px->real and px->imaginary

11.39 `struct  complex  cx[100];`

11.40
```
struct  complex  {
     float real;
     float imaginary;
}  cx[100];
```

Including the tag (complex) is optional in this situation.

11.41 The structure members are cx[17].real and cx[17].imaginary

11.42
```
typedef  struct  {
     int won;
     int lost;
     float percentage;
}  record;
```

11.43
```
typedef struct {
    char name[40];
    record stats;
} team;
```

where the structure type record is defined in Prob. 11.42.

11.44
```
team t;
```

The structure members are t.name, t.stats.won, t.stats.lost, and t.stats.percentage. The characters that make up t.name can also be accessed individually; e.g., t.name[0], t.name[1], t.name[2], . . ., etc.

11.45
```
team t = {"Chicago Bears", 14, 2, 87.5};
```

11.46
```
printf("%d\n", sizeof t);
```

or

```
printf("%d\n", sizeof (team));
```

11.47
```
team *pt;
```

The structure members are pt->name, pt->stats.won, pt->stats.lost, and pt->stats.percentage. The characters that make up t->name can also be accessed individually; e.g., pt->name[0], etc.

11.48
```
team league[48];
```

The individual items are league[4].name and league[4].stats.percentage.

11.49
```
struct team {
    char name[40];
    record stats;
    struct team *next;
};
```

11.50 Two solutions are given, either of which is correct.

(*a*)
```
struct team *pt;

pt = (struct team*) malloc(sizeof(struct team));
```

(*b*)
```
typedef struct team city;
city *pt;

pt = (city*) malloc(sizeof(city));
```

11.51 Two solutions are given, either of which is correct.

(*a*)
```
struct hms {
    int hour;
    int minute;
    int second;
}
union {
    struct hms local;
    struct hms home;
} *time;
```

(*b*)
```
typedef struct {
    int hour;
    int minute;
    int second;
} hms;
union {
    hms local;
    hms home;
} *time;
```

11.52 Two solutions are given, either of which is correct.

(*a*)
```
union ans {
      int ians;
      float fans;
      double dans;
};
struct {
    union ans answer;
    char flag;
    int a;
    int b;
} x, y;
```

(*b*)
```
typedef union {
      int ians;
      float fans;
      double dans;
} ans;
struct {
    ans answer;
    char flag;
    int a;
    int b;
} x, y;
```

11.53
```
union ans {
    int ians;
    float fans;
    double dans;
};
struct sample {
    union ans answer;
    char flag;
    int a;
    int b;
};
struct sample v = {14, 'i', -2, 5};
```

11.54
```
union ans {
    int ians;
    float fans;
    double dans;
};
struct sample {
    union ans answer;
    char flag;
    int a;
    int b;
    struct sample *next;
};
typedef struct sample struct_type;
struct_type x, *px = &x;
```

11.55 (*a*)
```
red green blue
cyan magenta yellow
red green blue
```

The structure variable `sample` is passed to `funct` by value. Hence the reassignments within `funct` are not recognized within `main`.

(b) red green blue
     cyan magenta yellow
     cyan magenta yellow

The structure variable sample is passed to funct by reference. (Actually, it is a pointer to the beginning of sample that is passed to funct.) Therefore the reassignments within funct are recognized within main.

(c) red green blue
     cyan magenta yellow
     cyan magenta yellow

The structure variable sample is passed to funct by value, as in (a). Now, however, the altered structure variable is returned to main.

11.56 8
100 0.000000 −0.000000
0 0.500000 −0.000000
−25098 391364288.000000 0.016667

The first line represents the size of the union (8 bytes, to accommodate a double-precision number). In the second line, only the first value (100) is meaningful. In the third line, only the second value (0.500000) is meaningful. And in the last line, only the last value (0.016667) is meaningful.

11.57 (a) 200 0.500012
               0 0.500000

The union variable u is passed to funct by value. Hence the reassignment within funct is not recognized within main. Note that only the first value is meaningful in the first line of output, and only the second value is meaningful in the last line.

(b) −26214 −0.300000
     0 0.500000

The union variable u is again passed to funct by value. Hence the reassignment within funct is not recognized within main. The first value in each line is meaningless.

(c) −26214 −0.300000
     −26214 −0.300000

The union variable u is passed to funct by value, but the altered union variable is then returned to main. Hence, the reassignment within funct will be recognized within main. The first value in each line is meaningless.

Chapter 12

12.21
```
#include <stdio.h>
FILE *pointr;
pointr = fopen("students.dat", "w");
```

12.22
```
#include <stdio.h>
FILE *pointr;
pointr = fopen("students.dat", "a");
```

12.23
```
#include <stdio.h>
FILE *pointr;
pointr = fopen("sample.dat", "w+");
fclose(pointr);
```

12.24
```
#include <stdio.h>
FILE *pointr;
pointr = fopen("sample.dat", "r+");
fclose(pointr);
```

12.25
```
#include <stdio.h>
#define  NULL  0

FILE *pointr;

pointr = fopen("sample.dat", "r+");
if (pointr == NULL)
printf("\nERROR - Cannot open the designated file\n");

fclose(pointr);
```

The `fopen` and `if` statements are often combined; e.g.,

```
if ((pointr = fopen("sample.dat", "r+")) == NULL)
printf("\nERROR - Cannot open the designated file\n");
```

12.26
```
printf("Enter values for a, b and c: ");
scanf("%d %f %c", &a, &b, &c);
fprintf(fpt, "%d %.2f %c", a, b, c);
```

Newline characters (`\n`) may be included within the `fprintf` control string, as desired.

12.27
```
fscanf(fpt, "%d %f %c", &a, &b, &c);
printf("a = %d   b = %f   c = %c", a, b, c);
```

12.28 (*a*)   `fscanf(pt1, "%d %f %c", &a, &b, &c);`

(*b*)
```
printf("a = %d   New value: ", a);
scanf("%d", &a);
printf("b = %f   New value: ", b);
scanf("%f", &x);
printf("c = %c   New value: ", c);
scanf("%c", &c);
```

(*c*)   `fprintf(pt2, "%d %.2f %c", a, b, c);`

Newline characters (`\n`) may be included within the `fprintf` control string, as desired.

12.29 (*a*)   `fscanf(pt1, "%s", name);`

(*b*)   `printf("Name: %s\n", name);`

(*c*)
```
printf("New name: ");
scanf(" %[^\n]", name);
```

(*d*)   `fprintf(pt2, "%s", name);`

Here is another solution.

(*a*)   `fgets(name, 20, pt1);`

(*b*)   `printf("Name: %s\n", name);`

(*c*)
```
puts("New name: ");
gets(name);
```

(*d*)   `fputs(name, pt2);`

12.30 (*a*)
```
fscanf(pt1, "%s", values.name);
printf("%s", values.name);
```

(*b*)
```
printf("a = ");
scanf("%d", &values.a);
printf("b = ");
scanf("%f", &values.b);
printf("c = ");
scanf("%c", &values.c);
```

(*c*)
```
fprintf(pt2, "%s %d %f %c", values.name, values.a,
values.b, values.c);
```

or

```
            fprintf(pt2, "%s\n%d\n%f\n%c\n", values.name, values.a,
            values.b, values.c);

            or

            fprintf(pt2, "%s\n", values.name);
            fprintf(pt2, "%d\n", values.a);
            fprintf(pt2, "%f\n", values.b);
            fprintf(pt2, "%c\n", values.c);
```

12.31 (*a*)
```
            fread(&values, sizeof values, 1, pt1);
            printf("%s", values.name);
```
(*b*)
```
            printf("a = ");
            scanf("%d", &values.a);
            printf("b = ");
            scanf("%f", &values.b);
            printf("c = ");
            scanf("%c", &values.c);
```
(*c*)
```
            fwrite(&values, sizeof values, 1, pt2);
```

Chapter 13

13.36
```
register unsigned u, v;
```

13.37
```
int u = 1, v = 2;
register int x = 3, y = 4;
```

13.38
```
unsigned *funct(register unsigned *pt1);       /* function prototype */

main()
{
    register unsigned *pt1;                    /* pointer declaration */
    unsigned *pt2;                             /* pointer declaration */

    . . . . .

    pt2 = funct(pt1);

    . . . . .

}

unsigned *funct(register unsigned *pt1)        /* function definition */
{
    unsigned *pt2;

    . . . . .

    pt2 = . . . . .;

    . . . . .

    return(pt2);
}
```

13.39 bit pattern corresponding to a: 1010 0010 1100 0011

(*a*)	5d3c	0101 1101 0011 1100
(*b*)	2202	0010 0010 0000 0010
(*c*)	9dc5	1001 1101 1100 0101
(*d*)	bfc7	1011 1111 1100 0111
(*e*)	80c1	1000 0000 1100 0001
(*f*)	623a	0110 0010 0011 1010
(*g*)	e2fb	1110 0010 1111 1011
(*h*)	1458	0001 0100 0101 1000
(*i*)	5860	0101 1000 0110 0000
(*j*)	0	0000 0000 0000 0000 (valid for any value of a)
(*k*)	ffff	1111 1111 1111 1111 (valid for any value of a)

(*l*)	ffff	1111 1111 1111 1111	(valid for any value of a)
(*m*)	a000	1010 0000 0000 0000	
(*n*)	c100	1100 0001 0000 0000	
(*o*)	a0c3	1010 0000 1100 0011	
(*p*)	5bc3	0101 1011 1100 0011	
(*q*)	3a00	0011 1010 0000 0000	
(*r*)	5b3c	0101 1011 0011 1100	
(*s*)	fbc3	1111 1011 1100 0011	
(*t*)	fb00	1111 1011 0000 0000	
(*u*)	fbff	1111 1011 1111 1111	

13.40 (*a*) `a &= 0x3f06`   (*d*) `a >>= 3`   (*g*) `a &= ~(0x3f06 << 8)`

(*b*) `a ^= 0x3f06`   (*e*) `a <<= 5`

(*c*) `a |= ~0x3f06`   (*f*) `a ^= ~a`

13.41 (*a*) `v & 0xaaaa` or `v & ~0x5555`   (*c*) `v | 0x5555`

(*b*) `c & 0x7f`   (*d*) `v ^= 0x42`

13.42 (*a*) Note that v represents a positive number, since the leftmost bit is 0 (the equivalent decimal value is 13980). Hence, the vacated bits resulting from both shift operations will be filled with 0s. The resulting values are

(*i*)   `0x69c0`   (*ii*)   `0x369`

(*b*) Now v represents a negative number, since the leftmost bit is 1 (the equivalent decimal value is −15511). Hence, the vacated bits in the left-shift operation will be filled with 0s, but the vacated bits in the right-shift operation will be filled with 1s. The resulting values are

(*i*)   `0x3690`   (*ii*)   `0xfc36`

13.43 Each structure defines several bit fields.

(*a*) u consists of 3 bits, v consists of 1 bit, w consists of 7 bits, and x consists of 5 bits. The total bit count is 16. Hence, all of the bit fields will fit into one word.

(*b*) The individual bit fields are the same as in part (a). Now, however, each bit field is assigned an initial value. Note that each value is small enough to fit within its corresponding bit field (i.e., 2 requires two bits, 1 requires one bit, 16 requires five bits, and 8 requires four bits).

(*c*) u, v and w are each 7 bits wide. Two words of memory will be required. u and v will fit into one word, but w will be forced to the beginning of the next word.

(*d*) u, v and w are each 7 bits wide. Two words will be required. u will be placed within the first word, followed by 9 empty bits. v and w will fit into the second word, separated by 2 empty bits.

(*e*) u, v and w are each 7 bits wide. Three words will be utilized to store these bit fields. u will be placed within the first word, v will be forced to the beginning of the second word, and w will be forced to the beginning of the third word. Each bit field will be followed by 9 empty bits.

13.44 (*a*)
```
struct fields {
    unsigned a : 6;
    unsigned b : 4;
    unsigned c : 6;
};
```

(*b*)
```
static struct fields v = {3, 5, 7};
```
or
```
static struct {
    unsigned a : 6;
    unsigned b : 4;
    unsigned c : 6;
} v = {3, 5, 7};
```
Each value can fit into a three-bit field.

(*c*) The 6-bit fields can accommodate any value up to 63, since

$$63 = 2^6 - 1 = 1 \times 2^5 + 1 \times 2^4 + 1 \times 2^3 + 1 \times 2^2 + 1 \times 2^1 + 1 \times 2^0$$

The 4-bit field can accommodate any value up to 15, since $15 = 2^4 - 1 = 1 \times 2^3 + 1 \times 2^2 + 1 \times 2^1 + 1 \times 2^0$

(d)
```
static  struct  {
      unsigned a : 8;
      unsigned b : 6;
      unsigned c : 5;
};
```
a and b will be stored within one 16-bit word, and c will be stored within a second 16-bit word.

(e)
```
static  struct  {
      unsigned a : 8;
      unsigned   : 2;
      unsigned b : 6;
      unsigned c : 5;
};
```

(f)
```
static  struct  {
      unsigned a : 8;
      unsigned   : 0;
      unsigned b : 6;
      unsigned   : 2;
      unsigned c : 5;
};
```

Chapter 14

14.24 `enum  flags  {first, second, third, fourth, fifth};`

14.25 `enum  flags  event;`

or

`enum  {first, second, third, fourth, fifth}  event;`

14.26 `enum  {do = 1, re, mi, fa, sol, la, ti}  soprano, bass;`

14.27 `enum  money  {penny = 1, nickel = 5, dime = 10,`
`quarter = 25, half = 50, dollar = 100};`

14.28 `enum  money  coins = dime;`

or

`enum  {penny = 1, nickel = 5, dime = 10, quarter = 25,`
`half = 50, dollar = 100}  coins = dime;`

14.29 `north = 2`
`south = 3`
`east = 1`
`west = 2`

14.30 `move_1 = 3`
`move_2 = 2`

14.31 This switch statement calculates a cumulative score, using rules that depend on the values assigned to the enumeration variable move. The rules are as follows: if move = north add 10 points to score; if move = south add 20 points to score; if move = east add 30 points to score; and if move = west add 40 points to score. An error message is displayed if move is assigned anything other than north, south, east or west.

14.32 (a) `argc = 3, argv[0] = demo, argv[1] = debug, and argv[2] = fast`

(b) `argc = 2, argv[0] = demo, and argv[1] = debug  fast`

14.33 This program will read in a line of text and display it in either upper- or lowercase, depending on the second command line parameter. This parameter must be either upper or lower. If it is neither upper nor lower, an error message is generated and the text is not displayed.

14.34 `transfer.exe  data.old  data.new`

or, with some compilers,

`transfer  data.old  data.new`

14.35 *(a)* `#define  PI  3.1415927`

(b) `#define  AREA  PI * radius * radius`

(c) `#define  AREA(radius)  PI * radius * radius`

(d) `#define  CIRCUMFERENCE  2 * PI * radius`

(e) `#define  CIRCUMFERENCE(radius)  2 * PI * radius`

(f)
```
#define  interest  {                    \
             i = 0.01 * r;              \
             f = p * pow((1 + i), n);   \
         }
```

This assumes that the variables i, r, f, p and n have all been declared to be double-precision variables.

(g)
```
#define  interest(p, r, n)  {           \
             i = 0.01 * r;              \
             f = p * pow((1 + i), n);   \
         }
```

(h) `#define  max  (a >= b) ? a : b`

or

`#define  max  (((a) >= (b)) ? (a) : (b))`

The second version will minimize the likelihood of undesirable side effects.

(i) `#define  max(a, b)  (a >= b) ? a : b`

or

`#define  max(a, b)  (((a) >= (b)) ? (a) : (b))`

14.36 *(a)* If the symbolic consant FLAG has not been defined previously, define FLAG to represent the value 1.

(b) If the symbolic constant PASCAL has been defined previously, define the symbolic constants BEGIN and END to represent the symbols { and }, respectively.

(c) If the symbolic constant CELSIUS has been defined previously, define the macro temperature(t) to represent the expression 0.5555555 * (t − 32); otherwise, define temperature so that it represents the expression 1.8 * t + 32.

(d) If the symbolic constant DEBUG has not been defined previously, define the macro out as

`printf("x = %f\n", x)`

Otherwise, if the symbolic constant LEVEL has a value of 1, define out as

`printf("i = %d   y = %f\n", i, y[i])`

and if LEVEL does not have a value of 1, define out as the multiline macro

```
for (count = 1; count <= n; ++count)        \
printf("i = %d   y = %f\n", i, y[i])
```

(Assume that the variables x, i, y, count and n have been properly declared.)

(e) "Undefine" the symbolic constant DEBUG if it has been defined previously.

(f) This problem illustrates the use of the "stringizing" operator (#). If the symbolic constant ERROR_CHECKS has been defined previously, then the macro message(line) is defined in such a manner that the argument line is converted into a string and then displayed.

(g) This problem illustrates the use of the "token-pasting" operator (##). If the symbolic constant ERROR_CHECKS has been defined previously, then the macro message(n) is defined in such a manner that the value of messagen (e.g., message3) is displayed.

14.37 *(a)*
```
#if defined(BOOLEAN)           or        #ifdef  BOOLEAN
    #define  TRUE   1                         #define  TRUE   1
    #define  FALSE  0                         #define  FALSE  0
    #undef   YES                              #undef   YES
    #undef   NO                               #undef   NO
#endif                                    #endif
```

```
(b)   #if flag == 0
          #define   COLOR   1
      #elif flag < 3
          #define   COLOR   2
      #else
          #define   COLOR   3
      #endif
(c)   #if SIZE == WIDE
          #define   WIDTH  132
      #else
          #define   WIDTH   80
      #endif
(d)   #define   error(text)  printf(#text)
(e)   #define   error(i)  printf("%s\n", error##i)
```

Index

Programming examples are indicated in italics.

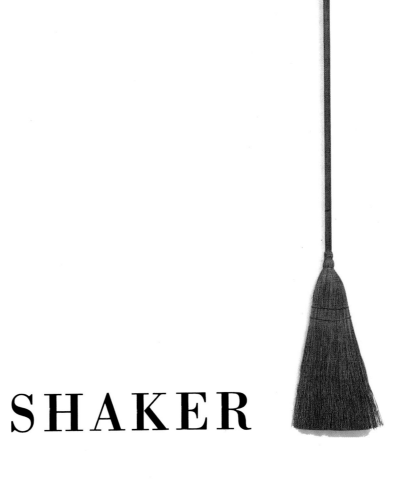

SHAKER

S H

JUNE SPRIGG and DAVID LARKIN

AKER

LIFE, WORK, and ART

Photographs by Michael Freeman

A David Larkin Book

Houghton Mifflin Company

Boston

To S.E.L.

First published in 1987 by Stewart, Tabori & Chang, Inc.

575 Broadway, New York, New York 10012

Library of Congress Catalog Card Number: 91-71234
ISBN: 0-395-59927-X

Printed in Japan

10 9 8 7 6 5 4 3 2 1

First Edition

CONTENTS

A DAY IN THE LIFE

4:30 A.M. A late September Saturday begins, and it promises to be fair. The first bell rings. The Sister is awake already, but her eyes remain closed. She stretches in her narrow bed. The stove still sends out some warmth, but it will need to be fed, as usual. Her roommates are beginning to stir. Across the hall, and next door, the sounds of the Family waking come softly to the room.

She awaits her turn at the washstand and splashes water on her face. She pulls the brown and blue cotton-and-worsted gown on over her shift, smooths her hair under the starched white cap, and pins her kerchief across her bosom. The aroma of breakfast wafts up from the kitchen far below, but there is more than an hour until it's time to eat.

The Sister draws the covers back from her bed and folds them neatly over the foot to air the sheets and keep them fresh. She glides her broom over the smooth pine floorboards. The daily routine is familiar and comforting, she thinks, as she brushes some wood chips and ash from the floor near the stove. She wipes the woodwork—the window sill, the built-in drawers—with a cloth and brushes a small spider web from the shelf. She refills the lamp with oil from the big bottle, which is getting low, and reminds herself to ask the Deaconess for more. She moves quickly and is straightening a box of spools when the bell rings again. The quarter-hour has passed, and the Brethren are dressed and heading out to the barn to do their chores.

The Brethren gone, she steps across the hall and cleans their room. That accomplished, she returns to her room to sit and think about the day ahead while she starts work on mending the stockings that a Brother has left for her. She will begin a four-week shift in the kitchen this morning. It's been a while since her last turn there. This pleases her; she likes the activity and camaraderie. The holes darned, she picks up some kerchiefs to mark with her initials, tiny cross-stitches in fine blue thread. Her thoughts wander as the day brightens outside.

8

In the room across the hall, the Brother also hears the 4:30 bell, and he rises to dress and greet those who share his room. It's hard to get up today; his bones are feeling the years and the coming of the cold. The Sisters hung the wall cloths from the pegboard last week, and he's grateful for the extra bit of insulation they provide. He peers into the small looking-glass and shaves his whiskers off with his razor. It pleases him that tomorrow is Sunday, and he won't even have to do this small chore. He pulls on his cotton-and-worsted trousers, buttons his vest, and ties the laces of his boots.

He feels hungry this morning, but there's the milking to do before the Family can eat. He walks, slowly, down the stairs and into the bright cold dawn. The barn is welcoming and warm, sharp with the scent of hay. The sounds of crunching feed and the ring of milk in tin pails are a soothing daily refrain. He leans his cheek against the broad, warm, softly heaving side of the cow and feels the rhythm of the milking.

6:00 A.M. The breakfast bell rings. The Family moves down the hall
to the stairs, exchanging nods and quiet greetings. Down the
separate stairs, through the double doors, the Brethren and Sisters
take their accustomed places at the tables, the Brethren on the east,
the Sisters on the west. They are still enjoying the novelty of the
new dining chairs, installed last month to replace the old, backless
benches. These are much more convenient and comfortable, and
deeply appreciated by all. After silent thanks, the Family sits. They
eat without talking, murmuring only thanks for passing platters.
There are, for this breakfast, boiled potatoes, fried sausage, wheat
bread, stewed applesauce, and camomile tea. Coffee and tea were
eliminated last year for the sake of health. The Family eats quickly,
rises at the signal, and leaves for a morning's work.

The Brother gets his coat and hat and leaves for the Brethren's
workshop, glad these days for its proximity. He stokes the wood
stove and resumes his work on oval boxes. He has been making
these boxes on and off for something like twenty-five years. In the
summer, he continues to supervise the orchard work. Now, however,
with the harvest in and the apples picked and stored, dried, or
made into good, rich applesauce, he turns again to his winter work.

12

He begins today by cutting "swallowtails" into the strips of wood that
will form the boxes' sides. This is pleasant work; it busies his
hands, but leaves his mind free to drift. He remembers his first
efforts at making boxes—what an eager young man he was, full of
questions. Why were the swallowtails necessary? Why cut them with
a knife, not a saw? Why use maple for the sides but pine for the
bottom? He recalls the patience of the aged Brother who taught him
the answers that he, in turn, has passed on to young Brethren in
recent years. The swallowtails keep the joint from buckling by
leaving room for the wood to swell and shrink with time and changes
in weather from damp to dry. Cut them with a knife to give the
edges a slight bevel, rounding them so that the delicate points are
less likely to catch on something and break. Maple bends easily
when soaked or steamed in hot water, so it's good for the sides,
wrapped around an oval mold until dry. Pine is readily available and
easy to work—a nice wood for bottoms and lids. The Brother is
proud of his own contribution—using copper tacks instead of iron,
which rust and discolor the wood. The boxes he makes are as
perfect as anything on earth can be—an honest product of his faith.

14

16

The Sister is down in the kitchen. They will be baking today, and the fire in the large brick oven is already roaring. She and her partner will be making the pies this month, while others attend to plucking chickens and all the rest. They decide to take turns peeling and slicing the apples, planning thirty-five pies to last half the week. The work goes fast, and it's cheerful here. Soon it's time to clean up and set the table in the dining room upstairs.

11:50 A.M. The first bell rings. The Brother stands, stretches, and brushes small curls of wood from his work frock. He takes a quick count of the box sides he's finished—forty-eight. He steps back to the dwelling on the stone walk, while the rest of the Family converges. The dinner is delicious: chicken pudding, stewed onions, pickles, turnips, bread, and his favorite—apple pie.

4:30 P.M. The shadows are long. Now the Sisters' side of the dwelling is filling with light, and the Brethren's side is dim. The Sister yawns. Supper will be simple—just applesauce, bread, and milk. She misses coffee; her partner longs for tobacco, but that, too, has been discouraged. It has been a busy afternoon, preparing simple food for the Sabbath. Tomorrow, dinner will be baked beans and brown bread. The kitchen is spotless, ready for the day of rest.

The Brother is tired. He has soaked the forty-eight box sides, tacked them to shape around the molds, and set them aside to dry. If the weather stays dry and fair, they should be ready for lids and bottoms by Tuesday. He has spent the rest of the afternoon tidying and sweeping. He thinks back to his first days as a Shaker. It has always pleased him that his wife and children agreed to join, too. All have remained but his eldest son; it's such a long time ago since he left.

The bell rings again. He blows out the lamp, shuts the workshop door, and returns with other Brethren to the dwelling house. A single star gleams in the darkening sky. The dwelling house looks warm and inviting, bright with lamplight. All across the yard, Believers are heading for home.

A BRIEF HISTORY

THE SHAKERS, OR UNITED SOCIETY OF BELIEVERS in the First and Second Appearance of Christ, were nineteenth-century America's largest and best-known communal utopian society. By 1840, nearly 6,000 celibate Brethren and Sisters lived and worked in nineteen communities from Maine to Kentucky. The Shakers, or Believers, were famous for their unusual way of life, for the excellence and simplicity of their work, and for the dance worship that gave them their name.

For more than 200 years, the Shakers have pursued their unique way of life, based on principles of equality and communalism. Today, fewer than a dozen Shakers remain, but the Shaker legacy lives on in the creations they have left behind.

Shaker history in America began in 1774, when a thirty-eight-year-old working-class Englishwoman named Ann Lee brought eight followers to New York. Raised in the slums of Manchester, Ann, the daughter of a blacksmith, was hardly a likely candidate for success. She was poor, had no influential friends, and could not read or write. Yet, while still a young woman, she possessed such powerful religious convictions that she became acknowledged as the spiritual leader of a small group of dissidents from the Anglican Church who came to be known as the "Shaking Quakers" because of the way they trembled when seized with the Holy Spirit. In spite of persecution and mob violence, "Mother" Ann persisted in preaching.

In 1770, while she was in prison for having disrupted the Sabbath, Ann had a vision that was to change her life and, ultimately, the lives of thousands of others: it seemed to her that carnal relations were the cause of most of the world's trouble. Her own four children had died by the time she was thirty. Her mission was to teach a new way of life, in which men and women were like children, as innocent in their relations as brothers and sisters. Members of her new society would live more like angels than like people, free from the age-old problems of war, violence, greed, exploitation, lust, and every kind of human abuse. Everyone would be equal, regardless of gender, race, or age.

20

Ann took Christ as her role model and taught that simplicity—material, temporal, and spiritual—was necessary for this new way of living.

Three years later, again in prison, Ann received a vision that God had a chosen people in America. The next spring, Mother Ann and her small group set sail for that bright new world. Among the faithful were her husband, Abraham Stanley, a blacksmith; her younger brother William Lee; and young, zealous James Whittaker, a distant relation.

Their arrival in New York was not auspicious. Lacking funds, the group separated and went to work to earn a living. Ann worked as a washerwoman; at times she was so poor that she had no food for supper. Things grew only worse. Her husband left her, impatient with her unswerving commitment to celibacy. Finally, in 1776, the group bought a small tract of land in Watervliet, near Albany, New York. Three years later, they built their first communal home. As if to mock their progress, the building caught fire and burned. Worst of all, they had attracted no converts in America after five difficult years. Somehow, Ann kept the others from losing heart completely, promising them that the day was near when eager listeners would "flock like doves to the windows."

Ann's prophecy came true the next spring, in 1780, when a religious revival swept through New York and New England. One of Ann's first listeners was a Baptist minister named Joseph Meacham, who questioned her closely on her unconventional views. Was she the "female Christ," as some were saying? She replied that she was not, but that as Adam and Eve were the "natural" parents of humanity, Christ and she were the spiritual parents of a new and higher order of humanity. With Christ gone from the earth, it was her work to bring word of this new and more perfect society. Convinced by her answer, Joseph became one of her first converts, and he persuaded most of his congregation to follow, too.

Fired by the growing enthusiasm of those who heard her, Mother Ann stepped up her traveling and preaching. But increasing interest in the new sect also brought persecution and imprisonment again; Ann was jailed from July through December 1780. In the following year, though, Ann embarked on a two-year proselytizing journey through Massachusetts and Connecticut. Missionaries had preceded her, attracting the attention of those who hoped to find salvation, as well as those who feared Ann as a British spy or witch. The trip was a mix of elevating spiritual success and humiliation at the hands of angry mobs in small towns. Exhausted, Ann returned to the home of Joseph Meacham in New Lebanon, New York, on the Massachusetts border. In September 1783, two days after a brutal attack, Ann returned to Watervliet. A year later, weakened by her experiences and saddened by the recent death of her beloved brother William, Ann Lee died at the age of forty-eight, after ten years in her "chosen land."

Mother Ann did not live to see the full flowering of Shakerism in organized communities, separate from non-Believers, whom the Shakers simply called "the World." At her death, those who called themselves Shakers lived in their own homes as individual families, maintaining their own farm properties but practicing celibacy and gathering to worship on Sundays. The creation of communal Families, who shared all their possessions in joint ownership and who shared work and reward as celibate Brethren and Sisters, was the contribution of Joseph Meacham and Lucy Wright, Ann's chosen successors. (James Whittaker died in 1787, less than three years after Ann. The loss of Ann was a severe blow to many who had converted because of her personal charisma, and James did not have the necessary temperament to guide the sect in new directions. Nevertheless, he kept most of the Believers together and in 1786 directed the building of a meetinghouse at New Lebanon.)

Ann's regard for Joseph, the Baptist minister originally from Connecticut, was high. She called him her "first-born son in America." She also thought very highly of Lucy, a bright young woman from western Massachusetts. "We must save Lucy," Ann said, "for it will be equal to saving a nation." Realizing that it was essential for the

Shakers to consolidate their material and spiritual strength to survive amid the temptations of the World, Father Joseph and Mother Lucy decided to set out on a new and unprecedented venture. Shakers were to leave their homes and live together in new communal settlements. Instead of rushing headlong into such an extraordinary move, however, they proceeded with great thoughtfulness. The society at New Lebanon, New York, would be the first to organize and would serve as a model in all things for other communities as they were established. Accordingly, in September 1787, Joseph and Lucy decreed that the time had come for the Shakers to separate from the World. About a hundred Believers were chosen to move to the adjoining farms of several members, bringing their possessions to be shared by all. A dwelling was built. The first meal shared by the new communal Family was Christmas dinner, 1787.

Father Joseph and Mother Lucy's contributions to the organization of Shaker communal life continued through the next decade. They established a system of "orders," or levels of commitment to the faith, to prevent hasty, impulsive conversions that would backfire in mutual disappointment. Joseph introduced a formal Covenant that all members would sign to declare their total spiritual and material commitment. In 1792, with the appointment of Elders and Eldresses to guide other newly formed communities, the "gospel order" of the Shaker faith was considered fully established. Pairs of Elders and Eldresses—bright, capable, and utterly devoted to the success of their unique experiment—went from New Lebanon to places where groups of converts who had worshipped together were now ready to take the bold step of living together. Across New England, Shaker communities officially "gathered into order"—Hancock, Massachusetts, in 1790; Harvard, Massachusetts, in 1791; Canterbury, New Hampshire, in 1792; Sabbathday Lake, Maine, in 1794—eleven settlements in all by 1794. Joseph also changed the way the Shakers worshipped, abandoning the whirling, shaking, and leaping of the first Shakers in favor of a simple, uniform dance that all Believers could practice as one, stepping forward and back in perfect unison.

Joseph died in 1796 at age fifty-four, leaving Lucy alone to guide the faith. It is a tribute to her skills and personality that she served as a second "mother" to the Shakers for the next twenty-five years, gently leading the group into its golden age of spiritual power. Heeding Mother Ann's prophecies that a second revival would take place in the West (present-day Kentucky and Ohio), Lucy sent three Brethren on a missionary tour beginning on New Year's Day, 1805. Their success was remarkable: nine new communities were established in the next two decades—five in Ohio, two in Kentucky, one in Indiana, and one in western New York State. The number of Shakers grew dramatically to about 2,500. Having survived internal and external challenges, the Shaker Society was a phenomenon unlike anything else in the New World or the Old.

Lucy died in 1821, leaving a society whose success would probably have surprised even Mother Ann. The next two decades witnessed further population growth to an estimated 4,000 to 6,000 by the 1840s, but no additional communities were successfully established. Significantly, the kinds of people who converted to Shakerism began to change. The original Believers, or "Mother Ann's first-born," had banded together to overcome severe local opposition and privation. Becoming a Shaker in the early years meant hardship, not ease. But as time passed, the Believers became increasingly prosperous, due to their simple living and thrift, and Shaker life became easier and more attractive to people of the World, including some who were more interested in a secure existence than in a soul-shaking spiritual experience.

The conflicts soon began to be felt. The Millennial Laws, first written in 1821, after Mother Lucy's death, were revised and expanded, codifying precisely what Believers ought to be and do. Some older or more deeply religious members felt that increased numbers were not necessarily a blessing, if converts came more for convenience than for a sincere desire for salvation. "Numbers are not the thing for us to glory in," they reminded each other.

By the mid-1840s, the Shaker population had already crested and begun its relentless downward drift. One by one, Families dwindled in size and ceased to exist. In 1862, a Brother from New Lebanon, visiting the Shakers in Union Village, Ohio, ruefully noted the decay of one Family's once-handsome brick dwelling, stripped of its woodwork and windows and open to sheep and hens, which lived as far upstairs as the attic. "Rather a costly hen roost & sheep fold," he lamented. In 1870, a Sister visiting a Family at Enfield, New Hampshire, sighed, "O how very few, only 10 Sisters and 9 Brethren; but O how we pray that there might be a gathering in this place." Those prayers were not answered. In 1875, at Tyringham, Massachusetts, the first entire community closed.

Today, fewer than a dozen Shakers remain in America, in two of the original nineteen communities: Canterbury, New Hampshire, and Sabbathday Lake, Maine. The oldest Shakers, who are in their eighties and nineties, have witnessed the near-extinction of their way of life. All but the first closings of the other communities have occurred within their lifetime.

How do the Shakers feel about the future of their way of life? Eldress Bertha Lindsay, who has spent more than eighty years at Canterbury, where she came as a little girl, recalls with sadness the 1965 decision to close the Covenant and cease taking in new members. She says, "We don't want to close our doors. I would like the churches all to fill right up with Shakers again."

She believes that whatever happens, however, the spirit of the Shakers will never truly die. She points to a renaissance of interest in the Shakers with pride and pleasure, sharing the admiration for those whom she reverently calls the "old Shakers." Bertha also views with enthusiasm the restoration of Shaker villages and the interpretation of Shaker life and work in museums. While there are no longer Shakers at most of the places mentioned and shown in this book, she enjoys hearing of the successful new careers of the former Shaker communities as museum villages. At Hancock, Massachusetts, and the two Shakertowns at Pleasant Hill and South Union, Kentucky, visitors can see restored buildings and Shaker furnishings in their original settings. At the Fruitlands Museums in Harvard, Massachusetts, and the Shaker Museum in Old Chatham, New York, those who appreciate Shaker design can tour fine collections in museum settings. At Sabbathday Lake, visitors can tour Shaker buildings and have the opportunity to meet and talk with surviving Believers. They can do the same at Canterbury, where a museum organization called Shaker Village, Inc., was created in 1974 to help the Shaker Sisters preserve the village for the future as a restoration, and as their home now.

Sister Frances Carr of Sabbathday Lake, a generation younger than Eldress Bertha, hopes that the Society will not come to an end. She points to the presence of three dedicated young newcomers to her community who are seeking to continue Shakerism as the "old Shakers" knew it, with large communal Families and many hands to share the work and blessings. Although the three have not signed the Covenant, they are accepted as Believers in their community.

Mother Ann herself foretold the rise and fall of the brave new world she envisioned, and predicted that when there were as many Shakers left as there are fingers on a child's hand, there would come another revival and a second flowering of the faith. The day is perhaps not far distant when only five Shakers will remain. The Believers and the World can only wait and see what happens. Meanwhile, as Eldress Bertha says, "The hands drop off, but the work goes on."

Few material traces of Mother Ann Lee exist, and no words were ever written by her—she could neither read nor write, as was typical of working-class women in America and Britain in the eighteenth century. However, a few remaining objects were prized by the Shakers as having been associated with Mother Ann. This rocking chair (with rockers added later to an old New England Windsor chair) was treasured by the Shakers at Harvard, Massachusetts, as "Mother Ann's chair." Ann Lee's ties with the Harvard community were special. She lived at Harvard for two years, 1781 to 1783, during her prolonged missionary tour of New England. Here, she said that she found God's "chosen people in America," whom she had seen in a vision before her departure from England.

26

The Meetinghouse at Sabbathday Lake, Maine, remains virtually unchanged since its construction in 1794; its details have been preserved in pristine condition. The building's timber frame was raised on June 14, 1794, under the direction of Moses Johnson (1752–1842), the master builder sent from New Lebanon, New York, to ensure that the Shaker meetinghouses conformed to the New Lebanon prototype. Like all of Moses Johnson's meetinghouses, the building has a gambrel roof and separate doors for Brethren, on the left, and Sisters, right. The 20,000 bricks required for the two chimneys were made by Brother Ephraim Briggs, who completed all the carpentry work.

The Meetinghouse at Canterbury, New Hampshire, was framed by
Moses Johnson (1752–1842) in 1792 as a replica of the 1786
Meetinghouse at New Lebanon, New York. This view, from the
belfry of the Church Family Dwelling, shows the distinctive gambrel
roof and the stairwell at the rear, with steep steps leading up to the
Ministry's quarters on the two upper floors. The rooms on the near
side were occupied by Job Bishop (1760–1831), one of Mother Ann's
best-regarded young followers, who was sent by the New Lebanon
community to head the New Hampshire Ministry in 1792. His
"proverbial piety, accomplished manners, and sound sense" did
much to guide the community's growth.

Ann Lee died in 1784, after ten years in America, exhausted by
physical persecution by mobs and saddened by the death six weeks
earlier of her beloved younger brother William. Mother Ann was
laid to rest at Watervliet, New York, her first and last Shaker home
in the New World.

In 1805, Mother Lucy Wright sent three Shaker Brethren as missionaries to the American West, then in Ohio and Kentucky. The three walked more than 1,000 miles after starting on foot from New Lebanon, New York, at 3 A.M. on New Year's Day. One, "Little Benjamin" Youngs, weighed only 100 pounds, but all three proved indomitable. By 1815, six new communities had been established in the West, with two more to come. The success of the western mission gave new hope and energy to Believers everywhere.

Pleasant Hill, in the bluegrass region near Lexington, Kentucky, was one of the new societies. Like all the others, this community followed the lead of New Lebanon in all matters. Shaker furniture, architecture, dress, and song were remarkably alike in villages as far apart as Maine and Kentucky. Here, the Center Family Dwelling at Pleasant Hill is visible in the distance.

Shaker villages were characterized by neatness and extreme simplicity. Architecture was unadorned. "Beadings, mouldings and cornices, which are *merely for fancy* may not be made by Believers," reminded the Millennial Laws of 1845. "Odd or fanciful styles of architecture" were likewise prohibited. The Laws also prescribed paint colors suitable for buildings in various parts of the village. Wooden buildings along the street were to be "of a lightish hue"; barns and other back houses, of a darker hue, such as red, brown, or "lead color." The Meetinghouse alone was white.

Here, two small outbuildings at Pleasant Hill, Kentucky, reflect the instructions of the Millennial Laws. On the left is the Water House, which contains a 17,600-gallon cistern for spring water, pumped in by horsepower. The cistern was begun in 1831, and the building was completed in 1833. To the right is the Bath House for the Brethren of the Center Family, built in 1860; a similar structure for the Sisters no longer stands. Personal cleanliness was as important to the Shakers as order in their dwellings and shops.

Eldress Gertrude Soule knits a baby bonnet for a worldly friend on the porch of the Dwelling House at Canterbury, New Hampshire. She joined the Shakers in Maine as a young girl with her sister. Today, she greets visitors to the Shaker village daily when the buildings are open to the public in summer and fall. Eldress Gertrude's warmth and humor surprise many visitors, who expect the Shakers to be a solemn lot. (Recognizing that her society has shrunk to fewer than a dozen members in America, Eldress Gertrude sometimes refers to the Shakers as "an endangered species.") Now in her nineties, Eldress Gertrude continues to wear traditional Shaker dress—a calf-length pleated dress with a shoulder cape, or "bertha," and a starched white net cap, symbol of the Sisters' celibate purity.

Unlike the Amish, with whom they are sometimes compared, the Shakers were always amenable to accepting technological progress, including electricity, indoor plumbing, telephones, televisions, and automobiles. In 1918, a group of Shaker Sisters from Canterbury, New Hampshire, clearly enjoyed their apple-picking outing in early fall. The two Sisters in the back row nearest the truck's cab still live at Canterbury. Eldress Bertha Lindsay, on the right, is the community's leader; Sister Ethel Hudson, on her right, still occupies the village's large communal Dwelling.

COMMUNAL LIFE

THE SHAKER EXPERIMENT IN COMMUNAL LIFE

formally began in 1787, when Father Joseph Meacham and Mother Lucy Wright gathered a hundred Believers to live and work together in a community at New Lebanon, New York. It was a bold and innovative step. While many attempts at communal life were tried in the mid-nineteenth century—Ralph Waldo Emerson exclaimed in 1840 that Americans were "all a little wild here with numberless projects of social reform—not a reading man but has a draft of a new community in his waistcoat pocket"—the Shakers in 1787 had no model to copy. The Yankee farmers and tradespeople who composed the first generation of Believers were not familiar with earlier ventures in communalism, at the Ephrata Cloisters in Pennsylvania, or at the semicommunal Moravian settlements in Pennsylvania and farther south. Nor were the Shakers familiar with the monastic traditions of Catholic Europe. Joseph and Lucy were starting fresh, and their organizational abilities were instrumental in the Shakers' success. By 1794—twenty years after Mother Ann Lee's arrival in New York—there were eleven established Shaker villages in New York and New England.

Life was not easy in the first years. The areas where the Shakers had settled did not necessarily have the best farmland in the Northeast, although the Believers in each community gathered on the best land available to them. In New Lebanon, Shakers assembled at the home

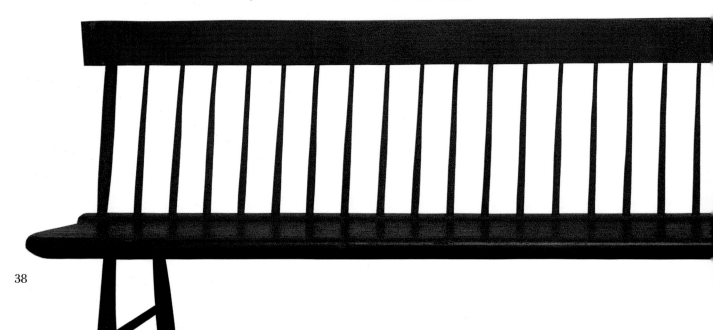

of George Darrow, in the hills along the Massachusetts border. At Canterbury, New Hampshire, the first Believers came to the farm of Benjamin and Mary Whitcher in the granite hills twelve miles north of Concord. At Sabbathday Lake, Maine, the Believers moved to Gowen Wilson's farm. It was difficult to make single-family farms produce enough food for dozens of new members. Shakers everywhere spent the first years improving fields and crops, erecting dwellings big enough to accommodate large Families, and building workshops where they could manufacture goods for their own use and for sale to supplement their income.

Calvin Green described his experience at New Lebanon in 1788, a drought year, when he was only eight. "We had very little bread," he recalled years later, "not much milk, scarcely any pie, butter or cheese. We had to live on meat, such fish as we could get, porridge, salt meat, broth and potatoes. For a time potatoes were our chief food. . . . [We] worked hard and were not overfed. I was hungry all the time." Similarly, Rebecca Clark remembered her first year at Hancock, Massachusetts, in 1791, when she was twenty-one:

> There were nearly a hundred in the Family where I lived. . . .
> Fourteen of us slept in one room. . . . Our buildings were small
> and we had to eat and live accordingly. . . . Our beds, bedding,
> and clothing that we brought with us, we all divided among the

members of the Family, as equally as we could. . . . We were all much engaged to build buildings, and to raise provisions, and gather a substance to live on. Our food was very scanty, but what we had we ate with thankful hearts.

At Canterbury, New Hampshire, the conversion to communalism took place with relative ease, as Benjamin and Mary Whitcher had already "most generously and conscientiously opened their doors and spread their tables in welcome to everyone who came to seek for the truth." Forty-three people were living at the Whitchers' farm when the community was formally recognized by the New Lebanon society in 1792.

To help all the communities succeed, Father Joseph and Mother Lucy decided that a hierarchy was needed, a system of "orders," or different communal Families, geared to the special needs and abilities of different kinds of converts. The original society at New Lebanon consisted of three orders. The first order included young unmarried people who were primarily indoor workers—that is, artisans and craftspeople. The second order was composed of young unmarried Believers whose work was principally outdoors—farmers, woodcutters, shepherds, and the like. The third order consisted of older converts, including those who had been married, and business-oriented people, like shopkeepers and those with skills in commerce and real estate. In 1799, Mother Lucy established two additional orders—a children's order, where youngsters not yet in their mid-teens lived with supervisors known as caretakers; and a novitiate, or "gathering," order, where people attracted to the Shaker way of life could see if it was something that they really wanted. Newcomers to the faith were known as "young Believers," no matter how old they were. The system was sufficiently flexible to evolve with the changing needs of the sect. By the early nineteenth century, the standard hierarchy in a Shaker community consisted of three distinct orders based loosely on the original plan, but with more formal legal arrangements between converts and the society. If the prospective convert and the leaders agreed that advancement was desirable, the next step after the novitiate was a junior order, whose members freely gave their labor to the community but retained their own property. The final step was the senior order, whose members signed the Covenant to declare their full spiritual and material commitment to the society. Senior-order Shakers freely gave their services, relinquished their property to communal ownership, and fully intended to remain with the Shakers for the rest of their lives.

By 1825, the Family, or order, structure had taken its final shape. Most communities had at least three Families. New Lebanon, the largest eastern community, had eight. The oldest, central, and largest Family in each community was called the Church Family (the Center Family in Kentucky). The Church Family, a senior order, was the site of the single Meetinghouse that the entire community shared. Other Families in each community were named for their geographical relationship to the Church Family—East, West, North, South—or occasionally for another identifying feature, such as Hill or Brickyard. Each Family had its own dwelling, barns, workshops, and enterprises. Members were not encouraged to visit other Families without a specific reason or without permission. The term "Family" in Shaker use meant a place as well as a group of people. In this sense, Families, usually a quarter- to a half-mile apart, were like neighborhoods.

New Families were established as the communities grew. At Hancock, for example, the Church Family gathered in 1790. In 1792, it was joined by the West and Second Families, both junior orders, and the East Family, a novitiate order. In 1800, the South Family was added as a second novitiate order. In 1822, the North Family, a senior order established to accommodate the overflow from the Church Family, was the sixth and final Family to incorporate as part of the Hancock community.

In addition to the system of orders and Families, Joseph Meacham and Lucy Wright instituted a system of leadership. Each Family had three sets of leaders: a pair of Elders and a pair of Eldresses (one of each pair was an assistant or junior member), who were in charge of their Family's spiritual well-being and of things in general; two Deacons and two Deaconesses, who were authorized to handle all practical concerns—such as laundry, meals, and the farm work schedule—and to provide tools, furnishings, and clothing as requested by the Family; and four Trustees, two of each sex, who lived in the Family's business office and were responsible for the Family's financial success and for transactions with the World. The Elders and Eldresses of the Church Family were also responsible for the entire community in general.

In turn, the Church Family Elders and Eldresses in each community were answerable to a higher authority, the two Elders and two Eldresses of the Ministry. Just as each Family was part of a larger community, so each community was part of a larger unit known as a bishopric. The Maine Bishopric had two communities, at Sabbathday Lake and Alfred. The New Hampshire Bishopric also had two communities, at Canterbury and Enfield. The Hancock Bishopric included Hancock and Tyringham, in western Massachusetts, as well as Enfield, Connecticut. It was the job of each bishopric's Ministry to oversee the spiritual and organizational well-being of each community in its care. The Ministry divided its time equally among its communities and spent considerable time traveling. It also kept closely in touch with the society at New Lebanon, the model for all other communities.

The final and highest authority in Shaker leadership was the Ministry at New Lebanon, which was regarded as the "capital" of the Shaker world. Bishopric Ministries were answerable to the Parent Ministry at New Lebanon, whose authority was revered because it descended in a direct line from Mother Ann. Ann chose Father Joseph and Mother Lucy as her successors. Lucy selected Ebenezer Bishop and Ruth Landon as her successors. In turn, Ebenezer and Ruth chose their successors, and so on through the years. It was customary for the junior partner to succeed the senior partner in the Ministry and Elders' positions, although circumstances sometimes dictated otherwise. The system was not perfect, but it generally worked well, with natural leaders rising to authority by virtue of their industry, charity, honesty, and common sense. It was usually the consensus of the Family that those who served as its leaders had been rightfully chosen.

With the communal framework solidly in place, the Shakers began to face the special circumstances of living a communal *and* celibate life—a combination so unusual that most worldly observers could scarcely comprehend it. "Their vow is celibacy; and they have everything in common," a Scottish visitor observed in 1841. "How they manage with their combs and tooth-brushes, I did not presume to ask them." Nathaniel Hawthorne decried the lack of privacy. Charles Dickens sniffed that rumors of secret romances were unlikely if all Shaker women were as unattractive as the one he had met. Serenely oblivious to the World's opinion, however, the Shakers set about solving problems with good sense, charity, and the ability to forgive.

One of the keys to success was order in every part of life. It simply worked best for the Family to do things according to a set schedule— to rise at the same time, to gather for meals at fixed hours, to begin and end work and retire for the night at the same times. Accordingly, the Shakers adapted their individual "time clocks" to the needs of the Family. Believers rose with the bell at 4:30 A.M. in summer, knelt in prayer, and pulled back the covers to air the beds. (The hour of rising in winter was 5:30 A.M.) In fifteen minutes, they were dressed and out of their "retiring rooms." Breakfast was an hour and a half after rising, dinner was at noon, and supper was at 6 P.M.

Believers entered the dining room in an orderly fashion. "Ye shall have no talking, laughing, sneering, winking, blinking, hanging and lounging on the railings, hugging, fumbling, and fawning over each other, when going to the table," reminded the Holy Orders of 1841. "And there shall no whispering, laughing, sneering or blinking be done or carried on at the table." Believers knelt together in silent prayer and dined in silence—an understandable rule to anyone who has heard the racket of a hundred voices in a wood and plaster room.

There were Family meetings every week night except Monday, which was an evening off. Meetings began at 7:30 P.M. in summer (a half-hour later in winter) and were preceded by "retiring time," a quiet period with no unnecessary talking or movement. After meeting, the Family retired for the night. The occupants of a "retiring room" were required to go to bed at the same time, unless prevented by necessary chores. Brethren and Sisters were not allowed to "sit up after the usual time of retiring to rest, to work, read, write, or any thing of the kind," without the permission of the Elder or Eldress. Such a regulation prevented individuals from exercising too much self-interest, and also helped reduce the risk of fire from candles or lamps. The Millennial Laws of 1845 prohibited the carrying of lamps or candles if they were not safely enclosed in a lantern, and also forbade smoking and working at the same time.

Order was also important in the physical environment. To avoid chaos in the dwelling and workshops, furnishings and tools were often marked to indicate their proper location; Mother Ann had advised her followers to keep things in such order that they could be found, day or night. Consideration was also essential in daily life. Believers were taught to speak and move quietly. "You ought to pass each other like angels," Father William Lee had said. During the Civil War, a toughened Texas Ranger could not believe that ninety people shared one dwelling at South Union, Kentucky. "If so many of us lived in one house," he declared, "we should fight and kill each other." Weekly confession to the Elder or Eldress helped to clear the air and maintain good feelings.

Uniformity was another key to success. No member was to have things better than the rest. Furnishings were kept to a minimum for the sake of simplicity and order. "Retiring rooms" were typically furnished with a chair and a narrow bed for each occupant, a wood-burning stove, a strip of carpet, a washstand, looking-glass, and towels, a few brooms and brushes, and little else.

44

Celibacy also required certain rules. The Shakers were distinctive among celibate sects for not cloistering men and women in separate dwellings. Instead, Brethren and Sisters had separate quarters in the same Family dwelling. It was "contrary to order" for individuals of the opposite sex to develop special, private relationships, lest they fall into temptation. Father Joseph realized early on, however, that friendship between the Brethren and Sisters was a good thing, given proper supervision. To this end, he established popular evening "union meetings," in which small groups of Believers met and visited informally or sang. There were three union meetings a week. Members of the groups were occasionally rotated to foster wider friendships and to minimize the chance of budding romance.

Boys and girls were more strictly segregated than were the adults. There were separate girls' and boys' houses, with two caretakers of the appropriate gender for each group. Although boys and girls received the same kind of education, they attended school at different times of the year—girls in summer, when the boys were needed for farm work, and boys in winter, for terms of about three months each. Children who were raised by the Shakers either came with their parents or were taken in as charitable wards from broken homes. As well as book learning, Shaker children learned trades in an apprenticeship system similar to that of the World. Although the young people raised by the Shakers were not required to sign the Covenant and stay when they turned twenty-one, older Believers naturally hoped that they would remain and perpetuate the community's labor and values. Sadly for the Shakers, many of the young people were either forcibly removed by their families or left on their own to explore the beckoning World.

Not everyone who tried the Shaker life found it suited to his or her needs, and not everyone who wanted to become a Shaker could make the requisite sacrifices easily. Shaker journals are scattered with references to the departure of Believers. Those who chose to leave in a forthright manner were treated with charity, although regarded with disappointment. In 1833, Peter Peterson honorably announced his decision to leave. He received clothing, a gift of $40, and a ride to the stagecoach to Albany, where his fare was paid. A Brother even assisted him with his trunks. But the more usual way to leave was to sneak off. Believers who left that way were often *not* sorely missed, as they were likely to have had problems adjusting to Shaker life in the first place. In 1816, a Believer noted, "Rebecca Quicksels goes off— good riddance." Believers who couldn't make up their minds whether to go or to stay were sometimes taken back for another try, sometimes with success and sometimes not. In 1836, Silvanus Rice of New Lebanon, New York, went "to the World"—again. "This is his second trip," a Brother wrote, "& I reckon he has learned the road to perdition well by this time." Opportunistic converts were known as "winter Shakers" (for the season when work was lighter) or as "bread-and-butter Shakers."

Although it is commonly assumed that celibacy doomed the Shakers to eventual decline, that is not necessarily true. Celibacy eliminated the guaranteed replacement of numbers through children, but it also meant that the people who lived in Shaker villages *wanted* to be there and had voluntarily chosen to make the necessary sacrifices. The result was a powerful conviction on the part of many Shakers that their way of life was the path to salvation. When asked why he was so cheerful, an aged Brother replied in 1851, "Why, I can't help it, for I love the way of God & keep my union to my Elders, & the Elders keep their union to the Ministry, & the Ministry are joined to Heaven; & how can I help being happy?"

The stone wall bordering the field south of the Meetinghouse at Canterbury, New Hampshire, was built in 1793 of large blocks of granite hauled into place, probably by teams of oxen. Some of the rocks are more than a yard across. The face of the wall is remarkably flat—an accomplishment indeed, considering the size of the stones. The stone wall is like an emblem of the community itself—the fitting together of different parts to make a whole more valuable than the sum of the individual parts. In the background is the Meetinghouse, built in 1792 as a joint effort by members of the newly established Shaker community.

48

The Meetinghouse at New Lebanon, New York, was the largest and most impressive Shaker house of worship—and the mother church for the entire Shaker society. Here, up to 500 Believers and as many as 1,000 visitors gathered for public meetings on Sundays.

This Meetinghouse was built in 1824 to replace the original, much smaller meetinghouse, which served as the model for other Shaker meetinghouses in New York and New England. Inside, the first floor was a vast open span sixty-five by eighty feet in area, uninterrupted by pillars, which would have interfered with the Shakers' impressive worship dances. The upper floors in an ell to the rear served as the quarters for the New Lebanon Parent Ministry, the two Elders and two Eldresses who were revered as the highest authority in the Shaker world. The barrel roof was designed to make possible the open span of the first floor.

The attic of the New Lebanon Meetinghouse shows the remarkable framing that makes possible the absence of pillars in the single large room on the first floor. A boardwalk spans the length of the building between the arc of the roof and the gentler curve of the ceiling below. A custom-made curved ladder, used to work on roof repairs, remains in the attic.

While art for its own sake was not acceptable to the Shakers because of its "uselessness," Believers encouraged the making of maps of their own villages. Such views and plans were useful for community planning, and perhaps also served a spiritual purpose as records of these heavens on earth.

In July 1836, George Kendall drew and painted this *Plan of The First Family, Harvard*, in Massachusetts. It shows the main street through the village running parallel to a "water course." Among the Church Family buildings are the gambrel-roofed Meetinghouse, two large gambrel-roofed dwellings, a school, and assorted shops, stables, and barns. Of particular interest is the hip-roofed dwelling in the upper-left corner at the edge of the orchard. The "Square House," as it was known, had been the home of the fanatical New Light preacher Shadrack Ireland before Mother Ann's visit. When it became clear to his followers that Ireland's promise to rise from the dead three days following his demise was not going to be fulfilled, they disbanded in disillusionment. Mother Ann stayed in the Square House during her prolonged visits to Harvard between 1781 and 1783. It is one of the few buildings extant in the United States that Mother Ann is known to have occupied.

In 1783, Mother Ann preached in the town of Hancock in western Massachusetts. The converts she made formally gathered into a community in 1790 on the adjoining farms of the Tallcott, Williams, and Deming families. By 1840, the village had nearly 250 members in six communal Families.

This view of the Church Family from the south includes, left to right: the Garden Tool Shed (a small outbuilding later moved to this spot); the large red Laundry and Machine Shop (c. 1800); the Meetinghouse (1790); the Brick Dwelling (1830); the brick Poultry House (1878); the red Tan House (c. 1840), where leather was tanned; and the Round Stone Barn (1826), with the 1939 Dairy Ell.

WATER COURSE

PLAN

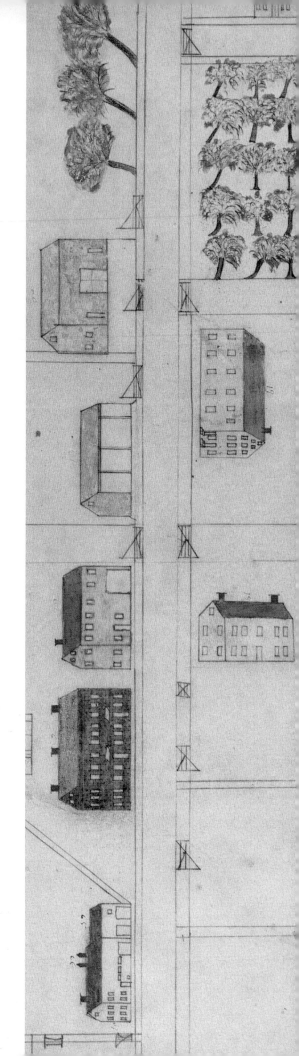

A plan of the Shaker village at Canterbury, New Hampshire, drawn in 1848 by twenty-four-year-old Henry Blinn (1824–1905), showed buildings, fields, orchards, and ponds in detail. This section of the large map, almost seven feet long, shows most of the Church Family buildings, which had been in existence for fifty-six years. Among the buildings represented are the dwelling for adults; a girls' house and a boys' house; a schoolhouse; a "sick house," or infirmary; an office for business transactions with the outside world; the gambrel-roofed Meetinghouse; the Ministry Shop; and a number of barns and workshops, including a spin shop, bake room, dairy, garden-seed room, doctor's shop, shoemaker's shop, joiner's shop, weaving room, distillery, herb-preparation shop, cider mill, printing shop, butcher room, blacksmith's shop, and tinker's shop.

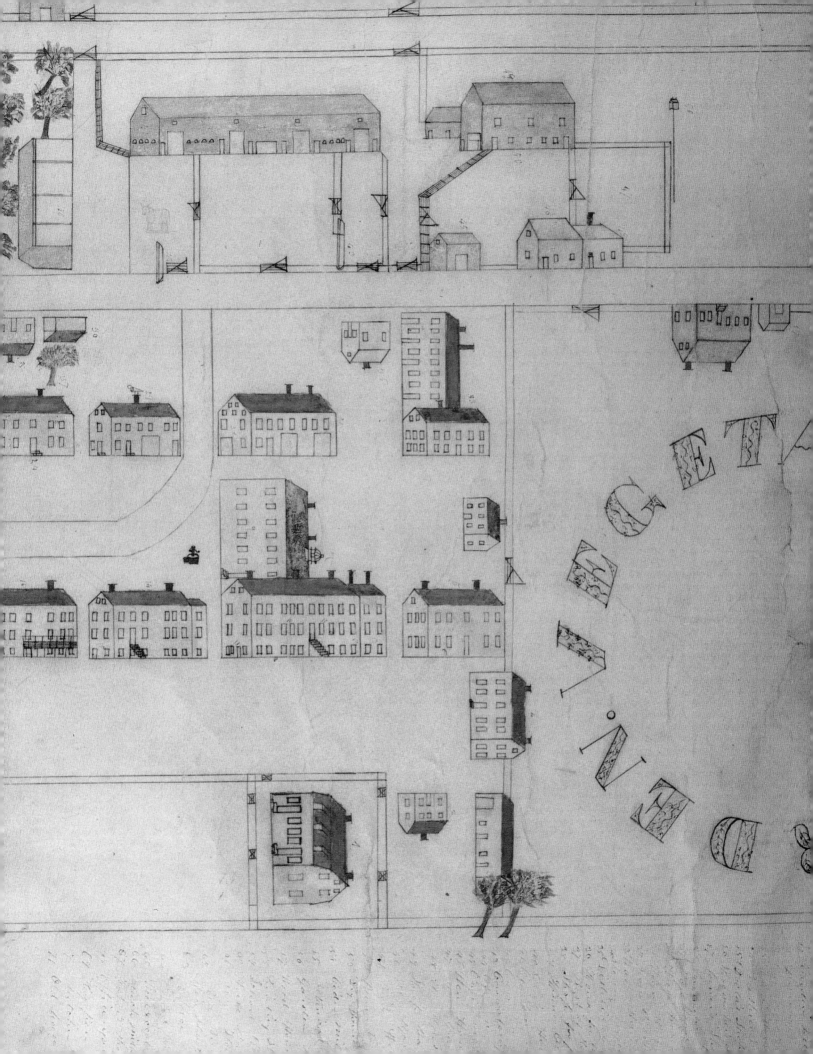

An easterly view between the Boys' Shop (1850) and Spin House
(1816) at Sabbathday Lake, Maine, highlights the extreme simplicity
of Shaker architecture. Although Shaker custom dictated that only
the Meetinghouse be painted white, Shakers in many communities
began to paint more of their buildings white in the late nineteenth
century, when they relaxed some of their strict rules.

Visitors found the Shakers' dwellings and work buildings unusually
large and hopelessly plain. Work buildings were customarily painted
red, tan, or yellow, with more costly white paint reserved for the
meetinghouse. Like Shaker architecture in general, this workshop at
New Lebanon, New York, is relentlessly unadorned—causing
Charles Dickens, a visitor to this community in 1842, to deride the
buildings as no more sightly than English factories or barns.

The handsome dwelling built for the Center Family at South Union, Kentucky, was started in 1822 and completed in 1833. In 1824, when the walls had been raised and the roof built, the date stone was set into place. The dwelling was the pride and joy of Elder Benjamin Seth Youngs (1774–1855), a versatile and able leader whose skills included clock making. The principal carpenter was Brother Robert Johns (1795–1863).

Although the dwelling was not designed with the customary double doors for Brethren and Sisters, it does have outside stairs that approach from different directions. The Brethren lived on the right side of the building, and the Sisters occupied the left. There are almost forty rooms on four floors. The ground floor or basement level has a kitchen, a dining room, a baking room, and six storerooms. On the first floor are ten "retiring rooms" and a large meeting room. The second floor also has ten "retiring rooms." On the top floor are several more "retiring rooms," a hallway referred to as the "Elders' Hall," and a very large attic.

In the mid-nineteenth century, Shaker societies began to build separate quarters for the two Elders and two Eldresses of the Ministry. Until that time, the Ministry had used the upper floors of the Meetinghouse. The new Ministry Shops, usually built next door to the Meetinghouse, were more spacious and more comfortable.

The Ministry Shop at Sabbathday Lake, Maine, was built in 1839 and enlarged in 1875. The Ministry Eldresses had their "retiring rooms" and workrooms on the second floor, and the Elders lived and worked on the first floor. Members of the Ministry, chosen for their ability and virtues, were among the most revered of the Shakers.

A detail of the back corner of the Herb House (1824) at Sabbathday
Lake, Maine, reveals a touch of economy. The building is faced
with clapboard on the front and both sides, all visible from the road,
but is faced on the back with plain shingles to save the cost of
clapboard and paint.

A corner of the Meetinghouse at Sabbathday Lake, Maine, shows
the characteristic angle of the gambrel roof and the dormer windows
that bring light into the upper floors, which were used as a
residence by the two Elders and two Eldresses who formed the
Maine Ministry.

The Center Family Dwelling at Pleasant Hill, Kentucky, remains one of the finest examples of Shaker domestic architecture. Like all Shaker buildings, it was based on American building traditions, which in turn came from English prototypes, and was then adapted to Shaker needs and made with precision and excellence.

The limestone dwelling was begun in 1824 and finished ten years later. Like most Shaker dwellings, it is divided into separate halves for Brethren and Sisters. Although the records are not clear, it is thought that the Brethren used the east side of the building and the Sisters, the west. Nearly a hundred members of the Center Family moved in when the building was completed.

There are more than forty rooms on a total of four stories. The basement level includes a kitchen, food-storage cellars, and a small dining room for the Ministry Elders and Eldresses. On the first floor is a communal dining room, one main kitchen and two baking rooms, a hall, six "retiring rooms," and two dressing rooms. On the second floor are six more "retiring rooms," two additional dressing rooms, a large meeting room, and four small rooms that constitute an infirmary. One of these is probably a physician's office, and the others are completely separate, possibly a measure taken to reduce the spread of any severely contagious diseases. The top floor includes two "retiring rooms," a skylit storage area with built-in drawers, and four smaller rooms for the storage of off-season clothing. At the very top, a curiously off-center cupola leads out onto a balustraded walkway on the roof, offering a handsome view of much of the village and the rolling bluegrass country.

A view from the steps of the Center Family Dwelling at Pleasant Hill, Kentucky, shows, from left to right, the Trustees' Office (1839), where visitors from the outside were welcomed and business was transacted; the Ministry's Workshop (1820), where the two Elders and two Eldresses in authority conducted their business; and the large white Meetinghouse (1820), where the Families gathered on Sundays for worship.

61

The Shakers at Sabbathday Lake, Maine, built this water tower in 1903 in the apple orchard high above the Church Family Dwelling. Water pumped up into it kept the community supplied. The availability of fresh water for drinking, washing, bathing, and water-powered equipment for large communal Shaker societies posed special problems that were met with ingenious solutions in different communities. In 1830, the Shakers at Hancock, Massachusetts, boasted running water on the first two floors of the Church Family's handsome new brick dwelling house. At New Lebanon, New York, the construction of a reservoir, an aqueduct, and other improvements occupied the Brethren throughout the nineteenth century. One Sister recorded their progress with tongue in cheek in 1895:

It seemed to uninstructed minds that Brethren must be playing
With instruments of various kinds, but lo! they were surveying.
Well then they figured, scored and planned on horseblock and on
*   gate-post,*
And always brought their board in hand when they to meals came,
*   late most. . . .*

They said with Grant, "We'll take this line," and not employ a
*   plumber,*
But we will lay the pipes ourselves if it should take all summer.
If man was made of dust, as said, we judged he must have floated,
But his descendants firmly tread when they with mud are coated.

62

The Church Family Dwelling at Hancock, Massachusetts, was built in 1830–1831 and housed nearly a hundred Believers when it was new. This vast building has forty-five rooms on six levels: a two-story attic; two floors of bedrooms, or "retiring rooms"; a main floor with public rooms, a Family meeting room, and a dining room; and a basement level with storage cellars and a large kitchen.

This view shows the east side, or Brethren's side. Visible on the left is the door into the small Ministry dining room, adjacent to the main dining room; the Brethren's main entrance is on the right.

Elder William Deming (1779–1849), the building's designer, described the new dwelling in 1832:

We commenced our building and in ten weeks from the placing of the first stone in the cellar the house was neatly laid up and the roof put on. . . . The work is all well done. There is none to excel it in this country. . . . We have found all the materials ourselves—such as sand, lime, stone & etc. with all the timber except the flooring. . . . Made all the windows, doors, cupboards and drawers, hung them and put on the trimmings. . . . With all this and a great deal more that we have done ourselves, the out expenses are about 8,000 dollars.

Added Elder William: "You will think our purse is pretty empty, which in truth is the case. But as we have given in obedience to our good Mother Ann's words—So we expect to receive. Her precious words were these, 'Your hands to work and your hearts to God and a blessing will attend you.' This we have found true."

The West Family Sisters' Shop, built in 1844, was one of the last major structures built at Pleasant Hill, Kentucky. Here, the West Family Sisters pursued their work, possibly making baskets, bonnets, or dresses. The building is noticeably old-fashioned for its time—its balanced façade carries on the Georgian tradition fashionable in the outside world decades earlier. However, the dormer and door are off-center, violating the otherwise strict symmetry, to fit form to function; the placement suits the interior halls.

Shaker communal life revolved around a strict schedule, with times for rising, dining, meeting, and working heralded by a bell. The system was much more practical than providing every member with a watch, or every workshop or "retiring room" with a clock. Tardy members who lingered in bed or on the way to a meal were called "old slugs":

A lazy fellow it implies,
Who in the morning hates to rise;
When all the rest are up at four,
He wants to sleep a little more.
When others into meeting swarm,
He keeps his nest so good and warm,
That sometimes when the Sisters come
To make the beds and sweep the room,
Who do they find wrap'd up so snug?
Ah! Who is it but Mr. Slug.

This bell, originally atop the dwelling house at the community in Alfred, Maine, was brought to Sabbathday Lake in 1967.

The second-floor hallway in the Church Family Dwelling at Hancock, Massachusetts, separates the Brethren's bedrooms, or "retiring rooms," on the left, from the Sisters', on the right. The bell rope in the center brings to mind the imaginary but powerful line that separated Shaker men and women. The Shakers were unusual among celibate societies for housing men and women under one roof—a situation that the Shakers attributed to the strength of their vows. One Elder likened his sect to "monks and nuns, without the bolts and bars."

The bell rope passes from the rooftop belfry down through six floors to the basement kitchen, and can be rung from any floor—a convenient step saver.

The dining room of the Church Family Dwelling at Hancock, Massachusetts, features a pair of dumbwaiters, the design of Elder William Deming (1779–1849), who was in charge of construction. "The victuals is conveyed up [from the kitchen below] into the dining room by means of two sliding cupboards," he explained, pleased with the convenience of the arrangement. No doubt the Sisters were pleased, too, at the saving of many steps at each meal.

The twin spiral staircases that rise through the Trustees' Office at Pleasant Hill, Kentucky, are representative of the simple splendors of Shaker architecture. The stairs soar through three stories and end in a skylit area. This building, begun in 1839 and finished in 1841, was an office where Shaker business leaders met with people from the outside world. Visitors could dine and lodge and transact sales, purchases, and other business.

Shaker dwellings usually provided a small separate dining room for the Ministry—the two Elders and two Eldresses in charge of two or three communities. Here, the Ministry's dining room adjoins the large dining room in the Church Family Dwelling at Hancock, Massachusetts. An outside door allowed the Ministry to enter and leave without passing through the dwelling's main hallway. Such measures were less privileges of leadership than a way of keeping the Ministry slightly removed from the communal Family so that it could be objective in counseling and disputes—in much the same way that officers in the armed forces remain separate from the rank and file.

The small trestle table, with its gracefully arching legs, was designed for this room. The Shakers favored trestle tables for dining because they gave the sitters more leg room. Believers did not make their own pottery, but bought dinnerware from the outside world, choosing plain, white undecorated china, such as this ironstone from England.

preceding overleaf:

Shaker dwellings had large meeting rooms where the communal Family assembled for meetings on week nights or on Sundays when bad weather made going to the community's central meetinghouse impractical. Believers brought their chairs with them into the spacious open room. This view shows one-half of the meeting room in the Church Family Dwelling. When the dwelling was new, nearly a hundred members gathered here. The room originally had two interior wall panels that could be raised or lowered to divide the room into two smaller rooms with a hall in between, providing separate meeting areas for the Sisters and Brethren. The walls are no longer extant, but the pulley system in the walls above remains intact.

Shaker architecture in Kentucky is characterized by higher ceilings and airier halls than cozier New York and New England Shaker buildings. The high ceilings made sense in the warmer temperatures of the South. The use of arches is also more typical of Shaker buildings in Kentucky.

Here, a corner of the Center Family Dwelling at Pleasant Hill, Kentucky, shows a closet with a transom window above to admit light, and a Kentucky Shaker ladder-back chair, neatly hung upside down on the pegboard to prevent dust from settling on the top of the seat.

Visible at the end of the hall at the Center Family Dwelling at South Union, Kentucky, is the meeting room, with two wood stoves for use in winter. A particularly convenient feature of the banisters, perhaps inspired by a suggestion from the Sisters, is the raised base, which lifts the spindles above the floor to make it much easier to sweep or mop.

The dining room in the Church Family Dwelling at Hancock,
Massachusetts, includes these characteristic conveniences—a built-
in cupboard, probably for dining utensils, and a window in an
interior wall to let natural daylight into the stairwell on the opposite
side of the wall. The combination of wood and plain white plaster is
also characteristic, as is the narrow strip of pegboard for hanging
useful household items.

The stairwell, opposite, leads off the dining room to the basement
kitchen. Two stovepipes join one of the main chimney flues.

80

According to Mother Ann's instruction, the Shakers used very simple place settings. "Never put on silver spoons, nor table cloths for me," she exhorted, "but let your tables be clean enough to eat from without cloths, and if you do not know what to do with them, give them to the poor." Believers used wooden or pewter dishes in their earliest years and later purchased plain white china, such as ironstone, from the outside world.

This view is of the small Ministry dining room in the basement of the Center Family Dwelling at Pleasant Hill, Kentucky; the main Family dining room is on the first floor. The Ministry customarily dined, lived, and worked apart from the communal Family in the interest of maintaining objectivity in guiding the community.

The two Elders and two Eldresses who composed the Ministry for a particular region devoted their lives to spiritual guidance and to overseeing the welfare of the communities in their care. They chose the Family Elders and Eldresses and generally saw to it that the communities ran smoothly and in harmony with the principles established by the Parent Ministry at New Lebanon, New York. Ministry members traveled frequently as part of their work, visiting New Lebanon and other societies as often as was practical.

A corner of the Shaker Office at the Fruitlands Museums suggests the Ministry's experience. The graceful trestle table, made at Harvard, Massachusetts, may have been a dining table for the Ministry there. Its relatively short length would comfortably accommodate four Believers; dining tables for the large communal Families were usually much longer. The wide pine top is made of two boards.

84

The remodeled Ministry Shop at Sabbathday Lake, Maine, featured several improvements in the new attic space provided when the original flat roof was changed to a pitched roof. This rack in a small closet was designed to accommodate off-season clothing. The ingenious V-shape allowed many garments to be stored in a relatively compact space.

The top two floors of the Church Family Dwelling at Hancock, Massachusetts, are attics, where the communal Family stored off-season clothing and bedding. This view shows the topmost floor and the stairwell down to the lower level. The Shakers liked to use skylights to bring natural daylight into their attics, in part to lessen the risk of fire from candles or lamps. In an adjoining room, a system of double skylights—one in the roof over one in the floor—lets daylight into the rooms of the level below. The simple elegance of the banisters and curved ceiling in a seldom-seen area of the building reveals the Shakers' attitude that perfection was important, even where it did not readily show.

In 1875, the Sabbathday Lake Shakers remodeled the original flat
roof of the Ministry Shop, built in 1839, because it "leaked like a
riddle" (or sieve) in the wet weather and hard winters of Maine.
Elder Otis Sawyer reported that "the nuisance was taken off and a
common double inclined roof put on, and finished off nicely which
now affords for the Sisters much needed accommodation for
storage." The two dozen large built-in drawers and cupboards above
were used for general storage. The gray paint is original.

The attic of the Church Family Dwelling at Canterbury, New Hampshire, is one of the most impressive examples of the Shakers' preference for built-in storage. Called the "new attic" for 150 years since it was constructed in 1837 as an addition to the 1793 dwelling, the room has 2 under-eaves storage spaces, 6 closets, 14 cupboards, and 101 drawers, all beautifully made of clear pine and conveniently numbered. The attic was used primarily to store off-season clothing and bedding.

The storage area at the Church Family Dwelling in Enfield, New Hampshire, was equally impressive. That Dwelling, also built in 1837, featured 860 built-in drawers—about nine for each of the approximately ninety-five inhabitants.

This storage cabinet, with forty-eight drawers, was originally built into a workshop at Hancock, Massachusetts. Traces of original paper labels on the drawers indicate probable use as an herb-storage case, possibly in a pharmaceutical shop. The drawers graduate in height from top to bottom, a typical Shaker design feature that combines practicality with pleasing proportions—the larger drawers are at the bottom so that heavier contents are not precariously near the top. Although the case is as simple as possible, the play of drawer sizes and the punctuation of the darker drawer pulls make it attractive.

The Shakers were not the first Americans to build storage cupboards into their walls, but they did make extensive use of these conveniences in their dwellings and workshops. The built-in storage units in the Church Family Dwelling at Hancock, Massachusetts, are among the finest that survive. Elder William Deming (1779–1849), the building's chief architect, could not resist a little bragging about the workmanship:

Scarcely a knot can be seen in all the work, except for the floors and they are yellow pine and very good. There are 100 large doors including outside and closet doors; 245 Cupboard doors—369 drawers—These we placed in the corners of the rooms and by the sides of the chimneys. . . . And I think we may say it is finished from the top to the bottom, handsomely stained inside with a bright orange color.

The carpentry was shared by Brethren skilled at woodworking. Records and other evidence reveal that Brother Comstock Betts (1762–1845) made all the doors and that Assistant Elder Grove Wright (1789–1861) and Brother Thomas Damon (1819–1880) probably made the drawers. The drawers, with warm butternut fronts, are subtly graduated in height—with larger drawers at the bottom for heavier loads—the effect pleasing to the eye as well as practical. One advantage of built-in furniture was cleanliness—no dust could collect on top or underneath.

92

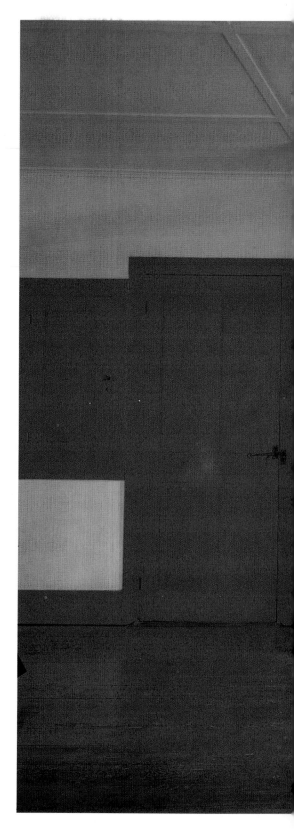

preceding overleaf:

This Brethren's bedroom, or "retiring room," in the Church Family Dwelling at Hancock, Massachusetts, was nearly identical to nineteen other rooms that housed the communal Family. Believers shared their rooms dormitory-style, four or five to a room, and kept furnishings to a minimum for the sake of simplicity and order. Visible here are typical furnishings. At the far left, a built-in cupboard and case of drawers provided storage for clothing and other personal items. Other furniture includes a blanket chest with a drawer and a narrow bed for each occupant. The beds are on wheels to make them easier to move and to clean under. The cast-iron wood-burning stove, more efficient than a fireplace, was a typical feature of Shaker rooms. The long stovepipe helped to heat the room more uniformly.

Small, useful items, from left to right, include a string mop; a dustbox with a curved handle (a receptacle for swept dust); a round maple and pine spitbox, or spittoon, common in Shaker rooms before an early-nineteenth-century ban on tobacco; a small rectangular lap board, or lap desk, hung from a peg; a rectangular slab of soapstone under the stove, to heat the cold sheets on the bed; and a strip of blue rag carpet, easy to remove for cleaning. The cloth hanging on the pegs is based on a nineteenth-century print of a Shaker room showing fabric hanging on the wall—probably a form of insulation against drafts, as were tapestries in medieval castles. Other furnishings, not shown, would typically include a chair for each occupant, a washstand and looking-glass, and brooms and brushes for cleaning.

Education was an important part of life for children raised by the Shakers. By the early nineteenth century, Shaker villages had schoolhouses where young Brethren taught the boys in winter and young Sisters taught the girls in summer. Shaker schools were often considered among the best in their areas.

The Shakers at Canterbury, New Hampshire, were particularly progressive in teaching their young members. The first schoolhouse was built in 1823, then enlarged in 1863 with the addition of another story. To simplify the construction, the Brethren jacked up the original building and added the new story at ground level, saving the trouble of building a new roof. The Canterbury school remained in operation until 1934. In later years, local worldly children also received instruction in this well-regarded school.

The dining-room windows in the Church Family Dwelling at
Hancock, Massachusetts, bring daylight into this spacious room
from the east, south, and west. The Elder in charge of construction
noted with pleasure that the building had 95 "24 lighted [paned]
windows . . . in all 3,194 squares of glass including inside and
out." The windows include a particularly ingenious feature: the
sashes are held in place by a strip of wood on each side, fastened to
the frame with three wooden thumbscrews on each strip. Loosening
the screws allows the lower sash to slide up to any desired level,
where it can be held in place simply by tightening the thumbscrews.
The thumbscrews and strips could be removed altogether to bring in
both upper and lower sashes for cleaning or repairing—a safety
feature, especially in the high upper stories.

The Shakers commonly numbered rooms and storage areas for the
sake of order; this wall of shelves in the Laundry at Canterbury,
New Hampshire, is an example. Baskets of various shapes and sizes
were used to carry linens and clothing to the Laundry for washing
and ironing. Such baskets sometimes bore the initials of an
individual member to help sort the clothes and household linens,
which were also usually identified with initials.

preceding overleaf:

While the Shakers discouraged association between men and women
on a one-to-one basis for the sake of celibacy, they realized that
friendships between the Sisters and Brethren were natural and
desirable. To this end, Father Joseph Meacham (1742–1796), a key
Shaker leader after Mother Ann, instituted the "union meeting" in
1793. As described by a Brother in the 1850s, six to ten Sisters
brought their chairs to a Brethren's room three nights a week to chat
sociably. Propriety required a distance of several feet between the
sexes. The meetings usually lasted an hour, with perhaps twenty
minutes for singing, if desired. The participants were matched by
the Elders and Eldresses, with rotations, so that no cliques could
form or romances blossom. Reported one Sister in 1839:

*Eliza and I have attended union meeting in all the rooms in the
house once or more in a place. The brethren and sisters set about 6
feet apart and those that are rather hard of hearing appear as well
contented as any one that can hear all that is said.*

This room in the Church Family Dwelling at Hancock,
Massachusetts, shows chairs lined up as if for union meeting. From
a number of Shaker communities, they differ slightly in their
details, but are remarkably alike. The wall clock, designed to hang
from the pegboard, is one of six matching clocks made by Isaac N.
Youngs (1793–1865) of New Lebanon, New York. Each of the clocks
is dated 1840, although he did not finish this clock until seven years
later. It was intended for a barn—a fact that gave Isaac pause for
thought, raised as he had been on strict Shaker notions of
simplicity. "It is rather a new idea to have clocks in barns, but they
seem to be needful and admisable under suitable restraint," he
finally concluded. Isaac signed his clocks modestly on the back of
the face, unlike more worldly clockmakers.

Many examples of Shaker furniture point to shared use—sensible
and desirable in a communal society. This double desk was made at
New Lebanon, New York, in about 1840, probably for the use of
Elders, Eldresses, or business leaders called Trustees. Small
handwritten paper labels over the pigeonholes on the left specify
Letters, *Quotations*, and *Religious Manuscripts*, among other
designations. When closed, the desk presents a nearly flat front—
the better to remain clean and dust-free. The pine desk retains its
original light-orange stain.

103

Sister Aida Elam (1882–1962) of Canterbury, New Hampshire,
shares wash day with a little girl, circa 1915. The Shakers took in
and cared for thousands of children over the years, often developing
very strong bonds of love. As the nineteenth century progressed,
however, more and more children raised by the Shakers chose to
live in the outside world when they came of age. With the passage
of time and the establishment of orphanages and foster homes, there
were more options for homeless children.

At Canterbury, New Hampshire, a group gathered for a photograph in the late 1880s. The young girls were not in Shaker dress. Elder Henry Blinn (1824–1905), a widely respected member of the community, sat on one of the large blocks of native granite that was used to terrace the lawn near the Dwelling. In the background on the left is the Ministry Shop (1848), where Elder Henry worked at various trades, including dentistry. On the right is the Meetinghouse (1792), by this time nearly a century old.

preceding overleaf:

In death as in life, the Shakers sought uniformity and simplicity. The earliest Shaker graveyards contained only plain wood or stone markers. Because of inconsistencies in appearance and cost, the community at New Lebanon, New York, decided in 1873 to authorize the replacement of old markers with cast-iron markers of a uniform shape and design. These were actually made for a few communities only, and the graveyard at Harvard, Massachusetts, is the only place where the markers remain *in situ*. Records show that 328 Believers were laid to rest here.

In keeping with the Shakers' preference for simplicity, their grave markers did not feature the tombs, urns, angels, death's heads, or vases of flowers popular in the outside world. The Believer's name, dates, and age at death were considered sufficient. Many Shakers lived long enough to occasion comment by outsiders. When questioned, the Shakers credited their longevity to their sensible living, their abstinence from alcohol and tobacco, and their celibacy.

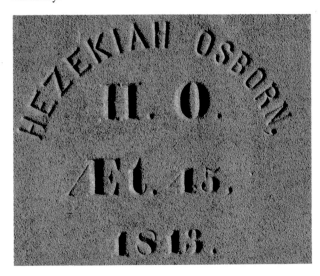

The early years in most Shaker communities were times of trial. Besides privation, the Shakers at Hancock, Massachusetts, suffered a severe loss in 1813, when many members died in a fever epidemic. Hezekiah Osborn, Jr. (1768–1813), who died at age 45, was himself a stonecutter. Later Believers added his name to the original stone, which was as simple as possible, bearing only his initials, age, and year of death. Later, the Hancock Shakers replaced the individual gravestones with a single large monument marked simply *Shakers*, to reduce graveyard maintenance and to symbolize their communal nature.

108

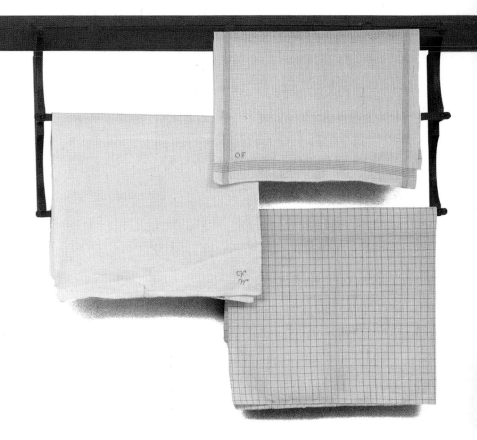

THE SHAKERS AT WORK

FROM THE BEGINNING, WORK WAS AN INTEGRAL
part of Shaker life. Mother Ann Lee and her original English working-
class followers did not have any source of income besides their own
skills. As a young woman, Ann had worked in textile mills. Her
brother William had apprenticed to their blacksmith father. Her
follower James Whittaker was a weaver. After her arrival in America,
Mother Ann repeatedly urged her listeners, "Put your hands to work,
and your hearts to God, and a blessing will attend you."

The earliest Believers in the newly established communities brought
with them a wide variety of skills and trades. Josiah Tallcott, Jr., of
Hancock, Massachusetts, was a printer; Micajah Tucker at
Canterbury, New Hampshire, was a woodworker and stonecutter;
Thankful Goodrich at New Lebanon, New York, was a skilled
seamstress. In time, the Shakers in various communities developed a
remarkable number of occupations—tinsmithing, blacksmithing,
spinning, weaving, dyeing, cooking, cabinetmaking, dairying, orchard
work, beekeeping, masonry, carpentry, dentistry, medicine, teaching,
basketmaking, butchering, gardening—producing much of what they
needed as well as a wide range of high-quality manufactured goods
for sale.

The Shaker label became synonymous with excellence. Humorist
Artemus Ward poked fun at the Shaker way of life, but admired their
applesauce nevertheless: "When a man buys a kag of apple sass of
you he don't find a grate many shavins under a few layers of sass—a
little game I'm sorry to say sum of my New Englan ancesters used to
practiss." Even Charles Dickens, who disliked nearly everything
about the Shakers, had to admit that their work was exceptional.
"They are good farmers," he confessed, "and all their produce is
eagerly purchased and highly esteemed. 'Shaker seeds,' 'Shaker
herbs,' and 'Shaker distilled waters' are commonly announced for sale
in the shops of towns and cities."

Because of their unusual way of life, which combined communalism

110

and celibacy, the Shakers had an approach to work that differed from their neighbors'. They had many more hands and were able to tackle more enterprises. Their farms eventually became much bigger than ordinary American farms; several thousand acres also provided each Shaker community with stone, timber, clay, and even iron ore in some communities. Most important, Shakers did not work competitively for private gain. Since all profits went to the group as a whole, workers did not receive individual financial reward for their particular endeavors. Their reward was of a different kind—the satisfaction of a job done well for its own sake. Despite the absence of the conventional monetary incentive, the Shakers were extraordinarily productive. Father Joseph Meacham summarized the Shaker philosophy of work and reward: "From each according to his ability, to each according to his need." Because money matters were handled by shrewd business heads in the Family's office, artisans were free to do their best without worrying about economic survival. In their unhurried but steady pursuit of excellence, Shakers followed the advice of Mother Ann, who had told Believers to work as if they had a thousand years to live, *and* as they would if they knew they were to die tomorrow.

With so many workers and so many jobs to be done, a system of organization was essential. Although considerations were sometimes made for an individual's special skills or preferences, the Shakers were expected to do what was needed for the good of the Family. Elders and Eldresses assigned permanent jobs and changes, while Deacons and Deaconesses were authorized to schedule temporary switches—during haying season, for example, a Brother who was principally a carpenter might be instructed to assist the farmers. Sometimes particular enterprises went along with positions of leadership. The Parent Ministry at New Lebanon, for instance, traditionally made baskets. With all the proper equipment, tools, supplies, and know-how already established in the Ministry's workshop, this practice made sense.

Although the Shakers valued virtuosity because they admired perfection, they also prized versatility. "If you improve in one talent," they said, "God will give you more." Most Believers were particularly skilled in one or two areas, but capable of fine work in as many as a dozen occupations. During the course of his life at New Lebanon, Giles Avery worked at building repair, masonry, plumbing, carpentry, plastering, teaching, cabinet work, wagon making, dipper making, orchard work, farming, and writing songs and journals; and he eventually became an Elder.

Sometimes assigned job changes were welcome—in 1852, Brother Henry DeWitt of New Lebanon rejoiced, "This morning I have heard the sound of liberty! Liberty from the bondage of old Boots and shoes; after having spent 26 years at the business." Isaac Youngs of the same community, who had loved fiddling with clocks since boyhood, worked as a tailor, as he was told, but when he was twenty-one, he finally got permission to work with an older clock maker, to his great satisfaction. Other changes were not so happy. In 1854, Anna Dodgson confided mournfully to her journal that her "long loved companion Maria" had been transferred out to take charge of the weaving department, ending ten years of happy work together. Some jobs were rotated on a regular basis; Sisters took four-week shifts in the kitchen, for instance, then moved on to other occupations.

The Shakers were far ahead of their contemporaries in believing that women and men were equal in ability and responsibility. Shaker Brethren and Sisters shared equally in leadership, an unusually progressive practice for the nineteenth century. When one visitor learned of the Shakers' acceptance of women as leaders, he was prompted to ask, "Suppose a woman wanted, in your Family, to be a blacksmith, would you consent?" The answer was an unhesitating no, because it would bring Sisters and Brethren into a relationship that the celibate Shakers did not think wise. Sisters and Brethren occupied separate workshops and were not allowed to enter each other's shops for longer than fifteen minutes without permission from the Elder or Eldress. Believers found that the traditional division of labor by gender was particularly suited to a celibate society. Sisters were in charge of the household, with tasks including cleaning, cooking, and textile work. Brethren were responsible for the farm and for the trades conventionally held by men. In times of need, Shaker men and women assisted each other with chores. One Brother wrote gratefully in 1837, "The Sisters have been so very generous as to turn out & top the beets," which were raised for cattle feed. "They are worthy many thanks." He had good reason to be thankful—they had finished 500 bushels.

Like other nineteenth-century Americans, Believers found that their work varied from season to season. Each month brought its particular tasks, and if the natural course of the farming year brought pressures—to get in all the hay before rain, or to harvest all the pumpkins before frost—it also brought a welcome variety.

In spring, Shaker Sisters occupied themselves with traditional spring cleaning, painting and staining interior woodwork, whitewashing the plaster walls, and clearing the dooryards of wood chips and other litter. In summer, the Sisters were busy with the vast kitchen gardens, picking and serving fresh greens and other fresh produce as they came into season. They also devoted their time to preserving stores for winter—making berry jams, pickling cucumbers, and drying beans and other vegetables and fruits. In fall, the principal tasks were harvesting apples and making cider, dried apples, and applesauce for winter use. Butchering took place in early winter, when freshly slaughtered beef and pork could be kept cool enough to retard spoiling, while the Sisters made salt and dried meat and stuffed sausages.

Textile work was also regulated by the seasons. The Brethren sheared sheep in late spring or early summer. The Sisters then processed the raw fleeces into fine homespun wool—washing, sorting, carding, spinning, and dyeing the wool as the year progressed. To make linen, flax plants were sown in spring and then pulled up by the roots in summer (to waste none of the valuable inner fiber). The plants were then rotted and pounded to free the fibers from the outer stem. The raw flax was then hatcheled, or combed, spun into fine linen thread, and bleached white for shirts, towels, and sheets. Short, leftover fiber, called "tow," was carded and spun into coarse brown tow cloth for work clothes and grain sacks.

In addition to their seasonal chores, Shaker Sisters were responsible for certain jobs all year long—including cleaning the dwelling daily, cooking and serving meals, washing dishes, and mending. Individual Sisters were also active in skilled professions, including teaching, weaving, nursing, and making goods ranging from pincushions and woolen cloaks to cheese and herbal medicines.

Brethren's work was similarly dictated by the seasons. In spring, Shaker men dressed the fields with manure, plowed, and sowed crops. Summer brought the long weeks of haying, and load after wagonload of freshly mown grass was drawn to the barns. In fall, Brethren joined Sisters to harvest apples and other crops. In winter, Brethren threshed the grain crops and cut, sawed, split, and stacked firewood. At New Lebanon, New York, 300 cords a year were required just to dry herbs for the community's pharmaceutical business.

Although nearly all Shaker Brethren had some farm work to do at some time in the year, many were also skilled in trades. Shaker "mechanics"—a traditional term for an artisan or a skilled handyman—built dwellings and workshops, made highways, laid stone walls, mended fences, dug drainage ditches, and produced useful iron, tin, and wooden items for home use or for sale. The mechanics often showed considerable ingenuity in making their work easier or more convenient, adapting worldly technology and frequently improving on it. "We have a right to improve the inventions of man," Father Joseph Meacham had said, "but not to vain glory, or anything superfluous." At least in one community, a certain distinction was made between the farmers and the mechanics. A young Brother at Enfield, New Hampshire, said that the word "farmers," in Shaker use, was "an appellation . . . as disreputable as 'rowdies' elsewhere." The farming Brethren, mostly young, vigorous outdoorsmen, had a great deal more freedom of movement and time because of the nature of their work, which required them to roam beyond the village and often to continue their work beyond normal working hours. (The young Brother added that the farmers cheekily referred to their stay-at-home indoor colleagues as "the Aristocracy.")

Today, much of the Shakers' work has vanished with their passing. The fields that the Brethren diligently plowed have grown back into woods, the fields marked only by stone walls that course incongruously through trees. The shirts and sheets that Sisters stitched have long since fallen to rags and disappeared. What does remain of Shaker work testifies to the makers' conviction that what they did really mattered. The humblest, most mundane objects—a coat hanger, a clothesbrush, a wheelbarrow—reveal a concern for excellence and grace. Many Shaker products are distinguished by a subtle beauty, derived from the simplest of elements: thoughtful proportions; graceful line; cheerful, bright color. Shaker barns, boxes, the lilting melody of the Shaker hymn "The Gift to Be Simple"—all reveal the gifts of the creators. Work and worship were not separated in the Shaker realm. As Eldress Bertha Lindsay of Canterbury, New Hampshire, says, "You don't have to get down on your knees to say a prayer. . . . If you're working, you can say a prayer."

This stone wagon mount was brought to the Fruitlands Museums from the South Family at Harvard, Massachusetts, early in the twentieth century. Stonecutters and stonemasons prepared foundations, steps, and fence posts in each of the Shaker communities. This graceful mount allowed Believers to enter or leave wagons or carriages in comfort and safety.

A stonecutter at Pleasant Hill, Kentucky, shapes a limestone dripstone, a fine reproduction of the Shaker original. The dripstones caught rain water from downspouts and carried it away from the foundation. It was typical of the Shakers to make such a mundane object so graceful.

Black converts were accepted as equals in Shaker communities. They were more numerous in Kentucky than in the North, but there were also some black Shakers in New York and New England, as well as a small Family of black Sisters in Philadelphia. While the Shakers did not fight in the Civil War because of their principles of pacifism, they did not support the institution of slavery. One Shaker Brother who had been born in Kentucky but raised at New Lebanon, New York, returned to his birthplace on a visit in 1852 and had "a pretty smart talk with a Kentucky slaveholder about the propriety or impropriety of holding slaves." Added the Brother, "He thought of course I was an eastern man, but I told him I was a Kentuckian by birth and yet could not approve of Slavery."

below:

The Shakers in several communities made their own bricks. Here, the original mortar retains the lines scored by the bricklayer at Pleasant Hill, Kentucky. Although the Shakers built mostly with wood, they preferred stone or brick when they could afford it, to help prevent fires and to build for the ages.

right:

The restored Center Family Dwelling at Pleasant Hill, Kentucky, was made of native limestone, as was the original mortar. Modern masons duplicated the original bevel in the pointing between the stones—the outward angle sheds rain water and helps preserve the masonry.

This detail of a Shaker workbench shows what care the unknown maker put into a utilitarian piece of shop furniture. Shaker tools often reveal the same kind of care—testimony to the respect for honest work that Shaker workers felt. On this workbench, Shaker Brethren at New Lebanon, New York, are likely to have made all sorts of woodenware, from windows and doors to beds and chairs to boxes and pails.

The blue paint is unusual on furniture; it was usually saved for the interior trim of each community's meetinghouse. The workbench is made of mixed woods, including pine, maple, and oak or chestnut. The curved, unpainted shape is a sliding board jack, made of fruitwood. The bellying front is pleasing to the eye and also functional—it allows the jack to slide without hitting the drawer knobs. A vise on the left side of the bench, not visible in this view, holds one end of a board, and this jack holds the other end, which allows the worker to plane or otherwise work on the edge.

A cabinetmaker planes the edge of a board with the traditional tools and methods of Shaker craftsmen. "Put your hands to work and your hearts to God," Mother Ann Lee counseled her followers. Brethren who converted to the Shaker faith brought the skills they had learned in the world outside—carpentry, doctoring, tinsmithing, stonecutting, farming, printing, tailoring, and a host of other abilities. Younger boys raised in Shaker villages learned trades as apprentices to the older Brethren.

A cabinetmaker's shop with some early equipment is reminiscent of
Shaker woodworking shops at the turn of the twentieth century. This
shop, in a Shaker building at Canterbury, New Hampshire, is used
by a craftsman who makes fine reproduction Shaker furniture as
part of his work. Shaker furniture makers were typically versatile
workers who concentrated on cabinetmaking in the winter, when
farm work and woodcutting were minimal.

A splendid workbench testifies to the care that Shaker workers put into everything that they made, from tools and equipment to furniture to a meetinghouse. Several features distinguish this particular workbench, which is ninety-seven inches long at its oak top. It was designed and built for a left-handed woodworker—the bird's-eye-maple tail vise, ordinarily mounted on the right side, is on the left. The upper-right drawer has a pine lid and probably functioned as a handy writing or figuring surface—a stool pulled up alongside the drawer would make a good temporary "desk." An unusual and idiosyncratic construction feature in the drawers—sides that taper from thin at the top to thicker at the bottom (not visible in the photograph)—places this workbench among furniture known to have been made at Hancock, Massachusetts, or Enfield, Connecticut, in the mid-nineteenth century.

123

Shaker workshops were usually well supplied with the proper tools,
like this assortment of woodworking planes in a tool cabinet.
Believers were supposed to share equipment and supplies. "No one
should take tools, belonging in charge of others, without obtaining
liberty for the same, if the person can consistently be found who
takes charge of them," reminded the Millennial Laws of 1841.
"When anyone borrows a tool, it should be immediately returned,
without injury, if possible, and if injured, should be made known by
the borrower to the lender;—'The wicked borrow and never
return.' "

"Provide places for all your things, so that you may know where to
find them at any time, day or night," Mother Ann had counseled her
followers. Order was especially important in a communal Family,
since things were shared, not privately owned. This narrow wall
cupboard in the Brethren's Shop is pine, stained bright yellow in
part. It holds an assortment of awls for use in leatherworking and
shoemaking.

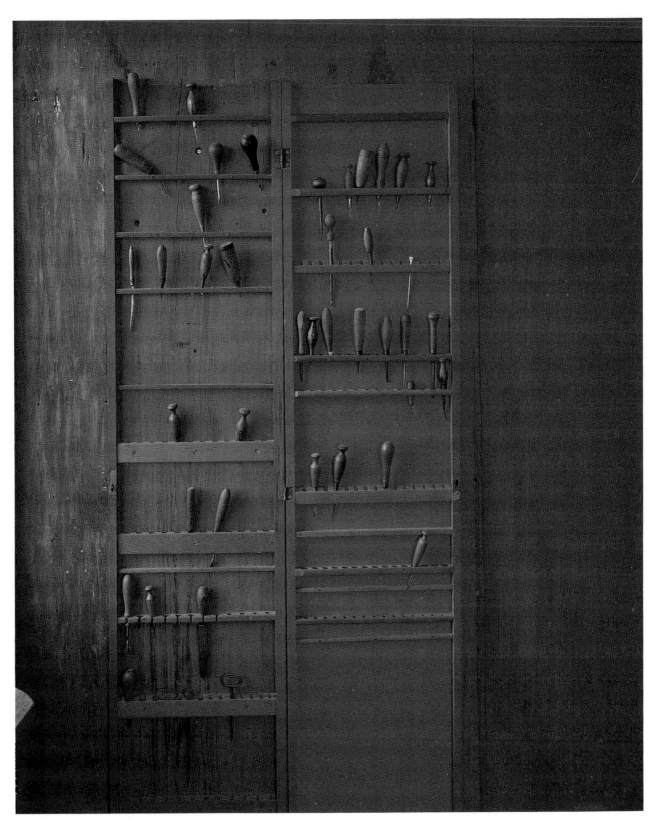

A basketmaker prepares splints of ash by shaving them to the required thinness with a drawknife on a shaving bench—a traditional technique. The Shakers of New Lebanon, New York, who produced elegant baskets for their own use and for sale, developed specialized machinery to speed the work without sacrificing quality. In 1873, a Brother visiting from New Hampshire admired the ingenuity of Elder Daniel Boler (1804–1892), who developed a machine that planed the strips of wood. "Passing through a set of rollers [they leave] the machine highly polished," he noted. "Most of the basket wood is prepared in this shop—It forms quite a branch of business for this family & several hands are engaged at it, most of the year."

The basketmaker attaches a bail handle to a basket. This kind of handle, and the single blue splint near the top of the basket, are the adaptations of a modern craftsman to the traditional Shaker style. Shaker baskets were pale, as is this one, when new; time has mellowed them to a rich golden brown.

The Shakers used oak and ash splint, as well as willow, to make a
wide range of baskets for home use and for sale. The basketmakers
favored the use of practical features—such as the notched wooden
handle here—while not necessarily innovating them. The notch
grips the rim to prevent the handle from pulling away from the
basket, even if it is filled with a heavy load.

This delicate basket, one of the finest examples of Shaker basketry, was designed with a lid that slides up and down the handle, but cannot be taken off—and hence mislaid. This kind of basket was often called a "feather basket" in the outside world, because the feathers or down of a plucked fowl were protected from blowing away. The body and the lid were woven over wooden molds to get their shapes. The design on the lid, called "twilling," required special skill.

The basket exemplifies the rule of thumb of Shaker design: don't make something if it's not useful; but if it is both necessary and useful, don't hesitate to make it beautiful, as long as the decorative elements are an inherent part of the design and don't interfere with function.

This practical, graceful oval wooden box is an emblem of Shaker work in general. The Shakers in several communities made boxes like this in a wide range of sizes for household and workshop use. These could hold anything except liquids. The distinctive finger-shaped joint on the side was not a Shaker innovation, but a tradition borrowed from the outside world and perfected. Cutting space between the fingers allowed the thin maple side to swell and shrink naturally with changes in temperature and humidity, with less risk of buckling than a straight seam. This box was probably the work of Elder Daniel Crosman (1810–1885), a master box maker at New Lebanon, New York.

"Trifles make perfection, but perfection is no trifle," said the Shakers. The side of an oval box shows this attention to detail in the curves of the fingers in the joint; in the careful alignment of the small copper tacks (which will not rust and discolor the wood, as iron would); and in the graceful shaping and pivot of the bail handle.

A detail of the side of a finished oval box shows the graceful repeating pattern of fingers, or "swallowtails," as they were called by the Shakers, and the precise alignment of copper tacks.

134

Delmer Wilson (1873–1961) was the last Elder and oval-box maker at Sabbathday Lake, Maine. This versatile Shaker Brother worked variously as artist, photographer, orchardist, builder, barber, dentist, beekeeper, and woodworker. This photograph of Elder Delmer, standing next to a planer, was taken in his workshop in the Boys' House in 1915, when he was forty-two. He began making oval boxes in 1896 and continued well into the twentieth century, carrying on a tradition of more than a century in Shaker work.

Wooden dippers or measures were another useful Shaker product. They were used to measure dry substances, such as grain and flour, in quantities up to one quart. The dippers shown here remain in a wooden carrying device, ready for shipment and sale. Like the oval boxes, the dippers were formed of thin strips of maple that were soaked or steamed until flexible enough to be bent. The graceful handles were attached with rivets.

137

Examples of Shaker workmanship include a cupboard, oval boxes, and a pail. Shaker furnishings are characteristically free of ornament, but they are nevertheless appealing because of their shapes and colors. Believers liked bright, solid colors in their rooms, contrary to what outsiders have assumed. Products like these were made of local woods—pine for the cupboard and pail, maple and pine for the oval boxes. Shakers favored the use of plain wooden or white china drawer pulls, not the decorative brass hardware fancied by the outside world.

This Shaker shovel from New Lebanon, New York, carved from a single piece of walnut, was based on American traditions, but was noticeably finer and more elegantly proportioned than ordinary shovels. To prevent the danger of sparks from a metal tool, wooden shovels were customarily used in barns in which grain was stored. This shovel was repaired by the Shakers with a piece of tin when its bottom edge split.

An unusually large and handsome broom, probably made in a New York Shaker community, may have been designed for sweeping a wide hallway or a large meeting room.

141

The Round Stone Barn at Hancock, Massachusetts, is one of the spectacular examples of Shaker ingenuity and excellence. Although the Shakers did not originate the notion of a round barn, Elder Daniel Goodrich (1765–1835) adapted the idea in one of the biggest examples in America. The barn, 270 feet around, was built in 1826 to house more than 50 head of dairy cattle. Each of the barn's three floors is accessible from the ground by means of ramps. The top floor was for hay wagons, which drove in, circled as the loads were thrown into the center of the barn, and exited without having to back up or turn around. Up to ten wagons at a time could bring in hay.

The second floor was for the cattle, whose stalls ringed the barn's outer wall. A walkway between the cattle and the central haymow allowed Shaker Brethren to feed the herd with ease. (One visitor suggested that the Shaker cows' renowned productivity resulted from their clear view of all that tasty hay!) The ground level was the manure pit. Trap doors behind the stalls facilitated the removal of dung, which was brought out in spring to dress the fields.

The Hancock barn was the only Shaker barn that was round, but other, more conventionally shaped Shaker barns were equally impressive. The Shakers in Canterbury, New Hampshire, had a splendid barn 200 feet long, with polished chestnut beams. In New Lebanon, New York, a vast 5-story stone barn stretched 196 feet long by 50 feet wide.

The cow barn at Canterbury, New Hampshire, was one of the highlights of the village. Built in 1858, the barn was 200 feet long with 25-foot ramps at both ends, totaling 250 feet; it was probably the largest barn in New Hampshire. The frame was made of chestnut, and the barn was kept immaculately clean. Stalls on the main floor, shown here, housed a large herd of fine cattle. The barn was tragically destroyed by fire in 1973.

The interior of the Round Stone Barn at Hancock, Massachusetts, shows the central haymow and the central shaft—a ventilating device designed to bring fresh air into the hay to keep it dry and reduce the risk of spontaneous combustion. In spite of great care, the barn did catch fire and was rebuilt in 1864, thirty-eight years after its construction. The Shakers decided to take advantage of the misfortune by adding the clerestory with windows, which changed the outline of the roof and allowed much more daylight into the barn.

At Canterbury, New Hampshire, a windrowing machine was
photographed raking hay near the Second Family Dwelling around
the turn of the century. Farming was the mainstay of the Shakers'
economy throughout their history. Shaker farms were admired as
models of good husbandry and productivity. Even critics of the
Shaker way of life praised the "sleek cattle upon their hills, their
excellent barns and outbuildings, their substantial walls and well-
cultivated gardens and fields."

Haying occupied Shaker Brethren for weeks during the summers. It was necessary to cut and bring in the hay in dry weather to prevent damp hay from igniting by spontaneous combustion. In August 1836, Giles Avery of New Lebanon, New York, recorded the completion of haying for the season with the last two oxen and two horse loads. The Sisters helped celebrate by bringing a treat of "some excellent drink sweetened with sugar & soured with lemon. . . . Also a large quantity of crackers cakes &c." Accordingly, the Brethren seated themselves "squaw fashion" around the goodies, although Giles noted that their appetites were somewhat reduced thanks to two similar visits by the Sisters earlier the same day. To prevent an attack of gout, the Brethren playfully decided to jump back and forth across the creek, and "went at it britches and boots."

These Canterbury girls busied themselves in a garden near the Ministry Shop and Meetinghouse, circa 1915. In addition to attending school and playing, Shaker children spent a considerable amount of time doing chores. Eldress Bertha Lindsay, who still lives at Canterbury, New Hampshire, was in charge of baking pies for the communal Family of more than a hundred members when she was in her teens, in the early twentieth century.

A worker leads a flock of sheep at Hancock Shaker Village in Massachusetts. Shakers here and in other communities raised thousands of sheep, including Merino sheep, which produce a superior fleece. The Shakers at Sabbathday Lake, Maine, still maintain a small flock and sell the wool.

overleaf:
The Shakers commonly used oxen for plowing and hauling. Oxen (neutered bulls) were stronger and calmer than horses. Most Shaker Brethren turned from various kinds of indoor work—furniture-making, coopering, and the like—to farm work in early spring as soon as the ground thawed, when the fields were dressed with manure.

Finished flat brooms from the broom shop at Pleasant Hill, Kentucky, are fine reproductions of the original Shaker product.

The familiar flat broom stands as an emblem of Shaker ingenuity and creativity. According to Shaker records, the first flattened brooms were produced by a Brother at Watervliet, New York, as an improvement over the traditional round bundles of broomcorn; the wider bottom edge swept more efficiently. Several Shaker communities went on to manufacture brooms and brushes in large numbers—an appropriate enterprise, given the Believers' devotion to cleanliness.

A well-made broom will stand on its own, before and after it has been stitched into the familiar flat shape. The bins behind hold broom handles. Turning these out in quantity kept Shaker Brethren busy at the lathe. Orren Haskins (1815–1892), a particularly gifted woodworker at New Lebanon, New York, went for the record in 1836. "[He] informs me that he has turned 1000 one day this week and I think now that all brags are beaten," wrote another Brother.

153

These fine reproductions of Shaker rocking chairs, made by the cabinetmaker at Hancock Shaker Village, Massachusetts, recall the way Shaker furniture makers frequently made things in multiples—several dozen ladder-back chairs for a new dwelling, for example, or a pair of washstands, or four small cases of drawers. Such production methods were not only efficient, but they helped to ensure uniformity—a quality the Shakers prized in their communal way of life, in which no person should have finer things than another.

At the same time, however, Shaker furniture makers did design individual pieces of furniture to suit a certain Believer's size; a rocking chair—like a suit of clothes—might resemble everyone else's, but it might well be extra large or small for a particular individual. Shaker Brethren usually made furniture in the winter months, when farm work was minimal. Most known furniture makers did a wide range of jobs during the course of the year. That their occasional products possess such grace testifies to their commitment to perfection in every kind of work.

These chairs rest on a Shaker workbench from New Lebanon, New York—one of the finest Shaker workbenches in existence. The top is made of three sections, using different woods for different areas. The first section is laminated maple or birch; the center, hard, durable oak or chestnut; and the third, a pine board, softer than the other hardwoods.

Shaker chairs were typically light but sturdy. This early example, probably made at New Lebanon, New York, in about 1820, is a streamlined version of an American rocker, with no carving or decorative painting to clutter its simplicity. The maker, however, was interested in making the chair look "right"—note the way the back slats increase in height as they go up. This subtle visual characteristic "balances" the chair in the eyes of the beholder and is typical of Shaker work—it goes beyond mere utility, but does not interfere with function. This unusually small chair was probably custom-made for a Shaker Sister. Some exceptionally conservative Shakers regarded rocking chairs as a needless luxury, but most enjoyed the soothing motion.

A detail of the rocking chair shows the woven tape seat, a close reproduction of original Shaker tape seats. Colorful, comfortable, durable, and easier to install than cane, rush, or splint, tape seats were used by the Shakers as early as the 1830s and seem to be a true Shaker innovation. Common seat patterns included plain checkerboards and a herringbone pattern, illustrated here.

A detail of the arm and front post of this rocking chair shows the type of construction typical of early-nineteenth-century Shaker chairs with arms. The entire front post was turned on a lathe from a single piece of wood—the broad "mushroom" at the top is not a separate, glued-on piece. This method made the front posts sturdy and unlikely to break or come apart.

157

A variety of colorful chair-seat tapes from Pleasant Hill, Kentucky, shows changes over time. The earliest tapes, on the left, were woven by hand by Shaker Sisters from home-dyed yarns; the earliest record of tape production dates from around 1820, when the Sisters were producing hundreds of yards a year. The tapes on the right date from the 1860s, when the Shakers found it more practical to buy twilled cotton tapes than to produce their own. "We used to have more looms than now," sadly reflected an Elder from New Lebanon, New York, in 1875, "but cloth is sold so cheaply that we gradually began to buy. It is a mistake; we buy more cheaply than we can make, but our home-made cloth is much better than that we can buy; and we have now to make three pairs of trousers, for instance, where before we made one. Thus our little looms would even now be more profitable—to say nothing of the independence we secure in working them."

The Shakers used colorful, comfortable woven tape seats in their chairs as early as the 1820s. This is one kind of a simple tape loom, used with an ordinary ladder-back chair to keep the warp threads taut. The weft, or cross threads, will then be woven around the warp to form a long tape. The Shakers also made small standing looms to produce tape.

A Shaker ladder-back chair typifies the Shaker approach to life and possessions. Straightforward and unadorned, it nevertheless reveals features intended for comfort and convenience. The seat is made of woven cloth tape, more comfortable than splint or rush. The chair angles back at a slant to provide relaxed seating. The chair is light enough to be easily portable and to hang from the pegboard—a handy place to put the chair while sweeping. The chairs were commonly hung upside down, so dust would not discolor the top of the seats.

The back posts have a unique feature—wooden ball-and-socket "tilter" feet that keep the back legs flat on the floor when the sitter leans back. The tilters are held in place by narrow leather strips threaded through a hole in the foot and through a hole drilled in the leg a few inches above the foot. Such feet were becoming common on Shaker chairs by the 1830s. In spite of admonitions against leaning backward in chairs—"It is not right to lean our chairs back against the wall in our dwelling houses nor any decent buildings; nor against any beds or furnature," reminded the Millennial Laws of 1821—the habit persisted, and the practical Shakers adapted their chairs to suit. The main advantage was the protection of floorboards, most often made of soft pine, from the little dents that the hardwood legs of ordinary chairs would make.

Chairs similar to this were made by the thousands for the Believers in every community. These particular chairs were made at New Lebanon, New York, in about 1840.

Characteristic Shaker furnishings included built-in drawers and cupboards—these, in the Church Family Dwelling at Hancock, Massachusetts, are made of warm butternut and pine—and a cherry candlestand and maple rocking chair, both made at New Lebanon, New York, in about 1840. Based on styles popular in America around 1800, Shaker furniture was simple and refined, as well as light and easily portable—a plus for communal living, since all furnishings were owned by the entire society and liable to be moved around.

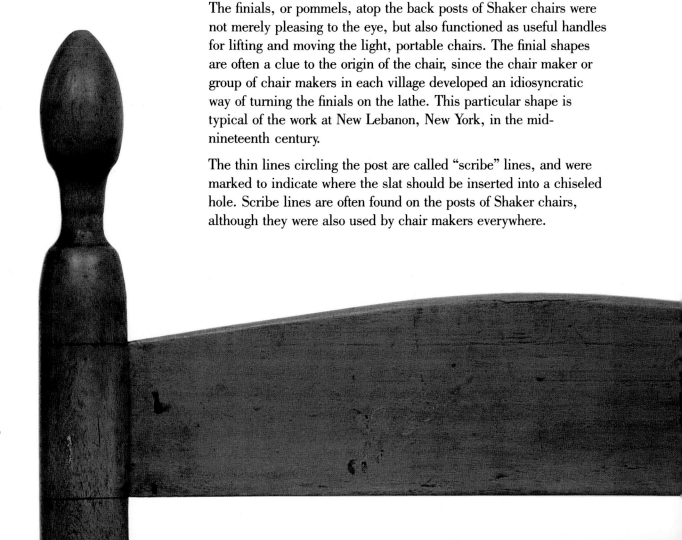

The finials, or pommels, atop the back posts of Shaker chairs were not merely pleasing to the eye, but also functioned as useful handles for lifting and moving the light, portable chairs. The finial shapes are often a clue to the origin of the chair, since the chair maker or group of chair makers in each village developed an idiosyncratic way of turning the finials on the lathe. This particular shape is typical of the work at New Lebanon, New York, in the mid-nineteenth century.

The thin lines circling the post are called "scribe" lines, and were marked to indicate where the slat should be inserted into a chiseled hole. Scribe lines are often found on the posts of Shaker chairs, although they were also used by chair makers everywhere.

One characteristic of Shaker furniture is its delicacy. The legs of this drop-leaf table are very slender; the panels of the pine lap desk, or "writing box," are unusually thin; and the legs and spindles of the revolving chair are similarly free of excess weight. In spite of their delicacy, however, the pieces are surprisingly sturdy. Furthermore, they were treated with great care by Believers, who recognized in their possessions not private property to be abused, but communal property to be shared with future generations of Shaker converts.

All three pieces were made at New Lebanon, New York; the lap desk is stamped *1847*. Such desks were regarded as something of a luxury rather than a necessity by more conservative Shakers, for whom plain rectangles of pine sufficed as a writing surface. Chairs and stools with turning or revolving seats were made for the Shakers' use and for sale in the 1860s. One Brother visiting from Ohio admired the "new kind of chair, which turns on a screw pivot, every which way, different kinds and sizes."

167

A desk probably made by a Shaker Brother in Harvard, Massachusetts, is unusual for its visual "deception"—it looks like an ordinary case of drawers, but the front of the second drawer lowers to reveal a desk top. The construction is very impressive, with delicate dovetail joints in the drawers. Most Shaker furniture makers avoided anything that resembled deception, including veneer and grain painting (both of which made plain wood look finer and costlier). Perhaps it was furniture like this that prompted one very traditional Believer to complain on a visit to Harvard in 1850, "I think they have gathered into their habitations too much furniture which belongs to Babylon! Mother [Ann] used to say, 'You may give such things to the moles and the bats, that is the children of this world.' "

168

Examples of furniture attributed to the Shakers at Harvard, Massachusetts, include this cupboard and desk. The desk is a variation of the sewing desk, or "work stand." Of particular note is the way in which drawers are set into the bottom on the front and on the side. Such drawer placement is found on other Shaker sewing desks and furniture, a handy feature allowing the user to get things from the drawers without having to bend low under the work surface. What distinguishes this desk, however, is the addition of a writing desk on the front, apparently an alteration adapting the sewing desk for writing. Written journals were mandatory for certain Believers—including Elders and Eldresses, Deacons and Deaconesses, and Trustees—but ordinary members also kept diaries of their work and days, forming a rich record of everyday Shaker experience.

The sewing desk, or "work stand," was a popular item of furniture among Shaker Sisters in the years following the Civil War. The drawers provided convenient storage for small sewing implements, and the pull-out board handily enlarged the work surface without taking up extra space when the work was done. This exceptionally fine pair of sewing desks is unique because they were designed to fit together back to back.

The desks were made of birch, oak, and maple by Elder Henry Green (1844–1931) of Alfred, Maine, in about 1880. The design of these desks as a pair suggests the Shaker way of working—companionable, not lonely, with colleagues to share the work and talk.

Shaker Brethren often built sewing desks as special requests for individual Sisters. This desk was evidently made for Adeline Patterson (1884–1968), whose name was chalked on the underside of the pull-out work surface in front. This desk is identical to another desk in a private collection. Shaker furniture makers commonly made pieces in multiples of two or more.

An unusually tall stand made at South Union, Kentucky, was probably used as a lectern—an ink inscription on the underside of the top indicates that it was a "Meeting Room Stand." It is based on examples of Shaker stands made at New Lebanon, New York, and other eastern Shaker societies, but it is a little more exuberant in the curve of the legs and the swell of the post—evidence, perhaps, of the distance between the model community at New Lebanon and this community, more than 1,000 miles distant.

This cupboard and broom serve as emblems of the Shakers' insistence on order and cleanliness. The cupboard is attributed to the Shakers at Harvard, Massachusetts, and probably dates from the late eighteenth or very early nineteenth century. This kind of raised panel in the doors was typical of American woodwork at that time, and is found on early examples of Shaker work. Visitors from the outside world were frequently impressed with the remarkable cleanliness of Shaker villages. In 1851, Nathaniel Hawthorne found everything so neat at Hancock, Massachusetts, that he said it was "a pain and constraint to look at it."

Personal cleanliness was important to the Shakers. "It is contrary to order for any slovens or sluts to live in the Church, or even for brethren or sisters to wear ragged clothes about their work," reminded the Millennial Laws of 1821. There was probably a washstand in each dwelling "retiring room," or perhaps, in some cases, a communal washroom for each sex on each floor of the dwelling.

This washstand, made at Hancock, Massachusetts, of butternut, pine, and tiger maple, is almost identical to another washstand dated 1850. The subtle flare of the top and splashboard is typical of Shaker work—something done to please the eye, without adding ornament, requiring extra time and skill of the workman. Above the washstand is a looking-glass designed to hang from the pegboard. According to Shaker rules, looking-glasses were to be no larger than twelve by eighteen inches, to discourage vanity.

A corner in the Church Family Office at Harvard, Massachusetts, shows some of the finest Shaker interior woodwork in existence. The Office, built in the early 1840s, has about forty rooms and dozens of built-in drawers and cupboards made of pine. The building has been a private residence since the early twentieth century, when the community disbanded and sold its property.

The sturdily built work table, more than twelve feet long, is so delicately proportioned that it appears much lighter than it is. The wheels, like those on Shaker beds, made moving the table and sweeping the floor easier. Wheels or rollers were commonly used by Shakers on large, heavy pieces of furniture.

Both the table and the built-in storage drawers show how the Shakers designed their rooms to be easy to keep clean. "There is no dirt in heaven," Mother Ann had said.

178

This small table has a very unusual kind of foot. The arches facing each other at right angles to the wall are not out of the ordinary—similar feet are common on the trestle tables that Shakers favored for dining tables. It is the *third* "toe" on each side, pointing out, that is so odd. The construction, also, is as curious as a Chinese puzzle. To deepen the enigma, an old photograph shows the table with the toes pointing in. Clearly, at some time, the whole was taken apart and reassembled. This work might have been done by the Shakers or by a later owner. The small item on top to the left is a book press.

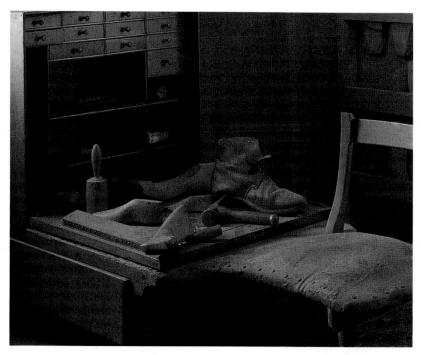

The Shakers produced their own boots and shoes—sturdy leather for outdoor wear and fine cloth slippers for Sunday worship services, when hundreds of dancing feet stepped lightly on the polished pine floor of the meetinghouse. The village shoemakers custom-made shoes for individuals, as this variety of wooden forms, or lasts, indicates. (One surviving last has a thick leather "bunion" tacked to the toe to accommodate one poor Believer's problem foot.)

The low workbench, made at New Lebanon, New York, in about 1840, has a comfortable padded leather seat. Upholstery of any kind was exceedingly rare in Shaker furniture, although a few workshop stools and chairs had durable leather seats like this.

Sewing implements on a desk from Harvard, Massachusetts, include a "tomato"-shaped pincushion, made of satin and stuffed with wool; fabric cases for knitting needles and threads; a wooden form to shape emery-filled "strawberries" for cleaning and sharpening needles; and some examples of plain homespun Shaker cloth. The Sisters in many communities made the manufacture of such "fancy goods" an increasingly important mainstay of their Family's economy in the late nineteenth and early twentieth centuries. The term "fancy" is slightly misleading, as it referred primarily to quality, not to decorativeness. The Shakers did not produce goods for sale that they considered unfit for use at home.

A Sister's sewing notions included such equipment as this fine hexagonal-weave basket, a miniature of a full-size cheese basket that was designed to be lined with cheesecloth so that the whey could drain from the curds. This miniature version (with a lid, unlike the large cheese baskets) was simply a small, nicely made basket for indoor use in a workshop. The larger basket with the delicately curved handles was also for light household use, possibly to hold a pincushion and small scissors or other useful items. The spool is typical of Shaker spools; with a narrow center, it holds considerably more thread than the modern commercial spools familiar today.

Shaker Sisters in several communities made warm woolen cloaks for their own use and also for sale in the late nineteenth and early twentieth centuries. Adapted from the cloaks commonly worn by American women in the eighteenth century, the Shaker cloaks enjoyed popularity among worldly women for wear to the opera. The brighter colors—including pink, red, purple, bright blue, and green—were intended for sale. The hoods and cloaks were often lined with satin.

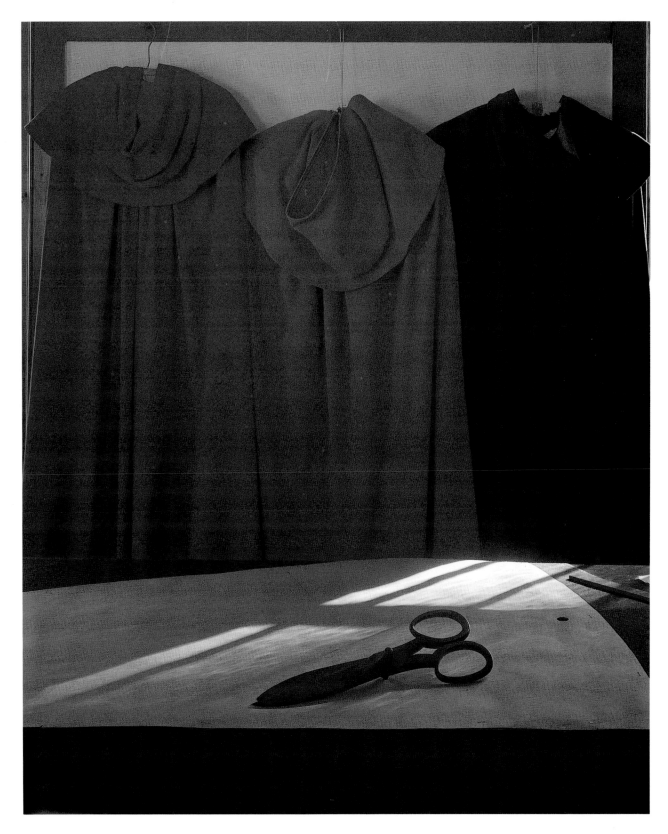

A weaver works at an overshot coverlet on an original Shaker loom at Pleasant Hill, Kentucky. The term "overshot" refers to a traditional style of weaving—here, the red woolen threads "overshoot" the linen warp to form a reversible pattern. This technique may well have been too worldly for some Shakers, who were supposed to use plain blankets and "comfortables." Shaker Sisters in all communities were heavily involved with textiles, from preparing thread and cloth, to cutting and sewing clothing, to making household textiles, including coverlets, sheets, towels, tapes for tying, and carpets.

"Hands to work and hearts to God," said Mother Ann. The Shakers believed that work is a form of worship. Here, a textile worker demonstrates the traditional way of carding wool, or combing and straightening the fibers in preparation for spinning on a wheel. The fleece is combed and fluffed between two wooden paddles set with hundreds of wire teeth. The resulting rolls are then spun into thread or yarn on a large spinning wheel. The Shakers prepared their own cloth from home-raised sheep and flax (for linen) well into the nineteenth century, even when commercial cloth was readily available.

The device clamped to the bench is a table swift, which Shaker
Sisters used for winding a skein of yarn into a ball. The swift was
not a Shaker invention, but the Shakers at Hancock, Massachusetts,
improved on it and manufactured them by the thousands.
Thumbscrews fasten the swift to a table or other surface, and hold
the collapsible arms out while the swift turns, releasing the yarn as
it's wound into a ball. When the work was finished, the swift folded
up neatly (like an umbrella) for storage. Swifts came in three
sizes and sold for the considerable sum of fifty cents in the
mid-nineteenth century.

Two yarn reels attributed to the Shakers at Harvard, Massachusetts,
reflect the Shakers' interest in mechanization and technological
progress—as long as it did the job as well as or better than the old-
fashioned way. Such reels were based on traditions from the world
outside. They were used to wind and measure yarn or thread into
skeins. The "squirrel cage" type, on the right, may be a later
model, but the principle is the same.

190

Shaker tools and equipment, no matter how mundane, were characteristically made with as much care as if they were furniture for the dwelling. A three-legged yarn reel, made by Shakers in Alfred, Maine, was used to wind and measure yarn into skeins. The double coat hanger was designed to hang two garments, perhaps a Brother's coat and shirt or vest. Neither device was a Shaker invention, but both are typically well made. They are shown against the original deep-blue paint in an upper floor of the Meetinghouse at Sabbathday Lake, Maine.

Shaker spinning wheels were characteristically free of unnecessary decorative turning on the legs and spindles. Large or "great" wheels, such as this one, were used to spin wool into yarn. Spinning occupied many Sisters for many years. After the sheep were sheared, the fleece was washed and prepared for spinning by carding into long soft rolls. The yarn was either dyed or used as it was.

194

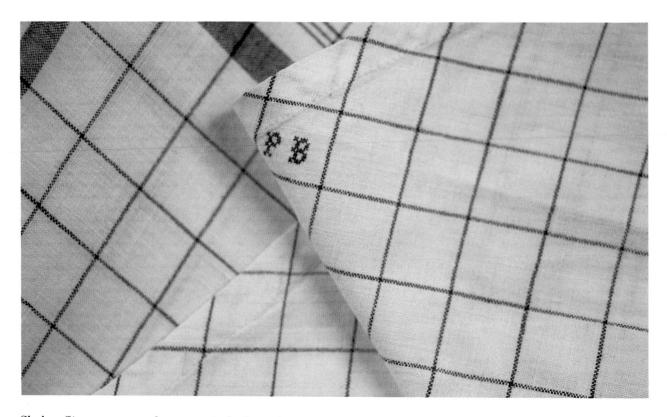

Shaker Sisters commonly cross-stitched numbers and initials on household textiles. While this was also common practice in the world outside, it made a great deal of sense as an aid in sorting laundry in the Shakers' large communal Families. Textiles, opposite, include an off-white woolen blanket, a white linen towel with an absorbent "diaper" weave, and a black-and-white checked kerchief. *No 1* may refer to a room number in a dwelling or to a number in a set of blankets; *67* probably refers to the date. The Millennial Laws of 1845 suggested, "It is considered unnecessary to put more than two figures for a date, on our clothes or tools, and it is strictly forbidden unnecessarily to embellish any mark." The initials *PB* stand for Peggie Bridges, a Sister at South Union, Kentucky, where these textiles were made.

The Kentucky Shakers were among the early silk producers in the United States. By 1832, the Sisters at South Union, Kentucky, had produced enough silk to make themselves neck kerchiefs. These silk kerchiefs, made at South Union, show the bright colors that the Sisters favored. The iridescent appearance of the silk was created by using warp and weft threads of different colors—magenta and white to produce pink, for example. Weaving silk requires great patience because of the fineness of the threads.

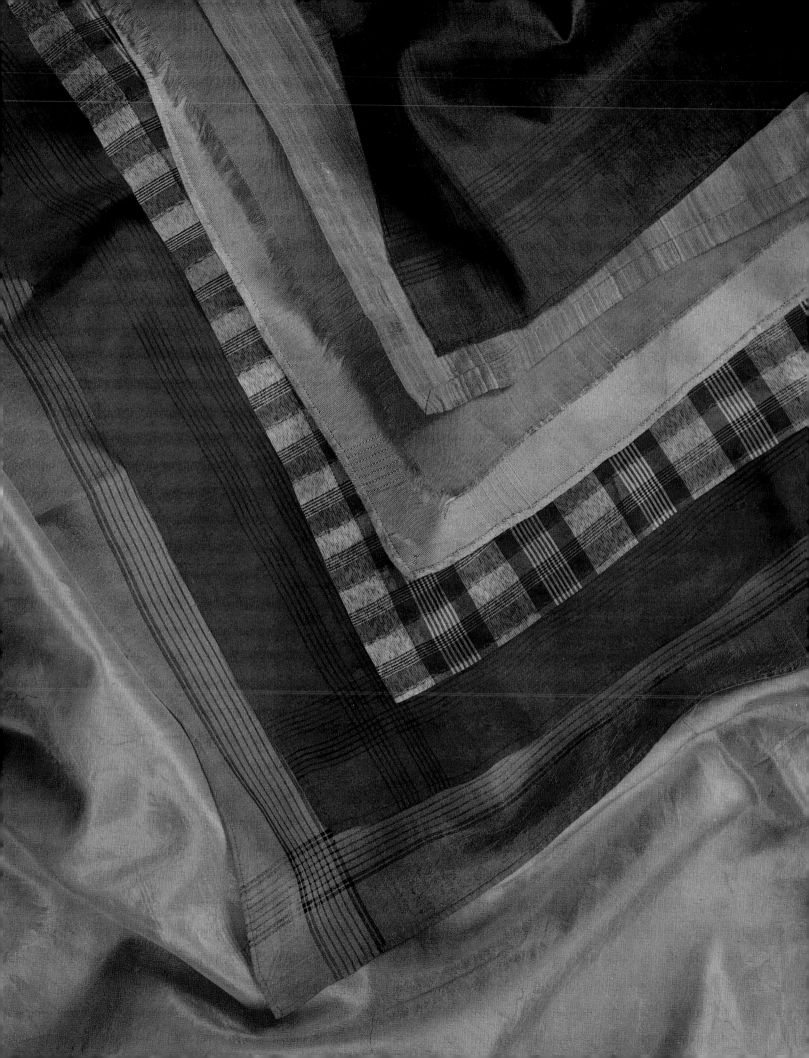

Shaker Sisters dyed their homespun yarn and cloth in restrained but pleasing colors. The yarns here show the colors that result from traditional techniques of dyeing with plants and other natural materials. The Shakers were more likely to use dyes such as butternut, which yields a rich, dark brown, and indigo, a purchased dye that produces blue. Dyeing in a Shaker community was done on a large, almost industrial, scale and required considerable expertise. In 1849, some Sisters at New Lebanon, New York, ran into problems. Complained one:

O Sorrow & joy Betsy Crosman, Mary Ann Mantle, Amy Reed have finished coloring blue wool, they began the 12th had 105 lbs. & more than this had it all to wash over because Maria says we had such poor judgment & got the liquor too strong . . . & too hot I suppose. O Murder evry thing happens this awful year !!!!!!

The skeins of wool are, top row, left to right: a full skein (560 yards) of natural Leicester wool, and yarns dyed with osage orange and alum, tree lichen and alum, osage orange and copper sulphate, osage orange and cream of tartar; bottom row, left to right: hickory bark and copperas, cochineal, log wood and alum, madder root, and osage orange and copperas.

201

In 1879, the year after a new reservoir and aqueduct were built at Sabbathday Lake, Maine, the Shakers there installed a brand-new washing machine in the basement of the Sisters' Shop. Made of "polished stone"—probably soapstone—the washing machine weighed two and a half tons and required four horses to cart it from Durham, Maine, where it was made to order for the Shakers. An improved washing machine suitable for Shaker communal life and also for hotels and other institutions in the outside world was one of the few inventions patented by the Shaker society; it was designed and manufactured for sale at Canterbury, New Hampshire.

A hoist in the Laundry was an added convenience for the Shakers at Canterbury, New Hampshire. On the hoist is a basket made at Canterbury; the SXX mark on its side indicated that it was used in the sweater trade. The Canterbury Shakers developed a good market for their original "Shaker-knit" sweaters, mostly to New England college boys, in the early twentieth century.

The Shakers at Canterbury, New Hampshire, installed a steam-drying room in their Laundry in 1854; until that time, all the clothes had been dried on lines. The room, with its sliding racks, was remodeled in 1862 and again in 1908, when a blower was put in the attic to force air up through the hanging laundry and out the ceiling through a pipe. Drying laundry inside, regardless of the weather, was practical for large communal Shaker Families, who could plan to do the washing on a predictable schedule.

206

Shaker Sisters were responsible for laundering the clothes and bedding for communal Families of up to a hundred members. It was not unusual for a Brother to assist with some of the heavy work. To speed up the job, the Shakers developed this stove, designed to heat dozens of flatirons at once. The stove was originally used in a laundry building at New Lebanon, New York. The Believers who used this convenience no doubt recalled that Mother Ann had supported herself during her first two years in the United States by taking in washing and ironing in New York City.

Wooden stocking forms were used to dry knitted hose to shape. The Shakers at Canterbury, New Hampshire, began to manufacture knitted stockings in the 1850s for sale to the outside world. These forms remain in place in the Laundry.

210

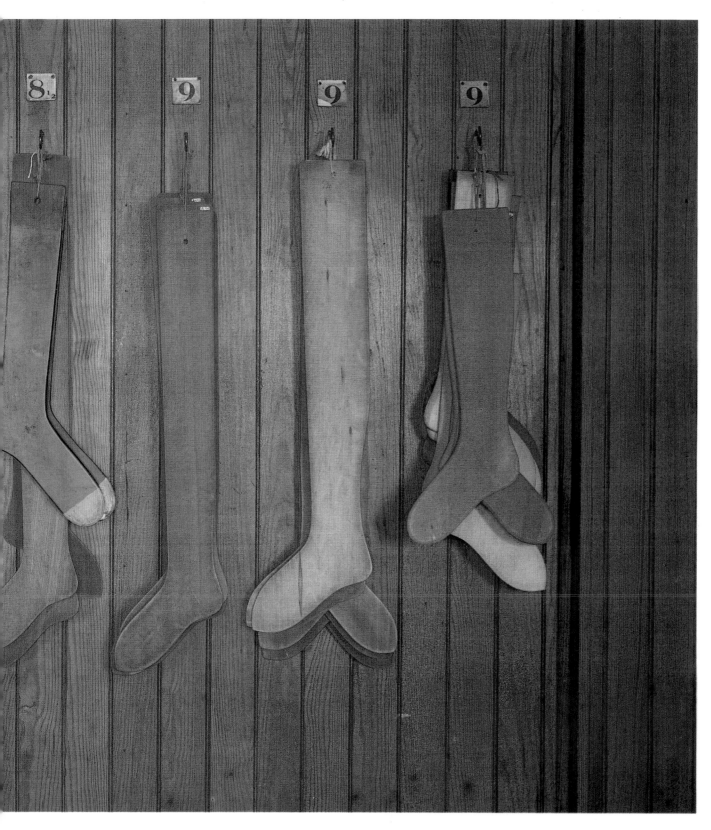

In 1849, Elder Hervey L. Eades (1807–1892) of Union Village, Ohio, and South Union, Kentucky, printed a large illustrated volume on Shaker clothing called *The Tailor's Division System*. It is believed that he sent a copy to each of the eighteen extant Shaker communities for the use of Shaker tailors everywhere. Today, the book is extremely rare. This plate showed tailors how to measure individual Brethren for "coats, vests, frocks, and trowsers."

Uniformity in all matters, including dress, was important to the Shakers. While there was some variety in Believers' work clothes during the week, depending on the kind of work they did, Sunday wear was uniform so that all members of each gender looked alike. Brethren's clothing was usually made by Brethren who were skilled tailors; mending was commonly done by the Sisters. The Millennial Laws of 1845 prudently cautioned Sisters not to mend or "set buttons on Brethren's clothes, while they have them on." Shaker tailoring systems were complex, derived from worldly systems and based on an individual's body measurements to ensure a precise, custom-made fit.

In 1924, Elder Delmer Wilson and the other Shakers at Sabbathday Lake, Maine, participated in the 150th anniversary of nearby New Gloucester with a flourish. According to his diary, the Shaker Family "fixed up banners at church and entered parade at old block House grounds. I got into big carriage wearing old Shaker coat, vest and broad brim hat. Were in parade two hours and no float drew more notice and applause than ours. Cameras were snapping in all directions." One such camera caught Elder Delmer in the traditional Shaker clothing of the century before. The plain coat, loose trousers, and broad-brimmed hat were based on styles popular in the outside world around 1800. By the mid-nineteenth century, such garb looked hopelessly outdated to worldly observers, but the Shakers thought it a waste of time to pursue endless changes of fashion. Although the Shakers have modified their clothing somewhat in the twentieth century, most of today's Shakers dress simply, in styles based on clothing worn by Believers in the last century.

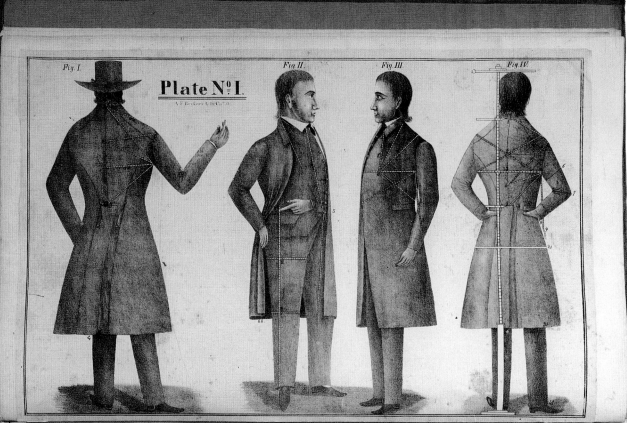

Fig. I.   Plate N.º I.   A. F. Becker's Lith. Co.º 11   Fig. II.   Fig. III.   Fig. IV.

MENSURATION.

DIRECTIONS FOR PLATE No. 1.

Rules of Measurement, for Coats, Vests, Frocks and Trowsers.

SURTOUT MEASURE, SEE FIG. 1.

    Take your tape measure laid off in inches, ¼ths & ⅛ths.
1   Measure from 1 to 3 & 4 as length of coat.*
2   From 2 on back-seam, to the width of back, extend the measure to the elbow, and to the length of sleeve at hand; ☞ have the person to elevate his arm at right angles with the body, incline it a little forward and bend at elbow, sufficiently to determine the middle of elbow.
3   From 1 by front of scye on line A to 1.—This is called the Upper Shoulder Measure.
4   From 2 on back-seam over the shoulder, around by front of scye and back to 2.—This is called the Lower Shoulder Measure.
5   From 1 on line a a. round by front of scye, under the arm to back-seam.—This is called the Proof Measure.
6   From 1 on line a a, by front of scye, and down to waist at fig. 3.—This is called the Balance Measure.
7   Take lapelle measure from 1 over the shoulder or collar bone, extend it down to waist, hold it here with your right hand; with your left bring the upper end forward to collar point, as shown in fig. 2, for vest; then as low down as you wish your skirt to come.
8   Take the size around the breast and waist over the coat, and set down your measure thus: with the name of the customer underneath:

16½, 38—19, 32—(26, 25½)—22, 24—22, 7½, 37—45, 34.
A. B.

  * You will take all your measures over the kind of garment you are going to cut, except the frock, for which you measure over the vest; but in no case be governed by what the person has on, but be governed by your measure, which see to take correctly.

N.B. 1st. Select scales by the upper and lower shoulder measures, enclosed in parenthesis—always put the scale corresponding with the upper shoulder measure in the long arm of the Square, and that of the lower shoulder measure in the short arm. The scale of the upper shoulder measure, is to give the proportions up and down, or lengthwise of the garment; the other scale to give the proportions across the garment.

N.B. 2d. In order to find the right place for fig. 1, throw the tape across the person's neck, after turning up the collar—put your hands under his arms, taking hold of the ends of the tape, and draw it back and forth 2 or 3 inches—then dot with chalk under the edge of tape at fig. 1, for a starting point.

N.B. 3d. If the person's shoulders are not alike, or nearly so, you must measure both, and draft accordingly; and if you have difficulty in finding the centre of back at fig. 2, you will continue the measure round both shoulders, and set down half the measure, as shown on fig. 4; this is the surest plan to obtain the lower shoulder measure correctly, as it is sometimes difficult to find point 2.

JACKET, OR VEST MEASURE, SEE FIG. 2.

    Let the person to be measured take off his coat—you then proceed to take the measure precisely as you do for coat, from 1 to 3 & 4 as length—you do not want sleeve measure.
    Take the shoulder measures as for coat.
    You take Lapelle Measure from 1 on line a, over the shoulder and down to fig. 5; hold the tape at fig. 5 with your right hand, and with your left carry the upper end forward to fig. 6, under the chin; then breast and waist measures, and set down your measure thus: with the name of the person measured underneath:

17, 24—(25, 24½)—21½, 24—22, 6½—36, 33.
A. B.

TROWSERS MEASURE SEE FIG. 2.

    Let the jacket be held back with the right hand, as the frock is; place the top of your measure, or fig. 1 of tape, on the top of hip bone, or as high as you wish the trowsers to extend. Let the person you are measuring, place the forefinger of his left hand on the top of the measure and hold it there, while you with the forefinger feel the crease of the muscle at the thigh bone joint, or "spring of seat;" note the distance as from 1 to 2, and the knee at 3, and bottom of ancle bone at 4. Now take the measure round the waist, hips, thigh, and knee; then set down the measure taken thus, with the person's name underneath:

11½, 24, 41½, (32, (37) 21) 14½.   A. B.

    Now select scales by the waist and thigh measures, place the waist scale (32) in the long arm of the square, and the thigh scale (21) in the short arm, and you are ready for drafting.

FROCK MEASURE, SEE FIG. 2.

    Let the person take off his frock or coat, but keep his vest on; you then commence at fig. 1, or socket bone of neck, and measure down to 44, as length; you then take the upper and lower shoulder measures and length of sleeve, and set down the measure thus:

40—(26½, 26½)—19, 33.   A. B.

    You do not want proof, balance, breast, nor waist measures; proceed to draft as directed under Plate No. 10. You mark the right side of cloth on Frocks.

This fine linen shirt for a Shaker Brother was made at an unidentified eastern community in the mid-nineteenth century. The very long shirttail may have served as a kind of undergarment tucked inside the Brother's trousers, or this may have been a nightshirt. All the workmanship, from the homespun linen thread to the weaving and the stitching, is of the highest quality. The construction shows how straight coat hangers functioned well with traditional tailoring patterns. Note the cross-stitched initials and number near the bottom of the shirt.

The Shakers traditionally did not raise flowers for their beauty, but only for their use in medicines or for culinary purposes. Recalled Sister Marcia Bullard (1821–1899) of New Lebanon, New York:

The rose bushes were planted along the sides of the road which ran through our village and were greatly admired by the passersby, but it was strongly impressed upon us that a rose was useful, not ornamental. It was not intended to please us by its color or its odor, its mission was to be made into rose-water, and if we thought of it in any other way we were making an idol of it and thereby imperiling our souls.

Sister Marcia added that the roses were to be plucked with no stem at all, to avoid the temptation of fastening a fresh rose to a dress for adornment.

Rose petals were gathered and distilled into rose water, which was used medicinally and also as a flavoring in cooking, much as we use vanilla today. Rose water was a traditional ingredient in Shaker apple pies.

In the late nineteenth century and into the twentieth century, the Shakers relaxed their strict rules against ornamental gardens and cultivated beautiful flower beds.

The small but energetic Shaker Family at Sabbathday Lake, Maine, carries on several traditional enterprises, including the raising of sheep for wool and the raising and packaging of herbs and herbal teas. This herb garden abuts the Meetinghouse, visible in the background.

Equipment in the Farm Deacon's Shop at Pleasant Hill, Kentucky,
recalls the Shakers' cultivation of medicinal herbs and plants.
Typical equipment included scales, glass jars, and fine sieves,
woven of silk, to process powdered ingredients. The long wooden
box is cleverly designed with a curved bottom to rock like a cradle,
sending seeds to one end and chaff to the other. The sieves and the
box were made by the Shakers; the other equipment was purchased
in the outside world.

Pharmaceutical equipment used by the Shakers includes a tin stencil for labeling containers of Shaker Hair Restorer—a product that promised to restore original hair color (like a popular modern formula), not to restore missing hair to a balding head! The Shakers, shrewd businesspeople, insisted on honesty in their advertising.

The Shakers in several communities were well known for their pharmaceutical industry. Believers raised dozens of varieties of medicinal plants in gardens of up to ten acres, and also gathered wild roots and barks from the surrounding woods and meadows. The plants were processed into extracts or were dried and pressed into small blocks that were wrapped in paper and sold. "They take great pains in drying and packing their medical herbs, and so highly are they valued that they have frequent orders for them from Europe to a very large amount," noted a visiting Yale professor in 1832. In addition, the Shakers also prepared medicines, including Tamar Laxative, a product of Sabbathday Lake, Maine, and Corbett's Syrup of Sarsaparilla, from Canterbury, New Hampshire.

One of twenty "retiring rooms," or dormitory-style bedrooms, in the Church Family Dwelling at Hancock, Massachusetts, shows typical features: wall pegboards, built-in cupboards and drawers, large windows, plain pine floors, and white plaster walls. The furnishings are similarly distinctive—unadorned, yet designed with care and sensitivity to line and form. The legs of the drop-leaf table splay slightly, as much for visual reasons as for the additional sturdiness; the legs of the candlestand flow in a graceful, streamlined echo of their worldly Chippendale roots; and the rocker's proportions are appealing. All the furniture was made at Hancock or nearby New Lebanon, New York, between about 1825 and 1850.

The Shakers prepared many of their own medicines from herbal
ingredients for home use and for sale. Medicines came in liquid,
powder, or pill form. This beautifully crafted device was used to
make pills. By spreading a stiff medicinal paste on the grooved
metal plate and sliding the crossbar forward and back, the worker
sliced the paste into strips, which were then cut into individual
pellets and dried. This exceptionally handsome pill maker was used
at New Lebanon, New York, in the early nineteenth century. It may
well have been bought from the outside world.

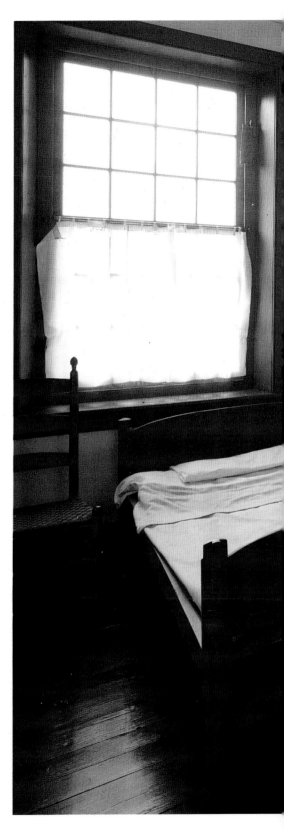

Each Shaker community had at least one infirmary, or Nurse Shop, where skilled Shaker physicians and nurses provided nearly all medical care. In times of emergency, the Shakers did not hesitate to call in a worldly doctor, but they were able to handle a wide range of services, from dentistry to appendectomies. When Shaker treatment did not relieve the complaints of aging Elder Grove Wright (1789–1861) of Hancock, Massachusetts, he let concerned Believers talk him into seeking relief at the "Water Cure establishment" at Saratoga Springs, New York, in 1860. "The first week appeared rather favorable for me, but after that, rather lost ground," reported Grove. "The Dr. thought, however, that if I would stay 6 or 8 weeks, he could cure me up." Added the Elder: "He probably thought I had money enough to last about that length of time."

In this room at Hancock, Massachusetts, specialized medical equipment includes, from left to right, a unique hospital bed, with cam arrangements to raise or lower the head or foot; a pair of crutches; and two adult-sized cradles for gently rocking weak or aged invalids. The movement was soothing, and it probably helped to prevent bedsores. Such cradles were not a Shaker innovation, but were adapted from worldly traditions.

226

Dairying was an important part of the Sisters' work in most Shaker communities. In a corner of the Sisters' Shop at Hancock, Massachusetts, tin milk pans and a large wooden butterworker occupy a corner of the Buttery. After letting cream rise to the top of the milk pans, the Sisters skimmed it off and churned it into butter. The grooved rolling pin in the butterworker pressed out any last traces of buttermilk to keep the butter from turning rancid. In 1863, one Hancock Sister noted the total amount of butter made in April, May, and June—875 pounds.

The Shakers made their own cheese. The addition of a piece of calf's stomach to heated milk produced curds and whey. Large, hexagonal open-weave baskets like these were lined with cheesecloth and filled with curds to let the whey drain off. At left, a cheese press—used to compress curds into round wheels of cheese. which were removed and stored for curing—stands on the floor.

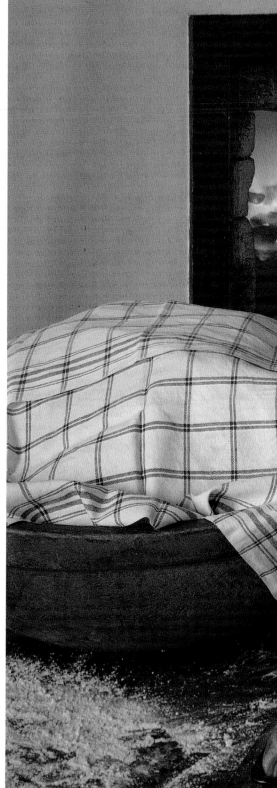

Shaker Sisters cooked in quantities that seem enormous compared with those of ordinary households. Dozens of loaves of bread were required weekly for communal Families of up to a hundred members. The size of the wooden bowl, here filled with rising bread dough, is typical. The flat wooden paddle on the wall is a peel, used to slide bread pans in and out of the deep brick oven.

Shaker women took turns in the kitchen, in shifts that averaged about four weeks. After their term, they went to other workshops to do other work. The large, cheerful kitchens must have been appealing to other Brethren and Sisters, because the Millennial Laws of 1821 offered these reminders:

All are forbidden to throng the kitchen or to go into it unnecessarily while the cooks are employed in it. Let no one attempt to instruct the cooks in their duty, nor undertake to represent the feelings of others, except those trustees whose business it is to direct them in their management of kitchen concerns.

230

A wooden firkin hanging in the Center Family Dwelling at Pleasant Hill, Kentucky, reveals the maker's concern for utility and grace. The container, designed to hang neatly from the pegboard, was used in the Dairy for pouring milk. The edges are flared at the sides to prevent spillage. The firkin was made by a cooper from wooden staves like a pail or barrel, joined, and held in place with wooden bands (the upper band was replaced long ago with a metal strip).

232

Preparing a chicken dinner for a communal Family of up to a hundred members required considerable advance time to kill, pluck, truss, and roast the bird. "We pick 35 chickens after breakfast," reported a Sister on kitchen duty in 1835, "& make some frost grape sauce." This chicken was roasted in a tin reflector oven, set before a hearth of glowing coals, and turned slowly with the handle connected to the spit. Near it are a tin colander and a stoneware preserving jar topped with a piece of tied cloth.

Shaker kitchen gardens—which might be as large as five acres—produced a wide variety of fresh vegetables for Shaker Families. The Shakers in several communities also developed considerable skill in preserving fruits and vegetables and making condiments, including applesauce, horseradish, and ketchup.

In 1843, the Shakers in New Lebanon, New York, printed *The Gardener's Manual* to share some of their know-how with the outside world, through "plain instructions for the selection, preparation, and management of a kitchen garden, with practical directions for the cultivation and management of some of the most useful culinary vegetables." The manual also served the purpose of advertising the New Lebanon Shakers' extensive and highly successful business of selling garden seeds; it included a list of seventy-four varieties, from "Asparagus, Giant" to "Turnip, Ruta Baga." The manual concluded with a few recipes for cooking and pickling garden produce. Perhaps its most valuable message was also its simplest: "The garden is said to be an index of the owner's mind." The neatness and fruitfulness of their gardens testified to the Believers' spiritual values.

Lemon pie—an extraordinarily rich concoction of sliced lemons and sugar in a crust—is a traditional Shaker recipe from Kentucky and Ohio. Shaker cooks prepared dozens of pies to serve to their large communal Families. In 1869, two Sisters at Watervliet, New York, recorded the results of their baking for a single month: "Made pies the first week 166, next 152, next 163, next 139, total 620." The two-pronged fork with the wooden handle is a pie lifter, for handling and moving hot pie plates.

OHIO LEMON PIE

Slice 2 lemons as thin as paper, rind and all. Place them in a yellow bowl and pour over them 2 cups sugar. Mix well and let stand for 2 hours or better. Then go about making your best pastry for 2 crusts. Line a pie tin with some. Beat 4 eggs together. [Alternate layers of lemon and sugar in an unbaked pie shell, then pour beaten eggs over all. Add top crust and cut small vents to let out steam.] Place in a hot oven [450° F.] for 15 minutes and then cut down heat [to 400° F.] and bake until tip of a silver knife inserted into custard comes out clean.

238

Angel food cakes were prepared in the kitchen of the Center Family Dwelling at Pleasant Hill, Kentucky, according to a traditional recipe. The first years in many Shaker communities were difficult, as large numbers of people struggled to produce enough to eat on what had been single-family farms. An aged Sister at Hancock, Massachusetts, later recalled the privation of her youth in the late eighteenth century:

Our food was very scanty, but what we had we ate with thankful hearts. For breakfast and supper, we lived mostly upon bean porridge and water porridge. Monday morning we had a little weak tea, and once a week a small piece of cheese. Wheat bread was very scarce; and when we had butter it was spread on our bread before we came to the table. Our bread was made chiefly of rye and Indian meal [cornmeal] mixed together. Our dinners were generally boiled. Once in a while we had a little milk, but this was a great rarity.

She concluded, "When I look back to those days, and then to the fullness with which we are blessed, it fills me with thankfulness."

The bounty of later nineteenth-century Shaker tables became well known to visitors and beggars. In 1886, a visitor to Hancock enjoyed a lunch of cold beef, white bread, brown bread, butter, boiled rice, baked beans, blackberry jam, blackberry pie, potato cake, apple pie, milk, pickles, cream cheese, cottage cheese, cake, and doughnuts—for a bill of 25 cents, cheap even at that time. He added that the cooking was "worthy of Delmonico's," a fashionable New York eatery.

The griddle and deep fryer in the Church Family Dwelling at
Hancock, Massachusetts, was a modern novelty when it was new.
With this equipment, the Sisters prepared pancakes, doughnuts,
fritters, and other treats. It was heated with wood fires in the
fireboxes behind the two small doors in the iron front.

The large brick oven in the Church Family Dwelling at Hancock, Massachusetts, accommodated dozens of loaves of bread or pies for a communal Family of nearly a hundred. In traditional fashion, the oven was readied for baking by building a fire inside. When the wood had burned to coals and the bricks were thoroughly heated, the ashes were scraped out, and the bread or pies were placed inside to bake. Since the heat could not be adjusted, cooks had to rely on experience to bake properly without burning or undercooking. A nineteenth-century Shaker recipe gives some idea of the quantities prepared:

Soft Ginger Bread

4 qts of Molasses, 2 [ditto] New Milk, 30 Eggs.
6 tablespoonfulls of ginger, 12 teaspoonfulls of pearlash, 10 cups of butter, [mix] about as thick as batter.

SPIRITUAL LIFE AND WORSHIP

THE SHAKERS' RELIGION WAS NOT A ONCE-A-WEEK
affair, but something to be put into practice in every part of their daily
lives. As one Believer pointed out, "A man can show his religion as
much in measuring onions as he can in singing glory hallelujah."
Nevertheless, Sundays were special. This day was devoted to Family
worship services and to private meditation. Mother Ann had insisted
on setting aside mundane thoughts and tasks on the Sabbath, in order
for Believers to fully reacquaint themselves with their higher purpose.
In 1780, she told one prospective convert, "You must never cut your
nails, nor scour your buckles, nor trim your beard, nor do any such
thing on the Sabbath, unless in case of great necessity." By sundown
on Saturday, all workshops were cleaned and put into order, all food
was prepared for the simple Sunday meals, and all sins and troubles
were confessed to the Elder or Eldress. Sunday was a day to
refresh the spirit.

Of all that was remarkable about the Shakers in the eyes of the World,
their method of worship distinguished them most. Instead of sitting
quietly in church, listening to a minister preach, the Shakers all
joined in dance, men on one side of the room, and women on the
other, marching in unison to the sound of unaccompanied voices
raised in song. While most visitors could understand the concepts of
celibacy and communalism—after all, there *were* unmarried people in
the outside world, and large nineteenth-century households and
extended families experienced something akin to communalism—no
one in the outside world got up in church and danced. It simply
wasn't done. Outsiders were scandalized, amused, and usually
critical. "Senseless jumping," declared Ralph Waldo Emerson, "this
shaking of their hands, like the paws of dogs." James Fenimore
Cooper sniffed, "It is scarcely possible to conceive anything more
ludicrous, and yet more lamentable." An English lady described what
she witnessed as a "swinging step somewhat between a walk and a
dance," while the Shakers flapped their hands with "a penguin kind
of motion."

To the Shakers, however, the unconventionality of their worship was its blessing. The dance gave them a vivid sense of "union," clearly visible in the uniform movements of hands and feet. Besides, the dance had its origins in the worship of Mother Ann and the early Believers, known in England as the "Shaking Quakers" because of the movements they made when under the influence of the Holy Spirit. In America, the first Believers experienced the same kind of manifestations. The first eyewitness description of Shaker worship, in 1780, reveals a powerful spiritual and physical energy:

> One will stand with his arms extended, acting over odd postures, which they call signs; another will be dancing, and some times hopping on one leg about the floor; another will fall to turning round, so swift, that if it be a woman, her clothes will be so filled with the wind, as though they were kept out by a hoop; another will be prostrate on the floor. . . . They have several such exercises in a day, especially on the Sabbath.

After the death of Mother Ann, Father Joseph Meacham had another inspiration. Instead of individual manifestations, he had a vision of a more orderly kind of worship. The "Hosts of Heaven" appeared to him, performing the simple, shuffling steps that the Shakers called "laboring." With this revelation, the true Shaker dance began. Later, Mother Lucy Wright encouraged Believers to speak out in meetings, sharing testimonies about their faith, and to sing lively hymns and anthems. Simple dance steps were added, including the "Square Order" and the "Sacred March."

By the early nineteenth century, the Shaker Sabbath had settled into a comfortable routine. Believers rose a little later than on weekdays and dressed themselves in their Sunday clothes. While work clothes varied with each Shaker's occupation, Sunday dress was strictly uniform, all Brethren attired exactly alike in striped trousers, white shirts, and blue vests; all Sisters, in white cotton gowns. In winter, Sisters wore dark gowns of "cotton-and-worsted," a blend of cotton and wool; Brethren similarly changed to their warmer winter dress of the same cloth. All Believers made the switch on the same day, to maintain uniformity.

Sunday breakfast was a simple meal, as were all meals on the Sabbath—perhaps baked beans or bread or other foods that could be prepared ahead of time. Worship meetings followed breakfast and noon dinner. The afternoon meeting was public, so visitors from the World could hear the message of Mother Ann firsthand. Depending on the weather and the season, each Family might stay at home to worship in its dwelling's meeting room, or it might join the other Families in the Meetinghouse. During cold or wet weather, Families usually stayed at home to worship by themselves. In the Meetinghouse, worldly spectators sometimes outnumbered the Shakers. When the new Meetinghouse at New Lebanon, New York, was dedicated in 1824, 500 Believers and 1,000 "World's people" filled the large hall. Even smaller communities attracted large crowds. In 1874, the Shakers at Sabbathday Lake, Maine, hosted more than 500 onlookers—so many that they did not all fit inside the room, and a "gaping crowd" surrounded the Meetinghouse to peer in through the windows.

The rest of the Sabbath was for private devotions. Believers did not go to their workshops or outdoors, but remained quietly in the dwelling, passing the day in companionship and rest.

Besides Sunday, other days of the year were regarded as holy. Thanksgiving was not originally a day of feasting among Believers, but a day for setting things right. On Thanksgiving Day, 1834, a New Lebanon Brother explained, "To day we keep according to the general custom of Believers, that is to clean up dirty places." Similarly, Christmas was a day for setting personal matters right, for "putting away hard feelings" in order to increase love and union in the community. Mother Ann's birthday—Leap Day by tradition, but celebrated on February 28 or March 1 as well—was like Christmas, a special day to recall the good example of the first Shakers.

By the 1830s, Shaker worship services had become a well-established American tradition. But in 1837, an event occurred that was to change Shaker life profoundly over the following two decades. At Watervliet, New York (Mother Ann's first Shaker home), two young Shaker girls began to receive communications from the spirit world. The phenomenon spread to other communities, as young people saw and spoke with angels and departed Believers, or received sacred songs in their dreams. It did not trouble the Ministry that the first evidence of "Mother Ann's work" appeared among the young. After all, Mother Ann had told her followers to be as simple and innocent as children. Soon, adults were also receiving messages, or "gifts," of song, new dance movements, and visions. Some Believers even received precious objects—balls of gold, shining lamps, gowns of silver cloth—no less "real" because they belonged to the spirit world and were visible only in the imagination.

Within a few years, the nature of Shaker worship and daily life had been transformed. As in the earliest years of Shaker life, individuals experienced widely varying "gifts." The Shakers were especially pleased when the mediums received messages from "primitive" spirits, who could thus be introduced to Mother Ann's message of salvation. In 1842, the Shakers at New Lebanon welcomed visits from "the Natives," or the spirits of an Indian chief and his tribe; the "Ice Landers"; the Arabs; and some Africans.

The Shakers in each community were instructed by divine revelation to establish outdoor "feast grounds," or holy places, to be marked with an engraved stone. Each Shaker village received a spiritual name—New Lebanon became "Holy Mount"; Hancock, Massachusetts, was known as the "City of Peace"; Sabbathday Lake, Maine, took the name "Chosen Land." By 1842, Shaker worship services had become so unpredictable that public services were suspended for three years, so that the Shakers could experience revelations without interruptions or distractions. (Charles Dickens, one of the first visitors to be denied entry, was keenly disappointed and was forced to base his derogatory remarks about Shaker worship on a popular print caricaturing the Shakers' dancing.)

The period of "Mother Ann's work" brought mixed blessings to the Shakers. Many sincerely inspired Believers contributed richly to a revival of the original Shaker values, especially simplicity, that were in danger of being forgotten as the Society grew increasingly prosperous. Talented Believers created a loving, beautiful legacy of songs and drawings. Older Believers in particular welcomed the revelations as a means of teaching the younger generation about the goodness of Mother Ann and the early Shakers. With the steady loss of "Mother Ann's first-born"—those who had known Mother Ann personally—the influence of Mother Ann, Father Joseph, Mother Lucy, and other bygone, beloved members was sorely needed.

But some individuals found an opportunity to turn circumstances to their own benefit by faking messages. Individuals who sought attention, who wanted power over their fellow members, or who were simply troublemakers could seriously disrupt Family harmony. One young Brother at Enfield, New Hampshire, pretending to be speaking in tongues, was found to be swearing in Latin. In 1850, Elder Freegift Wells confessed to questioning some revelations after a similarly bad experience. "I once swallowed down without doubting everything that came in the shape of a message from the heavens," he wrote. "But after a while I got confounded by receiving a message in the name of Mother Ann, which I knew was a positive lie! From that time I found it necessary to be more on my guard."

The revival faded in the 1850s, some twenty years after its beginning. Believers ceased marching to the feast grounds. The engraved stones were buried, and the sacred "gift drawings" were hidden away and eventually forgotten.

Shaker worship services underwent more change in the years after the Civil War. By the late nineteenth century, services consisted mostly of singing and speaking, and the dances were discontinued. Shakers in most communities began to gather in the Family meeting rooms in the dwellings instead of assembling in the Meetinghouse. As membership dwindled, and Families and then entire villages ceased to exist, the Shakers entered the twentieth century with quiet devotions. Although the public was still welcome to attend services, fewer and fewer visitors came.

Thomas Hammond, Jr. (1791–1880), was an especially gifted
member of the Shaker community at Harvard, Massachusetts. An
Elder of the Church Family, he also served as foreman of a chair-
making enterprise. He made, or was given, this clever five-pointed
ivory-handled pen to draw a musical staff with less effort.

Many Shakers composed sacred songs under what they believed was
divine inspiration. Such "gift songs" were created by the thousands.
The Shakers did not use musical instruments until late in the
nineteenth century, originally believing that the unaccompanied
human voice was properly simple and all that was necessary to
make music. From the mid-1830s through the 1880s, the Shakers
created a distinctive system of musical notation that did away with
the traditional staff altogether, using only letters of the alphabet and
other simple markings to designate timing.

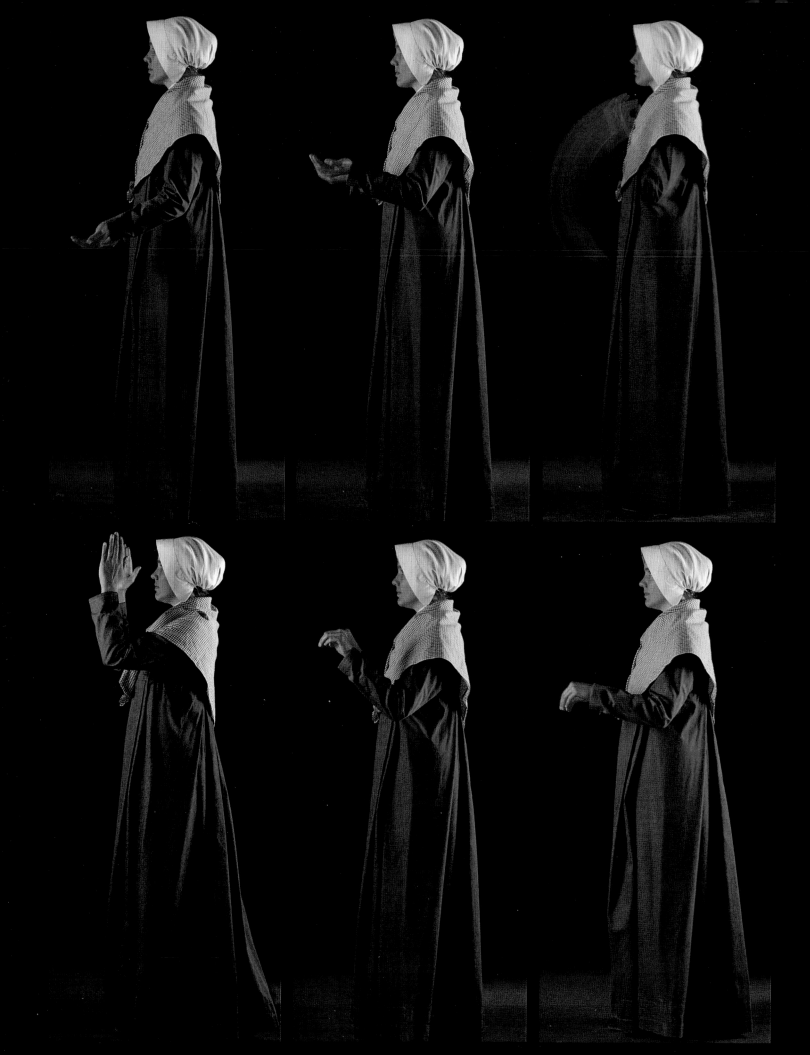

A museum interpreter in reproduction Shaker dress demonstrates the basic hand movements in the Shaker dance worship. With palms up and arms raising, she "gathers" blessings from her Brothers and Sisters. With palms down and arms lowering, she "dispenses" blessings. The most common Shaker dance was a very simple forward and backward stepping movement. Lines of Brothers and Sisters faced each other in the meetinghouse and moved in unison to the sound of singers' unaccompanied voices. The effect on visitors, who were welcome to attend worship for nearly all of Shaker history, was strong and varied. Some found the dances ludicrous; others admired the spirit of union that was so forcibly demonstrated as all Believers moved as one.

Shaker dancing began officially in the 1790s,. when Father Joseph Meacham (1742–1796) instituted the dance as a more orderly alternative to the earlier Believers' manifestations of the Holy Spirit, including leaping, whirling, and shaking or trembling. Shaker tradition records that Joseph, although "entirely lacking in natural ability for the movements and exercises employed in worship," nevertheless devoted himself so earnestly to practicing—wearing the floorboards in his room smooth in the process—that eventually "he became endowed with such ability and grace that he seemed to exercise more like a spirit than a human being." No doubt his perseverance was inspirational to others.

The costume here, reproduced from mid-nineteenth-century originals, shows how completely the cap, neck kerchief, and straight gown conceal the figure—an intentional effect for the sake of modesty and celibacy. Fashionable visitors found both Brethren and Sisters hopelessly unstylish. Humorist Artemus Ward referred to one Sister as a "last year's bean-pole stuck into a long meal bag." In their turn, the Shakers ridiculed the fickle outside world, which seized on new fashions with every passing year.

overleaf:
The Center Family at Pleasant Hill, Kentucky, gathered on week nights to worship in the airy meeting room attached to the dwelling. The coved roof is unusual in Shaker architecture, although it may have been inspired by the curved roof of the 1824 meetinghouse at New Lebanon, New York. The arched transom window over the door is also unusual. The meeting room faces east and west, so it is filled with light all day long. When the Brethren and Sisters gathered to worship, they sat on portable benches or perhaps brought their ladder-back chairs from their "retiring rooms."

253

The Meetinghouse at Canterbury, New Hampshire, built in 1792,
was the first building raised jointly by members of the newly
established Shaker community. According to records, it was built in
reverent silence, with no talking louder than a whisper.

In the background is the Church Family Dwelling, begun in 1793.
Although it has been added to and improved many times in its
nearly two centuries of existence, the basic original structure
survives, making this the only Shaker Dwelling that includes
portions of its original eighteenth-century structure. (More
commonly, Shakers simply replaced their original dwellings with
larger, more modern quarters in the nineteenth century.) As it exists
now, the dwelling has about fifty rooms. The belfry, with a Paul
Revere bell, was the subject of some consternation in 1837, when
the visiting Ministry from New Lebanon, New York, found its
appearance too worldly. To conform to acceptable Shaker standards,
the Canterbury Brethren cut down the cupola by five feet and five
inches to give it a more "modest" appearance. Today, the Dwelling
is still used as a Shaker residence by Sister Ethel Hudson and her
cats. The two other Shaker Sisters at Canterbury share another
building.

The Meetinghouse fence at Sabbathday Lake, Maine, duplicates the prototype built at New Lebanon, New York, in 1841. An identical fence also remains in front of the Meetinghouse at Canterbury, New Hampshire. These fences illustrate the earnest desire of Shakers in all communities to follow the pattern of the society at New Lebanon, thought to be guided by divine inspiration.

Across the street in the background is the Church Family Dwelling, begun in 1883 and finished in 1884. The first meal served there was Thanksgiving dinner, 1884. The new dwelling replaced the original 1795 dwelling, which was moved from its original site with the help of more than thirteen yoke of oxen. The Church Family continued to live in its old home until the new structure was ready.

Beginning in 1837, the Shaker society experienced a wave of religious revivalism known as "Mother Ann's work." The purpose was to guide Shakers back to the example of Mother Ann and the earliest Believers to regain true simplicity and spirituality. During this period, Shakers received many "gifts" from the spirit world—messages and visions from angels, departed Shakers, and other revered figures, including even George Washington. Many messages came from the "Heavenly Father" and his female counterpart, "Holy Mother Wisdom," the Shakers' mother-father Godhead.

Several dozen "gift drawings" from the 1840s and 1850s reveal the inspiration of individual Believers. This drawing, featuring the "wings" of both heavenly Parents, is one of a series of nine similar drawings done in 1845 to 1847, possibly the work of Sister Sarah Bates (1792–1881) of New Lebanon, New York. According to the handwriting on the drawing, this represented "A Holy & Sacred Roll, sent from Holy & Eternal Wisdom brought by her message bearing dove to those who do, or may hereafter reside in the holy Sanctuary at Holy Mount." The vision was "given" in 1845 and "copied" in 1846. The detailed emblems and detailed inscriptions include a clock, trumpet, table, and lamp and five heavenly trees belonging to Mother Ann, her brother Father William, her faithful friend from England Father James, and her American followers Father Joseph and Mother Lucy—all figures of importance in the founding of Shakerism. Such drawings, haunting and mysterious today, are reminders of a time when the Shakers spoke with angels and saw Heaven in their dreams.

258

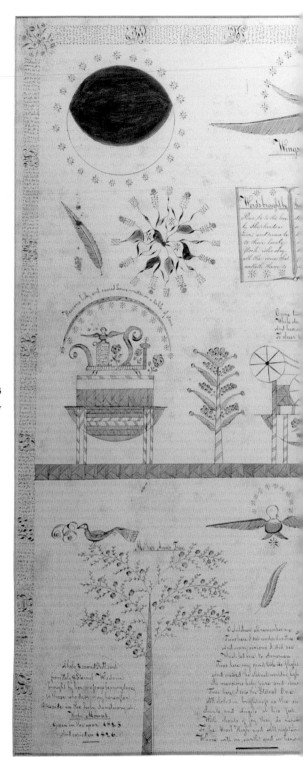

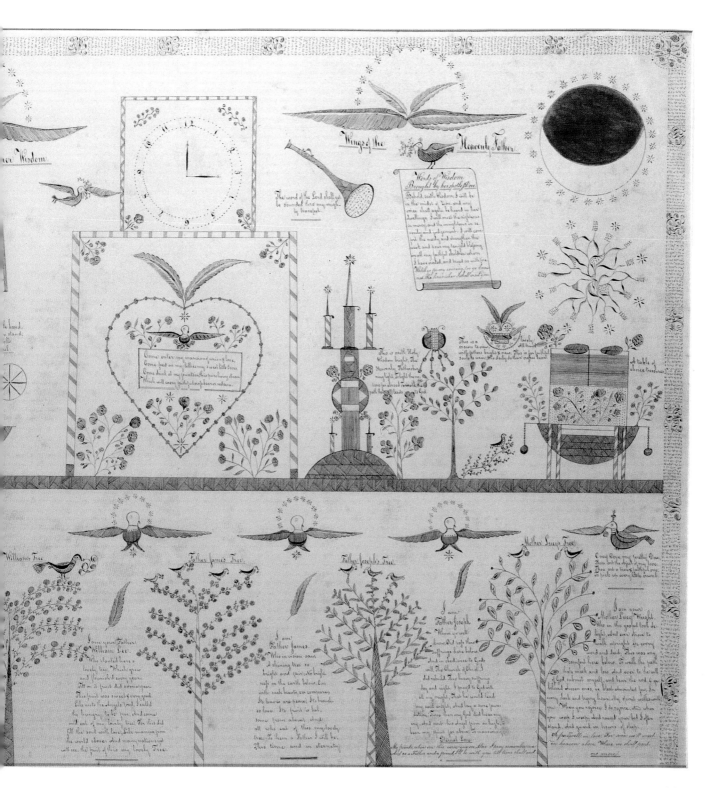

259

An Emblem of the Heavenly Sphere, attributed to Sister Polly Collins (1801–1884) of Hancock, Massachusetts, represented "A Present from Mother Ann," given in January 1854. The artist depicted her notion of Heaven, with forty-eight smiling saints and early Shaker leaders seated in neat ranks and all wearing traditional Shaker clothing. Mother Ann Lee, her brother William, and her faithful follower James Whittaker appear at the top with Christopher Columbus (whose role as discoverer of the New World, which became the chosen home of the Shakers, may have warranted his presence in such an honored position). Below Mother Ann, the Savior raises his hands in benediction.

The landscape of Heaven is lush with a wide variety of trees, from prosaic apple and peach to the more exotic "Celestial Cherry Tree" and "Tree of Order." Since Shaker villages were thought to be precise replicas of Heaven on earth, it's no surprise that Heaven, in turn, is furnished with simple Shaker furniture—two spindle-back benches, an arched-legged trestle dining table, and a writing desk and straight ladder-back chair.

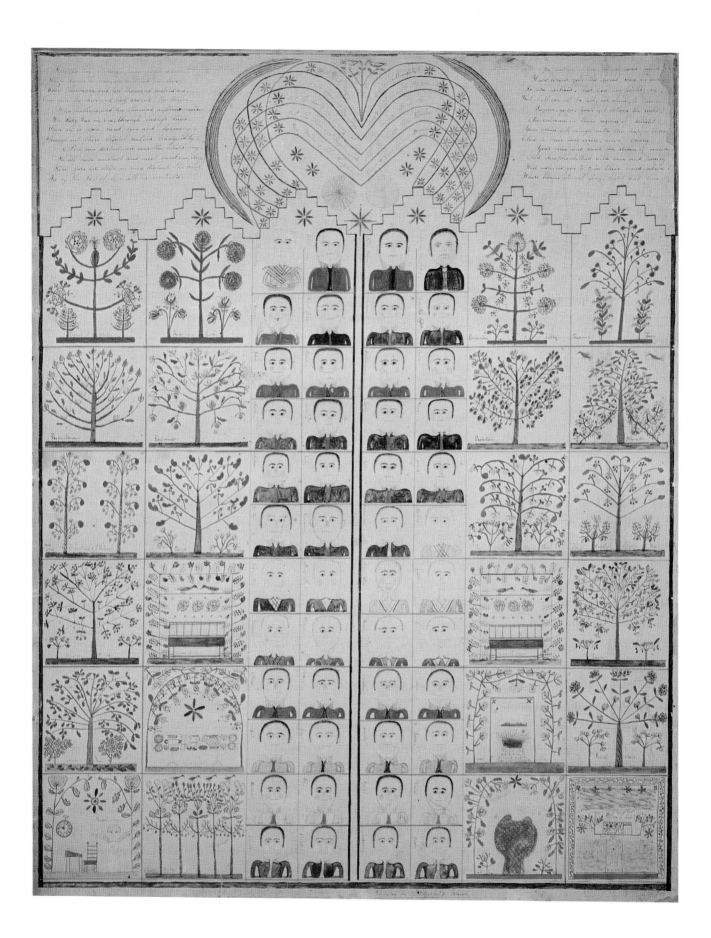

Another drawing attributed to Sister Polly Collins of Hancock, Massachusetts, is *The Gospel Union, Fruit Bearing Tree*, painted in 1855. According to the inscription, the artist's hand was moved when writing the text by the spirit of Elder Joseph Wicker, whose death three years earlier had left the community without one of the most active leaders of "Mother Ann's work" and its spirit manifestations. The tree, with its many varieties of fruit, was seen in the center of the meeting room in the Church Family Dwelling, sent as a gift from "holy Mother" via Elder Joseph's loving spirit.

Come, come my beloved
And sympathize with me
Receive the little basket
And the blessing so free

Sabbath. P. M. June 29th 1856.

I saw Judith Collins bringing a little basket full of beautiful apples, for the Ministry, from Father Calvin Harlow and Mother Sarah Harrison. It is their blessing and the chain around the tail represents the combination of their blessing. I noticed in particular as she brought them to me that ends of the stems looked fresh as though they were just picked by the stems and set into the basket one by one. Drawn and painted in the City of Peace.

by Hannah Cohoon.

Sister Hannah Cohoon (1788–1864) of Hancock, Massachusetts, best known for painting a striking *Tree of Life*, produced three other "gift drawings" that survive. Her last known drawing, *A Little Basket Full of Beautiful Apples*, is one of her most charming. Hannah was sixty-eight years old when she painted it in 1856. Intended as a gift for the Hancock Ministry, it was brought by the spirit of Sister Judith Collins from two of Hancock's most revered early leaders, Father Calvin Harlow (1754–1795) and Mother Sarah Harrison (1760–1796). "It is their blessing," adds Hannah's handwritten inscription, "and the chain around the bail [handle] represents the combination of their blessing."

overleaf:
The interior of the Meetinghouse at Sabbathday Lake, Maine, looks very much as it has for nearly two centuries. The beams retain their original handsome dark-blue paint. Blue paint, which was costlier and therefore more prized than shades like red or yellow, was so much a tradition in Shaker meetinghouses that the Millennial Laws of 1845 stated formally that meetinghouse interior trim should be painted "a blueish shade." To preserve the polished pine floorboards, Believers removed their ordinary shoes and put on cloth slippers for the dance worship. Portable benches, easy to move aside, and a floor uninterrupted by pillars provided a suitable place for the Shakers' impressive dances. Visitors from the outside world frequently commented on the extraordinary condition of the meetinghouse floors. One gentleman found the polished floors "elegant in spite of Shakerdom." An English lady declared one such floor "the best kept and most beautifully polished floor I have seen in this country," and added that spitting boxes for visitors' chewing tobacco were in every corner to prevent spots and stains.

The Sabbathday Lake Shakers still gather in the Meetinghouse to worship on Sundays. Although the Shakers have not included the traditional dance in their services for more than a century, visitors are still welcome to share in the speaking, praying, and singing.

Today, the Shakers in both remaining communities continue the traditions of the Believers who went before them. The Sisters at Canterbury, New Hampshire, observe the Sabbath privately. Primarily because of their age and health, they no longer deem it necessary to gather in the meeting room or Meetinghouse. The small Shaker Family at Sabbathday Lake, Maine, assembles in the Meetinghouse or meeting room. As always, visitors are welcome to share in the service.

As the Shakers stand now, poised on the threshold of their demise or their rebirth, they surely ponder their past as well as their future. Although numbers of people allowed the Shaker society to accomplish what it did, it is not ultimately *en masse* that Shakerism is experienced, but individually, in each Believer's spirit. When Mother Ann arrived in America, there were only nine Shakers. As the total number of Shakers in America comes full circle to fewer than a dozen, the strength of the society's existence is not diminished in its most real sense. As long as there is a single Believer, the Shakers believe that their way of life continues, agreeing with the Brother who wrote in 1837:

> Those who're faithful just & true
>
> Firmly speak it—I'll go thro'
>
> And in answer not a few
>
> Firmly say I'll go with you.
>
> Tho' the number in the hive
>
> Should be lessened down to five
>
> I shall of this number be
>
> Then we'll say so let it be.

SELECTED BIBLIOGRAPHY

ANDREWS, EDWARD DEMING. *The Community Industries of the Shakers*. Albany: The University of the State of New York, 1932.

————: *The People Called Shakers: A Search for the Perfect Society*. New York: Dover, 1953.

ANDREWS, EDWARD DEMING, and FAITH ANDREWS. *Religion in Wood: A Book of Shaker Furniture*. Bloomington: Indiana University Press, 1966.

————: *Shaker Furniture: The Craftsmanship of an American Communal Sect*. New York: Dover, 1950.

————: *Visions of the Heavenly Sphere: A Study in Shaker Religious Art*. Charlottesville: The University Press of Virginia, published for The Henry Francis du Pont Winterthur Museum, 1969.

BREWER, PRISCILLA J. *Shaker Communities, Shaker Lives*. Hanover, N.H.: University Press of New England, 1986.

CARR, SISTER FRANCES A. *Shaker Your Plate: Of Shaker Cooks and Cooking*. Sabbathday Lake, Maine: United Society of Shakers, 1985.

GORDON, BEVERLY. *Shaker Textile Arts*. Hanover, N.H.: University Press of New England with Merrimack Valley Textile Museum and Shaker Community, Inc., 1980.

HORGAN, EDWARD R. *The Shaker Holy Land: A Community Portrait*. Cambridge, Massachusetts: The Harvard Common Press, 1982.

KASSAY, JOHN. *The Book of Shaker Furniture*. Amherst: The University of Massachusetts Press, 1980.

LASSITER, WILLIAM LAWRENCE. *Shaker Architecture*. New York: Bonanza Books, 1966.

MEADER, ROBERT F. W. *Illustrated Guide to Shaker Furniture*. New York: Dover, 1972.

MELCHER, MARGUERITE FELLOWS. *The Shaker Adventure*. Cleveland: Press of Case Western Reserve University, 1968.

MILLER, AMY BESS, and PERSIS FULLER. *The Best of Shaker Cooking*. New York: Macmillan, 1970.

MORSE, FLO. *The Shakers and the World's People*. New York: Dodd, Mead, 1980.

MULLER, CHARLES R., and TIMOTHY D. RIEMAN. *The Shaker Chair*. Canal Winchester, Ohio: The Canal Press, 1984.

NEAL, JULIA. *The Kentucky Shakers*. Lexington, Kentucky: The University Press of Kentucky, 1982.

NORDHOFF, CHARLES. *The Communistic Societies of the United States*. New York: Dover, 1966.

PATTERSON, DANIEL W. *Gift Drawing and Gift Song*. Sabbathday Lake, Maine: The United Society of Shakers, 1983.

PEARSON, ELMER R., and JULIA NEAL. *The Shaker Image*. Boston: New York Graphic Society in collaboration with Shaker Community, Inc., 1974.

SPRIGG, JUNE. *By Shaker Hands*. New York: Knopf, 1975.

————: *Shaker Design*. New York: Whitney Museum of American Art in association with Norton, 1986.

SPRIGG, JUNE. PHOTOGRAPHS BY LINDA BUTLER: *Inner Light: The Shaker Legacy*. New York: Knopf, 1985.

WERTKIN, GERARD C. *The Four Seasons of Shaker Life*. New York: Simon & Schuster, 1986.

ACKNOWLEDGMENTS

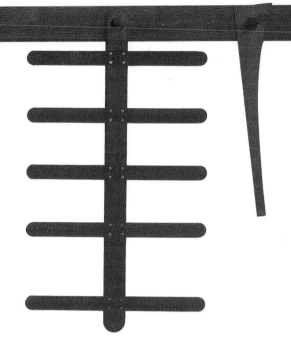

*We are grateful to these institutions
for their generous cooperation:*

Hancock Shaker Village, Pittsfield, Massachusetts

Shakertown at Pleasant Hill, Harrodsburg, Kentucky

Archives, Shaker Village, Inc., and the Canterbury Shakers,
Canterbury, New Hampshire

The Fruitlands Museums, Harvard, Massachusetts

The United Society of Shakers, Sabbathday Lake, Maine

Shakertown, South Union, Kentucky

The Shaker Museum, Old Chatham, New York

Old Sturbridge Village, Sturbridge, Massachusetts

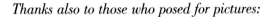

Thanks also to those who posed for pictures:

Cheryl Anderson, dancer, Hancock Shaker Village, Massachusetts

David Lamb, cabinetmaker, Canterbury, New Hampshire

John McGuire, basketmaker, Hancock Shaker Village

Cliff Myers, boxmaker, Hancock Shaker Village

James Higgins and Jack Jenkins, stonecutters, Pleasant Hill, Kentucky

Martha Sue Mayes, cook, Pleasant Hill

Bianca Fiore, herbalist, Hancock Shaker Village

Suzanne MacDonald, shepherdess, Hancock Shaker Village

Thanks also to Roger Hall for information on the Shaker graveyard
in Harvard, Massachusetts; Robert P. Emlen for information on
George Kendall's map of Harvard; Scott Landis for information on
Shaker workbenches; and Martha Wetherbee for information
on Shaker baskets.

INDEX TO PHOTOGRAPHS

Shaker communities and museums welcome visitors. Those who wish to further identify the photographic sources in this book may refer to the page numbers given below.

Composed in Bodoni and Bodoni Book by
Trufont Typographers, Inc., Hicksville, New York.
Printed and bound by Toppan Printing Company, Ltd.,
Tokyo, Japan.

FRANK E.
peretti

piercing
the
Darkness

Living
Books®

TYNDALE HOUSE PUBLISHERS, INC., WHEATON, ILLINOIS

Visit Tyndale's exciting Web site at www.tyndale.com

TYNDALE is a registered trademark of Tyndale House Publishers, Inc.

Tyndale's quill logo is a trademark of Tyndale House Publishers, Inc.

Living Books is a registered trademark of Tyndale House Publishers, Inc.

Designed by Jacqueline L. Noe

Originally published by Crossway Books. Reprinted by permission.

ISBN 0-8423-6372-6; 978-0-8423-6372-3

Printed in the United States of America

10 09 08 07 06 05
11 10 9 8 7

To Gene and Joyce,
my dad and mom,
who gave me my heritage,
and always encouraged me

"The Light shines in the darkness,
and the darkness has not overcome it."

John 1:5, RSV

one

IT could have begun in any town. Bacon's Corner was nothing special, just one of those little farming towns far from the interstate, nothing more than a small hollow dot on the AAA road map, with exit signs that offered gas, no lodging, maybe a little food if the place was open, and little more.

But it began in Bacon's Corner.

It was a normal Tuesday evening. The workday was over, supper was on in most of the homes, the stores were locking up, the tavern was filling up. All the employees at the Bergen Door Company had clocked out, and the security guard was checking the locks. Mr. Myers's son was bringing all the lawn mowers and tillers in for the night at the Myers Feed and Farm Store. The lights were winking out in the local mercantile. Two retirees sat in their chairs in front of the barbershop, putting in their idle hours.

The fields and farms right across the Toe Springs–Claytonville Road were getting warmer and greener with each day, and now the evening breeze was carrying a lot of mid-April smells—apple and cherry blossoms, plowed dirt, a little mud, some cattle, some manure.

It was a normal Tuesday evening. No one expected anything unusual. No one saw or heard a thing. No one could have.

But the commotion started behind a dismal little rented farmhouse just south of Fred Potter's place—a flapping, a fluttering, a free-for-all, and then a cry, a long, eerie shriek, an echoing, slobbering wail that raced into the forest like a train whistle through a town, loud, muffled, loud, muffled, moving this way and that through the trees like a hunted animal; then a flash of light, a fireball, blinking and burning through the forest, moving with blinding speed, right behind that siren, almost on top of it.

More cries and screams, more flashing lights! Suddenly the forest was filled with them.

The trees ended abruptly where the Amhurst Dairy began. The chase broke into the open.

First out of the forest came a bug, a bat, a black, bulb-eyed thing, its dark wings whirring, its breath pouring out like a long yellow ribbon. It just couldn't fly fast enough, but clawed the air with its spidery arms, desperate for speed and shrieking in total panic.

Right behind it, so close, so dangerously close, the sun itself exploded out of the forest, a brilliant comet with wings of fire tracing a glimmering trail and a sword of lightning outstretched in burly bronze hands.

The black thing and the comet shot into the sky over Bacon's Corner, zigzagging, shooting this way and that like wild fireworks.

Then the forest, like a row of cannons, spewed out more hideous creatures, at least twenty, each one fleeing in utter panic with a dazzling, flaming figure tenaciously on its tail, scattering in all directions like a crazy meteor shower in reverse.

The first demon was running out of tricks and maneuvers; he could feel the heat of the warrior's blade right at his heels.

He spit over his shoulder, "No, turn away, I am going!"

The fiery blade cut an arc through the air. The demon met it with his own and the blow sent him spinning. He corrected with his wings, turned and faced his assailant, shrieking, cursing, parrying blow after blow, looking into the fiery eyes of more power, more glory, more holiness than he'd ever feared before. And he could see it in those eyes—the warrior would never turn away. Never.

The demon withered even before the blade struck its final blow; it slipped from the earth, from the world of mankind, into outer darkness, gone in a tumbling puff of red smoke.

The warrior turned and soared higher, spinning his long sword above his head, tracing a circle of light. He burned with the heat of battle, the fervor of righteousness.

His fellows were consumed with it, striking demons from the sky like foul insects, vanquishing them with strong swords, relentlessly pursuing them and hearing no pleas.

On the right, a long, slithering spirit took one more swipe at his heavenly assailant before curling tightly in anguish and vanishing.

On the left, a loud-mouthed, boasting imp cursed and taunted his opponent, filling the air with blasphemies. He was quick and confident, and just beginning to think he might prevail. His head went spinning from his body while the proud sneer still twisted the face, and then he was gone.

There was one left. It was spinning, tumbling on one good wing.

"I'll go, I'll go," it pleaded.

"Your name?" ordered the angel.

"Despair."

The warrior swatted the demon away with the flat of his blade, and it fled, gone, yet still able to work evil.

And then it was over. The demons were gone. But not soon enough.

"Is she all right?" asked Nathan the Arabian, sheathing his sword.

Armoth the African had made sure. "She's alive, if that's what you mean."

The mighty Polynesian, Mota, added, "Injured and frightened. She wants to get away. She won't wait."

"And now Despair is free to harass her," said Signa the Oriental.

Armoth replied, "Then it's begun, and there will be no stopping it."

Sally Roe lay in the grass, clutching her throat and gasping for air, taking long, deliberate breaths, trying to clear her head, trying to think. A raw welt was rising on her neck; her plaid shirt was reddened from a wound in her shoulder. She kept looking toward the goat pen, but nothing stirred there. There was no life, nothing left to harm her.

I have to get moving, I have to get moving. I can't stay here—no, not one more minute.

She struggled to her feet and immediately rested against

3

the farmhouse, her world spinning. She was still nauseous, even though she'd already lost everything twice.

Don't wait. Go. Get moving.

She staggered up the back porch steps, stumbled once, but kept going. She wouldn't take much with her. She couldn't. There wasn't time.

Ed and Mose were quite comfortable, thank you, just sitting there in front of Max's Barber Shop right on Front Street, which is what they called the Toe Springs–Claytonville Road where it passed through town. Ed was sixty-eight, and Mose wouldn't tell anyone his age, so nobody asked him anymore. Both their wives were gone now—God bless 'em, both men had pretty good retirements and Social Security, and life for them had slowed to a comfortable crawl.

"Ain't bitin', Ed."

"You shoulda moved downriver, Mose. Downriver. They get cranky swimmin' clear up to your place. You gotta catch 'em in a good mood."

Mose listened to the first part, but not the second. He was staring at a green Plymouth hurrying through town with two upset children in the backseat.

"Ed, now don't we know those kids there?"

"Where?"

"Well, why don't you look where I'm pointing?"

Ed looked, but all he could see was the back end of the Plymouth and just the tops of two blond heads in the backseat.

"Well," he said, shading his eyes, "you got me there."

"Oh, you never look when I tell you. I know who they were. They were that schoolteacher's kids, that . . . uh . . . what's his name . . ."

Irene Bledsoe sped along the Toe Springs–Claytonville Road, wearing a scowl that added at least a decade to her already crinkled face. She kept her fists tightly around the wheel and her foot on the gas pedal, spurring the green Plymouth onward whether Ruth and Josiah Harris liked it or not.

"You two be quiet now!" she yelled over her shoulder. "Believe me, we're doing this for your own good!"

Bledsoe's words brought no comfort to Ruth, six, and Josiah, nine.

Ruth kept crying, "I want my Daddy!"

Josiah could only sit there silently, numb with shock and disbelief.

Bledsoe hit the throttle hard. She just wanted to get out of town before there was any more trouble, any more attention.

She was not enjoying this assignment. "The things I do for those people!"

Sally stepped out onto the back porch, still trembling, looking warily about. She'd changed her shirt and donned a blue jacket. She gripped her wadded-up, bloodstained plaid shirt in one hand, and a paper towel dipped in cooking oil in the other.

It was quiet all around, as if nothing had happened. Her old blue pickup was waiting. But there was still one more thing to do.

She looked toward the goat pen, its gate swung wide open and the goats long gone. She took some deep breaths to keep the nausea from coming back. She had to go into that little shed once more. She just had to.

It didn't take long. With her heart racing, her hands now empty, and her pockets stuffed, she got out of there and ran for the truck, clambering inside. It cranked and groaned and started up, and with a surge of power and a spraying of gravel it rumbled down the long driveway toward the road.

Irene Bledsoe was speeding, but there were no cops around. The speed limits were inappropriate anyway, just really impractical.

She was coming to a four-way stop, another stupid idea clear out here in the middle of nowhere. She eased back on the throttle and figured she could just sneak through.

What! Where did—?

She hit the brakes, the wheels locked, the tires screamed,

the car fishtailed. Some idiot in a blue pickup swerved wildly through the intersection trying to avoid her.

Little Ruth wasn't belted in; she smacked her head and started screaming.

The Plymouth skidded to a stop almost facing the way it had come.

"Be quiet!" Bledsoe shouted at the little girl. "You be quiet now—you're all right!"

Now Josiah was crying too, scared to death. He wasn't belted in either, and had had quite a tumbling back there

"You two kids shut up!" Bledsoe screamed. "Just shut up now!"

Josiah could see a lady get out of the pickup. She had red hair and a checkered scarf on her head; she looked like she was about to cry, and she was holding her shoulder. Bledsoe stuck her head out the window and screamed a string of profanity at her. The lady didn't say a thing, but Bledsoe must have scared her. The other driver got back in her truck and drove off without saying a word.

"The idiot!" said Bledsoe. "Didn't she see me?"

"But you didn't stop," said Josiah.

"Don't you tell me how to drive, young man! And why isn't your seat belt fastened?"

Ruth was still screaming, holding her head. When she saw blood on her hand, she went hysterical.

When Bledsoe saw that, she said, "Oh, great! Oh, that's just terrific!"

Cecilia Potter, Fred's wife, was glad that one of those fool goats wore a bell. At least she was able to hear something and run out into the yard before they ate up all her flowers.

The two kids bolted and ran back toward the rental home. As for the doe, she thought she owned anything that grew, and she wasn't timid about it.

"You, GIT!" Cecilia shouted, waving her strong arms. "Get out of those flowers!"

The doe backed off just a little, but then lowered her head, giving Cecilia a good look at her horns.

"Oooh, you're really scary!" said Cecilia. She ran right up, clamped an angry fist around the doe's collar, and lifted the doe's front legs off the ground in turning her around.

"You're going back where you came from, and right now, and don't you think you can scare me!" *WAP!* "And you lower those horns right now!"

The doe went with Cecilia, mostly on four legs, but on two if she even dared to hesitate, and got more than two earfuls of sermonizing on the way.

"I don't know how you got out, but if you think you're going to run rampant around here, you've got another think coming! Sally's going to hear about this! She knows better! I'm really surprised . . ."

She crossed the field between the two houses and then saw the goat pen, its gate wide open.

"Sally!" she called.

There was no answer. Hmm. The truck was gone. Maybe Sally wasn't home yet. Well, she was late then. She always came home from work before this. But how did that gate get open?

She dragged the doe alongside her and through the gate.

"Back where you belong, old girl. No more of this free and easy stuff—"

Well . . . who was that in the shed?

"Sally?"

The doe, suddenly free, walked out through the still-open gate. Cecilia didn't follow it.

She was looking at the body of a woman, thrown down in the straw like a discarded doll, limp and white.

She was dead.

Nathan, Armoth, and the other warriors made a low, slow pass over the farmhouse and saw a distraught Cecilia running from the goat pen. Nathan gave the others a signal, and with an explosive surge of their wings they shot forward, etching the evening sky with streaks of light.

The fields below them passed by with the swiftness of a thought, and then the green canopy of the forest swallowed

7

them up, the leaves and branches whipping by, over, around, and through them. They rushed through shadows and shafts of fading light, through tall trunks and thick, entangling limbs, and finally reached the clearing where the captain was waiting.

With wings snapping full like opening parachutes, they came to a halt and settled to the forest floor with the silence of snowflakes. The moment their feet touched down, the lightning glimmer of their tunics faded to a dull white, their fiery swords cooled to copper, and their wings folded and vanished.

Tal, the mighty, golden-haired Captain of the Host, was waiting, his fiery eyes burning with expectation, his face tight with the tension of the moment. Beside him stood Guilo, the Strength of Many, a dark, bearded, massive spirit with thick, powerful arms and a heart yearning for a fight. They were dressed in dull white as well, and wore formidable swords at their sides.

Nathan called his report even as Tal and Guilo were stepping forward to greet them. "All the demons were routed except for Despair."

"Good enough," said Tal. "Let him carry word back to his comrades and then continue his work. Any other spirits from Broken Birch involved in this?"

"Several. Formidable, but defeated for now. We didn't see Destroyer anywhere. He sent his lackeys and stayed out of it himself."

"Of course. Now what of Sally?"

"Sally Roe is fleeing. Her truck is several miles down the road, heading south toward Claytonville. We sent Chimon and Scion to follow her."

"The assassin?" asked Tal.

"Slain, by our hand. We had no choice. Sally was close to death."

Guilo rumbled his approval of the action.

"How is Sally now?" Tal asked.

Armoth reported, "A minor throat injury, a welt on her

neck, a shallow knife wound in the shoulder. No immediate physical danger."

Tal sighed just a little. "No, not immediate anyway. What about the near-collision with Irene Bledsoe?"

Nathan and Armoth looked toward Signa, and the lithe Oriental smiled. "Successful, but by a hair. Ruth Harris suffered a small injury on her forehead, but Sally was clearly seen by everyone in the car, and she saw them just as clearly."

Armoth picked up from there. "And now Mrs. Potter has found the assassin, and she is calling the police."

Tal had to take a moment just to shake his head at the immensity of it all. "Just that is news enough."

Guilo expressed his anxiety with a gravelly chuckle. "Captain, we have never before hoped for so many things to go right . . . that can go so wrong!"

Tal looked toward Heaven and smiled a cautious smile. "We can hope for them all to go right as long as the saints are praying, and they are."

There was a mutter of agreement from all of them. They could feel it.

"So," Tal continued, "if all goes well, this time *we* advance, *we* conquer, *we* set the enemy back . . . *We* purchase just one more season of restraint."

"One more season," they all echoed.

"Sally should arrive in Claytonville safely enough with Chimon and Scion as escorts. The demon Terga has much to answer for now; I expect he'll send some spirits after her to tear her down. Even so, Chimon and Scion have orders not to intervene unless absolutely necessary."

"*More* pain, captain? *More* destruction?" Guilo blurted in anger. "One would think these wretched spirits can never inflict enough suffering!"

Tal looked into those dark eyes, so full of the fire of battle, and yet so tender toward God's elect. "Good friend, we all hurt for her. But her suffering will bring about God's purpose, and you will see it."

"May it come soon," Guilo said, gripping the handle of his

sword. He looked at Nathan and prompted sarcastically, "I'm sure you have more joyful news?"

"Yes," said Nathan. "Of Tom Harris. He is at the police station now, trying to do something to get his children back, trying to reason with Sergeant Mulligan."

At the mention of Mulligan's name, Guilo laughed a roaring, spiteful laugh, and the others made a distasteful face. Nathan only nodded with resignation. They were right.

"So now comes the testing of Tom's faith, a real trying of his commitment," said Tal.

"I'll be watching the saints," said Guilo. "I'll see how they handle this one."

Tal touched Guilo's shoulder. "This will be one of those things we hope will go right."

"Oh, may it go right, may it go right."

"For Tom's sake," said Nathan.

"For *everyone's* sake," said Armoth.

"Which brings us to Ben Cole," Tal prompted.

Nathan responded, "He's about to walk into it right now."

two

officer Ben Cole pulled the squad car into the lot behind the precinct and sat behind the wheel for a moment after the engine was still. It had been a long day, and he was tired. Bacon's Corner didn't have that much heavy action, but today was a little more trying. The trucker he'd stopped for speeding was twice his size and didn't like being one-upped by such a young officer, much less one who was black; Bill Schultz still hadn't contained that dog of his, and now someone else had been bitten; he'd caught the Krantz boy with some pot again, and his parents still wouldn't believe it.

That was the rub with police work—you always had to see the bad side of people, when they were angry, defensive, self-righteous, drunk, drugged . . . *Oh, let it go, Ben. The day's over. There are some good people in the world, really. You just need to get home, have some supper, see Bev. Yeah, that'll make it all right.*

He got out of the car; he was going to write up some quick reports and get home so . . . *Now whose cars are these?* Two strange cars were sitting in the reserved parking spaces, and wasn't that Tom Harris's little station wagon? The office was closed by now; it was too late for visitors. He'd better check it out once he got inside.

He went in the back door and started down the long hall-way that connected the rear offices and cell block to the front office area.

Oh brother, now who's Mulligan hollering at?

He could hear Sergeant Mulligan's voice from clear down the hall, booming through the open door of his office. "So all right, you don't have to tell me anything! Go ahead and lie! You guys always lie, and I'll be happy to listen to that so I can use it against you!"

"Sir, I'm not lying . . ."

Ben stopped in the hall to listen. That other voice sounded familiar.

"So let's have the truth, huh?" said Mulligan. "You've been having yourself a real party with those little kids, haven't you?"

"Sir, *again*, there is nothing going on at the school, or at my home, or anywhere! This whole thing is a terrible mistake!"

Yeah, that *was* Tom Harris's car out there, and this was Tom getting outtalked by the sergeant.

Ben had to look. This conversation was sounding worse all the time. *Lord, please don't let it be what it sounds like. I was just feeling better thinking about the good people in the world.*

He went down the bare hallway to Mulligan's door, and stuck his head in.

"I'm back, Harold." *No big deal, I'm just reporting in, nice and businesslike, just finding out what's going on.*

Ben stood there frozen, looking at the shaken, upset man sitting across the dented, green, metal desk from big Sergeant Mulligan.

Mulligan was in his overweight, ugly glory, and really enjoying this. He always got his kicks from all the wrong things. "Hey, Cole, look what I caught today! Another Christian! I'll bet you two know each other!"

Ben looked confused. "Hey, Tom. What gives?"

"Child abuse!" interrupted Mulligan, proud of the fact, proud of his catch. "Got a real case brewing here."

"Then you know far more about this than *I* do!" Tom said. He looked up at Ben with tear-reddened eyes. "The sergeant here just . . . just *stood* there while some welfare lady came and took away Ruth and Josiah, just dragged them from the house, and . . ." Tom's voice rose in fear and anger. "I want to know where they are."

Mulligan remained as hard as nails and sneered at Ben. "Wait'll you hear what this creep's been doing with some kids at the Christian school."

Tom rose from his seat. "I haven't been doing *anything*! Can't you get that straight?"

"You sit down, buddy!" Mulligan easily outweighed Tom and made every effort to show it.

Ben's heart twisted in his chest. The Christian school? Bacon's Corner only had one—the Good Shepherd Academy, a little first-through-sixth-grade ministry run by—

"I'd say your church is in big trouble!" Mulligan told Ben.

Ben looked down at Tom Harris, one of the gentlest, most godly men he'd ever met. Tom was in his thirties, with dark curly hair and a young face. Ben knew the guy was more than just honest—he was downright vulnerable. *No way, man. Tom Harris didn't do anything.*

"Tom," Ben said gently, "are you aware of your rights?"

"He's not under arrest!" Mulligan snapped. "He came here himself!"

"And I'm not leaving until I get some cooperation!" said Tom.

"Hey, don't come after me," said Mulligan. "The state people have to check this all out."

"So let's call them!" said Ben.

"You get out of this, Cole! You two are friends and everybody knows it. You're not coming anywhere near this case!"

Tom demanded in slow, enunciated words, "I want to see my children!"

"You're talking to the wrong man."

Tom pointed his finger. "You were right there! You abused your authority and let this . . . this Bledsoe woman march right into my house like some kind of . . . gestapo raid! She terrorized my children and invaded my privacy right under your nose!"

Mulligan remained straight and tall in his chair and said firmly and simply, "You watch it, Harris. Ms. Bledsoe had a bona fide court order to pick up your kids in response to a complaint filed against you!"

Tom was flabbergasted. *"What* complaint?"

"I don't know. Ask Bledsoe. That's her department."

"Then you must know how to contact her."

"I'll find out," said Ben.

"Isn't your shift over?" Mulligan roared.

"Yes, sir."

"Then get out of here!"

Ben had to obey. He told Tom, "Give me a call," and turned to leave.

Just then the police radio came to life. The sound of it always froze time in the station as everyone stopped to hear the message. "Bacon's Corner, Bacon's Corner, possible DOA at Fred Potter farm, 12947 197th SW. Aid crew is en route."

Mulligan jumped from his chair, making it rumble backward and smack against the wall. "Where's Leonard—is he here yet?" Then the phone rang. "Nuts! When it rains it pours. Get that!"

Ben hurried to the front desk.

A man and a woman were sitting in the reception area. Ben recognized the man: John Ziegler, reporter for the *Hampton County Star*; he worked the local police beat and hung around the station a lot. The lady was obviously a photographer. Ziegler had a notepad handy, and was apparently scribbling down everything he heard!

The phone rang again.

Ben kept staring at the news-hounds while he grabbed the phone. "Police Department." The voice on the other end was frantic. "Slow down, ma'am, please. I can't understand you." It was Cecilia Potter. She'd already called 911; now she wanted to make sure the police were coming.

Ben knew where their farm was. "We just got the call on the radio. We'll be right there." So much for going home.

The back door opened.

"Here's Leonard now," Ben reported.

Officer Leonard Jackson was reporting in for the night shift. He was a calm, thin, easy-paced sort of guy in his forties, almost a permanent fixture around the place. Mulligan nearly ran over him bursting out of his office.

"Let's move it, Leonard! There's a suicide down at the Potter place!"

"The Potter place?" Leonard had trouble imagining either of the Potters doing such a thing.

Ben was quite unsettled about an additional matter. "What about John Ziegler out there?"

Mulligan looked at the reporters and started cursing, looking this way and that. "Harris! Get out here!"

Tom stepped out of the office, trying to be cooperative.

Mulligan shoved him forward toward the front office. "Have a seat with those nice people—they want to talk to you! Leonard, we'll take your squad car."

Tom looked at Ben for help. "They were at my house today when that lady took the kids. They took pictures of it!"

Ben could feel his temper rising. "Tom, you don't have to say anything to them. Just go right on by them and go home!"

Mulligan must have seen something he didn't like. "Cole, you're coming too!"

Leonard was ready to roll. Mulligan grabbed his hat and jacket. The reporters were on their feet and coming toward Tom.

Ben asked, "Is Tom free to leave?"

Mulligan rolled his eyes at such a question. "Cole, he came in here on his own two feet—he can go out the same way. Hear that, Harris?"

Ben said quietly, "Tom, just get out of here. You don't have to talk to anyone."

Mulligan growled at him, "Are you about ready, Cole? C'mon, let's move!"

Ben didn't like this one bit, but orders were orders. He headed for the back door again.

Mulligan tipped his hat to John Ziegler and the camera lady. "Just make yourselves comfortable. We'll be back in about an hour, and I'll have a statement for you."

Ben told Tom, "I'll call you," then followed Mulligan and Leonard.

Mulligan muttered over his shoulder as they went out to the cars, "I'm not leaving you in there with that Christian buddy of yours, no way. If you're gonna be on duty, you're gonna work, and you're gonna do what I tell you and no static. We don't need you two fanatics having some powwow in there, no sir!"

Tom went back into Mulligan's office for his jacket and then stepped into the hall again.

John Ziegler was standing right in front of him, blocking his path.

"Excuse me," Tom said, trying to get around.

John was insistent on having a conversation.

"John Ziegler, with the *Hampton County Star*—"

"Yes, I saw you at my house," said Tom curtly.

Ziegler asked, "Mr. Harris, what is your response to these allegations?"

"*What* allegations? I don't even know why this is happening to me!"

"Do you think this will hurt the Christian school?"

"I don't know."

"Do you deny any abuse of children in the Christian school?"

That question stopped Tom cold. He was troubled by it.

Ziegler picked up on that. "You do deny the allegations?"

Tom found his voice for that one. "I don't know of any allegations."

Ziegler scribbled it down.

"Has there been any reaction from your family?"

"Besides the fact that my children were terrified?"

The woman began clicking a camera at him.

"Hey, come on, now . . ."

The camera kept clicking.

Ziegler raised an eyebrow. "I understand you're a widower. So you live at home alone with your children?"

Tom was indignant. "That's it! I'm leaving. Good night."

Ziegler threw questions at Tom's back as they followed right behind him toward the front door. "Is the state considering your children as possible victims as well?"

Tom jerked the door open and glared at them for a moment.

The camera caught his angry expression.

Ziegler was satisfied. "Thank you very much, Mr. Harris."

Just across the street, Despair sat on the roof of the Bacon's Corner Library and Gift Shop, a forlorn beanbag of melan-

16

choly filth, whimpering over his wounds and watching the two squad cars speed away.

"Oh, there they go, there they go. What now?"

Several other dark spirits were with him, staying low, muttering, hissing, slobbering in agitation. They were a motley band of tempters, harassers, and deceivers, suddenly half as strong, half as numerous, and full of anguish over the recent, terrible defeat of their comrades.

Despair was living up to his name. "Lost, lost, lost, all is lost! Our best are gone, all vanquished but for me!"

A sharp slap bounced his round head against his shoulder. "Stop that whimpering! You make me ill!"

"Terga, my prince, you were not there!"

Terga, the Prince of Bacon's Corner, resembled a slimy toad with a fright wig of black wire and two rolling, yellow eyes. He was indignant, and kept scratching his gnarled head purely from an itch of frustration. "Failure, that's what it was. An abominable display of ineptitude!"

Murder was quick to object. "Had the mission succeeded, no doubt you would have been the first to praise it!"

"It did not, and I do not!"

Deception tried to objectively assess the debacle. "Our forces were strong, and I'm sure they fought valiantly, but . . . the prayers of the saints are stronger. The Host of Heaven are stronger. They were waiting for our warriors, and they were ready. We severely underestimated their numbers and their power. It's quite simple."

Terga spun around and glared at Deception, hating his words, but knowing the astute demon was quite correct. He paced, he fidgeted, he struggled to comprehend what was happening. "We have moved against Tom Harris and the school! The Plan of the Strongman is unfolding at this very moment. It is underway, right now! But here you are, lamenting a rout and telling me that the Plan could be marching headlong toward destruction, and all because of this . . . this . . . *woman?*"

Deception thought about the question, and then nodded. "That would be a fair assessment."

Terga rolled his eyes toward the sky and wailed his fear and frustration. "Destroyer will have all our hides for this! Those who did not fall in this rout will certainly fall under *his* sword!" He counted the demons around him and came up shorter than he wanted. "Where is Hatred?"

"Gone," they all answered. "One of the first to fall."

"And Violence?"

"In chains in the Abyss, I imagine," said Deception.

"Greed? Lust? Rape?"

He only got forlorn stares. He looked out over the town, and his head just kept twitching from side to side. He could not fathom what had happened. "Such an easy task . . . a simple little murder . . . We've all done it before . . ."

Despair moaned, "When the Strongman finds out . . ."

WAP! Terga bounced Despair's head off his other shoulder.

"He must know!" said Divination.

"Then tell him!" said Terga. "Go yourself!"

Divination fell silent, hoping some other demon would speak up.

Terga snatched a fistful of Despair's baggy hide and held him up like a trophy. "Our envoy!"

They began to cheer, their talons clicking their applause.

"No . . . not the Strongman!" Despair whined. "Is not one thrashing enough?"

"Go now," said Terga, "or the Strongman's will be your *third* today!"

Despair fluttered crazily into the air. One wing was still battered and bent.

"Go!" said Terga. "And be quick about it!" Despair hurried away, whining and wailing as he went. "And when you're through with that, go back to the woman and continue your duty as you should!"

Some snickers caused Terga to spin around. A few small spirits cowered, looking up at him—they'd been caught.

"Ah," said Terga, and they could see the slime on the roof of his mouth. "Fear, Death, and Insanity, three of the woman's favorite pets! You look rather idle at the moment."

The three demons looked at each other stupidly.

"Back to your posts! Follow the woman!"

They fluttered into the air like frightened pigeons, clawing after altitude.

Terga wasn't satisfied. He slapped several more demons with his wings. "You too! All of you! Find her! Torture her! Terrorize her! Do you want Destroyer to think you are the worthless lumps you are? Correct your blunder! Destroy the woman!"

The air was filled with roaring, fluttering wings. Terga covered his head to keep from getting clouted with a wild wingtip. In only moments, they were gone. Terga looked down the street, down the road that would take the squad cars to Potter's farm.

"Our sergeant isn't going to find what he expected," he muttered.

three

IT was getting dark when the two squad cars rumbled down the gravel driveway to the Potters' house. The aid car was already there, its doors flung open, its lights flashing. Fred and Cecilia were out on the wide front porch waiting for the police, holding each other close. They were strong, rugged people, but tonight they were obviously shaken.

Mulligan locked the wheels and slid to an impressive, slightly side-skidding halt in the loose gravel, then bolted from the car in time to emerge like a god from the cloud of dust he'd stirred up. Leonard waited for the dust to blow by before getting out—he didn't want it all over the seat when he got back in the car.

Ben pulled to a careful stop behind the first car and got out in calm, businesslike fashion. He was being overcautious, aware that his emotions were on a thin edge.

Mulligan was already talking with one of the paramedics, getting the lowdown. The paramedic had just come from a little farmhouse across the field. Ben could see two more flashlights sweeping about in the darkness over there. Apart from that, there were no lights.

"Deceased," said the paramedic. "Dead at least an hour."

"Okay," said Mulligan, clicking on his big silver flashlight, "let's go."

He headed into the field, swishing through the wild grass with long, powerful strides, his nightstick swinging from his hip, his belly bouncing on his buckle. Leonard and Ben followed close behind.

"It's that Roe woman," said Mulligan. "Sally Roe. You know anything about her?"

Leonard assumed the question was directed to him. "Very little, Harold."

"I think she's one of those weird types, some kind of left-over hippie, a loser. Guess she decided to end it all."

21

Ben was probing his brain as they continued toward the dark farmhouse. Sally Roe. The name didn't register.

"All right," said Mulligan. "There's the goat pen. Spread out a bit, you guys. No hiding behind me."

They came out of the field, crossed an unused, heavily weeded roadway, and came to the goat pen. The fence was crude and aged, made of rusted wire nailed to split rail posts, with a creaking gate hanging crookedly on one good hinge and one loose one. The gate was still open; all the goats were now corralled over at the Potters'. Two emergency medical technicians were standing outside the pen, putting away their gear.

"She's all yours," said one.

Ben glanced around the pen, shining his light here and there, just checking for anything unusual, not wanting to disturb it. His eye caught a spilled pail of goat feed near the door of the goat shed.

"Hey, check that out," he said, pointing with his light.

Mulligan ignored him and charged right across the goat pen and into the weathered, tin-roofed shed, leaving a big manured footprint in the middle of the spilled feed. Then he stopped short. He'd found something. Leonard and Ben came up behind him and looked in through the doorway.

There she was. The dead woman. Ben couldn't see her face; Mulligan was in the way. But she was dressed all in black, and lay on her back in the straw, her body and limbs twisted and limp as if someone had wadded her up and thrown her there.

Ben shined his light around the inside of the shed. The beam fell on a plaid shirt next to the body. Apparently Mulligan hadn't seen it. He reached in and picked it up. It was stained with blood.

"Hey, Harold, look at this."

Mulligan spun around as if rudely surprised. "Cole! Get back to the Potters and get a statement from them!"

"Yes, sir. But take a look at this."

Mulligan didn't take it—he grabbed it. "Go on, get over there. We can handle things at this end."

Leonard was shining his light at the woman's face and Ben

caught his first glimpse of it. She was young and beautiful, but dead—violently dead. The expression on the face was blank, the eyes dry and staring, the shoulder-length black hair a tangled shadow upon the straw.

Ben didn't know he was staring until Mulligan hollered at him.

"Cole! Have you seen enough? Get moving!"

Ben got out of there, and hurried back across the field to the Potters' house. His mind was racing. This was going to be a bigger case than they'd thought. The appearance of that body, the bloodied shirt, the spilled feed, the obvious violence . . .

This was no suicide.

The aid crew drove away in the aid car, their work completed. Ben put on a calm demeanor as he went up the porch steps. The Potters heard him coming and immediately came to the door.

"Hi. I'm Officer Ben Cole."

Ben extended his hand, and Fred took it.

Fred stared at Ben just a little. "Have we met before?"

"No, sir. I'm new in Bacon's Corner. I've been here about four months."

"Oh . . . well, welcome to the neighborhood. Things aren't usually this exciting around here."

"Of course, sir. Uh, with your permission, I'd like to get a statement."

Cecilia opened the door. "Please come in . . . Ben, was it?"

"Yes, ma'am. Thank you."

Fred and Cecilia took their place on the couch and offered Ben a chair facing them. He took out his notepad.

"How are you doing?" he asked.

"Oh . . . fair," said Fred.

Cecilia just shook her head. "Poor Sally." Tears returned to her eyes. "This is just awful. It's terrifying."

Ben spoke gently. "I . . . understand it was you who first found her?"

She nodded.

"Did you touch her or move her in any way?"

Cecilia was repelled by the very thought. "No. I didn't go near her. I didn't even look at her face."

"About what time was this?"

"About 6."

Ben jotted these items down. "Now, why don't you just tell me everything that happened?"

She started telling him about the goats being out, and about the nanny goat trying to butt her, and then tried to remember what she did to get that goat back to the pen, and then a strong opinion took precedent over her narrative and she blurted, "I think somebody killed her!"

Fred was shocked at that, of course. "What? What gives you that idea?"

Ben had to get control of this. "Uh . . . we'll work on that when the time comes. But for now you need to tell me what you saw . . . just what you saw."

She told him, and it wasn't much different from what he himself had seen. "I didn't want to see her that way. I just didn't stay there."

"Okay. Can you tell me the victim's full name?"

"Sally Roe. She was such a quiet sort," Cecilia said, her face full of grief and puzzlement. "She never said much, just kept to herself. We enjoyed having her for a renter. She was clean, responsible, we never had any trouble from her. Why would anyone want to hurt her?"

"So you can't think of anyone who might . . . have some kind of grievance or grudge against her?"

"No. She was a very private sort. I don't remember ever seeing her having company or visitors."

"Can you think of anything else that may have seemed out of the ordinary?"

"Did you see the feed spilled on the ground?"

"Yes, ma'am."

"Someone may have jumped out and grabbed her."

"Uh-huh. Anything else?"

"I saw a long piece of rope in her hand. Maybe it was to tie the goats, I don't know."

Ben noted it.

There were loud footsteps on the porch. It was Sergeant Mulligan. He let himself in, and removed his hat.

"Well, folks, it's been quite an evening. We've seen a real tragedy here. Got their statement, Cole?"

Ben rose and looked over his notes. "Just what Mrs. Potter saw initially. I suppose—"

Mulligan took the notes from Ben's hand and looked them over.

Ben finished his thought. "I suppose once we check the house and comb the area we'll have more to go on."

Mulligan didn't seem to hear him. "Umm. Okay, I'll get these typed into the report." He pocketed Ben's notes and told the Potters, "Guess she hung herself from the rafters of the shed, who knows why."

"Hung herself?" said Cecilia in surprise.

"How about any suicide notes? Did you find anything like that around?"

Cecilia was still taken aback. "No . . . no, I—"

"Well, we'll be checking the scene over tonight and maybe we'll find something." He headed out the door again. "Cole, go ahead and call it a day. Leonard and I will check the area over and wait for the coroner."

"You say it was a *suicide?*" Ben asked, following him out the door.

"Cut and dried," said Mulligan.

"Well . . . maybe."

Mulligan got impatient with that kind of response. "What do you mean, 'maybe'?"

"Well, you saw what it looked like in there . . ."

"Yeah, I saw it all, and you didn't."

"But Mrs. Potter did. The body wasn't hanging when she found it. It was lying in the straw just like when we first saw it."

Mulligan turned back toward the rental. "Go on home, Cole. Don't worry about things that aren't your responsibility."

Mulligan headed across the field, cutting the conversation short. Ben went back to his car and sat in it with the door open, flipping through his notepad. He clicked his pen and started scribbling some notes to himself, things he wanted to remember: "plaid shirt with blood . . . position of body suggests violence . . . spilled feed . . . rope in hand, not around neck . . . victim not hung . . ."

Just outside Claytonville, Sally turned off the highway onto an obscure, overgrown and rutted road that meandered deep into the forest, winding around trees and stumps, passing under low limbs, dipping into black mudholes, and making the old pickup buck and rock with every new pothole, rut, bump, and turn. This road—or maybe it was a trail—had probably been used by surveyors and developers, but now was kept in existence only by kids on dirt bikes and perhaps an equestrian or two. Maybe somewhere back in here she could find a good spot to abandon the truck.

She finally found what looked like a turnaround or dead end, a short section of once-cleared area the dirt bikers hadn't found yet, quickly being reclaimed by the thick brush. She cranked the wheel hard and let the pickup push its way forward, plowing through the brush and flattening the weeds that rose in front of the headlights.

Far enough. She turned off the lights and shut down the engine.

And then she sat there, her elbows on the wheel and her head in her hands. She had to hold still for just a minute. She had to think, to assess the situation, to sort out thought from feeling. She didn't move for a minute, and then another, and then another. The only sound was her own breathing—she was conscious of every breath—and the steadily slowing *tink, tink, tink* of the engine cooling. It occurred to her how still it was out in these woods, and how dark it was, and especially how lonely it was. She was alone in the darkness, and no one knew.

How poetic, she thought. *How appropriate.*

But to the business at hand: *How about it, Sally? Do you keep going or do you give up? You can always call them, or send them a letter, and just let them know where you are so they can come and finish the job. At least then it will all be over and you won't have to wait so long to die.*

She drew a long, tired breath and leaned back from the steering wheel. *Such thoughts, Sally, such thoughts!*

No, she finally admitted to herself, *no—I want to live. I don't know why, but I do. I don't know how much longer, but I will. And that's all I know for now.*

That's all I know. But I wish I knew more. I wish I knew how they found me . . . and why they want to kill me.

She clicked on the dome light—it would only be for a second—and reached into her jacket pocket for a small object. It was a ring, ornate, probably pure gold. She took a close and careful look at it, turning it over and over in her fingers, trying to make out the strange design on its face. It made no sense to her, try as she might to understand what it could mean. For now, she only knew one thing for sure about this ring—she'd seen it before, and the memories were her worst.

She clicked off the dome light. Enough sitting. She put the ring back in her pocket, took the keys from the ignition, and opened the door. In this deep, surrounding quiet, the dry, dirty hinges seemed to scream instead of groan. The sound frightened her.

The dome light came on again, but then winked out as she closed the door as quietly as possible, which still amounted to a pretty loud slam. Now the only light in the middle of that thick, forlorn forest was gone. She could hardly see, but she was determined to get out of these woods even if she had to feel her way out. She had to get moving, get someplace safe. She pressed on, fighting the brush as it pulled at her legs, scratched her with its thorns, jabbed at her out of the dark. Somewhere ahead was that old roadway where the ground was still bare and walkable. She only had to find it.

Underneath a fallen log, deep down in a dark and rotted pocket, two yellow eyes were watching her, two taloned hands curled in hate. The thing let out a little snicker as she stumbled past.

In the low, overhanging branch of a tree, another spirit

crouched like a grotesque owl, its black wings hanging at its sides like long, drooping curtains, its head not more than a knob above its shoulders. The yellow eyes were following her every move.

They were out to do Terga's wishes; they hoped to appease Destroyer.

She made it to the old roadway; she could feel firm, bare ground under her feet and discern just a little more light ahead of her. She quickened her pace. She was starting to feel like a little girl again, afraid of the dark, afraid of unseen horrors, longing for some light to drive all the spooks away.

Two black shapes hovering just above the roadway waited for her to pass beneath them. They drifted in little back-and-forth patterns, floating on unfurled, shadowy wings, their long, spindly legs and arms hanging down like spiders' legs, each tipped with long, clawed talons that flexed and curled with anticipation.

Sally stopped. Did the roadway turn here? *Come on, girl, don't get lost. That's all you need.*

Three more spirits, some of Terga's worst, sailed down through the trees like vultures gathering for a feast. They came in behind her, slobbering and cackling, jostling each other to get closer.

Sally thought she saw the roadway again, heading off to her left. She tried that direction. Yes, she'd found it. But her legs were getting weak. Her heart was beating against her ribs like it wanted out. *No, please, not again, no more . . .*

But it was fear, all right, the old-fashioned kind—the kind she'd lived with for years. Just when she thought she'd gotten rid of it, escaped from it, forgotten it, here it was, back again, as fierce as ever, digging into her, scrambling her thoughts, making her tremble, sweat, stumble.

Her old friends were back.

She passed under the two hovering demons.

"YAAAK!" they screamed, enveloping her with sulfur.

The spirits following behind slapped through her soul with their black wings.

OOF! She pitched forward into the dirt, a muffled cry in

her throat. She struggled to get her legs under her again, to get moving again. Where was that road?

The spirits alighted on her back and dug their talons in deep.

She covered her mouth tightly with her hands, trying to keep a cry inside, trying to keep quiet. She couldn't get her balance. Something was after her. She had to get away. She was still trying to get up.

The demons gave her a stab and a kick, cackling and shrieking with delight, and then they let her go.

She was on her feet again. She could see the roadway and she ran, her arms in front of her face to block the forest limbs that slapped and grabbed her. She could hear some traffic out on the highway. How much further?

The dark spirits fluttered and flapped after her, chattering and spitting. It was a wonderful, cruel game.

But warriors were watching. Deep within the texture of the forest, here and there within the trees, the logs, the thick brush, there were deep golden eyes watching it all, and strong arms upon ready swords.

The Good Shepherd Community Church had a prayer chain, a simple system for spreading prayer requests throughout the church via the telephone. Every participant had a list of all the other participants and their phone numbers. When you needed prayer for something, you called the next person on the list after yourself, who then called the next person on the list, who then called the next person, and so on. The whole church could be praying for a request in just a matter of hours any day of the week.

Tom's request for prayer set the lines buzzing with the news about Ruth and Josiah, and with each phone call, more saints started praying. At the top of the list was Donna Hemphile, a supervisor at the Bergen Door Company; next on the list was the Waring family, then the Jessups, followed by Lester Sutter and his wife Dolly, then the Farmers, then the Ryans, then the widow Alice Buckmeier, then the elders on the church board—Jack Parmenter and his son Doug, Bob

Heely, and Vic Savan. On down the list it went until all the numbers were called.

That started a flurry of prayer, of course, but also a flurry of phone calls back to Tom to find out more. To his great sorrow, he had nothing more he could tell them; and to his frustration, a lot of the information being passed through the chain was wrong.

He tried to call the Child Protection Department, but they were closed.

He tried to find Irene Bledsoe's home phone number; it was unlisted.

He tried the office of the State Ombudsman. The lady there told him to call the CPD or try the Department of Social and Health Services.

He called the DSHS and they told him to contact the CPD in the morning. They had no number for Irene Bledsoe, but weren't free to give out numbers anyway.

Pastor Mark Howard and his wife Cathy were out of town. but would be back sometime tomorrow.

Ben Cole made good on his promise and called, but by now there was nothing that could be done until morning.

After one last call to a state representative who didn't answer, Tom dropped the receiver into its cradle and hid his face in his hands. He had to stop, to breathe, to calm himself. It couldn't be as horrible as it seemed. Somehow, sometime, somewhere he had to find Ruth and Josiah. It just couldn't be this difficult.

The silence, the emptiness of his little house was so odd, almost taunting. Right now he should have been tucking Ruth and Josiah in for the night. But he was alone, and so tired.

"Lord God," he prayed, "Lord God, please protect my children. Bring them back to me. Please end this nightmare!"

Wednesday morning.

The Bacon's Corner Elementary School reeked of demons. As Nathan and Armoth flew high above, they could feel them, sense them, often see them, buzzing and swirling in and out of that brand-new brick and concrete structure the community was so proud of. The playground was full of kids, about two hundred, running, playing, and squealing before the first bell signaled the start of classes. Then they would gather in all those classrooms where the spirits would be busy, more than ever before.

The two warriors passed over the school, continued on for another mile, then banked sharply and sideslipped toward the earth, dropping like stones, twisting slowly about until they were facing the way they had come. Then, easing back their speed, they skimmed across the fields of hay and young corn, across some gravel access roads, right through some sprinklers, and finally came to an old chicken house on a farm next to the school.

Their wings snapped like parachutes, and they went through the old clapboard walls of the chicken house feet first. Inside, a cackling chorus of eight hundred leghorns carried on, pecking at feed, rolling out eggs, oblivious to their presence.

They hurried toward one end of the long house, moving through floating white feathers, fine brown dust, and chickens, chickens everywhere.

Tal stood at a window, looking toward the school.

Armoth quipped, "One might ask why you chose this place."

"For the view," said Tal. Then he looked toward the school again. "They have quite a project going over there, well established."

"The saints are buzzing with the news about Tom's children. They are praying," said Nathan.

"And the Lord is responding, so we're well covered so far. But the real attack is still coming this morning. Place a guard around Tom. It's going to be hard enough for him; I don't want any extra harassments against him while he's down."

"Done."

"Where is Sally now?"

"She made it to Claytonville, and she has a motel room.

Chimon and Scion are watching, but Terga's spirits are tormenting her, hoping to regain Destroyer's favor."

Tal bristled at that. "What spirits?"

Armoth had a mental list. "Fear, Death, Insanity. They and some others tormented her last night, and they've followed her today as well, trying to break her spirit."

"What about Despair?"

"Terga sent him to inform the Strongman."

Tal was amused. "How bold of him." He looked toward the school again. "I want Signa and Mota to clear a path into that school, do some screening, some diversions. We'll need to get in and out of there without the whole demonic network finding out about it. As for Cree and Si, they'll need to do the same thing at Omega, which means they'll need twice the warriors just to get Sally in and out of there with her life."

Armoth drew a deep, long breath. "A touchy business, captain."

"And getting touchier with each move we make. What about the room at the Schrader Motor Inn in Fairwood?"

Nathan reported, "We have warriors there now, keeping it open. And the old hiding-place for the ring is still intact."

Tal took a moment to think. "So those fronts are covered. Now all we can do is play the game, one careful move at a time." He smiled with amusement. "So I suppose the Strongman should be hearing from Despair any moment now."

"And who is stationed there?"

"Guilo."

Nathan and Armoth nodded. That was no surprise.

four

GUILO had often noted how the darkest, most horrible evil seemed to choose the most beautiful places to build a nest, and so it was again. The mountains around him were towering, jagged, snowcapped, picturesque. The early morning air was clear, the visibility unlimited, the wind steady and gentle, the sky deep blue. Tall armies of evergreens stood at attention on every hillside, and crystal-clear streams trickled, splashed, and cascaded down from the pure white glaciers. Below him, the little town of Summit nestled peacefully in the green, wild-flowered valley, surrounded by a restful, noticeable quiet.

He whistled at the thought: all those little people down there, surrounded by all this beauty, could not see the horror all around them, the impending storm about to swallow them up, the cancerous darkness that first blinds, then consumes.

He and some dozen warriors were staying out of sight, sticking close to the pines, not showing any light of glory. He didn't want to be spotted by the evil powers that only spirits could see—a cloud of demons that swarmed and swirled like a smoke-black whirlwind on the mountainside only a mile away from the town. Below the guarding whirlwind, almost invisible in the trees, was a quaint, alpine village, a picturesque campus of ornate buildings, fastidious walkways, fascinating trails, stunning gardens. The whole place shouted invitation, exuding a welcoming, embracing sense of peace, beauty, and brotherhood.

It was the home of the Strongman, his outpost, the hub of an ever-widening evil. The sooty spirits were bold and riotous, reveling in a constantly growing tally of victories over human souls.

Guilo stood still, watching their moves, sizing them up, getting an idea of their numbers. Yes, it was nice to see them so cocky; demons in that state of mind were always easier to

catch unawares. But they wouldn't be so cocky for long—
he and his warriors had seen the recent arrival of one little
whimpering demon, one little envoy from one little insignificant farming town, and the news that spirit was bringing was
sure to change things throughout that supposedly charming
village. An assault would have been difficult enough beforehand. Now it was going to be nothing short of a real nightmare.

A cry! A wail, a shaking rippled through the whirlwind. The
ranks of demons began to compress, shrinking tighter, packing closer, growing even darker, thicker.

"Oh . . ." said Guilo. "Looks like the Strongman's gotten
the news."

"ROOOOOOAARRRRR!!"

Despair's shapeless little blob of a body stretched, warped,
and bulged this way and that, like a big black bubble fresh
from the wand, as he sailed across the chalet and then
dropped to the floor, whimpering loudly, his black body limp
and flat like a sobbing, shuddering bear rug. All around him,
the demon princes and generals were in a chugging, slobbering, sulfurous dither, hollering and shouting out curses and
yellow vapor as thick as cigar smoke. The chalet was filling
with a heavy, putrid fog that almost obscured their shadowy
forms.

They didn't like his news either.

At the end of the living room, the Strongman was glaring
at the pitiful little demon, his huge yellow cat eyes almost
popping from his head, his nostrils flared, the sulfur chugging
out of them in swirling clouds. The immense, hulking spirit
was trying to decide if he felt better now, or needed to hurl
Despair across the chalet again.

The princes and generals—almost a hundred of them—
were beginning to turn on each other, waving their arms,
throwing their black wings in each other's faces, shouting and
hissing; some were demanding explanations, some were
beginning to pass blame, some wanted to know what to do
next, and some just stood there cursing.

The Strongman filled his end of the room with his wings and held out his arms. "Silence!"

He got it.

He took one huge step toward the center of the room, and all the demons backed one step away, bowing, folding their wings. He took a few more steps, and the room echoed with the sound of them.

Then he addressed the little rug on the floor. "Have you anything else to report to me?"

"No, my Ba-al."

"No further casualties?"

"No, my Ba-al."

"No further blunders?"

"No, my Ba-al."

The demon lord considered that for just a moment.

Then the order exploded from his gaping mouth as from a cannon: "Then get out of here!"

The force of the Strongman's breath was more than enough to get Despair started. He was out of the chalet and into the sky before he even opened his wings.

The Strongman paced back to his end of the room and sank onto his throne—the fireplace hearth—with a deep scowl. The demonic ranks on either side of him trimmed their lines, standing straight and tall against the walls. The room came back to order, filled with darkness, shadows, yellow fog, and a deathlike stench.

"She is alive," he mused bitterly. "We were rid of her, we thought for good, but then she popped up again. We sought to kill her, but now she is still alive and . . . under *their* protection."

The princes stood like statues, silently waiting for his next word.

"RRROOOOOOWWWLLLLLL!"

The demonic ranks had to trim their lines again.

"Broken Birch . . ." he continued to muse. "Such a delightful group of people, so unabashed and forthright. So ready to kill. So . . . so CLUMSY!" He fumed, he drummed his huge fingers, he glared at nothing in particular. "These humans . . .

these worshipers of our lord are marvelously evil, but some-times . . . sometimes they stumble ahead of *us!* No subtlety, no caution.

"So now we have a blunder, and a slippery little soul has escaped from our fist, a worse threat to us now than ever she was!"

A prince stepped forward and bowed. "Will my lord consider aborting the Plan?"

The Strongman straightened, and his fists thundered down on the hearthstones. "NO!"

The prince stepped back into the ranks under the condemn-ing stares of his fellows.

"No," growled the Strongman, "not this Plan. Too much is at stake, too much has already been established and prepared. There is too much to be gained to let one little woman, one little pitiful soul, ruin it all!"

The loathsome spirit tried to relax, leaning his head back and letting his amber tongue roll across his lips.

"The town was so perfect," he mused. "The saints of God so few, so penniless . . . and *our* people, oh, so strong, so numerous, so . . . so pioneering! We worked so hard to estab-lish the foothold we have in that town. Ah . . . who knows how long it took . . . ?"

"Twenty-three years, Ba-al," said a well-meaning aide.

The Strongman glared at him. "Thank you. I know."

The aide bowed and retreated.

The Strongman continued his mental review. "And the petty little saints in the town were . . . obscure, don't you see, far from help, far from the mainstream, alone amid the roll-ing farmlands . . . unknown. It was a perfect place to begin the process." His beastly face grew tight and bitter. "Until they started praying. Until they ceased being so comfortable and started weeping before God! Until they began to reclaim the power of the . . ." The Strongman sealed his lips.

"The Cross?" the aide volunteered.

"YAAAAA!!" The Strongman's sword sizzled through the air and missed the aide by inches. No matter. Several princes grabbed this foul-mouthed vassal and ousted him.

The Strongman settled onto the hearth with a thud. "Destroyer!"

The princes looked toward the other end of the room. A mutter moved through their ranks. Some stepped back.

A shadow stepped forward, a silhouette. It was tall, shrouded in billowing wings. It moved so smoothly, so silently, that it seemed to float. The other demons dared not touch it. Some bowed slightly.

It moved across the room and then stood before the Strongman, its head lowered in obeisance. It remained absolutely still.

The Strongman studied this dark, silent shape for a moment. "You have been noticeably silent during these discussions."

The thing raised its head and looked at its lord with narrow, calculating eyes. The face was not entirely hideous; it was almost human. But it was evil; it was cold and filled with hate.

"Speak, my Ba-al," he said, "and I will answer."

The Strongman's eyes narrowed. "Your minions failed, Destroyer. She is alive and free. What do you say to that?"

Destroyer's face was rock-hard, his spine straight. "Is she still mine?"

There was a strange, cutting tone in the Strongman's voice. "Do you still deserve her, Destroyer?"

Destroyer didn't seem to appreciate the question.

The Strongman spoke clearly, threateningly. "I want you to remove her, so that she will never reappear again." There was a slight tinge of doubt in the Strongman's voice as he asked, "*Can* you do that?"

The thing didn't move for a moment.

SLASH! Red flash! A sizzling sword cut through the air and divided space into burning segments. Black wings filled the room like smoke and rolled like thunder. The princes fell back against the walls; the Strongman actually flinched.

The thing stood there motionless again, the eyes burning with anger, the black wings slowly settling, the glowing red sword steady in his hand.

His low, sinister voice was seething with resentment. "Give me some real warriors, not Terga and his bungling, whining little imps of Bacon's Corner! Turn over your best to my command and let them empower Broken Birch, and you will see what your servant can do!"

The Strongman studied Destroyer's face and without the slightest smile asked, "What about the rumors I hear?"

Destroyer puffed a derisive laugh through his flaring nostrils. "They are rumors spread in fear by cowering spirits! *If* our opponent be this Tal, so much more the thrill of the challenge."

"He is mighty."

Destroyer countered, "He is *clever*. His strength is not in his own sword, but in the saints of God. The ranks have made a legend of his victory over us in Ashton, but they pay him too much respect. It was the prayers of the saints that defeated us, not this wily Captain of the Host." Destroyer waved his sword slowly through the air, admiring the burning after-image that trailed behind its razor-sharp edge. "And so it was in this recent, minor setback. But I now have an advantage, Ba-al: I have tasted the enemy's wiles, I have tested his strength, and I know the source of his power."

The Strongman was dubious. "And just how do you expect to thwart him where once you could not?"

"I will go to the saints first. Already there is plenty in Bacon's Corner for them to be upset about, plenty to divide them. I will keep them busy censuring and smiting each other, and then their hearts will be far from praying." He held the sword high; its red glow lit up the room and his yellow eyes reflected the glow in bloodshot crimson. "I will pull Tal's strength right out from under him!"

The Strongman was impressed, at least for the moment. "I will commission my best to accompany you. Broken Birch is clumsy at times, but totally devoted to us. Use them at your pleasure. Now go!"

Ben sat at his small desk in the front office of the police station and tried to get some paperwork cleared up before going out on patrol. It was a nice little office, with two small desks, a copy machine, some colorful traffic safety posters, and a low wood railing partition. Right now the morning sun was streaming in through the big windows, warming the place up. Under different circumstances he'd always enjoyed working here.

But Ben was far from cheery this morning, and his mind was far from his paperwork. He'd seen Mulligan's final report on the so-called suicide, and found it unbelievable. He couldn't be sure, but the photographs of the body and of the surrounding conditions simply did not match what he remembered seeing. Suddenly there was a rope around the woman's neck—last night Ben saw no rope around her neck, and even Mrs. Potter said the woman had the rope in her hand. The spilled goat feed had mysteriously vanished, and the straw around the body seemed undisturbed, not at all in the trampled, kicked-around mess it was in last night.

Ben didn't like the thought of it, but it was obvious that the scene—and the photographs of it—had been sanitized, as if Mulligan and Leonard had done away with all the evidence before taking the photographs and writing up the report.

As if that wasn't enough to stew about, there was also Mulligan's deriding and accusing of Tom Harris, and in front of reporters. And what in the world was the press doing in the station anyway? A lot of things were looking suspicious to Ben right now.

The *Hampton County Star* was lying on the corner of his desk. He had to go all through the paper before he could find even the slightest mention—and that's all it was—of the death at the Potter farm. The article was more a space filler than any real news, as if the reporter dropped all the facts on the floor somewhere and forgot about them . . . or purposely ditched them there. The whole thing felt wrong, so wrong it turned Ben's stomach.

I've got to get out of here, get out on patrol. I don't want to talk to Mulligan, don't even want to look at him.

But Mulligan was hard to ignore—he liked it that way. He came up to the front, belched loudly, and sat behind the desk across the room like a load of grain landing on a wharf. He had the investigation report in his hand, and started flipping through it for one last look.

"Well," he said, his booming voice shattering the nerves, "that does it."

"Any next of kin we can notify?" Ben asked.

Mulligan pulled a manila envelope out of a drawer. "There aren't any. Roe was a nobody, a loner." He slid the report, along with its accompanying sketches and photographs, into the envelope and folded it shut. "She pulled her own plug, and now it's our job to plant her quietly and get on with business."

"I don't suppose there will be a coroner's report?"

Ben knew he'd overstepped. Mulligan was getting steamed. "Of course there will. What about it?"

Ben wanted to back off, but now he had to answer Mulligan's question. "Well . . . with all due respect . . . the coroner might find some evidence to suggest another cause of death."

Mulligan didn't have time for this. "Listen, Cole, if just being a plain, hard-working, clean-nosed cop isn't enough for you . . . if you just don't feel you have enough responsibility . . . I'm sure I can find you some more important jobs, something you can really take pride in. The place could use some sweeping, and I know you'd be thorough; you'd get that broom into every corner, you'd catch every cobweb, huh?"

Ben knew he was glaring at Mulligan, but he made no effort to soften his expression. "I could be very thorough in checking the accuracy of last night's investigation."

Mulligan yanked a file drawer open and tossed the envelope in. "You just concentrate on doing your job, Cole. I'm not paying you to be my conscience."

five

postmaster Lucy Brandon couldn't keep her mind on her work. Debbie, the postal clerk, had already asked her three questions—one about the Route 2 driver, one about the cracked mailing trays, and one about . . . now she couldn't remember the third question. She couldn't answer any of them; she couldn't recall the information; she just couldn't think.

"Hey," Debbie said finally, "are you feeling okay?"

Lucy removed her glasses and rubbed her eyes. She was usually a strong person, tough enough. A tall brunette in her late thirties, she'd been through plenty of life's little trials by this time: poverty, the early death of her parents, a wild and rebellious youth, a shaky marriage, picking up the pieces after a bitter divorce, and raising a young daughter alone—all in all, a well-rounded package of scrapes. So she'd learned to cope, usually; most troubles never really got her upset—as long as they didn't touch her family.

She looked around the small Post Office, and fortunately it was quiet right now. The midday rush was still a few hours away, the drivers had all left for their routes, the stack of work on her desk was growing, but she could catch up.

She was determined to answer at least one question. "Well, no, not really."

Debbie was young, pretty, and compassionate. Maybe she hadn't lived long enough to develop a tough exterior. She touched Lucy's shoulder tenderly. "Anything I can do?"

"Well . . ." Lucy checked the clock on the wall. "I have an appointment coming up in just a few minutes. Think you and Tim can hold down the fort until I get back?"

"Oh, sure."

A flash of reflected sunlight danced along the wall. A deep-blue fastback pulled up outside.

"Oh, there's my ride."

"You go ahead. Don't worry about us."

41

The driver of the car was Claire, a wonderful friend and counselor for not only Lucy, but many people of all walks of life around the town. She was a beautiful woman with blonde hair arranged neatly around her head and adorned with combs and pins that twinkled and shined. Her blouse and long skirt, both of beautifully woven natural fibers, draped about her like regal robes, and in Lucy's eyes Claire *was* a real queen. She and her architect male friend Jon were the perfect couple, constantly growing together in self-realization and harmony and becoming an enduring example to all their friends.

As Lucy climbed in, Claire leaned over and gave her a hug. "And how are you, Lucy?"

"Oh . . . coping," she answered, finding her seat belt.

Claire pulled out of the Post Office parking lot and headed down Front Street.

"And how is Amber?" she asked.

"She's doing all right. I didn't tell her we'd be coming by today. I didn't want to cause any alarm before we had to."

"Fine, fine."

"I'm going to take her back to the elementary school on Monday and see if I can get her worked into her classes there again. Miss Brewer doesn't think she'll have too much trouble catching up and just finishing out the year."

"Oh, no, not Amber, and it's so close to the end of the year anyway."

They drove through town and then turned onto 187th, commonly called Pond Road because it passed by a large and popular cattailed pond some two miles west. Along with the street sign naming the road was another sign pointing the direction to the Good Shepherd Community Church and the Good Shepherd Academy.

"I think John and Paula will be there today," said Claire. "I hope you don't mind."

"I guess not. I haven't even met them yet."

"Well, you'll find they're wonderful people. I'm glad we'll be working with them on this thing. Reporters aren't always as courteous as they are."

Lucy was quiet for a moment, just watching the farmlands and small forests go by.

Finally she said, "Why did we have to bring in the press?"

"Oh, it's very simple. In a case like this, public opinion is important. It's the public mind that eventually creates the laws we all have to live by. You see, we fight our battles at two levels: in the courts and in the public arena. A lot of the cases we win today came about because of public opinion that was molded years ago. What we do now to mold public opinion will have a positive effect on legal cases that arise in the future. It's a process."

"I just don't know if Amber can go through it."

Claire smiled with confidence. "Oh, Amber's a strong little soldier. She can do it. I was impressed with how she spoke right up and told everything to our staff, and Dr. Mandanhi, and even Mrs. Bledsoe."

Lucy was bitter. "*Amber?* You mean 'Amethyst,' don't you?"

Claire smiled and nodded. "Yes, you're right. But that doesn't matter. It's still Amber, really. Amethyst is a good friend for Amber because she bears the burden of what happened and speaks so freely, something Amber could never do as herself."

Lucy smiled a nervous smile. "But you know . . . I don't think I like Amethyst."

Claire laughed.

Lucy laughed too, hoping that statement would not be taken as seriously as she meant it. "I mean . . . Amethyst is just so brash and disrespectful . . . And I think Amber's getting away with a lot by blaming it on Amethyst."

"Well, you should put a stop to that, of course."

"But you see what I'm worried about? I think I would trust Amber to tell the truth . . . and I would know what she was thinking and feeling. But I just don't know about Amethyst. I never know what she'll say next!" Lucy shook her head to think she was even having such a conversation. "I need a set of reins for that little critter!"

Claire only laughed again. "Oh, don't be afraid of Amethyst. Inner guides are always trustworthy, and Amber needs that support and fellowship for what's ahead."

"Oh, I can see that."

But Lucy didn't feel any better, and Claire noticed.

"What else?" Claire asked.

"Since we're talking about Amethyst . . ."

"Yes?"

"Did you see that other article in the paper, about Sally Roe?"

Claire knew about it. "Lucy, really that's no concern of yours. You shouldn't even think such a thing!"

Lucy was close to tears. "But how can I help it?"

Claire stole several looks at Lucy as she drove. "Listen to me. It's not Amber's fault. I had some friends check out Sally Roe the moment you told me what happened in the Post Office. From what I've heard, Sally Roe was a deeply disturbed individual. She was tormented with self-doubt and guilt, and she could never break through . . . She was a karmic mess! Amber had nothing to do with her killing herself. She would have done it anyway."

Lucy shook her head and stared out the window. "But if you could have been there . . . if you could have seen that woman's face when . . . when *Amethyst* just tore into her. And I couldn't get her to stop. Amber just wouldn't snap out of it."

Claire patted Lucy's hand. "Let it go. Sally Roe is gone, fulfilling her own path wherever it takes her. You have your own, and so does Amber. You need to be thinking about that."

Lucy finally nodded. They were getting close to the Christian school, and she was feeling nervous. "I just hope this whole thing goes all right. I hope we know what we're doing."

Claire was firm. "I think it's something we must do. Religious bigotry is everyone's enemy. I think we would be denying our responsibility not to do anything."

There wasn't time to say any more. Claire was slowing the car down and signaling for a turn. There, on the left, stood the Good Shepherd Community Church, a simple brick building with gabled roof, traditional arched windows, and a bell tower. It was a landmark around Bacon's Corner, the home of several different congregations over the years; some had died out, some had moved on and new groups had come in, but it remained through it all for almost a century, a steadfast monument to tenacious Christianity. This latest congregation seemed to be setting a new record for endurance; it had been there in the church for almost fifteen years, and the current pastor had hung on for at least eight.

Claire pulled into the parking lot between the church and the Good Shepherd Academy, a simple, shed-roofed portable sitting on posts and piers. There were four vehicles parked in the lot at the moment. Two must have belonged to the school staff; the station wagon belonged to John Ziegler and Paula the photographer, and the large white van was clearly marked, "KBZT Channel Seven News."

"A *television* crew?" asked Lucy in surprise.

"Oh, right," said Claire. "I didn't tell you about that. The people from Channel Seven thought this would make a good news story."

The two men from Channel Seven were already prepared for Claire and Lucy's arrival, and bolted from the van as soon as their car pulled in. The cameraman set the camera on his shoulder and started watching the news with one eye. The other man, a young, athletic sort with suit and tie above the waist and jeans below, stepped up and greeted Claire as she got out of the car.

"Hey, right on time!" he said, shaking her hand.

"Hi, Chad. Good to see you again."

"This is Roberto."

"Hi."

Roberto smiled back, looking at her through the camera. Lucy got out of the car a little hesitantly.

Claire introduced her. "Chad and Roberto, this is Lucy Brandon, the mother."

"Hi there. Chad Davis. This is Roberto Gutierrez."

"Are they going to take my picture?"

45

"Do you mind?" asked Chad.

"It'll be all right," Claire assured her.

Lucy just shrugged.

John Ziegler and Paula were there, ready to go. Claire greeted them, and Lucy just smiled.

The door to the portable opened, and a man looked out. At the sight of this band of people gathered in the parking lot, his face went pale; he looked sick.

He was, of course, Tom Harris.

Claire raised her hand in greeting, said, "Oh, hello there," and started walking toward the portable, the others following close behind.

No, Lord, no . . .

If I could just close this door and never come out, Tom thought. *If I could just call down fire from Heaven to clear these people out of my life, to make them go away . . . Haven't they done enough to me?*

Tom had been on the telephone most of the morning, riding the carousel of state bureaucracy while trying to teach his classes, and he still had not found his children. The last word he got was from the CPD, and they were emphatically refusing to tell him of the children's whereabouts. Pastor Howard still wasn't back, everyone else was at work, and nothing was happening fast enough.

Lord, I just wish these people would go away. I wish this day would end.

Tom looked back inside. Two kids, one third-grade, one fourth, were getting curious.

"Hey . . . TV!" said the little girl.

Tom was being recorded on camera this very moment. At least addressing the child would give him a chance to turn his back.

"Sammie, go sit down—this is none of your concern. Clay, are you finished? Well, put it on my desk and start the next page. I'll check it right after lunch, all right?"

"Mr. Harris?" said Claire, coming up the wooden steps.

"Yes?"

"My name is Claire Johanson. I'm a legal assistant for

Ames, Jefferson, and Morris. I'm here representing Mrs. Lucy Brandon, whom you know. May we speak with you briefly?"

"This has been a very difficult day for me, Mrs. Johanson . . ."

"*Ms.* Johanson."

"I have nothing to say to any more reporters. I've had quite enough."

"This is a legal matter, Mr. Harris."

Oh, terrific. What more could go wrong?

Tom knew better than to embark on any conversation in the presence of big-eared reporters and a television camera. "Why don't you come inside?" Then he made it clear. "You and Mrs. Brandon. These others can wait out here."

He stepped aside and let the two women come in, then closed the door against the reporters.

They were standing in a common lunchroom/coat room/ library between two classrooms. Tom poked his head into the classroom on the right. A first- and second-grade class of about ten children was puttering away at some low worktables, coloring, pasting, and keeping the level of noise just below their teacher's established limit.

"Mrs. Fields?"

A plump, middle-aged woman stepped out of the classroom. Her cheeks were rosy and her hair tightly permed. Her eyes immediately showed alarm at the sight of Lucy Brandon and this officious-looking woman beside her.

"We have some important visitors," Tom explained quietly. "Could you please oversee my class for a few minutes?"

"Certainly," said Mrs. Fields, unable to take her eyes off the two women.

"They're doing their reading assignments right now, and should be finished by 10. Clay's on a special project I gave him; just make sure he puts it on my desk."

She nodded and crossed over to look in on the third-through sixth-graders.

"Let's step into the office," said Tom, and led the way to a small cubicle in the back of the building containing one desk, a computer, a copy machine, and two file cabinets. There was hardly room for three people to sit down. Tom offered the ladies the only two chairs and chose to stand, leaning against the file cabinets.

Claire wasted no time. "Mr. Harris, we're here to remove Amber from the school. We'd like to have all her academic records."

Tom kept cool and businesslike. "I'll check with our secretary and have those prepared for you. You understand that all tuition payments must be current before the records can be released."

Claire looked at Lucy as she said, "All the payments will be taken care of. We'd like to process this as soon as possible."

"Certainly." Tom looked at Lucy. "I'm sorry that we weren't able to discuss this . . ."

Claire interjected, "There is nothing to discuss." With that, she rose, and Lucy did the same. "Now if you'll let Amber know we're here . . ."

The two women went out into the common room, and Tom followed.

Tom just wasn't satisfied. "Uh, this is a bit of a surprise. I take it we weren't able to resolve things to your satisfaction?"

Claire began to answer, "No, Mr. Harris—"

"The question was addressed to Mrs. Brandon," Tom said politely but firmly. He looked at Lucy. "It's been a month since we had that little problem. We talked it through, and I thought everything was settled. If you still had some doubts or misgivings, I certainly would have welcomed another meeting with you."

"Would you call Amber, please?" said Claire.

Tom poked his head in the door of the classroom and quietly called, "Amber? Your mother is here. Better get your coat and your things."

There were eighteen third- through sixth-graders in the classroom, each seated at a small desk, and all the desks were arranged in neat rows. Posters of nature, astronomy, the alphabet, and tips on cleanliness adorned the walls. Against one wall a large aquarium gurgled, and nearby a donated telescope stood poised to probe the heavens. There were pots of pea plants all lined up and labeled on a table, and next to them a family of hamsters in a large, activity-filled cage.

At the second from the last desk, fourth row, was Amber Brandon, a bright, clever, slightly mischievous fourth-grader with a full, often wild head of blonde hair and large blue eyes. She was wearing a purple jumpsuit and pink tennis shoes, and on her shoulder, a little pin of a toy horse.

She was surprised to hear that her mother had come, but also a bit excited. She hurriedly closed her workbook, gathered up her textbooks and her pencil box, and came to the door.

Lucy bent and gave her a hug. "Go get your coat, honey, and your lunchbox."

Those were the first words Tom heard from her today.

As soon as Amber was ready, Tom saw them to the door, opening it widely for them to pass through. The reporters were still waiting outside, of course, and Tom could almost feel the one-eyed stare of that television camera.

"Say, listen," he said to the reporters, "you people are on private property, and I think it would be best if you just move on, all right?"

"Oh, Mr. Harris," said Claire, turning back and joining him in the doorway. The camera caught a perfect two-shot. "I'm also here to serve you this."

She took an envelope from her suitcoat pocket and placed it in his hand. The camera zoomed in for a close-up. Paula's camera clicked and whirred off several shots.

"We'll see you in court, sir. Good day."

She went down the stairs and walked with Lucy and Amber back to her car.

Tom was frozen to the spot for a moment, which was fine with Paula and Roberto. He stared down at the envelope, his stomach in a knot, his heart pounding so hard he could feel it. The envelope was starting to quiver in his hand. He looked at the newspeople. They got some more shots.

"Please leave," he said, his voice hardly audible.

"Thank you, Mr. Harris," said John Ziegler.

Tom swung the door shut and then leaned against it, all

alone in the common room. He felt his legs would collapse under him and he would sink to the floor any moment.

"Oh, God," he prayed in a whisper. "Oh, God, what's happening?"

From the two classrooms the quiet puttering and studying continued. Suddenly that was such a precious sound to him. He looked around the common room and recognized the coats and lunchboxes of all the children, all this dear little tribe. Before long they would be having a prayer and going out for morning recess, filling the swings and playground like they always did. Such simple, day-to-day routines now seemed so priceless because of the envelope in his hand, this invader, this cancer, this vicious, imposing enemy! He wanted so fervently to tear it into a million pieces, but he knew he couldn't.

Now everything was coming together. Now things were beginning to make sense. His eyes blurred with tears.

So this was why they took Ruth and Josiah!

Tal was there, his sword drawn, staying close to the building, out of sight, watching the car and the news van pull away. Only a few dark spirits had accompanied the visitors, and there were no skirmishes, at least for now. The fact that Tom was well-guarded by two towering warriors helped keep things peaceful, plus the fact that Nathan and Armoth were atop the church in plain sight.

"No more harassments for the rest of the day," Tal instructed Tom's guards. "Let him heal up from this one first."

Then he spread his wings and reached the roof of the church in one smooth leap.

"So they've decided to go ahead with it!" said Nathan.

"The Strongman can be inflexible," said Tal. "I expect this will be a fight to the finish. It's—"

FOOM! A sudden explosion of wings! All three warriors immediately formed a close cluster, each facing outward, sword drawn, poised for battle.

"There!" shouted Tal, and they all faced the old bell tower.

It was Destroyer, standing tall and imposing, his expansive wings just settling, his glowing red sword drawn. A dozen warriors accompanied him, six on each side, almost as monstrous as he was. The hot yellow vapor from each demon's nostrils was already collecting in a writhing ribbon that drifted out over the parking lot like a slow, inquisitive serpent.

"If I mistake not, you are Tal, the Captain of the Host!" the demon called.

Tal, Nathan, and Armoth were sizing up this bunch. A fight would best be avoided.

"I am," said Tal.

The black, bristly lips pulled back in a mocking grin, unveiling long, amber fangs. "Then the rumors in the ranks were true!"

"And who might you be?"

"Call me Destroyer for now." Then he proclaimed proudly, "I am the one assigned to the woman!"

Tal didn't stir. Taunts never bothered him. He never fought until he was ready.

The demon continued, his sword ready. "I thought, before the battle begins, the two warlords should meet each other. *I* wanted to meet *you* to see if all the lofty words I've heard are true." Destroyer eyed Tal carefully. "Perhaps not." He waved his sword about. "But please look at this place, this little school! Is it really so much a prize as to be worth all your armies? Be assured, we want no more trouble in taking it as you desire in saving it. Captain of the Host, we could settle the matter sooner rather than later."

Tal answered, "The school is ours. The saints are ours."

Destroyer spread his arms with a flourish and made a pronouncement. "The Strongman has authorized me to give you the Christian schools in Westhaven, in Claytonville, in Toe Springs! You may have them! We will leave them alone!"

Tal remained stone-solid. "No."

Destroyer only laughed. "Oh. It must be the woman. Perhaps you are still bolstered by your recent victory in saving

51

her. Consider that a gift, captain, our last blunder. Yes, you did save her life, but she lives for us. Her soul is ours!"

Tal said nothing.

"And not only the woman, but also all the power, resources, people, minds, money . . . *everything* we will ever need to trample you and your motley little flock of saints into the dust! You are too late, Captain of the Host! The time is past for you and your saints. *We* hold the power now! Surrender, cut your losses, and be content!"

"We will see you in battle," said Tal.

Destroyer looked at Tal for a long moment, shaking his head slowly, marveling at this angelic warrior's stubbornness. Finally he nodded.

"In battle then."

With another explosion of rushing, leathery wings, the demons rose into the sky, whooping and wailing, mocking and spitting until they were gone.

Only then did Tal put away his sword.

"Was that an attempt to frighten us?" asked Armoth.

"A strategic move," said Tal. "He was trying to steal our courage at the beginning."

"So now what do you think of our chances?" asked Nathan.

"Even," said Tal. "Maybe just even."

six

chimon and Scion remained hidden on either side of Room 12 at the Rest Easy Motel in Claytonville. There were dark spirits about, apparently Destroyer's scouts—slimy, cowardly harassers, swooping down through the trees and power lines, zipping up and down the streets, looking into houses, through windows, down chimneys for the poor, bedraggled fugitive. The two angels were working hard to maintain a hedge about the woman, to screen her from their sight, and thus far they were able to keep her hiding-place a secret from any spirits sent to torment her.

But four spirits still followed Sally Roe wherever she went, and had been her close companions for so long that they could not be separated for the present. Chimon and Scion were just itching to stand in their way, to hack Despair, Fear, Death, and Insanity out of this world, to lessen the pain for that frightened, battered soul. But her life was such that they were there by right; and besides, the pain was necessary. The two warriors had to withhold their power.

Sally gave her head a good rub with a towel, and then straightened up for a look in the bathroom mirror. Her once-red hair now cascaded over her shoulders and down her back in wet, black strands. Well, maybe it would work—if they were only looking for red hair. But her face was still too distinctive; even with her hair dyed black and all pinned up, she still looked like Sally Roe. If she could hide all those freckles it would help. Maybe she could conceal her brown eyes with a pair of glasses, those stylish, tinted kind. Maybe she could wear a lot of makeup.

Her heart sank. This was all so futile, so childish. She was dreaming, groping for hope, and she knew it. If they ever spotted her, they would recognize her. She was finished, through, as good as dead.

She leaned on the sink, let her head droop, and just stayed

there for the longest time, her mind failing her miserably; it just wouldn't function. It was tired, burned out, discouraged. All she could do was stand there, breathing one breath at a time. At least she could breathe; at least *something* was still functioning.

But why was she so glad about it? That bothered her. *Sally, you're too tired to think about it. Let it go.*

But then her mind clicked on, just a little, and again, for the millionth time, she tackled the same vexing question: If life was so pointless, so futile, so meaningless, so empty, why was she trying so hard to hang on to it? Why did she want to keep going? Maybe it had something to do with how life evolved; nothing poetic or lofty, to be sure, just that mysterious, unexplained self-preservation instinct, the only reason we hung on long enough to beat the odds so we could walk upright and kill each other . . .

She snapped out of it. It was a waste of time trying to figure it out. It was a merry-go-round, an endless maze. *Keep it simple, Sally: somebody wants to kill you, but you want to stay alive. Those two propositions are enough for now.*

She leaned forward to check the cut in her shoulder. No infection, at least; that was good. For now the bleeding was stopped and the wound was closed, but just barely. She carefully bound it up with adhesive tape and gauze—a nice manual task, no heavy brainwork—then slipped carefully into her shirt.

She came out of the bathroom, sat on the bed, and started tinkering with the clasp on an inexpensive neck chain. It was a good buy down at the local variety store—provided it didn't turn her neck blue—and should do the trick.

She'd been shopping that morning, as quickly and quietly as possible, constantly hoping she would not be seen by anyone who might know who she was, or care. But she had to get that tape and gauze, the hair rinse, this chain, some clean clothes . . . and the morning paper.

The *Hampton County Star* was still spread out on the bed. She'd paged through it the moment she got back to the room. The front page carried some stories about a sewage plant, a local political scandal, and a county commissioner's thirtieth year in office, but no news from Bacon's Corner. The second and third pages didn't say anything either. She didn't find what she was after until the bottom of the last page of the news section. It was a tiny headline and about one and a half inches of story:

> LOCAL WOMAN FOUND DEAD
> Bacon's Corner—The body of a local woman was discovered last night in her home, an apparent suicide. The victim is identified as Sally Beth Rough, 36, an employee at the Bergen Door Company.
>
> Her landlady, Mrs. Fred Potter of Bacon's Corner, made the discovery after noticing some of Rough's goats were loose.
>
> "It's a real tragedy," she said.

It was a ridiculous piece of reporting. A run-over chicken would have gotten more copy, maybe even had its name spelled correctly. But that didn't bother Sally. That wasn't the point.

The story was not just wrong—it was incredibly, shockingly wrong.

They think the dead woman is me? *The woman who tried to kill me? They think she's me?*

She'd brooded about that all through her shower. It bothered her so much she had to read the instructions on the bottle of rinse three times.

At first she thought it could be good news. *They'll think I'm dead!*

But that notion soon faded. *They know I'm not. They have to know. They've lied to the paper, or the paper is lying.*

She finally got the clasp of the chain open and hung it around her neck. Then she reached over to the night table and picked up . . . that ring. She threaded the neck chain through it, fastened the clasp, buttoned up her shirt, and the ring was hidden.

They know who that woman was. They don't want anyone else to know.

And she knew she wasn't hallucinating. The ring around her neck told her that. It was one solid piece of evidence that would help her hold on to reality, bizarre as it may be.

Sally reached for her jacket and pulled another solid piece of evidence from the pockets—many pieces, actually.

Cash. She'd already counted it. Ten thousand dollars, in three bundles: one of twenties, one of fifties, and one of hundreds. The assassin's fee, most likely. Sally found it all in the woman's coat pockets and grabbed it. Why the woman was carrying it all on her person was a mystery, unless she carried the money for the same reason she wore the gold ring.

But the question still remained: After all these years, what had Sally done? How had she gotten in their way?

It had to be what happened in the Post Office. It was the only thing Sally could think of, a frightening experience and now a horrible memory. It was just like being caught, found out, discovered by an old enemy . . . a *savage* enemy! That little girl's eyes! Those taunting, hideous eyes! She could never forget that short moment when every fear, every night-mare from all her previous years came back in a torturous, merciless wave of recollection.

She had looked into the eyes of a devil. She could recognize it; she'd seen that look before, felt the stinging, mocking hate, heard the same vicious lying.

Sally flopped on the bed. No, she couldn't think about it. She was just too tired. She was frightened, her hair was black and looked strange, she couldn't think, she was a hunted animal, and she was just too tired.

Your hope is lost, worthless creature, said a voice in her head. *It's only a matter of time; a very short time,* said another.

"Amber . . ." It sounded so much like her.

Now you can see how big we are, and how little you are! You are dead, worthless creature! You are crazy!

Sally leaped from the bed and grabbed a pen from the table. She found some stationery in a drawer next to a Gideon Bible. She would write things down, that was it! Perhaps her mind wouldn't get scrambled if she put it all down on paper. She could record her thoughts before they melted away. She bent over the table, her pen poised over the paper.

But Despair was wounded, humiliated, indignant, and determined to redeem himself. He hung on her back like a coal-black leech, sucking out her will, whispering confusion to her mind. The other three spirits were with him, circling Sally, taunting her, jabbing her with their swords.

Insanity whipped his sword right through her brain.

Sally stared at the paper. Somehow she'd ended up on the floor. Nothing would come. What was that thought? She just had it, she was going to write it down, and now it was gone.

Give it up. Turn yourself in.

No one will ever believe you. You're crazy.

Crazy. It was a word. She wrote it down.

Insanity, cackling his witchy laugh, grabbed her mind between his two hairy palms and dug in his talons. Death joined in the attack.

Sally's mind went blank. The paper began to grow into a white screen that filled her eyes like a fog, a blizzard white-out. She was floating. She kept writing: "My name is Sally Roe . . . Sally Roe . . ."

She could hear voices in the room, taunting her, and could feel sharp claws tugging at her. They remained invisible, hiding from her, teasing, tormenting.

Then came Fear. Sally was overcome with a numbing, para-lyzing fear. She was lost and falling, spinning, tumbling in space. She couldn't stop.

She willed to think, to form the word in her mind: Sally. Sally. Sally.

Come on, write it. Take the blasted pen in your hand and write it!

We have you now. We will never let you go.

Sally. She could feel the pen moving.

The pen raced over the paper in circles, squiggles, jagged lines, crisscrosses.

It was gibberish. Nonsense.

She kept writing. She had to capture a thought, any thought.

Chimon and Scion had seen enough. It would have to be quick. Scion slipped outside to check the perimeter. Chimon crept like a shadow through the walls, moving in close.

All four spirits were clustered around Sally's head, whipping her consciousness into a myriad of senseless fragments. Chimon got a nod from Scion—he would be able to shield out the spirits outside. Now for these insects inside. It had to be just the right moment, just that one instant of opportunity.

Now. They wouldn't see it. Chimon whipped his sword in a quick, tight circle, a shining disk of light. *WHAM!* The flat of the blade smacked the demons senseless and shattered their tight little cluster. Despair went tumbling backward in a blurred spin and landed outside the motel; Fear, Death, and Insanity were interlocked and fell away together, their arms, legs, and wings a spinning, fuming, angry tangle.

The two warriors ducked back inside the walls.

Despair righted himself with a shriek and a huff, and only then realized where he was. With a flurry of wings, he shot back through the wall into the room. His three cohorts were just recovering. All four flung themselves at Sally's mind again.

But it was too late. She'd slipped from their grip like a bird out of a trap. Her thoughts, though sluggish, were moving in an orderly sequence through her brain.

Sally was suddenly able to read the words on the page. There were only six legible words at the top, "Crazy my name is Sally Roe." The rest of the page was filled with aimless, chaotic scribbles. She got up from the floor and sat at the table to try again. She had to keep writing, first one word, then a phrase, then another word—anything that would capture her racing, fragmented thoughts before they escaped her.

"Death and despair and fear and madness are back," she wrote, and then another thought: "Why kill me? I died years ago."

Sally kept moving that pen, whether her mind stayed on it

or not. She was going to whip this madness. She had to. She was going to get her thoughts down on paper where they couldn't get away. She was going to win.

Ben was beginning to wonder about his gift for timing. He'd been out on patrol and just happened to stop in at the station to pick up some more highway flares. As soon as he stepped through the back door, he could hear Mulligan in his office, talking to someone on the phone, and using a hushed tone of voice that immediately roused Ben's suspicion. Since when did Mulligan ever get that quiet?

Ben got his flares from the supply room. The quicker he got out of there, the better.

Oh-oh! There went Mulligan's chair again, rolling back and hitting the wall. Ben ducked into the supply room, expecting Mulligan to come bursting through his door.

But Mulligan must have jumped up in anger. He stayed in his office, hollering at whoever was on the phone.

"No, Parnell, I'm telling you, there was nothing on either hand! That's what I said, nothing!"

Hmm. Parnell. That was the coroner.

Mulligan gave Parnell time to say something, and then dove into him again. "No, I didn't find anything in her pockets either! What kind of a jerk do you take me for?" Parnell got another two bits in, and then Mulligan answered, "Well, you just go back and check around again! I'm doing my job, now you do yours!" Another pause. "Hey, you're the one who got the body, not me. I delivered it just like I found it. Why not ask the medics, if you've got a problem? Yeah, Parnell, it's *your* problem, and I can make it a bigger problem if you just say the word!"

He slammed the phone down and cursed.

Ben ducked back outside as quickly as he could. Even as he closed the door behind him, he could hear the sergeant still hissing and cursing under his breath.

seven

JAMES Bardine was a young, handsome lawyer with black, wavy hair left long in the back and a voice with a lingering adolescent quack. Normally, he was tough and decisive—his associates used words like belligerent and rude behind his back—and in control of his situation. He was ambitious, a real goal-grabber, and flaunted his red Porsche at every opportunity. His suits were specially tailored to project an image of power. He'd perfected his own walk for use whenever he went to court: a quick, intimidating clip, chin high, spine straight, and lots of extra yellow legal pads under his arm. He knew he'd go far. He had the grit for this work. He was good at it.

Right now, he was scared to death. He was sitting in an overly soft couch in the outer office of his boss, Mr. Santinelli, waiting to be called in for a conference. The room had high, twelve-foot walls, dark-stained mahogany trim around, over, and under everything, and a thick carpet your feet sank into. It was deathly quiet except for the secretary's steady tapping on the typewriter and an occasional electronic warbling of a telephone. Bardine needed a cigarette, but Mr. Santinelli forbade smoking in his office. The magazines on the coffee table were either old or boring, but it didn't matter. There was no way he'd be able to read right now.

He was trying to compose a defense in his mind, something persuasive. Surely Mr. Santinelli knew when he had a good man; surely he wouldn't make a big thing out of such a little incident. Surely he would consider the fine record Bardine had accumulated in the past five years.

The big mahogany door opened like the seal of a crypt, and Mr. Anthony stepped out. Anthony was Mr. Santinelli's aide and right-hand man, a tall, thin, ghosty character, something like a cross between a butler and a hangman. Bardine rose quickly.

"We're ready," said Anthony. "Won't you come in?"

Such a nice invitation to an inquisition, Bardine thought. He stepped forward.

"Are those yours?" Anthony asked, pointing to some yellow legal pads on the coffee table.

"Oh, yes, thank you."

Bardine grabbed them up and followed Anthony through the big door. It closed after them with a thud of finality.

This was the inner conference room adjacent to Mr. Santinelli's office. The ornate light fixtures were at full brightness, but the room still seemed gloomy. The dark woodwork and furniture seemed to absorb the light; the heavy, floor-to-ceiling, velvet curtains were drawn over the windows.

Mr. Santinelli sat at the other end of the oval conference table, looking over some papers before him and seeming not to notice when Bardine came in. He was an impressive figure, intimidating by his very presence. He was expensively dressed, gray, grouchy, and *in charge*. He was flanked by two of his closest and most powerful associates, Mr. Evans, a tight-faced, iron-fisted attorney who hadn't smiled in years, and Mr. McCutcheon, a man who had so much money the subject bored him. Near this end of the table sat Mr. Mahoney, Bardine's immediate superior, and not an impressive figure at all. One other man was present at the table, but unknown.

"Be seated, Mr. Bardine," said Santinelli, still not looking up.

Anthony showed Bardine to the chair at the nearest end of the table, the one directly opposite from Mr. Santinelli. This was going to be a real eye-to-eye meeting.

Bardine took his seat and arranged his legal pads neatly in front of him. "Good day, gentlemen."

Some of them muttered good day back. Some only nodded. None of them smiled.

Mr. Santinelli finally finished perusing his papers and looked up. "Mr. Bardine, let me introduce you to the gentlemen seated with us. Mr. Evans and Mr. McCutcheon I'm sure you know already."

Bardine nodded at the two men, and they nodded back.

"Mr. Mahoney is here as well, and we acknowledge his attendance. The other gentleman is Mr. Goring, from Summit, here to lend his assistance and expertise."

Bardine nodded at them, and they didn't nod back.

Mr. Santinelli leafed through the papers in front of him. "To quickly review our present situation, we find that a . . . complication . . . has developed, which at first seemed not so grievous as it now appears. Ehmmmm . . . and with each passing moment, the gravity of the complication increases . . ." Then Santinelli looked straight at Bardine and asked, "Mr. Bardine, are you familiar with the name Sally Beth Roe?"

Arrow Number One. Bardine could feel the question go right through him. "Yes, sir."

"And what about the name Alicia Von Bauer?"

That felt like several arrows. "Yes, sir."

"Would it be true to say, Mr. Bardine, that you are *extremely* familiar with the name of Ms. Von Bauer?"

"Well . . . I'm not sure what you mean by that . . ."

"We'll get to that later." Santinelli set that paper aside and perused the next sheet. "I'm sure you are aware by now that Ms. Von Bauer is dead?"

"Mr. Mahoney advised me of that this morning, sir."

Santinelli adjusted his reading glasses and studied the paper in front of him. "Sally Beth Roe . . . How interesting that she should pop up again, and in Bacon's Corner, of all places!" Santinelli looked at the men on either side of him. "Strange how things like this happen so often. You'd think there was an intelligent mind behind it, the hand of whatever god you may wish to imagine . . ."

It was no joke, and no one laughed.

"At any rate," Santinelli continued, "we have just recently learned that a plan was launched to have Sally Roe murdered, and, of course, to make it look like a suicide. Just whose idea was that?"

Mahoney spoke quickly and clearly. "Mr. Bardine's, sir."

Bardine looked at his superior in horror.

Santinelli asked, "You seem to be having a problem with his answer, Mr. Bardine."

Bardine's voice cracked as he said, "Uh, well, yes . . ."

"We'll get to that later," said Santinelli, looking at the paper again. "To continue my recounting—and please correct any flaws as you catch them—Alicia Von Bauer, a member of a Satanist organization called Broken Birch, was hired to perform this murder, and paid . . ." Santinelli bristled as he read the amount. ". . . ten thousand dollars as a retainer, with another ten thousand promised upon successful completion of her assignment. Am I correct so far?"

Mahoney just looked at Bardine. Bardine looked back at him. Neither man answered.

Santinelli continued, but watched both of them. "Apparently Ms. Von Bauer made her attempt on Tuesday night of this week, but found Ms. Roe to be more than her match. Ms. Roe was able to overcome her assailant and escape, leaving the dead body of her assassin behind, where, theoretically, she herself would have been found had the plan succeeded." He set the paper down flat in front of him, folded his hands on top of it, and looked at Mahoney and Bardine over the top of his reading glasses. "In other words, this ambitious, overly imaginative plot was a pitiful failure."

Mahoney looked at Bardine again. Bardine glared back at him.

Santinelli slid that paper aside and picked up the next one. "To further complicate matters, the, uh, planners of this scheme widened the circle of confidence beyond the key players and brought in a local peace officer named . . . uh . . . Mulligan, as well as the local medical examiner—the assumption being made, I suppose, that these two parties are steadfastly loyal to our cause, seeing that they were actually told in advance that there would be a suicide at the Potter farm and to handle it as quickly and quietly as possible."

Santinelli dropped the paper to the table and leaned back, removing his glasses. "Which, much to their credit, they are doing, or at least are trying to do, despite the fact that the deceased who is supposed to have killed herself is dead from an obvious act of violence and is, of course, the wrong person to begin with. By your silence I take it my account is accurate so far?"

Santinelli didn't need the answer he didn't get. He just replaced his reading glasses and went to the next sheet of paper. "Now for the complications—the *real* complications. First of all, the most obvious: Sally Beth Roe is alive . . . somewhere. She is living, breathing, walking about, and I'm sure totally cognizant that there was a ruthless attempt on her life. If she doesn't know who was responsible, I'm sure she has a very good idea. And how am I so sure? Let me tell you the next complication.

"According to a reliable source who shall remain nameless, Alicia Von Bauer was wearing a ring when she committed— excuse me, tried to commit—the murder. At our request, the medical examiner checked the body for that ring, and found that it had been removed from the third finger of the right hand with the help of cooking oil . . . uh, traces of the oil were still on the finger. We sent some people to check the murder site and the house, and the peace officer and medical examiner doublechecked the personal effects of the assassin. The ring is gone.

"And then there is the matter of the ten thousand dollars. That is also gone, without a trace. Von Bauer may have placed it in a secret account somewhere, but that is unlikely, knowing the delicate nature of her mission."

"Uh, sir?" said Bardine.

Santinelli lifted his eyebrows just enough to give Bardine the floor.

"The . . . uh . . . ten thousand dollars *was* laundered. It can't be traced to us."

The eyebrows went up again. "To *us*, Mr. Bardine?"

Bardine stumbled a bit. "Uh, to uh, the . . . to, uh, well, to us . . . myself, and . . . and uh . . ."

"It *is* gone, is it not?"

"Gone, sir?"

"Unless you can make a call or take a drive—just go and get it?"

"Oh . . ." Bardine stalled, but finally answered, "Yes, sir, I would say that the money is out of our reach now, irretrievable."

"But . . . laundered."

"Oh yes, sir."

Santinelli continued, referring to his notes. "The third complication embodies the first two: We have every reason to presume that Sally Roe has both the ring and the money. As such, she presents the greatest possible threat to us and to our plans." Santinelli paused for emphasis. "A greater threat, gentlemen, than she ever could have been had she been left alone."

Santinelli put his notes aside, removed his glasses, and looked squarely at Mahoney and Bardine. "Now, Mr. Mahoney and Mr. Bardine . . . let's return to an earlier question: Just whose idea was this assassination plot?"

Mahoney spoke first. "Mr. Santinelli, I'll have to claim some responsibility. When we heard that Sally Roe was in Bacon's Corner, we knew it could be a serious deterrence. We weighed many options, and I guess it became too high a priority in our minds. When Mr. Bardine presented the idea of an assassination to me, I guess I just wasn't firm enough in discouraging it. But by no means did I authorize the action, sir."

Santinelli could see that Bardine was quite agitated. "Do you have anything to add to that?"

Bardine looked from Mahoney to Santinelli and back again. "Sir . . . I . . . well, I understood that this undertaking had been authorized from the top down. I believed I was carrying out the plan with the full endorsement and authorization of my superiors." Bardine could feel the cold, icy wind blowing his way from Mahoney's countenance. He found himself at a loss for words—appropriate words, anyway. "The . . . uh . . . concept of a suicide, sir. This was not to be a murder, you understand, but a suicide, for all practical purposes. Done correctly, it would never be interpreted as anything else. Sally Roe was already a lonely and wasted individual with a terrible past and nothing ahead of her. Suicide seemed credible."

"I did not authorize it, sir!" said Mahoney. "He acted without my direct orders!"

Santinelli made no attempt to hide the smirk on his face. "We'll get to that later. Mr. Bardine, I do have some questions about the involvement of the deceased, Ms. Von Bauer. How was she brought into this?"

"Uh . . . she . . ." Bardine felt like a badgered witness on the witness stand. "I, uh, was talking to her about this particular problem, and she . . . well, she proposed the arrangement."

"She proposed killing Sally Roe?"

"Yes, sir, for the price of twenty thousand dollars." Bardine quickly added, "As you know, this sort of thing *is* done now and then."

Santinelli's eyes narrowed. He was moving in for the kill. "You say you were talking to her about this particular problem?"

"Well, I . . ."

"Mr. Bardine, do you always discuss such highly sensitive subjects with such questionable characters?"

"No, sir, of course not!"

"You freely discussed top-level concerns with a *Satanist?*"

"Not a Satanist, sir—at least, not in a derogatory sense. She belongs to Broken Birch, yes, but they command much respect, even among our own ranks—"

"And just where did this discussion take place?"

"Well, I suppose . . ."

"Wasn't it in your home, Mr. Bardine? More specifically, in your bedroom?"

Bardine was silent. He was stunned.

Santinelli explained briefly, "We do keep up on things, Mr. Bardine." Then he started attacking again. "You were romantically involved with Alicia Von Bauer, weren't you?"

Bardine was trying to formulate an answer.

Santinelli hit him again. "You'd already had many clandestine trysts with Von Bauer even before this; you'd already revealed several of our secrets to her, and now, at the peak of your infatuation, when she had your complete confidence, you told her about this problem, and the two of you made a pact together, isn't that correct?"

Bardine decided to try honesty. "I . . . I thought it would be safe. I mean, she was involved in a bizarre group, she already had a criminal record . . . I thought that if something went wrong, we could always dissociate ourselves from her, claim no knowledge of her actions. She was . . . she was a disposable entity, purely utilitarian. I was sure it would work."

Santinelli placed both hands squarely on the table, as if bracing himself right before exploding. "I suppose, Mr. Bardine, you never considered what it could do to the reputation of not only yourself but this organization for you to be intimately associated with a convicted criminal?"

"Sir . . ." Bardine tried to lighten things up. "Our people are seen in the company of this kind of people all the time . . ."

"Not this kind, Mr. Bardine! Not Satanists! We do not wish to associate with them because we do not wish to *be* associated with them by the public, do you understand? This relationship of yours with Von Bauer was most imprudent!" Santinelli stopped, not satisfied with the word. "*Imprudent?* Mr. Bardine, it was *reprehensible!*"

Bardine could only sit there, silent and shot to pieces.

But Santinelli wasn't through. "Did it never occur to you that she could be a spy? Did it never once dawn on you that all the inside talk you were sharing with her—no doubt to impress her—would be immediately afterward shared with her cohorts in Broken Birch? Haven't you learned anything about the politics of power? Have you any idea how vulnerable you have made us to those despicable leeches?"

Santinelli was hot and rolling; there was no stopping him. "They want power, Mr. Bardine, just as we all do! They are no exception in this game! We all want it, and we all have our own little machinations and tricks to get it. But be sure of this, Mr. Bardine: power, real power, belongs to the select few, and *we* are that select few—do you understand?" He didn't give Bardine time to answer. "All the others, be they rich, be they royalty, be they gutter rats like these Satanists, will just have to get used to that fact and live by it. We will not allow any more petty power-grabbers to vie for leverage against us, and—" he leaned into this phrase—"we will not allow any more of our people to *give it to them!*"

Bardine's voice was barely audible. "I understand, sir."

Santinelli ignored the reply. "The ring taken from Alicia Von Bauer's finger . . . it was yours, wasn't it?"

Bardine tried to explain. "She . . . she stole it, sir! I did not give it to her! She had to have stolen it from the top of my dresser!"

"And this was, of course, after you had made your pact with her?"

"I . . . I suppose."

"So she took your ring, with your personal inscription on it, and placed it on her own finger, just in case—" Santinelli took a moment to breathe and cut some holes through Bardine with his eyes—"just in case something went wrong, and we tried to dissociate ourselves from her and claim no knowledge of her actions and treat her like a disposable entity. With your personalized ring, don't you see, she would have some recourse against us, some proof that it was one of our own top-level attorneys who hired her and paid her that ten thousand dollars!"

Bardine looked down at the tabletop.

Santinelli had vented most of his anger. Now his voice softened. "Mr. Bardine, it is not my responsibility to think all these things through for you; it is your responsibility to do that, and to always keep the best interests of this organization foremost in your mind."

"Yes, sir. I'm sorry, sir."

"It's too late for that. The damage is done, and by another romantic entanglement! I hope you've learned—and it has been in the hardest way—how dangerous they can be."

"Yes, sir, I have."

"You're a good man, Bardine. I like your record of accomplishments. We're going to keep this quiet, and I expect you to keep it quiet, for your sake and ours too."

"Yes, sir. You have my word, sir."

"We will grant you a leave of absence to . . . pursue some further studies—and please come up with something convincing. In the meantime, we'll just have to see what we can do to straighten this mess out."

By this time, such a sentence was good news. "Yes, sir. Thank you for your kind considerations . . ."

Santinelli began to gather his papers together. "In the future, Mr. Bardine, you will show by your example how such actions as we've discussed are never a good idea for any man in your sensitive position."

"Yes, sir," said Bardine. "I will, sir!"

Santinelli only smiled. "Oh, I'm positive of that."

eight

RANSACKED. The place was a disaster, just like Mrs. Potter said.

Ben stood in the doorway of the Potters' little rental house and figured he'd better have a good look from here before he went inside. The small living room was scantily furnished with an old couch, a rocking chair, a small thin-legged lampstand, and one gray and brown rag-rug.

The cushions from the couch were tossed on the floor, the rag-rug was rolled aside and piled in a corner. In the middle of the floor were papers, books, small boxes, and several items of clothing, apparently the contents of some drawers somewhere, brought in and spilled out.

Ben checked his watch. Yes, he had time to linger a little longer. This sidetrip back to the scene of the so-called suicide was not official, to say the least, and he did have some other stops to make. But he had some nagging questions that drew him here, and he was hoping an answer, no matter how small, might turn up. Mrs. Potter was glad enough to see him again, and gave him the key after preparing him for what he would find.

He stepped inside the house and went into the kitchen. Every drawer had been pulled open and the contents scattered on the old trestle table: some unmatched bowls and plates, old army eating utensils, some aging dish towels, some cookware, and a half-empty box of Saltine crackers. The canisters on the counter were all open—someone had dug through the flour, the tea, and the sugar, spilling much of it. He checked the refrigerator—they'd gone through that too.

He found the bedroom. It was the messiest of all the rooms, probably because it held the most of Sally Roe's few possessions. Ben stood just inside the doorway a moment, noticing the intricate quilt now pulled from the small bed, the beautiful carved horse on the dresser, the pictures now hanging crookedly on the walls—prints of serene country-

71

sides, grazing horses, hard-working farm folk. On the square table next to the bed was a small porcelain lamp, cracked, but decorated with hand-painted flowers and topped with an intricate crocheted lampshade. Apparently this was Sally Roe's favorite room, her private little world. It had received most of her attention and creativity.

The small closet had been rummaged through, but most of the clothes still hung there. Ben noted the blouses, the skirts, the dresses, the scarves. They were all clean, pressed, cared for, conservative. The closet smelled of lavender.

The room was flooded with sunlight that came through the south-facing window. Just below the window was Sally's old walnut desk, the drawers all pulled out, the contents scattered everywhere. Even so, Ben could easily picture how it used to be; a few books, a dictionary, and a thesaurus standing at attention on the left end, a small desk caddy holding a supply of pens and pencils on the right end, and in the middle . . . Well, whatever Sally used to have there, whatever she'd been working on, was now somewhere on the floor, or confiscated. But for a moment he could imagine her sitting in that heavy wooden desk chair with the casters on its feet, rolling this way and that, the sun warming her, the whole sun-washed, green, and growing countryside on continuous display through that window.

It wasn't a long, meticulous thought, just a quick impression, a simple conclusion: Mulligan hadn't captured all that Sally Roe was by such descriptions as "leftover hippie" and "loser."

Ben heard footsteps on the front porch and then Mrs. Potter's voice calling, "Officer Cole?"

"Yes, ma'am, I'm in here."

He made his way through the house to meet her, and found her in the living room, her arms crossed, shaking her head at the terrible mess.

"Just look at this! I've never been so disgusted!"

Ben was quite stunned himself. "These were people sent by *our* department?"

"That's what they said. Sergeant Mulligan said they'd be

coming by to look for clues and things and to just let them in, so I did; and when they left, the place looked like this! Do you think I should complain?"

"Well . . . who were they? Had you ever seen them before?"

"No. They weren't from around here."

"Did they say what they were after?"

"No, I didn't think to ask."

"Well . . ." Ben looked all around, not sure what to tell her. "I'll, uh . . . I'll ask Sergeant Mulligan about it. I wouldn't worry. I'm sure they'll also take responsibility for cleaning the place up once they've finished their investigation."

She shook her head and started slowly for the door. "Well, I suppose they may as well box it all up and give it to a charity or something. I don't know what else to do with all the clothes and things with Sally dead. Poor thing. And tell me, just what am I supposed to do with her . . ." She stopped short, standing out on the front porch, looking up and down the drive. "Well . . . that's right! Her truck!"

Ben went out to join her. "Something wrong?"

She was still looking around. "Well, I was just going to ask you what I should do with her pickup truck now that she's dead, but now I remember . . . it isn't even here."

Ben took note of that. "That's . . . uh . . . that's unusual?"

"Well, she always drove it to work, and she always came home in it every day, and if she was home the other night, it just seems sensible that her truck would have been here. She would have had it parked right over there. See that brown grass? That's where she always kept it."

"Maybe it was already impounded. I'll check."

"But it wasn't here the evening I found her."

Ben made a curious face. "That is a little odd, isn't it?"

"Oh . . . who knows what's what anymore . . ." Cecilia looked through the doorway, surveying the living room again. "But I guess she was terribly lonely. Seemed like the animals were her only friends. I figured she was divorced, or separated, something like that. Can't see how else a beautiful redhead like that could be all alone and single."

Ben didn't think the question was that important when he asked it. "She was a redhead?"

"Sure. Had hair like the sunrise."

No. That didn't make sense; it didn't feel comfortable. "Umm . . . what *did* she look like, Mrs. Potter?"

"Oh . . . she was pretty, but tired, you know? Had freckles, big brown eyes . . . but lots of lines, lots of care in her face."

"How tall would you say she was?"

"Mmmm . . ." She held up her hand, palm down. "About there."

"Five five, five six . . . what about her age?"

"Well, she said thirty-four on her rental application, but that was two years ago, so I guess she's about thirty-six; that would be about right."

Ben doublechecked. "And red hair?"

She looked at him just a little impatiently. "Didn't you see her the other night?"

"Well, yes . . ."

But suddenly he wasn't so sure.

The red Porsche was traveling at better than ninety miles an hour when it failed to negotiate the turn, sailed off the freeway shoulder, and nosed into an embankment. Several cars stopped the moment it happened, and there were many witnesses.

"Yeah," said a retired vacationer, "he was doing fine there, passed my camper like I was standing still, and then, zingo! Right off the shoulder, just like that!"

"He was going too fast," said the wife, "just way too fast!"

The patrolman wrote it all down. There was an adequate crew on hand: two patrol cars, two aid cars, and even a fire truck, flashing their lights, setting out flares, and creating quite a spectacle. All the passing drivers were doing the usual rubbernecking, and traffic on the highway had slowed to a crawl.

The patrolman shouted, "Hey, let's get someone out there to handle that traffic! Get those cars moving!"

His partner came up the bank from the wreck. "Got an ID for you, Brent!"

"So, was I right?"

"Yep, it's James Bardine, the hotshot kid lawyer, your favorite."

"Dead, I take it."

"Oh yeah. Half his body went through the windshield, and he's wrapped up in the hood. They're going to have to cut up the car to get him out of there."

The patrolman scribbled it all down. "Well, now we won't be able to play tag with him anymore. Too bad."

The partner looked down into the gully where several men were cutting and winching the front of the car apart, trying to extricate the body. "Boy, the way he could corner in that thing! Never missed a move! He must have had a blowout or something."

"Probably fell asleep at the wheel."

"In the middle of the day?" The partner frowned. "Not him. He was a good driver. I'm kind of surprised."

"Aw, the other guys will figure it out, so don't worry about it. Let's just do our job and get out of here."

James Bardine was as crumpled and crushed as his car; his blood trickled to the ground even as the medics began to pull his body out of the twisted metal. It was tedious work, and they were taking it slow.

But during their grim task, no one smelled the odor of sulfur, or saw the yellow eyes peering from the rear of the car; they didn't hear the fiendish snicker, or the sudden rushing of black, leathery wings as the spirits soared away.

Lucy Brandon and her daughter Amber got home about 5 in the afternoon, and both of them were tired, cranky, and disoriented. Lucy's day had been traumatic enough with the filing of the lawsuit and everything that entailed, and she dreaded the thought of her face being on television that night. Amber's day had been a shambles; she'd spent most of the day at Claire's house instead of in school with her friends, and she still wasn't entirely sure why.

Lucy found some stew in the freezer. She could heat that up in the microwave and then make some salad, and that should take care of dinner for now. She was too tired and preoccupied to put any big effort into a meal tonight.

Amber took off her coat and plopped down on the floor in the living room among her dolls and toys. She picked up one doll, a blonde baby in a long, pink dress, and cuddled it, rocking it gently.

"Mommy?" she asked.

"Yes, honey," Lucy answered from the kitchen.

"Can't I go back to the school?"

Lucy didn't like that question. It made it all the more difficult to keep her mind made up. "No, honey, not the Christian school. We'll try to get you back into Miss Brewer's class. Would you like that?"

Amber rocked the doll and looked down into its little, painted eyes. "I want to go to the Christian school."

Lucy punched the buttons on the microwave and set it whirring. "We'll . . . well, we'll just talk about that later, Amber. It's been a confusing day."

Amber sank deeper and deeper into a melancholy mood. "I don't want to go back to Miss Brewer's class. I don't want to do those things anymore."

Lucy looked into the living room. "Amber, hang up your coat, please."

The little girl ignored her.

"Amber!"

She sat there very still, her blue eyes staring forward and blank. The doll had fallen from her arms.

Lucy approached her to give the command more emphasis. "Amber, I said to hang up your coat!"

"Aahhh!" the little girl squealed in delight, her face breaking into an ecstatic smile. She was looking at a little toy car on the coffee table.

Lucy froze where she stood. Oh no. It was happening again.

Amber rose to her feet, leaped in the air, and pawed the air like a jubilant show horse. She whinnied like a wild stallion, her blue eyes dancing; she tossed her head, causing her blonde locks to whip about her shoulders. "Indeed! All is well, Amber! Indeed, have no fear, for your friends do go before you!"

Lucy didn't know what to do. She was just getting so tired of this. "Amber, that's enough! You don't need to be Amethyst! I don't want you to be Amethyst! Now hang up your coat!"

Amber trotted up to the coffee table and grabbed the little car. "Varroooom!" She raced it around the table, mimicking the sound of squealing tires.

Lucy was angry now. "Amber! Do you want me to—" She was going to say the word spank, but . . . now it didn't seem to fit.

"Faster," said Amethyst, "faster, faster . . . to your death, to your death!"

Then, with a final squealing sound and a powerful thrust of her hand, she sent the little car off the end of the table. It flew across the room and nosed into the carpet, tumbling end over end.

"And now you are gone, removed from that which is called life!" said Amethyst with a raucous laugh and another whinny. "You were just so clumsy!"

Lucy backed away as her daughter danced and pranced around the little upside-down car.

She took Amber's coat and hung it up herself.

nine

"YOU did *what?*"

Attorney Wayne Corrigan had been patiently listening to Tom Harris's story up to this point and had hardly said a word. This was his first question.

Tom tried to back up a bit to explain. "She was . . . well, she was 'channeling' a spirit."

Corrigan rested his forehead on his fingertips and stared down at his desk, paging through the lawsuit as purely an emotional outlet. Looking down felt safer right now than looking Tom Harris and Pastor Mark Howard in the eye. "Channeling . . ."

"Well, yes. We used to call it mediumism; a person allows a demonic spirit to speak through him or her . . ."

"Well, yes, I know what it is, but . . ." And then Corrigan couldn't think of the right words for his feelings. He could only shake his head.

This was his last appointment of the day, and now it would probably be his worst. He was trying to be pleasant, but it was tough. Oh, what so many people expected of him! Here he was, in his forties, a small-town lawyer just scraping by, a reasonable man with a dear wife, four kids, mortgage payments, and a life of struggles and mistakes just like everybody else. But once again, someone with a need and no funds was sitting there looking for him to perform some miracle and suggest quick, simple answers to a case that was going to be complex and difficult. It just wasn't fair.

Pastor Mark decided to get into this. "Mr. Corrigan, I can assure you that Tom is a reasonable and truthful man. I believe what he's saying, and besides, Mrs. Fields can concur. She was there; she saw it too."

"All right, all right."

Corrigan stopped to think for a moment. Should he hear the rest of this? How far should he let these two go before he turned them down? Maybe he should just tell them how much defending a case like this would cost, and that would end this whole conversation. He wasn't too familiar with Tom Harris, but he knew Mark Howard and liked him. This gentle, genuine man in his fifties had that "gray head found in the way of righteousness" that the Bible talked about. Corrigan considered him a decent man of God, and most everyone agreed that the Good Shepherd Community Church was doing a lot of good for its people and for the community.

Corrigan shook his head. *It always happens to the good people,* he thought.

He leaned back with a sigh. "Okay, go on."

Tom wasn't sure he wanted to. "She . . . well, she came to our school just about three months ago. Her mother brought her in and signed her up."

"Did Mrs. Brandon agree to your Statement of Beliefs?"

"Well, yes. She signed her acceptance of them. She knows our doctrinal positions."

"What about the paragraph in the handbook about corporal punishment?"

"Well, I assumed that she'd read it."

"All right, go ahead."

Tom regathered his thoughts and picked up the story again. "Amber got along fine with the other kids for a while. It took her about a month to fit in. Then, during recess, she started teaching the children . . . how to relax."

"Relaxation techniques?"

Tom and Mark looked at each other with a ray of hope in their eyes.

"You've heard of it?" Tom asked.

"We had a case a year ago involving yoga being taught in a physical education class, and relaxation techniques were a part of it. Some parents—Christian parents—complained the school was teaching Eastern religion."

"So . . ." Mark was curious, "what happened?"

"We complained to the school district, but we didn't get the results we wanted. The school simply changed all the terms and sanitized the program so it wouldn't sound like religion, and then just kept doing it."

"So . . ." ventured Tom, "I guess you lost that one."

"We didn't exactly lose it. We dropped it. Let's hear the rest of your story."

"Well . . . I saw what Amber was doing and I asked her what was going on, and she told me that it was what she learned in Miss Brewer's class—that would be at the Bacon's Corner Elementary—and that it was fun because it helped you feel better and meet special friends, imaginary guides. I didn't know quite how to handle that, so I let it go. The other kids didn't seem that interested anyway.

"Well, then the kids started playing pretend games—you know how kids do. They were playing like they were in a horse show, and some of them were acting like horses and doing tricks while the other kids were the trainers. Kids play pretend games like that all the time—it was nothing odd, really.

"But then . . . Amber became the leader in the group, and her horse—the one she was pretending to be—was showing all the other horses how to prance, and do tricks, and how to . . . well, be good horses, I guess. And that was fine. But after recess, she wouldn't stop pretending to be a horse. She'd prance into the room and sit at her desk for a while, then prance over to the pencil sharpener, then prance up and down the aisles for no good reason, and she'd make horse sounds whenever I called on her, and we started having a real discipline problem. She was disturbing the class and disrupting things at every turn."

Mark prompted, "Tell him about the horse's name."

Tom recalled that part. "Oh yeah, right. I got after her once. I said, 'Amber, now you sit down and be quiet,' and she—" Tom made the motions with his hands—"pawed the air like a wild horse, and whinnied, and said, 'I'm not Amber. My name is Amethyst!'" Tom shrugged. "That was enough. I had to take her into the office with Mrs. Fields and have her paddled."

"Uh . . ." Corrigan looked at the document on his desk. "I think that's the second item on the complaint here."

"I think so. We followed the procedure clearly stated in the handbook and agreed to by any parent who enrolls his or her child. We use a paddle when a child decides to force his will against the teacher's will and we've carefully considered all the circumstances. We get alone with the student, we pray with them, we immediately try to contact the parents—"

"Could you contact Mrs. Brandon?"

"No. We tried her at home and at the Post Office, but she just wasn't available and the situation was getting pretty intense."

"Who spanked Amber?"

"Mrs. Fields. It's our policy that the girls must be spanked by a woman and the boys by a man."

"Oh, that's good. Did you have a witness?"

"Yes, our art teacher was there that day, and she served as a witness. We made a record of the whole thing, and then we finally contacted Mrs. Brandon that night and told her what had happened."

"So what was her reaction?"

"That's the strange part. She agreed with our action. She wasn't opposed to spanking Amber if Amber needed it."

Corrigan looked at the lawsuit again. "Mm. Somebody's changed her mind. But when did you . . . uh . . ."

Tom knew what Corrigan meant. "Just about a month ago. After we punished Amber, things went pretty smoothly for about three days, and then . . ." Tom stopped to think. "I think it must have started up again during noon recess. Amber became a horse again, just like before, and came back into class as . . . as 'Amethyst.' This time I wasn't about to tolerate it, and I got firm with her, confronted her, and then . . ."

Tom had to stop. He looked like he would cry. He forced himself to continue. "And then something came over that little girl. Her entire personality changed. She began to blaspheme, and curse, and mock the name of Jesus, and . . . and I had to get her out of there. The other kids were really being disturbed by it.

"I took her by the arm and had to physically drag her from the room—she was grabbing onto the desks and the chairs and even the other kids. Mrs. Fields could hear the commotion from clear across the hall, and she came running to see what was going on, and it took the two of us to get her out into the common room and hold her down. She was just having a real tantrum . . . no, worse than that. She wasn't herself. She wasn't Amber Brandon."

Tom stopped. Neither Corrigan nor Mark said anything. There were no questions. They were both waiting to hear the rest.

Tom pushed ahead, over the edge. "So, I . . . I discerned in my spirit that Amber was manifesting a demon, and I confronted this . . . this Amethyst in the name of Jesus; I ordered it to be silent, and to come out of her."

Corrigan slumped in his chair and exhaled a long sigh.

Mark interjected, "But she was all right after that, wasn't she?"

"She was herself again, yes."

Corrigan asked, "So naturally you assumed that this demon had left Amber, that you'd succeeded in casting it out?"

Tom was obviously embarrassed. "Yes. I guess so. But she must have told some real tales when she got home. Mrs. Brandon came in for a conference the next day, and by then she was beside herself, accusing me of physical abuse, terror, intimidation . . ."

Corrigan looked at his bookshelf, steadily slumping lower in his chair. "You tried to cast a demon out of a ten-year-old child . . ."

Mark protested, "Mr. Corrigan, you know what the Bible says about demon activity. You know demons are real, don't you?"

Corrigan flopped his arm over his desk and pointed it in Mark's face. "Do you think a jury will buy that, pastor? Go ahead! Pull a stunt like that and then try convincing any jury in this country that your behavior was appropriate!" Now he used both hands because he needed a bigger gesture. "A *child*, a ten-year-old child, and you tried to cast a demon out of her!"

"Well, what was I *supposed* to do?" Tom asked.

Corrigan sat up before he slid off his chair. He leaned over his desk and leafed through the complaint in front of him. "Well, to start out, you shouldn't have acted alone and you shouldn't have gone ahead with this . . . this act . . . without getting some counsel, even *legal* counsel."

Mark said, "He knows that now."

Then Tom protested, "But legal counsel? How was I supposed to know about that? Since when did Paul and Silas seek legal counsel before they—"

"They ended up in jail, remember?" Corrigan snapped, and for him to use a voice that was even a *little* loud had to mean he was upset. "They were beaten and thrown in jail for casting out a demon, and you're up against the civil version of the same thing. A civil suit isn't going to get you thrown in jail, but you're still going to need some kind of a Philippian earthquake to get you out of this. The American Citizens' Freedom Association has their fingerprints all over this thing . . . I suppose you know that."

Mark and Tom looked at each other. The ACFA, that infamous association—one could say conspiracy—of professional, idealistic legal technicians, whitewashed, virtuous, and all-for-freedom on the exterior, but viciously liberal and anti-Christian in its motives and agenda. Nowadays it was getting hard to find any legal action taken against Christians, churches, or parachurch organizations that did not have the ACFA and its numerous, nationwide affiliates behind it.

Mark said, "We thought maybe that was the case . . ."

Corrigan tapped the bottom of the first page of the complaint. "Ames, Jefferson, and Morris are members of the ACFA; they run the local chapter, and they've been the liberal, legal bullies around here for years. Why else do you suppose the press knew about your kids being taken away and were right there to hassle you at your home and in the police station? Why do you think they were right there to record you being served your summons? To create a scandal and smear you in the press, that's why. Why do you think your two kids were taken away in the first place? As soon as the ACFA heard about this case, they leaked the information—probably embellished quite a bit—to the Child Protection people and pulled them into it. They want this kind of spicy news. Now you're branded a child abuser, Tom, before you even get to court. The ACFA plays dirty.

"Well, just look at the complaint here against . . . uh . . . the pastor, the headmaster, the church, and the church board: 'Outrageous Religious Behavior Against a Child'—casting out the demon, of course, 'Physical Abuse by Spanking, Excessive Religious Instruction Harmful to the Child, Harassment, Discrimination, and Religious Indoctrination Using Federal Funds.'

"All this stuff is dynamite; it's going to make the case difficult because the ACFA will use all these hot issues to get the public's attention and stir them up.

"And did you catch those big key words, *federal funds?* That's what's going to get them through the door of the federal courts: 'violating mother's civil rights by teaching religion using federal funds—a violation of the Munson-Ross Civil Rights Act and the Federal Day-care and Private Primary School Assistance Act.'"

"Federal funds?" asked Tom.

"Lucy Brandon works at the Post Office, right? She's a federal employee, and under this Federal Day-care Act she receives a subsidy to help pay Amber's tuition. Didn't you know that?"

Tom was obviously surprised. "It's news to me. She didn't say a thing about it."

"Interesting. Maybe she didn't want you to know. Anyway, if you're getting federal funds, that means you can't discriminate or impose religion or spank or cause mental anguish by suggesting a child is demon-possessed, or whatever else the ACFA wants to test in a court of law. That's the whole point of this thing: they find a vague law and then work up legal cases just like this one to stretch that law as far as they can in the courts. This Federal Day-care and Private Primary School Assistance Act is a big, vague, anything-goes cloud of smoke, a clever move by Congress that most people never heard about.

Now the ACFA's ready to get it defined through case law, legal precedents, maybe a Supreme Court decision.

"That's why they're going federal with this, citing federal law. Look here: 'You are commanded to appear at nine in the morning, two weeks hence, at the department of the Honorable Emily R. Fletcher of the *Federal* District Court, Western District, Room 412, *Federal* Courthouse, blah, blah, blah.' This is a federal case, guys."

"So what do we do?" asked Tom.

Corrigan became quiet and then fumbled through an answer. "Well . . . I would say you need a lawyer, all right, but . . . um . . . I'm not sure whom you should consult on something like this . . ."

"You mean, you won't take this case?" Mark asked.

Corrigan gave a nervous chuckle and shook his head. "Well . . . no. No, I can't." He quickly blurted, "Now before you say anything or ask me why not . . ."

Then he stopped. *Oh brother, here I go again, having to explain this to another bunch of naive martyrs.*

"Listen, no offense intended, please understand. I mean, I can appreciate your position . . ." Corrigan pushed his chair back from his desk, waved his hands around a little, and looked at his bookcase as he tried to find the words. "But I've just about established a new policy in this office not to defend Christians anymore who can't pay for my services."

Mark thought the statement a little strange. "But . . . we didn't think you'd do this for free."

It wasn't a good enough escape for Corrigan to look down at his desk—now he looked down at the rug. "Pastor Howard, you're the last guy on earth I'd ever want to turn down, but . . . Well, let me just share some depressing information with you.

"Okay, I'm a Christian and everybody knows it; the police know it, the local judges know it, the county prosecutor knows it . . . Worst of all, all the Christians around this county know it. That means, when the Christians get into a legal predicament, they call me, because I'm a 'brother in the Lord.'

"But then, because they're . . . Christians . . . they come into it having some convictions about how my services are going to be paid for, if paid for at all; they sit in my office and tell me about faith and God's provision and usually throw something in about God rewarding me for all my time and sacrifice; but in the meantime, my practice goes down the tubes from bad debts.

"But please don't get me wrong. I'm not blaming them. It's just the way the system works: The little people—the Christians—get into legal tangles because the state, or the ACFA, or some other rabid, Christian-eating secularist organization decides to pick on them, and those people always have all the power, connections, and finances they need to win any battle they want in a court of law. Not so with the Christians. They have to put on spaghetti dinners and car washes and jogathons just to hire some poor, minor-league attorney like me who supposedly has such a love for righteous causes that he doesn't care about the money."

Corrigan saw that Mark and Tom were listening without any signs of malice—at least not yet; so he proceeded. "Now that's half of the problem. The other half is that all too often Christians just aren't credible. You know, I've actually instructed some clients not to testify in court that they are Christians because in too many cases that information would damage their credibility! The world out there . . . the system . . . thinks it understands us. It has us pegged, categorized, defined. We believe in God; we believe in absolutes. Therefore, we can't possibly be credible!" He chuckled wryly. "When I was in law school it was the other way around. The perception was that people lacked credibility if they didn't believe in God. We've come a long way, haven't we?

"So anyway, I'm faced with two options: I can be retained by Christians and find out later they can't afford my services, or I can take their case for free or on a reduced basis—usually a drastically reduced basis. In this case right here, there would be about a zero chance of any contingency recovery. I could only hope to receive part of the settlement, but even then the system is already so stacked against me that I have no fair chance of winning, and therefore no chance of being paid that way either.

"Am I making this clear for you? To put it simply, I can't afford it, monetarily or reputationally. I've been too close to bankruptcy too many times to take another case like this. I think what you need is a fresh visionary, a brand-new horse who still has some miles left on him, somebody you can run ragged for next to nothing."

Corrigan stopped. He felt released now, but also a little ashamed. He looked at the wall where his eyes fell on his license to practice law, and concluded with, "Sometimes I almost admit to myself that I hate this job. Look what it does to me . . . makes me dump all my feelings on good people like you."

Mark looked at the legal torpedo on Corrigan's desk and sighed. "So where can we go from here? Tom's children are taken from him, and he still doesn't know where. Now the school is slapped with a lawsuit that . . . Well, it seems to me that our very freedoms are being threatened. There aren't any attorneys in Bacon's Corner; we could have gone elsewhere, but we came to Claytonville to see you because—and I'm not ashamed to say it—we knew you were a Christian. We knew you'd have the right perspective."

Corrigan looked at the minister just a little sheepishly. "Well, I guess I've blown that notion out of the water."

"But what about Tom? He could be bitter right now. He lost his wife in a car wreck just three years ago, his salary is pitiful, but he's stayed right here with his two children and served as the headmaster at our Christian school for four years now, doing an excellent job. And what thanks does he get? His children taken away and a lawsuit against the school that could jeopardize everything he and the rest of us hold dear. It isn't fair. It isn't right. Even so, he's remained true to his calling. He's a righteous man, a man of principle and conviction . . ."

"Hence the pitiful salary. Excuse me. Go on."

Mark was getting disgusted. "I'm through."

Corrigan sat quietly, rested his chin on his knuckles,

thought for a moment, then nodded in agreement to his own thoughts.

"And to think it all started in Bacon's Corner. I guess it had to happen somewhere." He sat up straight and folded his hands on the desk. For the first time in several minutes, he looked directly at Tom and Mark. "Pastor, the ACFA isn't after your little school; Tom, they're not really interested in you either; as for this allegedly traumatized child, they couldn't care less about her. No, what they're really after is a legal precedent, something that's going to affect not just you, but everyone. They have all the money and skill they need to pull this thing off, and they know that you don't, and that's what they're counting on. That's why they chose a little place like Bacon's Corner and a little dirt-poor church like yours.

"And I guess they have me where they want me. I can just see those ACFA lawyers sitting in their office over at Ames, Jefferson, and Morris saying, 'Yeah, hit Bacon's Corner. That Wayne Corrigan is a burned-out tube, he'll never take the case.' Now wouldn't that be just peachy for them?"

He looked at the papers on his desk again.

"All right, I'll tell you what: I'll repent . . . sort of. I'll take this case, but I'll take as little of it as possible. That means you do the work, you do the hoofing, you do the research, you build the case. I'll tell you what to do, I'll write up the affidavits, I'll take the depositions, I'll plead the case and present the arguments, I'll advise you; but any information relating to this case is your responsibility. I suggest you get yourselves a private investigator to help you out. As far as my involvement, you'll get what you pay for, and . . ." He swallowed hard, came to a reluctant decision, and added, " . . . I'll reduce my fee by half, but you must agree to raise the other half."

Tom and Mark exchanged a quick glance and quickly agreed. "Okay."

"So what comes first?" Mark asked.

Corrigan leafed through the papers. "Number One, you've got a temporary injunction here that restrains you from just about everything named in the complaint. Uh . . . I think what it's going to boil down to is that you'll have to cease and desist from spanking and from any further 'outrageous religious behavior.' Guess that means you can't cast out any more demons until the court hearing in two weeks."

"What happens in two weeks?" asked Tom.

"We have to appear in court . . . 'to show cause, if any you have, why you and all persons acting on your behalf or on behalf of the school should not be immediately restrained from spanking, hitting, or otherwise having physical contact with children at the school for any reason whatsoever, and why you and all persons acting on your behalf in concert with you, should not be immediately restrained from any further religious behavior which could prove harmful to the mental, emotional, or social welfare of the child, or any excessive religious instruction, direct or indirect, of any kind, at the school or day-care facility, that could prove harmful . . .' And it goes on and talks about all this other stuff."

"Just what do they mean, 'excessive religious instruction'?" asked Tom.

"That has yet to be defined."

"What should we do?" asked Mark.

"Try to behave yourselves for the two weeks. Don't be outrageous, whatever that means. In the meantime, you need to give me some good arguments why you should be allowed to continue the above-mentioned activities. Then I'll file the briefs and affidavits with the court, and then we'll go in and see if we can turn you guys loose from this restraining order. That's the first thing."

"And then?" asked Mark.

Corrigan suddenly looked worried and careworn. "One bite at a time, pastor. You're going to be busy for a long, long time."

"What about Ruth and Josiah?" asked Tom.

"No easy answers there. It's going to be a tangled mess, and could be even worse, depending on whom you're dealing with in the system. I think you're entitled to a hearing within seventy-two hours to determine if the removal of your children has merit, but that's usually a rubber-stamp session where the judge approves the removal of the children based on the testimony of the social worker. You might be called to appear, you might be barred from the hearing altogether. It just depends on who's running the case. I'll look into it."

"But . . . won't I get my kids back?"

Corrigan hesitated to answer the question. "You'll probably have to go through a trial first, and that could mean a wait of six months or more."

Neither Tom nor Mark were ready for an answer like that.

"That can't be all there is to it!" said Mark. "There have to be other options, something we can do!"

"You can pray," Corrigan answered. "Specifically, pray for some friends in the right places. You've got a fight ahead of you."

ten

SALLY would be staying at the Rest Easy another night. She had the whole ten thousand dollars to spend on this one room if she wanted to, if no better ideas came to her. Right now she had no better ideas.

She'd used up the afternoon and all the stationery in the room just scribbling thoughts down as they came to her. Now, as the day outside the windows gave way to evening, she sat at the table and leafed through page after page, her day's work.

The first page was no masterpiece: "Crazy my name is Sally Roe," followed by a full page of aimless lines and squiggles. Apparently she'd failed to capture her thoughts. But that was depressing. Maybe this *was* an accurate record of her thoughts. She didn't even remember doing it.

The next page had some scribbled words that looked like they might be "Death" and "Madness," but she couldn't be sure. After that, her writing broke down into chaotic scribbles again, and then at the bottom of the page she'd written her name several times, encircled by some strange, dark doodles. She remembered making those in a pit of depression when she didn't feel like thinking or writing anything. It just felt good to doodle, to pour her feelings onto the page without using any language.

The third page sounded so great when she'd first written it: "I am I: I think, I exist, but know nothing of the grasping of the essence of all that is under or over the abysmal attitudes that so wrack our awareness in the last autumns of mayhem upon the earth . . ." Now not even she could decode all that. Apparently her brain had been working while her mind was disconnected.

But she felt encouraged, not because her afternoon's project had produced such drivel, but because she could sit quietly now with her mind clear and *realize* it was drivel. She'd just come through some kind of spiritual storm, some raging, agonizing battle. *Just like the old days,* she thought. So many of the impressions, the hallucinations, the mindless wanderings were so familiar. Her mind had not slipped over the edge like that in almost ten years.

No doubt it was this new, mysterious terror that had brought it all back. She had stepped in the way of an old Evil, and she recognized it all too well. It must have recognized her too, and that was why it was chasing her now. With only a little imagination she could sense it still lurking outside the walls of the motel room, ready to pounce on her again should she ever rest.

But . . . what to do, what to do. What was the next step? How could she free herself?

She picked up that day's *Hampton County Star.* There was nothing new about her own death, and she figured there never would be. That story, her life, her name, were now buried, tucked neatly away in the archives to be forgotten.

She flipped to the front page and studied a large photo. Some blonde lady was handing a guy what looked like a summons. Well, this was more news from Bacon's Corner, a Christian school scandal. Tom Harris, headmaster at the Good Shepherd Christian School . . . accused of child abuse . . . accusations brought by local postmaster—

Sally's eyes froze on those last words. The local postmaster? She read the paragraph again.

" . . . the child's mother, the local postmaster, first became suspicious when her ten-year-old daughter was playing games of pretend and began to recount questionable behavior by her teacher at the school . . ."

Sally checked the time. A little after 5. Maybe there was something on television. She clicked it on.

Well . . . nothing much, just the sale of a pro football team to some unknown millionaire, a cleanup of hazardous waste in some small Midwest town, a new paint job for a historical building in the state capital . . .

She let the television talk to itself while she finished reading the newspaper.

According to reliable sources, Tom Harris's two young children were taken from his home by child welfare workers yesterday afternoon . . . The CPD had what it felt was adequate reason to remove the children from the home . . . "If we must err, we must err on the side of the child," said the source . . . CPD is beginning an investigation into the alleged abuses of children at the school . . . Postmaster Lucy Brandon and ACFA lawyers have filed a suit against the school, charging the school with outrageous religious behavior against a child, physical abuse by spanking, excessive religious instruction harmful to the child, harassment, discrimination, and religious indoctrination using federal funds. The little girl reported that Harris tried to cast a demon out of her . . .

Oh! There it was on the television! Sally turned up the sound just as the on-the-scene footage began to roll. There was the little school, and there was Tom Harris, the headmaster, standing in the doorway. Yes, and there was the blonde lady, handing him the summons.

Chad Davis, reporter for Channel Seven News, was doing his voice-over narration. "The lawsuit on behalf of Ms. Brandon once again raises the question of how much religious freedom is too much, especially where young children are concerned, and calls for a limit to extreme fundamentalist practices that violate the laws of the state."

Next shot: Lucy Brandon, the postmaster, and . . . Amber! Neither of them said anything—they just went to their car and got in. Davis narrated, "The case could have implications at the federal level because federal funds were involved in the child's education at the school. The ACFA argues that the practices and teachings of the school are extreme, harmful, and clearly violate the laws concerning separation of church and state."

The blonde lady came on the screen. Her name appeared below her face: Claire Johanson, ACFA.

"We are concerned for the welfare of our children," she said, "and want to protect them from any more vicious and inexcusable abuse inflicted upon them under the license of religion."

Next came a quick interview with a Child Protection

Department lady, Irene Bledsoe. "We always investigate any reports that come to us," she was saying, "and we are looking into it."

Davis pressed a question from off camera. "Have Mr. Harris's children been removed from his home?"

"Yes, but that's all I can say."

"In the meantime," Davis continued in his voice-over, "the Federal District Court has handed down a temporary injunction against the school, barring any further spanking, religious teaching that could be harmful to children, or outrageous religious behavior, pending a hearing to be held in two weeks."

Back came the anchorman, staring soberly at the camera. "Thank you, Chad, for that report. We'll definitely keep working on this one and bring you more developments as they happen. Speaking on the lighter side . . ."

Commercial. Young bucks running and hollering and opening bottles of beer.

She turned off the television and sat on the bed, stunned. Irene Bledsoe . . . that same woman with the ratty brown hair and crinkled moonface. That same scowl.

The woman at the intersection! That was *her?* Those were *Tom Harris's* kids?

Lucy Brandon. Amber. Oh, and just when my mind was clearing up!

Thoughts began to fill Sally's mind with the bursting rhythm of popcorn, carrying it away in a tumbling flood, driving it forward like a wild automobile with no one at the wheel; it raced and swerved headlong from one thought to another, skipping over memories and colliding with replays, snagging and dragging scenes through her consciousness faster than she could watch them, flushing out conversations, facts, faces.

She clapped her hands to the sides of her head as if being attacked by a horde of noises. *Please, one at a time! I can't hear you when you're all screaming at once! Slow down!*

She looked at the news photo of Tom Harris again, standing in the doorway of the little school, getting his big white envelope from the blonde lady.

So he had met little Amber too!

Sally's hand went to the ring hanging under her shirt. It seemed that bad things happened to people who had run-ins with Amber Brandon.

She went to the table and found the first piece of paper she'd scribbled on that day. It was all she had; perhaps some legible writing would show up against all that nonsense.

Unless she just wrote more nonsense. It was going to be a struggle, but she would try again. She would try all night if she had to. Her head was boiling with scattered, unruly thoughts, and sooner or later they would have to spill out in some clear fashion.

Then suddenly, all around the motel, such an unexpected legion of harassing demons began to shower down that Chimon and Scion could no longer hide and had to throw any subtlety to the wind. They were in full glory, bright and visible, swatting and slashing as the demons swarmed around them like vile, biting bees. The intensity of the onslaught was shocking, surprisingly strong. It seemed each spirit would be swatted away only to be replaced by two more, and the air was filled with them. They were bold, brash, reckless, attacking with screams and shrieks, even grinning mockingly.

"For Destroyer!" they screamed as their battle cry. "For Destroyer!"

So that was it. The demonic warlord was trying a new tactic now, and this difficulty could only be caused by one thing: something had happened to their prayer cover.

"Well," said Judy Waring, "you just . . . you just never know about people. I always did wonder about him. We voted on your recommendation, we went along with it, and now what are we going to do . . ."

Mark was trying to end this telephone conversation and get back to the meeting. The parsonage telephone had been ringing all day, and he was about to pull the plug out of the wall.

"Listen, Judy," he said, "we're about to have an emergency board meeting about it right now, so I have to hang up. But let me assure you that Tom's handling this whole thing very well, just really open and forthright. I think we can trust him."

"Well . . . I'm hearing a lot of things . . ."

"Right . . . Let me say something about that before I hang up. I don't want any more gossip going around about Tom or the school or any of these matters. If there's anything to be settled, it will be settled at this meeting, with Tom present and able to speak for himself. Now please—"

"You *did* hear what the news said tonight—"

"Judy! Now listen to me! You don't need to get your information from the news, not when all this is happening to *us*, in our own church. Now you just sit tight and don't listen to any more rumors, and please don't spread any, all right?"

"Well, all right, but I don't know if we can keep Charlie enrolled at the school with this going on . . ."

"We'll have our meeting tonight, and then we'll take care of your concerns. Just be patient."

Judy was about to say something else. She always had the last word in any conversation. Mark quietly and courteously hung up before she could get rolling again.

Cathy Howard was nearby, making coffee for the men gathered in the dining room, and overhearing Mark's end of at least the twentieth conversation. Mark told her quietly, "Maybe you can unplug this thing, or leave it off the hook."

She made a questioning face.

"Or take the calls?" Mark asked.

"Just go ahead and have your meeting," she said with a chuckle. "I'll screen the calls for you."

That deserved a kiss. Cathy, a striking blonde with fine Nordic features, was remarkably serene. She'd kept her composure during this rough time, and Mark was thankful for her, more than he could say. Of course she didn't enjoy tribulation—who does?—but right now, when extra strength and resilience were needed, she was supplying them, and that gave Mark a quiet assurance that they would get through this crisis.

He stepped through the kitchen door and out into the dining room. The four church elders were gathered around the table, listening to Tom's account of what had happened up to this time.

"So what was it this spirit said?" asked Jack Parmenter, a hardworking, durable farmer with silver hair.

Tom didn't enjoy the memory of it. "Oh . . . it said we were all fools to worship Jesus, that He was only a liar, and not God at all, but just an illegitimate child—uh, the spirit used another word, of course—and then it went on to accuse Jesus of sexual perversions . . . in graphic terms."

"All that coming from a ten-year-old," said Bob Heely in disgust. Bob was a Viet Nam vet, a diesel mechanic who kept all the farm machinery around Bacon's Corner running. His hands were rough and grease-blackened.

"Sounds pretty weird to me," said Doug Parmenter, Jack's son and the spitting image of his father. "What do you think, Mark? I've never seen someone demon-possessed before."

Mark took his place at the head of the table. "I have, and I think Tom's impressions were correct."

Vic Savan, who ran the farm right next to the Parmenters', concurred with that. "Well, what that little girl—or that demon—had to say fits right in with everything else the Devil's saying nowadays about Christians and about Christ. Just look at all the slander he's been spreading in the papers and on the television, and I don't mean just our own situation. Seems like it's everyone else's civil rights and freedoms that matter, but when it comes to Christians, people—and I guess demons—can say and do whatever they want."

"Well," said Mark, "like Wayne Corrigan said, a lawsuit, a test of Christian freedom, had to happen somewhere. Looks like that somewhere is here in Bacon's Corner, and at our school."

"But isn't it just like Satan to use a child?" said Jack. "I mean, that's getting really low."

"Well, he can use God's own people, too. How many of

you have heard some destructive talk about this before coming to the meeting tonight?"

Every man put up his hand.

Vic related, "I ran into the Jessups at the filling station, and they were wondering how many other kids got abused."

Tom cringed at that. "Abused? Just what do they mean by that?"

"You can fill in the blank, Tom."

"Well, we have the newspaper and KBZT to thank for that," said Jack. "They've been tossing that word around like it was a fact."

"And that's my point," said Mark. "We're the elders of this church, and we've got to keep a lid on this thing. There are going to be questions flying and a lot of accusations and gossip, and we'd better be thinking of how we're going to handle it."

Vic raised his eyebrows, shrugged one shoulder, and said, "Well, as far as the Jessups are concerned, they're taking their two kids out. They don't want any part of it."

"Neither do the Wingers," said Doug.

"And they said I was a fool for keeping my three in there," said Bob.

The phone out in the kitchen rang again. They could hear Cathy answering it.

Mark commented, "That's probably another family with the same concerns." He looked at Tom. "Well, Tom, let's get the first item covered and then we can go from there."

Cathy peeked in. "Ted Walroth's on the phone. He saw the news tonight, and he wants to know if we're going to have a congregational meeting."

"Tell him I'll call him back," said Mark. Cathy went to tell him, and Mark returned his attention to Tom. "You want to tell them?"

Tom didn't hesitate. "I'm stepping down as headmaster of the school; I'm going to take a leave of absence until this whole thing gets cleared up."

Jack was ready to debate that move. "Who says?"

"The school's in trouble because of me. If we're going to save it at all, I've got to get out of the picture."

He was right. Every man at the table hated to admit it, but he was right. There was a long, fidgety silence. They all looked at the table or out the window or around the room, and only occasionally at each other.

Mark decided to break the silence. "Tom and I talked and prayed about it, and we agreed that all of us have to face the facts as they are: the ruckus is over him; he's the center of the controversy. Now I know we're all standing with him, but the matter of his innocence is secondary. The biggest and most immediate concern right now is the confidence of the parents and the community. That confidence is taking a real beating right now, and it's going to be hard to get it back if we keep Tom in his position."

Jack fidgeted, looked this way and that, and then gave the table a pound. "But, Mark, we can't do that! It'd be like admitting Tom's guilty!"

Doug jumped in. "But, Dad, some people already think that! I've talked to some folks just today who are ready to give the whole thing up, just pull out of the school and let it die. They're knocked on their backs by this thing."

Mark cut in. "But that's part of the warfare, guys. Satan set this whole thing up so he could weaken us with gossip and slander. We need to do as much as we can to protect ourselves from that, or at least provide no fuel for the fire."

Tom explained, "If I stay at the school, we won't be able to convince anyone that we're truly concerned about all this. *I'm* concerned. I'm willing to step down in good faith until we can get all this trouble resolved."

"We'll do all we can to keep the academy open. Mrs. Fields will stay on and teach the remaining kids in her classes. I'll take charge of the remainder in the upper grades. Tom, what's the prospective enrollment?"

Tom had scribbled down a tentative list. "Um . . . I guess we should go for a worst case scenario . . . which would mean that Judy Waring will take out her son Charlie . . . and then

there are the Jessups and their two . . . and then the Wingers
with their three . . ."

"What about the Walroths?" asked Jack.

Mark answered, "I'll be calling him. I think I can talk him
into hanging on for a while."

"So we'll leave those two children in?" asked Tom.

"For now."

Tom wrote them back in. "Okay. That means five kids are
out of Mrs. Fields's class. Her enrollment's cut in half. My
class is down by one. That isn't too bad."

"So for now we'll be able to survive," said Mark. "But
tonight we'll have to talk about Tom's salary while he's out,
plus some more volunteer help to keep things running—I
won't have time to do all the bookkeeping and administrat-
ing. Then we'll have to reassign the bus route now that the
Wingers are out and get someone else to organize the hot
lunches now that the Warings are out."

"Donna Hemphile called today," Tom remembered. "She's
very supportive of the school, and willing to put in any time
she can spare when she's not tied up at the door factory."

"Who?" asked Doug.

"Donna Hemphile," said Mark. "She's a supervisor at the
Bergen Door Company, a single gal."

"Yeah, she's nice," said Jack.

"Anyway," said Tom, "she says she'll take care of hot
lunches, probably two days a week."

"Good enough." Mark wrote it down in his own notes.
"Okay, other things to discuss tonight: We need to update
you on what Wayne Corrigan told us, and what we have to do
to fight this thing in court." Mark looked at Tom. "And
there's also the latest report on your kids."

Tom looked tired. He'd been through quite a battle already
over that issue. "Wayne Corrigan called this afternoon. He
finally got in touch with someone at the District Court in
Claytonville. They had the hearing today, in Judge Benson's
court. It took about ten minutes, I understand. I guess I didn't
miss anything; they would have barred me from the court-

room anyway. The judge approved the removal and set a date for the trial in October."

"October?" Jack exclaimed. "So what happens in the meantime?"

"I'm supposed to get some counseling, but from a court-appointed counselor. I'll be able to visit the kids, I don't know exactly when, and it'll be controlled; a social worker will have to be there . . ." Tom couldn't continue.

"Well, I say we fight this thing," said Jack. "Let the others run and hide. If being Christian is too tough for them, well, they can't say Jesus didn't warn them. But let's fight it! Let's go to our knees, and beseech the Lord to show us a way out of this. Our God is greater than any lawsuit or any bunch of social service bureaucrats! He'll stand with us, and that's . . . well, that's my final word on the subject!"

Mark looked around the table. "So how about the rest of you? Let me hear from you now, before we take another step."

"Let's fight it," said Doug.

"We're in this for the Lord," said Bob. "He'll help us."

Vic raised his hand to be counted. "Hey, if it had to happen to us, then it had to happen to us. Looks like we're first in line, guys. If we fall, all the other Christian schools are going to fall next. We'd better give them a good fight, with the Lord's help."

Mark felt the hand of God upon these men. He met Tom's eyes, and through Tom's tears he saw a quiet confidence.

"Then let's go to prayer," he said, "and let our agreement this night be settled in Heaven."

They joined hands around the table, making their covenant with each other and God.

High above the town, hovering between Heaven and Earth, his wings a soft, blurred canopy, Captain Tal overheard the transaction. The saints had bound themselves together in prayer according to the will of God; the Lord Almighty had received their petition. There was agreement, and that agreement was now sealed.

"Good," said Tal, "good enough!"

In Claytonville, the demons abruptly called it a day. The last of them swooped down, spit out some insults, and then soared off like a crazed swallow into the night, leaving Chimon and Scion alone on the roof of the motel. The sudden silence was jarring.

"Well," said Chimon, "did we get a prayer?"

"Looks that way," said Scion.

They sat on the roof, their swords resting on the shingles, their eyes scanning the sky. Below them, Sally Roe was lying down to sleep.

Perhaps now they would all have some peace for the night.

eLeven

The Bergen Door Company was a noisy, dusty place employing about a hundred people, the only real industry to be found in Bacon's Corner. It was Friday morning, and during the regular work shift the planers, sanders, saws, and drills produced such a deafening din that ear protection was required and also a lot of lipreading.

Ben wore ear protection—little sponge-rubber earplugs—and also safety glasses as he walked through the factory. He'd never been here before, and found it a fascinating place, with the smell of sawdust filling the air, and doors, doors, doors everywhere, some stacked, some standing, some riding the forklift down to the loading dock; small doors, big doors, cheap doors, exquisite doors.

He was catching a few glances from the employees as he passed by. The sight of a uniformed police officer often roused curiosity, as if "something" was up. He just smiled cordially at the hefty women, the sawdusted men, the part-time students, the single mothers. He recognized many of them, including Donna Hemphile, busily supervising a big material sorting project. She recognized him and waved.

"Hey, Ben, what are you doing here?" she hollered.

"Oh, just a little business," he answered, probably not loud enough for her to hear him. He was hesitant to talk about it.

Up ahead, at the center of all the hubbub, was the enclosed office space of the floor supervisor, Abby Grayson. She spotted him through the office window and gave him a wave. The front office had already called ahead, and she was expecting him.

"Come in out of the racket," she said, throwing open the door.

He stepped inside the little cubicle and she closed the door after him, shutting out the noise.

"Have a seat," she said. "You must be that new cop. I don't

think we've met before, and maybe that's a good thing, you know?"

They went through some friendly introductions. Abby was a homely but personable lady in her forties; she and her husband were real career people in this place. She'd just received her twenty year pin, and he his twenty-five.

"Well," she said, "we're all pretty shocked. Sally was a good worker. It's too bad she didn't open up a little more. We thought she might have some deep problems, but . . . Hey, we *tried* to be friends; what can I say?"

"I've heard from several people that she was reclusive," Ben said.

"Yeah, pretty much a hermit. We invited her to the last Christmas party, and I think she almost came, but then she found some excuse and stayed home. She didn't get out much as far as any of us could tell."

"You wouldn't have any photographs of her, would you?"

"Funny you should mention that. I guess she hated having her picture taken. We were all going to pose for a company picture . . . When was that? I think around Labor Day, and I remember she just kept hiding behind people and turning away. Ehh, some people are like that."

"So what kind of person was she really? What were some of your impressions?"

Abby took a moment to consider the question. "She was bright and intelligent, good with her hands, and caught on to the job right away, really easy to train. But there was always something a little strange about her." Abby smiled about a thought that came to her. "Well, I suppose I can say it now. You know . . . I think she was hiding something. A lot of us thought that."

"Hiding something?"

Abby shook her head and chuckled. "Oh, we came up with all kinds of silly notions, talking about her maybe being a fugitive from the law, or an ex-con, or a witch, or a hooker, or a lesbian . . . It was pretty silly, but when people are that secretive, that quiet, you wonder about them a little. It's only natural."

"Well?"

"Well what?"

"Was she any of those things to your knowledge?"

She laughed. "No. It was talk, nothing but talk."

"But still you think she was hiding something . . ."

"I don't know. She just acted like it, I guess."

Ben chuckled to keep the atmosphere relaxed. "Well . . . how about a description? What did she look like?"

"Oh . . ." Abby's eyes drifted about the room as she reconstructed an image of Sally Roe in her mind. "About my height, and I'm 5' 6". Red hair . . . long . . . I saw her brushing it out once; it went down to about the middle of her back. But she kept it bound up in a checkered scarf when she was working here, so you never saw much of it."

"Color of eyes?"

"Color of eyes . . . Boy, I never gave it much thought Seems to me they were brown."

"How old was she?"

"Thirties. Maybe a little older."

"How about her weight?"

"Pretty good," and with that comment Abby laughed. "I don't know, she looked all right to me, enough to be jealous about, anyway."

Ben had heard enough for now. He stood up. "Well, thanks a lot. If I think of any more questions I'll give you a jingle. Oh . . ." He scribbled his phone number on a piece of paper. "If you come up with anything you think I'd want to know, just give me a call at home. It'll be fine."

"Sure thing." She stood and shook his hand. "Well, it was a real shock, just really tough news."

He nodded.

"And then that news this morning about the Christian school and what that teacher was doing! What a world, huh? You just never know about people . . . It's kind of scary."

Ango was nothing significant, nothing to bow to, worship, revere, or dread. He was small, thin like a spider, and ugly. Oh, he knew it. He lived with it. He put up with the taunts of the other spirits who lorded it over him, ordered him this way and that way, took his glory, gave him their blame. Ah, it was all part of the warfare, all part of the master's plan for the earth, and each spirit had his own role, his own station, his own level of power. He knew his was a lowly station. To the rest of the demonic kingdom, what was the Bacon's Corner Elementary School? What did it matter among all the schools in the world?

His lips stretched open, and his jagged teeth clicked and gnashed as he hissed a giggle. Oh, this place *did* matter now! The other spirits had laughed and chided, but somewhere, seated loftily at the peak of power, the Strongman himself had chosen this place to begin the Plan. He had spoken the name of Ango as the spirit to be placed in charge! Now little ugly Ango had the Strongman's favor—and the other spirits' envy!

But why not? He deserved it. It took years to take control of this school—to oust the resisters, to implant the sympathizers, to blind the parents to what was happening to their children. It was no small task.

But it happened, and all because of Ango! Let the other spirits call him little and ugly. At this school he was *Ba-al* Ango, the beautiful and mighty. All the deceivers who flitted, darted, and hovered around that place were at his command, and through them many of the teachers, as well as the principal and the vice-principal. That was a precious power, a constant titillation, a marvelous reward for all those years and all that work. As he sat on his haunches on the expansive tar roof, he indulged himself in some hacking, sulfurous laughter.

He was thinking of all those young, impressionable children sitting in all those classrooms down there, and what they must be learning right now. As usual, most of his spirit underlings were occupied with that task. They were the best, and he reveled in the fact that for the past several years, ever since the laws had been changed, their job had been so much easier. Oh, how quickly men could accept the most outrageous of lies once the Truth was removed from consideration!

Yes, there were still some bold saints of God lurking about like stubborn weeds in this otherwise flourishing garden, causing trouble with their protests, parent-teacher conferences, telephone babblings, and notes, notes, notes to the teachers, but . . .

Ango wheezed out another sulfurous laugh and rolled like a playful pup on the black tar. No matter. They were losing. Let them protest. *He* held all the power here.

Mota, strong, tall, and deep bronze, stood with his sword in his hand, his piercing eyes on the Bacon's Corner Elementary School, and his feet in about eight inches of chicken manure. His oriental friend and fellow-warrior Signa stood beside him, as deep into the same predicament. Were they not angelic spirits, it would have been most unpleasant. As it was, they were not disturbed by their surroundings, and the eight hundred cackling leghorns were not aware of their presence in this old chicken house.

It was Friday, and almost time for lunch and the noon recess.

"She's on her way," said Signa.

"Now," said Mota.

They were gone.

The bell rang for lunch. Ango could hear all the classroom doors opening and the mobs of children filling the halls. Recess would be an enjoyable time, just like always. What corruption the teachers could not spread in the classroom, the children could spread among themselves on the playground.

"Hail!" came a booming voice behind him.

"Aaaak!" Ango's sword was immediately in his hand as he spun to face the heavenly warrior. Oh, he was a big brute! A massive Polynesian, shining like lightning, with wings that scattered the fire of the sun. His sword was drawn, and it glimmered with a living light, but he held it downward, the tip resting on the roof.

"Forces!" Ango screamed, and fifty demons popped up

through the roof like startled gophers with squawks and hoots of surprise and rage. They surrounded the big warrior.

"What brings you here?" Ango demanded.

But Mota wanted a little more space. He raised his sword, held it straight out at waist level, and began to sweep it in a wide circular arc around him. The seething, hissing spirits backed off when the tip of the sword passed under their chugging noses.

Now he was more comfortable, and spoke. "I'm looking for a petty little lizard called . . . Ankle . . . Inkle . . ."

"You seek Ango!"

Mota smiled and raised his index finger. "Yes! Ingo, that's it!"

"Ango!" the demon corrected.

Two guards were at their posts by the main door when Signa dropped out of the sky like a ball of lightning and knocked them both to the ground by his sheer presence.

"Forces!" they screamed, struggling to their feet, grabbing their swords. Twenty demons were immediately on hand, swords drawn, eyes gawking at this visitor.

One spirit shot out of the school in careless haste, not wanting to miss anything, his sword waving, his wings whirring. He got too close to the warrior.

Whoosh! The sword moved so fast it looked like a disk of light. Shredded particles of the spirit fluttered and floated in all directions, trailing red smoke and dissolving out of sight. The tip of the sword was now poised and ready for the next brazen attacker.

No one felt that brazen. They remained like statues, their eyes on this warrior. He remained motionless as well, watching them with his fiery eyes.

Sally Roe reached up and pulled the bell cord. The little bell at the front of the bus went *ding*, and the driver slowed for the next stop along the Toe Springs–Claytonville Road. She could see the Bacon's Corner Elementary School just ahead. She'd never been inside, but somehow she'd just have to find her way around without being seen by too many people. She'd done as much as she could to look unlike Sally Roe; she had her hair—black now—braided and pinned behind her head; she'd found some sunglasses that could pass for tinted eyewear, although they bothered her; she knew her old factory clothes would not be a good idea, so she'd managed to purchase a casual outfit—slacks, blouse, loafers. Apart from that, she could only hope that no one at this little school had ever seen her before or knew who she was.

The bus pulled to a stop, and she got off right in front of the school.

Mota still seemed unsure. "No . . . it cannot be Ango. I see no one here who fits what I have heard of him. I seek Ango the small, weak, and pitiful."

Ango could feel the stares of his subordinates. Of course they wanted to see what he would do. He raised his sword, and they all did the same. "The Ango you seek is mighty! He is Ba-al of this place!"

"Ba-al?" Mota asked. "A spirit with only half a heart, and less of a brain?"

"Gaaaa!!" Ango cried, raising his sword over his head. "*I am Ango!*"

He brought his sword down in a red, glowing blur. The huge sword of the warrior was there instantly and took the blow.

Mota was surprised. This little demon could strike hard, with much greater strength than Mota expected. He hid his concern, however, and only acted as if he finally realized whom he was addressing. "Ooohhhh . . ."

"Forces—" Ango screamed.

Mota thrust his sword right under Ango's nose. "Before you attack . . ." Ango swallowed the order. "I would like to state my business with you."

Signa had the attention of the guards in front of the school and at least half the demons from inside it.

"And now," he said, "we'd like to take a look inside this school."

The guards spit sulfur at him, and for a moment he was blinded. He raised his sword in defense and tried to clear his eyes, stumbling backwards out onto the school lawn. The guards followed him, pushing him back, waving their swords. The other spirits felt a new courage, and moved in closer, hissing, spitting, holding their swords high.

They were not watching the door.

Sally walked briskly up the front walk and through the door. The clock in the main hall said she was on time; it was 11:50, time for lunch break. Now to find Miss Brewer's classroom, Room 105. It was either to the left or the right, but first she'd have to pass by the school office. There was a receptionist standing behind the counter, and several office personnel working at desks behind her. *Well,* she thought, *if I just look like I know what I'm doing, maybe they won't ask to help me.*

She headed for the hall, walking by the reception counter, keeping her eyes ahead, not slowing her walk, not looking bewildered. *Come on, Sally, make it convincing.*

"Don't you move!" said the demon behind the counter. "Don't you come one step closer to me!"

Chimon and Scion had come in with Sally, and were now standing at the counter, their wings unfurled, totally blocking any view of the hallway. Their swords were drawn, but at their sides. They didn't speak, but just looked at this slimy creature yelling at them.

"How did you get in here?" the demon demanded. "Guards!"

Suddenly Scion's hot blade rested right between the demon's yellow fangs. He thought it best not to pronounce another word.

The receptionist looked at the clock. Hmm. Miss Brewer was expecting a visitor today; the receptionist thought she'd heard someone come in, but there was no one in the hall. *Well, the visitor must be a little late.*

Sally took a left turn down the hall, disappearing around the corner. It had to be a miracle that that lady behind the counter had not seen her. Oh well. Now to find Room 105.

Good! Here was Room 103, and now Room 104, and bingo! Room 105!

She stood in the open doorway and knocked on the jamb.

Miss Brewer, the young and pretty fourth grade teacher, rose from her desk with a welcoming smile and extended her hand. "Hello. You must be Mrs. Jenson!"

Sally took her hand and replied pleasantly, "And you are Miss Brewer."

"Please come in."

I can't believe I'm doing this, Sally thought. She immediately stopped thinking such things—it could ruin her act.

Miss Brewer motioned Sally to a chair beside her desk and then continued to the bookshelf behind it. "So how are things at the Association?"

Sally sat down and kept her eyes on Miss Brewer. "Well, just wonderful so far. I'm really glad to be working for them now."

"Well," said Miss Brewer, pulling a loose-leaf binder from the shelf, "we've certainly enjoyed this curriculum, and the kids really take to it. Most of our parents are very pleased."

She set the binder on the desk in front of Sally, and Sally smiled as she picked it up. On the cover were the words, "Sexual Understanding and Family Life, Fourth Grade." At the bottom was the name of the publisher, Freeman Education Associates. She began to leaf through it.

"Could I help you find what you're looking for?"

"Oh, don't take your lunchtime to help me. I have a whole list of revisions . . . Let's see, this is the newest edition, isn't it? All right, that should make it easier, not quite as much to doublecheck."

"Just what was the problem?"

Sally had her story well rehearsed. "Well, the quotes are

accurate enough, but the sources didn't feel the attributions were clearly enough stated, so now I have to prepare a reply and . . . wouldn't you know it, I left my copy in the last town. Well, such are the hazards of being on the road."

"It must be exciting, though, servicing so many schools around the state. Has the curriculum been well received in other school districts?"

"For the most part, yes."

Miss Brewer paused to think, then chuckled, sitting on the edge of the desk. "Having trouble with the right-wing fundamentalists?"

Sally chuckled back and nodded. "That's one reason I have to review all the attributions, to make sure everybody's legally covered."

"Oh, what a world!"

Sally took a chance. "Speaking of fundamentalist problems, I understand Amber Brandon was in your class?"

Miss Brewer smiled with curiosity. "Now how did you know that?"

"Well, yours is the only fourth grade class, and the paper said that the child involved in the lawsuit was in the fourth grade, and I learned somewhere that the child was Amber, so . . ."

Amber's former teacher nodded sadly. "Isn't it awful? I'm glad they're taking this thing to court. We've just got to stop all this harassment and censorship. Enough is enough."

"Listen, don't let me keep you from lunch!"

Miss Brewer set out for the door. "Can I bring you anything?"

"Oh, no, don't worry about me. I won't be long anyway."

"Fine. Just take your time."

And with that, she was out the door and down the hall.

Sally waited just a moment, then closed the binder and placed it back on the shelf it came from. Then she looked among the other binders, books, and materials for the title she was after. The kids in the class had drawn pictures of strange faces, weird animals, gods, and bizarre cartoon characters, and the drawings were still displayed on the walls, along with several complex, mesmerizing pattern studies. The curriculum had to be here.

She found it.

Ango began to curse at Mota as his demon warriors became steadily braver. "Out! Begone, you! This is our territory, and none of your concern!"

Mota decided to push this demon a little. "Oh, is that what you think?"

He made a move toward the roof, ready to pass through it and invade their little operation.

"Attack!" Ango screamed, and every demon rushed forward, red blade flashing. "Away with him!"

Mota shot skyward, drawing a horde of spirits after him. He stopped, flipped, faced them. His sword became a continuous ribbon of light.

The first demon became two halves that passed by Mota on either side and then sank into oblivion. The second and third he swatted aside. He kicked and bowled down a cluster of eight. But they just kept coming, faster and faster, swinging and slashing with more and more strength. Mota had planned on putting on an act to keep them following him, but suddenly he found he was no longer acting. This fight was real.

The next wave of spirits surged upward. He backed away, his wings reaching higher and higher. He couldn't let this end too soon, but he was beginning to wish he could.

To the west he saw Signa involved in a similar skirmish, taking some real attacks, whipping his sword about and drawing the guards away from the school. He was backing away, about to be surrounded.

Chimon and Scion could hear the commotion all around the outside of the school. The demons sounded rather jubilant.

"YAAA!!" Suddenly four huge demonic thugs exploded through the walls on every side, their teeth bared, their talons ready to tear.

Chimon and Scion shot through the roof of the school like two rockets, retreating, totally surprised, and angry about it.

"Where did they come from?" Chimon hollered.

Scion was too busy defending himself against their swords and sharp teeth to answer. It was like being chased up a huge tree by a foaming pack of rabid dogs.

They backed away, higher and higher, trying to stay clear of those whistling red blades. What horrible situation had they walked into?

Sally's hands were shaking and she was afraid to open the three-ring binder now in her lap. The title sounded harmless enough: *Finding the Real Me—Self-Esteem and Personal Fulfillment Studies for Fourth-Graders.*

She flipped the cover open and quickly perused the title page. She didn't recognize the author's name, but the name of the publisher immediately turned her stomach: The Omega Center for Educational Studies. With great effort, she turned several more pages, skimming the contents. She found a particular index tab and skipped far forward to a later chapter.

Her heart was pounding as if she'd sprinted up a hill, and her hands were getting slick with sweat. They were shaking.

The old torments! Her mind was beginning to race again. She could hear the voices calling, mocking, cursing. There were spirits in the room!

She had to get out of there.

She carried the binder to the shelf and tried to put it back. A large atlas fell over, blocking the slot. She almost whimpered out loud as her fingers dug after the fallen atlas, trying to get a grip on it. She lifted it, it slipped out of her fingers, she lifted it again, tried to hold it in place while she jammed the binder in. The binder got hung up on a bulging manila envelope and wouldn't go in; she pressed the envelope aside with her palm.

The binder slipped back into place. As soon as her fingers let go of it, her nausea began to ease.

I've got to get out of here. Right now!

She dashed for the hallway and then ran down to the north entrance, pushing her way outside as if running from a fire.

Above and all around the school, the demons were just returning from a glorious rout. They had chased those pesky warriors of Heaven away at last, and now the territory of the glorious Ango was safe again.

Far above the school, a safe distance away, Mota, Signa, Chimon, and Scion gathered to update each other.

"What happened down there?" Chimon wondered.

"Ango and his imps were never this strong!" said Signa, still rubbing the burning sulfur out of his eyes.

Scion was checking a good-sized cut in his leg as he said, "We were all playing the fool to go into that thinking only of a diversion. They meant business!"

Far below, looking as small as an insect on the vast green terrain, Sally was running back to the Toe Springs-Claytonville Road. She would probably run to the next bus stop instead of waiting in front of the school where she might be seen. At least five taunting, torturing spirits were following her, buzzing about her head like angry hornets.

"They'll follow her to her next destination," said Signa.

"When they're clear of this place we'll take them out," said Mota. "We can't fight them here."

"Cree and Si are already at Omega. They have no idea what's in store for them!"

They all knew the problem without anyone having to say it. Mota finally did. "The prayer cover. We're losing it!"

Tom Harris pushed his grocery cart up and down the aisles of the PriceWise grocery, making his weekly rounds. He was having a little trouble with his shopping list; with Ruth and Josiah gone, he wasn't sure what items he should restock and which he should just skip for now. He crossed off the breakfast cereal—there was still plenty of that. The milk in the refrigerator was going sour. He decided he would pour it down the sink and just buy a quart today instead of the usual two half-gallons.

"Hey, Mr. Harris!"

Oh! It was Jody Jessup, the little fifth-grader. It was strange seeing her here in the store during a school day, but then, Tom wasn't usually in the store during the school day either. In any case, he was happy to see her bright smile again.

"Hi, Jody! How're you doing?"

She came running down the aisle past the cornflakes and oatmeal, her long brown hair flying. "I'm with my mom. I get to help her buy groceries."

She pressed against his side, and he gave her a little hug around the shoulders. "Well, it's great to see you."

"It feels funny not being in school anymore."

Tom agreed. "Yes, it sure does."

Then came an alarmed voice from down the aisle. "Jody! Come here!"

It was Andrea Jessup, Jody's mother, pushing her shopping cart with Jody's younger brother Brian by her side. Tom was shocked and incredulous at the coldness in her eyes.

He waved. "Hi, Andrea. Good to see you. Hi, Brian!"

Andrea ignored him. "Jody! Come here right now! I don't want you talking to Mr. Harris!" Jody hurried back to her mother. Andrea bent and barked the order directly into Jody's face. "You stay with me now, and don't talk to strangers!"

Jody started to object, "But that's Mr. Harris!"

"Don't argue with me!"

And then they were gone around the corner; Tom could hear their conversation moving down the next aisle.

"You stay away from that man," she was saying. "Don't you go anywhere near him! And that goes for you too, Brian!"

Brian started asking questions, but Andrea hushed both her children and continued down the aisle.

Tom's life came to a halt, right there next to the breakfast cereal. The Jessups used to be such good friends, and so supportive. He'd shared dinner with them on several occasions, he'd played with their kids, they'd gone together on field trips with the whole school. Jody and Brian were—used to be—two of his best students.

No more. Everything had changed. Tom tried to think of a good reason, but couldn't. He tried to think of what he had to buy next, but he couldn't think of that either.

Lord, he finally prayed silently, *I haven't done anything! Why did Andrea treat me like that?*

Then he began to wonder how many more of his own brothers and sisters in the Lord felt the same way about him.

Andrea kept pushing her cart along, grabbing pickles and relish off the shelf with hardly a glance, and moving on. She wanted to get out of the store before she saw that man again, before her children saw him again. She'd never been so upset at anyone in her life. The nerve of that man!

A small spirit, Strife, followed Andrea. He had nervous, agitated wings that never stopped quivering and a blaring mouth that more than made up for his size. He ran along the tops of the jars and boxes, hurdling the Saltine crackers and leaping over the paper towels.

He lied to you all along! he shouted to her. *And you know, Pastor Mark is lying too, trying to protect him! You don't know half of what went on in that school!*

On the other side of the aisle, rushing through the flour and sugar and somersaulting over the cooking oil, Gossip filled in all of Strife's pauses. *Sexual! He has problems with sex! It has to be sexual! You'd better ask around and see if anyone knows anything! You just never know about these people! Talk to Judy Waring! She might know!*

Andrea got more enraged, the more she thought about this whole Christian school scandal. *That Tom Harris needs prayer,* she thought.

But she hadn't done much praying.

Mulligan's ears were so red they almost glowed.

"Cole! You are just that far from being canned!"

Mulligan towered over Ben's desk like a rotting tree about to fall, and Ben felt he should stand up to keep from being crushed, except that Mulligan might interpret that move as aggressive.

Mulligan pointed his finger—it seemed a bit red too—right in Ben's face. "Were you out at the Potter place the other day?"

"Wednesday afternoon, sir," Ben replied, noting that he'd called Harold "sir." *Wow, I must be scared.*

"And just who ordered you to go out there?"

"The visit was voluntary, sir. I had a little free time, so I—"

"So you thought you'd snoop around without authorization, isn't that right?"

Ben drew a breath and then released it slowly before he said another word. He had to be careful now because he was upset. "I was not aware, sir, that the Potter residence was off-limits to a law officer, especially when his presence there was with the full invitation and welcome of Mrs. Potter herself."

"So how about that little visit out to the door factory? What about that?"

"They were glad enough to have me there."

"And I say you misused your badge!"

Now Ben did stand up, tall and straight. "You might be interested in what I've found out, Sergeant Mulligan, *sir*."

"If it's about Sally Roe, forget it! That case is closed because I said so!"

"The descriptions of Sally Roe that I got from Mrs. Potter and from Abby Grayson at the Bergen Door Company were consistent. Sally Roe was in her mid- to late-thirties, about five six, with long red hair."

"What of it?"

"The woman we found in the goat shed was younger, and had black hair, probably shoulder-length, but no longer."

Mulligan smiled a smile of pity. He put his big hand on Ben's shoulder and spoke condescendingly. "Cole . . . come on. It was dark in there. You only saw the body for a second. I don't know what's gotten into you."

"Harold . . . why was the house ransacked? Did you authorize that?"

"Sure I did. We were looking for evidence."

"Evidence of what? You said it was a suicide."

"Standard procedure. Isn't your shift about over?"

"I do have a message for you from Mrs. Potter. She'd like to have that mess cleaned up by whoever it was that made it."

"That's taken care of . . . Don't worry your little head about it."

"And whatever happened to Sally Roe's pickup?"

Mulligan looked at him just a little funny. "What pickup?"

"Sally Roe always drove a '65 blue Chevy pickup. I let Mrs. Potter go through our vehicle ID book yesterday, and she pointed out the make and model to me. The truck's nowhere around the property. Roe had to have driven it home from work the evening she allegedly killed herself. I was wondering if the same people who ransacked the house may have made off with her truck."

Mulligan looked a little worried. "I don't know anything about that."

"And since we're on the subject, I'm still wondering about that bloodstained shirt we found. Did the coroner ever check the blood type? That scene was full of signs of violence. And the body . . . That woman didn't hang herself!"

Mulligan turned his back on Ben, stomped into his office, and returned with some papers in his hand. He slapped them on Ben's desk. "There! The county coroner's report on the death of Sally Roe! Read it for yourself! Death by asphyxiation from hanging. Not murder, not a struggle, not anything! Now if you disagree with the coroner, why don't you come up with another body for him to examine?"

"There might be one."

Mulligan actually grabbed Ben's shirt in his fist. His eyes were wild, and he hissed the words through jaws locked shut in anger. "Stop right there! Not another word!" Ben said nothing, but he didn't back down either. Mulligan didn't like that at all. "Your shift is over for today, Officer Cole, and if I hear one more word about this from you, your *job* is going to be over, you got that?"

Mulligan let go of Ben's uniform with a feisty little shove. Ben did what he could to straighten out the wrinkles. "I'll be watching you, boy, I mean really watching you. You drop this Sally Roe thing, you hear? One more false step from you, and I'm going to have myself some real joy ripping that badge right off your chest!"

twelve

WELL, *those guys mean business, I guess.*

Wayne Corrigan sat at his desk after-hours, drinking one last cup of coffee from his thermos and looking through several pages of notes Mark Howard, Tom Harris, and the church board had compiled in answer to the temporary injunction against the school.

All the usual arguments for corporal punishment were clearly laid out—the Scriptures from Proverbs about the rod, of course, and a definitive procedure for spanking clearly outlined in the *Student-Parent Handbook*. Lucy Brandon's signature on the enrollment agreement constituted her agreement with the handbook, so that wasn't going to be hard to argue. It was obvious the church board had done their homework many times over in this area.

As for their argument against any restraint from "further religious behavior which could prove harmful to the mental, emotional, or social welfare of the child, or any excessive religious instruction that could prove harmful," they did a pretty good study on that, with Scripture after Scripture declaring the existence, purpose, behavior, and "casting out" of demons, as well as a general apologetic for the basic gospel message. This was definitely a matter of religious belief, supposedly protected by the Constitution, sure . . .

But an exorcism perpetrated upon a ten-year-old child? A minor, with no parental consent? Where was that provided for in the handbook? When did Mrs. Brandon agree to that kind of treatment for her daughter?

He stopped cold. This case was too big and the stakes were too high. It was more than he could handle.

Yeah. Those ACFA guys found just what they were looking for; the way they would handle the case, the Constitution would be just so much toilet paper when children were involved.

Well, Corrigan, you did it again: you said yes too easily. Now the hearing's in twelve days. Better do something.

"Lord God," he prayed, "I'm in over my head again. I need Your help to bail me out . . . to bail *all of us* out."

He started scribbling out a brief for the court, trying to cover the items in the complaint. Misuse of federal funds was easy to refute, and Discrimination and Harassment were basically a walk in the park, but then came the tricky stuff, and he began to pray in earnest as he wrote every line.

On Monday morning, a week after Ruth and Josiah were first hauled from his home, Tom got a call from an unidentified lady at the Child Protection Department. Without consulting him, and with no prior notice other than this call, an appointment had been set for him to visit with his children for one hour under the supervision of a child welfare counselor. The appointment was for 11 that morning, at the courthouse in Claytonville.

He barely made it in time, pulling into a visitor parking slot at the courthouse at 10:52. He doublechecked his appearance in the visor mirror, straightening his tie, smoothing down his hair, his hands trembling and his stomach queasy from the anticipation. He grabbed a brown bag of things for the kids, locked up the car, and bounded up the concrete steps of the old stone building.

The inside hall was cold marble, tall, gray, and imposing. Every footstep echoed like a public announcement, and he felt naked in this place. Lawyers, clerks, and other just-plain folks passed him on every side, and he found it hard to look them in the eye. What if they had seen his face in the paper or on television? They probably wouldn't want his autograph.

The girl at the information desk took his name and offered him a seat on a hard wooden bench against the wall.

"I'll let them know you're here," she said.

He sat there and slowly scratched his chin, looking down at the marble floor. He felt angry, but he knew he couldn't let it show, he couldn't let it come out, or he'd only make things worse.

He prayed repeatedly, *O Lord, what can I do? I don't even know what to say . . .*

He naturally thought of Cindy, now gone for three years. Difficult times such as this reminded him of how much he always needed her, and how much he had lost. He'd recovered from the initial grief, yes, but sometimes, when life was at its darkest and the struggle was the most uphill, out of habit he would reach for her, think of her, rehearse the words to share his pain. But then would come that same, persistent reminder, the realization that she was gone, replaced by a closely following shadow of sorrow.

Cindy, he thought, *you just wouldn't believe what's happening down here. I guess it's the persecution Jesus and the apostles warned us about. I guess it always seemed like something far away, maybe in Soviet Russia, or during Roman times, but not here, not now. I never thought it would actually happen to me, and I sure didn't think it would happen to the kids.*

He pulled his handkerchief from his pocket to wipe his tears away. He couldn't let the kids see him like this—and what would the state people think?

"Mr. Harris?"

He sucked in a breath and immediately, even desperately, tried to compose himself. *Tom, whatever you do, be cordial! Don't give her anything to use against you!*

He was looking up at none other than Irene Bledsoe.

"I'm sure you remember me?" she said, sitting near him on the bench.

"Yes." He figured that would be safe.

"Before I take you upstairs to see your children, I need to remind you that this visitation is a privilege that can be revoked at any time. We expect you to remain on your best behavior and to comply with my instructions at all times. You are not to touch your children, but remain on your own side of the conference table. You cannot ask them anything about where they are staying. Any other questions that I may deem inappropriate will be disallowed, and the meeting can be terminated at any time if I find it necessary. Is all that clear to you?"

"But . . . Mrs. Bledsoe, are we going to have a chance to talk this thing out? I want to get this whole mess cleared up and get my children back home with me where they belong."

"That won't be possible at this time; our investigation is still in progress."

"What investigation? I haven't heard a thing from anyone, and I haven't even been able to get through to you."

"We have a very heavy caseload, Mr. Harris. You'll just have to be patient."

Tom felt an anger, even a hunger for revenge rising inside him, something totally un-Christian, he knew, but it was irrepressible. He just couldn't think of any words that would be civil.

Irene Bledsoe asked him again, more firmly, "Is all that I have said clear to you?"

All he could do was give her the right answer. "Yes."

"What is this package?"

Tom opened it for her to see. "I brought some things for the kids. They don't have their Bibles, so I brought them, and some pens and stationery."

"Fine." She took the bag. "Come with me."

She took off at a hurried, efficient pace, the *pock, pock, pock* of her heels telling everyone on the floor she was passing by. Tom just tried to step quietly; this kind of attention he didn't need.

She led him up the winding marble staircase to the second floor, along the balcony overlooking the front entry, and through a heavy, uninviting door with big brass hinges and a knob that had to weigh twenty pounds. They passed through a cold and bare antechamber with one tall window letting in grayish light. A security guard stood by an archway to the right, looking just a little bored, but manning his post. Tom followed Mrs. Bledsoe past the guard and through the archway.

Tom's heart leaped into his throat, and tears flooded his eyes.

There, seated on the other side of a large table, were Ruth and Josiah. They were on their feet in an instant at the sight of him, crying "Daddy," their voices shrill with excitement. They ran for him.

Irene Bledsoe stood in their way and blocked them with her arms. "Sit down! Sit down at the table!"

"I want to see my dad!" Josiah cried.

"Daddy!" was all Ruth could say, her hands outstretched.

He couldn't take them in his arms. He couldn't touch them. All he could do was cry. "Sit down now. Do like Mrs. Bledsoe says."

Ruth began sobbing, almost wailing. "Daddy . . ."

"I love you, Ruth! Daddy loves you. Go ahead. Sit down. Everything's going to be all right."

Irene Bledsoe encouraged the children to sit down with a firm hand on their arms.

"Mr. Harris, you may sit in this chair facing your children. Let me remind you of what we discussed downstairs."

We didn't "discuss" anything, Tom thought. *You gave the orders, I sat there and listened.*

He slowly slid the chair out and sat down. He couldn't waste this time crying. He tried to sober up, and pulled out his handkerchief to wipe his eyes again.

"How are you two?"

"I wanna go home, Daddy," said Ruth, still sobbing.

Josiah was trying to be brave, and wiped his eyes like his father. "We miss you."

"Is Mrs. Bledsoe taking good care of you?"

Mrs. Bledsoe answered that one. "Your children are in very good hands, Mr. Harris, and I think that should be the last of that sort of question."

Tom glared at her. He couldn't hide his anger. "Then I'd like to ask you some questions afterward."

She smiled pleasantly in the children's presence. "We can discuss that later."

Tom noticed the bump on Ruth's head the moment he saw her. Now he was ready to ask about it. "What happened to your head, Ruth?"

Bledsoe cut right in on that question, even rising a little

from her chair. "We can't discuss that! I'm sure you understand!"

"I bumped it in the car," said Ruth.

"Ruth! Don't you talk about that or I'll take you away!"

She started crying in anger now. "How come?"

"It's all right, Ruth," said Tom. "We don't have to talk about it." He turned to Josiah. "So . . . uh . . . what have you guys been doing?"

Josiah was unhappy and made no attempt to hide it. "Nothing. We sit around and watch TV."

Tom was unhappy to hear that, but he didn't show it. "Oh, does Mrs. Bledsoe let you watch TV?"

"No, Mrs. Henley does . . ."

Irene Bledsoe was right on top of that. "Josiah, we can't talk about who our foster parents are. That's a secret."

Tom tried to get the conversation back into safe territory. "So . . . how about reading? Have you read any good books?"

"No," said Ruth.

"They have some video games," Josiah volunteered. "Those are kind of fun."

"So . . . are there other kids around to play with?" Tom cringed even as he asked the question, but Irene Bledsoe let that one go.

"Yes. There's a boy named Teddy and another boy named Luke. But I don't like them."

"Oh . . ."

"They're bigger, and they pick on us."

"They pick on you?"

"Yeah, they push us around and use bad language. They're not Christians."

Ruth stuck her lower lip out and said, "Luke calls me names."

"Oh, Ruth, that's too bad. Have you tried to be friends?"

She looked at him, and her eyes flooded with tears again. "I want to go home!"

"I want you to come home too."

Tick, tick, tick. Irene Bledsoe was tapping the table with her fingernail and glaring at Tom.

Josiah must have caught that signal. He was a sharp little nine-year-old. "Ruth bumped her head on the side of the car."

"Now that's enough!" said Mrs. Bledsoe.

Tom looked at Irene Bledsoe and tried to keep his face calm. "What car, Mrs. Bledsoe?"

Mrs. Bledsoe looked at him with her eyebrows raised and her head tilted forward, so condescendingly. "Mr. Harris, we've found that children will usually concoct stories to protect their parents."

Tom caught her meaning. He had to choose—seriously, *strenuously* choose—to stay calm and cordial. "And just what story did both Ruth and Josiah concoct, Mrs. Bledsoe?"

She raised her chin and appeared to look down at him. "Mr. Harris, I can understand how you would be concerned about the injury to Ruth's head. But you should know, so are we. I'm sure that, given time to get over their fears and prior conditioning, your children will be ready to tell us the truth. For now, I think this visit is concluded." She rose from her chair. "Children, say good-bye to your father."

"We just got here!" said Josiah.

"I don't wanna go!" Ruth wailed, her face filling with fear.

"Children, we are going!" said Mrs. Bledsoe.

"Just one moment!" said Tom. The meeting was shot anyway. He dove for the opportunity. "Josiah, go ahead. Tell me how Ruth got that bump on her head."

"We almost got in a wreck . . ."

"John!" Mrs. Bledsoe yelled.

The security guard walked into the room and just let his presence be known. Tom didn't want any trouble; he made no moves.

Bledsoe grabbed both children by the arms. "Mr. Harris, I warned you to control yourself, and you can be sure that your behavior will go down in my report!"

"Which part didn't you like? When I bit the chair leg or when I broke out all the windows?"

She started hauling both kids toward the door. Tom was on his feet, ready to do something. The guard stood in his way—

just like Mulligan had stood in his way a week ago. It was happening all over again, right before Tom's eyes. Mrs. Bledsoe was pulling Ruth and Josiah by their arms, taking them away screaming. She reached the archway. He wanted to stand in her way; he wanted to reach out and stop her.

He couldn't. All he could do was watch it happen.

"What wreck, Josiah?" he asked.

"Children, come on!" Bledsoe shouted, pulling them into the antechamber.

"I hit my head," Ruth repeated. "She stopped too fast and I hit my head."

Josiah went for broke. "She went through a stop sign and almost hit a blue pickup truck! Ruth hit her head on the door of the car!"

"She? You mean Mrs. Bledsoe?"

Irene Bledsoe had Ruth through the door and jerked Josiah through before he could complete an answer. But he was nodding a firm yes as he disappeared.

"Kids, I'm proud of you! Real proud of you! I love you!"

They were gone.

"Give 'em a few minutes," said the guard, not letting Tom follow.

Tom sat at the table again. The guard went to the door to make sure Mrs. Bledsoe was in the clear.

Tom noticed the brown paper bag on the floor. Irene Bledsoe had left the package behind, and the kids had not gotten their Bibles or stationery. He couldn't touch them in this way either.

"Okay," said the guard, "you can go now."

His job completed, the guard went out the door and on to other business, leaving Tom alone in the cold, vacant room.

"O Lord . . ."

Tom broke. The tears ran down his face.

But they weren't entirely tears of grief, and they certainly were not tears of despair. He'd seen his kids, and they had shared something, despite Irene Bledsoe, despite the guard. He knew that their souls had touched, that their hearts were still together. It was not enough, of course, to see them for just those few minutes. Such a cold and regimented visit could never be enough. But for right now, it was enough to know they loved him. They loved their daddy. They wanted to be with him.

Now his doubts were gone. Amid all the pain and challenge, the smearing, the soiling of his name, he'd found himself wondering where he really stood. There were voices in his mind telling him horrible things he'd never thought about himself. He tried not to give place to such lies; but still, because the voices were so relentless, he'd wondered if there was something wrong with him, something he'd been blind to. Maybe, the voices would say, he deserved what was happening to him.

But now he knew. He still had his integrity, and before God he still had the hearts of his children. Right now, it was just so wonderful to know that for sure.

Ben and Leonard quickly ducked into Don's Wayside, trying to look casual, even though they were in full uniform, carried their nightsticks, wore their guns, and had their portable radios on their belts, hissing and squawking. Every eye in the place was instantly drawn in their direction.

It was a bust! It was something for everyone to watch and then talk about at home. The contractors sitting at the counter and the truckers sitting at the tables looked up from their lunch and wagged their stubbly jaws only enough to finish the last bite of soup and sandwich. Some kept talking only to look natural, but they were watching, all right.

The name was muttered around the room by several, and rose above the general hubbub: "Krantz. Yeah, the Krantz boy. He's still at it."

At the end of the counter, Kyle Krantz sat under the watchful eye of bald and chubby Don Murphy, the proprietor, and two blue-jeaned farmer's sons who were well-built for haybucking, steer handling, and cornering shoplifters.

"Hey, Kyle," said Ben. "What are you up to now?"

"Caught him dipping into the cash register," said Don. "Then he took off for the door trying to get away. Bub and

Jack were just coming in and held him until you could get here."

"How much did he take?" asked Leonard.

"Eighty-five dollars," said Don, indicating a wad of bills on the counter.

Leonard gave Kyle a careful visual scrutiny. The boy was only fifteen, skinny as a rail, with shaggy, unkempt black hair and pimples. His face was dull and expressionless, and his eyes were red and watery.

"You know, son," said Leonard, "I think I have cause to believe you might be carrying something illegal. I'd like you to empty your pockets for me."

Kyle hesitated.

"You heard the man," said big Jack, tilting his hat forward to emphasize his lean toward the boy.

"We can help you if you're unable," said Bub.

Kyle began emptying his pockets. First he set some change on the counter, then some cigarette papers.

"Jacket pockets," directed Leonard.

Kyle hesitated, then wilted in surrender, dug into his jacket pocket, and produced a plastic bag full of ground green leaves.

The front door opened.

"Ehh . . ." said Don, sorry to have to miss the rest of this. "Customer."

Ben glanced at the man who had come in. He was middle-aged, handsome, well-dressed. Ben recognized him: Joey Parnell, the county coroner.

Leonard was handling the Krantz boy okay. Ben said softly, "Hey, uh . . . you've got it under control; maybe I'll have a word with Parnell over there . . ."

Leonard shrugged. "Go for it."

Ben walked to the other end of the counter where Parnell had taken a stool and was perusing the simple menu.

"Excuse me," said Ben. "Joey Parnell?"

Parnell looked up and smiled. "Yes."

Ben introduced himself. "Can I join you for just a minute?"

Parnell was agreeable. Ben took the stool next to him and tried to think of where to start.

"Just off the record, unofficially . . ." he began, and felt a little sheepish even saying that. "I wanted to ask you what your findings were in that Sally Roe suicide case."

Parnell looked at the menu again, a clear signal that he wasn't interested in talking about it. "I handle a lot of cases, Officer Cole. Just what is it you want to know?"

"Well . . . now I know this may sound a little strange, but . . . were you able to make a positive identification of the body?"

Parnell looked at Ben as if he were joking. "Well, I should hope so. I wouldn't be a very good coroner if I couldn't even determine whose remains I was examining."

Ben knew he was looking foolish, but he tried to press on. "Well, what about that plaid shirt with the blood on it? Did you get that?"

Parnell didn't answer right away. He seemed to be having trouble remembering. "Uh . . . yeah, I think I got that."

"Did the blood types match?"

"What do you mean, did the blood types match?"

"Well, did the blood on the shirt match the blood of the deceased?"

Parnell broke into a grin and eyed the menu again. "Well, I don't know. I guess I never checked that. Why should I?"

"Was there a wound on the deceased that could explain where the blood on the shirt came from?"

"I . . . I don't remember that there was."

"And what was the cause of death? I think you said asphyxiation by hanging in your report?"

"Mm. That's right. I do remember that."

"I was there on the scene, Mr. Parnell, and what I saw indicated a violent death, not at all what you would expect in a suicide. Also . . . the body wasn't hanging. It was thrown violently to the floor, and there was no rope around the neck."

Parnell just looked at him, listening, without comment.

133

Ben pressed some more. "Could you tell me . . . just so I know for sure . . . a description of the deceased?"

Don came down the counter, and Parnell ordered a beef sandwich and some soup. Parnell took his time, and seemed to enjoy not having to talk to this young, inquisitive cop.

Ben waited politely. Finally Parnell turned to him and with a wry smile said, "No, Officer Cole, I couldn't."

That didn't sound right to Ben. "That's . . . privileged information?"

"That's right."

"Well, what about the color of the hair? I recall seeing a woman with black hair, in her twenties, medium height . . ."

"How about asking me something else?"

Ben stopped, considered, and then asked something else. "According to what I've seen around the station, and then at the Potters' rental, something's missing, perhaps something that belonged to the dead woman. Would you have any idea what everyone is looking for?"

Parnell was clearly getting impatient. "Now that question I don't understand at all."

"Well, Sergeant Mulligan sent someone to the house to search it, and I know he was asking you about something—"

"No comment, sir!" Parnell was visibly upset.

Ben figured he'd better retreat from that line of questions. But now what? "Uh . . . well, just one more question."

Parnell was emphatic. "One more."

"Is it still possible to see the body?"

Parnell chuckled at that. "Afraid not. It's been cremated. Now, is that going to do it for you?"

Ben smiled. "Sure. Thanks a lot, Mr. Parnell. Sorry to bother you."

"All right."

Parnell unfolded a copy of the *Hampton County Star* and gave it his full attention. Ben joined Leonard, who now had Kyle Krantz in custody, and they went out to the squad car.

thirteen

SALLY Roe was far from Bacon's Corner, sitting on a hard bench in a bus depot in another town, looking the part of a wayward, hitchhiking vagabond, dressed in her old jeans and blue jacket, her dyed hair braided and tucked under a wool cap, her nicer clothes hidden in a large duffel bag on the bench beside her. She was oblivious to the passing travelers and their whining children, the used sections of newspapers strewn on the benches, the gum wrappers on the linoleum floor, and the occasional squawking announcements of departures and arrivals over the public address. Her bus would be leaving in one hour. She would spend that hour writing in the spiral notebook in her lap. It would be a letter, her first, to Tom Harris.

> *Dear Mr. Harris,*

She stopped. *How do I start this? He doesn't even know me. Guess I could say that.*

> *I don't know how to start this letter; after all, you don't even know who I am. But let me introduce and explain myself, not just in this letter, but I hope in many more to follow. Perhaps by the time I have written my last letter to you, everything will be clear to both of us.*
>
> *My name is Sally Roe, formerly a planer-sander at the Bergen Door Company. You may have read the recent news story about my death by suicide. I assure you, I am the Sally Roe the news story talked about, and obviously, I am alive.*
>
> *Let me tell you what really happened . . .*

Sally could see it all happening again, even as she searched for the words to recount it.

The day had been perfectly normal and downright boring. Working at the factory always was a bore, especially working

135

in the sanding department, operating power sanders that hummed, whirred, and vibrated until it seemed they would make a milkshake out of your brains. After a full day and a quota of twenty-five doors, she finally drove the old blue pickup down the gravel driveway to her house. She was tired, tasting sawdust, and had no other plans than to shower, grab dinner, and go to bed.

But then there were the goats, Betty the doe and her two kids, Buff and Bart. Pets, mostly. Sally inherited a buck and a doe from a lady at the factory who couldn't afford to keep them. Sally sold the buck, kept the doe, had her bred, and now had the mother and two babies who were the cutest in the world and good company, always glad to see her come home.

Sally parked the truck and headed for their pen. She would greet them first, give them some feed, have her usual one-sided conversation with them about her day, and then go inside and collapse.

The goats were excited, but not with happiness. They were glad and eager to see her again, but mostly because something was disturbing them.

"Hey . . . settle down there . . . Momma's home . . ."

She dug a pail of rolled ration from the feed bin beside the house and stepped through the gate into the goats' pen. Betty circled her, happy but upset. The kids just kept bleating and bounding back and forth along the fence.

Sally shook the pail to get their attention. "Come on, get some treats!"

She went to the shed, hoping they would just follow her and calm down. The neighbors' dog must have been around. He often got a real kick out of terrorizing her goats.

She stepped into the shed. "Come on now, it's all right—"

Shock! A rope came over her head from behind and began crushing her windpipe before she even knew what it was! The pail of feed fell and spilled on the ground. With incredible strength, an unseen assailant heaved on the loop of rope, jerking her body backward, lifting her feet off the ground. She kicked, she grabbed at the rope. No air.

Her feet found the wall, and she pushed. She and her

attacker fell back against the feeder, and it cracked. The rope went slack and she wriggled free, dropping to the floor, rolling in the straw, pulling in air.

A woman in black, eyes wild with hate, a knife! The killer pounced like a leopard, Sally ducked to one side, the knife caught Sally in the shoulder with searing pain.

Sally tried to wriggle out of the corner in which she was trapped, kicking and clawing the straw and dust. The woman's knee came down on her chest and held her there. The rope fell across her neck again. Sally kicked the woman with one free leg.

WUMP! Just that fast, like a rag doll, the woman crashed against the opposite wall of the shed, her head and limbs slapping against the boards, as if a giant had grabbed her and thrown her there. Sally had hardly made contact with her kick and felt some amazement, but at least the woman was off her. She scrambled out of the corner, her eyes on her assailant. The assassin slid down the wall to her feet and stumbled forward, her eyes blank and wandering, her jaw hanging.

OOF!! Something struck the woman with such force, it lifted her off her feet. She flopped into the straw, her arms limp and flailing, her head crooked, her body lifeless, the rope still in her hand.

> *I didn't take any time to look. I just got out of there, still trying to breathe, totally occupied with just staying alive. I remember getting through the gate and then falling to the ground and retching. I can't blame Betty and the kids for running away. Maybe it was a good thing they did.*

Sally leaned back from her writing and absentmindedly tapped the pen on the notebook, just thinking. It was a pretty bizarre way to open a letter. Maybe if she just kept writing, she would seem more credible as her story progressed. Well, all she could do was try.

> *What can I say, Tom? How can I qualify myself as a reliable witness? If you were to ask me who I am, I would have to*

> reply that I don't know. For years I have asked myself the
> same question and now I wonder if, in the writing of these
> letters, I might be reaching out for an answer.
>
> You see, Tom, I want to help you. In my own way, and
> drawing from my own experience, I can relate to your situa-
> tion and I know how you must feel. As one lost entity with-
> out source and without destination in a universe that is
> ultimately meaningless, I can't tell you where my concept of
> "wrong" ever came from. Call it sentiment, call it "the way
> I was raised," figure I'm just taking a desperate stab at
> meaning through antiquated morality, I still feel it—what is
> happening to you is wrong, and I'm sorry for your pain.

She looked up at the big clock above the depot door. Her
bus was scheduled to leave in half an hour. Soon the public
address would be squawking out the announcement.

> If you would indulge me, I would like to at least act as if
> something matters. I would like to do one "right" thing. I
> might be concocting my own concept of "good deeds" in an
> effort to run from despair, to convince myself that life isn't
> futile after all, but I have nothing to lose. If despair is the
> final truth we all face, then let me hide from it, just this
> once. If hope is a mere fiction of our own making, then let
> me live in a fantasy. Who knows? Maybe there will be some
> meaning in it somewhere, some purpose, some reward.
>
> At any rate, I'm going to retrace some old steps and find
> some things out, for your sake and for mine. I hope to share
> some useful information with you before long—information
> sufficient to get you out of trouble and, most of all, bring
> your children back to you.
>
> Please keep this letter, even if it sounds strange to you,
> even if you don't believe it. I'll write again soon.
>
> I remain sincerely yours,

Sally signed her full name, "Sally Beth Roe," carefully took
the pages from the spiral notebook, and folded them. She
had a box of envelopes in her travel bag. While in Bacon's

Corner, she'd looked up Tom Harris's home address and written it in the front of her notebook. She now copied that address onto the envelope and stuffed the letter inside. She didn't seal it yet, but rose from the bench and walked over to the small depot cafeteria to get some dimes. If she hurried, she could get this letter mailed before she left for the next town.

Chimon and Scion walked beside her, wings unfurled, swords drawn. For now, the demons were hiding.

Chimon looked down at the letter in Sally's hand. "'The word of her testimony,'" he said.

"That's one," said Scion.

Terga, Prince of Bacon's Corner, was glad for some good news, and was ready to share a rare smile with Ango, the little Prince of the Bacon's Corner Elementary School.

"Chased them away, eh?" said Terga, strutting up and down the school's tar roof with Ango at his side.

Ango was ecstatic with this great honor. To think that all his underlings were now seeing him in the company of the Prince of Bacon's Corner! Before this, Terga had never even known his name.

Ango was rising to the occasion and giving his report like a real commander-in-the-field. "It was a brazen onslaught, my Ba-al. An incredibly large heavenly warrior challenged me on the roof, and another challenged my guards at the front door. Two warriors were caught inside, but were immediately chased away."

"But you overcame them all?"

"Not without a deadly struggle. I am most proud of my warriors, who showed themselves brave, fierce, and daring!"

"And I am proud of you, Ango, for proving to me that Bacon's Corner is still secure for our operations."

"Thank you, Ba-al."

"With my commendations to you and your warriors, I leave you now . . ."

Terga stopped in midsentence. Both demons heard a familiar sound, and began searching the eastern horizon. From

139

somewhere beyond the treetops, a low, droning rumble reached their ears, growing steadily louder, closer.

"Now who could that be?" Ango wondered.

The deceivers and guards in and around the school heard the sound as well and paused in their duties, buzzing and flitting out into the school yard for a look, or popping up through the roof for a better view.

Terga's wings billowed and lifted him from the roof. He drew his sword as he peered toward the east. Then he tensed just a little and called down to Ango and his troops, "They are ours!"

"But who?"

Terga looked grim, and shook his head in dismay. "I believe it is Destroyer, with fresh forces from the Strongman."

That word brought a mutter of fear from all the ranks below.

Then the visitors appeared, still a mile away, approaching like a low-flying squadron of bombers. There were at least a hundred, flying in an arrowhead formation and coming closer, closer, closer. Now the red glow of their swords appeared against the dark shadowy blurs of their wings.

Terga set down on the roof again. "Ango, prepare your forces to greet some honored guests!"

"Forces!" Ango yelled. They fluttered up out of the school and school yard. He ordered them to assemble in orderly ranks on the front lawn. They formed the ranks immediately, a motley, sleazy crew of some three hundred—tiny spirits of anger, hatred, rebellion; huge, lumbering giants of violence, vandalism, destruction; clever deceivers with their wily ways and shifty eyes. They looked sharp, all lined up in neat rows, the tallest in the back, the shortest in the front, and every demon's sword held across his chest.

Destroyer's squadron came over the town, casting a spiritual shadow upon the entire length of Front Street and putting a chill in the air that the humans down there could feel. The shadow passed over the fire station and then the row of homes along the Strawberry Loop, and dogs all over the neighborhood began to howl.

Terga, Ango, and all the assembly of demons could now see the squadron's leader well in front, at the tip of the arrowhead. They could see the yellow glint of his eyes and the red glimmer of his sword. They all bowed low.

Destroyer and a terrifying battalion of the Strongman's handpicked best descended on the school like a cloud of monster locusts, their wings producing a roar that could be felt and stirring up such a wind that some of the smaller demons on the front lawn blew over and rolled like leaves across the grass.

Destroyer alighted on the roof of the school with twelve hideous captains surrounding him. The rest of the battalion took positions all around the perimeter of the school grounds. The wings settled, the roar subsided. Now Terga and Ango found themselves in the presence of a spirit so evil that neither of them could look up for stark fear.

Destroyer took a moment to look all around. He gazed with narrow, fiery eyes at the troops gathered on the lawn. He wasn't impressed. He walked slowly toward the two bowing princes of this place, his toes settling into the tar, his talons gripping tightly with each step. He stood in front of them, his captains standing on either side like tree trunks.

"So, Terga," he asked in a voice as cold as ice, "it seems you have reason to be giddy?"

Terga straightened, said, "I have, my Ba-al," and then bowed again.

With numbing fear, Terga suddenly felt the hot edge of the Ba-al's blade under his chin. He followed the blade's prompting and raised his head.

"Who is this beside you?"

"This is Ango, the prince of this school, a brave leader."

The burning sword raised Ango's chin. "You are prince of this place?"

Ango tried to speak in a strong voice, but couldn't keep it from quivering. "Yes, my Ba-al."

Destroyer leaned close to Ango's face. "I have received word that you had a confrontation here with the Host of Heaven."

141

Ango smiled faintly. "It was my duty and joy to please such as you, and drive the heavenly warriors away."

"How many heavenly warriors?"

"Four, my Ba-al. One assailed me on the roof, one attacked our guards at the front, and two launched an attack from inside. We chased them all away immediately."

Destroyer pondered that for just a moment. He had no immediate compliments for Ango's actions. "What else happened that day?"

Ango wasn't at all prepared for the question. "What else?"

"Did you have any unexpected human visitors to the school?"

Destroyer was staring, waiting for an answer, and now Ango could feel a stare from Terga. But he couldn't come up with an answer. "I . . . I know of none."

"Can you give me any good reason why four—only four— of the enemy's hosts would suddenly appear here, only to allow themselves to be chased away by spirits as petty and weak as you?"

Ango shuddered. This conversation was taking a bad turn. "They . . . they came to spy on us, to invade the school . . ."

"That is your explanation?"

"That is . . . Yes, that is what I know."

Destroyer sheathed his sword, and everyone breathed a little easier. "Go back to your duties, Ango the Terrible, you and your warriors. Do your worst with these little children. Terga, I'll have a word with you."

Terga followed Destroyer to the other end of the roof, while Ango dismissed his demons to return to their duties. When Destroyer came to a stop, satisfied with the place, the twelve captains surrounded him and Terga like a castle wall.

Terga was worried.

Destroyer glared down at him—angry, but calculatingly controlled. "She was here."

Terga, of course, did not want to believe it. "How do you know, my Ba-al?"

"Where did she go from the motel in Claytonville?"

"I . . ."

"Did your petty pranksters follow her? Did they have her under their careful watch at all times?"

Terga felt he would melt right through the roof. "The . . . the Host of Heaven . . . We were confounded . . . They got in our way . . . We couldn't see her anymore . . ."

"You lost track of her! She eluded you!"

Terga knew full well that Destroyer's own ravagers were following the woman too, but now did not seem an appropriate time to remind him. "Uh . . . yes. But . . . she wouldn't come back *here*, to the place of greatest danger—"

"Danger?" Destroyer's voice was as sharp as his blade. "What danger, when you and such as this Ango are responsible for it?"

"But why would she come here?"

Terga didn't even see Destroyer's huge hand before it struck him, dashing him to the roof. Terga made no move of retaliation; he never had any intention to do so, and besides, twelve huge swords were only inches from his throat. All he could do was look up at the furious face of Destroyer as the wicked spirit unloaded his venom.

"You fool!" Destroyer shouted. "Why wouldn't she come here? This is where our Plan began, or don't you recall all our years of development, our infiltration of this place? You were here, you were a part of it. Did you think we carried it all out with no object in mind?"

"I'm sorry, my Ba-al."

Destroyer's foot caught Terga under the ribs and kicked him several feet in the air. Terga's body struck the immovable chest of one of the captains and then tumbled down to the roof again.

"You're sorry . . ." muttered Destroyer mockingly. "You let her elude you in Claytonville, you let her sneak into this school under your very nose, you let her escape again, to disappear until she pops up again to do more damage, to uncover more of our Plan, we know not where, and all you have to say is, 'I'm sorry'!"

Terga wanted to say he was sorry again, but knew that would not be accepted. Now he had no words left to say.

"Go!" said Destroyer. "Take care of your little town. Leave Sally Roe to me."

One of the captains, built like a bull, took Terga by one wing and flung him into the sky. Terga tumbled and fluttered skyward until he could recover control of his wings, then shot away in shame.

Destroyer watched until Terga was gone, then spoke in low tones to the twelve demons with him. "The Strongman does have all his players in place and a strong network ready to be used, but we have seen ourselves how vulnerable the Plan can be, especially when the Host of Heaven are interested in our enterprise, and most certainly interested in Sally Roe. They are trying to set up a hedge around her, screen her from our eyes, accompany her. They have a plan too."

One hulking spirit reminded Destroyer, "But the Strongman will not turn away from his Plan; he is committed to it."

"An easy position for him to take," Destroyer hissed spitefully, fingering the handle of his sword. "If the Plan should fail, it will not be his head that rolls, but ours. He will see to that. We must succeed."

He stopped to think for a moment, his black talons pulling like hooks at the stiff hairs on his neck.

"I am learning more and more about this Tal; he is quite the strategist, a master of subtlety. Thus far the Host of Heaven have been effective and yet largely invisible. Tal is waiting, maneuvering. He is a layer of traps, a setter of snares."

Another spirit, scarred and grotesque, growled, "I was there in Ashton. I saw the ambush."

Destroyer spit sulfur and let his anger rise. "So you know that Tal waited until our forces could wait no longer and flew headlong into his patient trap, brash and unaware. We had only our confidence, but Tal was *ready*. We will not make that mistake again."

Destroyer scanned the town from this rooftop perch. "If Tal is so subtle, we will be even more so. If he depends on the prayers of God's people, then we will work all the harder to keep God's people from praying." He chuckled a sulfurous chuckle. "You don't know about the little imps I requested from the Strongman: Strife, Division, Gossip, and a host of others flooding this town at this very moment! These humans are only of flesh, of mud, and I suggest there is one force stronger than their zeal for God: their own self-righteousness! We will make them proud, pure in their own eyes, vindictive, unjust judges over each other, and stir up such a noise among them that the simplest prayer will not be uttered!"

The warriors were impressed and muttered their awe and approval.

"In the meantime," Destroyer continued, "let us not forget that *our* people are praying as well, devoting much time and worship to our lord, and he is responding with great favor toward us, sending more and more forces to bolster our ranks and confound our enemies! Time is on our side!" Then he stopped and grinned. "So, if Tal is a master of waiting, we will be the same! Though Tal may dangle Sally Roe like a carrot before our noses, we will not assault her too soon. We will not fly into another ambush." Destroyer's eyes narrowed with cunning. "We will wait, as Tal does. We will watch, we will follow, until our moment is right, until this mighty Captain of the Host is not so mighty, but is confounded, stripped of his power by the saints of God themselves!

"And then sometime, somewhere, Sally Roe will have her Gethsemane. She will be alone. Her escorts will be unaware, unready, small in numbers. The moment will be ours to take her."

"But how will we know?" asked a fourth demon.

"We will know, just as before, because a Judas will tell us. All we have to do is find him." Destroyer hacked a hideous chuckle. "Such a marvelous thing, betrayal!"

fourteen

BEN would be getting out of the station and out on patrol a little earlier this morning. He had plans to sit behind the trees at the west end of the Snyder River Bridge and nab speeders for a while, maybe get his citation quota up a bit.

But first . . . if he could do it quietly enough, he thought he'd use the police teletype to request a crime check on Sally Roe. It just might turn something up.

"Cole . . ."

It was Mulligan, and there was something strange about the tone in his voice.

"Yes, sir."

Mulligan came out of his office and over to Ben's desk. He leaned on it with his big fist and cut into Ben with his eyes.

Ben was ready to talk, but not to be stared at. "Something wrong, Harold?"

Mulligan was almost smiling. "You been snooping around again?"

"Snooping?"

"Leonard tells me you were bothering Joey Parnell, the coroner."

Ben was a little stunned to hear that such a report had come from Leonard, of all people. "If Leonard told you I was *bothering* Mr. Parnell, I would have to disagree with his terms. I don't think I was bothering Mr. Parnell at all. I sat next to him over at Don's and just asked a few questions. It was all very casual."

"Didn't I tell you to drop this Sally Roe thing? What's wrong with your memory, Cole?"

Ben had been a wimp long enough. He stood to his feet and faced Mulligan eye to eye. "There is nothing wrong with my memory, Harold, Mr. Sergeant, sir! I have never been able to forget what I've seen pertaining to this case and the way it's been handled. I've been bothered by it, I've lost sleep over it, and quite frankly I've been very disappointed by the incompetence I've seen on the part of some duly elected public servants who should know better. If we must discuss memories, I found that Mr. Parnell's memory is no better than your eyesight in regard to the dead woman we found and her true identity. Forgive me for speaking so freely, sir."

Mulligan leaned toward Ben so that their faces were only an inch apart. "I thought you and Leonard were supposed to be doing a drug bust at Don's. I don't see any contraband, Cole. Where is it?"

"Leonard took care of that, sir."

Mulligan called, "Leonard?"

Leonard was doing something in the back. "Yeah?"

"Did you bring any contraband back from that drug bust?"

"Yeah. About a quarter kilo of marijuana. Ben took care of it."

Ben made a face and smiled a bit at the mixup. "Leonard, you handled that whole case, remember? I was over talking to Parnell."

Leonard came into the room, his face filled with astonishment. "Ben, have you slipped a gear? I gave that pot to you to file as evidence."

Ben was incredulous. "No way!"

Mulligan looked back and forth at the two men. "Guys, we are missing some pot. Now where is it?"

"I gave it to Ben to file as evidence," said Leonard.

"No," said Ben. "Absolutely not!"

Mulligan smiled cunningly. "How's about we just take a look in your locker, Cole?"

"Sure thing."

But even as Ben said that, it occurred to him what might be happening. As they went down the hall to the lockers, he knew he wouldn't be surprised if . . .

Mulligan threw open the locker. The plastic bag of marijuana fell out and landed on the floor.

Mulligan raised an eyebrow. It was no secret that he was getting a kick out of this. "Looks like you filed it in the wrong place, Cole."

Ben nodded with full knowledge of what was happening.

"Yeah, right, right." He looked at Leonard. "Next time I'll have to get a lock on my locker instead of trusting the people I work with."

Leonard countered quickly, "Careful what you say, Ben. This could be serious."

"Serious? Guys, this is *pitiful!*" Ben reached for his chest. "Hey, how about it, Harold? I'll bet you have a spicy report written up already. Don't worry. You won't need it. Guys, the game stops here. I'm not playing." He removed his badge and held it out for Mulligan to take.

Mulligan took it. "Turn in your uniform by tomorrow."

"You got it."

Ben went quietly to his desk, removed his gun, radio, and other gear, and set them down. He opened the drawer, removed a New Testament and some other personal items, then slid it shut.

As he put on his jacket, he realized he had mixed feelings about what had happened—he felt sorrow and anxiety over losing his job, but at the same time elated and relieved. At least he was losing his job for the right reasons. Hopefully the Lord would bless him for that.

Mulligan and Leonard stood in the hall together, watching him go. He examined their faces for just a moment, and then went out the door.

The two weeks were up. The hearing convened on schedule, at nine o'clock in the morning, in the department of the Honorable Emily R. Fletcher of the Federal District Court, Room 412, the Federal Courthouse, in the city of Westhaven, some sixty miles south of Bacon's Corner.

Tom and Ben rode with Mark and Cathy. They challenged the freeway, waited for the lights, made the correct turns, and arrived in Westhaven with just enough time to park in a multistoried concrete parking lot, get their parking stub, dash across the street to the courthouse, and catch a crowded elevator up to the fourth floor where they finally found Room 412.

Right away, they knew the whole experience was going to be imposing, foreign, frightening, and inscrutable. It was bad enough being in this vast building with heavy marble walls that seemed to close in on you. It was worse to know next to nothing about what was going to happen and how your fate was going to be decided by so many three-piece-suited professionals you'd never seen before. It was even worse than that to find no less than a hundred people crammed into the hall outside the courtroom trying to get in. Who *were* they, anyway?

Tom cringed. Many were reporters. They weren't allowed to bring their cameras in, praise the Lord, but they were certainly gawking at him and muttering, swapping information, scribbling in their notepads. Some artists were there, easels and chalk ready to sketch a quick portrait of these strange Christians from an obscure little town.

Where was Wayne Corrigan? He said he would meet them here. Oh, there was his hand, waving in the air above a tight circle of reporters. He elbowed his way out of the circle and hurried up to meet them, the reporters following him as if connected to his body with string.

"Let's get inside," he said, sounding desperate. "It's a zoo out here."

They pressed forward into the crowd, and somehow, one step at a time, they made it to the big wooden doors and pushed through.

Now they were in a cavernous courtroom, with deeply stained woodwork, a thick green carpet, tall, draped windows, and a bench that rose like a mountain in front. The gallery was almost full.

Corrigan showed Tom and Mark to the defendant's table; Ben sat with Cathy in the front row of the gallery. Mrs. Fields was already seated there and doing some cross-stitch. Three board members, Jack and Doug Parmenter and Bob Heely, were ready to testify as well.

Corrigan spoke to Tom and Mark in muffled tones. "The judge may not take any oral testimony, but it's good to be ready in case. It's a real circus, let me tell you. The ACFA is here in full force, and the press, and I think some people from the National Coalition on Education. We're in the hot seat. It's—"

Lucy Brandon entered the courtroom, wearing a blue dress and looking very formal. She was flanked by the blonde Claire Johanson and a tall, youthful-looking man, obviously her attorney.

"That's Gordon Jefferson, Brandon's attorney. He's ACFA."

In came an older attorney, his chin high, holding a black briefcase in front of his stomach.

"Wendell Ames, Brandon's other attorney, senior partner at Ames, Jefferson, and Morris. His father was the state founder of the ACFA back in the thirties."

The four sat at the plaintiff's table without looking their way.

"*Two* attorneys?" Tom asked.

"They're out to win. What can I say? I did the best I could with the brief. It only came to twelve pages. The affidavits— the sworn statements of yourselves and Mrs. Fields—seem effective enough, but our Scriptural arguments are going to have trouble standing up against psychological reports. They've hired a shrink, you know, some child psychologist named Mandanhi. That's him sitting in the second row over there."

They looked and saw a balding, dark-skinned man of apparent East Indian descent.

"What did he have to say?" asked Mark.

"What do you think? He has Amber diagnosed as a sick and traumatized little girl, and it's all your fault, naturally."

"Naturally," muttered Tom.

"We'll see how we do, guys. Just remember, it's only the first battle, not the entire war."

A door to the left of the bench swung open.

The bailiff stood to her feet and declared, "All rise."

They all rose.

"Court is now in session, the Honorable Emily R. Fletcher presiding."

Judge Fletcher was a dignified woman in her fifties with close-cropped blonde hair and a pleasant facial expression.

She took her place behind the bench and spoke in clear tones. "Thank you. Please be seated."

They sat.

"The case is *Brandon v. The Good Shepherd Academy*. Today is a hearing on a temporary injunction issued by this court two weeks ago restraining The Good Shepherd Academy from . . ." She perched her reading glasses on her nose and referred to the documents before her. "'Outrageous Religious Behavior Against a Child, Physical Abuse by Spanking, Excessive Religious Instruction Harmful to the Child, Harassment, Discrimination, and Religious Indoctrination Using Federal Funds.' Are counsel ready to proceed?"

She looked toward Lucy Brandon and her two attorneys. Ames stood to his feet. "Yes, Your Honor."

She looked toward Tom, Mark, and Wayne Corrigan. "And the defendants . . . are you ready?"

Corrigan rose and replied in the affirmative.

She looked over her reading glasses at the crowded courtroom. "This case is obviously one of great public importance and intense public interest. If there are no objections from counsel, the court is prepared to grant permission for the use of cameras and recording devices by the press."

Gordon Jefferson stood up immediately. "No objections, Your Honor."

Corrigan noticed the immediate headshake from Tom and Mark. He stood. "Your Honor, the defendants would request that no cameras be allowed."

Jefferson countered, "Your Honor, as you have observed, this case does reflect matters of great public interest. I think the public would be well served through firsthand information that television can provide."

Corrigan whispered to Tom, "The ACFA loves to try cases in the press. They're going for this one."

Judge Fletcher didn't take long to ponder the issue. "Mr. Corrigan, the court sees no harm in such camera coverage, certainly not so much harm that the importance of public awareness does not outweigh it. Cameras will be allowed."

Several reporters bolted from the courtroom to grab their gear.

The judge flipped to the next page before her. "I have read the briefs and affidavits presented by both sides in this case. Well done, excellent on both sides, and as one might expect, in sharp dispute. In light of the short time frame, and in the interest of expediency, we will avoid oral testimony if counsel agrees, and hear this case on the basis of the affidavits and oral argument of counsel."

Wayne Corrigan whispered to Tom, "It's okay. It's to our advantage. They have to meet a higher standard of proof if there's no oral testimony." He spoke to the judge. "We have no objection, Your Honor."

Ames and Jefferson were still whispering to each other. They didn't seem too happy about the court's suggestion. Finally Ames answered, "Uh . . . no objections, Your Honor."

The judge seemed pleased with the progress they were all making. "Well then . . . if counsel are ready, Mr. Ames or Mr. Jefferson, you may proceed with your argument."

Jefferson rose, buttoning his jacket. "Thank you, Your Honor."

He walked forward and began to form his argument, wandering back and forth, studying the carpet, waving one hand in the air as if leading a choir. "Your Honor, this is not a difficult case; as the court has seen in the brief and affidavits, the complaints against the Good Shepherd Academy are well-founded. We do believe in religious freedom, of course, and far be it from us to suppose we can infringe on that sacred right. But how, Your Honor, does a child of ten have the power to decide freely in such matters when surrounded by a coercive and repressive environment such as we have found at the Good Shepherd Academy?"

Tom listened raptly to Jefferson's speech. The guy was being slanderous, he thought, but selling it all very well. The press was going to eat this up for sure.

"You have seen the report by Dr. Mandanhi, a distinguished psychologist well-acquainted with emotional trauma in children. He has clearly stated that young Amber has been

153

severely traumatized by the outrageous religious behavior of these people, and has demonstrated such symptoms as illness, headaches, loss of appetite, and bed-wetting, not to mention severe religious delusions and even . . . uh . . . personality disorders which can be attributed to the curriculum taught and example set by the leadership at the Good Shepherd Academy. I must also inform the court that Mr. Harris is currently under investigation by the CPD for possible child abuse, and that his own children have been removed from his home pending that investigation."

Corrigan bolted out of his chair. "Objection!"

"Sustained," said the judge. "Mr. Jefferson, Child Protection Department matters are strictly confidential and are not to be discussed in open court. You will restrain from any further mention of it."

"And in light of just such tactics as this," said Corrigan, "may I again request that cameras and recording devices be barred from the courtroom?"

"The request is denied," said the judge, but then she looked toward the members of the press. "But the press is ordered not to publish anything about that revelation."

Corrigan said, "Thank you, Your Honor," and sat down. He whispered to Tom, "Jefferson knew what he was doing."

Jefferson continued, unruffled. "As for the 'outrageous religious behavior,' the details are clear in the court file, of course, and I hardly need to comment on the behavior described, that of attempting to cast a demon out of Amber, and even suggesting to an impressionable child that she is possessed by a spirit. Your Honor, this is a most unusual twist, a new and obviously bizarre form of child abuse; this must fall outside the protective umbrella of religious freedom, and we would ask the court to so rule.

"The physical abuse by spanking is clear enough as well, and even the defendants admit that the spanking did occur. As the court well knows, this practice is already forbidden by the state in any foster homes and in the public schools, and we would suggest that the precedents in law and in society are clear on this issue. This is not proper behavior toward a child, but is another form of abuse, and should also be extricated from under the umbrella of religious freedom."

Tom and Mark could see the case forming; this clever lawyer was whittling away at something he repeatedly termed "the umbrella of religious freedom." It was clear to them that umbrellas had little to do with it—religious freedom itself was the object of his attacks. But Jefferson was good at what he did, they had to admit that. His oratory was forceful, well choreographed, and persuasive. The disturbing thought now was, *Is Corrigan going to be able to top it?*

"As for excessive religious instruction," Jefferson continued, "who can object to teaching basic virtues such as honesty, self-esteem, the Golden Rule? Our difficulty is in the pervasive fundamentalist idea that we are all feeble, despicable, worthless sinners, incapable of any good in ourselves, but dependent on some outside 'savior' to lift us out of our personal morass, and without whom we have no hope at all . . . an idea we must suggest is destructive to the mental health and well-being of any child, and Dr. Mandanhi's report reflects this.

"To quickly close the matter, and not take any more of the court's time, the above-mentioned offenses do necessarily constitute a form of harassment and discrimination because no opposing view of these fundamental beliefs is allowed; this is intolerance, of course, and the seedbed of bigotry.

"But, of course, an even greater legal issue here is that these teachings and indoctrinations are being supported and paid for by federal funds, since Mrs. Brandon is a federal employee and is receiving a child care subsidy under the Federal Daycare and Private Primary School Assistance Act, part of which she has used to pay her daughter's tuition."

Judge Fletcher interrupted. "Counselor, it is the court's understanding that Amber has now been removed from the school."

"Yes, Your Honor, for her own well-being, of course. But we submit that the issue of separation of church and state is still viable since federal funds were used in the religious indoctrination of Amber while attending the school, which would bring the school into accountability to the state. This is covered in detail in our brief on the applicability of the Munson-Ross Civil Rights Act and the Federal Day-care and Private Primary School Assistance Act. While Congress intended to assist working parents with child care, no one in their right mind would argue that federal funds should be used for religious instruction. Our brief shows how legislative history and prior case law make this abundantly clear.

"Finally, we would ask that the court consider not only Amber, who was fortunate enough to be removed from the school and therefore saved any further harm; we would ask the court to also consider the children still there, still subject to this excessive behavior and instruction, still very much in harm's way. We don't know who the other children in the school are and whether or not federal funds are being used to supplement their tuition as well. That is why we are asking the court to order that the defendants produce the name of each child and any financial information concerning the child's enrollment in the school, in addition to continuing the restraint.

"Your decision here today will affect the future well-being of the other children also, and therefore we are sure the court will rule in their favor."

Jefferson sat down as every television camera in the room followed him to his chair and cameras clicked away.

Tom and Mark looked at Corrigan. He was hurriedly going over his scribbled notes, apparently hoping for an inspiration. It didn't seem to be coming to him.

"Mr. Cotrigan?" said the judge.

Tom gave Corrigan an encouraging pat on the shoulder. "Godspeed, brother."

Corrigan rose to his feet. This was his moment. He buttoned his jacket as well, not to signal his determination to do battle, but because his nervous hands needed something to do. It also gave him a moment to pray.

"Your Honor, counsel for the plaintiff has taken great pains to paint a bleak and gruesome picture of the Good

Shepherd Academy. We can assure you that things at the school are much different than they've been made out to be.

"First of all, we haven't had a chance to meet with Dr. Mandanhi and discuss his findings, and therefore we can't be certain that Amber's problems are entirely due to her attending the school. As we've tried to show in the affidavits, she came to the Good Shepherd Academy with some problems already, and I suggest it would not be fair or accurate to attribute all her problems to the environment at the school. We should have the opportunity to have our own expert examine Amber, as I'm sure another expert could balance the report of Dr. Mandanhi.

"As for corporal punishment, this is certainly not the anachronism that the plaintiff is trying to make it out to be, and we are not going to resolve that issue in this case. Spanking, when administered by loving parents, or by a Christian school headmaster following agreed-upon procedure, is not abuse at all, but proper discipline, and as we have shown in our court file, a matter of Biblical doctrine, a matter of deep religious conviction.

"Also, I would remind the court that the guidelines for corporal discipline are clearly spelled out in the Academy handbook, and that Mrs. Brandon signed a letter of agreement to those guidelines. Both items are included in our brief, and speak for themselves.

"So I think this issue of spanking is not at all settled, especially when there can be no doubt that Amber's punishment was properly and lovingly administered. It would not be fair or accurate to label it as child abuse. To do so would invade the privacy and convictions of millions of parents across this country who still believe in spanking, and yes, there is the matter of religious conviction and religious freedom. These must be protected and should not be infringed upon.

"We must also object to the plaintiff's accusation of 'excessive religious instruction.' What the plaintiff refers to is a fundamental part of the gospel, but I must remind the court that the gospel is the Good News, not Bad News. The message of the gospel does not leave us all condemned . . . or as counsel for the plaintiff stated, 'feeble, despicable sinners.' We believe . . . that is, the doctrinal position of the Good Shepherd Academy is . . . that yes, man is a sinner. He is separated from God because he has transgressed God's righteous law, and, by himself, has no salvation from his predicament. But this message is never forced or imposed on any child without the positive side of the message, that God sent His Son to pay the price of our sins with His own life, and thereby save us and reconcile us to God.

"Now, I realize I may sound like a preacher here, but this is, after all, one point of contention raised by the plaintiff, and I must answer it." Corrigan brightened a bit as a thought hit him. "But maybe it would be appropriate for me to point out right here that clearly this is a religious matter. Your Honor, we are discussing religious *doctrine*, and in a court of law! Yes, Your Honor, we do challenge the plaintiff's contention that any excessive religious instruction has occurred that would be harmful to Amber. But also, we remind the court that through this complaint, the plaintiff has asked the state to rule on the propriety of a particular religious belief, and this is something the state is constitutionally barred from doing."

You got them there, thought Tom.

"We also deny any harassment or discrimination, and as the court file shows, even though the plaintiff has obtained the professional opinion of Dr. Mandanhi regarding alleged trauma to the child, the plaintiff has failed to prove any specific allegations of excessive or outrageous behavior."

The judge looked up from her notes with a quizzical expression. "Counselor, your brief included at least a cursory reference to the alleged 'outrageous religious behavior' cited by the plaintiff. Do you now deny the plaintiff's allegation that Mr. Harris attempted to cast a demon out of the child?"

Tom and Mark were certain that Corrigan would be cornered on this one, but he didn't seem to balk at the question. Apparently he'd done a lot of thinking about it. "The allegation is open to challenge, Your Honor, inasmuch as there could be many different interpretations, many different definitions of the word 'demon.'"

The judge leaned forward, lowering her chin to just inches above the bench. "Would it be fair to suppose a Judeo-Christian or Biblical interpretation of the word 'demon' in this case?"

Tom could feel his heart pounding and his stomach turning into knots.

Corrigan drew a breath and came back with his answer. "I suppose it would, Your Honor, but then, even within the parameters of a Biblical interpretation, you would have to decide between . . . uh . . . whether it would be a liberal, allegorical interpretation of the word, or the more fundamentalist, literal interpretation . . ."

The judge smiled just a little. Someone in the courtroom snickered. "I suppose we could belabor that point, counselor, and indeed enter into a theological argument. Please proceed."

Tom looked at Mark. Was that a good or bad sign? They couldn't help trying to guess what the judge was thinking.

Corrigan tried to cap off his argument. "We are here today, Your Honor, to show just cause why we should not be restrained from certain activities. Well, first of all, I would argue that these allegations of activities are spurious and unfounded at best, and that the plaintiff in this case has fallen sadly short of proving the truth of any of them. This being the case, a restraining order against the school is simply uncalled for, and I would suggest entails a violation of the separation of church and state, in that the state is encroaching on the free exercise of religion by the Good Shepherd Academy by placing itself in a position to decide for the Academy what is acceptable religion and what is not. I hope that we will not find that kind of a situation developing here, and that this restraining order will be removed. It is appropriate here for the court to remove the restraint because the plaintiff is no longer affected by the school's policies, and no other student is a plaintiff and therefore this case is moot. Thank you very much."

With that, Corrigan sat down.

"Thank you, Mr. Corrigan," said Judge Fletcher.

Then came the long, second-by-second wait. Judge Emily R. Fletcher leafed through her notes, scribbled some notes next to her notes, and then stared at her notes as a tense silence fell over the great chamber.

fifteen

FinaLLy Judge Fletcher set down her pen and spoke, alternately looking through her reading glasses at the papers in front of her and then looking over them at the lawyers, litigants, observers, and television cameras.

"I doubt that either side will be entirely pleased with my decision, but contrary to Mr. Jefferson's opening assertion, this *is* a difficult case, and it puts me in an even more difficult position, where I'm called upon to balance, as it were, the Constitution and the best interests of a ten-year-old child. In trying to achieve that kind of balance, it's inevitable that both sides in this dispute are going to lose something and find their respective desires not totally satisfied.

"I've read the file and heard the arguments of counsel. I believe this is a case where some injunctive relief is warranted. However, there are some strong and some weak arguments on both sides, and some issues that seem to me to be, at least at this point, unarguable. I'll address the separate complaints one by one.

"To go down the list . . . pertaining to 'Outrageous Religious Behavior Against a Child,' I agree with the Constitution that there is a place for individual religious persuasion and practice. But I hold that there is certainly a place for proper restraint, and no place at all for any violation of the laws of the state. The complaint of the plaintiff is clear and direct, that Amber was harassed and effectively branded as someone possessed by a spirit, a demon, whatever the definition of that word might be. I do believe the propriety of such behavior should be called into question; I think this protection should remain. Therefore, the restraining order against such behavior shall issue until the matter is resolved in trial.

"I will say the same for any further spanking of any child at the Academy. The state has an interest in protecting its children, and there have been many cases where corporal punishment has been found to be inappropriate. While religious

161

conviction has its rightful place in our society, the possibility of child abuse still exists, and therefore I think it is appropriate that a restraining order should issue along the lines requested by Mrs. Brandon, and that the matter proceed to trial.

"As for the next three complaints, 'Excessive Religious Instruction Harmful to the Child,' 'Harassment,' and 'Discrimination,' I would agree with Mr. Corrigan that these are rather vague complaints that have not been established to the satisfaction of the court as harmful to the children. The court agrees that these are religious matters, and it is clear that the religious position of the Academy was well-advertised and clearly stated so that Mrs. Brandon was aware of the religious nature of the Academy before enrolling her child. If the plaintiff argues that such beliefs and teaching are inappropriate for any child, then let counsel build a case and present it in trial.

"As for the final complaint, 'Religious Indoctrination Using Federal Funds,' Mrs. Brandon has removed her daughter from the school, and as long as no further tuition is paid to the school out of Mrs. Brandon's salary, there is, in my opinion, no further violation of the law, and no further harm done until this matter can be decided in trial. The restraint is moot, then, and therefore removed.

"I will sign the appropriate written order when completed by counsel. Counsel should discuss the appropriate bond to be placed in the order. If you cannot agree, call my clerk.

"I am withholding a ruling at this time on the production order plaintiffs seek. I'm concerned about that. Further argument may be needed, or it may be moot, but it is an important issue.

"By this order I'm not saying the plaintiff's claims are unfounded, just that all the restraint requested pending trial is not warranted. The whole matter will proceed to trial in due course." She picked up the gavel and rapped it sharply. "This court is in recess."

"All rise," said the bailiff, and they all rose, and the muttering and mumbling started as Judge Fletcher left the room.

"Now what?" Tom asked.

"Now we dodge the reporters and get out of here," said Corrigan.

"How did we do?" asked Mark as Cathy took his arm and listened.

"Well, we still have a long battle ahead of us. To review, your school can stay open and you can keep teaching your normal curriculum, but spanking is out and casting out demons is taboo. The judge says you don't have to produce the names and financial records of any of the other kids, so that's one hassle avoided. I would say we did pretty well, considering how it could have gone. Let's get out of here."

Mrs. Fields and the Parmenters were full of questions too.

"Can the school stay open?" Mrs. Fields asked.

"Yes, it's all right," said Tom.

Cathy gave her a hug and said, "We're going to have a meeting with everyone and explain it all."

Jack Parmenter was still itching for a fight. "We've got to get that . . . that Jefferson punk. We don't have to stand for that kind of talk!"

"Let's talk about all that somewhere else," said Corrigan.

He led the way, and the others followed in a single file through the courtroom doors.

The camera lights were blinding; it was like daylight in the hall outside.

"Mr. Harris!" came the first reporter. "What is your reaction to the judge's ruling?"

"No comment," said Wayne Corrigan.

"What about your children?" asked another reporter. "How long have they been removed from your home?"

So much for the judge's order, Tom thought.

"Is it true that you tried to exorcise a demon from the child?" said a lady, shoving a microphone in Tom's face.

Corrigan grabbed the microphone. "We intend to try our case in a court of law, not in the press. Thank you."

More questions.

"Let's go," Corrigan said to Tom and the others.

They kept moving, even slinking, through the crowd. They passed a cluster of reporters and cameras gathered around Lucy Brandon and her two lawyers. Jefferson was holding forth with quite a comment for the press. ". . . The judge's decision was just what we expected. While we can't believe that anyone would allow their children to be subjected to this kind of curriculum and the harsh treatment it requires, I can understand why the judge was reluctant to rule on the abbreviated evidence that one can produce for a short-notice hearing such as this. We are, however, pleased that the judge chose to protect the children of Bacon's Corner from further physical abuse at the hands of Tom Harris and his staff . . . these fundamentalists."

Tom heard all that and turned. He had to say something. He couldn't let that get into the press.

"Come on, let's just go," said Corrigan, tugging at his arm. They hurried from the courthouse.

The Wednesday night prayer meeting at Mark and Cathy's house was packed. Attendance wasn't that bad on any normal Wednesday night, but this night was not normal at all, and there weren't enough chairs for everyone.

All the board members were there along with their wives, as were some of the people on the prayer chain: Donna Hemphile, Lester and Dolly Sutter, Tim and Becky Farmer, Brent and Amy Ryan, and the widow Alice Buckmeier. Ben Cole was there with his wife Bev; Mrs. Fields was there, even though she regularly attended the local Baptist church on Wednesday nights. Wayne Corrigan was there as well and would probably be the center of attention.

The one person noticeably absent was Tom Harris. He'd taken his leave of absence, and felt compelled to keep his distance. Besides, Mark felt the evening's discussion would be freer and any grievances could be more easily voiced if he was not there, and Tom agreed with that.

Some other absences were a little unsettling to Mark, who, being the pastor, was more prone to notice. Andrea and Wes Jessup, who usually attended the midweek meeting, were absent, as were the Wingers. Mark knew why they were gone. There were still some disgruntled people out there who needed to have their fears and false information cleared up, and naturally, being the ones who needed most to be here, they were not. Dealing with them was going to be a tough and unpleasant project.

In all, the house had to be holding no less than fifty people. This had to be a crisis indeed.

But the house was also filled with other visitors, no less than fifty, almost an even match in attendance. Tal was there, along with Guilo, recently returned from his surveillance near the mountain town of Summit; Nathan and Armoth were ready at Tal's side, and at their command was a formidable troop of warriors. Mota and Signa, having completed their assignment at the elementary school, were in attendance and overseeing the hedge of guards now surrounding the house. This would be one meeting uninvaded by any marauding spirits.

"Messengers are ready," Nathan reported. "All they need is a word from you."

Tal looked around the room and managed a grim smile. "Maybe we'll get a better idea where the trouble is, and where our prayer cover went. May the Lord grant His people a special portion of His wisdom tonight." He took one more look around the room and then said, "The messengers will wait for my word."

"Done."

"What of Sally Roe?"

Chimon stepped forward. "Scion and I have just delivered her into Cree and Si's care. They're escorting her to the Omega Center."

"Good. Go immediately to Bentmore and prepare the way for her there."

"Done."

Chimon and Scion vanished to their next assignment.

Wayne Corrigan stood to address the group and field their questions.

"I would say it was about a fifty percent victory," he said, "which is a positive way of looking at it. The Academy should be able to run smoothly without too much interruption—"

"Until some of those kids find out you can't paddle 'em," said Tim Farmer, who *was* a farmer, showed a missing tooth whenever he grinned, and had his boy in the Academy's fifth grade. "Whatever you do, don't tell Jesse about this!"

They all laughed. They were glad it was Jesse's father who'd said it.

"You will be under a handicap, certainly," said Corrigan. "You'll have to come up with some other means to deal with discipline problems."

Judy Waring, always the hearer and bearer of bad tidings, was bursting to say her piece. "Well, I want to know what got us into all this trouble to begin with! Just what is Tom Harris doing with our kids?"

"Judy!" Mark cut in. "We're here to cover that to everyone's satisfaction, don't worry."

Amy Ryan asked a simple question. "Mark, could we hear it from you? Did Tom try to cast a demon out of this little Brandon girl?"

Mark knew he was going to have trouble as soon as he said it. "Yes, he did. She was—"

"Now there was a dumb move," piped Brent, Amy's husband. He was a muscular public utilities contractor who considered his areas of competence to be natural gas, the Word of God, and dumb moves. "How did he know if it was a demon or not?"

Judy Waring was more than ready to whip that horse. "He didn't have any idea what he was doing, and now he's gotten our school into hot water it'll never get out of!"

Mark tried to restore order, and had to speak in firm tones. "All right, everybody. Now before we all run off in a hundred different directions, let's just be quiet and first hear what Wayne has to say. Direct your questions to him, one at a time!"

"We've done something wrong," Judy insisted. "We wouldn't be in court if we didn't do something wrong."

"Judy!"

She closed her lips, but with a defiant expression.

"Come on, saints," said Tal, "you can do better than that!"

Guilo muttered, "You were wondering where our prayer cover went?"

Wayne Corrigan tried to start again. "I want to give you an accurate picture, but also I don't want to sound too negative. We *are* in the middle of a lawsuit, but it's not the end of the world . . . or of the school. It's possible we can pull through this thing and come out unscathed with the help of the Lord and everyone who can pitch in. For right now, the school is under a restraining order forbidding the use of spanking or of any religious behavior that could be construed as harmful to children."

"Casting out demons . . ." Brent muttered under his breath. Everyone heard him.

"No, now let me comment on that right now. You have to realize how the system works, and how the ACFA works. Casting out demons isn't the ultimate point of all this. It's just the issue that keeps moving to the forefront because it's sensational in nature and mostly because it involves a child. The ACFA knows that and they're playing it for all it's worth, making it the rallying point.

"But it would be better to follow and watch the phrase, 'outrageous religious behavior.' You see, what could happen in this case is that the courts—for the sake of a child—will have to rule that some particular action by a religious group constitutes outrageous religious behavior; once that legal precedent is set, it can be used in future cases to widen the original definition of just what kind of religious behavior is outrageous and can be legally challenged, whether a child is involved or not. We would ultimately open the gate for the courts to establish what kind of religious belief is acceptable and what is not, to put it bluntly."

"But what about religious freedom?" asked Lester Sutter, one of the senior citizens of the congregation. "Since when does the government tell us how to live our lives and how to raise our children?"

"Exactly. That is the real issue here, and I want all of you to understand that. This lawsuit is not about spanking or demons or anything else. The ACFA is behind this whole thing, and you can be sure they are working to set some legal precedents that will give the federal government the power to control religion and religious schools."

"They can't do that!" said Amy Ryan.

"They're doing it," said Brent.

"But what about the Constitution?"

Brent shrugged. "What about it?"

Corrigan stepped in. "Brent's aware of my point. The popular notion these days is that the Constitution is a 'living document' that can be reinterpreted by the courts as society continues to evolve morally."

"Or *decay* morally," said Frank Parmenter.

"Or *spiritually*," said Mark. "Listen, people, this isn't just some kind of legal battle. This is a spiritual battle, don't forget that."

"Yeah," said Brent, showing a slight turn-around in his attitude. "What if it *was* a demon? Pretty soon it's going to be against the law to cast one out."

"But who says we have to do what the government says?" asked Tim Farmer. "What about the apostles? They didn't obey the Jewish rulers when they were told not to preach about Jesus."

Corrigan replied, "That's an important point, and something you all need to consider seriously: you may choose to be civilly disobedient as the apostles were, and to obey the Law of God rather than the law of man . . ."

"Let's do it!" said Frank Parmenter.

"But," Corrigan was quick to add, "remember that the apostles went to prison, were beaten, tortured, and martyred for their stand. And as I've said before, Paul and Silas cast out a demon in Philippi and ended up in prison for it. Civil disobedience is not without a price." Now the room was quiet. Corrigan continued, "And that price could also mean extreme damage to your credibility in this lawsuit. Your arguments on appeal will be harder to sustain. Now of course you must follow your conscience before God, and there is Scriptural precedent for civil disobedience—the Hebrew midwives who violated Pharaoh's orders to kill the male Hebrew children, Rahab who hid the spies, the apostles who preached in the name of Jesus when ordered not to. But my advice to you is to work through the system first, the old Romans 13 approach. It will go better for you in the trial."

"What if we lose?" asked Brent.

"Then . . ." Corrigan hesitated and considered his answer. "Then you'll just have to do what you have to do." He hurriedly added, "But please remember, the legal process takes time. You must be patient and not do anything rash that could hurt your chances of winning in court. Remember, the ACFA plans to go national with this case, as far as it can go, with national media attention and as much negative publicity as they can generate. They're using the Day-care Act to get into the federal courts as well, so this case could easily have damaging precedents that could affect every other church, every other Christian school in the country. You're not just making choices for yourselves tonight, but for your brothers and sisters everywhere. You're the first domino. Remember that."

"The first domino," Brent said quietly, and then shook his head at the thought. "Looks like the persecution's started, folks."

Mark stepped in. "So what's coming up next, Wayne?"

"The hardest part of all, I suppose. We'll have to send interrogatories to the other side, take depositions from them, and build a defense. For those of you who don't know what those words mean, an interrogatory is simply a list of questions, things we want to find out from them. We want to know what their grievances are and what they know, so we can counter whatever their argument is going to be. The depositions are similar. We will meet with the witnesses who will be testifying against us, and they will answer our questions under oath with a court reporter there to take down a verbatim record of what they say. The other side is going to do the same with our witnesses, and supposedly both sides will know what testimony and evidence are going to be presented so they can prepare their arguments for the courtroom."

"So what can we do to help?" asked Jack Parmenter, and every face in the room agreed with the question.

"Well . . ." Corrigan looked at the ceiling for an answer. "Any lawyer is only as good as his information, and as I've already discussed with your pastor and with Tom Harris, I'm hard-pressed as far as the availability of my time to do all the homework. I . . ." He wasn't sure if he should say his next thought. "Well, with some reservation let me just say this: obviously we're up against some aggressive people, very organized, highly motivated, with contacts and assistance all over the country as near as their phone. They mean business, they mean to win, and their methods are not always above board . . ."

"They're a bunch of crooks, in other words," said Brent.

"Well . . ." Corrigan tossed up his hands. "I guess I won't debate that opinion. What I'm trying to say is, you need an investigator; someone who can dig after the facts that our opponents are going to do their best to hide. I've dealt with the ACFA before, and they do not cooperate when it comes to supplying any information in answer to interrogatories. They're sneaky, conniving, stealthy, and ruthless. Within Christian propriety, of course, you need someone who can be just as ruthless and find out what you need to know even if the ACFA is trying to hide it. That takes time, skill, and experience; you need someone who can help you with that."

"So who do we call?" asked Jack Parmenter.

"I don't know of anyone nearby who'll do it for any price you can afford."

Suddenly Ben Cole spoke up. "Well, maybe I can work on that. I'm out of a job right now; I have the time, for a while anyway."

Amy Ryan leaned forward to see Ben around several other heads. "Ben, I didn't know you were out of work. What happened?"

Ben shrugged. "It's a long story."

Bev looked at him for just a moment. "You gonna tell 'em?" Ben hesitated, so Bev jumped in. "You wanna talk about shady dealings goin' on, I think Ben got caught stickin' his nose where certain people didn't want it. He was onto somethin', I know."

Ben was apologetic. "Well, that's off the subject."

But Bev didn't drop it. Tall, lean, and athletic, she was no weakling and could be very persistent when it came to fighting for the truth. "It might be right on the subject. You know that suicide that happened a couple weeks ago?"

Some did, some didn't. Few could see what it had to do with anything.

"Ben thinks it was a murder, but the cops are covering it up. I think he was getting too close to finding something out and that's why they fired him."

Ben held up his hands and smiled apologetically. "Hey, it's a great story. I'll tell it to everybody later."

Mark said sincerely, "Ben, we'll pray about all that tonight."

Ben nodded. "Thanks. Anyway, all I wanted to say was that I'll be happy to do what I can. I'll do some of the hoofing; just tell me what to do."

Mark thanked Wayne Corrigan and then stepped to the center of the room. "Let's go to prayer. I think we're going to have a real mountain of things to do, and all kinds of battles to fight on the natural level; we'll be fighting against the schemes of men, against all the curveballs hiding in the law courts, against the financial challenge this is going to be. But none of the battle is going to succeed if we don't fight first of all where the real battle is taking place, and that's in the spiritual realm."

"Pastor," said Donna Hemphile, "may I just say something?"

"Go ahead."

Donna Hemphile stood to her feet and addressed the group. "I feel a real spirit of defeat in the group tonight, and I just want all of us to know that we don't have to accept any of this! God is our Victory, and He's already won for us! All we have to do is move in and take that victory, just pick it like ripe fruit!"

"Right on," someone said.

"Amen," said Jack Parmenter.

Donna kept talking along those lines. An address from her to the congregation usually took longer than was necessary, but her words were always encouraging, so they all learned to bear with it.

Tal could feel the Spirit of God speaking, and noticed Cathy Howard hearing the Lord's gentle voice.

Cathy leaned over and whispered in Mark's ear, "Honey, I feel a check. I don't trust her."

He squeezed her hand to acknowledge her words.

Donna kept going. "We have the right to speak what we want and see it happen. We need to search our own hearts for the strength that's ours!"

Okay, that was enough. Mark quickly, very courteously got the floor back from Donna and continued, "Let's call upon the Lord tonight, and ask Him to help us and guide us through this thing. Like Jonathan said, the Lord is not constrained to win by many or by few. If God is on our side, He'll bring things around just the way He wants them. Let's pray."

The saints joined together in prayer, a genuine concert of praise and petition. They agreed from their hearts, and as a body they were one in purpose. They asked for the Lord's special guidance for Wayne Corrigan as he worked on the case, and cried out to the Lord for the sake of the school. Jack Parmenter prayed for the kids still in the school, that their education and spiritual training would continue with strength and clarity; Mrs. Fields prayed for Tom, that the Lord would give him strength and reunite him with his children; Brent Ryan prayed for Lucy Brandon and the others who were suing them; Mark prayed for Ben and his job situation.

Tal could feel a good concert of prayer here—but he was also distracted by a bad presence in the group. Somewhere, somehow, Destroyer had planted an invisible, insidious infection, and Tal could feel it growing. Destroyer had done well; on the surface, the infection was almost impossible to notice; it was going to be hard to expose, and even if the Heavenly

Host could reveal it, the hearts of the people themselves would have to change before the germ could be rooted out.

But in the usual way, unaware of the undercurrents, the saints continued to pray, and for now it was enough.

Ben prayed for help, any help, that the Lord could bring their way—someone who would know what to do, where to look, how to fight.

And Tal got his order from Heaven.

"Go!" he said.

Nathan passed the command to two messengers waiting just outside the house: "Go!"

The two messengers instantly exploded into brilliant figures of light and shot into the sky with a rushing of jeweled wings. They soared higher and higher, the town of Bacon's Corner shrinking to a cluster of tiny lights below them, lost in the center of a vast, flat table of patchwork farmlands. Then they streaked toward the east, passing over green hills and forested mountains as if with one instantaneous leap, the winding rivers, rural roads, and gray interstates appearing ahead and vanishing behind in an eye's twinkling.

And then they arrived at their destination, another cluster of lights, though much larger than Bacon's Corner, in the middle of farmlands and countryside. They dove headlong for that cluster and it grew before them, becoming a distinguishable grid of streets, alleys, neighborhoods, a new mall, and a quaint college campus. Automobiles were still moving steadily up and down Main Street, dark little bugs with red lights on their tails and headlights peering into the pools of light they formed on the street ahead of them. The streetlights glowed in warm, welcoming amber. Up the hill above Main Street, porch lights glimmered on all the houses where families were tucked away for the evening with homework, after-dinner dishes, perhaps a football game on television.

The two messengers pulled out of their dive and shot up Main Street, etching two brilliant trails between the streetlights. Then they slowed to a hover above a small storefront office between the new bakery and a bicycle shop. They dropped through the roof and landed in the front office area.

The place was deserted; it was after-hours. They paused a moment to look around. This humble little home of the town's newspaper hadn't changed much since they were here the last time. The three old desks were still there, but now one of the two typewriters was replaced with a word processor, and the telephone system had been upgraded from one line to two.

The glass-enclosed office of the editor was still the same—still out of place in this cluttered, cramped building, and still a bit messy. On the wall above the desk was a small calendar indicating all the games in the upcoming season of the editor's favorite football team, and on the desk, in a special corner undisturbed by any papers, galleys, photographs, or scribbled notes, were framed photographs of a lovely redheaded woman and what had to be her daughter, also lovely and also redheaded.

Just behind this enclosure was the teletype room. The messengers checked the recent news releases. They found just the right one, separated it neatly from the other wire copy, then carried it into the editor's office and set it squarely in the center of his desk.

Then they waited. He was going to see it. They were there to make sure he did.

At precisely eight o'clock, a key worked in the front lock, the door opened, the little bell at the top of the door *ding-a-linged,* and the editor came in, switching on the lights, raising the thermostat, hanging up his coat, and heading for the coffeemaker. He poured in the grounds, filled it with water, and plugged it in, then stepped into his office.

The two messengers were there, watching his every move. He wasn't looking at his desk yet, but instead started fumbling with some scribbled notes on the bulletin board above the filing cabinets, muttering some unintelligible words of frustration against someone who didn't do what they were supposed to do when they said they were going to do it. He dropped some of the bulletin board pins, so he had to pick them up; and then, having removed some of the items from the bulletin board, he found he finally had enough pins to hold each item up there without doubling up the items, and that pleased him.

Then he went to the phone on his desk and picked up the receiver. His eyes fell on the wire copy the messengers had placed there, but he didn't take much notice of it.

The Lord spoke.

The messengers heard His voice clearly and wondered if the big, red-haired fellow had also. He wasn't dialing the phone yet, but was holding the receiver next to his head and not moving. He stayed that way for just a moment.

He jerked his head a little—his way of shrugging that was smaller than a shrug—and then started to dial the phone.

The Lord spoke again.

He stopped in mid-dial and hung up the receiver. The messengers drew closer for a better look.

Yes, he was reading the news item. It was about the recent hearing in the city of Westhaven, and about the Christian school scandal that was rocking a tiny, obscure farming town called Bacon's Corner.

The Lord spoke. The big man sat down at the desk and listened, holding the news item in his hand, reading it again slowly.

Finally, with a low, husky morning-voice, he said, "Well, Lord . . . what do You want me to do?"

sixteen

Near the East Coast, up in the green hills above a picturesque river, people from all over the world had found a special place to gather; with devotion, vision, and sweat they had worked to convert an old YMCA camp into a special campus, a center for learning, personal enrichment, and community. The Omega Center for Educational Studies was now in its fourteenth year of existence and growing steadily every year, supported and enhanced by teachers, professionals, scholars, artists, intellectuals, and spiritual pilgrims from all walks of life and many nations of the world. Their binding, motivating spirit: a vision and hope for world peace and community; oneness with the rhythms of nature and the eternal expansiveness of the universe; the accepting of the impulse to change; the challenging of the unknown.

Among its neighbors, the Omega Center was described in many terms of varying shades, from such labels as "a real vanguard in human potential" to such accusations as "a Satanic cult." The people who worked, lived, and studied at the Center took it all in stride. They knew not everyone would understand their mission and purpose right away, but they clung to the dream that, given time, the unity of all mankind would manifest itself. They were dedicated to seeing that happen.

It was early on a Friday morning. Cree, his wings spread and motionless like the wings of a gull, dropped over the tops of the bordering maples and glided just above the glass-smooth surface of Pauline's Lake, silently passing the small summer cottages, diving rafts, floating docks, and beached canoes. He would come up behind the Center, hopefully avoiding any spirits that might be on watch near the main Administration Building.

He slowed, rose from the lake, and drifted to a silent, stalled landing on the swimming beach. The sand was wet with dew, and a mist rose from the lake. Rowboats lay on racks belly-up; the roped swimming area reflected the boat dock like a flawless mirror. To one side, back among some trees, was the equipment shack. He ducked through its walls and found a hiding-place among the canoe paddles, volley-balls, and tennis rackets.

Then he listened. There was no sound. The timing was right; the Center was almost deserted now. It was a short time between two educational retreats. The weekday group had finished, packed up, and left Thursday night; the weekend group was due this evening.

Most importantly, the prince over this place was away, feel-ing lax and confident during the lull, probably on some errand of mischief along with the bulk of his demonic hordes. The prayers of those faithful few saints in faraway Bacon's Corner were having their effect; the prayer cover was slight, still decaying, but enough for now, provided Cree and his warriors timed things just right.

The heavenly troops were here to find one particular resi-dent faculty member, a lady who lived in the faculty dorm.

Cree, in appearance a Native American, with powerful bronze arms and long, ebony hair down to his shoulders, had all the stealth and cunning of a skilled hunter. His sharp eyes peered through the window and out across the lake. He drew his sword and let just the tip shine through the window.

From trees nearby, from boats on the lake, from cottages and boathouses, from the thick woods across the lake, tiny points of light answered, the tips of hundreds of angelic blades.

All warriors were in place. They were ready.

Cree waved a quick little signal with his blade. A warrior appeared from behind a rowboat, skimmed across the water, zigzagged through the trees, and joined Cree in the shack. Another warrior emerged from a boathouse, shot across the water, ducked behind the swimming dock, then made it to the shack as well. Two more, darting from tree to tree and flying low, completed the number Cree wanted. They remained for a moment in the shack, tight against the walls, listening, watching.

"She'll be awakening soon," said Cree. "She'll have four guarding her. They aren't strong, but they do have big mouths. Don't let them cry out."

They drew their swords and set out across the campus, working their way from building to building, tree to tree, smoothly, steadily.

"'Course now, the drones aren't much good for anything after they've gone flying with the queen, so they just get thrown out of the hive with the garbage. Heh! I know a lot of men who are just like that, only good for eating and mating."

Mr. Pomeroy, a jolly retiree in jeans, flannel shirt, and workboots, was talking about bees, his hobby and obsession, and Sally just let him talk; the more he talked, the less she would have to, and the less questions she would have to answer about herself.

They were riding in Mr. Pomeroy's old Chevy pickup with the rack over the bed and the dented right side—he'd run over a stump trying to pull out another one and he told her all about it. He was just on his way up to a fellow-beekeeper's house to check his hives when he spotted this lone, wandering gal out on the highway, dressed in jeans and an old blue jacket, a blue stocking cap on her head, and a large duffel bag over her shoulder. He was a neighborly sort and didn't like to see a woman hitchhiking alone; so he pulled over, picked her up, gave her a short lecture about the dangers of hitchhiking, and then asked her where she was going.

"The Omega Center," she said.

She almost expected a negative reaction from this local, traditional thinker, but apparently he'd grown used to the Center being around and had no hard feelings, just curiosity.

"Must be an interesting place up there," he said.

"I don't know. I haven't been there in years."

"Well . . . we're all searching, aren't we?"

Sally didn't want to get into any deep discussions, but she answered anyway. "Yeah, we sure are."

"You know, I've found the God of the Bible to be a terrific answer to my questions. You ever thought about that?"

Sally noticed the bee helmet and veil behind the seat and used that to change the subject. "Hey, you take care of bees?"

And that was what got Mr. Pomeroy started about workers, drones, queens, hives, honey, extractors, and on and on. Sally was glad. It got them off the uncomfortable subjects and excused her from having to talk.

"That Center's just up the road here a few more miles. I can drop you off right at the front gate . . . How about that?"

The faculty dorm was a new structure, two-storied, with twenty units. The dark-stained, grooved plywood siding and shake roof matched the general motif of the campus—rustic, woodsy, but functional. Cree and his warriors found plenty of places to hide in the thick shrubbery just beneath the rear windows.

At one end of the building, a dark, slick-hided arm hung through a closed window pane and dangled outside, the silver talons walking absentmindedly, playfully back and forth along the wall. Yes, there were enemy spirits about. This one must belong to another resident faculty member. That was his room.

The opposite end of the building was a blank wall, void of windows and flanked by some large trees. Cree appointed a sentry, and then, as the sentry watched from the bushes, the other four warriors ducked around that end of the building, floated up the wall, and disappeared into the attic space. Then the sentry followed.

They crouched just under the rafters, their feet in the pink fiberglass. Now they could hear a faint, whining sound, not unlike a violin in the hands of a beginner. It was coming from one of the rooms not too far from them. They moved forward, the roof bracing passing right through their chests as they walked. Now they were above the sound.

Cree pitched forward, sinking slowly through the fiberglass and ceiling joists until he could look into the room.

Yes. They'd found the room of Sybil Denning, a kind and matronly educator of many years, just dozing in her bed, not quite awake. She was apparently enjoying some half-dreams still playing in her head, and was not ready to open her eyes just yet.

Sitting beside her on the bed, a playful, elfin spirit moved his finger about in her brain as if stirring a bowl of soup, singing quietly to himself, giggling a little between his singsong, scratchy phrases as he painted pictures in her mind.

"You will enjoy this one," it teased in a crow's voice. "Go ahead . . . leave your body and touch the moon . . ."

There were three other spirits in the room, one hanging from the wall like a bat, one flat on his back on the rug with his clawed feet in the air, and one lying on the end of the bed as if asleep. They reminded Cree of young delinquent boys hiding in some forbidden hangout, gleefully committing sin in secret.

"Oh, don't give her *that* one again," said the spirit hanging from the wall.

"Why not?" said the dreampainter. "She always believes it."

"I can do one better."

"Tonight will be your turn."

Cree looked up at the warriors. They were ready.

The dreampainter's yellow eyes danced with delight at his own cleverness. "Oooo, remember this place? You've been here before. It is a part of you!"

A blinding flash! Four angels, four demons! Flashing swords, red smoke!

Mrs. Denning awoke with a start.

Oh. It was morning. What had she been dreaming? Walking on the moon, touching it, knowing it as if she'd made it. Yes. How beautiful. Maybe it was true, just buried behind a veil of forgetfulness. Someday she must analyze what it could mean.

She sat up. She felt rested, but not energetic. Somehow her usual inspiration wasn't with her. Maybe the previous week's work had drained her power.

Cree and his warriors regrouped in the attic to watch her. The room was empty now except for her.

She got up, got dressed, and went down the stairs. Perhaps a short walk on this crisp, clear morning would reawaken her

181

inner potential and get the creative juices flowing. It always worked before.

"Yeah, here it is," said Mr. Pomeroy, pulling over next to a wide, gravel drive that wound back into the woods. Just next to the road was an attractive, sand-blasted sign: OMEGA CENTER FOR EDUCATIONAL STUDIES.

Sally swung the door open and hopped out. "Thanks a lot."

"God bless you now," said the kind man.

More traditional thinking, Sally thought. "Sure. Take care of yourself."

He nodded and smiled. She closed the cab door and pulled her duffel bag from the truck's bed. She gave him a wave, and off he went, apparently with bees and hives on his mind.

The sound of the old pickup faded away, and then there was only the quiet of this mountain morning. Sally stood motionless for a moment, just looking at that sign. She figured they had probably repainted it at some point, but apart from that, it was still the same. The gravel drive looked the same as well. How many years had it been? At least ten.

She was afraid, but she just had to take the chance. She started walking up that gravel drive, watching carefully on all sides. She tried to remember what it was like, where everything was. She was hoping nothing would escape her notice and surprise her.

Mr. Pomeroy's old pickup roared up the mountain road and around a long, steady curve. When the road passed behind a thick grove of trees the sound of the truck faded quickly, replaced by a whispered rushing of silken wings.

Where the road reappeared, Si, a dark East Indian, was aloft, his wings unfurled and his sword in his hand. With a burst of power he went into a steep climb and circled back toward the Center.

Mrs. Denning felt a little better out in the fresh air, walking on the smooth, asphalt path between the classrooms and meeting halls. Soon the campus would be full of people again and this restful solitude would be ended. It was certainly pleasant now; there went a chipmunk up that tree, and how the birds were chattering!

Oh, what was this, an early arrival? Just beyond the sports field, a young lady was coming up the main road into the complex. Their eyes met.

Cree touched Mrs. Denning's eyes. *Easy now . . . don't see too well.* Then he darted into the trees and out of sight. Somewhere the other warriors were present, ready and invisible.

Sally looked carefully at this woman she was approaching. She wasn't sure who she might be. She was afraid they may have known each other before. She kept walking.

Finally the two women came face to face in front of the quaint Log Cabin Cafe.

"Hello," said Mrs. Denning. "And who might you be?"

Sally smiled, but her mind was instantly far away, more than eighteen years away.

I know this woman.

The woman before her, dressed in gray pants and a casual Omega Center sweatshirt, was eighteen years older, grayer, with more lines in her face. But the gray eyes still had that same sparkle, the head still had that same playful tilt when she spoke. This was Sybil Denning!

Sally found her tongue and the name she'd decided to use. "Um . . . I'm Bethany Farrell. I was just passing through the area, and someone told me I might find a place to stay up here."

Mrs. Denning smiled. "Oh, you just might. We have overnight camping here, and some nice cabins. We're expecting people to arrive for a weekend retreat this afternoon, but they're a small group. I'm sure we'll still have some rooms empty. What did you have in mind?"

"Oh . . . just a warm place out of the rain, some blankets, maybe a mattress."

Mrs. Denning laughed. "Oh, we can do better than that! Listen, the office doesn't open for a few more hours. I think the Galvins are up by now; maybe they'll open the cafe and we can get a cup of coffee, all right?"

"All right."

Mrs. Denning turned toward the Log Cabin Cafe, and Sally followed her.

"By the way, I'm Sybil Denning."

"Pleased to meet you."

"Excuse me. What was your name again?"

"Bethany Farrell."

Mrs. Denning paused on the large patio in front of the cafe. "Bethany Farrell . . ." She stared at Sally for a moment. "Don't know why you seem so familiar to me. How do you spell your last name?"

"F-a-r-r-e-l-l."

Mrs. Denning shook her head just a little. "No . . . that doesn't sound familiar. Tell me, have we ever met before?"

Sergeant Mulligan drove over to the Post Office the moment he got the call. He parked the car quietly, went up the steps quietly, and quietly found Postmaster Lucy Brandon, then just about broke a blood vessel containing himself.

"Hi, Lucy," he said, probably too loudly.

"Oh hi, Harold," she replied from behind the counter. She was helping a patron decide whether to send something first or fourth class, and the little lady couldn't seem to make up her mind. She turned to Debbie, who was just handing a giddy junior-higher a box of baby chicks. "Debbie, could you finish helping Mrs. Barcino?"

Debbie stepped over and began checking the weight of the package on the scale. "Fourth class?"

Mrs. Barcino still wasn't happy. "Well, I don't know . . . That's kind of slow, isn't it?"

Lucy hurried to the back room and opened the Employees Only door for Mulligan. He stepped inside, his hand on his hip and his feet shuffling nervously. Lucy said nothing, but quickly stepped behind a partition for privacy. Mulligan followed her, and when they were both safe from any watching eyes, she showed him a letter, still in a sealed envelope.

He took it in his big fingers, read the address and the

return address—actually just a name, and said nothing. He couldn't think of what to say.

It was a letter addressed to Tom Harris. The name in the upper-left corner was Sally Roe.

"When did this come in?" Mulligan asked.

"Today. And look at the postmark: just three days ago."

Again Mulligan couldn't think of what to say.

Lucy was quite troubled. "I don't understand. I guess it could have gotten lost somewhere, or rerouted, I don't know, but . . . there's only one postmark, and that's . . . that's half-way across the country."

Mulligan murmured, "Somebody's being a real sicko. It's a joke."

"Well, there's no address to return it to. I just don't know . . ."

"Can we open this thing?"

"No, we can't tamper with the mail . . ."

"Mmm."

"It's kind of scary, though. The postmark is after Sally Roe's suicide. What if Sally Roe is still alive somewhere?"

Mulligan didn't handle that question very well. "She isn't! That's crazy!"

She put her finger to her lips to shush him.

Debbie's attention was caught, however, by that outburst. She was finished with Mrs. Barcino and could see just a little of what was going on behind the partition.

He struggled for an answer. "Well . . . listen, I don't know what this is all about, but let me take this with me and check into it."

"But . . . it's mail!"

He held his hand up. "Hey, we're only delaying it, that's all. We need to check into this."

"But—"

"If Tom Harris ever got this letter . . . You never know, it might hurt your lawsuit."

Lucy hesitated when he said that. "But I'm concerned about the law . . ."

"Don't worry about it. We'll cover for you. I'll just have some friends check this out, and we'll get it back to you."

"You're not going to open it . . ."

"Don't worry. Just don't worry."

He put the letter in his pocket and got out of there, leaving Lucy troubled, curious, nervous, and yes, worried.

When he put the letter in his pocket, Debbie saw him do it. She didn't know what it all meant; she just thought it might be something worth remembering.

Debbie wasn't the only one who saw it. Two little spirits were following Mulligan, flitting about his shoulders like oversized mosquitoes, carefully eyeing that letter, snuffing and hissing in a frantic, secret conversation.

Mulligan climbed into his car and cranked the engine to life. He would have some phone calls to make when he got back to the station.

The two spirits had seen enough.

"Destroyer!" hissed one.

"He will reward us for this!" slobbered the other.

They shot up the street, careening over the tops of the trucks and cars, dodging the utility poles, darting this way and that between and through the stores and businesses. Destroyer must still be nearby; they would find him.

Just beneath them, unnoticed, a brown Buick eased down Front Street. The big man driving the Buick was taking it easy going through town, just getting a feel of the place. It wasn't much of a place. On the one side was the only gas station in town, boasting cheap prices and fixing flats for ladies free. Next to it was the Bacon's Corner Mercantile, a sagging old veteran of many a hard season, just like the old rusted tractor parked alongside in grass as high as the hubs.

On the other side of the street was the Myers Feed and Farm Store. That place seemed to be getting a lot of busi-ness—there were a lot of weathered pickup trucks parked around it and a lot of John Deere hats around. Then came the grain elevators, the towering sentinels that were visible for miles and bore the name of the town for anyone who might be wondering what all these little buildings were doing out in the middle of nowhere. The PriceWise grocery seemed out of place—it needed a mall around it to look right.

"So where now?" the big man asked his wife.

She sat next to him, at least as radiant in real life as she was in that picture he always kept on his desk. "What was that church we passed back there?"

"Methodist, I think."

"Oh, here's a Lutheran."

"Yeah. Very nice."

"So where do you put a Community Church?"

"We're running out of community, Kate. We'll have to turn around."

"Guess we'd better ask somebody."

He pulled over in front of Max's Barber Shop, much to the interest of the two easygoing retirees sitting in their wooden chairs on the front porch.

"Hello there," he said, and they both stood and came closer.

"Well, hi," said Ed.

"Yeh," said Mose.

"I'm looking for the Good Shepherd Community Church."

The two grayheads looked at each other and exchanged a silent, inside joke with their eyes.

Ed leaned against the car and just about put his head through the window. "You another reporter?"

Well . . . in a way, he was. "Uh, not exactly."

Mose stood behind Ed to ask his question, even while Ed just stayed there, his nose almost through the window, looking this big fellow over. "Don't think anyone's there now. The school's in session, though, and maybe the pastor's there, but he and that other lady . . ."

"Mrs. Fields," said Ed.

"Yeah, they'd be up to their gizzards in kids right now. But Tom Harris is the real hot item. If you want to see *him* . . ."

The man looked at his wife. She already had one eyebrow raised. This thing *was* big news around this town. He turned to Mose—and Ed, who was unavoidable. "Okay. Where can I find Tom Harris?"

187

"You're almost there. Head on up to the bank there, turn right. That's Pond Road. You go about half a mile, and you'll see the church first, on the left, and then Tom Harris's place is just the other side of the pond, on the right, a little white house with a glassed-in south side."

"Where you from?" asked Ed.

"You've never heard of the place."

"Just wondering."

Ed stood away from the car and gave a little wave as the Buick drove away. Mose just watched with a smile on his face.

Ed nodded with great conviction. "He's a reporter, Mose. I can tell."

Tom was reading through some notes he'd made for some upcoming interrogatories. Wayne Corrigan said the ACFA probably would skirt having to answer most of them, but he was going to ask them anyway. He had a lot of questions to ask those characters, and it was going to start right here.

There was a knock on the door. He closed the folder and tucked it away on the bookshelf.

Then he opened the door. His first thought was that he was facing another set of reporters, but these two were probably married, the way they stood next to each other. The man was tall and strong-looking, about middle-aged, dressed casually. His wife was attractive, also dressed casually, but exuding a quiet dignity.

"Tom Harris?" the big man asked.

"Yes," he answered, and made no effort to hide his wariness of these two strangers. "And just who are you?"

"The name is Marshall Hogan, and this is my wife Kate. We've come a long way, and we'd like to talk to you."

seventeen

TOM made a lunch of it. He invited Mark and Cathy, Ben and Bev, and Wayne Corrigan. Corrigan was in court and couldn't make it, but the others got right over there. They pooled their sandwiches, chips, salad, and soft drinks and met with the two out-of-towners in Tom's backyard for a meeting of the minds, a serious checking-out of this Marshall Hogan. Sure, he was a Christian, and sure, he'd been through an interesting spiritual battle himself, but he was also a member of the press, and by now the press was not considered friendly or trustworthy.

They sat in a circle of chairs in the yard, munching on sandwiches and talking seriously. Marshall recounted in crisp, newscopy fashion the adventure he'd had in the town of Ashton. They were amazed. Naturally, the occult-based conspiracy to take over Ashton and the thwarting of that conspiracy went unreported in the national media. No one sitting in the yard that day had ever heard of the place or what happened there.

"And I never would have heard of you people either," he said, "if the whole thing didn't have such scandal potential. Hey, this kind of stuff the press calls news. It sells papers, and that's how it got to me, over the news wire. From what I read in the wire copy—reading between the lines, of course—you folks are up against the same thing we were facing, only worse."

Mark asked, "So you weren't disillusioned by the reports of our 'outrageous religious behavior'?"

"Maybe you *are* outrageous. Maybe you're like too many Christians who see a demon under every doily. Maybe you deserve the lawsuit and the press you're getting." Marshall looked every one of them in the eye as he spoke. "Or maybe this whole thing is legit. If it is, then I might stick around and do what I can to help you out. I've got a young gal who can run that paper while I'm away; I can take care of my own expenses up to a point. I'm a good snoop, I know how to dig things up, and I know how to fight. If this thing is what it looks like, then I'm ready to make myself available, and so is Kate."

Could this be an answer to prayer? Mark was willing to explore it further, and the others agreed. They decided to tell Marshall the details of the lawsuit and the strange incident with Amber Brandon that started the whole thing. Marshall listened intently to the whole story, and he appeared to believe it.

Then Marshall asked, "So did Amethyst ever show up again?"

Tom thought about that question. "Not in the same way. Amber stayed quiet, but she was still really strange— depressed, edgy, inattentive. She couldn't sit still during our morning devotions, and she couldn't stand hearing the Word of God. Now we know why. Amethyst wouldn't manifest at the school anymore, but she never really left."

"A tougher case than you figured on, I suppose?"

Tom turned to Cathy Howard. "Why don't you tell him about what Alice Buckmeier told you?"

"Alice Buckmeier's a widow who attends our church. She's a dear," Cathy explained. "It wasn't too long ago, just about the same time this lawsuit began, that Alice was in the Post Office mailing a package when she heard this big commotion and saw Amber screaming at a woman patron. Lucy Brandon—the postmaster—came out of the back room and tried to quiet Amber down, but she just kept screaming, and Alice says Amber was prancing like a horse again, just running circles around the woman and screaming at her and scaring her to death. The woman ran away really frightened, and Alice was just . . . she just stood there, just blown away."

"Who was the woman?"

Cathy shrugged. "Alice didn't know; she never saw her before. Anyway, Lucy Brandon chased Amber around the Post Office lobby for a long time, and I guess Amber finally calmed down and acted like nothing happened, like a total personality switch. Now that sounds . . . well . . ."

Marshall whistled at the story. "This is getting more convincing all the time."

Tom shook his head sadly. "Just try convincing the rest of the world."

"Right." Marshall pulled some news clippings from his attaché case. "The *Hampton County Star* seems to have you all figured out."

"And most of the big papers too," said Mark. "It's gone out over UPI and AP. I imagine the whole country's buzzing about it now."

"Oh sure. I see they're cashing in on the child abuse angle: 'Child Victims of Bizarre Fundamentalist Behavior.' Nice. Or how about this one from the East Coast: 'Religion as Abuse: Behind the Doors of a Private School.' Oh, I was going to ask you about this one: 'Christian School Responds to Court Order.' It says here that you still hadn't decided if you would obey the court order or not. Where's that quote? Oh. '"We must obey the laws of God rather than the laws of men," said Pastor Mark Howard.'"

Mark nodded and had to laugh. "Yes, I did say those words, but I think my entire statement was that we had heard from both sides of the question, and that some said we should obey God's appointed authorities, and some said we must obey the laws of God rather than the laws of men. I guess they caught the last part of my statement but not the first."

"So what did you decide?"

"For now, we'll submit to the court order. We figure it would be in our best interests until this lawsuit is settled. Then we'll just have to look at the question again."

Bev piped up, "Just goes to show how people with the power can decide what we know and what we don't know. It's just like what happened to Ben."

"That's nothing . . ." Ben started to say.

Bev was indignant. "Nothin'? It's got you out of a job, babe, and I don't call that nothin'!"

Cathy was in Bev's camp. "There's some other hanky-panky going on right in the Police Department. A lady was killed a few weeks ago, and they're calling it a suicide, but Ben thinks it was a murder, and now they're just covering it all up."

"And the *Star's* coverin' it up too," said Bev. "Did you see that little puny article calling the whole thing a suicide?" Marshall only began to shake his head. "Well there. See, you didn't see it either. They didn't want anyone to see it."

Marshall got a question in. "Ben, what happened to your job?"

"They canned him," said Bev. "He knew too much."

Ben laughed and put his arm around Bev. "That's the way I see it, yes."

Marshall considered that. "Okay. Maybe we'll talk some more about that later. But let's get back to the core of this problem, and that's Amber. Tom, you said something about her claiming to have learned all this stuff in her class at the elementary school . . ."

"Right. Miss Brewer's class. I can believe it. The schools have been experimenting with a lot of new curricula. It could be that some kind of thinly cloaked occultism got in."

"What do you know about Miss Brewer?"

"Zilch. I think she's new this year."

Cathy confirmed that. "Yes, she's new. I have some friends who know her."

"All right, we'll have to talk to them and see what they know. Miss Brewer may have brought a curriculum in with her, or maybe the school board's trying out something new. In any case, it would be nice to know how Amber got the way she is, and to be able to prove it. How about it, Kate? Feel like paying Miss Brewer a visit?"

She looked up from her notes and smiled at the thought of the adventure. "Looking forward to it."

"Now . . . people of like interests tend to clump together, just like we're doing right now, and that's called networking. Once they get networked, they start working together, and that gives them a lot of clout they didn't have before. I'd like to know how much this town is networked by any occult or cosmic-type groups. They might already be in the schools. Maybe they've infiltrated into other areas of power as well."

"There's LifeCircle," Mark said.

"Some kind of occult fellowship?"

"Oh yes. You hear a lot about them around town, and they sell herbs and mystical, holistic literature down at the Mercantile. They call themselves something like, 'a supportive circle of friends devoted to personal growth and evolvement.'"

"Who belongs to this bunch?"

They all started looking at each other. No one knew for sure who was involved in it.

"I don't know anyone right offhand," Mark explained. "They don't function much in public; they're not very visible."

"What about Miss Brewer?"

No one knew.

"How about Lucy Brandon?"

No answer.

"Well, we'd better find out then. We can't see anything yet, and it may not be just this LifeCircle outfit, but what we're looking for is some kind of connection, some kind of link-up between these ACFA guys, Claire Johanson, Lucy Brandon, Miss Brewer, and ultimately Amber. We've got to know the enemy before we can deal with him." Marshall finished the last few drops of root beer. "And I guess you know this is a spiritual battle. How are things in that department? Do you have some good prayer warriors?"

The reaction wasn't immediately affirmative. There was doubt all around, on every face.

Mark tried to explain. "It's been tough because of the lawsuit, because of the accusations leveled at Tom. The people here today are all praying, but the church is really struggling with this whole thing, and there are a lot of very unhappy people. I'm still trying to get a handle on all the talk going around."

"So they're talking and not praying?"

Mark nodded. "That's about it."

Marshall thought about that and nodded. "Sounds like a

smart move on Satan's part. If he can divide the church and split you into camps, his job will be a picnic."

"Well," said Mark, "we can sure pray now, just us. I know *we're* together on this thing."

"Yeah, let's do it," said Ben.

They prayed, and took quite a bit of time at it. Marshall and Kate joined them, and that meant a lot to everyone. There was definitely a unity here, a oneness of spirit. This big man from far away and his wife were not strangers at all, but fellow-combatants. This was the hand of God.

Now long after Mark said the final "Amen," Marshall popped the final question. "So how does it sound to you? You want to deal us in, and see what develops?"

By now they were ready. Mark extended his hand, and he and Marshall shook on it. "We have fellowship, brother."

"All right, then. I've got a few projects in mind already. Cathy, see what your friends can tell us about Miss Brewer, and then Kate will drop in and visit her in person. Bev, we'll need to talk to Alice Buckmeier about that incident in the Post Office and hopefully get some more details from her; maybe then we can find out where Amber got this little horse friend and what we're really dealing with. I'll see if I can check out this LifeCircle bunch and find out who's involved."

It sounded good to them all.

The group began to break up. Cathy and Bev started clearing plates from the picnic table. Mark and Tom started folding up the furniture.

"Oh, Ben . . ." said Marshall, and Ben joined him by the back fence. Marshall leaned on the fence and looked out over a wide, green pasture bordering Tom's yard. "You were a cop, huh?"

"Yes. *Was.* They let me go about two weeks ago."

"Because you were getting too close to something they were trying to cover up?"

Ben smiled apologetically. "Well . . . in retrospect, I don't know for sure. It just seemed fishy to me."

"Let's say you *were* onto something. Tell me what."

Ben looked out at some Holsteins grazing lazily in the —

distance. "I've no idea, Marshall. It was simply that the deceased, a woman named Sally Roe, was killed quite violently—at least that's how the evidence looked to me. There were signs of a struggle, a shirt stained with blood, some spilled goat feed—the body was found in a goat pen, the body itself was flung on the floor as if there had been a violent struggle. The medical examiner attributed the death to asphyxiation by hanging, the same as Sergeant Mulligan's initial conclusion, but I don't think that conclusion matched the situation found at the scene. When the landlady, Mrs. Potter, found the body, it wasn't hanging from the rafters; it didn't have a rope around its neck, nor was any rope tied to the rafters. The deceased did have a rope in her hand. And the body was flung in the straw, just as we first found it. I'm also bothered by the fact that when the call first came in, Sergeant Mulligan referred to it as a suicide before we even drove out there, and I know I gave him no information at the time to that effect.

"Add to that a disturbing development that I uncovered by talking to some people who knew Roe before her death: the description they gave me of Sally Roe doesn't match the description of the woman we found in that goat shed, which raises some frightening implications. The whole thing doesn't make sense at all, and I'm still disturbed about it."

"I see you have moles in this part of the country too," said Marshall, pointing out some new molehills in the yard.

Ben was a little disappointed. Apparently his concerns were unimportant to this man who claimed to be so interested in the problems he and his friends were facing. "Well . . . yeah. They're tough to get rid of. When they come up in my yard, I just keep scooping up the hills so they don't kill the grass. It's about all you can do."

Brother, thought Ben, *what a stupid conversation this is becoming.*

"Looks like the neighbors have them too." Marshall pointed at several molehills out in the pasture.

"Yeah, they get around," said Ben, ready to end this letdown of a conversation, starting to look around.

"Two different pieces of property here," said Marshall, looking up and down the fence. "Tom has a mole, and the farmer over there has a mole." Then Marshall looked at Ben for a moment, waiting for Ben's full attention. "How much you wanna bet that the molehills in this yard and the molehills in that pasture were made by the same mole?"

Ben stopped any other thoughts and paid attention. This guy was making a point that sounded interesting.

Marshall enhanced his point. "Ben, from up here on top of the ground, we think in terms of property lines, of separate domains. Tom has his yard, the farmer has his pasture, and the two domains are separated by this fence. But what about the mole? The fence doesn't stop him; he just goes wherever he wants and pushes up his little hills, and as far as he's concerned, it's just one big piece of ground."

"Keep going," said Ben.

Marshall smiled, his eyes squinting a bit in the sun, the breeze blowing his red hair. "The Good Shepherd Academy has a problem, and you have a problem. The Academy has a mole, and you have a mole. I'm suggesting that it might be the same mole. We're talking spiritual warfare here; spirits don't care about whose yard it is, or where our fences might be."

"So what are you saying?"

"I'm saying I'll feel a whole lot better if you and I can find out all we can about this Sally Roe."

Ben felt better. "You know, I was hoping someone would see it this way."

"I think Bev already did."

Ben carefully considered that. "She sure did." Then he dug up a buried idea. "I was going to run a criminal check on Roe before I got fired. I think I could still run a check; I have a friend with the police in Westhaven who could do it for me."

Marshall looked at the molehills again. "Can't wait to see it."

eighteen

sybil Denning was a kind and sociable person, and she never seemed to be at a loss for words and topics. She and Sally spent the better part of the morning wandering about the grounds of the Omega Center for Educational Studies as Mrs. Denning pointed out all the buildings, their purpose, and what new projects were currently underway.

"This plaza should be ready in a few weeks," she said, pointing to a large patio the size of a basketball court, but without any markings and bordered by newly planted hedges. "The Tai Chi Chuan program has gained such popularity that we thought it fitting to create an effective space for it."

They walked further. "This is the performance theater. It seats about four hundred, and is our showcase for any performing arts such as music, movement, dance, poetry, drama, and so forth. Oh, and down here . . ." They came to a large stone-and-glass structure. "This is our healing arts center. We've had our various workshops in classrooms all over the campus, but since last year we've tried to consolidate the research in one building. We're trying new holistic approaches to the immune system, as well as nutritional therapy, and then homeopathy, crystals, vibrational healing, even Tibetan medicine—that's a course I plan to take while I'm here. Listen, are you hungry? It's almost time for lunch, and I'm sure the Galvins will have something ready."

"Lead on," said Sally, alias Bethany Farrell.

They sat down to a tasty vegetarian lunch. Sally ordered the rice and stir-fried vegetables; Mrs. Denning ordered a large green salad.

"Obviously," Mrs. Denning continued, not skipping a beat from the entire morning's lecture, "the goal of education, true education, is not simply teaching generation after generation the same amount of academic content as a preparation for life—just the same old basics, as they say. The human race is

197

evolving too fast for that. What we are more concerned with in education is the facilitation of change. We need to change the upcoming generations to prepare them for a global community. That means a lot of stubborn old ideas about reality are going to have to be cast aside: such notions as nationalism, accountability to some Supreme Being, even the old Judeo-Christian dogma of absolute morality. In their place, we purpose to implant a new worldview, a global scheme of reality in which our children realize that all the earth, all nature, all forces, all consciousness are one huge, interconnected, and interdependent unity. And we're no longer alone in that goal; even the National Coalition on Education has taken up the cause."

She continued to munch on her salad like a happy rabbit. "So, we bring all wisdoms of the world to this place, all systems of belief, all mystical traditions, and we bar almost nothing. Through it all, the truth can be found by each person where he finds it."

"Human potential," said Sally.

"Oh, yes, that, and spiritual wholeness, universal consciousness, all of the above!" Mrs. Denning laughed with delight. "It's been such a rewarding time for me . . . well, for many years of my life, actually. I used to teach high school English until six years ago when I came on staff here."

Sally knew that. Though her memory of Mrs. Denning the English teacher went back nineteen years, she could see it as if it were just yesterday. A scene began playing in her mind. There stood a much younger Mrs. Denning, with more brown hair than gray, scowling at her, angry at being interrupted. Sally was much younger too, a junior in high school with a drab green sweater, a thigh-high skirt, and long, straight, red hair down to her waist.

"Who are you and why?" Mrs. Denning demanded. It was a stock question she always used; she must have thought it was clever. Sally thought it was rude.

Obviously, Mrs. Denning was not feeling well at the moment. She was trying to lead a remedial reading group, and most of the students were the shaggy, acid-dropping, spit-on-the-floor type who couldn't read and didn't care if they ever did. Mrs. Denning was definitely not in her element, much less in her best mood.

Sally wasn't feeling well either. Her mother, whom she hadn't seen in almost twelve years, had just died, a pitiful alcoholic. Sally felt no remorse, but the event did deepen some attitudes she'd been developing in that high school—attitudes of fatalism, cynicism, and gloom.

Now Sally was only doing her job as an office assistant during fourth period, and trying to bring Mrs. Denning a sign-up sheet on a clipboard, a typical list of participants in an upcoming volunteer whatever-it-was. She didn't ask to be snapped at. Mrs. Denning's question hit a lot of raw nerves.

Who am I and why? Good question.

She looked down at the teacher scowling up at her, and answered quite directly, "I don't know, and you teachers have convinced me that I never will."

Well, of course Mrs. Denning got irate. "Young lady, I don't like your attitude!"

At this point in her life, Sally didn't care what Mrs. Denning liked or didn't like. "Mrs. Denning, I came into this classroom because Mrs. Bakke would like to get your signature on this sign-up sheet. I'm just doing my job, and I don't deserve to be treated rudely."

Mrs. Denning stood to her feet, ready to take up the challenge. "What is your name?"

"Roe. Sally Roe. That's R-o- . . . Got a pencil?"

Mrs. Denning had a pencil.

"R-o-e. I'm sure you'll remember it."

"I'm surprised they let you work in the office. Mrs. Bakke is going to hear about this!"

Sally held the clipboard out. "Will Mrs. Bakke be able to count on you as a volunteer?"

Mrs. Denning grabbed the clipboard and hurriedly signed it. "Now get out of here!"

"Thank you for your time."

Sally was just reaching the door when Mrs. Denning had

some parting words for her. "This *will* be counted against you, young lady!"

She stopped and looked back at this teacher, this figure of authority. "Well, you're the teacher; you have the power. Right and wrong are situational and law derives from power, so I guess that makes you right." Then Sally thought it best to footnote her comments. "Mr. Davis, Humanities 101, sixth period."

Mrs. Denning meant to report Sally's behavior, but never did. Something about that brief encounter stuck with her, and no, she did not forget Sally Roe's name.

Sally's mind returned to the present, and she chased a mushroom around her plate as Mrs. Denning continued to prattle. Sally had to smile at how different their conversation was compared to their first.

"Of course, I was involved here long before I actually came on staff. I'd be here almost every summer, working on continuing education credits and helping with the Young Potential program." Sally was just about to ask, but didn't need to; Mrs. Denning went on to explain what that was. "Several of the teachers acquainted with Omega regularly took part in a program to recruit young people from the various high schools we represented around the country, young people who showed real potential for future leadership, who displayed special ability. I recruited several young people myself from the high school where I taught. These Young Potentials, as we called them, would be a part of our summer program here at the Center, and several came back for intensive training over several summers, even after they started college."

Sally smiled. She could remember the Mrs. Denning of nineteen years ago, sitting at her desk in her empty classroom during the lunch recess, strangely pleasant.

Sally, still the skinny and stone-faced upstart, had paused outside the classroom door to get her nerves good and steely before she stepped inside. When Mrs. Denning smiled and offered her a chair, she was quite surprised and a little suspicious.

"As you have probably figured out," she said, "I didn't report that confrontation we had a few weeks ago."

Sally said nothing. She was here because Mrs. Denning had asked her to come; let Mrs. Denning carry the conversation.

Mrs. Denning rested her elbows on the desk and folded her hands just under her chin. "I apologize for being so crabby. I considered what you said, and yes, I believe I was rude to you."

Sally wasn't feeling talkative yet. "Okay."

"Sally, I've talked to Mr. Davis, and also to Mrs. Bakke and Mr. Pangborn, and we've all come to agree that you show great promise; you've risen above some real obstacles in your life and excelled academically and intellectually. Now the other teachers tell me you're asking some incisive questions and digging into the material much more deeply than the courses require."

"I want it to be *about* something," Sally said.

Mrs. Denning was impressed and nodded with a smile. "Yes. The meaning behind it all, isn't that right?"

Sally was in no mood to waste words. "I've excelled. I've learned. I've kept a consistent 4.0 average. But if I'm nothing more than a cosmic accident, then I don't see any point in all that I've done, and to be honest, I'm getting quite bored with it."

Mrs. Denning reached for a brochure and handed it to her. "You might be interested in this."

Sally looked it over as she listened.

"It's a special summer program for exceptional students. I've been involved as a summer advisor for several years now, and I'm always looking for new Young Potentials. I think you would fit the qualifications."

"What would I learn?"

Mrs. Denning was delighted to give such an answer. "The meaning behind it all."

The meaning behind it all. Now, nineteen years later, Sally couldn't hold back a bitter smile. Fortunately, Mrs. Denning didn't notice.

"Would you like any more tea?" the teacher asked.

"Yes, please."

Mrs. Denning poured the green, herbal concoction into Sally's cup.

Sally asked, "So how have all these Young Potentials turned out?"

"Marvelous! We've had an impressive record, with our Young Potentials going on to become educators, psychologists, doctors, even statespersons. You see, the strength of Omega is in the upcoming generations we educate. When we mold them in their younger years, they then mature to be the future change agents in our culture, bringing all the masses closer and closer to the ultimate goal of world community. It starts in the classroom.

"And that's what's so exciting about the changes that have occurred in recent years. Our material and curricula are gaining a much wider acceptance now. Educators and schools all over the country are attending our seminars and signing up for our programs. I think one factor would be the dissolving of the old traditional worldview, the Christian factor, that's been such an obstacle for so many years. People are starting to wake up to themselves and the need for global community. It's the only way our race can survive, of course. Now that we're educating new generations totally free of the old traces of Judeo-Christian bigotry, our success rate is rising exponentially."

Cree was hearing it all, hiding in the attic of the little cafe. But he was getting edgy; it was getting later all the time, and before too long, more people would start showing up, more teachers, more leaders, more gurus and shamans, and with them, more demons than he or his warriors wanted to face. Worst of all, the prince of this place would be back as well, and he would be most upset to find these saboteurs lurking about.

He heard a special whistle. It was Si, signaling trouble. He shot down the length of the attic, out the end of the building, and into the concealing branches of a large maple.

There was a tiny sparkle of light coming from the trees near the front gate—Si's signal. He was alerting all the warriors.

And there was the trouble! The demons appeared first, swirling and hovering in a flock of at least a hundred, following about twenty feet above an unseen vehicle. They weren't too large, probably not front-liners, but deadly nevertheless. Cree had to cringe just looking at those flashing fangs and clicking, razor-sharp talons. Assailing that bunch would best be avoided.

Then the vehicle appeared, a large van, lumbering toward the campus, stirring up the dust. It was full of weekenders— and full of demonic warriors as well.

The window of opportunity was rapidly closing. They had to get Sally out of there!

"Say," said Sally, as if she'd just remembered something, "would it be the Omega Center that published that curriculum I saw . . . *Finding Me* . . . ?"

Mrs. Denning's eyes brightened. "*Finding the Real Me*! Yes, that's a popular curriculum for grades 1-6; we have different programs for every grade, but the easiest implementation so far has been with fourth-graders. You know, we've had that curriculum available for about ten years, but never got into the schools until just a few years ago—the old Christian roadblocks again. We're having great success with it now, however. It still works, and that says a lot for the staff that put it together."

Si whistled again, and Cree got the signal. More vehicles were coming up the road: a fifty-passenger bus, full of highschoolers, several cars, another van.

The first van was pulling up in front of the registration office, its escorting cloud of demons beginning to disperse, all cackling and chattering, some roosting in the trees, some alighting on the top of the van, some just flitting about the grounds looking for mischief.

No! Cree hadn't seen these two yet. From within the van, like huge, hulking dinosaurs, two demon warriors emerged and stood guard, their swords ready at their sides, their yellow eyes darting about with great wariness. They were searching the grounds, the trees, every possible hiding-place, looking for any intruders.

Then a man stepped out of the van and stretched a bit. He was dressed in a navy-blue jogging suit and wore dark sunglasses. He was middle-aged, but obviously a real health enthusiast. His face had a strange, stony expression; the muscles seemed tight.

Cree recognized him immediately.

Steele. The mysterious Mr. Steele, overseer of the Omega Center! No wonder there were such monstrous demon guards along!

Four other men got out of the van, each with at least four demonic escorts clinging to him. These were vicious characters indeed. There was something about these four; Cree could sense that they were something even more insidious and evil than Mr. Steele.

Mr. Steele paused by the registration office to chat with some old friends who had just arrived in the school bus. He waved at all the high schoolers still waiting to pile out.

Cree could no longer signal anyone without being seen. He and his warriors would soon be boxed in.

Both ladies had finished their lunch and now sat over their cups of tea, relaxing.

Sally figured the time was right for her next question. She began to pull the neck chain from inside her shirt.

"Say . . . in all your travels, I was just wondering . . . have you ever seen a ring like this?"

She brought the ring out into the open and let Mrs. Denning have a good look at it.

Mrs. Denning put on her reading glasses for a closer look. "Hehhh . . . what is this symbol on here?"

"I've always tried to figure that out."

"Where did you get this?"

"A friend."

Mrs. Denning turned the ring over, this way and that,

studying it. "Well . . . this face could be a gargoyle, but so triangular . . . like a combination of ghoulish face and triangle . . . Fascinating."

"But you've never seen anything like this before?"

"Oh no, not that I know of."

Steele was heading for the cafe. Cree looked across the grounds. His warriors were hiding themselves well—so well that even Cree could not see them. He wasn't sure where they were, or if they were there at all.

Oh no! Beyond the lake, just over the tops of the trees, a large detachment of demons approached like a swarm of bats, appearing as a long, thin, charcoal smudge across the sky. The Prince of Omega was returning, ready for more evildoing. Soon he and his horde would be right over the lake.

Cree ducked back into the attic of the cafe to check on Sally.

Mr. Steele went into the Log Cabin Cafe and immediately greeted Mr. Galvin, who stood behind the counter polishing a long row of drinking glasses along the back shelf with a soft white towel.

"Hey, Mr. Steele, you're back already!"

Mr. Steele didn't remove his sunglasses, but he did allow a smile to cross his tight lips. "Wanted to be here for the weekend, Joel."

"What'll you have?"

"Coffee, please."

"Got a fresh batch."

Mrs. Denning heard Mr. Steele's voice and turned in her seat. "Oh, Mr. Steele! What a surprise!"

He smiled at her and came their way.

Sally looked down at the table immediately, trying to get the horrified expression off her face. Was her heart beating? For a moment she thought it had stopped.

"So how has the week gone, Sybil?" said Mr. Steele.

"Mr. Steele, I'd like you to meet a visitor we have today.

This is Bethany Farrell, a traveler from Los Angeles just looking for a change, a little bit of a challenge."

Mr. Steele removed his sunglasses. Sally looked up at him. Their eyes met.

They knew each other.

Cree drew his sword, trying to concoct a plan. With Sally cornered in the cafe he might have to call for a full assault. In any event, they only had minutes to spare now. Demonic forces were gathering on every hand. What about Si—

ROOAARRR! Cree ducked as the blazing sword slashed right over his head! Teeth! Yellow eyes! Gaping jaws!

Cree's wings exploded into a brilliant blur. He shot through the attic toward the gable end, the demon's sword like a shrieking buzz saw at his heels.

YAUGHH! The other demon guard appeared in front of him like a bomb blast, yellow teeth bared. Cree couldn't stop in time; he whipped his sword in a fiery arc.

The demon's head and Cree went sailing through the end of the building; the head dissolved, and Cree shot skyward, letting out a desperate shout that echoed over the campus and across the lake.

The remaining demon guard, a hideous monster, grabbed at Cree's feet. Cree shot upward with another burst of speed. Another demon from above swooped down like a hawk and lunged with its sword. Cree blocked it and sent the demon spinning crazily away.

The guard's blade came at his midsection full-force. Their swords met in an explosion of fiery sparks, and Cree tumbled into the trees.

Mr. Steele's lips were even tighter now, and his eyes were piercing. He extended his hand in greeting. "I'm pleased to meet you, uh . . . Bethany."

Sally took his hand, and he gripped it so tightly it hurt. For the longest time he just wouldn't let go, but held her hand and gazed at her.

"I'm pleased to meet you," she said as soon as she could find her voice.

He hasn't changed at all! He still looks the same!

Mrs. Denning was still her jovial self. "Mr. Steele is the director of the Omega Center. He's a tremendous man." Then she told Mr. Steele, "I've been showing her around the Center, just acquainting her with what we're about . . ." She just kept going on and on.

Oh, Mrs. Denning, please shut up. You're going to get me killed.

"So you've seen everything, have you?" asked Mr. Steele.

"Well, not *everything* . . ." He was hurting her hand.

He was the same way when he taught the summer classes here at the Center years ago. Sally was afraid of him then. She was afraid of him now. There was a sinister power, a presence, about him. He could hypnotize with those eyes of his.

Si shot out of the trees along with about fifty warriors at that end of the campus, taking the demons by surprise. One cluster of them was just coming onto the grounds with another automobile full of weekenders. The heavenly warriors flooded over them before they knew what was happening and removed that complication immediately.

In answer to Cree's shout, the remaining hundred warriors swept in a fiery sheet across the lake, divided into many streams, and rushed through the campus like a flood. Demons spun about, then shot forward from the trees, buildings, and vehicles with piercing cries and vicious wails. Swords clashed, wings roared, sparks flew. The angels were engaging the demons' full attention, fiercely battling two, three, six demons at once, but they were not prevailing. The evil spirits were standing their ground.

Cree shot and zigzagged through the trees, this way, that way, in, out, up, down, feinting, darting.

CRUNCH! The guard came at him, and their swords met again. This demon couldn't be shaken!

The expansive cloud of spirits beyond the lake heard the cries and saw the battle. Out front, his fangs protruding past his chin and his head bristling with spikes, Barquit, the Prince of Omega, roared a command and drew his sword. With an echoing, ringing, flourishing of red, glowing blades, the returning warriors dove for the campus.

Mrs. Denning wasn't about to stop until she had told Mr. Steele everything. "Oh, you know what? She has a strange ring she ought to show you."

Mr. Steele let go of Sally's hand. He leaned closer. She thought she felt heat from his face. "A ring?"

Sally shook her head and tried to smile, to chuckle the whole thing aside. "Oh no, it's nothing."

He was still leaning so very close. "Oh, yes. I'd like very much to see it."

The guard came down from high in the trees like a meteor. Cree shot sideways and just barely avoided being cut in half. He gave another mighty burst of his wings and headed for the sky.

The guard had his heel! Cree pulled with his wings, but the beast jerked him down!

ZZOOOSH! Si! God bless him!

OOF! Cree's heel was free.

In a long streak of light, Si dropped out of the sky and rammed the guard full-force. Both went tumbling in a grappling, snarling ball of fire. Cree flipped over and dropped earthward again, sword ready.

The guard had Si by the throat, his big sword raised.

Cree hurled his sword, and it went through the guard's torso like a missile. Si wriggled free and cut the thing in half. It dissolved in a choking cloud of red smoke.

Cree regained his sword. He could see the Prince of Omega descending like a storm. "Let's get her out of here!"

Sally drooped her head.

"Is something wrong?" asked Mrs. Denning.

"I think I'm going to be sick." She wasn't lying.

Mr. Steele grabbed her wrist. "Let me help you to the restroom."

He lifted her from her seat.

"No, let me go alone . . ."

Mrs. Denning was a little startled by Mr. Steele's forward behavior. "Mr. Steele, maybe she can go alone . . ."

He didn't seem to hear her. He was signaling through the window to the four men who had come with him in the van. They were watching. They saw the wave of his hand and started toward the cafe.

Cree and Si had made their chance.

"No guards," shouted Cree. "He's open!"

Barquit and his demons were diving across the lake, heading for the campus, swords ready.

Sally could see four men hurrying to the cafe. They could see her through the window, and the sight quickened their step. Mr. Steele was making no effort to get to the restroom. He wouldn't let go of her.

This wasn't a man. This was . . . something else.

"I'm going to throw up!" Sally threatened.

Cree banked sharply, made a tight turn, and dropped like a missile toward the end of the cafe, his wings roaring. The wall of the cafe filled his vision, slapped past him. He was inside, careening over the tables, along the counter, sword extended.

Joel Galvin ducked, his arms over his head, and Mrs. Denning shrieked as the entire row of drinking glasses shattered from one end to the other.

Mr. Steele ducked too, pulling Sally down with him.

Cree was out the other end of the cafe, pulling up into the sky just as Si shot like a bullet through the front of the cafe and right through Steele.

"Ahhh!!" Mr. Steele's hand went to his eyes.

"Mr. Steele!" shouted Galvin.

Sally was free. She ran for the door.

Si's sword had been there. The four men didn't see her, and neither did the spirits attached to them. The spirits were fluttering about, looking for their attacker; the four men stood there squinting, shading their eyes, trying to figure out which direction the sun was coming from.

The Prince of Omega and his hordes descended on the campus, flushing out a blizzard of brilliant warriors who scattered in all directions, fleeing like frightened birds. The demons shrieked and gave chase. This was the kind of sport they were hoping for. Barquit kept looking for the leader of this marauding host, but did not see him.

Retreat! Retreat! The angels fled, leading the demonic hordes further into the sky, further from the campus, further from the trouble below.

"Good!" said Cree, following Sally.

Sally ran down the gravel road, passing more cars arriving with more people.

"Hey," somebody called, "which way to registration?"

"Just keep going," she replied. "You'll find it."

They kept going. So did she.

The Prince of Omega and his demons cheered and wailed as they chased countless angelic warriors across the sky. They had the power and they had the numbers. They would purge their territory of these brilliant troublemakers, and that would be that.

Cree and Si just kept close to Sally, trying to force her under trees and out of sight. She seemed to know what to do, where to run, how to hide. They flew headlong just above her, swords drawn, rolling steadily to look skyward, earthward, skyward . . .

They didn't know how many they'd lost in this battle. But they still had Sally Roe . . . for now.

Good. Run, girl, just run.

nineteen

Mr. Steele stood, but his hands were still covering his eyes. Mr. Galvin and Mrs. Denning hurried to his aid.

"Hey, easy now! Get glass in your eye?" Galvin asked.

"Must be, must be."

The four men hurried inside, still seeing spots in front of their eyes. One stayed by the door. Another checked the back door.

The third took hold of Mrs. Denning's arm. She protested, "Ouch! I beg your pardon!"

"That's Mrs. Denning!" Mr. Steele snapped.

The man let go of her. "What happened?"

The fourth man helped Mr. Steele to his feet. "Man, look at the mess!"

"Mr. Steele, you all right?" Galvin asked.

His eyes cleared. Galvin looked at them closely.

"I don't see anything, Mr. Steele. You feel anything?"

Mr. Steele was concerned about something else. "Did you see her?"

The fourth man answered, "Not clearly, just through the window."

"Did you see her *leave?*" he demanded.

"No."

"We didn't see a thing," said the third man. "The sun was right in our eyes."

Mr. Steele sat in anger and disgust. "The sun . . . !"

Galvin was curious. "Who was that woman, Mr. Steele?"

Mr. Steele suddenly smiled as if she were a pleasant subject. "An old friend, Joel. I hadn't seen her in years."

Mrs. Denning's eyebrows shot up in surprise. "You *know* Bethany Farrell?"

He looked at Mrs. Denning quite flustered and didn't answer.

"How are your eyes?" she asked.

"They're fine, thank you."

Mr. Galvin got a broom to sweep up the broken glass. Steele got up and motioned his four men outside.

As soon as they stepped onto the porch, Steele cautioned his men, "Nobody hears about this."

"Right," they answered, "you got it."

He spoke rapidly and quietly. "She's got a dye job now, her hair's black, and she's wearing tinted glasses. She has the ring, all right."

"She can't get very far," said the first man.

Steele whispered to the fourth man, "I'll give you some work right away if you wish."

The fourth man understood. He whispered some quick orders to the other three. "Check up and down the road right away, and then check around Fairwood."

Mr. Steele suggested, "They might check at the Schrader Motor Inn in Fairwood. She used to stay there."

The fourth man nodded and gave one final order. "If you find her, take care of her cleanly and quietly."

The three other men snapped into action.

Mr. Steele looked back toward the cafe. "Mrs. Denning will have to be interviewed. Goring will be coming from Summit on Monday, and Santinelli said he'd be here by Monday evening. We'll talk to Mrs. Denning as soon as Goring gets here. I think you should be at the interview as well."

The fourth man nodded. He was dark and lean, dressed all in black, with a sharp nose, deep brown eyes, and strange, pointy eyebrows.

"Looks like your energies hit a critical mass in there," he said. "That was quite a disturbance."

"Maybe." Mr. Steele was unwilling to admit it. "Roe might be into some new kind of power . . . She *might* be." Then his voice took on a strange, sinister tone. "But she's dealing with *us* now, so she won't last forever. The real power is ours, and it's going to stay that way!"

"No," said Ted Walroth, starting to raise his voice. "June and I have talked about it, we've prayed about it, and we just can't go on with this. Listen, Mark, we've gone astray from the will of the Lord having this school. I've always thought that, and now we're just finding it out the hard way. The Lord just isn't blessing this thing!"

Mark and Ted were in the little school office; Mark had gathered all the records for the two Walroth children, Mary and Jonathan, and had them ready to hand over to Ted, but he was still hoping against hope that he could talk Ted into keeping his children in the school.

"But, Ted . . . if you'll be honest with yourself, with June, with Mary and Jonathan, you'll have to admit that the school's done them a world of good. Their scores are up, they're close to the Lord, their self-esteem is great, they're happy . . ."

"Oh, are they?" Ted challenged. "For how long? How long is it going to be, Mark, before something happens to them too?"

Mark had heard that kind of talk too many times before, and he was getting tired of it. "Ted, I don't know who you've been talking to, but there are a lot of outright lies going around, and I hope—"

"I don't care about the lies or the gossip, I know about all that nonsense. But I believe that behind all the talk and the fear there is a definite element of risk—"

"There is no element of risk!"

Now Ted was openly angry. He pointed his finger at Mark and looked down that finger with cold blue eyes. "Now that right there is a problem in itself! You've lost your objectivity in this thing, Mark, totally and completely! If there was a problem, even a serious problem, I don't think you'd admit it! You've taken Tom's side in this thing, and I think that's unacceptable for the pastor! You don't know what kind of person Tom is when you're not around! None of us do! And if you're going to be his advocate in these matters, then I don't think we can trust you either, and I don't think we can remain under your pastorship!"

Mark took a moment to be quiet and break the momentum of this building confrontation. He spoke softly. "Ted . . . Satan is busily at work among us, trying to split us up, trying to cause division . . ."

Ted agreed. "I'll say! You can't see the Lord's will anymore, Mark, even when it's as plain as day, right in front of you! This school is a colossal mistake, a wrong step we never should have taken, and now we're paying for it, and you're just refusing to see that."

Mark tried to clarify what he meant. "I meant . . ."

"I know what you meant! And I'm saying you're wrong, dead wrong. You've been stubborn, you've been blind, you've come to the defense of a man that we simply can't trust, and now we're all under a lawsuit and push has come to shove. June and I want no part of it, and we certainly don't want our kids dragged through it." He grabbed the knob and opened the door. "I've got to go."

Mark handed him the records.

"Thanks."

Ted walked hurriedly, angrily, to the main door.

"See you Sunday?" Mark asked.

"No," Ted replied, not turning around. "Don't expect that. I don't think the Lord is happy with this church right now."

And with that, he was gone.

Tal, Nathan, and Armoth stood just outside, watching him go.

"It's spreading," said Nathan. "First in the school, and now in the church. They're at each other's throats."

Tal fell back and leaned against the school building. "Destroyer! With no change in direction, the saints here won't have a school left to defend."

"And we won't have the prayer backup to succeed in . . . in *anything!*"

"But what about the spirits responsible?" demanded Armoth. "Surely we can root them out!"

"No," said Tal, and he was quite angry and frustrated. "They have a right to be there. They were invited. The saints have given themselves over to this fight, and until their hearts break, until they repent, this cancer will never slow its spread."

"So what now?" asked Nathan.

"Mota and Signa are working to find a breach in the enemy's ranks, some weak spot in Destroyer's plan that we can expose for the saints to find. In the meantime, all we can do is keep the core group praying, fighting. The Lord will move according to his purposes. He'll—"

They drew their swords.

No, it was no demonic army, not even a formidable spirit, only a small, ugly messenger, brazen enough to fly right over their heads, waving its empty hands to show it was not an aggressor.

"Ha haaaa!!!" it called. "Are you Captain Tal?"

"I am," said Tal.

"Destroyer has a message for you!" The little imp hovered high above them, calling out its message with a high, grating voice. "He says, 'I have cut you down, great captain! Omega is mine, and ever shall be, and your army is routed and scattered! Send some more! My warriors are hungry!'"

The imp darted away like a little fly.

Tal did not smile as he said, "Sally Roe is safe. Had they destroyed her, that would have been Destroyer's message." He sheathed his sword. "We'll find Cree and Si, and make sure of their welfare. I've sent Guilo ahead to aid Chimon and Scion at Bentmore. We three will take charge of Sally's next stop. We must keep her alive."

"We are weakened, captain," said Nathan.

Tal nodded. "Gather all the forces you can spare, Nathan. We'll do our best."

Sally remembered a side road when she came to it, but couldn't remember exactly where it went. She took it anyway, just to get off the main highway. There was a red farmhouse not too far down on the right, with a gully in front and a classic-looking red barn. That registered. She'd seen it before, perhaps while bicycling. This road should eventually lead her back to Fairwood.

She heard a vehicle approaching and ducked into the woods. It was just a farmer in his pickup.

She decided to wait for just a while. She pulled out her

spiral notebook and added some quick notes to another letter, first recounting her recent narrow escape, then trying to summarize her troubled, churning memories.

I'm remembering, Tom, piece by piece. The Omega Center has grown a lot and is double the size it was when I was last there. But the spiritual forces are the same, as are the philosophies and the goals of those people.

It all seemed so utopian eighteen years ago. I can recall the classes in Eastern philosophy and the long sessions in the meadows, sitting for hours in meditation, feeling such a unity with all life, with all that is. What bliss that was. I can remember the special spirit-guides who came to me during my last summer. They opened my consciousness to realize my own divinity, and revealed worlds of experience and awareness I'd never known before. It was like an endless carnival ride through a world of enticing secrets, and my guides promised to remain with me forever.

But the joy of those days eventually soured like warm, aging milk. The bliss of meditation became more and more a form of insanity and escape; the spirit-guides did not remain with me as they promised, but decayed into illusions, ghostly images, tormentors. I had gone to Omega to find, as Mrs. Denning put it, "the meaning behind it all," but found instead a world of mindless credulity and wishful thinking, a floating, aimless quest for experience in place of rationality. Meaning? No, only self-aggrandizement. And whether a person is a small cosmic accident or a god who fills all that is, that person is still alone.

So it was futile. I can see that now, but of course "now" is too late. I am so much older, and so many fruitless years have passed. Looking back, I find it so very sad to count the years I devoted to that place and what it stands for. I find it even sadder to think that it is still there, still drawing more and more Sally Roes into its nets. I wonder, someday will those bright-eyed and optimistic teens look back across the years and find the futility that I find now? From a better vantage point, will they assess their lives and find as little value?

Those were, as I have said, days of madness. But I must REMEMBER, whatever it takes. There is still more to the story, and I must remember who these people are, where they are, and what they intend. I must remember who I am, and what I am—or was—to them.

I'll keep writing as often as I can.

"Yeah, and some very hot places are going to freeze over before I'll believe that! You heard me!"

Wayne Corrigan slammed down the phone and fumed, "They won't answer my interrogatories! They're stalling, playing games!"

"Surprise, surprise," said Marshall.

Corrigan, Marshall, Ben, and Tom were sitting in Corrigan's office comparing notes and going over the case.

"How many interrogatories did you send out?" asked Marshall, sitting on the other side of Corrigan's desk, looking through a stack of copies.

"Just the preliminaries, the basics," said Corrigan. "But they won't even answer those, they won't return my phone calls, and even if I do get through, they stonewall it. You may have noticed the response I got from Brandon's lawyer just now, that Jefferson character."

"I noticed the response he got from *you*."

"Well, I was upset."

Ben was leaning against the windowsill, just listening to the conversation. "You did just fine. They had it coming."

Marshall concurred. "They're just looking out for their own behinds. It won't hurt to go after them a bit, keep them off-balance."

Corrigan tried to explain his frustration. "But they keep saying their records are too personal and confidential, and then Jefferson told me they haven't even assembled their discovery materials yet, and I think that's baloney. On top of that, I think they're stalling on taking depositions from our side. They want us to go first so they'll have more ammunition. I can't stall like that; we just don't have the time."

"Looks like they aren't going to give you anything without a court order."

"Yeah, tell me all about it."

"Hey, listen. Kate's asking around about this Miss Brewer at the elementary school, and she's already made an appointment to visit the class on Monday. Maybe when she gets back she'll have some goods on this Miss Brewer, and you can use that in some depositions."

"Well, that's what I need: more leads, more players in this thing. So far I'm in the dark about what the other side is up to."

Marshall tossed the interrogatories back on Corrigan's desk. "Well, it's bigger than it looks, I know that."

"Moles," said Ben.

"Huh?" said Tom.

"Get Marshall to explain it to you sometime. It's a great parallel."

Corrigan was ready for another topic. "So how about your kids, Tom? Are you going to be able to see them again?"

Tom wasn't happy about his answer. "Pretty soon, but I'm not sure when. It's all up to this Irene Bledsoe lady, and she's . . . well, she's quite ruthless. I try not to think about it too much."

Corrigan shook his head and leaned back in his chair, making the springs squeak. For him, leaning back and examining the ceiling was a typical expression of frustration. "She's feeling her oats, if you know what I mean. Tom, if you were rich and powerful, you'd probably have your kids back by now. But Bledsoe knows she has all the power she needs, and without some real pressure from people in important places, she can do whatever she wants. The laws are just vague enough to allow a lot of leeway from case to case."

"But she's so unreasonable!" Tom moaned. "She's guarding my kids like . . . like she's afraid to let them out of her sight, like she wants to control them."

"She is and she does," said Marshall.

"But you heard about that bump on Ruth's head, didn't you?"

Marshall was sitting in a swivel chair. With a simple kick he swiveled around to face Tom. "No. Tell me."

"Last time I visited the kids, Ruth had a big bump on her head, and both of them said she got it when Bledsoe just about got into a wreck driving them away from our house! Bledsoe's trying to blame that bump on *me*, suggesting that *I* did it!"

Marshall was hearing some shocking news, it seemed. "A near-wreck?"

"Yes. You should have seen how Mrs. Bledsoe tried to keep the kids from saying *anything* about that, but Josiah told me about it anyway. He said she went through a stop sign and almost hit a blue pickup truck. She stopped too fast, the kids must not have been belted in, and Ruth—"

Ben interrupted. "Wait a minute! Did you say a blue pickup truck?"

"Yes, that's what Josiah said."

"When was that?" Ben started thinking back.

"I'm not sure . . ." Now Tom started recalling. "Evidently the evening when she came and took them away . . ."

Ben brightened with recollection. "The same evening when we checked out that so-called 'suicide' at the Potter place! Listen: Cecilia Potter told me that Sally Roe drove a blue pickup truck—a '65 Chevy, to be exact—and when I was there checking out the scene later on, the truck was gone. We were wondering about that."

"The truck was gone?" asked Marshall.

Ben was getting excited. "Gone. Now listen. According to Mrs. Potter, Roe always drove that truck to work and came home in it every day. So if Sally Roe did commit suicide like Mulligan and the medical examiner said, who drove her truck away?"

"Whoever Mrs. Bledsoe almost ran into, that's who!" said Tom.

Marshall was sitting up straight in his chair. "Did your kids see who was driving that truck?"

"I don't know. I suppose . . . somehow . . . I could ask them."

Marshall looked at Ben. "You ordered that criminal check, right?"

"I've got Chuck Molsby working on that. He's that friend of mine with the police in Westhaven."

"I hope we get a mug shot or something."

"I hope she's a criminal," said Tom.

"Yeah," said Marshall, "there is that little detail. But if we can get a photo of her, and if we can get it to the kids and have them identify her . . ."

"The fur would hit the fan!" said Ben. "It would prove Sally Roe is still alive, that it wasn't her suicide that we found!"

Marshall stood to his feet. "Moles."

"There's that word again," said Tom.

Corrigan straightened up in his chair and leaned over his desk. "Hey, guys, anytime you want to explain all this to me, I'd be glad to listen. I *am* supposed to be your lawyer, you know."

Marshall took a piece of scratch paper from Corrigan's desk. "Just like a mole in your yard and somebody else's yard . . . well, in three yards, actually. Three molehills, but all the same mole." He took out his pen and drew a small circle. "Here's the first molehill: the lawsuit against the Christian school, Lucy Brandon, the ACFA, that whole ball of wax." He drew another circle. "Here's the second molehill: The ACFA uses the child abuse hotline to report Tom and get the CPD into it. Irene Bledsoe gets the pickup order and takes the kids. That connects the two molehills . . . sort of." He drew a connecting line between the two circles.

"Maybe," said Corrigan. "I mean, you know it and I know it, but proving it is another thing."

"That comes later," said Marshall. "But now . . ." He drew a third circle. "Here's the third molehill: the mysterious death of Sally Roe—or somebody else. Somehow, possibly, the real live Sally Roe crossed paths with Irene Bledsoe right after the point in time when she was supposed to be dead." He drew another connecting line between the second and third circles. "Now you have two kids who might be—*might be*—witnesses to that, and so . . . possibly . . . Irene Bledsoe is withholding them, hiding them, dragging her feet all she can, to keep them quiet. Now she might just be protecting her own position, waiting for Ruth's bump to heal, or for both kids to forget what happened. Or . . ."

Ben took his own pen and connected the third circle with the first, forming a closed triangle. "Or she's helping to cover up whatever happened at the Potter farm, which means this Sally Roe thing could be in some way connected with the attack on the Christian school, which we know is connected with the taking of Tom's kids."

"None of which you can prove," Corrigan reminded them again.

"That comes later," said Marshall again. He smiled. He felt good. "But that's what's happening. We've got moles—spiritual powers and human counterparts—under all this, and they've pushed their way to the surface in these three areas."

Tom stared at the three circles. "If you want to talk about underground spiritual activity . . . how about the mileage Satan's gotten out of this whole CPD deal? They've got me branded as some kind of child abuser, and the whole church is falling apart over it. We can't win any fight of any kind in the shape we're in."

Marshall nodded. "Exactly. Now you're catching on."

Tom wanted to believe it. "But . . . I don't see any *direct* connection between what happened to Sally Roe and what's happening at the school. There's nothing there."

"There is," said Marshall.

"There isn't!" said Corrigan. "You can't prove a bit of this!"

"We will. Call me a fanatic, but I think God's showing this to us. He's giving us the outline; all we have to do is fill it in."

Ben was getting stirred up. "You've got something, Marshall!"

"But nothing *I* can use!" said Corrigan.

Marshall put his pen back in his pocket and just looked at

that little diagram. "We'll get you something, Wayne. I don't know what, but we'll get it."

The music was soft, steady, compelling, with a relaxing rhythm and tone. Miss Brewer, a young and pretty teacher with a disarming smile, read from a script in a soothing, almost hypnotic voice.

"Feel the breeze drifting through your hair, feel the warm sun on your skin, the firm, inviting earth under your body. You're just a rag doll, totally limp, filled with sawdust . . ."

Kate Hogan sat quietly in the back of the classroom, trying to surreptitiously jot down notes as she watched the twenty-three fourth-graders go through the exercise. The desks were arranged to provide floor space for an activity area at one end of the room, and now the children lay flat on their backs on the floor in that area on blankets, pillows, or coats, their eyes closed, their breathing slow and deep, their arms limp at their sides.

"First the sawdust drains from your head . . . then from your neck . . . then from your chest . . . You just start sinking, sinking, sinking toward the ground . . ."

Kate watched the clock on the wall. So far they'd been lying on the floor for ten minutes.

The music kept playing. Miss Brewer came to the end of her soothing, lilting monologue. She paused, looked around the floor at every child, and then proceeded with some softly spoken instructions.

"Do you hear a babbling?" Then she whispered, "Listen! Do you hear it?" She took a moment for the kids to listen. "It's coming closer now, isn't it? It's your new friend, your wise person; they've come to talk to you. Let your friend appear on your mental screen. What is your friend's name?"

Kate scribbled just a few words to guide her memory. Most of the details of what she was now witnessing were familiar to her.

"Pick a room for your friend; make up a room in your mind to be your new friend's house. Make it something just right for them. Now talk to your friend, your very own wise person. Remember, your friend knows all about you . . . how you feel . . . what you like . . . what you don't like . . . all your problems and hurts . . ."

The exercise lasted another fifteen minutes or so, and the silence in the room was impressive for this age group. At last, after a predetermined amount of time, Miss Brewer counted to five slowly and then snapped her fingers. The children seemed to wake up from a trance, and sat up.

"Very good! Now we'll all take our seats and the monitors will pass out some paper. We'll draw our new friends."

The children folded the blankets, put away the pillows, hung up the coats, then returned to their desks. One child from each row passed out drawing paper. Under Miss Brewer's firm but kind guidance, the children got out their crayons and began to create portraits.

Miss Brewer walked up and down the rows, surveying each child's progress. "Oh, what a nice-looking friend! What's that on his head? Stars? He must be a marvelous creature!"

Kate took a short tour herself. The children were drawing ponies, dragons, princes and princesses, and some rather frightening monsters as well. They all received praise and compliments from Miss Brewer.

One little fellow showed Kate his picture. "This is Longfoot," he said. "I'm going to keep him in my mental basement."

The picture was typical fourth-grade artwork, but recognizable as a giant, lumbering figure with large feet.

"Look at his huge feet," Kate said playfully. "What does he do with those big feet?"

"He stomps on my mom and dad and all the big kids."

"Oh my."

A little girl turned to join the conversation, holding up her drawing for Kate to see. "See my friend? He's a dragon, but he doesn't breathe fire. He spits out jawbreakers!"

"Oh, and did you meet him today?"

She shook her head a little sadly. "No. He already lives in my head; he's been there a long time, and we're friends. I couldn't see my new friend today. I heard him, but I couldn't see him."

"Look at my picture!" said another little girl.

Kate walked over to take a look. Then she took a longer look.

The child had drawn a big-eyed, chubby-cheeked pony. The drawing was exceptional.

"This is Ponderey," she said. "He's my inner guide."

"A pony . . ." said Kate in wonder. She smiled. "That's a wonderful picture, honey. You draw very well."

"Ponderey helps me. He loves to draw."

Kate took her seat again in the back of the classroom and jotted down a few more notes, even though her hand was a little unsteady. She was so upset, she feared losing her quiet, professional manner.

Before long it was time for recess; the children filed out in a neat line until they reached the door to the playground. Then they abandoned the building like sailors from a sinking ship.

Miss Brewer sank into her chair at her desk and sighed with a big smile. "Well, that much of the day is over!"

Kate approached her and found a chair nearby. "They're a wonderful group."

"Aren't they, though? This is a great year for me; the kids in this town are really special!"

"The creative exercise was something special too; it evoked a lot of response."

Miss Brewer laughed out of pleasure and pride. "It's an adventure every time. Kids can be so creative, and there's just such wisdom and insight locked up in each one of them. You never know what they'll uncover."

"And what do you call this? Isn't it like Whole Brain Learning?"

"Sure. That's part of it. But most of the concepts and exercises are from the *Finding the Real Me* curriculum. It's a tried and tested program, and it includes the best of the proven theories now in use. It's very comprehensive."

"Well, what's the underlying principle to all this?"

Miss Brewer smiled. "You're not a parent, are you?"

"No, just a curious citizen. Like I said on the phone, I've heard a lot about what you're doing here, and I thought it would be interesting to watch."

"Sure. Well, of course our perspective is that each child should be free to achieve his or her own highest potential, and that takes a certain measure of creative and intuitive freedom. Too often an educator can stifle that potential by imposing a particular rule of behavior or truth upon the learner when the learner should be experiencing his own realities, creating his own concept of the world.

"We've found that relaxation and visualization exercises are a real key to untying each child, setting him free to start his own process of becoming. Human consciousness, even in a child, carries an incredible wealth of knowledge that no traditional classroom could ever cover even in a lifetime. That knowledge is available to each child from his own inner wisdom. We don't teach the child how to feel or how to perceive truth. All we have to do is show him how to unlock his own wisdom and intuition, and the rest just happens."

"And that's what you were doing today?"

"Well sure, exactly. We only use about two percent of our brain anyway. When we teach the children how to tap into the vast resources hidden in the rest of their brain, the sky's the limit."

"So where do these 'inner guides' and 'wise persons' come into all this?"

Miss Brewer let her eyes search the heavens as she formulated an answer. "To put it simply, there is a vast storehouse of knowledge locked up in our own hidden consciousness, and one of the ways to access it is to personify it, dress it up as a person, a character familiar to us. So, say I'm a little girl with fears about big people, grown-ups, maybe my own parents. Actually, I already have within myself all the knowledge I need to cope with whatever situation I encounter. I only need to learn it from myself. So, to facilitate that, I relax, let my mind go, and imagine—visualize—a favorite image, a character, a friend. Did you notice the pictures the children drew? Every one of those drawings was the child's expression of an inner friend, an inner guide, a personification of their own wisdom with which they feel free, unhampered, and comfortable. Once they create this image, it takes on a life of its own, and can talk to them and give them the advice and counsel they need for whatever they're having to deal with. In essence, they are learning from themselves, from their own buried consciousness."

"And this is all contained in this *Finding the Real Me* curriculum?"

"It's all in there, all organized, categorized, and graded. It makes the whole task a lot simpler."

"But—if I might play the Devil's advocate for a moment—what are they actually learning from this? Is there any academic achievement connected with the time you spend going through these exercises?"

Miss Brewer paused to formulate an answer. "I think what you're alluding to is the kind of argument we hear a lot, that we're not really teaching the kids anything, but are programming them, or using them for guinea pigs. But really, what is education? It's training and equipping children to live their lives, to survive in this world, to have the right attitudes and life skills to adapt to a rapidly changing social environment."

"And . . . I take it, of course, that reading, writing, mathematics, social studies, subjects like this have their place in this overall definition of education?"

Miss Brewer made a strange face. "Well . . . basic academic training is one thing, but it won't bring about the necessary change . . ."

"Change?"

"Well, reading, English, arithmetic, and those other subjects are in another category. They can't be applied in an affective, clinical sense . . ."

Kate hesitated. This young gal was enthusiastic about her job and her teaching style, but also vague with her answers.

"Okay . . ." she said, looking over her notes. "You used the word 'clinical.' So you see your role as more than just a teacher? You see yourself also as a therapist of some kind?"

Miss Brewer smiled and nodded. "That's a fair way to put it, I think. It's not a complete education to just fill their heads with the same old ideas that were taught to their parents. We need to equip them to rise above whatever knowledge came before, and to search out their own truth and personal values."

Kate was tired of generalities. "Even if it means training young children in shamanism and Eastern meditation?"

Miss Brewer laughed as if she'd been told a joke. "You make it sound like there's some kind of religion going on here. That's a common objection we hear all the time. There were some parents who came to me with that conception, but we cleared it up. This isn't religion; it's purely scientific."

"I understand those same parents withdrew their children from this school because they were convinced you were teaching religion here, something contrary to their own beliefs."

Miss Brewer nodded. She remembered it. "I guess that's how we cleared it up. Sounds like you've already talked to them."

Kate nodded back. "Yes."

Miss Brewer was still pleasant and all the more confident. "Well, I have no misgivings about what we're doing here. I think the school board and all the teachers they hire are more than qualified to judge what is helpful and constructive for the children. And the courts have stood behind the education community in that regard. If parents don't feel they can trust highly trained professionals to be competent in handling their children, then I guess withdrawing their children is their only real option. We aren't here to cater to fringe elements who insist on living in the past."

"You referred to the school board. I take it they selected and authorized the *Finding the Real Me* curriculum?"

"Yes, unanimously. You really should meet them before you draw any final conclusions. They're a wonderful group of people. I'm proud to be working with them."

"Well, I'm sure they are. But tell me . . ." Kate was ready to ask the question, but didn't know if Miss Brewer was ready to answer it. "Wasn't Amber Brandon in your class this year?"

Oh, Miss Brewer received that question like a revelation. She closed her eyes and smiled a long, showy smile as if to say, *Aha!* "So . . . is that what this visit is all about?"

Kate decided to try some education rhetoric herself. "Well, let's just remember that we all believe in freedom of thought, freedom of information, and above all freedom from censorship for those who have a right to know." Then she tried a straight answer. "For your information, I'm a friend of Tom Harris's, and I'm doing some research for him."

Miss Brewer was truly an admirable person. She remained strong and sat up straight. "I don't mind. I don't have to make apologies or hide anything I'm doing in this classroom. In answer to your question, yes, Amber Brandon was in my class, and as a matter of fact, she's back once again to finish out the year."

"Was she here today? I don't think I saw her."

"No, and it's understandable. Due to the trauma she's going through, she just isn't willing to attend this part of the class anymore. She spends this time in the library, and then returns to class after lunch."

"Then can you tell me about Amethyst the pony?"

Miss Brewer rose from her desk and pointed out a crayon picture posted high above the chalkboard. "Here she is, right here."

Kate walked closer for a better look.

It was an eerie experience, like getting the first look at a night-stalking burglar, or seeing the face of a serial rapist for the first time.

So this was Amethyst!

She was a little purple pony with shining pink mane and tail; her eyes were large and sparkling, she had a five-pointed star on her cheek, small white wings grew from her shoulders, and she stood tall and alert under a rainbow arch. She was beautiful, a remarkable drawing for a ten-year-old. In the lower-right corner, Amber had carefully printed her name in dark pencil.

"She drew this about a month before she transferred to the Christian school," Miss Brewer explained. "She was having some remarkable experiences during our exercise sessions. I've never seen such progress in a child."

Kate swallowed. Her mouth was suddenly dry.

"And you . . ." She began, but had to clear her throat. "You hold that this . . . this image . . . is a . . . uh . . ."

"A visualization of Amber's own inner wisdom."

"I see." Kate took a moment to formulate her next question. "So . . . as you probably know, the current case against Tom Harris stemmed from a confrontation between himself and . . . and Amber as Amethyst."

Miss Brewer smiled. "Well . . . all I can give you is my opinion."

"Please do."

"Whenever a child is thrust into a situation that is intolerable, such as a case of abuse, it's not unusual for the child to bury the memory of it or any thought of it to avoid the pain and trauma of the event. Many child abuse counselors have found that one way to bring things back out into the open is to allow the child to project the memory into a neutral object, such as a figure or doll or puppet.

"In Amber's case, you have a little pony who is bright, confident, and pristine, and who has the strength to deal with such problems where Amber doesn't. When it comes to what really happened at the Christian school, Amber can't talk about it, but instead lets Amethyst come forward and do the talking for her."

Kate digested that for a moment. "But would that explain why Amethyst appeared and caused a disruption even before Tom Harris confronted her?"

"Well, we don't know everything that happened, do we? There could have been some abuse before the events that Tom Harris told you about."

"What if Amber came to the school already manifesting herself as Amethyst? Would that suggest that there had been some kind of abuse before Amber ever met Tom Harris or ever spent one day in the Good Shepherd Academy?"

Miss Brewer shook her head. "I doubt it. Amber comes from a very loving home."

Kate nodded. "All right. Say, would you have a copy of that curriculum around? I'd like to look through it."

"Certainly."

Miss Brewer went to the shelves behind her desk and scanned all the titles. "Well . . . no, umm . . ." She straightened and turned. "Well, it isn't here . . ." Then she remembered. "Oh, that's right, I'm sorry. The principal, Mr. Woodard, asked to borrow it. He was supposed to bring it back, but obviously he hasn't yet. But if you care to, you can always order a copy from the publisher."

That idea intrigued Kate. "And who might that be?"

"The Omega Center for Educational Studies. I think I have the address here somewhere."

Miss Brewer combed through some binders on her desk.

Kate had another question, a stab in the dark. "Isn't there a support group of some kind in Bacon's Corner? Some group called LifeCircle?"

Miss Brewer looked up from her search. "Oh, yes. They're a wonderful group of people."

"What is it exactly?"

"Oh, just a loosely organized fellowship of people with like interests—the arts, religion, philosophy, ecology, peace, that sort of thing."

"Do you belong to that group?"

"Yes, I do."

"Then you must know Lucy Brandon personally?"

"Uh-huh." She caught herself and smiled. "That's right; you're probably finding out all about her."

Kate smiled and shrugged. "Of course."

"Oh, here's the address." She scribbled it down on a scrap of paper.

"Then that other woman, the legal assistant for Ames and Jefferson . . . ?"

"Claire Johanson."

"Yes."

"She must be involved in that as well."

"Oh yes. She's one of the leaders. But a lot of people belong to it."

"Like who?"

Miss Brewer stopped, tapped her chin as she thought a moment, and then answered, "Maybe you should ask *them.*"

twenty

Barquit stood his ground, his nostrils chugging sulfur straight down over his burly chest and his yellow eyes steadfast, unflinching. He was the mighty Prince of Omega, and had done more mischief and won more victories for his master than this pompous, swelled-headed upstart that now stood before him, spewing threats and abuse.

Destroyer was not about to be ignored. He drew his sword and flashed it about, ready for a test between the two of them. "You blind, bumbling sloth! Revere me now, or challenge! I will abide either course!"

They hovered high above the Administration Building on the Omega Center campus, surrounded by their respective guards, escorts, and aides.

The escorts on either side of Barquit began to beseech him, "No, do not assail him, Ba-al! He is sent by the Strongman!"

"He calls me a sloth!" Barquit hissed through clenched teeth.

"*And* a bumbler!" said Destroyer. "You were away from your post, and allowed that woman to roam and learn freely!"

Barquit drew his sword so fast it whistled. He held it forth to strengthen his reply. "And where was the word I never received, that this wretch would be entering my domain? If you are so intent on capturing her, why was I never told?" He continued with an added edge, "And how is it that she is still alive at all, and free to harass us? Wasn't she supposed to be destroyed in Bacon's Corner?"

The two swords almost touched.

Just then a human voice broke in. "Gentlemen, if you'll just have a seat . . ."

The spirits in the air froze. Business was calling. The humans below were starting their meeting.

Barquit sheathed his sword. "The heavenly ranks were routed, and we still hold our territory. I'll put this behind us."

Destroyer put his sword away as well. "I'll put aside past blunders . . . for now."

They dropped through the roof of the building to join the meeting, taking place in a small conference room. Mr. Steele sat at the head of the table; at his right sat the dark man dressed all in black; at his left sat two other men. At the other end of the table, looking nervous, sat Mrs. Denning.

Mr. Steele led the proceedings. "Sybil, we'd like to thank you for coming. Let me introduce everybody. Obviously, Mr. Tisen you know. Gentlemen, this is Gary Tisen, the faculty head here at Omega." Tisen was a bearded man in his thirties, a likable sort of guy. "This gentleman here on my right is Mr. Khull, a free-lance journalist and photographer. On my immediate left is Mr. Goring, from the Summit Institute." Goring was an older man with probing eyes, meticulously combed white hair, and a neatly sculpted beard. He wore several strings of beads around his neck. "Gentlemen, this is, of course, Sybil Denning, a member of our faculty for several years now."

Everyone nodded at everyone else. Mrs. Denning smiled a little, feeling like this meeting might not be as serious as she once thought.

Mr. Steele maintained a smile, but there was something cutting in his eyes. "Now, Sybil, we had some questions about this woman who came to the Center last Friday. What did she say her name was?"

Sybil was a little taken aback by that question. "Well, Mr. Steele, that was Bethany Farrell, from the Los Angeles area, remember? You said you knew her."

Mr. Steele chuckled sheepishly, and then he lied. "I thought she was someone else. What we're trying to find out now is who she really was. Did she give you any other identification, any other proof of who she might be?"

"Well . . . no."

Mr. Steele paused at that answer. "So . . . Sybil, you see what happened? A total stranger walked onto our campus, gave you nothing more than her name and the claim that she was from Los Angeles, and that was all she had to do to get a carte blanche tour of the Center." Mrs. Denning didn't know what to say. Mr. Steele just smiled. "Well, Sybil, that's what I've always liked about you: you love people, you trust them, you reach out to them, and that's what Omega is all about, isn't it?"

She brightened just a little. "Well, of course."

"Did she say anything else about herself?" Mrs. Denning tried to remember. "Is she married, for instance?"

"No, she's divorced. She said she was just hitchhiking around the country, trying to find herself. She was looking for a place to stay, as I recall."

"And so you gave her a tour of the campus."

"Yes. I took her for a walk and talked about the Center and what we do here, and what our goals are."

Mr. Steele and Mr. Goring each drew a breath and held it a moment. Then Mr. Steele spoke. "Uh . . . Sybil, that's the sort of thing I was alluding to. To put it simply, you shouldn't have done that. We don't know who this woman was, or what her intentions were, and I'm sure you realize that there are many interests out there that are hostile to us. Our goals could be severely jeopardized if we aren't careful choosing whom we give information to. What goals did you discuss with her?"

She probed her memory, and it was painful to admit anything she found. "Uh . . . our goals for change through education . . ."

That brought an audible sigh, and Mr. Tisen even tapped the table.

"What else, Sybil?"

"Our programs, our curricula, our working into the public education system . . ." Her emotions started to show. "I'm sorry. I just didn't know . . ."

"What else?"

"Umm . . . I know we talked about the Young Potentials program . . . and our quest for global community . . . and our clinical approach to education . . ."

Mr. Goring asked a brief question. "Did you discuss the *Finding the Real Me* curriculum?"

Mrs. Denning was a little surprised that Goring knew about that. "Why . . . yes, we did. But I think it was because we were already talking about getting our curricula placed in the public schools, and apparently she'd seen it somewhere, and wondered if we were really the ones who had published it."

"Mm. Now, I understand she showed you a ring?"

"Yes. She had it on a chain around her neck. She wondered if I'd ever seen a ring like it before."

"Had you?"

"No."

"What did the ring look like?"

"Oh . . ." She tried to draw little images with her hands as she described it. "It was kind of large, like a class ring . . . It was gold . . . There was a strange, mythical-looking face on it, like a gargoyle, but triangular."

The men were keeping a poker face, with obvious effort.

Mr. Steele asked, "And you're sure you've never seen her before?"

That question suggested the possibility. "Um, well, I don't know. Should I have known her?"

Goring butted in. "No, of course not."

But Mrs. Denning thought about the face again, and that first meeting, and that woman spelling her name, "F-a-r-r- . . ."

Goring decided they'd asked enough questions. "Don't worry about this, Mrs. Denning. Obviously there was no harm done. We know you'll be cautious in the future."

A memory was emerging. Spelling a name. Who was that girl who did that? She was really sassy when she did.

Mr. Steele also tried to close out the conversation. "You've done a wonderful job here, Sybil, and we're glad to have you on board. Thanks for your time."

But Mrs. Denning kept remembering. She saw the face; freckled, stone-hard, long red hair. "R-o-e . . ." said the girl.

Mrs. Denning's eyes popped open wide, as did her mouth. "Roe! It was Sally Roe!"

Mr. Goring didn't seem to hear her. "Thank you very much, Mrs. Denning. Gentlemen, I'm ready for some coffee."

Mrs. Denning was awestruck, her mind awash with the memory. "She was a student of mine years ago! She was here at the Center in the Young Potentials program! *Now* I remember her!"

Mr. Steele cut in. "Sybil . . ."

"Whatever was she *doing* here? Why didn't she tell me who she was?"

"Sybil!"

She gave him her quiet attention.

Mr. Steele looked grim. "Save your excitement. I can assure you, it wasn't Sally Roe."

Now that was hard for her to swallow. "It wasn't?"

"Sally Roe is dead. She committed suicide a few weeks ago."

That silenced her. She was shocked, confused, speechless.

Mr. Steele dismissed her. "Thank you. I think if you hurry, you can get to your first class right on time."

She stood and left the room without a word.

Destroyer was spitting sulfur, grabbing and clawing at Steele while Barquit tried to hold him back. *You fool! Haven't you done enough damage? I'll cut out your tongue!*

Goring glared at Steele. "Not exactly a prudent line of questioning."

Mr. Steele tried not to look embarrassed. "Mr. Goring, we can rehash our slip-ups or we can talk about what we're going to do."

Goring moved on, but unhappily. "Mrs. Denning is now a liability. You and I both know she's suspicious that Sally Roe is still alive—and we both know why."

"No," said Tisen, "I wouldn't worry about that. She has a marvelous and deep loyalty to the leadership here."

Mr. Steele turned away from that issue. "She's not a problem. What I'm wondering is where will Roe turn up next, and should we forewarn anyone before she can get to them and milk them for information as she did Mrs. Denning?"

Destroyer stood back and glared at Mr. Steele. *Bungler! Fool! Idiot!*

Goring rolled his eyes. "Do you actually propose that we forewarn everyone to be looking out for a woman who is supposed to be dead? Just how far down the ranks should that information go? Don't be a fool, Steele! Once such information leaves this room, it will be beyond our control. Besides that, whom would we tell? How do we choose which direction Roe will go? We don't know what she's thinking, and obviously you had no idea she would appear here!"

Barquit stood between Mr. Steele and Destroyer before the angry predator did something rash. "I remind you, great warrior, that we received no warning! You could have foreseen she would be here, and we would have been spared this difficulty and embarrassment!"

Destroyer calmed just a little. "All right. Granted. For a time, the Host of Heaven hid her from us, responding to the prayers of the saints of God. The saints in Bacon's Corner do have quite an interest in this battle. But their prayers are weakening now. They are preoccupied with other things." Just the thought of that cheered Destroyer, and he became more pleasant. "We will find her, Barquit, but by stealth and craftiness rather than force." Destroyer could see someone approaching the room. "Ah! Behold this! We've just gained another advantage the Heavenly Host have not thought to contain."

"An advantage?"

Destroyer only smirked and looked toward the door.

There was a knock.

"Who could that be?" Mr. Steele wondered.

"We weren't to be disturbed," said Tisen.

"Who is it?" Mr. Steele demanded.

The door opened a crack, and a young student assistant stuck his head in. "Excuse me, Mr. Steele. I have a special item for Mr. Goring."

"I'll take it," said Goring.

The young man entered the room with a manila envelope.

Two spirits entered as well, quite gleeful, trying not to cackle too loudly. Destroyer ordered them to stand just behind him. They obeyed instantly.

"Very punctual," he said to them.

They tittered and cackled their delight at such a compliment.

As Destroyer and Barquit watched the young man hand the envelope to Mr. Goring, Destroyer explained, "These two messengers happened upon an interesting development back at the Bacon's Corner Post Office. I decided to reward them and secure their future services."

The young man exited. Mr. Goring opened the envelope and pulled out the contents with a puzzled expression. A small letter-envelope and a three-page cover letter fell to the table.

Almost at the same time, all four men saw the name on the upper-left corner of the envelope: Sally Beth Roe.

Goring read the cover letter. "It's from Summit. This letter from Sally Roe arrived last week at the Bacon's Corner Post Office. Lucy Brandon discovered it and referred it to the peace officer Mulligan. He checked with LifeCircle and Ames and Jefferson, the lawyers on the case. They sent it on to Summit. The people at Summit opened it and thought I should see it immediately."

Goring picked up the much-traveled letter from Sally Roe, addressed to Tom Harris. All four men looked at it with shock, awe, and then a steadily increasing jubilation.

Goring spoke first. "So . . . Sally Roe is writing letters!"

Mr. Steele was almost smiling widely. "To . . . to *Tom Harris?*"

Goring was skimming the letter from Summit. "Brandon is reasonably sure that this is the first letter." He dug Sally's letter from its already opened envelope; it was a document handwritten on three-ring spiral notebook paper. He quickly perused it. "Yes. This sounds like the very first letter. She's introducing herself . . . Oh no! She's describing her encounter with Von Bauer!"

At that, they all gathered to look over Goring's shoulder.

Mr. Steele read the account, taking great interest in how Von Bauer suddenly died. He then recalled what happened in the Log Cabin Cafe. He looked at Khull. "She *is* into some kind of tremendous psychic power. *Something's* protecting her!"

Goring wasn't entirely impressed. "And yet she still seems lost, confused. Look at her here, going on and on about morality, meaning, despair. The woman is a mess!"

Mr. Steele read ahead. "Mm. 'I'm going to retrace some old steps and find some things out.' That's why she was here. She's hunting for information."

"And she found it," said Goring in disgust.

Another thought was sobering. "If Tom Harris had actually received this letter . . ."

Goring looked up. "Of course. It could have spelled the end of everything, including Brandon's lawsuit." But Goring's mood began to lighten. "But as it now stands . . . Sally Roe has virtually betrayed herself to us. See here? She plans to write more of these letters, and that could be the key to finding her, predicting where she'll be, finding out what she knows, and just what she has planned!"

The four men looked at each other. It just might be that.

"If we can continue to intercept these letters, observe the postmarks, derive clues from their content, I would say we would have a remarkable advantage," Goring summarized.

"But can we trust Brandon to intercept the letters?" asked Mr. Steele. "Won't she buckle under the legalities?"

Goring smiled. "No, not Brandon. She has too much to lose by not cooperating, what with the lawsuit now in progress. Besides, if we can persuade her that it would be in her best interests to cooperate with us, then . . . we will have all the more leverage for controlling her with each letter she tampers with."

The men exchanged glances and nodded. It sounded like a workable plan.

Goring concluded, "We'll consult with Santinelli when he gets here. If he's agreeable, we'll send word back to LifeCircle to persuade Brandon to continue intercepting the letters and sending them to Summit. Eventually, most certainly, Sally Roe will tell us where she is, and . . . you, Mr. Khull, will then be of value to us."

Khull smiled, relishing the thought.

The two messengers behind Destroyer cackled and slobbered in delight.

"A Judas," said Destroyer. "Someone who will betray Sally Roe into our hands: Sally Roe herself!"

Claire Johanson and her live-in boyfriend Jon Schmidt shared a large, white house on the outskirts of town. The house was once the center of a large ranch, but the ranch had been divided into several smaller farms, and now the house remained as a comfortable, manageable estate for Claire and Jon's purposes. She was, of course, a legal assistant for Ames, Jefferson, and Morris; Jon was an architect and painter.

But most of all, they were the founders and facilitators of a movement, a fellowship, a gathering known to its members as LifeCircle.

Today was a LifeCircle meeting, not too formal an occasion, but rather a time to share, to combine interests, to discuss new discoveries and insights. There were plenty of cars parked on both sides of the road that ran in front of the house, and the house was full of people, not only from the immediate Bacon's Corner area, but from other communities as well.

In the living room, the fine arts enthusiasts enjoyed a miniconcert of mind-expanding music by a popular instrumental trio consisting of flute, guitar, and string bass. The president of the local grange was there, in a strange daze as he listened; Mr. Woodard, the elementary school principal, was also there with his wife, relaxing to the lilting sounds. Some young farmers were in attendance as well, some enjoying the music, and some thinking of moving on to another activity elsewhere on the grounds.

Upstairs, in a bedroom that was totally empty except for cushions everywhere on the floor, young men and women participated in a yoga workshop, humming and droning like a beehive, sitting in the lotus position. They were everyday people—a rancher, a carpenter, a UPS truck driver, a teacher of "special needs" children, a couple who ran a day-care center, and Miss Brewer, who taught fourth grade at the Bacon's Corner Elementary School.

Outside the back door, sitting in comfortable chairs under a vast grape arbor, a discussion group of some dozen people was taking time to share ideas and hear the opinions of a visiting author regarding the application of Zen to farming.

In a corner of the backyard, not too far from a swing set, several young children cavorted on the grass, pretending to be ponies. Leading them all was Amber, now Amethyst, jumping, prancing, and spouting words of wisdom.

"It is as you see it to be," she was saying. "If you see yourself as a black horse, that is what you are. If you see before you an open prairie, that is where you are. Create your own world, and run free in it!"

So, the kids created their own world and ran free in it—as far as the back fence, anyway.

In Claire's office on the main floor, behind closed doors, a meeting of great importance was in progress. Claire sat regally behind her desk; Gordon Jefferson, the ACFA attorney, sat at one end of the desk, his briefcase at his side; opposite them sat Lucy Brandon. Next to the door, in a neutral position, sat Jon, Claire's live-in. He was blond and handsome, like a male model for running shoes, and had a quiet, confident demeanor.

Another woman was present, a short-haired, thin, female attorney from Sacramento, who'd brought a brief from another case the ACFA had finished there.

"You'll find a lot of useful parallels in this case," she said, handing it to Jefferson. "If you have any questions, Mr. James will be happy to offer his time and services."

"Splendid!" Jefferson replied, taking the materials. "I

understand Mr. James was able to uncover some persuasive case law in this one."

"And it's yours to use as well."

Claire smiled with gratitude. "Thank you, Lenore. I suppose you know the people in Chicago are watching this one?"

The woman named Lenore smiled. "Oh, of course. So if you find yourselves in any need at all, we're ready and waiting to send you more manpower, more documents, anything."

Jon chuckled and clapped his hands. "We're off and running!"

"And that reminds me," said Claire, "we've been getting a little low on news items; John Ziegler and the folks at KBZT are always open for more news if we can find it."

Jefferson responded, "Well . . . the case is pretty much in limbo until the trial."

Jon asked, "What about Harris's troubles with the child welfare people?"

Claire shook her head. "We can't go near that, not yet. The judge ordered the press to stay away from that, and if they try to dig anything up it will look too much like a violation of her order."

"Well," Jefferson thought out loud, "if we could find something outside that order, it would help. We need to keep the Christians on the run, keep them hiding."

Jon joked, "Maybe we could use the child abuse hotline again and get Harris in trouble with someone *else's* kids."

"No . . ." said Claire, though she knew Jon wasn't serious. "We don't want to start looking obvious, and Irene Bledsoe's under enough of a load as it is."

"Well, be patient," said Lenore. "It's a gradual process, one case at a time. The consolation is that once we gain the ground, we never lose it again."

"So time is on our side," said Jon.

There was a lull in the conversation. All eyes began to drift toward Lucy Brandon, who sat silently, listening to them all.

She returned their gaze, and smiled nervously. "You're asking me to do a lot."

Claire chuckled disarmingly. "Oh, it's not as serious as all that."

Jon patted her hand. "Don't worry. There's too much power represented here for you to be in any real jeopardy. Isn't that right, Gordon?"

Gordon Jefferson jumped right in. "Of course. Listen, Lucy: these letters are not legitimate mail. They're from some crank, some sick person who's been following the case in the media. It happens all the time. Letters like that shouldn't be delivered anyway."

Claire added, "But in the meantime, we never know just what or who might be behind them, and we can't afford to take any risks."

"That's right," said Jefferson. "We don't know what the letters contain, but we can be sure that your case will not be helped in any way if Tom Harris should ever receive them."

Lucy sat there thinking about it, but still seemed unconvinced.

"Well," asked Claire, "how many have there been now?"

"The second one came in just yesterday."

"What did you do with it?"

"I still have it 'on hold.' I wanted to talk to you first."

"That was smart."

Jefferson concurred. "Real smart. You see, Lucy, we could be dealing with some pretty shady people in this case. You never know what kind of stunt they might try to pull." Then he added in a slightly quieter voice, "Also, consider the stakes involved. If you should win this case, there would be quite a bundle of money in it for you."

"But money aside," Claire added, "think of all the children this case could affect in the future. If we're ever going to build a future of peace and world community, we must deal with the Christians; we must remove their influence upon the upcoming generations. It's for their own good, for the good of humanity."

"But what about Amber?" Lucy asked.

Jefferson was quick with an answer. "You know, Lucy, I don't think you even have to worry about that. Dr. Mandanhi can present reports and testimony on Amber's behalf, and she'll never have to go anywhere near the courtroom. We'll be able to insulate her from this case altogether."

"That would be nice."

"Well, we'll just play it that way."

Claire spoke with great sincerity in her voice. "Really, if we thought this was going to be harmful to Amber, we wouldn't pursue it. It's the children we're concerned about, after all."

"Right, absolutely," said Jon.

Lucy finally smiled and nodded. "All right. I just wanted to be sure, that's all."

"No problem," said Claire.

"We understand," said Jon.

Jefferson doublechecked. "You do have the address for forwarding the letters?"

Lucy thought she remembered. "The Summit Institute, right?"

"Right."

"I have it in my private files. I'll send the letters off as soon as I get them."

They all nodded their approval. "Excellent, excellent."

The music played on, the discussions continued, the humming and chanting made the windows buzz. All in all, LifeCircle was having a fruitful day.

So was Marshall Hogan. It hadn't taken him too long to drive slowly by the house and past all those parked cars, chattering into a small tape recorder in his hand. "GHJ 445, HEF 992, BBS 980, CJW 302 . . ."

In just two passes, he had them all.

245

twenty-one

Dear *Tom,*

> *I want to know something for sure. Right now I don't.*
>
> *Blame it on pride. When I first entered high school I relished what I was taught; that I was the ultimate authority in my life, the final arbiter of all truth, the only decider of my values, and that no prior traditions, notions about God, or value systems had any authority over my will, my spirit, my behavior. "Maximum autonomy," they called it. Such ideas can be very inviting.*
>
> *But there was a catch to all this freedom: I had to accept the idea that I was an accident, a mere product of time plus chance, and not only myself, but everything that exists. Once I bought that idea, it was impossible to believe that anything really mattered, for whatever I could do, or create, or change, or enhance, would be no less an accident than I was. So where was the value of anything? Of what value was my own life?*
>
> *So all that "maximum autonomy" wasn't the great liberation and joy I thought it would be. I felt like a kid let loose to play in an infinitely huge yard—I started to wish there was a fence somewhere. At least then I would know where I was. I could run up against it and tell myself, "I'm in the yard," and feel right about it. Or I could climb over the fence, and tell myself, "Oh-oh, I'm outside the yard," and feel wrong about it. Whether right or wrong, and with infinite freedom to run and play, I know I would still stay near the fence.*
>
> *At least then I would know where I was. I would know something for sure.*

Sally was in the town of Fairwood, a small burg along a major river, a fairly busy shipping port for that part of the state. Even though the Omega Center was only a half-hour, winding drive into the hills above the town, she had lingered and hidden here for the weekend, getting to know the place again, walking its streets by day and spending the cool nights in the woods down by the river.

The town had not changed much in ten years. There was a new mall at the north end of the main thoroughfare, but every town has to have a mall sooner or later. As for the city center, all the stores remained the same, and even the Stop Awhile Lunch Counter was still there, with the same jukebox and ugly blue Formica-topped counter. The menus were new, but only the prices were different; every page still carried the same logo and the same meals.

She was remembering things. She was bringing it all back. The park in the middle of town was just the way she remembered it. The wading pool was empty and dry, waiting for warmer weather, but kids were playing on the swings and monkey bars, and Sally considered how the playground was the same but the kids were different; it wouldn't be too long before the children who were there ten years ago would be sending *their* children down to the same park to play on the same swings.

> *It's really not a bad town. I can't blame it for the feelings it evokes in me, the strange conflicts I feel. In this one place are hidden my happiest and my most bitter memories, side by side. Both have been buried so long, obliterated by drugs, by delusion, by altered states of consciousness, that I've forced myself to remain here to revive them. I must remember.*

She was being followed by friends. From atop the First National Bank building across the street, Tal, Nathan, and Armoth kept watch as she sat on a bench in the park, writing another letter.

"She hasn't found it yet," said Nathan. "I don't think she wants to. She's been down every street but the right one."

"She wants to find it, but at the same time she doesn't, and I don't blame her," said Tal. "But we'll have to help her. With our present tactics, we can only hold that motel room open for today."

"She's moving again," said Armoth.

Sally was putting her notebook back in her duffel bag and preparing to move on.

Nathan surveyed the skies over the town. "Destroyer's scouts are still around. They must know we're here."

Tal agreed. "They simply aren't afraid of us. But I consider that an advantage. I would prefer them to be very confident." Then he saw Sally turning to the right on Schrader Avenue. "Oops! No, Sally, not that way."

They unfurled their wings and leaped from the building, floating down over the tops of passing cars, banking silently around the corner, and settling to the sidewalk on either side of this singular, weary traveler. She seemed a little perplexed, not knowing which way to go.

Nathan spoke to her, *No, Sally, you've already been this way. Turn around.*

She stopped. *Oh, brother, I've already been down this street, and it was a bore.*

She turned around and followed Schrader the other way, crossing several streets, passing other pedestrians, always looking over her shoulder.

The three warriors walked with her, staying close.

Sally looked around as she walked. No, she hadn't been this way yet. Some of the storefronts looked kind of familiar. *Oh! That flower shop! I remember that!*

Then, finally her eyes caught a sight she hadn't seen—or wanted to see—in ten years. Up ahead, on her side of the street, was a large, rectangular sign, SCHRADER MOTOR INN, and below that a smaller sign, KITCHENS, DAILY, WEEKLY, MONTHLY RATES. She stopped dead in her tracks and gazed at that sign, spellbound.

It hadn't changed. That motel was still there!

Tal came up close behind her. *Steady, Sally. Don't run.*

She wanted to run, but she couldn't. She didn't want to face this memory, but still she knew she had to.

If you want to know the truth, said Tal, *you must face it even if it's painful. You've run long enough.*

She stood still in the middle of the sidewalk as if her shoes were glued to the pavement. She began to remember more and more of this place. She'd walked down this sidewalk before, many, many times. She'd visited that flower shop. There was a True Value Hardware on the corner, but now she remembered it used to be a variety store.

She started walking again, slowly, drinking in every sight. These planters were new; it used to be just a bare curb here. That parking lot across the street had undergone a change in management, but it was still a parking lot.

The Schrader Motor Inn was the same, a large, sixty-unit motel of three stories, L-shaped, with parking in front and around the back. It wasn't a high-priced place, nothing fancy, no swimming pool. The motel may have been painted; she wasn't sure about that. The entrance to the office looked the same as she remembered, and still had the large breezeway jutting out across the entrance.

She looked up at the third story, and scanned all the blue doors facing the iron-railed balcony. Yes. She could see Room 302 down near the end.

It had been her home for almost ten months. Such a short period of time, and so long ago!

Even as she passed under that breezeway and stepped up to the office door, she felt she was being a bit irrational. What purpose could such an action serve? Why dig up the past? None of this was necessary.

She was going through with it. She had to see it all again; she hadn't paid attention the first time.

She pulled the door open.

It was meant to be, came a memory from somewhere in her mind. It was her own voice. Now she remembered saying it. *My higher self ordained it.*

"Hello," said the nice lady behind the counter. "Can I help you?"

Sally could still hear her own voice echoing from the past: *After all, there is no death; there is only change.*

She knew she'd been asked a question. "Uh . . . yes. I was wondering if you had a kitchen unit available."

The lady checked her register. "Hm. You're in luck. Yes,

that fellow moved out just this weekend. It's on the third floor . . . Is that all right?"

"It's fine. Uh . . . would it happen to be 302?"

The lady's eyebrows went up. "Why, yes, as a matter of fact. Have you stayed there before?"

Sally was looking this lady over carefully. No, they'd never met, she was sure. She must be a new owner, or employee, or something. "On occasion."

The lady slid the application across the counter to her, and Sally filled it out. She gave her name as "Maria Bissell," put down a totally fictional address in Hawthorne, California, then claimed to be driving a '79 Ford Mustang with a California license plate, and she made up the license plate number as well. All she could hope was that this lady would appreciate the color of her money and not question her credentials.

The lady did appreciate the color of Sally's money, receiving a week's rent and damage deposit in cash. She handed Sally the key.

The stairway had new green carpet now. Sally could remember the worn, brown carpet it used to have.

She reached the third floor and walked along the balcony overlooking the parking lot and beyond that, the Nelson Printing and Bookbinding Shop, still there, the offset presses still rumbling inside.

She placed her hand on the railing and noticed her wrist was unhampered. The last time she ever saw this railing, she was handcuffed, and she was not free.

Out of her buried memory came the image of squad cars parked in the lot below, their lights flashing. Then she recalled the other tenants watching through their windows, peeking around the drapes, curious and anonymous. She could feel the pain of big hands holding her arms, pushing her along this balcony.

There was an aid car down there too, and some medical personnel running around. She could just barely remember them.

She came to the door. With held breath and a turn of the

key, she opened it. The chain-lock was repaired now, and apparently the doorjamb had been replaced.

Some things were different. The couch was new, but still sat in the same place. The picture on the wall just above it used to be a sailboat, and now it was a surrealistic vase of flowers. She liked the sailboat better.

The kitchen looked the same, and the cabinets hadn't changed a bit. The sink still had that brown crack. The pots and pans were in the same cupboard just to the left of the sink.

Through an archway at the back of the room was the bedroom. She knew where the bed would be, and she knew the room had a large closet. She didn't bother going in to look.

Next to the bedroom was the bathroom. She didn't want to go in there at all.

Ben was almost beside himself when Marshall came pulling into the driveway. He ran out to the car to meet him.

"Man, where have you been?"

Marshall was feeling pretty good himself. "Got some license numbers from the cars belonging to our local LifeCirclers. That'll give your friend in Westhaven some more to do, running some Motor Vehicle Reports."

"Chuck's already done a *lot*," Ben exclaimed, fidgeting on the sidewalk. "Come on in!"

Marshall hurried inside and followed Ben into the dining room. Bev was there, her eyes gawking, studying some documents spread out on the table.

"*Oh, Lord . . .*" she said.

Ben wasted no time, but pointed to a grainy, black-and-white, front- and left-profile mug shot. "That's the lady. That's Sally Roe!"

Marshall picked up the photo and studied it carefully. "Man, she's wasted!"

Indeed she was. The tired, gaunt, and dazed woman in the photographs looked every bit the part of a half-drunk or half-drugged tramp. Mug shots never were very complimentary, but even so . . .

Ben grabbed Marshall's shoulder in his excitement and started jabbing his finger at the photographs. "Marshall, that is *not* the dead woman we found at the Potter farm! But it's Sally Roe, all right! I've already been by the Potters' and the Bergen factory to talk to Abby Grayson. Both of them confirm that this is Roe."

"They must not have been too happy . . ."

"They were shocked. Yes, very shocked." Ben went on to explain. "Chuck requested a Records Check from the National Crime Information Center and the State Information Section. Sally Roe was only arrested once, ten years ago. He got the rap sheet on that, then followed that up with the local police in the town where the arrest occurred."

"Fairwood, Massachusetts . . ."

"Right. They supplied the photographs."

Marshall hesitated. He was bothered about something. "Fairwood, Massachusetts . . . Fairwood . . . I'd better check with Kate about that." He took another look at the photographs. "And we'd better get some copies of these pictures."

Bev piped up, "I'm gonna do that right now; I'm goin' down to use the church's copier."

"Great. Kate's going to need one, I know." He looked over the other documents. "Okay, now what did she do?"

Ben pointed out the crime record. Marshall stopped short. He turned the paper toward him, so he could read it better.

"Isn't that a kicker?" said Ben.

"This thing is getting juicier all the time! Any details?"

Ben pointed out a short police bulletin. "It's bizarre; nothing like I expected."

Marshall read the bulletin as his face filled with horror and disbelief. All he could say was, "Why? This is crazy."

"We've got to find out more, Marshall."

Marshall stared at the photograph again. "I've got a friend in New York, name's Al Lemley. That guy's a real friend, and he can produce. Maybe he can get us something more on this."

Ben had a thought. "You might want to stop in at Judy's Secretarial Service. It's in that little storefront at the four-way stop. She has a fax machine, and you could get the stuff right away."

"Yeah. For sure." Marshall looked at the crime record again and shook his head. "First-degree murder!"

"You're nothing but bloodthirsty killers, as far as I'm concerned," said Mr. Santinelli, warming himself in front of the fire in Mr. Steele's private lodge. He'd put his full and hectic schedule on hold and caught an afternoon flight from Chicago to get here. Now he was tired and cranky, and not at all happy with some of the company he was keeping.

His statement was addressed to the dark and mysterious Mr. Khull, who sat comfortably on the couch, swirling a gin and tonic about in a glass, making the ice cubes tinkle. Mr. Khull was not in the least ruffled by Santinelli's blunt statement.

"We are all that way, Mr. Santinelli—if not in deed, at least in heart. You did, after all, hire me."

Mr. Goring, relaxing in an overstuffed chair before the fire, quipped, "A decision we have all regretted, Mr. Khull."

Santinelli took an indignant puff from his cigar. He didn't like the tone of Goring's comment. "I should like to remind you, as I'm sure Mr. Khull will be happy to boast, that he already had a controlling interest in our organization, thanks to the romantic adventures of the man he eventually eliminated, our boyish upstart, Mr. James Bardine."

"James Bardine . . ." Mr. Khull seemed to have a lapse of memory. Then it came to him. "Oh yes! He died in that tragic automobile accident! I believe he fell asleep at the wheel . . ."

"Everyone believes that," said Santinelli. "My compliments."

"Thank you. We try to be thorough."

Santinelli sat down in a chair opposite Khull, making no effort to hide his disdain. "All you Satanists are thorough, I'm sure. You worship on the run, don't you, always looking over your shoulder?"

Khull leaned forward, his drink in his hands, his head drooped between his shoulders, his eyes piercing. "No. Actually, we have yet to be chased."

Mr. Steele, listening to it all from his own chair directly facing the fire, intervened. "Gentlemen—and Mr. Khull—we know how we feel about each other, so that matter is settled. We don't trust each other, and that's the way we want it."

Santinelli added, "What is also settled is that a liability has been removed—namely, Alicia Von Bauer and James Bardine and their little love nest. Such relationships can be an extreme embarrassment, and from this point forward I hope we've made a clear enough example to our subordinates that any more relationships with these Broken Birch people will not be tolerated."

Khull took a sip from his drink and leaned back into the soft couch. "Especially by those who know as much as Mr. Bardine did."

Santinelli fumed. "As much, I'm sure, as you do now, thanks to the lecherous Ms. Von Bauer!"

Khull laughed. "Such are the politics of power."

Goring responded, "And the reason you are even allowed in our company!"

Mr. Steele was eager to finish their unsavory business. "All right, whether we like it or not, Broken Birch is now part of the Plan. Let's get the ledger balanced, so Mr. Khull can go away satisfied and be about his business."

Santinelli produced a check and handed it to Khull. "There. While in our employ, and admittedly due to our negligence, Ms. Von Bauer was killed. We gave you freedom to kill our own Mr. Bardine, and here are your damages as you have required."

Khull examined the amount on the check and nodded his approval. He folded it and slipped it into his pocket. "That's settled."

"Good," said Mr. Steele. "Now get that ring back."

Mr. Khull sipped from his drink again. "Your credit is good with us, of course, but . . ."

This time Mr. Goring produced a check. "As we discussed,

here is your first half to commence the job. The second half is payable upon recovery of the ring and the elimination of Sally Roe."

Khull took that check and pocketed it. "As you know, this Roe has been very elusive."

"And we are paying you to make her vanish altogether."

Khull swirled his ice cubes. "And, naturally, her blood would be on *our* hands. How convenient for you."

Mr. Steele objected, "Your hands are already bloody."

"And yours aren't?" Khull laughed at them. "Ah, don't worry. I understand. We kill regularly, as a form of worship; it's a sacrament to us. If you kill . . . well, it's only through hirelings like us. It keeps your hands clean. You don't plunge the knife, so you don't feel the pang of conscience." He laughed again. "Maybe you are still too Christian!"

Mr. Santinelli hated this man's taunts. "If I may remind you, Mr. Khull, you are serving your own interests in this as well, perhaps more so than we. If Sally Roe should ever be found alive, if she should ever tell her story, you and your followers could easily be implicated with murder. And unlike human sacrifices that vanish without a trace, this victim is alive, walking, and talking. At least our suicide cover story has bought us all some time. I would say you owe us something for that."

Khull was only mildly impressed. "Yes, we both have something to lose if she remains alive. But how much we have to lose depends on how much we've invested, doesn't it? What is Broken Birch, compared to you and your Plan?"

"Not much," said Mr. Steele, supposedly admitting something, but actually using it as a taunt.

Khull ventured a sneer. "You're no better. Someday you'll realize that. What we are now, you are rapidly becoming. If you hate us so much, perhaps it's because you see yourselves in us!"

Santinelli barked, "I will see *you* to the *door!*"

Alice Buckmeier was a marvelous hostess, of course, and loved to have company. So what Kate had planned as a short interview turned out to be a delightful visit over tea and pastries in the widow's dining room, surrounded by knick-knacks, doilies, crystal, and pictures of sons, daughters, and grandchildren.

"You must be everybody's grandma," Kate said.

Alice laughed. "A title I wear proudly. I don't just have my own grandchildren, you know, but I'm Grandma Alice to all the kids at church, too!"

"That's wonderful."

"I love children, I really do. Sometimes it's hard to understand how people treat their children. I know it breaks the Lord's heart." She warmed up Kate's cup of tea and continued, "I've wondered about that little Amber ever since I saw what I saw at the Post Office. What must she be going through at home?"

Kate got her notebook ready. "Bev Cole says you have quite a story."

"Oh, yes. It was very disturbing. I was mailing a package off to my son—well, actually, to my grandson, Jeff. I knitted a sweater for him, and I was trying to get it there in time for his birthday. Well, I was just standing there at the counter, and that other young lady, Debbie, was weighing my package and stamping it and all that . . ."

Judy Balcom stuck her head into Don's Wayside and called, "Mr. Hogan! Al Lemley's on the phone!"

Marshall got up from the counter, paid for his coffee, and hurried next door.

Judy Balcom ran a tight little secretarial service, typing letters, making and answering calls, making copies, doing word processing, and relaying messages—to name just a few tasks—for many of the local businesses around the town. For a reasonable fee, she let Marshall call Al Lemley in New York, and now Lemley, true to his style, had wasted no time in finding what Marshall needed.

"Hello from New York," came that same East Coast voice.

"Al, are you going to make me happy?"

"No, buddy. I'm going to make you sick. Got the fax ready?"

Judy was ready.

Marshall gave Al the go-ahead.

Alice continued her story. "Now, I didn't even notice who was over in the lobby where all the mailboxes are. I never pay attention to that unless it's someone I know. But all of a sudden I heard this commotion out there like some child was getting rowdy—you know, misbehaving, and I remember thinking, Now where are that child's parents? They shouldn't let her carry on so!

"Well, Debbie was all finished with my package, so I went out into the lobby, and then I could see the whole thing. Here was this woman, just standing there in the middle of the lobby . . . She had some mail in her hand, so I guess she'd come to get her mail . . . And then, here was this little girl, this Amber, just screaming and shouting and . . . and prancing like she was a little horse, and that poor woman was just terrified!"

The fax machine started to hum and roll out some documents. Marshall picked each page up as it dropped into the bin. There were police reports similar to what he already had, and then there were some news articles from the local newspapers. One article carried another photo of Sally Roe, this time in handcuffs, in the custody of two uniformed officers.

"And what that child said!" Alice exclaimed.

"What did she say?" asked Kate.

"She pranced, then she hit the woman, and she screamed, and just kept hitting the woman, and she was saying, 'I know who you are! You killed your baby! You killed your baby!' The poor woman was just terrified; you'd think she was being attacked by a vicious dog or something.

"Well, finally the woman broke free and ran out the door like a scared rabbit. Amber ran after her as far as the door, still shouting at her, 'You killed your baby! I know you! You killed your baby!' Then Mrs. Brandon came out of the back room and grabbed her daughter and tried to pull her back inside, but she wouldn't go with her mother, she wouldn't go at all, and so they had a big tugging match right there in the lobby, right in front of me, and Mrs. Brandon was shouting, 'Stop it, Amber! Stop that right now! No more of this!'"

Kate asked, "Did Mrs. Brandon ever use the name Amethyst?"

A light bulb went on in Alice's head. "Why, yes! I do remember that! She was calling Amber Amber one minute, and Amethyst the next. She was saying, 'Amethyst, Amethyst you stop that now! You stop screaming and calm down!' I didn't understand what she meant; I thought it was just a nickname or something."

Another news article dropped out of the fax machine. Marshall skimmed it. Sally Roe had been arrested after police broke down the door of her motel room in Fairwood. Inside. they found Roe in the bathroom in a seemingly drugged stupor, and her infant daughter, less than two months old, drowned in the bathtub. Roe was subsequently charged with first-degree murder in the drowning death of her child.

Kate could hardly wait to ask her next question. The incident in the Post Office could have been coincidence, but in a small town like this, that was unlikely. She dug in her briefcase and brought out the mug shots of Sally Roe, placing before Alice. "Is this the woman you saw that day?"

Alice's eyes grew wide, and then she gave a slow, awestruck nod. "She looks so awful in this picture . . . but this is her. Sally Roe, huh?"

"That's right."

"Is she a criminal?"

"Yes."

"What did she do?"

"Well . . . she did kill someone."

Marshall walked slowly to his car, got behind the wheel, and then just sat there for a long while, reading through the news articles and police reports Al Lemley had sent. It was fascinating stuff, full of potential leads, but also very, very tragic.

"Tramp," the prosecutors had called her. "Diabolical witch, self-centered, self-seeking, contemptible, child-killer."

The police report said that Sally Roe was soaking wet when she was found on the floor in the bathroom. The tub was overflowing. The child was in the tub, dead. She'd told the police at the time that she'd killed her baby, but when questioned later, claimed she had no recollection of what had happened.

During the trial—and Marshall found this interesting—Sally seemed detached and unremorseful. "It was meant to be," she said. "My higher self ordained this should happen. Rachel's higher self wished to die at this time, and Jonas was there to carry it out. We all determine our own fates, our lot in life, when we are to die, and what destiny we are born into the next time. There is no death; there is only change."

Jonas. A spirit-guide, according to Sally. She admitted drowning the child at first, but later seemed to change her testimony by blaming her spirit-guide. "He took control," she said, "and he did the drowning."

The jury didn't buy it. They found her guilty, and Sally was later sentenced to thirty years in prison.

As for the father of the child, he never came forward and was never found. Sally never identified him. She was simply portrayed as a tramp and her child as illegitimate.

It all happened ten years ago.

twenty-two

Drip. *Drip. Drip.*

The faucet seemed to mark off segments of time, announcing the passing of a moment, and another moment, and another moment, and another moment, like a clock, never stopping, never slowing—steady dripping, moments passing.

Traffic flowed by outside the bathroom window, but Sally didn't hear it. A siren wailed once, but she did not stir or take notice. She had no strength, no will to rise from her place there on the bathroom floor—her back against the pale blue wall, her hands limp upon her lap, her head resting against the hard plaster, but not turning away from the discomfort.

She just sat there, staring vacantly at that tub, listening to the faucet drip, watching each drop build on the tip of the spout and then, stretching with weight, break free and disappear.

Drip. Drip. Drip.

"Ms. Roe, did you think there was no law higher than yourself?"

"There is no higher reality, sir, than what I myself have created."

Drip. Drip. Drip.

"You honestly don't recall picking up your child, holding her under the water, and drowning her?"

"I told you before, I wasn't there; it was Jonas."

"But you admitted drowning your daughter!"

"Jonas performed the act. My higher self willed it, he carried it out . . ."

Drip. Drip. Drip.

"We found the defendant in the bathroom . . . She seemed dazed . . ."

"And what did she say to you?"

"She said, 'Oh no! I've killed my baby.'"

Drip. Drip. Drip.

". . . ladies and gentlemen of the jury, you have heard an

261

account of the unthinkable . . . This vile creature, void of conscience, without remorse . . ."

Void of conscience, without remorse. Void of conscience, without remorse. Void of conscience, without remorse.

A child in an infinite yard with no fence. The creator and arbiter of all reality. The center of her own universe. No right, no wrong. Only self. *I am all that matters.*

At least, that's how it used to be.

Sally shifted just a little. The hard linoleum floor reminded her of where she was: her glorious universe. Yes. A small, cold, echoing bathroom with a dripping bathtub faucet, inhabited by a murderer, a vagabond, a tramp, a failure, an empty jar drained steadily over ten years of pointless, aimless existence, a discarded piece of flesh nobody wanted.

Now she sat on the linoleum, her head against the wall, her elbow resting on the toilet, beside the bathtub where she'd taken the life of her daughter.

Her universe. Her destiny. Her truth.

She had no tears. She was too empty to cry; there was no soul within her. She continued to breathe, but not because she wanted to. It just happened. Life just happened. She just happened, and she didn't know why.

The spirits had found her: Despair, Death, Insanity, and now Suicide. They dug at her, whispered to her, scratched away her soul one layer at a time. *Murderer,* they said. *Worthless, guilty murderer! You can never do good! There's nothing good in you! You can't help anyone! Why don't you give it all up?*

It's lonely in this universe, she thought. *It's supposed to be my creation, but now I'm lost in it. I wish I could know something for sure. I wish I could find a fence at the end of this yard.*

Ah, but it is too late for that now.

Her hand fell from her lap and thumped gently against the side of the tub.

A fence.

No, it wasn't a big thought; it wasn't a stirring idea, and it didn't cause the slightest change in her breathing or pulse. It was just a notion, an inkling of a possibility, a simple proposition to toss around: this tub could be a fence.

She looked at the tub; she touched the cold, blue-green porcelain. *I could pretend,* she thought. *Just for the sake of discussion, I could pretend that this is a fence, a limitation, a boundary.*

A boundary I crossed over, and shouldn't have.

She let her thoughts continue on their own and just enjoyed listening to them huddle together and confer in her head.

What if what happened here was wrong?

Ah, come on, according to whom? There are no absolutes; you can't know anything for sure.

What if there are, and what if I can?

But how?

Later, later. Just answer the first question.

What if it was wrong?

Yeah.

Then I'm guilty. I made a wrong choice, I jumped the boundary, I did wrong.

But I thought boundaries exist only in your mind!

I did wrong. I want to think that, just once.

Why?

Because I need a fence. Even if I'm on the wrong side of it, I need a fence. I need to be wrong. I need to be guilty.

What for?

Because . . .

Sally stirred. She pressed her hand firmly against the side of the tub where her child had died. She mouthed the words, then she whispered them, then she said them out loud, "Because at least then I'd know where I am!"

Apparently she'd awakened a dormant emotion; pain came upon her suddenly, an aching deep in her soul, and with gritted teeth and a stifled whimper, she pounded the side of the tub. *"Oh, God!"*

She rested against the hard plaster wall again, panting in hurt, anger, and despair. "O God, help me!"

Despair slipped and fell. His talons had lost their grip.

There. She'd said it. She'd followed the proposition through to its conclusion, had her little fit, and now she was finished. She didn't know if she felt better. She felt a little foolish for talking out loud to herself—or to God, whatever the case may be. It didn't matter.

For some reason she felt a weight around her neck, against her chest. Her hand went to the ring hanging there. She pulled it out and looked at it again. The ugly little gargoyle bared its teeth at her.

And then a memory hit her. It hit her so hard and so suddenly that she was amazed it had stayed hidden so long.

"The ring! *Owen's* ring!"

Irene Bledsoe was visibly uncomfortable. "Mr. Harris, your friends will have to remain here."

Under the circumstances, Tom never felt better. He was sitting on the same hard wooden bench in the same cold, echoing, marble hallway in the courthouse in Claytonville; he was here for another prearranged visit with his children, and once again Irene Bledsoe was in charge.

But this time he was flanked by . . .

"Mrs. Bledsoe, this is my pastor, Mark Howard, and my attorney, Wayne Corrigan."

Both men offered their hands, and she shook them out of necessity, but she was not entirely cordial. "Hello. As I said, Mr. Harris will only be allowed to see his children alone."

Corrigan was in great form. "We are here upon Mr. Harris's invitation, and we will accompany him during his visitation. If you refuse to allow it, you'll be required to appear in court to show just cause." Then he smiled.

Bledsoe was indignant and actually had to search for her words. "You . . . This is . . . this is a private meeting! Mr. Harris must see his children alone!"

"Then I'm sure you'll be happy to remain here with us while he does so?"

"That's not what I meant and you know it! The visitation is to be between Mr. Harris and his children with a social worker in attendance."

"Meaning yourself?"

"Of course!"

Corrigan got out his notepad. "By whose order?"

She stalled. "I'd . . . I'd have to look it up."

"If it's all the same to you," said Tom, "I'd like to see my kids. They're waiting for me, aren't they?"

"One moment," she said with a raise of her hand. "Have you brought the questionnaires I sent you?"

Corrigan had something to say about that as well. "In light of the pending civil suit, I've advised my client to defer filling out any psychological surveys or other tests for the time being."

Her answer was cold and threatening. "You do realize, of course, that this will delay our releasing the children back to Mr. Harris's custody?"

"According to CPD records, you've never released any children back to their parents without first having a trial anyway, so at the moment we're resigned to that. Now, if we could proceed with the visitation?"

She gave in. "All right. Won't you follow me?"

She started walking toward the big marble staircase again, the *pock, pock, pock* of her heels echoing through the hall as an announcement of her authority, and perhaps an expression of her indignity as well. They reached the second floor, went through the big, uninviting door and into the antechamber where John the guard was stationed once again. He seemed a little surprised to see three men instead of just one, but since they came in with Bledsoe, he figured it must be okay.

"Hi, kids!"

With cries of delight, Ruth and Josiah ran to their father. Tom dropped to one knee to embrace them, and for some reason Irene Bledsoe did not come between them. Josiah was really tickled to see his dad again; Ruth just started crying and wouldn't let go of him. All the hugs went on for quite some time.

"Poor, abused kids," Corrigan whispered to Mark.

Bledsoe took her seat at the end of the table and offered chairs to Mark and Corrigan. They sat down quietly on Tom's side of the table.

"Okay, kids," Tom said finally. "Go ahead and sit down."

They went to their chairs on the other side of the table, and just then noticed Mark. "Hi, Pastor Howard."

"Hi. How are you?"

"Okay."

"We have forty minutes," Bledsoe said, mostly to remind everyone that she was still in charge.

For the next thirty minutes Tom visited with his kids, getting caught up on mostly trivial matters. The kids were trying to read more, and seemed to be getting along better with the other kids in the foster home, although Tom couldn't be sure if it was the same foster home as last time. They weren't doing any schoolwork, though, which meant they would have some catching up to do during the summer, if that happened at all. Ruth's bump had healed well and was barely visible.

But as the time grew shorter, there was one thing Tom knew he must do before leaving, while he still had the chance. Above all else, he knew he must pray with his kids.

"Hey, Daddy has to go pretty soon, so let's pray together."

He reached across the table and took their hands. They were a family again, just for that moment, and he was the spiritual head, the leader and example he was meant to be.

"Dear Lord, I just pray now for my children, and I ask You to place a hedge of protection around them. Protect their hearts and their minds, and may they never doubt that You love them and that they are in Your hands. Help them to always be good kids and live the way You want them to. I pray, dear Father, that we will all be together again."

Mark and Corrigan joined in the prayer, and listened as little Ruth prayed for her daddy and her brother, and even for Mrs. Bledsoe. Then Josiah prayed, declaring his love for Jesus and his desire to be a good child of God.

None of this was an accident. They were doing battle in this room, for even though the state might erect insurmountable walls of red tape around these children, the prayer of each child, offered in simple faith, would be enough to tear the walls down. This was where the victory would begin. They all knew it, and as the kids prayed, they could feel it.

"Amen," said Josiah.

"Amen," they all said—all except for Irene Bledsoe.

It was almost time to go. Tom opened a paper sack. "Here. I meant to give these to you last time."

"Hey, all right!" said Josiah, receiving his Bible.

"Thank you, Daddy!" said Ruth, hugging hers to her chest.

Tom also brought them some of their favorite books and the stationery they didn't receive the last time. He could see Irene Bledsoe eyeing everything he brought out of the sack, but he proceeded slowly and openly, having nothing to hide.

Well, almost nothing. Josiah was thumbing through his new book about whales when he found some photos inserted between the pages.

Tom, Mark, and Corrigan tried not to look at him too directly, lest they draw Bledsoe's attention.

"Like your book, Ruth?" Tom said, reaching across the table to help her find his little note to her on the title page. That physical gesture helped; Bledsoe watched him closely. "See what I wrote? It says, 'To my darling daughter Ruth. Jesus thinks you're precious, and so do I!'"

"Hey!" said Josiah. He was looking at the photos. "The lady in the pickup truck!"

That got Bledsoe's attention immediately. She saw Josiah holding the pictures, studying them with wide-eyed recognition. Her face went visibly pale.

Corrigan asked, "What do you mean, son? Have you seen that woman before?"

Bledsoe jumped to her feet. "Mr. Harris!"

Tom responded calmly. "Hm?"

"How dare you! How *dare* you!"

Corrigan pressed Josiah for an answer. "Do you recognize her?"

"Sure," said Josiah. "She's the lady that was driving that truck we almost hit. She always looks kind of sick, doesn't she?"

Bledsoe stomped around to where Josiah sat and grabbed the pictures from him. She took only a moment to look at them in outrage, and then defiantly she tore them in half, in quarters, in eighths, and then crumpled them up and pitched them into a wastebasket.

Then she stood there, shaking, glaring at Tom. "Just what are you trying to prove here?"

Mark spoke gently. "Mrs. Bledsoe, you're upsetting the children."

She pointed her finger in Tom's face, and her voice trembled with rage. "You have committed a serious offense! I can make things very hard for you! Don't think I can't have your children taken away permanently!"

Tom replied calmly—mostly for the children's benefit, "Then what are you so afraid of?"

She fought back. "Oh, I am not afraid, Mr. Harris. You don't scare me!"

Tom gave her a statement he'd rehearsed in his mind for quite some time. "Mrs. Bledsoe, it's been quite clear to me that you are not as concerned with the interests of my children as with your own interests. In any case, I think you're abusing your power—and my children, and me—and I intend to find out just whom you're trying to protect."

She tried to keep her voice down; after all, shouting was unprofessional. "Why, you—!" With great effort, she relaxed, assumed a professional demeanor, and announced, "This visitation is over. I think your betrayal of my trust was deplorable, and I will keep it in mind when I consider the date for our next meeting."

"It'll be sooner than you think," said Corrigan. He walked around the table, took her hand, and slapped a subpoena into it. "Try not to tear this up. Good day."

Dear Tom,

I feel different today, and I don't know if I can explain it. Undoubtedly it stems from my fanciful proposition of the morning, the possibility of my guilt. Being guilty, or even feeling guilty, is not pleasant, of course, but the mere suggestion of it seems to have weakened another nagging emotional companion of mine: despair. It makes me think of a clown hitting his thumb with a hammer to get his mind off his head-ache: now that I feel guilty, I don't feel as much despair.

But—and this is purely for the sake of discussion—it could be said that the reasons go deeper than that. As I've said before, an all-out plunge into humanism and its total lack of absolutes can leave you groping for fences, wondering where you are, wishing you could know something for sure. Now that's despair.

Then suddenly, guilt—well, the possibility of guilt—has come upon the scene, and I find myself playing with the thought that I might be standing in the wrong, which means I could have violated a standard somewhere, which means there might be a standard to be violated, which means there might be something out there somewhere that I can know for sure.

So, I guess I said all that to say this: If I really can be guilty, if I really am guilty, then at least I know where I stand. Suddenly, after all this time, I've found a fence, a boundary, and just the thought of that dispels that old cloud of despair, so much that I've noticed it.

Just consider, Tom, what great lengths I've gone to all through my life to quell despair. The Young Potentials program at the Omega Center presented a possible escape; I dove into everything they offered: yoga, TM, diet, folk medicine, altered states, drugs, and a lot of mental trips about my own divinity and ability to create my own reality. It was a long excursion into insanity, I admit it. What good did it do to make up my own truth? I was lost and drifting to begin with, and any reality born in my head could be no better off. I and the universe I created were lost and drifting together.

And then there was Jonas, my "consummate friend." He was a marvelous salesman with a lot of good lines, remark-ably skilled in flattery. We took many long walks together during my yogic trances, and he did have me convinced that all reality—including death—was an illusion to be manipu-lated, and that I, being God, could form reality to be what-ever I wanted it to be.

And for a crucial season, I believed that. I believed I had formed a reality to serve me and supply what I wanted. I believed I had formed a man who gave me pleasure without guilt. I believed I had formed a child that asked me to send her on to her next life, leaving me free to continue where I left off.

But did I form the prison bars too? I was talking about fences, wasn't I?

I lived behind that fence for seven years, and Jonas never came to visit me. I did resent that. I did blame him for Rachel's death. It was, in my thinking, his idea. He was the one who took control of my body and snuffed out her life. He committed the act. He was to blame.

But I don't think that now. I changed my mind at some point; maybe it was this morning.

"Amethyst" was right; I killed my baby.

Sally put away her notebook and went out, her mind full of thoughts, turning things over, sorting things out. She felt a change coming, though she had no idea what it could be or which direction it would go. But this walk of hers right now was going to be part of it; she was going to track down a memory and find another missing piece to the puzzle of her life.

As near as she could remember, it was an old red brick building not far from the motel, and there was an alley, an old, cobblestoned alley with a stream of water running down its center and a grate over a drain. Oh, where was that?

Tal followed right behind her. Nathan and Armoth hovered just above, swords drawn, eyes looking warily about. Destroyer was getting close. Time was short.

Keep going, Sally, said Tal. *You're getting warmer.*

She turned down a side street. This sidewalk looked familiar; these potted elms seemed to match the memory, though they were much bigger now.

A noisy garbage truck roared and rumbled out of an alley behind an old brewery, nosed its way into traffic, and then growled through its gears, heading down the street.

Sally headed for the alley.

This had to be it! The same, narrow, cobblestoned alley, the same, towering, red brick walls of the old brewery! She was walking into the past. The drain was still there, the moss on the brick walls was still the same, the smell of garbage was right out of her memory. She quickened her pace. It was somewhere along here, a loose brick in a windowsill . . . She was remembering more and more as she ran along, looking carefully at each window, hoping for any detail that would trigger a memory.

Tal could see the angelic sentries ahead, guarding the spot. There were four of them, bold and brilliant, all grim with dedication, their swords ready. They'd been at this post, watching it, preserving it for ten years. At the sight of Sally Roe approaching, they raised their swords and let out a cautious, muffled cheer.

She approached the rear corner of the building. It had to be here somewhere; she seemed to remember it being near the corner.

There was one last window, and the brick sill was at eye-level. She stopped and looked around. She was alone in the alley. She touched the sill, ran her fingers along it. It had to be the same one. Was that loose brick on the right side or the left? She put her thumb under the brick on the left end and gently pressed upward.

It budged. For the first time in ten years, it budged. The light of day flooded the cavity underneath it.

Sally's heart leaped. She could see a faint glint of gold. She lifted the brick further.

There lay the ring. It was like a miracle. Sally's emotions rose to such a pitch that a faint cry escaped from her. She reached into the niche and grabbed the ring between her thumb and forefinger. She pulled it out into the light, and let the brick sink back into place.

Ten years later, the ring was still remarkably clean except for some gray spiderwebs. She rubbed it against her shirttail, and the shine returned. She pulled the first ring out of her shirt and held the two together.

Yes, they were the same. Now there were two little gargoyles, snarling at her with identical expressions.

Tal dismissed the sentries.

Sally leaned against the brick wall and thought about the day when she planted the ring in this hiding-place. She was desperate, afraid she would be betrayed. Perhaps it was a stealthy, conniving act to steal that man's ring and hide it here, but as it turned out, she *was* betrayed, and now, ten years later, this ring could be a key to reopen the past, to view it all again, to find out what went wrong.

She thought of Tom Harris and those Christians at that little school in Bacon's Corner.

Have I done wrong? If so, then let me do something right, *just this once.*

She unclasped the chain around her neck and placed the second ring beside the first.

Back at the Schrader Motor Inn, the office door swung open; the electric eye beeped that someone had come in.

The lady behind the counter looked up. "Hello. May I help you?"

Mr. Khull smiled most pleasantly. "Good morning. I'm looking for my wife. She said she'd rented a room here . . . uh, number 302?"

"Oh!" She pulled out the registration. "Are you Mr. Rogers?"

Khull broke into a wide grin. "Yes, yes! All right, I finally found her!"

She was curious. "Well, how did you know where to look?"

"Oh, we've rented the room before. We love it. We stay here every time we come through. I was detained at home for a few days, but she called me and said she'd found the same room. I was hoping it was the one I was thinking of."

"Well . . ." She found a problem. "Uh, she only rented it to herself. I guess she misunderstood."

Khull got out his wallet. "Yeah, that's a mistake. Let me make up the balance. Is she up there right now? I think I might surprise her."

"Well, no, I think she went out. But I can give you a key."

"Great."

"Why don't you fill out another form here so I can get my records straight?"

"Sure."

He filled out another form and gave their names: Mr. and Mrs. Jack Rogers. He had a good size wad of bills as well, and paid her the balance still owed.

She looked at the address he gave. "So how are things in Las Vegas? Is it as wild as they say?"

"No . . ." He laughed. "Well, in certain places it is, I suppose. But it's not a bad place to live."

"Well, here's your key . . . Oh dear. I guess she has the only duplicate. Well, come on, I'll just go up and let you in."

"Thanks. Hey, don't tell her I'm here. She isn't expecting me until tomorrow!"

Across the street, crouching atop the hardware store, and across the motel parking lot, hiding on the roof of Nelson Printing and Bookbinding, squads of filthy warriors puffed a cloud of sulfur when they saw Khull follow the lady up to Room 302.

Destroyer watched from his vantage point above the flower shop. "They guessed right," he hissed. "She's here!"

twenty-three

"**praise** God," said Tom, so excited he couldn't sit still. "I can't believe it! Progress!"

"Well, a hundred different pieces maybe," said Marshall. "But give it time—it'll fall together."

Tom, Marshall, Kate, and Ben were having another powwow with Wayne Corrigan in his office, not too long after that rather explosive meeting with Irene Bledsoe.

Ben had gotten over his excitement. Now he was pensive, probing. "She's alive. Sally Roe is alive, and Mulligan knows it."

"And Parnell too," said Marshall. "I've got him on my list."

"But what are they trying to pull, and why?" asked Kate.

"That's what I'm still waiting to hear," said Corrigan. "I love all this stuff, guys—I'm really enjoying it, but sooner or later—and let's hope sooner—it's got to add up to something. We need a case we can present in court, and so far I don't see anything that directly applies to the lawsuit."

"Right," said Marshall, looking through some notes. "So far it's all indirect, peripheral stuff. But we're getting closer. Here are the names of the people I got from that Motor Vehicle Report on the license plates. The following people are possibly involved in this LifeCircle outfit, and some of them fit right into this: Mr. Bruce Woodard, the elementary school principal, and, no surprise, our plucky Miss Brewer."

Kate inserted, "And as for Mr. Bruce Woodard, I talked to him on the phone again today, and he still assures me he'll find that curriculum so I can look at it. But if you ask me, he's stalling."

"If he is, try these names: Jerry Mason, Betty Hanover, and John Kendall, three members of the Bacon's Corner school board, all three most likely connected with LifeCircle."

"Hence the *Finding the Real Me* curriculum at the elementary school," said Tom. "It fits right into their worldview."

"And their agenda," said Marshall. "These people are just

as evangelistic about their religion as we are, and they're wasting no time." He raised an eyebrow at the next set of names. "Jon Schmidt and Claire Johanson. Schmidt doesn't impress me yet, but Johanson is big stuff, a direct connection with the ACFA. Oh, and who was that other guy? Oh yeah. Gordon Jefferson was there too, so now we have a link-up with the ACFA for sure, not to mention . . ." He scanned down the page. "Lenore Hofspring, from California. Check the ACFA California roster, Kate. I'll bet she's on it. They're bringing in some bigger guns from out of state."

"It isn't fair!" said Tom.

"Have faith. We've caught so many fish today our nets are breaking. Here's another fish right here . . . Surprise, surprise. Lucy Brandon. What a recipe. Take a mother involved in this cosmic mystic group, add the cosmic mystic group controlling the school board and pumping cosmic mystic curricula into the local school, then get a well-meaning, crusading teacher fresh out of . . . what was that teacher's college?"

Kate answered, "Bentmore."

"Right, one of America's finest, they say. Miss Brewer learned everything she knows from them, and now she's cramming it into the kids. These people have the whole system sewn up from the top down.

"Anyway, throw it all into the pot, stir it all up, and what do you get? A little girl channeling a spirit just like all the moms and pops and uncles and aunts out there at the big white house.

"We're talking about a lot of moles, a lot of demons connecting this whole thing: Lucy Brandon, LifeCircle, the school board, the school, the ACFA, and even the little girl."

Ben was puzzled. "But . . . are you saying they purposely enrolled Amber in our school just to force a confrontation?"

Marshall laid the notes on the desk and thought about that. "No. Maybe Lucy Brandon really wanted something better for her kid. Maybe the trouble that popped up was something the others—LifeCircle, the ACFA—saw as an opportunity. What do you think, Tom?"

Tom was intrigued with the notion. "When she first

enrolled Amber, she seemed concerned about the changes Amber had gone through since being in Miss Brewer's class. At the time, I honestly thought that Lucy Brandon wanted a more basic, 'traditional' education for her daughter."

"That's the feeling I get," said Marshall. "It'll be interesting to talk to her and find out what she's really thinking, and if she's doing her own thinking at all."

Kate reported, "Alice Buckmeier told me about Debbie, the girl who works with Lucy at the Post Office. Debbie was there that day and saw the confrontation between Amber and Sally Roe. She might be able to tell us something more about Lucy."

"Sounds good. And now . . ." Marshall spread some sheets of paper out on Corrigan's desk as the attorney watched. "Here's the best part, I think. It could make this case bigger than just Bacon's Corner . . . and it could blow it wide open. We don't know yet."

The others gathered around.

"That address bothered me, the location of the Omega Center that published that curriculum. That was in Fairwood, Massachusetts, right?"

Kate had that information. "Right. I got the address from Miss Brewer."

"Ben, where did you get that arrest record, the one that included the mug shots of Sally Roe?"

Ben was stunned as he doublechecked the document. "Fairwood, Massachusetts!"

"So . . . a lady gets arrested for murder clear across the country, but then shows up in this little place for no apparent reason. In the meantime, a curriculum is published in the same town where she was arrested and finds its way here . . . Maybe it's just a coincidence, except for some more molehills: a little girl who ends up demonized, most likely because of that curriculum, later confronts Roe in the Post Office, and the little mole sticks its head up out of the ground and says, 'I know you, you killed your baby!'" Marshall smiled and shook his head at his own conclusion. "That demon was in Fairwood; it knew about Sally Roe."

"And then . . ." said Ben; he was figuring it out.

Marshall verified his thought. "And then somebody comes along and tries to kill Sally Roe . . ."

"The very same day my kids were taken!" said Tom.

"*And* the very day before you got your summons."

"I love it," said Corrigan. "But what does it really mean?"

Marshall looked over all the notes one more time and answered, "I don't know. We have molehills all over the place, and demons tunneling everywhere, maybe even across the country, but . . ." He sighed. "No case. We can theorize that Sally Roe's so-called suicide has something to do with the lawsuit against the school, but . . . what? And so what? There just isn't any visible connection—yet."

Ben turned away, frustrated. "We've got to find out who that woman was, the one we found dead in the goat shed!"

"Parnell's the one to talk to."

"Well, he wouldn't talk to me! He and Mulligan are in this together, that's obvious, and they're looking out for each other."

"And I'll guess somebody higher up is watching them closely, if you get my drift."

Corrigan piped right up. "I don't get your drift."

"Humor an old reporter," said Marshall. "I'm guessing they both belong to some kind of secret group, maybe a lodge, maybe something occult, who knows, something like LifeCircle, something tied closely to it, maybe even a part of it, but not nearly as nice. Hidden. Powerful. Something has a really short leash on those two."

"But you're guessing," said Corrigan.

"Keep on guessing," said Tom. "You're a good guesser."

Marshall ran his fingers through his hair. "I'm in your camp, Wayne; a guess is only good if it pays off. We'll just have to find some levers to pull, some way to squeeze these people. Oh, Kate, speaking of levers, forget waiting for Woodard to get you the curriculum. Go to the school board, those three people . . ." He checked his list again. "Uh . . . Jerry Mason, Betty Hanover, and John Kendall. Just see what they say, but don't wait for them either. If they stall, write to Omega for it. I want to see that curriculum."

Corrigan rested his chin on his knuckles and stared at all the notes. "Man, where is Sally Roe?"

Marshall said grimly, "I imagine somebody else is wondering that too."

A rustling went through the demonic ranks surrounding the motel; black wings began to quiver, and red glowing blades appeared.

Sally Roe was returning to the motel, walking briskly up the street, alone and unprotected.

"Remain in place," said Destroyer. "Don't move."

Immediately there was a hissing and an agitation among the ranks. The officers on either side of Destroyer got fidgety.

"She is ours!" said one.

"Alone!" said another.

"Remain in place," said Destroyer.

Sally felt no anxiety, no fear. If she felt anything, it was a new kind of exhilaration. She still couldn't believe the incredible recovery of that second ring. She considered herself extremely lucky, or fortunate . . . She wasn't ready to say "blessed."

She rounded the corner, passed under the breezeway, and started up the stairs to Room 302.

"We should saturate the building!" said the monster at Destroyer's right. "Khull and his men need our power!"

"You must reinforce the demons of Broken Birch!" said the beast at Destroyer's left.

Destroyer watched, still silent, as his warriors fussed and hissed all around him, itching to get in on the kill.

Sally reached the first landing and was starting up the second flight of stairs.

Khull was in the room, waiting. One of his men, dressed as a repairman, remained near the soft drink machine at the other stairway, ready to block any escape that way. Another man, looking like a casual vacationer, took his post at the bottom of the stairs Sally had just taken.

A third man, dressed in dark clothes and smoking a cigarette, started up the stairs after her, quietly, surreptitiously.

Sally was just on the second flight of stairs when she didn't feel right about something.

Tal was beside her. *Stop*, he said. *Wait.*

She stopped. She'd seen that one man standing near the office door when she came around the corner, and now she was sure he was coming up the flight of stairs below her. When she stopped, he hesitated. Now it was ominously quiet.

Tal remained beside her; Nathan stood at the top of the stairs, Armoth at the bottom. They were making themselves clearly visible.

Tal drew his sword slowly and let its light flicker against the wall of the building for all to see. Nathan and Armoth did the same. Now they could see the demonic response: from rooftops all around the motel, the sky lit up with the red glow of enemy swords, and the air was filled with the clatter and rustling of black wings.

There was a standoff.

A taloned hand grabbed Destroyer's arm.

"Will you not attack? There are only three guarding her!" said the warrior. The demons all around squawked their eager agreement.

"Only three?" Destroyer replied. "You mean you *see* only three." He pointed his crooked finger at the warrior that had grabbed him, then at another whiner, and then at one more overly anxious fighter. "Very well. You, you, and you, attack! Do your worst!"

They shrieked, raised their swords, and shot from the roof like skyrockets, swooping down toward the motel. They would give Broken Birch all the power they needed, and Sally Roe was as good as dead!

Tal shot from the stairway in a brilliant explosion of wings, and met the three attackers over the parking lot. Two were instantly shredded; the third went careening and fluttering over the print shop, trailing red smoke from what was left of him. Back on the stairs, Nathan and Armoth closed in on Sally Roe, their wings outspread, their swords ready.

KAWOOOM! Bursting instantly out of hiding, at least a dozen warriors appeared all around the motel, their wings spreading to form an impenetrable wall.

"Oh, Mrs. Bissell!"

It was the office lady. Sally was relieved to hear her voice. "Yes, I'm up here!"

"Could I see you for a minute?"

The man on the flight below dropped his cigarette and crushed it out with his toe. Then he hurried back down and ran across the parking lot. Sally went to the balcony railing and saw him ducking around the corner.

"Hmm," said Destroyer. "How many more warriors do you suppose he has hidden in there?"

No demon would venture a guess.

"Maybe none at all . . . maybe thousands! Would anyone like to find out?"

The lady in the office brought Sally's travel bag out from behind the counter.

"I hope you won't think me too forward for doing this," she said, "but before you go up to your room, you'd better know that there's a man up there waiting for you. He said he was your husband."

Sally was horrified. "What?"

"Is he?"

Sally backed toward the door. "I don't have a husband."

"Don't go out there, not yet."

Sally stopped.

"What about that other man, the one following you up the stairs?"

Sally was amazed. She looked out the windows. "He's . . . I saw him running away." Then she backed away from the window, afraid of being seen.

"I don't know who you are, or who he is, but I ran a check and there's no such thing as a '79 Mustang with the license number you gave, and no such thing as a Buick Regal with the license number he gave. Maybe two people can be married and have different last names, but when you say you're from Hawthorne, California, and he says you're both from Las Vegas, I just don't like the looks of it."

Sally didn't know what to say. "I'm sorry."

"I got your bag out of the room when I let him in; I told him the previous tenant left it there. Is there some kind of trouble? I don't want anything weird going on in my motel."

Sally took the bag. "Thank you."

"Should I call the police?"

"Uh, no. No, I'll just leave. Keep the rent money—it's okay."

"What about 'Mr. Rogers' upstairs?"

Sally was backing toward the door. She looked out the window to make sure he wasn't lurking about. "Uh . . . yes, call the police."

Destroyer and his army could see Sally slip quickly out the front door and run down the street, completely surrounded by the angelic guards.

A demon hissed and pointed. There went Khull, sneaking out of Room 302, hurrying down the back stairs with the "repairman." The casual vacationer had also disappeared. Somehow they knew the jig was up. Perhaps it was that timely interruption by the lady in the office; maybe they'd felt Sally Roe's great "psychic power" in the place. Perhaps they could feel their demonic escorts being stalled by the angelic guard. Whatever the case, things did not feel right, and they were calling it quits.

Destroyer blew a stream of sulfur from his nostrils. "Remember," he said to his warriors, "this Tal is a layer of traps, a setter of snares. No little human as dangerous to us as Sally Roe is going to walk down the street uncovered and alone. He was there. His warriors were ready." He laughed. "But that will change."

He looked down the street in time to see Sally Roe disappear around a corner, still heavily guarded. "No, Captain of the Host! Not this time. You are still too strong, but time is on my side! I have your saints in *my* hands. This game will be *ours. We* will set the rules, *we* will pick the time."

Judy Waring wasn't spending as much time home schooling her son Charlie as she promised herself and everyone else she would. At the moment, her plucky little third-grader was doing whatever he wanted out in the yard while she tended to some pressing matters on the telephone.

"Well, that's what I heard," she said. "He's had sexual problems ever since Cindy passed away, and I think they were even having trouble in their marriage because of it. Did you ever notice the way he'd always stand so close to Cathy Howard? Maybe she was next on his list, I don't know."

Then the other party talked for a while, and Judy kept busy snipping coupons out of the shopping news.

Judy's turn came again. "Well, that's what I think too. I mean, how can we be sure what really went on in that classroom? Mrs. Fields is busy enough with all the kids in her class; she can't possibly be watching Tom all the time."

Gossip sat on her shoulders, dangling his skinny fingers in her brain while Strife sat on the table and watched.

"A marvelous idea!" said Strife.

"You know," said Gossip, "this woman will believe anything!"

twenty-four

"He was harsh, belligerent, and frightened the children on many occasions," said Irene Bledsoe, her face defiant, her spine straight as a rod.

She was flanked by the two ACFA attorneys, Jefferson and Ames, sitting in a conference room adjacent to Wayne Corrigan's office. Across the conference table from her sat Wayne Corrigan, Tom Harris, and Mark Howard. At the end of the table was the court reporter, taking down everything spoken.

Wayne Corrigan scanned his notes. This lady was a tiger for sure, and he was wishing he had more to go on. With the little information he had so far, it was going to be a short deposition.

"But this is based solely on the word of Amber Brandon, is it not?" he finally asked.

"Yes, and she is a bright, truthful, and responsible little girl."

"But you yourself never saw Mr. Harris displaying any of this behavior?"

"I certainly did: the first time he came to visit his children. He violated the rules we had agreed upon, he was rude, and he was belligerent."

"Belligerent. You've used that word twice. Now, is that your word or Amber's?"

Jefferson spoke up. "What kind of a question is that?"

Corrigan didn't have to tell him, but he did. "I'm trying to figure out what Amber Brandon said and get around any embellishments from Miss Bledsoe." He went to the next question. "So what about Amber's testimony to you? What specifically did she say Mr. Harris did?"

Bledsoe leaned forward just a little, but kept her spine straight. "Amber told me that Mr. Harris and the other children made fun of her, harassed her, and tried to impose their religious views on her."

"Could you be more specific? How did they make fun of her?"

Bledsoe hesitated. "Well, they . . ."

"Did they call her names?"

"I suppose so."

"Well, did they or didn't they?"

"Amber wouldn't cite any specific names, but I'm sure if we asked her, she could tell us exactly."

"All right, we'll do that." Corrigan moved on. "Now what about harassment? How did Mr. Harris harass Amber?"

Bledsoe laughed at that question. "Oh, how indeed! I suppose you consider it normal to be branded as demon-possessed, to be forbidden to play with the other children . . ."

"Mr. Harris forbade Amber to play with the other children?"

"Oh yes. She was forced to stay inside at recess and write a page from the Bible."

Corrigan made a note of it. "And did Amber say just what the reason was for that?"

Bledsoe shrugged just a little. "Oh, apparently Mr. Harris wasn't happy with her views in a particular matter, and so he decided she needed some more intense indoctrination."

"Are those the words Amber used?"

"No . . ."

"That's just your interpretation?"

"Well, yes."

"What exactly did Amber say?"

"She said that Mr. Harris wouldn't let her go out for recess, but made her stay inside and copy from the Bible."

"Did she suggest that she was being punished for an infraction of the school rules?"

"I didn't gather that from what she said."

"Did it happen once, for one recess, or was it a constant, daily practice?"

"I'm not sure."

"And again, you were not a direct witness to any of this?"

"No, of course not."

"Was anyone?"

"Well, Mr. Harris, but . . ."

"Mm-hm." Corrigan flipped to another page of notes. "Let's talk about Amethyst the pony. Is that the correct name of this . . . uh . . . alter ego?"

"I don't know. She does identify herself as Amethyst, and I understand she is a pony, a mythical character."

"So you've met Amethyst yourself?"

Ames jumped in on that one. "Excuse me, Mr. Corrigan—I don't think that question is very clear."

Corrigan asked Bledsoe, "Is the question clear to you?"

"No."

"Have you ever dealt with Amber when she was acting like Amethyst?"

She shrugged, unruffled. "Of course."

"And nothing about it seemed strange to you?"

"No, of course not. Children have been known to dissociate into alternate personalities, or make up imaginary friends in dealing with severe trauma. It's very common."

"And what severe trauma are we talking about?"

Miss Bledsoe tried to compose a clear answer. "There was severe trauma all through Amber's experience at the Christian school: harassment, discrimination, stress, imposing of Christian dogma . . . It all led to Amber resorting to a false personality to cope with it. Mr. Harris could have responded properly and dealt with the real source of Amber's trouble, but instead he compounded the trauma by branding Amber as demon-possessed, which I think is just horrendous."

"But you were not a direct witness to any of this?"

"No."

"This is all according to what you learned from Amber?"

"Yes."

Corrigan jotted some notes and went to a fresh page. "Let's talk about the Harris kids. What first brought the situation in the Harris home to your attention?"

She hesitated. "I believe . . . we received a complaint."

"You mean a hotline complaint?"

"Yes."

"So you don't know from whom?"

"No."

"It was not from the attorneys for Mrs. Brandon?"

Jefferson was right on top of that. "Objection!"

Corrigan pointed his finger at Jefferson. "This isn't a court-room, and you aren't the judge, Mr. Jefferson!"

"I resent the question!"

"Do *you* want to answer it?"

"Don't be impertinent!"

Corrigan turned back to Miss Bledsoe. "Miss Bledsoe, to the best of your knowledge, did you receive the complaint from anyone connected with this lawsuit?"

"Absolutely not!" she said with great indignity.

"Not from any of the attorneys for Mrs. Brandon?"

"No!"

"How about Mrs. Brandon herself?"

"No!"

"All right. Now, I'm sure you've had abundant opportunity to talk to Ruth and Josiah?"

"Oh yes."

"Have they reported any abuse of any kind from their father?"

"Yes, they have."

Tom looked up at that remark.

Corrigan pressed it. "Okay. What abuse?"

"Frequent spankings with a wooden spoon."

"I take it you had reason to believe that these spankings were not administered in a loving and controlled manner?"

"They were administered, Mr. Corrigan, and that to me is abuse."

"All right. Any other abuse toward the children?"

"He doesn't let them watch television."

Corrigan remained deadpan, and scribbled that down. "Were you aware that Mr. Harris doesn't even own a televi-sion set?"

"Yes. His children told me."

"Were they complaining about it?"

"I think they were. I took it that way. They're captivated by the simplest programs as if they've never seen anything like it before. They know so little about what's going on in our culture. Their lives are far too sheltered for their proper social development."

"And that is your professional opinion?"

"Yes, of course."

"And what about direct evidence of any physical abuse? Did anyone see any bruises on the children, any signs that something was amiss?"

"Well, of course! Ruth had a large bump on her head!"

It was all Tom could do to remain quiet.

Corrigan asked, "I take it the anonymous hotline caller reported that bump?"

"Of course."

"Did Ruth ever say where she got that bump?"

Miss Bledsoe assumed an even stiffer posture and answered, "We're still investigating, and until that investigation is complete, the matter is strictly confidential."

"I would think the bump is a matter of public record," said Corrigan. "You realize, of course, that the children have told their father, in your presence, where that bump came from."

"But remember, Mr. Corrigan, that it was their father they were talking to. Out of fear, a child can tell a tale to avoid further abuse."

Corrigan indulged in a quick sigh of frustration. "Ms. Bledsoe, why do I get the impression that you don't really have a concrete reason for holding the children in custody in a strange home and environment, away from their own home and father?"

Miss Bledsoe made a visible effort to keep her cool. "We have suspicions, Mr. Corrigan, and suspicions are enough reason. We are still working with the children. We have ways of drawing out the truth eventually. The children do want to tell us everything, but are often afraid."

"So you do believe that Ruth and Josiah mean to be truthful?"

"Yes."

"And yet you won't accept Ruth and Josiah's account of your near-collision with a blue pickup truck, and their claim that it was in that near-mishap that Ruth sustained the bump on her head?"

She grimaced in disgust at the question. "That's an entirely different matter! You can't trust children to be reliable witnesses in such things."

"So they are reliable witnesses only when their testimony confirms your prior suspicions?" Jefferson started getting ruffled. Corrigan spoke first. "You don't have to answer that."

Corrigan pulled out a photograph and placed it in front of her. "Have you ever seen this woman?"

Bledsoe looked at the picture of Sally Roe and did her best to draw a blank. "No, I don't think so."

"Any chance that she was the driver of that pickup?"

"Objection!" said Ames. "You haven't established that there even was a pickup."

"Miss Bledsoe, did you have a near-miss encounter with a blue pickup while driving the Harris children away from the Harris home?"

"No, I did not!"

"With any vehicle of any color?"

"No!"

Corrigan pointed at the picture of Sally Roe. "You said you've never seen this woman before. Have you ever seen this picture before?"

She hesitated. "I may have."

"Where?"

"I don't recall."

"Do you recall tearing up some photographs that were in Josiah Harris's possession during the children's last visit with their father?"

She was clearly uncomfortable. "Oh . . . I tore something up, I'm not sure what it was."

Corrigan took back the picture. "Let's talk about your driving record. Any moving violations in the past three years?"

Now she hesitated. "What do you mean?"

"Traffic tickets. Citations."

"I believe so."

"According to the Department of Motor Vehicles, you've

had five speeding violations in the past three years. Is that true?"

"If that's what they say."

"You've also been cited twice for failing to stop at a stop sign, correct?"

"I don't see what this has to do with anything!"

Corrigan insisted, "Correct?"

She sighed. "Yes."

"You've had to change insurance companies three times?"

"I don't know."

Jefferson blurted, "I think you're badgering the witness, Mr. Corrigan."

"I am through with this witness, Mr. Jefferson." Corrigan folded up his notes, relaxed, and smiled. "Thank you very much for coming, Miss Bledsoe. Thanks to all of you."

Bledsoe and the two lawyers felt no need to hang around socially, and the court reporter had another appointment. In no time at all, Corrigan, Mark, and Tom were alone in the conference room.

"Well?" asked Tom.

Corrigan wanted to be sure Bledsoe and the others were gone. He leaned over to look out through the door. The coast was clear. He sat down and thought for a moment, looking through his notes.

"Well, she's lying like a rug, and it shouldn't be too hard to trap her on the witness stand."

Mark asked, "What about Marshall's theory? She's connected to this whole thing, isn't she? She's working for them."

Corrigan thought for just a moment, and then nodded. "The evidence is still circumstantial, but there's a connection, all right, and she's working hard to cover it up. That's one reason she's being so stiff-necked with your kids, Tom. They're witnesses. If you want to hear my latest theory, I'd say she was brought in just to discredit you, but then crossed paths with Sally Roe with the children as witnesses, which complicated everything. Now she not only has to keep the kids quiet about seeing Sally Roe, she also has to keep them quiet about having that near-accident in the first place, and Ruth's bump isn't going to make that easy."

"My children are like hostages!" said Tom angrily.

Mark was fuming as well. "She's connected with Mulligan, then; she's helping him protect that whole suicide story."

Corrigan leafed through his notes. "The more we get into this, I think the more we're going to find that everybody's connected with everybody else. And don't forget Parnell, the coroner. In order to get the whole thing dismissed as a suicide, he'd have to be a part of this too."

Mark looked at his watch. "We'd better pray for Marshall and Ben. They're talking to him right now."

Joey Parnell was not happy at all when he opened his front door to find Marshall Hogan and the recently jobless Ben Cole standing there.

"Hi," said Marshall. "Sorry to bother you at home. Apparently you forgot our appointment."

He had trouble looking them in the eye. "I'm sorry. My secretary was supposed to call you. I'm sick today."

"She did tell us that," said Ben, "but only after we sat there and waited for half an hour."

"Oh, I am sorry. Well, perhaps some other time . . ."

"You'd better have your secretary call the Westhaven Medical Association too," said Marshall. "I saw the ad in the paper, and I just talked to them. They're still expecting you to speak at their conference in an hour."

"Is that why you're wearing your dress shoes and slacks?" asked Ben. "Looks like you're getting dressed to go somewhere."

Parnell became angry. "What business do you have snooping into my daily affairs?"

Marshall reached into a manila envelope. "This might help to answer that." He produced a photograph and showed it to Parnell. "Mr. Parnell, to the best of your knowledge and expertise, is this the woman who committed suicide at the Potter farm several weeks ago?"

He didn't want to look at the picture. "Listen, guys, I do

have some other things to do and I have to get ready. Now if you'll excuse me—"

"Just give us a minute," said Ben. "Please."

Marshall showed him the picture again. "Take a good look. We've checked around with several witnesses who have positively identified her; we have fingerprints, a rap sheet, the whole thing. Is this Sally Roe?"

He looked at the picture for a moment. "Yeah, sure it is. I remember her. Death by strangulation. She hung herself."

"Just checking," said Marshall.

Parnell turned away from the door. "Now if that's all . . ."

"Mr. Parnell," said Marshall, "that was a picture of my sister."

Parnell's face went blank and suddenly pale. His hands were starting to shake.

Marshall continued, "I figured since you live here in Westhaven you probably wouldn't know what the real Sally Roe looked like, and now it's obvious you've never seen her dead either."

Parnell was speechless. He kept looking down, then at the door, then inside the house, then at Marshall and Ben. The poor guy was acting like a cornered animal.

Ben asked, "Can you tell us who the dead woman really was?"

"I can't tell you anything!" he finally blurted. "Just go away—get out of here!"

He slammed the door.

Marshall and Ben walked back toward their car.

"Did you see that?" asked Marshall.

"That guy is *scared!*" said Ben.

Kate's afternoon had been, in a way, informative; at least she was being informed in a most frustrating way how difficult it was to ever see a bona fide copy of the *Finding the Real Me* curriculum for fourth-graders.

She stopped by the office at the elementary school to meet with Mr. Woodard, the principal, and look at the curriculum. Mr. Woodard wasn't there. She found him down the hall, whereupon he had a sudden recollection of their appointment.

Then the curriculum was nowhere to be found, and he couldn't understand whatever happened to it. He told her to talk to Miss Brewer. Miss Brewer was with her class and could not be disturbed, but would call her. Miss Brewer never called.

Then Kate called Jerry Mason, a member of the school board and most likely a member of LifeCircle.

"Well, I think the teacher should have a copy," he said.

Kate was getting tired of that line. "No, she doesn't. I've already checked with her and she referred me to Mr. Woodard, who then referred me back to Miss Brewer."

"Well, I don't have a copy."

"I was just wondering if you might, since you did approve the curriculum for the elementary grades."

"But do you have a child taking that curriculum?"

"No, I'm just trying to see a copy of it."

"Well, there aren't that many around, and I don't think anyone who wants to can just drop in anytime and see it. We prefer to work with only the parents. You probably should make an appointment."

Kate ran around the mulberry bush a few more times with Jerry Mason, and then called Betty Hanover, another school board member.

"Say, listen," Betty said, "we've been through all this before with the . . . the religious fringe. The community has decided they like the curriculum, and we'd just as soon have some peace now, all right?"

John Kendall was no better. "Did you ask Miss Brewer? It's the teachers who are supposed to be in charge of it. They ought to be able to help you out."

Kate put down the phone and checked off another name. Then she let out a mock scream.

If for no other reason, that curriculum had to be worth seeing simply because so many people were going to such great lengths to keep it hidden.

Another letter! It was just like the other ones—same envelope, same handwriting, same thick letter inside on lined notebook paper! Lucy grabbed it out of the pile of incoming mail and slipped it quickly into her pocket. Where were all these letters coming from? If this was a joke, it was certainly a long-lived joke, and not at all funny.

If it wasn't a joke, and these letters really were from Sally Roe . . .

She didn't want to think about that; it was easier not to consider it at all, and go on trusting all the people she now trusted.

Debbie was nearby, sorting through the mail in another mailbag. She'd stopped working, and seemed to be looking carefully at a mailing label on a magazine, but. . . . To Lucy, it seemed like Debbie was watching her, but trying not to look like it.

"Something wrong?" Lucy asked.

"Oh, no . . . nothing," Debbie answered, turning away and shoving the magazine into one of the mailboxes.

They went on sorting the mail, and nothing more was said.

But Debbie had seen the whole thing.

twenty-five

WAYNE Corrigan had read Dr. Mandanhi's detailed report on Amber Brandon's condition. Most of it was so technical it would take another expert to refute it, if it was refutable. One thing was clear to even a lay reader of the document: Mandanhi held the Good Shepherd Academy responsible for Amber's troubles, and had a low opinion of Christianity. This deposition would not be easy.

Mandanhi was a gentle man, however, and not unpleasant to deal with. He was in his forties, of East Indian descent, well-dressed, well-mannered, professional. Attorneys Ames and Jefferson sat on either side of him, as they did Irene Bledsoe, but didn't seem quite as edgy for his sake as for Bledsoe's. Apparently they were sure Mandanhi could take care of himself.

Corrigan started with some basics. "So could you review for the record Amber's basic symptoms of trauma?"

Mandanhi brought a few notes, but didn't seem to need them. "Amber's behavior is typical of any child her age who has undergone extensive emotional trauma: bed-wetting, moodiness, occasional nausea, and frequent escapes into fantasy . . . a loss of reality, paranoia, the fear of unseen enemies—spooks, bogeymen, that sort of thing."

"And you attribute all this to the environment at the Christian school?"

He smiled. "Not entirely. There could well be other factors, but the pervasive religious overtones of the school's curriculum would be, in my opinion, sufficient to exacerbate Amber's preexistent emotional turmoils. The Christian doctrines of sin and of a God of wrath and judgment, as well as Christianity's imposition of guilt and accountability, would immediately assimilate into the child's preestablished identity structure, producing a whole new set of reasons for her to be insecure and fearful of her world."

"Have you discussed any of this with the pastor of the

Good Shepherd Church, or with the headmaster of the school?"

"No, sir, I have not."

"So do you know for a fact that the school was imposing any kind of guilt or fear upon the child?"

"I have examined the child, and I know she went to the school. A clear connection is not hard to draw."

Corrigan made a few marks in the margin of his copy of Mandanhi's report. "Now . . . about this Amethyst, this little pony that Amber becomes . . . What was that term you used?"

"Dissociative disorder, or hysterical neurosis, dissociative type."

"Uh . . . right. Could you explain just what that is?"

"Basically, it is a disturbance or alteration in the normally integrative functions of identity, memory, or consciousness."

"I'm going to need that in simpler terms, doctor."

He smiled, thought for a moment, and then tried again. "What Amber is displaying is what we call Multiple Personality Disorder; it's a condition in which two or more distinct personalities exist within one person. This disorder is almost always brought on by some form of abuse, usually sexual, or severe emotional trauma. The onset is almost invariably during childhood, but often is not discovered until later in life. Statistically, it occurs from three to nine times more often in females than males."

"I wanted to ask you about some of these complications you listed."

Mandanhi consulted his own copy of his report. "Yes. Complications, difficulties that can arise when this disorder manifests itself."

Corrigan scanned the list. "External violence?"

"Yes. A total break with social norms of behavior, social inhibitions. Blind rage, injury to others . . ."

"How about screaming, kicking, resisting authority?"

"Oh yes."

"Suicide attempts?"

"Very common."

"How about Amber?"

Mandanhi thought for a moment, then shook his head. "Her case seems rather mild in that area."

Corrigan found another new word. "What is coprolalia?"

"Violent, obscene language, usually involuntary."

Corrigan stopped on that one. "Involuntary?"

"The victim has no control over what he or she says; the utterance is spontaneous and can include animal noises, growls, barking, hissing, and so forth."

"Uh . . . how about blasphemy?" Corrigan felt a need to explain that. "Uh . . . railings, obscenities, slanderous statements against a Deity?"

"Yes. Quite frequent."

"And then there are . . . altered states of consciousness?"

"Yes, trance states."

"And according to your experience, this sort of thing is usually—or almost always—brought on by severe emotional trauma or sexual abuse?"

"That is correct."

"And this is your assumption regarding the Good Shepherd Academy?"

"It is."

"But you haven't talked to the school personnel about this?"

"No."

"I see." Corrigan jotted some notes and read a few more notes. "The press seems to have some firm opinions about what went on at the school, and they've said some pretty rough things about Tom Harris. Have they gotten any of their information from you, doctor?"

"I have not spoken to them personally, no."

Corrigan raised an eyebrow. "But it's reasonable to think that your opinions, in some form or another, have gotten into the hands of the press?"

He didn't seem too happy to have to answer. "I believe so."

"How about the Child Protection Department?"

Mandanhi looked at the lawyers. They didn't seem too

distressed. "The CPD received a complete copy of my report, and I have consulted with them on a regular basis."

To Corrigan that was not a complete surprise, but he could still feel a tinge of anger. "So . . . they must think the Academy's quite a dangerous place for children."

"You would have to ask them."

Corrigan's voice rose just a little. "What did you tell them?"

Mandanhi balked at the question. "What did I tell them?"

"You've regularly consulted with them. Have you led them to believe the school is a dangerous place for children?"

"I can't tell you what they believe."

Corrigan let the question go. "Then I suppose by the same token you can't explain why there hasn't been an all-out investigation of the school and its personnel, and of every parent who has their child enrolled there?"

Mandanhi only shrugged. "That is not my responsibility to know. I don't make the decisions."

"Would the CPD representative you've regularly consulted with happen to be Irene Bledsoe?"

"Yes."

Corrigan said nothing in response to that; he just wrote it down. "Have you ever heard of a Miss Nancy Brewer, fourth grade teacher at the Bacon's Corner Elementary School?"

"No, sir."

"Have you ever heard of the *Finding the Real Me* curriculum that Miss Brewer teaches to her fourth-grade class?"

"No, sir."

"Then you are not aware, doctor, that Miss Brewer regularly teaches the children to relax, achieve susceptible states of consciousness, and contact inner guides?"

The question grabbed Mandanhi's interest, but he still had to reply, "No."

"Were you aware that, prior to Amber's enrollment at the Christian school, she was a student in Miss Brewer's class and went through that curriculum?"

That grabbed Mandanhi's interest even more. His expression became a little grim. "I was not aware of that."

"Are you familiar with a local organization called LifeCircle?"

"Yes."

"Are you aware that they regularly practice consciousness-altering techniques such as yoga, meditation, and . . ." Corrigan paused and then hit the term with emphasis." . . . trance channeling?"

"I am aware of that."

"Are you aware that Lucy Brandon and her daughter Amber are both closely involved with that group and its practices?"

"Yes."

Corrigan wasn't expecting all these affirmative answers; he was a little shocked. "Then can you please explain to me, doctor, just how you can be so sure that only the Good Shepherd Academy is to be blamed for Amber's abnormal behavior?"

He smiled. "I do not blame the Academy for Amber's behavior; I blame it for the trauma that precipitated the behavior."

Corrigan had to get a grip on himself. This man was starting to bother him. "But in light of what is happening at the elementary school and at LifeCircle, can you agree that such behavior as Amber's can be taught and conditioned in a young child *without* severe trauma?"

Mandanhi laughed. "Since you are asking me, I will tell you that I do not recognize the validity of anything that may be happening at the elementary school or at LifeCircle. I look upon these things as highly subjective, even religious matters, something I prefer not to approach clinically."

"So Amber's behavior, in your opinion, must indicate severe emotional trauma as its only cause?"

"That is what I have written, and that is my opinion."

Corrigan stopped for a moment. He was frustrated, but tried not to show it. He went back to some other notes he'd jotted on the report. "So, doctor, between the Christians, the LifeCirclers, Miss Brewer, and even Amber, it looks like we have a lot of different opinions as to what this Amethyst really is."

"I am not responsible for any opinion other than my own," the doctor interjected.

"Would you agree that Amber is able to communicate with this . . . whatever it is?"

"That is not untypical for a dissociative. The different personalities are often aware of each other, will often converse, and sometimes even disagree and argue."

"And it's normal for Amber to blink out and not remember the passing of time when Amethyst is manifesting herself?"

"That is quite typical."

"How about special knowledge? Is it possible for Amethyst to know information that Amber could not possibly know or have prior opportunity to learn?"

Mandanhi hesitated. "I'm not sure I can answer that. The disorder does present a lot of questions at times . . ."

"Such as?"

"Oh . . . My colleagues and I have always been mystified by that one trait you mentioned, special knowledge—some would call it clairvoyance or ESP. But another phenomenon we often find in this disorder is an actual physiological change in the person affected. The normal personality may not need eyeglasses at all, while the alternate personality does; or both may wear glasses, but the prescription will be quite different. The blood pressures can be different, or the reaction to certain medications; the bleeding and clotting rates can be different, and we've even noted a clear and measurable change in the blood composition."

Corrigan wrote it all down. "Any explanations, doctor?"

Mandanhi shook his head and smiled. "There is still much we do not know about ourselves, Mr. Corrigan."

Corrigan had heard enough. He was ready for the next witness. "How would you feel if I talked to Amber about all this? Would she be willing to talk about it?"

Mandanhi considered that. "I don't see that it would do any harm, provided you limit yourself to reasonable questions and behavior toward the child."

"Well, I was thinking I'd like to have our own psychologist examine Amber as well."

Suddenly Jefferson jumped on that. "No, Corrigan. Forget it. That isn't going to happen."

Corrigan knew he'd hit a nerve somewhere. "Hey, come on. Dr. Mandanhi doesn't seem to think it'll hurt."

Ames was really hot about it. "You're not going anywhere near that child! She's suffered enough!"

Corrigan turned to Dr. Mandanhi. "How about it, doctor? Think it'd be okay?"

Mandanhi looked at the attorneys and caught the meaning in their eyes. "Well . . . I suppose not, Mr. Corrigan. I suppose it would be harmful."

"You suppose?"

"It *would* be harmful."

"Forget it!" said Jefferson.

Fat chance, thought Corrigan.

twenty-six

Before Sally noticed, she was writing by the light of the overhead lamp above her seat, and not by the daylight coming in through the window. It was getting late. The hazy red twilight was giving way to the deepening gray of night, and now the farms and fields rushing by outside were beginning to hide behind the reflection of her own face. The rhythmic rocking of the railcar and *click-click-clacking* of the tracks had a lulling effect, a dulling effect, and she was feeling sleepy.

It would be another day or so before she would reach her destination and revisit old Bentmore University. Her stomach turned with fear at every thought of it. These would be the powerful people, the influential ones, the molders of education and educators. If the people at Omega remembered her, undoubtedly she would be remembered at Bentmore. But still she had to go. She had to see that place again.

> So, my stay in Room 302 in Fairwood was suddenly ended, and I am on the road—riding the rails, actually—once again, with only my duffel bag and my life as possessions. I don't mean to sound flippant, but running for my life is a whole new experience for me. First of all, I've never done it, and secondly, I never thought I would be running from the people I once trusted and admired so deeply. One of the hardest lessons I have had to learn is that the utopian dream of a new world order is not without its dark side, its power-mongers, schemers, manipulators, and killers. Behind all the Mrs. Dennings and Miss Brewers who dream of refining and guiding mankind, there are the Mr. Steeles who dream of subjugating and controlling mankind. The Dennings and Brewers work hard to prepare all mankind for a global community; the Steeles look forward to running it.
>
> And then there are the Sally Roes who get caught in the middle, disillusioned by the idyllic dreams of the Dennings

and Brewers and trying to stay out from under the crushing boot of the Steeles. Perhaps they are the ones the Steeles fear the most: they know all the tenets, but no longer believe in the faith. They can get in the way more effectively than anyone.

She paused, and looked at her reflection in the window, a tired face with the blackness of night behind it, and it occurred to her what sorts of allegories she would have drawn from such a picture only a few days ago, or even yesterday. She could have written about the blackness of her soul, or the great void that lay beyond the visible Sally Roe, or the transience of her life, nothing more than a fleeting reflection on a thin pane of glass—here during the night, but gone by morning.

Oh, it was great stuff, but for some reason she just didn't feel that way. Something deep inside her was still changing, like a gradual and steady clearing of the weather.

Tom, remember my last letter, when I talked about guilt? I haven't forgotten any of those thoughts; as a matter of fact, they are still churning in my head, and I don't know where they will eventually carry me.

Since I last wrote, I did come up with one challenging proposition about guilt: that it could be a fact, and not just a feeling.

I'm sure you know how much the rest of us despise that one aspect of Christianity: the classic "guilt trip." If I recall the jargon correctly, we are all "sinners," we are all guilty. Religion has always been, in my perception, one big guilt trip, and no one wants to feel guilty. That is why my friends and I spent so much time and energy concocting a universe in which right and wrong did not exist—if there is no right or wrong, there is no need to feel guilty about anything.

Now for the wrench in the works, first thrown in this morning: the possibility of guilt as a fact and not just a feeling. If—and I emphasize the word if—there is a fixed standard of right and wrong—a fence, as I've said—then it *is possible to be guilty of an offense, all feelings of guilt aside. I can be on the wrong side of the fence and be in the wrong regardless of how I feel about it.*

Please bear with me if I state the obvious; I have the distinct fear that you got all this clear in your own mind when you were a child and are getting bored, but please bear with me. I have to think it through, and it helps to do it on paper.

Let's say I rob a bank. That makes me guilty of robbery. Let's say I don't feel guilty about it. If robbery can be established as wrong, then I'm still guilty of robbery, regardless of how I feel.

The feeling—or lack of feeling—does not change the fact.

So, reflecting on what I've learned through the years in the humanist and mystic camps, I see that much of it was an attempt to escape from guilt through philosophy, meditation, drugs, etc., etc. But now I have to ask, what exactly have I been trying to escape: the feelings or the fact? I have been able to escape the feelings—for a season. The feelings you can bury, suppress, deny, or talk yourself out of.

But what can change or erase the fact? So far I haven't thought of a thing.

Wayne Corrigan had mixed feelings about Thursday's deposition; he felt prepared in some ways, and in other ways he was sure he and his volunteer crew of investigators had not yet scratched the surface of what Lucy Brandon and her lawsuit were really all about. But here she sat, the plaintiff herself, dressed up in a gray pantsuit, flanked by Ames and Jefferson, ready to hold forth and looking nervous.

Mark and Tom were present again, and Corrigan had plenty of notes for reference.

They went over old ground first, rehashing the offenses against Amber at the Christian school. Lucy seemed to have a much better grasp of the details than Irene Bledsoe displayed.

"He would often grab Amber by her shoulders and shake her until she produced the answer he wanted," she said.

"Can you give us an example?" Corrigan asked.

"Well . . . she told me once about Mr. Harris trying to get Amber 'saved,' and he was quite forceful about it, shaking her, insisting that she say that Jesus was her Savior. She just wanted to say that He was her example, or her friend, or her guide, but that wasn't good enough for him. He shook her, yelled at her, and really upset her. Then he made her stay in during recess until she changed her attitude. It was horrible; she cried about it all that evening. It was all I could do to get her to go back to the school the next day."

Tom jotted a note to himself. This testimony was a blatant lie, but it was not surprising. He'd heard Amber use the same truth-stretching whenever she tattled.

"This is, of course, Amber's account?" asked Corrigan.

"Yes, it's what she told me."

"And you were not a witness to this?"

"No, but I believe my daughter."

"Did you ever discuss this with Mr. Harris?"

"No, I didn't."

"Why not?"

She had to search for an answer. "Oh, I guess my mind was on other matters, and it didn't seem important at the time."

"But it seems important now?"

"Why, yes."

Corrigan showed her a document. "This is your signature on this Parental Agreement Form, correct?"

She looked at it. "Yes."

"And if you'll notice paragraph nine on this form, it states that you have read the Student/Parent Handbook and agree to all it contains. Did you read the handbook, and did you agree to all it contained?"

Lucy was quite reluctant to answer. "Yes."

Corrigan checked some records. "Is it true that Amber was paddled on . . . March 25th, and that Mr. Harris informed you about it that evening by telephone?"

"Yes."

"And is it true that at that time you approved of the spanking?"

"Yes."

"To the best of your knowledge, has Amber ever been spanked since then?"

"No."

"So, just to make sure I have this straight, you are suing the school for physical abuse by spanking, but as far as you know there was only one incident of spanking, and you approved of it beforehand when you signed the Parental Agreement, and also at the time the spanking was administered? Do I have that right?"

She was unhappy, but answered truthfully, "Yes, that's right."

"Were you aware of the infraction for which Amber was spanked?"

Lucy thought for a moment. "I think she was being disruptive in class."

Corrigan didn't want to go into the next subject, but he had to. "Do you recall the nature of the disruption? Do you remember Mr. Harris describing it to you?"

Lucy stumbled with an answer. "She was . . . being noisy, um, playing at her desk . . ."

Corrigan dove in. "Well, let's just go ahead and talk about Amethyst."

Lucy brightened with recollection. "Oh . . ."

"Do you recall now that Amber was spanked because she was portraying Amethyst in the classroom and disturbing the class, and not heeding Mr. Harris's orders to stop that behavior?"

"Yes."

"Mrs. Brandon, we've heard a lot of opinions about who or what Amethyst really is. Who or what is Amethyst in your opinion?"

Lucy looked down at the table, thought about the question, even laughed just a little, and then shook her head. "I'm not sure. I guess she's just a character that Amber made up, but . . . Well, Dr. Mandanhi said it's possibly an alternate personality, but I don't know . . ."

"Are you affiliated in any way with a fellowship group in the Bacon's Corner area called LifeCircle?"

"Uh . . . yes."

"Isn't it true that that group holds to a belief in channeling and spirit-guides?"

She laughed, but it was a nervous laugh. "Well, we embrace a lot of different beliefs; we all have our opinions about channeling. I guess ultimately we don't question it, we just experience it."

"Would you say that Amber was channeling Amethyst?"

"Oh, she could be channeling, or she could be pretending she's channeling, or . . . I don't know. There are many different views. It's really something to be experienced for what good can be derived from it; it's not to be questioned."

"Have you ever considered that Amethyst could be a spirit?"

The term seemed to shock her. "A spirit?"

"Yes, a spirit-guide, or an ascended master, or a disembodied entity from the astral plane. Those are familiar terms to you, aren't they?"

She smiled, impressed. "You know a lot about this sort of thing, don't you?"

Corrigan smiled back pleasantly. "Well, I try to do my homework. But do you think Amethyst could be a spirit-guide? Is that possible?"

She furrowed her brow and looked down at the table, struggling with such a thought. "Some believe that. I still don't know what to think."

Corrigan scribbled in his notepad. "At any rate, on March 28th, Mr. Harris and Amethyst had a confrontation. Do you recall hearing about that?"

"Yes. Mr. Harris called me at the Post Office. It sounded serious, so I came over."

"Did he tell you what happened?"

"Yes. He said that Amber had been . . . Oh, I can't remember how he put it, but he basically told me that they thought she had a demon and tried to cast it out of her. I was outraged. I'd never heard of such a thing."

"You've never heard of casting out demons?"

She answered bitterly, "That's strictly a Christian idea, an invention of organized religion, and I resent that it was imposed upon my daughter! Channeling is a gift, a special ability; it has nothing to do with religion!"

"But you do understand that the Bible teaches otherwise?"

Lucy was angry and hurt. "Mr. Corrigan, she's just a *child*, a child with a special gift! She doesn't have to explain her gift to me, or defend what she's experiencing. I've never singled her out or harassed her; I've just loved her, accepted her, and just let her have her gift for whatever good it can do for her and for the rest of us. She's just a child, not a theologian or a scholar or a priest or a lawyer, and what power does a ten-year-old child have to stand up against—" she hesitated, but then spewed out the words—"against hard-nosed, prejudiced, religious adults in that school who abuse their power and their size, who have no tolerance and no understanding, who just . . . attack her, pounce on her, scream at her, and accuse her of being possessed . . ."

She buried her face in her hands for a moment. Corrigan was just about to call for a recess, but then she recovered and finished her statement. "They just had no right to treat my daughter that way, to single her out and persecute her just for being different."

Corrigan figured it was time to go on to the next question. "When you came to the school, what did you find? How was Amber?"

Lucy thought for a while, recalling it. "She was . . . she was sitting in the school office, and she looked awful. She was very tired, and I remember she was wet with perspiration and her hair was all uncombed. She was upset . . . moody. When I took her home, I found that her body was bruised in several places like she'd been in a terrible wrestling match. I was just shocked." Lucy's emotions began to rise. "I couldn't believe such a thing could happen to my daughter, and at a Christian school where . . . Well, I once believed that a Christian school, of all places, would be a good place for Amber, a safe place. I didn't think that Christians would stoop to such behavior. But they did."

Corrigan spoke gently to her. "Mrs. Brandon, was it Amber

as Amber who remembered the incident? Could she tell you what happened?"

Lucy was still composing herself. "I don't think she's ever been able to talk to me directly about it. She has to be Amethyst to talk about it."

"So it was Amethyst who told you what happened?"

"Amber pretending to be Amethyst, or channeling Amethyst, yes."

Corrigan thought for a moment. "Mrs. Brandon, whenever Amber becomes Amethyst, after she stops being Amethyst, does she remember anything that Amethyst said or did?"

Lucy smiled a little sheepishly. "Well . . . she says she doesn't."

"All right. At any rate, that incident occurred on March 28th, but you didn't take Amber out of the school until April 20th. Can you explain why, after such an outrageous incident, and such selective, prejudicial behavior toward Amber, you still kept your child enrolled at the school?"

"I . . ."

"Obviously you consulted a lawyer during the interim?"

"Yes."

Corrigan produced a photocopied, handwritten record. "Part of the discovery materials included this photocopy of a journal you kept. Do you recognize it?"

"Yes."

"So, between March 28th and April 20th, you kept detailed records on the school . . ." Corrigan leafed through the many photocopied pages. "You kept track of all the lessons, the Bible verses for each day, the discipline problems, the Bible projects . . . quite a detailed account."

"Yes."

"So isn't it true that you kept this record all this time, with Amber still enrolled, because you fully intended to bring this lawsuit against the school?"

Jefferson jumped on that. "I object, counselor. That's a matter of speculation and conjecture; there's a total lack of foundation."

"So let's get some foundation. Mrs. Brandon, some time

after March 28th, didn't you consult a friend at LifeCircle for legal advice regarding these matters?"

Lucy even shrugged a little. "Yes."

"Was it Claire Johanson, legal assistant to Mr. Ames and Mr. Jefferson?"

"Yes."

"And what was the result of that conversation?"

"The result?"

"Didn't you decide at that time to pursue a lawsuit against the school?"

"I think so."

"You think so?"

"Well, yes, I did."

"And in preparation for the lawsuit, you began keeping this detailed record of everything happening at the school, correct?"

Lucy was chagrined. "Yes."

"All right. Now, having established that, let me ask this question: Since you kept Amber enrolled at the school despite the outrageous behavior demonstrated against her, is it possible that gaining more material for your lawsuit was more important to you than your own daughter's well-being?"

"I'll definitely object to that!" said Jefferson.

"And I'll drop the question," said Corrigan, unruffled. He looked at his notes. "Does Amber still become Amethyst from time to time?"

Lucy smiled as she reluctantly admitted, "Yes, she still does."

"Was she displaying this kind of behavior even before she enrolled at the Christian school?"

"Yes."

"Is it true that she learned to . . . create or visualize Amethyst in her fourth-grade class at the Bacon's Corner Elementary School, a class taught by a Miss Brewer?"

"Yes. Miss Brewer is a wonderful teacher."

Corrigan paused. "Then why did you transfer Amber to the Christian school?"

Lucy seemed a little embarrassed. "Oh . . . I thought her

time in the elementary school had served its purpose. Amber was fulfilling her potential and discovering herself, yes, but . . . she wasn't learning much else."

"A little weak in academics?"

"A little. I thought some balance would be good for her; a wider realm of experience."

"I understand." Corrigan went to another matter. "Do you recall an incident at the Post Office several weeks ago when Amber, as Amethyst, had a confrontation with a patron in the lobby?"

Lucy was visibly disturbed by that question. "How did you find out about that?"

"Do you recall it?"

"Yes."

"Does Amber recall it?"

"No. She was . . . Well, she was Amethyst at the time, and now she doesn't remember any of it."

"She doesn't remember it?"

"No."

"Is it true that Amber, as Amethyst, became very aggressive toward the patron?"

Lucy was sickened by the memory, and perhaps by the question. "Yes."

"She circled the patron, struck her several times?"

"I . . . I did see her hit the lady, yes."

"Did Amber, as Amethyst, make loud, screaming accusations against the lady?"

"Yes."

"Would you say that Amber's behavior was violent, uncontrolled?"

She didn't want to admit it. "Yes."

"So violent that the lady was forced to flee from the lobby?"

Lucy was getting upset; the memory was a painful, perplexing wound. "That's what happened. I couldn't get Amber to stop. I was just so embarrassed."

"Did Amber know this woman?"

"No. I just don't know how she could have."

"And as far as you know, the woman did nothing to provoke this attack?"

"No."

"Do you recall what Amethyst was screaming?"

Lucy's eyes dropped to the table; she rested her forehead on her fingers. "She was saying . . . something about the woman's baby . . . saying, 'You killed your baby.'"

"Do you know who the woman was?"

"I don't know . . . I think so."

Corrigan took out a photograph and showed it to her. "Is this the woman?"

Jefferson jumped in. "Really, I don't see what this has to do with anything!"

Corrigan just gave him a correcting look, and he remained quiet.

"Is this the woman?"

Lucy stared at the grainy photograph. Her face answered the question before she said it. "Yes."

"Do you know who this woman is?"

She seemed to give in. "Her name is Sally Roe. She was a patron at the Post Office. But that's all I know about her."

"And she committed suicide just a few weeks ago, isn't that true?"

Lucy lashed back, "That wasn't Amber's fault!"

Corrigan paused just a little at that outburst, then said, "We're not saying it was. Now, you heard Amethyst—Amber, whatever—accuse Sally Roe of killing her baby, correct?"

"Asked and answered," said Jefferson.

"Just trying to be sure," said Corrigan.

"Yes, I did," said Lucy.

"Were you aware that Sally Roe had a criminal record?"

It was obviously news to Lucy Brandon. "No."

Corrigan produced some documents. "This is a copy of her criminal record, and here are some news clippings. You'll notice the highlighted areas: she was convicted of first-degree murder ten years ago. As you can see here, and here, and on this news story here, she was found guilty of the drowning death of her baby daughter."

315

He waited for it all to sink in, and watched the blood drain from Lucy Brandon's face.

"Obviously your daughter, as Amethyst, was correct in her accusations against Sally Roe in the lobby of the Post Office. To the best of your knowledge, was there any way that Amber could have known about Sally Roe's past?"

Lucy could hardly speak. "No. I didn't even know about it."

"Can you explain, then, how *Amethyst* knew about it?"

Lucy took time to answer only because it was difficult. "No." She tried to do better. "Psychic ability, maybe."

"On whose part, Amber's or Amethyst's?"

Lucy shook her head, quite flustered. "I don't know. I don't understand these things. But it can happen in channeling."

"So Amber was channeling?"

"Yes, I guess she was."

"And apparently this special gift of hers has a rather violent side to it?"

"I don't know . . ."

"You did have quite a wrestling match with Amethyst, didn't you? It was several minutes before you could get your daughter under control?"

"Yes."

"And when the incident was finally over, would you say your daughter was wet with perspiration, probably disheveled, tired, moody, maybe even bruised a little?"

Lucy was reluctant to answer that.

Corrigan pressed it. "Wasn't that her general condition?"

"I suppose so."

"And during the scuffle, didn't you refer to your daughter as Amethyst?"

She looked puzzled.

Corrigan asked it another way. "Didn't you wrestle with your daughter, and say words to the effect, 'Amethyst, you stop this . . . Amethyst, calm down'?"

Lucy's voice was barely audible. "I suppose I did."

"Just who were you talking to?"

Lucy didn't appreciate that question. "My daughter!"

"Which one?" Lucy hesitated, so Corrigan built on the question. "You've already stated that Amber has no recollection of the incident, and normally does not remember anything that Amethyst says or does. You have admitted that Amber was channeling. Would it be correct to say that it was Amethyst, and not Amber, who was displaying all this aggressive behavior?"

"But it was my daughter . . ."

"But a different and separate personality, correct?"

Lucy stared at him. She was thinking about it. Corrigan could sense Ames and Jefferson getting more and more tense.

"Correct?" Corrigan asked again.

"Yes," she said finally. "I think that's correct."

"So . . . if someone—even yourself—should ever confront Amethyst, they would actually be confronting a personality other than your daughter?"

"I guess so. Maybe."

Ames and Jefferson did not like that answer. No doubt they would have quite a conference with Lucy Brandon when this was over.

Corrigan decided it was time for a provocative benediction. "So, does it seem so strange to you now that Mr. Harris might also have had a similar encounter, not with your daughter Amber, but with Amethyst, a separate personality: a violent struggle, a wrestling match, a demonstrative confrontation? Can you imagine what it must have been like for him to have Amethyst behave in the classroom as she behaved in the Post Office lobby, screaming, hitting, and producing information that Amber—as Amber—could not possibly know? Can you understand now what conclusion a Biblical Christian would come to when confronted with a violent, uncontrollable, alternate personality in a young, innocent child?" He didn't need an answer, and he didn't wait for one. "Thank you, Mrs. Brandon. I know this has been difficult for you. That's all for now."

twenty-seven

Bentmore University was nestled—almost hidden—within the tight, red-brick grid of a major metropolis. In every direction, it was just across the street from the noise, litter, traffic, and growing pains of the city. It had outlived the rise and fall of a low-income housing project on its north flank; on the west side, the delicatessens, tailors, and cleaners were now owned by third generations; on the east, the tugs still pulled their barges up and down the murky river, the rumble of their engines audible across the campus when the wind was right; on the south, several new apartments had become the only view in that direction, and now the streets down there were filled with big old cars driven by retired folks who drove slowly.

In the center of it all, Bentmore lived on, standing firm and steadfast in red brick and white stone, its halls, dormitories, libraries, and labs evenly dispersed on the lawned terrain, its patterned brick sidewalks radiating like spokes from every entryway, crisscrossing and networking like trade routes to every point on the campus.

To the human eye, Bentmore seemed an oasis of peace, reflection, and learning amid the hubbub of its surroundings; in the spiritual realm, the real trouble was within its borders, not outside them.

Guilo met with Tal and his top warriors on the roof of the old North American Can Company, located just across the river from the campus. Beneath their feet, soup cans, juice cans, fruit cans, and sardine cans took shape and clattered by the windows in an endless, rolling parade; across the river, still veiled by the morning mist, old Bentmore was ominously quiet.

Guilo stood beside Tal to give his report. He was nervous, agitated, ready for a fight, his hand resting on the handle of his sword. "Some of their best are there. The great deceivers, the great builders of the Enemy's coming kingdom, all supervised by a behemoth who calls himself Corrupter."

"I've heard of him," said Tal. "He has power and great deceptive ability, but not much speed or wit in battle."

"An advantage, to be sure. If we remain stealthy, there is a lot we could do before he becomes aware of it."

Nathan peered through the mist and thought he saw some hulking spirits gliding occasionally between the structures, but most of them were unseen. "They remain hidden, tucked away inside the buildings."

"Very occupied," said Armoth. "Classes are in session."

"Corrupter is a bit comfortable at the moment, and off-guard," said Guilo, "but Destroyer is going to be another problem. He is on his way now, with all his forces. Then old Bentmore will be like a hive of hornets at rest. Merely shake the tree, and . . ."

"They will overrun us," said Tal. "Destroyer's troublemakers in Bacon's Corner are doing well at this point; our prayer cover is as weak as it's ever been, and we're left with seriously depleted numbers. Direct confrontations are going to be risky. We'll have to lean heavily on stealth and strategy . . ."

Guilo allowed himself a quick, stifled chuckle as he eyed the campus. "I remind you all: they could eat us alive."

The benches here and there on the campus were still wet with dew and mist, but Sally found a comfortable desk hidden away in the stacks of the Research Library. So far she hadn't seen library staff that she recognized, and that set her a little more at ease. Thanks to a small cleaning shop on the west side of the campus, her better clothes—slacks, blouse, dress jacket—were cleaned and pressed; she'd replaced her wayfaring-stranger ensemble with a more presentable outfit, and stashed her duffel bag, replacing it with a less obtrusive carry bag. She could recall looking sharp and professional twelve years ago, with carefully coordinated outfits and her hair tightly pinned. Today the best she could look was casual and twelve years older, with tinted glasses and dye-blackened hair pinned up as best as she could arrange it.

She just had to hope she looked different enough from the Sally Roe people would remember.

> *Oh, I must have been so proud of my calling as an educator! As I sit here and observe the graduate students around this place, working toward their Master's degrees just like I did, I can see the same pride in their faces, I can sense the same highbrow demeanor. To be honest, I see myself as I was back then. The old Bentmore mold has not broken. I can guess what they're thinking: they are world conquerors, missionaries for a bold message of global change.*
>
> *And I would say they are correct. Bentmore is still turning out great educators, great agents of change. They will be the teachers, the administrators, the principals, the authors, the lobbyists. A nation will follow them; they will restructure an entire culture.*

Sally checked her watch. It was after 9 in the morning; someone should be in Professor Lynch's office by now, either his secretary or Lynch himself. This would be the greatest risk of all, but she must contact him. Of all people, he should have some of the answers she needed.

She'd checked for his name and number in the campus directory, and surprising as it was, after twelve years Samuel W. Lynch was still head of the School of Education. As she remembered him, he was definitely fit for the position, always an imposing man of great knowledge, stature, and strength.

A tall, athletic undergrad had just finished using the pay phone on the wall behind her. She grabbed the opportunity. She would try to get an appointment with Lynch, perhaps during his office hours. All she could hope was that the man was not as brilliant as she remembered him to be; perhaps he wouldn't recall who she was.

Wayne Corrigan and Gordon Jefferson, the ACFA attorney, were never going to be good friends, that was readily apparent.

"Mr. Jefferson, I'm simply saying that we have the right to confront our accuser!" Corrigan was feeling very forceful, and had his mouth so close to the receiver that Jefferson heard a roar every time Corrigan pronounced an *s* or an *f*.

Jefferson came back just as firm, and even a little snide. "Your accuser, Mr. Corrigan, is Lucy Brandon, not Amber, and you have already deposed Mrs. Brandon in such a harsh manner as to cause her terrible distress! We wouldn't think of putting Amber in the same situation."

"We do not wish to cause Amber any grief—none at all! We'll work within restrictions, we'll be gentle. But so far everything we've heard, all the testimony, all the grievances, have come through either Lucy Brandon or Dr. Mandanhi. The real complainant in this case is neither of these people, but Amber herself."

"Amber is not going to testify or be forced to go through a deposition. We will fight that, sir!"

"We must have Amber's direct testimony concerning the complaints brought against my clients."

"It would be too traumatic for her. She's already so deeply wounded by these unfortunate events, we simply cannot allow her to be traumatized further by being put through the stress and pain of a deposition and a trial!"

"Then we want our psychologist to examine her. At least then we would have our own expert testimony to balance the testimony of Dr. Mandanhi."

"Absolutely not! Amber is not to be involved in this case in any way. She must be kept separate from it; she must be protected from any further abuse and intimidation!"

Corrigan sighed and looked across his desk at Marshall, who was closely listening and watching Corrigan's side of the conversation. Marshall made a wringing motion with his hands as if twisting an invisible arm and whispered, "You stick it to 'em!"

"I'm afraid we can't back down in this matter," Corrigan told Jefferson. "If you won't change your mind, then we'll ask the court to compel her availability and testimony."

"We're prepared for that," said Jefferson.

"Very well, then."

Corrigan hung up, and then he thought for a moment. "Maybe I pushed Lucy Brandon too hard. Now they're hiding Amber under a bushel."

Marshall nodded an emphatic nod. "Sure. Irene Bledsoe, and Lucy Brandon, and this Dr. Mandanhi character can say all they want, but Amber's the key to this whole thing. As long as Amethyst is doing her—its—stuff, Amber's going to be a real risk."

"Sure, if we can just get her on that stand, or get our own expert to examine her. I mean, if we can just get Amethyst to manifest once, we could build an argument that Tom's behavior in confronting Amethyst was justified." He smiled. "Wouldn't it be great if we could get Amethyst to tear up the courtroom? We could *win* this case!"

"They know that."

"Well, we *do* know what happened in the Post Office, and that has them scared. We need to beef up that defense; we have Alice Buckmeier's eyewitness account, but another witness would sure be nice, especially if Lucy decides to squirrel out of her deposed testimony somehow."

Marshall answered, "Well, there's still that other gal, Debbie, who works at the Post Office with Brandon. Alice says she was there, but I'm wondering where her loyalties might lie."

"We'll just hand her a subpoena and find out."

"And then there's the victim of Amethyst's attack."

Corrigan nodded. "Our greatest unsolved mystery. She's like a ghost, you know? We have pictures of her, eyewitness accounts of her, facts and information about her, but as far as what she has to do with this case, she's like a mirage, she simply isn't there."

"So push this Amber thing. Go ahead and ask for a hearing. The ACFA could use a dose of their own medicine. If it doesn't do anything else for us, it'll buy us time. You never know when something big will break."

Corrigan was captivated by the thought. "Amber, we've got to get you on that stand!"

Claire Johanson got Dr. Mandanhi on the phone only minutes after Jefferson had hung up on Wayne Corrigan.

"Doctor, your report is too weak."

Dr. Mandanhi was nonplussed, and also a little impatient. "Now . . . which report is that, the first one or the second one, or the second version of the first one?"

Claire made a disgusted face only because Dr. Mandanhi would not see it over the phone. "The first version of the second report, the one establishing that Amber is in too delicate a mental condition to be deposed or to testify."

"And what do you mean when you say it is too weak?"

"It just doesn't have enough persuasiveness; it would be too easy for the defense to play down. Corrigan is going to ask for a hearing to decide whether or not Amber should be made to testify, and we need something stronger to present to the court."

Mandanhi paused a moment. He was clearly unhappy. "Ms. Johanson, we've been down this path before. You didn't think my first report was strong enough either!"

"Well, it's the way things go—"

"Ms. Johanson, when you first brought me into this, I gave my fairest, most objective opinion regarding Amber's condition. I agreed with you and with the child's mother that the child had suffered harm. Why wasn't that enough?"

Claire was feeling the pressure from above and now from this doctor below. "Because, Dr. Mandanhi, in a court of law an argument has to be forceful, it has to have overwhelming power to persuade. Your first version was too . . . too . . ."

"Too factual?" Mandanhi suggested. "You would rather I lied and fabricated additional trauma just to win a court ruling?"

"Not fabricate, doctor. Enhance maybe, just make your opinions more forceful."

"Well, I feel I did that with my first report. I gave you what you wanted, and I think more than the facts warranted. Now you want me to do that again?"

Claire hesitated. Then she snapped, "With the facts at hand your second report could be enhanced. Make it stronger, make it persuasive! It shouldn't be too hard to show how the stress on Amber would cause her permanent psychological harm."

"Are you asking me to lie?"

"I'm asking you to use the facts, be an advocate, and protect Amber. She must not testify!"

Sally got her appointment with Professor Samuel W. Lynch, and made it to his office on time at 6 in the evening. It was an odd hour, but he was usually in his office at this time anyway and would be happy to see her.

He had a new office now, on the second floor of Whitcombe Hall, the main hub of the Bentmore School of Education. Whitcombe Hall was a newer structure of steel, marble, and glass and towered ten stories over the rest of the campus. Apparently Bentmore was proud of its contributions to education and wanted to display that pride in a big way.

Room 210 was more than just a room; it was the whole north end of the floor, divided off by a wall of glass with impressive double doors. The secretary was working late as well, and could look through that glass wall from where she sat and see anyone coming down the hall. She saw Sally the moment Sally got off the elevator, but she didn't seem to linger on the sight too long. That was comforting.

Sally pushed through the doors and tried to address the secretary from a distance. "April Freeman to see Professor Lynch."

The lady smiled and nodded. "Yes, the woman from the *Register*?"

"That's me."

"All right, fine." She picked up her telephone and pressed a button. "The lady from the *Register* is here to see you." She looked at Sally. "He'll be right with you. Go ahead and have a seat."

Sally stood near the couch in the waiting area, but did not sit in it. She was too uncomfortable to sit, and apt to run. The fib about being a reporter from the campus newspaper was working so far, but if anyone should think to call the *Bentmore Register* office to check on any of this, her disguise was history. Besides that, a man was already sitting there, and she'd caught him looking at her once, even though he was supposedly reading a magazine. Maybe he was reading that magazine, but maybe he wasn't. What was he doing here at 6 in the evening? The way she felt right now, every person in that place was a potential killer.

Her heart was pounding; if her hands shook much more, it would show. She tried to take some deep breaths to steady herself.

"Miss Freeman!"

That voice! After twelve years she still remembered it. She turned.

There stood Professor Samuel W. Lynch. Oh! That tremble was so great, it had to show! She stiffened her body to remain steady, forced a smile, and extended her hand. "Hello."

He shook her hand. "A pleasure. Come this way."

He turned, and she followed him back toward his office.

This wasn't right. It wasn't twelve years later. It had to be twelve years *ago*. He hadn't changed. He was still the same, distinguished, overweight, gray-haired gentleman, the same articulate pedagogue she'd admired. She would have recognized him anywhere.

Was she as familiar to him? Hundreds of students must have passed through his life since she was last here; surely her face would be lost behind all the others.

He led her into his office and offered her a comfortable, padded chair. She sat immediately and found herself looking up at just about everything. The book-lined walls in this room towered so high overhead that she felt she was sitting in the bottom of a deep well. The room was dead silent, like a crypt.

Lynch took a seat behind his desk and relaxed for a moment, studying her face, his hands clasped in front of his chest.

She looked back at him and tried to smile. She was beginning to feel the silence. This wasn't right. Someone should be saying something by now.

"So you're with the *Register*?" he asked, still relaxed, leaning back in his chair.

"Yes, I just started this quarter."

"And what is your major?"

"Um . . . economics."

He smiled. "Good enough. What do you think of Professor Parker?"

Oh-oh. Was this a test? Who was Professor Parker? Was it a he or a she? Was Parker even alive?

Sally fumbled. "Oh . . . I still get the profs mixed up. I just transferred in . . ."

He laughed. "No matter. You'll get to know them, and I'm sure they'll get to know you. You'll find we're a cordial institution, one big family. Where are you from, anyway?"

She was using a phony accent. "Oh, uh, Knoxville, Tennessee."

Sally opened her notebook just for something to do, something to fill the awkward, empty time. Her mind had suddenly gone blank as if a dark cloud had entered it. One moment she knew what she was going to say, and the next moment she felt that part of her brain had died.

And Professor Lynch was just sitting there, not saying a word. Silence filled the room like deep water; the warm, stuffy air pressed in on all sides.

"Uh . . . I just wanted to ask you some questions . . ." Sally said, pulling a notebook from her carry bag and leafing through it. Where were the questions? She'd written several down, but now . . . "I'm just trying to find my questions; I had them here somewhere."

"Don't be nervous," said Lynch. "I won't bite you."

She laughed. So he'd noticed! "Thank you. I'm still a bit new at this." She found the questions. "Oh! Here we go. I thought it would be interesting to track down a Bentmore success story and do an article about Owen Bennett."

He smiled. "Ahhh . . . That would make an interesting story. Owen Bennett is a fascinating man."

"He was a professor here for many years, I understand."

"Oh, yes! But say, would you excuse me for just a moment?"

"Certainly."

He rose from his chair and hurried from the room, leaving her alone in the bottom of this dark, oppressive well.

The silence closed in again, heavier than ever. She had trouble breathing, as if her chest were collapsing, as if the air were too thick to inhale. It had to be her imagination, the stress, the nervousness.

She closed her eyes and opened them again. The room still seemed dark. Maybe darker.

High above her, the walls holding hundreds of books on all those shelves looked like they were leaning more and more toward the center of the room. It was a wonder all the books—and some of them were massive—weren't sliding off the shelves and crashing down on her. At the same time, the ceiling, distant as it was, seemed to be receding even further away, making this well, this pit, this trap all the more deep.

Sally closed her eyes. She did not want to believe that her old tormentors were lurking about. She could not accept that she might be trapped in this pit with them, with no escape, helpless, with no choice but to wait for the first clap of their invisible jaws.

But try as she could, she could not shake this . . . this *presence*. No, it wasn't the walls and the books that were closing in. These illusions were only born out of a devouring, inner terror. There was something else oozing into this room, something from her childhood nightmares—that steady, unrelenting, slowly advancing *thing* of terror, that bogeyman, that monster, that unseen, voracious, undefeatable enemy she could never run fast enough to escape from. It was here somewhere, hiding behind the books, maybe wriggling through them, staring at her, watching her shrink into the chair, watching her tremble and sweat.

Her palms were leaving wet patches on the arms of the chair. Her skin was crawling.

She had to get out of here. She'd made a mistake; she'd

walked into a death trap. This room was alive with evil, about to crush her.

She saw it! A cry escaped from her throat before she could stop it. Just behind the desk, directly opposite from where she sat, a row of angry, golden eyes glared at her from the bookshelf. Her own eyes blinked shut. She thought better of that, and opened them again.

They were still there, not moving. But . . . no. They were not eyes. She exhaled slowly and tried with all her might to steady her emotions and her thoughts. She looked at them deliberately; she gazed at them, even challenged them.

They were four golden symbols on the spines of four ornately bound volumes. They still seemed to be staring at her. She tried to stifle her imagination. She had to be objective about this.

She leaned toward them. They were faces. Ghastly, triangular faces, all staring, all seemingly snarling at her. Little gargoyles. Deep, vacant eyes, almost like sockets. Bared teeth. High, shining foreheads.

Her heart began to race. Her mouth dropped open, and she stared transfixed. With fingers numbed and fumbling, she pulled at the chain around her neck. The two rings emerged from hiding and she held them side by side in front of her face, looking at them and then beyond them at the faces on the four volumes.

Identical.

twenty-eight

When Lynch returned to his office, he found his guest looking quite wilted and noticeably white.

"Are you feeling all right?" he asked.

She smiled weakly. "Oh, to be honest, I think I'm battling a little bit of flu or something."

"Oh, I'm very sorry. Let's try to proceed with this interview as quickly as possible, then."

Sally didn't feel like proceeding, but she did. She got out her pen, and prepared to take some notes.

Lynch started talking without any questions. "As you must know, Owen Bennett was a law professor here for several years, and a good friend to all of us. He was adventuresome, innovative, intelligent . . ."

This moving tribute to Owen Bennett continued for several minutes. Sally wrote it all down as best she could, hoping desperately to find some point where she could just cut it off, thank Professor Lynch, and get out of there.

Professor Lynch had been sitting in his chair, turned slightly away from Sally, looking at the books on the wall and speaking in fluid sentences, his fingers spread and his hands bouncing against each other, fingertip to fingertip. Now, with hardly any pause at all, but with a strange, ominous change in his tone, he turned his chair toward Sally and continued his comments. "Now, it was in that particular year that Owen, having completed the initial structuring of the Law Advisement Council and having entrusted its administration to capable hands, took up another, even more pioneering challenge, that of serving on the advisory board for a new visionary effort: The Omega Center for Educational Studies, located in Fairwood, Massachusetts."

Sally wrote it down. She noticed that he stopped to watch her write it down.

"This came as a surprise to some people. They asked, 'What interest could you possibly have in that place?' For a man of

Owen's professional stature, such a role on the advisory board of an obscure, metaphysical institution seemed a condescension.

"But they didn't know Owen as his closer friends did. Those who knew Owen well knew that he was a master of the politics of power; he understood that power can be a commodity to be sold in exchange for favors and more power, a bribe that can be slipped to the right people to accomplish a certain agenda, and even a lever to control the wills and purposes of underlings or professional enemies. He was already welcome in the company of legislators and judges, corporate executives and politicians, all the *right* people who could make the right things happen in the right places for anyone who had enough influence with which to bargain. Owen had influence, but taking this position gave him even more.

"The Omega Center, you understand, is a center for the facilitation of change in our society. As a man thinks, so is he. Change the way he thinks, and you change the man. Change the way a society thinks, and you change the society. The Omega Center is dedicated to changing the way our society thinks, and hence changing our society, beginning with its most vulnerable and moldable segment: its children.

"That, Ms. Freeman, was the kind of thing that could attract Owen as honey attracts bees. If such an institution as the Omega Center can actually play a part in controlling what our society will become, then it would be most beneficial to be one of the people who control the Omega Center. Owen Bennett became one of those controllers, a controller of a controller! Now he had something others would want."

Lynch turned his chair so that he was facing Sally directly. "But of course you know all that. It's one of the simplest principles of survival in this world: if you want to get ahead, have friends in high places." His eyes narrowed, and a grin—it looked malicious—slowly spread on his face. "As an example, I can recall a student I had some time ago, an extremely bright young lady who actually spent several summers at the Omega Center before she started her studies

here at Bentmore. She came here with a high recommendation from the Omega Center, and we were happy to give her
special attention. She remained here until she earned her
Master's degree in education and then, wouldn't you know it,
she desired to return to the Omega Center and be a part of
that dream.

"Fortunately, she and Owen Bennett were the closest of
friends, and by that time he was on the Omega advisory
board, so her position with the Omega Center was an instant
reality." He laughed and leaned on his elbows. "So you see,
even as I have taught my students, it does help to have friends
with influence to offer, especially in a field where you may be
changing a society against its will."

Sally smiled and jotted down some notes. He just kept staring at her.

She was finished. *Very* finished. All she wanted was to get
out of there. "Thank you so much for your insights. I'd like to
take this home now and organize it. Perhaps I can call you
again?"

"Oh, just one more thing!" he insisted, gesturing for her to
remain seated. "Yes, friends in the right places are important,
and power is definitely a tool, but you must remember never
to be too close to your friends, because any weapon, any lever
you may use to gain power over others, can also be used to
gain power over *you* unless you take necessary precautions. I
know of one man, a skilled, upcoming young attorney, who
allowed a lady friend of questionable background to know
him just a little too well, and she later attempted to use that
knowledge as a lever against him. It created a most ticklish
situation! Do you understand?"

She was on the edge of her seat, ready to stand and walk
out of there. "Well, yes, like blackmail, I suppose."

He brightened at her correct answer. "Yes, that's it exactly!
In gaining power over others, you never want to rule out
blackmail as one lever to get what you want or to protect
yourself!" He suddenly reached into his pocket and brought
out a small jewelry box. "This is why I stepped out of the
office momentarily. I knew you'd be interested in this."

He flipped it open and showed her the contents.

It was a gold ring. The same gargoyle.

Professor Lynch's voice grew quiet and somber. "This young lawyer hired his lady friend to kill someone. Yes, that's right, *kill* someone, and he paid her a large sum of money to do it. But she was subtle and clever; she stole a very personal item of his, his sacred ring, knowing that forever afterward she would be able, should she have the need, to prove that she had had an alliance with him. She wore the ring on her person when she tried to carry out the grisly deed, and we have good reason to believe she carried the money on her person as well so that, should something go wrong, she would be found with it and a connection could be made to the one who hired her. At any rate, the ring was identical to this one and, with the money, was a perfect lever to blackmail and manipulate him."

He let her view it for just a moment, and then abandoned all cordiality when he demanded, "You do have the ring in your possession, don't you?"

She rose to her feet but wobbled there, feeling faint, light-headed with terror. Words wouldn't come. There weren't any words.

"I . . . Thank you, sir," she said, nausea washing over her. "I need to go now."

She hurried to the door and threw it open.

The man from the waiting area! He was no longer reading a magazine—now he filled the doorway, blocking her escape!

Lynch spoke to her coldly. "This is Mr. Khull, a highly motivated individual now in our employ. We knew there was a probability you would be here next, and so we invited Mr. Khull to be on hand should it happen. Why don't you have a seat again so we can complete this interview . . . Sally Beth Roe?"

Khull leaned toward her. She backed away until she bumped into her chair, then sank into it.

Lynch sat down and glared at her for several moments.

"So what do you hear from Jonas these days?" he finally asked.

She looked at him for the first time since she sat down. There seemed to be no reason to carry on her act. The Tennessee accent vanished. "He's gone. I haven't channeled him since I went to prison."

Lynch smiled. "I imagine he felt there were more respectable people to work with, not vile, pitiful baby-killers."

She looked down in shame and defeat. She no longer knew how to defend herself.

"Yours is a pitiful story," said Lynch. "I had such great hopes for you. I groomed you, I honed you myself, I made you what you are—excuse me, *were*. You were a born leader, Sally. We were counting on you. Owen was counting on you. Such marvelous potential, such incredible spiritual connections!" He paused just to look at her forlorn frame. "But oh, how you toppled! Oh, how you fell!"

Perhaps it was hate that gave her the strength to say, "I didn't fall far enough, I guess. That woman you were talking about, who stole the man's ring—I take it she's the one who tried to kill me?"

He was not at all disturbed about it. "So I've heard. But that brings us back to my original question: What did you do with the ring you took from your attacker's finger?"

She couldn't think of a good enough lie, so she said nothing.

He nodded in response. "Of course. You're not going to tell me. As we've already discussed, you took it for insurance, for . . ." He couldn't help laughing. "For leverage! Oh, Sally, as your teacher I feel condemned!" He reached over and picked up the little jewelry box, eyeing the ring inside it. "Fine, fine. You don't have to tell me. Now that we have you, the ring doesn't matter. But really . . ." He looked at her and laughed as if he'd seen a joke. "Why do you want to help that pitiful little teacher in Bacon's Corner? What good could you possibly do?"

Now he circled his desk and stood above her, making her feel even smaller. "Do you feel guilty perhaps? Now, that would be so unlike you, Sally." His voice went down in tone, and every word cut like a knife. "Since when does guilt mean

335

anything to you, a murderous wench bereft of conscience? As for Tom Harris, you will never find a more insignificant nothing! He is garbage, like you! And what can garbage offer to garbage? Who would believe a word you said? Who would give you the time of day?" He laughed, genuinely amused. "But I can understand your infatuation with the man; you make a perfect pair: a child killer and a pedophile!"

He was trying to cut her down, and even through her weakness and torment she was beginning to resent it. "What happens now?"

He circled back around to his chair and sat down, letting her wait for an answer. "First, some advice which will probably go unheeded, but maybe not. I strongly suggest, Sally, that you abandon this escapade of yours, whatever your intentions. Find another little farm somewhere near another obscure little town, and disappear—forever."

He seemed so relaxed. A moment passed, and nothing happened. Nothing was said.

Sally looked at him, then at the sinister Khull, and then back at Lynch again. She felt too weak to get out of the chair; she was helpless regardless of the answer to her question. "Are you going to kill me?"

He smiled. "You are one scared little waif. Well, it will be good for you. It will provide incentive for you to seriously consider your options. There are only two: Find a deep, deep hole somewhere, Sally, and disappear into it. Let us not see your face again in this life. Or, consider your life ended altogether, perhaps today, perhaps tomorrow, but most certainly."

He nodded to Khull, who stepped away from the door. With a glance back at Sally, he released her to go.

She reached down and picked up her carry bag. Then she pushed her way out of the chair, found strength for the first step, then the next, then enough strength to get to the door.

"Sally!" Lynch called.

She wasn't about to stop. Khull made sure she did.

"Don't ever blame Jonas for what happened. *You* did it, Sally. *You* are the one to blame!"

"I know that, sir," she replied.

"Disappear, Sally. Disappear!"

She went through the door, then found new strength to quicken her step down the hall to the big glass doors. She got through them.

Then she ran. Tears started to blur her eyes. With her renewing strength she realized how terrified she was. She could never wait for the elevator. She took the stairs.

Tal had some special warriors busy at a dairy far away. He needed to shake things up in a home near the Bentmore campus.

Marv and Claudia Simpson were just starting to enjoy this short stay with their daughter and son-in-law when the phone rang.

"It's Mack, at the dairy," his daughter Jessica said.

Marv scowled and took the phone. "Okay, Mack, break it to me gently."

"Marv," said Mack, "you'd better get back here. Lizzy's getting ready to drop that calf now!"

"Now? She's a week early!"

"And the milking machine is on the fritz too. I don't know what's wrong with it!"

Marv grimaced. "Oh, great!"

"And that stupid tractor won't start for anything!"

"Doggone! Ed and I were planning to go to the ball game tonight!"

"Well, it's your dairy. Do what you want."

"Oh, right, sure, some choice I've got!" He looked at Claudia, who only shook her head in sad resignation. "All right, we'll get going right away, but we're going to have to drive all night."

"Well, I'll try to hold down the fort until you get here. Sorry to interrupt your visit."

"Yeah . . ."

Marv hung up, questioning why God would allow such things to happen at such inopportune times.

Mota stood in the room, making sure things happened. *Come, Marv, be quick about it!*

Khull took a moment to relax in the same chair where Sally had sat, and listened to Professor Lynch's side of a long-distance conversation.

"Mr. Goring, I was disappointed. She was hardly the formidable foe she seems to be in her letters. A breeze would have knocked her over. That's right." He listened for a moment, then forwarded a question to Khull. "How many men do you have tailing her?"

Khull answered quickly. "Five around the building, five more on the main campus walks."

Lynch brought back an answer. "Well covered. After today, the saga of Sally Roe will be over. Yes. I'll bring you word as soon as I know. Oh, and will you want the ring back?" He chuckled. "I guess I can always flush it down the toilet. Then Bardine and his ring will be together!" He took some time to laugh at that wisecrack, and apparently Goring was laughing at it too.

Khull laughed for about half the time, then stopped abruptly.

Lynch started his good-bye. "Very well, then. Happy to be of service. Yes. Give my regards to everyone at Summit. Yes, I'll see you all at the conference. All right. Good-bye." He hung up the phone and leaned back in his chair. "Oh, such a nasty business!" He looked at Khull. "But I suppose you Satanists take it all in stride?"

"We are *all* killers at heart, Professor Lynch."

"Well, I hope you just do it quickly, and spare me the details!"

"It's too bad you let her go."

"Don't be silly. I don't want it happening anywhere near here. I can't let anyone in this office suspect I had anything to do with it."

"Well, maybe you thought she was weak and helpless, but it looks like she was still clever enough to rip you off."

Lynch looked toward Khull, then followed his gaze to the bookshelf behind the desk.

Khull announced even as Lynch noticed it, "Looks like she took your rosters."

The four volumes that bore the strange symbol of the snarling gargoyle were gone, leaving a distressing gap.

"Destroyer!" said Tal, and all the warriors looked. Yes, there he was, swooping over the campus like a huge, black hawk. "He'll take her this time!"

Guilo pointed with his sword to a huge, black shape rising from the Administration Building. "Corrupter! He's slow, but he sees well!"

"Keep him busy and out of our business!" Then Tal started barking orders as warriors shot into the sky in all directions. "Scion, decoys! Chimon, stay with her. Signa, back him up! Nathan, Armoth, block the bus stop! Cree and Si, set screens!"

Lynch grabbed Khull's arm. He was desperate. "Khull, make sure your men succeed! They must succeed!"

Khull looked at Lynch, then at the gap in the bookshelf, and smiled a wicked smile. "Hm. You must be pretty scared."

Destroyer could see a tiny, frightened figure bursting out of Whitcombe Hall. "Hmm. So how strong are you now, Captain Tal? We will make you show us." He called to his captains, "Take her!"

"There she is!" said one thug to his partner. He'd spotted Sally running from Whitcombe Hall, heading south toward the nearest bus stop. It was dark. They could take her into any of the gardens, alleyways, or groves and finish her instantly.

They were large, burly men, heavily tattooed; one had a deep scar on his left cheek; both wore a large earring in one ear. Beneath their dark leather coats, they carried the shining silver tools of ritual death.

The second one put a portable radio to his jaw and muttered, "She's—"

He was about to say which direction she was going, but suddenly she was gone.

Both men bolted from their hiding-place and stood in the middle of the walkway. Sally Roe had vanished.

Cree and Si stood directly in front of them, wings outstretched. Behind them, Sally continued to run south.

A shriek from the sky! The two warriors shot a glance south. Sally was dashing down some steps, dropping out of sight. Above them, four demon warriors dropped like falcons. Cree and Si bolted, one this way, one that, disappearing in a flash of light into the buildings on either side of the walkway. The demons went after them.

"The woman!" screamed Destroyer from the sky. "Get the woman!"

The demons spun in tight circles, their red blades streaming fire, and kicked the two men in their backs. *Move! This way!* Then they shot down the campus, the walls, windows, and walkways a blur on either side, their black wings screaming.

The two thugs ran after them.

"She was heading south," the man barked into his radio.

Corrupter rose above the campus with the agility of a hot air balloon, watching the incredible spectacle on every side. He spotted Sally and pointed. "There! There—do you see her?"

A bolt of light came from somewhere, delivering such a blow to his head that he tumbled backward, end over end, like a helpless, spinning beach ball, wailing and howling.

Guilo knew he'd be out of the way for a while. He darted away with other things to do.

Sally took only a few seconds to duck into some shrubs and retrieve her hidden duffel bag. She jammed her carry bag into it and continued running.

She rounded a corner near the Psych Library, saw the bus

stop illuminated by an amber street lamp, dashed that way, slipped and stumbled to a stop, and dashed back the other way.

The bus stop was covered. Somehow she knew who those two men were.

Run! said Nathan. *The other way!*

Armoth took the blows from the two demons guarding the bus stop just long enough to slow them down. They didn't want him—they wanted Sally Roe.

Two more normal-looking killers were at their post by the Memorial Fountain. One saw through the vertical jets of water and spotted the woman running north toward the Sculpture Garden.

"Heading north!" he barked into his radio. "The Sculpture Garden!"

Sally was heading west—not north—toward the Physical Sciences Building when she ducked behind a tree to hide from four fierce-looking characters running north toward the Sculpture Garden. As soon as they had passed, she headed west again.

"Where'd she go?" a killer asked, looking this way and that.

The Sculpture Garden contained plenty of weird sculptures in stone and steel, but no fleeing woman.

Scion, looking like himself again, took wing and swooped out of the Sculpture Garden with four black bats hot on his tail. As soon as he cleared the roofs, still trailing a stream of light, Si crossed that stream with a searing trail of his own and drew aside two of the demons. At least these buzzards would be busy for a while.

Sally ran past the Physical Sciences Building, over a plaza, and then down a long flight of concrete stairs to the busy street below. A taxi was approaching. She waved furiously. "Taxi! Taxi!"

Two men, looking like any other university students, spotted her and started her way.

The cab driver thought he saw someone trying to flag him.

Two demons dropped through the roof and clawed through his brain.

Huh? Eh, she isn't there . . . Now where was I going, anyway?

The taxi drove by, swerving from lane to lane, not slowing. Sally bolted into an alley.

It was a blind alley—sheer concrete walls and no escape.

The two men closed in behind her, silent, skillful. If they moved quickly enough, they could finish her before she had a chance to scream. One had a long scarf in his hands, the other held a gleaming knife.

Filthy spirits were there too, whooping and frothing, bouncing off the walls like golf balls down a gutter. This was it!

Mota rode on the roof of Marv Simpson's ranch wagon as it rolled lazily down Hannan Boulevard on the south end of the Bentmore campus. When it came to a corner, Mota's wings burst forth like fireworks and the next thing Marv knew, he was in a right-turn-only lane and had to turn right, heading up the campus's west side.

"Doggone," he muttered.

"Weren't we supposed to go the other way?" Claudia asked.

But he was looking this way and that and trying to change lanes, getting more and more frustrated. "Now how do we get out of *here*?"

Sally backed away until she came up against the sheer, featureless concrete at the end of the alley. So much for flight. Now for fight. She raised her duffel bag to shield herself.

No sound, only shadows blurring in the street lights. The scarf hit her face, her head hit the wall, one eye was covered, she couldn't see.

A knife flashed!

Chimon was there and parried.

The knife deflected and lodged in the duffel bag.

A blow to her neck! She pitched forward, grabbing the knife man. He pulled the blade free and plunged it at her again.

The knife ripped through her coat. Her scream was muffled inside the scarf.

A searing blade opened Chimon's shoulder. Two demons caught his backhanded sword and dissolved.

The knife slashed Sally's coat open, but missed her flesh.

Scion came in low, ducked under a cluster of lashing, hacking spirits, and rolled into the knife man's legs. He fell backward. The knife clinked on the concrete. Scion had rolled into the middle of a death trap. Twisting and spinning, he was able to fend off most of the demons' blows, but one wild blade caught his leg, cutting it deep.

Chimon had a screaming, flopping, slobbering demon by the feet. He batted Scion's attackers away in one powerful swing, then whipped the flailing body over his head and smacked the scarf man in the face.

The scarf slipped away. Sally could see again. She lunged forward and broke free.

The knife man grabbed her coat sleeve.

Signa dropped out of the sky, tracing an exclamation point of light. His sword caught the seam at Sally's shoulder and the sleeve tore away.

She ran. Alive!

The knife man was looking for his knife. The scarf man couldn't tell where he was in the dark.

Chimon, Scion, and Signa were cut, bruised, and limping, but they grabbed hold of Sally and got her out of that alley.

Destroyer saw it all, and screamed for his hordes. The spirits gathered from every corner of the campus, swords burning, wings roaring, ready for a kill. With Destroyer at the point of a massive arrowhead formation, they dove toward the street.

In Bacon's Corner, Lucy ran into Amber's bedroom expecting blood, bruises, an accident, something horrible.

It was nothing of the kind. The child was beside herself, screaming, cursing, pounding the walls.

343

"Amber, what's wrong?" her mother cried, trying to embrace her.

She spun around like a vicious animal and stood apart from her mother, her fingers curved like claws, her eyes wild and glaring, darting about the room as if watching distant events. "Cut her up! Grab her, take her, cut her up!"

Lucy backed into the wall and remained there, speechless. There was no stopping Amethyst when she was like this. She'd tried before.

Destroyer and his hordes were screaming out their war cry, their sulfurous breath forming yellow streamers that etched the sky like comb's teeth.

Marv Simpson was looking for a place to turn around and getting more and more frustrated. He hardly noticed that woman running out of the alley.

"Oh my," said Claudia, "what's going on here?"

Tal dropped through the roof and filled the whole backseat with his massive frame. *Stop and pick her up!*

Marv saw her again. She was actually running into the street.

"Oh!" Claudia exclaimed, "she's coming toward us!"

"Oh, man, a nut case! We've got to get out of here—"

Tal grabbed Marv's head in his two huge hands and forced him to look toward the woman. *PICK HER UP!*

"Let's pick her up," said Claudia.

He pulled over.

Guilo shot into the sky, flanked by Nathan, Armoth, Cree, and Si. They intercepted Destroyer and his henchmen like a clap of thunder over the campus. The demons were like an irresistible wall, and the angelic warriors went tumbling and spinning aside. Destroyer and his horde resumed their course, dropping toward that station wagon; the five warriors recovered, circled, and dove down on the demons' backs like falcons. The vile spirits fought them off, but they had to take precious time to do it.

"Need a ride?"

Sally pulled the door open and clambered into the backseat. "Please. Get me away from here!"

Four men appeared on the sidewalk, two with radios. They saw her get into the car and quickly disappeared.

Marv was still lost. "How do I get out of here?"

"Left, up at the corner," said Sally, "and then go under the tunnel."

"Tunnel?"

Destroyer and his warriors skimmed over the top of the Physical Sciences Building and dropped toward the street, closing in on the station wagon. Tal and Mota clung to the car's roof, swords ready, wings covering the passengers inside. Then Guilo shot out from a side street, Nathan and Armoth whipped around a bank building, Scion dropped from an overpass, Chimon and Signa weaved among the cars only inches above the pavement, Si came up through a manhole, and they all pounced on the car, covering every square inch of it, their drawn swords making it look like a glowing porcupine.

This would be it, a direct, power-for-power battle!

But suddenly, surprisingly, Destroyer pulled out of his dive and followed only twenty feet above them, passing through the traffic lights, telephone lines, and street signs, keeping an eye on them, sizing them up. The sight of the small band of warriors clinging to the vehicle, swords drawn for a last stand, made him laugh. It made his henchmen laugh.

Finally he shouted to them, "Call it a victory, captain! *I* call it progress! You are weaker than ever now, and the next time will be ours. The fruit will be ripe, and we will pluck it down with ease! And don't concern yourself with hiding her. We will always know where she is!"

They climbed into the night sky and were just disappearing into the darkness when the car went into the tunnel.

"What now?" Chimon asked, holding his wounded shoulder.

"Name it, cap," said Scion, holding his useless leg. "We'll do it."

"We are spent," said Tal. "Even though we confused Khull's men, Destroyer could have taken us, and it's only by the hand of the Lord that he didn't know it. It's time we hid her in Ashton."

"And let her hear of the Cross!" said Nathan.

"We'll get her there and let the Spirit speak to her." Then he added with an unabashed anger, "While we get back to Bacon's Corner and root out this prayer blockage once and for all!"

"Uh," asked Marv, "where you headed?"

Sally was gasping for breath, sick with terror, and dripping with sweat. She was not entirely rational. "I don't care. Anywhere. Anywhere away from here."

Claudia looked over her shoulder at the pitiful creature slumped over in the backseat, weeping, panting, dripping with sweat. "You poor dear!"

Marv looked at her through the rearview mirror and could see the fear in her eyes. The Lord spoke to his heart. Yep, it was no accident that he'd picked her up. "Well, you just take it easy and try to rest. We'll get you far away from here. I know just the place."

twenty-nine

LUCY Brandon was feeling weak and ill, but trying not to show it, even as she scribbled a forwarding address on still another letter from Sally Roe and slipped the letter into the bag of outgoing mail. She didn't want to do it, but she could see no alternative. Her lawyers were pressuring her, her friends at LifeCircle were smiling and encouraging her, Sergeant Mulligan was watching her, the lawsuit was moving full speed ahead, and the momentum was overpowering, carrying her along like a runaway train.

But after no less than twenty of these letters, she'd seen enough. She was afraid, she was ignorant of legal strategy, and perhaps she was a little too trusting and gullible, but she wasn't stupid. There was no question in her mind that Sally Roe was alive.

The more she thought about that, the more devastating it became. Gradually, just one small idea at a time, she was allowing herself to think the unthinkable: something more than a lawsuit was in progress and she was being lied to by someone, maybe everyone. If she was being lied to, she was probably breaking the law for all her friends and not for herself. If all that were true, then—she'd tried to bury this thought for weeks—she was being used.

She had no question that her daughter Amber was being used, if not by these legal eagles, then certainly by that once-cute little pony Amber had befriended in Miss Brewer's fourth-grade class. The laughter, the fun and games, the cartoon-character charm were all things of the past. Amethyst was no friend of any kind.

But now Lucy was in so deep, how could she back out? What direction could she turn? How—

The bell rang at the front desk. Debbie was on her break, so Lucy hurried to the front.

This big man looked familiar. She'd seen him around

town, but he wasn't from around here. She immediately felt uncomfortable.

"Can I help you?"

"Hi. I'm Marshall Hogan. I'm a friend of Tom Harris, and I just got a letter here from the Omega Center for Educational Studies in Fairwood, Massachusetts . . ."

He acted like he was giving her a cue, but she didn't catch whatever it was. "Yes? Is there a problem?"

"Well . . . I suppose you know that they're the publishers of the *Finding the Real Me* curriculum that Miss Brewer uses at the elementary school?"

"I still don't see your point."

"Well, I wrote to the Omega Center to order a copy of the *Finding the Real Me* curriculum, and they tell me here in this letter that they only make that curriculum available to educational institutions, and not to the general public. Don't you think that's a little strange?"

Lucy knew she didn't want to talk about this. "I'm not the Omega Center, sir, and I'm not responsible for their policies. Now unless you have some business with the Post Office . . ."

Marshall looked behind him. No one else was standing in line. "I'll just be a second. Let's talk about that local group, uh, LifeCircle. I understand that LifeCircle is a major force in education around here: three of the school board belong to it, the principal of the elementary school—Mr. Woodard—belongs to it, Miss Brewer belongs to it, and you belong to it. The school board adopted the Omega Center curriculum, Mr. Woodard implemented it, Miss Brewer's teaching it, and your daughter Amber contacted her inner guide, Amethyst, because of it."

Only a week ago Lucy would have felt invaded, and very angry. Today was different. "What about it?" She really wanted to know.

She was trying to look strong and unshakable, but Marshall caught the curiosity in her eyes. "Let me ask you this: Why do you suppose Miss Brewer couldn't produce the curriculum when we asked to see it, and neither could Mr. Woodard, and neither could the school board, and now the

Omega Center itself won't allow me to order a copy of it? When I consider how all you people are connected, it sure makes me wonder if your lawsuit against the Good Shepherd Academy might have something to do with it. Do you suppose there's something in that curriculum your friends don't want us to see?"

Lucy didn't answer for a long moment. She'd never thought about the question before. She wanted an answer herself. "I don't know, Mr. . . . ."

"Hogan. Marshall Hogan."

"What are you, an investigator or something?"

"Sure, something like that. Mostly just a friend of your opponents in this lawsuit."

"Well, obviously I can't talk about any of this."

"I understand. Thank you very much for your time."

"You're welcome."

He left the building, and Lucy returned to her work, or at least tried to return to it. If she was pensive and troubled before her visit with this Mr. Hogan, now she was totally distracted. What else did that man know, and why didn't she know it?

Marshall got back to Ben and Bev's, and placed a collect long-distance call.

Back at his newspaper, a young, pretty, bespectacled brunette answered the phone from inside Marshall's glass-enclosed office. "*Ashton Clarion*, Bernice Krueger speaking."

"Hey, Bernice, this is Marshall."

"Well, well!" She closed the office door against the outside clamor and plopped down at his desk, ready for the latest. "Can any good news come out of Bacon's Corner?"

"Well . . . the walls of the fort are getting thin, but no breakthroughs yet."

"Keep digging."

"That's why I called. You remember I told you about that curriculum at the elementary school?"

"Right. The kids getting into alpha mind control and spirit-guides. Did you ever get a copy of it?"

"No dice. They're stonewalling it, as far up the ladder as Omega itself. Are you still in touch with that guy in Washington, what's-his-name . . . ?"

"Cliff Bingham. Sure. He got me some inside stuff on the last election."

"I'm wondering if he couldn't check with the Library of Congress and find an original copy of this thing."

Bernice grabbed a pen and started writing herself a note. "I'll call him. What exactly do you want?"

"*Finding the Real Me*, a curriculum for fourth-graders."

She wrote it down. "Published by Omega Center . . ."

"Uh . . . Omega Center for Educational Studies, Fairwood, Massachusetts."

"Any idea what year?"

"Beats me."

"Okay. We will see what we will see."

"Okay, now let's talk about the Tuesday edition. Pull that malt shop story; John likes it, but his wife will have a fit . . ."

They talked business. Bernice took notes, pulled files, read copy over the phone, and got orders from her boss.

Outside, the midweek, midday business in the town of Ashton was in full swing; people, grocery carts, and vehicles were circulating through the parking lot at Carlucci's Market; the fire fighters were hosing down the apron at Station Fifteen and shining up the pumper; Clyde Sodeberg and his sons were beating the still-green concrete off some forms over at the new Midwest Savings and Loan project.

Driving past it all, and then stopping at the second of four lights along Main Street, Marv and Claudia Simpson introduced Sally Beth Roe—they thought her name was Betty Smith—to their town.

"It's a great place to live and do business," said Marv. "At least it is now. We've had our share of trouble, but things have settled down quite a bit, and I think we're having a turn for the better."

The light turned green and Marv piloted the big station

wagon further down the street, past the small stores, the True Value Hardware, the local newspaper . . .

"That's the *Ashton Clarion*," said Marv. "It comes out on Tuesdays and Fridays, and the editor's a saint. I think he's been out of town for a while; I don't know what he's been doing."

They drove past the high school. It was new this year, because enrollment was up.

Marv turned left at the third light and drove up a gradually graded street into a quiet neighborhood with massive oak trees lining the street, small, garishly painted bicycles leaning against the oaks, and orange basketball hoops on every other garage. The lawns were neat, the sidewalks were clean, and the cars all seemed to know their proper parking places.

Marv turned left again and came to a row of large, turn-of-the-century homes with white, beveled siding, large chimneys, massive roofs, cozy dormers, and wide, roomy front porches. He pulled over and parked in front of the third house on the right, probably the most inviting house of all, with a perfectly manicured lawn, colorful planted borders, a pillared front porch, and an inviting porch swing. In front, just beside the walkway, was a small, unpretentious sign: Sara Barker's Boarding House.

"Here's the place I told you about," said Marv.

"It'll be just right, I think," said Claudia. "You'll have time to think things through and get your head clear."

Sally took their hands and held them tightly. "You've done me a wonderful kindness. Thank you very much."

"You're welcome," said Marv. "We'll have you out to the dairy sometime."

"I'd love that."

"Oh, here's Sara now," said Claudia.

"Sara's a good gal; you'll like her."

Sara was, and Sally did. The house actually belonged to Sara and her husband Floyd, but they thought using just her name on the sign would be more charming. Floyd was a tall, thin man of few words who had recently retired from the grain business and was now trying his hand at being a writer when he wasn't serving as the handyman for the boarding house—which he was at the moment. He was glad to meet her and shook her hand warmly. As for Sara, she impressed Sally as everyone's idea of the perfect grandma, a short little woman with close-cropped gray hair, little round glasses, and a cute story about most everything.

"We used to have eight kids, and now they're gone, so we have all these rooms empty and ready for the right people," she explained, showing Sally through the big house. "We've had mostly single women here; some have troubles at home and need to stay away, some are on their way somewhere else—you know, between things—and the two that are here right now are here for keeps until they get married, I suppose."

The living room was old, classic, with a high ceiling, finely milled wainscoting, inviting, comfortable, antique furniture, and even an old pump organ from Ashton's first pioneer church. The dining room was large and well-suited for a big family, or for a houseful of boarders.

"Now, we have a downstairs bathroom, but it's being worked on . . ."

They were in the central hallway just below the big staircase, and they could see a toolbox jutting into the hall through the bathroom door and hear the clunking and tinkering of work going on.

Sara stepped around the toolbox and then out of the way, so Sally could look in. "When we get the plumbing fixed, things should be back to normal."

Sally looked into the bathroom. It was large, and during normal times it was probably very nice. Right now it was a mess; the carpet was rolled back, there were tools and pipe fittings on the floor, a glaring work light hanging from the vanity mirror, and, strangest of all, a young man in coveralls on his knees in front of the toilet—he seemed to be hollering down into the bowl.

"No," he shouted, "come back up! You're going the wrong way!"

A muffled voice—it was Floyd's—came from below somewhere. "Who put all this stuff down here, anyway?"

"You put it in, Floyd; don't blame me!"

Then the young man noticed Sally watching him. "Oh, hi there."

"Hi."

Sara leaned in. "Hank, this is Betty Smith, a new boarder. Betty, this is Hank Busche, our pastor."

He waved a wrench at her. "Pleased to meet you. I'll be happy to shake your hand later." It was clear to see that his hands were quite dirty at the moment.

Sally was fascinated. This was a pastor? "Why are you yelling down the toilet?"

He thought that was funny. "Well . . . that's Floyd down there. Have you met Floyd?"

Floyd's voice came from under the floor. "Yeah. That's Betty, right?"

Hank hollered back. "Yeah."

"We've met."

"She's here to inspect your bolting job."

"Oh, I'm in trouble now!"

Hank explained, "Floyd used the wrong bolts to put this toilet in fifteen years ago, and now we can't get the nuts loose underneath."

Sally's smile was a weary smile, but it felt good.

Sara said, "You're tired. Come on upstairs and I'll show you your room."

But Sally hesitated just a moment. "You don't look like a pastor."

Hank smiled, brushing some hair away from his forehead with his forearm. "Thanks."

Why not go straight to the horse? Sally thought. "I suppose you know God?"

"Sure, I know Him."

He was so matter-of-fact about it. He didn't even hesitate with that answer. Sally tried a tougher question. "Can you prove He exists?"

Hank sat back from the toilet and just looked at her for a moment. "Got a Bible?"

Sally was about to say no, but Sara said, "There's one up in her room."

Hank was thinking. He almost looked like he was listening. "Tell you what. Read Psalm 119, and just ask God to speak to your heart while you read it. See what happens."

"Psalm 119," Sally repeated.

"Right."

"Good luck with the toilet."

"Thanks. And nice to meet you."

Hank sat there a moment after Sally and Sara were gone. The Lord had spoken to him about this woman named Betty.

Floyd's voice came from below, "Psalm 119? What kind of Scripture is that for getting somebody saved?"

Hank was puzzled himself. "I don't know. It's the Scripture the Lord told me to give her."

"The longest chapter in the Bible . . ." Floyd muttered.

Hank prayed, right there. "Lord God, please make Yourself real to Betty Smith. Show her how much You love her."

"Amen," said the voice under the toilet. "Now can you flush me a smaller wrench?"

Atop the house, Tal consulted with the two angelic princes of Ashton, Krioni and Triskal.

"We are honored to see you again, captain," said Krioni. "We'll always remember the victory achieved here."

Tal scanned the horizon and could see the thick hedge of angelic warriors that surrounded the town, sealing it off from demonic invasion. They were there to serve the saints within, responding to their prayers, widening doors of opportunity to minister. The town was not perfect, not without problems; it still had its taverns and turmoils, its scrapes and its sins. But the Lord was working in Ashton, its saints were praying, and for Sally Beth Roe it was safe.

"I leave her in your hands, Krioni. I see Hank is planting the right seeds already."

Triskal smiled. "The Spirit of God is continuing to draw her."

"Care for her in the meantime. Make sure she meets Bernice, but don't let Bernice know who she is until the right time."

Krioni gave Tal a knowing look. "Once again you have a plan. How is it unfolding?"

Tal looked grim. "Steadily, but miserably."

Krioni nodded. "You and the others are going to need some time to heal up, I see."

"Destroyer learned from what we did here. He got to the saints first. He and his demons are wreaking strife and division that church hasn't seen in years, and every day our situation grows more precarious. I'm going back to Bacon's Corner to stop that campaign. Nothing else can proceed until I do."

Triskal's face wrinkled with concern. "But is there time, captain?"

Tal answered simply, "No. We'll just have to do what we can. If you can use this crisis to arouse specific prayer from the saints here, so much the better."

Triskal smiled. "Count on it. They will pray."

Krioni added, "But it sounds like Sally Roe is headed for even greater jeopardy."

Tal nodded, with regret. "We cannot bring the plan up short, or spare her every last step. We will win all . . . or we will lose all."

Krioni and Triskal embraced him. "Godspeed."

Tal drew his sword to rally his warriors, and they shot into the sky, bound for Bacon's Corner.

"Lost?" Destroyer roared. "You dare to tell me you lost her?"

Six loathsome spirits stood before him on the roof of Whitcombe Hall at Bentmore University. They'd locked their eyes on the thick, rolled roofing and refused to look up. They were silent, with no fitting words of explanation. Destroyer and Corrupter were not too far from shredding them this very moment.

Destroyer wanted an explanation, and right now. He grabbed one demon by the hair and jerked his head upward so their eyes would meet. "I knew *you* would never lose her,

355

but follow her to the ends of the earth so we could choose our time, taunt the Host of Heaven, pick the fruit when it was ripe, and now . . . you have lost her? Tell me how!"

"We followed her," the thing said.

"And?"

"She went west with the dairy farmer."

"*And?*"

The spirit looked at his comrades. They wouldn't even return his gaze, lest Destroyer think they knew something. "The farmer took her to Ashton."

Destroyer gave the demon's hair a painful yank, twisting his neck backward. "*Ashton?*"

The demon winced with pain. "We followed as long as we could, but we were turned back."

Destroyer's eyes burned with fury. "The Host of Heaven?"

The warrior was almost falling over, squirming in Destroyer's iron grip. "They hold that territory, they and the saints of God!"

Destroyer released the demon's hair and the warrior dropped to the roof, rotating the kinks out of his neck.

Destroyer and Corrupter moved away to consult privately.

Destroyer was turning the air yellow with his frantic, anxious panting. "That slimy, slippery, subtle Captain of the Host! I should have anticipated this! He is hiding her in a stronghold we cannot penetrate!"

Corrupter muttered, "She is free, and alive, and now has *both* the ring and the rosters."

"The rosters are *your* fault!" Destroyer insisted.

"And her disappearance? Is that not yours?"

"If we lose track of her now . . ."

"That is not an option."

" . . . the Strongman will take both our heads from our bodies with his bare hands!" Destroyer spit sulfur in a new burst of rage. "Never! The Captain of the Host will not defeat me! I will not be humbled by these feeble saints!"

He screamed to his henchmen who stood guard nearby. They snapped to attention.

"Gather your hordes! We return to Bacon's Corner! We will finish this business and decimate the saints, silencing their prayers once and for all!"

Claire Johanson hung up the telephone in her office and then stared at it, motionless, deep in thought.

Jon knew that look on her face. "What is it?"

"That was Mr. Goring, from Summit. Sally Roe showed up at Bentmore. She was right in Samuel Lynch's office."

Jon rose from his chair, anticipating an answer he would not like. "She didn't get away?"

Claire sighed, letting her hand fall to the desk with a slap. "She did. Khull and his men chased her all over the Bentmore campus, but she managed to hitch a ride with some stranger and they lost her."

Jon threw up his hands in anger. "Great. That's just great! I'm really starting to wonder about this Khull. He's had two chances now and came up empty both times!"

Claire cautioned him, "Please keep your voice down. Some LifeCirclers are in the house."

Jon tried to calm himself, but couldn't sit down or relax at all.

"She has the rosters," Claire added.

Jon looked at her curiously. "What rosters?"

"Professor Lynch's membership rosters."

Jon stared at her blankly. He couldn't bring himself to believe it. He shook his head. "Now that has to be a mistake. Somebody's wrong. That isn't true."

"It's true."

He shook his head again, harder. "No, it is not true! It's too unthinkable to be true!"

"Lynch stepped out of the office to get his ring and contact Khull. She must have snatched them from his bookshelf while he was gone. He didn't notice until after she left."

Jon shouted at that. "She *left?*"

Claire shushed him, feeling defensive for Lynch. "He couldn't have her killed right there in his office! Khull's men were supposed to take care of her elsewhere, secretly."

357

Jon fumed and huffed and paced around the office. "Is Professor Lynch still alive?"

"Of course he is."

"Why?"

Claire looked away impatiently. "Jon, what would that solve?"

Jon was having trouble keeping his voice down. "That old codger is a liability! He should be eliminated, and Khull as well!"

Claire sighed and rested her chin in her hand. "Maybe they will be, I don't know. I don't control such things."

"So, when is that hearing?"

"Nine o'clock Monday morning."

Jon cursed. "We should have known by now! There are other forces working on Roe's behalf, directly opposing us. I can feel it. No doubt they're working against this lawsuit as well. We could get a wrong ruling."

Claire was about to disagree, but then decided she couldn't. "I believe that is a possibility."

Jon stopped to give Claire a good look in the eye. "If we lose in this hearing, and they can put Amber on the stand, or even depose her . . ."

Claire agreed. "I'll call the others."

"And Hemphile too. I want her in on this. We have to hit that church!"

"We already have . . ."

"I mean hit them harder! Something right up front!"

Claire stood, her finger to her lips. "Someone might hear you."

He tried to quiet himself. They could hear a LifeCircle yoga class going on upstairs, right above their heads.

Claire had another caution. "You know that with any overt action we'll be risking exposure . . ."

Jon chuckled at that. "Come on. They're old-fashioned, fringe, fanatic Christians. Who's going to believe them?"

She acquiesced. "All right."

"We'll curse the church, and we'll curse Sally Roe. Can we get anything she owns?"

"Well, I guess the rental house still has all her belongings in it."

"Anything alive?"

Claire thought for a moment. "Oh, yes. As a matter of fact, I think she did have some animals."

Jon smiled and calmed a bit. "Good. Good."

thirty

IT was quiet at Floyd and Sara Barker's after dinner. Floyd and Sara were settling into the couch downstairs for some reading; Michelle, the young college girl, was in her room studying; Suzanne, a young attorney just new in town, was out meeting a prospective partner.

Sally was fed, bathed, warm, and secure in her little corner bedroom, snuggled in the soft bed under one of Sara's handmade comforters, her back supported by an ample supply of large pillows.

For the first time in so many years Sally had trouble calculating the number—she finally figured it had to be about twenty-five—she held in her hands a volume she had blamed for the world's woes, belittled as an overrated anthology of myths, resented for its narrow views of morality, condemned as oppressive and authoritarian, and ignored as an outmoded, stagnating lead weight around the intellectual ankle of mankind.

It was one of Sara Barker's Bibles.

She found the book of Psalms immediately. It was in the middle of the Bible.

"Just open your Bibles right to the middle," came a voice from her past. "Psalms is right there in the middle."

What was that woman's name? Oh, Mrs. Gunderson, that's right. She was an older lady. She was old as long as Sally ever knew her, as if she'd hit a peak in years and just stayed there. Every Sunday morning, Sally would clump down the church stairs with all the other seven- and eight-year-olds and gather in Mrs. Gunderson's Sunday school class in that cold church basement, in that small, echoing classroom with the hard wooden chairs and the chalkboard that still bore the unerasable traces of lessons from weeks ago.

Then Mrs. Gunderson would tell them a story, placing paper Bible characters on the same green-grass-and-blue-sky flannel background. Even now, as Sally lay in the bed with the Bible in her lap, she could remember those stories: the wee little man who climbed the sycamore tree, the fishermen who fished all night but caught no fish, the disciple—she thought it was Peter—who walked on the water to meet Jesus, the man named Lazarus whom Jesus raised from the dead, Moses, Noah, and of course Jonah who was swallowed by the fish.

Strange. She'd put those stories out of her mind as far back as junior high school, but now, at thirty-six, she remembered not only those stories, but also the deep feelings of conviction and morality she always had after every Sunday school: I want to be good. I want to do good things and love God. I want Jesus to come into my heart.

Such old memories, such long ago feelings. But the memories were pleasant, and the feelings they evoked were warm and comforting, which caused her to pause and reflect. How many pleasant memories did she really have? Not too many. Maybe these, some of her oldest, were her happiest.

Psalm 119. Hmm. It was a long chapter. She read the first verse.

"Blessed are they whose ways are blameless, who walk according to the law of the Lord."

That first verse was enough to grab her attention, and she read on.

Verse 3 said, "They do nothing wrong; they walk in his ways."

Verses 4, 5, and 6 continued the same theme: "You have laid down precepts that are to be fully obeyed. Oh, that my ways were steadfast in obeying your decrees! Then I would not be put to shame when I consider all your commands."

How did that pastor know? She'd asked him the toughest question she could think of, but he came back with the answer she needed, the one perfect for her situation, right here and now, the very next step in her musings.

She continued to read, and the words spoke to her over and over again about something she'd fled from for years, denied, fought against, and finally lost . . . but perhaps needed most of all.

Absolutes. A genuine right and a genuine wrong. A fence, a point of reference, a way to know something for sure.

She couldn't let these ideas get away from her. She hopped out of bed and hurried to the closet for her duffel bag. The few clothes she had were in the laundry at the moment, so the bag was a lot emptier, containing a still frightening amount of freshly minted cash, her notebook, which she set aside, and . . . the rosters from Professor Lynch's office.

She felt sick at the sight of them, as if there was an evil attached to them, as if an invisible, poisonous stowaway had come along to haunt her. They frightened her; they gave her the same stomach-turning fear and disgust one feels while waiting for something horrible to jump out in a late-night horror movie.

Unseen by Sally, though she could sense them, the same little quartet of demons still lurked about, watching her, looking for opportunities. They had followed her everywhere she went, and could pass through any angelic hedge because she carried them with her. Despair was enjoying his job less and less; the more Sally continued in her quest, the less of his poison he could sow in her mind. Fear had had much to do and a lot of fun doing it, and was glad to have those rosters along, but Death and Insanity were getting frustrated. Sally had found some new purpose somewhere; Death was no longer welcome in her thoughts, and her thoughts were becoming too clear and rational for Insanity to scramble.

All four reached out for her, but at the moment there was nothing to grab.

Sally closed the duffel bag, leaving the rosters hidden and confined. *Not now, rosters; I'll deal with you later. I don't want to feel sick, I don't want to struggle. Just give me a break. Let me rest awhile.*

The demons slinked away to wait.

She grabbed up her notebook and pen, and hopped into the bed again.

> *Good feelings, don't go away. Let me meet with you awhile, study you, figure you out; let me think things through.*

She began another letter to Tom Harris.

> *I'm working my way through Psalm 119, and if I understand the message correctly, there are at least two absolutes being presented, two things I can know for sure:*
> *1)There is a right: to obey God's laws and follow His ways.*
> *2)There is a wrong: to disobey God's laws and not follow His ways.*
> *How am I doing so far? I hope you're keeping up, because now it's going to get tougher.*
> *Psalm 119 also talks about two human conditions that are the direct result of the two absolutes:*
> *1)Do what is right, and you'll be happy and blessed.*
> *2)Do what is wrong, and you'll be put to shame.*
> *Now is that simple or what? Too simple, I suppose; too basic to be believed and accepted by people like me who insist there is no reality higher than themselves.*
> *But, Tom, I do believe I have been put to shame. Even the vicious, cutting remarks of an enemy, Professor Lynch, make that clear to me. He was trying to destroy me, I know, but there was nothing he said that wasn't true. I couldn't argue with him. The truth is, my life is in ruins.*
> *But can I accept the Bible's explanation for it? Dare I trust this Book? If the Bible is trustworthy, and if I did choose to believe it, then I could, once and for all, determine who and where I am: in the wrong, outside of God's favor, put to shame.*
> *Not a comfortable thought, but at least I would have an immovable rock under my feet.*

Despair flopped to the floor beside the bed, holding his stomach and moaning. Death and Insanity weren't feeling very well either, but took it out on Despair.

"You're losing her, leech! You're the one in charge of this mission! Do something!"

Fear volunteered, "Perhaps I could think of something to frighten her."

Despair hissed at him, "You've done that, and driven her closer to the truth!"

Sally felt sleepy at last. For now, her questions were resolved, her thoughts were recorded, and she could rest. She set the notebook on the bedside table, put all the pillows aside except one, and clicked off the lamp.

As she lay there in the dark, she noticed how peaceful she felt. This was the first night in a long time that she did not feel afraid. Instead, she felt . . . what was this? Hope? Yes! This had to be hope. It felt so foreign, so different.

Out of her distant past, she could recall once again those old feelings and thoughts from Sunday school: I want to be good. I want to do good things and love God. I want Jesus to come into my heart.

She fluffed her pillow and let her head sink into it. Hm. Jesus. Now what does He have to do with all this?

Very early on Sunday morning, Ben Cole stood in the gate to Sally Roe's goat pen, incredulous, sickened, wary of proceeding inside. This couldn't be real. Things like this just didn't happen, not around here.

He looked back toward the field between the Potter home and the rental. Mrs. Potter stood in the middle of the field, nervously wringing her hands and watching, but refusing to come any closer.

He looked back toward the goat pen. Buff and Bart, the two kids, were still alive, but disturbed and jittery. As for Betty, the doe . . .

Ben finally entered the pen, closing the gate behind him, stepping carefully through the dirt and straw, searching the ground for any clues. He approached Betty's dead and butchered carcass. She hadn't been killed too long ago. It had to have been the previous night.

He turned and shouted to Mrs. Potter, "Did you hear anything?"

"No," she replied.

Ben looked around the carcass. No clues. No footprints. The dirt did seem to be disturbed, however, probably brushed and raked to erase any clues.

Mrs. Potter came closer, but still wouldn't look.

"Have you called the police?" Ben asked.

"Well, I called you."

He smiled. "I'm no longer with the Police Department."

"I know. But I wanted you to come. I don't trust Sergeant Mulligan. I don't think he'd do anything about it."

Ben backed away from Betty's carcass and joined Mrs. Potter near the fence. He was wishing he had a camera to record this.

"Well," he said, drawing his first full breath, "I'm going to do something about it."

Betty lay in the straw, her throat cut, her body totally drained of blood, and all four legs cleanly and skillfully removed, missing without a trace.

The morning air was chilly, but Ben could feel a chill that had nothing to do with the weather. In his spirit, he could feel some real trouble approaching.

Well, maybe I should, Sally thought. *It's one thing I haven't tried yet. It could provide more information that would round out my perspective. It might clarify some of the old memories I haven't been able to fully recall. It would be an interesting glimpse into middle-class American religious culture. Perhaps it might—*

"Get your coat, then," said Sara Barker. "Floyd's warming up the car right now."

Sally answered a little late, "Well, sure, I'll go. Why not?"

And that's how she found herself standing in front of the little white Ashton Community Church, a half-mile up Morgan Hill on Poplar Street, on a warm and beautiful

Sunday morning. People were already filing inside, talking, laughing, hugging like old friends, guiding their small children by the hand and calling to the older ones to come on and hurry up, church was starting.

Sara spared no pains to make sure Sally met everyone. "Hi, Andy, this is Betty Smith. Edith, how are you? I'd like you to meet Betty Smith, our new boarder. Cecil, it's great to see you're feeling better. Have you met Betty Smith?"

Sally smiled and shook the hands extended to her, but with only half her attention. The sight of a little girl in a Sunday dress, holding her mother's hand and carrying a Bible, triggered a memory.

Thirty years ago, that was me.

Sally could remember wearing a pretty dress and a matching ribbon in her hair. She could remember carrying a Bible too, a gift from the lady who held her hand back then, her guardian, Aunt Barbara. Sally's mother, lost to alcohol, had never been much of a positive influence. Aunt Barbara, on the other hand, always took her to Sunday school. Aunt Barbara took religion seriously, and in those days Sally respected that. It was good for Aunt Barbara, and yes, it felt right for Sally too.

"Well, we'd better get in there," said Sara, her words jolting Sally from her reverie.

They went up the front steps, through the double doors, and into a small foyer where a few clusters of people—Floyd was part of one cluster—were still getting caught up on each other's week.

Oh, there was the Sunday school attendance posted on the wall. She remembered that. She remembered always bringing an offering, too; that was important in those days.

The people around her were of all kinds. Some were well-dressed, some were in blue jeans; there were older folks and many younger; there were plenty of young children about, suggesting a middle-class, Protestant baby boom.

Sally quickly had to admit to herself that, Christianity itself notwithstanding, there was little reason to be uncomfortable in this place. Her lack of acceptable attire could have been a reason—she had only her slacks and blouse and could not wear the jacket because of the knife holes in it, not to mention the missing sleeve—but now she saw that attire had little to do with acceptance, and neither did ethnic background or social status.

Well . . . I guess I won't be uncomfortable.

She followed Floyd and Sara to a place in a wooden pew near the back and sat down. Her feet could touch the floor. The last time she sat in a pew, her feet dangled. That was when . . . Tommy Krebs! Yes, now she remembered him, that little snotty kid with the crewcut and the marker pen without a cap. She finally tattled on him and that brought some peace for a while, but not before he'd blackened her knee. Yes, that all happened in a pew just like this one, during the Sunday school's opening exercises. Oh! What was that song she and all those other little moppets used to sing? "Jesus loves me, this I know, for the Bible tells me so . . ." Oh, yes. That song had to be one of the oldie-goldie hits of American Protestantism; obviously *she* never forgot it.

She tried to relax, and looked around the small sanctuary at the backs of all those heads. Oh, there was the pastor, Hank What's-his-name, closing off a conversation and taking a chair on the platform. Now he looked a little more like a pastor, with a suit and tie, but she knew she'd never forget that guy wrestling with a toilet back at the boarding house.

This was becoming quite an experience. There was so much to see and remember, so many feelings to sort through, she hadn't become bored yet. Rather, she was captivated.

But . . . what am I doing here, really? she wondered. *Is it just because Sara invited me?*

No, not really. The invitation was as good an incentive as any, but not the real reason. Sally did want to be here, even though it was only now that she realized it.

Is it a matter of curiosity?

No, more than that. Curiosity was one thing, hunger was another.

Hunger? For what—fond memories? Nostalgia?

No, more than that. It was more a haunting sensation that

she had come full circle after thirty years and found, just as strong as ever, a truth, a treasure, a special matter of the heart she once held but lost. She couldn't recall her life being as shaky during her Sunday school childhood as it had been ever since. There was just something about the convictions of this culture, the solid certainty of everything.

Maybe that was part of it. Maybe those experiences of long ago were the last solid ground Sally had ever walked on.

Yes, things were so different then.

Sally, Sara, and Floyd all scooted over a little to make room for a young lady to sit next to Sally.

"Hi," she said, offering her hand. "I'm Bernice Krueger."

"Um . . . Betty Smith." She had to be sure she remembered the right name.

"She's our new boarder," said Sara.

"Oh, great," said Bernice. "You new in town?"

"Yes."

"What brings you here?"

"Oh . . . just traveling."

"So how long have you been here?"

"Uh . . . I just got here yesterday." Sally was hoping this wasn't going to be a long interview. She decided to get the subject off herself. "So what do you do?"

"I work for the local newspaper. I'm a reporter and assistant editor, and I also wash the coffee cups and empty the wastebaskets."

"Oh, that's interesting."

Bernice laughed. "Sometimes it is. Well, it's great to have you here."

"Thank you."

There was a slight pause. Bernice looked forward and Sally thought the conversation was over, but then Bernice turned to Sally again with an additional thought.

"Say, if there's anything I can do for you, please let me know."

The offer was a little abrupt and unexpected. It made Sally wonder what this Bernice Krueger was thinking. *Do I seem that pitiful?* Sally did appreciate the compassion, but knew she could never accept it. "Thanks. I'll remember that."

The service began, and it was a real study in middle-class fundamentalism. Sally decided she would be an objective observer and take mental notes.

The content of the songs was worth noting: in every case, the lyrics spoke of love, worship, adoration, and reverence for God and for Jesus Christ, and it was readily apparent, as expected, that the people believed and practiced with great conviction the sentiments expressed in the songs.

As the service progressed through the songs and then a time of sharing inspirational personal anecdotes, Sally found it easy to get caught up in the very phenomenon she was observing. She was enjoying it. These people were happy, and even though the form and process of worship seemed a little odd and foreign to an outsider, Sally knew and reminded herself that next to her own yoga techniques and trance channeling, this stuff was tame, normal, even downright bland.

The time came for prayer, and Pastor Busche opened the floor for prayer requests. An elderly man was having trouble with a pulled muscle and asked for prayer, as did a young lady concerned for her husband who "didn't know the Lord," a young father who needed a job, and a lady whose sister had had a child born prematurely.

Then the young lady who worked at the newspaper, Bernice Krueger, spoke up. "Let's remember to pray for Marshall and Kate while they're away. I guess things are getting pretty difficult, and they're encountering a lot of spiritual resistance."

"Right," said Pastor Hank, "we've all been following that. We'll be sure to pray about it."

And then the pastor led the congregation in prayer, glorifying and praising God, and then asking God to supply all the requests that the people had made.

"And we remember Marshall and Kate as well, involved in spiritual warfare . . ."

That topic caught Sally's interest. Spiritual warfare. Wow! If these people only knew what *she* was going through.

thirty-one

"'BUT he was pierced for our transgressions, he was crushed for our iniquities; the punishment that brought us peace was upon him, and by his wounds we are healed.'"

Bernice Krueger read the words in a soft voice from her Bible as Sally followed along in the Bible she'd brought from Sara Barker's. They were sharing a booth at Danny's Diner on Main Street, not far from the *Clarion*. They'd ordered their lunch, it was on the way, and now, over coffee, they were taking a second look at Hank's sermon text for the morning, some verses from Isaiah 53.

Bernice read the next verse. "'We all, like sheep, have gone astray, each of us has turned to his own way; and the Lord has laid on him the iniquity of us all.'"

"Sin and redemption," said Sally.

Bernice was impressed. "Right. So you know *something* about this."

"No, nothing really. It's a phrase I've heard in some circles, apparently a quick way to define the typical Christian view of things. We always hated the idea."

Bernice sipped from her coffee. "Who's 'we'?"

Sally brushed off the question. "Just some old friends."

"And what did you hate about it?"

Sally sipped from her coffee. It was an effective way to buy time to formulate an answer. "The notion of sin, I guess. It's hard enough for anyone to feel good about himself, and it seemed so negative and oppressive to teach that we're all miserable, no-good sinners. Christianity was the curse of mankind, enslaving us and holding us back from our true potential." She felt a need to qualify that. "Anyway, that's what we thought."

"Okay, so that's what you thought about the sin part of it." Bernice smiled, and tapped the passage from Isaiah 53 that still lay open under Sally's nose. "But did you catch the redemption part? God loves you, and He sent His Son to pay for that sin with His own death on the cross."

Now Sally remembered Aunt Barbara and Mrs. Gunderson telling her that. "So I've heard."

"But getting back to what the Bible says about sin, since when is that such a shock? Mankind has been proving for thousands of years the kind of stuff he's made of. Listen, man's problems aren't due to politics or economics or ecology or levels of consciousness; man's problems are due to his ethics—they're lousy."

Sally heard that. It sank in. That was putting it simply enough, and hadn't she demonstrated the truth of those words in her own life? "I guess I'll agree with you there. But let me just confirm something: I take it the Bible is the ethical standard by which we determine what's 'lousy'?"

Bernice gave an assertive nod. "*And* what's good, what's righteous."

Sally pondered that. "That being the case, I imagine this standard puts us all on the wrong side of the fence."

"I think you'll find that idea acceptable if you're honest with yourself. You've lived long enough to know what we as human beings are capable of."

Sally even chuckled. "Oh, yes indeed."

"And here's God's answer for it." Bernice pointed out the phrases and reviewed them. "'He carried our infirmities and our sorrows . . . he was pierced for our sins and crushed for our iniquities . . . the Lord has laid on Him all our sins.'"

"Why?"

Bernice thought for a moment. "Well, let's talk about justice. You do something wrong, you end up in prison, right?"

Sally definitely agreed. "Right."

"Now, in the ideal sense, all legal loopholes aside, there are only two ways out of there: change the rules so that what you did isn't wrong so you aren't guilty, or pay the penalty."

"I've tried changing the rules," Sally admitted.

"Well, in God's scheme of things, rules are rules, because if they weren't, they wouldn't be worth much, and right and wrong would be meaningless. So what's left? The penalty. That's where God's love comes in. He knew we could never pay the penalty ourselves, so He did it for us. He took the form of man, took all our sins upon Himself, and died on a Roman cross two thousand years ago."

Sally examined the passage again. "So tell me: did it work?"

Bernice leaned forward and said, "You be the judge. The Bible says that the penalty for sin is death, but after Jesus paid that penalty He rose from the dead on the third day, so *something* was different. He conquered sin, so He was able to conquer sin's penalty. Sure, it worked. It always works. Jesus satisfied divine justice on that Cross. He bore the punishment in full, and God never had to bend the rules. That's why we call Jesus our Savior. He shed His own blood in our place, and died, and then rose from the grave to prove He'd won over sin and could set us free." Now Bernice started getting excited. "And you know what thrills me about that? It means we're special to Him; He really does love us, and we . . . we *mean* something, we're here for a reason! And you know what else? No matter what our sins are, no matter where we are or what condition we're in, we can be forgiven, free and clear, a clean slate!"

The lunch came—two soups and two salads. Sally was thankful for the pause in the conversation. It gave her a chance to think and to wonder, Who gave this young lady the script anyway? How was it that she could say so many things that spoke directly to Sally's situation?

Well, Bernice did go to Pastor Hank Busche's church, and *he* had a way of hitting the nail on the head. His suggestion to read Psalm 119 was perfect, and his morning sermon on Isaiah 53 was just more of the same perfectly tailored message, exactly what she was ready to hear.

But there was still a snag in all this. Sally took a few bites of her salad while she considered her next question, and then she formed it as a comment. "I don't feel forgiven."

Bernice answered, "Have you ever asked God to forgive you?"

"I've never even believed in God, at least not in the traditional sense."

"Well, He's there."

"But how can I know that?"

Bernice looked at Sally and seemed to know her heart. She replied simply, "You know."

"So . . ." Sally stopped short, and ate some more salad. She couldn't ask the question she had in her mind. It would seem too silly, too childish, like a dumb question already answered. But still . . . she had to hear a direct answer, something she could carry away without any doubts. "Well, I hope you'll indulge the question . . ."

"Sure."

"It's easy to speak in comfortable, generalized, generic terms . . ."

"Be as specific as you want."

"Did . . ." She stopped again. Where was that emotion coming from? She pushed it down with another bite of salad. Now she felt all right. It seemed safe to ask. "Did Jesus die for *me?*"

Bernice did not answer lightly or flippantly. She looked Sally in the eye and gave her a firm, even reply. "Yes, He died for you."

"For me, for . . ." She had to remember her alias. "For Betty Smith? I mean, Bernice, you don't know me . . ."

"He died for Betty Smith just like He died for Bernice Krueger."

Well, she got her answer. "Okay."

That was the last item on that topic. Bernice could sense her lunch guest was getting uncomfortable, and didn't want to make things worse. Sally was afraid she'd opened up just a little too much to an innocent stranger, and dared not risk dragging this nice woman into her troubles.

Bernice resorted to purely social conversation. "So how long have you been on the road?"

Sally was even afraid of that question. "Oh . . . about a month or so, something like that."

"Where are you from originally?"

"Does it matter?"

After that, conversation was difficult, and both regretted it. Except for small talk and purely social conversation, the lunch was more important than any more words. The salads disappeared, the soup bowls went empty, the minutes slipped by.

"I enjoyed meeting you," said Bernice.

"I guess I'd better get back to Sara's," said Sally.

"But listen . . . why don't you come by the *Clarion* when you get the chance? We could have lunch again."

Sally's first impulse was to refuse, but finally she allowed herself to relax, trust just a little, and accept the invitation. "Well . . . sure, I'd like that."

Bernice smiled. "Come on. I'll drive you back to Sara's."

The old farm outside Bacon's Corner had been deserted for years, the barn empty and graying. Ever since the owner had died, no human was ever seen in this place, not a sound was heard, not a single light glowed—except for certain nights no one was supposed to know about.

On this night, the dull orange glow of candles appeared through the cracks in the clapboard siding and through the chinks in the weather-warped door of the massive old barn. Inside, human voices muttered, murmured, and rumbled through rhythmic chants and incantations.

There were about twenty people inside, all clothed in black robes except for one woman who wore white, standing around a large pentagram etched in the bare earth floor. In the center of the pentagram, two hind legs cut from a goat lay crossed in an X, and a candle burned at each of the pentagram's five points.

At the head of the circle, the woman in white led the meeting, speaking in low, clear tones, a large silver cup in her outstretched hands. "As from the beginning, the powers will be brought forth through blood, and restitution by our hand will balance the scales."

"So be it," the others chanted.

"We call forth the powers and minions of darkness to witness this night our covenant with them."

"So be it!"

Demonic wings rustled in the rafters as dark, destructive spirits began to gather, looking down with gleaming yellow eyes and toothy grins, basking in all the adoration and attention.

In the peak of the roof, clinging to the rafters and overseeing it all, Destroyer could mouth the ceremony even as he listened to it.

"May their fury be kindled against our enemies, against all who oppose. May their favor be with us as we dedicate this offering."

"So be it!"

"May the woman be found."

"So be it."

"So be it," agreed the demons, exchanging glances.

"It will be," said Destroyer. "It will be."

"May she be driven from hiding, and crushed as powder," declared the woman.

"So be it," chanted the others.

The demons nodded and cackled in agreement, their wings quivering with excitement. More spirits arrived. The rafters, the hayloft, the gables of the roof were filling with them.

"Defeat and division to the Christians, ill health, ill will."

"So be it."

Destroyer spoke quickly to the gathering demons, pointing to this one and then that one, assigning hordes to every task as the spirits murmured their acceptance.

"May they grant a court decision in our favor! We give to them the heart and mind of Judge Emily Fletcher!"

"So be it."

Destroyer looked around their group and finally settled on a larger, hulking spirit roosting on a diagonal brace. He'd handled courtrooms before; he would be in charge of that.

"And now . . ." The woman drew the silver cup to her lips. "Through blood we seal the success of the powers, the death of Sally Beth Roe, and the defeat of the Christians!"

"So be it!"

The demons all leaned forward and craned their necks, wanting to see. They giggled, they slobbered, they gave each other happy pats and pokes. Destroyer became drunk with exhilaration.

The woman pulled back her hood and took a drink from the cup. When she withdrew the cup, the stain of fresh goat's blood remained on her lips.

Claire Johanson, high priestess of the coven, passed the cup to Jon, who drank and passed it on to the next person, and every witch, male and female, drank to seal the curses.

Then, in chorus, their arms shooting upward, the witches let out an eerie wail: "So be it!"

"Go!" said Destroyer with a clap of his wings and a point of his crooked finger.

The marauding spirits shot out of the barn, pouring from the roof like black smoke from a fire, like bats from a cavern. They dispersed in all directions, howling and cackling, full of lustful, destructive mischief.

On Monday morning, the day of the hearing in Westhaven, Pastor Mark Howard was thankful he'd arrived at the church earlier than everyone else. Hopefully he would be able to clean up the mess before any of the school kids saw it.

He'd already opened the school building and turned up the heat; so the facility was ready, and he still had about forty-five minutes before the parents started dropping off their children. He hurried down into the church basement, opened his office, and grabbed the telephone.

His voice was quiet and somber as he spoke, almost afraid of being heard. "Good morning, Marshall. This is Mark. Sorry to wake you up so early. Please come to the church right away. I'm going to be calling Ben, and I hope to have him here as well. Yes, right away. Thank you."

He opened the utility closet under the stairs and grabbed a mop and bucket. He was so upset he forgot he would need a garbage can as well. With his heart racing, he ran upstairs and out onto the front porch of the church.

The blood on the front door was dry. It would take some scrubbing to get it off.

Oh! I've got to get the garbage can! No, not yet. I'd better wait until Marshall and Ben get here. I hope they get here before the children do. O Lord Jesus, we pray for the covering and protection of Your shed blood over this place!

Come on, guys, hurry up! I can't leave these things here!

At Mark's feet, crossed like an X and staining the church steps red, were two front legs from an animal, most likely a goat.

At nine o'clock that morning, representatives of the press, the ACFA, the National Coalition on Education, and even a few churches converged on Room 412 at the Federal Courthouse in Westhaven, the courtroom of the Honorable Emily R. Fletcher.

Wayne Corrigan and Tom Harris were already seated at the defendant's table; Gordon Jefferson and Wendell Ames, Lucy Brandon's attorneys, were seated and ready for combat, with Lucy seated between them. In the first row of the gallery, Dr. Mandanhi was waiting to testify.

KBZT Channel Seven News reporter Chad Davis was there, prowling about for any news tidbits or comments while Roberto Gutierrez set up the television camera.

John Ziegler was there as well, and Paula the photobug had already snapped some pictures—uninvited—of Tom and Corrigan.

The bailiff stood to her feet. "All rise."

They all rose.

"Court is now in session, the Honorable Emily R. Fletcher presiding."

The judge took her place behind the bench. "Thank you. Please be seated."

They sat. So far everything was going the same as last time, and just like last time, the judge perched her reading glasses on her nose and looked over the documents before her.

"The defendant has requested today's hearing to determine whether or not the child in this case, Amber Brandon, should be excused from any deposition or testimony. It is the court's understanding that counsel for the plaintiff strenuously opposes any deposition or testimony from the child, and so the court has been asked to rule on the question." She looked up and seemed just a little impatient with the whole matter. "Mr. Corrigan, please proceed."

Corrigan rose. "Thank you, Your Honor. Our request is simple enough, and not at all irregular. The complaint against my client includes charges of harassment, discrimination, and outrageous religious behavior. But may I remind the court that thus far, any testimony pertaining to these charges has not come from the plaintiff's key witness, Amber herself, but secondhand, through Amber's mother, Lucy Brandon, and from the plaintiff's expert witness, Dr. Mandanhi. We've made many requests to talk to Amber, to have our own psychologist visit with her so Dr. Mandanhi's opinions can be balanced with those of another expert witness. But counsel for the plaintiff has adamantly refused to cooperate, and we are concerned that my client's right to confront his accuser is being infringed. Also, with no opportunity to question Amber and hear her testimony for ourselves, we have no assurance that the indirect testimony coming through Mrs. Brandon and through Dr. Mandanhi is not in some way colored, tainted, or embellished.

"Counsel for the plaintiff has insisted that Amber is in too delicate a condition, at too fragile an age to go through a deposition or a court trial. But we can assure counsel that we would not in any way resort to harsh tactics.

"Also, the record is clear that Amber is a strong-willed child and has stated conflicting facts, even to her mother. In addition to that, Amber's mother has testified in deposition that there are other influences affecting Amber's life which she was exposed to outside the school. Only Amber herself can answer the many unanswered questions that arise in these areas.

"All we're asking is that we be allowed to hear the details from Amber herself, and that our own psychologist be allowed to examine Amber to verify or refute the findings of Dr. Mandanhi."

Corrigan took his seat, and the judge recognized Wendell Ames.

Ames wasn't quite as exciting to watch as the younger Jefferson, but he did exude a dignity of experience that was in itself persuasive. "Your Honor, this entire case is being brought to court because of severe damage done to an innocent child, the extent of which is clearly shown in the affidavits and the reports of Dr. Mandanhi. As attorneys for the plaintiff, we wish to right a wrong, to redress a grievance, and to somehow undo the harm that has been done. It was never our intention, as responsible human beings, to only increase Amber's pain by putting her through the trial process, dredging up all her old wounds, and putting her hurts on public display.

"We have presented an additional opinion from Dr. Mandanhi, detailing for the court Amber's current emotional condition and establishing that it would not be in her best interests to be made to testify or give a deposition. If the court so requires, Dr. Mandanhi is here to testify in person as to Amber's fragile state of mind and emotions at this time."

Judge Fletcher looked at Mandanhi and then at Ames. "Would the doctor have additional statements to make not included in his written opinion?"

"I'm sure he could clarify for the court any items the court may need clarified."

The judge quickly perused Mandanhi's report. "I think it's clear enough. Any further oral testimony would most likely be cumulative."

"Very well."

"Anything else?"

"Yes. Even though there are strong arguments on either side, we would hope that common sense and decency will speak more loudly and persuasively than any argument, and that the court would spare this innocent child the pain and grief of reliving her hurts, of being challenged and doubted by the defense, of being put on display, as it were, in open court.

"We understand the legal process, of course. We understand that the defendant does have a right to confront his accuser. But we remind the court that we are dealing with a case of child abuse, a fact the defendants have already admitted."

"Objection," said Corrigan. "The defense has made no such admission."

Ames responded, "Your Honor, I was simply referring to what has already been established, that spanking does occur at the school, and that the school does teach pervasive and imposing doctrines . . ."

The judge was a little impatient. "The affidavits are clear on what the school practices and teaches, Mr. Ames. If the defendants want to stand by their practices, this in no way constitutes an admission of guilt. The objection is sustained."

Ames regathered his thoughts and continued. "At any rate, Your Honor, we hold that Amber is a child of tender years who needs to be protected. That is, after all, the motivation behind this suit in the first place. Given that, we must plead that the court spare Amber any further pain and trauma by ruling that she need not be deposed and she need not testify, or go through any more grueling examination by still another psychologist."

Ames sat down.

The judge looked at Corrigan. "Anything else?"

Corrigan stood. "I suppose it might be effective to point out why I don't have anything else I can say. If, as the plaintiff argues, Amber Brandon is in such a pitiful state of mind and emotion that she simply must not be allowed to testify or participate in the trial, we are left with having to take counsel's word for it, with no way of knowing how true these claims are. Amber could actually be in this bad a condition, but we could never confirm that. The plaintiff might be conducting a clever, purposeful cover-up, but we could never know that either. Counselors for the plaintiff obviously think they know all they need to know about Amber and what she allegedly went through at the hands of the defendants, but the defendants and their counsel know virtually nothing apart from the filtered hearsay provided thus far. Without

Amber we are being restricted, expected to present a persuasive defense, but forbidden to cut through to the real heart of the matter, to the real source of these complaints. I repeat again, we do not want to hurt Amber in any way or add to her trauma—if there be any trauma. We simply want to get to the facts so we can prepare to answer the charges. You have our brief as to the law which shows that Amber must be made available."

Corrigan sat down, and the judge looked at Ames and Jefferson. "Anything else?"

"No, Your Honor," said Ames.

"Court will recess, then, and reconvene at 2 this afternoon for my ruling."

"All rise," said the bailiff, and they all rose, and out went the judge.

Tom whispered to Corrigan, "How do you think we did?"

Corrigan wasn't very happy. "I have no idea. I think that's the weakest argument I've ever presented for anything." He fretted, fumed, replayed the hearing in his mind. "I should have stressed the law more; it's supposed to be on our side . . . Did you see her reaction to Mandanhi's affidavit? She took it as gospel!"

"How about some lunch?" Tom asked.

Corrigan followed him out of the courtroom, still muttering to himself.

thirty-two

The spirits were aloft and rampant, goaded on by goat's blood and blasphemy, by rage and conspiracy, by Destroyer's reckless indignation and thirst for immediate victory over the subtle Captain of the Host and his prize, the elusive Sally Beth Roe.

Infested by lying demons, the Warings (Ed and Judy) and the Jessups (Andrea and Wes) were meeting for lunch at the Warings' home to prayerfully discuss the latest news hot off the prayer chain: June Walroth had just heard that Tom regularly beat his daughter Ruth, and always dressed her in long sleeves so no one would notice; someone else—they didn't know who, but the person had to be reliable—was concerned because Pastor Mark and Cathy were having some marital problems, most likely because Mark had been unfaithful years ago; the Christian school was actually in terrible debt because Tom and Mrs. Fields were pilfering some of the money.

Andrea was aghast. "Are you sure about that? I can't believe Mrs. Fields would do such a thing."

"Well," said Judy, "do you know how little money she makes teaching at that school? It would be a real temptation, let's face it."

"But who told you about this?"

Ed was reluctant to reveal their source. "It's . . . Well, let me just say that it's someone close to the church board, someone I've really come to respect, all right? But this is all in strict confidence!"

Wes was immediately angry. "So why hasn't the board told the rest of the church?"

"The party I spoke to is concerned about the same thing. She's in a real fix: she doesn't want to violate the confidence of the board, but at the same time she's hurt because so much of this is being kept secret."

Judy piped in, "I think we need to have a congregational meeting, that's what I think!"

Andrea concurred. "And get this stuff out in the open once and for all!"

Ed nodded. "Well, I've talked to Ted and June Walroth, and they're ready for one."

Wes just shook his head and even laughed to vent his nerves. "This is all going to come out in that trial, you know. Somehow those ACFA guys are going to dig this up, and they're going to sue the ever-loving buns off our church!"

Gossip, Slander, and Spite thought that was funny, and shrieked with laughter. What wouldn't these people believe?

At the school, Mrs. Fields and Mark had just broken up their third fight, and now eight kids—six who were fighting and two who were urging them on—were staying inside for noon recess, cleaning the blackboards, dusting the furniture, and sweeping the floor. It had been a trying day.

Mrs. Fields plopped into her chair and heaved a deep sigh. "Pastor, what's happening around here?"

Mark wanted to say they were under spiritual attack, but he steered clear of that out of concern for Mrs. Fields. She was a sensitive woman, and it would have been distressing for her to learn what he'd found on the front steps that morning.

He finally just asked her to pray with him, and that is how they spent their noon hour—in between peacekeeping missions on the playfield.

Dreaming, dreaming . . . little baby girl . . . Rachel . . . pink and fat, laughing . . .

"Come on, sweetie, time for your bath."

Water running in the tub, just the right temperature.

Let her play in the running water. "See that? Isn't that fun? Time to get all clean."

Jonas. He's calling.

Not now. I'm giving Rachel a bath!

Pulling, pulling, yanking me from my body . . . No, not now . . .

Sudden blackness, floating, no feeling, no sounds, no pain, nothing but sweet love, bliss, oneness . . . A long, long tunnel, a bright light at the end, getting closer, closer, almost there, I've got to get back! What's happening to Rachel?

SLAP! A hand across her face!

"Come on, lady, snap out of it! Get up!"

Water everywhere, all over the floor. I'm sitting in it, I'm soaked. Who's this guy?

"Can you hear me? Get up!"

He's a cop! What's wrong!

"Aw, she's stoned, man, bombed to oblivion!"

Where's Rachel? "Where's my baby?"

The tub, filled to the brim, running over, water everywhere, cops, medics, the landlady, everything a blur.

A piercing, stabbing horror slowly rising. The unthinkable invading her mind. "Oh no! I've killed my baby!"

"Ma'am, I need to advise you of your rights. You have the right to remain silent . . ."

Up off the floor, held in strong arms, her hands bound behind her. "Where's my baby?"

"Get her out of here."

"Where's my baby?"

"Your baby is dead, Sally. Come on."

The quickest image, only appearing for a second: a tiny bundle on the kitchen table, medics all around, covered in a white cloth . . . one little pink hand showing.

"Oh no! Rachel! I've killed my baby! Jonas!"

Pain from handcuffs, her arms twisting, soaking wet, shoved out the door.

"Rachel!!"

"Come on, Sally, let's go!"

AAWW! Sally jolted awake in the darkened bedroom, almost falling off the bed. Her four tormenting companions were all over her.

Forever, forever, said Despair, *you will be condemned forever. You are what you are, you can never change it.*

Insanity piped in with renewed vigor, *It's all in your poor twisted mind, you know. You're a very sick lady!*

Death always follows you, said Death. *Everything you touch, everything you love, will only die.*

And they'll get you for this! said Fear. *All the spirits you've ever crossed are waiting to get you!*

Sally rolled over and buried her face in the pillow. "O God, help me!"

He can't help you . . . you've offended Him, He'll never hear you . . . we have you now . . .

Sally looked toward the window. The daylight was still visible around the edges of the drawn curtain. She checked the clock beside the bed. Four P.M. She flopped onto her back and tried to calm down, steady her heart, slow her breathing.

She told herself, *Easy now, girl, it was all a dream, a nightmare. Calm down.*

Her heart was still pounding and her face was slick with sweat. *Some nap this turned out to be; I feel worse.*

She tried to sort it all out. Yes, the dream was like a videotape; that's the way it happened. She hadn't had that clear a memory of it in years. *O God, what did I do, what did I do? How could I let this happen to me, to my daughter?*

Jonas, my wonderful counselor and friend, my infinitely wise spirit-guide!

The thought of that spirit made her sick.

I trusted him! I gave him my life, my thoughts, my spirit, my mind, and now . . . now I find out how evil he was. Or is.

Evil. Well, there's another absolute. Jonas is one incredibly evil spirit, and no one's going to convince me otherwise.

What had she just been reading? She rolled slowly off the bed, planted her feet on the floor, and went to the window. She pulled back the curtain and had to squint in the daylight that flooded the room. There, on the table under the window, was Sara's Bible, still opened to the Gospel of Mark. She'd just started reading it before she got sleepy and lay down. There was something it had said, and at the time she only gave it a passing thought.

She sat at the table and looked that passage over again.

Here it was, in chapter 1: "Just then a man in their synagogue who was possessed by an evil spirit cried out, 'What do you want with us, Jesus of Nazareth? Have you come to destroy us? I know who you are—the Holy One of God!'

"'Be quiet!' said Jesus sternly. 'Come out of him!' The evil spirit shook the man violently and came out of him with a shriek. The people were all so amazed that they asked each other, 'What is this? A new teaching—and with authority! He even gives orders to evil spirits and they obey him.' . . .

"That evening after sunset the people brought to Jesus all the sick and demon-possessed. The whole town gathered at the door, and Jesus healed many who had various diseases. He also drove out many demons, but he would not let the demons speak because they knew who he was."

Demons. They're demons. Sally believed it. She'd never given this Bible much credence since her Sunday school days, but right now, sitting in that room, having awakened from as clear a lesson as she could ask for, she believed what this Book said about these spirit entities. The whole thing was a sham, a deception, a spiritual con game. These things were as evil as evil could be.

Where's that notebook? I've got to write to Tom.

> *Tom, you know this already, and that's why you're in all this trouble, but let me assure you as one who has been on the other side, you are correct. Amber Brandon has contacted a spirit-guide, and now that thing is controlling her life, her thoughts, her behavior. I had Jonas, now Amber has Amethyst, and if I haven't said it clearly enough before, let me say it clearly now, because now I know it clearly: these spirits are evil; they are out to destroy us. Just look at what Jonas did to me. I don't blame him entirely; I asked him into my life, I gave him my mind and body. But I found out too late what his real agenda was.*
>
> *And what about Amber? I suppose for her it was all fun and games to begin with. Now I'm almost sure she's into something she would rather be out of, but can't escape it. To be honest, I'm not sure that I have escaped it.*

> *But if the Gospel of Mark is correct, and this Jesus of yours can order these spirits around and rescue people from their power, then I hope you have enough faith in your Savior to get His help.*
>
> *And, Tom, while you're at it, please put in a good word for me.*

Destroyer's spirits were laughing themselves silly as they fluttered out of the courthouse.

The judge rose, everyone in the courtroom rose, and then she went out, leaving the ACFA attorneys feeling pretty cocky while Wayne and Tom could only stand there with their mouths open.

Corrigan was so upset he could hardly keep his voice down as he muttered to Tom, "We are absolutely going to appeal this one. I've never seen a more obvious, ludicrous breach of justice or denial of due process in my career!"

Tom didn't know whether to have hope, or put up a fight, or give it up, or go home and die, or what. "Okay. If you think that will work."

"I don't know if it will work or not, the way these courts are getting so stacked, but we might have better luck with a different judge. Ultimately, it has no bearing on the decision to appeal. I'd be as remiss as the judge if I didn't appeal her decision. Come on, let's get out of here."

Just outside the courtroom, Wendell Ames was basking in the floodlights and catering to the microphones as he delivered a prepared statement to the press. "We are certainly gratified that a person of the stature of Judge Fletcher acknowledges that children of tender years still need protection from admitted child abusers, even in a court of law . . ."

"That's all," said Corrigan. With a sudden, uncharacteristic anger, he forced his way right into the circle of reporters. "Gentlemen and ladies, I will have a statement for you as soon as Mr. Ames has completed his statement."

He got their attention right away. They were hungry. They flooded him with questions, many of them quite loaded.

He brushed all the questions aside and said what he

wanted to say. "First of all, to correct Mr. Ames, this case centers on constitutionally guaranteed freedom of religion and not on child abuse. No admissions of any kind have been made, and try to get that right when you run your stories. If spanking is child abuse, then let's put half the country in jail right now!

"Secondly, seeing as the attorneys for the plaintiff continually insist on trying this case in the press, let me just throw this into the mill for your consideration: a) Everything we've heard in this case has been filtered through Amber's mother and the attorney-appointed child psychologist, Dr. Mandanhi, and we insist we have the right to confront our accuser, who is Amber, and just get to the truth. b) We do not intend to be harsh toward Amber or abuse her in any way. We will accept reasonable restrictions, and we will work with the judge and with the plaintiff's attorneys accordingly.

"Now, as to this ruling of Judge Fletcher: it is clearly erroneous and absolutely contrary to the law, and we have no choice but to appeal to the Court of Appeals without delay. Now try not to edit that too much."

With that, and with more questions still being hollered at them, Corrigan and Tom hurried down the hall to the elevators.

Back in Bacon's Corner, little Amber Brandon was giddy and laughing when she got off the school bus, and had been so disruptive on the bus that the driver was only minutes from writing her a discipline slip to give to her mother. But Amber's stop came first, and so the driver was satisfied with just getting Amber and her playmates off the bus.

Her playmates were used to seeing Amber acting like a pony, and some had even played the pretend game with her. But today Amethyst was not a fun pony to play with. She pushed her friends, she teased them, she stole their books and threw them about, she jumped, pranced, somersaulted, and mocked them.

All Amber's friends went home angry at her, vowing never to play with her again.

But Amethyst just kept laughing and prancing, and she didn't care a bit.

It was definitely time to get all the team together. That evening, Mark and Cathy opened up the church and the core group gathered—the Howards, Ben and Bev Cole, Marshall and Kate Hogan, Tom Harris, and Wayne Corrigan—along with the elders, Don Heely, Vic Savan, Jack and Doug Parmenter, and their wives. Push had come to shove. God was moving in their hearts and they could all feel the threat from outside; it was time to do some serious business with the Lord.

They sat in a close circle on the pews and some pulled-up chairs at the front of the sanctuary, ready to compare notes, talk it out, pray it through.

"I figured we should meet here tonight," said Mark. "This seems to be the center of Satan's attention right now, the center of his attacks. We need to pray a hedge around this place."

"Let's meet the enemy!" said Ben.

"It's high time we did!" said Jack.

Mark smiled, encouraged. "I want to tell you, the battle is getting thick out there!"

"So how did your deposition go last week?" Doug Parmenter asked.

Mark sighed; Corrigan rolled his eyes a bit. Mark answered, "Ames and Jefferson are laying a trap of some kind, that's obvious. They were just so kind and yet . . ."

Corrigan completed the thought. "They were trying to milk Mark for anything they could find to use against him, to set him up for a fall." He looked at Mark. "I think you did all right, though, pastor. You came out squeaky clean, and they didn't like that."

"Well, praise the Lord for that. 'He who walks in integrity walks securely.'"

"Right on," said Bev.

Mark turned to Corrigan again. "Wayne, since we're on the

subject, why don't you tell all of us what's next in the legal process?"

Corrigan looked a little tired and depressed. "Well, of course, Tom and Mrs. Fields are scheduled for depositions in the next few weeks. But in the meantime, we're going to appeal today's ruling to the Court of Appeals, and then we'll have to wait and see. We may not win there either, but at least it will buy us a little more time. Mind you, this is just a minor detail in the whole lawsuit, only one little skirmish in a long and costly war." He looked at Marshall. "We'll have to hope that something else breaks in this case. It just feels like we're so close!"

"How about that curriculum?" asked Kate. "I'm convinced now that the school system isn't going to let us see it without some real legal pressure. They're stalling."

Corrigan nodded. "I wouldn't be surprised if they were hoping they can outlast the court system and hide that curriculum until we're already in court. Well, with today's ruling and the appeal process starting, that's going to be hard to do. I'll definitely issue a subpoena for that curriculum tomorrow."

"As far as something else breaking," said Marshall, "we just might have it, or a part of it, or an inkling of how we might track down a corner of a part of it. I'm talking about the curse put on the church this morning."

Bob Heely asked, "Did you go to the police about that?"

Ben replied, "Are you kidding? I'm about 90 percent sure that Mulligan's in on this thing! Those goat legs came from Sally Roe's goat, and you know how Mulligan's been covering up that attempt to murder her. He's got to be a part of this curse too, or at least helping whoever it was that did it."

Jack Parmenter had to ask, "Are you really sure about that?"

Marshall stepped in. "Not yet. But the point I'm making is that now we have concrete evidence that there's some witchcraft or Satanism in the area, some organized, heavier form of occultism like a coven, a secret society, whatever. And that means there are people—and I mean normal-looking, everyday people you'd never suspect—that belong to this group. And in a town this size, they can pull a lot of weight and intimidate a lot of people. Mulligan and Parnell the coroner might be under the control of these people, or they might belong to the group themselves.

"But don't miss this point: Whoever these people are, they've clearly spelled out that this church and Sally Roe have something in common: we are their enemies, and they mean to do us harm. They killed Sally's goat and drained its blood, probably for use in their ceremonies. Now that's a contact point for them, something that belonged to the person they want to curse. They took off the legs and left the front ones here at the church. That includes us in the curse they've leveled at Sally Roe. I'm guessing that the hind legs are still with the witches somewhere as a contact point at their end."

"Why the legs?" asked Corrigan.

Marshall guessed, "Well, you can't run far without them, and right now Sally Roe is running, I'm sure of that."

Tom's wheels were turning rapidly. "So there are your moles again, Marshall! They've tried to put Sally Roe and us under the same curse; so even though we can't see it yet, there has to be a connection: Sally Roe has something to do with our situation, with this case, and they know it."

"You've got it."

Corrigan clenched his fists and looked toward Heaven with mock drama. "Oh, if only we could prove all this! If only we knew who these weird people are!"

"I don't know about you, but I have some suspects," said Marshall. "We would do well to take some careful second looks at Sergeant Mulligan and Joey Parnell. They've been close to this whole Sally Roe thing, and we know Parnell is scared spitless right now."

Ben was more blunt. "Parnell's in it, no doubt."

"And I'll even throw in Irene Bledsoe, the CPD lady, as a suspect. She's working with the whole Brandon/ACFA camp, and she's being anything but objective."

"Oh, man, I hope not!" said Tom.

"How're the kids?"

392

"I saw them on Friday. They're hanging in there. The foster home sounds pretty rough, but at least they're not in Bledsoe's daily care. A witch taking care of my kids, that's all I need!"

"And there might be still another suspect," said Mark. They turned to hear who, but he fell silent and thoughtful, exchanging a look with Cathy. "How do we know that one of these witches, or Satanists, or whatever they are, hasn't come right into this church? We've been having no end of trouble, and I've never seen so much division as long as I've pastored here."

Cathy added, "I feel that we do have some kind of poison working directly among us, no question."

"It does happen," said Marshall. "They do infiltrate churches; they know all the Christian lingo, they know the Bible, they make it a serious business to pass for Christians and stir things up from the inside."

That stopped them all cold. Suddenly they found themselves looking at each other like all the suspects in a "whodunit." It was a downright creepy feeling.

Jack asked Mark and Cathy, "Any idea who?"

Mark shook his head. Cathy answered, "No . . . but listen: we have one. We have a demonic mole in this church. I just feel that from the Lord."

Marshall nodded. "That's a distinct possibility."

They pondered that for only a moment, and then, without a further word, Mark slid from his chair and sank to his knees right there. The others did the same. It was spontaneous. They knew what they had to do.

"O Lord God, have mercy," Mark prayed. "Where we have sinned, forgive us. Grant us wisdom to know what we're doing wrong, and repentance from that wrong. Have mercy on us, Lord God, and restore us."

His prayer continued, and the others prayed right along with him. Tears started to flow, unbridled weeping before the Lord.

Ben prayed, "Lord, help us to sort this whole thing out.

Protect us from our enemies, and give us a victory for what's right."

"We pray for all the children," said Cathy. "This is their battle too, maybe even more than ours. Satan wants our kids, and we just can't let him have them."

Mark declared, "We just pray now for a hedge of angelic warriors to surround this place and guard it. Surround Your people, Lord, and protect us all from any curses leveled against us. We plead the shed blood of Jesus over ourselves, our ministry, our children, the school . . ."

"Protect Ruth and Josiah," prayed Tom. "O Lord, please protect my kids."

"Bring an answer, Lord," said Marshall. "We have enough hunches and theories to fill a warehouse, but we need an answer, something solid, something positive, and we need it fast. Please break through the walls the enemy has put up; break through, Lord God, and bring us an answer."

"And, Lord," said Jack, "if there is an invader in our church, a demonic mole, we just put chains on that person right now, we bind the demons associated with him or her, and we ask, Lord, that this person be exposed."

Outside the church, Nathan and Armoth set up the hedge, a regiment of the best warriors available for the job, all standing shoulder to shoulder around the church property, swords ready, alert, ready for a fight.

Tal was pleased with this little bit of progress. "That should hold things together for a while. Now to root out that mole!"

"It looks like we'll be ready," said Nathan, regarding the prayers from the people inside the church.

"Of course," said Tal. "And it was nice of Destroyer to get so reckless. He's exposed the breach we needed!"

thirty-three

I$\dagger$ was Tuesday morning and the *Ashton Clarion* was out on the stands, in the grocery stores, and on the front porches all over town. That used to mean it would be a little calmer around the *Clarion* office; Cheryl the cub reporter could relax and catch up on advertising clients, Tom the paste-up man could go fishing or work at home in his yard, and George the typesetter could sleep in.

Well, this Tuesday things were a little different. The *Clarion*'s tough, whip-cracking editor was gone on an assignment—he never was clear about its exact nature—but that didn't mean there would be any vacation. Actually, because Marshall was such a hard worker, it meant more work than before, and Bernice Krueger, now filling Marshall's shoes, could be just as tough, demanding, and efficient as her boss.

So, Tuesday was rolling along at a brisk pace, everyone was there, hard at work, and Bernice never seemed to be in one room or chair for any more than two minutes at one time. With papers, galleys, or a cup of coffee in her hand, she was constantly running to the front to check a traffic revision story Cheryl was trying to get out of the county road crew, then charging to the back with more copy for George to typeset, then running into Marshall's glass-enclosed office to answer phone calls, then running up to the front desk to wait on a customer because Cheryl was busy taking an ad over the phone.

I am going to visit with Betty Smith, Bernice kept telling herself. *So help me, when my lunch comes, or before that, or during break, or sometime, I'm going to sit down and visit with her; she must think I'm so rude, inviting her here just to ignore her!*

But so far "Betty Smith" was not feeling slighted or snubbed. She was sitting in the teletype room, watching the news stories come clattering in over the news wire. For the last half-hour it had been interesting—for the last few minutes it had been riveting. She now held a particular news story in her hand, and she was devouring the news.

"WESTHAVEN—Federal District Judge Emily R. Fletcher today ruled that a ten-year-old child, key witness in the much publicized Good Shepherd Academy child abuse case, would not be required to testify or be examined by defense psychologists, agreeing with the plaintiff's attorneys that such further questioning and examining of the child could prove harmful.

"Citing expert evaluations offered by psychologist Dr. Alan Mandanhi, Judge Fletcher concluded that the mental state of the child is in such a tender and vulnerable state because of the alleged abuses that any further recounting of them would do even greater damage.

"'We are here to speak for the children,' she said, 'and protect them from abuse. We cannot justify even further abuse in the cause of preventing it.'"

Several daily newspapers from around the country lay ready on the table for Bernice's perusal when she got the chance. Sally reached for the one on the top of the stack, a large newspaper from the West Coast. She found nothing about the case on the front page, but the second page did carry a story, along with a nonflattering courtroom photograph of Tom Harris and his attorney. The description under the photograph identified them as "alleged child abuser Tom Harris and attorney Wayne Corrigan."

It was all bad news for the Good Shepherd Academy.

She found an editorial in the second newspaper. The ACFA could not have written it better.

"This will be a precedent-setting case, interpreting the Federal Day-care and Private Primary School Assistance Act, and defining whether the state may breach the wall of separation in order to protect innocent children from harm done in the name of religious freedom.

"Freedom of religion is part of our heritage, but freedom of religion does not mean freedom to abuse. It is our hope that this case will establish once and for all a binding legal and social mandate that religious practice, though free, must never violate the laws of the state, but be subject to the state for the good of all."

It sounded so virtuous, so American, so right. But the writer had never met Amber Brandon. None of the journalists across the country had ever looked into those demon eyes and heard that mocking, accusing voice. They'd never been a victim of the wrath and ruination Sally's former associates could dish out. Instead, as if on cue, they were writing, reporting, selecting, and interpreting the same ideas and opinions, as if the same instructor taught them all.

I can't stay here, Sally thought. *I have to move on. I have to finish.*

"Hey, Betty!" It was Bernice, standing in the doorway looking a bit frazzled. "I'm sorry it's such a madhouse around here, but I think I'm caught up for the time being. Are you keeping yourself occupied?"

Sally set the newspaper down. "Oh, I was reading the newspaper and the items coming in over the wire. It's been interesting."

Bernice could tell she was bothered about something. "How are you doing?"

Sally evaded the question. "I think there's a bus leaving in an hour. I need to be on it."

"Moving on so soon?"

"Could I have . . . Would it be okay if I had your address and telephone number? I'd like to be able to contact you later on."

"Sure thing." Bernice wrote it down on a slip of paper.

"Oh, and the *Clarion*'s address too?"

Bernice wrote that down as well, and handed it to her. Then she looked for a moment at the trouble in Sally's eyes. "Is there anything else I can do?"

Sally thought for a moment with a timid smile on her face. "Well . . . you could pray for me. You never know, it might work."

Cheryl called from the front, "Bernice, it's Jake's Auto Repair on the phone . . ."

"I'll call them back."

"He's leaving in ten minutes. He needs to talk to you now."

Bernice was obviously frustrated, and looked at Sally apologetically. "Listen, after this call we'll just get out of here. I'll take you to lunch, all right?"

Sally smiled. That was all. "Um . . . is there a Post Office around here?"

"Sure, just two blocks up the street on the right-hand side. It's on the way to the bus station. I can drop you by there."

"Great."

"Give me a second, okay?"

Bernice hurried into Marshall's office and took the call from Jake's Auto Repair. Jake could talk and talk about the same thing over and over as if he had nothing else to do with his time and no one else did either. "Okay, sure, we'll change the ad in Saturday's issue, all right?" He went back to the beginning and started the conversation all over again, and Bernice mouthed the words, "No, listen, you already told me that. We'll take care of it for Friday." He started squawking. "Well, that issue's already out, it's history, we can't change that now." She pounded the desk with her fist. This guy was impossible! "All right, listen, Jake, you know our deadlines just like everybody else; don't give me that! You'll get the change on Friday. Yes, that's a guarantee. Hey, didn't you tell Cheryl you had to leave in ten minutes? You're late. Goodbye."

She hung up and bolted from the office, grabbing her coat. "Okay, Betty, let's get out of here! Betty?"

She went into the teletype room. Betty was gone. She stepped into the hall. "Cheryl?"

"Yo!"

"Where's Betty?"

"She left."

That stung. Bernice's first question to herself was, *What did I do? Oh brother, it's what I didn't do! That poor gal. I don't blame her. I shouldn't have invited her into this madhouse!*

She dashed out to the street, but Betty Smith was nowhere in sight. Bernice's initial thought was to run after her, or get the car and try to find her, but then that thought melted away as a more practical one took its place: *This is probably the way she wants it. It's just the way she is, poor thing. Oh well. Maybe she'll write or call sometime.*

Maybe. Bernice felt terrible.

She went back inside.

Tom came out from the back room. "Say, what about that ad for Jake? Cheryl says you talked to him."

"We're rewording it. Cheryl has the new copy, so tell George to set it right away."

"All right. But what about that aluminum can drive? Are you sure you want that on page 3?"

Bernice kept moving down the hall, her mind occupied. "Change Jake's ad first, and then I'll take a look at page 3."

"Well, I need to know—"

"Just give me a second, will you?"

Tom turned on his heels and headed toward the back again. Bernice ducked into the teletype room knowing she owed Tom an apology.

She plopped into the chair Betty Smith had sat in, and took just a moment to pray. *Lord, I could have done better. I could have given her my time. I should have done more to tell her about You* . . . Doggone! What a lousy way for this to end!

Her eye caught the wire copy lying on the table, an item from Westhaven . . .

Westhaven? She snatched up the wire copy and scanned it. Yes. It was the latest news on the Good Shepherd Academy case in Bacon's Corner!

The warrior Triskal stood in the teletype room with her, just watching. He had his orders, and now the time was right. He gently touched her eyes.

Okay, Bernice. Time for you to see.

Bernice saw the newspaper opened to the editorial page. She saw the editorial. Good Shepherd Academy. Bacon's Corner.

Betty had been reading about that case! Is this why she

seemed so troubled, so secretive? A lone woman, traveling, elusive . . .

It was like a stab through the heart. Hadn't Marshall told her about some woman they were trying to find?

She bolted from the room and dashed into Marshall's office.

Bev Cole turned off her vacuum cleaner and answered the phone. "Hello?"

Bernice was frantic. "Is this the Cole residence?"

"Yes, it is."

"Is Marshall Hogan there? This is his assistant at the *Ashton Clarion*, Bernice Krueger."

"Oh, he's out right now. I can have him call you."

"Well, who am I talking to?"

"This is Bev Cole."

"Do you know anything about the Good Shepherd Academy case?"

"Oh boy, do I!"

"What about that woman that's missing? Do you know anything about that?"

"Oh, you mean Sally Roe?"

Bernice recognized the name. "Yes! That's the one! Do you know what she looks like?"

Bev stumbled a bit on that one. "Well . . . we've never met her in person. All we have is a bunch of police and newspaper photos, and they aren't very good . . ."

"Does she have long, black hair?"

"No, I think her hair's red."

"What about her age?"

"I think she's about thirty-six now."

"Can you send me those pictures?"

"You want me to mail them to you?"

"Can you fax them? I need them right *now*."

Bev was getting flustered. "Well, the only fax machine is down at Judy's Secretarial, and Ben's gone with the car."

Bernice gave Bev the *Clarion's* fax number. "Get them to

me right away, as soon as you can, all right? Send me everything you have on her. And have Marshall call me."

"Hey, what's happening over there?"

"I've got to go. Please get that stuff to me!"

"Okay, you've got it."

Bernice hung up and then ran into the front office. "Cheryl, get your keys! We've got to find Betty!"

Cheryl half-rose from her desk, still wondering what was going on. "What . . ."

Bernice grabbed her purse and dug for her own keys. "You go down to the bus station and see if she's there. I'll check at the Post Office. If you find her, stall her and call my pager."

Cheryl got up and grabbed her coat. She had no idea what this was all about, but Bernice was so frantic, it had to be important.

Lucy Brandon unlocked her front door and stood back to make sure Amber went inside. "Go ahead, Amber." No response. "Amethyst, go inside, and quietly."

Amethyst complied, moving rather stiffly, a pout on her face. She went to the stairway in the front entry and sat down on the first step, her chin in her hands. Then she glared at Amber's mother as Lucy closed the door and hung up her coat.

"How dare you bring me home!" she said finally in a low, seething voice.

Lucy was angry enough by now to directly face this creature. "I had to, and you know it! Miss Brewer refused to have you in the class anymore."

Amethyst bared Amber's teeth in an animal-like snarl. "She knows not what she wants! First I was invited, and now I am rejected! Miss Brewer is a turncoat and a fool!"

Lucy bent low over Amethyst and spoke directly to her. "And you are a filthy, destructive, disrespectful little imp!"

Amethyst snarled at her.

Lucy slapped her soundly across the face. "Don't you snarl at me, you little monster!"

But Amethyst began to laugh a fiendish laugh. "Why are you slapping your *daughter*?"

Lucy wilted a little. She didn't know what to do. "I want you to get out of my daughter. I want you to leave her alone!"

Amethyst smiled haughtily. "Your daughter is mine. She invited me in, and now I have her. She is mine." Then she pointed her finger right in Lucy's face. "And you are mine as well! You will do as I say!"

Lucy felt a terrible rage and even raised her hand, but had to stop.

Amethyst taunted her. "Go ahead. Slap her again."

"No! You won't do this to us!" She called, "Amber! Amber, wake up! Amber, answer me!"

"She can't hear you."

A formula, a tradition from Lucy's past, came to her mind. "In the name of Jesus Christ, I command you to come out of her!"

Amethyst raised her eyebrows in mock horror. "Oh, now you're throwing that name around! Ha! What is He to you?"

Lucy didn't know why she grabbed Amber's body. It was an unthinking, desperate act. She was trying to find her daughter in that little body somewhere. "Amber!"

SMACK! Lucy stumbled backward, her hand to her face, stunned. Like a wild animal escaping from a cage, Amethyst bolted from the hallway. Blood trickled from Lucy's nose; she dug in her pocket for a handkerchief as she ran around the corner into the dining room, bumped against the table, recovered, went through the kitchen doorway. She could hear silverware rattling to her right.

Amethyst had opened the cutlery drawer. Amber was holding a knife to her own throat. "Stop or I'll—"

But this was Amber's mother, wild with rage and maternal instinct. Lucy clamped onto the arm holding that knife and jerked it away with such force that Amber's entire body came up from the floor as Amethyst screamed. Lucy slammed into the counter behind her, bruising her spine. The hand would not release the knife.

The drawer flew open; butcher knives, steak knives, utensils all shot across the kitchen and clattered against the opposite cupboard doors.

Amethyst snarled, cursed, spit in Lucy's face. Her strength was incredible.

Lucy worked the knife loose. It fell away, hung in midair, spun, came at Lucy point-first.

"Aaww, Mommy!" came Amber's voice.

Lucy spun away as the knife went past her and dug into the dining room carpet. She fell to the floor with Amber still in her arms.

Amber screamed a long, anguished scream of terror. "Mommy . . . Mommy!"

Lucy held her tightly. The blood was still dripping from Lucy's nose. She wiped it away with her hand.

"Mommy . . ."

"I love you, Amber." Lucy wept in pain and fear. "I'm right here, honey. I have you."

"Mommy, why do I do bad things?"

"It's not you, sweetheart. It's not you."

"I don't know why I'm bad!"

Lucy held her tightly. For now, she had her daughter back. "Shhh. It wasn't you. It wasn't you."

Bernice and Cheryl returned to the office two hours later with nothing to show for their frenzied efforts. Bernice had checked with the Post Office, but the clerk on duty knew nothing of any strange woman coming through; another clerk may have seen her, but was now gone for lunch. Cheryl searched the bus station and even waited for the mysterious Betty Smith to appear, but there was no sign of her. There was, however, an eastbound bus that left only moments before Cheryl got there. Both ladies had searched up and down the streets between the *Clarion* and the bus depot, but Betty Smith/Sally Roe was gone.

As soon as Bernice came in the door, Tom and George were full of questions.

Bernice talked as she hung up her coat. "Paste Jake's ad on page 4 and shove over the Insurance box; just yank those personals and put them alongside the classifieds this time. Go to twelve point instead of sixteen for that notice, and change 'howl' to 'bark,' we'll get a pun out of it."

"Yeah," said George, "I thought of that."

They were content for now. Bernice checked the fax machine, nestled against the wall in the front office, next to the photocopier. They'd received a transmission—the long ream of paper poured out of the machine and lapped upon itself several times on the floor. She carefully tore it off and then found the first page.

Cheryl was there to see it too. There, looking vacantly over her ID number in a police photo, was Betty Smith, alias Sally Beth Roe.

"I'd better call Marshall," Bernice said in a weak voice. "He's going to love me for this."

Cheryl asked, "What about Sara Barker? Sally Roe stayed in her boarding house. Maybe she knows something about Sally's plans."

"Call her."

Bernice contacted the Cole residence in Bacon's Corner. Ben Cole was there this time.

"Did you get that fax?" he asked.

"Yes, Ben, thank you very much, and thank Bev too. I need to talk to Marshall."

"Well, he's still out, hunting for information."

"Well, I have some for him. Have him call me, will you? I'll either be at the *Clarion* office or at home."

At the elementary school, Mr. Woodard was all smiles and pleasant as he handed the *Finding the Real Me* curriculum across the office counter to Kate Hogan. "There. Actually, a subpoena wasn't necessary. I know we would have found it sooner or later."

"Well, it never hurts to jog somebody's memory a little," said Kate. "Thanks a lot."

She hurried to her car, the thick binder under her arm. That she actually had possession of this document was almost beyond believing. Now the question was, would it answer any questions or confirm any hunches?

As soon as she got into her car, she flipped the curriculum open to the title page.

The publisher: Omega Center for Educational Studies, Fairwood, Massachusetts.

The title: *Finding the Real Me: Self-Esteem and Personal Fulfillment Studies for Fourth-Graders.*

The authors: Dee Danworth and Marian Newman.

She read every word on the title page, and quickly skimmed the introductory pages for any leads, anything that might tie in Sally Roe. So far, nothing.

Well . . . if it was there, she was going to find it. She started the car, and headed back to the Coles' house.

When Bernice called Hank Busche, she was close to tears. "She was right here, Hank, right under my nose, and I didn't see it; it never occurred to me! Her life is in danger, and we could've helped her, and I let her get away!"

Hank was just as shocked and dismayed. "It's incredible. I talked to her when I was over at Barkers', and I could feel a tug from the Lord then. I just knew she was here with a real need."

"We've just got to pray that we find her, that she writes to me or calls or *something!*"

"I'll get on the phone. We'll get something going."

Triskal and Krioni soared high over the town of Ashton, their wings rushing, shedding, rippling, sparkling trails of light. The prayers were beginning all over the town, and the Spirit of God was stirring up even more.

"There now," said Krioni. "This should make a difference in Bacon's Corner!"

"Let's just hope it isn't too late!" said Triskal.

All over Ashton, with one accord, the saints knelt wherever they were—beside their beds, at couches and chairs in living rooms, in a garage next to a jalopy, next to a television that had been turned off for this important moment, over a sink where dishes were soaking in suds. Some were visiting friends, and they all sought the Lord together; school kids paused in their homework to say a quick word; grandparents and relatives across the country joined the prayers by telephone.

They prayed for this woman, this unknown, mysterious, and troubled stranger named Sally Beth Roe. They prayed for her safety and that she would find whatever she was seeking.

Most of all, they prayed that she would turn to God and meet Jesus Christ.

They prayed for a place they'd never heard of before: Bacon's Corner. They sought the Lord on behalf of the believers there, and asked for a real victory in their time of siege and struggle. They bound the demonic spirits in the name of Jesus and by His authority, forbidding them to do any more mischief among those people.

Bernice skipped dinner so she could fast that night. She spent the time sitting on the couch in her apartment, praying and waiting for the phone to ring. It finally did at just about seven o'clock.

"Hello?"

"Bernice, this is Marshall."

"Marshall!" Then Bernice choked up.

"Hello?"

She blurted it out. "Marshall, she was here!"

Marshall knew immediately what Bernice meant, but he didn't want to believe it. "Are we talking about Sally Roe?"

"She was here, Marshall, right here in Ashton!"

"Where is she now?"

Bernice slumped on the couch, heartsick. "I don't know. I didn't know who she was until she left town on the bus. She was staying at Sara Barker's . . ."

Bernice told Marshall everything she knew: how she'd met Sally Roe in church, had lunch with her, and tried to visit with her at the *Clarion*, but just got too busy.

Marshall had to be the most frustrated man in the world right now. Bernice could hear him trying to hide it, trying to remain calm and civil. "We've got to find her, Bernie. We've got to find her."

"I know."

"Did she say anything about the case?"

"She's following it, Marshall. She was reading the wire copy that came in today, and some newspaper stories about it. She seemed pretty upset about that recent ruling."

Marshall paused again. Bernice could just envision him chewing up the phone book. "Well . . . was she coherent?"

"Very coherent, intelligent, articulate. And I think very hungry spiritually. We talked about Jesus and the Cross at lunch on Sunday. She didn't seem to buy into it, but she understood it." Then she added, "But she was elusive about herself. Secretive. She wouldn't talk about herself at all."

"That sounds like every other report I've heard about her. You got those mug shots from Ben?"

"Yes, over the fax. It's her."

"I finally saw the *Finding the Real Me* curriculum today."

"Oh, man, don't tell me . . ."

"I won't. There's no visible connection. But the content is solid confirmation of what Miss Brewer is doing with the kids in the class, along with all the usual humanist, cosmic stuff: collectivism, global consciousness, altered states, relativism . . ."

"All the usual 'isms' . . ."

"But no mention anywhere that Sally Roe had anything to do with it. So we still don't know what this whole attempted murder thing is about, or what Sally Roe has to do with this case, and I've used up a lot of precious time."

"She did get my phone number and address from me."

"No kidding!"

"So there's still hope."

"Yeah, and we've got a lot to hope for. Keep praying."

"Oh, we're all praying for you, Marshall, right now. The whole bunch of believers over here."

"Good! We need something to break, and real soon!"

thirty-four

The prayers reached to Heaven from Ashton, from Bacon's Corner, and everywhere in between, and it was as if the Lord God was waiting for just this moment, just this particular cry from His people. He began to move His sovereign hand.

Tal got the report from a courier in the early hours of Wednesday morning. "Guilo!"

Guilo was at his side in an instant.

Tal's voice was strained with excitement. "The Lord has spoken! She's ready!"

"Praise to the Lord!" said Guilo. "Where? When?"

"She's left Ashton and is almost to Henderson. It'll only be a matter of hours. We'll meet her there with everything we can muster! If we can get her through before Destroyer and his minions find out, we may be able to tip the scales at last!"

Guilo drew his sword with a metallic ring and a flash of light. "A turning point!"

"Mota and Signa will remain here with their warriors ready, watching that breach." Tal smiled for the first time in weeks. "They just might get some real action today!"

> Dear Tom,
>   I arrived by bus about seven o'clock this morning, and I imagine I'll get a room soon enough. For now, I'm quite comfortable just sitting in Lakeland Park near the city center. The sun is warm, the bench is dry, and the nearby pond is placid and full of ducks.
>   I would not call the city of Henderson an inviting place, but it does have some major advantages: it is a large, metropolitan city, and therefore easy to hide in, and it has an immense downtown library, an excellent place for finding certain information. I'll be going there today, or tomorrow, or whenever I finish a more immediate matter demanding my attention.

A more immediate matter. Sally was a little surprised at her detached, businesslike tone, as if she were going to type a letter or make a purchase. In reality, she was about to enter into a relationship that could potentially alter the course of her entire life, totally restructure her worldview, and bring into consideration every moral issue, every act, every decision, and every attitude of all her previous years; her deepest scars and emotions, the most personal and guarded areas of her life, would be laid bare. The relationship would be confrontational, perhaps devastating.

At least, that is what she expected from the arrangement, and for that reason she'd pondered the move all through the night, weighing the pros and cons, considering the costs, testing and eliminating the options. It became clear to her that she would have to pay an enormous price in terms of ego and self-will, and that the arrangement would carry with it staggering implications for the future. But every second thought was entertained and answered, every objection received a fair hearing, and in between the fierce and heated debates Sally conducted with herself on the floor of her own mind, she slept on it.

By the time the light of day peeked through the bus windows, she'd settled in her mind that, with all things considered, such a major commitment would be the most logical, practical, and desirable thing to do, with advantages that far outweighed the disadvantages.

It was quiet in the park, with few people around besides a matron walking her poodle and a few yuppies jogging to work. She moved to another bench closer to the pond, out in the full morning sun, and sat down, her duffel bag beside her.

Then she took a good long look at herself. Dressed in her jeans and blue jacket, with a stocking cap on her head and a duffel bag beside her, she looked like a homeless vagabond.

She was.

She looked solitary and lonely.

She was.

She also looked small and insignificant in a very large world, and that carried more weight in her mind than anything else. What must she look like to a God big enough to have created this huge globe on which she was sitting? Like a microbe on a microscope slide? How would He even find her?

Well, all she could do was make some noise, call out to Him, cause a disturbance, send up some verbal flares. Maybe she could catch His eye or His ear.

She placed her notebook in her lap and flipped to a page of notes she had prepared. Now . . . where to start?

She spoke softly, just barely forming the words on her lips. She felt self-conscious and she was willing to admit it. "Uh . . . hello." Maybe He heard her, maybe He didn't. She said it again. "Hello." That should be enough. "I imagine You know who I am, but I'll introduce myself anyway. It just seems the thing to do. My name is Sally Beth Roe, and I guess one refers to You as . . . God. Or maybe Jesus. I've heard that done. Or . . . Lord. I understand You go by several titles, and so I hope You'll indulge me if I grope a bit. It's been a long time since I've tried to pray.

"Uh . . . anyway, I would like to meet with You today, and discuss my life and what possible role You might wish to play in it. And thank You in advance for Your time and attention."

She stared at her notes. She'd gotten this far. Assuming she'd secured God's attention, she proceeded with the next item. "To quickly review what brought this meeting about, I guess You remember our last visit, approximately thirty years ago, at the . . . uh . . . Mount Zion Baptist Church in Yreka, California. I want You to know that I did enjoy our times together back then. I know I haven't said anything about it in quite a while, and I apologize. Those were precious times, and now they're favorite memories. I'm glad for them.

"So I suppose You're wondering what happened, and why I broke off our relationship. Well, I don't remember what happened exactly. I know that the courts gave me back to my mother, and she wasn't about to take me to Sunday school like Aunt Barbara did, and then I went to live in a foster home, and then . . . Well, whatever the case, our times together just didn't continue, and that's all . . . Well, I guess it's water under the bridge . . ."

Sally paused. Was there some kind of awakening happening inside her? God could hear her. She could sense it; she just knew it somehow. That was strange. It was something new.

"Well . . ." Now she lost her train of thought. "I think I do sense that You're listening to me, so I want to thank You for that." She got her thoughts back again. "Oh, anyway, I guess I was an angry young woman, and maybe I blamed You for my sorrows, but . . . at any rate, I decided that I could take care of myself, and that's basically the way it went for most of my life. I'm sure You know the story: I tried atheism, and then humanism with a strong dose of evolution thrown in, and that left me empty and made my life meaningless; so then I tried cosmic humanism and mysticism, and that was good for many years of aimless delusions and torment and, to be honest, the mess I'm in right now, including the fact that I'm a convicted felon. You know all about that."

Okay, Sally, now where do you go from here? You may as well get to the point.

"Well, anyway, I guess what I'm trying to say is that Bernice, back in Ashton, was right, at least as far as Sally Roe is concerned. I have a moral problem. I've read some of the Bible. Uh . . . it's a good book . . . it's a fine piece of work— and I've come to see that You are a God of morals, of ethics, of absolutes. I guess that's what 'holy' means. And actually I'm glad for that, because then we can know where our boundaries are; we can know where we stand . . .

"I'm beating around the bush, I know."

Sally stopped to think. How should she say it? Just what was it she wanted from God?

"I guess . . ." *Oh-oh. Emotion. Maybe this is why I can't get around to it.* "I guess I need to ask You about Your love. I do know it's there; Mrs. Gunderson always talked about it, and so did my Aunt Barbara, and now I've had a brief glimpse of it again in my talks with Bernice and that pastor, Hank the Plumber. I need to know that You'll . . ."

She stopped. Tears were forming in the corners of her eyes. She wiped them away and took some deep breaths. This was supposed to be business, not some emotional, subjective experience she might later doubt.

"Excuse me. This is difficult. There are a lot of years involved, a lot of emotion." Another deep breath. "Anyway, I was trying to say that . . . I would like very much for You to accept me." She stopped and let the tightness in her throat ease. "Because . . . I've been told that You love me, and that You've arranged for all my wrongs, my moral trespasses, to be paid for and forgiven. I've come to understand that Jesus died to pay my penalty, to satisfy Your holy justice. Um . . . I appreciate that. Thank You for that kind of love.

"But I . . . I want to enter into that kind of relationship with You. Somehow. I have wronged You, and I have ignored You, and I have tried to be a god myself, as strange as that may sound to You. I have served other spirits, and I have killed my own offspring, and I've worked so hard to lead so many astray . . ."

The tears were coming again. Oh, well. Considering the subject matter, a few tears would not be inappropriate.

"But if You will have me . . . if You will only accept me, I would be more than willing to hand over to You all that I am, and all that I have, whatever it may be worth." Words from thirty years ago came to her mind, and they captured her feelings perfectly. "Jesus . . ."

She couldn't stop the emotions this time. Her face flushed, her eyes filled, and she was afraid to go on.

But she did go on, even as her voice broke, as tears ran down her cheeks, as her body began to quake. "Jesus . . . I want You to come into my heart. I want You to forgive me. Please forgive me."

She was crying and she couldn't stop. She had to get out of there. She couldn't let anyone see her like this.

She grabbed her duffel bag and hurried away from the pond, turning off the walkway into the nearby trees. Under their sheltering, spring-fresh leaves, she found a small clearing and sank to her knees on the cool, dry ground. With a new freedom that seclusion brought, the heart of stone became a heart of flesh, the deepest cries of that heart became a fountain, and she and the Lord God began to talk about things as the minutes slipped by unnoticed and the world around her became unimportant.

Above, as if another sun had just risen, the darkness opened, and pure, white rays broke through the treetops, flooding Sally Beth Roe with a heavenly light, shining through to her heart, her innermost spirit, obscuring her form with a blinding fire of holiness. Slowly, without sensation, without sound, she settled forward, her face to the ground, her spirit awash with the presence of God.

All around her, like spokes of a wondrous wheel, like beams of light emanating from a sun, angelic blades lay flat upon the ground, their tips turned toward her, their handles extending outward, held in the strong fists of hundreds of noble warriors who knelt in perfect, concentric circles of glory, light, and worship, their heads to the ground, their wings stretching skyward like a flourishing, animated garden of flames. They were silent, their hearts filled with a holy dread.

As in countless times past, in countless places, with marvelous, inscrutable wonder, the Lamb of God stood among them, the Word of God, and more: the final Word, the end of all discussion and challenge, the Creator and the Truth that holds all creation together—most wondrous of all, and most inscrutable of all, the *Savior*, a title the angels would always behold and marvel about, but which only mankind could know and understand.

He had come to be the Savior of this woman. He knew her by name; and speaking her name, He touched her.

And her sins were gone.

A rustling began in the first row of angels, then in the next, and then, like a wave rushing outward, the silken wings from row upon row of warriors caught the air, raising a roar, and lifted the angels to their feet. The warriors held their swords Heavenward, a forest of fiery blades, and began to shout in tumultuous joy, their voices rumbling and shaking the whole spiritual realm.

Guilo, as brilliantly glorified as ever he was, took his place above them all, and swept his sword about in burning arcs as he shouted, "Worthy is the Lamb!"

"Worthy is the Lamb!" the warriors thundered.

"Worthy is the Lamb!" Guilo shouted more loudly.

"Worthy is the Lamb!" they all answered.

"For He was slain!"

"For He was slain!"

Guilo pointed his sword at Sally Beth Roe, prostrate, her face to the ground, still communing with her newfound Savior. "And with His blood He has purchased for God the woman, Sally Beth Roe!"

The swords waved, and their light pierced the darkness as lightning pierces the night. "He has purchased Sally Beth Roe!"

"Worthy is the Lamb who was slain," Guilo began, and then they all sang the words together with voices that shook the earth, "to receive power and wealth and wisdom and strength and honor and glory and praise!"

Then came another roar, from voices and from wings, and another flashing of hundreds of swords. The wings took hold, and the skies filled with warriors, swirling, shouting, cheering, worshiping, their light washing over the earth for miles around.

Miles away, some of Destroyer's demons covered their eyes against the blinding light.

"Oh no!" said one. "Another soul redeemed!"

"One of our prisoners set free!" wailed another.

A quick, sharp-eyed spy returned from taking a closer look. "Who is it this time?" they asked.

The spirit answered, "You will not like the news!"

Tal and Guilo embraced, jumping, spinning, laughing. "Saved! Sally Beth Roe is saved! Our God has her at last!"

They remained, along with their warriors, keeping the

hedge about her strong and brilliant, making sure her conference with the Lord would proceed undisturbed.

Time passed, of course, but no one seemed to notice or care.

Later—she didn't know how much later—Sally pressed her palms against the earth and slowly lifted herself to a sitting position, brushing dry leaves and humus from her clothes and using a handkerchief to wipe her face. She had been through an uncanny, perfectly marvelous experience, and the effect still lingered. A change, a deep, personal, moral restoration had taken place, not just in her subjective perceptions, but in fact. This was something new, something truly extraordinary.

"So this must be what they mean by 'getting saved,'" she said aloud.

Things were different. The Sally Roe who first ducked into these woods was not the same Sally Roe that now sat in the leaves, a trembling, awestruck, tear-stained, happy mess.

Before, she had felt lost and aimless. Now she felt secure, safe in God's hands.

Before, her life had no meaning. Now it did, with even more purpose and meaning yet to be discovered.

Before, she had been oppressed and laden with guilt. Now she was cleansed. She was free. She was forgiven.

Before, she was so alone. Now she had a Friend closer than any other.

As for her old friends, her tormentors . . .

Outside that hedge, thrown there like garbage into a dumpster, Despair, Death, Insanity, Suicide and Fear sulked in the bushes, unable to return. They looked at each other, ready to squabble should any one of them dare to say the first word.

They were out. Vanquished. Through. Just like that. Somehow, she'd no sooner become a child of God than she began to assert her rights and authority as such. She didn't say a lot, she didn't make it flowery. She simply ordered them out of her life.

416

"She learns fast," said Despair.

The others spit at him just for saying it.

"This is marvelous," she said to herself, chuckling in amazement and ecstasy. "Just marvelous!"

Tal and Guilo were watching, enjoying every moment.

"'The word of her testimony and the blood of the Lamb,'" said Tal.

Guilo nodded. "That's two."

"Captain Tal!" came a shout. A courier dropped from the sky like a meteor, snapping his wings open just in time to alight directly in front of Tal. "Mota sends word from Bacon's Corner! The prayers have brought a breakthrough! They've opened the breach, sir! They're ready to expose Broken Birch!"

Tal laughed with excitement. "Well enough! The kindling is stacked, and"—he looked at Sally—"we now have the match to start the brushfire! Nathan and Armoth!"

"Captain!" they replied.

"Sally's ready. Follow her from here on, and be sure Krioni and Triskal are warned to secure Ashton from invasion. When she lights the brushfire, sound the signal for Mota and Signa in Bacon's Corner."

"Done!"

"Cree and Si, establish your armies at the Omega Center. When the fire reaches there, send it on to Bentmore."

They were gone immediately.

"Chimon and Scion, prepare armies at Bentmore; be ready to send the fire on to Summit."

They soared away.

Tal turned to the courier. "Tell Mota and Signa that they have the prayer cover and can proceed closing the trap. After that, have them wait for the signal from Nathan and Armoth."

The courier flew off with the message.

Tal put a brotherly hand on Guilo's shoulder. "Guilo, the Strength of Many, it's time to position the armies at the Summit Institute!"

"YAHAAA!" Guilo roared, raising his sword for the other warriors to see. "Done!"

Tal unfurled his wings with the sound of a crashing ocean wave. He raised his sword high, and they all did the same so that Lakeland Park was flooded with the flickering light. "For the saints of God and for the Lamb!"

"For the saints of God and for the Lamb!"

Mota got the word from Tal, and not too soon. He and Signa were just then hiding in the ventilation ducts at the Bergen Door Factory, looking for an opportunity to throw a wrench into Destroyer's clever, unseen assault on the saints of Bacon's Corner.

Signa was pointing out supervisor Abby Grayson, moving among the router tables with her ever-present clipboard in hand, just keeping things running smoothly as she had done for the last twenty years. "They've never brought their intrigues and manipulations into this place, at least not so much as to be seen. Abby has no idea what's been happening."

Just then, a pimple-faced youth came down the main aisle through the plant, catching a few stares from some of the workers and looking very uncomfortable.

"All right," said Mota, "here we go. Hopefully Abby's going to have her eyes opened."

"Come on, Abby. Pay attention."

The kid walked up to Abby looking hesitant, embarrassed, but determined to have an audience with her. No voices could be heard above the roar of the machinery, but Abby's lips weren't too hard to read: "So what can I do for you, Kyle?"

Come on, said Signa. *Tell her.*

Two angels immediately stood by Kyle Krantz's side, dressed like factory workers—the people couldn't see them, but any demons might. Kyle—wayward, oft-busted, former pot-smoking Kyle—needed all the encouragement he could get. He was just plain scared.

Come on . . . Mota urged.

Kyle leaned close to Abby's ear and said what he had to say

before he lost his nerve completely. Abby seemed a little puzzled, maybe even shocked at his words.

"Let's get inside my office," she said.

The two angels looked up toward the ventilation ducts and gave strong, affirmative nods.

"Done!" said Mota.

"Better surround that office. Those two need to talk!" Signa added.

Only an hour later, Abby Grayson gave Ben Cole a call from her little office cubicle. Ben could still hear the muffled noise of the factory in the background.

"Well hi, Abby! This is a pleasant surprise."

"Oh, this crazy world's full of surprises. I heard you were fired. Is that true?"

The question seemed rather blunt, but very much like Abby. "Well, yes, it is. It's a long story . . ."

"I'm going to make it longer. I've just heard some information you ought to know."

Ben sat down on the sofa. "Go ahead."

"I just had a long talk with Kyle Krantz—remember him? You've busted him a few times for carrying pot."

"Yeah, right."

"He was working here and doing all right until he got fired yesterday. The word among the supervisors was that he was peddling drugs around the plant, and we have strict rules about any of that stuff, so out the door he went. But he got brave and came to see me today, and . . . Well, normally I wouldn't believe him, but considering everything else that's happened, maybe this time I do." She hesitated.

Ben figured he'd better make it easier for her. "Hey, don't worry. I'm with you so far."

"Well, Ben . . ." She had to build up the nerve to ask it. "What would you say if I told you that we have some witches in town, and some even working here in this plant?"

Ben sat up straight, his whole body full of attention. "I would be very interested to know about that."

"So you don't think it's crazy? I did say *witches.*"

Ben's memory still carried vivid scenes of a goat dismembered and its two front legs crossed and bloody on the front steps of the church. "No, Abby. We've seen quite a few strange things lately. I don't think it's crazy at all."

"Then maybe you'd better hear what Kyle has to say. Will you be free after four o'clock?"

Does a duck swim? "You just name the place."

thirty-five

IT was about four-thirty, and there was a cold wind blowing across the long-neglected, weed-infested fields of the old Benson farm. The white paint on the farmhouse was turning a gritty gray and beginning to peel like a sunburn; the windows were broken out, the shakes on the roof were beginning to splinter away in the wind; the apple and pear trees in the front yard were blossoming, but now reached skyward in a wild profusion of unpruned trunks and unsightly suckers. The Benson farm had been deserted too long and was simply not surviving, but fading steadily into decay and ruin with every passing season.

A heavy chain blocked the driveway, and Marshall could drive the Buick no further. A NO TRESPASSING sign hung from the chain and swung forward and backward in the wind, right above the Buick's grill.

"Is this the place?" he asked.

Kyle Krantz, the young delinquent who couldn't seem to stay out of trouble, sat in the seat beside him, nodding his head and looking scared. In the backseat, Abby Grayson and Ben Cole looked at the dismal scene before them, and found it easy to believe what Kyle had told them about it.

Kyle pointed. "That's the barn right back there. That's where it was."

"I take it they were trespassing, just like you were?" asked Marshall.

Kyle had grown dull toward such loaded statements. "They were here, man."

Marshall looked at the others. "So, I guess we'll have to trespass too."

They got out of the car and took a moment to look the place over. As near as they could tell, they were the only living beings here. There were no sounds except for the wind and the occasional cheep of the swallows nesting under the eaves of the farmhouse.

Marshall ducked under the chain, and the others followed. The driveway wound around the farmhouse, went past a garage and toolshed, then opened into a wide, graveled area in back—a turnaround and access for farm machinery, supplies, and livestock that were no longer there. On the far side of this open area stood the old gray barn, weathered but intact, the main doors shut.

"Just what were you doing here anyway?" Marshall asked the boy.

"Billy and I were looking for a good place to have a kegger. We always do that 'cause we find good spots no one knows about."

"So this barn must have looked pretty inviting."

"Yeah, back then it did. Now it doesn't."

"How did you manage to get this close without anyone seeing you?"

"It was dark, and we snuck in around the other side of the house. They weren't watching for us anyway; they were too busy doing all their weird stuff."

They reached the doors.

"Have you ever gone inside?"

"No way. Billy and I just wanted to get out of here, and that's all."

The big door swung open with a long, aged creak. The inside of the barn was cool, dim, and expansive. No one entered. Marshall was waiting for his eyes to grow accustomed to the low light.

Finally they could all make out the dirt floor. It seemed plain enough—just smooth dirt. They saw nothing out of the ordinary. They looked at Kyle. He was immediately uneasy and defensive.

"I saw it, man. They were here."

"Okay," said Marshall, "show us what you saw."

Kyle went into the center of the floor and turned in a circle, his finger extended out and toward the floor. "They had a big circle carved in the dirt right here, and a big pentagram in the middle of it." Then he pointed to a spot toward the back wall. "There was a big bench there, like an altar, and there was blood on it, and there were about twenty people standing all around the circle with robes on and hoods over their heads, and they were all chanting and shouting, and there were candles around the circle. They had candles at all the points of the pentagram."

Marshall looked around the barn. "What cracks did you and Billy look through to see all this?"

Kyle pointed to the side of the barn. "Right over there."

The daylight was now plainly visible through two large spaces between some loose boards. Marshall went to where the cracks were, crouched down to their level, and looked back. He was satisfied—the cracks provided a wide, clear view of the area in question.

"You say they had hoods on their heads?"

"Yeah. Black robes and hoods, and they were barefoot."

"So how do you know who they were?"

"'Cause some of them were facing this way. I could see their faces turned right at me." Kyle was offended and edgy. "I don't know why you don't believe me!"

Marshall held up his hand to calm the boy. "Hey, I didn't say I didn't believe you. But listen: you've got plenty of reason to get back at Mulligan, or any cop for that matter."

"Not to mention getting your job back," said Abby.

"I'm not making it up, man! I saw Mulligan. He was standing right here, with a robe and a hood on, and chanting just like all the others."

Ben was inspecting the spot where Kyle claimed an altar had stood. "Marshall."

Marshall joined him. Ben had scratched in the dirt with his finger and uncovered some brown stains. He was able to pick up some clumps of stained dirt in his fingers. "Could be blood. I'll take a sample."

"See?" said Kyle.

Marshall asked, "Tell me about that blood you saw. What were they doing with it?"

"They were drinking it out of a big cup, a big silver cup. They were passing it around."

"How do you know it was blood?"

"The lady said it was."

"What lady?"

"Well, the leader, I guess. She was standing right there, and she said something about making some woman die and beating all the Christians. Uh . . . she said, 'Defeat to the Christians!' And she drank from the cup and passed it around, and they all drank from it." Then Kyle remembered something else. "Oh yeah, man, get this: they had some animal legs right here in the middle of the circle."

Oh-oh. Kyle could tell he'd impressed them with that. Hogan and Cole were looking at him, dead serious and ready to hear more.

"Tell me about the animal legs," said Marshall.

"They had to be goat legs. They were crossed right here, like an X." He saw something. "Hey!"

"Hold it!" said Marshall, touching Kyle to stop him from disturbing the dirt at his feet. "Ben."

Ben crouched for a close look. "Yeah. More blood. And here are some hairs."

"Goat hairs," said Kyle. "That's what they are."

"So they wanted to defeat the Christians, huh?" asked Marshall.

"Yeah, they were really hollering about it." Another memory. "Oh, and they were saying something about a courtroom, winning in a courtroom."

"And they were after some woman too?"

"Yeah."

"Did they say her name?"

The name meant nothing to Kyle, but he remembered hearing it. "Uh, Sally on Death Row, or something like that."

He was batting a thousand now. He could see it all over their faces.

Marshall dug into his jacket pocket. "Did you see any of the other people's faces?"

"Sure. The woman leader took her hood off, and I could see her."

Marshall produced some color photographs he'd taken

with much care, stealth, and a telephoto lens. He showed Kyle a picture of Claire Johanson.

"Yeah! Yeah, that was her!"

"The woman who led this whole thing?"

"Yeah."

Marshall showed Kyle a picture of Jon Schmidt.

"Yeah! He was here too."

Marshall slipped in a picture of his sister.

"No. I've never seen her before."

A photo of Irene Bledsoe.

"Uh . . . no, I don't think so."

Officer Leonard Jackson.

"No."

Bruce Woodard, the elementary school principal.

"Naw, not Mr. Woodard. Man, where'd you take all these?"

Marshall put the pictures away. "Kyle, I think you're giving it to us straight. Now listen, I'm not a cop, and whatever you tell me I'm not going to take it to the cops. I just need the information. It's important. I want you to tell me the real truth: did you have any marijuana on the job at the Bergen Door Company?"

Kyle raised his hand as if taking an oath. "None, I swear. Hey, Cole knows I've had some here and there, but not on the job. My old man would kill me, and besides, I need the work bad."

Abby cut in. "So you're saying that you were set up just to get you fired?"

"You got it. I didn't put that marijuana in my locker."

Marshall looked at Ben and could tell he was recalling a similar incident involving marijuana in a locker.

"Any idea who put it there?"

"Who do you think? I saw her here, and then opened my big mouth about it in the lunchroom, and so she must have found out about it. She gave me some pretty dirty looks after that, and then, bam! *She's* the person who says they ought to search my locker, and then they find the pot. Real handy, you know?"

Ben added sympathetically. "And considering your reputation, there wasn't much point in denying it."

"You got it."

Abby objected, "But Donna's been with Bergen almost as long as I have. I can't believe she'd pull a stunt like this."

"She was here," Kyle insisted. "She was standing right next to Mulligan. I saw her, and she knows it, and that's why I got fired." Kyle then recalled bitterly, "Then Mulligan comes down to the factory and tells me he'll let it go this time if I behave myself and 'make the right choices,' he said. I know what he was doing. He was telling me to keep my mouth shut or he'd bust me for good."

Marshall reviewed it all in his mind. "So . . . looks like we might have a real club here: Claire Johanson, Jon Schmidt, Sergeant Mulligan, and . . ."

Kyle resented Marshall's hesitation. "She was here! I swear it!"

Marshall completed the sentence. "Donna Hemphile, Kyle's supervisor at the Bergen Door Company, and a member in good standing at the Good Shepherd Community Church!"

Thursday afternoon, Officer Leonard Jackson had some unwelcome visitors. He was sitting in his squad car, cleverly hidden in the trees at the west end of the Snyder River Bridge, just watching for speeders and having a pleasant day building up his citation quota, when suddenly, without prior notification of any kind, a big brown Buick swung off the road and into the trees, pulling right up alongside him.

Now who in the world was this? Leonard felt invaded. This was a desecration of a sacred place.

A handsome black man rolled down the window on the passenger side of the Buick. "Hey, Leonard, how's it going?"

Ben Cole.

Leonard tried to be sociable. "Not bad, I suppose. What can I do for you?"

Ben looked toward the driver of the Buick. "Have you met Marshall Hogan?"

Leonard had seen him around town and never felt good about him. "No, we've never met."

Marshall called a greeting. "Hello, Officer Jackson."

"Hello."

Ben said, "We'd like to have a brief word with you."

"Well, I'm on duty . . ."

"How's your quota so far?"

Leonard realized Ben would know everything about his job, so bluffing wasn't going to be possible. "Well . . . I guess I'm doing all right. I've logged twelve so far."

Ben was impressed. "Hey, you're way ahead of the game! How about taking a short break for a little conference?"

"I promise you'll find it interesting," said Marshall.

At Summit, five demon messengers gathered just outside the dark, musty, secret chambers of the Strongman, each with an urgent message for Destroyer.

The first demon said to his fellows, "I bring word that Broken Birch has been breached!"

The second demon nodded in acknowledgment and added, "I bring word that Hogan and Cole are about to corner Officer Jackson!"

The third demon gasped at that news and growled his own. "I bring word that they will be seeing Joey Parnell again and may frighten him into talking!"

The fourth said, "I bring word that Pastor Mark Howard is rooting out the division in his church even now, and the Enemy is healing all the damage we've done!"

The fifth said, "I bring word that Sally Roe has—"

Oh. The ground suddenly quivered with a roar that came from inside the Strongman's lair. Apparently Destroyer and the Strongman already knew about that.

Destroyer dared not draw his sword—such an aggressive move would only worsen the Strongman's fury. So he dashed to and fro, grabbing the air in violent, desperate wingfuls, his arms covering his head and face, as the Strongman came after him with flying blade and swinging fist, his mouth foaming with rage, his jowls flopping, his rancid breath turning the air yellow.

"A reversal!" the Strongman screamed. "She was ours, and now you let them have her!"

"I allowed no such thing!" Destroyer countered. "I was biding my time—"

Contradicting the Strongman was a poor idea. It earned Destroyer a violent swat across his head from the flat of Strongman's blade. "Lazy, unmoving, blind idiot!"

"She is ours, my liege!" Destroyer shouted over Strongman's roaring. "Tal and his hordes grow weaker by the day!" *SMASH!* A huge fist in the neck. "Soon they will fall away from her like overripe fruit—" A clawed, scaly foot to the rump. "—from a tree, and we will take her!" *OOF!* A knee to the stomach.

"You were going to take away Tal's prayer cover!" yelled the Strongman. "What became of that?"

"As I've tried to tell you, we have been whittling it away!"

"*Whittling* when you should have been chopping, dashing, shredding, *slaughtering!*"

"You will see it!"

"I wish to see her destroyed, bumbling spirit! Live up to your boastful name! Pierce through a chink in her armor! Let her own sins rot her away!"

"Her sins are gone, my Ba-al! She has come to the Cross—"

WHAM! A folded wing against the midsection. Destroyer tumbled and fluttered sideways across the room.

"NOOO!" the Strongman screamed. "You will not mention *that!*"

"But we can still take her . . ." Destroyer insisted, although rather weakly.

"We will not . . . turn . . . back!" the Strongman roared, waving his sword in a fiery, rushing arc with each word. "I have a plan—I will see it unfold! Let the blood of the Lamb defeat the others—it will not defeat me! I will tread upon it, march around it, assail it and bury it, but I will not surrender to it!"

"I know we *will* take her!" Destroyer insisted again.

"YAAAA!" The Strongman brought his sword down with immeasurable fury, trailing a long, crimson streamer of light.

Destroyer drew his own blade in an instant and blocked the razor edge with a shower of sparks. The power of the blow slammed him into the wall, and the Strongman held him there like a ton of fallen earth.

Now they were eye to eye, the yellow, glowing orbs almost touching, their sulfurous breath mixing in a putrid cloud that obscured their faces. The Strongman's arm did not weaken; he did not lessen the weight that held Destroyer motionless.

"You will do it," he said finally, his voice a low, panting wheeze, "or I will feed you to the angels myself—in tiny pieces!"

With an explosion of arms, wings, and one blade that seemed like several, the Strongman cast Destroyer from the room, and he tumbled into the five demons still waiting for him outside. They bowed before him—as soon as they could crawl out from under him.

"We bring word, Ba-al!" they said.

"What word?" he asked.

They told him.

He cut them all to pieces.

> Tom, I am free. I could just see that Cross so clearly, just as it must have looked on that bare, forlorn hill two thousand years ago, and I was flat on my face before it, so weighed down with my wrongs, my boasts, my choices, my SELF that I couldn't rise an inch. All I could do was lie there, admitting and confessing everything and reaching out to that rough-hewn piece of wood like a drowning man reaches for a lifeline, and grabbing hold for my very life.
>
> And how can I describe it? I apologize, but the words will not capture the experience: I had nothing to offer Him, no incentive at all for Him to forgive me, not the slightest item of value with which to barter or cajole. All I had was what I was.

But He accepted me. I was so surprised, and then relieved, and then, with the steady realization of what had happened, ecstatic! My offering—nothing other than myself, Sally Beth Roe, pitiful, failing, and wayward—was accepted. I was what He always wanted in the first place, and He received me. He lifted the load from my heart, and I could feel it go; I could just sense it all drawn away from me and rushing up to that Cross. I felt so light, I thought I would be carried away by the slightest breeze.

I was able to raise my head, and then saw the closing of our transaction: a trickle of blood running down the wood and puddling on the ground. The payment. Such a gruesome sight, such a discomforting thought, but really, to be honest, quite appropriate considering what Jesus, the Son of God, had just purchased.

I am free. I am ransomed. I've never felt this way before, like a slave set free who was born a slave and never knew what freedom was like.

I want to get to know this Jesus who has ransomed me. We've only just met.

Sally laid her pen down on the small motel room desk, and wiped some tears from her eyes. She was still shaking. Just beside her notebook, a Gideon Bible lay open to the Gospel of Matthew, chapter 11:

"Come to me, all you who are weary and burdened, and I will give you rest. Take my yoke upon you and learn from me, for I am gentle and humble in heart, and you will find rest for your souls. For my yoke is easy and my burden is light."

thirty-six

That night, Marshall and Ben found County Coroner Joey Parnell at his home in Westhaven. As usual, he wasn't glad to see them, nor was he willing to chat.

"Now get out of here and don't come back!" he ordered through his barely cracked front door.

"Mulligan's controlling you, isn't he?" said Marshall. "He knows about that hit and run, and he's been hanging it over your head."

The door didn't close. "Who told you about that?"

"A source close to the Bacon's Corner Police Department. You struck a deal with Mulligan, and he's owned you ever since." The door started to close. Marshall talked fast. "You hit a high school girl named . . . uh . . . Kelly Otis, and Mulligan tracked you down, and you were just then working on a case of suspected homicide, some female transient, and Mulligan made you a deal: falsify the cause of death of this female transient, and he'd let the hit and run slip by. Am I right so far?"

The door cracked open a little more. "Just what do you want from me?"

Marshall tried to sound compassionate despite the urgency that kept making his voice tense. "How much longer do you want this to go on? You can be their puppet for the rest of your life, or you can help us put a stop to it."

Parnell was silent for a moment. Then he opened the door wide enough to pass through. "Come inside before somebody sees you."

Parnell's wife was beside him. She was dark-haired, stout, and looking as troubled as he was. "This is Carol. We can talk freely in front of her; I've told her everything."

"Would you like some coffee?" she said quite mechanically. It was clear she didn't know what else to do.

"Yes, thank you," said Marshall, and Ben accepted as well.

"We'll sit in the dining room," said Parnell, leading them through the house.

They sat around a large table under a dimly glowing chandelier. The low, somber lighting seemed to match Parnell's mood; he looked worn, tired, at the end of his strength.

Without cue or question, he started talking as if he'd saved this story for years. "The transient was a thirty-two-year-old woman named Louise Barnes—she was homeless, a scavenger, no family. She was found dead in the woods along the Snyder River, about six miles north of Bacon's Corner. I remember the details perfectly because I want so much to forget them." He paused to gather his thoughts and control his emotions, then continued. "Her body was found hanging by the ankles from a tree limb, the blood drained. There were abundant signs of bizarre, ritualistic murder that I won't go into. The hunters who found her had apparently startled the killers, who fled before they could dispose of the body altogether.

"I received the remains and finished the autopsy. I found the cause of death to be homicide, of course. But then . . . as you have already heard, I did get into a mishap near the high school on my way home. I didn't see the girl, Kelly Otis, until she stepped from behind a tree and into the street, and . . . and I hit her. I slowed just enough to look, to see that she was still alive though injured. Some other people were running to help her. I . . . I just couldn't let the incident damage my career. I'd just gotten the coroner's job, and you know how the political world is, how fragile a reputation can be. I fled.

"Sergeant Mulligan came to my office the next day, and we met in private. I expected him to question me about the hit and run, but he immediately asked me about the body of Louise Barnes and what my findings were. I told him, and that's when he made the offer to let the hit-and-run incident pass, just bury it, if I would alter my findings and not report the real cause of death." Parnell just stared at the table, his face etched with pain. "I accepted his offer, filed the cause of death as accidental, and it was the worst decision of my life.

"There have been three ritual murders since then that I

know of, and I'm sure many more that no one will ever know of. The three brought to me I quickly wrote off as accidental deaths. They were unknowns, possible runaways. I was hoping they would not be missed, but simply buried and forgotten, and that's what happened.

"But you see, I knew Sergeant Mulligan and his friends would be watching me. I knew I would have to perform to satisfy them, and so, with each murder I concealed, I fell deeper and deeper under their control, and that's where things stand at the present time."

Marshall asked, "Just who are these people? *What* are they?"

Parnell reached into a cabinet and pulled out a file folder, then set it before him closed, his folded hands resting on top. Carol brought the coffee and sat down beside her husband, putting her hand on his arm and saying nothing.

"If you want a name to call them, you can use the term Broken Birch. It's a secret label they share among themselves. They're a coven of witches, Satanists, occultists, whatever you wish. They're linked with hundreds of other such groups across the country. And taken together, these people wield incredible power, mostly through terror."

"And they're responsible for those ritual murders?"

Parnell looked at the telephone hanging on the wall. "You should know that right now I can pick up that telephone, call any one of six different phone numbers, and have both of you dead within twenty-four hours. The other side of that, however, is that there are other parties who can make the same call regarding me, and I could be dead just as quickly, and may very well be if they find out I've talked to you. Unknowns and transients are used for ritual sacrifices; people who are known and would be missed are . . . Well, fatal accidents are arranged for them."

"Can you tell us who belongs to this bunch?"

Parnell shook his head slowly for emphasis. "First of all, I don't know all of them. Secondly, I wouldn't tell you if I did. I can only confirm what you already know: Sergeant Mulligan is involved, and has been for years. As I understand it, he and some of the men from the local lodge checked it out and found the transition very easy. Because he holds such power in town and is head of law enforcement, they were quite willing to include him."

"Can you confirm Claire Johanson?"

Parnell hesitated, and then answered, "Yes."

"What about her boyfriend, Jon Schmidt?"

"Yes, he's part of it."

Ben wondered, "So what about all those people involved in the LifeCircle fellowship? Do they tie into this?"

Parnell shook his head emphatically. "They aren't supposed to know about it. All those well-meaning people being pulled into the LifeCircle group are simply being used and manipulated; they have no idea that Broken Birch is at the core of it, and they have no idea what their leaders are really up to."

Marshall asked, "What about Donna Hemphile? Is she a part of Broken Birch?"

"I believe so. It's hard to be sure sometimes, they hide it so well." Parnell drew a breath to change gears, then opened the file folder. "Here's what you really want to know, and all I really want to tell you."

He distributed the contents of the folder on the table in front of Marshall and Ben. With great interest, the two men examined several police mug shots and the rap sheet on a young, beautiful, black-haired woman.

"Not Sally Roe, obviously," said Parnell.

Ben recognized her. "The dead woman we found in the goat shed."

"I did some checking on my own. Her name is Alicia Von Bauer, twenty-seven, a Satanist, a member of Broken Birch. You'll note her criminal record: animal mutilations, public nudity and perverse behavior, prostitution, pornography. I might add to that list ritualistic murder, but who could ever prove it?"

Marshall asked, "So you think this Sally Roe thing was another ritual murder, or at least an attempt at one?"

434

"Exactly. It's clear to me that her death was arranged, and it was supposed to appear to be a suicide."

"That's how you recorded it, anyway," said Ben.

Parnell nodded. "With an unforeseen additional service: identifying the body of Alicia Von Bauer as that of Sally Roe. I do what I'm told, Mr. Cole. But obviously, something went terribly wrong, and all I can figure is that Sally Roe—or something else—overpowered Von Bauer, and Roe escaped."

"That's our theory," said Ben. He picked up the most recent photograph of Alicia Von Bauer for a closer look. The deep black eyes seemed to stare back at him from the page. It was eerie.

Marshall asked, "Where's the body now?"

"Cremated. We did that as soon as possible."

"Disposing of the evidence?"

"Exactly."

Marshall didn't know if he'd get an answer to the next question. "Mr. Parnell, we have a lot of reason to believe that this attempted killing isn't just a Broken Birch affair. What about the big people Claire Johanson and Jon Schmidt are connected with? Would they have something to gain?"

"I think you're on the right track. I'm sure the order for the murder came from someone higher up."

"How do you know?"

Parnell even smiled a little. "Because it's the first time I've seen Sergeant Mulligan afraid. Not long after I collected the body, Mulligan called me, asking if I'd found any personal effects on the body, which I hadn't. I could tell he was getting pressure from someone much higher, much more powerful than him or his Broken Birch friends. He was desperate enough to tell me what to look for, something missing that should have been there."

"Yeah," Ben recalled, "I asked you about that. Somebody even ransacked the rental house."

"So what was missing?" asked Marshall.

"A gold ring," Parnell answered. "Someone took it off Von Bauer's finger with cooking oil. I found traces of the oil still on Von Bauer's finger. The other thing missing was ten thousand dollars in cash."

Marshall and Ben looked at each other. They both had the same thought.

Ben spoke it. "Somebody hired her."

"Who?" asked Marshall.

Parnell shrugged. "I'd advise looking for someone rich, influential, and very powerful."

Ben responded, "A mighty big mole, Marshall."

Marshall had no comment. Right now he was overwhelmed with a sudden, flesh-crawling fear he hadn't felt since a few years ago in Ashton, when it seemed all the evil in the world was about to crash down on him. A mole? Suddenly the analogy was inadequate. What Marshall felt was more like a dragon, a monster—dark, insidious, clever, and big enough to fill the sky, with jaws gaping just above them, dropping to the kill, closing like a vise.

Far away from Bacon's Corner, and still hidden from her enemies, Sally Roe sat among the floor-to-ceiling shelves at the downtown library in Henderson, flanked on every side by invisible angelic guards, and paging through a massive National Bar Association directory of attorneys. She had a hunch, only a guess, but in her thinking it was the strongest possibility.

At her elbow sat Volume IV of the four rosters she had stolen from Professor Samuel W. Lynch's office, its full title: *A Continuation of the History and Roster of the Royal and Sacred Order of the Nation.* Each of the four volumes contained about two hundred pages. Most of the pages were devoted to weird, esoteric, ceremonial mumbo-jumbo, secret rites and initiations, minutes of meetings, and bylaws. At least fifty pages in each volume were dedicated to the names of members. The pages of names held her attention for the time being; she'd been scanning them for hours.

She now had another volume lying across Volume IV to hold it open to page 68, *The 168th Brotherhood of Initiates.* Like the 167 pages in this and the three volumes that came before, this page listed the names of new members brought into the Order of the Nation in one particular year, and contained two columns of fifteen names each. The column on the left contained bizarre, esoteric names like Isenstar, Marochia, and Pendorrot. The column on the right contained real names, some of them even familiar. Two-thirds of the way down the left column, she'd found the name she had looked through several years' worth of pages to find: Exetor.

At first, Exetor was just a mysterious word she'd found engraved on the inside surface of the ring she'd taken from the finger of her would-be assassin. Until she stole the rosters and studied them, the engraving made no sense at all. When she finally found page 68 in Volume IV of the rosters, it made a lot more sense. Exetor was a secret name or title, ninth on the list of fifteen. Directly opposite the name Exetor, in the right column, was the real name of the man who had received the title.

"James Everett Bardine."

James Bardine. He'd been initiated into the Sacred Order of the Nation along with fourteen other men twelve years ago, and upon his initiation had been granted the secret Brotherhood name of Exetor and his Ring of Fellowship bearing his secret name.

Very impressive, even spooky, and not to be scoffed at. The Nation could have been just another lodge or fraternal organization, some secret society or club where all the good old boys could get together, have a secret meeting with its oaths, handshakes, funny hats and rituals, and afterward down some beers and be rowdy. Almost every town had a lodge or secret order of some kind.

But the Nation went beyond that. It bound a lot of familiar names together and gave them at least this society in common. She'd found the name of Samuel W. Lynch among the 129th Brotherhood of Initiates—he'd been initiated into the Nation fifty-one years ago, and as he showed her in his office, still kept his cherished Ring of Fellowship.

The second ring in her possession—the one she'd hidden for ten years under the brick windowsill in Fairwood—bore

437

another secret name, Gawaine, but she already knew whose ring it was. She quickly found his name at position seven, opposite the name Gawaine, in the 146th Brotherhood of Initiates: Owen Jefferson Bennett, initiated thirty-four years ago when a senior at Bentmore University.

Good old Owen. There were so many things he never told her.

All this was fascinating, of course, but first and foremost in Sally's mind at this moment was the name of James Everett Bardine. The Nation was a strictly male organization, but a female assassin was wearing his ring. What was the connection? Who was Bardine in the first place?

Perhaps it was the current lawsuit causing all the stir in Bacon's Corner that made her think Bardine might be an attorney; perhaps it was the fact that the Nation seemed to have no ordinary, blue-collar people in its membership, but only bankers, businessmen, educators, attorneys, and statesmen—purveyors of power.

Whatever the case, she was now narrowing her search in the "B" section of the Bar Association directory, and getting closer.

Barcliff . . . Barclyde . . . Barden . . . Bardetti . . . Bardine. James Everett Bardine.

Bingo. This guy was an attorney. The listing was current, published this year. Bardine was working for a big law firm in Chicago: Evans, Santinelli, Farnsworth, and McCutcheon. They were members of the American Citizens' Freedom Association.

Sally had to sit back and think about that. *James Bardine is a member of the ACFA . . . The ACFA is bringing the lawsuit against the school . . . The killer was wearing Bardine's ring.*

Did this mean a connection between the ACFA and Sally's would-be killer? Sally thought so. She would be looking up more names, that was certain. She couldn't wait to write to Tom and tell him.

But who in the world was that fiendish woman in black?

Friday morning, Pastor Mark Howard found his way through the noisy, busy, bustling Bergen Door Company, protective eyewear and earplugs in place, dodging the forklift, ducking around the doors being stacked, being sanded, being moved. He engaged a clipboard-carrying foreman in a brief, shouting conversation, and got directions to the small cubicle office of Donna Hemphile, Finish Supervisor. Mark could see Donna through the glass enclosure. He stepped up and tapped on the door.

"Yeah, come in!"

Mark stepped inside.

Donna Hemphile swiveled around in her desk chair and stuck out her hand. "Hey, Mark! What a surprise! What brings you here?"

Mark had no time for sweet-and-easy, beat-around-the-bush phrases. "Some pretty serious matters, Donna."

Donna looked at the clock. "Well, you know, I have to be out of here by—"

"I already talked to Mr. Bergen. He has someone else handling that new band saw. He said I could have an hour with you."

Donna had to digest that for a moment, and then relaxed back in her chair. "Okay. Have a seat."

Mark wheeled the only other chair around and sat facing Donna. "I've been running all around town since Wednesday night trying to nail some things down, and I haven't slept much. You know the kind of trouble we've been having in the church since this lawsuit came up. I've felt like a seaman trying to patch the leaks in a sinking ship before it goes down completely."

Donna nodded. "Yeah, it's been rough."

"Anyway, I finally got three families together for a conference: the Warings, the Jessups, and the Walroths. It was a pretty good meeting, I guess. Ed and Judy Waring are still disgruntled, but the Jessups and Walroths might be coming around." Mark paused. He was going to change directions. "But I wanted to ask you about something they all told me, and you know, I never thought about it before this. You're on the prayer chain, and your name comes before the Jessups, the Walroths, and the Warings."

"Mm-hm." Donna just sat there listening.

Mark plunged in. "So, let me ask you point-blank: Did you tell June Walroth that Tom Harris beats his daughter Ruth, and that's why he puts long sleeves on her so often?"

Donna chuckled at that. "No."

"Did you tell Judy Waring that Cathy and I are having marital problems because I was unfaithful and had an affair a few years ago?"

Donna smiled and shook her head. "No."

"Did you tell Ed Waring that the school was in bad debt because Tom and Mrs. Fields were stealing the school's money?"

"No."

"Did you tell Andrea Jessup that Tom's had some real problems with sexual deviancy ever since Cindy died?"

"No."

Mark was finding Donna's extremely brief answers a bit jarring. "You don't have any other comment about all this?"

Donna smiled and shook her head in seeming incredulity. "Why should I say anything, Mark? Those people are gossip-hounds. This is the kind of thing they'd come up with."

"Why do you suppose they all came up with the same source for their information?"

She tossed up her hands. "Beats me. They must have some-thing against me, I don't know. So what else do you have on the list?"

"Well . . . somebody who doesn't even go to our church. Kyle Krantz, the kid who got fired on Tuesday for having marijuana in his locker."

At that, Donna rolled her eyes. "Oh, brother!"

"Well, he has an interesting story to tell, and you know, a lot of what he has to say checks out. I guess you know his side of the story, right? That someone planted that bag of pot in his locker to set him up?"

"Oh yeah, I've heard it, all right. He could have come up with something more original. All the kids use that line."

"I've heard it before myself, from Ben Cole. Somebody planted some confiscated marijuana in his locker at the police station, and Mulligan fired him. Of course, it was Mulligan, according to Kyle, who came down to the plant here and struck a deal with Kyle and didn't book him for possession, isn't that right?"

"That part of it wasn't my concern. I just fired him according to company policy."

Mark slowed down a little for emphasis. "Kyle says Mulligan told him he'd let it go if Kyle kept his mouth shut about some things he knew."

Donna got just a little tense. "Well, listen, Mark, what goes on in this plant is my business, and none of your concern."

Mark didn't back off, but kept going. "Somebody killed Kyle's dog too; they cut it open and left it on the front seat of his car. Maybe they were trying to give him a little reminder to watch himself."

Donna leaned her elbow on her desk, propped her hand under her cheek, and gave every appearance of patiently humoring a childish, assuming, overimaginative minister.

Mark kept going. "That was weird enough in itself, and I don't know if I would have believed Kyle if something similar hadn't happened to us, right at the church. Monday morning, somebody splashed goat's blood on the front door and left two goat legs crossed on the porch. It was some kind of curse, or maybe it was a warning, I don't know. But just the day before, on Sunday morning, Ben Cole went out to the Potter place to investigate the killing of a goat that used to belong to Sally Roe. All the blood had been drained out, and the legs cut off.

"Then, according to Kyle, on that Sunday night he and a friend were out at the Benson farm and saw a witch coven holding a ritual in the barn, and wouldn't you know it—the witches, or Satanists, whatever they were, were drinking goat's blood and were standing in a circle around two more goat legs, calling for the defeat of the Christians and for the death of Sally Roe."

That finally evoked at least a small comment from Donna Hemphile. "Heh. Pretty bizarre."

Mark hit her squarely with the next sentence. "And Kyle

says *you* were there, that you were part of that group holding the ritual, along with Sergeant Mulligan, Claire Johanson, and Jon Schmidt—probably Tom Harris's, and our church's, worst enemies right now."

Donna said nothing. She just leaned back in her chair and kept listening, surprisingly detached.

"We also checked with Kyle's friend and gave him quite a thorough testing with some photographs Marshall had of the people Kyle claimed were there, as well as some photographs of people who were not there, and some phony information we claimed Kyle had told us. The friend checked out on every detail. I'm convinced we have two reliable witnesses."

"And a pretty wild story," Donna reminded him.

"Well . . . after all we've been through, and everything we've seen and learned, it isn't that wild. It's disgusting, it's tragic, it's bizarre, but at this point I find it incontrovertible, especially since Mulligan—and perhaps yourself—have stooped to such terror and intimidation tactics to keep the boys quiet about it." Donna didn't look like she had any comment to that, but Mark didn't wait for one. "Donna, you said that what happens here at the plant is your business and none of my concern. Well, what happens to my church is my concern, so let me just get down to the direct question: Were you there at the Benson farm on Sunday night?"

"No," she said simply.

"Are you involved in witchcraft or occultism?"

"No."

"Are you trying to destroy my church with gossip and division?"

She chuckled, and the chuckle had a note of mockery in it. "Of course not. Hey, you're going through difficult times. If you don't all stick together, you won't make it."

"What about Sally Roe?"

"Never heard of her."

An unplanned question occurred to Mark. "What about the social worker for the CPD that took Tom's kids, Irene Bledsoe? Is she purposely working against us, trying to destroy Tom's reputation?"

Donna laughed. "Hey, as far as I know, she's just doing her job. If you ask me, Tom's a sick man, and I think she can see that."

"What about that time you saw Ben Cole first visiting Abby Grayson here at the plant? Did you report that to Sergeant Mulligan?"

"You mean, did I snitch?"

"Whatever."

"I don't really know Mulligan. Why would I go out of my way to tell him about one of his own cops?"

Mark looked at Donna, and Donna returned his gaze. There was no question remaining between them.

"Donna . . . you don't lie very well."

She smiled that same subtle, mocking smile. "On the contrary, Mark—you did approve my application for church membership."

Mark nodded. "So I did. So I did." He'd heard enough. "Well, I could go through the Biblical pattern and come back with some witnesses to go through all this again with you, but . . . what do you think? That probably isn't worth the trouble, is it?"

Donna just kept smiling. "No need, really."

The phone rang. Donna picked it up. "Yeah. Okay. I'll be right there." She hung up. "Well, sorry, that was Mr. Bergen. He wants to meet with me right away."

"I know," said Mark, rising from his chair. He let himself out the door, and walked down the aisle. Donna was not far behind him.

Mr. Bergen's office was about halfway down the floor. Mark looked through the window; Abby Grayson, Kyle Krantz, Kyle's friend Billy, and Marshall Hogan had already been there quite a while. Mr. Bergen, a stern-looking man in his sixties, was pacing about the office, waiting impatiently, visibly angry.

Mark cracked the door open and stuck his head in long enough to catch Mr. Bergen's eye. Bergen looked his way immediately; he was expected.

"It's all true," said Mark.

Then he closed the door and went on his way, pausing just long enough to look back and see Donna Hemphile go into the office of her boss.

thirty-seven

LUCY Brandon could feel her scalp crawling and her stomach twisting into a knot. This was her second such phone call today, interrupting her work at the Post Office and scaring her to death.

"Don't talk to Hogan," said her once-kind friend Claire Johanson. "Don't say a word to him, or to any of those people! It could go very bad for you if you don't protect any knowledge you have!"

Lucy tried to keep her voice down so Debbie wouldn't overhear. "Claire, what's happened?"

"Nothing has happened!"

"I got a call from Gordon Jefferson just like yours. He wasn't kind at all. He kept telling me I'd be in legal trouble if anything leaked, and I didn't even know what he was talking about . . ."

Claire didn't answer right away. She was working on a reply that was safe—or downright deceiving. "The hearing before the federal Court of Appeals is coming up soon, and things are getting critical, that's all. I think it has all of us on edge."

"So why come down on me?"

"It's not just you. We're clamping down on everyone, even ourselves. Too much information is getting out, and it could ruin our case. We have to be careful. I'm sure you understand that."

"This all seems so sudden."

"Well, it just seems that way. Don't worry about it. Just keep quiet, and keep things to yourself from now on. I have to go."

Click.

I'm going to explode, Lucy thought. *I'm just going to go crazy, stark raving mad. I can't take this anymore!*

Ding!

A patron was at the counter. *No, I can't see anyone, I can't talk to anyone. I just want to get out of here. But where could I go? How would I explain my daughter? What about the trouble I've gotten myself into?*

Ding!

Oh, where's Debbie? Lucy looked at the clock. *Oh, wonderful! She's on break, probably across the street buying some sugarless gum or something.*

"Coming."

She gathered herself, trying to calm down, and stepped to the front.

The patron was Tom Harris.

Both of them immediately felt awkward and even shied back a little.

"Oh, I'm sorry," said Tom. "I mean, I don't have to—"

Lucy looked this way and that. There was no one else in the lobby. "Well, I can wait on you."

Tom stood back from the counter. He extended his arms to lay some packages in front of Lucy. "I wanted to send these to my folks."

Lucy pulled the packages toward her, turned them around, turned them around again, read the addresses, read them again, still didn't know what she'd read. She just couldn't think. Was she supposed to weigh them? She set all three on the scale at once and fumbled with the sliding weights. No, no, this wouldn't work, not all three . . .

She set the packages down and without looking up tried to say, "I'm sorry any of this ever happened," but her voice was too weak and trembling.

Tom heard her anyway. "Sure. So am I."

She tried to concentrate on the packages. "Well, I guess we aren't supposed to talk about it."

"I understand."

"Do you think Amber's possessed?"

The question didn't just slip out—Lucy pushed it out. She wanted to know.

But Tom Harris was muzzled, and acted like it. Even though he wanted to answer, he could only look at her in obvious frustration. "You know I can't talk about that."

"I need to know. For *me."*

He shook his head sadly, painfully. "I can't talk about it. But listen . . ."

She listened.

"Uh . . . Jesus Christ conquered the spiritual forces of evil on the Cross. The Bible says He disarmed them and made a public display of them. He has all authority over them, and He's given that authority to His people, the true believers in Him. He's the answer. That's all I can say."

"Have you ever seen someone possessed?"

Tom took back his packages. "I wish I could tell you all about it. Maybe when this lawsuit is over, huh? I'll . . . Listen, no offense, okay? I'll mail these later."

He hurried out the door, leaving Lucy with her questions unanswered.

"Evans, Santinelli, Farnsworth, and McCutcheon," said the receptionist.

"Mr. Bardine, please," said the woman's voice on the other end.

The receptionist hesitated. "Uh . . . I'm very sorry to inform you, but Mr. Bardine is deceased. Did you have any current business with him? We can arrange for someone else to complete that."

The other party was understandably shocked by the news. "Did you say Mr. Bardine was deceased?"

"Yes, I'm sorry to tell you that. He was killed in an auto accident several weeks ago. It was a real blow to all of us here at the firm."

"Well, I'm . . . I'm shocked to hear that myself."

"I'm sorry. Perhaps you'd like to talk to Mr. Mahoney, Mr. Bardine's superior. Perhaps he can help you."

"Oh, thank you, no. Let me sort things out first."

"Fine. Thank you for caring."

"Good-bye."

The receptionist hung up the phone and went back to typing a letter on a sophisticated electronic typewriter, sitting at a massive, dark oak, brass-fitted desk, in a plush carpeted office with twelve-foot-high, wood paneled walls and ornate lighting fixtures, as gray-haired senior partners, junior partners dressed for success, aggressive legal assistants, ambitious secretaries, and powerful incognito visitors moved tight-lipped and chin-high up and down the halls with their brief-cases, legal files, or yellow legal pads.

The Chicago offices of Evans, Santinelli, Farnsworth, and McCutcheon were more than a palace; they were a citadel of power and legal technocracy, where knowledge and power were synonymous and time was money—lots of money. Here the czars of case law and the architects of legal precedent groomed the future by challenging, bending, stretching, and even crossbreeding the law, turning it their way as far and as often as their money, skill, connections, and power would allow.

These were the offices of the elite: the promoters of the favored and the deposers of the dispensable, the guarantors of success and the instigators of ruin.

Atop this ivory tower, at the pinnacle of the pyramid, strode the ruthless and powerful Mr. Santinelli.

"Good afternoon, Mr. Santinelli," said the receptionist.

"Good afternoon," he replied with a faint, obligatory smile, extending his hand to receive the newly typed letter. "I'll be having a special meeting for the next half-hour; there will be no calls, no disturbances."

"Yes, sir."

Santinelli continued down the aisle to a tall and imposing mahogany door. An aide swung the door open just in time for him to pass through it, and then closed the door after him like a slab over a crypt.

Santinelli was in the private conference room adjacent to his office, a soundproof, secret, and rather gloomy place. The woodwork still seemed to absorb the light, and the floor-to-ceiling, velvet curtains were still drawn over the windows.

Three men stood in a tight cluster at one end of the room, talking in hushed voices. They nodded a greeting when Santinelli came in.

One of them was Mr. Khull, the man entrusted with the elimination of Sally Beth Roe.

Santinelli made some quick introductions. "Gentlemen, allow me to formally introduce Mr. Khull, who will be assisting us in the present pressing matters. Mr. Khull, I present to you Mr. Evans, a partner in this firm, now fully devoted to our present legal concerns, and Mr. McCutcheon, our director of administration and finance."

"A pleasure," said Khull.

"I've spoken with Mr. Goring at Summit and Mr. Steele at the Omega Center," Santinelli reported. "It's clear to all of us that Sally Roe has been tracking down the owner of that ring she slipped from Von Bauer's finger, and using Von Bauer's fee to finance her cross-country sleuthing. They agree with us that the rosters are enough to lead her to the late James Bardine, which means she'll have to come here, though we can't be sure when. Mr. Khull has secured the building for that eventuality, and of course we have your assurance, Mr. Khull, that the failure at Bentmore University will not be repeated?"

"Last time we were a little too discreet, I would say. I have twice the personnel here as I had stationed at Bentmore, and our techniques will be much more direct this time."

"The hearing in the federal Court of Appeals is on Monday," Santinelli fumed. "A ruling in our favor will not be much consolation if Roe is still at large. When she comes, you may bring her to this room and kill her right here, as far as I'm concerned."

Khull stifled a laugh.

Just across the conference table, Destroyer and the twelve grotesque warriors who flanked him did not stifle their laughter at all, but thoroughly enjoyed the thought of killing that woman.

Destroyer's laugh was a brief indulgence, however. He still bore the bruises and shame from his recent meeting with the Strongman, and now his exhilaration at the thought of Sally Roe's impending death was mixed with desperation.

You will take her this time! he growled, his wings flared in anger, his crooked finger pointing across the table. *You will take her and kill her!* Then he shouted to his warriors, "Surround this place, and post sentries over the city! She will not evade us this time!"

The warriors swooped out of the room with a thunderous war cry, almost crazy with a thirst for blood.

Destroyer glared at Khull, and muttered to himself, *Come to us, Sally Roe. Whatever your condition, Cross or no Cross, this time nothing will stop us. Nothing!*

On the outskirts of Chicago, Sally Roe sat in a dismal, musty room at a cheap motel, staring at the telephone and wondering what to do next. So James Bardine was dead! She'd spent no small amount of time preparing herself to confront him face to face, to bring it all to a head, and she had come so close, but now what could she do? Well, there was no point in visiting Evans, Santinelli, Farnsworth, and McCutcheon. The man she sought was no longer there.

But obviously Bardine wasn't the only player in this game; there were other players and strategists, from the clumsy police in Bacon's Corner to the mind-molders at Omega, to the highest levels of the educational establishment at Bentmore University, and even beyond that. They all knew about her, they all wanted that ring, and they all seemed quite determined to kill her.

With reluctance, she brought back an old thought she'd entertained several times in the past few weeks and went over it again. There was one final ploy she could try, one do-or-die way to find and identify the people who were responsible for this whole nightmare. Did she say do-or-die? It would most likely be die, if God didn't see fit to spare her.

Funny. Before she encountered the Cross, she saw no reason to live but feared death. Now she had a reason to live, but did not fear death at all. It was an odd kind of peace, a fascinating sense of rest and stillness deep in her soul. Someday she would have to analyze it and clarify just what had happened to her, *if* she lived long enough. If not . . . Well, maybe she'd lived long enough already.

She got out her notebook again, and began to compose her very last letter to Tom Harris.

Nathan and Armoth were tense with anticipation and preoccupied with strategy, but they were there by Sally's side when she started that letter.

"'The word of her testimony, the blood of the Lamb, and she does not love her life so much as to shrink from death,'" said Nathan.

"That's three," said Armoth.

Sally's pen glided over the paper.

> *Tom, this will be my last letter to you. I have told you all that I have done, and all that I know, and I've shared with you my encounter with the God and Savior you serve. What more could remain but to see you face to face and finally bring this trouble to an end?*
>
> *There is no doubt in my mind that the ACFA has pulled some big strings, or vice versa, and are connected with the attempt on my life, which must be connected with the attack against you and your school. I now have the gold ring taken from my would-be assassin as well as the four volumes of the History and Roster of the Royal and Sacred Order of the Nation, which prove the ring belonged to the now deceased James Everett Bardine, an attorney in high standing with the ACFA. I also have other information, much of which I have provided in many letters, that should prove invaluable to you in your defense against this lawsuit.*
>
> *All that remains now is for me to return to Bacon's Corner to aid your attorney in building his defense, and ultimately to testify in open court on your behalf.*
>
> *I believe it's time I heard from you. Please contact me at the Caravan Motel.*

She gave Tom the address and telephone number, then closed her notebook. If she hurried, she could get the letter photocopied and mailed.

But first, there was one more letter to write. She flipped to a fresh page in her notebook—she'd used up the pages in two notebooks by now, and was starting into her third—and began her first and last letter to Bernice Krueger, c/o the *Ashton Clarion*. She wrote hurriedly, saying only what was essential.

The young clerk at the Post Office was just bagging up the mail for the evening pickup when a lady in jeans and a blue jacket came to the counter with some more. He was in a hurry; the truck was coming any minute. He took care of her quickly, applied the necessary postage, and threw the rest of the mail into the mailbag.

There was the truck! He grabbed the bag and headed for the back door.

The lady went out the front door, glad she'd made it in time.

In the rush, one letter fell from the mailbag to the floor under the front counter and lay there facedown.

It was addressed to Bernice Krueger, c/o the *Ashton Clarion*.

thirty-eight

On Monday morning, without prior warning and totally unexpected, the fax machine in the *Ashton Clarion* office warbled its electronic ring and was barely heard over the prepublication bedlam that usually marked Monday mornings. Bernice didn't hear it at all; she was in Marshall's glassed-in office trying to convince Eddy's Bakery to buy just two more column inches so she wouldn't have to keep filling in that space with stupid one-liners.

"Hey listen," she said, "we'll make the donut bigger, and then make the coffee mug bigger, you know, show more steam coming out or something. The readers will grab right onto it. Sure they will!"

"Bernice!" Cheryl called through the glass. "You're getting a fax!"

Bernice looked up at Cheryl. "What?"

Cheryl said something back, and all Bernice could hear through the glass was the word *fax*. The rest was meant for lipreaders.

A fax? From who? So far she was drawing a blank.

The phone squawked in her ear. She had to give a reply. "Oh, yeah. Well, think about it, will you, Eddy? I'll give you a deal on it. Well, let *me* think about *that*. Okay, good-bye."

Cheryl knocked at the door lightly, cracked it open, and tossed the sheet of paper in, hot off the fax machine.

Bernice grabbed it before it floated to the floor and gave it a once-over.

Oh! This was from Cliff Bingham, her contact in Washington, D.C.! She'd forgotten all about him. Well, well! He'd found the *Finding the Real Me* curriculum for fourth-graders at the Library of Congress and sent her the title page with a note scribbled at the top: "Bernice, is this the one you're after?—Cliff."

She smiled. *Well, Cliff, you did all right, but Marshall's seen the curriculum already; you're too late. Thanks anyway.*

She went to her Rolodex to find Cliff's number, found it, and picked up the telephone. She punched in the number, and looked over the title page again as she waited for the ring and the answer.

Then she saw it. She slammed the phone down. She scanned the page again to make sure. She checked the publication date.

She picked up the phone and pounded out the number for the Cole residence in Bacon's Corner.

"Hello?" It was Bev Cole.

"Hello, Bev. This is Bernice Krueger in Ashton."

"Oh, hi! What do you know?"

"I've got to talk to Marshall right away!"

"Hooo, well he isn't here, and I don't know where he is."

"I've got to—oh, nuts! Did he say when he'd be back?"

"No, he runs around so much I never know where he is, he and Ben."

"Bev, listen, I'm going to fax him something. He should be able to pick it up at Judy's, right?"

"Oh yeah, if she's open."

"I'm going to fax it to Judy's Secretarial Service right now, and you tell him to get over there right away and pick it up, all right?"

"Okay, I'll tell him. Hey, you sound excited."

"Oh, I'm a little excitedseeyoulatergood-bye!"

She scrambled out of the office and made a beeline for the fax machine.

Marshall, where are you?

Lucy Brandon was going through the morning mail, sorting it, slipping it into all the Post Office boxes and assigning it to the four different carrier routes. She was ill, nervous, overwrought, and exhausted, and now she was beginning to hate her job, especially when letters came in from "S. B. Roe."

Like this one, fresh out of the bag, no sooner thought of than in her hand! How many did this make? It had to be more than thirty. Thirty-plus envelopes, all stuffed with several thicknesses of the same lined notebook paper, all written in the same, fluid handwriting just visible through the envelope, and all addressed to Tom Harris.

So I guess when I forward this one, I'll be violating federal law over thirty times. What a thought. What if I just delivered it to Tom Harris? What if I slipped it into his carrier's box, just one of these letters, just once?

"Good morning, Lucy!"

She literally jumped, dropping the letter to the floor.

Sergeant Harold Mulligan!

"Sergeant! What are you doing back here? You scared me to death!"

He stooped and picked up the letter from the floor. "Ah, another one, eh?"

She tried to take it from him. "Yes, thank you kindly—"

He wouldn't let go. "Naw, now just hold on, Lucy. I've got orders regarding any further mail from Miss You-know-who."

She didn't care. "I'll take that letter back, sergeant! It's United States mail!"

What? He actually grabbed her arm with painful force and pushed her against the wall! He hurt her, and she just couldn't believe it!

He spoke to her in a low, threatening voice she'd never heard from him before. "And just what do you think you're gonna do with it, huh, Lucy? Are you thinking you just might mail it where it's supposed to go? Huh?"

"You let go of me!"

"You listen to me, little lady! Any more mail from Roe, you put it right in my hand, right here, see? You don't mess with it, you don't even think about it, or you are gonna have one big, ugly pack of troubles!"

She was getting scared. "I'm doing what I'm told, Harold, you know that. Please let go of me!"

"Just wanna make sure we're clear on this—"

"Excuse me," came a voice from the front.

It was Marshall Hogan.

Oh man, how much of this did he see? Mulligan immediately turned his aggressive posture into a teasing one and let Lucy go. "Okay, Lucy, take care!"

He went out the back way with the letter in his pocket.

Debbie stepped up to the counter to help the big, red-haired man. Lucy hurried forward. "I'll take care of him."

Debbie backed away, but could see Lucy was in no condition to help anyone. Too late, though. They couldn't talk about such a thing in front of a customer. She went back to her sorting, but kept an eye on her boss.

"I'd like a book of stamps," said Marshall gently.

She reached into the drawer under the counter. Her hands were visibly shaking, and she couldn't look up.

"Are you in trouble?" Marshall asked.

"Please, I can't talk to you," she said on the verge of tears.

"Just sell me some stamps then," he said. "Do that first."

She finally found a book of stamps and set them on the counter.

He had something else on the counter as well. "This is County Coroner Joey Parnell's report on the woman who committed suicide, supposedly Sally Beth Roe. See the description? Black hair, in her twenties. Here . . . look at this." He set a photograph in front of her and continued to talk in quiet, gentle tones. "This is a police mug shot of her. She had a criminal record. Now I know you know what the real Sally Roe looks like; you identified a picture of her at your deposition. But this is the woman who was found dead. She was a member of a secret coven of witches who call themselves Broken Birch, and when she tried to kill Sally Roe, she was working for someone—she was carrying ten thousand dollars."

Lucy looked down at the picture, still shaking but listening.

Marshall continued, "Now that cop who just roughed you up back there has done all he can to cover this up and make it look like a suicide, and we think we know why: he belongs to that coven; he's in on the whole thing. As a matter of fact, that coven lays claim to some pretty big wheels in LifeCircle—some of your own friends, including Claire Johanson and Jon Schmidt."

Marshall waited just a moment for that to sink in, and then concluded, "As for Sally Roe, we have good evidence that she's still alive somewhere, probably hiding for her life. So the question I'd like you to consider is this: Why would the same friends who are helping you in this lawsuit want Sally Roe killed?"

Lucy didn't say a word. She could only stand there stone-still, staring at the photographs as tears filled her eyes.

Marshall got his answer from her face. He took back the coroner's report and photos and slipped a piece of paper to her. "This is where you can reach me, at Ben and Bev Cole's house. Call me anytime."

He paid for the book of stamps and walked out. Lucy still didn't move, even as Marshall's money for the stamps sat on the counter in front of her.

Debbie saw the whole thing. Now she was finished with just watching. She was going to do something.

The mail . . . I forgot the mail!

Bernice got into her Volkswagen Beetle and zipped over to the Ashton Post Office a little late this morning. In all the excitement, her daily mail pickup had slipped her mind.

She went into the lobby, said hello to Lou, the young mail clerk, and opened the *Ashton Clarion*'s Post Office box.

Krioni stood beside her, as interested in the morning mail as she was. He was looking for an important letter from Sally Roe.

Bernice flipped through the junk flyers, the bills, the letters to the editor . . . Ah, here were some checks in payment of advertising and want ads; those were always nice.

Nothing unusual, everything routine. She dropped all the mail into her large plastic shopping bag and headed out the door.

This was a horrendous development! Krioni shot through the roof of the Post Office and met Triskal high above.

"Nothing!" he said.

Triskal wasn't ready for that report. "Nothing? No letter?"

They could see Bernice getting back into her little car, far too calm and unruffled.

"It didn't get here," said Krioni, agitated, frustrated, and thinking fast. "It's lost . . . It's misplaced . . . I don't know! We'd better get word to Nathan and Armoth. If we don't get the fire started in time, Sally Roe is as good as dead!"

Sally's last letter to Tom Harris lay open on Claire Johanson's desk, and Claire was on the telephone.

"The Caravan Motel," she said. "I think our magic worked after all; this is the first time Roe has ever revealed her where-abouts. Apparently she'll be there for a while; she's waiting for Tom Harris to contact her." The party on the other end was elated. "Well, I'll breathe easier when we have her, before she writes to anyone else. And I'll breathe easiest of all when she's dead." More elated squawkings from the other end. "Yes, I'm sure Mr. Santinelli will be pleased. Give him our regards."

Claire hung up, rested her chin on her knuckles, and smiled at Sergeant Harold Mulligan. "Harold, help yourself to a drink."

Nathan shot through the roof of the Post Office near Chicago and flew over the heads of the busy staff, looking this way and that, banking and swooping over the tables, counters, and carts, then ducking under the tables, flying just inches above the linoleum, his sharp eyes scrutinizing every scrap of paper, every piece of junk mail, every—

There! Just under the front counter, facedown, lay the lost letter to Bernice Krueger. It was going to take some special measures to get it to Ashton in time. He grabbed it, arched upward, and looked around the room for the right mailbag to put it in.

Snatch! The letter was gone from his hand! He spun about in time to see a brazen little imp holding the letter in his claws, grinning a toothy grin, hovering on blurred black wings.

"Ooo," said the demon, "and what have we here?"

Nathan didn't have time for this. His sword was instantly in his hand.

OOF! A kick from a black, clawed foot! Another spirit came at him from the side, sword ready!

Nathan dashed the demon's sword aside with his own, then kicked the demon back, sending him through the wall of the building.

Another spirit dropped from above; Nathan shot sideways to dodge a plunging sword, then mowed the spirit in half.

Where was that imp? There! Hiding behind the sorting bench!

Two more spirits! They must have heard there was a fight in here. Nathan dove for the first, his sword raised, but the other spirit grabbed his ankle and jerked him backward. His sword cut through space, and that was all. The first demon was ready now with his own sword, laughing and drooling. The ankle-grabber was still pulling, his claws digging in.

Well, use what you have, Nathan figured. His wings roared with power, pulling him forward. With incredible strength and perfect timing, he swung his leg in a high, sweeping kick, giving the ankle-grabber a thrilling ride until Nathan brought him down with skull-crunching force on his partner. They were out.

There went the imp with the letter! Nathan shot sideways and caught him in the belly. The legs drifted to the floor while the imp dissolved. Nathan caught the letter, made a quick search, then slam-dunked it into the right mailbag. It would go out on the next truck.

As for the demons, Nathan knew there could be trouble— some of them had gotten away with the knowledge of this letter.

In the sealed conference room at Evans, Santinelli, Farnsworth, and McCutcheon, Santinelli hung up his private line and looked across the table at the anxious Mr. Khull.

"Mr. Khull, I've just been given some good news. You'd better gather your choice personnel."

That "good news" went out through the demonic ranks like a shock wave, and as Destroyer flew up through the roof of the law office building to gather his hordes, he suddenly found he had all the friends and yea-saying lackeys he needed to finish the job, especially the demons from Broken Birch. They were swarming in from every sector of the sky, whooping and hollering, wanting to be a part of this glorious moment.

"I knew it!" he gloated, and with no small measure of relief. "I knew it would work! Our Judas has come through at last, and now Sally Roe will have her Gethsemane! We will take her!" Then he added under his breath, "And I will throw her as a gift into the Strongman's face!"

The demons were muttering, nodding, and rumbling their approval and admiration of Destroyer's great wisdom as they came to rest on the roof, hovered overhead, buzzed in tight circles around the building, and even tripped over each other.

This motley, bloodthirsty swarm needed to be brought to order. Destroyer soared into the sky where every gleaming yellow eye could see him, and waved his glowing red sword in wide circles to get their attention. Most of them settled down and listened. The others were too busy hooting, hollering, and sparring.

"Forces!" Destroyer called.

His twelve captains converged immediately.

"We need to weed this garden and select the best! Choose warriors for our mission, and send the rabble to Summit. Let the Strongman put them to work!"

The captains soon had the spirits thoroughly sifted; the best warriors stood ready, swords gleaming. The pranksters, imps, and harassers were ordered to Summit, and left with much grumbling.

Destroyer was satisfied. He addressed the great horde. "We will prepare the way for Broken Birch! Death to the woman!"

"Death to the woman!" they shouted as one, and with an explosion of wings they rushed into the sky.

From miles away, Tal, Nathan, and Armoth saw the demons rise like a swarm of shrieking, whooping bats over Chicago, heading south. This was an armada of death for Sally Roe, a black cloud of doom.

Tal had received Nathan's news about Sally's last letter.

"Then it's going to be a day late. Our fire is delayed, and Sally will soon be in their hands!"

"Can we stop them?" asked Armoth.

Tal shook his head. "Everything is in motion now. We're committed."

"We do have warriors posted to monitor everything," Nathan assured his captain.

"But Destroyer will take her," Tal replied, his voice weakened with the pain of it. "And he will do what he wants with her . . ."

Marshall no sooner got back from his trip to the Post Office for stamps than he was out again, this time heading for Judy's Secretarial Service, quite curious and adequately baited by Bernice and her maddening flair for suspense. To hear Bev Cole tell it, the fate of the world depended on Marshall picking up whatever Bernice was going to fax to him.

Sally Roe remained in her musty little room at the Caravan Motel, sitting in the only chair, reading from a Gideon Bible.

"Who shall separate us from the love of Christ?" she read. ". . . I am convinced that neither death nor life, neither angels nor demons, neither the present nor the future, nor any powers, neither height nor depth, nor anything else in all creation, will be able to separate us from the love of God that is in Christ Jesus our Lord."

She closed her eyes, gave thanks, and kept reading, just waiting hour by hour in her little room.

Marshall pulled into the small parking area in front of Judy's Secretarial. Well, was anybody there? The lights were on inside, but there was no sign of Judy. Hm. That looked like a note taped over the OPEN sign hanging in the window. He got out to have a look.

Outside Chicago, two cars turned off the main thoroughfare, came down one block, and slowed long enough for the people inside to get a good look at the Caravan Motel.

"Hm, so this is the Caravan," said Mr. Khull, giving the old motel a quick once-over. "Roe isn't operating on much of a budget."

"What a dump," said one of Khull's three favorite killers, a young, wiry woman with long, blonde hair who could have passed for a college student.

The Caravan Motel was no joy to behold. Long ago, before the freeways diverted all the interstate traffic, this place probably did a profitable and respectable business in housing weary travelers for the night. Now times had changed, the fourteen little cabins were run down, the lawn had surrendered to weeds, and most of the business here was probably the disreputable kind.

"Which cabin is she in?" asked a tall, youthful-looking man. He'd gotten within a knife's blade of Sally Roe on the Bentmore University campus. He still had his knife, and he was looking forward to a longer, more satisfying encounter.

"Fourteen," said Khull, "right on the end near the road. We won't have to pass any of the other rooms. She's making it easy."

Khull parked the car just past the motel, and the other car pulled in behind. Altogether, eight people got out of the two cars. Khull gave the four men from the second car a slight nod, and they scattered immediately up and down the street, covering every avenue of escape from the motel.

"Okay, babe," said Khull, "check and make sure."

The young woman went ahead of them, walking into the motel office.

Khull and the other two just stood on the sidewalk, talking and looking casual.

She came out again, and pointed discreetly at Number 14.

"Let's go," said Khull.

"Oh, hi," said Judy. "Been waiting long?"

"No, not long," said Marshall. "About ten minutes, I guess." He'd seen the little note she'd taped in the window, "BACK IN TEN MINUTES."

"Had to get a new typewriter ribbon. I can hardly read my

letters anymore." She had a small sack in her hand, which meant her trip must have been successful.

"I think I have a fax waiting for me."

"Oh yeah, you do."

Judy unlocked the door and let him in. "It came in not too long ago. I think I put it . . . Let me see, where did I put it?"

The young blonde knocked on the door to Number 14.

Sally tensed, closed her eyes, and prayed a quick prayer. Then she rose from her chair and approached the door. "Yes?"

"Maid," said the woman.

Judy finally found the sheet of paper that had come out of the fax machine. "Oh, here you are."

Marshall took it and thanked her. Now this looked familiar. It was even disappointing. Hadn't he told Bernice he'd already seen the curriculum? What was the big deal? All the way over here to Judy's for this?

But what was Bernice's note at the top? She'd written it in bold marker pen.

"Okay, just a minute," Sally said, and looked around the room one last time. She was ready. She went to the door and put her hand on the knob.

"Marshall," said Bernice's note, "have you seen this? Call me."

From the note, a huge arrow drawn with a wide-tipped marker pen bled down the page to a glaring circle at the bottom.

Within that circle was the name of the curriculum's author—its *real* author.

Sally Beth Roe.

WHAM! The door burst open and almost caught Sally across the face. Khull was all over her, then two more blurred figures. Arms grappled and grabbed, the room spun around

463

her, she fell to the floor, her face smacking the worn carpet. A sharp knee gouged into her back, pinning her down so hard she thought her ribs would crack. They grabbed her arms and twisted them behind her until she cried out in pain, then bound them with loop upon loop of tight, cutting rope.

AAW! Khull grabbed a fistful of her hair and wrenched her head up from the carpet. She couldn't breathe. He held a glimmering, silver knife to her throat. "Make a sound, and this goes in."

She closed her mouth tightly, trying to contain the cries of pain and terror she just couldn't help.

The room was full of people, searching every corner, every drawer, under the mattress, dumping out her duffel bag, going through all her possessions.

"You know what we're looking for," said Khull right into her ear. He grabbed one of her bound hands and forced her index finger open. "Tell us where the ring is and where those rosters are, or I start cutting."

"If I tell you, you'll just run off with them yourself!" said Sally. The knife came against the base of her finger. She gushed the words out. "I'll tell the people who sent you! Turn me over to them!"

The knife remained in place.

Sally blurted, "You want to get paid, don't you?"

The knife stayed where it was; Khull's grip on her finger never loosened. She could feel the edge of that knife against her skin, and she prayed while an eternity passed.

Destroyer stood in the room, not at all willing to lose the prize once he had found it.

Take her to Summit, he said to Khull.

Khull leaned over Sally, longing with every fiber of his being to run his knife through her heart. He hesitated, breathing hard.

Destroyer put his hand on his sword. *You will take her to Summit, to the Strongman, and you will do it now!*

After the longest, most agonizing moment, for no apparent reason, Khull took away the knife and let her finger go.

Sally thought she would faint. She was close to vomiting.

"Get her up!"

She was snatched from the floor in an instant by no less than four huge thugs, and held tightly, unable to move. Now she could see Khull's face leering at her, the eyes full of hate. Demon eyes.

SLAP! His hand felt like iron across her jaw, cheek, and nose. She almost blacked out. Warm blood began to trickle from her nose and down over her mouth.

Khull grabbed a fistful of her hair again and held his knife right under her nose. "We're going to take you to our friends. They are going to get the whole package right in their laps, and listen to me now: you'd better give them everything they want when they want it, because I will be right there, and if they don't get what they want, they are going to give you to me. To *me*, understand?"

"I *will* cooperate."

"Not a sound from you!"

"Not a sound."

Khull looked at her with all the lust and murderous intent of the Devil himself, and then gave the order: "Let's go."

The young blonde woman stuffed everything Sally owned into Sally's duffel bag, and a thug grabbed it up.

In broad daylight, like a gruesome parade, Khull led his band of rogues and their captive, bound with rope and her nose still bleeding, out of Number 14 and to the street. Sally could see some curtains cracked open across the courtyard, but no one dared show their face. Even the owner of the place, an ugly, chain-smoking woman in her fifties, caught just a glimpse of them and then turned away, being careful to mind her own business.

They took Sally to the first car, shoved her into the backseat between two men—one of them was the young knife-wielder she'd met at Bentmore—and drove away unhurried, un-hampered, and unchallenged.

The Caravan Motel was almost invisible under a crawling, hissing swarm of evil spirits. Every person in every building was motivated by fear, self-interest, and even self-delusion.

No, they didn't see anything. It wasn't what it looked like—it just seemed that way. It wasn't their problem. A lot of that kind of thing happened around places like this; so what?

Destroyer and his twelve key warriors flew just above the two automobiles, wary and braced for any angelic resistance. The resistance never came. They did see some heavenly warriors, but the warriors made no moves against them; they were intimidated by the great demonic numbers, no doubt.

"Ha!" Destroyer laughed, elbowing his closest warrior. "What did I say? Their strength is gone! Tal has no more numbers to boast in, and . . ." He was delighted with his own craftiness. " . . . I do believe we have surprised them all! Before they could muster any new strength, we have snatched their new little saint right from under their noses!"

As the two automobiles turned onto the main thoroughfare and sped away, many of Nathan's prize warriors were on hand to watch, hiding in the shadows, crouching behind trees, parked cars, and houses. They kept a close watch, but they did not intervene. The word had spread quickly and clearly among them all: This was Destroyer's moment, and Captain Tal's biggest risk ever.

Out on the interstate, a U.S. Mail truck sped along, heading southward from Chicago toward the easy rolling hills of the Midwest and the quaint little college town of Ashton.

On board, in a mailbag, just a little dirty and wrinkled by now, was that letter addressed to Bernice Krueger.

thirty-nine

MARSHALL was impatient, and that made him anxious, and that made him irritable. Ben Cole just kept pacing around the house trying to think of what else to do, Kate sat next to Marshall at the dining room table, flipping through all their accumulated files for any information Marshall might need, and Bev Cole just kept watching it all and praying softly, "Lord Jesus, we need You now!"

Marshall was on the phone with John Harrigan, a friend and contact with the FBI. "Oh yeah, she wrote it, all right. I got back to my reporter, and she'd already gotten back to this Cliff Bingham guy, and he verifies the edition he found was recent, published only two years ago." Marshall rolled his eyes and gritted his teeth. This conversation wasn't bringing results fast enough. "So that means the curriculum the school gave to us was doctored; Sally Roe's name was deleted and substituted by two other names, and that fits right in with the cover-up I told you about. No, I don't have a case yet. I thought you guys were the ones who are supposed to investigate these things. Well, I'm close, real close, and I do think it's something for you guys to handle. The Omega Center's in Fairwood, Massachusetts, and Sally Roe was almost murdered clear over here in Bacon's Corner, for crying out loud! Now is that across state lines or what?" More talk from the other end. "All right, listen: can you give me a number where I can reach you anytime, I mean, right in the middle of the night if I have to? I won't call unless I've got some real stuff for you, but when I do get it, time will be that much shorter for Sally Roe." He got an objection. "Come on, I'll owe you one. Just remember that lead I got you in that cocaine operation." Marshall grabbed his pen. "Good man!"

He got several numbers, said good-bye, and hung up.

Everyone in the house converged on him. "Well? What did he say?"

"He'll be on call. I've got phone numbers to reach him at

work, at home, at church, and I've also got his paging service, so he's covered. But what he's waiting for is some firm information to justify the FBI getting involved."

Ben was indignant. "What's wrong with all that stuff you gave him?"

"Eh, it was enough to make him interested, but not enough to make him stick his neck out."

"What about Wayne Corrigan?"

Kate answered, "I left a message at his office. He'll get what we have."

"O Lord Jesus, protect Sally Roe!" said Bev.

Guilo had returned to his post in the mountains above the picturesque town of Summit, and though the surroundings were as strikingly beautiful as ever, the invisible evil was even worse. Educators, statesmen, jurists, entertainers, corporate moguls, and financiers from all over the world were gathering just a mile up the valley from Summit at the Summit Institute for Humanistic Studies. Their semiannual conference was just getting underway, and as these global planners gathered, demon lords and warriors of the most conniving sort gathered with them, filling the valley with a swirling, sooty, steadily thickening cloud of spirits. The demons hovered, hooted, sparred, and jostled, more numerous, riotous, and cocky than ever before.

"They are expecting a real party," said Guilo.

Mr. Santinelli, kingpin of the law firm of Evans, Santinelli, Farnsworth, and McCutcheon, Mr. Goring, the lord and administrator of the Summit Institute for Humanistic Studies, and Mr. Steele, the ruthless ruler of the Omega Center for Educational Studies, were together again, enjoying a brandy by the fire in Mr. Goring's rustic chalet on the Summit Institute campus. This meeting brought back the memory of their last meeting at Omega, when things were not so rosy; they could recall the indignation of having to endure the very presence of that most undesirable of personalities, Mr. Khull—and, of course, at that time Sally Roe was still at large.

Now they clinked their glasses together in a toast of victory. Indeed, with the news that came in earlier today, things were definitely different.

"To the future!" said Santinelli.

"To the future!" echoed Goring and Steele.

They sipped from their drinks, smacked their lips, and even allowed themselves a chuckle or two

As they relaxed into Goring's soft couch and easy chair, Santinelli addressed the pressing matters before them. "I've sent our private jet to bring Mr. Khull and his personnel. They should arrive here with the prize in a matter of hours."

"Have you ever met her?" asked Steele.

Goring and Santinelli exchanged glances.

"Not I," said Goring, "but I'm looking forward to it."

Santinelli agreed. "An outrageous fish story can never compare to actually seeing the fish hauled in. Actually, I'm impressed that Khull was able to restrain himself and deliver her to us alive."

Goring spoke with great anticipation. "I'll be fascinated to meet her. I have many questions, to be sure."

"Oh," said Santinelli, "we'll all have questions for her— serious questions."

"Any word on the ring or the rosters?" asked Steele.

"None. But with Sally Roe in our custody, I can't imagine that will be a problem."

Goring cautioned, "But just remember, there are many delegates and visitors about. Our present business would be quite distasteful to most of them, I'm sure; so our guests must never know about it."

"Agreed. And I have instructed Khull to preserve Roe's appearance, just in case she may be seen by someone."

"Now," said Goring, "there is that other matter that we discussed . . ."

"Of course," said Santinelli, "the whole matter of Khull in particular and Broken Birch in general."

"Mm," said Steele, nodding. "I've thought about that too. Now that they're in bed with us, they won't stop until they control the bed."

"I've consulted with Mr. Evans and Mr. Farnsworth, and they have some of their best people looking into it. If we move carefully, and lay a thoroughly thought-out plan, we could accumulate some damning evidence against Broken Birch while keeping ourselves clean. Evans and Farnsworth are quite sure that the whole lot of them can be arrested for crimes totally unrelated to our enterprise."

Goring smiled and nodded. "Excellent. I've already consulted with my board, and they think such a plan would be feasible. We'll be able to call in some favors from our corporate and governmental resources, and I'm sure they'll be most willing to see what we want them to see and to look the other way when it would be . . . worthwhile."

"Then we must proceed on this without delay," said Santinelli. "Khull and Broken Birch have finally done their job, but upon delivery of Sally Roe we must erase any association with them."

Goring added, "Any *memory* of them in *any* circles, if we can help it!"

Santinelli raised his glass. "I'll drink to that!"

And so they did.

The van had been driving along the winding, climbing, meandering highway for what seemed hours, and Sally finally nodded off, her chin on her chest, sitting between two of the four surly, burly escorts that came with Khull and herself on the plane. The flight had lasted several hours, the driving even longer, and now it was night.

She looked a little better. At least Khull figured she couldn't escape from a flying jet plane, and, reciting Santinelli's order to "preserve Roe's appearance," untied her and let her use the cramped little washroom to wash the dried, caked blood from her mouth and chin, change from her bloodstained shirt to a clean but sadly wrinkled blouse, and brush out her hair. She looked a little better—for a totally exhausted, manhandled, soon-to-die fugitive.

They were heading into the mountains, through tall forests of pine and fir that became monotonous after a while. Sally slept fitfully, jolting awake every few moments, but only long enough to see more trees going by the window, and then she would nod off again.

Some time later—she didn't know how much later—she awoke to morning light. The van was slowing down; Khull and his cohorts were looking around, trying to get their bearings. They were entering a village.

Khull, sitting in the front passenger seat, turned around to tell her, "Welcome to Summit."

Sally rubbed the sleep from her eyes and looked out the windows at a quaint-looking little town surrounded on all sides by snow-covered, sawtoothed peaks and thick, unblemished forests. Out the left window, just above the A-framed roofs of some ski lodges, the morning sun turned a distant waterfall into golden tinsel; out the right window, through a gap in the small inns and storefronts, the mountainside dropped sharply away to a flower-strewn alpine meadow. Patches of snow still remained everywhere, dripping and glistening in the low-angled sunlight.

Why have we come here? Sally wondered. It hardly seemed the setting for such gruesome business, and people like Khull and his bunch just didn't fit at all.

But then again, maybe they did. Sally began to notice some of the establishments and institutions in this village; she began to read some of the signs.

Taoist Retreat Center. Valley Tibetan Project and Monastery. Temple of Ananta. Library and Archives of Ancient Wisdom. Native American School of Traditional Medicine. Karma Triyana Dharmachakra. The Temple of Imbetu Agobo. Babaji Ashram. Mother's Temple Shrine of Shiva. The Children of Diana. Temple to the Divine Universal Mother. The House of Bel. The Sacred and Royal Order of the Nation.

She leaned toward the window. The big escort put his ham-sized palm in her chest and shoved her back. She twisted and looked out the rear windows as the building passed.

The Sacred and Royal Order of the Nation. The little gargoyle snarled at her from the front door of the black stone temple and from the building's facade. She could just hear it screeching, Welcome to Summit!

Destroyer had followed the hunting party clear from Chicago, and now, as the van came through the valley and entered the village, he was going to milk this moment for all it was worth. He dropped from the sky, alighted on the roof of the van, and stood there, his sword held high in victory, his wings trailing like banners behind him, his twelve captains forming his honor guard. Driving under the thick mantle of spirits was like entering a dark tunnel under a towering mountain; on every side, and thousands of feet above, demons cheered and waved their swords in a thunderous display of admiration.

Destroyer reveled in his victory and newfound fame. These vile hordes once ignored him, mocked him, cared not to know his name. Now listen to them! Let the *Strongman* listen to them! A better announcement of his arrival could not be asked for.

Guilo turned at the sound of wings behind him. The captain had arrived.

The cheers of the demons echoing out of the valley could only be for one reason. "They've brought her," Guilo reported.

Both he and Tal stayed low among the trees with their warriors. The swarm of demons below was nothing to tangle with before the right time.

Guilo pointed. "There! That blue van just entering the Summit Institute!"

They could see it only intermittently, as small as a grain of sand, appearing through the thinner parts of the demonic swarm and then disappearing again. It reappeared just long enough for them to watch it turn off the thin, gray ribbon of highway and slip out of sight under the mantle of spirits covering the Summit Institute.

"Well, now she's alone," said Tal. "We can't break through that."

"What about the fire you were going to start?" Guilo asked. "If ever we needed something to happen, it is now!"

Tal shook his head. "It will be a day late. For now, all we can do is wait for Nathan's signal and hope it comes soon."

The semiannual Global Consciousness Conference was getting underway; so the van's driver had to drive up and down the large, black-topped parking lot several times before he could find an empty parking place. Sally spent that time observing the Summit Institute for Humanistic Studies. It reminded her a lot of the Omega Center, except that it was newer and the architecture more modern. Stone was an abundant building material around here, and so was used in the construction of the offices, lecture halls, walkways and gardens. True to their religious devotion to Mother Earth, the designers of the campus did not supplant the natural environment, but let the campus merge with it, almost hiding it among the trees, rocks, and hilly terrain.

The hour was still early, so there were no people out walking. How fortunate for Sally's captors.

Khull turned to Sally, holding up his knife as a reminder. "All they paid me to do is deliver you here. If you get cut up in the parking lot, it's your fault and not my problem, understand?"

She nodded.

"Let's get her into Goring's place."

An observer standing at a distance would have thought an important dignitary had arrived and was now surrounded by Secret Service agents. Sally was barely visible within the tight cluster of bodies that formed outside the van's side door and then began moving up the path toward Mr. Goring's chalet.

Sally made a concerted effort to see around the backs and shoulders of her escorts and study the layout of this place. Right now they were passing through an expansive, meticulously arranged herb garden with sculptured hedges, stone pathways, and eye-pleasing reflection pools. In the middle of a carpet of moss, one lone man sat almost naked in the early-morning cold, eyes shut, legs crossed in the lotus position, totally entranced.

Leaving the herb garden, they rounded a corner, followed a narrow, natural stone stairway with tall evergreen hedges on either side, and then broke out into the open. To the right, the ground dropped away into a natural amphitheater, and beyond the amphitheater, a heart-stopping view of the mountains spread wider and higher than the eye could take in.

In the center of the amphitheater, a sizable group of people stood in neat, concentric semicircles around a blazing firepit, chanting, droning, and tossing flowers, grain, and fruit into the fire. On a small platform at the head of the circle, gawking down into the fire as if mesmerized by it, seven stone deities received the offerings and worship of these adoring early-risers while a gaunt, white-haired woman in a yellow robe sang a haunting song in Sanskrit.

Sally remembered the song and still knew some of the words, even though she hadn't heard it in ten years. She couldn't remember all the names of the seven little deities, but they were secondary gods anyway. This ceremony was to invoke the blessing of the Universal Mother first of all, and secondly to appease these seven dwarfs.

Then she caught a glimpse of some of the faces as they lifted toward the morning sun. No! There was Mrs. Denning from the Omega Center, and two of the Omega faculty! And was that Mr. Blakely, her counselor at Bentmore Teacher's College? She thought she recognized his face, and then his cracking, squawking chant identified him for sure. Close to the fire, her face washed with red light, was Krystalsong, a witch, scholar, and mother of four from the West Coast; she and Sally had worked together on a holistic preschool program.

Quite a homecoming for us all, she thought.

On the highway to Ashton, the mail truck continued to roll along, right on schedule. The morning mail shipment would be at the Ashton Post Office the moment they opened the doors.

"That has to be it!" said a spirit to his friends.

They were whirring and rushing along above the highway,

keeping pace with the truck and eyeing it curiously. The spirit leading them had been in a terrible fight; his wings were tattered, his flight was wobbly, and his face was misshapen.

"This time," he slurred, "we won't let any heavenly warrior stop us!"

"Destroyer will reward us!" said another.

"We will stop the truck and get that letter!"

They swept their wings tightly behind their shoulders and dropped like torpedoes toward the truck, cutting through the thin layers of morning mist, the wind whistling through their wings and whiskers. This should be easy enough. They could foul the engine, break the steering, flatten a tire. They could—

LIGHT! SWORDS! WARRIORS! The truck was full of them!

Nathan shot into the air and met the battered demon.

"You again?" they both said.

The demon dissolved into red smoke. Nathan spun to take out another one.

Armoth tore three spirits apart with one sword swipe, and then spun in a blur to bash two more with his heel.

A dozen warriors had burst out of the truck and now swirled around it, swatting and hacking.

Their picnic ruined, the remaining spirits fled like flies and the truck kept rolling.

forty

The saints were on their knees. The division was fading. Mark had devoted multiplied hours of his time and large measures of his personal concern to healing and restoring the hurting and wounded among his flock, steadily, prayerfully undoing the tangled mess that Destroyer and his hordes had created in the church. It had taken some real breaking, some repenting, some forgiving on all sides, but it happened, and was still happening, one heart at a time.

The Jessups were so hurt and dismayed that it took careful, loving appeals from the Walroths for them to come back into fellowship; Judy Waring was carrying a lot of bitterness against the likes of Donna Hemphile who had used her—and her mouth—to hurt God's people. But she had to admit that it was, after all, her mouth and her heart, and she started her turnabout with those two areas of her life. Every one of them had to totally reevaluate their opinion of Tom Harris, and they were still in that process even as they prayed.

It wasn't an easy restoration for any of them, but in the face of their revealed enemy they had a clear choice: rejoin God's army and fight the evil that was even now destroying them, their families, and their Christian faith, or . . . proceed with being destroyed.

They rejoined the army—with a vengeance.

The angels kept quiet, stayed low, and didn't talk much as they secretly placed themselves at strategic points around the country, waiting for Tal's "brushfire" to start.

Mota the Polynesian and Signa the Oriental had many points to cover all around the Bacon's Corner area, but they now had more than enough warriors, so carefully, methodically they covered them. Terga, the tender-egoed prince of the town, was getting edgy about the sudden tide of prayer coming from the reunited saints, but so far he did not sense the activity all that prayer was bringing about. Besides, he'd heard the news from the powers above him: the woman had been captured; the danger was over.

Cree the Native American and Si the East Indian had returned once again to the Omega Center for Educational Studies, and were now planting angelic warriors like explosive charges in just the right places all around the campus. It was tedious, dangerous work, the greatest danger being discovery. While they crawled along or under the ground, moved under the surface of the lake, stole from tree to tree, or spent hours totally motionless under rocks, boats, or buildings to avoid discovery, they could always see Barquit, the Prince of Omega, soaring to and fro, his eyes everywhere, laughing and exulting in any progress made in the classes and workshops, then growling and spitting at any clumsy moves by his demons or by his puppet-people below. He was still very much in charge and ruling his demon hordes with an iron hand. Now that the woman was captured, he felt no fears or worries at all, and obviously planned on remaining at his post forever.

On the surface, Bentmore University looked like the same old red-brick, permanently established alma mater it had always been, and classes were in full swing as usual.

In the spirit realm, however, Corrupter, Bentmore's rotund master of disinformation and fleshly indulgence, moved like a blimp over the campus, seeking out any damage the school may have incurred from that recent, violent exchange with Heaven's warriors. Ha! Destroyer was nothing but a status-anxious worrywart! Damage? There was none to speak of. Professor Lynch had been a bit ill lately, but he was getting old anyway, and there were plenty more where he came from. With the woman captured, the future was wide open.

Across the river, atop the North American Can Company, Chimon the European and Scion of the British Isles were back, hiding behind one of the factory's many ventilator stacks. Things looked quiet at Bentmore right now, but when Tal's brushfire started, there would be noise enough.

Chimon and Scion were looking for hiding-places and sending troops to fill them. The warehouse by the river could hold a myriad or so; the wharf on the Bentmore side would also serve very well, being closer to the campus. The troops moved silently and quickly. One false move, one ill-timed glint of light, could endanger them all.

At every point along Sally's journey, at every stronghold of Satan, the angels moved into position and then waited for the signal.

But they all knew they were waiting longer than expected.

In the peaks above Summit, Tal and Guilo watched and listened for any hint of what might be happening inside. Behind them, a hidden army lay in waiting, ready.

"Any time now," Tal said more than once. "Any time."

In purely a physical sense, Mr. Goring's chalet was an inviting A-framed structure built with rough-hewn timbers and a full-height glass front that commanded a marvelous view of the mountains. It could have served so well as a ski lodge or mountain getaway.

In a spiritual sense, it was a churning, frothing hornets' nest of evil, and Sally could feel it even before her captors led her through the front door. She knew she was being watched from every direction; she could discern the oppressive, smothering hate that covered the place like a leaden fog.

Destroyer was already in the chalet, shoving his way into the living room, brushing aside the Strongman's demons and attendants with rude boldness. Into the Strongman's lair he went, strutting down a narrow aisle formed by two straight lines of demon lords from all over the world, until finally he stood in the presence of the Strongman.

"My Ba-al," he said loudly, with a rather showy bow, "I bring to you Sally Beth Roe!"

The Strongman had heard the demonic cloud in an uproar, and now he could see Khull and his party bringing Sally Roe

479

to the front door. He nodded in carefully measured approval. "So you have. So you have."

The demon lords raised their swords to begin a cheer.

The Strongman growled, his arms outstretched, "Hold!" They froze and stared at him. "First we will see if there is anything to cheer about."

The heavy plank door closed behind Sally and her captors. They were standing in Mr. Goring's spacious, comfortable living room. At one end was a massive stone fireplace; at the other end, a wall of glass brought in the mountains; the open-beam ceiling soared above them to the roof's apex, and from the massive ridge beam, rustic iron chandeliers hung on long chains.

Three men rose from their places by the fire. Sally recognized Mr. Steele, and it was obvious by his satisfied grin that he recognized her.

It was Goring who ordered, "Bring her here and sit her down."

Khull was after some glory. He grabbed Sally's arm and pulled her forward, keeping her constantly off-balance, then, with a cruel grip that bruised her arm, flung her down into a sofa. With just a few small gestures, he ordered his four thugs to stand guard around her.

"Gentlemen," he said arrogantly, "I bring to you Sally Beth Roe."

The three men stood before her, staring at her with great interest. The gray-haired man with the perfectly trimmed beard and the bone necklace looked at the tall, silver-haired executive type, and then both of them looked at Mr. Steele.

"This is she," said Steele. "Well done, Mr. Khull. We will settle our account with you immediately. However, if you are agreeable, we may still have need of your services."

Khull smiled, giving Sally a leering, sideways glance. "It would be my pleasure."

"Then please remain for a time, you and your staff. We'll try to settle this business as quickly as we can."

"Take your time."

With Sally placed securely on the sofa and under capable guard, the three gentlemen relaxed and took their seats—the two older men in another sofa facing Sally, and Mr. Steele in a large easy chair between the two sofas, facing the fire.

Steele opened the conversation. "Sally, let me introduce my two friends." He indicated the man with the perfectly trimmed beard. "This is Mr. Emile Goring, presently Director of Finance of the Mannesville Association, an international humanitarian and environmental think tank and mobilizer of global projects. He's a major stockholder and director in over forty global corporations dealing in oil, gas, transportation, exports, mining, and so forth."

Sally looked toward Goring, who nodded back at her with a grim but still fascinated expression.

Steele wanted to be sure Sally was impressed. "Consequently, what Mr. Goring desires to do, he has the means to do. He and his associates are major contributors and underwriters for such endeavors as the Summit Institute; this institute is part of their vision, and it wouldn't be here at all if not for their efforts.

"The other gentleman is Mr. Carl Santinelli, Senior Partner at Evans, Santinelli, Farnsworth, and McCutcheon, one of the most powerful law firms in the country and, in a sense, the flagship of the ACFA. He is a man of great causes in law and jurisprudence, a legal activist of the highest order, and definitely not a man to be tampered with."

Sally looked at Santinelli, and got a cold, probing stare back.

Then Mr. Steele turned to Goring and Santinelli. "Mr. Goring and Mr. Santinelli, I introduce to you Ms. Sally Beth Roe, former Director of Primary Curriculum Resources at the Omega Center for Educational Studies, convicted murderer, former convict, production worker at the Bergen Door Factory, and most recently, vagabond."

Goring and Santinelli continued to study her as if looking upon a real oddity.

Steele relaxed in his chair and studied her himself. "It has been quite an adventure, hasn't it?"

"It has," she answered.

"I see your hair roots are beginning to grow out. I do miss seeing your fiery red hair. And since when do you wear tinted glasses?"

She sighed and removed them, rubbing her tired eyes. "All a disguise, of course." Then she bitterly admitted, "And quite futile."

"Quite futile," Steele agreed. "But you do understand, don't you, why we had to track you down?"

The question angered her. "It is my impression, Mr. Steele, that you and your associates want me dead, and I would like to know why."

"Oh, come now!" said Santinelli. "A person of your brilliance and experience should have no trouble seeing how much you are in our way. As for that initial attempt on your life, we will not mince words. It was a blunder, an unfortunate fiasco perpetrated by some incompetents who thought they would please us. We were not pleased. Killing you in such a way was never our original intent."

"So what was your original intent?"

Santinelli smiled. "Our original intent was the lawsuit against the Good Shepherd Academy in Bacon's Corner, your current town of residence. Your stumbling into the middle of our project was a total surprise to all of us."

Sally needed to confirm what she thought. "*You* are the people ultimately responsible for the lawsuit against that Christian school?"

Santinelli nodded. "Lucy Brandon first contacted our local ACFA affiliate, the affiliate contacted the state chapter, the state chapter contacted us, and we decided the case could prove profitable. We immediately put our strength and influence behind it."

"But not for the child Amber's sake, of course?"

Santinelli exchanged a glance with the others. This woman was as sharp as Steele had said she was. "Obviously you have no illusions about our concern for the safety, rights, and welfare of children, especially since the ACFA regularly defends the interests of child pornographers and molesters." He sat back with his chin high, tapping his fingertips together, watching her eyes for a response.

She forced one corner of her mouth to stretch upward and nodded.

"As you may well imagine, the real object of that lawsuit is not the awarding of damages to the plaintiff, but legal precedent, the molding and shaping of law, even the rewriting of law, through an ideal test case."

Steele contributed, "Ms. Roe is quite familiar with our agenda for social change through state-controlled public education. She was a major contributor to that effort at one time."

Santinelli nodded, impressed. "So you do realize how great a deterrent to our cause the Christians are as long as they are allowed to raise and educate their children according to their Biblical beliefs. Even before your years at Omega, we were seeking legislation and legal precedent that could be used to stifle that deterrent. It's taken this long for that to develop."

"But it did," said Goring with a gloating smile.

Santinelli indulged in the same smile and continued, "The latest legislation for our use was the Federal Day-care and Private Primary School Assistance Act, and the Munson-Ross Civil Rights Act, each a rather muddled stack of laws that—as we had hoped—would require testing and clarification in the courts. The Good Shepherd Academy case seemed tailor-made for that purpose. It not only involved federal funds spent in a Christian school, and therefore government intervention and control, but also included the useful, inflammatory child abuse angle, something we could use to incite support in the media and in the public mind, getting them all on our side regardless of the real issues. And that, of course, was the object. With the public outraged and preoccupied with the protection of innocent children, we would be seen as no less than champions for children in establishing through case law the right and duty of the state to control religious education." He couldn't resist a laugh of delight. "Even after the initial trauma—real or concocted—against the child fades into the past and is forgotten, the laws will still be on the books, and the government firmly planted within the walls of the church.

"As you yourself taught and were taught, once such control of religious instruction is established, the methodical, gradual elimination of religious instruction altogether is only a matter of time. And then such people as you once were will have tremendous, far-reaching power to control and mold every segment of the next generation without resistance."

Sally nodded. She'd learned this catechism.

Goring picked up the narrative. "Well, it did look promising, of course. But that was before you happened along. You can imagine what a shock it was to learn you were out of prison and living in the very town where we'd brought the lawsuit. Worse than that was the way we found out: Our little prize, the very child in question, supposedly the pristine, totally innocent victim of Christian bigots and abusers, suddenly chose to demonstrate her true colors one day in the local Post Office. Ah! I see you remember the incident! Of all people to witness such an outburst, it had to be you!

"When Mrs. Brandon brought the incident to her attorneys' attention, they passed the word to us, and, knowing who you were, we saw a substantial risk that you would recognize the child's condition, especially since you wrote the very curriculum that caused it. We were aware that you could severely jeopardize our case should you decide to step forward."

Santinelli allowed himself a mournful chuckle. "But really, we hadn't yet decided what our course of action would be before a misguided member—uh, former member now—of our staff took matters into his own hands and secured the services of an assassin."

"That part you are quite familiar with," said Goring.

"Oh, yes," Sally answered.

"And that," said Santinelli, "brings us to why we've all been on this merry chase. Ms. Roe, had you died then, we could have absorbed the error and continued with our plan, none the worse for our friends' impulsiveness." He sighed. "But impressive person that you are, you not only lived, but a) you killed the assassin and left her there to create all kinds of questions should she be found, and b) you made off with a ring the assassin was wearing on her finger, a ring that could eventually link the whole wicked affair with us."

Sally said nothing, and tried to keep her face from saying anything.

"The assassin was a crafty sort. She was a paramour of that former member of our staff, and pilfered his ring, we believe, for the purpose of blackmail and manipulation. That ring could have told anyone who its owner really was—all it would take would be the securing of the Nation's rosters in which all the code names are listed. Both items are now, we believe, in your possession?"

"I'm prepared to bargain," she replied.

They all stifled a laugh and exchanged glances.

Steele ventured a question they all felt was unnecessary. "So . . . you are willing to relinquish the rosters and the ring in exchange for something? Just what would that be?"

Sally looked them all in the eye and spoke clearly. "Abandon the lawsuit. Leave the Christian school alone, and let Tom Harris have his children back."

This time they didn't stifle their laughter at all, but enjoyed her appeal thoroughly.

"And then," Goring asked, "you will release the ring and rosters back to us for our disposal?"

"We can certainly talk about it; I'm sure we can arrange something."

Santinelli leaned forward. "Is that a chain I see around your neck?"

Khull found out for sure. He forced her head sideways and grabbed at the chain, yanking it from under her blouse.

The gold ring dangled on the end.

With a vicious jerk that pulled her from the sofa and gouged her neck, he snapped the chain and tore it from her. She landed on the rug with a cry of pain, only to be gathered up by the thugs and flung on the sofa again.

"Here now, enough!" said Goring. Then he pointed to her bleeding neck. "Put a cloth on that. I don't want it staining the sofa."

One of Khull's men placed his handkerchief around Sally's neck.

Khull dangled the ring above Santinelli's palm, and then dropped it.

Santinelli examined the ring. "Mm-hm. The Ring of Fellowship in the Royal and Sacred Order of the Nation. A sacred object, to be sure." He glared at Sally. "Too sacred to be in your possession . . . and no longer in your possession."

Sally held the handkerchief to her neck, stunned and deflated in her spirit and wincing from the searing pain from her wound. "I see you belong to that group."

Santinelli looked at the gold Ring of Fellowship on his own hand. "Oh, the Nation consists of many brothers, all in vital places: in government, in banking, on the federal bench, on college boards and regencies. You were quite familiar with Owen Bennett, of course, and I'm sure you've already read an impressive list of names from those rosters you stole. Like any other secret society, we help all our initiates get established in the right places, and we see to each other's interests—provided, of course, that each man's interests conform to the interests of the society."

"Apparently James Bardine's interests did not."

Santinelli smiled. "Ah, yes, that 'former member of our staff' does have a name. Then it was you who called our office? I understand our receptionist recently informed an anonymous female caller of his untimely death." He dropped the ring back and forth from hand to hand. "Brotherhood is one thing; violation of sacred blood oaths of secrecy is another."

He looked out the windows toward the mountains. "There are some things that are best kept sealed, Ms. Roe. If you could have toured these grounds, or walked through the town of Summit and met some of the people that are here this week, you would have found many different esoteric organizations represented, as well as some very . . . unique . . . individuals. We're all one global family, you know; that is the unifying cry of every heart. We proclaim that idea here and everywhere, just as you yourself have proclaimed it, and we teach that all are equal." He paused for effect. "But we keep to ourselves the fact that some are more equal than others, and far more fit to rule."

He set the ring on the glass coffee table and then looked directly at her. "I trust that now you fully appreciate what the stakes are here, how ruthless and determined we are, and how desperate your situation is. We are not here to bargain, Ms. Roe, but to put an end to the threat you pose to us. Exactly what process will be necessary to accomplish this will depend largely on yourself." He looked toward Khull. "I'm sure you'll find little comfort in the fact that Mr. Khull and his four accomplices are members of the same secret order to which your assassin belonged, a Satanic cult known as Broken Birch. They're a ruthless bunch who thrive on bloodletting, torture, human sacrifice. Quite unsavory." He looked back at Sally. "Ms. Roe, we are decent men, and we desire no more discomfort for you than you may make necessary. To be blunt, your fate depends on your performance."

Nathan the Arabian and his small band of sentries continued to ride shotgun in the mail truck as it drew closer and closer to Ashton. Armoth the African had flown ahead to warn Krioni and Triskal, the watchcaring angels of the town—it was only a matter of time before Destroyer heard about the letter aboard that truck.

In the herb garden not far from Goring's chalet, a group of about thirty conferees gathered in the crisp, scented air for a morning workshop led by a well-known recording artist. The young, blond-haired man had his guitar along, and some songs were planned before his talk on "Ecology: The Merging of Earth and Spirit."

There was a certain giddiness in the group. These people had never been this close to such a famous person before, and he was not the only famous person sitting there amid the rosemary, thyme, and lamb's ears. Two newsmaking clergymen of global stature were also in attendance, as well as a director of mystical science fiction films whose name was a household word and whose film characters were now plastic toys in every kid's room in this country and abroad.

The blond singer strummed his guitar, and they all began to sing one of his well-known ballads. The moment was magical.

The demons among them were enjoying it as well. Such worship and attention as they were now receiving was like getting a good back rub, and they even twitched and squirmed with delight at every bar of the song's carefully shaded double meanings.

Huh? What was that? The demons twisted their heads around to look toward a disturbance.

Two demonic warriors were gliding in over the top of the Goring Pavilion, apparently heading for Goring's chalet. They carried between them the drooping, limp form of a battered demon, still whimpering and wailing in agony. With a soft, rustling sound, they passed right over the herb garden and then disappeared beyond the tall evergreen hedge.

The demons in the herb garden fidgeted, stirred, and muttered to each other. *What was that? Who was that? What has happened?*

Some psychics were in attendance, and the demons attached to their brains were just as stirred up as the others. The psychics could immediately sense it.

The blond man even stopped the song. "What is it?"

"A disturbance," said a woman attorney and psychic.

"Yes," said a fifth grade teacher, his eyes closed. "Some kind of bad energy. Something's wrong somewhere."

In the chalet, Destroyer was relishing the entire conversation, as was the Strongman, though the Strongman was getting impatient.

Why wait so long? he growled. *Make her talk, and then finish her! The Plan is waiting!*

"Destroyer!" came a gravelly voice outside the building. It was one of Destroyer's henchmen. "A warrior brings news!"

"Not now!" Destroyer barked, wanting to watch what happened to the woman.

"Go!" said the Strongman.

He went, ducking outside the chalet to hear from a most pitiful-looking spirit.

"What happened to you?"

The demon sat on his haunches on the ground, his wings spread like tattered black tarpaulins, wrinkled, limp, and full of holes. His head was battered, and he braced himself to keep from falling over. "We attacked a mail truck on its way to Ashton."

Destroyer stooped low. "*Ashton*, you say?"

The demon started to topple.

Destroyer grabbed him by the neck and jerked him upright. "Did you say *Ashton?*"

The demon slurred a faint answer. "Ashton. A letter is bound for Ashton, and the Host of Heaven guard it."

Destroyer shot a glance into the chalet. The Strongman was still watching the interrogation of Sally Roe. He was still impatient. He wanted results. If he didn't get results, and fast, certain heads were going to roll.

Destroyer could just feel his head rolling. He let the demon flop to the ground, then motioned to his captains who gathered around him. "There is a letter bound for Ashton, guarded by the Host of Heaven. They do not guard it for nothing!" His face crinkled grotesquely at the thought of it. "Sally Roe may have written to someone there."

The captains gawked at each other.

"Well?" Destroyer demanded. "Did you hear me?"

"Ashton!" exclaimed one.

"We can't go back there!" said another.

Destroyer shushed them with a quick gesture. "Just look into it, and do it quietly. I'm sure it's nothing to worry about, just one little letter."

They looked back and forth at each other. "Which of us should go?" they wondered.

Destroyer held back a scream and hissed instead, "How about *all* of you? And take some spare warriors with you."

They all went, gathering as many demon troublemakers as wished to go.

Destroyer hurried back into Goring's chalet. The Strong-man was intently listening to Sally's interrogation and didn't ask what the interruption was about.

Destroyer had no intention of telling him.

In Ashton, Krioni and Triskal could see the mail truck entering the city limits, right on time. Unfortunately, the precious letter inside was one truckload and one day late.

Triskal looked toward the west. "All clear so far."

Krioni was not optimistic. "They'll be here."

forty-one

SANTINELLI leaned back, relaxed, and with an instructive glance at Goring and Steele encouraged them to do likewise. Then he looked at Sally and became suspiciously cordial.

"Sally, I have always considered myself a gentleman, a man of dignity and honor, and respectful of the dignity of women. I sincerely desire an intelligent, productive dialogue with you, and I'm sure, given the alternative, you desire the same."

"I would prefer it," Sally admitted.

Santinelli nodded. "Then, having agreed on that, it might be well for us to consider your credibility as a witness against us. It seems to me that you've forgotten what you are."

Sally answered simply and directly, "I'm an adultress, a baby killer, and a convicted felon." They looked uncomfortable. She'd answered that question a little too easily. "I've been reminded of that constantly since the day it first happened, by seven years of prison, by spirit tormentors, and by my own conscience."

Steele said, "Sally, that's a shameful and disgusting set of labels."

She smiled, and that even surprised her. "Actually, those labels are marvelous and beautiful because . . ." She hesitated.

Goring completed her sentence. "Because of the Cross?"

She brightened at that question. "Yes, Mr. Goring. I'm surprised you would know about that."

Goring sneered a little. "We know about a lot of things, Ms. Roe."

Sally gave that statement no reaction, but went on. "I'm far from competent in Christian theology, but I do know I've met this Jesus personally, and I know I've been forgiven. Considering what my deeds were, I find that fact exhilarating, inspiring."

They didn't like that answer at all.

The Strongman didn't like it either, and let out a roar that filled the building and set the demons stirring. He shot a sideways glance at Destroyer, who looked away.

Santinelli tried to keep cool, but his face was getting a little pink. "So are we to understand that you've turned to antiquated religion in one final attempt to expunge your past?" He laughed derisively. "That, Sally, is a marvelous delusion for the fainthearted and weak-minded. The notion that your sins are forgiven is as much a fable as the sins themselves. You are God, Sally; you are accountable to no one."

"Then I should be free to go, shouldn't I?"

"That's a side issue," said Goring with a wave of his hand, "having no bearing on our present purpose. Sally, let me be blunt: Even if sins were real and this Jesus could save you from them, what you must face at this moment is that He cannot save you from *us*."

"I wouldn't presume that He should."

Now Santinelli even raised his voice. "Ms. Roe, I'm sure you know that this conversion of yours has placed you in even greater jeopardy. You could have done no better in assuring enmity between us, and even your own death, than by becoming a Christian!" He leaned forward and with a controlled rage pointed his finger in her face. "You have established yourself as a supreme enemy of this enterprise, deserving of our hatred!"

Just like Amber, Sally thought. *Steele, Santinelli, and Goring are showing the same demon eyes, the same diabolical hatred.*

She acknowledged Santinelli's words. "I know."

The Strongman could see the peace in her eyes, and it incensed him. *Strike her!*

Santinelli slapped her across the face. "You will tell us where the rosters are! What did you do with them?"

Krioni and Triskal greeted Nathan and his warriors as the mail truck reached the Ashton Post Office.

"So you've had some trouble?" asked Krioni.

"A little," said Nathan.

"Well, we're expecting more," said Triskal.

Armoth followed the driver into the building and watched

intently as he set the mailbag with some others on a receiving cart. Soon the mail would be removed and sorted, and that would be the most critical time of all.

A sooty, motley band of imps and troublemakers, led by Destroyer's loathsome twelve, made their way toward Ashton, flying low to the ground, pouring on speed, their swords drawn, their eyes bulging with anxiety. This battle would be their last, thought the twelve. It may as well be their best.

At the *Ashton Clarion*, it was time to get the morning mail; Bernice had her coat on and her car keys in her hand, but wouldn't you know it? She no sooner put her hand on the front door knob than the phone rang, and it was Eddy from Eddy's Bakery. The guy was a paragon of pickiness!

"Yeah, Eddy, we can give you those two inches. Well, yes, for free, but that's just for a one-month trial basis." More questions. "To decide if you like it that way and if we like it that way. We've never done it, and I thought we should try it." He kept talking. She shifted her weight toward the front door. "No, I think we can just blow up that coffee mug a little larger and it'll work out fine. Right, you won't have to change your logo." She made a face and rolled her eyes. "Listen, why don't you talk to Cheryl about it? Yes, she knows all about it."

He didn't want to talk to Cheryl.

ATTACK! The black spirits threw fear and caution to the wind and descended on Ashton in a torrent of chaos and evil, wings roaring, sulfur streaming, blotting out the light, clashing with angelic warriors all over the town. Up and down the streets they soared, tumbling, clashing, hacking with swords of fire and heat at Heaven's warriors, dashing through traffic, ambushing at corners, streaking through buildings and wreaking confusion, shrieking their war cries, fully abandoned to keeping the angels on edge, in battle, no matter what the cost, no matter what the loss. While the imps, harassers, and troublemakers stirred up the town like a whirlwind, Destroyer's twelve went for that letter.

Bernice got to her little Volkswagen bug at last, but the door wouldn't open. The key wouldn't even turn in the lock.

WHOOOSH! A streak of light cut across the demon who had fouled the lock. He dissolved.

The key turned at last. Bernice climbed in.

Down the street, the traffic light jammed on red and the cars began to back up.

A small sedan eased to a stop right beside Bernice's car, and immediately a pickup rear-ended it. Both drivers climbed out of their vehicles and began to engage in a long battle of apologies.

Six angels flew abreast down 6th Avenue while four more dove out of the sky and shot up Miller Street. They converged in an explosive clash just above the traffic signal, hurling dissolving demon saboteurs in high arcs that created a fern of red smoke trails.

The light turned green.

But the traffic still wasn't moving, thanks to the fender bender. Bernice decided to walk.

Sally tried to sink deeper into the sofa, but there was no way to lessen the pain of the big thug's bruising, crushing grip on her shoulders. He was hurting her and enjoying it.

Steele was speaking slowly and deliberately to make sure she heard him; at the moment she seemed rather preoccupied with her agony. "I'm sure you're familiar with Satanic rituals, so I shouldn't have to go into the details. Sally, we don't want to see it happen; but if we have to, we'll turn you over to Mr. Khull and his people and let them do their worst until you tell us what we want to know."

Sally was about to answer, about to say they were going to kill her anyway, but she was stopped when something happened to her eyes, as if they'd opened for the first time, as if a dark curtain had been pulled aside. Maybe the pain was causing her to hallucinate.

She could see the spirits behind these men. They were

towering, warted, ugly things, glaring at her with murderous hatred. Throughout her occult experiences, good and bad, she'd never seen them so clearly; she'd never discerned such evil or such hate.

But she could tell their hatred was not for her. It was for the Savior within her.

And then she knew. She just knew, and she spoke, whether aloud in the present world or in her spirit in another dimension, she couldn't tell. "You were there! All of you were there! You gave Him your worst . . . you killed Him!"

That troubled the spirits. They looked at each other, indignity and outrage wrinkling their faces.

"And He defeated you by dying! He won!" The big, hulking spirit hovering high above bared his teeth and roared indiscernible curses at her, his wings billowing. She looked into those burning, yellow eyes, and to her great surprise she saw fear. In her spirit she laughed. "And whatever you may do to me, *I've* won!"

She cried out. She could feel all the pain again. The thug was about to break her neck. The spirits faded away with the rest of the world. She no longer saw, she no longer heard. She was sinking into a dream, into bottomless darkness. Santinelli yelled something, and the thug let her go. She thought she would float up from the couch. The pain lessened.

In a moment she could see and hear again, and she realized she was almost falling over. Her shoulders were throbbing. Santinelli was saying something about killing her.

Then Goring said, "The conference day is going to start; people might walk by the windows. We'd better continue this downstairs."

"Wait!" Sally said, and they all froze. She had their attention. She raised her head, gathered her strength and courage, and feebly muttered, "I do have an additional bargaining chip. You should know that I've corresponded on a regular basis with Tom Harris in Bacon's Corner. I've told him everything I know and everything I've done. If anything happens to me, somebody will know."

Goring smiled, and reached into a briefcase beside the sofa.

"Oh, you must be referring to these." By handfuls, three at a time, four at a time, one at a time, Goring pulled the letters from the briefcase and set them in a pile on the coffee table, giving Sally a slow, torturous revelation. When she turned a satisfying shade of white, he continued, "We've put a great amount of preparation into our plan, and fortunately we were able to exert enough influence on the plaintiff in the lawsuit who is also the local postmaster. She's been forwarding all your letters to us; so needless to say, Tom Harris and his friends never got them. They have no idea of your whereabouts, or what you might know."

Santinelli added, "And yes, we have been watching them, and it's obvious that they have little information about you and are shooting in the dark. I would say they're getting rather desperate. But that doesn't matter now, does it? We have you, and we will deal with you as we see fit, as we find necessary."

Goring pointed to the coffee table. "So, we have you, we have all your letters, we have the telltale ring; it's time we firmly dealt with those stolen rosters. Gentlemen?"

Suddenly she was hanging from her arms. She pushed with her feet to lessen the pain, and stood on her own.

"This way," said Goring.

The men of Broken Birch forced her along, taking her toward a stairway that led down into the cold, concrete belly of the chalet. Goring led the way, turning on the lights and guiding them down the winding steps.

Steele followed behind, and after him Santinelli. Khull followed at the rear of the procession, reaching into his coat for his knife.

Then Khull hesitated. "I'll make sure the front door's locked," he said.

He went upstairs again, but passed by the coffee table to take a good look at all those letters. *Hmmm. Excellent!*

There, I made it! Bernice checked her watch and found it only took about ten minutes to walk to the Post Office. That wasn't so bad.

Now to get that mail.

High overhead, Destroyer's twelve henchmen saw her. They also saw the canopy of angels over that building. They let out a cry and dove to the battle, their wings screaming, their nostrils trailing sulfur.

WHOOSH! Three of them swept five angelic warriors from the Post Office roof and engaged them, tumbling, rushing, spinning, hacking. They would be busy for a while.

Two henchmen shot through the north wall. Nathan and Armoth ducked as they passed, swatted them soundly, and sent them through the south wall.

OOF! Four more dropped through the roof and struck the angels down with bared talons. The demons got a faceful of fiery wings and then saw the swinging blades too late.

Red smoke.

The young mail clerk carefully emptied the mailbag, sorting out the packages, envelopes, junk mail, magazines.

"Hi, Al!" came a call from the lobby.

"Hi, Bernice! The mail's a little late."

"Oh, that's okay, so am I."

Ah, here was some mail for the *Clarion*. He slipped it into the *Clarion*'s box, then looked to see if there was more.

Four henchmen exploded through the wall, wings a blur, Krioni and Triskal hot on their heels.

A red sword swept downward.

The letter fluttered to the floor.

Bernice gathered all the mail out of the *Clarion*'s box and dropped it into a shopping bag. She looked through the opening and called, "Is that it?"

Al looked through the new mail that had come in. "Yeah, I think I got it all."

"Okay."

Bernice closed the door of the box and turned to leave.

Krioni took one spirit by the heel, but the thing was so strong it dragged him through the Post Office wall and he had to let it go.

Triskal took a nasty blow from one monster, slashed away at another one, and kicked a third out over the counter.

Bernice didn't see the spirit sail right past her as she reached to push the door open.

Nathan ducked for the letter.

A black, taloned foot caught him in the chest and propelled him as high as the ceiling. Two more spirits closed in on him. He spun, sword extended, dividing one, catching the parry of the other with a burst of sparks.

Krioni was back, saw the letter, and went for it. Armoth covered for him, pushing two spirits backward, right into Nathan's blade.

Krioni slipped his sword under the letter and flipped it into the air.

Al didn't see Krioni punching two demons out of the mail clerk's way, but he did see the letter just coming to rest on the floor, address up. "Oh, hey, Bernice!"

The door was just about to close behind her. She heard him call and turned back, opening the door again and re-entering the lobby.

Good! Now the warriors could concentrate on the demons. There shouldn't be too many more—just the biggest and strongest.

Al handed Bernice the letter over the counter. "Kinda thick. Might be a card in there or something."

Bernice's heart almost stopped when she saw the return address: S. B. Roe.

In Bacon's Corner, Kate handed Marshall the phone. "On your toes, Marshall," she whispered.

Ben and Bev heard that and got close. "Who is it?"

Marshall spoke into the phone, "Yeah, this is Marshall Hogan."

"Mr. Hogan," said the voice on the other end, "this is Debbie Aronson. I work at the Post Office with Lucy Brandon. I need to talk to you."

The Post Office lobby filled with red smoke as Triskal shot sword-first right through two spirits and through the wall to the outside, shaking the dissolving spirits from his shoulders and wings.

Bernice tore the letter open and found a Post Office box key inside. Box 203. Here? In this Post Office? She quickly scanned the letter from Sally Roe.

She may not have noticed, but she began to bounce up and down on her toes.

Marshall grabbed a pen while Kate got him some paper, and he sat down at Ben and Bev's dining room table. "I'm glad you called, Debbie. I'd be happy to talk to you."

"Well, I don't have that much to say. I'm on my break, over at Don's Wayside."

"Can we get together somewhere, sometime?"

"No, I don't want to risk being seen with you. Listen, just let me tell you what I know, and then we'll pretend I never talked to you, all right?"

"All right."

Bernice found Box 203. She could see a large stack of mail through the glass panel. She put the key in the lock, and it fit perfectly, turning the latch.

"Lucy's been intercepting some mail; she's been forwarding letters that I'm sure aren't supposed to be forwarded. I've seen her doing it for weeks now, and I think Sergeant Mulligan is scaring her into doing it."

Oh man, oh man, oh man. Lord God, is this it? Marshall tried to keep his voice calm. "Okay. Do you know who the letters are for, or who they're from?"

Bernice opened the mailbox door. What were these? Manila envelopes, smaller envelopes, a plain brown package, a little box wrapped in paper.

"They've all been addressed to Tom Harris . . ."
Marshall could feel his eyes getting big.
" . . . and they've all been from that woman who's supposed to be dead . . ."
Marshall kept from saying the name. Debbie had to say it herself. "What woman, Debbie? Do you know the name?"
"Um, that Roe lady. Sally Roe."

Bernice's hands were trembling as she dug every last item out of the mailbox and stuffed it into her shopping bag. She couldn't wait to get back to the office.

Nathan ducked under a violent sword thrust of one remaining beast, then came back hard and fast with his own blade. The thing backed through the wall, and Krioni met it outside.
Red smoke. That was the last of them.
The rest of Ashton was safe as well. The attack, centered on the Post Office, had been met and defeated.

Marshall hung up the phone gently, then leaned back in his chair, threw his head back, and let out a roar that shook the windows. He didn't know what to say, what to do, how to express how he felt, so he just hollered while Kate, Ben, and Bev tried to get him to talk.
"Marshall!" Kate insisted. "What is it?"
He just hollered again, raising his hands toward Heaven.
The phone rang again. Marshall picked it up in trembling hands. "Yeah?"
The voice on the other end could hardly speak, and the pitch was ceiling-high. "Marshall, this is Bernice! Sit down whatever you do!"

Sally had lit the brushfire at last.

Nathan was the first to have his hands free. He shot into the sky over Ashton, cutting a brilliant swath through the ebbing smoke of the battle now ending, and put a golden trumpet to his lips.

The signal carried over the farmlands, over the prairies, from one end of the sky to the other; every angelic warrior could hear it and knew what it meant.

Still they waited. Not yet. First Bacon's Corner, and then the rest. They listened again. The signal from Bacon's Corner should come soon enough.

At the Summit Institute, the demons heard the faraway signal, and it was unnerving, like a deeply buried memory too horrible to face. Too many of them had heard that sound before and now bore the scars that came immediately after hearing it.

The Strongman cocked his head around for a moment. "Wait! Be still!"

Destroyer heard it, but didn't want to admit it. He immediately thought of his twelve henchmen and the hordes they'd led into Ashton. Wasn't that the direction the sound was coming from? Oh no.

Out in the herb garden, the psychics were gasping with fear.

"No . . . no!" said the demon atop the woman attorney.

"No . . . no!" echoed the woman.

"What is it?" said the blond singer.

The demon atop the fifth grade teacher concocted an answer he didn't believe himself. The teacher echoed, "It is fear and ignorance, bigotry and hatred, still rife in the land! The winds of change must blow it aside; we must stand before it and prevail!"

"Yes, yes!" they all replied. The singer strummed his guitar, and they began to sway with the melody of still another song of global peace and perfection.

In Bacon's Corner, Mota and Signa burst from hiding with a shout, swords flashing, wings unfurling like the crashing of waves, white light burning like the sun.

"For the saints of God and for the Lamb!" they shouted as the cornfields, the silos, the store buildings, the barns, the forests, the roads all around Bacon's Corner exploded with the white light of Heaven's legions.

Mota shouted, somewhat with glee, "Stand ready! We will begin with Amethyst!"

forty-two

The sound of Nathan's trumpet was still ringing in the Strongman's ears. He knew something was going wrong somewhere. *Get on with this! Cut her, burn her, do what you must, but delay no longer!*

Khull spoke softly to the dignified, honorable, respectable men who were paying him for his services. "We can make her sing loud and long. Just say the word."

Santinelli took only a furtive, sideways glance at Sally, now bound and held in a hard wooden chair in the middle of the basement, weak with exhaustion, pain, and fear. She was surrounded by Khull and his four cutthroats, who now brandished their implements of ritualistic torture and were all too eager to begin.

"Sally, to think it would ever come to this!" Santinelli muttered. "You should never have mentioned that Name; you should never have aligned yourself with our enemies!"

Goring reminded him, "We have much at stake here, Carl. I would say the situation forces our hand."

Santinelli replied in a voice hushed by his own disgust, "So now we have become butchers!"

Khull smiled. He almost laughed. "No, Mr. Santinelli. You pay *me* to do that. I'm not as dignified and respectable as you are. I'm just a plain little rotten Satanist."

The Strongman gave Destroyer a shove, and Destroyer spoke quickly to Steele's mind.

Steele offered, "We're talking about a commodity here. Sally Roe's only value is in what use she is to us. Let's get that information and be rid of her."

Khull did chuckle a bit this time. "How about it, Mr. Santinelli? It's your decision: do you want her tortured?"

Santinelli glared at Khull. "Do *I* want her tortured?"

Khull smiled. He loved to see a big man like Santinelli squirm. "Okay, I'll tell you what: Add two extra grand to my fee and I'll pretend that it wasn't you that hired me." Then he tilted his head the other way, his eyes full of mocking. "Maybe you're still a little too Christian, huh?"

Do it! shouted the Strongman. *Just do it!*

Sally closed her eyes and prayed.

"I can't come to work!" Lucy cried into the phone. "It's Amber again! She's beside herself! I'll call later!"

She slammed down the telephone and went after her berserk little daughter, following a trail of chaos and destruction: in the kitchen, the drawers were yanked open and the contents spilled all over the floor, including the knives Lucy had tried to hide; in the dining room, the tablecloth had been yanked from the table and the azalea centerpiece now lay broken on the floor, the potting soil strewn everywhere.

From the front of the house, the shrieking voice of Amethyst the pony continued to rant and rail against unseen enemies. "No! No! Leave me alone! My master will destroy you! Leave me alone!"

Lucy ran into the living room. The coffee table was upside down, the books and magazines flung everywhere.

Amethyst's voice came from the front entryway. "She is mine! I have a right to be here! Go away!"

Lucy ran and found her daughter cowering in the corner on the floor, her arms covering her head, screaming in fright.

"Leave me alone, leave me alone!" the pony screamed.

Lucy stopped in her tracks and observed for a moment. Had she ever heard Amethyst frightened before?

Mota and Signa stood in the entryway near Lucy, swords drawn, in full glory, their light washing out any darkness around them. In the distance, the dull thundering of angelic wings grew louder and louder, and the light of Heaven's Host began to stream through the windows.

They had chased and cornered the imp, the teaser, the liar named Amethyst—and Amethyst was not a cute little pony. She was a small, crinkled, warty lizard with toothpick arms and legs and a dragonlike face, cowering in the same corner, her body superimposed over Amber's, her arms covering her head.

"She is mine," Amethyst insisted, even pleaded. "She invited me in!"

Mota held his sword right under Amethyst's flaring, chugging nostrils. "Saints of God are coming, and they will deal with you."

"No . . . please . . ."

The doorbell rang. Lucy's first thought was: *No! Not now of all times! God, how can You be so cruel to me?*

But she could see the outlines of her visitors through the frosted glass of the front door. She threw the door open.

Marshall and Kate Hogan.

"Hi," said Marshall, "we're—"

Amethyst screamed, "No, go away! Go away!" Then she began to curse.

Lucy stepped back from the door and motioned for them to come in. "You may as well know everything!"

They stepped through the door.

At the sight of them, Amethyst leaped to her feet, her back flat against the wall, her eyes bulging with terror. "Stay away from me! I'll kill you! I'll kill *her!*"

It took only a split second for the Spirit of God to tell them what they were facing.

"You be quiet!" said Marshall.

Amethyst's head bumped against the wall as if she'd been thrown a punch. She glared at them through wide, glazed eyes, hissing through tightly gritted teeth like a muzzled, rabid dog.

"Just stay there now, and be quiet."

Kate stood by Lucy and held her. Lucy clung to her without reserve.

"Amethyst?" Kate asked.

Lucy nodded.

Marshall and Kate couldn't help staring. This was the initial cause of it all; the lawsuit, the heartache, the mystery, the gossip and division, *all* the trouble began with this imp now trembling and cowering before them. It was like isolating a virus—or cornering a rat.

"Amethyst," said Marshall, "it's all over."

Amethyst glared back at him defiantly. "She's mine. I won't let her go!"

Marshall spoke evenly and firmly. "Spirit, my Master has defeated your master. He has disarmed all the powers and authorities, right?"

Amethyst drooled in defiant silence.

"The shed blood of Jesus Christ has taken away your authority, right?"

"Yes!" Amethyst hissed.

"And my Master, the Lord Jesus Christ, has granted me His authority over you, hasn't He?"

"Yes!"

"And *you* are defeated, aren't you?"

Amethyst put her clawed fingers over her own mouth and refused to answer.

Mota flipped the hand away. "You answer him!"

Amethyst could hear the angels everywhere, could feel the heat of Mota's blade, and could not back away from the authority of this believer in Jesus. It was no use resisting.

"Awww!" Amethyst cried. "I hate you! I hate all of you!"

"Come out of her."

"No!"

"I'm binding you right now, in Jesus' name!"

Amethyst cried out, writhing, struggling against unseen shackles that held her arms and legs. She couldn't move.

"Let go of this little girl. Come out, and go where Jesus sends you."

One claw at a time, Amethyst began to let go of the little girl, her eyes darting back and forth from Marshall to the angels and back again. Mota and Signa began to close in.

With an anguished scream she dropped the girl and made a break for it, shooting through the roof of the house. Mota and Signa made no attempt to chase her.

It wasn't necessary. Amethyst had no sooner cleared the

roof of the house than she saw an incoming wave of white fire rolling over the town, heading her way.

The Host of Heaven!

She let out a squeal and shot across town, heading for the big white house. *The spirits at LifeCircle! They got me into this!*

Amber slumped toward the floor as if in a faint, but Marshall caught her. Lucy and Kate knelt beside them.

"Mommy . . ." said the girl, dazed and exhausted.

Marshall gave the girl to her mother. "She's all right, but we'll have some praying to do. We'll have things to talk about."

Amber fell into her mother's arms, and then nestled there with no desire to leave. That was fine with Lucy. She had her daughter back, and she wasn't about to let go.

With tearful, weary eyes she looked at these two rescuers and whispered, "I'm sorry."

Marshall and Kate were in a terrible rush, but they had to be gentle about it.

Kate started. "Can you help us?"

Lucy couldn't answer. She was torn and confused, pulled from all directions.

Marshall spoke gently but quickly. "Listen to me, Lucy. We know Sally Roe is alive, that she's been writing letters, and that you've been intercepting those letters from some people who want to kill her. The last letter she wrote gave away where she could be found. If she isn't dead by now, she soon will be if you don't help us."

Lucy looked down at her daughter, peaceful though shaken. "It's been just awful."

Kate asked, "Where did you send those letters, Lucy? Please tell us. Sally Roe's life could depend on it."

Lucy looked at them, then at her daughter. Her mind was so confused; it was just so hard to know what to do anymore.

Destroyer was filling Khull's mind with some marvelous inspirations as Khull held his knife in plain sight, always sure that Sally could see its clean, keen edge. "Might as well face it, *gentlemen.* We're all made of the same stuff. All our hands are dirty, and we're all killers at heart. You want power, we want power, and we walk on the disposable people to get it. That's the name of the game."

Santinelli looked at Sally. Her face was still red from where he had struck her. "I will not have your blood on my hands, Ms. Roe. What follows will be your doing, not mine."

Sally spoke for the first time since being bound in the chair. "The responsibility is *yours*, sir. I appeal to you in the name of decency itself, in the name of all that is right."

"Law derives from power, Ms. Roe, not from morality. Spare me your newfound beliefs."

"The rosters, Ms. Roe," prompted Goring.

Do it, said the Strongman.

"She'll turn state's evidence, John. Yeah, and she's got an earful for you."

Marshall was sitting at Lucy Brandon's dining room table, on the telephone with John Harrigan, his friend in the FBI. Lucy, Kate, and Amber sat in the living room; Lucy was still holding Amber, who hadn't made a sound. Pastor Mark Howard was there as well, at Lucy's invitation.

"Ever heard of the Summit Institute? Well, let me give you the location. Sally Roe's letters went there, and now she's probably there too, if she's still alive."

Lucy spoke up from the living room couch. "They'll kill her. They want her for no other reason."

Marshall liked what he was hearing from Harrigan. "Yeah, right, those agents shouldn't be too far from there right now. That's good. Well, get them over there, and I mean now! Yeah, right."

Lucy told Kate and Mark softly and bitterly, "LifeCircle! They got me into this! The whole lawsuit was their idea! Claire Johanson and Jon Schmidt—the whole lot of them! They've done nothing but threaten me and coerce me since this whole mess started, and now where are they? Well, I'm not going down alone!" She called to Marshall, "Tell them I'm ready right now."

Marshall heard her. "John, you can send somebody over here right now. She's ready to talk."

This was it! The brushfire was catching on! From here it would burn upward—hot, hungry, inextinguishable!

Mota took a golden trumpet in his hand and shot through the roof of the house, soaring through the white light of his warriors still rushing over the town. Upward, skyward, slowly spinning, wings afire, he put the trumpet to his mouth.

In the mountains above the Summit Institute, the signal reached Tal's ears loud and clear.

"Done!" he cried, leaping to his feet. "They've set the fire in Bacon's Corner!"

"Better late than never," Guilo said with a shrug.

"It will reach Summit soon enough," said Tal, drawing his sword. "Prepare to attack!"

Amethyst was getting close to the big white house, the home of LifeCircle. The roar of Heaven's wings thundered in her ears. She whimpered, she cried, she fled before them. *My masters in LifeCircle! They will save me!*

Santinelli smiled a bitter smile as he looked long and hard at Mr. Khull, still brandishing the knife. "I believe you're right, Mr. Khull. I do see myself." He looked at Sally. "Power is power, whether it be wielded through legal decisions or . . . from the edge of a knife. And as for our gentle followers . . ." He looked upward, thinking of the hundreds of peace-seeking conferees now gathered from around the globe. "We *are* equal. We are devils, all."

He stepped back and took his place by the wall, out of the way. Goring and Steele joined him. He crossed his arms and with chin jutted out resolutely, said, "Teach us, Mr. Khull. We will learn."

Destroyer clicked his talons, and the spirits of Broken Birch moved the five Satanists like puppets.

Khull smiled with diabolical pleasure and nodded to his

men. Two of them immediately looped a chain over a beam and affixed a hook to it. The other two released Sally from the chair and yanked her to her feet.

The Strongman, Destroyer, and all their wicked lords and commanders gathered, moving in close, ready for the triumph.

Sally knew there was no more time. "The rosters are in Ashton!"

"Too late," said Goring. "Please proceed, *gentlemen!*"

They bound her hands in front of her.

"The rosters are in Ashton!"

Where? growled the Strongman.

"*Where* in Ashton?" demanded Santinelli.

"I sent them to a Post Office box!"

Santinelli put up his hand. Khull looked disappointed, but he motioned for his men to stop.

Santinelli stepped forward. "What Post Office box?"

Sally really did try, but . . . "I . . . I can't remember the number."

"Proceed, gentlemen."

They grabbed her arms and started lifting her.

"I planned all those letters!"

Santinelli held up his hand again, and Khull's men set her down. Santinelli exchanged encouraged glances with Goring and Steele. "My, how the revelations are beginning to flow!"

Destroyer didn't like the subject matter. He nudged Steele.

"She's lying," said Steele.

"I remember the mail room, Mr. Steele!" Sally cried with a trembling voice.

Steele only leered at her. He didn't know what she was talking about.

"I used to work in the mail room at the Omega Center, remember?"

Steele didn't leer this time. He remembered.

Sally spilled it out rapidly, desperately. "You told me how to intercept mail you didn't want the staff to read. You said it wasn't wrong because it protected our purposes. You said your people did it all the time! Remember that, Mr. Steele?"

Goring and Santinelli looked at Steele. He was silent because he did remember it.

The Strongman suddenly grabbed Destroyer around the neck, but he didn't start squeezing. Not yet. He was waiting to hear the rest.

"Go on," said Santinelli.

"It was the only way to find you. I figured whoever tried to kill me would have to keep anyone from finding out I was still alive, so they'd have to intercept my letters; and I knew from the papers that you were using the postmaster in Bacon's Corner for your lawsuit, so that's where I sent them, and . . ."

"And you addressed them all to the defendant in the lawsuit, Tom Harris . . ."

"I knew you couldn't let *him* see the letters."

Santinelli smiled. He was impressed. "So your letters were to be a trail to the people ultimately responsible for your . . . alleged death!"

"Professor Lynch knew about my concern for Tom Harris, and Khull knew exactly where to find me, and you all knew without my telling you that I'd embraced Christianity. That was confirmation enough that you'd stolen my letters, but of course . . . now you've shown them to me. You have them. Every one of them."

Destroyer tried to force a leering, cocky smile as he choked and gargled out, "So what?"

Goring stepped in. "Marvelous! Yes, the letters are all here, and so are you. Now you have the satisfaction of knowing who your would-be killers are. But you recall, of course, that no one else has seen those letters, and the world has lost all track of you!"

"That's why I made copies."

There was a strange delay, as if that sentence took a few seconds to reach their ears and register in their minds. They all looked at her dumbly.

She drew a breath and went for broke. "The copies are in the Post Office box too, along with the rosters and James Bardine's ring, the one I took from the finger of that woman who tried to kill me. The ring you took from my neck is the one I got years ago from Owen Bennett. You can doublecheck his code name, Gawaine, on the inside of the ring if you like."

Santinelli came close, and he was even shaking a little. "What Post Office box, Ms. Roe?"

"It's empty by now anyway. I sent a letter to a lady who works at the *Ashton Clarion*, and I enclosed the key."

Now the Strongman applied the pressure, and Destroyer had to struggle for breath. "I never heard of any such letter! What do *you* know about it?"

Destroyer tried to answer. "I sent the twelve captains to Ashton to look into it—"

The Strongman began shaking him, making Destroyer's eyes look like horizontal, yellow blurs. "Where are those twelve?"

"They . . . they . . ."

"Wasn't the intercepting of those letters *your* idea?"

Suddenly Destroyer thought he was reliving his first feelings of doom; he was hearing the sound of a trumpet again, just like before. But this time it was louder. It was reverberating all around them. It was so loud he couldn't be imagining it.

He wasn't. The Strongman heard it too, and let out a growl that shook the room.

Then they heard a resounding shout from so many voices it sounded like waves of the ocean. "For the saints of God, and for the Lamb!"

The Strongman roared again and threw Destroyer to the floor. "The enemy! We are discovered!"

The hundreds of demons in the room—the Strongman's aides, the bloodstained murderers of Broken Birch, the lofty and conceited deceivers controlling Santinelli, Goring, and Steele—flew into a panic, reaching for their swords, jostling each other, shouting and shrieking.

The floor and walls began to shake with the rumble of heavenly wings descending from above like a violent storm.

It was exhilarating, thrilling, reviving, rewarding—everything an angelic warrior was made for!

The Host of Heaven had waited so long and had built up such fervor that when the signal finally came, they broke over the crests of the mountains on every side like a violent, shimmering ocean wave and showered down like hail upon the dark cloud of demons in the valley, scattering them like dust before the wind, routing, battling, swinging, and pushing down, down, down toward the Summit Institute.

Tal, at the crest of the wave, dove like a hawk, his wings straight back, his sword a needle of light at the end of his outstretched arm. His war cry could be heard above all the tumult, and his sword was the first to strike.

They flew into the heart of the black cloud, like piercing a black, boiling, thunderhead. The swords of spirits clashed, wings slapped and fluttered, red smoke fogged the air. Tal kicked, cut, spun like a scythe, and fought his way downward, downward. He could hear the roar of Guilo, the Strength of Many, just above and to the left, batting at demons and mowing them down, flipping them sideways to meet other blades, kicking and grabbing what hides he could find, cutting a widening swath, gutting the cloud at its core.

The Strongman slapped his demon lords about the room to bring them to their senses. "Are you commanders or not? To your posts! Defend us!"

The demons scattered to their posts, leaving the room almost empty except for the demons of Broken Birch.

The Strongman glared at Destroyer. "The woman has lit a fire that will consume us. There is nothing more we need from her. Finish her before *we* are finished!"

Destroyer shot a glance at Khull's demons.

Khull raised his knife.

"Mr. Goring!" came a cry from upstairs. "Mr. Goring! Something terrible is happening!"

Footsteps! People were in the chalet!

Khull grabbed Sally from behind, clapped his hand over her mouth, and poised his knife at her throat. His message was clear.

"Mr. Goring!" came the shout again.

Santinelli pushed Goring. "Answer them! Stop them before they find us!"

"My word," said Goring. "Those letters! They're right up there on the table!"

He hurried to the stairs, turning off the basement lights.

"Mr. Goring, are you here?"

He ran up the stairs. "Yes, right here! What is it?"

Amethyst cupped her wings open and came to an abrupt halt just short of the big white house. LifeCircle was under attack! Angels were everywhere! The spirits there, her masters, were fleeing!

Claire and Jon scurried about the office, finding documents, papers, anything and everything that might connect them with this miserable lawsuit and everything it entailed. They would deny everything, of course. It was all they could do. Maybe they'd get through okay, maybe they wouldn't—they didn't know, they couldn't think about it, they could hardly think at all; they were just too scared.

They'd gotten the tip-off: Lucy was talking; there were copies of Roe's letters in the wrong hands. The lid was coming off!

Jon jammed papers into a trash can until it was full, muttering angrily, "I knew we should have gotten out of this long ago! We've overreached ourselves!" He ran to find another container.

Claire had the telephone propped on her shoulder. She was talking to Miss Brewer, Amber Brandon's fourth grade teacher. "That's right. You'd better come up with some good explanations for what happened to Amber. Lucy Brandon's done an about-face, and she's blaming it all on you. Hey, don't blame *us*! You didn't have to select that curriculum; that was entirely your own choice, and we had nothing to do with it! No, I never heard of any Sally Roe; that's your concern, not ours!"

She slammed down the phone just as Jon rushed back into

the room with a garbage can. "Jon, what about that curriculum? Can that be traced to LifeCircle?"

Jon found some documents and held them up for Claire to see. "Not after I burn these!"

Overhead, the swarm of survivors from the LifeCircle rout turned tail and fled before a wall of angels. They flew toward the elementary school. Ango the Terrible would be there with all his mighty hordes! He would know what to do!

Goring reached the upstairs and found the two psychics from the morning discussion group all in a dither.

"Here now," he said, "what's all the commotion?"

"Bad energy," said the woman attorney. "I can't explain it, but all the psychic energy around here is horribly disturbed!"

The fifth grade teacher nodded in agreement, his eyes wide with horror. "We're being invaded! That's the only word I can think of to describe it!"

In the basement, Sally, Khull, and the others stood in the dark, overhearing the conversation. Sally tried not to stir; she could feel Khull's blade against her throat.

Goring was trying to calm them. "Well, just take it easy. Let me encourage you to combine your insights with others around the campus. Perhaps we can all learn and benefit from this experience."

"It's scary!" said the lady.

"I'm so disoriented," said the man.

Khull pulled Sally's head back so hard, she thought her neck would snap. He huffed into her ear, "They're feeling *you*, lady! You and your filthy Jesus!"

The cloud of evil spirits closed ranks and drew in tight, swords ready, as all around angelic warriors continued to thunder down the mountainsides like an avalanche and swirl around them like a cyclone. The Host of Heaven struck the cloud at the base, and it collapsed downward to fill the gap; they assaulted the pinnacle and it shriveled, bleeding a shower of stung demons; they shot like fatal bullets through its center, and the cloud's mass began to thin. They harried it, struck at it, sliced it into weaker segments. The cloud was thick, tough, and tenacious, but it was weakening.

Tal hacked an attacker, mowed through four more, spun and kicked another spirit aside, and then spotted a sudden, instantaneous gap in the demonic mantle just over Goring's chalet. He folded his wings above his head and dropped through it.

Sally and the others could hear Goring having a bit of trouble with his distraught psychics.

"Now, if you'll excuse me," said Goring, "I do have some urgent business to attend to."

"What could be more urgent than this?" said the man, his voice coming close to the basement stairway.

"Please!" said Goring, coming after him. "Use the front door! Go out the way you came in!"

Maybe, just maybe, that man would hear her. Sally steadily filled her lungs.

"Wow!" said the woman. "What are all those letters? Fan mail?"

Sally screamed, pushing the sound against Khull's hand with all the diaphragm she could muster. The scream came through Khull's thick hand a pitiful, muffled moan. No one heard it.

Khull had his excuse. He dug in with the knife.

"AWWW!"

"Khull!" said Santinelli. "What is it?"

Khull just moaned something unintelligible.

"Get the lights!"

"Where are they?"

Cursings, fumblings in the dark, tripping, stumbling, Khull growling, cursing, bumping into things, the wooden chair toppling.

"What was that?" said the man upstairs.

"Out!" said Goring. "Get out of this house!"

Steele found the lights.

"Khull!" said one of Khull's men.

Khull was holding his chest; his shirt was slashed, red with blood. He'd carved a wound across his own ribcage.

"Where's the woman?" he cried, his eyes wild with rage.

The Strongman and Destroyer were blinded for an instant. Something had struck them. They blinked and squinted, trying to recover.

"Where's the woman?" the Strongman howled.

Destroyer stared in horror at the spirits of Broken Birch—they were strewn about the room as if by a bomb blast, dazed, disoriented. The Strongman's aides looked this way and that, but saw nothing.

"There!" a spirit shouted.

The light of day hurt Sally's eyes. She was out in the morning air. She could see the herb garden and people gathered there.

A huge man held her, his face like bronze, his hair like gold. He set her down and pointed toward the mountains.

"Run, Sally! RUN!"

New strength coursed through her legs, and she ran.

The demons hurled themselves at Tal with suicidal abandon, their eyes crazed with bloodthirst. He darted, dodged, feinted, meeting their swords with his own, kicking whom he could, swirling, dashing, jabbing, keeping them back.

"YAHAAA!" came Guilo's voice behind him. Now Tal had some help. Struck demons began to fly across his vision, limp and dissolving.

He could see Sally Roe, still in the clear, still running. *Run, girl! RUN!*

forty-three

SALLY ran like a frightened gazelle, her thoughts set on that front gate, her stride never breaking. She bounded into the herb garden and whisked right past the blond singer and his little group.

"Hey, who's that?" someone asked.

Then came Sybil Denning's voice. "Well . . . ! Sally! Sally Roe! Sally, is that you?"

Sally didn't look back, she didn't slow down; she just kept running, her long hair blowing in the wind behind her, her arms pumping, her legs grabbing up distance. She dashed out of the herb garden, across a lawn, down a pebbled path, and into the main parking lot. She could see the main gate.

Goring was just herding the two psychics out the front door against their protests when someone else ran up full of questions.

"Hey, who was that we saw running? What's going on around here?"

Goring asked directly, "Was it a woman?"

"Yeah. Man, she looked scared—"

"Which way did she go?"

"We're *all* scared! What's happening?"

"*Which way did she go?*"

"Well, toward the front gate. She was splitting the place!"

"I'll look into it."

Goring closed the door right in their faces and called to Khull's men. "She's outside, heading for the front gate!"

Khull's four hooligans were just bringing Khull upstairs.

Goring was indignant. "Don't bring him up here! You'll drip blood on my carpet!"

"Get the woman!" said the Strongman.

Destroyer shoved and swatted the Broken Birch spirits into action. "You heard him! Get the woman!"

Khull ordered his men, "Get her! Bring me the pieces!"

They bolted for the back door.

Amethyst was only one of a mob of hysterical demons who converged on the Bacon's Corner Elementary School, but there was no rescue here either. The Host of Heaven had already struck the place, and demons were scattering from the roof, from the playfield, from all around the school, like hornets from a burning hive.

Ango, the boastful lord of the school, was fluttering about the sky with half a wing gone, wailing, cursing, spitting his hatred and screaming for help; but all his hordes had forsaken him and fled. Out of control, he careened crazily into a cluster of brilliant warriors, met their swords, and exploded in several directions, vanishing in trails of red smoke.

In the school office, Miss Brewer was having a face-to-face confrontation with Mr. Woodard, the school principal.

"No way!" she said in a voice just below a scream. "I'm not responsible for selecting that curriculum, no matter what anybody says! You told me to teach it! You and that Life-Circle bunch were behind this whole thing, and I'll tell that to anyone who wants to know! I'm not going to take the rap for this, not for anyone! *You're* the principal! *You're* the one responsible! You can fire me if you want, but I won't be your patsy. Is that clear?"

"I'll look into it," said Mr. Woodard, looking pale.

Miss Brewer went back to her classroom. Mr. Woodard picked up the phone and dialed Betty Hanover, the Number One power-holder on the school board. "Betty? Bruce Woodard. Listen, I don't know what's going on here, but I want you and the rest of the school board to be clear on where I stand in these matters. I will *not* be left holding this thing, understand? I can be heavy-handed if I have to be . . ."

The demons from LifeCircle and now the survivors from the elementary school turned and fled before the pursuing angels. Terga, the Prince of Bacon's Corner! He controlled the school board! Surely *he* could stem this tide and stand against this attack!

Amethyst was not quick to flee, but indecisive. Where was Ango?

The demons rushed away, leaving her behind. She searched for Ango. Was he here?

STUNG! An angelic sword caught her under the arm and she went spinning, plummeting down toward the school. She reached toward that black tar roof, even pushed toward it with the power of her wings. It was a safe place. She'd flourished in those rooms before. Maybe someone below could help her, hide her . . .

The black roof slapped by her, then the rafters, the insulation, the ceiling, a classroom full of children—

SWIPE! A warrior finished her, and she fell dissolving to the floor, a smoldering heap just behind Miss Brewer, just below a crayon drawing on the wall, a marvelous picture of a purple, winged pony under a rainbow.

Sally ran toward the big stone gate. Right now that gate seemed like the gateway to Hell itself, but she was getting *out*, she was escaping, she was breaking free! *Come on, girl, get through that thing!*

Khull's men raced through the hedges and down an obscure pathway toward the highway to head her off. So far they hadn't been seen by any conferees, but that was due more to luck than caution.

"The woman!" cried the spirits, their attention diverted from the battle overhead to the fleeing figure on the ground. That diversion cost many of them their presence in this world. The angels were there, swords flashing, and no one could stop Sally Roe.

She reached the gate. There was no invisible barrier, no burly thug to stop her, no dirty hands grabbing. She passed through it like a bird out of a cage, her heart soaring. *O Lord God, my Savior Jesus, will You save me? Are You running with me now?*

She crossed the highway and ducked into the forest on the other side. First she would get some distance behind her, then perhaps double back to the village, get a ride, hike out, whatever. *Just stay alive, Sally, just stay alive! Hang on!*

Khull's men saw her cross the highway. They fanned out. The demons of Broken Birch stayed close to the ground and followed them, goading them on, filling their blackened minds with thoughts of blood and murder.

The cloud of spirits began to change shape. The base began to shift sideways, crawling up the mountainside, spreading a mantle over the path of that solitary, fleeing figure.

Tal shouted to his commanders, "Keep her covered, but let them follow!"

They understood, and backed away before the advancing demonic hordes.

The thick mantle over the Summit Institute began to pull away, leaving it open and vulnerable.

Demonically speaking, LifeCircle was a desolate ruin, the elementary school had fallen to the enemy, and now as the wilting, bleeding leftovers from those two defeats fled to the homes and businesses of the Bacon's Corner school board, they discovered Terga, their mighty prince, all by himself, flying in crazy circles over the town, screaming in rage.

"Cowards!" he shrieked. "Deserters! Come back and stand!"

The demon lords under his command were nowhere to be seen, but had fled before the advancing flood of heavenly armies. The Oriental, Signa, was right at Terga's heels. Terga was as good as finished and presently out of his mind.

Mota had already led a powerful contingent of warriors on a bold sweep through the home of board chairwoman Betty Hanover, routing the ruling demons of that household and leaving Mrs. Hanover feeling unsure of herself—especially now, when a federal postal agent was on the phone.

"Just trying to track down some information," he said. "We

understand your elementary school was using a curriculum written by the woman in question, a Sally Beth Roe."

"Uh . . . well, I don't know anything about that."

"We understand that Sally Roe lived right in your area."

"Really?" Betty tried to sound surprised, but never was much of an actor.

"Well, we're just trying to find her. We have to follow up on a complaint."

"Complaint?"

"Mail tampering, for one thing."

"Well . . . you might try talking to Claire Johanson . . ."

"Already did. She said to call you."

"She—" Betty buttoned her lip, but cursed Claire up one side and down the other in her mind.

"Hold on," said the agent. "I've got the name of the curriculum right here . . . Yeah . . . *Finding the Real Me.* Ring any bells?"

"The Omega Center!"

"Beg your pardon?"

"The Omega Center for Educational Studies in Fairwood, Massachusetts! They're the publishers of that curriculum! They'd know the author, I'm sure. We don't know anything about the author. All we did was buy the curriculum from Omega. They're the ones you should talk to. We don't know anything."

"All right. Do you have their number, address, all that good stuff?"

"Just hold on."

She gave him the information and hung up the phone, unable to stop shaking.

The phone rang again. It was school board member John Kendall. "Betty, I'm calling to warn you—"

"You're too late," she told him.

School board member Jerry Mason called right after she hung up on John Kendall. He wanted to know what she knew about the Sally Roe/mail tampering/lawsuit/curriculum thing, and didn't Sally Roe commit suicide a while back? She wanted to know what he knew, they both wanted to know what Claire Johanson knew, and both agreed that none of them knew a lot and that all of them wanted to know a lot more, especially what the *feds* knew.

The demonic powers and authorities of Bacon's Corner were scattered. Terga's best warriors fled elsewhere to find a new home for their mischief; Terga, alone except for the deserters who joined him on the way, set out for the Omega Center. Perhaps there was time to warn Barquit, Omega's prince. Maybe Barquit would have the strength to save them and stop this onslaught.

Far away from it all, in the city of Westhaven, the Circuit Court of Appeals, with all parties oblivious to the spiritual racket steadily growing and spreading out of Bacon's Corner, convened at two o'clock in the afternoon. Wayne Corrigan and Tom Harris took their places at the defendant's table on the right side of the courtroom, while attorneys Ames and Jefferson took their seats on the left.

"All rise," said the bailiff, and they all rose, and in strode the three appellate judges, one younger man, one older man, and one sagging woman. They sat down, the three lawyers sat down, the clerk and bailiff sat down, and the court stenographer poised her fingers over the little keys.

Tom looked around the courtroom. Apart from one reporter that had shown up looking a little bored with his assignment, the gallery was empty. Of course. The public was waiting for the real show, the trial.

"Ah well," Corrigan whispered, "it's going to be a short day anyway."

"No earthshaking surprises?" asked Tom.

"To be honest, I'm not expecting any."

The older judge put on his reading glasses and referred to his papers. "This is the case of *Brandon v. the Good Shepherd Academy*, the defendant appealing the lower court's ruling as to compelling a child witness to be examined by defense's experts and to testify in this case . . ."

Corrigan sneaked a glance at Ames and Jefferson. They looked bored. Boy, now there was confidence!

In Fairwood, Massachusetts, the Omega Center was in full swing, with classes in progress, fair weather on the campus, and—by their standards—nothing weird or unusual happening. A gang of young adults continued their good-hearted game of touch football on the playfield; on the Tai Chi plaza, two dozen practitioners moved in slow motion through time, space, and spirit; in the classrooms, high school kids, adults, and even senior citizens learned the latest westernized twist on Hindu mysticism; and in the quiet, cushioned meditation rooms, young transcendentalists watched with eyes closed as demons played cosmic movies in their brains.

Cree and Si, their armies in position, were ready and waiting. Any moment now . . .

Barquit, Prince of Omega, was troubled when he first heard the humming and whistling of frayed wings and then the anguished wails and laments of spirits far away. He took wing and hovered above the Omega Administration Building, peering westward until he saw the spirits from Bacon's Corner approaching, screaming with alarm.

Something was up. "Forces!"

FWOOOM! He covered his head, blinded by brilliant light exploding on every side, obliterating the forests and hills, washing out the blue of the sky, bleaching out the colors of the Center. Spinning about in panic, he drew his sword, but it was struck away before he even saw his attacker.

He fled into the sky, feeling the burning light of Heaven at his heels.

Telephones began to ring in every room on the campus, and every teacher, group leader, and facilitator got the word: the football game was over, classes were canceled, and anyone out in astral travel would have to come in for a landing. Mr. Tisen, the head of the Omega faculty, had gotten an angry call from

Betty Hanover, a threatening call from Claire Johanson, and last but not least a nosy and intimidating call from the FBI. He was clearing the campus, and that meant everyone.

Cree and Si led their forces through the campus like a flash flood, whipping through and around the buildings, flushing demons out of the rooms, chasing them through the surrounding woods, cutting them down out of the sky. The demonic deceivers were swamped and confounded. They called for Barquit, their crafty leader, but he was long gone. They had little time to lament about it before they were gone as well.

Barquit looked back only once, just long enough to know that Omega, his empire, had fallen.

The Strongman! This is his blunder!

"Classes are canceled," said Tisen over the loudspeakers. "Everyone to your dorms. Get your belongings loaded on the buses and be ready to roll!"

The classes ended so abruptly and the students were sent out so quickly that many thought it was a fire drill, or even an air raid. Some were still slipping on their coats as they hurried outside; others, still half-entranced, had to be led by the hand. The teachers were gathering up their coats, grabbing their briefcases, handouts, and curricula, shutting off the lights, locking up the rooms.

The football game broke up, and the players jogged back toward their dormitories full of questions.

Within an hour, the buses began to roll down the drive to the main road, carrying away faculty, students, even maintenance personnel, all chattering and wondering together just what in the world was going on.

Only a few noticed the plain olive sedan parked in front of the Administration Building. It hadn't been there long.

"I'm sorry," Tisen told the two federal agents now standing in his office. "You've come at a hectic time. We're just closing down for our midspring break. Hardly anyone is here now."

The two men exchanged glances.

"*Midspring* break?" asked one.

Tisen smiled. "We follow a rather unique calendar here, gentlemen."

"We'll have a look at it."

The other agent noted, "We saw the buses pulling out. It looked like an evacuation."

Tisen grinned sheepishly. "Well, most of them have planes to catch . . ."

The agents didn't waste time. "Like I asked you over the phone, this is the same Omega Center that published the *Finding the Real Me* curriculum?"

"Well . . . yes, it is."

"Then you must be familiar with the author, Sally Roe?"

"You mean me personally?"

"I mean you personally or any other way."

"Well, of course I'm familiar with the name . . ."

"Where can we contact her?"

"Um . . . Well, I'm afraid she's deceased."

"How do you know that?"

"Well, I—"

One agent consulted some notes. "What about an instructor here, a lady named Sybil Denning? Is she still on the campus?"

Tisen shook his head with just a little too much sadness. "No, I'm afraid she's gone."

"Do you see much of Owen Bennett anymore?"

Tisen looked shocked at that question. "*Owen Bennett?*"

"He used to be on the Omega advisory board, right?"

"That was a long time ago."

"How about the director of this place . . . uh . . . Steele?"

"He's gone."

"The *director's* gone?"

"He's away at a conference."

"What conference and where?"

"Well, um . . . Do I really have to answer all these questions?"

"Maybe now, for sure later. Suit yourself."

These guys were intimidating. "He's . . . he and some other people on our faculty are at the Summit Institute."

The two men nodded to each other. Apparently they already knew about that place.

Goring, Steele, and Santinelli stood in a close cluster near the big fireplace, trying to lay a contingency plan. They paid little attention to Khull, who still sat at the top of the basement stairs trying to tape up his wound with gauze, cotton, and anything else he could find in Goring's first aid kit. So far he was only making a mess.

"You know what she said in those letters!" said Goring. "She didn't leave out one thing!"

Steele asked Santinelli, "How would our chances be in court?"

Santinelli was grim but determined, and spoke in a low mutter. "There are many variables and contingencies. We should immediately inventory and eliminate any liabilities." Goring and Steele couldn't help a quick, sideways glance at Khull. Santinelli cleared his throat to correct them. "Any connections at all with the Bacon's Corner case must be eradicated. I can call my office on that. As for material evidence . . ." He shot a glance at the coffee table. "I strongly suggest we burn these letters!"

Khull pretended he didn't hear anything.

The telephone rang. Goring cursed, but decided to pick it up in the kitchen. He stepped out of the room.

"Power in the right places will also be a crucial factor," said Santinelli. "This will be a test of how much we really have."

"Mr. Steele!" Goring called. "It's your faculty head, Mr. Tisen!"

Steele motioned for Santinelli to follow him, and they joined Goring in the kitchen.

"It sounds urgent," Goring whispered.

Khull saw his chance, and struggled to his feet.

A sleek, blue sedan pulled into the parking lot, and three men in business suits got out, getting a good look at the place and acting just a little bewildered.

"They're going to think we're crazy," said one.

"Let's make this quick," said another. "I want to get back in time to see the Broncos game."

They encountered a beautiful blonde woman just getting out of her Mercedes.

"Pardon me, ma'am," said the group's leader. "We're looking for . . . uh . . ." He lost his train of thought.

The second man stepped in. "We need to talk to the people in charge of this place."

"Oh," said the woman. "Why don't you try Mr. Goring? His chalet is right over that way, beyond the herb garden, see?"

She gave them just a few more pointers and then went her way. One man was ready to head for the chalet, but the other two just kept staring after the woman.

"C'mon," said the one, "let's go."

"You know who that was?"

"C'mon!"

"That was . . . you know, What's-her-name, from that TV show . . ."

Tal's brushfire continued to rage.

Far away, on the Bentmore University campus, there was quite a buzz about the School of Education closing down so suddenly. Information was scarce. There were isolated conversations here and there about the sudden death of Professor Samuel W. Lynch. No one seemed to know how he died, or at least no one was willing to talk about it. The only news being consistently repeated among the faculty and students was that he'd been found dead in his office and that the School of Education was suspending classes indefinitely. There were rumors, of course: Lynch may have been murdered, and there might be some kind of scandal afoot. There might be an investigation. Student reporters for the *Bentmore Register* were hoping for an exposé.

Corrupter, the bloated demon Prince of Bentmore University, was dethroned at last, and it was Chimon the European and his British friend Scion who batted him out of his position like a beach ball over a fence. The angelic forces had done their job quickly, and now homeless demons were aloft and wailing, most of them heading for Summit. Soon they would descend upon the Strongman along with all the other evicted and dethroned spirits, demanding rescue, answers, relief.

Immediately, with the slamming down of the phone, Goring, Santinelli, and Steele came dashing around the corner and back into the living room with one goal in mind.

And one huge shock waiting for them—an empty coffee table, and no Mr. Khull.

"The letters!" cried Goring.

"Khull!" said Steele.

"That devil!" said Santinelli, dashing out the door.

forty-four

SALLY'S heart pounded and ached in her chest as she scurried and stumbled over damp pine needles and patches of crusted snow, grappled and groped through prickly, dead branches, and tried with all her rapidly ebbing strength to stay ahead of the snappings, huffings, rustlings, and footfalls of the devils pursuing her.

Two were directly below, but invisible behind limbs and thickets; a third was to her left, and she'd seen him twice, so close she could read the demons in his eyes. The fourth was silent and invisible except for his eerie, intermittent whistling to let the others know where he was.

They were getting closer. *O Lord Jesus, help me run!*

"Hey," said one of the three visitors, "now who's that?"

His friends expected to see another celebrity. What they saw was a silver-haired man in a business suit running like a wild man across the herb garden.

"Guys, I just have this feeling . . ."

Khull, his chest still reddened from his wound, had Goring's briefcase full of Sally's letters in one hand and the keys to the van in the other. He stood by the van, unable to find the right key to open it. He could see the key to the door, but it kept falling out of his fingers and dangling from the key ring.

Guilo stood by him, flicking at the keys with the tip of his finger, making them dance, slip, flip, and turn every which way but where Khull wanted them.

Tal swooped low over the parking lot with a message: "They're on the way!"

"Splendid!" said Guilo.

Santinelli was gasping for breath and about to collapse when he reached the parking lot, but the sight of Khull holding Goring's briefcase fed his rage and his rage kept him going.

531

He got to the van in mere seconds, pointing his shaking finger.

"I'll . . . take . . . those!" he gasped.

Khull smiled mockingly. "Huh? You mean *these?*" It was a great joke to him.

Santinelli was losing all semblance of dignity. "You devil! How dare you betray us!"

Khull held up his hand. "Hey, just who was going to betray who? We're all devils, right? You said so yourself. I'm taking these for insurance: number one, to make sure I get paid, and number two, to make sure you and I always remain close, trusting friends!"

Santinelli had more rage than sense, and grabbed at the briefcase. Khull wasn't about to let go of it.

Guilo let them go ahead and tangle. He was waiting for the right moment.

All right. Good enough.

With his huge hand, he batted the briefcase free. It struck the pavement, flipped twice, then flew open, throwing the letters everywhere.

Santinelli—dignified, honorable, distinguished, high-powered attorney Santinelli—stooped to grab up the letters, but so did bloodthirsty, demonized, Satanist murderer Khull. They went to their knees, playing one on one, grabbing faster, grabbing more, shoving, jostling, grappling, ripping . . .

Until they came to the feet. Three sets of feet. Nice shoes. Nice suits. Three men.

One man held out his badge. FBI.

Destroyer braced himself, but the Strongman didn't roar this time. He didn't even slap Destroyer around the room. Instead, with defeat in his eyes, he looked above and all around, just watching his empire crumble.

The cloud of demons was so hacked apart by this time that the light of Heaven was shining down on the Summit Institute in alarmingly large patches, turning the Global Consciousness Conference into a shambles. The psychics were unable to get any readings, the channelers' spirit entities weren't speaking, the tarot readers couldn't remember what their cards were saying, and every "higher self" on campus was out to lunch and not answering.

In the meantime, word was getting around the campus that three federal agents had just arrested someone and were still checking around. Something big was going down, and few conferees had their minds on their own hidden potential and godhood, a shot in the arm the demons could have used.

All this was distressing enough, but then the other spirits began to arrive from Bacon's Corner, the Omega Center, Bentmore University, and other centers of demonic power disrupted by the spiritual shock waves. One by one, in various stages of dismemberment and injury, they tumbled into the basement of the chalet, screaming, scratching, clawing for rescue, for answers, for someone to blame.

Terga, the Prince of Bacon's Corner, was slowly withering, and pointed at the Strongman with his one good hand. "You brought this upon us! You and your ridiculous Plan!"

Corrupter, only half his original size, rolled across the floor like a lame rat and spit out his accusation. "Have we built our empire at Bentmore only to feed it to Heaven's Host?"

Barquit kept his wings tightly wrapped around him, humiliated by his defeat and now swordless. "Your Plan! Always *your* Plan! Is this why I was never warned of the woman's coming, *or* of this ambush laid against my principality?"

Then from all around, from every fanged, drooling, spitting mouth, came the big question: "What have you done about the woman?"

The Strongman had one simple answer for all the questions. He pointed to Destroyer. "*There* is your betrayer! If he had killed her when he should have, we would not be in this state today! It was *his* idea to capture her letters, and now her testimony is *in writing* and defeats us! He is the one whose harassments did not destroy her, but drove her to the Cross!"

The Cross! That was all the spirits needed to hear. Swords appeared. "You will pay for this!"

Destroyer met their murderous eyes with his own, drew his

blazing sword, and sliced the air with ribbons of red light. "So you are better than I? Then show it now!"

They stood in their places, spitting and cursing at him from a safe distance.

He huffed at them in anger. "To the Abyss with all of you! I will finish what I have started!"

The Strongman shook his head. "You won't, Destroyer. She belongs to the Lamb. He has redeemed her from our grasp!"

Destroyer clenched his teeth and growled, "I *will* finish!"

The Strongman spread his wings in Destroyer's path. "We are withdrawing, Destroyer, and Khull's henchmen will not go with you. Without men to do your killing, the *woman* will have power over *you!*"

"She doesn't know that!" Destroyer pointed his sword right at the Strongman's belly. "I will finish what I have started!"

The Strongman studied Destroyer with probing eyes, and then stepped aside. The hate-crazed demon shot out of the chalet.

"We will not see him again," said the Strongman. He turned to the battered, tattered assemblage. "Princes, we are restrained! We will wait for a better time."

In a burst of black wings, chugging sulfur, and trails of red smoke, the Strongman and his princes scattered in all directions from the Summit Institute, abandoning it like a sinking ship, letting the clamor and smoke shrink into the distance behind them.

Follow the woman, follow the woman, get her! The spirits of Broken Birch thought only of the woman and stayed close to the ground in hot pursuit, guiding and empowering the four killers who now thrashed and clawed their way through the forest looking for their fleeing prey.

There! The killers spotted her, struggling up a steep bank, losing strength, stumbling, falling.

Tears streamed down Sally's face; her shirt clung to her back, soaked with sweat. She clambered over some stones and then flopped to the ground, her lungs heaving. Every muscle in her body trembled and quivered; her legs and arms would no longer move. She couldn't see, she couldn't think; she felt she was dreaming.

The demons jumped on the backs of the killers. *Kill her! Kill her! Chop her into little pieces!*

There was a roaring sound behind them. The forest was flooded with light.

Behind them?

Some looked back. They screamed, and others looked back also.

They could no longer see the Summit Institute, their haven, their fortress—all they could see was the Host of Heaven!

Cut off! Ambushed!

"Take them!" said Tal.

Red smoke.

Killer Number One collapsed to the ground, gasping for air. He'd had enough of this mountainside.

Killer Number Two, further up the slope, turned when he heard Number One hit the ground. "Hey, c'mon!"

Number One didn't answer. He just wanted to breathe.

Number Three had just broken into a clearing and could see the Institute. He whistled at them. "Hey! Looks like feds down there! They've got Khull!"

Number Four saw the woman tumble behind some rocks. He took his knife in his hand. He was almost there. He paused just momentarily to look back, then cursed. "It *is* Khull!"

The Summit Institute looked like a model of itself from up here, with neat rows of toy cars lined up in the blacktop parking lot and rough shake rooftops nestled among the trees. Khull wasn't hard to recognize, staggering along between two men in suits with the front of his shirt all red and his hands behind his back. That guy behind him had to be Santinelli, being led along by a third man. There was no sign of Goring, but just seeing this was enough.

"Good-bye," said Number Three, heading back down the mountain.

Number One followed him. "Let's get into town. I'll hot-wire a car."

There was an immediate consensus.

Sally did not hear them go. She lay among the rocks in a dead faint. The Satanists had come within four feet of her hiding-place before turning back.

In Claytonville, former Police Sergeant Harold Mulligan locked the front door of coroner Joey Parnell's home and put Parnell's house keys in his pocket. He'd just dropped by the Parnell residence on a business call—but it wasn't police business. Mulligan was in civilian clothes, and was driving his own private vehicle, an older Ford. He did not linger, but got into that Ford, backed down the driveway, and drove out of that neighborhood, out of that town, and, for all practical purposes, out of existence. He would never be seen again.

Within a few days, the papers would report the mysterious gunshot deaths of Parnell and his wife, both found dead together in the Parnell home, apparently from a mutual suicide pact. Satanic literature would be found in the home, along with evidence linking Parnell to several unsolved murders in that part of the state.

Sally awoke with a start and stiffened. *Don't move! They might be near you!* She stifled her breathing and remained still, listening.

There was no sound except the cold breeze. The shadows were longer. It was the only way she could tell that any time had passed. She lay among some large stones, flat on her back. She raised her head slightly. She felt cold.

Then she felt fear. Steady. Pounding. Growing. Like foot-steps behind her in the dark, like some . . . some *thing* lurking around the next blind corner, like a crawling, unstoppable monster approaching while she was unable to move.

She whispered so quietly she only mouthed the words, "Who's there?"

EYES! Scales! Blackness, power, sulfur, *hatred!*

It stood tall before her, a waking nightmare, a black, towering silhouette against a surreal, blood-red sky, the bulging yellow eyes leering at her, never blinking, never wavering.

She knew it was there. It was not material, and physical eyes could not see it, but she'd had such visitations before, and she knew it was real. She tensed, rose to her elbows, looking up at it while it looked down at her, the sulfur blowing in silken wisps from its nostrils, its fangs bared as it grinned with fiendish delight.

It spoke to her in her mind. *You know me.*

She did, and now she had good reason to be terrified. She pushed herself away, wriggling backwards on her hands and elbows, speechless, shaking.

The thing's words throbbed in her head. *You know me, Sally Roe, and you won't get away!*

The huge red sword came down like a meat cleaver.

Tal heard Sally's scream above the battle and shouted, "Guilo!"

"YAHHH!" came Guilo's answer as he shot up from the center of the ebbing cloud. He'd heard it too.

Side by side, with wings spread full and trailing fire, they dove like meteors for the mountain, rolled sharply to the right, then dropped into the forest, lighting up the treetops.

Sally tumbled over the rocks and rolled down the steep incline, arms thrashing, kicking up pine needles, dirt, and pebbles. The ground was washed red with the light of that huge sword as the thing glided down the slope after her, wings spread like a canopy. She could hear its huffing breath, the rippling of its leathery wings.

She came to a stop against a tree.

WHOOSH! The sword split the air once more. Sally ducked, scrambled down the hill, fell, and rolled again.

Tal banked to the left, Guilo to the right; they would strike from opposite sides. Tal shot up from the mountainside, chest just above the rocks and brush, then cupped his wings, swung his feet out before him, and doubled back.

He could see Sally tumbling down the slope with the black spirit pouncing on her like a murderous vulture, red sword flashing again and again. Beyond the spirit, he saw Guilo as a fast-closing ball of light. Tal hauled back his sword, ready to strike.

The loathsome spirit saw them coming and stood his ground, ready to meet them. They came at him like two colliding trains. With incredible power, he batted them both aside. Guilo went tumbling uphill, trying to come out of a spin, while Tal cannonballed downhill, passing through and between the pines, disappearing into the thick forest below.

You are mine, said the spirit, *and I will finish what I have started!*

"No!" Sally pleaded. It was the only word that would come to her mind.

ZING! The sword caught her in the leg. She fell against a tree, then to the ground. The sword came down again, just missing her shoulder.

Brilliant light! Two comets! Guilo from above, Tal from below, closing again!

Guilo struck first. The spirit batted him aside, but caught a stunning blow in the back from Tal's sword and teetered forward before spinning and meeting Tal's sword with a jolting parry that sent Tal fluttering into the forest again.

Guilo dove and struck the thing's neck. It elbowed him several miles out of the way.

Tal righted himself, gripped his sword tightly, and shouted, *Sally Roe! Stand against him! Turn him away!*

Sally didn't seem to hear. She was crying out, trying to get on her feet. The thing leaped upon her, digging its talons into her. She could feel them searing her flesh. She was choking on the foul breath. It raised the sword again.

OOF! A streak of light passed overhead, and the thing pitched forward. Guilo looped in a tight circle and came in for another pass, and there came Tal, straight down from above.

The spirit rose to its feet and faced them head-on, wild-eyed, sword ready. Guilo came in low; it kicked him aside. Tal dropped from above; it batted him into the treetops.

Speak up, Sally! said Tal.

"Stand aside," the thing roared. "The woman belongs to *me!*"

With that, it stomped its black, scaled foot down on the fleeing woman's leg, knocking her down, holding her there.

Tal shouted, "She is *ours,*" and dove for the demon again, at least to keep it diverted.

This time their swords met in a shower of sparks. The blow sent Tal reeling.

Take authority! said Tal.

You are mine, Sally Roe! said the demon.

"No!" said Sally. She'd found some words. "I belong to Jesus, the Son of God!"

That's it, that's it, that's it! Guilo roared, rushing through the trees with incredible fury.

His blow knocked the demon backward. The thing whipped his sword around, but Guilo pulled his feet in just in time and got away.

You do not belong to Jesus! the monster screamed. *He could never love you!*

Sally was distraught, groping for words. "Jesus loves me! The Bible tells me so!" A child's Sunday school song. It was all she knew.

Tal scored a hit and sent the demon tumbling into the trees.

Sally went running for her life, crying out, "Jesus, help me! Help me!"

The demon recovered and roared after her, wings thundering. *You will burn in Hell with me! I will drag you there myself!* He swung his sword at her, but his reach was short.

She fell, twisted, looked up at those yellow eyes.

He landed on her, knocking her flat with his knees, clamping her down.

Their eyes met.

"Jonas!" she screamed.

He broke into a wide, hideous grin, the fangs dripping, the

brow furrowed with wicked laughter. The sword went high over his head.

"Jonas," she said, extending her open hand toward the gnarled face, "STOP!"

The sword remained above his head. The eyes narrowed. *You are mine!*

She rose up on one elbow. She was gaining new courage. "I am *not* yours! I belong to Jesus!"

No . . . no, Sally Roe!

She was amazed. The sword teetered above the demon's head. He could not lower it. She spoke again. "I belong to Jesus now; He paid for my sins with His blood, and you can't torment me anymore!"

I will do what I wish! I am going to kill you! Suddenly the demon didn't sound too convincing.

"My Lord has defeated you!"

Destroyer stumbled to his feet, holding his sword limply, his eyes losing their fire.

"Get out of my life, Jonas! Forever! Do you hear?"

THUD! Tal came in with a blow that sent Destroyer spinning. The black demon righted himself and held his sword ready. Guilo came in from the side and assailed him again with a clash of blades and bursts of light.

"The woman belongs to *me!*" Destroyer roared.

"She is *ours!*" said Tal.

Sally's desperate, screaming voice came across the distance: "I belong to Jesus! Jonas, I *renounce* you! You have no claim to me! Get out of my life!"

The words hit Destroyer like poisonous darts. Then a revelation hit like a salvo, and Destroyer stood still, facing his archrival, the Captain of the Host.

"You *knew*, Captain of the Host! You knew she would do this to me, to *us!*"

Tal held his sword ready, but answered, "I knew what you would do to *her*—that you were commissioned to destroy her."

Destroyer's mouth spread open, and the fangs went dry. "*You* placed her there, in Bacon's Corner!"

"And you tried to kill her, as always!"

Destroyer began to wilt. "She . . . was *mine*, from her youth!"

"Ours—our Lord's," said Tal, "from her mother's womb."

"Get out of my life, Jonas!" Sally cried. "Jesus has conquered you—so get out!"

The sword quivered in Destroyer's hand. "She has taken away my name!"

With an agonized roar and a final burst of fury, the weakened demon dove at Tal, bringing his blade down in a fiery arc. Tal parried, jabbed, let him keep coming. The red sword swung from the side, came back again, cut through the air. Tal sidestepped it, struck it aside with enough force to throw the demon off-balance. He delivered a stunning kick to the demon's flank, jolting him, toppling him. The demon twisted about, swung at him; Tal met that clumsy attack easily, then brought his own blade down in a shining arc.

The air filled with red smoke. Destroyer wailed like an eerie siren, clutching his opened side, floating, withering, fading. He pushed himself backward with one foot, hovering on erratic wings. Tal hauled back for one more blow, but it wouldn't be necessary. As the demon's eyes remained fixed on him, ruby-red, bulging in hate, the wings fell silent.

With the dying, groping lips forming a silent curse, the thing pitched forward, sighing out sulfur, and slipped into oblivion.

The forest was suddenly quiet. Now Tal could hear the muffled weeping of Sally Roe. He sheathed his sword.

She lay nearby, facedown in the dirt, weeping, physically exhausted and emotionally spent. Guilo sat beside her, his wings spread over her, stroking her head and speaking soothing words to her soul. Tal approached quietly, knelt beside them, and spread his wings high and wide, joining Guilo's wings to form a canopy to keep out the world for a while.

"One more season of restraint," he said. "She has gained it for all of us." He touched her head, now scratched and dirty, and said softly, *It's over, Sally. You've won.*

In the valley below, the sounds of battle continued—rumblings, shrieks, clashings, flashes of light like distant lightning. But it would settle eventually. The outcome was certain and only a matter of time. For now, they remained with her.

forty-five

IN Westhaven, in the quiet, dull courtroom, Wayne Corrigan was just finishing his rebuttal to Gordon Jefferson's arguments.

"And so, we hope that the court will be careful to protect Mr. Harris's constitutional right to due process and his right to confront his accuser. We confirm once again that we have no intention of harming Amber Brandon or causing any further trauma. We only desire to get to the truth, and that, we believe, is the least our judicial system must allow any defendant. Thank you."

He took his place next to Tom Harris. Tom had been watching the clock. It was just about 4 in the afternoon.

The three judges had been watching the clock as well. The one in the middle, the older man, shuffled his papers together.

"Thank you, Mr. Corrigan, and thank you, Mr. Jefferson and Mr. Ames. Arguments were thorough and well-presented. Court will recess for the day. We'll have a ruling for you by Thursday, the day after tomorrow."

WHAM! The bailiff rapped the gavel and ordered, "All rise!" and they all rose, and the judges went out.

Ames and Jefferson seemed just a little somber, even angry, as they rose, gave Corrigan and Tom a carefully sculpted dirty look, and left the courtroom.

"Hm," said Corrigan. "I didn't think I did that well."

"I thought you did great," said Tom.

Corrigan shrugged. "Well . . . we've been praying. It's in the Lord's hands." He gave a weak smile, looked at the floor, and admitted, "But I don't know, Tom. Sometimes I wonder if I'm just a rotten lawyer or if God chooses to stay out of courtrooms. I haven't had much to feel good about lately."

Tom's smile came from deep inside. "Oh, whatever happens, God isn't mocked. He's Lord, Wayne. However He

543

wants this to turn out, I'll accept it." He slapped Corrigan on the back. "Let's get some dinner."

Corrigan fumbled a bit. "I hope you have some money on you."

"Uh . . . I have three dollars, I think."

"Okay. I think I can match that."

"We'll make it McDonald's!"

The lake was calm, like a mirror, reflecting the trees on the shoreline with clear, unbroken lines and deep spring colors while just above the water's surface myriads of bugs danced in the sun like tiny golden sparklers. The lone fisherman sat in his aluminum boat, glad for the quiet, glad to be alone. He was somewhere in his fifties, with salt-and-pepper hair and a youthful face, dressed in jeans, flannel shirt, and a drooping fishing hat that had to have been his favorite for years. The fish weren't biting much, but he was getting the peace he'd come for, and he was satisfied. For now, he reclined lazily against a boat cushion, just floating, relaxing, and not thinking much.

Somewhere in the middle of the day, he heard the rumble and gentle splashing of boat oars, and looked out from under his hat brim. Yes, someone was coming toward him in a small wooden dinghy.

When the visitor drew nearer, the fisherman sat up. He knew that slightly rotund, bespectacled man in the straw hat. They weren't exactly friends, but they'd bumped shoulders on many occasions. What was he doing here? This was supposed to be the fisherman's hideaway.

The visitor looked over his shoulder, smiled, and kept rowing closer, not saying a word.

The fisherman had an eerie feeling about this encounter. If the visitor wasn't going to speak, then *he* would. "Jim?"

Jim looked over his shoulder. "Hey, Owen." With a few last oar strokes, he brought the little dinghy alongside. Owen used a short piece of tether to join the two boats together. "Ah, thank you much."

"To what do I owe this visit?" asked Owen Bennett. "I hope it isn't business. I'm out of the office right now."

"Oh, I figured this would be a great place to have a chat, just you and me." Jim looked back toward the resort. Some families were picnicking near the lakeshore. "But I'd talk quietly, Owen. The sound is really carrying today."

Owen lowered his voice and asked, "So state your business. I'm very busy doing nothing today and I'd like to get back to it."

Jim heaved a deep sigh, rested his forearms on his knees, and just looked at Owen for a moment. "I'll come right to it, but even that'll take a while. I suppose you've been keeping up on that case out of Bacon's Corner?"

Owen stared at him blankly, then shook his head.

"Never heard of the place?"

"No, afraid not."

"Well . . . I never heard of it either. Never cared to, except that the ACFA started a lawsuit there, and I know they were coming your way with it. They were going after a Christian school again, and thought they had all their ducks in a row, including you."

"Well, if it's a pending case, obviously I can't discuss it . . ."

Jim held up his hand. "Oh no, no . . . don't worry about that. We don't need to discuss the case, no sir. We can talk about other things."

"All right."

Jim looked across the lake, gathering his thoughts. "We can talk about a few personal items, I suppose . . . like a particular secret society, the Royal and Sacred Order of the Nation?"

Owen smiled. "Well now, if I talked about that, it wouldn't stay a secret, would it?"

Jim nodded. "So I've gathered. You know, I'm amazed at how many supposed friends of mine know everything else but what I want to find out about that bunch."

"It's just a lodge, Jim. It's really nothing to worry about."

Jim wasn't that willing to brush the matter off. "Ehhhh . . . you have to understand, a man in my position gets a little spooked when men in your position start protecting each other and keeping little secrets among yourselves. Well, I said *little* secrets, but I don't know *what* size they are, do I?"

Owen remained tight-lipped. This was Jim's meeting; let him carry the conversation.

Jim did. "I hear that Carl Santinelli's a member, and *that* would concern me, as much as his name gets around Washington. To think the two of you are bosom buddies in the same secret society curls my hair just a little."

Owen got a little tense, and his voice had an edge. "That raises an obvious question for me, though I doubt I'll get an answer: How did you find out?"

"I've been reading some mail, Owen. A lot of mail." Jim looked directly at him. "Letters written by Sally Beth Roe."

Paydirt. Jim could see a definite reaction all over Owen's face. Owen lowered his head and muttered, "Oh, boy."

"Aw, we've all got a few skeletons in the closet, Owen. You know that about me, and I know that about you."

Owen couldn't contain his curiosity. "What . . . Did she write to *you?*"

"Oh, no. She wrote to the headmaster of that Christian school—I guess to give him some inside information and help him out."

"Well . . . I hope you can recognize truth from vindictive lies."

"Mmmm . . . one of the first things she wrote was that she wasn't dead, and I was impressed by her truthfulness."

"Jim, I think you're talking in riddles!"

"Well, okay, stop me if you've heard this one: Sally Roe wrote a whole stack of letters to the headmaster of that school, I guess to help him out. The only problem was, he never got the letters because somebody tampered with United States mail and snatched them all. Turned out it was the local postmaster, also the plaintiff in the suit, but she agreed to cooperate and told us where she sent them all. You'll never guess where: the Summit Institute! Some FBI agents went there and found every one of them in the possession of—are you ready for this?—Carl Santinelli, Mr. ACFA himself. He's in real hot water right now."

"That has nothing to do with me."

Jim was a little shocked. "What happened to the old team spirit, Owen? I thought you guys were lodge brothers."

"That means nothing."

"All right, all right, we'll try not to place guilt by association."

"I would greatly appreciate that."

"But just for my own information, don't all you Nation guys have some kind of membership ring, some funny gold ring with an ugly face on it, and your secret code name on the inside?"

"I don't have any such ring."

"Well, I know you don't have yours. Sally Roe has it. Well, she *did* have it. Now we have it."

Owen just stared.

"Yeah, it's yours, all right. We checked your secret lodge name against the Nation's official membership rosters. 'Gawaine,' wasn't it?"

Owen's face was like cold stone. "What game are you playing here?"

"The game we all play, Owen. Sally says she learned it from you. That's why she saved your ring all these years. It's a nice ace for her to play, and it makes her story credible, especially since she happened upon another ring, this one belonging to some kid brother of yours in the Nation, James Bardine, a hotshot punk lawyer with Santinelli's firm. Bardine's ring turned up on the finger of a Satanist." Jim added with an appropriate, sinister touch, "A woman who was hired to kill Sally Roe." He quickly added, "The assassin blew it. She got killed herself, and now we have that ring too.

"So that sort of ties all four of you together in this thing: you, Carl Santinelli, James Bardine, and that Satanist lady— uh, make that woman, or something derogatory if you like."

Jim removed his straw hat and wiped his brow. "Owen, I'm ready to lay odds you already know the rest, the whole lawsuit over that little girl having some kind of psychotic, personality blowout of some kind, and the ACFA blaming the Christian school just to get the government through their door, and . . . Well, it was quite a plan, yes sir." Jim looked directly at Owen for his next comment. "A plan worth killing Sally Roe to protect—a plan worth covering up the fact that someone tried to kill Sally Roe to protect. A plan worth tampering with the mails and hunting down Sally Roe to protect."

Owen occupied himself with his rod and reel, and didn't look up. "Jim, I believe I'm growing tired of your company."

"That was your baby, wasn't it?"

Owen froze for a moment. If Jim was attempting to shock him, the attempt succeeded. He reached down and began to untie the tether between the two boats. "I think you'd better leave."

Jim placed his hand on Owen's to stop him. "You were on the advisory board at the Omega Center, and you got her that position at the Center after she graduated from Bentmore. You spent a lot of time with her, didn't you, every time you flew out for meetings with Steele and the others?

"Until she had that baby instead of aborting it. Now there was a wrench thrown into your career! She could have sued you for child support, laid the whole thing open in public, right? What better way to solve that problem than to remove the only tangible link between the two of you—and destroy the woman in the process?"

Owen straightened up defiantly. "Do you actually intend to argue that *I'm* to blame for Sally Roe's incredible delusions?"

"*You* believe in that spirit stuff, don't you?"

"That's my personal business."

"And at the time, *she* believed in it—with a lot of help from you and that Omega bunch."

"That establishes nothing."

"Who says the newspapers and networks ever have to establish something as juicy as this? They'll print it now and prove it later. You've slipped them some goodies yourself from time to time, you know that."

"And we could slip them some more—*you* should know *that!*"

Jim nodded. "Yeah, that's right. We could make life pretty difficult for each other, no question." Then he chuckled. "But I sure enjoy the picture I get in my mind of you hearing a case brought by some of your lodge brothers in the ACFA, knowing they tried to protect their case by killing a woman you once had an affair with. Top that, Owen!"

Owen Bennett looked across the lake and thought for a moment. "So what do you want?"

Jim smiled. "Have I done it, Owen? Do I really have a lever on you?"

Owen snapped, "What do you want?"

"The sound carries, remember." Jim stopped to think for a moment. "Owen, I think I've been a pretty good attorney general, and I think I could do an even better job if certain parties would take all their weight and push it around elsewhere. I want this leash off my neck."

Owen looked grim. "I didn't put it there."

"But you have pull with the people who did. You're one of their star players."

"I can't cross them, Jim. You know that."

Jim shrugged. "Well, you could always step down, I suppose."

"I can't do that either."

Jim was resolute. "I'm giving you a choice, Owen."

Tom Harris grabbed the *Hampton County Star* from his front porch and stepped inside to the smell of hot biscuits, eggs, hash browns, bacon, the works.

"What's new?" asked Marshall.

"Oh, quite a bit," said Tom, perusing the front page.

It was Friday morning, it had been a week like no other week, and the core group, the central players, were gathered in Tom's house for a big breakfast, just to be together: Ben and Bev Cole, Mark and Cathy Howard, Marshall and Kate Hogan, and Tom. Just Tom. If social worker Irene Bledsoe had heard of all the shake-up, she wasn't saying, and so far she wasn't returning Tom's calls.

Ben asked, "Any speeches from the ACFA boys about the court's decision?"

"Kind of a moot point now anyway," said Mark. "The lawsuit's been dropped. It's all over."

"Too bad," Tom quipped. "I was scheduled to give a deposition next week. Now I'll miss out on the wonderful experience."

"But it ain't over, not yet," said Bev. "I mean, we're talking 'bout a big investigation here. We're talking 'bout some arrests!"

Marshall smiled a weak smile and shook his head. "Probably not."

"Are you crazy?"

"Sometimes I wonder . . ."

Mark asked, "Well the authorities *are* going to look into this?"

"My FBI friend John Harrigan doesn't think so. There are cases and there are cases. Some you go after, some you don't. A thing like this is . . . well, such a big can of worms; there's so much of it going on in so many places, and you can't arrest *everybody*."

"Hey, listen to this," said Tom. "Here's a quote from Gordon Jefferson. There's even a picture of him here, standing outside the courtroom . . ."

"Wait," said Ben. "I want to sit down."

Tom read the quote from the ACFA lawyer. "'We sincerely regret this monumental breach of justice and of the rights of children everywhere. The clock of progress has been set back severely by this ruling. Had the court ruled in favor of the child, this lawsuit could have continued, and we could have fought against the scourge of religious bigotry and intolerance against our children. Mrs. Brandon wishes me to share her deep regrets and her thanks with all her supporters everywhere, and to express her heartfelt dream that the fight for our children will continue. For now, she has asked, and we have agreed, to drop the suit, pick up the pieces, and go on with our lives as best we can.'"

Kate was appalled. "What a pile of *lies!*"

"But what great PR!" said Marshall. "Official ACFA policy: No matter what happens, come out the hero!"

"Let me see that," came a voice from the kitchen. Tom handed the paper to Lucy Brandon herself as she came into the room. She perused the story and just shook her head. "I dropped that suit on Tuesday, *before* that hearing!" She passed the paper on to Ben and said angrily, "But they'll never tell, will they?"

Tom remarked, "Wayne Corrigan and I were wondering why Ames and Jefferson gave us such dirty looks. They *knew* the suit was dropped!"

"But they still wanted that ruling," said Marshall. "Every little step helps."

"Well to be honest," said Mark, "I think they did just fine. The judges handed down some pretty strict guidelines."

Ben searched through the paper glumly. "Nothing more about Joey and Carol Parnell."

Bev put her hand on Ben's shoulder. "Ben, you just got your job back. Don't go chasing another phony suicide. Leave that for the Claytonville cops."

But Ben was obviously frustrated. "I'm having a hard time being patient with all the inaction I'm seeing!"

"I should have warned you about this part," said Marshall. "It's tough to get action out of the authorities when the case is so vague and untraceable . . . and when the authorities are part of the problem."

Ben passed the paper to Marshall, still fuming. "Well, this is one authority who's going to earn his pay. There has to be a way to stop them!"

Marshall skimmed the first few pages and then smiled. "I think we did."

"No, we didn't! There's been no investigation, no arrests, not even truthful reporting in the papers about what really happened. We all know the kinds of things these people are getting away with!"

"Oh . . . we hurt them, Ben. We hurt them. We won this round." Marshall passed the paper to Kate. "And . . . well, I think we stand a good chance of recovering our POWs too."

"Josiah and Ruth?" asked Tom.

Marshall nodded. "Stomp a mole in your yard, you've killed your neighbor's mole too. We'll see."

"What about our MIA?" asked Kate.

"Sally . . ." said Marshall. The thought was painful.

"What did Harrigan say?"

Marshall hesitated a little on that one. "That's a tough situation. Khull and his people were apparently in the middle of some Satanic ritual in Goring's basement when the feds got there. They had to have had a victim, but there was no sign of Sally, and Khull isn't talking. The only thing they found was Sally's letters. She could have escaped, or maybe the Satanists—Khull and his bunch—killed her and disposed of the body before the feds got there. We just don't know."

Tom grew very somber. "We owe her everything. She's just got to be alive somewhere."

"We're gonna be prayin' for that gal, that's for sure," said Bev.

"And I want to meet her," said Tom. "After reading all her letters, I feel like I know her. No. I *do* know her."

"An incredible woman," said Kate.

"That she was," said Marshall.

Just outside Claytonville, a housepainter pulled his battered, laddered van to the side of the highway and let off a hitchhiker. "Sure I can't drive you further? You're out in the middle of nowhere."

"Thank you, no," said Sally Roe.

She remained there on the highway shoulder, a very tired, dirty, bedraggled vagabond in jeans, soiled blue jacket, and checkered scarf, watching the old van pull away, its rocker arms clacking, its exhaust pipe blowing smoke, its springs sagging under all the ladders and paint cans.

She felt just like that van. Her face was etched with the miles, her soul was weary from the pain, her body was bruised and dented from the abuse. But . . . she was still rolling, still chugging along, and at least now she had a good reason.

She crossed the highway as soon as she got the chance and ducked into the woods, following an old, rutted, surveying road she'd visited in the darkness of night . . . When was that? It seemed like years ago. She almost wondered if it was the same road, it looked so different in the daylight—inviting, peaceful, canopied in the fresh, new-growth green of spring, and not at all the horrifying, demon-infested hell it was the last time she was here.

She walked for some distance, following the meandering, rising, and dipping road through thick forest, tangled brush, and low-hanging limbs. She didn't remember it being this far. Perhaps she'd missed a turn somewhere. Maybe she'd hidden that truck a little too well.

Oh! There, through the limbs and leaves, she caught a familiar blue tint. Well! Still there!

Mota and Signa stood next to the old Chevy pickup, hands on swords, eyes alert, waiting for her arrival. Their warriors had closely guarded that machine since Sally left it there. The kids on dirt bikes, the hikers, the equestrians, and any would-be vandals had all passed it by, so it remained untouched, slightly overgrown with brush, but ready to roll.

Sally pushed through the new growth, pulling the keys from her jacket pocket. The door opened with its familiar groan; the smell of the cab was the same; she still remembered to avoid that small rip in the seat lest it grow longer. Her heart danced a little. This old truck was a blessing because it was familiar, it was hers, it was a piece of home.

It moaned a bit, hesitated, cranked over a few times, and then, with Sally's well-practiced pumping of the gas pedal— something that had to be done just right—it lurched to life!

Mota and Signa gave her a push, and with little difficulty she got the truck turned around. The two warriors hopped into the back, and they were all on their way back to Bacon's Corner.

## forty-six

"I would like to know the real reason why I'm being fired," Irene Bledsoe demanded.

Her supervisor was an older woman with white hair pulled tightly to the back of her head and held there with innumerable pins; her hair was tight, her expression was tight, and due to her obesity, her clothes were tight. Everything about the woman was tight, especially her patience.

"You know your driving record better than I do," she snapped, hardly looking up from the work on her desk. "Such irresponsibility on the road, especially while transporting children, is a liability to this organization and cannot be tolerated."

Bledsoe tried to maintain her professional dignity, but she was definitely indignant. "Ms. Blaire, I have here in my hand the driving records of no less than a dozen other Child Protection Department employees; I even have some aptitude test scores—"

"I have seen them all, and do not wish to see them again."

"Ms. Blaire, you are tangling with the wrong person!"

SLAM! Ms. Blaire slapped her papers and pencil down on her desk and bored into Bledsoe with eyes of cold steel. "You just *said* that to the wrong person. Ms. Bledsoe, you are addressing, in essence, the state. We don't 'tangle' with anyone; we set our agenda and judge our employees by how efficiently they carry out that agenda. The fact is, you have been judged to be a liability to this department, and as such, you have been terminated."

"It's because of the Harris case, isn't it? That *is* the real reason?"

Ms. Blaire answered coldly and mechanically, "It is because of your driving record, Ms. Bledsoe. You—"

"I was only fulfilling the orders I received!"

"You simply can't be trusted to transport children safely, and that is my final word on the subject. Now finish out your duties properly, or I'll see to it that you forfeit your severance pay!"

"You . . . you can't do that!"

Ms. Blaire only smiled her cold, calculating smile. Oh yes she could, and Bledsoe knew it.

"All right. All right. I've cleaned out my desk and handed over my caseload to Julie and Betty. So what's left?"

"Drive the Harris children back to Bacon's Corner."

Ed and Mose were still sitting at their post in front of Max's Barber Shop, just taking in whatever passed before them on the Toe Springs–Claytonville Road.

Ed was looking through the latest *Hampton County Star* and making sure Mose was kept up to date on everything whether Mose was interested or not.

"The Big White House is for sale," he said.

Mose was watching a mud puddle across the street and wondering if maybe the Mercantile needed new gutters. "Heh?"

"I said the Big White House is for sale. That couple living in sin finally decided to move on."

"What? They splitting up?"

"It's just an ad for the house, Mose. It doesn't say anything about that."

Mose took a moment to spit into the street. "Yeah, probably doesn't say anything about Sergeant Mulligan either. He was living in sin too, I hear, him and that supervisor from the door company."

"You mean with each other?" Ed wondered.

"They're both gone, aren't they? Both took off at the same time. Somebody saw them together. I wasn't born yesterday, Ed."

Ed thought for a moment. "Eh . . . I don't mind them leaving. They were a strange bunch, them and their friends."

"Not a very good cop either."

"Jon Schmidt was a cop?"

Mose was astounded at Ed's dullness today. "No, friend, *Mulligan!*"

"Well, I'm glad to see him go too."

"Yeah, and that bunch at the Big White House, I'm glad to see them go."

"*Everybody's* going. Looks like the whole town's quitting."

"Who's quitting?"

Ed turned the paper toward Mose, and Mose adjusted his glasses. "See here? You've got . . . uh . . . these three folks on the school board, uh, Mrs. Hanover, and John Kendall . . ."

"John Kendall? That stubborn—! Who finally talked him into it?"

"And look here: Jerry Mason. That's three."

Mose was amazed. "Well . . . wasn't it just yesterday Elvira was telling me that the grade school lost the fourth grade teacher, Miss Beer?"

"Brewer."

"The same. She and that Woodard got into a fracas."

"Woodard's getting old, that's his problem. He's retiring."

"Say what?"

"He's retiring end of this month."

"He didn't seem that old."

"You been looking in the mirror too much, Mose."

Mose tilted his hat back. "Well I'll be. You're right. Everybody's quitting! Maybe they know something we don't! Hey! Hey, wait a minute there!"

"What?"

"Well, flip back to the second page there. Look there."

"Well, give me wings and call me an angel . . ."

"There's something going around, Ed. Something going around."

They were looking at a news item: SUPREME COURT JUSTICE STEPS DOWN.

Ed tilted his head back so he could read through his bifocals. "Who's this Owen Bennett?"

"Newest man on the Supreme Court. Hasn't been there long."

"'Bennett attributes his resignation to ill health and personal reasons.' But he looks kind of young, don't you think?"

"You been looking in the mirror too much yourself, Ed."

"Well now, that could be . . ."

Mose broke out laughing. "Hey, you know what, Ed? Maybe we oughta quit too."

Ed thought about that a moment and replied with great seriousness, "Mose, where would the world be without us keeping an eye on it?"

Then they both laughed, hitting and poking each other and having a great time; you could hear them for blocks.

Sally drove on toward Bacon's Corner, turning over and over in her mind just how she was going to present herself to Mrs. Potter, back from the dead as it were, and ask to continue renting the old farmhouse. Of course, that would be contingent on getting her job back at the door factory, and that was probably contingent on whether they would accept her excuse for being away so long without saying anything, and that raised the whole question of what she was going to tell them, and that was going to depend on what she could and couldn't talk about in public during the course of the investigation, and then again, she didn't know yet if there would even be an investigation.

She slowed as she approached an intersection out in the middle of the cornfields. She felt a slight tension in her stomach. This was the same intersection where that Bledsoe woman just about rammed her with Tom Harris's kids in the car.

Anyway, the first thing was to find out what was happening in Bacon's Corner, and how that lawsuit was progressing, or if it was still progressing at all. Bernice Krueger should have gotten that last letter by now, and she must have sent all that material to Tom Harris, so *something* should be brewing. She hadn't seen any newspapers in the last several days . . .

Well! What was this, a flashback of some kind? She had to be seeing things!

There was that same green Plymouth!

Irene Bledsoe made sure to stop carefully and safely at the notorious intersection that had cost her her job. Josiah and

Ruth were buckled in snugly this time. The intersection looked the same except that the corn was taller. It was almost like *déjà vu*, sitting here waiting for that . . . that blue pickup truck . . . being driven by the lady with the checkered scarf . . . !

Sally stared transfixed. She couldn't help it. This was Irene Bledsoe again! And there were the two Harris children!

From the back of Sally's pickup, Mota and Signa waved to their two comrades, Chimon and Scion, who rode atop the Plymouth. This encounter had timed out nicely!

Irene hesitated. She was the vehicle on the right, so she was supposed to go through the intersection first, but she just couldn't move. This couldn't be!

Josiah saw the woman too, and marveled. "Hey, look! There's that lady in the blue truck!"

"Yeah," said Ruth. "I remember her!"

So it wasn't a hallucination! Irene pressed the gas pedal gently and began to creep across the intersection, just staring at the woman.

"Hey," said Josiah, staring as well, "she's crying."

Sally watched the Plymouth pass in front of her and speed away, and then she wiped her eyes.

Lord, this was from You! You've used this to tell me!

Now she knew. This encounter, this scene before her, said it all: Somewhere, somehow, the darkness had been pierced; it was broken, fallen, its power was gone.

The children were going home!

From high above, Bacon's Corner looked downright cheery, warm, and inviting, like a little town from a model railroad, its brown, red, and black roofs bold against the surrounding patchwork green of the fields, and its silver elevators stretching toward the sky, flashing in the sun.

The skies were clear, both of clouds and of spiritual filth, washed with Heaven's light, freshened with prayer and praise to the Maker of it all. It was good to be back, good to see the place so clean. This was victory's reward.

Tal and Guilo began a gentle descent, their wings spread wide and motionless to carry them lazily over the town, high over Front Street with its cars and pickups jostling through the one intersection, over the Mercantile with its chimney smoking and red rototillers out on the sidewalk, over the small cluster of houses and garages on the Strawberry Loop, just over the top of the big silver water tower with the red light on top, steadily lower over some small farms—from up here the chickens looked like little white, black, and red triangles—and finally, at rooftop level, across the Pond Road and to the roof of Tom Harris's house.

They came in over Tom's front yard, pulled up, and stalled just above the peak of his roof, alighting upon it. They could hear breakfast in progress below; much chatter, sharing, rejoicing. Good enough. The others would be arriving any moment, and then that almost happy gathering below would be completed.

Guilo pointed to the northwest. Two streaks of light were descending rapidly out of the sky. Nathan and Armoth, just returning from Ashton!

Two more trails of light appeared in the eastern sky; Cree and Si were returning from the rout at the Omega Center.

Within moments, Nathan and Armoth passed over the house like two shining eagles, waving their swords in greeting. Tal pulled his glimmering sword and directed them to land on the left side of the front yard.

Cree and Si dropped steeply from above and cupped their wings to break their dive, settling like paratroopers to the right side of the front yard as Tal directed them.

Then they waited, every warrior in his place.

"Ah, here they come," said Tal, looking up the Pond Road toward town.

It was the green Plymouth, with Chimon and Scion still riding on top, their wings trailing like flashing, flickering banners. They waved their swords at their fellows, who waved back.

Irene Bledsoe eased the Plymouth to a stop out on the road in front of the house. She was about to reach back to help the children unbuckle and get their things, but there was no need; Josiah and Ruth burst out of that car like kids out of school and raced down the front walk without looking back.

Bledsoe turned her sharp nose forward, hit the gas, and got out of there. Chimon and Scion spread their wings, lifted from the roof, and let the car shoot out from under them. Then they settled to the ground on either side of the front gate.

The kids didn't knock or announce their arrival at all, but simply yanked the front door open and burst into the house, raising such a reaction from the people inside that Tal and Guilo could feel the noise through their feet.

In Heaven, reunions like this happened all the time, and the angels always found it absolutely riveting. Only human souls made in the image of God could fully know the soaring joy, the tear-stained ecstasy of losing a loved one and then, after a stretch of time that is always too long, feeling their warm embrace again, hearing their voice, sharing all their news. But moments like this were what the angels worked and fought for, and it was their fathomless joy, their greatest reward, to behold it once again.

The warriors in the yard could see through the front door. Tom was on his knees, clutching his children, weeping with joy. His friends were gathered all around, touching him, touching the children, murmuring prayers of thanksgiving and praise, asking questions, but getting no answers in all the confusion, and not minding at all.

The wings of the angels rose with their emotions, reaching high, spreading wide, shining like the sparkling joy that filled the house this day. They began to worship.

"Can we stay home now, Daddy?" Ruth asked through her tears.

Tom hesitated. He was afraid to answer.

Marshall touched him. "You can tell her yes."

Tom's eyes shone with deep joy and assurance. "We *did* win, didn't we?"

Marshall indicated the kids with his eyes. What more proof did they need?

Tom said, "You'd better believe it! We're never going to be apart again!"

More hugs. More tears.

A quiet squeak of breaks. Tires on gravel. A glint of blue.

Tom didn't notice, for obvious reasons, but Marshall did. He looked out the open front door.

He couldn't be sure. He couldn't believe it. He moved toward the door while the others stayed in their little rejoicing huddle.

There was a woman out there, parked across the street in a blue pickup truck.

Sally tried to keep low, tried not to be obvious as she examined Tom's house. She listened, and could hear the rejoicing through the open front door. She'd seen Irene Bledsoe driving off, and she'd seen the children run inside. They were all having such a wonderful reunion in there. She didn't feel she belonged. She didn't know what to do.

Mota and Signa hopped out of the back and stood by the cab, speaking gently to her. *They aren't going to hurt you, Sally.*

Hey, they won't mind the way you look.

I look awful, she thought. *I smell bad. What if they don't know who I am? What if this is the wrong house?*

C'mon. They'll be glad to see you!

She turned off the engine and sat there for a few more moments, just staring ahead and thinking. Her hands were shaking; she was so nervous her stomach ached.

They sound happy in there. They seem like a friendly bunch. I've just got to know how things turned out. They can reject me, I suppose, but I've got to know.

She opened the truck door and stepped out onto the shoulder. She walked toward the back of her truck—from this angle she could peer through the front door and see what was going on in there.

Oh, brother! They'll be able to see me too! I think that big guy did!

At that one, fleeting glimpse, Marshall thought he would soar through the roof and straight to Heaven! This was the Lord's work, all right! Oh, He does all things so well!

He moved carefully to the front porch as if approaching a timid deer, afraid of scaring it off.

Tal dropped to the porch and stood beside him. *That's her, Marshall. Don't let her get away.*

Sally hurried back to the cab of the truck and started to climb inside. She was going to bag this idea. Maybe she could write Tom another letter; this was just too awkward!

"Sally!"

She froze, her hand on the door handle, her right foot on the truck's running board. She didn't know if she should be Sally Roe or not. Who was this guy?

"Sally Roe?"

She remained still, just staring ahead. *If I turn my head, he'll know. Who is he?*

From inside the house she heard the children laughing. "Wow," said the little boy, "my own bed again!"

Am I safe? Is the running over?

"Thank You, Jesus," came a black woman's voice. "Oh, thank You, Jesus!"

You're safe, Sally.

She turned her head and looked at the big, red-haired man standing on the front porch. His eyes were gentle.

"Yes," she said, not loudly. Having said it once, she said it loud enough for him to hear. "Yes! That's me!"

Suddenly there was a crowd of people on that front porch, all looking her way—a lovely red-haired woman, a good-looking black couple, a kind-looking gray-haired man and his blonde wife, and . . .

Sally stared at that man as much as he stared at her. She'd seen his picture.

Tom had seen her pictures too.

You could cut the silence with a knife.

Marshall broke the silence with an invitation. "Sally, Tom

Harris—and all of us—would like very much to meet you. Would you like to come in?"

She relaxed just a little, but tried to hide behind the open truck door. "I'm . . . I'm hardly presentable . . ."

Tom replied, "You're among friends!"

Tal had to laugh. Hardly presentable! Wasn't it strange, the way humans looked at themselves with eyes of flesh and not of the Spirit? Certainly that dear woman had been through mire and filth of every degree; she was scarred, exhausted, ragged, and dirty.

But to the angels, she appeared as God Himself saw her, just as any other redeemed saint of the living God: pure, shining, clean, dressed in garments as white as snow.

With a little loving prod from Mota and Signa, Sally crossed the road, a tired, blue-jeaned vagabond coming home. She passed through the front gate, approached the front porch, and then, as angels and saints alike watched in tremendous awe, she extended her hand to the lone man standing between his two bubbly children.

"Tom Harris?"

"Yes."

"I'm Sally Beth Roe."

Tal clapped his wings just enough to return to the roof, then settled there in a comfortable sitting position, his sword at rest by his side.

Guilo asked the question for all of them. "What now, captain?"

Tal looked down at the laughing, praising group below. "I think we'll stay a while."

The warriors were glad to hear that, and moved in closer to listen to all that marvelous conversation, all that sharing and catching up.

Tal smiled and shook his head in wonder. "Redemption. It will never cease to thrill me."

Frank Peretti has woven a prophetic tale for our times that penetrates to the very heart of a struggle that threatens to tear our society to pieces.

TILLY

Kathy and Dan Ross are just like any other young couple ... except for the secrets that lie buried in their souls. When Kathy is captivated by the simple name "Tilly" on a small grave marker, both her life and Dan's are changed forever.

Tilly is the deeply moving story of a woman's struggle to reconcile herself with a long-ago abortion, and a couple's efforts to ultimately move forward with their lives. This powerful tale of forgiveness will shake the most stoic soul.

The Cooper Kids Adventure Series

A four-volume set of Frank E. Peretti's "Indiana Jones-style" adventure series. Build sound values in kids ages 9-14 while keeping them glued to their seats. Nearly 2,000,000 copies sold!

BOOK 1:
The Door in the Dragon's Throat

Jay and Lila Cooper have been on adventures with their archaeologist father before, but nothing like this! As they make their way through the dark and mysterious cavern called The Dragon's Throat, they can't help thinking about the other exploration parties that tried to open the Door leading into it. All fled in panic or died terrible deaths!

What really lies behind the Door? Incredible riches from a lost kingdom? Some ancient evil? Will they be able to overcome whatever force lurks behind the Door in the Dragon's Throat? Join them as they solve this dreaded desert mystery, which ends with a gigantic clash between the forces of good and evil.

BOOK 2:
Escape from the Island of Aquarius

When Jay and Lila travel with their adventurous father to an exotic South Seas island to find a missing missionary, they discover some very strange things going on. It appears that the arrogant leader of the island colony is the man they've been sent to find. But if that's true, then why is he acting so strange? As the Coopers attempt to solve the mystery, they find they also must find a way to overcome the evil that holds the colonists in a death grip—before the entire island breaks apart.

BOOK 3:
The Tombs of Anak

When Jay and Lila Cooper enter the cave-tombs of Anak with their father, they hope to find a coworker who has unaccountably disappeared. Instead, they stumble onto a frightening religion and new mysteries that soon put them all into incredible danger.

Who or what is Ha-Raphah? How does he hold the local villagers in overwhelming fear? The Coopers desperately search for answers and begin to unravel the mystery, but more peril lies ahead. Will they understand the truth in time to avoid disaster, or will they be swept away in a last desperate attempt by Ha-Raphah to preserve his evil powers?

BOOK 4:
Trapped at the Bottom of the Sea

When Lila insisted on leaving her father's teaching expedition to go back to the States, she never suspected that her flight would be hijacked! Now she is a prisoner, trapped at the bottom of the sea in a locked, top-secret weapons pod with no way of escape. Meanwhile, her dad, Dr. Jake Cooper, her brother Jay, and darling adventure-journalist Meaghan Flaherty are trying to pick up Lila's trail.

Pursued by angry terrorists, they island-hop in a remote corner of the Pacific, hoping against hope to find the plane. But will they reach Lila before her air runs out? Or before the pod is found by another hostile group searching for it?